OLPH COUNTY
FROM GUILFORD 1779

NALL'S CROSS ROADS

MORAVIA SETTLEMENTS

YADKIN ROAD 1754

OLD SALEM

TO COX'S R

GRASSY CREEK

SALEM OR

CROSS CREEK ROAD 1754

WILLIAMS'S CREEK

BEAR CREEK

BEAR

BLADEN-ANSON BOUNDARY ESTABLISHED 1749

WOLF CREEK

MECH.

CABIN CREEK

WET CREEK

DRY CREEK

TILLIS'S MILL CREEK

HORSE CR.

SING'S CREEK

TO WADESBOROUGH

JOEL ROAD

1764

CLA

SOUTHERN BOUNDARY LORD GRANVILLE GRANT   ESTABLISHED 1747

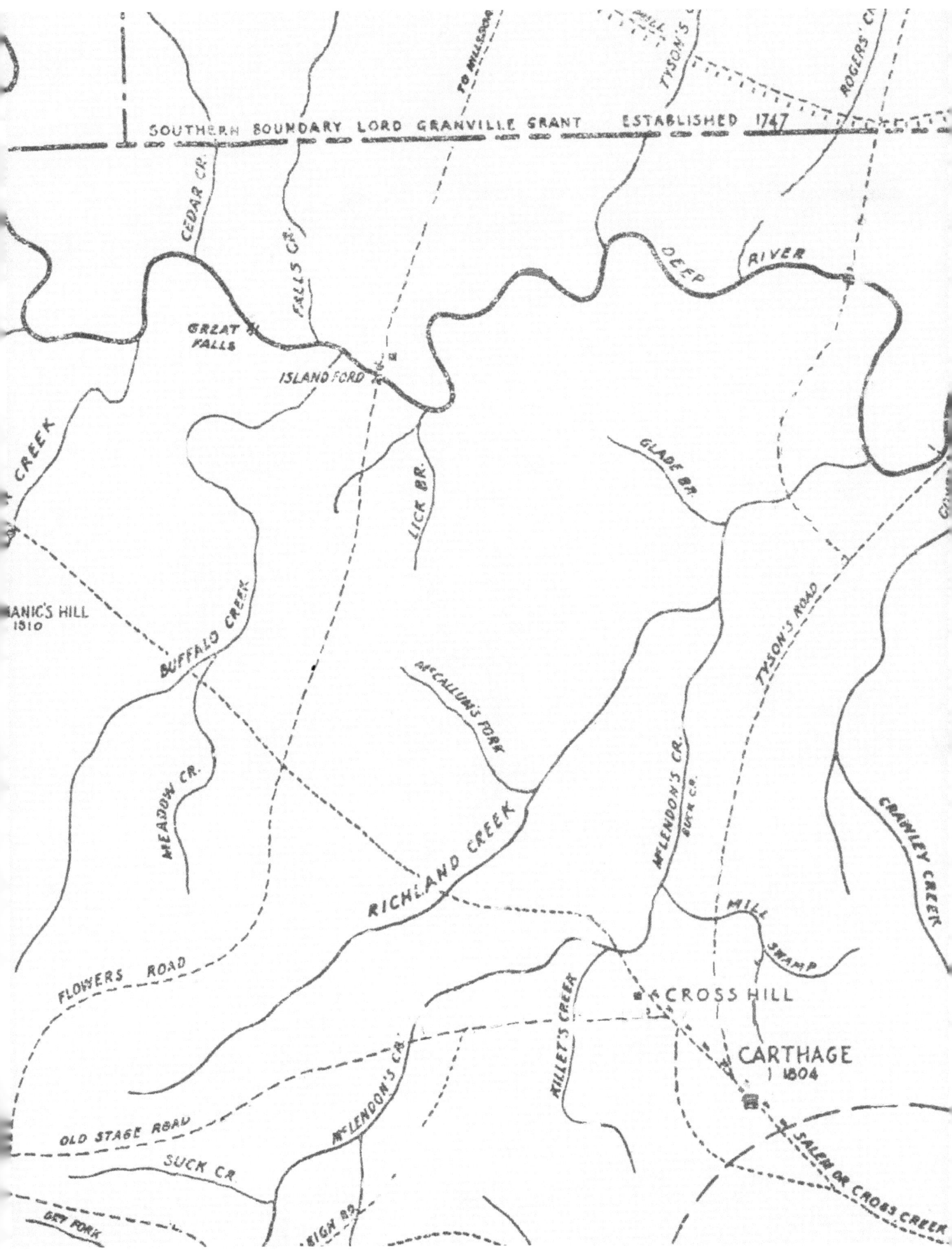

TO MILLSBORO

TYSON'S

ROGERS CR.

CEDAR CR.

FALLS CR.

DEEP   RIVER

GREAT FALLS

ISLAND FORD

GLADE BR.

CREEK

LICK BR.

...ANIC'S HILL
1810

BUFFALO CREEK

M?CALLUM'S FORK

TYSON'S ROAD

MEADOW CR.

McLENDON'S CR.

BUCK CR.

CRAWLEY CREEK

RICHLAND CREEK

MILL SWAMP

FLOWERS   ROAD

CROSS HILL

KILLET'S CREEK

CARTHAGE
1804

OLD STAGE ROAD

McLENDON'S CR.

SUCK CR.

SALEM OR CROSS CREEK

GET FORK

SIGN RD.

The Families of Northern Moore County:
Abstract of Miscellaneous and Rare Records
Volume I
1746-1830

Researched and
Compiled by

Morgan Jackson
www.MooreCountyWallaces.com

Inside Front & Back Covers: Northern Moore County from a portion of a map created by Rassie E. Wicker
Courtesy of the North Carolina Maps Digital Collection at UNC-Chapel Hill
Call Number MC.068.1956w
http://dc.lib.unc.edu/cdm/ref/collection/ncmaps/id/3432

ISBN 978-0-578-41447-8
ISBN (ebook) 978-0-578-21206-7

Published by Morgan Jackson
Raleigh, North Carolina
www.MooreCountyWallaces.com
morganjackson_1997@yahoo.com
919-624-7281

Printed by IngramSpark
www.IngramSpark.com

For my grandfather Mallie Wallace. You sparked a lifelong love of family and a burning desire to find out more about who we are and where we came from. You are missed every single day.

To my mother, Pat Wallace Jackson. Thank you for the many years of unconditional support, advice and love. And for supporting and nourishing the spark that Pop created. And for being my lifelong Editor!

And to my family...Shawn, thank you for everything, for it all. Nothing in our life happens without you. Emsley and Colt, I hope that my lifelong study of where we came from will help you keep your feet firmly on the ground and your eyes aimed at the sky.

Table of Contents

Maps

Introduction

My grandfather, Mallie Wallace, loved his family and loved to tell tales of the "old Wallaces". Many of these stories had been passed down to him from his grandfather, Emsley Wallace. Over thirty years ago, my grandfather said, "it's about time somebody started writing this down." As the youngest of his eleven grandchildren, that fortunately became my task. My love of genealogy, history and stories of long ago began with him and we spent the better part of his last twenty years writing it all down. He passed away in 2002 at 92 years old but continues to live on in our hearts and minds. We always planned to write a book on the Wallaces but I suffered from that familiar foil of most genealogists in that I could never reach a point where I felt it was truly finished. So in 2009, I launched *www.MooreCountyWallaces.com* to achieve the goal of publishing the work that he and I started and be able to keep it continually updated with new information. The website, while dedicated and named for our Wallace family, explores and attempts to document all of the families of northern Moore County, NC. As it turns out, the saying, "if you are related to one family, you're related to them all", couldn't be truer. If you descend from the families who resided in or near the towns of Robbins [formerly Hemp and Mechanic's Hill], High Falls or Eagle Springs or current/former communities of Westmoore, Spies, Needham's Grove, Parkwood, Hallison, Putnam, Carter's Mills, Gold Region, Big Oak, Caledonia, Prosperity, Noise, Quiet, Rise, Horners or for that matter anywhere in Bensalem, Ritters, Sheffields, Deep River or Carthage townships or communities in neighboring counties like Candor, Biscoe, Star, Seagrove, Whynot, Bennett or Carbonton, your ancestors can likely be found in this book and at *www.MooreCountyWallaces.com*.

Along the way, the search for family histories led to the search for proof and for the facts. This collection is that, *just the facts*.

Moore County, NC has long been a challenging place to do genealogical research, even more so if your family lived in Northern Moore County. Due to the immense loss of records in the 1889 Moore County courthouse fire combined with Northern Moore's large mix of Scotch-Irish, German, Swiss, English and other settlers who often kept to themselves and left very little evidence behind – genealogical and historical research on these families generally leaves researchers with no shortage of dead ends, brick walls and ancestors who disappear into genealogical black holes.

With this series, I hope to shine a light on these families and piece together the records that survived the fire and the test of time. It is my sincere hope that readers will be able to fill in a gap of knowledge, prove an oral tradition or at the minimum add to what they already know.

Utilizing over thirty years of personal research and a multitude of information from numerous sources, the following pages are a collection of abstracts of miscellaneous and hard to find records relating to the families of northern Moore County including land grants, deeds, church records, obituaries, school records, wills, estates, tax lists, military service and pension records, family bibles, newspaper accounts, marriage, death and court records. I've excluded census records on purpose as they would make this work too voluminous and these records are readily available and accessible. There are records from Moore County and surrounding counties as well as records from these families as they migrated west to Tennessee, Georgia, Alabama, Mississippi and Texas.

This first volume abstracts thousands of these records in a timeline format from the first 85 years of recorded history beginning in 1746 including several hundred images and hard to find maps. A full name index includes over 5,000 individuals and over 750 place names. Each individual entry is denoted by an item number and the index refers to the item number rather than the page. Often a letter will follow a number – this happened as more records were added post the initial round of indexing. So, sequencing may be as follows: 1211, 1211a, 1212. All items numbers and letters appear in the completed index. Due to the large number of misspellings of surnames in these ancient records, where possible, I have utilized the most popular spelling in the index rather than listing each individual spelling. For instance, Cagle, Cagel, Kagle, Keagle, Kegel and other variations are all located under the proper spelling - Cagle.

Theses abstracts were collected over many years from courthouses, libraries, state archives and other researchers as well as from *Ancestry.com*, *Familysearch.org* and other amazing web-based repositories. I have strived to be as accurate as possible, but readily admit that there are likely errors and omissions. Please contact me at ***morganjackson_1997@yahoo.com*** and I will gladly make any corrections to future editions, paper and online.

This collection was inspired by and I hope continues to add to the volumes of genealogical research that came before. No discussion of Moore County, NC history and genealogy can be complete without paying tribute to *Miscellaneous Ancient Records of Moore County, NC* by Rassie E. Wicker; *A Guide to Moore County Cemeteries* by Anthony E. "Tony" Parker; *Moore County 1747-1847* by Blackwell Robinson and *Moore County 1847-1947* by Manly Wade Wellman. Finally, a special praise and word of thanks to my longtime friend, mentor, and master genealogist James Vann Comer, whose volumes of work have documented too many families, communities and institutions across Central North Carolina to list them all here. His *Moore County Bible Projects Vol. I-III*, *Old Moore County Vital Statistics* and *Central North Carolina Vital Statistics* were direct inspirations to this collection.

Morgan Jackson – December 1, 2018
www.MooreCountyWallaces.com

> *Moore County, NC was formed from Cumberland County, NC in 1784 and Cumberland County, NC was formed from Bladen County, NC in 1755. Therefore, the earliest Moore County records are located in Bladen and Cumberland Counties.*
>
> *Similarly, the earliest Randolph County, NC records are found in Orange and Guilford Counties as Randolph was formed from Guilford County in 1779 and Guilford was formed from Orange in 1771. Chatham County, NC records prior to 1771 are located in Orange County records. Prior to 1779, Montgomery County records are located in Anson County.*

1. 1746, Jun 26 -- Land Grant #277 & 983, Bladen County, NC
   Thomas Armstrong received 300 acres located south of Deep River about one mile above the mouth of Buck Creek. [*Editor's Note: **Armstrong** --> **Robert Dickinson** 150a --> **James Dickinson** 1762 --> **Mary Dickinson** 1768 --> **Willis Dickinson***]

2. 1746, Jun 26 -- Land Grant #338 & 1046, Bladen County, NC
   Thomas Armstrong received 300 acres located south of Deep River. [*Editor's Note: **Joseph Elkins** deeded **Emanuel Stevens** 150a 1759 --> 150a **James** and **Mary Finley** 1759 --> 150a **Conner Dowd** 1762 --> **John Hancock Jr.** 1771 --> 100a **Willis Dickenson** 1780*]

   A. 1746, Nov 26 -- Land Grant #1090, Bladen County, NC
   John Collson received 400 acres located north of the Great Pee Dee above the mouth of Little River adjoining **Nicholas Smith** and **Jacob Collson**.

3. 1747, Oct 1 -- Land Grant #364 & 1074, Bladen County, NC
   Gabriel Johnson (in name of **Edward Griffith**) received 7,654 acres located on Deep River in four adjacent tracts: [1] 2,344 acres located east of Deep River and adjoining Earl of Granville line; [2] 2,560 acres; [3] 1,680 acres adjoining Grist Mill Creek; [4] 1,070 acres adjoining **John Richardson**. [*Editor's Note: willed to **Saml. Johnson** and **John Johnson** 1761 --> **Samuel Johnson** deeded ½ interest to **George Blair** 1763 --> **Blair** and **Johnson** deeded 4,000 acres to **Phil Alston** 1772; B&J deeded 150 acres to **Joshua Hancock** 1763; B&J deeded 450 acres to **Powell Benbow** 1765; B&J deeded 400 acres to **Starling Carroll** 1765; B&J deeded 383 acres to **Cornelius Tyson** 1765; B&J deeded 122 acres to **Elisha Hunter** 1765; B&J deeded 118 acres to **Cornelius Tyson** 1768; B&J deeded 100 acres to **Joseph Gilbert** 1772*] --- See map on the following page

4. 1748, Sep 30 -- Land Grant #259 & 965, Bladen County, NC
   John Tyson received 250 acres located north of Deep River below the Meery Maid Camp about five miles from the plantation where **Thomas Richardson** lives. [*Editor's Note: **John Tyson** of Beaufort County, NC deeded to **Cornealus Tison** 1752 --> 150a [part of 2 tracts to] **Robert Cheek** 1765; **Cornelius Tyson** 200a --> **John Shearin** 1763 --> son **Charles Shearin** 1766 --> **Samuel Temple** 1780*]

5. 1748, Sep 30 -- Land Grant #260 & 966, Bladen County, NC
   Joel McClendon received 300 acres located south of Deep River two miles above Buck Creek on Rocky Ford. [*Editor's Note: deeded to **James Barton** 1754 --> 270a on Cannon Landing to **James Russell** 1756 --> **James** and **Mary Russell** deeded 220a to **Gabriel Harden** 1762; **James Barton** deeded 80a to **James Muse Sr.** 1755 --> **Charles Findly** deeded 80a to **Sterling Carroll** 1762 --> **Gabriel Harden** 1764 at Rocky Ford --> **John Hardin** 1770*]

6. 1748, Sep 30 -- Land Grant #401 & 1111, Bladen County, NC
   Jacob McClandon received 300 acres located at the mouth of McLendons Creek. [*Editor's Note: deeded to **Joel McClendon** 1754 --> **Dennis McClendon** deeded 100a to **John Overton** 1756 and 200a to **Sterling Carroll** --> **Sterling Carroll** deeded to **John Carroll** 1767 --> **John Overton** 1773*]

7. 1749, Sep 31 -- Land Grant #394 and 1104, Bladen County, NC
   George Fagin received 200 acres located on Deep River four miles above the Great Falls. [*Editor's Note: **George** and **Elizabeth Feagon** deeded to **Abel Lee** 1757--> **Frederick Gregg** and **Richard Lyon** 1769*]

   A. 1748, Oct 5 -- Land Grant #267 and 973, Bladen County, NC
   Nicholas Smith received 400 acres located west of the Great Pee Dee 1/4 mile above **Isaac Denson**.

B. 1749, Mar 3 -- Deed Book A Page 20-21, Anson County, NC
Nicholas Smith (of Bladen County) deeded **Nathaniel Hillen** (of Anson County) half of the tract of 400 acres located north of the Great Pee Dee. **C. Robinson** and **Chas. Robinson Junr**. were witnesses.

8. 1749, Oct 10 -- Land Grant #01347, Bladen County, NC
Francis Mackilwean received 200 acres located on Bear Creek ten or twelve miles above the mouth. [*Editor's Note: Never granted*]

Earliest Land Grants on Deep River 1747
Near Glendon and the *House in the Horseshoe*

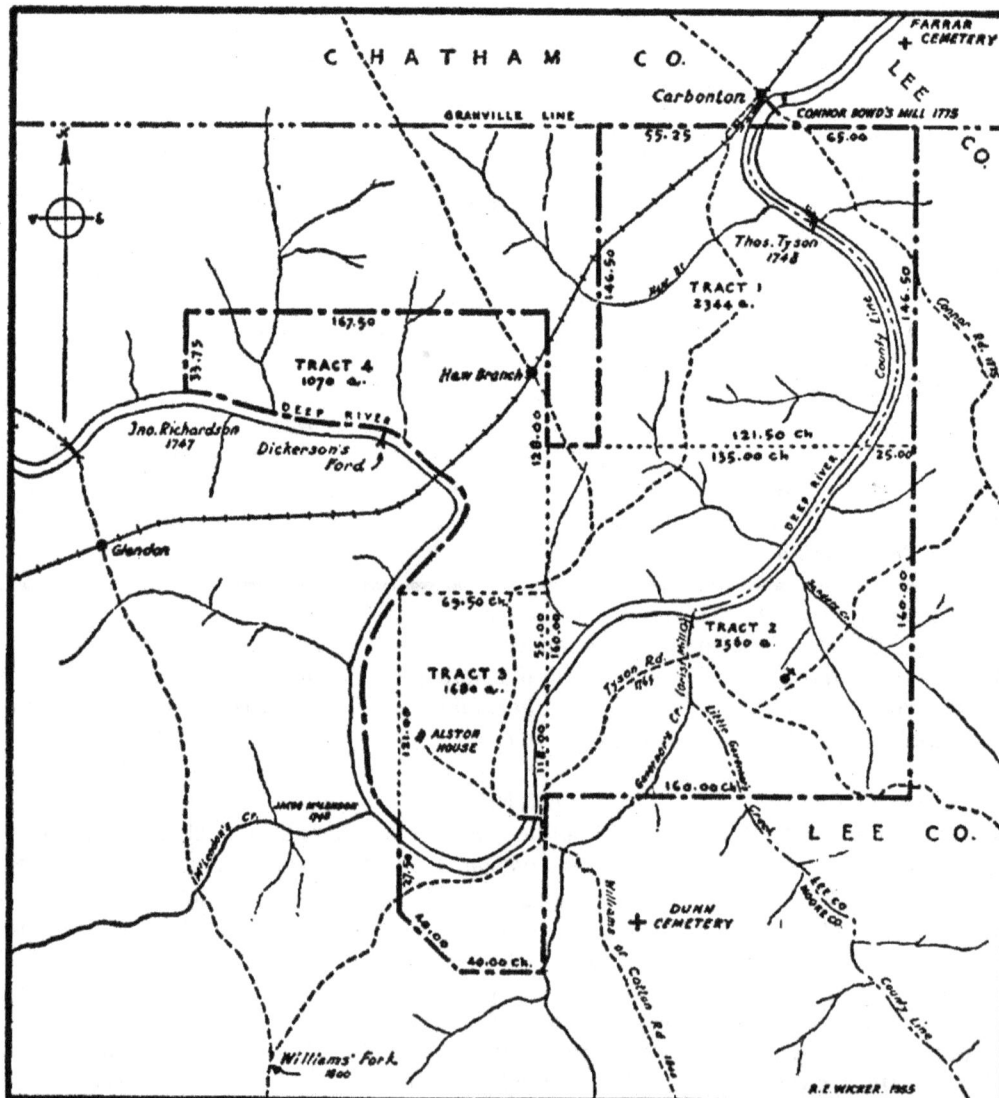

MAP SHOWING LOCATION OF GRANTS FROM THE CROWN TO
EDWARD GRIFFITH, OCTOBER 1, 1747

Map by Rassie E. Wicker from *A History of Moore County 1747-1847* by Blackwell P. Robinson

9. 1749, Oct 13 -- Land Grant #339a & 1047, Bladen County, NC
Benjamin Foreman received 147 acres located north of Deep River about ¼ mile above the mouth of Buck Creek opposite to the upper end of Hobby's Island adjoining the Governor's line (**Gabriel Johnson**). [*Editor's Note: deeded to William Ainsworth 1754 --> James Patterson Ainsworth deeded 50a to Isaac Ramsey and Robert Moore 1760; William Ainsworth deeded 50a Joseph Dunham 1761*]

A. 1749, Oct 13 -- Land Grant #339 and 1048, Bladen County, NC
Nicholas Smith received 200 acres located south of Great Pee Dee and above the mouth of Little River 1/2 mile above the Waggon Ford.

10. 1749, Nov 16 -- Land Grant #0385, Bladen County, NC
Martin Caswell received 100 acres located on Bear Creek at a place called the Hazle Neck. [*Editor's Note: Never granted. Similar tract granted to Richard Caswell in 1759*]

"Hazel Neck"

The first known survey near the current town of Robbins. The name arises from the confluence of Bear Creek and Cabin Creek [*listed as Eastern prong in survey*]. Later renamed as Mechanic's Hill, Hemp, Elise and finally Robbins. The above survey was a speculative survey and wasn't granted to Martin Caswell. In 1759, Governor Richard Caswell received a similar grant which he deeded to James Cheney in 1760 and later to John Cagle in 1761. Adjoining tracts later comprised the Cagle Gold Mine.

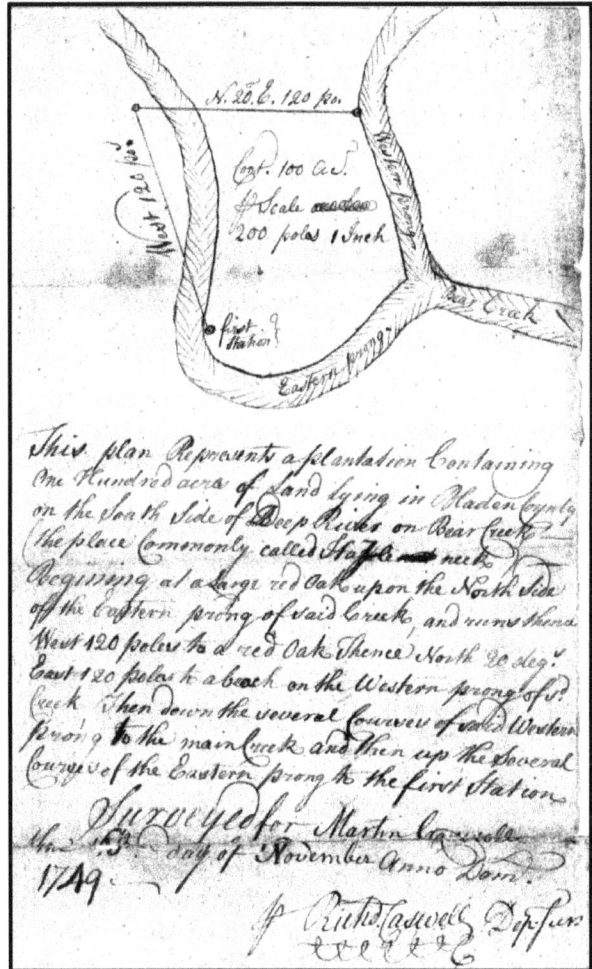

A. 1750, Jun 11- Deed Book A Page 40-41, Anson County, NC
Nicholas Smith (of Bladen County) deeded **Robinson Townsend** (of Anson County) 200 acres located north of the Great Pee Dee and above Little River. **Chas. Robinson Senr.** and **Chas. Robinson Junr.** were witnesses.

11. 1751, Apr 1 -- Land Grant #305 and 1012, Bladen County, NC
Nicholas Smith received 450 acres located at the mouth of McLendons Creek. [*Editor's Note: deeded to Thomas Collins 1754 --> 225 acres to Robert Dickinson 1758 --> Robert and Mary Dickinson to John Overton 1772; Thomas Collins deeded 225 acres to John Overton 1759*]

12. 1751, Apr 2 -- Land Grant #363 and 1072, Bladen County, NC
John Smith received 140 acres located on both sides of Bear Creek [Wet Creek]. [*Editor's Note: deeded to Thomas Holmes 1754*]

13. 1752, Mar 25 -- Land Grant #1240, Bladen County, NC
Thomas Armstrong received 300 acres located south of Deep River.

14. 1752, May 10 -- Deed Book 2 Page 16, Cumberland County, NC
Nicholas Smith deeded **Thomas Collins** 450 acres located south of Deep River on Buck Creek. **Robert Love** and **Thomas Richardson** were witnesses.

15. 1753, Sep 11 -- 1752-1758 Court of Pleas and Quarter Sessions, Orange County, NC Page 35
James Muse Senr. deeded his son **James Muse Junr.** his entire

estate. **Giles Tillet**, **Charles Seal** and **Alexander Going** were witnesses.

16. 1753, Sep 26 -- Land Grant #444 and 1154, Bladen County, NC
James McCallum received 300 acres located on both sides of Deep River including the place where **Jacob Barnes** lives. [*Editor's Note:* **William Pugh**, *Administrator of* **James McCallum**, *Dec'd. deeded 210 acres to* **Jacob Barns** *1755 -->* **Jacob Barnes** *deeded 100 acres* **John Phillips** *1756;* **Jacob** *and* **Mary Barns** *deeded 110 acres to* **Jacob Rogers** *1761*]

17. 1753, Nov 17 -- Land Grant #464 and 1175, Bladen County, NC
James McCallum received 300 acres located on Juniper of McLendons Creek adjoining **William Odom**'s improvement and the path from **Thomas Anderson** to **John Smith** [*Editor's Note:* **William Pugh**, *Administrator of* **James McCallum**, *Dec'd. deeded to* **Joel McClendon** *1756 -->* **Edward Cox** *1774*]

1754 -- Cumberland County, NC formed from Bladen County, NC

18. 1754, Feb 20 -- Land Grant #0458, Bladen County, NC
Joseph Elkins received 100 acres located west of Deep River adjoining his own line. [*Editor's Note: Never granted*]

19. 1754, Feb 27 -- Land Grant #525 & #1237, Bladen County, NC
Howel Brewer received 200 acres located northeast of Deep River 3 miles above Tices Creek at the mouth of a gutt. [*Editor's Note:* **Howel Bruer** *deeded to* **Zacharia Green** *1758 -->* **Green** *deeded 100a to* [**Frederick**] **Gregg** *and* **Richard Lyon** *1769 -->* **William Campbell** *1773;* **Green** *and wife* **Jeresth** *deeded 100 acres to* **John May** *1769 --> **Richard Lyon** & Co. *1772*]

20. 1754, Apr 13 -- Deed Book 2 Page 27, Cumberland County, NC
Jacob McClendon deeded **Joel McClendon** (both of Craven County) 300 acres located south of Deep River at mouth of Buck Creek. Patented to **Jacob McClendon** 1748. **James Barton Jr.** and **James Barton** were witnesses.

21. 1754, Apr 13 -- Deed Book 2 Page 29, Cumberland County, NC
Joel McClendon (of Craven County) deeded **James Barton** 300 acres located south of Deep River at Rocky Ford. Patented to **Joel McClendon** 1748. **Jacob McClendon** and **James Barton Jr**. were witnesses.

22. 1754, May 16 -- Land Grant #1267 and 1407, Bladen County, NC
Howell Brewer received 200 acres located on Deep River adjoining his own line. [*Editor's Note:* **Howel Bruer** *deeded to* **John May** *1767 -->* **Richard Lions** *1771*]

23. 1754, May 17 -- Land Grant #1263 & 1403, Bladen County, NC
Warner Coleman received 200 acres located on a branch of McLendons Creek. [*Editor's Note: deeded to* **Isaac Odom** *1754 --> 100 acres to* **William Killet** *1754*]

24. 1754, Jun 3 -- Deed Book 2 Page 5, Cumberland County, NC
Benjamin Foreman deeded **William Ainsworth** 147 acres located north of Deep River ¼ mile above mouth of Buck Creek at opposite end of Hobby's Island adjoining **Governor Gabriel Johnston** and granted to **Benjamin Foreman** 1749. **James Barten** and **William Ainsworth Jr**. were witnesses.

25. 1754, Jul 27 -- Deed Book 2 Page 74, Cumberland County, NC
Warner Coleman deeded **Isaac Odom** 200 acres located on a branch of McLendons Creek where **William Kellet** now lives and granted to **Warner Coleman** 1754. **Warner Coleman**, **Cornelus Tyson** and **Henry Yeats** were witnesses.

26. 1754, Jul 27 -- Deed Book 2 Page 75, Cumberland County, NC
Isaac Odom deeded **William Kellet** 100 acres located on a branch of McLendons Creek where **William Kellet** now lives and granted to **Warner Coleman** 1754. **Cornealus Tyson** and **William Kellet** were witnesses.

27. 1754, Sep 25 -- Land Grant #61 and 220, Cumberland County, NC
Isaac Horser received 200 acres located on McLendons Creek. [*Editor's Note:* **Isaac Horser** *and wife* **Mary** *deeded to* **John McNeill** *1772*]

28. 1754, Sep 28 -- Land Grant #1279 and 1423, Bladen County, NC
John Teer received 200 acres located on Wet Creek of Bear Creek adjoining the place where **Wm. Quinn** lived below the path from **John Smith**'s to **Nicholas Smith**'s. [*Editor's Note: deeded to **James Cheney** 1760 --> **John Walsh** deeded to **William Hooper** 1769 -- > **John Walsh** deeded to **Nicholas Newton** 1784*]

29. 1754, Oct 19 -- Deed Book 2 Page 53-54, Cumberland County, NC
John Smith deeded **Thomas Holmes** 140 acres located on both sides of Bear Creek [Wet Creek]. **Timothy Claven** and **Thos. Jones** were witnesses.

30. 1755 -- Tax List, Cumberland County, NC [selected residents]
James Barns 2 white polls; **Jacob Barns** 2 white polls; **John Carrol** 1 white poll; **Thomas Collins** 1 white poll; **Robert Dixson** 1 white poll; **Joseph Elkins** 1 white poll; **Saml. Elkins** 1 white poll; **George Fegin** 1 white 1 black poll; **William Kallit** 1 white poll; **William Morgan** 1 white poll; **Joseph Morgan** 1 white poll; **James Muse Senr.** 1 white poll 3 black polls; **James Muse Junr.** 1 white poll; **Isaac Odom** 1 white poll; **Mark Phillips** 1 white poll; **John Phillips** 1 white poll; **Cornelius Tyson** 1 white poll; **Christopher Yiew** 1 white poll.

31. 1755 -- Tax List, Orange County, NC [selected residents]
John Kogle 1 white poll; **Robert Milton** 2 white polls; **William Sercy** 1 white poll; **Enoch Spinks** 1 white poll.

32. 1755, Jan 21 -- Deed Book 2 Page 65, Cumberland County, NC
James Barton deeded **James Muse Sr.** 80 acres located south of Deep River at Cannon Landing. Patent to **Joel McClendon** 1748 and sold to **Barton**. **Timothy Claven** and **Joseph Elkins** were witnesses.

33. 1755, Jul 15 -- Deed Book 1 Page 29-31, Cumberland County, NC
James Muse Jr. deeded **James Muse Sr.** all the estate formerly deeded by **James Muse Sr.** to **James Muse Jr.** **Jacob Blocker** and **James Nicol** were witnesses.

34. 1755, Aug 9 -- Land Grant #74 and #232, Cumberland County, NC
Jonathan Evans received 100 acres located on Richland Creek. **Moses Tomlin** and **Timothy Cleaver** were chain carriers. [*Editor's Note: deeded to **Joseph Dunn** 1764*]

35. 1755, Oct -- 1755-1759 Court of Pleas and Quarter Sessions, Cumberland County, NC
Thomas Collins, **Thomas Anderson** and **Rob. Dickison** appointed road commissioners for the road from Deep River to the Yadkin Road near **Wm. Gilmores**.

36. 1755, Oct -- 1755-1759 Court of Pleas and Quarter Sessions, Cumberland County, NC
John Smith, **John Hurd**, **Archd. McKay** [crossed out] and **William Gilmore** commissioners of the Yadkin Road from the upper part of the county leading to Newberry Mill.

37. 1755, Oct -- 1755-1759 Court of Pleas and Quarter Sessions, Cumberland County, NC
William Pugh free to sell the perishable estate of **James McCallum**, Dec'd.

38. 1755, Oct 23 -- Deed Book 1 Page 79, Cumberland County, NC
Wm. Pugh, administrator of **James McCallum** Dec'd. deeded **Jacob Barnes** 210 acres on both sides of Deep River being the place where **Jacob Barnes** lives and part of the 300 acres granted to **James McCallum** 1753. **James Nicol**, **Wm. Dawson** and **Thos. Armstrong** were witnesses.

39. 1756, Jan 23 -- 1755-1759 Court of Pleas and Quarter Sessions, Cumberland County, NC
Petition granted for a road from Deep River at **Robert Dickasons** to a road leading to the Wagon Road near **William Gilmores**.

40. 1756, Jan 23 -- Deed Book 1 Page 147, Cumberland County, NC
Jacob Barnes deeded **John Phillips** 100 acres north of Deep River adjoining **Jacob Barnes**. **E. Richards**, **Walt. Dickinson**, **William Killet** and **Thomas Collins** were witnesses.

41. 1756, Feb 25 -- Deed Book 1 Page 166, Cumberland County, NC

Christopher Yow and wife **Christian** deeded **John Underwood** 200 acres southwest of Cape Fear River adjoining **John Davis**, **Hugh** and **David Smith**. Patented by **John Martileer** 1740 and sold to **Yow** 1747. **Joseph Rainboult** and **William Hearing** were witnesses.

42. 1756, Mar 19 -- Land Grant #85 and 243, Cumberland County, NC
Nicholas Smith received 100 acres located on Buffalo Creek. [*Editor's Note: deeded to* **Henry Guest** *1757 -->* **John Smith** *1758 -->* **Isaac Hill** *1764 -->* **Zachariah Smith** *1783*]

43. 1756, May 1 -- Land Grant #203, Orange County, NC
William Searcy received 640 acres located on both sides of Deep River adjoining his own line. **William Reed** and **John Burd** were chain carriers.

44. 1756, May 1 -- Land Grant #205, Orange County, NC
William Searcy received 640 acres located on both sides of Deep River. **William Reed** and **John Burd** were chain carriers. [*Editor's Note:* **William Searcy**'s *two land grants were located in the southeast corner of present day Randolph County on the Moore County border and near the Chatham County border.* **William Searcy** *ran a ferry across Deep River during the Revolutionary War period.* **Edmund Waddell** *received permission to operate a ferry here in 1802. Originally the area was known as Searcy's Ford, then Searcy's Ferry and in the 1800's Waddell's Ferry.*]

45. 1756, Jun 16 -- Land Grant #0176, Cumberland County, NC
George Feagin received 200 acres located on Buffalo Creek of Deep River including **Coleman**'s improvement. **Jno. Smith** and **Charles Seales** were chain carriers. [*Editor's Note: Never granted*]

46. 1756, Jul 15 -- Land Grant #96 and #254, Cumberland County, NC
Thomas Mathews received 200 acres located on McLendons Creek. [*Editor's Note:* **Thomas Matthews Sr.** *and wife* **Mary** *deeded to son* **Thomas Matthews, Jr.** *1765 -->* **Josiah Williamson** *1773 -->* **Thomas Elet** *1774 -->* **Thomas** *and wife* **Eleanor Elet** *deeded to* **Elexander MacLeod** *1774*]

47. 1756, Jul 10 -- Deed Book 1 Page 116, Cumberland County, NC
James Barton and wife **Anne** deeded **James Russell** 270 acres located south of Deep River at Cannon Landing. Patent to **Joel McClendon** 1748 and sold to **Barton** 1756. **Thomas Collins**, **James Barnes** and **James Own** were witnesses.

48. 1756, Jul 21 -- 1755-1759 Court of Pleas and Quarter Sessions, Cumberland County, NC
Marks and brands of **Francis Bettis**, **John Bettis**, **Elijah Bettus**, **Elisha Bettis** and **Jonathn Evans** recorded.

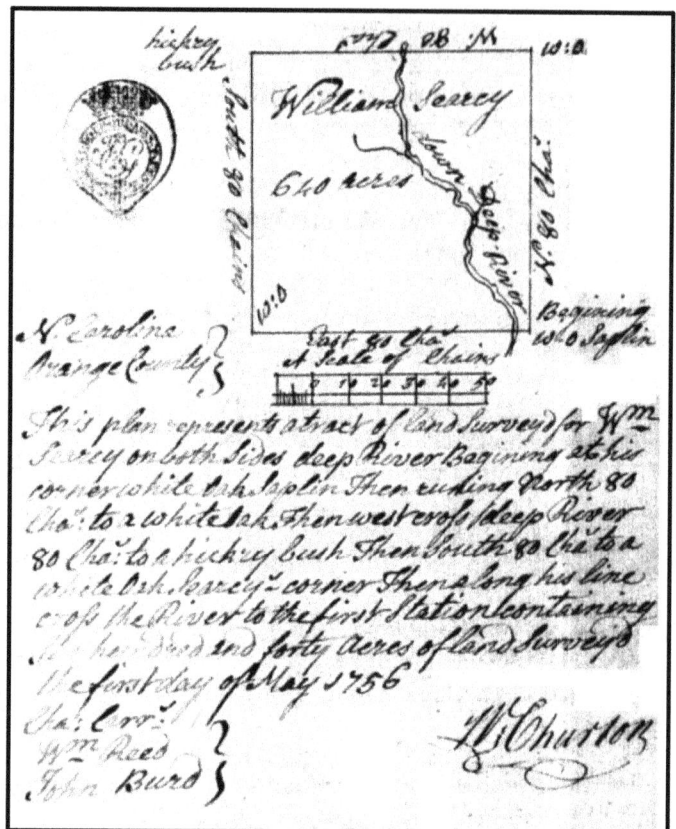

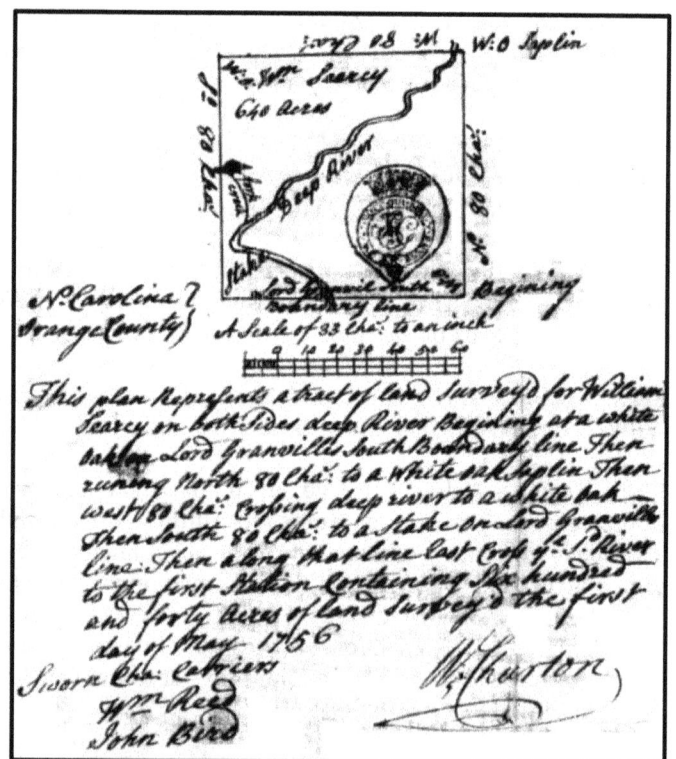

49. 1756, Oct 20 -- Deed Book 1 Page 161, Cumberland County, NC
Wm. Pugh, administrator of **James McCallum** Dec'd. deeded **Joel McClendall** 300 acres on Buck Creek or Juniper originally granted to **James McCallum** 1753. **Thomas Bennett**, **Nicholas Cavenah** and **Rebecca Joanes** were witnesses.

50. 1756, Oct 23 -- Deed Book 1 Page 202, Cumberland County, NC
Cornelius Tyson deeded **Robert Cheek** 150 acres located north of Deep River at mouth of a gully at the Island Ford. **Randolph Cheek**, **George Hendry** and **Thomas Collins** were witnesses.

51. 1756, Nov 4 -- Granville Land Grants, Orange County, NC
Robert Melton entered a 640 acre Land Grant located north of Haw River below red field at the Great Falls and above the mouth of Second Branch. **Robert Patterson** and **John Collins** were chain carriers. Warrant issued 14 May 1757 and surveyed 25 Oct 1759. The warrant was deeded to his heir **Nathan Melton** and he received 391 acres of the original entry on Jul 30, 1760.

52. 1756, Nov 6 -- Land Grant #146, Orange County, NC
William Reed received 480 acres located on Bush Creek of Deep River. **Thomas Graves** and **Richard Curtis** were chain carriers.

53. 1756, Nov 6 -- Granville Land Grants, Orange County, NC
William Reed received 640 acres located below the mouth of Richland Creek, called the Haw Fields, on both sides of Crooked Creek including **Josiah Wallace**'s improvement. Entered 13 Dec 1755 and warrant issued 3 Feb 1756.

54. 1756, Nov 9 -- Deed Book 1 Page 178, Cumberland County, NC
Denis McClendon deeded **John Overton** 100 acres located below the mouth of Buck Creek adjoining **Nicholas Smith** and is part of **Jacob McClendon**'s former tract. **Thomas Collins** and **James Underwood** were witnesses.

55. 1757, Jan 10 -- Deed Book 1 Page 204, Cumberland County, NC
George Feagon and **Elizabeth Feagon** deeded **Abel Lee** 200 acres located on Deep River 4 miles above the Great Falls. **Thomas Collins** and **William Owen** were witnesses.

56. 1757, Jan 29 -- Deed Book 1 Page 174, Cumberland County, NC
Nicholas Smith deeded **Henry Guest**, **Jr.** 100 acres located on Buffalo Creek. **Jacob McClendon**, **Joel McClendon** and **Abraham Richardson** were witnesses.

57. 1757, Apr 19 -- 1755-1759 Court of Pleas and Quarter Sessions, Cumberland County, NC
Conner Dowd licensed to keep an ordinary tavern at the house of **John Overton** with securities **John Heard** and **Samuel Howard**.

A.   1757, May 11 -- Land Grant #696, Orange County, NC
Stephen Howard received 530 acres located on the mouth of Indian Creek and Deep River opposite the Pocket.

58. 1757, May 25 -- Land Grant #23 and #386, Cumberland County, NC
John Smith received 200 acres located on branch of Bear Creek. **Wm. Arrington** and **Adam Rouse** were chain carriers. [*Editor's Note: **John** and **Sarah Smith** deeded to **William Morris** 1763 --> **William** and **Anne Morris** to Thomas Leonard Cotton 1771*]

59. 1757, Nov 5 -- Land Grant #412 and 838, Cumberland County, NC
Jemima McClendon received 200 acres located on McLendons Creek including **Jacob Newton**'s improvement. [*Editor's Note: **Benjamin Dumas** and wife **Jemima** sold to **Jacob McClendon** 1765 --> **Donald McDonald** 1773*]

60. 1757, Nov 5 -- Land Grant #59 and #218, Cumberland County, NC
Moses Tomlin received 200 acres located on Richland Creek. [*Editor's Note: deeded to **John Overton** 1758 --> Elijah Bettis 1769*]

61. 1757, Nov 6 -- Land Grant #410 and 840, Cumberland County, NC

Joel McClendon received 200 acres located on McLendons Creek about 1 mile below **Abraham Richardson**'s improvement. [*Editor's Note: deeded to **Thomas McClendon** 1770 --> **Thomas** and **Levisa McClendon** to **Joel McClendon Jr.** 1775 --> **John McClenden** deeded 100 acres to **William Barrett** 1779 and 100 acres to **Robert Graham** 1787*]

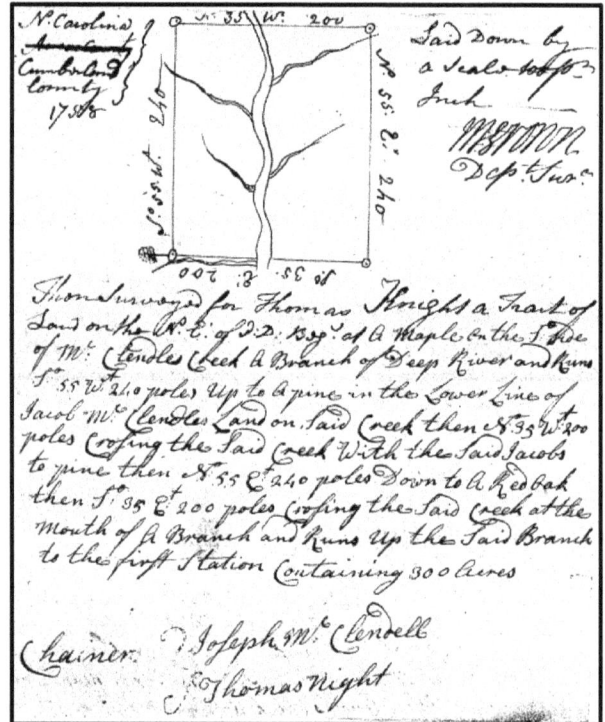

62. 1757, Nov 15 -- Land Grant #0487, Cumberland County, NC
Cornelius Tyson received 200 acres located south of Deep River adjoining **Cheek**. **Moses Tomlin** and **Thomas Colince** were chain carriers. [*Editor's Note: Never granted*]

63. 1757, Dec 30 -- Deed Book 1 Page 334, Cumberland County, NC
Will of **William Ainsworth** Dec'd. Heirs: sons **William Ainsworth**, **Leven Ainsworth** and **James Patterson Ainsworth**; wife **Jeannette Ainsworth**. Executors: wife **Jeannette Ainsworth** and son **Leven Ainsworth**. Witnesses: **E. Richards**, **Thomas Collins** and **James Barton**. Proven Jan 1760.

64. 1758 -- Land Grant #294, Cumberland County, NC
Thomas Knight received 300 acres located south of McLendons Creek adjoining **Jacob McClendle**. **Joseph McClendell** and **Thomas Night** were chain carriers. [*Editor's Note: deeded to **Jacob McClendon** 1762 --> **Isaac Sewell** 1772*]

A.   1758, Jan -- Land Grant #441, Orange County, NC
Joseph Carruthers received 456 acres located on Deep River and the mouth of Line Creek adjoining **Lord Granville**'s line and **Nathanl. Powell**.

65. 1758, Feb 21 -- Deed Book 1 Page 308, Cumberland County, NC
Thomas Collins deeded **Robert Dickinson** 225 acres located on Buck Creek (part of **Nicholas Smith**'s former tract). **E. Richards**, **James Underwood** and **Cornelius Dowd** were witnesses.

66. 1758, Mar 30 -- Deed Book 1 Page 241-242, Cumberland County, NC
Will of **James Muse**, Dec'd. Heirs: wife **Sophia**, son **James Muse** [*negro girl **Penelope***], daughter **Liddy Ceal** [*negro **Benjamin***], son **Thomas Muse** [*negro **Nell***], son **Daniel Muse** [*negro **Lucy***], daughter **Anne Muse** [*negro **Belinda***], daughter **Annabarbury Muse**, daughter **Sophia Pope Runnels** and her son **William Ceal Muse**. Executors: wife, son **James Muse** and **Charles Ceal**. Witnesses: **Robert Dickinson**, **James Bain** and **Isaac Dickinson**.

67. 1758, Apr 6 -- Deed Book 1 Page 274, Cumberland County, NC
Henry Guest deeded **John Smith** 100 acres located on Buffalo Creek. **Thomas Franklin** and **Joel McClendon** were witnesses.

68. 1758, May 23 -- Granville Land Grants, Orange County, NC
Joseph Walker received 468 acres located north of Haw River. **Robt. Melton** and **Nathan Melton** were chain carriers. Surveyed 2 Apr 1756.

69. 1758, Jun 8 -- Land Grant #268, Cumberland County, NC
Christopher Ewe received 400 acres located on Gares Creek of Upper Little River west of the Northwest River.

70. 1758, Jun 9 -- Land Grant #0153, Cumberland County, NC
William Killet received 150 acres located on Mill Branch of McLendons Creek including the old mill place. **James Reed** and **John Wear** were chain carriers. [*Editor's Note: Never granted*]

71. 1758, Jun 10 -- Land Grant #413 and 837, Cumberland County, NC

John Smith received 200 acres located on Mill Creek on the Arkin[Yadkin]/Waggon Road being the place he now lives including his mill. [*Editor's Note: **John (Sandhill)** and **Sarah Smith** deeded to **Richard Tillis** 1765 --> **Elizabeth, Temple** and **Willoby Tillis** to **Isaac Sanders** 1780--> **Lewis Sowell** 1786*]

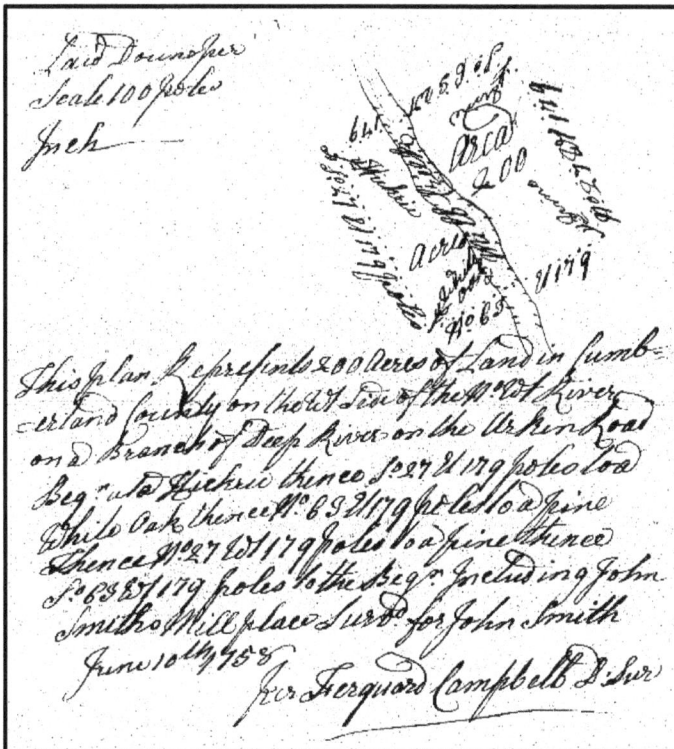

72. 1758, Jul 19 -- 1755-1759 Court of Pleas and Quarter Sessions, Cumberland County, NC
Will of **James Muse** proven by **Robert Dickeson**. **Sopha Muse**, Executrix, granted letters testamentary. On motion of **Sophia Muse** by her attorney, **Plunkett Ballard**, the following receipt was allowed to be recorderd: received of my mother, **Sophia Muse**, one negro girl **Pennallopy**, right and title, and I acknowledge her to be my full part of my father's estate. **James Muse** 1 Jul 1758. Witnesses: **Robert Dickinson** and **James Barnes**.

73. 1758, Jul 20 -- 1755-1769 Court of Pleas and Quarter Sessions, Cumberland County, NC
Thom. Donaho appointed constable in the district where **Joseph Durham** formerly served and **William Harrington [Arrington]** from the upper part of the county to the district where **Thomas Donaho** was to serve.

74. 1758, Aug 29 -- Deed Book 1 Page 337, Cumberland County, NC
Howel Bruer (of Orange County) deeded **Zacharia Green** 200 acres located on both sides of Deep River including place where **Zacharia Green** dwells adjoining his own line. **Thomas Collins**, **Robert Cheek** and **Charles Campbell** were witnesses.

A.   1758, Sep 14 -- Land Grant #1448/#1957, Anson County, NC
Thomas Ward received 200 acres located on both sides of Little River including his own plantation. **John Jeffery** and **Isaac Lukes** were chain carriers.

75. 1758, Sep 19 -- Deed Book 1 Page 268, Cumberland County, NC
Moses Tomlin deeded **John Overton** 200 acres located on Buck Creek including the land **Moses Tomlin** lives on. Granted to **Tomlin** 1754. **Thomas Collins** and **Frances Farris** were witnesses.

76. 1758, Oct 1 -- Land Grant #423 and 827, Cumberland County, NC
William Powell Esq. received 640 acres located on Deep River.

77. 1758, Oct 9 -- Estate, Cumberland County, NC
Inventory of the estate of **James Muse Senr.** including slaves **Benajmin, Belinda, Lucee, Penellupee** and **Elenor.**

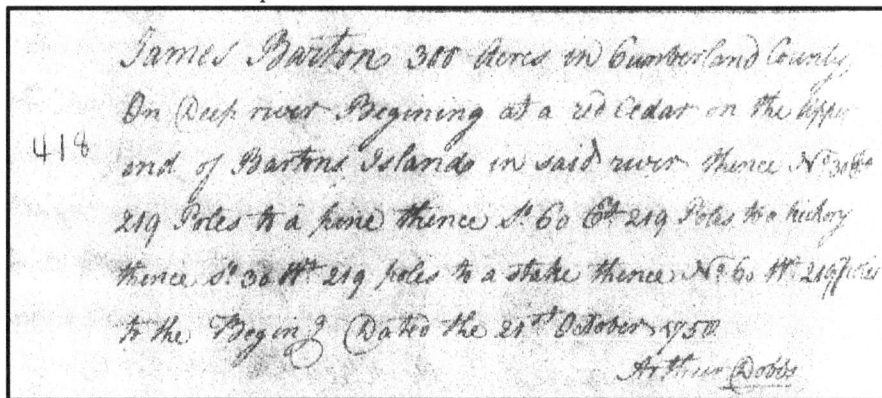

78. 1758, Oct 21 -- Land Grant #418 and #832, Cumberland County, NC
James Barton received 300 acres located on Deep River including Barton's Island. [*Editor's Note: deeded to **Samuel Williams** 1760 --> 250 acres to **Francis Treadwell** 1761; 50 acres to **Abel Lee** 1761--> **John Garner** and **John May** 1771 --> **Abel** and **Ann***

Lee to David Stroud 1771 --> 250 acres to Thomas Tucker 1773 except John Garner 50 acres --> William England 1784]

---

79. 1758, Oct 21 -- Land Grant #422 and #828, Cumberland County, NC
Joel McClendon received 100 acres located west of Deep River. [*Editor's Note: deeded to William Smith 1761 a place called Golden Grove*]

80. 1759, Apr 19 -- Deed Book 1 Page 309, Cumberland County, NC
Joseph Elkins deeded **Emanuel Stevens** 150 acres located south of Deep River. **Thomas Collins** and **Nicholas Smith** were witnesses.

81. 1759, Apr 24 -- Will, Orange County, NC
Will of **Robert Melton**, Dec'd. Heirs: eldest son **James Melton**, son **Nathaniel Melton**, sons **Nathan, Iseum** and **Ancel Melton**, younger son **Archelius Melton**. Executor: son **Nathan Melton**. Witnesses: **Richard Parker, Mary Stratten** and **James Sellars**. Proven Jun 1759.

82. 1759, May 9 -- Deed Book 1 Page 332, Cumberland County, NC
Thomas Collins deeded **John Overton** 225 acres located on Watery Branch (part of **Nicholas Smith**'s former tract). **Cornelius Dowd** and **William Hood** were witnesses.

83. 1759, Jun (2nd Tues) -- 1752 - 1762 Court of Pleas and Quarter Sessions, Orange County, NC Page 23,183
Will of **Robert Melton**, Dec'd. exhibited by **Nathan Melton** was proven by **Richard Parker**. Other witnesses **James Sellers** and **Mary Stratton** to be summoned to appear next Superior Court.

84. 1759, Jun 22 -- Land Grant #108 and #266, Cumberland County, NC
Edward Scarborough received 150 acres located on Richland Creek. [*Editor's Note: deeded to John Rasberry 1767 --> Malcolm McNeill 1775*]

85. 1759, Jun 22 -- Land Grant #117 and #275, Cumberland County, NC
John Overton received 100 acres located on McLendons Creek adjoining his own line and **Thomas Colince**.

86. 1759, Jul 18 -- 1759-1765 Court of Pleas and Quarter Sessions, Cumberland County, NC
William Ritchison served jury duty.

87. 1759, Jul 20 -- 1759-1765 Court of Pleas and Quarter Sessions, Cumberland County, NC
On or about the 19th or 20th of Jul, **Thomas Collins** lost a pocketbook containing a deed from **Suffia Muse** to **Charles Findley**.

A. 1759, Aug 4 -- Cane Creek [Quaker] Meeting Records (1756) Vol. 1 Page 21, Alamance County, NC
Cornelius Tyson received into membership by request.

88. 1759, Sep 1 -- Land Grant #426 and #824, Cumberland County, NC
Andrew Killett received 200 acres located on the drains of McLendons Creek. [*Editor's Note: Andrew Killett and wife Mary deeded to Frances Stribling 1766 --> 15a to Daniel McDonald 1772; Francis Stribling deeded 200a to James McDonald 1775 --> James Fry 1783*]

89. 1759, Sep 12 -- Deed Book 1 Page 376, Cumberland County, NC
Emanuel Stevens deeded **James Finley** 150 acres located south of Deep River adjoining **Robert Dickinson**. **Stephens** purchased from **Joseph Elkins** the ½ of 300 acres that **Joseph Elkins** purchased from **Thomas Armstrong**. **Thomas Collins** and **William Collins** were witnesses.

90. 1759, Oct 12 -- Land Grant #130 and #288, Cumberland County, NC
Farquard Campbell received 150 acres located on Richland Creek including **Jonathan Richeson**'s improvement. [*Editor's Note: deeded to James Muse 1762*]

91. 1759, Oct 15 -- Granville Land Grants and Land Grant #160, Orange County, NC
Luke Smith received a 222 acre Land Grant located on both sides of the Fork of Brush Creek. **John Kagle** and **Archibald Smith** were chain carriers.

92. 1759, Oct 22 -- Deed Book A1, Page 40, Johnston County, NC
Dixon Pearce deeded to **John Kilercas** 200 acres located south of Little River being where **Dixon Pearce** now lives adjoining **Edmond Smith**. This represents part of a tract that was granted to **Windsor Pearce** Apr 13, 1755 and sold to **Dixon Pearce** Oct 5, 1757. **Benjn. Crawford** and **William Raiford** were witnesses.

93. 1759, Nov 14 -- Land Grant #184 and #342, Cumberland County, NC
John Smith received 250 acres located on both sides of Deep River including **Abraham Richeson**'s plantation. **Vinson Yow** and **John Morgan** were chain carriers. [*Editor's Note: **John (Sandhill)** and **Sarah Smith** deeded to **John Stanton** 1764 --> **John** and **Abigail Stainton** to **Edward Moore** 1771*]

94. 1759, Nov 17 -- Land Grant #0445, Cumberland County, NC
Charles Seale received 300 acres located on both sides of Deep River including the place **James Barton** now lives adjoining **Duncan Buey**. **Moses Tomlin** and **Thomas Collince** were chain carriers. [*Editor's Note: Never granted*]

95. 1759, Nov 30 -- Land Grant #823, Cumberland County, NC
Richard Caswell received 120 acres located on Hasel Neck Fork of Bear Creek. **Farn Green** and **Joel McLendon** were chain carriers. [*Editor's Note: deeded to **James Chaney** 1760 --> **James** and **Mary Cheney** deeded to **John Cagle** 1764*]

A.   1759, Dec 1 -- Cane Creek [Quaker] Meeting Records (1756) Vol. 1 Page 21, Alamance County, NC
Jacob Barns received into membership by request.

96. 1759, Dec 10 -- Deed Book 1 Page 384, Cumberland County, NC
Will of **Robert Dickinson**, Dec'd. Heirs: wife **Mary** [*plantation I now live on*], son **James** [*150 acre plantation on Deep River he now possesses*], son **Michael** [*plantation on Little River where **Thomas Donahoe** now lives*], son **Willis** [*under age 18*], daughter **Charity** [*under age 18*], daughter **Sarah** [*under age 18*], son **Robert** [*under age 18; plantation I now live on after Mother's decease*] and mentions unnamed Father [*lifetime maintenance*]. Executors: wife **Mary**, son **Michael Dickinson** and **Thomas Collins**. Witnesses: **James Dickinson** and **Thomas Collins**. Proven Nov 1760.

97. 1759/1760 -- 1756-1785 Inventories, Sales and Accounts of Estates, Orange County, NC Page 25-27
Estate of **Robert Melton**, Dec'd. by Administrator **Nathan Melton**. *Items purchased by the following*: **Christian Kirksey**, **William Goffey**, **Henry Brown**, **William Borden**, **Ancel Melton**, **Robert Patterson**, **Robert Sellars**, **Hercules Melton**, **Henry Bauson**, **William Griffen**, **Nathan Melton**, **Alfred Davis**, **Oneal Melton** and **James Patterson**.

98. 1760, Jan 16 -- 1759-1765 Court of Pleas and Quarter Sessions, Cumberland County, NC
Will of **William Ainsworth** offered by **Jennet Ainsworth**, wife of the deceased, and **Leaven Ainsworth**, proven by **Thomas Collins**, Esq. Ordred that **Jennet** and **Leaven Ainsworth** have letter of administration on the estate.

A.   1760, Mar 1 -- Cane Creek [Quaker] Meeting Records (1756) Vol. 1 Page 22, Alamance County, NC
James Barns, **Robert Cheek** and **Jeremiah Barnes** received into membership by request.

99. 1760, May 28 -- Deed Book 1 Page 362, Cumberland County, NC
James Patterson Ainsworth deeded **Isaac Ramsey** 50 acres located Deep River ¼ miles above mouth of Buck Creek at opposite end of Hobby's Island adjoining **Governor [Johnston]**, patented to **Benjamin Foreman** and deeded to **William Ainsworth** 1754 and by will of **William Ainsworth** Dec'd. to **James Patterson Ainsworth**. **Wm. Ainsworth** and **Charles Lindly** were witnesses.

100.   1760, May 28 -- Deed Book 2 Page 106, Cumberland County, NC

Richard Caswell (of Dobbs County) deeded **James Cheney** 120 acres located on a fork of Bear Creek called the Hasle Neck. **Thomas Gibson** and **James Davis** were witnesses.

101.   1760, May 28 -- Deed Book 2 Page 107, Cumberland County, NC
John Tear (of Craven County) deeded **James Cheney** 200 acres located on a prong of Bear Creek [Wet Creek] adjoining the place where **Wm. Quinn** lived below the path from **John Smith**'s to **Nicholas Smith**'s. **Richd. Caswell** and **Patrick McCabe** were witnesses.

102.   1760, Jun 15 -- Land Grant #131 and #289, Cumberland County, NC
Farquard Campbell received 200 acres located on Richland Creek including **Moses Tomlin**'s improvement.

103.   1760, Jul 12 -- Land Grant #181 and #339, Cumberland County, NC
Cornelius Tyson received 100 acres located north of Deep River adjoining **Robert Cheek**. [*Editor's Note: Cornelius Tyson deeded to Robert Cheek 1765 (part of two tracts)*]

A.   1760, Aug 5 -- Land Grant #108, Orange County, NC
Nathaniel Powel received 700 acres located on the mouth of Indian Creek and Deep River adjoining **Stephen Howard**.

104.   1760, Aug 16 -- Land Grant #175 and #333, Cumberland County, NC
Robert Cheek received 100 acres located north of Deep River adjoining **Cornelius Tyson**.

105.   1760, Aug 16 -- Land Grant #179 and #337, Cumberland County, NC
Robert Cheek received 150 acres located south of Deep River below the mouth of the Island Ford.

106.   1760, Aug 17 -- Land Grant #157 and #315, Cumberland County, NC
John Donahue received 200 acres located on Lick/Leek Creek. [*Editor's Note: should be Wet Creek -- deeded to Nicholas Newton 1764 --> Bartholomew Dunn 1773*]

107.   1760, Aug 19 -- 1759-1765 Court of Pleas and Quarter Sessions, Cumberland County, NC
Wm. Ritchison served jury duty.

108.   1760, Aug 20 -- Granville Land Grants #6596, Orange County, NC
Josias Wallace entered 700 acres located on Fork Creek of Deep River including the plantation where **Enoch Spink** now lives.

109.   1760, Aug 22 -- 1759-1765 Court of Pleas and Quarter Sessions, Cumberland County, NC
Ordered that **Thomas Knight** be appointed constable in place of **Jonathan Ritchison**.

110.   1760, Nov 14 -- Land Grant #149 and #307, Cumberland County, NC
Conner Dowd received 128 acres located south of Deep River adjoining **Governor Johnston** and **John Overton**. [*Editor's Note: deeded to John Hunnicutt 1769*]

111.   1760, Nov 17 -- Deed Book 1 Page 441, Cumberland County, NC
James Barton deeded **Samuel Williams** 300 acres located on both sides of Deep River at the upper end of Barton's Island. **John Smith**, **William Ritchison** and **Abel Lee** were witnesses.

112.   1760, Nov 19 -- 1759-1765 Court of Pleas and Quarter Sessions, Cumberland County, NC
William Ritchison served jury duty.

113.   1760, Nov 20 -- 1759-1765 Court of Pleas and Quarter Sessions, Cumberland County, NC
Will of **Robert Dickeson** proven by **James Dickeson**. Deceased names his wife **Mary Dickeson** executrix and **Michael Dickeson** and **Thomas Collins**, executors, they being granted letters testamentary.

A.   1761, Feb 5 -- Land Grant #616, Orange County, NC
Capt. John Gardner received 500 acres located on Richland Creek and Deep River. **John Lawence** and **John Needham** were chain carriers.

B.   1761, Feb 7 -- Cane Creek [Quaker] Meeting Records (1756) Vol. 1 Page 23, Alamance County, NC

James Cheek received into membership by request.

114.　　1761, Feb 19 -- 1759-1765 Court of Pleas and Quarter Sessions, Cumberland County, NC
Ordered that a road be laid from the mouth of Fork Creek to **Captain Collins'** road near **Joseph Dunham's** and the following appointed commissioners: **Wm. Morgan, Thomas Knight, James Muse** and **Abel Lea**.

115.　　1761, Mar 8 -- Land Grant #153, Orange County, NC
Enoch Spinks received 225 acres located on Fork Creek of Deep River. **Jno. Lawrence** and **Jas. Latham** were chain carriers.

116.　　1761, Mar 24 -- Deed Book 1 Page 436, Cumberland County, NC
William Ainsworth deeded **Joseph Dunham** 50 acres located north of Deep River being land that was granted to **Benjamin Foreman** and deeded to **William Ainsworth** Dec'd. **John Goodwin** and **Leaven Ainsworth** were witnesses.

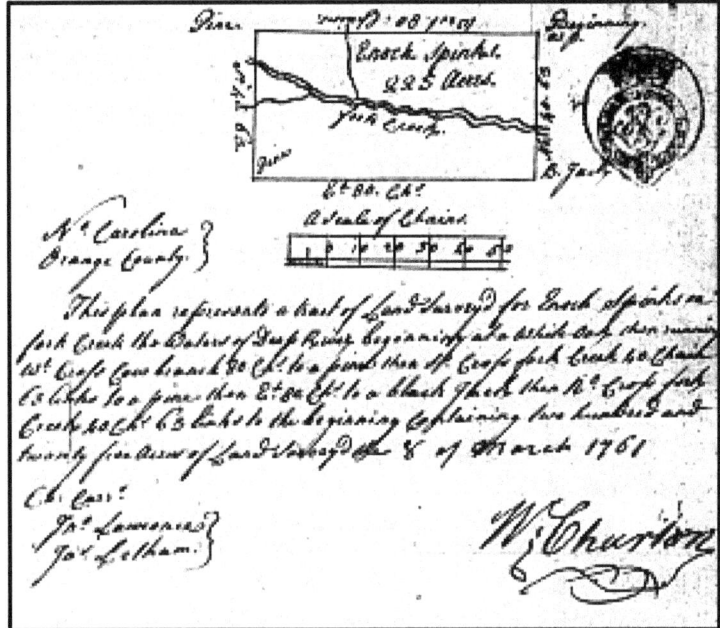

117.　　1761, Apr 10 -- Land Grant #142, Cumberland County, NC
William Key received 200 acres located on Wet Creek.

118.　　1761, May 21 -- 1759-1765 Court of Pleas and Quarter Sessions, Cumberland County, NC
James Muse appointed constable from Beaver Creek to McClendons Creek and **Wm. Arrington** appointed constable from McClendons Creek to the upper bounds of the county including all within the Yadkin Road.

119.　　1761, Jun 6 -- Land Grant #166 and 324, Cumberland County, NC
Leonard Hard [Hart] received 200 acres located on Grassy Creek.

120.　　1761, Jun 6 -- Land Grant #162 and #320, Cumberland County, NC
John Williamson received 300 acres located on Grassy Creek including his own improvement.

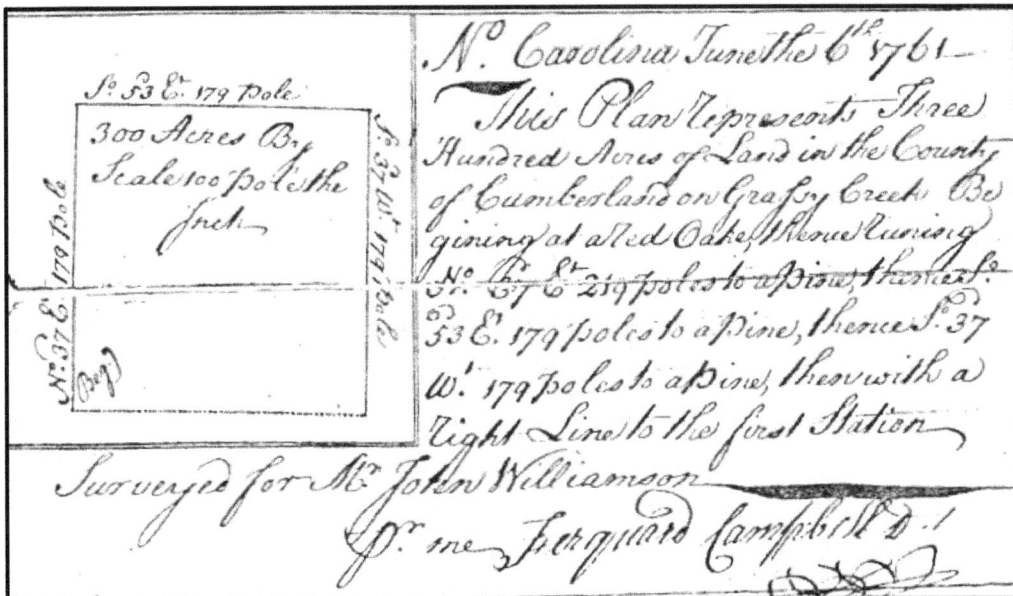

121.　　1761, Jun 6 -- Land Grant #201, Cumberland County, NC

John Haire received 200 acres located on Wolf Creek.

122. 1761, Jun 9 -- Land Grant #159 and #317, Cumberland County, NC
John/Thomas Donahue received 200 acres located south of Smith's Creek [Mill Creek] on the Yadkin Road including **Arenton**'s Cabin.

123. 1761, Jul 11 -- Deed Book 1 Page 138, Cumberland County, NC
Michael Dickinson deeded **John Pate** 100 acres on Lower Little River including plantation where **John Pate** lives. Patent by **Charles Heard** 6 Mar 1759. **James Ainsworth** and **John Overton** were witnesses.

124. 1761, Aug 4 -- Land Grant #154 and #312, Cumberland County, NC
Conner Dowd received 150 acres located south of Deep River adjoining **Governor Johnston** and **Lord Cartret**'s line.

125. 1761, Aug 10 -- Deed Book 1 Page 470, Cumberland County, NC
Jacob and **Mary Barnes** (of Orange County) deeded **Jacob Rogers** 110 acres on Deep River adjoining **John Phillips**. Part of 210 acre patent to **James McCallum** then sold by administrator **Wm. Pugh** to **Jacob Barns**. **Robert Smith** and **Richard Mauldin** were witnesses.

126. 1761, Sep 16 -- Deed Book 2 Page 120, Cumberland County, NC
James Patterson Ainsworth deeded **Robert Moore** 50 acres located Deep River ¼ miles above mouth of Buck Creek at opposite end of Hobby's Island adjoining **Governor [Johnston]** and **Robert Moore**, part of 147 acres patented to **Benjamin Foreman** and deeded to **William Ainsworth** 1754 and by will of **William Ainsworth** Dec'd. to **James Patterson Ainsworth**. **Isaac Ramsey** and **Leaven Ainsworth** were witnesses.

127. 1761, Oct 1 -- Deed Book 2 Page 324, Cumberland County, NC
Samuel Williams deeded **Francis Treadwell** 250 acres located north of Deep River, part of the 400 acre Land Grant to **James Barton** 21 Oct 1746 including the upper end of Barton's Island. **Abel Lee**, **William Morgin** and **Robert Lee** were witnesses.

A. 1761, Oct 6 -- Deed Book 6 Page 154, Anson County, NC
Joel Phillips (of Anson County) deeded **Nicholas Smith** (of Cumberland County) 200 acres located southwest of Pee Dee River and Gould/Gold's Fork adjoining **Wm. Powell**. **Wm. Reed** and **Chas. Robinson** were witnesses.

128. 1761, Oct 20 -- Granville Land Grants, Orange County, NC
William Wilborn Jr. received a 375 acre Land Grant located on McEntires Creek of Deep River. **Isaac Starns** and **Charles Cagle** were chain carriers. Surveyed Jul 18, 1761.

129. 1761, Nov 6 -- Deed Book 2 Page 144, Cumberland County, NC
Joel McClendon deeded **William Smith** 100 acres located west of Deep River, a place called the Golden Grove. **Thos. Collins** and **Niclus Nuton** were witnesses.

130. 1761, Nov 8 -- 1759-1765 Court of Pleas and Quarter Sessions, Cumberland County, NC
John Dunahoe's mark and brand recorded. **John Dunahoe** licensed to keep a tavern at his dwelling house.

131.   1761, Nov 21 -- 1759-1765 Court of Pleas and Quarter Sessions, Cumberland County, NC
John Overton appointed commissioner of roads in place of **Robert Dickeson**, Dec'd.

132.   1761, Dec 18 -- Land Grant #620, Orange County, NC
Thomas Graves received 700 acres located on both sides of Deep River adjoining **William Searcy**. **Thomas Jones** and **John Graves** were chain carriers.

133.   1762, Feb 12 -- Deed Book 2 Page 102, Cumberland County, NC
James Dickinson deeded **Mary Dickinson** 150 acres located south of Deep River 1 mile above mouth of Buck Creek. Part of the 300 acres patented to **Thomas Armstrong** 1747 and 150 acres sold to **Robert Dickinson**. **Michael Dickinson, Charles Findley** and **Levin Ainsworth** were witnesses.

134.   1762, Feb 19 -- Deed Book 2 Page 180, Cumberland County, NC
Dennis McLendon (of Craven County) deeded **Sterling Carroll** 200 acres located on fork of Deep River and McLendons Creek. **Thomas Knight, Joel McClendon** and **Francis McClendon** were witnesses.

135.   1762, Feb 25 -- Cane Creek [Quaker] Meeting Records (1756) Vol. 1 Page 17, Alamance County, NC
Jonathan Barns of Cumberland County and **Sarah Steell** of Cumberland County were married at the Deep River. **Cornelius Tison, Thos. Branson, Gidean Gilbert, Powell Benbow, Mary Hall, Elizabeth Chason, Easther Smith, John Jones, James Barns, Jacob Barns, Elesebeth Barns, James Russell, Elisha Hunter, Margret Hunter** and **Mary Russell** were present and served as witnesses.

A.   1762, Apr 9 -- Deed Book 3 Page 1, Anson County, NC
Nicholas Smith (of Cumberland County) deeded **Benj. Thompson** (of Anson County) 200 acres located south of Pee Dee River and Gould's Fork adjoining **Wm. Powell**. **John Thompson** and **John Leverett** were witnesses.

136.   1762, Apr 24 -- Land Grant #169 and #327, Cumberland County, NC
Samuel Jackson received 100 acres located on Jacksons Branch of Drowning Creek.

137.   1762, Apr 28 -- Deed Book 2 Page 123, Cumberland County, NC
James Russell deeded **Gabriel Harden** (of Lunenburg County, VA) 220 acres located south of Deep River. **Sterling Carroll, Charles Finley** and **Susan Finley** were witnesses.

138.   1762, May 3 -- Deed Book 2 Page 140, Cumberland County, NC
James Findly and **Mary Finley** deeded **Conner Dowd** 150 acres located south of Deep River being part of 300 acres that formerly belonged to **Thomas Armstrong**. **Sterling Carroll, Samuel Elkins** and **Hart. Hunnicut** were witnesses.

139.   1762, May 15 -- Deed Book 2 Page 121, Cumberland County, NC
Charles Findly deeded **Sterling Carroll** 80 acres located south of Deep River at Cannon Landing being land that formerly belonged to **James Barton**. **James Muse** and **Isaac Ramsay** were witnesses.

140.   1762, May 17 -- Deed Book 2 Page 139, Cumberland County, NC
Farquard Campbell deeded **James Muse** 150 acres located on McLendons Creek including **Jonathan Ritchinson**'s improvement. **John Overton** was a witness.

141.   1762, May 19 -- 1759-1765 Court of Pleas and Quarter Sessions, Cumberland County, NC
Ordered that **Jonathan Ritchison** be appointed constable from McClendons Creek to the upper boundary of this county including all within the Yadkin Road. **Joshua Collins** appointed from Cranes Creek to McClendons Creek. **Christopher Yeaw Jr.** from Dobbins Road including the branches of Upper Little River to Deep River.

142.   1762, May 20 -- 1759-1765 Court of Pleas and Quarter Sessions, Cumberland County, NC
Ordered that **Poll Pigg**, orphan girl aged 13, shall live with **John Donahoe** for 3 years.

143.   1762, May 21 -- 1759-1765 Court of Pleas and Quarter Sessions, Cumberland County, NC
Ordered that constables **Joshua Collins** and **Jonathin Ritchison** make list of taxables for Justice **Thomas Collins**, Esq.

A.   1762, Jun 30 -- Land Grant #492, Orange County, NC
Thomas Choist [Cash/Cosht] received 240 acres located on Reedy Creek and Fork Creek.

144.   1762, Jul 25 -- Deed Book 2 Page 150, Cumberland County, NC
Thomas Knight deeded **Jacob McClendon** 300 acres located on both sides of McLendons Creek adjoining **Jacob McLendon**. Patented to **Thomas Knight** 1760. **John Grehum** and **Joel McClendon** were witnesses.

145.   1762, Sep 2 -- Land Grant #630, Cumberland County, NC
Jacob Kerringer received 200 acres located west of Deep River adjoining **William Morgan** and **Leonard Haird**.

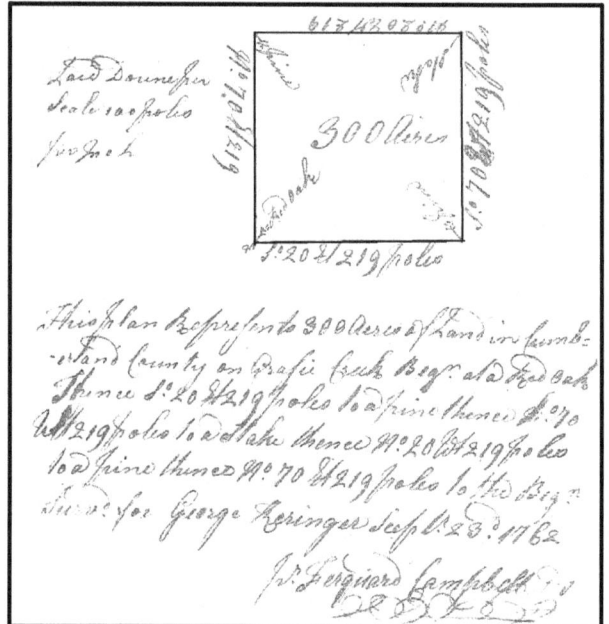

146.   1762, Sep 2 -- Land Grant #484 and #664, Cumberland County, NC
Edward Cox received 150 acres located on the head of McLendons Creek including where he now lives. [*Editor's Note: **Edward** and wife **Margaret Cox** deeded to **John Campbell** 1774*]

147.   1762, Sep 23 -- Land Grant #626, Cumberland County, NC
George Keringer received 300 acres located on Grassy Creek adjoining **Leonard Haird**.

148.   1762, Sep 24 -- Land Grant #705, Cumberland County, NC
Owen Carpenter received 250 acres located on Falling Creek adjoining the Earl of Granville's line and including his own improvement.

149.   1762, Sep 24 -- Land Grant #0261, Cumberland County, NC
Robert Cheek received 300 acres located south of Deep River adjoining **James McCallum**. [*Editor's Note: Never granted*]

150.   1762, Sep 24 -- Land Grant #752, Cumberland County, NC
John Mires received 200 acres located on Buffalo Creek.

151.   1762, Sep 26 -- Land Grant #196 and #354, Cumberland County, NC
Aron Burleson received 150 acres located on Richland Creek adjoining **John Cooper**.

152.   1762, Sep 28 -- Land Grant #194 and #352, Cumberland County, NC
John Graham received 150 acres located on McLendons Creek adjoining **Edward Cox**, **Thomas Matthews** and the Poplar Springs. [*Editor's Note: deeded to **John Cox** 1770*]

153.   1762, Oct 20 -- Land Grant #174 and #332, Cumberland County, NC
Thomas Minard received 200 acres located on Richland Creek. [*Editor's Note: **Thomas** and **Mary Minard** deeded to **Joseph Carr** 1767*]

154.   1762, Nov 25 -- Cane Creek [Quaker] Meeting Records (1756) Vol. 1 Page 20, Alamance County, NC
Joseph Gilbert, son of **Gidean** and **Mary Gilbert**, of Cumberland County and **Sebarah Tison**, daughter of **Cornelius** and **Gean Tison**, of Cumberland County were married at the Deep River in Cumberland County. **George Hendry**, **Powell Benbow**, **Abigail Pike**, **Sarah Barns**, **Rachell Mainer**, **Joell Sanders**, **Cornelius Tison**, **Gidean Gilbert**, **Jean Tison**, **James Barnes** and **Jacob Barns** were present and served as witnesses.

155.   1762, Dec 8 -- Land Grant #482, Orange County, NC
Robert Cheek received 241 acres located on Tices Creek of Deep River and the [Moore] county line. **Randolph Cheek** and **Jacob Barns** were chain carriers.

A.   1762, Dec 30 -- Land Grant #99, Orange County, NC

Nathaniel Powell received 688 acres located on Deep River adjoining the King's line and his own line.

156.   1763, Jan 1 -- Land Grant #1625, #1814 & #0145, Cumberland County, NC
Peter Toncannon [Voncannon] received 100 acres located on Wolf Creek 2 miles above the mouth adjoining Hare. Jacob Hartley and Martin Off [Ott] were chain carriers.

A.   1763, Jan 15 -- Land Grant #562, Orange County, NC
Conner Doud received 302 acres located on Deep River and Smiths Creek adjoining the King's line and Nathl. Powell.

157.   1763, Jan 27 -- Land Grant #154, Orange County, NC
Enoch Spinks received 455 acres located on Fork Creek of Deep River. Thos. Gant and Jno. Higgins were chain carriers.

158.   1763, Feb 18 -- 1759-1765 Court of Pleas and Quarter Sessions, Cumberland County, NC
John McFarling appointed overseer from his house to Thomas Donahues; John Donahue appointed overseer of the road from Thomas Donahue's to Sandhill Smith's; John Smith appointed overseer of the road from Sandhill Smith's to the upper end of the county; John Overton appointed overseer from the upper end of the county to Dunhams Creek.

159.   1763, Feb 24 -- Deed Book 2 Page 607, Cumberland County, NC
Cornelius Tyson deeded John Shearin 200 acres located north of Deep River received from John Tison. William Sesson, Wm. Thompson and Robert Wilkins were witnesses.

160.   1763, Mar 8 -- Land Grant #492 and #673, Cumberland County, NC
Nicholas Newton received 100 acres located west of Dry Creek adjoining James Cheney. David Baldwin and William Smith were chain carriers.

161.   1763, Mar 9 -- Land Grant #186 and #344, Cumberland County, NC
Edward Morris received 100 acres located on Cabin Creek. Joseph Murphy and William Lukeus were chain carriers. [Editor's Note: Edward and Sarah Morris deeded to Ephraim Pender 1767]

162.   1763, Mar 10 -- Land Grant #0490, Cumberland County, NC
Francis Tidwell received 100 acres located on Dry Creek adjoining own improvement. William Keys and Luke Whitfield were chain carriers. [Editor's Note: Never granted]

163.   1763, Mar 20 -- Land Grant #189 and #347, Cumberland County, NC
Joseph Murphy received 100 acres located on Fork of Cabin Creek. Edward Morris and William Lukeus were chain carriers. [Editor's Note: Joseph and Valentine Murphy deeded to James Jeffreys, Sr. 1767]

164.   1763, Apr 7-- Land Grant #0494, Cumberland County, NC
William White received 50 acres located east of Wolf Creek. Hugh Johnston and Enoch Spinks were chain carriers. [Editor's Note: Never granted]

165.   1763, Apr 22 -- Land Grant #359, Cumberland County, NC
John Hare received 200 acres located on Wolf Creek.

166.   1763, Apr 22 -- Land Grant #187 and #345, Cumberland County, NC
John Goldman received 200 acres located on Rocky Creek. [Editor's Note: deeded to John Smith 1767 --> John and Frances Smith to Lewis Sowell 1780]

167.   1763, Apr 22 -- Land Grant #188 and #346, Cumberland County, NC
William Garner received 150 acres located on Bear Creek adjoining Michael Heart and including John Goalman's improvement that he bought. Hugh Johnston and Peter

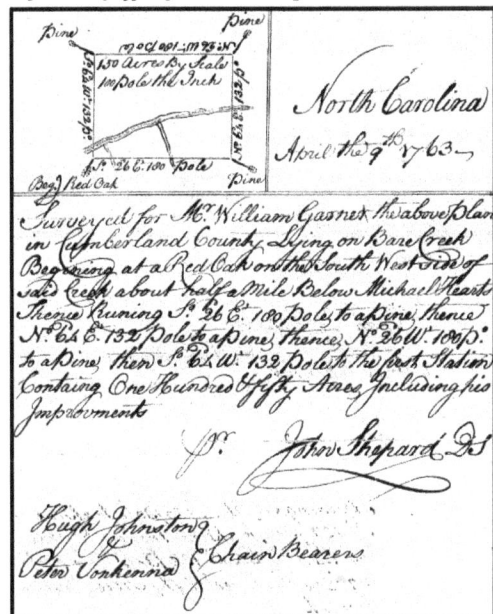

Vonkenna were chain carriers.

168. 1763, Apr 22 -- Land Grant #197 and #355, Cumberland County, NC
Robert Cheek received 300 acres located south of Deep River adjoining **James McCallum.**

169. 1763, Apr 22 -- Land Grant #1586 and #2096, Anson County, NC
John Donahue received 100 acres located west of Cabbin Creek.

170. 1763, Apr 22 -- Land Grant #190 and #348, Cumberland County, NC
John Donahoe received 100 acres located on Bear Creek including **Gunroad Goldman**'s improvement. [*Editor's Note: deeded to **Michael Heart** 1764 --> **Vincent Gardner** 1772*]

171. 1763, May 3 -- 1762 - 1766 Court of Pleas and Quarter Sessions, Orange County, NC Page 30
Road to be opened from Island Ford on Haw River to Childsburg by: **Joseph Kirk, Wm. Copeland Sr., Jon Ricketts, Joseph Copeland, Nathaniel Milton, Benjamin Clemens, Robert Patterson, John Edwards, John Bracey, James Haygood, Christopher Kirksey, William Griffin, Wm. Long, James Craig, Wm. Bynum, James Ballard** and **Wm. Salley**

172. 1763, May 18 -- 1759-1765 Court of Pleas and Quarter Sessions, Cumberland County, NC
Ordered that **Willm. Narrimour** appointed constable from Cranes Creek to McClendons Creek; **Jonathn Ritchison** be appointed constable from McClendons Creek to the upper boundary of this county including all within the Yadkin Road.

173. 1763, May 19 -- 1759-1765 Court of Pleas and Quarter Sessions, Cumberland County, NC
Ordered that constables **Thomas Tucker, Wm. Narrimour** and **Jonatn. Ritchison** make list of taxables for Justice **Thomas Collins**, Esq.

174. 1763, Aug 1 -- Deed Book 2 Page 279, Cumberland County, NC
John Smith and **Sarah Smith** deeded **William Morris** a tract located on a branch of Bear Creek [Wet Creek]. **Wm. Morris, Edward Morris** and **Henry Horn** were witnesses.

175. 1763, Aug 2 -- 1762 - 1766 Court of Pleas and Quarter Sessions, Orange County, NC Page 52
Mourning Milton, daughter of **Robert Milton,** Dec'd. to be committed to the care of Mr. **Robert Cate,** Jr. Bondsman **Thomas Cate.**

176. 1763, Aug 16 -- 1759-1765 Court of Pleas and Quarter Sessions, Cumberland County, NC
Ordered that **Joel McClendol**'s grist mill on McClendons Creek be a public mill.

177. 1763, Aug 18 -- 1759-1765 Court of Pleas and Quarter Sessions, Cumberland County, NC
John Williamson appointed overseer of the road from Buffalo Creek to the Orange County [Chatham or Randolph County] line.

178. 1763, Sep 23 -- Land Grant #876, Cumberland County, NC
Joseph Duckworth Junr. received 195 acres located on Deep River about ½ mile above McLendons Creek adjoining **John Carroll. Joseph Duckworth Senr.** and **John Carroll** were chain carriers. [*Editor's Note: deeded to **John Harden** 1774 --> **Philip Alston** 1778*]

179. 1763, Sep 27 -- Land Grant #472 and #652, Cumberland County, NC
Richard Worrell received 160 acres located on McLendons Creek adjoining **Horser.** [*Editor's Note: deeded to **Patience Barrett** 1765*]

180. 1763, Dec 20 -- Land Grant #446, Cumberland County, NC
George Carringer received 300 acres located on Grassy Creek.

181. 1763, Dec 20 -- Land Grant #448 and #628, Cumberland County, NC

Joel McClendall received 100 acres located on McLendons Creek adjoining his own line and **Hezekiah Horser**. [*Editor's Note: deeded to **Thomas McClendon** 1770 --> **Thomas** and **Luvisa McLendon** deeded to **John Martin** 1775*]

182. 1763, Dec 21 -- Land Grant #450, Cumberland County, NC
Jacob Carringer received 200 acres located west of Deep River adjoining **William Morgan** and **Leonard Hart**.

183. 1763, Dec 21 -- Land Grant #445 and #625, Cumberland County, NC
John Smith received 200 acres located west of Mill Creek adjoining his own line (mill land) and **Donaho**. **John Goldman** and **Edward Morris** were chain carriers. [*Editor's Note: **John (Sandhill)** and **Sarah Smith** deeded to **Richard Tillis** 1765*]

184. 1763, Dec 23 -- Land Grant #456 and #636, Cumberland County, NC
Enoch Spinks received 250 acres located on both sides of Deep River including where **Joseph Morgan** lived. [*Editor's Note: **Enoch** and **Amy Spinks** deeded to **John Gardner** 1764*]

185. 1764, Feb 3 -- Deed Book 2 Page 326, Cumberland County, NC
James Chiney deeded **John Kegill** 120 acres located in the fork of Bear Creek, a place called the Hasel Neck. Patented to **Richd. Caswell** and sold to **James Chiney** 10 May 1760. **Francis Tredwell**, **William Searcy** and **John Chiney** were witnesses.

186. 1764, Feb 13 -- Deed Book 2 Page 323, Cumberland County, NC
William Narrimour deeded **Edward Narrimour** 100 acres located on Lower Little River. **William Mears** and **Nicholas Smith** were witnesses.

187. 1764, Feb 14 -- Deed, Orange County, NC
Harman Husbands deeded **Peter Givet** 250 acres. **Henry Cagle** was a witness.

188. 1764, Feb 20 -- Deed Book 2 Page 321, Cumberland County, NC
John Smith deeded **Isaac Hill** 100 acres located on Buffalo Creek. **Henry Smith**, **Mary Smith** and **William Morgin** were witnesses.

189. 1764, Feb 22 -- 1759-1765 Court of Pleas and Quarter Sessions, Cumberland County, NC
[Deeds] **John Smith** to **Isaac Hill** proven by **Wm. Morgin**
James Cheney to **John Kegell** was proven by **Francis Teedwell**
Mary Cheney, wife of **James Cheney**, Esq. to **John Kegell** for right of dower to 120 acres

190. 1764, Feb 25 -- 1759-1765 Court of Pleas and Quarter Sessions, Cumberland County, NC
Joshua Hencock appointed road overseer in place of **John Overton**.

191.   1764, Mar 24 -- Deed Book 2 Page 352, Cumberland County, NC
Jonathan Evans deeded **Joseph Dunn** 100 acres located on Richland Creek. **William Maultsby** and **Theophilus Evans** were witnesses.

192.   1764, Apr 24 -- Land Grant #478 and #658, Cumberland County, NC
Abel Lee received 300 acres located on both sides of Deep River. [*Editor's Note: Abel and Ann Lee deeded to David Stroud 1771*]

193.   1764, Apr 25 -- Land Grant #482 and #662, Cumberland County, NC
Thomas McClendel received 150 acres located on both sides of McLendons Creek. [*Editor's Note: deeded to James Caddell 1767*]

194.   1764, May 14 -- Deed Book 2 Page 358, Cumberland County, NC
Sterling Carroll and deeded **Gabriel Harden** 80 acres located on the Rocky Ford of Deep River.

195.   1764, May 14 -- Deed Book 2 Page 361, Cumberland County, NC
Edward Narrimour deeded **Nicholas Smith** 100 acres located on Lower Little River. **Wm. Mears** and **Wm. Narrimour** were witnesses.

196.   1764, May 15 -- Deed Book 2 Page 360, Cumberland County, NC
Mary Cheney, wife of **James Cheney**, deeded **John Kigell** her 1/3 dowry right in the 120 acres in the fork of Bear Creek, a place called the Hasel Neck. Purchased by **James Cheney** from **Richard Caswell** and sold by him to **John Kigell** 3 Feb 1764. **Richd. Grove** and **Richd. Stringfield** were witnesses.

197.   1764, May 17 -- Deed Book 2 Page 355, Cumberland County, NC
Enoch Spinks and wife **Amy** deeded **John Gardner** 250 acres located on Deep River including the plantation where **John Gardner** lives. **Richd. Grove** was a witness.

198.   1764, May 18 -- 1759-1765 Court of Pleas and Quarter Sessions, Cumberland County, NC
Ordered that **James Muse** be appointed constable in place of **Jonathin Ritchison**.

199.   1764, May 19 -- 1759-1765 Court of Pleas and Quarter Sessions, Cumberland County, NC
A road to be laid off from **Sandhill Smith**'s to **Joel McClendon**'s mill, thence to Deep River Road about three miles below Dunhams Creek.

200.   1764, Jul 4 -- Land Grant #700, Cumberland County, NC
John Williamson received 100 acres adjoining his own line.

201.   1764, Jul 4 -- Land Grant #616 and #799, Cumberland County, NC
John Overton received 100 acres located on McLendons Creek adjoining **Tomlin**.

202.   1764, Jul 5 -- Land Grant #1430, Cumberland County, NC
David Caygill received 100 acres located on Flat [Flag] Creek about ¼ mile from **John Caygill**'s plantation. [*Editor's Note: David and Catharine Kegle deeded to William Smith 1769 --> Charles Sowel --> Jeremiah Williams, Thomas Williams, James Williams and Bartholomew Dunn deeded to William Williams 1823*]

203.   1764, Jul 6 -- Land Grant #0101, Cumberland County, NC
John Hunsucker received 150 acres located on Deep River adjoining **Stephen Ellis** improvement. [*Editor's Note: Never granted*]

204.   1764, Jul 6 -- Land Grant #0337, Cumberland County, NC
William Morgan received 200 acres located on Wolf Creek adjoining **William White**. [*Editor's Note: Never granted*]

205.   1764, Jul 7 -- Land Grant #499 and #680, Cumberland County, NC
Richard Dunn received 300 acres located on both sides of Wet Creek including the place where he now lives.

206. 1764, Jul 8 -- Land Grant #545, Cumberland County, NC
Leonard Herde [Hart] received 200 acres located on Grassy Creek adjoining **Jacob Keringer** and his own line.

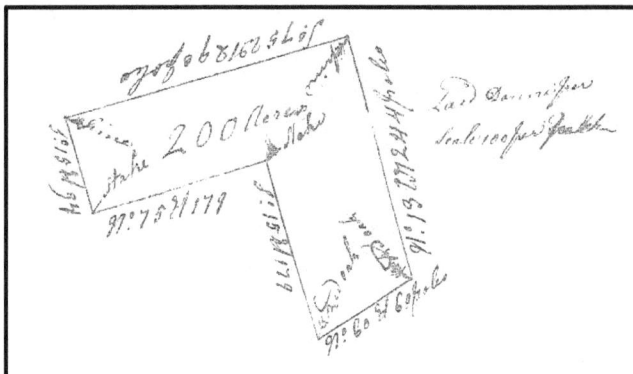

207. 1764, Jul 9 -- Land Grant #500 and #681, Cumberland County, NC
Charles Seal received 150 acres located on both sides of McLendons Creek. [*Editor's Note: deeded to James Muse 1766*]

208. 1764, Aug 4 -- Deed Book 2 Page 439, Cumberland County, NC
John Donahoe deeded **Michael Heart** 100 acres located south of Bear Creek. **Stephen Gilmore** and **Hugh Gilmore** were witnesses.

209. 1764, Aug 7 -- 1762 - 1766 Court of Pleas and Quarter Sessions, Orange County, NC Page 223
Ordered that twelve of the following persons meet and lay out a road from Rowan [current Davidson County/Randolph County] line opposite Fraziers Road to the best and nearest road leading to Cross Creek:
Windsor Pierce, Jeffrey Beck, Christopher Monday, John Needham, John Williamson, James Pittman, James Graves, Ralph Hinwelt, Charles Strange, Solomon Morgain, John Purslay, Peter Funcanon, William Searcey, Henry Smith, Adam Andrews, John Garner, John Lawrence and **Jno. Rodes**

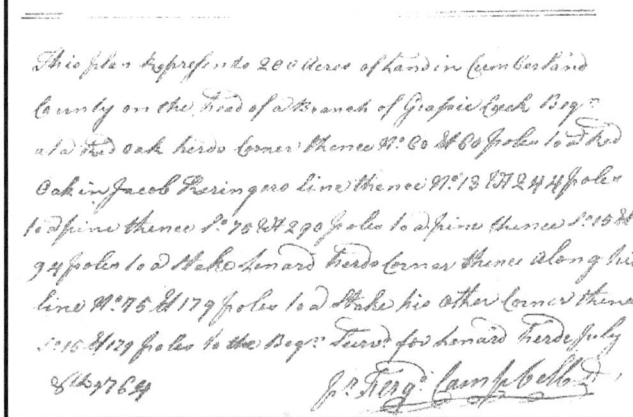

210. 1764, Aug 11 -- Land Grant #1539, Cumberland County, NC
John Brownlow received 150 acres located on Bear Creek about 1/2 mile above the mouth adjoining **John Kagil**. **Jacob Tiem** and **William Manes Junr**. were chain carriers.

211. 1764, Aug 23 -- 1759-1765 Court of Pleas and Quarter Sessions, Cumberland County, NC
A road to be laid off from **Sandhill John Smith**'s to **Joel McClendon**'s mill to Deep River Road about three miles below Dunhams Creek. **Joel McClendon** and **Jacob McClendon** to be overseers.

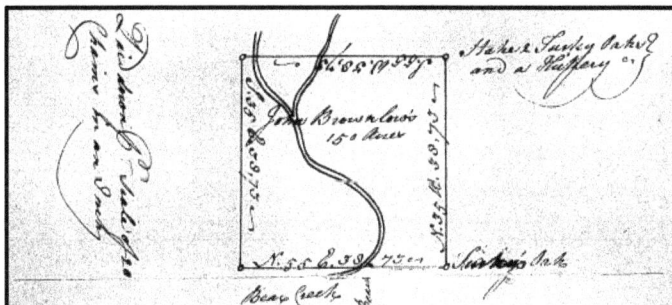

212. 1764, Aug 23 -- 1759-1765 Court of Pleas and Quarter Sessions, Cumberland County, NC
Conner Dowd granted license to keep an ordinary tavern at his dwelling house.

213. 1764, Sep 4 -- Deed Book 2 Page 476, Cumberland County, NC
John Smith (**Sandhill**) and wife **Sarah** deeded **John Stanton** 250 acres located on both sides of Deep River where **Stanton** now lives. **James Cheney** and **William Morris** were witnesses.

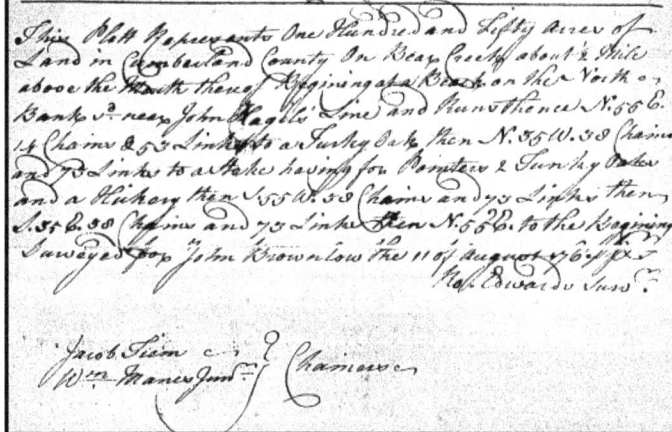

214. 1764, Sep 24 -- Land Grant #513 and #694, Cumberland County, NC

John Dunn received 150 acres located on Richland Creek 2 miles above **Benjamin Dunn**. Jonathan Richeson and **Joseph Dunn** were chain carriers. [*Editor's Note:* **John Walsh** *deeded to* **John Overton** *1769 -->* **Alexr. Morrison** *1773*]

215.   1764, Sep 24 -- Land Grant #517 and #698, Cumberland County, NC
Joseph Dunn received 50 acres located on Richland Creek and the Waggon Road adjoining his own line (formerly **Jonathan Evans**). **John Dunn** and **Jonathan Richeson** were chain carriers.

216.   1764, Nov 9 -- Land Grant #491 and #672, Cumberland County, NC
William Smith received 50 acres located east of Dry Creek. **David Baldwin** and **Nicholas Newton** were chain carriers.

217.   1764, Nov 9 -- Land Grant #493 and #674, Cumberland County, NC
Joseph Morgan received 100 acres located on Cabin Creek including his own improvement. **John Donaho** and **Luke Whitfield** were chain carriers. [*Editor's Note:* **Joseph Morgan** *(of SC) deeded to* **William** *and* **Mary Morgan** *1771 -->* **Ewel Watkins** *1774*]

218.   1764, Nov 9 -- Land Grant #498 and #679, Cumberland County, NC
James Muse received 250 acres located on McLendons Creek.

219.   1764, Nov 16 -- Land Grant #509 and #690, Cumberland County, NC
James Muse received 150 acres located west of McLendons Creek and west of the Cane Patch adjoining his own line.

220.   1764, Nov 21 -- 1759-1765 Court of Pleas and Quarter Sessions, Cumberland County, NC
A road to be laid off from **Sandhill Smith**'s and the following hands were ordered to work: **John Kigel, Wm. Smith Sr., Jno. Goleman, Jno. Smith, Nicholas Smith, Nicholas Nuton, Jacob McClendol, Joel McClendol, Thomas Ward, Jetson Ward, John Weare** and **Wm. Gillit [Killett].**

221.   1764, Nov 21 -- 1759-1765 Court of Pleas and Quarter Sessions, Cumberland County, NC
A road to be laid off from Bear Creek to **Shuffill**'s path to join **Spinx**'s road. **John Williamson** appointed overseer of the jury as follows: **John Williamson, John Gardner, Enox Spinx, Leonard Hart, John Shuffill, Wm. Garner, Abel Lee, Jno. Huntsucker, Wm. Kee, Jno. Kigell, Jas. Johnston** and **Mic. Heart.**

222.   1764, Nov 21 -- 1759-1765 Court of Pleas and Quarter Sessions, Cumberland County, NC
Joshua Handcock appointed road overseer in place of **John Overton.**

223.		1764, Nov 23 -- 1759-1765 Court of Pleas and Quarter Sessions, Cumberland County, NC
A road to be laid off from **Williams'** Mill to the Yadkin Road. **Saml. Jackson** appointed overseer and the following to meet **James Cheney**, Esq. at **Jackson**'s house on the second Saturday in January to qualify: **William Burt, Richd. Burton, Saml. Jackson, Andw. Bates, Henry Williams, John Henry, Natl. Ashley, Malcom Munroe, Wm. Berringtine, Saml. Williams, Joel McClendol** and **John Cox.**

224.		1764, Dec 9 -- Land Grant #494 and #675, Cumberland County, NC
William Morgan received 200 acres located on both sides of Deep River. [*Editor's Note:* **William and Mary Morgan** *deeded 150a to* **Solomon Morgan** *1767 -->* **Soloman Margin** *and* **Mehitable Ludlam** *to* **William Savory** *1771;* **William Morgan** *deeded 50a to* **John Garner** *1767*]

225.		1765, Feb 4 -- Deed Book 2 Page 520, Cumberland County, NC
John Smith (Sandhill) and **Sarah Smith** deeded **Richard Tullos** 200 acres and a mill located on a branch of the Deep River on the Yadkin Road. **James Cheney, David Baldwin** and **James Muse** were witnesses.

226.		1765, Feb 7 -- Deed Book 2 Page 563, Cumberland County, NC
George Blair and **John Johnston** (of Edenton) deeded **Starling Carroll** 400 acres located on Deep River and mouth of Governors Creek being part of the **Governor Gabriel Johnston** four grants bequeathed to **Samuel Johnston** and **John Johnston** who sold his share to **George Blair. James Russell, Elisha Hunter** and **John Carrell** were witnesses.

227.		1765, Feb 7 -- Deed Book 2 Page 595, Cumberland County, NC
George Blair and **John Johnston** (of Edenton) deeded **Joshua Hancock** 150 acres located on Deep River adjoining **David Bartram** being part of the **Governor Gabriel Johnston** four grants bequeathed to **Samuel Johnston** and **John Johnston** who sold his share to **George Blair. Elisha Hunter** and **Conner Dowd** were witnesses.

228.		1765, Feb 7 -- Deed Book 2 Page 612, Cumberland County, NC
George Blair and **John Johnston** (of Edenton) deeded **Cornelius Tison** 383 acres located on Deep River and [Chatham] County line being part of the **Governor Gabriel Johnston** four grants bequeathed to **Samuel Johnston** and **John Johnston** who sold his share to **George Blair. James Barns, Isaac Barns** and **Powell Benbow** were witnesses.

229.		1765, Feb 8 -- Deed Book 2 Page 613, Cumberland County, NC
George Blair and **John Johnston** (of Edenton) deeded **Elisha Hunter** 122 acres located on Deep River adjoining **Ainsworth** being part of the **Governor Gabriel Johnston** four grants bequeathed to **Samuel Johnston** and **John Johnston** who sold his share to **George Blair. Conner Dowd** and **John Hunnicut** were witnesses.

230.		1765, Feb 9 -- Deed Book 2 Page 504, Cumberland County, NC
George Blair and **John Johnston** (of Edenton) deeded **Powell Benbow** 450 acres located Deep River and the [Chatham] County line adjoining **Cornelius Tyson, William Hall** being part of the **Governor Gabriel Johnston** four grants bequeathed to **Samuel Johnston** and **John Johnston** who sold his share to **George Blair. Cornelius Tison** and **Conner Dowd** were witnesses.

231.		1765, Feb 9 -- Deed Book 2 Page 611, Cumberland County, NC
George Blair and **John Johnston** (of Edenton) deeded **James Barns** 663 acres adjoining **Benbow** being part of the **Governor Gabriel Johnston** four grants bequeathed to **Samuel Johnston** and **John Johnston** who sold his share to **George Blair. James Russell, Cornelius Tison** and **Thos. Smith** were witnesses.

232.		1765, Feb 19 -- 1759-1765 Court of Pleas and Quarter Sessions, Cumberland County, NC
Jotn. Ritchison served jury duty

233.		1765, Feb 20 -- 1759-1765 Court of Pleas and Quarter Sessions, Cumberland County, NC
James Muse ordered to return two negroes to **Susannah Lawson** that he had taken from her unlawfully.

234.		1765, Feb 22 -- 1759-1765 Court of Pleas and Quarter Sessions, Cumberland County, NC
James Muse recorded his brand and mark.

235. 1765, Feb 23 -- 1759-1765 Court of Pleas and Quarter Sessions, Cumberland County, NC **Joseph Carr** appointed road overseer in place of **James Muse**.

236. 1765, Feb 24 -- Deed Book 2 Page 522, Cumberland County, NC **Richard Worrill** deeded **Patience Barret** 160 acres located on both sides of Buck Creek adjoining **Horser**, **Thomas Matthews** and **Richard Worrill**. **Jacob McClendon**, **Saml. Williams** and **Joel McClendon** were witnesses.

237. 1765, Apr-Apr 1769 -- Deed Book 7, Dobbs County, NC Page 138 - **Jesse Ritter** to **Drury Alldridge**

238. 1765, Apr 23 -- Deed Book 2 Page 544, Cumberland County, NC **James Muse** secured a mortgage with **John Overton** for the following properties: 2 plantations on McLendons Creek in 2 surveys; 150 acres that was patented to **Farqd. Campbell** including **Jonathan Rittenhouse**'s improvement; tract of land where **James Muse** now lives, patented to **Muse**; 150 acres on on Killetts Creek including mouth of Mill Swamp, patented to **Charles Seal**; 150 acres on upper plantation of the creek; 200 acres on Killetts Creek patented to **James Muse**. Security was negro girl named **Pinnillipe**. **Joseph Stubbs** and **John Carroll** were witnesses. Paid Sep 24, 1767.

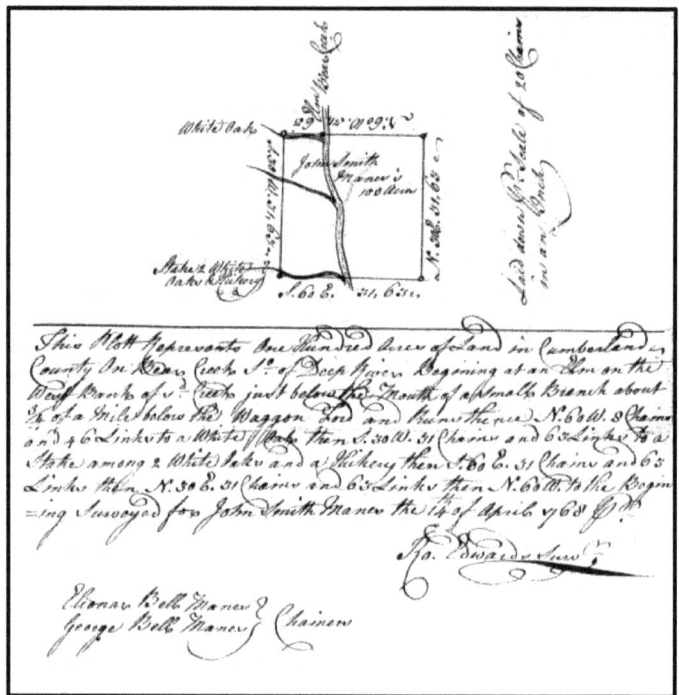

239. 1765, Apr 14 -- Land Grant #0424, Cumberland County, NC **John Smith Maness** received 100 acres located on Bear Creek. **Eleonar Bell Maness** and **George Bell Maness** were chain carriers. [*Editor's Note: Never granted*]

240. 1765, Apr 23 -- Land Grant #533 and #714, Cumberland County, NC **John Overton** received 100 acres located on both sides of Governors Creek and Wolf Branch including mouth of Benis/Bones Lock Branch.

241. 1765, Apr 24 -- Land Grant #532 and #713, Cumberland County, NC **John Overton** received 200 acres located on both sides of Governors Creek including **Hartwil Hunicut's** improvement.

242. 1765, May -- 1762 - 1766 Court of Pleas and Quarter Sessions, Orange County, NC Page 360 Orderd that **Windsor Pierce** be appointed Constable in the room of **John Carson**.

243. 1765, May 11 -- Deed Book 2 Page 521, Cumberland County, NC **John Smith** (**Sandhill**) and **Sarah Smith** deeded

Richard Tullos 200 acres located west of Mill Creek adjoining his old survey called the Mill land near **Donahoe**'s line. **James Cheney** and **James Muse** were witnesses.

244.　　　1765, May 21/22 -- 1759-1765 Court of Pleas and Quarter Sessions, Cumberland County, NC
Wm. Manus was appointed constable for Capt. Cheney's District. **Leaven Ainsworth** appointed constable for Capt. Carroll's District.

245.　　　1765, May 22 -- 1759-1765 Court of Pleas and Quarter Sessions, Cumberland County, NC
John Morgin was appointed road overseer in place of **John Smith**.

246.　　　1765, May 24 -- 1759-1765 Court of Pleas and Quarter Sessions, Cumberland County, NC
Wm. Smith appointed overseer in place of **Joel McClendon** and **Thos. Wadsworth** appointed overseer in place of **Jacob McClendon**.

247.　　　1765, May 24 -- 1759-1765 Court of Pleas and Quarter Sessions, Cumberland County, NC
Wm. Manus listed among constables being fined. **Wm. Manus** ordered to report list of taxables to magistrate **Richard Lyon**, Esq.

248.　　　1765, Jun 2 -- Land Grant #564 and #745, Cumberland County, NC
Farquard Campbell received 100 acres located on both sides of McLendons Creek adjoining **Jerom Miller**.

249.　　　1765, Jun 19 -- Land Grant #555 and #736, Cumberland County, NC
Cornelius Tyson received 150 acres located on north of Deep River adjoining Lord Granville [line]. [*Editor's Note: deeded to **Robert Cheek** 1767*]

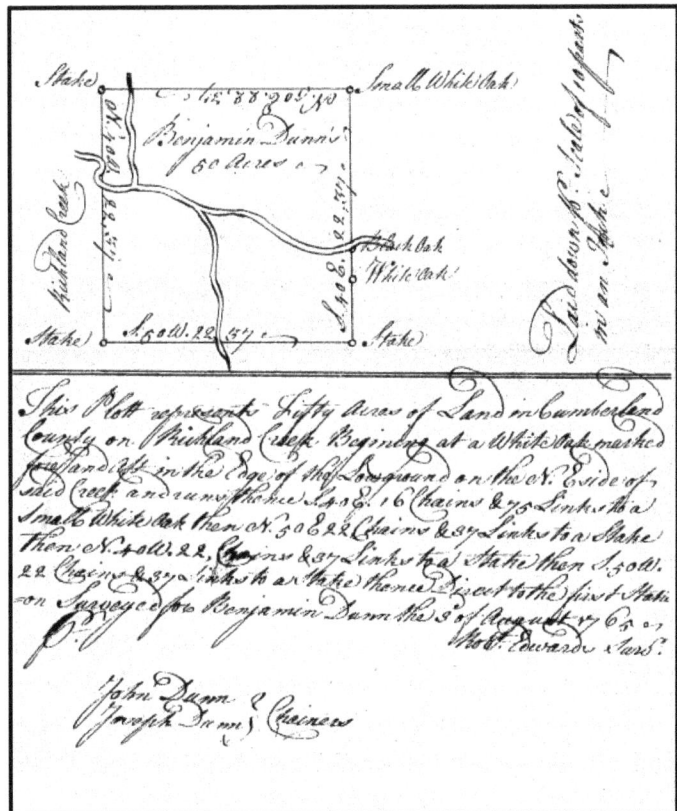

250.　　　1765, Aug 3 -- Land Grant #561 and #742, Cumberland County, NC
Benjamin Dunn received 50 acres located northeast of Richland Creek adjoining his own line and **Farquard Campbell**. **John Dunn** and **Joseph Dunn** were chain carriers. [*Editor's Note: **Benjamin** and wife **Sarah Dunn** deeded to **John Stevens** 1768*]

251.　　　1765, Aug 5 -- Land Grant #1429, Cumberland County, NC
Jesse Pearce received 50 acres located on McCallums Fork of Richland Creek adjoining **Joseph Dunn**. **John Keadle** and **Joseph Dunn** were chain carriers. [*Editor's Note: deeded to **Michael Hunsucker** 1770 --> **John Brownlow** 1772*]

252.　　　1765, Aug 6 -- Land Grant #1449, Cumberland County, NC
Henry Atkinson received 100 acres located on Richland Creek adjoining **Aaron Burleson**, his own line and **John Wier**. **Richard Upton** and **Thos. Atkinson** were chain carriers. [*Editor's Note: deeded to **Benjamin Atkinson** 1769 --> **Joseph Cheston** 1770 --> **Kenneth Campbell** to **Alexr. MacLeod** 1774*]

253.　　　1765, Aug 9 -- Deed Book 2 Page 561, Cumberland County, NC
William Narremore deeded **George Folds** 100 acres located in the Fork of Lower Little River including **Elizabeth Mins'** plantation. **Wm. Mears** and **Nicholas Smith** were witnesses.

254.　　　1765, Aug 9 -- Land Grant #0465, Cumberland County, NC
Richard Upton received 100 acres located on Locust Branch of Richland Creek. **James Smith** and **Joseph Dunn** were chain carriers. [*Editor's Note: Never granted*]

255.   1765, Aug 13 -- 1762 - 1766 Court of Pleas and Quarter Sessions, Orange County, NC Page 409
Ordered that the following lay out a road from the Redfields Ford on Haw River to New Hope Chapel: **Nathaniel Milton**, **Luke Bynum**, **Robert Cellars**, **James Cellars**, **Christopher Kirksey**, **Anson Milton**, **Robert Patterson**, **William Griffin**, **Vachel Clarke**, **James Rigsby**, **Thomas Durham**, **John Price**, **James Hogwood**, **Isaac Kirksey** and **John Gunter**.

256.   1765, Aug 13 -- Deed, Orange County, NC
Harmon Husband deeded **Luke Smith** 640 acres. **John Cagle** was a witness.

257.   1765, Aug 22 -- 1759-1765 Court of Pleas and Quarter Sessions, Cumberland County, NC
Wm. Manus, constable, ordered to attend May court.

258.   1765, Sep 28 -- Deed Book 3 Page 71, Cumberland County, NC
Benjamin Dumas and wife **Jemima** deeded **Jacob McClendon** 200 acres located on Buck Creek. Patented to **Jemima McClendon** 1758. **Joel McClendon** and **James McClendon** were witnesses.

259.   1765, Oct 2 -- Deed Book 3 Page 64, Cumberland County, NC
John Gilmore deeded **Thomas Maples** 150 acres located on Lower Little River three miles above Crane's Settlement. **Thomas Tucker** and **William Manes** were witnesses.

260.   1765, Oct 4 -- Deed Book 3 Page 166, Cumberland County, NC
John Goolman deeded **John Smith** 200 acres on a branch of Bear Creek called Rocky Creek. **John Jeffreys**, **William Spencer** and **Thomas Ward** were witnesses.

261.   1765, Oct 10 -- Deed Book 2 Page 606, Cumberland County, NC
Cornelius Tyson deeded **Robert Cheek** 150 acres located north of Deep River at Island Ford in two tracts [1] patent to **John Tison** 1748 and sold to **Cornelius Tyson** [2] patent to **Cornelius Tyson** 1762. **Conner Dowd**, **Randal Cheek** and **Charles Shearin** were witnesses.

262.   1765, Oct 30 -- Land Grant #538 and 719, Cumberland County, NC
Michael Hart received 200 acres located on Fork of Bear Creek known as Reedy Branch adjoining the Earl of Granville's line. [*Editor's Note: **Michael** and **Barbara Hart** deeded to **John Needham** 1767 --> **John** and **Susannah Needham** to **Henry Caster** 1771*]

263.   1765, Oct 30 -- Land Grant #552 and #733, Cumberland County, NC
Jerom Miller received 100 acres located on both sides of McLendons Creek. [Editor's Note: deeded to **William Killett** 1766]

264.   1765, Oct 30 -- Land Grant #544, #725 and #0488, Cumberland County, NC
Cornelius Tyson received 400 acres located on both sides of Deep River adjoining **Howel Brewer** and **Wm. Powell**. [*Editor's Note: **Cornelius Tyson** deeded 100 acre at Cane Patch to **John Thornton Senr.** 1774; deeded 300a to **John Carrel** 1774*]

265.   1765, Oct 30 -- Land Grant #563 and 744, Cumberland County, NC
Hartwell Hunnicutt received 250 acres located on McLendons Creek adjoining **Overton** [*Editor's Note: deeded to **John Overton** 1766 --> **Elijah Bettis** 1769*]

266.   1765, Oct 30 -- Land Grant #574 and #755, Cumberland County, NC
Michael Hart received 200 acres located on Fork of Bear Creek. [*Editor's Note: deeded to **Vincent Garner** 1772 --> **William Wright** 1774*]

267.   1765, Oct 30 -- Land Grant #575 and 756, Cumberland County, NC
Jacob McClendel received 100 acres located on both sides of Richland Creek adjoining **Benjamin Dunn**. [*Editor's Note: deeded to **William Cain** 1766*]

268.   1765, Oct 30 -- Deed Book 2 Page 579, Cumberland County, NC
Thos. Matthews Sr. and wife **Mary** deeded **Thomas Matthews Jr.** 200 acres located on McLendons Creek. **Stephn. Gilmore** and **Jno. Matthews** were witnesses.

269. 1766, Apr 10 -- Land Grant #1460, Cumberland County, NC
William Maness received 200 acres located on Bear Creek below the Waggon Road. **John Smith Maness** and **Eleanor Bell Maness** were chain carriers. [*Editor's Note: Nicholas Nall* built a grist mill on this land in 1788 where the Cross Creek to Salem Road crossed Bear Creek. It was known as Carter's Mill from the 1850's to early 1900's.]

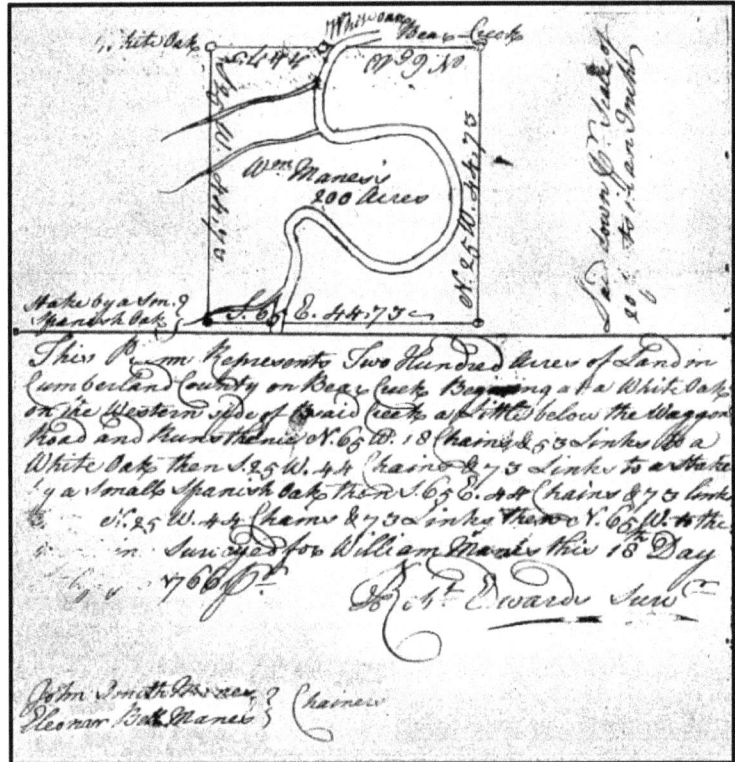

270. 1766, Apr 12 -- Land Grant #1431, Cumberland County, NC
John Madlin received 100 acres located on Richland Creek adjoining **Joseph Dunn**, **Wier** and **Henry Atkinson**. **John Dunn** and **John Keadle** were chain carriers. [*Editor's Note: deeded to Joseph Dunn 1769*]

271. 1766, Apr 12 -- Land Grant #1456, Cumberland County, NC
Joseph Dunn received 50 acres located on McCallums Fork of Richland Creek adjoining **Jesse Pearce**. **John Dunn** and **Jno. Keadle** were chain carriers.

272. 1766, Apr 15 -- Land Grant #1455, Cumberland County, NC
James Muse received 250 acres located on Killetts Creek adjoining his own line. **Jacob McClendall** and **John Howel** were chain carriers. [*Editor's Note: deeded to John Howell 1769*]

273. 1766, Apr 16 -- Land Grant #1490, Cumberland County, NC
John Williamson received 100 acres located on Grassy Creek adjoining his own line. **Leonard Hart** and **Wm. Williamson** were chain carriers.

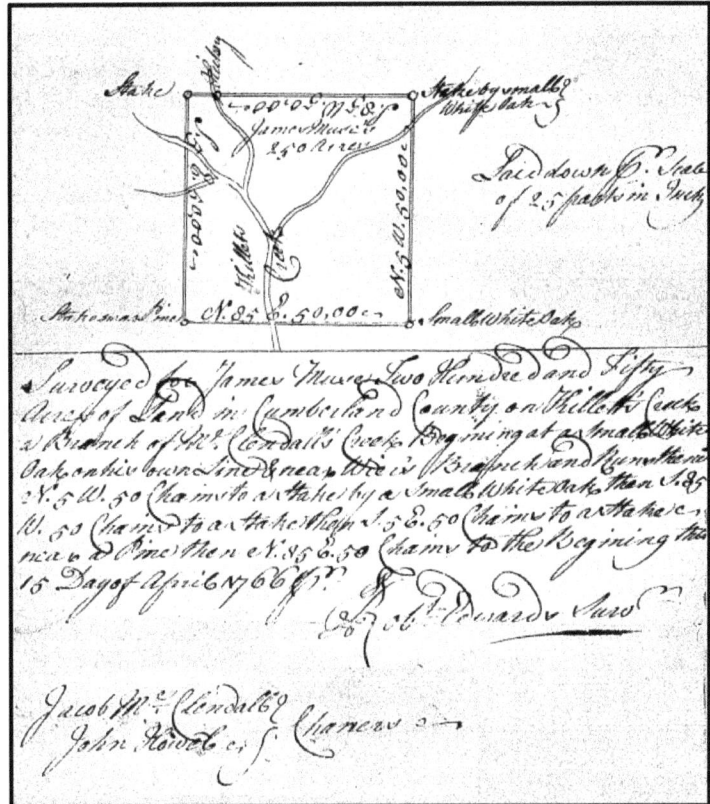

274. 1766, Apr 17 -- Land Grant #771, Cumberland County, NC
Lewis Sowell received 100 acres located between Dry and Horse Creek. **Robt. Edwards** and **Saml. Sewell** were chain carriers.

275. 1766, Apr 19 -- Land Grant #1484, Cumberland County, NC
John Overton received 250 acres located on McLendons Creek adjoining **Widow Dickerson**. **Robt. Edwards** and **Wm. Dickerson** were chain carriers.

276. 1766, May 11 -- Land Grant #1450, Cumberland County, NC
Owen Carpenter received 200 acres located on Wolf Creek adjoining **John Shuffel**. **John Williams**[on] and **Owen Carpenter** were chain carriers. [*Editor's Note: Owen and Caterin Carpenter deeded to John Sheffield 1771*]

277. 1766, Jul 10 -- Deed Book 3 Page 59, Cumberland County, NC

Cornelius Tyson deeded **Conner Dowd** 83 acres located on Deep River and [Chatham] County line being part of the **Governor Gabriel Johnston** four grants bequeathed to **Samuel Johnston** and **John Johnston** who sold his share to **George Blair** who sold to **Cornelius Tyson**. **Richard Lyon** and **John Carroll** were witnesses.

278.   1766, Jul 10 -- Deed Book 3 Page 61, Cumberland County, NC
Powell Benbow deeded **Conner Dowd** 250 acres being part of the **Governor Gabriel Johnston** four grants bequeathed to **Samuel Johnston** and **John Johnston** who sold his share to **George Blair** who sold to **Powell Benbow**. **Richard Lyon** and **William Tompson** were witnesses.

279.   1766, Jul 21 -- Deed Book 3 Page 30, Cumberland County, NC
John and **Sarah Overton** deeded **Frederick Gregg** and **Richard Lyon** 200 acres located on both sides of Governors Creek including **Hartwell Hunnicut's** improvement. Granted to **Overton** 30 Oct 1765. **Conner Dowd** and **Hartwell Hunnicut** were witnesses.

280.   1766, Jul 21 -- Deed Book 3 Page 31, Cumberland County, NC
Hartwell Hunnicut deeded **John Overton** 250 acres located on McLendons Creek adjoining **Overton**. **Conner Dowd** and **Cornelius Tison** were witnesses.

281.   1766, Aug 17 -- Deed Book 3 Page 35, Cumberland County, NC
Andrew and **Mary Killet** deeded **Frances Stripling** 200 acres located west of Deep River and drains of McLendons Creek. **William Boyuss**, **Walter Kickson** and **William Killet** were witnesses.

282.   1766, Aug 19 -- Deed Book 3 Page 27, Cumberland County, NC
Charles Seale deeded **James Muse** 150 acres located on both sides of McLendons Creek. **Richard Grove** and **William Seale** were witnesses.

283.   1766, Sep 23 -- Land Grant #579 and 760, Cumberland County, NC
James Muse received 300 acres located on McLendons Creek adjoining **William Killett** and **John Wear**. [*Editor's Note: deeded 100 acres to* **William Mears** *1767 adj* **George Feagan, Francis Stripling, John Wears** *-->* **James Muse** *1772 --> 100 acres to* **Donald McDonald** *1772*]

284.   1766, Sep 23 -- Deed Book 3 Page 111, Cumberland County, NC
Jerome Miller (of Anson County) deeded **William Killet** 100 acres located on both sides of McLendons Creek. **John Howell**, **William Miller** and **Robert Miller** were witnesses.

285.   1766, Sep 26 -- Land Grant #785, Cumberland County, NC
Henry Atkinson received 189 acres located on Richland Creek adjoining **James Mainyard** and his own line.

286.   1766, Sep 26 -- Land Grant #786, Cumberland County, NC
Henry Atkinson received 75 acres located on Richland Creek adjoining **Jonathan Evans** and **James Mainyard**. [*Editor's Note: deeded to* **Joseph Kerr** *1770 -->* **Alexander McRae** *1775*]

287.   1766, Sep 26 -- Land Grant #597 and #778, Cumberland County, NC
Jonathan Evans received 100 acres located on McCallums Fork of Richland Creek adjoining **Pearce** and **Joseph Dunn**. [*Editor's Note: deeded to* **George Evans** *1768 -->* **Theophilis Evans** *deeded to* **Donald McRae** *1784*]

288.   1766, Sep 26 -- Land Grant #599 and #780, Cumberland County, NC
Solomon Morgan received 100 acres located on Buffalo Creek at Honey Ridge and near the Richlands.

289.   1766, Sep 26 -- Land Grant #604 and #787, Cumberland County, NC
William Richardson received 200 acres located on both sides of Buffalo Creek. [*Editor's Note:* **William Richardson, Sr.** *deeded to* **Drury Richardson** *1768*]

290.   1766, Sep 29 -- Will, Cumberland County, NC
Will of **Henry Shamborger**, Dec'd. Heirs: daughter **Christina**, son **Peter Shamborger**, Executor: son **Peter**

Shamborger. Witnesses: **Jacob Laudermilk**, **Maria Elisabeth Garner** and **William Garner**. Proven May 1767. [*Editor's Note: written in German and English. German "HS" mark below*]

291.　　　1766, Nov 15 -- Deed Book 3 Page 53, Cumberland County, NC
James Barns deeded **Jacob Barns** 350 acres located on Deep River and [Chatham] County line being part of the **Governor Gabriel Johnston** four grants bequeathed to **Samuel Johnston** and **John Johnston** who sold his share to **George Blair** who sold to **James Barns**. **Thomas Hill** and **James Russell** were witnesses.

292.　　　1766, Nov 15 -- Deed Book 3 Page 92, Cumberland County, NC
Sterling Carroll deeded **James Russell** 100 acres located on Deep River being part of the **Governor Gabriel Johnston** four grants bequeathed to **Samuel Johnston** and **John Johnston** who sold his share to **George Blair** who sold to **Sterling Carroll**. **McLearin** and **Doud** were witnesses.

293.　　　1766, Nov 18 -- Deed Book 3 Page 74, Cumberland County, NC
Jacob McClendon deeded **William Cain** 100 acres located on both sides of Richland Creek adjoining **Benjamin Dumas'** plantation. Patented to **Jacob McClendon** 1765. **Stephen Gilmore** and **John Dobbin** were witnesses.

294.　　　1766, Dec 2 -- Deed Book 3 Page 119, Cumberland County, NC
John Shearin (of Bute County) bequeaths his son **Charles Shearin** 200 acres located north of Deep River at the mouth of a creek. Deed from **Cornelius Tyson** to **Shearin**. **William Tison**, **Cornelius Tison** and **Conner Dowd** were witnesses.

295.　　　1767 -- Tax List, Cumberland County, NC [selected residents]
Henry Atkinson 2 white polls; **Powell Benbow** 1 white poll; **James Barnes** 1 white poll 1 black poll; **Jacob Barnes** 2 white polls; **Elijah Bettis** 1 white poll 1 black poll; **Lenierer Brewer** 3 white polls; **Nehemiah Brewer** 1 white poll; **John Brownloe** 1 white poll 1 mulatto 1 black poll; *James Caddell 2 white polls; Owen Carpenter 1 white poll; Sterling Carrol 2 white poll; John Carrol 2 white poll 1 black poll; Robert Cheek 1 white poll; Joseph Chason 1 white poll; James Collings 1 white poll; Edward Cox 3 white poll;* **Francis Didwell [Tidwell]** 1 white poll; **Thomas Dunaho** 3 white polls; **Connor Dowd** 4 white poll 2 black poll; **Joseph Duck** 1 white poll; **Joseph Dunn** 1 white poll and 3 black polls; **John**

Dunn 2 white polls; **Jacob Dunn** 1 white poll; **Benjn. Dunn** 1 white poll; **William Dunn** 4 white polls; **Jonathan Evans** 2 white poll 5 black poll; **Edward Fagan** 1 white poll; **George Fagan** 2 white polls and 1 black poll; **John Garner** 2 white poll 2 black poll; **John Hincock** 3 white polls; **John Hincock** 1 white poll; **Leonard Harte** 2 white polls; **Michl. Hart** 2 white polls; **Isaac Hill** 1 white poll and 1 black poll; **James Hill** 1 white poll and 1 black poll; **Hartwell Hunnicutt** 1 white poll; **John Hunnicutt** 1 white poll; **Jacob Huffman** 1 white poll; **Abraham Hunsuker** 3 white polls; **John Hunsuker** 3 white polls; **James Jeffry** 3 white polls; **William Killet** 1 white poll; **John Keagel** 1 white poll and 1 black poll; **Leonard Keagel** 1 white poll; **Henry Keagel** 1 white poll; **John Keys** 1 white poll; **William Keys** 2 white polls; **David Lawson** 1 white poll; **Thomas McClendon** 1 white poll 1 black poll; **James Muse** 1 white poll 1 black poll; **Francis McClendon** 2 white polls and 7 black polls; **Joel McClendel** 1 white poll and 3 black polls; **Jacob McClendel** 2 white polls and 1 black poll; **Francis McClendon** 1 white poll; **William Menus** 1 white poll; **William Menus Jun.** 1 white poll; **John Morgan** 1 white poll; **James Morgan** 1 white poll; **William Morgan** 2 white polls; **George Morgan** 1 white poll; **Nicholas Nudon** 1 white poll; **John Overton** 1 white poll 6 black poll; **John Phillips** 1 white poll; **John Phillips Senr.** 1 white poll; **William Richardson** 2 white polls; **Lambert Reed** 1 white poll; **Drury Richeson** 1 white poll; **Charles Seale** 1 white poll; **Charles Shearing** 2 white poll; **Thomas Seale** 1 white poll; **William Seal** 2 white poll; **Frances Stribling** 1 white poll 2 black poll; **John Shuffield** 2 white polls; **William Shuffield** 1 white poll; **John Smith** 1 white poll; **Nathaniel Smith** 1 white poll; **Nicholas Smith** 3 white polls; **William Smith** 1 white poll; **William Smith Jr.** 1 white poll; **James Stevens** 1 white poll; **Cornelius Tyson** 3 white poll; **John Trap** 1 white poll; **Richard Tillis** 1 white poll; **Richd. Upton** 1 white poll; **John Wadsworth** 1 white poll 1 black poll; **Thomas Wadsworth** 2 white poll; **James Wadsworth** 1 white poll; **Jason Wadsworth** 1 white poll; **John Williamson** 3 white polls; **Christopher Yew** 1 white poll.

1747-1847 Map of Moore County by Rassie E. Wicker

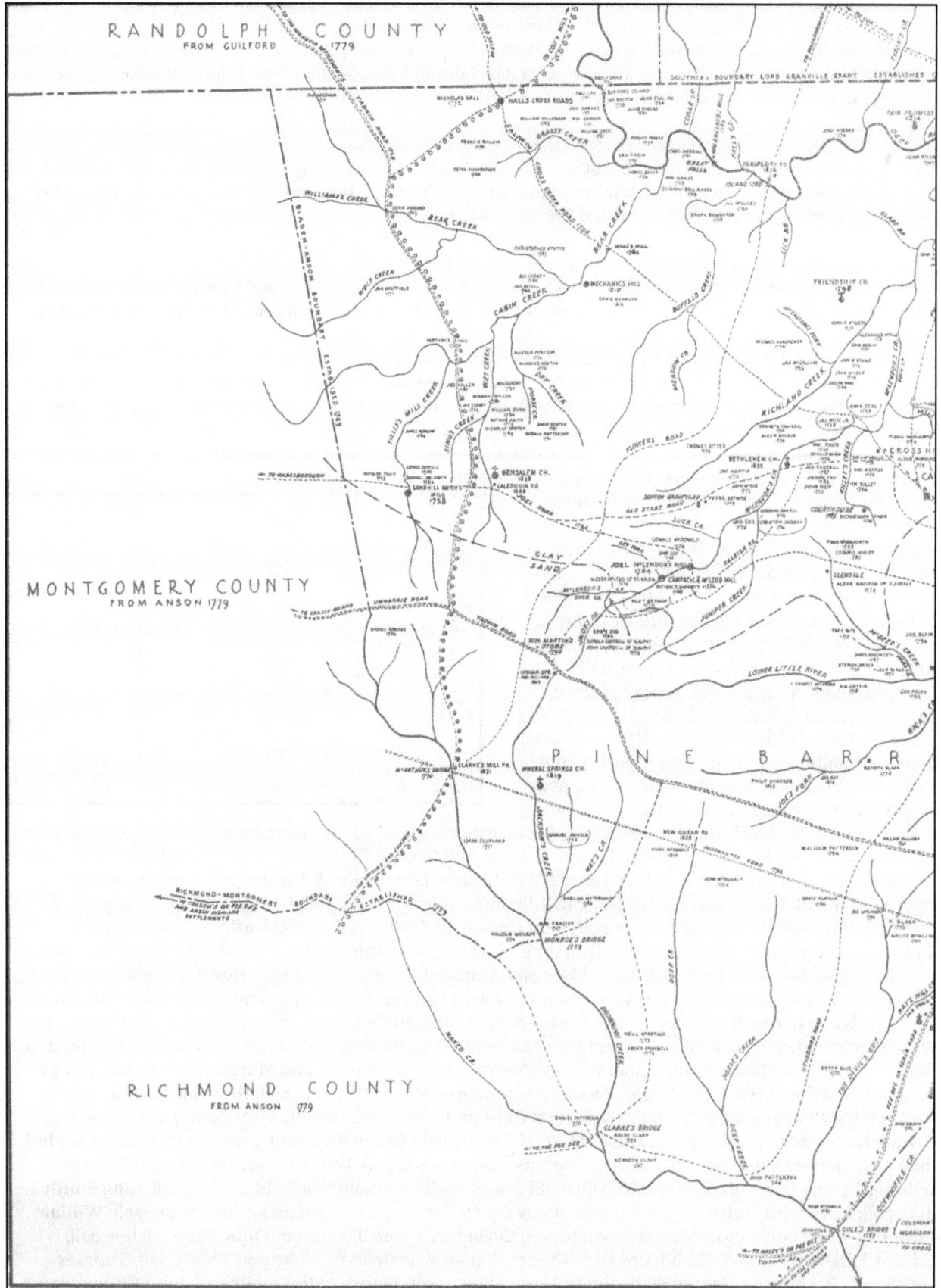

MAP OF THE REGION OF

MOORE COUNTY
1747 TO 1847

SHOWING STREAM NAMES & ROAD LOCATIONS

SCALE
MILES

COMPILED & DRAWN BY R. E. WICKER IN 1956

MILITARY MOVEMENTS 1776 - 1781

LT. COL. DONALD McDONALD	FEB. 1776	
GEN. HORATIO GATES	JUL. 1780	
LORD CORNWALLIS	MAR. 1781	
'LIGHTHORSE HARRY' LEE	MAR. 1781	
BARON DEKALB	JUN. 1780	

296.   1767, Jan 14 -- Deed Book 3 Page 142, Cumberland County, NC
Sterling Carroll deeded **John Carroll** 200 acres located south of Deep River at mouth of Buck Creek. **John Hunnicut** and **Randolph Hunnicut** were witnesses.

297.   1767, Jan 27 -- Deed Book 3 Page 166, Cumberland County, NC
Edward Scarborough deeded **John Rasberry** 150 acres located on Richland Creek. Patented to **Scarborough** 1759. **Jacob McClendon**, **Joseph Rasberry** and **Alexander Shepherd Jr.** were witnesses.

298.   1767, Feb 6 -- Deed Book 3 Page 167, Cumberland County, NC
Cornelius Tyson deeded **Robert Cheek** 150 acres located north of Deep River at Lord Granville's line. **John Carroll** and **Conner Dowd** were witnesses.

299.   1767, Apr 4 -- Land Grant #1441, Cumberland County, NC
James Muse received 200 acres located on McLendons Creek on the land ridge ½ mile below mouth of Mill Creek [Mill Swamp]. **James Muse** and **Robt**. **Edwards** were chain carriers. [*Editor's Note: deeded to* **Jacob Duckworth** *1771*]

300.   1767, Apr 4 -- Cane Creek [Quaker] Meeting Women's Minutes Page 54, Alamance County, NC
Ruth Dunn produced a certificate for herself and two daughters, **Sarah** and **Ann**, from Dunn's Creek monthly meeting and was accepted.

301.   1767, Apr 11 -- Cane Creek [Quaker] Meeting Marriages Vol. 1 Page 39, Alamance County, NC
James Barnes of Cumberland County and **Sarah Dunn** of Cumberland County were married at the Barnes Meeting House on Deep River in Cumberland County. **Jeremiah Barnes**, **Jonathan Barnes**, **Thomas Smith**, **Mary Barnes**, **Richard Dunn**, **Joseph Dunn**, **Ruth Dunn**, **John Jones**, **Cornelius Tison**, **Jane Tison**, **Abigail Pike** and **Eve Crafford** were present and served as witnesses.

302.   1767, Apr 22 -- Land Grant #619, Cumberland County, NC
John Sheffield received 200 acres located north of Wolf Creek adjoining **Owen Carpenter**.

303.   1767, May 2 -- Deed Book 3 Page 116, Cumberland County, NC
Thomas Minard and wife **Mary** deeded **Joseph Carr** 200 acres located west of Richland Creek. **William Seale** and **James Muse** were witnesses.

304.   1767, May 18 -- Deed Book 3 Page 113, Cumberland County, NC
William Gilmore deeded **Nicholas Smith** 100 acres located on a branch of Cranes Creek. **William Mears** and **Thomas Collins** were witnesses.

305.   1767, Jun 16 -- Deed Book 3 Page 137, Cumberland County, NC
John Donahoe deeded **Joseph Hough** 500 acres located on both sides of the Yadkin Road. Patented 24 Apr 1754. **Samuel Williams**, **Jacob McClendon Jr**. and **Sampson Williams** were witnesses.

306.   1767, Jun 27 -- Deed Book 3 Page 124, Cumberland County, NC
William Morgan and wife **Mary** deeded **Solomon Morgan** 150 acres located on Deep River. **Owen Carpenter** and **John Garner** were witnesses.

307.   1767, Jun 27 -- Deed Book 3 Page 124, Cumberland County, NC
William Morgan and wife **Mary** deeded **John Garner** 50 acres located on Deep River. **Owen Carpenter** and **Solomon Morgan** were witnesses.

308.   1767, Jul 3 -- Deed Book 3 Page 131, Cumberland County, NC
Thomas McClendon deeded **James Caddell** 150 acres located on both sides of McLendons Creek. Witnesses were **William Seale**, **George Feagin Sr**. and **Edward Feagin**.

309.   1767, Jul 22 -- Land Grant #1479, Cumberland County, NC
Elisha Hunter received 100 acres located north of Deep River adjoining **James Barnes** and **Jacob Barnes**. **Jacob Barnes** and **Joseph Cheston** were chain carriers. [*Editor's Note: deeded to **James McDonald** 1773 --> **James Collens** 1783 --> **Thomas Tyson** 1783*]

310.   1767, Jul 22 -- Land Grant #1488, Cumberland County, NC
Robert Cheek received 25 acres located north of Deep River on Tyson Creek including **Joshua Pain**'s improvement. **Robt. Cheek** and **Robt. Edwards** were chain arriers.

311.   1767, Jul 23 -- Land Grant #1514, Cumberland County, NC
John May Junr. received 200 acres located on Deep River. **John May Junr.** and **Charles Shearing** were chain carriers. [*Editor's Note: deeded to **Frederick Gregg** and **Richard Lyon** 1769*]

312.   1767, Jul 23 -- Land Grant #1517, Cumberland County, NC
Cornelius Tyson received 144 acres located on Deep River adjoining **John May** and **Zachariah Green**. **John May**, **Charles Shearing**, **Presley Wrenn** and **Ro. Edwards** were chain carriers. [*Editor's Note: deeded to **Frederick Gregg** and **Richard Lyon** 1769*]

313.   1767, Aug 9 -- Land Grant #1491 and 0489, Cumberland County, NC
Francis Tedwell received 200 acres located between Dry Creek and Horse Creek. **Thomas Key** and **Samuel Tedwell** were chain carriers.

314.   1767, Aug 10 -- Deed Book 3 Page 138, Cumberland County, NC
Howel Brewer (of Orange County) deeded **John May** 200 acres located northwest of Deep River above the mouth of Tices Creek. Patent to Brewer 1754. **Jacob Rogers** and **Thomas** [illegible] were witnesses.

315.   1767, Aug 10 -- Land Grant #1497, Cumberland County, NC
Richard Grove received 100 acres located on Wet Creek about a mile above the mouth. **Thomas Key** and **Samuel Tidwell** were chain carriers.

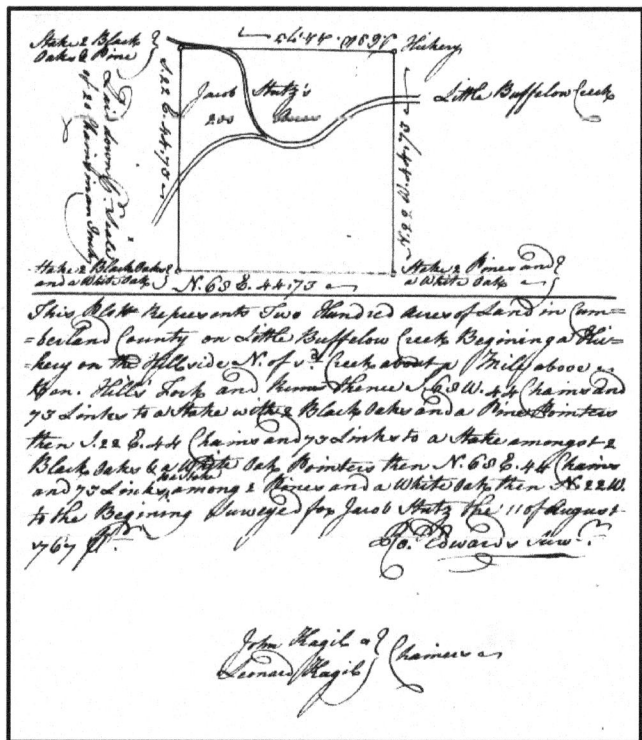

316.   1767, Aug 11 -- Land Grant #1500, Cumberland County, NC
Jacob Stutz received 200 acres located on Buffalo Creek about a mile above **Ben. Hill**'s fork. **John**

Kagil and **Leonard Kagil** were chain carriers.

317. 1767, Aug 11 -- Land Grant #0138, Cumberland County, NC
Charles Cagil received 100 acres located on Buffalo Creek adjoining **Jacob Stutz**. **John Kagill** and **Leonard Kagill** were chain carriers. [*Editor's Note: Never granted*]

318. 1767, Aug 11 -- Land Grant # 919, Dobbs County, NC
David Shurley received a 150 acre Land Grant located north of the Nuce [Neuse] River, east of lower Falling Creek and west of Clarks Bank adjoining **Jesse Retter**, **Stanley** and **Shurley**'s own line (formerly **Clarks**).

319. 1767, Aug 13 -- Land Grant #1358, Cumberland County, NC
Michael Hunsaker received 100 acres located on McCallums Fork of Richland Creek being the same once surveyed for **Jacob Tiem**. **Jacob Tiem** and **Robert Edwards** were chain carriers.

320. 1767, Aug 13 -- Land Grant #1513, Cumberland County, NC
Jacob McClendon received 150 acres located below the mouth of Juniper Branch of McLendons Creek. **Jacob McClendon** and **William Seale** were chain carriers. [*Editor's Note: deeded to **Obediah Sowell** 1772 --> **Thomas Armstrong**, Sheriff deeded to **John Cox** 1782*]

321. 1767, Sep 17 -- Deed Book 3 Page 176, Cumberland County, NC
Joseph Murphy and **Valentine Murphy** (of Anson County) deeded **James Jeffreys Sr.** 100 acres located in the fork of Cabin Creek. **Edward Morris**, **John Jeffreys** and **Thomas Suggs** were witnesses.

322. 1767, Sep 24 -- Will, Cumberland County, NC
Will of **Elisha Bettis**, Dec'd. Heirs: wife [*land **Alice Blanchfield** gave him at marriage on Great Road near **William Moris***], **Elija Bettis**, **Irvine Bettus** and **Francis Bettis**. Executor: brother **Elija Bettis**. Witnesses: **Thomas Hadly**, **Robt. Cochran** and **William H. Mills**. Proven Aug 1767. [*Editor's Note: Proven date is prior to will date.*]

323. 1767, Oct 16 -- Deed Book 3 Page 174, Cumberland County, NC
Edward Morris and **Sarah Morris** (of Anson County) deeded **Ephraim Pender** 100 acres located north of Cabin Creek. **John Jeffreys** and **Joseph Jeffreys** were witnesses.

324. 1767, Oct 17 -- Deed Book 3 Page 146, Cumberland County, NC
James Muse deeded **William Mears** 100 acres located on a branch of McLendons Creek adjoining **Francis Striplin** and **John Mairs** including **George Feagan**'s plantation at ford of **Anderson**'s old path. **George Feagan**, **Henry Dean** and **Thomas Rutherford** were witnesses.

325. 1767, Oct 26 -- Land Grant #1486, Cumberland County, NC
John Mears received 200 acres located on Buffalo Creek adjoining **Benjamin Smith**. [*Editor's Note: **John** and **Susannah Mayers** deeded to **Henry Cagle** 1768*]

326. 1767, Oct 27 -- Deed Book 3 Page 290, Cumberland County, NC
Leavin Ainsworth deeded **James Collins** 50 acres located north of Deep River adjoining **Governor [Johnston]** and **Moore**. **James Muse** and **Conner Dowd** were witnesses.

327. 1767, Nov 18 -- Deed Book 3 Page 149, Cumberland County, NC
Michael Hart and wife **Barbara** deeded **John Needham** (of Orange County) 200 acres located on Earl of Granville line crossing Bear Creek. **Robert Cochran** and **James Lathrum** were witnesses.

328. 1768, Mar 11 -- Deed Book 3 Page 266, Cumberland County, NC
George Blair (of Edenton) and **John Johnston** (of Bertie County) deeded **Cornelius Tyson** 118 acres adjoining **Benbow** being part of the **Governor Gabriel Johnston** four grants bequeathed to **Samuel Johnston** and **John Johnston** who sold his share to **George Blair**. **Elisha Hunter**, **Conner Dowd** and **John Carroll** were witnesses.

329. 1768, Mar 11 -- Deed Book 3 Page 298, Cumberland County, NC
Sterling Carroll deeded **James Russell** all his personal property bonded by **George Blair** and **John Johnston** (of Edenton). **Elisha Hunter** and **John Johnston** were witnesses.

330. 1768, Apr 10 -- Land Grant #802, Cumberland County, NC

John Shuffle received 200 acres located on Bear Creek adjoining **Carpenter**. **John Williamson** and **Owen Carpenter** were chain carriers.

A. 1768, Apr 14 -- Land Grant #2541, Anson County, NC
Joseph Allen received 100 acres located on Wolf Creek and Crawford Road. **Elizabeth Allen** and **Ann Allen** were chain carriers.

B. 1768, Apr 14 -- Land Grant #2490, Anson County, NC
Edward Morris received 150 acres located on Dicks Creek and Little River adjoining Mouth of 3 spring branches, 600y below mouth of Dicks Creek. **Edward Morris** and **Robert Edwards** were chain carriers.

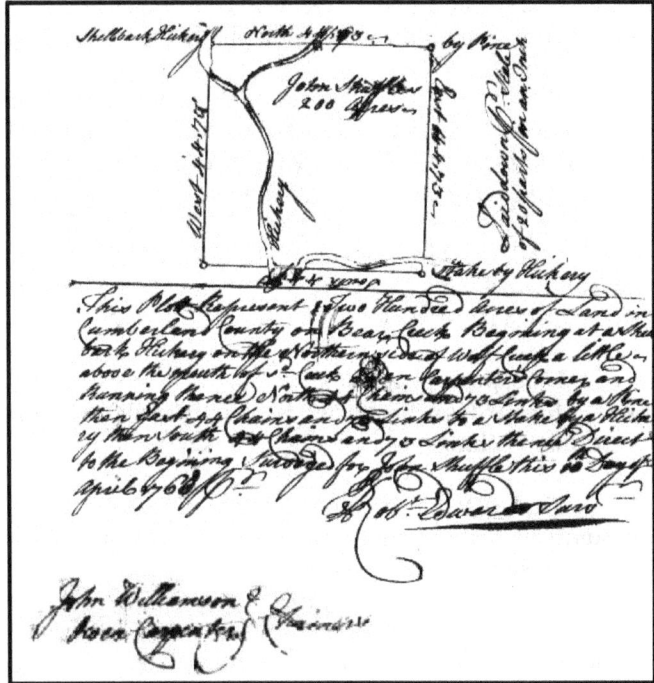

331. 1768, May 4 -- Deed Book 3 Page 362, Cumberland County, NC
Jonathan Evans deeded **George Evans** 100 acres located on Richland Creek. **Theophilus Evans** and **James Maultsby** were witnesses.

332. 1768, Jul 20 -- Deed Book 3 Page 227, Cumberland County, NC
Mary Dickenson deeded **Willis Dickinson** 150 acres located south of Deep River, a mile above Buck Creek. Part of the 300 acres patented to **Thomas Armstrong** 1747 and sold to **Robert Dickinson** Dec'd. **Robert Dickinson** and **James Muse** were witnesses.

333. 1768, Jul 25 -- Deed Book 3 Page 244, Cumberland County, NC
William Mears deeded **Thomas Bullard** 87 acres located on Lower Little River including **Elizabeth Mins'** plantation. **John Mishoe** and **Nicholas Smith** were witnesses.

334. 1768, Aug 2 -- Deed Book 3 Page 298, Cumberland County, NC
Elisha Bettis Dec'd. by his will [24 Sep 1767] bequested to his wife **Catharine**, what **Alice Blanchfield** gave to him at marriage the plantation where **Alice Blanchfield** lately live in the Great Yadkin Road adjoining **William Morris**. **Elisha** appointed his brother **Elijah Bettis** Exr. and he paid **Hugh Pattsull** and wife **Catharine** [former wife of **Elisha Bettis**]. **Archibald McKay** and **Arthur Wright** were witnesses.

335. 1768, Aug 17 -- Deed Book 3 Page 289, Cumberland County, NC
Elijah Bettis deeded **William Mears** 100 acres located on a branch of McLendons Creek adjoining **Francis Striplin** and **John Mairs** including **George Feagan**'s plantation at ford of **Anderson**'s old path. **George Feagan**, **Henry Dean** and **Thomas Rutherford** were witnesses.

336. 1768, Sep 17 -- Deed Book 3 Page 284, Cumberland County, NC
John Bettis deeded **John Patterson** 260 acres on branch of Raft Swamp by Juniper Branch by Wiggins Branch. Patent to **Francis Bettis** 26 Sep 1753 and sold to his son **Elijah Bettis** 14 Nov 1763 and conveyed to **Elijah** by last will and testament of his brother [**Elisha Bettis**]. **William Black**, **John McPherson** and **Duncan Patterson** were witnesses.

337. 1768, Sep 19 -- Deed Book 3 Page 267, Cumberland County, NC
John Brown deeded **Arthur Taylor** 100 acres located on Lower Little River that was patented to **George Foles** and then sold to **Archibald McDuffie** and then to **John Brown**. **William Mears**, **Archibald McDuffie** and **Nicholas Smith** were witnesses.

338. 1768, Sep 23 -- Land Grant #1164, Cumberland County, NC
John Hunnicut Junr. [assignee of **John Carroll**] received 100 acres located on Deep River adjoining **Gabriel Hardin** or **Joel McClendon** and **Joseph Duckworth Junr.** [*Editor's Note: deeded to **Philip Alston** 1775; similar deed from **Hunnicut** to **John Hardin** 1775*]

339.   1768, Sep 24 -- Land Grant #920, Cumberland County, NC
Joseph Dunn received 100 acres located on McCallums Branch of McLendons Creek adjoining his own line and **Jesse Pearce**. **Joseph Dunn** and **Joseph Cheston** were chain carriers.

340.   1768, Sep 27 -- Land Grant #862, Cumberland County, NC
Robert Edwards received 250 acres located on McLendons Creek adjoining **Thomas McClendon** and **James Muse**. **William Seale** and **George Feagin Senr.** were chain carriers. [*Editor's Note: **Moses Edwards** (of Cumberland County) deeded to **Asa Sowell** 1806*]

341.   1768, Sep 29 -- Land Grant #884, Cumberland County, NC
Robert Edwards received 150 acres located on Buffalo Creek adjoining **Jacob Stutz**. **Henry Cagill** and **Jacob Stutz** were chain carriers.

342.   1768, Oct -- Deed Book 3 Page 296, Cumberland County, NC
William Richardson, Sr. deeded **Drury Richardson** 200 acres located on Buffalo Creek. **Thomas Rutherford** and **Stephen Gilmore** were witnesses.

343.   1768, Oct 14 -- Deed Book 3 Page 275, Cumberland County, NC
Benjamin and wife **Sarah Dunn** deeded **John Stevens** 50 acres located on Richland Creek. **John Elwell** and **Richard Elwell** were witnesses.

344.   1768, Oct 24 -- Deed Book 3 Page 286, Cumberland County, NC
John Mayers and wife **Susannah** (of Orange County) deeded **Henry Kegle** 200 acres located east of Little Buffalo Creek on Smith's Fork. **William Minzes** and **William Garner** were witnesses.

345.   1768, Dec 7 -- Land Grant #864, Cumberland County, NC
Christopher Yow Junr. received 50 acres located on Lick Creek adjoining **Alexander Campbell**.

346.   1768, Dec 22 -- Land Grant #843, Cumberland County, NC
Terrance Brannon received 150 acres located on McLendons Creek adjoining **John Graham**.

347.   1768, Dec 22 -- Land Grant #850, Cumberland County, NC
Leonard Cagle received 200 acres located west of Buffalo Creek. [*Editor's Note: **Leonard** and **Susana Cagle** deeded to **Stephen Richerdson** 1775*]

348.   1768, Dec 22 -- Land Grant #851, Cumberland County, NC
Nathan Smith received 200 acres located on Rocky Branch of McLendons Creek adjoining **Campbell**. [*Editor's Note: **Nathan** and **Ann Smith** deeded to **Levi Pennington, Sr.** 1771 --> **Levi** and **Martha Pennington** deeded to **John McLeod** 1772*]

349.   1768, Dec 22 -- Land Grant #854, Cumberland County, NC
Charles Seale received 150 acres located on Mill Creek of McLendons Creek. [*Editor's Note: **Joseph Collins** deeded to **Richard Lyon** and Co. 1774*]

350.   1768, Dec 22 -- Land Grant #855, Cumberland County, NC
James Muse received 150 acres located on Killets Creek.

351. 1768, Dec 22 -- Land Grant #857, Cumberland County, NC
Edward Feagin received 300 acres located on Toms Creek of McLendons Creek. [*Editor's Note: deeded 150 acres to* **John McLendon** *1773;* **Francis Rasbury** *deeded remaining 150 acres to* **John Morrison** *1773*]

352. 1768, Dec 22 -- Land Grant #866, Cumberland County, NC
Thomas McClendon received 125 acres located on McLendons Creek adjoining **Jerom Miller** and **Farquard Campbell**. [*Editor's Note: deeded to* **William Richardson** *1769 -->* **William** *and* **Elisabeth Richardson** *deeded to* **Evan McSwine** *1772*]

353. 1769, Mar 7 -- Land Grant #1004, Cumberland County, NC
Francis Stribling received 300 acres located on drains of Killetts Creek adjoining **Andrew Killett**. **Thomas Seale** and **George Feagin Junr**. were chain carriers. [*Editor's Note: deeded to* **James McDonald** *1775 -->* **James Fry** *1783*]

354. 1769, Mar 7 -- Land Grant #1020, Cumberland County, NC
John Stevens received 150 acres located south of McLendons Creek on Dry Creek of the Juniper ½ mile above the mouth. **Thomas Seale** and **Moses Bland** were chain carriers. [*Editor's Note: deeded 70a to* **Donald Shaw** *1770 adjoining* **Demsy Watson**]

355. 1769, Mar 20 -- Deed Book 3 Page 403, Cumberland County, NC
John Medlin deeded **Joseph Dunn** 100 acres located on Richland Creek adjoining **Joseph Dunn**, **Weir** and **Henry Atkinson**. **James Muse** and **Benjamin Atkinson** were witnesses.

356. 1769, May 4 -- Land Grant #881, Cumberland County, NC
William Manes Junr. received 100 acres located southeast of Bear Creek.

357. 1769, May 4 -- Land Grant #882, Cumberland County, NC
Martin Ott received 400 acres located on Bear Creek three miles below the Yadkin Road. [*Editor's Note: deeded to* **William Gardiner** *1770*]

358. 1769, May 4 -- Land Grant #885, Cumberland County, NC
Robert Edwards received 150 acres located below the mouth of Juniper Branch of McLendons Creek adjoining **Ferquhard Campbell** and **Jacob McClendon**.

359. 1769, May 4 -- Land Grant #886, Cumberland County, NC
William Seale received 250 acres located on Juniper Branch. [*Editor's Note: deeded to* **Christian Jackson** *1774*]

360. 1769, May 4 -- Land Grant #888, Cumberland County, NC
Terrance Brannon received 100 acres located on McLendons Creek adjoining **Graham** and **Thomas Matthews**. [*Editor's Note:* **Elisabeth Brannon** *deeded to* **Robert Graham** *1774*]

361. 1769, May 4 -- Land Grant #890, Cumberland County, NC
William Smith Junr. received 100 acres located on Richland Creek adjoining **Nathan Smith**.

362. 1769, May 5 -- Land Grant #903, Cumberland County, NC
John Overton received 200 acres located on both sides of Governors Creek.

363. 1769, May 5 -- Land Grant #905, Cumberland County, NC
John Overton received 100 acres located on both sides of Governors Creek adjoining **Governor [Johnston]**.

364. 1769, May 20 -- Deed Book 3 Page 538, Cumberland County, NC
Abel Lee deeded **Frederick Gregg** and **Richard Lyon** 200 acres located on Deep River. **John Hile** and **Conner Dowd** were witnesses.

365. 1769, May 25 -- Deed Book 3 Page 381, Cumberland County, NC
John Donahoe deeded **Nicholas Newton** 200 acres located on Wet Creek. **Samuel Williams**, **Jesse Riter** and **Thomas Keys** were witnesses.

366. 1769, Jun 1 -- Deed Book 4 Page 239, Cumberland County, NC
Joshua Hancock deeded **Randolph Cheek** 150 acres located on Deep River adjoining **David Bartram** being part of the **Governor Gabriel Johnston** four grants bequeathed to **Samuel Johnston** and **John Johnston** and then to **George Blair** and then **Joshua Hancock**. **Elisha Hunter** and **Jacob Barnes** were witnesses.

367. 1769, Jul 6 -- Land Grant #1060, Cumberland County, NC
William Gardner received 50 acres located on Bear Creek opposite the mouth of Williams Creek adjoining **Martin Ott**. **William Gardner** and **Mark Shuffield** were chain carriers.

368. 1769, Jul 7 -- Land Grant #1002, Cumberland County, NC
William Morgan Senr. received 200 acres located on Wolf Creek about 200 yards east of the Yadkin Waggon Road. **James Morgan** and **William Morgan** were chain carriers.

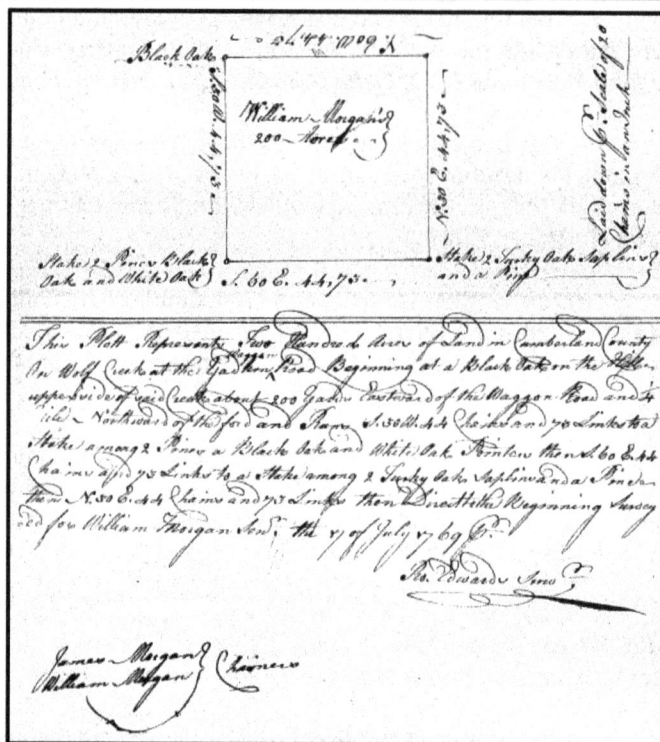

369. 1769, Jul 20 -- Deed Book 3 Page 437, Cumberland County, NC
David Kegle and wife **Catharine** (of Rowan County) deeded **William Smith** a tract of land located on both sides of Flat [Flag] Creek including a plantation. **John Kegle**, **Simon Hart** and **George Kegle** were witnesses.

370. 1769, Jul 22 -- Deed Book 3 Page 409, Cumberland County, NC
John Overton deeded **Elijah Bettis** 250 acres located on McLendons Creek. Patented to **Hartwell Hunnicutt** 1765 and sold to **Overton** 1766. **William Seale** and **John Hunnicutt** were witnesses.

371. 1769, Jul 24 -- Deed Book 3 Page 411, Cumberland County, NC
John Overton deeded **Elijah Bettis** 200 acres located on McLendons Creek. Patented to **Moses Tomlin** and sold to **Overton** 1758. **William Seale** and **John Hunnicutt** were witnesses.

372. 1769, Jul 24 -- Deed Book 3 Page 426, Cumberland County, NC
Conner Dowd deeded **John Hunnicutt** 128 acres located south of Deep River adjoining **Governor Johnston** and **John Overton**. **John Johnston** and **George Blair** claim an older title to land and dispute the sale. **James Russell** and **Benjamin Shield** were witnesses.

373. 1769, Jul 26 -- Deed Book 3 Page 346, Cumberland County, NC
John Walsh Esq., coroner deeded **John Overton** 150 acres located on Richland Creek including **John Dunn's** plantation. Sold to satisfy judgment from **John Pain** v. **John Dunn** suit. **Duncan Mackey** and **Thomas Rutherford** were witnesses.

374. 1769, Jul 29 -- Deed Book 4 Page 329, Cumberland County, NC
Zachariah Green and wife **Jeresth** deeded **John May** 100 acres located south of Deep River part of a grant to **Howell Brewer**. **James Collins** and **William Green** were witnesses.

375. 1769, Aug 31 -- Deed Book 4 Page 45, Cumberland County, NC
John Walsh Esq., coroner deeded **William Hooper** (of New Hanover County) 200 acres located on Wet Creek including the Lawyer's Path. Seized from **James Cheney**. **Richard Lyon** and **F. Richards** were witnesses.

376. 1769, Sep 16 -- Deed Book 3 Page 427, Cumberland County, NC
Thomas McClendon deeded **William Richardson** 125 acres located on both sides of McLendons Creek adjoining **Jerome Miller** and **Farquard Campbell**. **John Stewart** and **James Muse** were witnesses.

Cumberland County circa 1770

Moore County is located in the upper portion of Cumberland County, northwest of Cross Creek [Fayetteville].

I've annotated the map with approximations of the locations of <u>Robbins</u> and <u>Carthage</u> as well as the <u>Cross Creek to Salem Road</u> to provide a better understanding of the map based on the 1770 survey. The Cross Creek to Salem Road was a major thoroughfare that ran directly through Moore County.

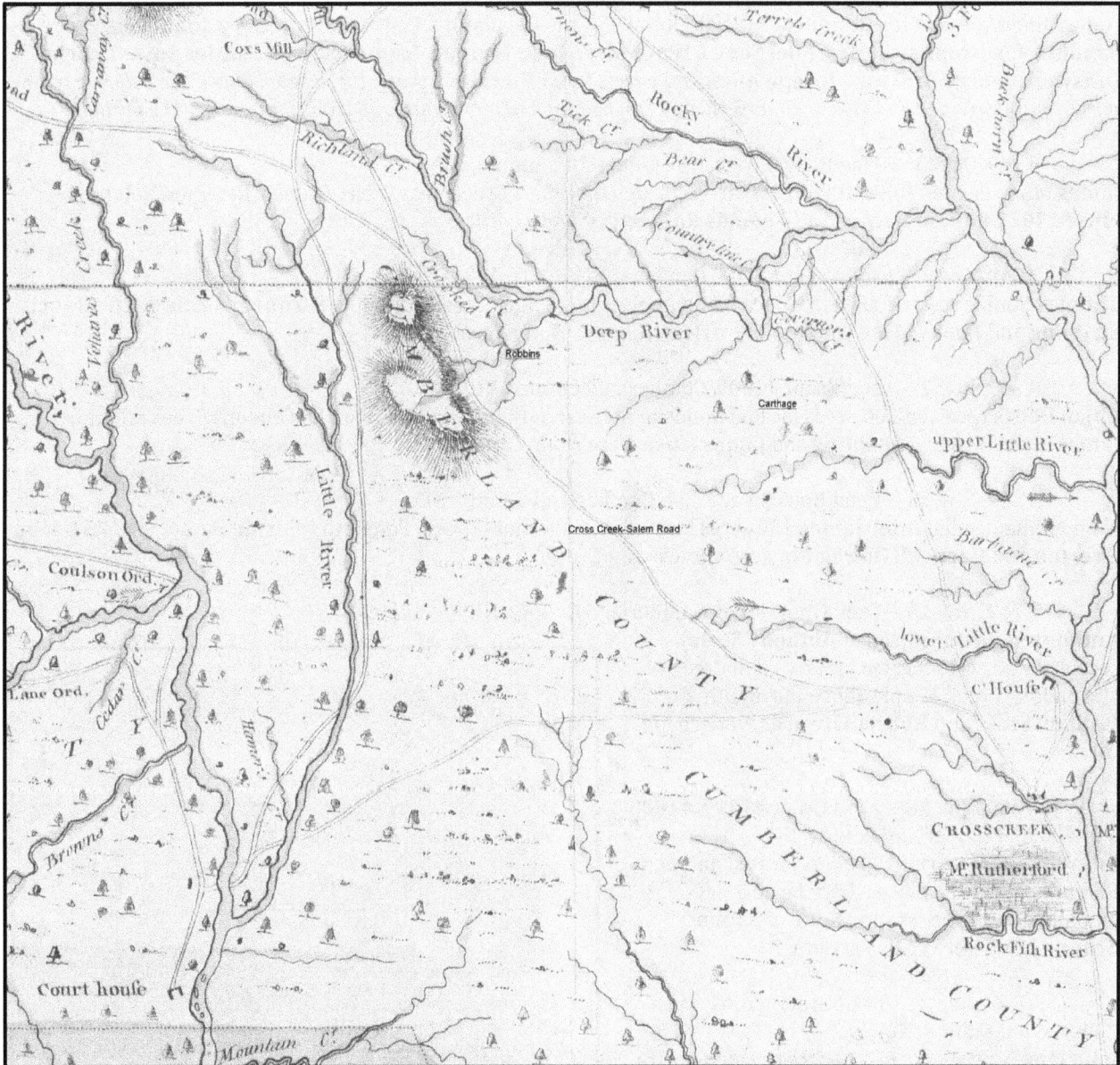

1770 Map of North Carolina by John Collet, J. Bayly and Samuel Hooper.
[Courtesy of the North Carolina Maps Digital Collection at UNC-Chapel Hill, Call Number CK.272]
http://dc.lib.unc.edu/cdm/singleitem/collection/ncmaps/id/467/rec/110

377.   1769, Sep 22,24 -- Will Book C Page 57-58, Mecklenburg County, NC
Will of **Henry Furrer**, Dec'd. Heirs: Eldest son **John Furrer**, second son **Paul Furrer**, wife **Rosena** and mentions other children "as they come of age". Executors: **Rosena Furror** and **Valetine Weaver**. Witnesses: **John Phifer**, **Paul Barringer** and **Valentine Weaver**.

378. 1769, Sep 28 -- Land Grant #1003, Cumberland County, NC
William Mears received 100 acres located west of Killetts Creek and on Quarry Branch of McLendons Creek adjoining **James Muse** and **Killett**. **John Howel** and **James Muse** were chain carriers. [*Editor's Note: deeded to Donald McDonald 1772*]

379. 1769, Sep 29 -- Land Grant #889, Cumberland County, NC
John Cagill received 100 acres located between Cabin and Bear Creek adjoining his own line. **Jacob Stutz** and **Jacob Cagill** were chain carriers.

380. 1769, Oct 9 -- Petition, Anson County, NC
The following individuals were among the Anson County [Montgomery County] residents signing the petition concerning taxes and fees for public officials. Known as the Regulator's Petition: **Jno. Jeffery**, **John Smith Sandhill**, **Christopher Butler**, **John Sowel**, **Wm. Sowel**, **John Morgan**, **Samuel Sowel**, **Charles Sowell**, **Richd. Braswell**, **George Braswell**, **Joseph Allen** and **Lewis Sowell**. [*Editor's Note: those listed above are believed to be past or future residents of Moore County, NC and can be found in numerous land transactions over the period.*]

381. 1769, Oct 23 -- Deed Book 4 Page 19, Cumberland County, NC
James Muse deeded **John Howell** 250 acres located on Killets Creek near Weirs Branch. Patented to **James Muse** 1767. **William Garner** and **Thomas Rutherford** were witnesses.

382. 1769, Nov 7 -- Land Grant #0444, Cumberland County, NC
Thomas Seale received 150 acres located on upper side of Buck Creek adjoining **Ferquhard Campbell**. **Francis Stribling** and **James Muse** were chain carriers. [*Editor's Note: Never granted*]

383. 1769, Nov 7 -- Land Grant #1000, Cumberland County, NC
Elijah Bettis received 200 acres located opposite of the mouth of Lick Branch on McLendons Creek adjoining **James Muse**. **Francis Stribling** and **James Muse** were chain carriers.

384. 1769, Nov 13 -- Deed Book 3 Page 534, Cumberland County, NC
John Misha deeded **Anne James** 150 acres located on Governors Creek. Patent to **John Misha** 24 Apr 1764. **John Overton** and **Hartwell Hunnicutt** were witnesses.

385. 1769, Nov 16 -- Land Grant #996, Cumberland County, NC
Anthony Seale Junr. [son of **Anthony Seale**] received 200 acres located on Cox's Mill Creek of McLendons Creek ¾ mile above the mouth. **William Seale** and **Robert Edwards** were chain carriers.

386. 1769, Nov 18 -- Land Grant #1619, #1808 and #0473, Cumberland County, NC
John Trapps received 150 acres located on Deep River including the place where he now lives adjoining **Lee**. **John Trapps Senr.** and **John Trapps Junr.** were chain carriers.

387. 1769, Nov 21-- Land Grant #1061, Cumberland County, NC
John May Junr. received 150 acres located north of Deep River on Fall Creek about 1.5 miles above the mouth. **Drury Richeson** and **John Trapps Senr.** were chain carriers. [*Editor's Note: John and Elisabeth May deeded to David Stroud 1772*]

388. 1769, Nov 21-- Land Grant #0392, Cumberland County, NC
Robert Phillips received 200 acres located on Earl of Granville's line east of Tyson's Creek. **Robert Phillips** and **Robert Cheek** were chain carriers. [*Editor's Note: Never granted*]

389. 1769, Dec 16 -- Land Grant #910, Cumberland County, NC
John Hunsucker received 200 acres located on Reedy Creek.

390. 1769, Dec 16 -- Land Grant #919, Cumberland County, NC
John Morgan received 100 acres located on Cabin Creek.

391. 1769, Dec 16 -- Land Grant #936, Cumberland County, NC
Joel McClendon received 200 acres located on Juniper of McLendons Creek adjoining his own line. [*Editor's Note: deeded to* **Edward Cox** *1774*]

392. 1769, Dec 16 -- Land Grant #938, Cumberland County, NC
James Muse received 150 acres located on Quarry Branch of McLendons Creek adjoining his own line.

393. 1769, Dec 16 -- Land Grant #939, Cumberland County, NC
James Muse received 150 acres located on Killetts Creek of McLendons Creek adjoining his own line.

394. 1769, Dec 16 -- Land Grant #944, Cumberland County, NC
John Overton received 200 acres located south of Deep River on a prong of the Goshen adjoining his own line.

395. 1769, Dec 16 -- Land Grant #945, Cumberland County, NC
Robert Cheek received 125 acres located on Tysons Creek.

A. 1769, Dec 16 -- Land Grant #2564, Anson County, NC
John Wilkins received 200 acres located on Wolf Creek in both Anson [Montgomery] & Cumberland [Moore] County.

396. 1769, Dec 21 -- Deed Book 3 Page 539, Cumberland County, NC
Cornelius Tyson deeded **Frederick Gregg** and **Richard Lyon** 144 acres located on Deep River adjoining **John Mays** and **Zack Green**. **Conner Dowd, Richard Moulden** and **Zachariah Green** were witnesses.

397. 1769, Dec 21 -- Deed Book 3 Page 541, Cumberland County, NC
John May deeded **Frederick Gregg** and **Richard Lyon** 200 acres located on Deep River. **Conner Dowd, Richard Moulden** and **Cornelius Tyson** were witnesses.

398. 1769, Dec 21 -- Deed Book 3 Page 542, Cumberland County, NC
Zachariah Green deeded **Frederick Gregg** and **Richard Lyon** 100 acres located north of Deep River. **Conner Dowd, Richard Moulden** and **Jeramiah Barnes** were witnesses.

399. 1769, Dec 22 -- Deed Book 4 Page 16, Cumberland County, NC
Henry Atkinson deeded **Benjamin Atkinson** 100 acres located on Richland Creek and Weirs Branch adjoining **Aaron Burleson**. **James Muse** and **Joseph Cheasten** were witnesses.

400. 1770 -- Deed Book 4 Page 386-387, Cumberland County, NC
Abel Lee and wife **Ann** deeded **David Stroud** two tracts [1] 300 acres located on both sides of Deep River above the mouth of Bear Creek [2] tract on both sides of Deep River and the upper end of Barton's Island adjoining **John Garner**. **John Garner** and **James Collins** were witnesses.

401. 1770, Feb 1 -- Deed Book 4 Page 13, Cumberland County, NC
Jesse Pearse deeded **Michael Hunsucker** 50 acres located on McCallums Fork of Richland Creek adjoining **Joseph Dunn**. **James Muse** and **Thomas Seale** were witnesses.

A. 1770, Feb 3 -- Cane Creek [Quaker] Meeting Records (1756) Vol. 1 Page 42, Alamance County, NC
Robert Cheek disowned for behaving in a warlike manner.

402. 1770, Feb 13 -- Deed Book 4 Page 339, Cumberland County, NC

Joel McClendon (of Anson County) deeded Thomas McClendon 100 acres located on McLendons Creek adjoining McClendon and Ezekeriah Horser. Patent to Joel McClendon 1763. Jacob McClendon and Samuel McClendon were witnesses.

403.   1770, Feb 13 -- Deed Book 4 Page 340, Cumberland County, NC
Joel McClendon (of Anson County) deeded Thomas McClendon 200 acres located on McLendons Creek. Patent to Joel McClendon 1758. Jacob McClendon and Samuel McClendon were witnesses.

404.   1770, Feb 22 -- Cane Creek [Quaker] Meeting Marriages Vol. 1. Page 45, Alamance County, NC
Cornelius Tison, son of Cornelius and Jean Tyson, of Cumberland County and Arcada Benbow, daughter of Powel and Elizabeth Benbow of Cumberland County were married at the Barnes Meeting House on Deep River in Cumberland County. James Barns, Thomas Tison, Jacob Barns, Cornelius Tison, Jean Tison, Powel Benbow, Elizabeth Benbow, Elizabeth Cheston, Richard Tison, Benjamin Tison and Sabra Gilbert were present and served as witnesses.

405.   1770, Mar 29 -- Deed Book 4 Page 11, Cumberland County, NC
Henry Atkinson deeded Joseph Kerr (of Orange County) 75 acres located on Richland Creek adjoining Jonathan Evans and Minyard. James Muse and Benjamin Atkinson were witnesses.

406.   1770, May 14 -- Deed Book 5 Page 44, Cumberland County, NC
Sterlin and Amy Carrel deeded James Russel 300 acres located west of Deep River on Governors Creek part of land bought from George Blair and John Johnston. John Carrel, John Hunnicutt and Randalph Hunnicutt were witnesses.

407.   1770, Jun 8 -- Deed Book 4 Page 31, Cumberland County, NC
Thomas Bennet deeded Jonas Johnston 100 acres located in the Fork of Lower Little River. Nicholas Smith, Christopher Darlington and Archibald Best were witnesses.

408.   1770, Jun 8 -- Deed Book 4 Page 33, Cumberland County, NC
Jonas Johnston deeded Nicholas Smith 100 acres located on Lower Little River including the plantation Thomas Starling lives on. William Seal, Thomas Starling and Winfred Seale were witnesses.

409.   1770, Jul 4 -- Land Grant #1058, Cumberland County, NC
William Seale received 50 acres located on Juniper of McLendons Creek. George Feagin Senr. and George Whitley were chain carriers. [Editor's Note: deeded to Christian Jackson 1774]

410.   1770, Jul 4 -- Land Grant #1084, Cumberland County, NC
William Killett received 200 acres located Wiers Spring Branch and Killetts Creek of McLendons Creek adjoining **Warner Coleman. George Feagin Senr.** and **Epaphroditis Whitely** were chain carriers.

411.   1770, Jul 4 -- Land Grant #1086, Cumberland County, NC
Andrew Killett received 120 acres located on McLendons Creek adjoining **Thomas McClendon** and **Jerom Miller. George Feagin Senr.** and **James Cadwell** were chain carriers. [*Editor's Note: deeded to **Daniel Muse** 1775*]

412.   1770, Jul 4 -- Land Grant #1057, Cumberland County, NC
William Seale received 150 acres located on Dunhams Creek. **William Seale** and **Robt. Edwards** were chain carriers.

413.   1770, Jul 5 -- Land Grant #1059, Cumberland County, NC
Anthony Seale Junr. [son of **Anthony Seale**] received 100 acres located west of Governors Creek adjoining **Sterlin Carroll. William Seale** and **Robt. Edwards** were chain carriers.

414.   1770, Jul 6 -- Land Grant #1008, Cumberland County, NC
Robert Edwards received 150 acres located on Long Meadow of Buffalo Creek adjoining **John Miers** and his own line. **Robert Edwards** and **James Muse** were chain carriers.

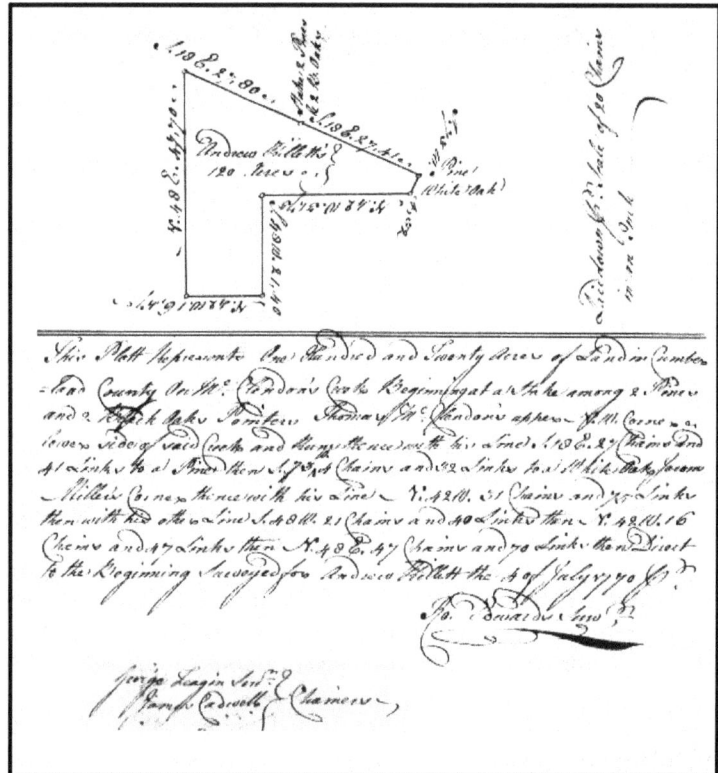

415.   1770, Jul 6 -- Land Grant #1017, Cumberland County, NC
Abraham Hunsucker received 200 acres located north of Grassy Creek adjoining **George Carringer. Leonard Heart** and **George Carringer** were chain carriers. [*Editor's Note: **Abraham** and **Katharine Hunsucker** deeded to **George Carringer** 1775*]

416.   1770, Jul 7 -- Land Grant #1018, Cumberland County, NC
Peter Shamburger received 200 acres located on Grassy Creek adjoining **John Williamson. John Williamson** and **Elisabeth Shamburger** were chain carriers.

417.   1770, Jul 16 -- Deed Book 3 Page 524, Cumberland County, NC
John Cagle, Henry Sides, Casper Clob, Peter Sides and **Doratha Elizabeth Sides** appointed **Simon Hart** as their attorney to recover from **John Waginer** and **Michael Heller** of Sorkney, PA their part of the estate of **Andrew Felsinger**, Dec'd. together with the part of **Doratha Sides**, which she left and granted the attorney to recover. **William Manes, Joseph Williams** and **George Cagle** were witnesses.

418.   1770, Jul 24 -- Deed Book 3 Page 545, Cumberland County, NC
John Graham deeded **John Cox** 150 acres located on McLendons Creek. Patented to **John Graham** 1762. **Duncan Mackie** and **Thomas Rutherford** were witnesses.

419.   1770, Aug 4 -- Deed Book 4 Page 128, Cumberland County, NC
Nicholas Smith and **Sarah Smith** deeded 100 acres to **Josiah Williamson** located on both sides of the south Fork of Crains Creek. **William Seale, George Feagin** and **William Manes** were witnesses.

420.   1770, Aug 8 -- Deed Book 4 Page 301, Cumberland County, NC
John Hunnicut deeded **Conner Dowd** 128 acres located south of Deep River adjoining **Governor Johnston** and **John Overton. Reuben Shields** and **Randolph Hunnicut** were witnesses.

421.   1770, Aug 18 -- Will, Cumberland County, NC
Will of **James Barnes**, Dec'd. Heirs: wife **Sarah** [*lower half of land and negro Will*], daughter **Elizabeth**, cousin **Joshua Barnes**, cousin **James Barnes**, cousin **Abigal Barnes**, cousin (and brother to **Abigal**) **Jeremiah Barnes**. Executors: wife **Sarah**, her father **Joseph Done [Dunn]** and **Cornelius Tison**. Witnesses: **Michael Russell**, **Gabriel Harden** and **James Russell**. Proven Oct 1770.

422.   1770, Sep 20 -- Deed Book 4 Page 226 Cumberland County, NC
Nicholas Smith deeded **Andrew Ingram** 100 acres located on both sides of Lower Little River. **John Stewart** and **William Ingram** were witnesses.

423.   1770, Sep 23 -- Will, Cumberland County, NC
Will of **John Hancock**, Dec'd. Heirs: wife **Susanna** [*plantation where I now live*], son **John Hancock** [*100 acres of the 150 that he now lives on*], sons **Robert**, **Clement** and **William Hancock** [*equal share of land of their mother's at her death*]. Executors: **Cornelius Tison** and **Conner Dowd**. Witnesses: **Jacob Roggars**, **Willis Akinson**, **Benjamin Owens** and **John Carrell**. Proven Jul 1772.

424.   1770, Sep 29 -- Land Grant #1014, Cumberland County, NC
John Overton received 50 acres located north of Deep River adjoining **Governor [Johnston]**. **John Overton** and **Joseph Duckworth Junr.** were chain carriers.

425.   1770, Oct 1 -- Land Grant #1010, Cumberland County, NC
Jacob McClendon received 150 acres located on Dry Fork of McLendons Creek adjoining **Thomas Matthews**. **Isaac Horser** and **William Barrett** were chain carriers. [*Editor's Note: deeded to **William Barrett** 1773*]

426.   1770, Oct 1 -- Land Grant #1011, Cumberland County, NC
Jacob McClendon received 150 acres located on McLendons Creek adjoining **Thomas McClendon**, **Jamima McClendon** and **Joel McClendon**. **Thos. McClendon** and **Jaml. McClendon** were chain carriers. [*Editor's Note: Jacob and Martha McClendon deeded to Donald McDonald 1773*]

427.   1770, Oct 2 -- Land Grant #1006, Cumberland County, NC
John Morgan received 100 acres located on Cabin Creek about ¾ mile above the mouth of Mill Creek. **George Morgan** and **William Morgan Junr.** were chain carriers.

428.   1770, Oct 9 -- Deed Book 4 Page 233, Cumberland County, NC
Benjamin Atkinson deeded **Joseph Cheston** 100 acres located on Richland Creek and Weirs Branch. **James Muse** and **Elizabeth Cheston** were witnesses.

429.   1770, Oct 15 -- Deed Book 4 Page 84, Cumberland County, NC
Christopher Ewe [Yow] Sr. and wife **Christian** deeded daughter **Sarah Ewe** 100 acres of a 400 acres tract patented by **Ewe** 1760. **Henry Gaster** and **Arthur Boyse** were witnesses.

430.   1770, Oct 18 -- Deed Book 4 Page 162, Cumberland County, NC
Martin Ott deeded **William Gardiner** 400 acres located on Bear Creek. **Owen Carpenter** was a witness.

431.   1770, Oct 20 -- Deed Book 4 Page 96, Cumberland County, NC
Gabriel Hardin deeded **John Hardin** 80 acres located on Deep River and the Rocky Ford. **Thomas Rutherford** and **James Russell** were witnesses.

432.   1770, Oct 26 -- Deed Book 3, Page 552, Orange County, NC
Abraham Richeson and wife **Sarah** (of Bladen County) deeded **Lambert Reed** (of Orange County) 50 acres located on the mouth of Buffalow Branch and Deep River adjoining **William Searcy** and **Lambert Read**. **Solomon Morgin** and **William Moore** were witnesses. Proven Jul 1771 by **Soloman Morgan**.

433.   1770, Dec 11 -- Land Grant #994, Cumberland County, NC
Elijah Bettis received 300 acres located on McLendons Creek ½ mile above the mouth of Richland Creek adjoining **Hartwell Hunnicut**. **Elijah Bettis** and **Primus Bettis** were chain carriers. [*Editor's Note: See grant #955 on microfilm as the grant was filmed in incorrect location*]

434. 1771, Jan-Jan 1772 -- Estate, Cumberland County, NC
Inventory of Estate of **James Barnes**, Dec'd. by Executor **Joseph Dunn**. **Benjamin Oens** indebted to estate.

435. 1771, Jan 23 -- Deed Book 4 Page 227, Cumberland County, NC
John Stainton and wife **Abigail** deeded **Edward Moore** 250 acres located on both sides of Deep River where **Stainton** formerly lived and **Moore** now lives. Patent by **John Smith** and sold to **Stainton**. **James Muse** and **William Richardson** were witnesses.

436. 1771, Feb 11 -- Deed Book 4 Page 307, Cumberland County, NC
Abel Lee deeded **John Garner** and **John May** 50 acres located on both sides of Deep River including upper end of Barton's Island. **William Garner** and **Owen Carpenter** were witnesses.

437. 1771, Mar 3 -- Deed Book 4 Page 306, Cumberland County, NC
Owen Carpenter and wife **Catherin** deeded **John Sheffield** a tract of land on Wolf Creek adjoining **John Sheffield**. **William Garner** and **Thomas Rutherford** were listed as witnesses.

438. 1771, Mar 21 -- Will, Cumberland County, NC
Will of **Richard Tullos** Dec'd. Heirs: wife **Elizabeth**, youngest sons **Temple** and **Wllloughby**, daughter **Sarah** and son-in-law **James Morgan**, son **John**, son **Tapley**, daughter **Elizabeth Bunell**, **Jane Gwyn** and son **Richard Tullos**. Executors: **John Lawrence** and son **John Tullos**. Witnesses: **James Sanders**, **Joseph Buchanan** and **William Morris Junr**. Proven Oct 1771.

439. 1771, Apr 3 -- Deed Book 4 Page 305, Cumberland County, NC
John Needham and wife **Susannah** deeded **Henry Gaster** 200 acres on north Fork of Bear Creek and Granville line. **Owen Carpenter** and **John Shiffield** were witnesses.

440. 1771, May 7 -- Deed Book 4 Page 430, Cumberland County, NC
Conner Dowd deeded **John Hancock Jr**. 150 acres south of Deep River being ½ of 300 acres that belonged to **Thomas Armstrong**. **Cornelius Tyson** and **Charles Shearin** were witnesses.

441. 1771, Jul 20 -- Deed Book 4 Page 428, Cumberland County, NC

Nathan Smith and wife **Ann** deeded **Levi Pennington, Sr.** 200 acres located on Rocky Branch of McLendons Creek adjoining **Campbell**. **John Stevens** and **Isaac Pennington** were witnesses.

442. 1771, Aug 13 -- Deed Book 4 Page 409, Cumberland County, NC
James Muse deeded **Jacob Duckworth** (of Chatham County) 200 acres located south of McLendons Creek in a gut, east of a place called the Sand Ridge. Patent to **Muse** 1767. **John Overton** and **Joseph Duckworth** were witnesses.

443. 1771, Sep 8 -- Deed Book 4 Page 361, Cumberland County, NC
Joseph Morgan [of South Carolina] deeded **William Morgan** 100 acres located on Cabin Creek. **Jepthar Medford**, **John Medford** and **George Morgan** were witnesses.

444. 1771, Sep 28 -- Deed Book 4 Page 410, Cumberland County, NC
Nicholas Smith deeded **Henry Smith** 100 acres located on the Fork of Little River. **Kenneth Black** and **John Black** were witnesses.

445. 1771, Sep 28 -- Deed Book 5 Page 17, Cumberland County, NC
Christopher Ewe [Yow] Sr. and wife **Christian** deeded **Malcolm Buie** 100 acres on Gares Creek of Little River adjoining **Gare**'s line. Patented by **Ewe** 1761. **John Campbell** and **Archd. Buie** were witnesses.

446. 1771, Oct 26 -- Deed Book 4 Page 215, Cumberland County, NC
Robert Rowan, Sheriff deeded **Peter Messer** 200 acres located northeast of Cape Fear River being the land of **James Boon**, Dec'd. in hands of **Robert Johnston**, Administrator. **John Leggett** and **William Manes** were witnesses.

447. 1771, Nov 4 -- Deed Book 4 Page 419, Cumberland County, NC
John May deeded **Richard Lions** and Co. 200 acres located northeast of Deep River at mouth of Tices Creek. **Conner Dowd** and **Edward Griffin** were witnesses.

448. 1771, Nov 5 -- Deed Book 4 Page 420, Cumberland County, NC
Soloman Margin and wife **Mehitabel Ludlam** (of Chatham County) deeded **William Savory** (of Guilford County) 150 acres located east of Deep River. **Conner Dowd** and **John Galston** were witnesses.

449. 1771, Nov 10 -- Deed Book 6 Page 213, Cumberland County, NC
Powel Benbow deeded **Joseph Gilbert** 15 acres located on Haw [Deep] River adjoining **Conner Dowd**. **Cornealus Tison** and **Benjamin Doutey** were witnesses.

450. 1771, Nov 23 -- Deed Book 4 Page 414, Cumberland County, NC
Nicholas Smith deeded **John Black** 60 acres located on Lower Little River. **Archibald McDuffie** and **Malcolm Patterson** were witnesses.

451. 1771, Nov 25 -- Deed Book 4 Page 426, Cumberland County, NC
Nicholas Smith deeded **John Black** 100 acres located on Lower Little River. **Archibald McDuffie** and **Malcolm Patterson** were witnesses.

452. 1771, Dec 7 -- Deed Book 5 Page 108, Cumberland County, NC
William Morris and wife **Anne** deeded **Thomas Leonard Cotton** (of Anson County) 200 acres located on a branch of Bear Creek [Wet Creek]. Patent to **John Smith** and sold to **William Morris**. **James Cotton**, **Thomas Ward** and **James Gibson** were witnesses.

453. 1772, Jan -- Deed Book 4 Page 432, Cumberland County, NC
William Mears deeded **James Muse** 100 acres located on McLendons Creek including **William Mears'** plantation adjoining **Francis Stribling** at the ford of **Anderson**'s path, **John Weir** and **John Weaver**. Patent to **James Muse** 1756. **Thomas Rutherford** and **William Seale** were witnesses.

454. 1772, Jan 7 -- Deed Book 4 Page 429, Cumberland County, NC
Jacob McClendon deeded **Isaac Sewell** 300 acres located on Richland Creek adjoining **Jacob McClendon**. Patent to **Thomas Knight** 1760. **Isaac McClendon** and **John McClendon** were witnesses.

455.   1772, Jan 7 -- Deed Book 4 Page 440, Cumberland County, NC
Jacob McClendon deeded **Obediah Sowell** 150 acres located on McLendons Creek below mouth of Juniper Branch. **Isaac McClendon** and **John McClendon** were witnesses.

A.   1772, Jan 22 -- Land Grant #2883, Anson County, NC
Rasha Suggs received 200 acres located on Suggs Creek. **John Bowling** and **Thomas Suggs** were chain carriers.

B.   1772, Jan 22 -- Land Grant #3646, Anson County, NC
Rasha Suggs received 50 acres located west of Suggs Creek adjoining his own line.

456.   1772, Jan 23 -- Deed Book 5 Page 171, Cumberland County, NC
Michael Hart deeded **Vincent Gardner** 100 acres located south of Bear Creek. **John Walsh** and **Robert Sims** were witnesses.

457.   1772, Jan 28 -- Deed Book 6 Page 334, Cumberland County, NC
Francis Stribling deeded **Daniel McDonald** 200 acres located on McLendons Creek. Patented to **Thomas Mathews Sr.** 1757 and sold to his son **Thomas Mathews Jr.** and sold to **Josiah Williamson** who sold to **Thomas Elit**. **Josiah Williamson** and **John Kenney** were witnesses.

458.   1772, Jan 29 -- 1771-1776 Court of Pleas and Quarter Sessions, Cumberland County, NC
A Deed from **Michael Hunsucer** to **Jas. McDonald** was proven by **William Manus**

459.   1772, Jan 30 -- 1771-1776 Court of Pleas and Quarter Sessions, Cumberland County, NC
[Deeds] **Solomon Morgain** and **Mehitabel Ludlam** to **William Savory** proven by **Conner Dowd**
Jacob McClendon to **Isaac Sowell** acknowledged
Nathan Smith and wife **Ann** to **Levi Pennington Sr.** was proven by **John Stephens**.

460.   1772, Jan 30 -- Deed Book 6 Page 256, Cumberland County, NC
William Mears deeded **Donald McDonald** 15 acres located south Springs Branch of McLendons Creek adjoining **Stribling**, part of the plantation where **William Mears** now lives, patented to **Andrew Killet** 1759. **James Muse** and **Jacob MacClendon** were witnesses.

461.   1772, Jan 30 -- Deed Book 6 Page 257, Cumberland County, NC
James Muse deeded **Donald McDonald** 100 acres located on Quarry Branch, Killets Creek and Striblings Creek adjoining **Stribling**. **Elisha Hunter** and **John Walsh** were witnesses.

462.   1772, Jan 31 -- 1771-1776 Court of Pleas and Quarter Sessions, Cumberland County, NC
Ordered that **Peter Shamburger** bring into court an orphan girl named **Ann** so she can be bound by the court.

463.   1772, Jan 31 -- 1771-1776 Court of Pleas and Quarter Sessions, Cumberland County, NC
Inventory of the estate of **James Barns**, Dec'd. given into court by **Joseph Dunn**.

464.   1772, Feb 19 -- Deed Book 5 Page 48, Cumberland County, NC
Isaac Horser and wife **Mary** deeded **John McNeill** 200 acres located on a branch of McLendons Creek 4 miles from the Wagon Road. Patent to **Horser** 1754. **Hector McNeill**, **Malcom Paterson** and **Alex McMillan** were witnesses.

465.   1772, Feb 22 -- Deed Book 6 Page 333, Cumberland County, NC
Elisha Hunter deeded **Philip Alston** 122 acres located on Deep River adjoining **Ainsworth**. **John Carrell** and **Willm. Harden** were witnesses.

466.   1772, Feb 24 -- Deed Book 5 Page 30, Cumberland County, NC
Mary Dikinson and **Robert Dikinson** deeded **John Overton** 225 acres located on Buck Creek being ½ of the land purchased from **Nicholas Smith** by **Thomas Collins** and sold to **Robert Dickinson**. **John Carrol** and **Randh. Hunnicutt** were witnesses.

467.   1772, Feb 25 -- Land Grant #1238, Cumberland County, NC
James Muse received 300 acres located on Killetts Creek of McLendons Creek 250 yards below Cabo Branch adjoining his own line. **William Mears** and **Henry Dean** were chain carriers.

468.   1772, Feb 26 -- Land Grant #1109, Cumberland County, NC **Powell Benbo** received 100 acres located north of Deep River adjoining **Johnston** and **Elisha Hunter**. **Powell Benbo** and **Jacob Barnes** were chain carriers.

469.   1772, Feb 26 -- Land Grant #1114, Cumberland County, NC **John Hancock** received 150 acres located south of Deep River adjoining **Thomas Armstrong**. **Robert Hancock** and **William Hancock** were chain carriers.

470.   1772, Feb 26 -- Land Grant #1121, Cumberland County, NC **John Overton** received 50 acres located on McLendons Creek.

471.   1772, Feb 26 -- Deed Book 5 Page 174, Cumberland County, NC **John May** deeded **John Garner** his share of the land and mill purchased from **Abel Lee**. **James Garner** and **Mariah Garner** were witnesses.

472.   1772, Feb 27 -- Land Grant #1104, Cumberland County, NC **Joseph Howell** received 200 acres located on Killetts Creek adjoining **James Muse**. **James Singleton** and **Hardy Howell** were chain carriers.

473.   1772, Feb 28 -- Land Grant #1222, Cumberland County, NC **Niel McGathy** received 150 acres located on McLendons Creek adjoining **Robert Edwards**, **Thomas McClendon**. **James Muse** and **William Mears** were chain carriers.

474.   1772, Feb 28 -- Land Grant #1226, Cumberland County, NC **James Caddle** received 200 acres located on McLendons Creek adjoining **Thomas McClendon**. **James Muse** and **Joseph Carr** were chain carriers.

475.   1772, Mar 7 -- Land Grant #1182, Cumberland County, NC **Isaac Hill** received 100 acres located on Long Meadow adjoining **Robert Edwards**. **Drury Richardson** and **Henery Kagill** were chain carriers.

476.   1772, Mar 9 -- Land Grant #1112, Cumberland County, NC **Simon Heart** received 100 acres located on Bear Creek adjoining **William Manes Junr**. **John Cagill** and **Simon Heart** were chain carriers.

477.   1772, Mar 9 -- Land Grant #1117, Cumberland County, NC **Everitt Smith** received 200 acres located on the waters of Cabin Creek

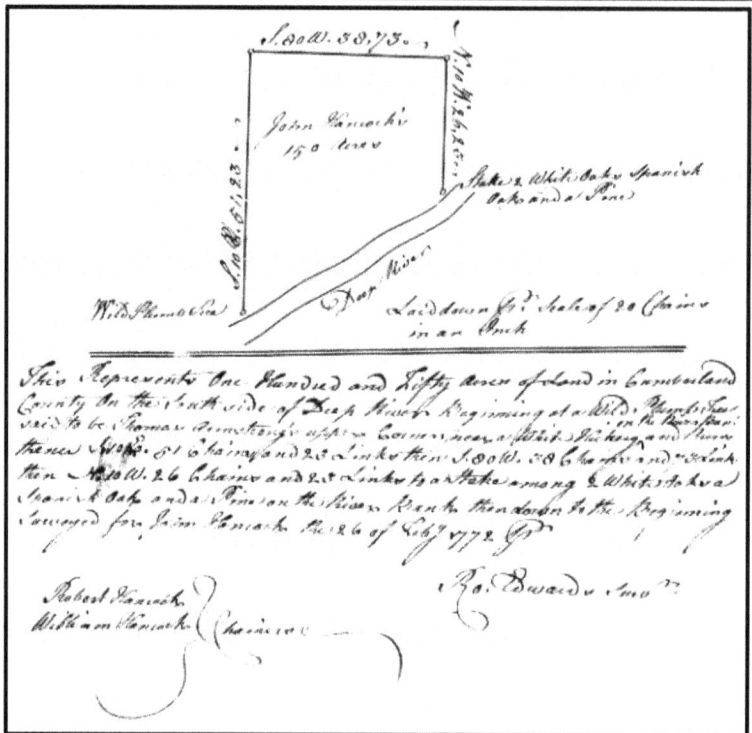

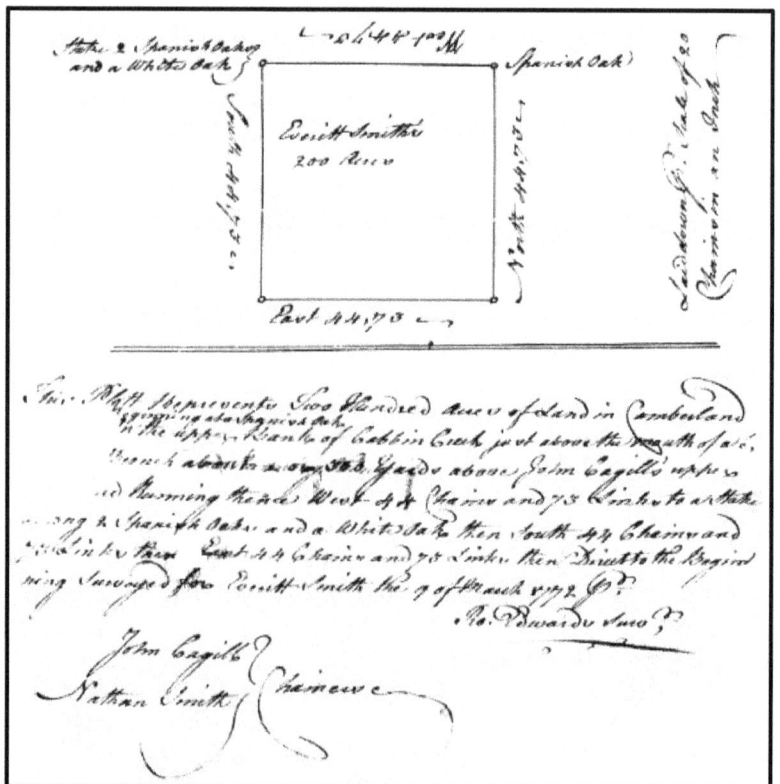

adjoining **John Cagill. John Cagill** and **Nathan Smith** were chain carriers. [*Editor's Note: deeded 50a to Burrel Deaton 1800 --> John Needham 1802*]

478.   1772, Mar 9 -- Land Grant #0405, Cumberland County, NC
David Stroud received 200 acres located on Deep River adjoining **George Feagin**, his own line (formerly **Abel Lee**). **Thomas Briggs** and **John Trapp** were chain carriers. [*Editor's Note: Never granted*]

479.   1772, Mar 10 -- Land Grant #1123, Cumberland County, NC
Adam Comer received 100 acres located on Williams Creek about 1 mile above Bear Creek. **John Shuffield** and **Adam Comer** were chain carriers.

480.   1772, Mar 10 -- Land Grant #1167, Cumberland County, NC
John Shuffield received 100 acres located on Bear Creek adjoining his own line. **William Shuffield** and **Henry Jackson** were chain carriers.

481.   1772, Mar 11 -- Land Grant #1163, Cumberland County, NC
Martin Johnston received 200 acres located on Eastern prong of Bear Creek on the Earl's [Randolph County] line. **William Hunsucker** and **John Lawley** were chain carriers.

482.   1772, Mar 11 -- Land Grant #1168, Cumberland County, NC
James Gilmore received 200 acres located on Bear Creek adjoining **Michael Heart**. **William Hunsucker** and **John Lawly** were chain carriers.

483.   1772, Mar 20 -- Will, Guilford County, NC
Will of **Enoch Spinks**, Dec'd. Heirs: wife **Amy** [*negro man Sampson*], daughters **Martha** [*lot of land including the storehouse that Southerland is posessed with*] and **Sarah**, sons **John** [*150 acres on Deep River and negro man Adam*], **Enoch** [*land on Fork Creek*], **Lewis** [*land and plantation I now live on*], **Rowley** and **Garrett**. Executors: **John Larrance, John Needham** and **Amy Spinks**. Witnesses: **John Lawrence, William Comb Jr.** and **Windsor Pearce**. Proven May 1772.

484.   1772, Mar 23 -- Deed Book 5 Page 130, Cumberland County, NC
Michael Hart and wife **Barbara** deeded **Vincent Garner** 200 acres located on both sides of the south prong of Bear Creek. **James Garner** and **Mekear Garner** were witnesses.

485.   1772, Apr 7 -- Land Grant #1102, Cumberland County, NC
Benjamin Atkinson received 100 acres located on the drains of Richland Creek between Locust Branch and McCallums Branch. **James Smith** and **Joseph Dunn** were chain carriers. [*Editor's Note: deeded to Richard Lyon and Co. 1772*]

486.   1772, Apr 29 -- 1771-1776 Court of Pleas and Quarter Sessions, Cumberland County, NC
Christian Jackson granted letters of administration on the estate of **Samuel Jackson** with **Edward Cox** and **Jacob McClendall** as securities.

487.   1772, Apr 29 -- 1771-1776 Court of Pleas and Quarter Sessions, Cumberland County, NC
Will of **Frances McClendall**, Dec'd. proven by **George Fagen**. **Jacob McClendall** and **Joel McClendall** qualified as executors.

488.   1772, Apr 30 -- 1771-1776 Court of Pleas and Quarter Sessions, Cumberland County, NC

Edward Cox appointed overseer of the road that leads from **Thomas Donahoe**'s to **Sandhill Smith**'s and have the following hands to work: **Jacob McLendall, Thos. Moore, Wm. Barrett, Wm. Smith Sr., John Kees, Archibd. Gibson, Nick Newton, Richd. Dunn, Robt. Grahams, Jas. Grahams, Francis Tedwell, John Cocks, Andrew Ingram, Willm. Ingram, Joel McLendall, Thos. Kees, Jas. Gibson** and **Robt. Cocks.**

489.   1772, May 16 -- Civil Actions, Cumberland County, NC

Phillip Alston claimed that **James Collins** has taken up a stray mare owned by **Alston. Elisha Hunter** summons **Alston** and **Collins** to appear. **Conner Dowd** is security for **Collins. Wm. Seale, James Muse, William Harden, John May, Josep Furr, Charles Shearin, Clem Hancock, Willis Dickerson, John Carrell, Starlin Carrell, James Phillips, James Russell** and **Phillip Colling** are also listed. Unclear if they were witnesses, jury or other.

490.   1772, Jun 4 -- Land Grant #1217 and 1732, Cumberland County, NC

James Cotton Junr. received 100 acres located on Cabin Creek adjoining **John Smith. Edwd. Gregory** and **Henry Smith** were chain carriers.

491.   1772, Jul 11 -- Deed Book 5 Page 71, Cumberland County, NC

Michael Hunsucker deeded **John Brownlow** 50 acres located on McCollums Fork of Richland Creek adjoining **Joseph Dunn. James Muse** and **Connor Dowd** were witnesses.

492.   1772, Jul 11 -- Deed Book 5 Page 100, Cumberland County, NC

John May deeded **Richard Lyon** and **Co.** 100 acres located south of Deep River. **Elisha Hunter** and **Conner Dowd** were witnesses.

493.   1772, Jul 11 -- Deed Book 5 Page 113, Cumberland County, NC

Benjamin Atkinson deeded **Richard Lyon** and Co. 100 acres located on Richland Creek on a ridge between Locust and McCallums Branch. **James Muse** and **Connor Dowd** were witnesses.

494. 1772, Jul 28 -- 1771-1776 Court of Pleas and Quarter Sessions, Cumberland County, NC
A Deed from **Michael Hunsucker** to **John Brownlow** was proven by **Conner Dowd**.

495. 1772, Jul 29 -- 1771-1776 Court of Pleas and Quarter Sessions, Cumberland County, NC
Christian Jackson returned an inventory on the estate of **Samuel Jackson** Dec'd.

496. 1772, Jul 29 -- 1771-1776 Court of Pleas and Quarter Sessions, Cumberland County, NC
Conner Dowd granted license to keep a tavern at his dwelling house.

497. 1772, Jul 30 -- 1771-1776 Court of Pleas and Quarter Sessions, Cumberland County, NC
Jamima Grimes, a boy aged 3, was apprenticed to **Michael Hunsucker**.

498. 1772, Jul 29 -- 1771-1776 Court of Pleas and Quarter Sessions, Cumberland County, NC
Wm. Burt, **William McCachie** and **John Paterson** appointed to value the estate of **Samuel Jackson** Dec'd.

499. 1772, Aug 7 -- Deed Book 6 Page 379, Cumberland County, NC
John May and wife **Elisabeth** deeded **David Stroud** 150 acres located south of Fall Creek. **John Garner** and **Windsor Pearce** were witnesses.

500. 1772, Sep 2 -- Land Grant #1645, Cumberland County, NC
Richard Dunn received 100 acres located east of Wet Creek adjoining his own line. **Richd. Dunn Senr.** and **Richd. Dunn Junr.** were chain carriers.

501. 1772, Sep 9 -- Land Grant #1644, Cumberland County, NC
Christopher Butler received 300 acres located west of Dry Creek including his own improvement. **Richard Dunn** and **Christopher Butler** were chain carriers. [*Editor's Note: **Christopher** and **Elizabeth** **Butler** deeded to **Robert Paterson** 1778*]

502. 1772, Oct -- Estate, Cumberland County, NC
Inventory of the estate of **John Hancock** Dec'd. by Administrator **Conner Dowd**. *Notes held on the following*: **Moses Bland**, **John Hunnicutt Senr.**, **John Hunnicutt Jun.**, **James Russell**, **Jacob Rogers**, **Joshua Hancock**, **Willm. Hancock** and **Rich. Lyon** & Co.

503. 1772, Oct 15 -- Deed Book 6 Page 216, Cumberland County, NC
John Johnston (of Bertie County), **Josiah Granbery** and **Samuel Johnston**, executors of will of **George Blair** Dec'd. (of Chowan County) deeded **Joseph Gilbert** 100 acres located on Haw [Deep] River adjoining **Conner Dowd** and **Powel Benbow**. **Ja. Milner** and **Jos. Jno. Alston** were witnesses.

Land granted in northern Moore County by 1775

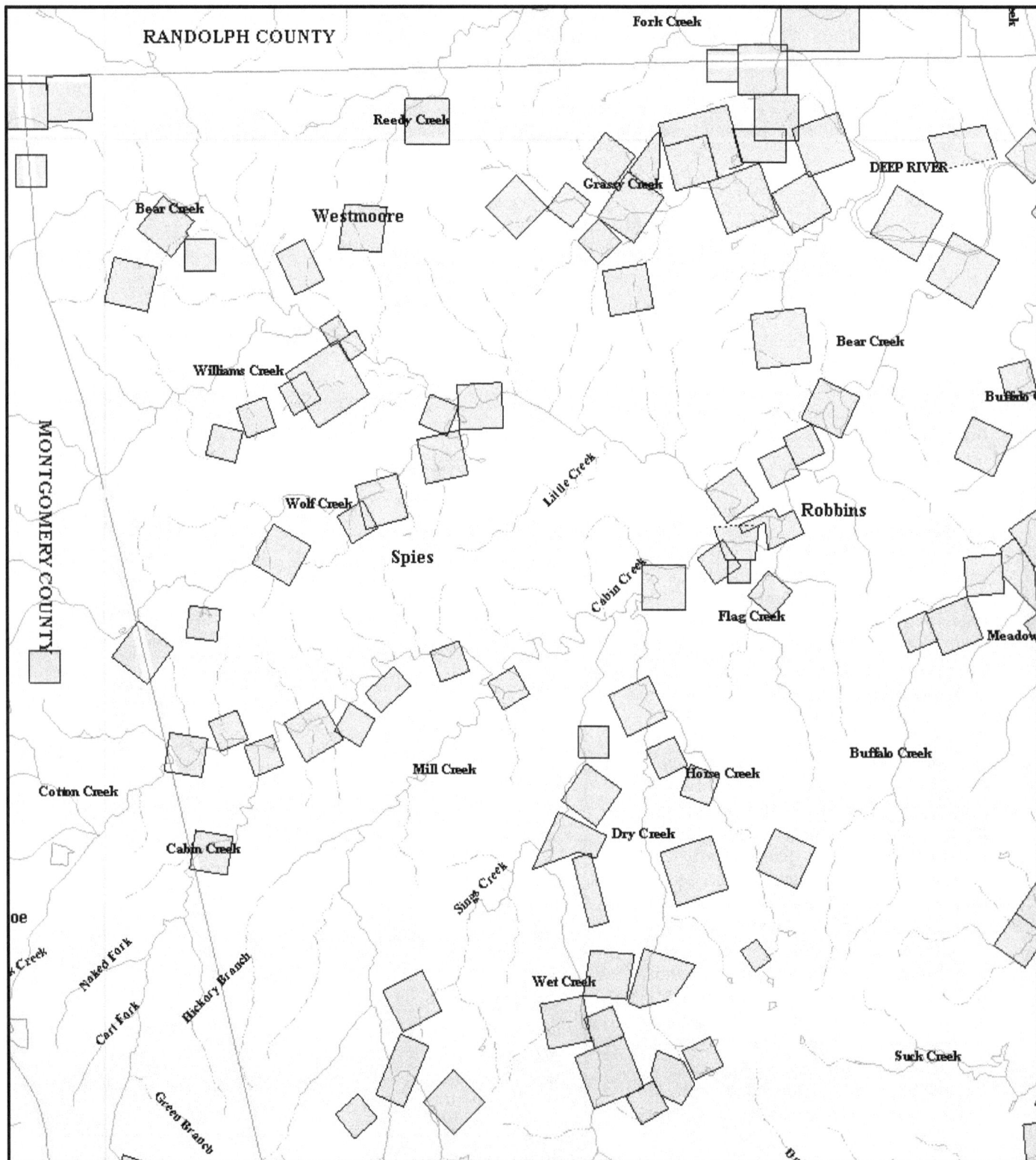

Map prepared utilizing early land grants
from Cumberland and Bladen counties.
For more information see www.MooreCountyWallaces.com

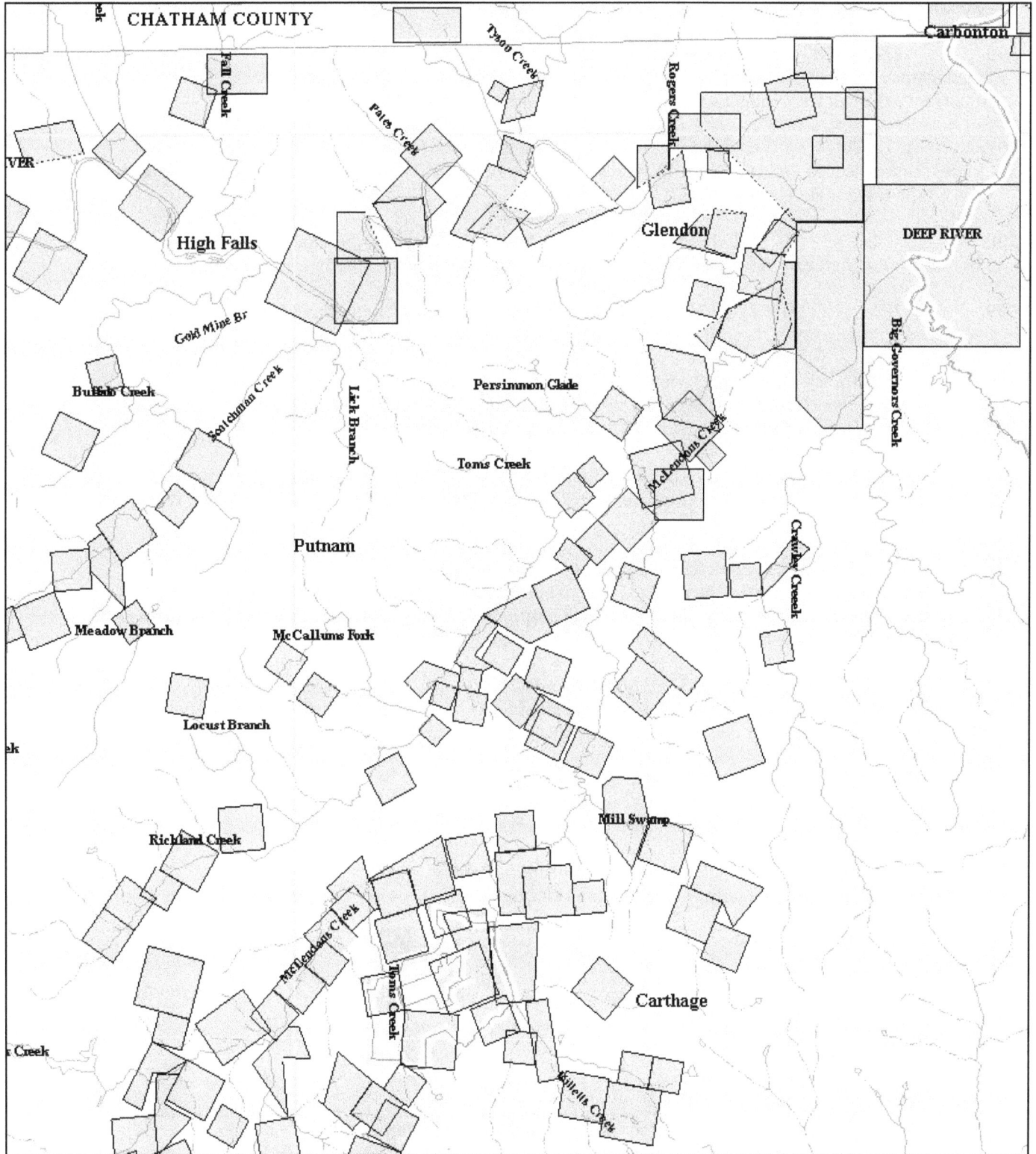

504.   1772, Oct 15 -- Deed Book 6 Page 246, Cumberland County, NC
John Johnston (of Bertie County), **Josiah Granbery** and **Samuel Johnston**, executors of will of **George Blair** Dec'd. (of Chowan County) deeded **Phillip Alston** 4000 acres in two tracts [1] located north of Deep River adjoining **Elisha Hunter, James Barns, Jacob Barns, Powell Benbow, Gilbert** and **Michael Russel** [2] located south of Deep River at mouth of Governors Creek and Sanders Branch adjoining **James Russell** and **Cornelius Tyson. Ja. Milner** and **Jos. Jno. Alston** were witnesses.

505.   1772, Oct 24 -- Land Grant #1220, Cumberland County, NC
Alexander McKay received 150 acres located on McLendons Creek adjoining **Elijah Bettis. James Muse** and **Robert Edwards** were chain carriers.

506.   1772, Oct 24 -- Land Grant #1237, Cumberland County, NC
James Muse received 200 acres located on Waggon Road 1 ¼ mile below McLendons Creek. **Jacob McClendon** and **Henry Howell** were chain carriers. [*Editor's Note: deeded to* **Alexr. Morison** *1774*]

507.   1772, Oct 27 -- Deed Book 5 Page 129, Cumberland County, NC
James Russel deeded **Conner Dowd** 400 acres located on Deep River and Governors Creek. **Benjamin Shields** and **Elisha Hunter** were witnesses.

508.   1772, Oct 29 -- 1771-1776 Court of Pleas and Quarter Sessions, Cumberland County, NC
The road from **Caster's** to **Wm. Seals'**, whereof **Henry Caster** was overseer, to be discontinued.

509.   1772, Oct 29 -- 1771-1776 Court of Pleas and Quarter Sessions, Cumberland County, NC
Wm. Seal granted a tavern license with security **James Muse**.

510.   1772, Nov 2 -- Deed Book 1, Page 188, Guilford County, NC
Josiah Carr and wife **Jane/Jean** deeded **Jennings Thompson** 200 acres located on Flat Creek of Deep River adjoining **Carr** (formerly **James Graves**). **Willm. Searcy** and **Windsor Pearce** were witnesses.

511.   1772, Nov 4 -- Deed Book 6 Page 214, Cumberland County, NC
Powel Benbow deeded **Cornelius Tison** 185 acres adjoining **Joseph Gilbert** and **Conner Dowd. Phillip Alston** and **John Wilkins** were witnesses.

512.   1772, Dec 4 -- Deed Book 6 Page 26, Cumberland County, NC
Levy Pennington and wife **Martha** deeded **John McLoud** 200 acres located on Richland Creek including the plantation where **Pennington** now lives adjoining **Campbell**. Patent to **Nathan Smith** 1768. **James Muse** and **John Martin** were witnesses.

A.   1772, Dec 7 -- Land Grant #3471, Anson County, NC
James Campbell received 400 acres located on the mouth of Crooked Creek and three spring branches adjoining **Edward Morris. Adryan Hix** and **Richd. Campbell** were chain carriers.

513.   1773, Dec 15 -- Deed Book 6 Page 89, Cumberland County, NC
John Overton deeded **Alexr. Morrison** 150 acres located on Richland Creek patented to **John Dunn** 1764. **Randh. Hunnicutt** and **Normand Morrison** were witnesses.

514.   1773, Dec 20 -- Deed Book 6 Page 175, Cumberland County, NC
Elisha Hunter (of Chatham County) deeded **James McDonald** 100 acres located north of Deep River adjoining **James Barns** and **Jacob Barns. Conner Dowd** and **Edw. Griffin** were witnesses.

515.   1772, Dec 31 -- Deed Book 6 Page 60-62, Cumberland County, NC
William Richardson and wife **Elizabeth** deeded **Evan McSwine** 125 acres located on both sides of McLendons Creek adjoining **Jerome Miller** and **Farquard Campbell. James Munk** was a witness.

517. 1773, Jan 4 -- Deed Book 6 Page 330, Cumberland County, NC
Thomas Mathews Jr. and wife **Sarah** deeded **Josiah Williamson** 200 acres located on McLendons Creek. Patented to **Thomas Mathews Sr.** 1757 and sold to his son **Thomas Mathews Jr.** 1763. **John Gilmore** and **Donn Thornton** were witnesses.

518. 1773, Jan 6 -- Deed Book 6 Page 9-10, Cumberland County, NC
Jacob McClandon deeded **Donald McDonald** 200 acres located on Buck Creek. Patented to **Jemima McLandon** 1758. **John Martin** and **James Graham** were witnesses.

519. 1773, Jan 6 -- Deed Book 6 Page 42, Cumberland County, NC
Jacob McClandon and wife **Martha** deeded **Donald McDonald** 150 acres located on Buck Creek adjoining **Joel** or **Thomas McLenden** and **Jemima McClendon**. Patented to **Jacob McLendon**. **John Martin** and **James Graham** were witnesses.

A. 1773, Jan 23 -- Land Grant #3003, Anson County, NC
Francis Jordan received 100 acres located on Dicks Creek. **John Sowell** and **Francis Jordan** were chain carriers.

520. 1773, Jan 27 -- 1771-1776 Court of Pleas and Quarter Sessions, Cumberland County, NC
Drury Richardson was appointed overseer of the road from **James Muse** Esq.'s to **Isaac Hill**'s.

521. 1773, Jan 28 -- 1771-1776 Court of Pleas and Quarter Sessions, Cumberland County, NC
A deed from **William Richardson** and wife **Elizth.** to **Evan McSwine** was proven by **James Cadel.**

A. 1773, Jan 29 -- Land Grant #3465, Anson County, NC
James Jeffrey received 150 acres located on Cabin Creek in Anson and Cumberland counties including his own improvement. **James Saunders** and **John Jeffrey** were chain carriers.

522. 1773, Jan 30 -- 1771-1776 Court of Pleas and Quarter Sessions, Cumberland County, NC
James Cadwel served jury duty

523. 1773, Mar 4 -- Deed Book 1, Page 225, Guilford County, NC
Jennings Thompson and wife **Elizabeth** deeded **Joseph Carr** 200 acres located on Flat Creek of Deep River. **William Searcy Senr.**, **Wm. Searcy Junr.** and **Windsor Pearce** were witnesses.

524. 1773, Apr-May 1775 -- Deed Book 10, Dobbs County, NC
Page 420 - **Jessee Ritter** to **Moses Ritter**

525. 1773, Apr 19 -- Deed Book 6 Page 221, Cumberland County, NC
Nicholas Nuton and **Melonay Nuton** deeded **Bartholomew Dunn** 200 acres located on Wet Creek. Patent to **John Doneho** 1765. **Joseph Williams** and **Thomas Green** were witnesses.

526. 1773, Apr 23 -- Deed Book 6 Page 215, Cumberland County, NC
Jacob McClendon deeded **William Barrot** 150 acres located on McLendons Creek adjoining **Thomas Mathes**. **Donald Shaw** and **Isaac McClendon** were witnesses.

527. 1773, May 5 -- Land Grant #1280, Cumberland County, NC
John Martin received 350 acres located

between McLendons and Richland Creeks including **James Hill**'s improvement. **Jacob McClendon** and **John Martin** were chain carriers. [*Editor's Note: deeded 150a to* **John McRae** *1775*]

528.   1773, May 7 -- Land Grant #1233, Cumberland County, NC
Dempsey Watson received 150 acres located on Dry Creek of Juniper adjoining **John Martin**. **John McNeil** and **Saml. McClendon** were chain carriers.

529.   1773, May 7 -- Land Grant #1279, Cumberland County, NC
John Martin received 250 acres located on Dry Fork of Juniper Creek adjoining **Dempsey Watson** and **George Whitley**. **John McNeil** and **John McClendon** were chain carriers. [*Editor's Note:* **John Martin** *and* **Meron McLeod** *deeded to* **Murdock McQueen** *and* **John Shaw** *1774*]

530.   1773, May 8 -- Land Grant #1230, Cumberland County, NC
John McNeil received 150 acres located on Toms Creek and McClendons Creek adjoining **Edward Feagin**. **John McNeil** and **John McClendon** were chain carriers.

531.   1773, May 8 -- Land Grant #1278, Cumberland County, NC
John Martin received 150 acres located on Richland Creek adjoining his own line, **William Smith** and **Reuben Taylor**'s cabin. **John Martin** and **Jacob McClendon** were chain carriers.

532.   1773, May 11 -- Land Grant #1235, Cumberland County, NC
Owen Carpenter received 100 acres located on Williams Creek ¼ mile southwest of the Yadkin Road. **William Shuffield** and **James Ludlow** were chain carriers.

533.   1773, May 11 -- Land Grant #1363, Cumberland County, NC
Henry Castor received 100 acres located on the drains of Bear Creek adjoining **Michael Heart**.

534.   1773, May 11 -- Land Grant #1587 and #1776, Cumberland County, NC
James Ludlow received 100 acres located on Williams Creek below the Yadkin Road adjoining **Adam Comer**. **Adam Comer** and **William Shuffield** were chain carriers.

535.   1773, May 12 -- Land Grant #1699, Cumberland County, NC
George Caringer received 300 acres located south of Grassy Creek on the Waggon Road between his house and Bear Creek. **Conrad Hunsucker** and **Thomas Wilkerson** were chain carriers.

536.   1773, May 20 -- Deed Book 6 Page 209, Cumberland County, NC
Robert Hancock (of Chatham County) deeded **William Hancock** undivided third tract where **John Hankok** Dec'd. formerly lived and that will pass to **Robert Hancock** on the death of **Susannah Hankok**, widow of **John Hankok**. **Conner Dowd**, **Edwd. Griffin** and **Daniel Brown** were witnesses.

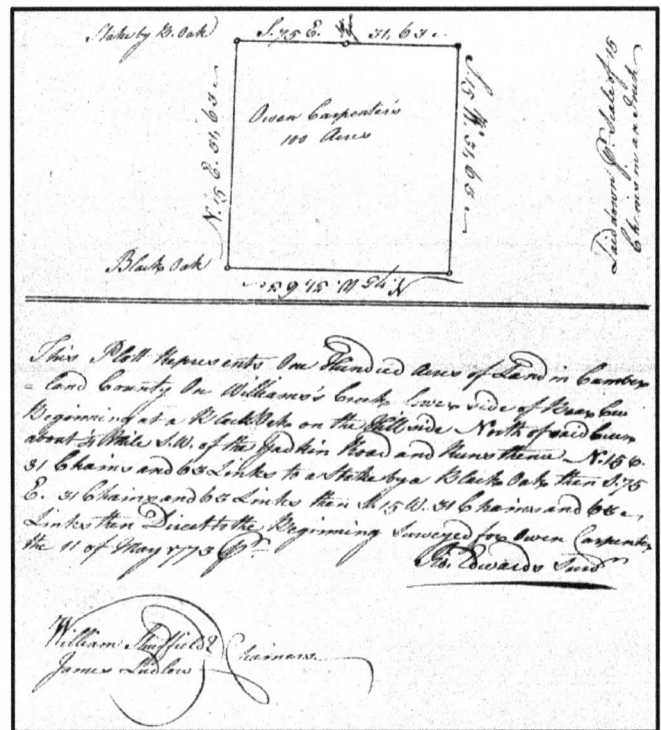

537.   1773, May 24 -- Land Grant #1218, Cumberland County, NC
Jesse Rutter received 200 acres located on Wet Creek adjoining **Jas. Chaney** and **Nicholas Newton** [*Editor's Note: deeded to* **Nathan Smith** *1774 --> * **Anson Melton** *1786*]

538.   1773, May 24 -- Land Grant #1223, Cumberland County, NC
William Garner received 50 acres located on Bear Creek adjoining his own line.

539.   1773, May 24 -- Land Grant #1232, Cumberland County, NC

George Kagill received 150 acres located on Bear Creek adjoining Simon Heart. John Cagill and Simon Heart were chain carriers.

540. 1773, May 24 -- Land Grant #1234, Cumberland County, NC
John Kagill received 50 acres located south of Cabin Creek adjoining Richard Caswell.

541. 1773, Jun 10 -- Deed Book 6 Page 218, Cumberland County, NC
David Strowd deeded Thomas Tucker (of Chatham County) 300 acres located on both sides of Deep River at the upper end of Barton's Island and adjoining John Garner. Patent to James Barton 1758 and sold to Garner and May. Jacob Hardeson and Mary Hill were witnesses.

542. 1773, Jun 11 -- Land Grant #1595, 1784 and 083, Cumberland County, NC
John Brownlow received 200 acres located on Horse Creek. John Kagill and Samuel Tidwell were chain carriers.

543. 1773, Jul 23 -- Deed Book 6 Page 180, Cumberland County, NC
Edward Feagin (schoolmaster, of South Carolina) deeded John McClendon 150 acres located west of Toms Creek of McLendons Creek. Part of 300 acre patent to Edward Feagin 1768. William Bevill and Richardson Feagin were witnesses.

544. 1773, Aug 10 -- Land Grant #3677 & 0142, Anson County, NC
James Cotton Jr. received 100 acres located on Cabin Creek adjoining the [Moore/Cumberland] county line. Edwd. Gregory and Henry Smith were chain carriers.

545. 1773, Sep 2 -- Deed Book 6 Page 229, Cumberland County, NC
Francis Rasbury (of Dobbs County) deeded John Morrison 150 acres located on Toms Creek of McLendons Creek including George Folk's improvement. Part of 300 acre patent to Edward Feagin (schoolmaster in South Carolina) 1768. Alexr. Morison, Donald Shaw and John Martin were witnesses.

546. 1773, Sep 24 -- Deed Book 6 Page 230, Cumberland County, NC
John Stevens deeded Donald Shaw 70 acres located on McLendons Creek. Part of 150 acres patented to John Stevens 1770 excepting 80 acres of Damsy Watson. Wm. Seale and James Muse were witnesses.

547. 1773, Oct 4 -- Land Grant #0107, Cumberland County, NC
John Hayes received 200 acres located on Bear Creek adjoining John Shuffle, Wm. Garner. William Sheffield and James Cotton were chain carriers. [Editor's Note: Never granted]

548. 1773, Oct 8 -- Land Grant #1686, Cumberland County, NC
Nicholas Newton received 148 acres located east of Wet Creek adjoining Chaney, Jno. Shepherd and including John McPherson's improvement and John Smith's improvement. Richard Dunn Junr. and Nicholas Newton were chain carriers. [Editor's Note: deeded to George Hunsucker]

549.   1773, Oct 11 -- Deed Book 1, Page 241, Guilford County, NC
William Reade Senr. deeded son **Arthur Read** 150 acres located north of Deep River adjoining **Winsor Pearce** and **Searcy**. **Wm. Searcy** and **Windsor Pearce** were witnesses.

550.   1773, Nov 2 -- Land Grant #1647, Cumberland County, NC
James Morgan received 100 acres located on Wolf Creek. [*Editor's Note: deeded to* **John Hunsucker** *1787*]

551.   1773, Nov 17 -- Land Grant #1608 and 1798, Cumberland County, NC
Laughlin Betton received 100 acres located on drains of Suck Creek between Richland and McLendons Creek adjoining **John Martin** and **Donald McDonald**. **John Martin** and **Neil Nicholson** were chain carriers.

552.   1773, Nov 18 -- Land Grant #1636, Cumberland County, NC
John McNeil received 50 acres located on McLendons Creek adjoining his own line. **John McClendon** and **Thomas Wadsworth** were chain carriers.

553.   1773, Nov 18 -- Land Grant #1637, Cumberland County, NC
John McNeil received 50 acres located on Juniper Branch of McLendons Creek including **Bland's** improvement. **John McClendon** and **Thos. Wadsworth** were chain carriers.

554.   1773, Nov 18 -- Land Grant #1703, Cumberland County, NC
John McClendon received 100 acres located on Juniper of McLendons Creek adjoining **Donald McDonald**. **Isaac McClendon** and **Thos. Wadsworth** were chain carriers.

555.   1773, Nov 19 -- Land Grant #1706, Cumberland County, NC
James Muse received 100 acres located on McLendons Creek adjoining his own line and **Howel. Moses Bland** and **William Bland** were chain carriers.

556.   1773, Nov 20 -- Land Grant #1663, Cumberland County, NC
Elijah Bettis received 200 acres located on Richland Creek adjoining **Evans**. **Joseph Cheston** and **William Dunn** were chain carriers.

557.   1773, Nov 20 -- Land Grant #1664, Cumberland County, NC
Elijah Bettis received 100 acres located on both sides of Lick Branch of McClendons Creek near the Poles Bridge. **Thomas Seal** and **Elijah Bettis** were chain carriers.

558.   1773, Nov 22 -- Land Grant #1352, Cumberland County, NC
Aaron Phagan received 100 acres located on both sides of Killets Creek adjoining **Stribling, Richardson Phagan** and **Killett. Francis Stribling** and **Arthur Davis** were chain carriers.

559.   1773, Nov 22 -- Land Grant #1408, Cumberland County, NC
Anthony Seale received 150 acres located on both sides of Mill Swamp of McClendons Creek adjoining his own line. **Francis Stribling** and **Arthur Davis** were chain carriers.

560.   1773, Nov 22 -- Land Grant #1409, Cumberland County, NC
Anthony Seale received 200 acres located on north fork of Mill Swamp of McClendons Creek adjoining his own line. **Francis Stribling** and **Arthur Davis** were chain carriers.

561.   1773, Nov 22 -- Land Grant #1716, Cumberland County, NC
Richardson Phagan received 100 acres located on both sides of Killets Creek adjoining **Aaron Phagan** and **Stribling. Francis Stribling** and **Arthur Davis** were chain carriers.

562.   1773, Nov 23 -- Land Grant #1707, Cumberland County, NC
Thomas Seale received 100 acres located on McLendons Creek adjoining **John Overton** and including his own improvement. **James Muse** and **John Tollison** were chain carriers. [*Editor's Note: Deeded to* **Ann James** *1782*]

563.   1773, Nov 24 -- Land Grant #1557/1746, Cumberland County, NC
Robert Melton received a 100 acre Land Grant located on a prong of Governors Creek adjoining **Russel's** line. **James Russell** and **Nunn Clark** were chain carriers.

564. 1773, Nov 25 -- Land Grant #1585 and #1774, Cumberland County, NC
David Lawson received 100 acres located on both sides of Buffalo Creek including where he now lives. **George Harden Junr.** and **Mary Lawson** were chain carriers.

565. 1773, Nov 27 -- Land Grant #1410, Cumberland County, NC
William Seale received 75 acres located on Dunhams Creek adjoining his own line, **William Killet**, **Cox** and **Dunham**. **Stephen Herd** and **Dann Thornton** were chain carriers.

A. 1773, Dec -- General Assembly Session Records
Petition to move the Guilford County, NC courthouse toward the center of the county. The signers included: **Ransom Southerland, James Lethem, John Needham, Josiph Carr, William Searcy, John Larrance, William Needham, John Hunesucker, William Reade Senr., Windsor Pearce, William Searcy Junr., Cornelius Lathem Senr., Corneleus Latham Junr., Arthur Reade, Bartholmew Dun, William Reade Junr., Abram Hunsucker, Konrad Andrews** and **William Hardin**. [*Editor's Note: These were inhabtants of southern Guilford County [now Randolph] petitioning that they had to travel 40-50 miles to the courthouse. Some of the signers were likely Moore County residents.*]

566. 1773, Dec 2 -- Land Grant #1361, Cumberland County, NC
Robert Cox received 100 acres located on the drains of McLendons Creek adjoining **Edward Cox** including his improvement. **Edward Cox** and **George Cox** were chain carriers. [*Editor's Note: deeded to **Donald Campbell** 1776*]

567. 1773, Dec 4 -- Deed Book 1, Page 240, Guilford County, NC
Arthur Read and wife **Martha** deeded **Ransom Southerland** part of manor plantation deeded to **Arthur** and **Martha Read** by Will of **Enoch Spinks** Dec'd. **Wm. Searcy Junr., Wm. Searcy** and **Thos. Cox** were witnesses.

568. 1773, Dec 14 -- Deed Book 1, Page 248, Guilford County, NC
Soloman Morgan and wife **Mehetabel** deeded **Lombard Reade** 100 acres located north of Deep River adjoining **Richeson**. Granted to **William Searcy** 1761. **William Searcy** and **Windsor Pearce** were witnesses.

569. 1773, Dec 17 -- Land Grant #1349, Cumberland County, NC
Neil McNeill received 150 acres located on Juniper of McLendons Creek adjoining **Seale**. **John McNeil** and **Neil McNeil** were chain carriers.

570. 1773, Dec 23 -- Deed Book 6 Page 109, Cumberland County, NC
John Carrel deeded **John Overton** 200 acres located above mouth of Buck Creek adjoining **Jacob McClendon**. Patented to **Jacob McClendon**. **Hartll. Hunnicutt** and **Randh. Hunnicutt** were witnesses.

571. 1774, Jan 1 -- Land Grant #1354, Cumberland County, NC
William Bastin Whitford received a 100 acre Land Grant located on Governors Creek adjoining **Connor Dowd**. **William Bastin Whitford** and **David Melton** were chain carriers.

572. 1774, Jan 2 -- Land Grant #1705, Cumberland County, NC
James Muse received 300 acres located on McLendons Creek adjoining his own line, **John Howell** and **Morrison**. **Daniel Muse** and **Richardson Feagin** were chain carriers.

573. 1774, Jan 8 -- Land Grant #1591 and #1780, Cumberland County, NC
James McDonald received 200 acres located north of Deep River adjoining **Elisha Hunter** and **Barnes.**, **Elijah Hooton** and **John Hooton** were chain carriers. [*Editor's Note: deeded to **James Collens** 1783 --> **Thomas Tyson** 1783*]

574. 1774, Jan 10 -- Land Grant #1618 and #1807, Cumberland County, NC
Frederick Gregg received 100 acres located north of Deep River adjoining **John/Jacob Rogers** and **Randolph Cheek** and including **John Phillips Junr.**'s improvement. **John Phillips** and **Robert Cheek** were chain carriers.

575. 1774, Jan 11 -- Land Grant #1617 and #1806, Cumberland County, NC

Randolph Cheek received 250 acres located north of Deep River adjoining **Frederick Gregg**, **Cheek** and **Governor Johnston** and including **Joshua Hancock**'s improvement. **John Phillips** and **Randolph Cheek** were chain carriers.

576. 1774, Jan 11 -- Land Grant #1698, Cumberland County, NC
John Gardner received 100 acres located on Grassy Creek adjoining **Enoch Spinks**, **Owen Carpenter** and his own line. **Owen Carpenter** and **David Stroud** were chain carriers.

577. 1774, Jan 11 -- Land Grant #1719, Cumberland County, NC
Thomas Briggs received 300 acres located on Deep River near the mouth of Buffalo Creek adjoining **John Trapp** and including **Barton**'s improvement. **David Stroud** and **John Trapp** were chain carriers.

578. 1774, Jan 12 -- Land Grant #1700, Cumberland County, NC
Richard Bird received 150 acres located on Buckhorn Branch south of Deep River adjoining **John Williamson** and **Owen Carpenter**. **William Williamson** and **William Bird** were chain carriers.

579. 1774, Jan 12 -- Land Grant #1701, Cumberland County, NC
John Williamson received 200 acres located on the drains of Grassy Creek including the meadows adjoining his own line. **William Williamson** and **William Bird** were chain carriers.

580. 1774, Jan 12 -- Land Grant #1552 and #1741, Cumberland County, NC
Leonard Heart received 100 acres located on the drains of Grassy Creek adjoining **John Williamson** and **Richard Bird**. **William Williamson** and **William Reed** were chain carriers.

581. 1774, Jan 12 -- Land Grant #0417, Cumberland County, NC
William Smith received 50 acres located at the mouth of Cabin Creek adjoining **David Kagill**, **John Kagill**, own improvement. **Jesse Ritter** and **Jacob Cagle** were chain carriers. [*Editor's Note: Never granted*]

582. 1774, Jan 13 -- Land Grant #1359, Cumberland County, NC
James Stevens received 100 acres located on Horse Creek adjoining **Lewis Sowell**. **Jesse Ritter** and **Robert Edwards** were chain carriers.

583. 1774, Jan 13 -- Land Grant #0418, Cumberland County, NC
William Smith received 100 acres located on Buffalo Creek adjoining **Leonard Kagill**. **Jesse Ritter** and **Isham Smith** were chain carriers.

[*Editor's Note: Never granted*]

584. 1774, Jan 14 -- Land Grant #1356, Cumberland County, NC
Donald McDonald received 150 acres located on Suck Creek of McLendons Creek adjoining **Jacob McClendon** and **Jamima McClendon**. **John Martin** and **Murdock McQueen** were chain carriers.

585. 1774, Jan 14 -- Land Grant #1356, Cumberland County, NC
Daniel Shaw received 100 acres located on Dry Creek and Juniper adjoining **John Stevens** and **Dempsey Watson**. **John McClendon** and **John McLeod** were chain carriers.

586. 1774, Jan 15 -- Land Grant #1610 & #1800, Cumberland County, NC
Joel McClendon received 200 acres located on Dry Creek of Juniper Branch of McLendons Creek adjoining his own line and **John Stevens**. **Isaac Sowell** and **Obediah Sowell** were chain carriers. [*Editor's Note: deeded to Edward Cox 1774*]

587. 1774, Jan 15 -- Land Grant #1611 & 1801, Cumberland County, NC
Joel McClendon received 200 acres located on McLendons Creek adjoining his own line and **Jacob McClendon**. **Thomas McClendon** and **William Barrett** were chain carriers.

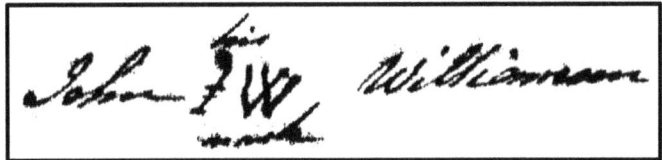

588. 1774, Jan 18 -- Deed Book 6 Page 352, Cumberland County, NC
John Williamson Sr. and **Jamimma** deeded his son **William Williamson** 100 acres located north of Grassy Creek adjoining **Leonard Hart**. **Windsor Pearce** and **Richard Bird** were witnesses.

589. 1774, Jan 20 -- Land Grant #1357, Cumberland County, NC
Thomas Collins received 150 acres located on McLendons Creek adjoining **Charles Seale**. **Richardson Feagin** and **Daniel Muse** were chain carriers.

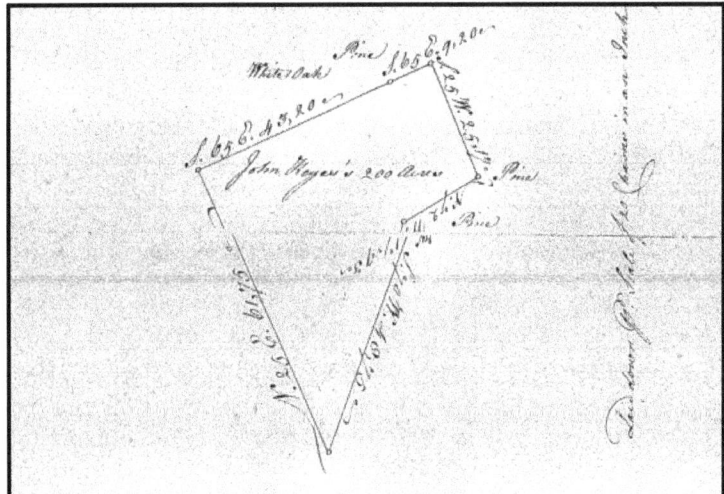

590. 1774, Jan 22 -- Land Grant #1714, Cumberland County, NC
John Smith received 100 acres located on Wet Creek ½ half mile above **Richard Dunn**'s Mill including the Hoop Pole Thicket. **Thomas Moore** and **Richard Dunn** were chain carriers. [*Editor's Note: **John and Easter Smith** deeded to **Richard Dunn** 1784 --> **Richard** and **Deborah Dunn** to **Alexr. McIver** 1784*]

591. 1774, Jan 22 -- Land Grant #1715, Cumberland County, NC
John Smith received 100 acres located on Wet Creek adjoining **Richard Dunn**. **Thomas Moore** and **Richard Dunn** were chain carriers.

592. 1774, Jan 26 -- Land Grant #1708, Cumberland County, NC
John Keyes received 200 acres located east of Wet Creek adjoining **William Keyes** and **Hugh Waddle**. **Thomas Moore** and **Joseph Williams** were chain carriers.

593. 1774, Feb 5 -- Land Grant #1594 & #1783, Cumberland County, NC

David Milton received a 100 acre Land Grant located on Governors Creek adjoining **Governor Johnston**'s line. **Sterling Carroll** and **James Collins** were chain carriers.

594.   1774, Feb 8 -- Deed Book 6 Page 225, Cumberland County, NC
Edward Cox and wife **Margaret** deeded **John Campbell** 150 acres located on head of McLendons Creek. Patented to **Edward Cox** 1764. **John Bethune, Donald McDonald** and **John Martin** were witnesses.

595.   1774, Feb 14 -- Deed Book 6 Page 272, Cumberland County, NC
Joel McClendon deeded **Edward Cox** 200 acres located on Juniper Branch of McLendons Creek adjoining **Jacob McClendon**. Patented to **Joel McLendon** 1769. **Thomas McClendon** and **James Graham** were witnesses.

596.   1774, Feb 14 -- Deed Book 6 Page 273, Cumberland County, NC
Joel McClendon deeded **Edward Cox** 300 acres located on Buck Creek or Juniper. Patented to **James McLendon** 1753. **George Cox, Thomas McClendon** and **James Graham** were witnesses.

597.   1774, Feb 16 -- Deed Book 6 Page 303, Cumberland County, NC
Josiah Williamson deeded **Thomas Elet** 200 acres located on McLendons Creek. Patented to **Thomas Mathews Sr.** 1757 and sold to his son **Thomas Mathews Jr.** and sold to **Josiah Williamson**. **John Kenney** and **John Gilmore** were witnesses.

598.   1774, Feb 16 -- Deed Book 6 Page 328, Cumberland County, NC
Thomas Elet and wife **Eleanor** deeded **Elexander MacLeod** 200 acres located on McLendons Creek. Patented to **Thomas Mathews Sr.** 1757 and sold to his son **Thomas Mathews Jr.** and sold to **Josiah Williamson who** sold to **Thomas Elit. Josiah Williamson** and **John Kenney** were witnesses.

599.   1774, Feb 17 -- Deed Book 6 Page 171, Cumberland County, NC
Cornelius Tison deeded **John Thornton Sr.** 100 acres located on Deep River and the Cane Patch adjoining **Howell Bruer** patented to **Tison** 1765. **Conner Dowd** and **Edw. Griffin** were witnesses.

600.   1774, Mar 7 -- Deed Book 6 Page 94, Cumberland County, NC
Christopher Yow and wife **Susannah** deeded **Alexr. Johnston** 50 acres on Lick Creek adjoining **Alexr. Campbell**. Patented by **Yow** 1768. **George McKay** and **Alexr. Allen** were witnesses.

601.   1774, Apr 27 -- 1771-1776 Court of Pleas and Quarter Sessions, Cumberland County, NC
William Burt and **Andrew Bates** appointed to appraise the estate of **Saml. Jackson** Dec'd. and divide the same amongst the kin.

602.   1774, Apr 28 -- Deed Book 6 Page 308, Cumberland County, NC
James Muse deeded **Alexr. Morison** 200 acres located northeast of the Wagon Road 1.25 mile below McLendons Creek. Patented to **Muse** 1773. **Donald Shaw** and **Normand Morrison** were witnesses.

603.   1774, Jun 19 -- Will, Cumberland County, NC
Will of **Jacob Rogers** Dec'd. Heirs: wife **Ruth**, daughter **Elizabeth Hancock**, daughter **Sarah Rogers**, daughter **Mary Ann Rogers**, sons **John** and **Enoch Rogers**. Executors: wife **Ruth** and **James Muse**. Witnesses: **William Manes, Charles Shearin** and **William Hancock**. Proven Oct 26, 1774.

604.   1774, Jun 11 -- Deed Book 6 Page 167, Cumberland County, NC
Kenneth Campbell deeded **Alexr. McLeod** 100 acres located north of Richland Creek and Weirs Branch adjoining **Aaron Burleson** patented to **Henry Atkinson** 1767. **Donald Morison** and **Donald MacLeod** were witnesses.

605.   1774, Jul -- 1774-1784 Trial and Appearance Docket, Cumberland County, NC
#12 **John Marsh** v. **Barthelomew Dunn**
Owen Carpenter and **Willm. Manus** listed as bail

606.   1774, Jul 2 -- Land Grant #1670, Cumberland County, NC
Phillip Alston received 300 acres located south of Deep River adjoining **Willis Dickson, Gabriel Hardin** and **Duke**.

607. 1774, Jul 8 -- Deed Book 6 Page 279, Cumberland County, NC **Jesse Ritter** deeded **Nathan Smith** 200 acres located on Wet Creek adjoining **James Chainey** and **Nicholas Newton**. **Thos. Branford** and **William Manes** were witnesses.

608. 1774, Jul 14 -- Deed Book 6 Page 270, Cumberland County, NC **William Seale** deeded **Christian Jackson** 50 acres located on Juniper Creek. **Frans. Stribling**, **William Jackson** and **Archibald McDonald** were witnesses.

609. 1774, Jul 14 -- Deed Book 6 Page 271, Cumberland County, NC **William Seale** deeded **Christian Jackson** 250 acres located on Juniper Creek. **Frans. Stribling**, **William Jackson** and **Archibald McDonald** were witnesses.

610. 1774, Jul 15 -- Deed Book 6 Page 353, Cumberland County, NC **Cornelius Tyson** deeded **John Carrel** 300 acres located south of Deep River adjoining **Thornton**. **Benjamin Tyson** and **Conner Dowd** were witnesses.

611. 1774, Jul 16 -- Deed Book 6 Page 170, Cumberland County, NC **Jonathan Williams** (of Chatham County) deeded **Moses Williams** 65 acres located south of Lower Little River. **James McDonald** and **William Manus** were witnesses.

612. 1774, Jul 16 -- Deed Book 6 Page 207, Cumberland County, NC **Vincent Garner** deeded **William Wright** 200 acres located on south fork of Bear Creek. **Lewis Meredith** and **Conner Dowd** were witnesses.

613. 1774, Jul 21 -- Land Grant #1277, Cumberland County, NC **John Martin** received 150 acres located on Richland Creek including the School House Ridge adjoining his own line. **Jacob McClendon** and **John Martin** were chain carriers.

614. 1774, Jul 23 -- Land Grant #1646, Cumberland County, NC **James Jeffry** received 150 acres located southwest of Cabin Creek.

615. 1774, Jul 23 -- Land Grant #3677, Anson County, NC **James Cotton** received 100 acres located on Cabin Creek near top of a hill near the [Cumberland] county line.

616. 1774, Jul 25 -- Land Grant #1665, Cumberland County, NC
William Burt received 300 acres located East of Drowning Creek adjoining **Samuel Jackson** and **Archibald Campbell**.

617. 1774, Jul 25 -- Land Grant #1676, Cumberland County, NC
Alexander McKay received 150 acres located between Buffalo Creek and Richland Creek.

618. 1774, Jul 25 -- Land Grant #1729, Cumberland County, NC
James Gibson received 100 acres located on Dry Fork of Tillis or Smith Creek including his own improvement. **Richard Dunn** and **Robert Edwards** were chain carriers. [*Editor's Note: deeded to* **Robert Cox** *1779*]

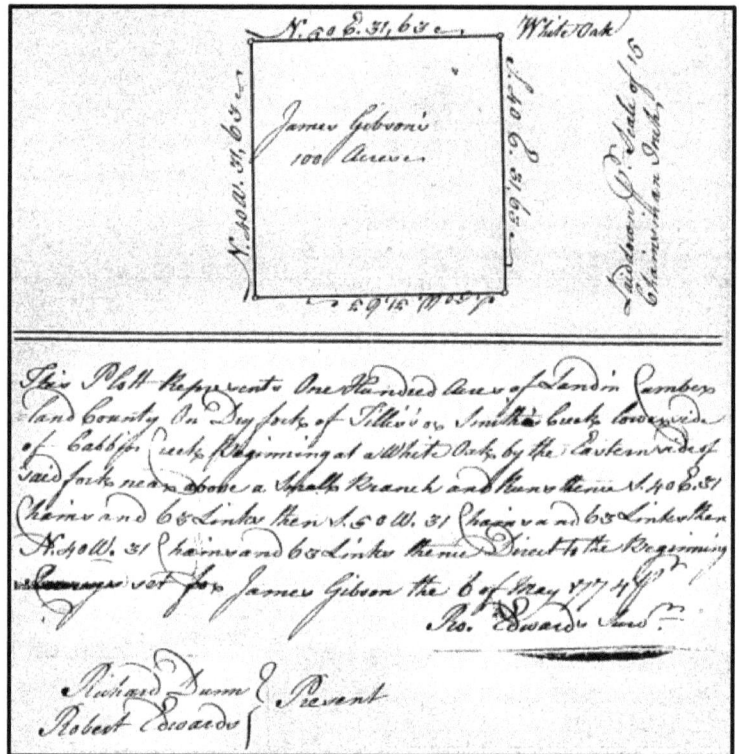

619. 1774, Jul 26 -- 1771-1776 Court of Pleas and Quarter Sessions, Cumberland County, NC
[Deeds] **Jacob McClendon** to **William Barret** proven by **Donald Shaw**
Nichelus Newton and wife to **Bartholomew Dunn** proven by **Thomas Green**

A. 1774, Aug 24 -- Land Grant #3236 and #3796, Anson County, NC
John Sowell received 100 acres located on Dicks Creek including his own plantation. **William Sowell** and **Thomas Dennis** were chain carriers.

620. 1774, Oct 24 -- Cane Creek [Quaker] Meeting Marriages Vol. 1 Page 62, Alamance County, NC
Benjamin Tison, son of **Cornelius** and **Jane Tyson**, of Cumberland County and **Ann Mayner**, daughter of **Henry** (Dec'd.) and **Jane Mayner** of Chatham County were married. **Jeremiah Piggott**, **Abigail Pike**, **Thomas Vestal**, **Mary Brooks**, **Margery Buckingham**, **Cornelius Tison**, **Jane Tison**, **Jane Mayner**, **Rachel Piggott**, **Sarah Bray**, **Sarah Tyson**, **Thomas Tyson**, **Richard Tyson** and **Katharine Tyson** were present and served as witnesses.

621. 1774, Oct 18 -- Deed Book 6 Page 296, Cumberland County, NC
William Morgan and wife **Mary** deeded **Ewell Wadkins** 100 acres located west of Cabin Creek below **Joseph Morgan**'s improvements. Originally granted to **Joseph Morgan** 9 Nov 1764 and sold to **William Morgan**. **James Jeffery** and **Temple Tullus** were witnesses.

622. 1774, Oct 21 -- Deed Book 6 Page 255, Cumberland County, NC
Joseph Collins (of Anson County) deeded **Richard Lyon** & Co. 150 acres located south of McLendons Creek on Mill Creek ¼ mile from the mouth patented to **Charles Seale** 1768. **Thos. Collins** and **William Crane** were witnesses.

623. 1774, Oct 24 -- Deed Book 6 Page 298, Cumberland County, NC
Joseph Dukeworth Jr. deeded **John Harden** 195 acres located south of Deep River adjoining **John Carrell**. **James McDonald** and **Levi Pennington** were witnesses.

624. 1774, Oct 25 -- 1771-1776 Court of Pleas and Quarter Sessions, Cumberland County, NC
[Deeds] Two deeds from **Wm. Seal** to **Christian Jackson** proven by **Wm. Jackson**
Jesse Ritter to **Nathan Smith** was proven by **William Manes**

625. 1774, Oct 27 -- Deed Book 6 Page 278, Cumberland County, NC

Elisabeth Brannan deeded Robert Graham 100 acres located on both sides of Buck Creek adjoining Graham and Thomas Matthews. Patented to Tarrance Brannan. John Campbell and Jams. Graham were witnesses.

626.   1774, Oct 29 -- 1771-1776 Court of Pleas and Quarter Sessions, Cumberland County, NC
John Overton appointed guardian to John, Jesse, Moses and David Overton, orphans of Aaron Overton with securities John Houton and Robt. Cheek.

627.   1774, Dec 10 -- Land Grant #1607 and 1797, Cumberland County, NC
John Cox received 100 acres located on McLendons Creek adjoining his own line. Nathl. Denis and John Cox were chain carriers.

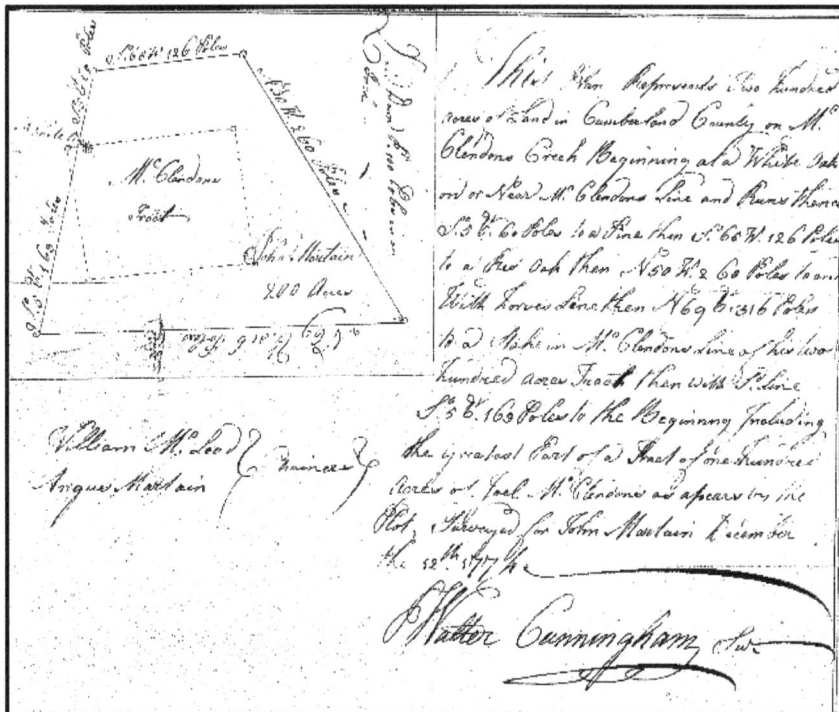

628.   1774, Dec 12 -- Land Grant #1563 and 1752, Cumberland County, NC
John Martin received 200 acres located on head of Locust Branch of McLendons Creek adjoining Horser, Joel McLendon and Murdo Martin. William McLeod and Angus Martin were chain carriers.

629.   1775, Jan 10 -- Deed Book 6 Page 293, Cumberland County, NC
Leonard Cagle and wife Susana Ceagle deeded Steven Richerton a tract of land west of Little Buffalo Creek. Bartholomew Dun and William Garner were witnesses.

630.   1775, Jan 12 -- Deed Book 6 Page 327, Cumberland County, NC
Thomas and Luvisa McClendon deeded John Martin 100 acres located on McLendons Creek adjoining John Martin. Patented to Joel McLendon 1763 and sold to Thomas MacClendon. Donald McDonald and Joel McClendon were witnesses.

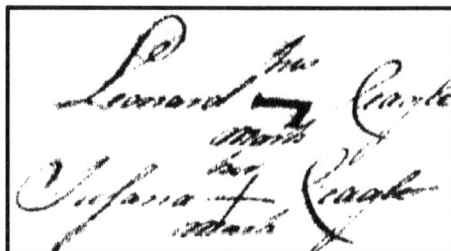

631.   1775, Jan 12 -- Deed Book 6 Page 397, Cumberland County, NC
John Hunnicutt Jr. deeded Philip Alston 100 acres located south of Deep River adjoining Joel McLendon, Gabril Hardin and Joseph Ducksworth Jr. William Douglass and Joseph Gordon were witnesses.

632.   1775, Jan 24-25 -- 1771-1776 Court of Pleas and Quarter Sessions, Cumberland County, NC
[Deeds] Leonard Keagle and wife Susanna Keagle to Steven Richerton proven by Bartholomew Dun
Wm. Morgan and Mary Morgan to Ewell Wadkins proven by Temple Tullas

633.   1775, Jan 25 -- 1771-1776 Court of Pleas and Quarter Sessions, Cumberland County, NC
Inventory of the estate of Jacob Rogers Dec'd. returned by executors James Muse and Ruth Rogers.

634.   1775, Jan 25 -- 1771-1776 Court of Pleas and Quarter Sessions, Cumberland County, NC
John Martin granted leave to have his gristmill on his land on McLendons Creek be recorded as public.

635.   1775, Jan 27 -- 1771-1776 Court of Pleas and Quarter Sessions, Cumberland County, NC
Gabriel Harden and Phillip Heron appointed patrollers from James McDonald's on Deep River to James Muse's.

636.   1775, Jan 30 -- Deed Book 6 Page 289, Cumberland County, NC

Thomas McClendon and **Levisa McClendon** deeded **Joel McClendon Jr.** 200 acres located on McLendons Creek. Patented to **Joel McLendon** 1758 and sold to **Thomas McClendon** 1770. **John Martin** and **Donald McDonald** were witnesses.

637.　　1775, Feb 14 -- Deed Book 1, Page 336, Guilford County, NC
Windsor Pearce and wife **Mary** deeded **Ransom Southerland** 100 acres located south of Deep River adjoining Pearces Creek and Read's Island. Granted to **William Searcy** 1761 and deeded to **Mary Pearce**. **John Lawrence** and **Jacob Shepherd** were witnesses.

638.　　1775, Feb 14 -- Deed Book 1, Page 338, Guilford County, NC
William Searcy Senr. deeded **Ransom Southerland** 37.25 acres located south of Deep River adjoining **Mary Pearce** and Read's Island. Granted to **William Searcy** 1761 and deeded to **Mary Pearce**. **John Larrance** and **Jacob Shepherd** were witnesses.

639.　　1775, Feb 16 -- Deed Book 6 Page 303, Cumberland County, NC
Josiah Williamson deeded **Thomas Elet** 200 acres located on McLendons Creek. Patented to **Thomas Mathews Sr.** 1757 and sold to his son **Thomas Mathews Jr.** and sold to **Josiah Williamson**. **John Kenny** and **John Gilmore** were witnesses.

640.　　1775, Feb 27 -- Land Grant #3279 and #3708, Anson County, NC
James Cotton received 200 acres located east of a Branch of Cabbin Creek.

641.　　1775, Mar 4 -- Land Grant #3230 & #3790, Anson County, NC
John Fowler received 200 acres located west of Cabbin Creek on the Crawford Road adjoining **John Donahue**.

642.　　1775, Mar 14 -- Deed Book 1, Page 352, Guilford County, NC
James Graves deeded **John Needham** 300 acres located on both sides of Deep River adjoining **William Searcy**, **Thomas Graves**, **Joseph Carr** and **John Spinks**. Granted to **Thomas Graves** 1762 and deeded to son **James Graves**. **Ransom Southerland** and **John Moon** were witnesses.

643.　　1775, Mar 22 -- Deed Book 6 Page 341, Cumberland County, NC
Francis Stribling deeded **James McDonald** two tracts [1] 200 acres located on drains of McLendons Creek [2] 300 acres located on Killets Creek adjoining first tract and **Andrew Killet**. **Wm. Seale** and **Thos. Mathews** were witnesses.

644.　　1775, Apr 3 -- Deed Book 6 Page 455, Cumberland County, NC
John Hunicutt deeded **John Hardin** 100 acres located south of Deep River adjoining **Joel McLendon** or **Gabriel Hardin** and **Joseph Duckworth Jr. Randh. Hunnicutt** and **William Harden** were witnesses.

645.　　1775, Apr 17 -- Deed Book 6 Page 374, Cumberland County, NC
Joseph Carr (of Guilford County) deeded **Alexander McRae** 75 acres located north of Richland Creek adjoining **Jonathan Evans** and **Minyard. Alexr. Morison** and **James Muse** were witnesses.

646.　　1775, Apr 22 -- Deed Book 6 Page 351, Cumberland County, NC
John Martin deeded **John McRae** 150 acres located between McLendons Creek and Richland Creek including plantation where **Martin** formerly lived adjoining **Peter Bethune**. Part of 350 acre patent to **John Martin** 1774. **Joel McClendon** and **Will. McLeod** were witnesses.

647.　　1775, Apr 27 -- 1771-1776 Court of Pleas and Quarter Sessions, Cumberland County, NC
Willis Dickinson appointed road overseer in place of **John Overton**.

648.　　1775, Apr 27 -- Deed Book 6 Page 343, Cumberland County, NC
Andrew Killet (of Dobbs County) deeded **Daniel Muse** 120 acres located on McLendons Creek adjoining **Thomas McClendon** and **James [Jerome] Miller. James Muse** and **John Elwell** were witnesses.

649.　　1775, Jul 14 -- Deed Book 1, Page 345, Guilford County, NC

William Searcy Senr. deeded **Ransom Southerland** 75.75 acres located south of Deep River adjoining **Windsor Pearce**. **Windsor Pearce** was a witness.

650.   1775, Jul 22 -- Deed Book 6 Page 384, Cumberland County, NC
John Martin and **Meron McLeod** deeded **Murdock McQuien** and **John Shaw** 250 acres located between west of Dry Fork of Juniper of McLendons Creek adjoining **Dempsay Watson**. Patented to **John Martin** 1774. **John Campbell** and **Murdock Martin** were witnesses.

651.   1775, Sep 16 -- Deed Book 7 Page 510, Cumberland County, NC
John Rasbury (of Dobbs County) deeded **Malcolm McNeill** 150 acres located on Richland Creek. **Francis Rasbury** and **Norman Morison** were witnesses.

652.   1775, Sep 19 -- Deed Book 6 Page 392, Cumberland County, NC
Abraham and **Katharine Hunsucker** deeded **George Karenger** 200 acres located above Grassy Creek adjoining **Karenger**. **Christopher Yow** and **Christopher Caringer** were witnesses. [*Editor's Note: signed in German*]

653.   1775, Oct 3 -- Deed Book 6 Page 453, Cumberland County, NC
John Overton deeded **John Dunlap** 50 acres located on McLendons Creek adjoining **John Overton**. **Thos. Agarton** and **Arthur Wilsonbrown** were witnesses.

654.   1775, Oct 23 -- Deed Book 6 Page 454, Cumberland County, NC
John Overton deeded **John Dunlap** 100 acres located on McLendons Creek being part of the land **Overton** bought from **Thomas Collins**. **Thos. Agarton** and **Arthur Wilsonbrown** were witnesses.

655.   1775, Oct 26 -- 1771-1776 Court of Pleas and Quarter Sessions, Cumberland County, NC
A Deed from **Abraham Hunsucker** and wife to **George Karenger** was proven by **Christopher Caringer**.

656.   1775, Nov 16 -- Will, Chatham County, NC
Will of **John Brown**, Dec'd. Heirs: children **John Brown** [*manner plantation of 100 acres*], **Abner Brown** [*125 acres adjoining adjoining brother John*], **William Brown** [*125 acres adjoining his brother Abner*], **Ambrose Brown** [*125 acres adjoining brothers William and Jesse*], **Jesse Brown** [*125 acres adjoining brother William*] and **Mary Ashcroft**, wife of **John Ashcroft**. Executors: **Isaiah Hogan** and **James Bell**. Witnesses: **Joseph Stewart** and **William Riddle**. Proven Feb 1776.

657.   1776, Feb 4 -- Will, Guilford County NC
Will of **William Searcey**, Dec'd. Heirs: wife **Kezia**; son **William Searcy**; daughters **Keron**

Searcy [*tract of land called Morgan's Neck*] and **Mary Pearce**; granddaughter **Mary Pearce**. Witnesses: **Arthur Smith**, **James Whittel** and **Adam Marmosh**. Proven May 1776.

---

658. 1776, Aug 7 -- Deed Book 7 Page 91, Cumberland County, NC
Robert Cox deeded **Donald Campbell** 100 acres located on the drains of McLendons Creek adjoining **Edward Cox**. Patented to **Cox** 1774. **James McDonald** and **John Cox** were witnesses.

659. 1776, Oct 6 -- Deed Book 1, Page 51, Randolph County, NC
John Needham deeded **Joseph Carr** 100 acres located on Deep River adjoining **Thomas Graves**. **Hamon Sutherland** and **Jacob Sheppard** were witnesses.

660. 1776, Nov 9 -- Will Book A Page 205, Orange County, NC
Will of **Robert Holloway**, Dec'd. Heirs: Wife: **Martha** (third wife). Sons: (eldest) **Samuel**, **Steven**. Daughters: **Elizabeth Horner**, **Brigett**, **Mary Readen**. Children from third wife **Martha**: **Priscilla**, **Susannah**, **Ann**, **Steven**, **Rachell**, **Ruth**, **Jane**, **Litici**[?]. Executrix: wife **Martha**. Witnesses: **Joseph Baker**, **Mary Baker**, **John Baker**. Proven Nov 1778.

661. 1777 -- Tax List, Cumberland County, NC, **Captain John Cox**'s District [all residents]
Name and amount of taxable property: **John Gardner** $100; **Christopher Yow** $300; **George Caringer** $350; **Owen Carpenter** $500; **Richard Dunn** $176; **William Williamson** $150; **John Keys** $176; **Richard Dunngaune** $100; **Thomas Keys** $160; **William Manus** $150; **Bartholomew Dunn** $176; **William Lee** $176; **William Manus** $160; **Isaac Dunn** $100; **Alexr. Aurty** $100; **Jesse Reter** $100; **John Hodges** $100; **Arthur Manus** $100; **Henry Jackson** $100; **Alexr. Furgerson** $124; **William Dun** $100; **Robert Cox** $150; **Stephen Richardson** $136; **William Jackson** $192; **Frances Tidwell** $150; **James Jeffry** $300; **James Jeffry Jr.** $150; **James Morgan** $146; **Neill Wadkins** $136; **William Morgan** $160; **John Morgan** $130; **John Shufell** $400; **Peter Shamberger** $174; **Richard Bird** $120; **George Cagle** $120; **Jacob Statuet [Stutts]** $150; **John Cagle** $310; **Robert Grimes** $245; **Pashons Baront** $176; **William Smith** $336; **Nathan Smith** $166; **Andrew Bates** $238; **Henry Cagle** $150; **William Barot** $100; **Daniel Campbell** $200; **John Cox** $603; **Nicholas Newton** $546; **John Williamson** [not valued].

662. 1777 -- Tax List, Cumberland County, NC, **Captain Jacob Duckworth**'s District [selected residents]
Name and amount of taxable property: **Susannah Hancock** $488.16; **George Brewer** $100; **John Hancock** $263.15; **Joel Phillips** $100; **Gabriel Harden Junr.** $100; **John Phillips** $219.30; **John Dunlap** $225; **Gabriel Harden Senr.** $575; **John Harden** $675; **Randolph Cheek** $836.12; **Drury Richardson** $237; **William Richardson** $220; **Abraham Richardson** $180; **Joseph Furr** $100; **John Overton** $5680; **John Hunnicutt Junr.** $104; **Thomas Seale** $100; **Conner Dowd** $7447; **James Muse** $2435; **Anthony Seale** $100; **Isaac Hill** $444; **David Lawson** $135; **William Hancock** $100; **Hartwell Hunnicutt** $201; **Robert Cheek** $1200; **James Collins** $100; **Joseph Duckworth** $400; **Elijah Beatis** $1500; **John Golston** $100; **Near Brewer** $100; **Benjn. Shealds** $100; **David Melton** $100; **Isaac Pennington** $500; **Edward Moore** $150; **William Dunn** $200; **Joseph Dunn** $1100; **Richard Upton** $100; **Benjn. Atkinson** $200; **James Harden** $100; **Nathan Manus** $100; **Thos. Atkinson** $100; **Joseph Gilbert** $600; **Thomas Tyson** $300; **Benjn. Tyson** $300; **Cornelius Tyson** $1000; **Danl. Muse** $100; **Peter Graves** $100; **Phillip Alston** $6936; **John Carrol** $700; **Jacob Duckworth** $370; **Willis Dickerson** $536.

663. 1777 -- Tax List, Cumberland County, NC, **Captain William Seale**'s District [selected residents]
Name and amount of taxable property: **Capt. William Seale** $482.17; **Christiania Jackson** $620; **Obed Sowel** $200; **Francis McClendon** $150; **James Hill** $100; **Richd. Fagens** $100; **Aaron Fagons** $100; **John Kadwell** $100; **James Kadwell** $100; **Danl. Muse** $100; **Farq. Beaton** $100; **Peter Beaton** $100.

664. 1777, Nov 1 -- 1777-1778 Court of Pleas and Quarter Sessions, Cumberland County, NC
The following be appointed in **Capt. Jacob Duckworth's** District: [Assessors] **John Overton**, **Jacob Duckworth** and **Willis Dickerson** [Justice] **Wm. Seale** Esq. [Constable] **John Weightat**. The following be appointed in **Capt. John Cox's** District: [Assessors] **John Cox**, **Nichelas Newton** and **John Williamson** [Justice] **Wm. Seale** Esq. [Constable] **William Manus**.

665. 1777, Nov 1 -- Cane Creek Meeting [Quaker] Minutes Vol. 1 Page 66, Alamance County, NC
William Dunn, son of **Joseph Dunn**, complained of [in Sep] for being guilty of appearing in a warlike manner and marrying outside of unity and after the usual labor extended, this meeting now disowns him.

666. 1778 -- Tax List, Cumberland County, NC, **Captain John Cox**'s District [all residents]
Name and amount of taxable property: **William Keys** $300; **Richard Dunn** $450; **John Keyes** $300; **Richard Dunn Jr.** $200; **James Jeffery Senr.** $250; **James Jeffery Junr.** $730; **Jesse Ritter** $230; **Isaac Dunn** $100; **John Hodges** $100; **William Manus** $250; **John Manus** $100; **William Smith** $100; **Alexr. Furgerson** $100; **Nathan Smith** $400; **William Barrot** $160; **James Stevens** $100; **William Dunn** $100; **William Jackson** $400; **Elizabeth Tullis** $150; **Andrew Bales** $500; **Robert Graham** $300; **Patience Barrot** $200; **George Morgan** $100; **George Brazel** $160; **Charles Sowel** $100; **Jeptha Medford** $100; **William Morgan** $200; **John Cagle** $800-3200; **Henry Cagle** $400-1200; **Jacob Stutts** $400-1200; **Alexr. Otrey** $100-400; **Bartholomew Dunn** $250-1000; **William Smth Senr.** $500-2000; **Francis Tredwell** $250-1000; **William Smith Jur.** $100-400; **Averet Smith** $200-800; **John Smith** $100; **Isom Smith** $100; **James Morgan** $300; **Uel Wadkins** $150; **John Field** $100; **Sampson Williams** $100; **Lenord Cagle** $250; **Saml. Tedwell** $100; **William Shuffle Sr.** $150; **James Ledlo** $150; **John Shuffle Jur.** $100; **John Shuffle Senr.** $800; **Adam Comer** $150; **Peter Shamburger** $300; **William Hunsucker** $100; **George Cagle** $300; **Danl. Manos** $100; **William Williamson** $300; **Christopher Carringer** $100; **George Carringer** $400; **Simon Hart** $100; **Henry Jackson** $100; **Solomon Barrot** $150; **John Carpenter** $100; **Thomas Godfrey** $100; **Stephen Richardson** $200; **Norman McLeod** $100; **Angus Stewart** $100; **John Funelson** $100; **Neil Matthewson** $100; **John McLeod** $300; **Angus Campbell** $100; **Allen Martin** $100; **Lochlin McCurry** $100; **Colin Baton** $100; **Farho Baton** $100; **Angus McMurray** $100; **John McNeil** $1500; **William Simmons** $100; **Richard Bird** $248; **John Morgan** $350; **John Garner** $4000; **Owen Carpenter** $1000; **Christopher Yow** $200; **William Manus Jr.** $150; **Danl. Campbell** $250; **William Gibson** $100; **Arch. Munk** $100.

667. 1778 -- Tax List, Cumberland County, NC, **Captain Jacob Duckworth**'s District [selected residents]
Names and amount of taxable property: **Susanna Hancock** $618.15; **Elizabeth Philips** $100; **William Richardson** $145; **John Goldson** $100; **John Hancock** $302.12; **David Lawson** $100; **Peter Graves** $100; **George Brewer** $100; **Joel Phillips** $100; **Abraham Richardson** $116; **William Hancock** $100; **Joseph Furr** $100; **John Phillips** $341.40; **Sterling Carrel** $193; **Anthony Seals** $100; **David Melton** $172; **Edward Moore** $411; **Reuben Shields** $100; **Robert Moore** $100; **Jas. Hardin** $100; **Aaron Feagon** $145; **Jas. Muse** $2812; **John Dunlap** $378; **Phillip Alston** $8363; **John Overton** $7454; **Elijah Beates** $1867; **Isaac Hill** $715; **Drewry Richardson** $464; **Hartwell Hunnicutt** $353; **Conner Dowd** $10850; **James Collins** $373; **John Hunnicutt Junr.** $400; **Cornelius Tyson** $6000; **Joseph Duckworth** $2000; **Joseph Dunn** $6000; **William Dunn** $800; **Richard Upton** $400; **John Carrol** $4000; **Gabriel Hardin** $2800; **William Hardin** $400; **Randolph Cheek** $2400; **Robert Cheek** $6000; **Benjamin Tyson** $1200; **Thomas Tyson** $1400; **Joseph Gilbert** $2000; **Benjamin Shields** $400; **Thomas Atkinson** $400; **Benjn. Atkinson** $400; **Isaac Pennington** $1600; **John White** $400; **Jesse Collins** $400; **Levy Askins** $400; **William Moore** $400; **William Davis** $400; **Danl. Muse** $400; **Jacob Duckworth** $370; **Thos. Seale** $100; **Willis Dickerson** $536.

668. 1778 -- Tax List, Cumberland County, NC, **Captain William Seale**'s District [selected residents]
Name and amount of taxable property: **Capt. William Seale** $825; **Joel McClindon** $704; **Isaac Sowel** $640; **Francis McClindon** $250; **Richardson Fagons** $400; **Christiania Jackson** $1240; **Peter Baton** $100; **James Cadwell** $1425; **James Hill** $100; **James Cadwell** $100; **Obed Sowell** $300; **Angus Beaton** $300; **Murdock Baton** $100.

Cumberland County Tax Districts 1770's-1780's

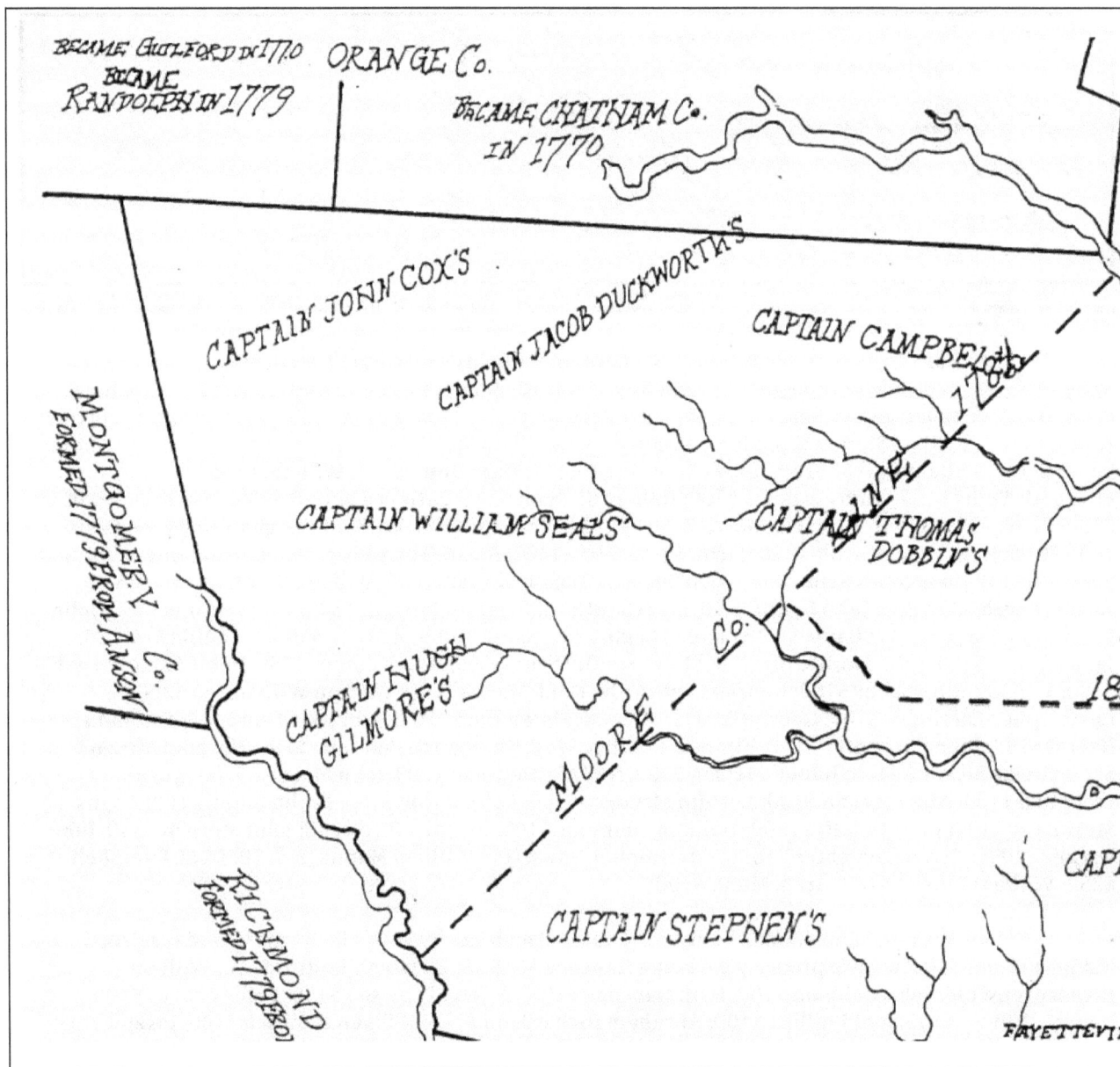

Created by Cumberland County Genealogical Society
Published in *Cumberland Chronicles* Vol. XVII, No.1, March 2002

669.   1778, Jan 30 -- 1777-1778 Court of Pleas and Quarter Sessions, Cumberland County, NC
Jeptha Medford was appointed constable in the place of **Wm. Manos.**

670.   1778, Mar 17 -- Deed Book 6 Page 480, Cumberland County, NC
John Harden deeded **Philip Alston** two tracts [1] 80 acres located below Rocky Ford adjoining **John Harden** and **John Hunicutt** [2] 195 acres located south of Deep River. **Jno. Gordon, John Hunnicutt** and **Daniel Gould** were witnesses.

671.   1778, Apr 2 -- 1777-1778 Court of Pleas and Quarter Sessions, Cumberland County, NC
Isaac Hill was appointed constable in the place of **John Williamson.**

A.   1778, Apr 10 -- Deed Book B Page 129, Chatham County, NC
John Brown deeded **Charles Stewart** 100 acres located north of Haw River including the house and improvement where **Abner Brown** now lives and being part of the tract that **John Brown Sr.** purchased from **Nathan Melton**. **Abner Brown** and **Mary Brown** were witnesses.

672.   1778, Apr 28 -- 1777-1778 Court of Pleas and Quarter Sessions, Cumberland County, NC
William Hancock was appointed road overseer in the place of **Willis Dickerson**. **Robert Cheek** was also appointed road overseer in the place of **Willis Dickerson**.

673.   1778, Jul -- 1777-1778 Court of Pleas and Quarter Sessions, Cumberland County, NC
The following signed the Oath of Allegiance to the State: [selected signers] **Thomas Kees**, **Bartholomew Dunn**, **William Dunn** and **William Meanus**.

674.   1778, Aug 10 -- 1777-1778 Court of Pleas and Quarter Sessions, Chatham County, NC Page 149
Ansell Melton appointed guardian to **Jesse Brown** and **Ambrose Brown**, having given bond with **Robert Patterson** and **John Thomas** in $L100 each guardianship.

675.   1778, Sep 14 -- 1778-1795 Land Entries, Cumberland County, NC
#118 **Joseph Wright** entered 300 acres located south of Deep River below the Cow Ford adjoining Cane Break and including the old **Barton** improvement.

676.   1778, Sep 14 -- 1778-1795 Land Entries, Cumberland County, NC
#119 **John Barton** entered 200 acres located north of Deep River including the Great Falls and three improvements.

677.   1778, Sep 14 -- 1778-1795 Land Entries, Cumberland County, NC
#120 **Isaac Pennington** entered 500 acres located on both sides of Deep River adjoining **John Carrell** and **Joseph Duckworth** above the mouth of White Lick Branch.

678.   1778, Sep 14 -- 1778-1795 Land Entries, Cumberland County, NC
#121 **Isaac Pennington** entered 200 acres located on both sides of Deep River at the head of the Big Island including an old improvement.

679.   1778, Oct 26 -- 1778-1795 Land Entries, Cumberland County, NC
#143 **David Argoe** entered 150 acres located north of Deep River adjoining **Trap**.

680.   1778, Oct 26 -- 1778-1795 Land Entries, Cumberland County, NC
#144 **David Argoe** entered 200 acres located on both sides of Cedar Creek near Chatham County line including **William Moore**'s improvement.

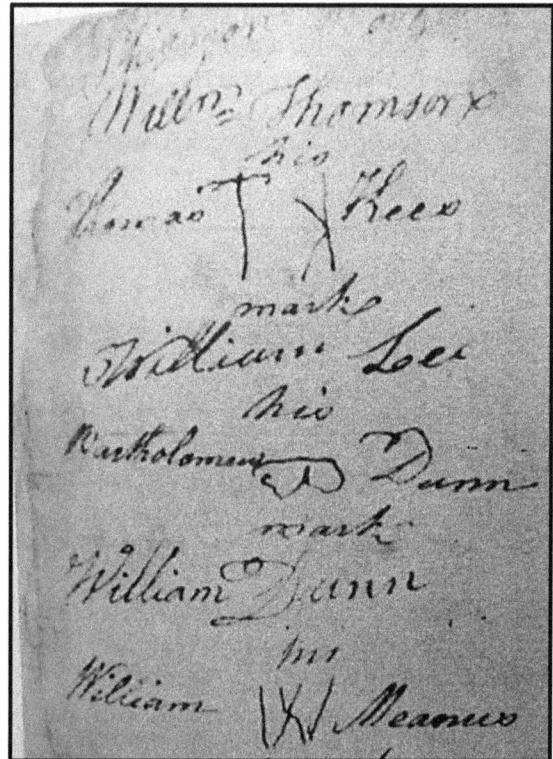

A.   1778, Nov 2 -- Land Grant #3511, Anson County, NC
Henry Smith received 400 acres located on Williams Creek adjoining **John Sheffield**. **James Sanders** and **Charles Sowel** were chain carriers.

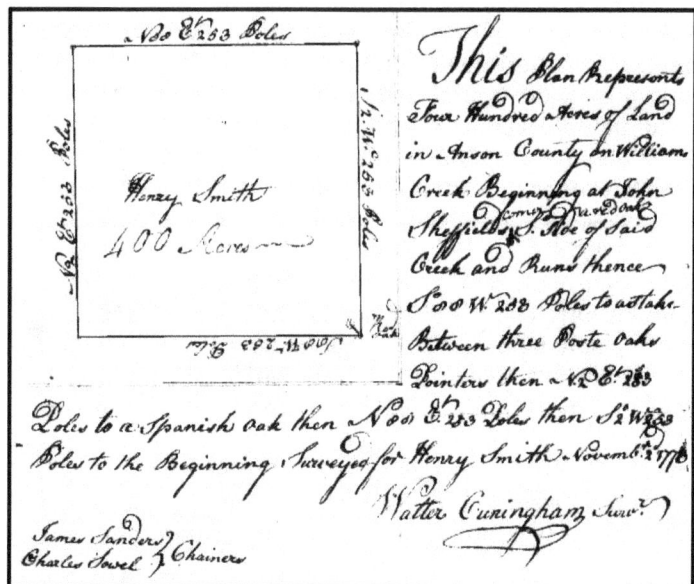

681.   1778, Nov 12 -- 1774-1779 Court of Pleas and Quarter Sessions, Chatham County, NC Page 167
Ansell Melton for **Brown**'s Orphans v. **Bendall Strawn**

682.   1778, Nov 28-- Deed Book 6 Page 521, Cumberland County, NC
Christopher Butler and wife **Elizabeth** (of Anson County) deeded **Robert Patterson** (of Chatham County) 300 acres. **Elias Butler**, **Henry Morris** and **Mathew Ledbetter** were witnesses.

A.   1778, Dec 5 -- Cane Creek [Quaker] Meeting Records (1756) Vol. 1 Page 75, Alamance County, NC
Jacob Barns' family obtained a certificate from this meeting to the monthly meeting in Wrightsborough in Georgia.

683.   1778, Dec 9 -- 1778-1795 Land Entries, Cumberland County, NC
#162 **Levy Pennington** entered 150 acres located on Buffalo Creek adjoining **David Lawson** and including the improvement where **Nathan Mainus** formerly lived.

A.   1778, Dec 15 -- Land Grant #110, Chatham County, NC
William Barber received 639 acres located on Indian Creek adjoining his own line. **Wm. Roberts** and **Peter Yates** were chain carriers.

> *1779 -- Montgomery County, NC formed from Anson County, NC*
> *Randolph County, NC formed from Guilford County, NC*

684.   1779 -- Tax List, Cumberland County, NC, **Captain John Cox**'s District [all residents]
Names and amount of taxable property: **Willm. Menos** $1000; **John Garner** $16000; **Stuffle Yow** $3000; **Owen Carpenter** $4000; **John Williamson** $4210; **George Carriner** $5010; **Batholimy Dunn** $1560; **Frances Tidwell** $1500; **Willm. Williamson** $1000; **Richard Bird** $2050; **John Cagle** $2600; **Alexander Otry** $500; **William Kees** $1600; **John Kees** $1510; **Nicolas Newton** $2010; **David Richardson** $1410; **Rebacah Copelan** $8050; **Ansel Melton** $1760; **Robert Patterson** $2000; **Willm. Richardson** $100; **Willm. Dunn** $620; **John Cox** $2500; **Patience Barret** $844; **Willm. Smith** $200; **Andrew Bates** $1500; **Richard Dunn Jr.** $750; **Richard Dunn** $700; **Isaac Dunn** $640; **Isakiah Dunn** $400; **Angush Stewart** $400; **Daniel McLoud** $800; **Norman Morrison** $800; **Jeffry Medford** $740; **Newil Watkins** $940; **John Held** $650; **James Morgan** $2000; **George Braswell** $440; **Willm. Morgan** $2800; **John Morgan** $3000; **Adam Comer** $2050; **James Ledlow** $1600; **Nathan Smith** $1440; **Willm. Smith** $1800; **Evrit Smith** $3200; **James Smith** $900; **John Smith** $800; **Lenard Kegle** $3100; **George Keagle** $1900; **Henry Keagle** $2400; **Jacob Stuts** $2000; **Willm. Smith Jr.** $2300; **Willm. Barrinton** $400; **Daniel McDonald** $230; **Daniel Campbell** $300; **John Buchanan** $450; **Kenith McDonald** $440; **Daniel McLoud** $420; **Robrt. Cox** $900; **John Carpenter** $1000; **Thos. Grimes** $400; **Soloman Barret** $400; **Simon Hart** $300; **Hardy Davis** $930; **Arthur Leadbeter** $100; **Henry Jackson** $620; **John Jenkins** $300; **John Shuffle Jr.** $300; **John McLoud Jr.** $400; **Willm. Jackson** $1300; **John Jackson** $1200.

685.   1779 -- Tax List, Cumberland County, NC, **Captain Joseph Duckworth**'s District [selected residents]
Names and amount of taxable property: **Joseph Furr** $260; **Randolph Hunicut** $220; **Will. Dickeson** $1610; **John Phillips** $1020; **Rubin Sheals** $987; **Gabril Harden** $2000; **Benjamin Sheals** $220; **Willm. Hancock** $400; **Susanah Hancock** $1500; **John Carrill** $3800; **John Hunicut Jr.** $300; **John Overton** $1500; **Elijah Bettis** $7000; **Edward Moore** $1200; **Isaac Hill** $3200; **Phillip Alston** $25600; **Coner Dowd** $21750; **David Melton** $450; **Hartwell Hunicut** $450; **John Dun** $1200; **Joseph Duckworth** $6010; **James Moore** $200; **Phillip Cheek** $800; **Demsey Phillips** $800; **William Harden** $250; **Lewis Laughan** $200; **George Brewer** $200; **Richard Cheek** $780; **Isaac Penington** $2960; **Willm. Harden** $1700; **Levy Askins** $200; **Cornelius Tyson** $1700-6800; **Benjamin Tyson** $570-2280; **Joseph Gilbert** $1100-4400; **Robert Cheek** $800-3200; **Benjamin Atkinson** $200-800; **Jesse Upton** $780-3120; **Willm. Dunn** $240-960.

686. 1779 -- Tax List, Cumberland County, NC, **Captain Hunnicutt**'s District [selected residents]
Name and amount of taxable property: **Richard Fagan** $510; **Aaron Fagins** $135; **Jonathan Cadwell** $100; **Angus Beaton** $460; **Francis McClendon** $430; **Peter Beaton** $320; **James Cadwell** $1660; **Wm. Seale** $1497; **Christian Jackson** $3450; **Jas. Muse Sr**. $6510.

687. 1779 -- Tax List, Montgomery County, NC [selected residents]
Richard Bean; Jonathan Carpenter; Jesse McClendon; Joel McClendon; William Morgan; John Smith; Charles Sowel. [_Editor's Note: those listed above are believed to be past residents of Moore County, NC and can be found in numerous land transactions over the period._]

688. 1779 -- Tax List, Randolph County, NC, **Windsor Pierce**'s List [selected residents]
Name and acreage: **William Searsey** 640 acres; **Adam Andrews** 300 acres; **Cornelius Lathem Sr**. 100 acres; **Coorod Andrews** 100 acres; **Aron Hill** 500 acres; **Thomas Cost** 440 acres; **John Foushee Garner** 250 acres;

John Vandiford 250 acres; **James Lathem** 235 acres; **James Graves** no acreage; **Thomas Needham** no acreage; **Vincent Garner** no acreage; **Cornelius Lathem Jr.** no acreage; **Stephen Searsey** no acreage; **Windsor Pearce** 100 acres; **John Needham** 200 acres; **James Garner** 250 acres; **John Spinks** 150 acres; **Amy Spinks** 150 acres; **John Kerr** listed but didn't return taxable property.

689.　　1779 -- Tax List, Randolph County, NC, **John Hind**'s List [selected residents]
Name and acreage: **Isaac Readfarn** 100 acres; **Joseph Kerr** 700 acres; **Robert Kerr** 6 acres improved; **William Argo** 200 acres; **Joseph Hix** 10 acres improved; **William Reid Sr.** 30 acres improved; **Charles Golson** 100 acres; **Arthur Smith** 8 acres improved; **William Reid Jr.** 275 acres; **William Needham** 20 acres improved.

690.　　1779, Jan 23 -- Will, Randolph County, NC
Will of **Joseph Kerr**, Dec'd. Heirs: brothers **John Kerr**, **William Kerr**, **James Kerr** and **Nathaniel Kerr** and sister **Mary Dougan**. Executors: brother **Nathaniel Kerr**. Witnesses: **Jno. Collein** and **John Ryan**. Proven Mar 1779.

691.　　1779, Jan 26 -- General Assembly Session Records
Petition to divide Guilford County, NC. **William Searcey**, **William Searcy** [likely Sr. and Jr.], **Windsor Pearce**, **Nicholas Nall** and **William Read, Jun.** were among the signers. [Editor's Note: Petition resulted in the formation of Randolph County from Guilford County.]

692.　　1779, Jan 27 -- 1778-1779 Court of Pleas and Quarter Sessions, Cumberland County, NC
Jas. Muse was appointed overseer in the place of **Jas. McDonald**.

693.　　1779, Jan 29 -- 1778-1779 Court of Pleas and Quarter Sessions, Cumberland County, NC
Insolvents allowed by the court in **Jacob Duckworth's** district: [selected names] **John Harden**, **Jesse Collins**, **Benja. Elkins**, **Lennear Brewer**, **James Harden**, **Peter Graves**, **John Womble**, **Danl. Muse** and **Wm. Davis**.

694.　　1779, Feb 3 -- 1778-1795 Land Entries, Cumberland County, NC
#280 **John Dunlap** entered 250 acres located east of Buck Creek adjoining **John Overton**.

695.　　1779, Feb 3 -- 1778-1795 Land Entries, Cumberland County, NC
#281 **Robert Cobb** entered 250 acres located near Alligator Pond on Deep River including the improvement where **David Melton** lives.

A.　　1779, Feb 5 -- Deed Book B Page 172, Chatham County, NC
Abner Brown deeded **Thomas Bell** 125 acres on Haw River and Second Creek adjoining **Charles Stewart**. **Mark Cooper** and **John Brown** were witnesses.

696.　　1779, Feb 6 -- 1778-1795 Land Entries, Cumberland County, NC
#291 **Charles Sherring** entered 200 acres located on the head of the Persummon Glade Creek.

697.　　1779, Feb 16 -- 1778-1795 Land Entries, Cumberland County, NC
#320 **John Burt** entered 300 acres located on Pocket Creek on **Connor Dowd's** road including the **David Milton**'s improvement.

698.　　1779, Mar 1 -- Land Grant #1832, Cumberland County, NC
William Seale received 50 acres located on Dunhams Creek adjoining **McMullen**. **Ralf Davis** and **Charles Seals** were chain carriers.

699.　　1779, Mar 6 -- Land Grant #1948, Cumberland County, NC
Joseph Wright received 300 acres located south of Deep River below the Cow Ford and Cane Brake

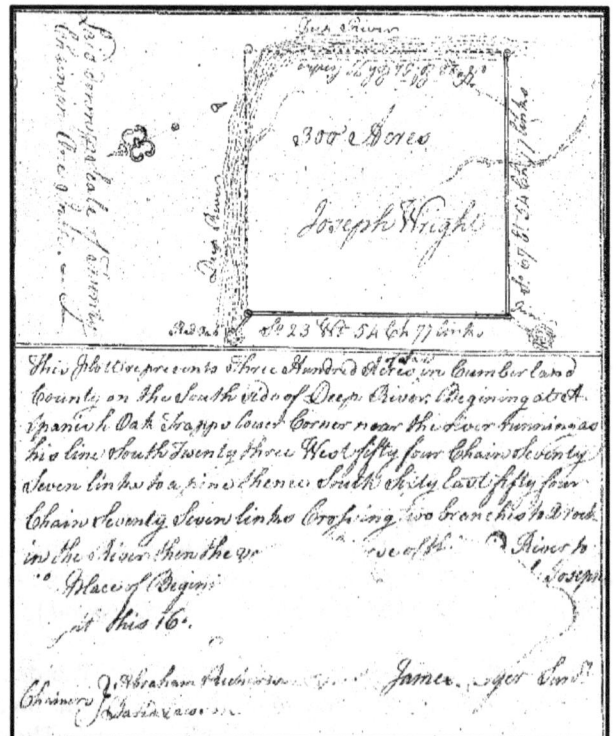

adjoining **Trapp** and including **Barton**'s improvement. **Abraham Richardson** and **David Lawson** were chain carriers.

---

700.   1779, Apr 29 -- 1779-1782 Court of Pleas and Quarter Sessions, Cumberland County, NC
Nicholas Newton, **John Cox** and **John Williams[on]**, assessors in **Capt. Cox**'s district be allowed $5 each.

701.   1779, May 8 -- Deed Book 7 Page 11, Cumberland County, NC
James Gibson deeded **Robert Cox** 100 acres located on the Dry Fork of Tillis or Smith Creek on lower side of Cabin Creek. **John Cox** and **Edward Cox** were witnesses.

702.   1779, May 9 -- Deed Book 1, Page 16, Randolph County, NC
Lambert Reed deeded **John Johnston** 50 acres located at the mouth of Bufelow Creek of Deep River adjoining **William Sercy**. **Charles Goldston** and **Joseph Carr** were witnesses.

A.   1779, Jun 27 -- Land Grant #391, Wake County, NC
Joseph Britt received 640 acres located north of Middle Creek and both sides of Juniper Branch adjoining **Hardy Sanders**, **John Myatt** and including his own improvement. **Mills Bearfield** and **Thomas Etheridge** were chain carriers.

703.   1779, Jul 7 -- Land Grant #546, Chatham County, NC
William Deaton received 400 acres located on both sides of Cedar Creek. **John Powers** and **James Deaton** were chain carriers. [*Editor's Note: **Nathan Deaton** deeded 200a to **William Needham** 1787 --> **William** and **Sary Needham** deeded to **John Vandiford** 1788 ; **Nathan** and **Margaret Deaton** deeded 200a to **James Deaton** 1787*]

704.   1779, Jul 7 -- Land Grant #551, Chatham County, NC
William Deaton received 300 acres located on both sides of Cedar Creek. **John Powers** and **James Deaton** were chain carriers. [*Editor's Note: **Nathan Deaton** deeded to **John Powers** 1786*]

A.   1779, Jul 15 – Land Grant #572, Chatham County, NC
Jeremiah Melton received 300 acres located on Little Indian Creek and the Cumberland [Moore] County line adjoining **Powell**. **Sterling Carroll** and **Levi Doughty** were chain carriers.

705.   1779, Jul 29 -- 1778-1795 Land Entries, Cumberland County, NC
#373 **Robert Paterson** entered 50 acres located on Wet Creek adjoining **Anson Milton** and including **William Dunn**'s improvement.

706.   1779, Jul 29 -- 1778-1795 Land Entries, Cumberland County, NC
#374 **Robert Paterson** entered 100 acres located on Horse Creek including the improvement where **James Stevens** lives.

707.   1779, Jul 29 -- 1778-1795 Land Entries, Cumberland County, NC
#375 **John Cox** entered 100 acres located on McLendons Creek including the improvement where **William Smith** lives.

708.   1779, Jul 29 -- 1778-1795 Land Entries, Cumberland County, NC
#376 **John Cox** entered 100 acres located on Flag Creek including the improvement where **Leonard Furr** formerly lived.

709.   1779, Jul 31 -- 1779-1782 Court of Pleas and Quarter Sessions, Cumberland County, NC
The following were appointed: Capt. Jacob Duckworth's District -- [Justice] **Thomas Matthews**; [Assessor] **John Gordon**; [constable] **John Weightat**. Capt. John Cox's District -- [Justice] **Thomas Matthews**; [Assessor] **Willis Dickerson**; [constable] **Wm. Manus / Wm. Dunn**.

710.   1779, Aug 9 -- 1778-1795 Land Entries, Cumberland County, NC
#380 **Joel McLendon** entered 400 acres located on McLendons Creek adjoining his own line.

A.   1779, Aug 9 -- 1779-1781 Court of Pleas and Quarter Sessions Page 195, Chatham County, NC
Jesse Brown, orphan of **John Brown** Dec'd. being formerly bound to **Jeduthan Harper**, Esq. being now brought

into court, ordered that he be bound to **Lewis Kirk** to learn the Trade of a Hatter 'till lawful age being now sixteen years old.

B.　　　1779, Aug 13 -- Land Grant #347, Wake County, NC

Joseph Britt received 378 acres located north of Middle Creek and both sides of Guffies Swamp near the Mill Branch adjoining **Simon Turner**, his own line and **Thomas Etheridge**. **Joseph Britt** and **John Turner** were chain carriers.

C.　　　1779, Sep 4 -- Wrightsborough [Quaker] Meeting Records (1772-1793) Vol. 1 Page 39, McDuffie County, GA

A certificate was produced here for **Jacob Barns** and his wife **Mary** and their children: **Elizabeth**, **Mary**, **James**, **Olive**, **Abigail**, **Jacob**, **Jeremiah** and **Samuel** from Cane Creek monthly meeting in North Carolina.

711.　　　1779, Sep 6 -- Land Grant #1986, Cumberland County, NC

Isaac Pennington received 500 acres located on both sides of Deep River above the mouth of White Lick Branch adjoining **John Carrell** and **Jacob Duckworth**. Abraham Richardson and **David Lawson** were chain carriers.

712.　　　1779, Sep 13 -- Land Grant #1870, Cumberland County, NC

David Argo received 200 acres located on both sides of Cedar Creek and Chatham County line including **William Moore** improvement. **Isaac Pennington** and **John Johnson** were chain carriers.

713.　　　1779, Sep 14 -- Land Grant #1827, Cumberland County, NC

David Argo received 150 acres located on Deep River adjoining **Trap**. **Isaac Pennington** and **David Argo** were chain carriers.

714.　　　1779, Sep 14 -- Land Grant #1842, Cumberland County, NC

John Barton received 150 acres located north of Deep River including the mouth of Fall Creek and the Great Falls. **John Johnson** and **David Argo** were chain carriers. [*Editor's Note: **William England** built a grist mill on this property in 1780. Later became High Falls.*]

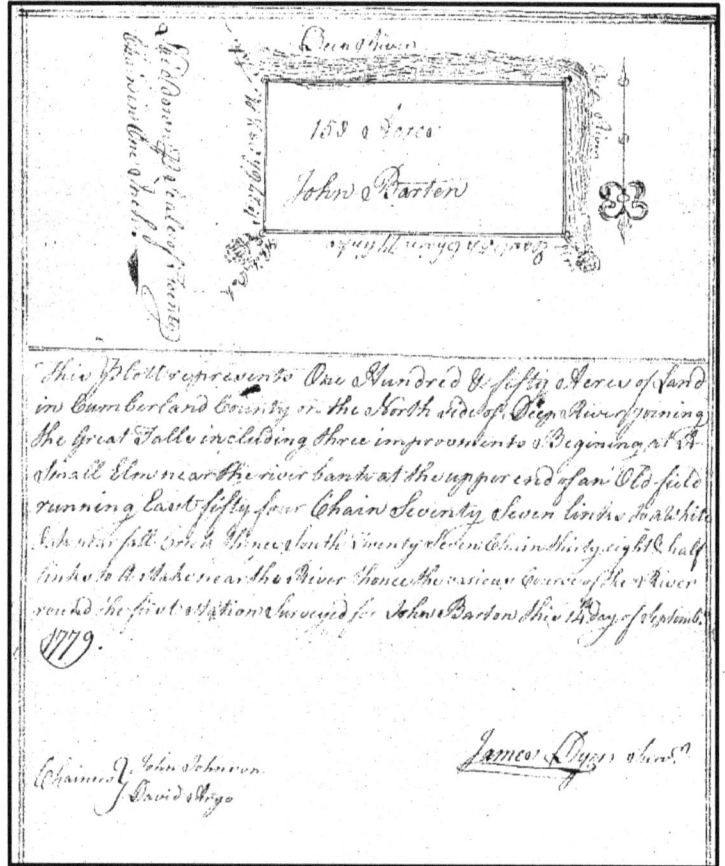

715.　　　1779, Sep 14 -- Land Grant #1843, Cumberland County, NC

Levi Pennington received 150 acres located on both sides of Buffalo Creek adjoining **David Lawson** and an improvement where **Nathan Manos** formerly lived. **Joseph Chason** and **David Argo** were chain carriers.

716.　　　1779, Sep 14 -- Land Grant #1879, Cumberland County, NC

Isaac Pennington received 200 acres located at the head of the Big Island on both sides of Deep River. **John Johnson** and **David Argo** were chain carriers.

717.　　　1779, Sep 18 -- Land Grant #1883, Cumberland County, NC

Joseph Chason received 100 acres located on Morter Glade of Buffalo Creek adjoining **Drury Richardson**. **Isaac Pennington** and **David Argo** were chain carriers.

718.　　　1779, Oct 4 -- Land Grant #1859, Cumberland County, NC

Charles Herd Gilmore received 100 acres located south of Deep River adjoining the Cain Brake where **Isaac Pennington** now lives and **Malcolm McNeill**. **Isaac Pennington** and **Hugh Gilmore** were chain carriers.

719. 1779, Oct 9 -- Land Grant #1824, Cumberland County, NC
Hugh Gilmore received 100 acres located north of Deep River adjoining **Conner Dowd**, **McNeill** and the place where **John Golston** now lives. **Isaac Pennington** and **Charles Herd Gilmor**e were chain carriers.

720. 1779, Oct 20 -- 1778-1795 Land Entries, Cumberland County, NC
#399 **Joseph Cheston** entered 100 acres located on Morter Glade Branch.

721. 1779, Oct 20 -- 1778-1795 Land Entries, Cumberland County, NC
#400 **Richard Dunn** entered 100 acres located east of Wet Creek adjoining his own line.

722. 1779, Oct 20 -- 1778-1795 Land Entries, Cumberland County, NC
#401 **Isaac Dunn** entered 100 acres located northwest of Wet Creek adjoining **Richard Dunn** and **Bartholomew Dunn**.

723. 1779, Oct 26-- Deed Book 7 Page 93, Cumberland County, NC
Joel McClenden (of Montgomery County) deeded **William Barrett** 100 acres located on McLendons Creek. Patented to **Joel McClenden Sr.** 1758 and sold to **Joel McClenden** 1775. **Solomon Barrott** and **Patience Barrett** were witnesses.

724. 1779, Oct 28 -- 1779-1782 Court of Pleas and Quarter Sessions, Cumberland County, NC
James Cadwell ordered to serve jury duty next term

725. 1779, Oct 29 -- 1778-1795 Land Entries, Cumberland County, NC
#406 **Robert Cox** entered 100 acres located on Tan Trough Branch adjoining **John Dunnahoe**'s old line and including **Angus Stewart**'s improvement.

726. 1779, Dec 16 -- 1778-1795 Land Entries, Cumberland County, NC
#432 **Richardson Feagin** entered 150 acres located on the head of McLendons Creek adjoining **Killet** and **Aaron Feagen**.

727. 1780 -- Tax List, Cumberland County, NC, **Captain John Cox**'s District [all residents]
Name and amount of taxable property: **William Menis Jur.** 200 acres/$450; **John Gardner** 580 acres/$3600; **Owen Carpenter** 350 acres/$1250; **Stifle Yow** 500 acres/$1350; **John Williamson** 500 acres/$1800; **George Carrner** 800 acres/$2250; **Betholimy Dunn** 200 acres/$450; **Francis Tidwell** 200 acres/$450; **William Williamson** 100 acres/$270; **Richard Burd** $150/$270; **Peter Shamburgar** 100 acres/$270; **John Cagle** 260 acres/$900; **Alexander Otrey** (horses and cattle only); **William Kees** 200 acres/$450; **John Kees** 200 acres/$450; **Nicolas Newton** 248 acres/$900; **David Richerson** 400 or 100 acres/$450; **Rebecah Coplain** 200 acres/$180; **Ansell Melton** 200 acres/$720; **Robert Paterson** 300 acres/$720; **William Richeson** (cattle only); **William Dunn** 50 acres/$180; **John Cox** 350 acres/$450; **Patience Barret** 160 acres/$270; **Alexander Kenady** (horses and cattle only); **John Shuffle** (horses only); **William Barret** 300 acres/$720; **Lachlon McCurrey** (horses and cattle only); **Ferquard Beaton** 100 acres/$90; **Lachlon McKennan** 150 acres/$135; **Angush Fletcher** (horse and cattle only); **Daniel McSwean** 50 acres/$90; **Angush McCurrey** 100 acres/$90; **Robert Graims** 200 acres/$225. *Not given in:* **Wm. Smith** $100-400; **Andrew Neats** $780-3120; **Richd. Dunn Jr.** $375-1300; **Richard Dunn Sr.** $350-1400; **Isaac Dunn** $320-1280; **Izekiah Dunn** $200-800; **Angush Stewart** $200-800; **Daniel McLeod** $400-1600; **Norman Morrison** $400-1600; **Jeffry Medford** $360-1440; **Newel Watkins** $470-1880; **John Felds** $325-1300; **James Morgan** $1000-4000; **George Braswell** $220-880; **Wm. Morgan** $1100-4400; **John Morgan** $1500-6000; **Adam Comer** $1050-4200; **James Leadlow** $805-3220; **Nathan Smith** $720-2880; **Wm. Smith** $900-3600; **Everit Smith** $1600-6400; **Isom Smith** $450-1800; **John Smith** $400-1600; **Lenard Kegle** $1550-6200; **George Kegle** $980-3920; **Henry Kegle** $1020-4080; **Jacob Stuts** $1000-4000; **Wm. Smith Sr.** $1160-4640; **Wm. Barrenton** $200-800; **Daniel McDonald** $100-400; **Daniel Campbell** $400-1600; **John Buchanan** $225-900; **Keneth McDonald** $220-880; **Daniel McLoud** $210-840; **Soloman Barret** $400-1000; **Simon Hart** $150-600; **Hardy Davis** $485-1940; **Arthur Leadbetter** $100-400; **Henry Jackson** $310-1240; **John Jenkins** $100-400; **John Shuffle Jr.** $150-600; **John McLeod** (single man) $400-1600; **Wilm. Jackson** $650-2600; **John Jackson** $600-2400; **Robert Cox** $450-1800; **John Carpenter** $500-2000; **Thos. Grimes** $400-1600.

728. 1780 -- Tax List, Cumberland County, NC, **Captain Jacob Duckworth**'s District [selected residents]
Name and amount of taxable property: **Joseph Furr** (horses and cattle only); **Randolph Honicut** (horses and cattle only); **Willis Dickason** 250 acres/$1125; **John Phillips** 100 acres/$360; **Rubin Sheals** 100 acres/$225;

Gabril Harden 200 acres/$900; **Benjamin Sheals** (horses and cattle only); **Wm. Hancock** (horses and cattle only); **Susannah Hancock** 200 acres/$630; **John Carril** 310 acres/$1350; **John Hunicut Jr.** 200 acres/$225; **John Overton** 2050 acres/$4500; **Elijah Bettis** 1250 acres/$1350; **Edward Moore** 200 acres/$360; **Isaac Hill** 200 acres/$540; **Phillip Alston** 2500 acres/$9000; **Conner Dowd** 3559 acres /$10000; **David Melton** 100 acres/$90. *Not given in:* **Hartwell Hunicut** $250-1000; **John Dunlap** $600-2400; **Cornelius Tison** $900-3600; **Joseph Duckworth** $315-1260; **James Moore** $100-400; **Benjamin Tison** $310-1240; **Joseph Gilbert** $555-2220; **Robert Cheek** $400-1600; **Phillip Cheek** $400-1600; **Demsey Phillips** $400-1600; **Willm. Harden** $120-480; **Lewus Laughan** $100-400; **George Brewer** $100-400; **Richard Cheek** $400-1600; **Benjamin Atkinson** $100-400; **Jesey Upton** $400-1600; **Wm. Dunn** $120-480; **Isaac Penington**; **Willm. Harden**; **Levi Askins** $100-200;

729.   1780 -- Tax List, Cumberland County, NC, **Captain William Seale**'s District [selected residents]
Name and amount of taxable property: **Isaac Sowell** 300 acres/$360; **James Cadwell** 65 acres/$108; **James Hill** 50 acres/$135; **Richardson Fagin** $200 acres/$135; **Antony Seal** 200 acres/$270; **Charity Muse** 1700 acres/$1350; **Charles Seal** 100 acres/$180; **Francis McLendon** (horses and cattle only); **Wm. Seal** 230 acres/$225; **Thos. Seal** (horses and cattle only); **Aaron Fagin** (horses and cattle only); **Angush Beaten** 200 acres/$270. *Not given in:* **Obediah Sowell** $350-1400; **James Muse** [lined out]; **Cristian Jackson** $3400-13600.

730.   1780 -- Tax List, Montgomery County, NC [selected residents]
Mark Allen; Christopher Butler; Jonathan Carpenter; James Cotton; Joel McClendon; William Morgan; Jesse Ritter; John Smith; Samuel Williams. [*Editor's Note: those listed above are believed to be past/current residents of Moore County, NC and can be found in numerous land transactions over the period.*]

731.   1780, Jan 1 -- Deed Book 7 Page 47, Cumberland County, NC
John Hancock deeded **Willis Dickenson** 100 acres located South of Deep River at the mouth of Big Branch adjoining **Willis Dickenson** and his own line. Part of 300 acre patent to **Thomas Armstrong**, Dec'd. and sold to **Conner Dowd** who sold to **Hancock. Conner Dowd, Reuben Shields, John Hunnicut** and **Randh. Hunnicut** were witnesses.

732.   1780, Jan 24 -- 1778-1795 Land Entries, Cumberland County, NC
#446 Joseph Wright entered 50 acres located on Deep River adjoining his own line opposite the Great Falls.

733.   1780, Feb 10 -- Deed Book 7 Page 299, Cumberland County, NC

Elizabeth Tillis, Temple Tillis and Willoby Tillis deeded Isaac Sanders 200 acres and a grist mill on a branch of the Deep River on the Yadkin Road. Patented by John Smith 1758. Lewis Sowell Sr., Shadrick Sowell and Lewis Sowell Jr. were witnesses.

734.   1780, Mar 16 -- Civil Actions, Randolph County, NC
John Beck and William Searcy sign bond that John Beck will appear in court Jun 1780. Windsor Pearce was a witness.

735.   1780, Mar 31 -- Land Grant #460, Chatham County, NC
Ansell Melton received a 150 acre Land Grant [for Orphans of John Brown] adjoining Jesse Brown. James Sellars and James Ballard were chain carriers. Entered 16 Feb 1779. Surveyed Apr 26, 1779. [Editor's Note: Ambrose Brown deeded to John Ferrington 1787]

736.   1780, Mar 31 -- Land Grant #450, Chatham County, NC
Ansell Melton received a 100 acre Land Grant [for Orphans of John Brown] adjoining Robert Patterson, James Sellars and John Brown. James Ballard and James Sellars were chain carriers. Entered 17 Feb 1779. Surveyed Apr 26, 1779. [Editor's Note: Jesse Brown deeded to John Ferrington 1787]

737.   1780, Apr 12 -- 1778-1795 Land Entries, Cumberland County, NC
#532 James Moore entered 250 acres located west of Waggon Branch adjoining the land where Jno. Golston lives.

A.   1780, Apr 15 – Land Grant #550, Chatham County, NC
Jeremiah Barnes received 200 acres located on mouth of Desolate Branch where Ezekial Hilliard now lives adjoining his own line. Joel Lawhorn and William Capps were chain carriers.

B.   1780, Apr 15 – Land Grant #0-3, Chatham County, NC
Jeremiah Barns received 640 acres located south of Indian Creek including his own improvement where he now lives adjoining Myrick. Ezekial Hilliard and Joel Lawhorn were chain carriers.

C.   1780, Apr 21 -- Land Grant #699, Chatham County, NC
William Goldston received 100 acres located on Fall Creek including Robert Hancock's plantation. Joseph Stephens and Robert Hancock were chain carriers.

D.   1780, Apr 22 -- Land Grant #694, Chatham County, NC
William Goldston received 200 acres located on Fall Creek adjoining Widow Powers's plantation. Robert Hancock and Bradley Powers were chain carriers.

E.   1780, Apr 22 -- Land Grant #662, Chatham County, NC
Conner Dowd received 300 acres located south of Fall Creek adjoining Goldston and including Edward Griffin's improvement. Henry Powers and Sampson Brown were chain carriers.

F.   1780, Apr 23 -- Land Grant #696, Chatham County, NC
Fox Palmer received 240 acres located on Fall Creek adjoining Elliott. Sampson Brown and Henry Powers were chain carriers.

G.   1780, Apr 23 -- Land Grant #697, Chatham County, NC
John Elliott received 400 acres located on Ocony Branch of Fall Creek. Robert Hancock and Sampson Brown were chain carriers.

H.   1780, Apr 24 -- Land Grant #692, Chatham County, NC
Charles Shearing received 200 acres located on Rattlesnake Branch of Tyson's Creek adjoining Benjamin Elkins. Vintsent Davis and William Patterson were chain carriers.

I.   1780, Apr 24 -- Land Grant #707, Chatham County, NC
Charles Shearing received 640 acres located on Richland Fork of Tysons Creek. William Phillips and Vintsent Davis were chain carriers. [Editor's Note: deeded to John Record 1798 > Bryan Boroughs 1805 > 320a to Zacheus Boroughs 1817]

J.   1780, Apr 25 – Land Grant #664, Chatham County, NC
Conner Dowd received 300 acres located on Flaggy Branch of Indian Creek including the improvement where **Edward Griffin** now lives adjoining **Duncan**. **Thos. Wilkerson** and **Jeremiah Phillips** were chain carriers.

K.   1780, Apr 25 – Land Grant #709, Chatham County, NC
Joseph Robertson/Robson received 250 acres located on Deep River north of Tysons Road. **William Capps** and **Ezekial Hilyard** were chain carriers.

738.   1780, Apr 27 -- 1779-1782 Court of Pleas and Quarter Sessions, Cumberland County, NC
John Williamson appointed overseer of the road from Bear Creek.

739.   1780, Apr 28 -- 1779-1782 Court of Pleas and Quarter Sessions, Cumberland County, NC
William England granted permission to build a grist mill on the Great Falls of Deep River on his land.

740.   1780, Apr 29 -- 1779-1782 Court of Pleas and Quarter Sessions, Cumberland County, NC
The following were appointed: Capt. **Hunnicutt's** District -- [Justice] **Wm. Seale**; [constable] **Chs. Seale**. Capt. **Duckworth's** District -- [Justice] **Phillip Alston**; [constable] **Wm. Popplin**. Capt. **Cox's** District -- [Justice] **Phillip Alston**; [constable] **Wm. Dunn**.

741.   1780, Jun 10 -- Will, Cumberland County, NC
Will of **James Muse**, Dec'd. Heirs: wife **Charity** [*Maner plantation where I now live and negroes Jo and Pen*], son **Daniel Muse** [*300 acres and 150 acres*], son **James Muse** [*plantation where he now lives and 150 acres joining Striblings Folly*], daughter **Ferriba Seale** [*200 acres where she now lives and negro girl Chloe*], son **Jesse Muse** [*the old plantation and 150 acres joining the Cain Patch*], son **Thos. Muse** [*150 acres at the mouth of the Mill Swamp formerly Charles Seal's and 150 acres between John Howell's and my old place*], daughter **Mary Muse** [*negro girl Venis*], daughter **Charity Muse** [*under age 16 -- negro girl Rachel*], daughter **Lidda Muse** [*200 acres joining Anthony Seal and taken up by Anthony Seal of Virginia and next child of negro women Pen*], daughter **Elizabeth Muse** [*under age 16 - 150 acres on the Mill Swamp joining Anthony Seal and taken up by Anthony Seal of Virginia and 300 acres on Road joining Morison*], son **Kindred Muse** [*Maner plantation where on he now lives -- at his Mother's death*] and daughter **Martha Muse** [*under age 16 - negro girl Luce*]. Executors: wife **Charity** and sons **Daniel** and **Jesse Muse**. Witnesses: **John Howell** and **Hannah Dun/Dean**. Proven 1782.

A.   1780, Jun 10 – Land Grant #807, Chatham County, NC
Joseph Stevens received 244 acres located on both sides of Fall Creek adjoining **William Goldston**. **Wm. Stevens** and **Thos. Simson** were chain carriers.

742.   1780, Nov 14 -- Deed Book 7 Page 89, Cumberland County, NC
John Smith and **Frances Smith** (of Montgomery County) deeded **Lewis Sowell** (of Montgomery County) 200 acres on Rocky Branch of Bear Creek. **William Gibson** and **John Carpenter** were witnesses.

743.   1780, Nov 30 -- Deed Book 7 Page 183, Cumberland County, NC
Charles Shearin deeded **Samuel Temple** 250 acres located north of Deep River adjoining **Robt. Cheeck** the land where **Corn. Tyson Sr.** formerly lived. **John Thompson**, **William Goldston** and **Daniel Gould** were witnesses.

744.   1781-1782 -- Memoir, Narrative of Colonel David Fanning, Page 19-21
Names of Loyalist Companies in Randolph County: Company 1: **John Spinks**, Ser. Maj. Company 3: **Wm. Finnacon**, Capt. (still in NC); **Richd. Bird**, Lieut. (still in NC); **Cornelius Latham**, Ensign, (still in NC). Company 6: **Stephen Walker**, Capt. (Murdered); **Frederick Smith**, Lt. (Hanged at Hillsboro for his loyalty); **Wm. Hunsucker**, Ensign

(Hanged at Hillsboro for his loyalty). Company 7: **Benj. Shields**, Lt. (still in NC). *Names of Loyalist Companies in Chatham County*: Company 12: **Wm. Deaton**, Capt. (killed in battle on the day after rebel **Gov. Burke** was taken [Sep 13, 1781]). *Names of Loyalist Companies in Cumberland County*: Company 16: **John Cagle**, Capt. (Hanged by rebels at P.D.); **Jacob Mauney/Maness**, Lieut. (still in NC); **Wm. Dunn**, Ensign. Company 17: **Reuben Shields**, Lt. (still in NC), **Wm. Hancock**, Ens.

745.   1781, Jan 6 -- 1779-1782 Court of Pleas and Quarter Sessions, Cumberland County, NC
Willm. Searcy allowed $100 for services as patroller in 1780.

746.   1781, Feb - Mar 7, 1783 -- 1781-1922 Miscellaneous Records, Randolph County, NC Confiscation Act
Wm. Golston, JP made oath that **William Searcy** claimed and reserved his property at **Cornelous Lathem Senr.**'s. [Editor's Note: **Cornelius Lathem** served with Col. **Davd Fanning** and much of his property was confiscated after the War.]

747.   1782, Jan 29 -- 1779-1782 Court of Pleas and Quarter Sessions, Cumberland County, NC
Jesse Muse was appointed the road overseer from Dunhams Creek to McClendons Creek. **Henry Cagell** was appointed the road overseer from McClendons Creek to Bear Creek. **Wm. Williamson** appointed overseer of the road from Bear Creek to the upper end of the county. **Willis Dickerson** was appointed the road overseer in place of **William Handcock**.

748.   1782, Jan 29 -- 1779-1782 Court of Pleas and Quarter Sessions, Cumberland County, NC
The following were appointed: Capt. **Hunnicutt**'s District -- [Justice] **Wm. Seale**; [constable] **Willis Dickerson**. Capt. **Cox**'s District -- [Justice] **Thos. Matthews**; [constable] **Wm. Cox**. Capt. **Seale**'s District -- [Justice] **Wm. Seale**; [constable] **Jonathan Cadwell**.

749.   1782, Jan 30 -- 1779-1782 Court of Pleas and Quarter Sessions, Cumberland County, NC
Will of **James Muse** proven by **John Howell**.

750.   1782, May 16 -- Land Grant #297, Montgomery County, NC
Jesse Ritter received 156 acres located on Densons Fork adjoining **William Haltom**. **Spencer Altom** and **Robert Stephens** were chain carriers.

751.   1782, May 22 -- Deed Book 7 Page 71, Cumberland County, NC
Mary James deeded her brother **John James** 150 acres including dwelling house and plantation where our father **Francis James** lived. Also signed by **Frederick Smith**. **Thos. Agarton** and **Thos. Seal** were witnesses.

752.   1782, Jun 15 -- Deed Book 7 Page 108, Cumberland County, NC
Thomas Seale deeded his daughter **Ann James** 100 acres including his dwelling house where he formerly lived on Overtons Road adjoining **Mary James** and **John Overton's** Gooden field. **Thos. Agarton** and **William Cockerham** were witnesses.

753.   1782, Oct 20 -- Deed Book 7 Page 211, Cumberland County, NC
Thomas Armstrong, Sheriff deeded **John Cox** Esq. 150 acres located on McLendons Creek below the mouth of Juniper Branch formerly the property of **Obediah Sowell** and sold to satisfy debts. **J. Campbell** and **John Jackson** were witnesses.

754.   1782, Nov -- Deed Book 7 Page 169, Cumberland County, NC
David Melton deeded **William Poplin** 100 acres located east of Governors Creek near **Johnston's** line. **Mathis Davis** and **Robbert Hunnicut** were witnesses.

755.   1782, Nov 4 -- Land Grant #3a, Randolph County, NC
William Searcy and **Charles Goldston** received 640 acres located on Deep River adjoining his own lines. **Richard Cheek** and **Seth Hill** were chain carriers.

756.   1782, Nov 4 -- Land Grant #1122, Guilford County, NC
William Sercy received 500 acres located north of Deep River adjoining **Charles Goldston**, **Reed** and his own line. **Seth Hill** and **John Pierce** were chain carriers.

757.   1782, Nov 5 -- Land Grant #1, Randolph County, NC

Windsor Pearce received 100 acres located on Pearce Creek including Buffalo Ford. **Seth Hill** and **William Mallit** were chain carriers.

758.   1782, Nov 6 -- Land Grant #1030, Guilford County, NC
Joseph Carr received 600 acres located on Flat Creek adjoining **Robert Carr**'s improvement and **John Powers'** improvement. **Robert Carr** and **James Garner** were chain carriers.

A.   1782, Nov 11 -- 1781-1785 Court of Pleas and Quarter Sessions Page 17, Chatham County, NC
Administration of the estate of **William Deaton** Dec'd. granted to **Sarah Deaton** with **James Deaton** and **Stephen Powel** as securities.

759.   1783 -- Tax List, Cumberland County, NC, **Captain John Cox**'s District [all residents]
Names and amount of taxable property: **John Garner** $210; **Owen Carpenter** $300; **Hardy Davis** $130; **John Williamson** $240; **Jepha Medford** $35; **Adam Commar** $70; **Wm. Williamson** $90; **John Morgan** $90; **Rich. Bird** $70; **George Carrner** $75; **Chrtr. Yow** $160; **Peter Shamburger** $100; **Robert Bird** $50; **Wm. Menis** [no amount]; **Alexr. Kenady** $45; **John Keyes** $70; **Wm. Menis Senr.** $75; **Danl. Menis** [no amount]; **Fras. Tidwell** $70; **John Manis** $25; **Drury Richardson** $70; **George Cagle** $90; **Jas. Ledlow** $120; **Leonard Cagle** $120; **Saml. Tidwell** $30; **Simon Hart** $70; **Henry Cagle** $100; **Jos. Cockman** $10; **Seth Menis** $5; **John Cagle** $140; **Jacob Stuts** $120; **E. Smith** $90; **Wm. Elmore** [no amount]; **Michl. Hill** $70; **Richd. Dunn** $260; **N. Newton** $190; **Alexr. Autery** $60; **Wm. Ashley** $110; **Jesse Riter** $210; **John Hare** $70; **Rebecah Coplin** $20; **Nathan Smith** $150; **Wm. Morgan** $70; **B. Dunn** $70; **Wm. Dunn** $60; **Susana Smith** $70; **Isom Smith** $40; **Alexr. McIver** $60; **B. Dunn Senr.** $70; **Ansell Milton** $70; **Danl. McKinsey** $20; **Isaac Dunn** $20; **John Fields** $70; **Stephen Richardson** $130; **John McCalley** $50; **Danl. McDonald** $35; **Alexr. Martin** $70; **Danl. McSwain** $70; **John McQueen** $10; **Kenth. McLoad** [no amount]; **Lenard Furr** $10; **Murdoch Beaton** $30; **Henry Jackson** $70; **Neill Mathewson** $50; **Wm. Moore** $30; **Norman Morrison** $50; **Wm. Smith** $50; **Allen Morrison** $40; **John Finelson** $20; **Thomas Keyes** $120; **Danl. Mathewson** $10; **Hezekia Dunn** $15; **Angus Campbell** $30; **David Richardson** $70; **John Shuffle Jur.** $60; **John Shuffle** $120; **Danl. McLoad** $70; **H. McLoad** $30; **John Buchannan** $20; **Keneth McDaniel** $30; **Reubin Freeman** $15; **Peter Hart** $210; **Robt. Stephens** $20; **Joseph English** [no amount]; **Norman McLain** $20; **Danl. McLoad** $40; **Hector McLain** $50; **Malcolm Morrison** $50; **Norman McLoad** $20; **Wm. Smith** $20; **John McDaniel** $30; **Solomon Barret** $40; **Thos. Jenkins** $40; **Robert Graham** $120; **John Cox** $450; **Patience Barrett** $70; **Thos. Graham** $30; **Angus Campbell** $20; **Wm. Barret** $100.

760.   1783 -- Tax List, Cumberland County, NC, **Captain John Hunnicut**'s District [selected residents]
Names and amount of taxable property: **J. Overton** $2060; **J. Phillips** $130; **G. Hardin** $125; **Wm. Hardin** $209; **J. Furr** $23; **J. Dunlap** $107; **J. Duckworth** $224; **J. Hunnicut Jur.** $133; **E. Bettis** $720; **W. Dickison** $225; **H. Hunnicut** $100; **R. Dickison** $30; **W. Dunn** $130; **R. Davis** $20; **B. Shields** $100; **W. Hardin** $10; **T. Tyson** $222; **C. Muse** $650; **L. Smith** $140; **L. Askins** $3; **R. Cheek** $300; **S. Hancock** $207; **P. Alston** $29015; **R. Hunnicut** $100.

761.   1783, Jan 24 -- Deed Book 7 Page 176, Cumberland County, NC
Isaac Hill deeded **Zachariah Smith**

100 acres located on Buffalo Creek. Patent to **Nicholas Smith** and conveyed by **John Smith** (his heir) to **Hill**. **Mary Richerson**, **Ritterell Doughty** and **Wm. Danielly** were witnesses.

A. 1783, Mar 10 -- Land Grant #756, Chatham County, NC
John Williams received 250 acres located on a branch of Tice's Creek, Cox's Road and the Cumberland [Moore] County line adjoining **Benj. Elkins**. **Benjamin Elkins** and **William Phillips** were chain carriers.

B. 1783, Mar 10 -- Land Grant #757, Chatham County, NC
Willis Phillips received 250 acres located on Seals Mare Branch of Tice's Creek and Cox's Road adjoining **Sheron**. **Benjamin Elkins** and **William Phillips** were chain carriers.

762. 1783, Mar 13 -- Deed Book 7 Page 139, Cumberland County, NC
Thos. Bullard deeded **Jonathen Caddel** 65 acres. **Jason Wadsworth** and **James Wadsworth** were witnesses.

763. 1783, Mar 31 -- Deed Book 7 Page 134, Cumberland County, NC
James McDonald deeded **James Fry** (both of Montgomery County) 2 tracts [1] 200 acres on drains of McLendons Creek, patented to **Andrew Killet** who sold to **Francis Stripling** who sold to **James McDonald**; [2] 300 acres located on drains of Killets Creek adjoining **Andrew Killet**. **Joel McClendon**, **John Morris** and **Richardson Fagin** were witnesses.

A. 1783, Apr 1 – Land Grant #737, Chatham County, NC
Joseph Stevens received 250 acres located on Fall Creek adjoining **William Goldston**. **Wm. Stevens** and **Thos. Simson** were chain carriers.

764. 1783, Apr 15 -- Deed Book 7 Page 127, Cumberland County, NC
James McDonald (of Montgomery) deeded **James Collins** 2 tracts [1] 100 acres located north of Deep River adjoining **James Barns** and **Jacob Barns** [2] 200 acres located north of Deep River adjoining **Elisha Hunter**. **Richardson Fagin** and **Thos. Collins** were witnesses.

765. 1783, Apr 22 -- Land Grant #3350, Mecklenburg County, NC
Jacob Cagle received 50 acres located on both sides of the Rocky River adjoining including **John Asly**'s improvement, **Doighles Winchester** and **Andra Mathews**. **Andra Mathews** and **Robert Bigger** were chain carriers. Entered Jun 3, 1779.

766. 1783, Apr 25 -- Land Grant #3382, Mecklenburg County, NC
David Caigle received 150 acres located west of Rocky River adjoining **Henry Smith**, **James Foleman**, **Paul Barringer**'s Waggon Road and **Lenard Furr**. **Jacob Haglor** and **John Haglor** were chain carriers. Entered Oct 22, 1779.

767. 1783, May 23 -- Deed Book 2, Page 10, Randolph County, NC
William Reed Junr. deeded **Richard Bird** 200 acres adjoining **Carr**. **Winsor Pearce** and **John Spinks** were witnesses.

768. 1783, May 23 -- Deed Book 2, Page 12, Randolph County, NC
William Read Senr. deeded **Richard Bird** 100 acres adjoining **Arthur Read** and **Nanion Sutherlan**. **Winsor Perce** and **John Read** were witnesses.

769. 1783, Jul 16-Mar 19, 1784 -- North Carolina Revolutionary Army Accounts, Vol. V Book 11
The following individuals appear on a longer list of people who applied in the Wilmington District for claims for revolutionary service: **Owin/Owen Carpenter**, **John Phillips**, **Tho. Seale**, **Chs. Seale**, **John Overton**, **Randle Cheek**, **Rob. Cheek**, **Jesse Muse**, **Wm. Seale**, **John Garner**, **Adam Comer**, **Isaac Hill**, **Jno. Williamson**, **George Carriner**, **Leonard Cagle**, **Henry Cagle**, **Jacob Stutts**, **Obediah Seawell**, **Isaac Seawell**, **Christian Jackson**, **John Sheffield**, **Bartho. Dunn**, **Charity Muse**, **George Cagle**, **John Dunlap**, **Solomon Barret**, **Gabriel Harden**, **Cornelius Tyson**, **Ben. Tyson**, **Col. Phil Alston**, **Tho. Tyson**, **John Morgan**, **Wm. Williamson**, **Wm. Smith**, **Wm. Barret**, **John Smith**, **Richard Byrd**, **Isaac Dunn**, **Willm. Dunn**, **Ever. Smith**, **John Cagle** and **Pr. Shamburger**. Wilmington Auditors Allowances to Militias from No. 5701 and 6016, Book. No.3: Capt. **John Cox**, **John Carpenter**, **Hezekiah Dunn**, **Isaac Dunn**, **Richard Dunn** and **William Dunn**. [*Editor's Note: the appearance on these lists does not necessarily mean they served in the militia during the Revolutionary War, but it is a good guidepost for further research.*]

770. 1783, Jul 25 -- Deed Book 7 Page 130, Cumberland County, NC
James Collins deeded **Thomas Tyson** 2 tracts [1] 100 acres located north of Deep River adjoining **James Barns** and **Jacob Barns** [2] 200 acres located north of Deep River adjoining **Elisha Hunter**. Thos. Collins and **William Dickinson** were witnesses.

771. 1783, Jul 26 -- Deed Book 7 Page 132, Cumberland County, NC

Charity Muse deeded **William Dunn** 250 acres located on both sides of McLendons Creek. **Jesse Muse** and **Nathl. Norwood** were witnesses.

772. 1783, Jul 26 -- Deed Book 7 Page 133, Cumberland County, NC
Charity Muse deeded **William Dunn** a tract located on both sides of McLendons Creek. **Jesse Muse** and **Nathl. Norwood** were witnesses.

773. 1783, Oct 25 -- Land Grant #144, Randolph County, NC
Ransom Southerland received 300 acres on Cow Branch of Fork Creek, the Moravian Road and the Salisbury-Cape Fear Road adjoining **Spinks** and including his own improvement. **Enoch Spinks** and **Johnston Leathim** were chain carriers. [*Editor's Note: deeded to Henry Couch 1796 --> 150a to Lewis Spinks 1797 and 150a to John Needham 1797*]

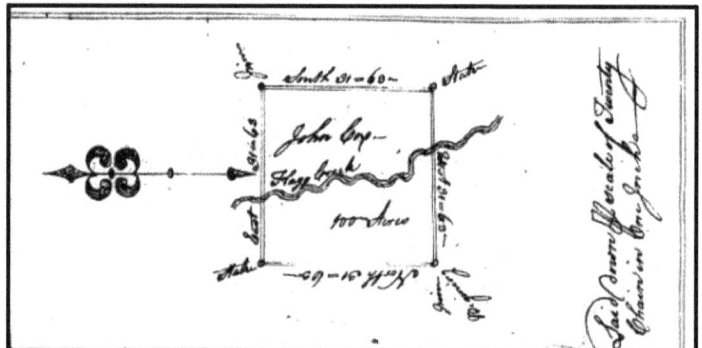

774. 1783, Nov 1 -- Land Grant #2063, Cumberland County, NC
John Cox received 100 acres located on Flag Creek including improvement where **Leonard Furr** formerly lived. **Thomas Penn** and **Richard Crooper** were chain carriers.

775. 1783, Nov 2 -- Land Grant #2049, Cumberland County, NC
William Seal received 50 acres located on Dunhams Creek including the plantation where he now lives adjoining **John Kinney** and **Charles Seal**. **Thomas Gilmore** and **William Seal Junr.** were chain carriers.

776. 1783, Nov 9 -- Land Grant #3353, Mecklenburg County, NC
Charles Cagle received 100 acres located on Adams Creek including **Henry Lengle**'s improvement adjoining **Conrad Coughy**. **Andra Stouth** and **Henry Hartsell** were chain carriers. Entered Jun 13, 1779.

A. 1783, Nov 11 -- Deed Book C Page 14-15, Chatham County, NC
Roger Griffith, Sheriff deeded **Nicholas Nall** 400 acres located on both sides of Ceder Creek. **Jo. Rosser** and **Charles Goldston** were witnesses. [*Editor's note: Confiscated property of William Deaton Dec'd. for his loyalty to King of England and to settle judgement from Randolph County, NC for damages against William Searcy.*]

777. 1783, Nov 16 -- Land Grant #1032, Guilford County, NC
Cornelius Latham received 100 acres located on Rock Creek adjoining **Sercy**. **William Sercy** and **John Pierce** were chain carriers.

778. 1783, Nov 16 -- 1778-1795 Land Entries, Cumberland County, NC

#4 **Jesse Rittar** entered 100 acres located on Buffalow Creek including **Matthew Leadbetter**'s improvement.

779. 1783, Nov 17 -- 1778-1795 Land Entries, Cumberland County, NC
#17 **John McAwalay** entered 100 acres located on Wet Creek adjoining **Archd. McKay** and **Richd. Dunn**.

780. 1783, Nov 17 -- 1778-1795 Land Entries, Cumberland County, NC
#18 **Malcolm Morrison** entered 200 acres located on Dry Creek adjoining **Ancel Milton** and the **Hill** Place now in possession of **Danl. McSween**.

781. 1783, Nov 17 -- Land Grant #2060, Cumberland County, NC
Robert Cox received 100 acres located on Tan Troff Branch adjoining **John Dunahoe** and including **Angus Stewart**'s improvement. **James Cotton** and **John Carpenter** were chain carriers.

782. 1783, Nov 18 -- 1778-1795 Land Entries, Cumberland County, NC
#19 **Allan Morrison** entered 100 acres located on Sings Creek adjoining **John Smith** or **Waddel**.

783. 1783, Nov 18 -- 1778-1795 Land Entries, Cumberland County, NC
#20 **Norman McLeod** entered 105 acres located on Sings Creek adjoining **Lewis Sowell**.

784. 1783, Nov 19 -- Land Grant #2066, Cumberland County, NC
Richard Dunn received 100 acres located on Wet Creek adjoining **Bartholomew Dunn** and his own line. **Hezekiah Dunn** and **Bartholomew Dunn** were chain carriers.

785. 1783, Nov 20 -- Land Grant #2059, Cumberland County, NC
Robert Patterson received 50 acres located on Wet Creek adjoining **Bartholomew Dunn, Anson Malton, Chinia** and including **William Dunn**'s improvement. **Hezekiah Dunn** and **Bartholomew Dunn** were chain carriers. [Editor's Note: **Jesse Sanders** sold to **Joseph Deaton** 1848]

786. 1783, Nov 29 -- Land Grant #2064, Cumberland County, NC
John Cox received 100 acres located on McLendons Creek adjoining whereon **William Smith** now lives. **Daniel McKinsey** and **Collin McClendon** were chain carriers.

787. 1783, Dec -- Deed Book 7 Page 162, Cumberland County, NC
John James deeded **John Overton** 100 acres located west of Overtons Road on drains of McLendons Creek including the improvements and adjoining **Overton**. **Wm. Seal** and **Ralph Davis** were witnesses.

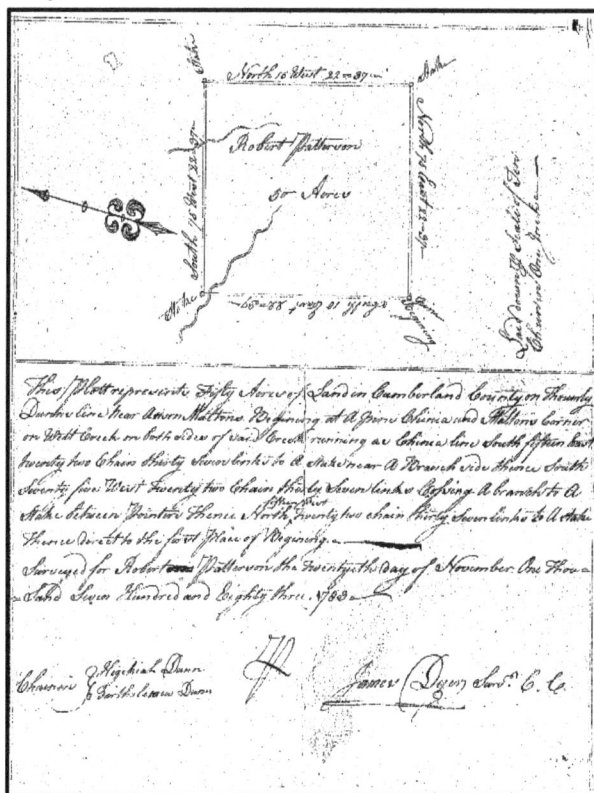

788. 1783, Dec 10 -- Land Grant #1025, Guilford County, NC
William Hughlit and **William Sercy** received 300 acres located on both sides of Little River. **Elijah Williams** and **William King** were chain carriers.

789. 1783, Dec 10 -- Land Grant #1124, Guilford County, NC
William Hughlit and **William Sercy** received 200 acres located on Fork Creek. **Elijah Williams** and **James Presnall** were chain carriers.

1784 -- Moore County, NC formed from Cumberland County, NC

790. 1784, Jan 3 -- 1778-1795 Land Entries, Cumberland County, NC
#34 **John McSween** entered 100 acres located on McLendons Creek adjoining **Farquard Campbell** and his own line.

791. 1784, Jan 4 -- 1778-1795 Land Entries, Cumberland County, NC
#35 **Hactor McLean** entered 50 acres located on Dry Creek adjoining **Norman McLean**.

792. 1784, Jan 19 -- 1778-1795 Land Entries, Cumberland County, NC
#48 **John Overton** entered 640 acres located on McLendons Creek of Deep River adjoining his own line and an improvement between McLendons Creek and Governors Creek.

793. 1784, Jan 26 -- 1778-1795 Land Entries, Cumberland County, NC
#67 **Kenneth McKenzie** entered 100 acres located on Buffalo Creek adjoining **Joseph Duck[worth]** and **Drury Richardson**.

794. 1784, Jan 29 -- 1784-1787 Court of Pleas and Quarter Sessions, Cumberland County, NC
Jas. Cadwell served jury duty.

795. 1784, Jan 29 -- 1784-1787 Court of Pleas and Quarter Sessions, Cumberland County, NC
Wm. Searcy, constable, allowed for attendance at Jul 1783 court.

796. 1784, Jan 31 -- 1784-1787 Court of Pleas and Quarter Sessions, Cumberland County, NC
John Jackson appointed to gather taxes for districts of **John Cox**, **Wm. Cox** and Capt. **Hunnicutt** for 1783.

797. 1784, Feb 1 -- 1778-1795 Land Entries, Cumberland County, NC
#70 **William Barrett** entered 50 acres located east of Drowning Creek including his own improvement.

798. 1784, Feb 1 -- 1778-1795 Land Entries, Cumberland County, NC
#71 **William Barrett** entered 50 acres located in middle prong of Drowning Creek about a mile from mouth of prong where there was a cabin.

799. 1784, Feb 1 -- 1778-1795 Land Entries, Cumberland County, NC
#72 **William Barrett** entered 100 acres located on Richland Creek adjoining **Daniel McQueen**.

800. 1784, Feb 9 -- 1778-1795 Land Entries, Cumberland County, NC
#77 **Robert Graham** entered 100 acres located east of McLendons Creek adjoining **Patience Barrett**.

A. 1784, Feb 10 -- 1781-1785 Court of Pleas and Quarter Sessions Page 60, Chatham County, NC
Ambrose Brown be bound to **Lewis Kirk** to learn the trade of hatter until he comes to lawful age he now being seventeen years of age.

801. 1784, Feb 14 -- 1778-1795 Land Entries, Cumberland County, NC
#84 **John McKennon** entered 100 acres located on Richland Creek.

A. 1784, Mar 3 -- Land Grant #734, Chatham County, NC
William Phillips received 150 acres located on Tysons Creek adjoining the Hay Meadow north of **Harmon Cox**'s Road. **William Phillips** and **Willis Phillips** were chain carriers.

B. 1784, Mar 4 -- Land Grant#793, Chatham County, NC
Jeremiah Phillips received 400 acres located on Blue Branch and Indian Creek adjoining **Caaps** and **Ezekial Hilliard**. **Joel Philips** and **Ezekial Hilliard** were chain carriers.

802. 1784, Mar 5 -- 1778-1795 Land Entries, Cumberland County, NC
#96 **Niell Matthews [Matheson]** entered 100 acres located on Dry Creek adjoining **Daniel McSween** and **Nicholas Newton**.

803. 1784, Mar 8 -- Land Grant #31, Moore County, NC
John McKinnon received 100 acres located on Richland Creek of McLendons Creek adjoining **Farquard Campbell** and including his own improvement. **William Cook** and **Alexander McIver** were chain carriers.

804. 1784, Mar 10 -- Criminal Actions, Randolph County, NC
Summons for **Windsor Pierce** to appear on a charge of profane swearing.

805. 1784, Mar 18 -- 1778-1795 Land Entries, Cumberland County, NC
#107 **John McKinnon** entered 100 acres located between McLendons Creek and Richland Creek adjoining **Farquhard Campbell** and including his own improvement.

806. 1784, Mar 20 -- Land Grant #2057, Cumberland County, NC
Isaac Dunn received 100 acres located east of Wet Creek adjoining **Richard Dunn**. **Hezekiah Dunn** and **Bartholomew Dunn** were chain carriers.

807. 1784, Mar 24 -- 1778-1795 Land Entries, Cumberland County, NC
#117 **Angus McIver** entered 50 acres located on a branch of McLendons Creek adjoining **John McNiell**, **Malcolm Shaw** and **Alexr. McLeod** and including his own improvement.

808. 1784, Mar 24 -- 1778-1795 Land Entries, Cumberland County, NC
#118 **John McKay** entered 100 acres located on Flag Creek adjoining **John Cox** and including **Henry Jackson**'s improvement.

809. 1784, Mar 24 -- 1778-1795 Land Entries, Cumberland County, NC
#119 **John McKay** entered 100 acres adjoining **Milton**.

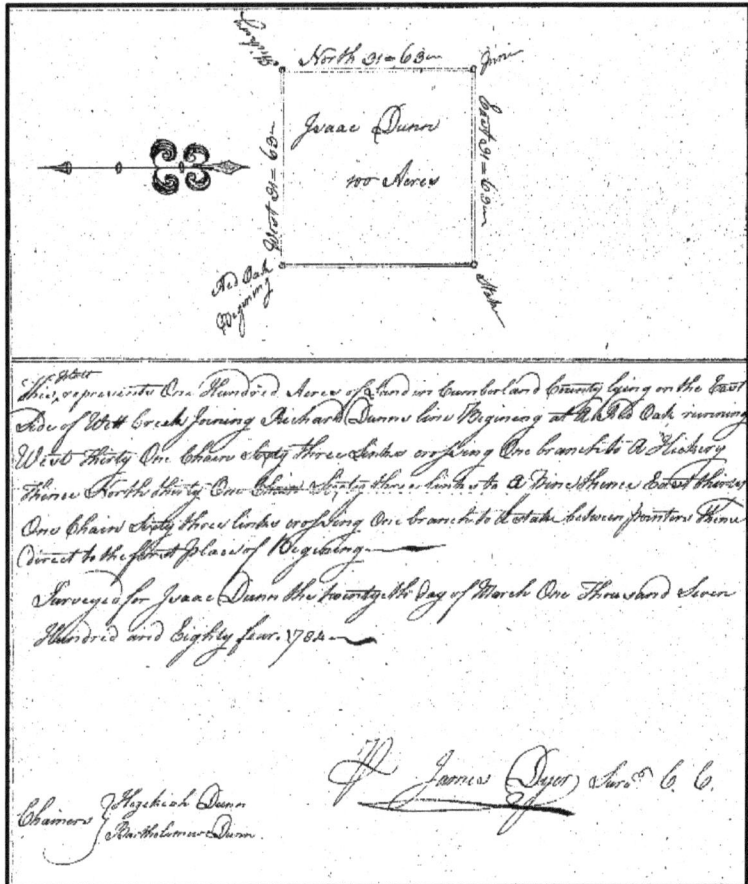

810. 1784, Mar 25 -- 1778-1795 Land Entries, Cumberland County, NC
#120 **John McKay** entered 50 acres located on Suck Creek including **York**'s cabin.

811. 1784, Mar 25 -- 1778-1795 Land Entries, Cumberland County, NC
#122 **Robert Graham** entered 50 acres located on a branch of McLendons Creek adjoining his own line and **Terrence Brannon**.

812. 1784, Mar 25 -- 1778-1795 Land Entries, Cumberland County, NC
#123 **John Cox** entered 150 acres located on both sides of Mill Creek including **Francis Fields'** improvement.

813. 1784, Mar 25 -- 1778-1795 Land Entries, Cumberland County, NC
#124 **John Cox** entered 100 acres located on both sides of Mill Creek including **Wm. Morgan**'s improvement and mill.

814. 1784, Apr 5 -- Land Grant #280, Randolph County, NC
John Needham received 640 acres south of Deep River on Fork Creek including his own improvement and adjoining **Cost**. **William Needham** and **William Larrence** were chain carriers.

A. 1784, Apr 12 -- Land Grant #574, Chatham County, NC
Moses Mirick received 400 acres located on Poplar Branch of Indian Creek adjoining **William Barber**. **Starling Carrel** and **Richard Barber** were chain carriers.

B. 1784, Apr 24 -- Land Grant #663, Chatham County, NC

Benjamin Elkins received 150 acres located on Tysons Creek and the Cumberland [Moore] County line. **John Williams** and **Vinsent Davis** were chain carriers.

815.   1784, Apr 26 -- Deed Book 7 Page 357, Cumberland County, NC
Theophilis Evans Esq. deeded **Donald McRae** 100 acres located on Richland Creek. **John McRae** and **Kenneth Murkinson** were witnesses.

816.   1784, Apr 27 -- Deed Book 7 Page 178, Cumberland County, NC
John Walsh deeded **Nicholas Newton** 200 acres located on Wet Creek where **James Cheny** lived on Lawyers Path. **Jesse Muse** and **Samuel Dunn** were witnesses.

817.   1784, Apr 28 -- 1784-1787 Court of Pleas and Quarter Sessions, Cumberland County, NC
Deed from **David Milton** to **Wm. Poplin** proven by **Mathis Davis**

818.   1784, Apr 30 -- 1784-1787 Court of Pleas and Quarter Sessions, Cumberland County, NC
[*jury duty - selected participants*] **Leonard Cakel**, **John Morgan**, **Nathan Smith** and **Jas. Morgan** were summoned.

819.   1784, May 1 -- 1778-1795 Land Entries, Cumberland County, NC
#159 **Thomas Armstrong** entered 100 acres located on Williams Creek including **William Freeman**'s improvement.

820.   1784, May 1 -- 1778-1795 Land Entries, Cumberland County, NC
#162 **Murdock Bethune** entered 70 acres located east of McLendons Creek near **Martin**'s Mill and including his own improvement.

821.   1784, May 5 -- Cane Creek Meeting [Quaker] Minutes Vol. 1 Page 528, Alamance County, NC
Samuel Dunn was disowned for marrying outside of unity.

A.   1784, May 10 -- Deed Book N Page 246-248, Chatham County, NC
Roger Griffith, Sheriff deeded **John Powers** 300 acres on Ceder Creek. **Jo. Rosser** and **T. Harper** were witnesses. [*Editor's note: Confiscated property of **William Deaton** Dec'd. for his loyalty to King of England and to settle judgement from Randolph County, NC for damages against **William Searcy**.*]

822.   1784, May 18 -- Land Grant #2541, Cumberland County, NC
Daniel Gold received 300 acres located north of McClendon Creek adjoining **John Carrolds** and **Overton**.

823.   1784, Jun 9 -- Deed Book 7 Page 249, Cumberland County, NC
John and **Easter Smith** (of Bladen County) deeded **Richard Dunn** 100 acres located on both sides of Wet Creek about ½ mile above **Richard Dunn**'s Mill. **Malcolm McNeill** and **William Smith** were witnesses.

824.   1784, Jun 14 -- 1778-1795 Land Entries, Cumberland County, NC
#178 **Robert Graham** entered 100 acres located east of McLendons Creek adjoining his own line.

825.   1784, Jun 14 -- 1778-1795 Land Entries, Cumberland County, NC
#179 **Daniel McDaniel** entered 100 acres located on a branch of McLendons Creek including his own improvement.

826.   1784, Jul 26 -- 1778-1795 Land Entries, Cumberland County, NC
#224 **Solomon Barrett** entered 100 acres located on McLendons Creek adjoining **John McNeill** and **John Martin**.

827.   1784, Jul 26 -- 1778-1795 Land Entries, Cumberland County, NC
#225 **Solomon Barrett** entered 200 acres located adjoining **Michael Hill** and land that **Wm. Smith** formerly owned.

828.   1784, Jul 26 -- 1778-1795 Land Entries, Cumberland County, NC
#226 **Solomon Barrett** entered 100 acres located on both sides of Camp Branch adjoining **Widow McLeod** and **Patience Barrett**.

829.   1784, Jul 27 -- 1778-1795 Land Entries, Cumberland County, NC
#237 **Solomon Barrett** entered 100 acres adjoining **William Smith**.

830.   1784, Jul 26 -- 1778-1795 Land Entries, Cumberland County, NC
#240 **Hector McNeill** entered 50 acres located on Buffaloe Creek on both sides of the Ridge Path including his own improvement.

831.   1784, Aug 17 -- 1784-1797 Land Entries, Moore County, NC
#2 **Nicholas Nall** entered 300 acres on Deep River adjoining the [Randolph] county line and including the crossroads.

832.   1784, Aug 17 -- 1784-1797 Land Entries, Moore County, NC
#7 **Thomas Gimore** entered 100 acres on Cabbin Creek adjoining **John Carpenter** and including **James Jeffery**'s improvement.

833.   1784, Aug 17 -- 1784-1795 Court of Pleas and Quarter Sessions, Moore County, NC
[jury duty next court -- selected participants]: **William Williamson**, **James Morgan**, **Peter Shamburger** and **Drury Richardson**.

834.   1784, Aug 17 -- 1784-1795 Court of Pleas and Quarter Sessions, Moore County, NC Page 3
Ordered that **Jonathan Caddwell** be appointed Constable in **Captain John Cox**'s District.

A.   1784, Aug 17 -- 1784-1795 Court of Pleas and Quarter Sessions, Moore County, NC Page 6
Ordered that **Thomas Gillmore** be appointed overseer of the road from **Connor Dowds** Road to **William Seals** Esq.

835.   1784, Aug 17 -- 1784-1795 Court of Pleas and Quarter Sessions, Moore County, NC Page 6
Ordered that **Isaac Harden** be appointed overseer of the road from the Chatham County line to **John Overton**'s.

836.   1784, Aug 17 -- 1784-1795 Court of Pleas and Quarter Sessions, Moore County, NC Page 6
Ordered that **John Overton Jr.** be appointed overseer of the road from **John Overton Senr.**'s to the fork of Muse's Road.

837.   1784, Aug 17 -- 1784-1795 Court of Pleas and Quarter Sessions, Moore County, NC Page 6
Ordered that **Jesse Muse** be appointed overseer of the road from the widow **Muse**'s to Dunams Creek.

838.   1784, Aug 17 -- 1784-1795 Court of Pleas and Quarter Sessions, Moore County, NC Page 6
Ordered that **William Dun** be appointed overseer of the road from the widow **Muse**'s to Bear Creek.

839.   1784, Aug 17 -- 1784-1795 Court of Pleas and Quarter Sessions, Moore County, NC Page 6
Ordered that **George Kagle** be appointed overseer of the road from Bear Creek to the Randolph County line.

840.   1784, Aug 17 -- 1784-1795 Court of Pleas and Quarter Sessions, Moore County, NC Page 9
Ordered that **Josiah Maples** be appointed overseer of the road in place of **John Overton** from McClendons Creek to the fork of the road and have the following hands to work: **Phil Alston, John Overton, John Blanchett, Anthony Street, Phill Cheek, Randolph Hunnicutt, William Pain, James Moore, Joseph Horser, John Carrell, Elijah Bettys, John Dunlap, William Poe** and **Theophelus Petty.**

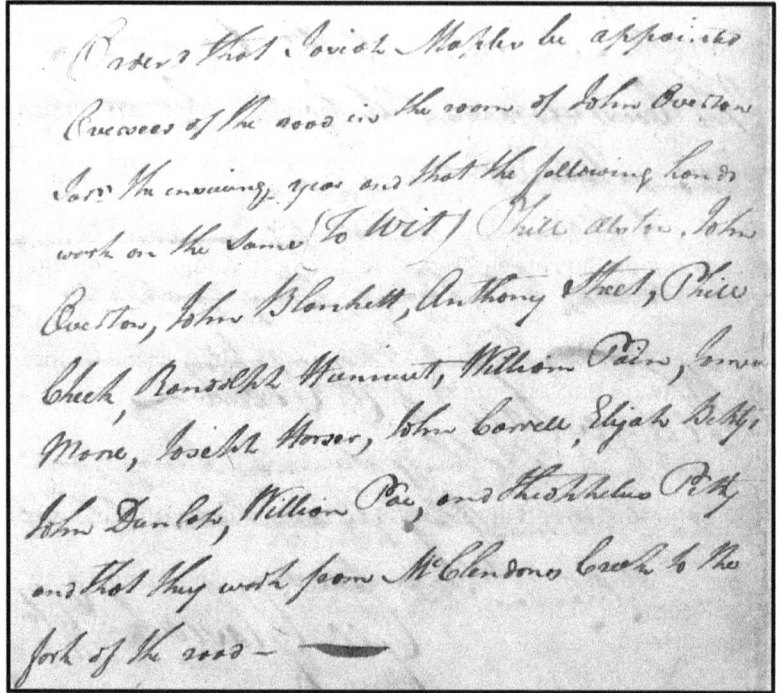

841.   1784, Aug 31 -- 1784-1797 Land Entries, Moore County, NC
#8 **Kenneth Murcheson** entered 200 acres on McLendons Creek adjoining **John Martin** and **John McNeill.**

842.   1784, Sep 4 -- Deed Book 3 Page 66-67, Orange County, NC
George Horner and wife, **Elizabeth Horner,** deeded **George Horner Junior** 250 acres on the west side of Mountain Creek adjoining **Wm. McCulloh** and **Stephen Wilson** (formerly **Wm. Ray**). **James Hunter** and **Wm. Johnston** were witnesses. Proven Feb 1785.

843.   1784, Sep 10 -- 1784-1797 Land Entries, Moore County, NC
#12 **Nicholas Newton** entered 100 acres on Wet Creek adjoining **Richard Dunn** and his own line.

844.   1784, Sep 10 -- 1784-1797 Land Entries, Moore County, NC
#13 **Nicholas Newton** entered 50 acres on Wet Creek adjoining his own line.

845.   1784, Oct 24 -- 1784-1797 Land Entries, Moore County, NC
#17 **Robert Bird** entered 150 acres between the head of Grassie Creek and Reedy Creek including his own improvement.

846.   1784, Oct 26 -- 1784-1797 Court of Pleas and Quarter Sessions, Cumberland County, NC
Deed from **John Smith** to **Richd. Dunn** was proven by **Wm. Smith.**

847.   1784, Oct 26 -- Land Grant #78, Moore County, NC
Robert Grimes received 100 acres located east of McLendons Creek adjoining his own line and **Patience Barrett. Thomas Grimes** and **Angus Campbell** were chain carriers.

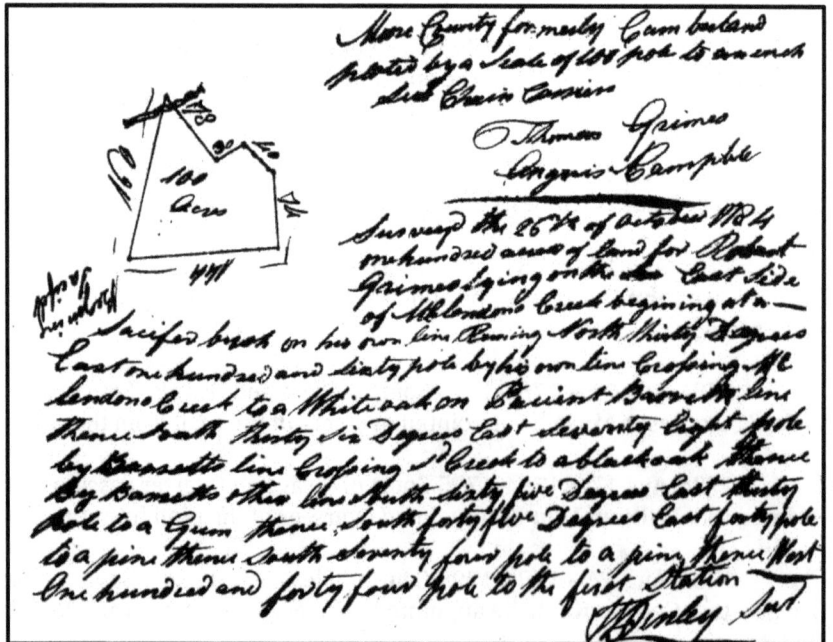

848.   1784, Oct 26 -- Land Grant #155, Moore County, NC
Robert Grimes received 50 acres located east of McLendons Creek adjoining his own line, **John Cox** and **Terrance Brannon. Thomas Grimes** and **Anguish Campbell** were chain carriers.

849.   1784, Oct 26 -- Land Grant #185, Moore County, NC
Jesse Ritter received 100 acres located on both sides of Buffalo Creek including **Matthew Ledbetter**'s improvement. **John Ritter** and **Thomas Ritter Junr.** were chain carriers.

850.   1784, Oct 27 -- Land Grant #144, Moore County, NC
William Barrett received 50 acres located on the middle prong of Drowning Creek about a mile from the mouth of said prong where there was formerly a cabin. **Thomas Grimes** and **Allen Martin** were chain carriers.

851.   1784, Oct 27 -- Land Grant #153, Moore County, NC
William Barrett received 100 acres located on both sides of Richland Creek adjoining **Daniel McQueen**. **Thos. Grimes** and **Daniel McQueen** were chain carriers.

852.   1784, Oct 27 -- Land Grant #179, Moore County, NC
William Barrett received 50 acres located on north prong of Drowning Creek including his own improvement. **Thomas Grimes** and **Allen Martin** were chain carriers.

853.   1784, Oct 28 -- Land Grant #62, Moore County, NC
Mary McDonal received 100 acres located on McLendons Creek adjoining **Daniel McDonald**'s plantation. **John Adkins** and **James Collins** were chain carriers.

854.   1784, Nov 8 -- Land Grant #1033, Guilford County, NC
William Sercy received 100 acres located on Rock Creek of Fork Creek adjoining his own line.

855.   1784, Nov 8 -- Land Grant #1034, Guilford County, NC
William Sercy received 200 acres located on Rock Creek of Fork Creek.

A.   1784, Nov 10 -- 1781-1785 Court of Pleas and Quarter Sessions Page 89, Chatham County, NC
Johnathan Barnes have leave to keep a public ferry on Deep River at **Conner Dowd's** Mill and enter into bond with **John Montgomery** Esq.

B.   1784, Nov 12 -- 1781-1785 Court of Pleas and Quarter Sessions, Chatham County, NC Page 92
William Tucker, **Willis Phillips**, **William Phillips Junr.**, **Benjamin Sanders**, **William Phillips Senr.**, **James Deaton**, **John Powers**, **Sampson Brewer**, **Thomas Younger**, **William Dunkin**, **Nicholas Nall** and **Charles Goldston** lay off a road from the **Widow Nall's** on Bear Creek to the Randolph County line near the Ceder Ponds crossing Deep River at **Gardner's** Ford.

856.   1784, Nov 15 -- 1784-1795 Court of Pleas and Quarter Sessions, Moore County, NC
[jury duty next term - selected participants] **Nichl. Newton**, **William Handock**, **Zach Smith**, **John Key**, **Thos. Key**, **Richard Dun Senr.**, **Willis Dickerson**, **Thomas Collins Junr.** and **Thomas Collins Senr.**

A.   1784, Nov 16 -- 1784-1795 Court of Pleas and Quarter Sessions, Moore County, NC Page 8
Ordered that **William Hardin** known by the name of **Buck** be appointed constable in Captain **Hunnicutts** District.

857.   1784, Nov 19 -- 1784-1797 Land Entries, Moore County, NC
#22 **James Hill** entered 100 acres on McLendons Creek adjoining **Muse** and **McLeod**.

858.   1784, Nov 24 -- Land Grant #2133, Cumberland County, NC
Mary McDonald received 100 acres located on Killetts Creek/Quarry Branch of McLendons Creek adjoining **Danl. McDonald** plantation. **Solomon Cox** and **William Cox** were chain carriers.

859.   1784, Dec 1 -- 1784-1797 Land Entries, Moore County, NC
#26 **John McNeil** entered 100 acres south of McLendons Creek adjoining his own line.

860.   1784, Dec 1 -- 1784-1797 Land Entries, Moore County, NC
#27 **John McNeil** entered 100 acres north of McLendons Creek adjoining his own line.

861.   1784, Dec 4 -- Land Grant #33, Moore County, NC

Murdock Beaton received 70 acres located on McLendons Creek including his own improvement near **Martin**'s Mill . **Thomas Graham** and **Solomon Barrett** were chain carriers.

862.   1784, Dec 7 -- Land Grant #32, Moore County, NC
Solomon Barrett received 100 acres located on McLendons Creek adjoining **John McNeill** and **Beaton**. **Thomas Grayham** and **Samuel Barrett** were chain carriers.

863.   1784, Dec 7 -- Land Grant #51, Moore County, NC
Solomon Barrett received 100 acres located on both sides of the Camp Branch adjoining **Widow McLeod**, **Patience Barret** and **McNeill**. **John Sowell** and **Thos. Graham** were chain carriers.

864.   1784, Dec 14 -- 1784-1797 Land Entries, Moore County, NC
#31 **Jesse Muse** entered 50 acres on McLendons Creek adjoining **Muse** and **Conner Dowd**.

865.   1784, Dec 14 -- 1784-1797 Land Entries, Moore County, NC
#32 **Jesse Muse** entered 50 acres on Mill Swamp Branch of McLendons Creek adjoining **Muse**.

866.   1784, Dec 15 -- 1784-1797 Land Entries, Moore County, NC
#33 **Angus McIver** entered 100 acres on Suck Creek adjoining **Widow McDonald**.

867.   1784, Dec 20 -- 1784-1797 Land Entries, Moore County, NC
#34 **Nicholas Newton** entered 100 acres on Horses Creek on the **Grove** path from his house.

868.   1784, Dec 20 -- 1784-1797 Land Entries, Moore County, NC
#35 **William Smith** entered 50 acres on Wet Creek including his own house and mill.

869.   1785 -- Tax List, Randolph County, NC, Capt. **Garner**'s District [selected residents]
Names and acreage: **John Lowrance** 1 white poll, 2 black poll 300 acres; **John Needham** 1 white poll, 4 black poll, 940 acres on Fork Creek; **John Spinks** 1 white poll, 150 acres on Deep River; **Enoch Spinks** 1 white poll; **Mary Leathm** 100 acres on R. Creek; **Cornealus Leathm** 1 white poll; **John Read** 1 white poll; **Amy Spinks** 125 acres; **Owen Carpender** 1 white poll; **Wm. Argo** 1 white poll, 217 acres; **William Searsy** 1 white poll, 1495 acres; **Jesse Upton** 1 white poll; **Richard Upton** 1 white poll; **David Andrew** 1 white poll; **Joseph Carr** 1 white poll 2 black polls 700 acres; **Robert Carr** 1 white poll 400 acres; **John Vandiford** 1 white poll 250 acres; **Winser Pirce** 1 white poll, 2 black polls 100 acres; **John Pierce** 1 white poll 250 acres; **Richard Bird** 1 white poll 275 acres; **Arter Reed** 1 white poll 150 acres; **Will. Reed** 1 white poll 75 acres.

A.   1785 -- General Assembly Session Records
Petition to erect a courthouse in the center of Randolph County, NC. [selected signers]
Richard Bird, William Bird, Nimrod Brewer, Arther Reade, Isaac Redfarn, Jas. Ledlow, Jas. Lathem Junr., Wm. Reade Junr., Jno. Williamson, Wm. Needham, Math. Deaton, Eldrig Deaton, Windsor Pearce, Joseph Hix, Arther Smith, Michall Andrews, Howell Brewer Sen., Wm. Richeson, Jno. Lathem, Wm. Lathem, Drury Richeson, Jas. Needham, William Smotherman, Cornelias Lathom, Thoms. Cost Sen., Thos. Cost Junr., Jas. Lathom Senr., Johnson Lathom, William Searcy, Joseph Carr, Wm. Neadom, John Garner, Rolle Spinks, John Pearce, John Read, Wm. Argo, Robt. Carr, John Deaton, John Spinks, Lewis Spinks, Garrot Spinks, Enoch

Spinks, **William Read, Adam Andrews, Davis Andrews, Charles Stewart, William Pearce, Thos. Waddill, Dennis Carpender, John Needham Senr.** and **Wm. Smith.**

870.　　　1785, Jan 6 -- Deed, Book 2 Page 197, Orange County, NC
George Horner Senr. deeded **George Horner Junr.** 80 acres on Mountain Creek adjoining **Charles Dunnagan** and **Edward Wothern. Richard Rhodes Jr.** and **Henry Moore** were witnesses. Proven Feb 1786.

871.　　　1785, Jan 20 -- Land Grant #143, Moore County, NC
Daniel McDonald received 100 acres located on McLendons Creek adjoining **William Barrett. Thos. Graham** and **Alen McDonald** were chain carriers.

872.　　　1785, Jan 29 -- Deed Book 3, Page 58, Randolph County, NC
Ransom Sutherland deeded **William Bowden** 100 acres located south of Deep River adjoining Pearces Creek and Reads Island. Two tracts conveyed by **William Searcy** Dec'd. to daughter **Mary Pearce** and **Winsor Perce** [27.5 acres] and to **Ransom Sutherland** [75.75 acres]. **William Poseat** and **Francis Bowden** were witnesses.

873.　　　1785, Feb 17 -- Deed, Will Book A Page 354-355, Orange County, NC
George Horner deeded son **James Horner** the plantation where **George Horner** now lives. **Thomas Hunter** and **George Horner Jur.** were witnesses. Proven May 1785.

874.　　　1785, Feb 21 -- 1784-1795 Court of Pleas and Quarter Sessions, Moore County, NC
[*jury duty - selected participants*] **Thos. Key, John Key, James Cadwell, James Collins, James Muse, Jesse Muse**
[*jury duty next court - selected participants*] **Zacha. Smith, William Dun, William Smith, Drury Richardson, James Muse, William Williamson.**

875.　　　1785, Feb 22 -- 1784-1795 Court of Pleas and Quarter Sessions, Moore County, NC Page 14
Thos. Key records his mark as a cross in the right and slit in ear.

876.　　　1785, Feb 22 -- 1784-1795 Court of Pleas and Quarter Sessions, Moore County, NC Page 15
John Keys records his mark as a lash in the left and a slit in the right.

877.　　　1785, Feb 22 -- 1784-1795 Court of Pleas and Quarter Sessions, Moore County, NC Page 16
George Cagle records his mark as a cross and 2 slits in left and niche in right.

878.　　　1785, Feb 22 -- 1784-1795 Court of Pleas and Quarter Sessions, Moore County, NC Page 17
Ordered that **Isaac Harden** be appointed overseer of the road from Chatham County to the fork in the road and have the following hands to work: **Robert Davis, Hezekiah Johnston, Benjn. Seal, Amos Cheek, Jams. Cheek, Chas. Shiran, Burwell Phillips, Mark Phillips, Lewis Phillips, John Rogers, Enoch Rogers, Joell Phillips, John Cheek, William Handcock, Levy Askins, Jams. Collins, Wm. Malone, John Blanchett, William Poe** and **Moses Myrick.**

879.　　　1785, Feb 22 -- 1784-1795 Court of Pleas and Quarter Sessions, Moore County, NC Page 18-19
[Deeds] **Cornelius Tyson** to **John McRea** was acknowledged
Joel McClendon to **Wm. Barrett** was proven by **Patience Barrett**
Henry Keagle and wife to **Zach. Smith** was proven by **William Mithoson**
Phill Alston to **Michael Russell** was proven by **Moses Myrick**
Two deeds from **Anthony Seal** to **James Muse** were proven by **Daniel Muse**

880.　　　1785, Feb 22 -- 1784-1797 Land Entries, Moore County, NC
#52 **Danl. McQun** entered 100 acres on Locust Branch including his own improvement.

881.   1785, Feb 23 -- 1784-1795 Court of Pleas and Quarter Sessions, Moore County, NC Page 20
Ordered that **Nicholas Nall** have leave to keep a taven at the crossroads near the Randolph County line where he now lives. **Phill. Alston** was a security.

882.   1785, Feb 23 -- 1784-1795 Court of Pleas and Quarter Sessions, Moore County, NC Page 24
Jacob Cagle was appointed Constable in **Capt. John Cox**'s District.
Ordered that **Jesse Muse** be appointed Constable in place of **Jonathan Cadwell**.

A.   1785, Feb 23 -- 1784-1795 Court of Pleas and Quarter Sessions, Moore County, NC Page 24
Ordered that **William Beazeley** be appointed overseer of the road in room of **Jesse Muse**.

883.   1785, Feb 23 -- 1784-1795 Court of Pleas and Quarter Sessions, Moore County, NC Page 24
Administration of the estate of **Isaac Sowell** is granted to **Mary Sowell** with **William Barrett** Esq. as security.

884.   1785, Feb 23 -- 1784-1795 Court of Pleas and Quarter Sessions, Moore County, NC Page 25
[Deeds] Two deeds from **Henry Gaster** to **Hardy Davis** was proven by **Jesse Muse**
Anthony Seal to **James Muse** was proven by **Daniel Muse**

885.   1785, Feb 24 -- 1784-1795 Court of Pleas and Quarter Sessions, Moore County, NC Page 28
Ordered that the following persons be appointed to lay out a road from the Montgomery County line at Burton's Ford on Drowning Creek to the Cross Creek Road to **William Seals** Esq.: **Edwd. Cox**, **Robert Grimes**, **Thos. Grimes**, **Daniel McCloud**, **John Cox** Esq., **Richardson Feagen** Esq., **Jos. Fry**, **Solomon Cox**, **Peter Salter**, **Jesse Muse**, **Benjn. Fry**, **Daniel Jones**, **William Cox**, **William Barrett**, **Jason Wadsworth**, **John Jackson**, **David Lewis** and **James Hill**.

886.   1785, Feb 28 -- Land Grant #169, Moore County, NC
William Finley received 50 acres located south of Bear Creek adjoining **Cagle**. **John Hinson** and **Thos. Bullen** were chain carriers.

887.   1785, Feb 28 -- Land Grant #180, Randolph County, NC
William Searcy received 120 acres located on Fork Creek adjoining his own line, **John Pierce** and **John Hankins**. **William Argo** and **Rolley Spinks** were chain carriers.

888.   1785, Feb 30 -- 1784-1797 Land Entries, Moore County, NC
#59 **Jesse Muse** entered 25 acres on a branch of Richland Creek and on both sides of the Waggon Road including Porch Corn Hill.

889.   1785, Mar 2 -- Land Grant #59, Moore County, NC
John Jackson received 100 acres located on Juniper Creek adjoining **Widow Jackson** and his own line. **George Jackson** and **Samuel Jackson** were chain carriers.

890.   1785, Mar 3 -- Land Grant #72, Moore County, NC
Nicholas Newton received 50 acres located on Dry Creek adjoining his own line. **Samuel Barrett** and **William Newton** were chain carriers.

891.   1785, Mar 3 -- Land Grant #79, Moore County, NC
William Smith received 50 acres located on Wet Creek including his own house and improvement. **Thos. Grimes** and **John Hare** were chain carriers.

892.   1785, Mar 3 -- Land Grant #81, Moore County, NC
William Dunn received 50 acres located on Wet Creek adjoining **Bartholomew Dunn, Ansel Melton** and **Chaney**. **Thos. Dunn** and **Samuel Barrett** were chain carriers.

893.   1785, Mar 4 -- Land Grant #239, Moore County, NC
Benjamin Fry received 40 acres located on Killetts Creek adjoining his own line. **James Fry** and **Joseph Fry** were chain carriers.

894.   1785, Mar 5 -- Land Grant #1, Moore County, NC

Nicholas Nall received 300 acres located on the waters of Grassy Creek adjoining the Randolph County line including the crossroads that come by **Widow Spinks** and crosses Deep River at **Searcy**'s. **Robt. Bird** and **Marten Nall** were chain carriers. [*Editor's Note:* **Nicholas Nall** *built a grist mill on this property that was located at the crossroads that later became known as the community of Needham's Grove.*]

895. 1785, Mar 5 -- Land Grant #178, Moore County, NC
Robert Bird received 150 acres located between the head of Grassy Creek and Reedy Creek adjoining his own improvement. **William Searcy** and **Robert Ellison** were chain carriers.

896. 1785, Mar 7 -- Land Grant #91, Moore County, NC
Hector McLean received 100 acres located on Wet Creek adjoining **Norman McLeod**. **Thos. Grimes** and **Murdock McLeod** were chain carriers.

897. 1785, Mar 8 -- Land Grant #55, Moore County, NC
John McKoy received 100 acres located on Flag Creek including **Henry Jackson**'s improvement and adjoining **John Cox**. **John Reed** and **John Smith** were chain carriers. [*Editor's Note: deeded to* **Thomas Graham** *1795 -->* **William Williams**]

898. 1785, Mar 8 -- Land Grant #92, Moore County, NC
John McKay received 100 acres located on Lick/Suck Creek including **York**'s cabin. **William Cook** and **Alexander McIver** were chain carriers.

899. 1785, Mar 19 -- 1784-1797 Land Entries, Moore County, NC
#64 **William Grove** entered 50 acres on Richland Creek adjoining his own line.

900. 1785, Apr 3 -- Land Grant #101, Moore County, NC
Charles Shearing received 200 acres located on Persimmon Glade adjoining **Joseph Duckworth** and **Hardin**. **James Thornton** and **Gabriel Hardin** were chain carriers.

901. 1785, Apr 8 -- Land Grant #141, Moore County, NC
William Barrett received 170 acres located on McLendons Creek adjoining his own line and **Widow McDonald**. **Thomas Graham** and **Math Carrboro** were chain carriers.

902. 1785, Apr 8 -- Land Grant #149, Randolph County, NC
Edmon Mash received 350 acres located on Fork Creek adjoining **Sutherland** and including his own improvement. **Luke Dempsey** and **John Lowdermilk** were chain carriers.

903. 1785, Apr 9 -- 1784-1797 Land Entries, Moore County, NC
#71 **Jesse Ritter** entered 50 acres located on Richland Creek adjoining **Ferquhard Campbell**.

904. 1785, Apr 10 -- 1784-1797 Land Entries, Moore County, NC
#72 **Leonard Furr** entered 50 acres located on Buffalow Creek adjoining **Richard Bean** and including his own improvement.

905. 1785, Apr 10 -- 1784-1797 Land Entries, Moore County, NC
#73 **Joseph Cockman** entered 50 acres located on Long Meadow of Buffalow Creek adjoining **Michael Hill**.

906. 1785, Apr 10 -- 1784-1797 Land Entries, Moore County, NC

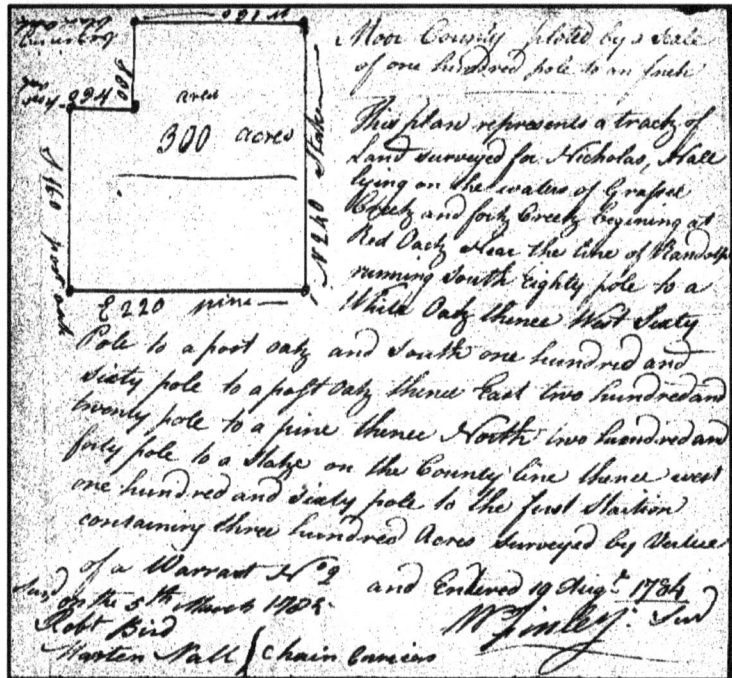

#74 **William Dunn** entered 50 acres on Long Meadow fork of Buffalow Creek adjoining his own line and **Michael Hill** and including his own improvement.

A.   1785, Apr 12 -- Deed Book Land Grant#387, Montgomery County, NC
Jeremiah Manascon received 100 acres on a branch of Cabbin Creek including **Charles Sowell's** improvement. **Joseph Parsons Esq.** and **William Trent Jr.** were chain carriers.

B.   1785, Apr 12 -- Land Grant #345, Montgomery County, NC
Christopher Butler received 100 acres located on Duck [Dicks] Creek. **Littleberry Hicks** and **Francis Jorden** were chain carriers.

C.   1785, Apr 13 -- Land Grant #360, Montgomery County, NC
Temple Carpenter received 100 acres located on Cabin Creek adjoining his own line. **Jonathan Carpenter** and **William Gibson** were chain carriers.

907.   1785, Apr 16 -- Land Grant #94, Moore County, NC
Richardson Fagan received 150 acres located on Killetts Creek adjoining **William Fagan**, **Killett**, own line and **Wier**. **John Salley** and **Peter Sarton** were chain carriers.

908.   1785, Apr 22 -- Land Grant #70, Moore County, NC
John Phillips received 150 acres located north of Deep River including his own improvement. **Shedrick Elkins** and **Burrell Phillips** were chain carriers.

909.   1785, Apr 22 -- Land Grant #100, Moore County, NC
Charles Shearing received 160 acres located on both sides of the Poplar Springs Branch of Deep River. **James Thornton** and **Gabriel Harden** were chain carriers.

A.   1785, Apr 23 -- Land Grant #11, Moore County, NC
Charles Shearing received 200 acres located on both sides of Watery Branch including Holly Spring. **James Thornton** and **Gabriel Harden** were chain carriers.

B.   1785, Apr 23 -- Land Grant #21, Moore County, NC
Charles Shearing received 200 acres located on Cain Patch Creek. **James Thornton** and **Gabriel Harden** were chain carriers.

910.   1785, May -- Will Book A Page 338, Moore County, NC
Estate of **Isaac Sowell**, Dec'd. by Administrator **Mary Sowell**. Mentions 300 acres on land. _Items were purchased by_: **Mary Sowell**, **Margrett Sowell** and **Richardson Feagan**.

911.   1785, May 8 -- 1784-1797 Land Entries, Moore County, NC
#75 **William Barrett** entered 50 acres on a branch of Deep Creek including his own improvement.

912.   1785, May 8 -- 1784-1797 Land Entries, Moore County, NC
#76 **Daniel McLeod** entered 50 acres between Tillis Branch and Sings Creek on the road from **Newton's** to **Tillis'** old Mill.

913. 1785, May 8 -- 1784-1797 Land Entries, Moore County, NC
#77 **Daniel McLeod** entered 50 acres on Sings Creek adjoining **Norman McLeod**.

914. 1785, May 8 -- 1784-1797 Land Entries, Moore County, NC
#78 **William Finley** entered 50 acres south of Bear Creek.

A. 1785, May 9 -- 1781-1785 Court of Pleas and Quarter Sessions Page 108, Chatham County, NC
Benjamin Sanders appointed overseer of the road from Anson Road to the Moore County line and have the following hands to work: **John Powers, Henry Brewer, Sampson Brewer, Nathan Phillips, Wm. Phillips, Willis Phillips, Howell Brewer, James Deaton, Nathan Deaton, Mathew Deaton, Widow Deaton, Wademn Commer, Wm. Phillips, Joel Phillips, Benjamin Elkins, William Caps, Ambrose Smith, John West** and his hands, **Samuel Moore, Samuel Hilleard** and **Jeremiah Phillips**.

915. 1785, May 16 -- 1784-1795 Court of Pleas and Quarter Sessions, Moore County, NC
[*jury duty - selected participants*] **Zach Smith, William Smith, William Dun, Drury Richardson, James Cadwell, Anson Melton, Jonathan Cadwell, Solomon Barrett, Jesse Muse, John Overton Senr., Thos. Collins Senr., Thos. Collins Junr., William Seale Jr.** [*jury duty next term - selected participants*] **Nicholas Newton, Richd. Dunn, John Morgan, James Morgan, William Williamson, Christopher Yow, William Hardin, Chas. Shearing, John Dunlap, Robert Cheek, Gabriel Harden Junr.**

916. 1785, May 16 -- 1784-1795 Court of Pleas and Quarter Sessions, Moore County, NC Page 31
Jeane Tedwell was appointed Administrator of **Frances Tedwell**, Dec'd. **Everit Smith** was named security.

917. 1785, May 17 -- 1784-1795 Court of Pleas and Quarter Sessions, Moore County, NC Page 32-33
[Deeds] **John Williamson** to **William Williamson** was proven by **Vincent Davis**
Simon Hart to **William Reed** was acknowledged

918. 1785, May 17 -- 1784-1795 Court of Pleas and Quarter Sessions, Moore County, NC Page 35
Ordered that a dedemus be issued to Montgomery County to examine **Frances Jordon** and **Littleberry Wicker, Jeffod Medford** and **John Butler** to prove the two deeds from **James Jeffrey** and one Deed from [*blank*] **Jeffrey** to **John Carpenter** and **Catherine/Chatham**[?] **Carpenter**.

919. 1785, May 17 -- 1784-1795 Court of Pleas and Quarter Sessions, Moore County, NC Page 36
Ordered that **Nicholas Newton** be appointed overseer of the road from **Tillis'** old mill leading into the new road from **Richardson Feagan**.

920. 1785, May 19 -- 1784-1795 Court of Pleas and Quarter Sessions, Moore County, NC Page 44
Deed from **Jams. Muse** and wife to **James Cadwell** was acknowledged

A. 1785, May 19 -- 1784-1795 Court of Pleas and Quarter Sessions, Moore County, NC Page 45
Ordered that **John Carrell** be appointed tax collector in **Hunnicutt's** District; **John Cox** in **John Cox's** District.

921. 1785, May 19 -- 1784-1795 Court of Pleas and Quarter Sessions, Moore County, NC Page 46
Ordered that **Geo. Braswell** be appointed overseer of the road from the Randolph County line at Adkin [Yadkin] Road and from there below **Tillis'** old mill to the fork of Montgomery County road.

922. 1785, Aug 15 -- 1784-1795 Court of Pleas and Quarter Sessions, Moore County, NC
[*jury duty - selected participants*] **William Williamson, Christopher Yow, Richd. Dun, Solomon Barrett, Anson Melton, William Cadwell, John Cadwell, Johnathan Cadwell, Chas. Shearing, Jesse Muse, Gabriel Harden, Thomas Collens, William Harden Senr., James Muse, Robert Dickenson** [*jury duty next term - selected participants*] **James Morgan, Zacha. Smith, William Smith, Drury Richardson, Nicholas Newton, George Cagle, Everett Smith**.

923. 1785, Aug 16 -- 1784-1795 Court of Pleas and Quarter Sessions, Moore County, NC Page 50
Ordered that **Jean Tedwell** have leave to sell the estate of **Francis Tedwell**, Dec'd.

924. 1785, Aug [undated estimate] -- Estate, Moore County, NC Will Book A, Page 339
Inventory of the Estate of **Frances Tedwell**, Dec'd. by Administrator **Jeane Tedwell**. Items purchased by the

following: **Jeane Tedwell**, **Richd. Bean**, **Saml. Tedwell**, **Averett Smith** and **Richardson Feagan**. [*Editor's Note: No date given on actual inventory, but the date was estimated using County Court Minute reference above.*]

925.   1785, Aug 16 -- Land Grant #279, Randolph County, NC
Thomas Cost received 100 acres on Fork Creek adjoining his own line and **John Needham**. **Wm. Larrence** and **Wm. Needham** were chain carriers.

926.   1785, Aug 17 -- 1784-1795 Court of Pleas and Quarter Sessions, Moore County, NC Page 54
Ordered that the whole of the estate of **James Muse** Dec'd. be restored to **Cathrin [*Charity?*] Muse** and children.

927.   1785, Aug 18 -- 1784-1795 Court of Pleas and Quarter Sessions, Moore County, NC Page 56
Jacob Cagle was appointed constable in **Capt. John Cox**'s District

928.   1785, Aug 18 -- 1784-1795 Court of Pleas and Quarter Sessions, Moore County, NC Page 56, 59
[Deeds] **Thos. Collins** to **Kenneth Morrison** was proven by **Randolph Hunnicutt**
Lenard Hart and wife to **Christopher Yow** was proven by **Geo. Garrenor [Carrigner]**.
William Dun to **Jesse Muse** was proven by **Catherine Muse**

929.   1785, Aug 19 -- 1784-1797 Land Entries, Moore County, NC
#82 **Thos. Matthews** and **J. Hinson** entered 200 acres located on Buffalow Creek adjoining **Cockman**, **Furr** and **Cagle**.

930.   1785, Aug 19 -- 1784-1795 Court of Pleas and Quarter Sessions, Moore County, NC Page 59
Ordered that **Edwd. Moore** be exempt from paying a poll tax for 1785.

931.   1785, Aug 19 -- 1784-1795 Court of Pleas and Quarter Sessions, Moore County, NC Page 62
Ordered that **Alexr. Cannady** be exempt from paying a poll tax for 1785.

932.   1785, Aug 20 -- 1784-1797 Land Entries, Moore County, NC
#80 **William Barrett** entered 100 acres on Wet Creek and the head of Sings Branch adjoining **John McKay**, **John McAuley** and **Kiah Dunn**.

933.   1785, Aug 20 -- 1784-1797 Land Entries, Moore County, NC
#84 **George Graham** entered 100 acres east of McLendons Creek including **Cox**'s cabin.

934.   1785, Oct 7 -- Land Grant #160, Moore County, NC
Allen Morrison received 100 acres located on Sings Creek adjoining **John Key**, **Waddle** and **John Smith**. **Alexr. Morrison** and **Murdoch Baton** were chain carriers.

935.   1785, Oct 7 -- Land Grant #170, Moore County, NC
William Grove received 60 acres located on Wet Creek adjoining his own line and **Thomas Keys**. **Murdock Baton** and **Alen Morrison** were chain carriers.

936.   1785, Oct 9 -- Land Grant #9, Moore County, NC
Jesse Ritter received 50 acres located on Richland Creek adjoining **Campbell**. **William Manes** and **Thos. Ritter** were chain carriers.

937.   1785, Nov -- Marriage Licenses, Will Book A Page 382, Moore County, NC [selected licenses]
John Stinson and **Sarah Tyson** were granted a marriage license. **James Thornton** was the surety.
John Overton and **Christian Jackson** were granted a marriage license. **John Overton Senr.** was the surety.
Jesse Been and **Cloey Ritter** were granted a marriage license. **Richd. Been** was the surety.
Geo. Baker and **Covil/Cesie Carriner** were granted a marriage license. **Geo. Carriner** was the surety.
Ambrose Manis and **Katherine Hunnicutt** were granted a marriage license. **Geo. Carriner** was the surety.
Jon. M. Glascock and **Polly Caddle** were granted a marriage license. **Geo. Glascock** was the surety.
Martin Nall and **Dolly Garner** were granted a marriage license. **Wm. Williamson** was the surety.
Jams. Collins and **Sarah McKeysick** were granted a marriage license. **Richardson Feagan** was the surety.
David Williams and **Tabitha Harden** were granted a marriage license. **Willian Harden (B)** was the surety.
William Newton and **Molly Patterson** were granted a marriage license. **William Barrett** was the surety.
Jesse Brown and **Mary Melton** were granted a marriage license. **William Barrett** was the surety.

John Caddle and **Mary Keys** were granted a marriage license. **William Caddle** was the surety.
John Spivey and **Susanna Smith** were granted a marriage license. **Leonard Furr** was the surety.
John Stutts and **Bathoney Spivey** were granted a marriage license. **Leonard Furr** was the surety.
Owen Carpenter and **Sarah Smith** were granted a marriage license. **Nathan Smith** was the surety.

938. 1785, Nov 4 -- Deed Book 2, Page 187, Randolph County, NC
William Searcy deeded **Nicholas Nall** 100 acres located on Deep River. Land Granted to **William Searcy Sr.** and deeded to **William Searcy Junr. William Findley** and **James Latham** were witnesses.

939. 1785, Nov 21 -- 1784-1795 Court of Pleas and Quarter Sessions, Moore County, NC
[*jury duty - selected participants*] **James Muse, Nicholas Newton, Drury Richardson, Geo. Cagle, William Manis, Wm. Smith, Zach Smith, Everett Smith, John Cadwell, John Comer, Johnathan Cadwell, Solomon Barrett, William Morgan, Edward Moore.** [*jury duty next term - selected participants*] **Adam Comer, Peter Shamburger, Leonard Cagle, Christopher Yow, Hardy Davis, James Morgan, James Cadwell.**

A. 1785, Nov 21 -- 1784-1795 Court of Pleas and Quarter Sessions, Moore County, NC Page 69
[Deed] **James McDonald** to **Thos. Fry** was proven by **Jas. Fry**

B. 1785, Nov 23 -- 1784-1795 Court of Pleas and Quarter Sessions, Moore County, NC Page 69

Molly Seal, wife of William Seal came into court and took the oath of peace against him and William gave William Seal Junr. and Josiah Maples as security for good behavior.

940.　　1785, Nov 24 -- 1784-1795 Court of Pleas and Quarter Sessions, Moore County, NC Page 70
Ordered that Robert Bird be appointed overseer of the road from Searcys by Nich. Nalls towards Marts Toney on Pee Dee.

941.　　1785, Nov 24 -- 1784-1795 Court of Pleas and Quarter Sessions, Moore County, NC Page 71
Ordered that William Garner be appointed overseer of the road from Bear Creek towards Pee Dee.

942.　　1785, Nov 24 -- 1784-1795 Court of Pleas and Quarter Sessions, Moore County, NC Page 72
Ordered that Mary Sowell have leave to sell the estate of Isaac Sowell Dec'd.

A.　　1785, Nov 24 -- 1784-1795 Court of Pleas and Quarter Sessions, Moore County, NC Page 72
Ordered that the following hands work on the road from the Wolf Pit to Seals Road under Jos. Fry as overseer: Peter Salter, Benjn. Fry, Daniel Jones, Nathan Fry, John Tailor, Jacob Harwick, Alexr. McLoud, Neel McLoud, John Caddle, Jams. Caddle Junr., Benjn. Caddle, Daniel Caddle, Solomon Cox, Samuel Jackson, George Jackson, Christian Jackson hands, John Jackson hands, Anguish Campbell, Thomas Harmon Senr. and Thos. Harmon.

943.　　1785, Nov 24 -- 1784-1795 Court of Pleas and Quarter Sessions, Moore County, NC Page 73
Ordered that Richd. Bean be appointed constable in John Cox's District.

A.　　1785, Nov 25 -- 1784-1795 Court of Pleas and Quarter Sessions, Moore County, NC Page 74
Ordered that George Glascock Esq. be appointed to take the number of citizens in Capt. Jams. Collins' District; William Barrott Esq. in Capt. John Cox's District.

944.　　1785, Nov 24 -- 1784-1795 Court of Pleas and Quarter Sessions, Moore County, NC Page 75
Ordered that Wm. Dunn and Wm. Beazely overseers of the Muses Road build a bridge across McLendons Creek near Charity Muses.

945.　　1785, Nov 24 -- 1784-1795 Court of Pleas and Quarter Sessions, Moore County, NC Page 75
Ordered that Peter Shamburger be appointed overseer of the road in place of Geo. Cagle.

946.　　1785, Nov 30 -- Land Grant #98, Moore County, NC
Malcolm Morrison received 200 acres located on Dry Creek adjoining Ancel Melton and Daniel McSwain (formerly the Sandhill Place). Isaac Dunn and Richd. Dunn were chain carriers.

947.　　1785, Nov 30 -- Land Grant #128, Moore County, NC
Neil Matheson received 100 acres located on Dry Creek adjoining Nicholas Newton and Donald McSwine. Isaac Dunn and Richd. Dunn were chain carriers.

948.　　1785, Dec 1 -- Land Grant #25, Moore County, NC
Robert Paterson received 100 acres located on Horse Creek including where James Stevens formerly lived. Ansel Melton and John McQueen were chain carriers.

949.　　1785, Dec 3 -- Land Grant #41, Moore County, NC

John McAulay received 100 acres located on Wet Creek. **Farquard Bethune** and **Norman Morison** were chain carriers.

950.   1785, Dec 3 -- Land Grant #138, Moore County, NC
John McKay received 100 acres adjoining **Melton**. **Bartholemy Dunn** and **Ansel Melton** were chain carriers.

951.   1785, Dec 3 -- Land Grant #188, Moore County, NC
Norman McLeod received 105 acres located on Suggs [Suck?] Creek adjoining **Lewis Sowell**. **Farquard Bethune** and **Norman Morison** were chain carriers.

952.   1785, Dec 12 -- 1784-1797 Land Entries, Moore County, NC
#88 **Moses Myrick** entered 100 acres north of Deep River adjoining **Hunter**, **McDonald** and **Barnes**.

953.   1785, Dec 22 -- Land Grant #140, Moore County, NC
Nathaniel Norwood received 100 acres located on Killets Creek adjoining **Peter Salter**, **Jas. Muse** and including his own improvement. **Jas. Muse** and **Geo. Fry** were chain carriers.

954.   1785, Dec 22 -- Deed Book 2, Page 195, Randolph County, NC
William Read deeded son **John Read** 75 acres located on Deep River adjoining **Richard Bird** and **Carr**. Granted to **William Searcy** and sold to **William Read**. **Arthur Read** and **Richard Bird** were witnesses.

955.   1785, Dec 28 -- Will Book A Page 303, Moore County, NC
Robert Dickerson sold **Willis Dickerson** several goods. **Hartwell Hunnicutt** and **Roling/Boiling Hunnitcutt** were witneses.

956.   1785, Dec 30 -- Land Grant #111, Moore County, NC
Jesse Muse received 50 acres located on Mill Swamp of McLendons Creek adjoining **Muse**. **Jas. Muse** and **Uyle Duckman** were chain carriers.

957.   1785, Dec 30 -- Land Grant #184, Moore County, NC
Jesse Muse received 50 acres located on McLendons Creek adjoining **Jas. Muse** and **Dowd**. **Thos. Muse** and **Ethro Boles** were chain carriers.

958.   1786, Jan 2 -- Estate, Cumberland County, NC
Inventory of the estate of **James Muse** Dec'd. by **Charity Muse**

959.   1786, Jan 4 -- Land Grant #204, Moore County, NC
Christian Bathune received 50 acres located on McLendons Creek adjoining her own line. **Murdak McAuley** and **Daniel McLeod** were chain carriers.

960.   1786, Jan 7 -- Land Grant #3548, Mecklenburg County, NC
Charles Cagle received 200 acres located on Dutch Buffalo Creek and east of Rocky River including his own improvement adjoining **Charles Hart**, **Paulser Ness** and **Jacob Mayer**. **John Clay** and **John Cagle** were chain carriers. Entered Mar 1, 1779.

961.   1786, Jan 24 -- Land Grant #114, Moore County, NC
William Barrett received 100 acres located on Wet Creek and the head of Sings Creek adjoining **McKay** and **Dunn**. **Dempsey Sowell** and **Bartholomew Dunn** were chain carriers.

962.   1786, Feb -- 1785-1868 Index to Trial Docket, Moore County, NC Page 9
Aaron Feagin v. **Nathl. Melton**

963.   1786, Feb 4 -- Land Grant #453, Randolph County, NC
Jno. Needham received 50 acres on Fork Creek adjoining his own line and **Thomas Cost**. **William Larrence** and **William Needham** were chain carriers.

964.   1786, Feb 13 -- Land Grant #39, Moore County, NC

Thomas Gilmore received 100 acres located on Cabin Creek including **James Jeffrey**'s improvement adjoining **John Carpenter**. **John Cox** and **Thos. Graham** were chain carriers.

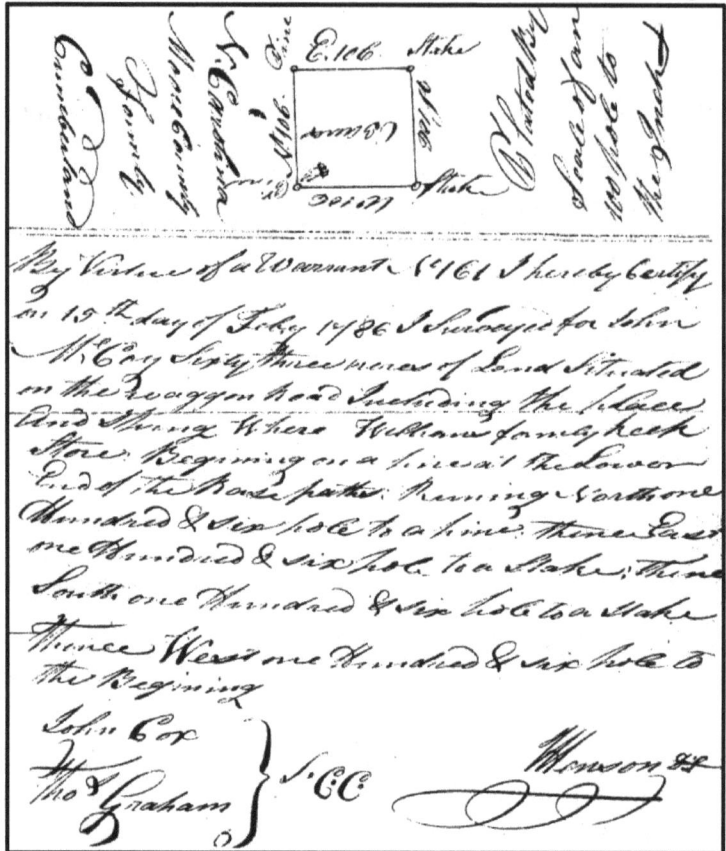

965.　　　1786, Feb 13 -- Land Grant #163, Moore County, NC
John McNeill received 100 acres located south of McLendons Creek adjoining his own line. **John Jackson** and **Neill McLeod** were chain carriers.

966.　　　1786, Feb 14 -- Land Grant #235, Moore County, NC
William Hardin received 200 acres located south of Deep River on both sides of Buffalo Creek adjoining **McNeill** and **England**. **William Richardson** and **Drury Richardson** were chain carriers.

967.　　　1786, Feb 15 -- Land Grant #24, Moore County, NC
John Cox received 150 acres located west of Mill Creek including his own improvement. **Thos. Graham** and **John Morgan** were chain carriers.

968.　　　1786, Feb 15 -- Land Grant #125, Moore County, NC
John McKoy received 63 acres on the Waggon/Adkin Road adjoining the place and spring where **Williams** formerly kept store. **John Cox** and **Thos. Graham** were chain carriers.

969.　　　1786, Feb 16 -- Land Grant #133, Moore County, NC
Thomas Armstrong received 100 acres located on Williams Creek of Bear Creek adjoining **Peter Hair** and including **Reuben Freeman**'s improvement. **Peter Hair** and **John Cox** were chain carriers.

970.　　　1786, Feb 20 -- Will Book A Page 302, Moore County, NC
Thomas Collins sold **James Collins** two negroes [*Bess and Searoh*]. **Willis Dickerson** and **Mary Dickerson** were witnesses.

971.　　　1786, Feb 20 -- 1784-1795 Court of Pleas and Quarter Sessions, Moore County, NC
[*jury duty - selected participants*] **James Morgan, James Caddle, Christopher Yow** [*jury duty next term - selected participants*] **Thos. Key, William Morgan, Peter Shamburger, Jacob Stutts, Nicholas Nall, Geo. Cagle, Drury Richardson, Zach. Smith.**

972.　　　1786, Feb 20 -- 1784-1795 Court of Pleas and Quarter Sessions, Moore County, NC Page 80
Deed from **Thomas Cotton** to **Richard Dunn** was proven by **Benj. Simmons**
Deed from **John Blanchett** to **Jos. Duckworth** was proven by **Ezekial Johnson**

973.　　　1786, Feb 20 -- Land Grant #135, Moore County, NC
Angus McIver received 100 acres located on both sides of Suck Creek adjoining **Widow McDonald**. **Obideah Sowell** and **Dempsey Sowell** were chain carriers.

974.　　　1786, Feb 21 -- 1784-1795 Court of Pleas and Quarter Sessions, Moore County, NC Page 81
Aaron Feagen v. **Nathl. Melton**

975.　　　1786, Feb 21 -- 1784-1795 Court of Pleas and Quarter Sessions, Moore County, NC Page 82
Ordered that negro **Will** the property of **Jams. Barnes** Dec'd. be freed pursuant to his will and **Thos. Tyson** be security for good behavior.

976. 1786, Feb 21 -- 1784-1795 Court of Pleas and Quarter Sessions, Moore County, NC Page 83
Jesse Writter records his mark as a swallow fork in the right ear and a slit in the left.

977. 1786, Feb 22 -- 1784-1795 Court of Pleas and Quarter Sessions, Moore County, NC Page 83, 87, 88, 93
[Deeds] **Phillip Alston** to **Jos. Gilbert** was acknowledged
Richardson Feagen to **John Williams** was proven by **John Carrell**
John Thorton to **William Harden** was proven by **Benjn. Shields**
Two deeds from **Richardson Feagan** to **John Overton** were proven by **Benjn. Shields**
Jams. Thornton to **Thomas Mathews** was proven by **Anthony Street**
Farquard Campbell to **Thos. Mathews** was proven by **John Barganeer**
Deed of bargain sale from **Robert Dickenson** to **Willis Dickenson** was proven by **Hartwell Hunnicutt**
Bill of sale from **Thos. Collins Senr.** to **James Collins** was proven by **Willis Dickenson**

978. 1786, Feb 22 -- 1784-1795 Court of Pleas and Quarter Sessions, Moore County, NC Page 87
John Cagle and **Simon Hart** be exempt from paying poll Tax for 1785.

979. 1786, Feb 22 -- 1784-1795 Court of Pleas and Quarter Sessions, Moore County, NC Page 89
Ordered that **Nicholas Nall** have leave to keep a tavern at his dwelling house with **Geo. Glascock** as security.

A. 1786, Feb 22 -- 1784-1795 Court of Pleas and Quarter Sessions, Moore County, NC Page 91
Account of the sale the estate of **Isaac Sowell** Dec'd. be recorderd

980. 1786, Feb 28 -- 1784-1797 Land Entries, Moore County, NC
#18 **Ferquhard Campbell** entered 100 acres east of Richland Creek adjoining his own line.

981. 1786, Feb 28 -- 1784-1797 Land Entries, Moore County, NC
#19 **John McAuley Jr.** entered 50 acres on the head of Sings Creek adjoining **Archibald McKay** and where **Angus McAuley** now lives.

982. 1786, Mar 1 -- Land Grant #132, Moore County, NC
William Handock received 100 acres located south of Deep River adjoining **Cheek** and his own line. **Howell Handock** and **Enock Rogers** were chain carriers.

983. 1786, Mar 1 -- Land Grant #186, Moore County, NC
Phillip Alston received 200 acres located south of Deep River adjoining his own line and **Hardin**. **Wm. Popplin** and **Leonard Surratt** were chain carriers.

984.   1786, Mar 3 -- Land Grant #197, Moore County, NC
Charles Shearing received 50 acres located south of Deep River adjoining **Robert Cheek** and **James Coleman**.
Wm. Poplin and **Shedrick Atkins** were chain carriers.

985.   1786, Mar 3 -- Land Grant #35, Moore County, NC
Nicholas Newton received 50 acres adjoining his own line and **Matheson**. **Samuel Barret** and **William Newton**
were chain carriers.

986.   1786, Mar 3 -- Land Grant #44, Moore County, NC
Nicholas Newton received 100 acres located on Horse Creek on the **Grove** path from his own home. **Samuel**
Barret and **Wm. Newton** were chain carriers.

A.   1786, Mar 4 – Deed Book D Page 133, Chatham County, NC
William Phillips deeded **Benjamin Saunders** 150 acres located on Tysons Creek and the Hay Meadow.
Sampson Brewer and **Willis Phillips** were witnesses.

987.   1786, Mar 10 -- 1784-1797 Land Entries, Moore County, NC
#23 **Solomon Barrett** entered 50 acres on McLendons Creek adjoining **John McNeill**.

988.   1786, Mar 11 -- Deed Book 1, Page 107, Randolph County, NC
William Argo and wife **Kenekappuck** deeded **Edmond Waddle** 200 acres located north of Deep River adjoining
Charles Goldson and the [Chatham] County line. **Windsor Perce**, **Mary Perce** and **Jesse Perce** were witnesses.

989.   1786, Mar 20 -- Deed Book 3, Page 64/Deed Book 8 Page 86, Randolph County, NC
William Searcy deeded **Elizabeth Alston**, daughter of **Philip Alston** two tracts: [1] 200 acres located south of
Deep River adjoining **Nall** and **Bowdon**. [2] 600 acres located north of Deep River adjoining **Argo**, **Searcey** and
Arthur Reed. **William Needham** and **Nicholas Nall** were witnesses.

990.   1786, Mar 20 -- Land Grant #60, Moore County, NC
James Moore received 250 acres located on Waggon Branch of Deep River adjoining the land where **John**
Goldson now lives. **Ewd. Moore Senr.** and **Ewd. Moore Junr.** were chain carriers.

991.   1786, Mar 20 -- Land Grant #96, Moore County, NC
John Cox received 100 acres located on both sides of Mill Creek adjoining **Morgan**'s improvement and mill.
Thos. Graham and **John Morgan** were chain carriers.

992.   1786, Mar 20 -- Land Grant #166, Moore County, NC
John Phillips received 25 acres located north of Deep River adjoining his own line. **Burrell Phillips** and **Dennis**
Phillips were chain carriers.

993.   1786, Mar 20 -- 1784-1797 Land Entries, Moore County, NC
#93 **Christian Bathune** entered 50 acres on McLendons Creek adjoining her own line.

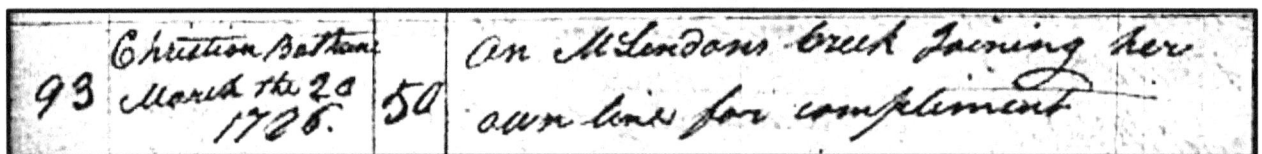

994.   1786, Mar 25 -- Land Grant #28, Moore County, NC
Anthony Seal received 100 acres located on Runnels Branch adjoining **Wm. Cox** and **Danl. McNeill**. **Thos.**
Egerton [Agerton] and **Ralph Davis** were chain carriers.

995.   1786, Mar 28 -- Land Grant #77, Moore County, NC
Kenneth Murchison received 200 acres located on McLendons Creek adjoining his own line, **John Martin** and
John McNeill. **Angus McIver** and **Jno. McDonald** were chain carriers.

A.   1786, Mar 31 -- Will, Chatham County, NC

Will of **Moses Teague**, Dec'd. Heirs: wife **Rachel** [*negro Abraham*], children: **Moses Teague, Esebell Wellborn, Abraham Teague, Isaac Teague, Jacob Teague, Wm. Teague, Elizabeth Jonson, Susanah Marly, Hannah Hornidy, David Teague** and **Charity Ray**. Executors: wife **Rachel Teague** and son **David Teague**. Witnesses: **Jacob Teague** and [faded] **Lawler**. Probated Aug 1799.

996.   1786, Apr -- Land Grant #108, Moore County, NC
Charles Seal received 100 acres located on Seal's Mill Creek adjoining his own line. **Thos. Gilmore** and **Jos. Perthys** were chain carriers.

997.   1786, Apr 3 -- 1784-1797 Land Entries, Moore County, NC
#29 **Angus McAuley** entered 50 acres on Tan Trough Creek of Mill Creek.

998.   1786, Apr 3 -- 1784-1797 Land Entries, Moore County, NC
#30 **William Barrett** entered [blank] acres between Sings Creek and Wet Creek adjoining **McKay** and **John McAuley**. [*Editor's Note: this entire entry was crossed out*]

999.   1786, Apr 4 -- Land Grant #117, Moore County, NC
Leonard Furr received 50 acres located on Buffalo Creek adjoining **Richard Bean** and including his own improvement. **John Viner**(?) and **Stephen Richardson** were chain carriers.

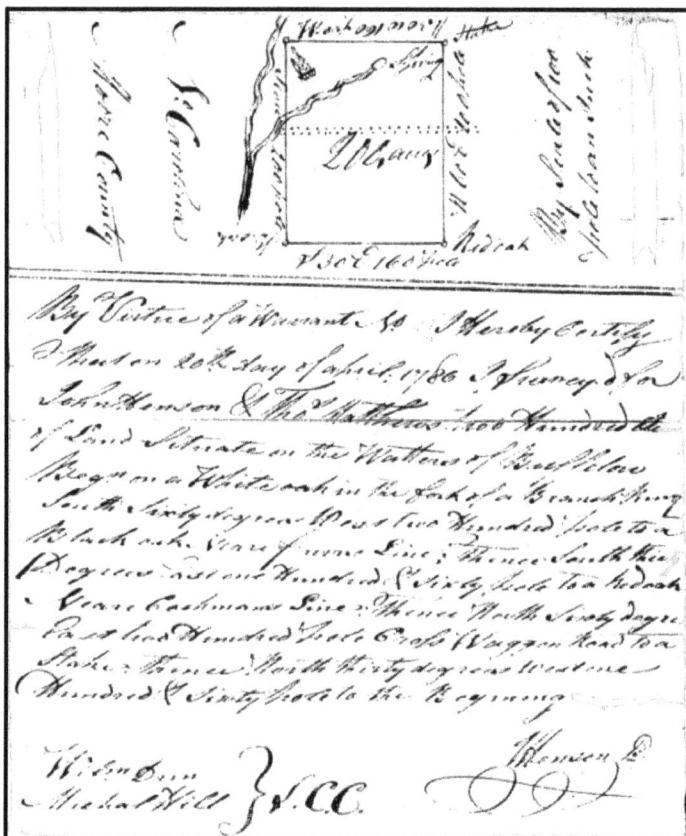

1000.   1786, Apr 20 -- Land Grant #148, Moore County, NC
John Henson and **Thomas Matthews** received 200 acres located on Buffalo Creek and the Waggon Road including the fork that goes to **Cagle**'s Bridge adjoining **Furr** and **Cockman**. **Wilm. Dunn** and **Michal Hill** were chain carriers.

1001.   1786, May 4 -- 1784-1797 Land Entries, Moore County, NC
#33 **John Dunlap** entered 50 acres adjoining **John Overton** and **Elijah Bettis**.

1002.   1786, May 5 -- 1784-1797 Land Entries, Moore County, NC
#35 **Richardson Feagan** entered 100 acres on both sides of **Edward Moore**'s Road including the flat land near **Golston**'s old place on the branches of Deep River.

1003.   1786, May 15 -- 1784-1795 Court of Pleas and Quarter Sessions, Moore County, NC
[*jury duty - selected participants*] **John Key, Thos. Key, Wm. Morgan, Jacob Stutts, Drury Richardson, Zach. Smith, Peter Shamburger, Nicholas Nall, Richd. Bean, Johnathan Caddle, Jos. Dun, Solomon Barrett.**

1004.   1786, May 15-16 -- 1784-1795 Court of Pleas and Quarter Sessions, Moore County, NC Page 94-95,97
[Deeds] **John Overton Senr.** to **Theophelous Petty** was acknowledged
Solomon Morgan to **John Caddle** proven by **Drury Richardson**
John Warner to **James Caddle** was proven by **John Caddle**
Robert Leavenston to **Robert Cheek** was proven by **Wm. Mares**
Thos. Armstrong to **Thos. Overton** was proven by **Robert Cheek**
James Muse to **Geo. Glascock** was proven by **John Jackson** Esq.
William Searcy to **Wm. Picken** was acknowledged

1005.   1786, May 15 -- 1784-1795 Court of Pleas and Quarter Sessions, Moore County, NC Page 94
Ordered that **Geo. Cagle** be exempt from jury duty

1006. 1786, May 15 -- 1784-1795 Court of Pleas and Quarter Sessions, Moore County, NC Page 95

Ordered that **Lewis Sowell** have leave to build a grist mill on the waters of Bear Creek formerly called **Tillis'** Mill on the old Askin [Yadkin?] Road near the fork.

1007. 1786, May 16 -- 1784-1795 Court of Pleas and Quarter Sessions, Moore County, NC Page 99
The following hands were appointed to work on the road from **Morgan**'s Mill to the old Yadkin Road:
Wm. Morgan, Geo. Brazwell, Richd. Dunn, James Morgan, Wm. Morgan Jr., Lewis Fields, Nathan Morgan, John Medford, John Morgan, Isaac Dun, Norman McLoud and **Robert Cox**.

1008. 1786, May 16 -- 1784-1795 Court of Pleas and Quarter Sessions, Moore County, NC Page 100
William Morgan have leave to build a grist mill on Tillis Mill Creek where a mill had formerly been built.

1009. 1786, May 16-18 -- 1784-1795 Court of Pleas and Quarter Sessions, Moore County, NC Page 100-102
Ordered that **John Williamson, Saml. Dun, Edwd. Moore** and **Bartholomew Dun** be exempt from paying poll tax for 1786.

1010. 1786, May 16 -- 1784-1795 Court of Pleas and Quarter Sessions, Moore County, NC Page 102
John Sowell and **Dempsey Sowell** brought into court suspected of stealing cattle and horse were examined and acquitted.

A. 1786, May 17-Aug 23 -- 1784-1795 Court of Pleas and Quarter Sessions, Moore County, NC Page 103, 111
Ordered that **John Overton, Thos. Overton, William Seale** and **Jos. Robson** be appointed to divide the estate of **Martin Johnston**, Dec'd. between widow **Sarah Johnston** and children **Mary Johnston** and **Catharine Johnston**.

B. 1786, May 18 -- 1784-1795 Court of Pleas and Quarter Sessions, Moore County, NC Page 104
Ordered that the following justices be appointed to take list of taxes in the following districts: **John Carrell** District 1; **John Cox** District 2, **William Barrott** District 3; **William Seale** District 5.

1011. 1786, May 30 -- Land Grant #34, Moore County, NC
John Jackson received 100 acres located on Jackson Creek adjoining **Bates**. **Andrew Bates** and **John Cox** were chain carriers.

1012. 1786, May 30 -- Will Book A Page 306, Moore County, NC
Josiah Maples sold **John Overton Senr.** negro **Jesse** and her children **Cherry, Jude** and **Isaac. John Dunlap** and **Sarah Dunlap** were witnesses.

1013. 1786, Jun 24 -- Deed, Moore County, NC
Mary Sowell and **John Sowell** deeded **William Barrett** 300 acres located on McLendons Creek adjoining **John Cox**, **Widow McDonald** and including plantation where **Mary Sowell** now lives. **John Jackson**, **Thomas Graham** and **George Jackson** were witnesses. [*Editor's Note: Original located in Herbert Floyd Seawell Sr. Papers at East Carolina University, Greenville, NC*]

1014. 1786, Aug 12 -- 1784-1797 Land Entries, Moore County, NC
#44 **William Dunn** entered 100 acres east of Wet Creek adjoining **Bartholomew Dunn**.

1015. 1786, Aug 12 -- 1784-1797 Land Entries, Moore County, NC
#94 **Ferquhard Campbell** entered 100 acres on Richland Creek adjoining his own line.

1016. 1786, Aug 12 -- 1784-1797 Land Entries, Moore County, NC
#95 **Murdock Bathune** entered 150 acres on Wet Creek adjoining **Morrison** and **Key**.

1017. 1786, Aug 19 -- Deed, Moore County, NC
Mary Sowell and **John Sowell** deeded **Margaret Sowell** 300 acres located on McLendons Creek adjoining **McDonald**. **Wm. Barrett**, **Jesse Ritter** and **Solomon Barrett** were witnesses. Proven by **Jesse Ritter** Feb 1787. [*Editor's Note: Original located in Herbert Floyd Seawell Sr. Papers at East Carolina University, Greenville, NC*]

1018. 1786, Aug 21 -- 1784-1795 Court of Pleas and Quarter Sessions, Moore County, NC
[*jury duty - selected participants*] **Hardy Davis, Peter Shamburger, David Richardson, John Caddle, Jesse Ritter, Leonard Furr, William Dunn, Zach Smith** and **Wm. Smith**. [*jury duty next term - selected participants*]
William Williamson, John Morgan, Nathan Smith, James Ledlow, Adam Comer, John Shuffle, James Key, Alexdr. Autery, Anson Melton, Lewis Sowell and **Hezekiah Dun**.

1019. 1786, Aug 21 -- 1784-1795 Court of Pleas and Quarter Sessions, Moore County, NC Page 109
Ordered that **James Caddle** be exempted from paying poll tax in the year 1786.

1020. 1786, Aug 21 -- 1784-1795 Court of Pleas and Quarter Sessions, Moore County, NC Page 109
Ordered that **Nathan Smith** be appointed road overseer in the place of **Geo. Brazwell**.

1021. 1786, Aug 21-23 -- 1784-1795 Court of Pleas and Quarter Sessions, Moore County, NC Page 109
Ordered that **James Hill, Geo. Cagle** and **Owen Carpenter** be exempt from poll Tax for 1786.

1022. 1786, Aug 21 -- 1784-1795 Court of Pleas and Quarter Sessions, Moore County, NC Page 109
Ordered that **William Davis**, an orphan age 9 years, be bound to **Hardy Davis** and learn the trade of a weaver.

1023. 1786, Aug 21 -- 1784-1795 Court of Pleas and Quarter Sessions, Moore County, NC Page 111
Ordered that **Christopher Yow** be appointed overseer in place of **Peter Shamburger**.

1024. 1786, Aug 22 -- 1784-1795 Court of Pleas and Quarter Sessions, Moore County, NC Page 111
James Caddle v. **Daniel Jones**

1025. 1786, Aug 22 -- 1784-1795 Court of Pleas and Quarter Sessions, Moore County, NC Page 112
Ordered that **John Caddle** be appointed overseer in place of **Jos. Fry**.

1026. 1786, Aug 22-24 -- 1784-1795 Court of Pleas and Quarter Sessions, Moore County, NC Page 110, 113, 117, 118
[Deeds] **Nathan Smith** to **Anson Melton** was proven by **Jesse Brown**
Tarply Tulles and wife to **Bartholomew Dunn** was proven by **William Dunn**
Isaac Saunders to **Lewis Sowell** was proven by **William Dunn**
Wm. Scoggin to **Jesse Muse** was proven by **James Muse**

1027. 1786, Aug 23 -- 1784-1795 Court of Pleas and Quarter Sessions, Moore County, NC Page 115
John Caddle v. **Chas. Shering**. Depositions ordered for **John Howell** and **James Caddle**.

1028. 1786, Aug 23 -- 1784-1795 Court of Pleas and Quarter Sessions, Moore County, NC Page 116
Benjn. Cadle v. **Solomon Cox**

1029. 1786, Aug 24 -- 1784-1795 Court of Pleas and Quarter Sessions, Moore County, NC Page 117
Ordered that a road be laid from **Morgan**'s Mill Path to **Morgan**'s Mill in the old Yadkin Road.

1030.   1786, Aug 24 -- 1784-1795 Court of Pleas and Quarter Sessions, Moore County, NC Page 120
Ordered that the following lay off a road from the courthouse to **Jesse Muse**'s and from there to Deep River and Dunhams Creek have the following hands to work: **Jos. Fry**, **John Caddle**, **Alexdr. McCloud**, **James Hill**, **James Caddle**, **Benjn. Fry**, **Neel McLoud**, **Leonard Thos.**, **James Caddle**, **John Black**, **William Beazley** and **John Beazley**.

1031.   1786, Aug 24 -- 1784-1795 Court of Pleas and Quarter Sessions, Moore County, NC Page 120
Ordered that **Jams. Muse** be appointed overseer of the road in place of **Thos. Maples**.

1032.   1786, Aug 24 -- 1784-1795 Court of Pleas and Quarter Sessions, Moore County, NC Page 121
Ordered that **Thos. Collins** be appointed overseer of the road in place of **John Adkins**.

1033.   1786, Aug 29 -- Deed Book 3, Page 73, Randolph County, NC
William Searcy deeded **James Bowdon** 16 acres adjoining **Bowdon**, **William Read** and **Spinks**. **Winsor Perce** and **Shadrach Dimo** were witnesses.

1034.   1786, Sep 3 -- 1784-1797 Land Entries, Moore County, NC
#3 **Christian Bethune** entered 50 acres on McLendons Creek adjoining **Campbell**, **McLeod** and **McDonald**.

1035.   1786, Sep 19 -- Deed Book 3, Page 84, Randolph County, NC
William Searcy deeded **Nicholas Nall** 160 acres located on Deep River and Fork Creek adjoining **John Perce** and **Edmond Waddil**. Granted to **William Searcy Senr.** and deeded to son **William Searcy**. **J. Knight**, **Winsor Pearce** and **Cornelius Latham** were witnesses.

1036.   1786, Sep 22 -- 1784-1797 Land Entries, Moore County, NC
#45 **William Barrett** entered 20 acres on Suck Creek adjoining **Angus McIver**, **Thomas Graham** and admitting a mill place.

1037.   1786, Sep 24 -- 1784-1797 Land Entries, Moore County, NC
#47 **George Glasscock** entered 100 acres on McLendons Creek adjoining **Hodges**.

1038.   1786, Oct 2 -- Land Grant #201, Moore County, NC
John Phillips received 50 acres located north of Deep River adjoining his own line. **Burrell Phillips** and **Dennis Phillips** were chain carriers.

1039.   1786, Oct 3 -- Land Grant #20 and 66, Moore County, NC
Donald McLeod received 50 acres located between Tillis' Creek and Sings Creek on the road that goes from **Newtons** to **Tillis'** Mill adjoining **Norman McLeod**. **Murdoch Baton** and **John McAuley** were chain carriers.

1040.   1786, Oct 3 -- Land Grant #76, Moore County, NC
James Hill received 100 acres located on Killets Creek adjoining **Daniel Muse** and **McLeod**. **Daniel Jones** and **Jesse Muse** were chain carriers.

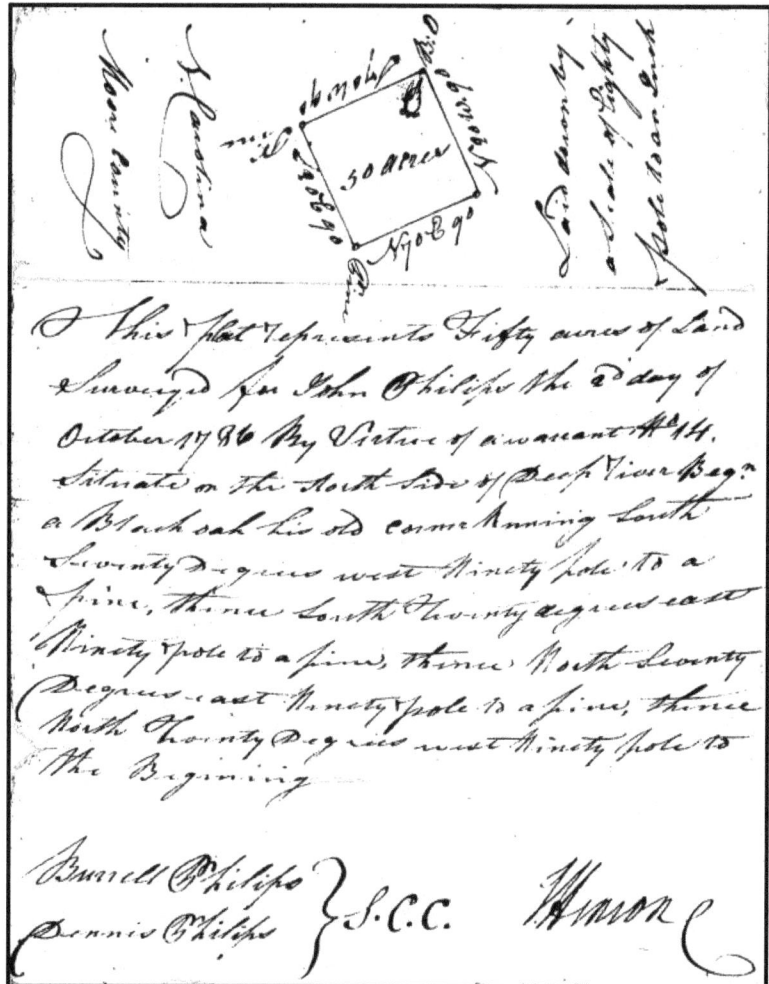

1041. 1786, Oct 6 -- Land Grant #86, Moore County, NC
Alexander McIver received 100 acres located on White Oak Branch of Wet Creek adjoining his own line. **Murdoch Baton** and **John McDonald** were chain carriers.

1042. 1786, Oct 10 -- Land Grant #174, Moore County, NC
Leven Hinsworth received 50 acres located on Deep River near Lick Creek adjoining **Hardin, Joseph Duckworth** and **John Carrel**. **Joseph Duckworth** and **Harmon Brewer** were chain carriers.

1043. 1786, Oct 10 -- Will Book A Page 311, Moore County, NC
Joseph McGee mortgaged 200 acres on Deep River to **William Harden Senr**. **John Carrell** and **Joseph Robson** were witnesses.

1044. 1786, Oct 16 -- Will Book A Page 308, Moore County, NC
Thomas Wade, Sheriff of Anson County sold **Thomas Muse** a negro boy named **Ben**, age 6 to resolve the matter of **John Garner** v. **James Mews** Exec.

1045. 1786, Nov 2 -- Land Grant #95, Moore County, NC
Solomon Barrett received 100 acres adjoining **Michael Hill** and the land **William Smith** formerly owned. **Thomas Graham** and **Richard Bean** were chain carriers.

1046. 1786, Nov 2 -- Centre [Quaker] Meeting Records (1775-1930) Page 55, Guilford County, NC
Aaron Tyson, son of **Cornelius** and **Jane Tyson**, of the Cane Creek Meeting and **Lydia Beals**, daughter of **William** and **Rachel Beals**, of Centre Meeting were married at the Centre Meeting House in Guilford County. **Matthew Ozburn, Robert Hodgson, Samuel Stanton, Aaron Coffin, Mary Ozburn, Rachel Green, Elizabeth Dicks, Robert Lamb, Joseph Macy, Benjamin Coffin, Daniel Worth, William Hoggard, Susanna Beal, Mary Reynolds, Mary Gilbert, Jane Tyson, Benjamin Tyson, John Beals, James Dicks, Hannah Hoggard, Jane Womble** and **Margaret Hoggard** were present and served as witnesses.

1047. 1786, Nov 3 -- Land Grant #85, Moore County, NC
Solomon Barrett received 100 acres adjoining **Hill** and the land **William Smith** formerly lived on. **Jacob Cagle** and **Michael Hill** were chain carriers.

1048. 1786, Nov 14 -- Land Grant #142, Moore County, NC
Joseph Cockman received 50 acres located on Long Meadow adjoining **Michael Hill**. **Leonard Furr** and **Michael Hill** were chain carriers.

1049. 1786, Nov 20 -- 1784-1795 Court of Pleas and Quarter Sessions, Moore County, NC
[*jury duty - selected participants*] Hezekiah Dun, Lewis Sowell, William Williamson, Nathan Smith, Adam Comer, John Shuffle, Alexdr. Attery, Jesse Ritter, Jos. Dun, Hardy Davis, Saml. Dunn, John Caddel, Zach. Smith, Bartholomew Dun. [*jury duty next term - selected participants*] Jas. Morgan, Peter Shamburger, Zach. Smith, John Key, William Dunn (Buffalo), William Dunn, Isaac Dunn, Thos. Keys, Jacob Stutts, Edwd. Moore, Bartholo. Dunn Senr., Nicholas Newton.

1050. 1786, Nov 20 -- Will Book A Page 309, Moore County, NC
Indenture between **Martha Cotes** and **Simon** and wife **Margreet Hart**. **Famariah Cotes** [age 10 years on Aug 20] to be bound to **Simon** and **Margreet Hart** until age 18. **Vincent Davis** and **Benjn. Stewart** were witnesses.

1051. 1786, Nov 21 -- 1784-1795 Court of Pleas and Quarter Sessions, Moore County, NC Page 123
William Barrett Esq. came into court and entered himself security to prevent **Nathan Barrett** and **George Barrett**, orphans of **Saml. Barret** Dec'd. from becoming charges of the county.

1052. 1786, Nov 21 -- 1784-1795 Court of Pleas and Quarter Sessions, Moore County, NC Page 123
Ordered that the court lay out a road beginning at **Morgans** Mill path and thence to **Morgans** Mill into the old Yadkin Road and all the hands who worked on the old road now work on the new road.

1053. 1786, Nov 21 -- 1784-1795 Court of Pleas and Quarter Sessions, Moore County, NC Page 123
Ordered that **Robert Davis** be appointed overseer of the road in place of **James Moore**.

1054. 1786, Nov 21 -- 1784-1795 Court of Pleas and Quarter Sessions, Moore County, NC Page 124-125
Mary Sowell v. **Wm. Caddle**

1055. 1786, Nov 21 -- 1784-1795 Court of Pleas and Quarter Sessions, Moore County, NC Page 124
[Deeds] **William Gardner** and wife to **Leonard Cagle** was proven by **Nathan Smith**.
John Barton to **William England** was proven by **John Williams** Esq.

1056. 1786, Nov 21 -- 1784-1797 Land Entries, Moore County, NC
#53 **Hezekiah Dunn** entered 50 acres on head of Mares Branch adjoining his own line.

A. 1786, Nov 21 -- 1784-1795 Court of Pleas and Quarter Sessions, Moore County, NC Page 118
Ordered that **George Carringer** and **Alexr. Autery** be exempt from paying poll tax for 1786.

1057. 1786, Nov 22 -- 1784-1795 Court of Pleas and Quarter Sessions, Moore County, NC Page 125
Ordered that **John Overton Sen.**, **Robert Cheek** and **Geo. Glascock** be appointed to lay off and divide the estate of **James Muse** Dec'd. to **Charity Muse**.

1058. 1786, Nov 22 -- 1784-1795 Court of Pleas and Quarter Sessions, Moore County, NC Page 126
Administration of the estate of **Chas. Shearing** granted to **Elizabeth Shearing** with **Willis Dickenson** and **James Collins** as securities.

1059. 1786-1787 [undated estimate] -- Estate, Moore County, NC Will Book A, Page 340
Inventory of the Estate of **Chas. Shearling**, Dec'd. Mentions 200 acres whereon he lived and died and 1150 acres in Chatham County. [*Editor's Note: No date given on actual inventory, but the date was estimated using County Court Minute reference above.*]

1060. 1786, Nov 22 -- 1784-1795 Court of Pleas and Quarter Sessions, Moore County, NC Page 126
Ordered that **William Beazley** be appointed overseer of the road from **Muse**'s to Moore Court and have the following hands to work: **John Beazley, Benjn. Fry, James Caddle Jur., Jesse Muse, Alexd. McLoud, Neel McLoud, James Muse, Hyman Hill, Thos.[?] Muse, Benjn. Caddle** and **Daniel Caddle**.

1061. 1786, Nov 23 -- 1784-1795 Court of Pleas and Quarter Sessions, Moore County, NC Page 128
Ordered that the sheriff summon a jury to resolve a land dispute between **John Keys** and **Murdock Bethune**.

A. 1786, Nov 24 -- Land Grant #980, Chatham County, NC
Edward Stuart received 40 acres located on Cain Creek adjoining **William McPherson, Braxton** and his own line. **Enoch McPherson** and **William McPherson** were chain carriers.

1062. 1786, Nov 25 -- 1784-1797 Land Entries, Moore County, NC
#55 **Donald McLeod** entered 60 acres on Old Yadkin Road adjoining **Lewis Sowel** and **Archd. McKay**.

A. 1786, Nov 30 -- Deed Book D Page 320, Chatham County, NC
Nathan Deaton deeded **John Powers** 300 acres located on both sides of Ceder Creek. **Sampson Brewer** and **John Reed** were witnesses

1063. 1786, Dec -- Criminal Actions, Randolph County, NC
Presentment of **Winser Pierce** on a charge of common drunkenness and profane swearing to the evil example of youth and to dishonor of society.

1064. 1786, Dec 2 -- Deed Book H Page 9-10, Wake County, NC
Joseph Britt, Blacksmith deeded **William Bridges** 270 acres located east of Little Creek on both sides of Guffey's Swamp adjoining **Benjamin Britt**. **Benjamin Britt** and **Rials Britt** were witnesses.

1065. 1786, Dec 7 -- Deed Book 3, Page 71, Randolph County, NC
William Searcy deeded **Arthur Reed** 100 acres located north of Deep River adjoining **Arthur Reed** and **Richard Bird**. **John Pearce** and **Lewis Spinks** were witnesses.

1066. 1786, Dec 8 -- Land Grant #47, Moore County, NC
Solomon Barrett received 100 acres located on McLendons Creek adjoining **William Barrett, Robert Grimes, John Cox** and **Widow McLeod**. **Thomas Graham** and **Solomon Barrett** were chain carriers.

1067. 1786, Dec 8 -- Will, Wayne County, NC
Will of **James Bradbury**, Dec'd. Heirs: Wife, son **Jacob Bradbury**, daughter **Hannah Ritter**, son **George Bradbury**, daughter **Mary Bele**, granddaughter **Elizabeth Bele**, son **Thomas Chambers Bradbury**, daughter **Rhoda Stanly** and

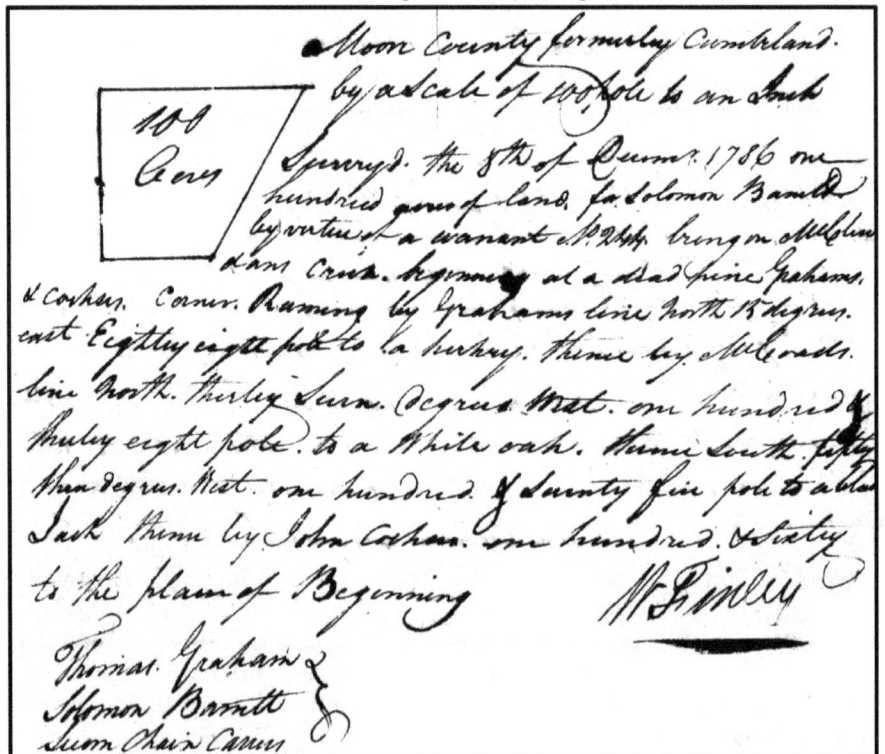

her eldest son **James Stanly**, son **James Bradbury**, daughter **Elizabeth Grantham**, son-in-law **Thos. Grantham**, grandson **James Bradbury Ritter** and grandson **Aron Ritter**. Executors: **William McKinne**, **Richard McKinne** and **Stephen Stanly**. Witnesses: **Wm. McKinne Junr.**, **Michel Buell/Bauell**, **Thos. Costettor** and **Elizabeth Auly/Orrly**. Proven 1787.

1068.   1786, Dec 23 -- Deed Book 3, Page 111, Randolph County, NC
William Searcy deeded **John Garner** 30 acres located on Deep River and Fork Creek adjoining **Nicholas Nall** and the county line. **John Pearce** and **James Husey** were witnesses.

1069.   1786, Dec 23 -- 1784-1797 Land Entries, Moore County, NC
#59 **Nicholas Nall** entered 200 acres north of Bear Creek and on the head of Ceedar Branch.

1070.   1786, Dec 23 -- 1784-1797 Land Entries, Moore County, NC
#60 **Bartholomew Dunn Jr.** entered 60 acres on Mill Creek in between the fork of the Dry Fork and the Wet Fork.

1071.   1786, Dec 25 -- Land Grant #421, Randolph County, NC
Nicholas Nall received 300 acres located on Fork Creek adjoining **Andrews**. **William Moore** and **Micajah Henry** were chain carriers.

1072.   1786, Dec 26 -- Land Grant #387, Randolph County, NC
Jno. Needham received 100 acres on both sides of Fork Creek and Meadow Branch adjoining his own line, **Spinks** and **James Lathem**. **Enoch Spinks** and **William Needham** were chain carriers.

1073.   1787 -- Marriage Licenses, Moore County, NC Will Book A Page 382 (selected licenses)
Wm. Cagle and **Mary Barrett** were granted a marriage license. **William Cockman** was the surety.
Nathaniel Melton and **Fereby Barrett** were granted a marriage license. **Nicholas Newton** was the surety.
John Ritter and **Elizabeth Richardson** were granted a marriage license. **Jesse Ritter** was the surety.

1074.   1787, Jan 1 -- Deed Book 3, Page 87-88, Randolph County, NC
William Searcy deeded **Aaron Hill** two tracts: [1] 640 acres located on Deep River on Moore County line adjoining **Charles Goldston**, **Argo** and the Chatham County line. [2] 30 acres located on Deep River adjoining **Nicholas Nall**. **John Powers**, **Winsor Pearce** and **John Pearce** were witnesses.

1075.   1787, Jan 13 -- Land Grant #196, Moore County, NC
Kenneth McKenzie received 100 acres located on Buffalo Creek adjoining **Joseph Duckworth** and **Drury Richardson**. **William Richardson** and **Robert Richardson** were chain carriers.

A.   1787, Jan 19 – Deed Book D Page 210, Chatham County, NC

Jeremiah Barns deeded **Joseph Gilbert** (of Moore County) 600 acres located south of Indian Creek adjoining **Myrick**. **Seth Barns** and **William Roberds** were witnesses.

1076. 1787, Jan 22 -- 1784-1797 Land Entries, Moore County, NC
#70 **Ambrose Brewer** entered 100 acres on Bear Creek adjoining **Edwards** and including his own improvement.

1077. 1787, Jan 22 -- 1784-1797 Land Entries, Moore County, NC
#71 **John Askins** entered 100 acres on both sides of Buffalow Creek adjoining **Isaac Pennington** and including the Steep Bottom Ford.

1078. 1787, Feb7 -- Will Book A Page 310-311 Moore County, NC
Geo. Glascock, **John Overton** and **Robert Cheek** appointed to allot the dowry to **Charity Muse**, widow of **James Muse** Dec'd.

1079. 1787, Feb 8 -- Will Book A Page 310, Moore County, NC
Hartwell Hunnicutt appointed **James Collins** and **Willis Dickerson** as power of attorney. **Geo. Glascock** and **Jon. Milton Glascock** were witnesses.

1080. 1787, Feb 13 -- Bible of **Edward Stuart** and **Mary McPherson**, Moore County, NC
Edward Stuart and **Mary McPherson** were married

1081. 1787, Feb 19 -- 1784-1795 Court of Pleas and Quarter Sessions, Moore County, NC
[*jury duty - selected participants*] **William Dun, Isaac Dun, Edwd. Moore, John Keys, Jacob Stutts, Zach. Smith, Thos. Keys, Bartholomew Dun, Saml. Dun, Nicholas Newton, Jesse Ritter, William Smith, Nathan Smith** and **James Caddle.** [*jury duty next term - selected participants*] **James Hill, William Smith, Everitt Smith, Anson Melton, Adam Comer, John Morgan, James Morgan, Nicholas Newton, Leonard Furr** and **Isam Smith.**

1082. 1787, Feb 19-22 -- 1784-1795 Court of Pleas and Quarter Sessions, Moore County, NC Page 132,139,140,143,145
[Deeds] **James Morgan** and wife to **John Hunsucker** was proven by **Leonard Cagle**
Richardson Feagan to **Benjn. Sheilds** was proven by **Geo. Glascock**
Geo. Glascock to **Benjn. Fry** was acknowledged
Mary Sowell and **John Sowell** to **Margaret Sowell** proven by **Jesse Ritter**
Richardson Feagan to **Cornelius Dowd** and **John Shepard** was proven by **Archd. Dalrymple**
William Smith to **Mary Hines** was proven by **Jesse Ritter**
Richdson. Feagan to **William Hancock** was proven by **Benjn. Shields**
Richardson Feagn to **John Epperson** was acknowledged
Richdson. Feagan to **Chas. Coffind** was proven by **John Love**

1083. 1786, Feb 19 -- 1784-1795 Court of Pleas and Quarter Sessions, Moore County, NC Page 132
A power of attorney from **Hartwell Hunicutt** to **Jams. Collins** and **Willis Dickinson** proven by **Geo. Glascock**.

1084. 1787, Feb 20 -- Land Grant #192, Moore County, NC
George Glascock received 100 acres located on McClendons Creek adjoining **Morrison. Murdoch Bathune** and **Julias Glascock** were chain carriers.

1085. 1787, Feb 20 -- 1784-1795 Court of Pleas and Quarter Sessions, Moore County, NC Page 134
Mary Sowell v. **James Caddle, Sr.**

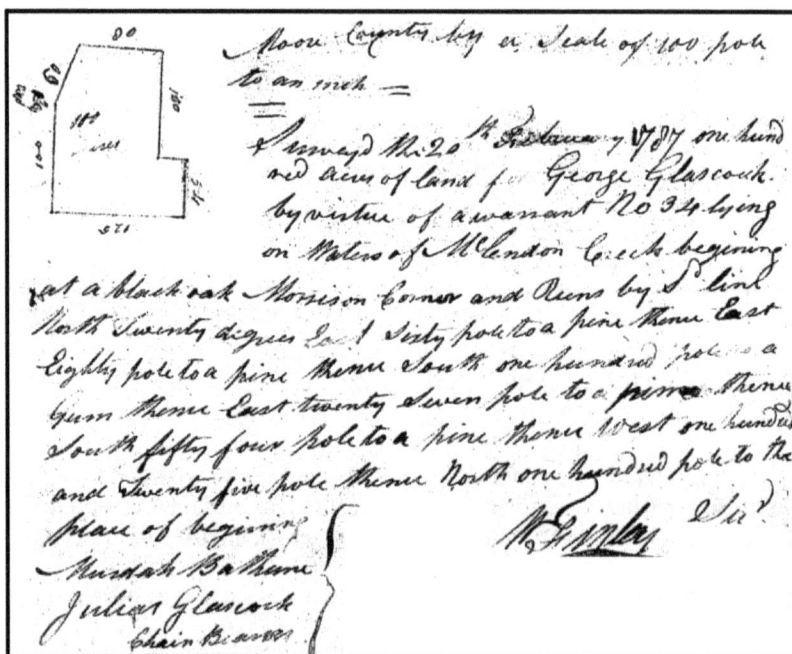

1086. 1787, Feb 20 -- 1784-1795 Court of Pleas and Quarter Sessions, Moore County, NC Page 134
Administration of the Estate of **Robert Moore** granted to **Sterling Carrell** with bond given with **John Blanchett** and **John Carrell**. Administration granted to **Betty Moore** has been struck through.

1087. 1787 [undated estimate] -- Estate, Moore County, NC Will Book A, Page 340
Inventory of the Estate of **Robert Moore**, Dec'd. Mentions 100 acres on Deep River. [*Editor's Note: No date given on actual inventory, but the date was estimated using County Court Minute reference above.*]

1088. 1787, Feb 20 -- 1784-1797 Land Entries, Moore County, NC
#75 **Niell McLeod** entered 60 acres adjoining **Murdock McAuley** and the fork of Mill Creek.

1089. 1787, Feb 21 -- 1784-1797 Land Entries, Moore County, NC
#79 **Samuel Perry** entered 50 acres including **John Golston**'s improvement.

1090. 1787, Feb 21 -- 1784-1797 Land Entries, Moore County, NC
#80 **Samuel Perry** entered 50 acres including improvements.

1091. 1787, Feb 21 -- 1784-1797 Land Entries, Moore County, NC
#82 **Jesse Muse** entered 25 acres on both sides of McLendons Creek including his own improvement.

1092. 1787, Feb 21 -- 1784-1797 Land Entries, Moore County, NC
#83 **Samuel Dunn** entered 25 acres on Richland Creek including **William Dunn**'s improvement.

1093. 1787, Feb 22 -- 1784-1795 Court of Pleas and Quarter Sessions, Moore County, NC Page 141
Ordered that **Zach. Smith** be appointed overseer of the road from the foot of **Charity Muse**'s Bridge to Bear Creek in place of **Benjn. Barrett**.

1094. 1787, Feb 22 -- 1784-1795 Court of Pleas and Quarter Sessions, Moore County, NC Page 141
Ordered that **Adam Comer** be appointed overseer of the road from Bear Creek to **William Garners** to the County line.

1095. 1787, Feb 23 -- 1784-1795 Court of Pleas and Quarter Sessions, Moore County, NC Page 146
Ordered that a road be laid off from Chatham County line about **Teague**'s Waggon road leading to Bear Creek near the **Widow Muses**.

1096. 1787, Feb 23 -- 1784-1795 Court of Pleas and Quarter Sessions, Moore County, NC Page 146
Ordered that the old road formerly laid out from **Jesse Muse**'s to the courthouse begin at the old road leading by **Jesse Muse**'s to the courthouse and from thence to the old road and work the following hands: **John Bezeley**, **Saml. Bezeley**, **Benjn. Fry**, **Alexdr. McLoud**, **James Caddle Jur.**, **Benjn. Caddle**, **Daniel Caddle**, **Hiram Hill**, **Thos. Harrington**, **Neal McLoud** and **Wm. Caddle**.

1097. 1787, Feb 23 -- 1784-1795 Court of Pleas and Quarter Sessions, Moore County, NC Page 147
Ordered that the following hands work on the road from the post at **Muses'** bridge to **William Seales**: **Jesse Muse**, **Geo. Glascock**'s hands, **Thos. Muse** and **Hiram Hill**.

1098. 1787, Feb 23 -- 1784-1795 Court of Pleas and Quarter Sessions, Moore County, NC Page 147
Ordered that **Betty Seal** orphan of **Peggy Seal** be bound to **John Adkins** until she reaches lawful age.

1099. 1787, Feb 23 -- Land Grant #193, Moore County, NC
William Davis received 255 acres located on Fall Creek adjoining **Lanear Brewer** and including the improvement where **James Elkins** formerly lived. **Samuel Person** and **Lanear Brewer** were chain carriers.

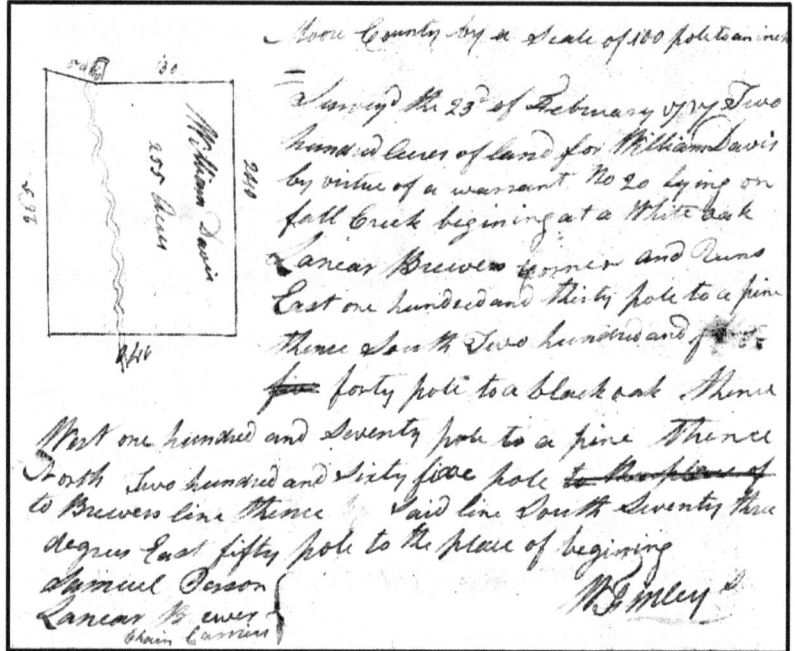

1100. 1787, Feb 23 -- Land Grant #200, Moore County, NC
Robert Cobb received 316 acres located on Fall Creek north of Deep River on the [Chatham] County line adjoining **Leanear Brewer**. **Samuel Person** and **Leanear Brewer** were chain carriers.

1101. 1787, Mar 4 -- Land Grant #265, Moore County, NC
John McSween received 100 acres located on McLendons Creek adjoining his own line and **Farquard Campbell**. **John Bethune** and **Angus McDonald** were chain carriers.

1102. 1787, Mar 10 -- Land Grant #283, Moore County, NC
Donald McQueen received 100 acres located north of Locust Branch adjoining **Kain** and including his own improvement. **Duncan McIntosh** and **Donald McQueen** were chain carriers.

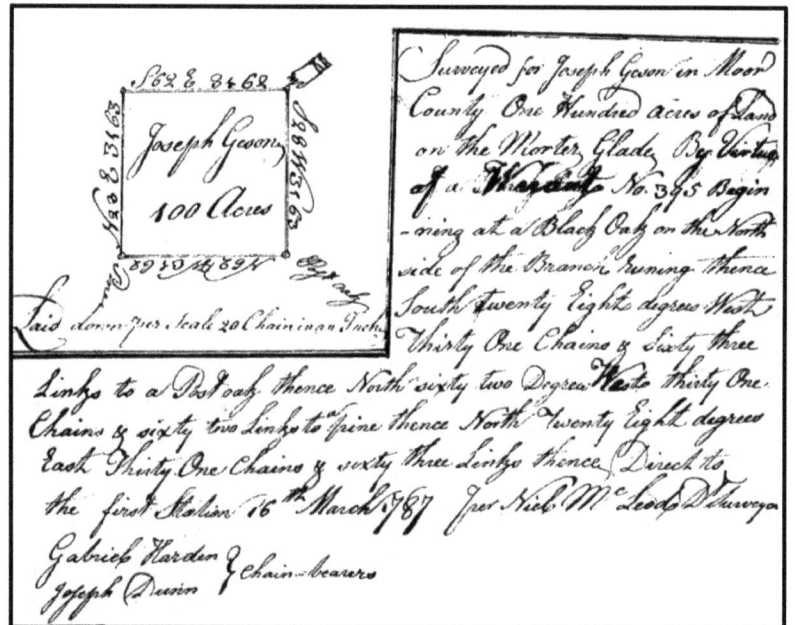

1103. 1787, Mar 16 -- Land Grant #264, Moore County, NC
Joseph Geson received 100 acres located on the fork of Lick Creek adjoining his own line including where **Geson** now lives. **Gabriel Hardin** and **Joseph Dunn** were chain carriers.

1104. 1787, Mar 16 -- Land Grant #284, Moore County, NC
Joseph Geason received 100 acres located on Morter Glade. **Gabriel Harden** and **Joseph Dunn** were chain carriers.

A. 1787, Mar 20 -- 1784-1795 Court of Pleas and Quarter Sessions, Moore County, NC Page 138
Ordered that the following be appointed to take the number of inhabitants: **John Carrell** Esq. – District #1; **John Cox** Esq. – District #2; **Geo. Glascock** – District #3

B. 1787, Mar 26 – Land Grant #973, Chatham County, NC
Samuel Seegar received 640 acres located on prong of Indian Creek. **John McVay** and **Lewis Phillips** were chain carriers.

1105. 1787, Apr 13 -- Land Grant #236, Moore County, NC
Richardson Feagen received 100 acres located north of Deep River on both sides of **Edward Moore**'s Road including the flat land near **Golston**'s old place. **Samuel Perry** and **William Cook** were chain carriers.

A. 1787, May 1 -- Deed Book D Page 253-254, Chatham County, NC
Ambrose Brown deeded **John Ferrington** 150 acres adjoining **Jessy Brown**. **John Ramsey** was a witness.

B. 1787, May 1 -- Deed Book D Page 256, Chatham County, NC
Jesse Brown deeded **John Ferrington** 100 acres adjoining **Patterson**. **Daniel Burnett** and **Hardy Owen** were witnesses.

1106. 1787, May 10 -- Will Book A Page 312, Moore County, NC
John Jackson sold **Christian Jackson** a negro named **Jim**, age 20. **Geo. Jackson** was a witness.

1107. 1787, May 14 -- 1784-1797 Land Entries, Moore County, NC
#99 **William Barrett** entered 50 acres north of McLendons Creek adjoining **McSwain** and **Ferquhard Campbell**.

1108. 1787, May 15 -- Land Grant #29, Moore County, NC
John Overton received 640 acres located on Deep River adjoining his own line, **Phillip Alston** and **Dowd**.

1109. 1787, May 15 -- Deed Book D Page 282, Chatham County, NC
Joseph McGee (of Moore County, NC) deeded **Joseph Taylor** (of Granville County, NC) 389 acres located in Chatham County on White Oak Creek of New Hope adjoining **Pheman**, **Joseph Taylor**, **William Davis**, **Pitts** and the [Wake] County line. **B. Ridley** was a witness.

1110. 1787, May 18 -- Land Grant #245, Moore County, NC
William Dunn received 100 acres located on Wet Creek adjoining **Bartholomew Dunn**. **Esekiah Dunn** and **Bartholomew Dunn** were chain carriers.

1111. 1787, May 18 -- Land Grant #257, Moore County, NC
Ezekiah Dunn received 50 acres located west of Wet Creek and the head of the Mirery Branch adjoining his own line. **William Dunn** and **Bartholomew Dunn** were chain carriers.

1112. 1787, May 21 -- 1784-1795 Court of Pleas and Quarter Sessions, Moore County, NC
[*jury duty - selected participants*] **James Hill, Everett Smith, Anson Melton, John Morgan, William Smith, Richd. Dunn, Adam Comer, Nicholas Newton, Leonard Furr, John Keys, Jesse Ritter, Wm. Dunn, Nathan Smith, Thos. Keys, Saml. Dunn, Geo. Cagle, Jos. Dun** and **Zacha. Smith**. [*jury duty next term - selected participants*] **Edwd. Moore, James Caddle, Drury Richardson** and **Alexr. Autery**.

A. 1787, May 22 -- 1784-1795 Court of Pleas and Quarter Sessions, Moore County, NC Page 153
Ordered that the following Justices be appointed to take the list of taxable property for 1787: **Thos. Tyson** Esq. – District #1; **Nicholas Nall** Esq. – District #2; **William Barrott** – District #3

1113. 1787, May 22-25 -- 1784-1795 Court of Pleas and Quarter Sessions, Moore County, NC Page 153, 157, 160, 162-163
[Deeds] **John Overton** to **William Payne** was acknowledged
John Overton and wife to **Richd. Street** was proven by **Thos. Overton**
John Overton and wife to **Alexd. McMillan** was proven by **Thos. Overton** and **John Overton Jr**.
Richardson Feagan to **Robert Cheek** was acknowledged
Richardson Feagan to **Robert Davis** was acknowledged
Richardson Feagan to **Thos. Mathews** was acknowledged
Richardson Feagan to **Donald Munk** was acknowledged
Richardson Feagan to **James Collins** was proven by **Geo. Glascock**
[Bill of Sale] **Jos. McGee** to **William Harden** was proven by **Jos. Robson**
[Bill of Sale] **John Jackson** to **Christian Jackson** was acknowledged

A. 1787, May 23 -- 1784-1795 Court of Pleas and Quarter Sessions, Moore County, NC Page 159-160
Ordered that **Fox Farmer** who was brought before the court under the charge of being one of the party under the command of **David Fanning** who burnt the houses of **Edward Cox** and **John Cox** and for the murder of **William Jackson** and **Robert Law** be commited to district goal [jail] of Wilmington and remain there until discharged. Brought into court on second examination and ordered released and acquitted.

B.   1787, May 23 -- 1784-1795 Court of Pleas and Quarter Sessions, Moore County, NC Page 159
Ordered that **Reuben Shields** be appointed Constable in Capt. Dowd's District with **Cornelious Dowd** and **Willis Dickerson** as securities.

1114.   1787, May 23 -- 1784-1795 Court of Pleas and Quarter Sessions, Moore County, NC Page 159
Ordered that **Jos. Duckworth** be appointed overseer of the new road from Chatham County line to where it crosses Deep River.

A.   1787, Jun 29 -- Deed Book D Page 394-395, Chatham County, NC
Nathan Deaton deeded **William Needham** a portion of 200 acres located on Ceder Creek adjoining **James Deaton**. **James Deaton** and **John Powers** were witnesses.

B.   1787, Jun 29 -- Deed Book D Page 404-405, Chatham County, NC
Nathan and **Margaret Deaton** deeded **James Deaton** a portion of 200 acres located on Ceder Creek. **John Powers** and **Windsor Pearce** were witnesses.

1115.   1787, Jul 6 -- Land Grant #275, Moore County, NC
John McLeod received 100 acres located on Juniper east of Wet Creek adjoining **Richard Dunn** and **Alexr. McIver**. **Niel McLeod** and **John McLeod** were chain carriers.

1116.   1787, Jul 13 -- 1784-1797 Land Entries, Moore County, NC
#102 **Joseph McGee** entered 350 acres south of Deep River adjoining **John Carrold** and **Joseph Duckworth**.

1117.   1787, Jul 14 -- Land Grant #262, Moore County, NC
John Askins received 100 acres located on Buffalo Creek including the Steep Bottom Ford and adjoining **Isaac Pennington**. **Loven Hensworth** and **Gabriel Harden** were chain carriers.

1118.   1787, Jul 14 -- 1784-1797 Land Entries, Moore County, NC
#105 **William Hardin** entered 200 acres south of Deep River on both sides of Buffalo Creek adjoining **McNeill** and **England**.

1119.   1787, Jul 14 -- 1784-1797 Land Entries, Moore County, NC
#106 **Kenneth McLeod** entered 50 acres on Mill Creek adjoining **Archibald McKay** and **Dunn**.

A.   1787, Jul 20 -- Land Grant #502, Montgomery County, NC
William Allin received 100 acres located on Williams Creek adjoining **Smith**. **Jesse Smith** and **Joseph Allin** were chain carriers.

1120.   1787, Jul 30 -- Land Grant #216, Moore County, NC
Batholomew Dunn Junr. received 50 acres located between the Wet Fork and Dry Fork of Mill Creek adjoining **Thomas Dunn**. **William Dunn** and **Thomas Dunn** were chain carriers.

1121.   1787, Jul 30 -- Land Grant #286, Moore County, NC
Angus McAulay received 63 acres located on Tan Trough Branch of Mill Creek adjoining **McKay**. **Murdock McAulay** and **Donald McLeod** were chain carriers.

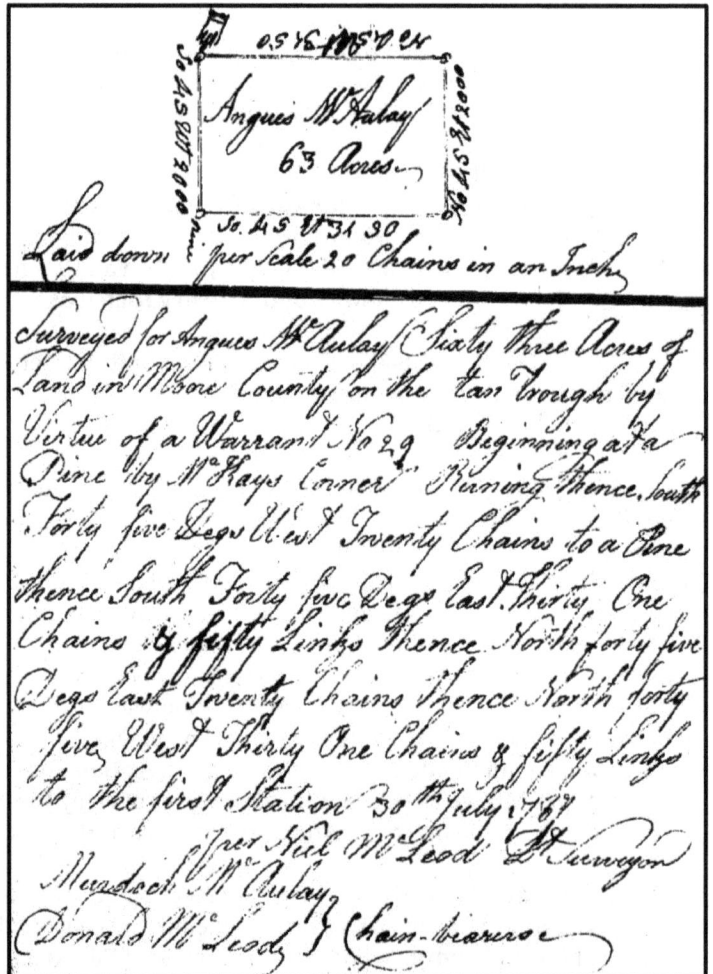

1122.　　　1787, Jul 30 -- Land Grant #475, Randolph County, NC
Nathan Dillon [Deaton] received 200 acres located on Deep River adjoining his own line, **Smith, Joseph Jackson**, **William Bell**, **Nicholas Ledford** and **Francis Wallace**. **Joseph Hill** and **Richard Wallace** were chain carriers.

1123.　　　1787, Jul 31 -- Land Grant #240, Moore County, NC
Nicholas Newton received 50 acres located on Sings Creek adjoining his own line and **Morison**. **Lewis Sowell** and **Allen Morison** were chain carriers.

1124.　　　1787, Jul 31 -- Land Grant #289, Moore County, NC
Donald McLeod received 60 acres located on Mill Creek adjoining **Archibald McKay** and **Lewis Sowell** on the old Atkin [Yadkin] Road/near the Waggon Road. **Murdock McAulay** and **Angus McAulay** were chain carriers.

1125.　　　1787, Aug 10 -- 1784-1797 Land Entries, Moore County, NC
#109 **Niell McLeod** entered 50 acres on Dry Fork of Mill Creek.

1126.　　　1787, Aug 20 -- 1784-1795 Court of Pleas and Quarter Sessions, Moore County, NC Page 167
Ordered that **Daniel Manus** be appointed overseer of the road in place of **Christopher Yow**.

1127.　　　1787, Aug 20-22 -- 1784-1795 Court of Pleas and Quarter Sessions, Moore County, NC Page 167,168
[Deeds] **Peter Smith** to **Robert Dickinson** was acknowledged
Robert Dickinson to **John Montgomery** was acknowledged
William Smith to **Neil McLeod** was acknowledged

1128.　　　1787, Aug 23 -- 1784-1795 Court of Pleas and Quarter Sessions, Moore County, NC Page 169
Ordered that the property of **Eliz. Brannon** now in the hands of **Jason Wadsworth** be delivered to **John Cox** and he keep her from being a county charge.

A.　　　1787, Aug 23 -- 1784-1795 Court of Pleas and Quarter Sessions, Moore County, NC Page 169
Ordered that **Melton Glasscock** be appointed overseer of the road in place of **James Muse**

1129.　　　1787, Aug 23 -- 1784-1795 Court of Pleas and Quarter Sessions, Moore County, NC Page 169
Administration of the estate of **George Glasscock** Dec'd. given to **Patty Glasscock** with **Benjn. Sheals** and **William Finley** as securities.

A.　　　1787, Sep 11 -- Deed Book D Page 579-580, Chatham County, NC
Samuel Stuart deeded **Jacob Cashat** 350 acres located on Pine Hill Creek of Cane Creek. **Edward Stuart** and **James Woolason** were witnesses.

1130.　　　1787-1788 [undated estimate] -- Estate, Moore County, NC Will Book A, Page 341-342
Inventory of the Estate of **Geo. Glascock**, Dec'd. by Administrator **Paty Glascock**. [*Editor's Note: No date given on actual inventory, but the date was estimated using County Court Minute reference above.*]

1131.　　　1787, Aug 23 -- 1784-1795 Court of Pleas and Quarter Sessions, Moore County, NC Page 170
Administration of the estate of **Theophilus Petty** Dec'd. given to **Thomas Graham** with **James Collins** and **Thomas Mathews** as securities. **James Collins**, **John Overton Senr.** and **Edward Moore** be appointed to lay off thirds for the widow.

1132.　　　1787-1788 [undated estimate] -- Estate, Moore County, NC Will Book A, Page 343
Inventory of the Estate of **Theophs. Petty**, Dec'd. by Administrator **Thomas Gilmore** Esquire. [*Editor's Note: No date given on actual inventory, but the date was estimated using County Court Minute reference above.*]

1133.　　　1787, Aug 23 -- 1784-1795 Court of Pleas and Quarter Sessions, Moore County, NC Page 170
Administration of the estate of **John Apperson** Dec'd. given to **Richardson Fagin** with **James Collins** and **Thomas Mathews** as securities.

1134.　　　1787-1788 [undated estimate] -- Estate, Moore County, NC Will Book A, Page 345
Inventory of the Estate of **Jno. Apperson**, Dec'd. by Administrator **Rich. Feagan**. [*Editor's Note: No date given on actual inventory, but the date was estimated using County Court Minute reference above.*]

1135. 1787, Aug 27 -- Land Grant #271, Moore County, NC
Joseph Dunn Junr. received 50 acres located on Mill Creek and the Waggon Road adjoining **McDonald**. **Samuel Dunn** and **Jesse Opton** were chain carriers.

1136. 1787, Aug 27 -- Land Grant #0245, Moore County, NC
Samuel Dunn received 25 acres located west of Richland Creek adjoining **Joseph Dunn**, **Brimlow** and **Wm. Dunn**'s improvement. **Jesse Opton** and **Joseph Dunn** were chain carriers. [*Editor's Note: Never granted*]

1137. 1787, Aug 30 -- Land Grant #483, Randolph County, NC
Isaac Redfern received 200 acres located on Flat Branch of Brush Creek and the County line adjoining **William Needham** and **Edwards**. **Mayness Teague** and **John Argo** were chain carriers.

1138. 1787, Sep 3 -- Land Grant #256, Moore County, NC
Neil Matheson received 50 acres located on Dry Creek adjoining **Nicolas Newton** and his own line. **Hector McLean** and **Normand Matheson** were chain carriers.

1139. 1787, Sep 20 -- 1784-1797 Land Entries, Moore County, NC
#110 **Jamey Murray** entered 200 acres north of Deep River between the Little and Big Cedar Creek on the Chatham County line adjoining **Argo** and **James Moore**.

1140. 1787, Sep 20 -- 1784-1797 Land Entries, Moore County, NC
#111 **Niell McLeod** entered 150 acres north of Deep River adjoining **England**, **Gilmore** and **George Feagan**.

1141. 1787, Sep 22 -- Land Grant #208, Moore County, NC
Ambrus Bruer received 100 acres located on Bear Creek including his own improvement. **William Barret** and **William Cox** were chain carriers.

1142. 1787, Sep 24 -- Land Grant #292, Moore County, NC
William Barret received 50 acres located west of McLendons Creek adjoining **Farquard Campbell** and **McSween**. **Stephen Richardson** and **John McCaskill** were chain carriers.

1143. 1787, Oct 2 -- Deed Book 3, Page 251, Randolph County, NC
William Searcy deeded **John Johnston** 300 acres located on Deep River near the head of Buffalo Branch adjoining **William Argo**, **William Searcy** (Dec'd.) and **Charles Goldston**. **John Pierce** and **William Argo** were witnesses.

1144. 1787, Oct 3 -- Land Grant #215, Moore County, NC
Robert Davis received 170 acres located south of Deep River below the Poplar Spring Branch adjoining **John Blanchard** and his own line. **Robert Cheek** and **Amos Cheek** were chain carriers.

1145. 1787, Oct 10 -- 1784-1797 Land Entries, Moore County, NC
#113 **James Riddle** entered 127 acres on Bear Creek of upper Little River adjoining his own line.

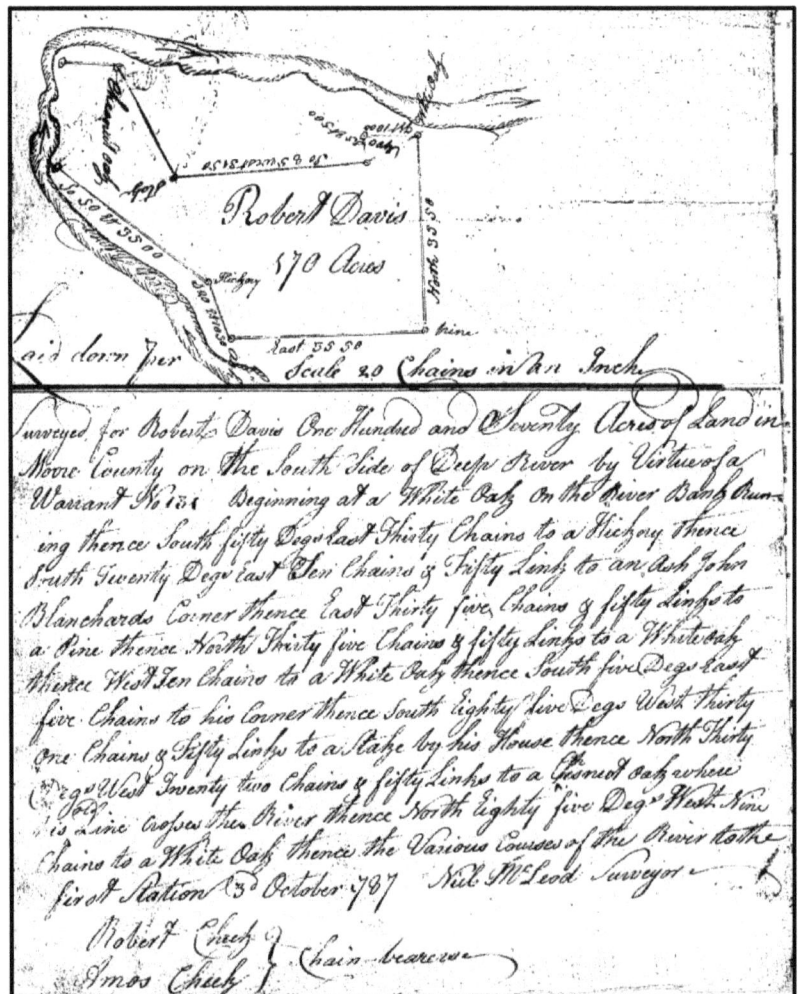

1146.   1787, Oct 12 -- Land Grant #195, Moore County, NC
Moses Myrick received 100 acres located north of Deep River adjoining **Hunter**, **McDonald** and **Barnes**. **William Hardin** and **Francis Myrick** were chain carriers.

1147.   1787, Oct 12 -- Land Grant #198, Moore County, NC
Joseph Gilbert received 100 acres located on the Haw Branch and the [Chatham] county line adjoining **Tyson**. **William Harden** and **Francis Myrick** were chain carriers.

1148.   1787, Oct 13 -- Land Grant #268, Moore County, NC
Richardson Feagan received 50 acres located on Killetts Creek adjoining his own line. **Nathan Fry** and **Joseph Fry** were chain carriers.

1149.   1787, Oct 13 -- Land Grant #274, Moore County, NC
Richardson Feagan received 50 acres located on Killetts Creek adjoining his own line and **Joseph Fry**. **Nathan Fry** and **Joseph Fry** were chain carriers.

1150.   1787, Nov 15 -- Land Grant #2, Moore County, NC
John Overton received 480 acres located on both sides of Pocket Creek being part of confiscated property of **Greg** and **Dowd**.

1151.   1787, Nov 15 -- Land Grant #3, Moore County, NC
Griffith John McRee and **Curtis Ivey** received 100 acres located west of McLendons Creek being part of confiscated property of the estate of **Laughlen Beaton**.

1152.   1787, Nov 15 -- Land Grant #4, Moore County, NC
Griffith John McRee and **Curtis Ivey** received 200 acres located on both sides of McLendons Creek being part of confiscated property of the estate of **John McNeal**.

1153.   1787, Nov 15 -- Land Grant #7, Moore County, NC
Melton Glass[**John Melton Glascock**] received 100 acres located on both sides of Juniper Branch of McLendons Creek being part of confiscated property of the estate of **John McNeal**.

1154.   1787, Nov 19 -- 1784-1795 Court of Pleas and Quarter Sessions, Moore County, NC
[*jury duty - selected participants*] **James Caddle, Richard Dunn, Edwd. Moore, Drury Richardson, Saml. Dunn, Joseph Dunn, William Dunn, Jacob Cagle, William Smith**. [*jury duty next term - selected participants*] **John Kee, Thomas Kee, Isaac Dunn, William Dunn** (**B.C.**), **William Dunn** (**W.C**), **Edward Moore, William Williamson**.

1155.   1787, Nov 19-21 -- 1784-1795 Court of Pleas and Quarter Sessions, Moore County, NC Page 172-173, 179
[Deeds] **Richard** and **Judy Dunn** to **Isaac Dunn** was acknowledged
Joel McClendon to **Robert Graham** was acknowledged
James Cotton to **Joseph Allen** was proven by **Wm. Morgan**
Nathan and **Ann Brady** to **Alexander Autery** was proven by **Darius Ramage**
William Morris, executor of **John McLendon** to **Christian Jackson** proven by **John Jackson**
[Bill of Sale] **Charles Seal** to **Betsy Seal, Molly Seal** and **John Seal** was proven by **Thomas Gilmore**, Esq.

1156.   1787, Nov 20 -- 1784-1797 Land Entries, Moore County, NC
#114 **John Ridder** entered 50 acres located on Locust Branch of Richland Creek.

1157.   1787, Nov 20 -- 1784-1795 Court of Pleas and Quarter Sessions, Moore County, NC Page 174
William Searcy v. **William Colyer**
William Pearce v. **Mathew Davis** and **Josiah Maples**

1158.   1787, Nov 20 -- 1784-1795 Court of Pleas and Quarter Sessions, Moore County, NC Page 174
Ordered that **Solomon Cox** be appointed overseer in place of **John Caddle**

1159.   1787, Nov 20 -- 1784-1795 Court of Pleas and Quarter Sessions, Moore County, NC Page 175

Ordered that **William Handcock** be appointed overseer in place of **Robert Davis**

1160.   1787, Nov 21 -- 1784-1795 Court of Pleas and Quarter Sessions, Moore County, NC Page 175
William Mears returns Inventory of Estate of **William Manus**, Dec'd.

1161.   1787, Nov 21 -- 1784-1795 Court of Pleas and Quarter Sessions, Moore County, NC Page 176
Ordered that a tract of land attached by **Reuben Shields** the property of **Isaac Pennington** at the suit of **Joseph McGee** be sold to satisfy judgement given by **John Cox**.

1162.   1787, Nov 21 -- 1784-1795 Court of Pleas and Quarter Sessions, Moore County, NC Page 178
Administration of the estate of **Robert Handcock** Dec'd. be given to **Eliz. Handock** with **James Collins** and **John Blanchet** as securities.

1163.   1787, Nov-Dec [undated estimate] -- Estate, Moore County, NC Will Book A, Page 344
Inventory of the Estate of **Robt. Hancock**, Dec'd. by Administrator **Elizabeth Hancock**. [*Editor's Note: No date given on actual inventory, but the date was estimated using date from above Court of Pleas and Quarter Sessions*]

1164.   1787, Nov 25 -- 1784-1797 Land Entries, Moore County, NC
#116 **Drury Richardson** entered 50 acres southeast of Bear Creek below the Waggon Ford.

1165.   1787, Nov 25 -- 1784-1797 Land Entries, Moore County, NC
#117 **Joseph Dunn Jr.** entered 50 acres on McCallums Fork called Mills Creek.

1166.   1787, Nov 25 -- 1784-1797 Land Entries, Moore County, NC
#120 **William Richardson** entered 100 acres on Holly Branch of Buffalow Creek.

1167.   1787, Nov 27 -- 1784-1797 Land Entries, Moore County, NC
#123 **John McAuly** entered 60 acres west of Wet Creek adjoining his own line.

1168.   1787, Dec 14 -- Criminal Actions, Randolph County, NC, 1787-B
Capias for **Winsor Pierce** on a charge of nusance and profane swearing. **Joseph Clark** and **James Roberts** were witnesses.

A.   1787, Dec 19 -- Land Grant #478, Montgomery County, NC
Little Berry Hicks received 20 acres located on the head of Dicks Creek. **Wm. Trent** and **Berry Hicks** were chain carriers.

1169.   1787, Dec 20 -- Deed Book 3, Page 244, Randolph County, NC
William Sercy deeded **James Presnal** 300 acres located on Little River of P.D. **N. Nalls**, **William Harvey** and **William Wright** were witnesses.

1170.   1787, Dec 20 -- Bible of **Lewis Phillips Jr.** and **Nancy Edwards**, Moore County, NC
Lewis Phillips Sr. and **Charity Dickerson** were married.

A. 1788, Jan 12 – Land Grant #1052, Chatham County, NC
William Caps received 100 acres located on Rogers Creek adjoining **Mullins'** old field and his own line. **Ezekiel Hilliard** and **William Caps Junr.** were chain carriers.

1171. 1788, Jan 26 -- Marriage Bond, Wake County, NC
Joseph Britt to **Olive Swanson**. **Richd. Swanson** was bondsman and **J. Rice** was witness. [*Editor's Note: Date of marriage occurred on or after date of marriage bond.*]

1172. 1788, Jan 29 -- Deed Book 4, Page 19, Randolph County, NC
William Searcy (of Montgomery County) deeded **William Pearce** 200 acres located north of Fork Creek and Rocky Creek adjoining **Adam Andrews** and **Widow Andrews**. **William Bowdon** and **John Pearce** were witnesses.

1173. 1788, Feb 5 -- Land Grant #1051, Chatham County, NC
Henry Persons received 100 acres located on Ceder Creek. **Richd. Vanderford** and **Matthew Daton** were chain carriers. [*Editor's Note: deeded to* **Minty Vanderford** *1793*

A. 1788, Feb 5 -- Land Grant #1061, Chatham County, NC
Samuel Persons received 250 acres located on Fall Creek. **Henry Persons** and **John Harden** were chain carriers. [*Editor's Note: deeded to* **Ely McManus** *1793*]

B. 1788, Feb 5 -- Land Grant #1065, Chatham County, NC
Samuel Persons received 150 acres located on Fall Creek. **Henry Persons** and **John Harden** were chain carriers.

C. 1788, Feb 5 -- Land Grant #1070, Chatham County, NC
John Argo received 250 acres located on Cedar Creek and the Moore County line. **Henry Person** and **Robert Harden** were chain carriers. [*Editor's Note: deeded to* **Zachariah Smith** *1793 > 100a to* **Eli Lawler** *1794; 100a to* **Isaac Teague** *1794*]

1174. 1788, Feb 9 -- Will Book A Page 235-236, Moore County, NC
Will of **William Davis**, Dec'd. Heirs: son **William Davis**, son **John Davis** [*320 acres in Wake County*], son-in-law **Benj. Cooper**, son-in-law **Henry Person**, grandson **Willis Davis** [*250 acres when he comes of age*], wife **Sarah Davis** [*rest of estate*]. Executors: son **William Davis** and **Benj. Sheales**. Witnesses: **Benjn. Sheales** and **Sarah Cooper**. [*Editor's Note: No proven date but surrounding wills proven in 1803 and 1804*]

1175. 1788, Feb 12 -- Land Grant #288, Moore County, NC
Willis Dickinson received 200 acres located south of Deep River on Leek Creek adjoining **Alston** and his own. **Patrick Dowd** and **William Hardin** were chain carriers.

1176. 1788, Feb 13 -- Land Grant #219, Moore County, NC
Kenneth McLeod received 60 acres located on Mill Creek adjoining **Thomas Dunn**, **Bartholomew Dunn** and **McKay**. **John McAulay** and **Donald McLeod** were chain carriers.

A. 1788, Feb 13 -- Deed Book D Page 537, Chatham County, NC
William and **Sary Needham** deeded **John Vandiford** a portion of 200 acres located on Ceder Creek adjoining **James Deaton**. **John Argo** and **James Deaton** were witnesses.

1177. 1788, Feb 14 -- Land Grant #285, Moore County, NC
William Richardson received 100 acres located on Holly Branch of Buffalo Creek. **Robert Richardson** and **Drury Richardson** were chain carriers.

1178. 1788, Feb 15 -- Land Grant #246, Moore County, NC
Drury Richardson received 50 acres located southwest of Bear Creek below the Waggon Ford adjoining **Nall**. **William Richardson** and **Robert Richardson** were chain carriers.

1179. 1788, Feb 19 -- 1784-1795 Court of Pleas and Quarter Sessions, Moore County, NC

[*jury duty - selected participants*] **Wm. Williamson, John Kee, Wm. Dunn (WC), Isaac Dunn, Thos. Kee, John Cadwell, Edwd. Moore, Jacob Stutz, Wm. Manus, Drury Richardson, Jas. Cadwll.** [*jury duty next term - selected participants*] **Alex. Autery, John Morgan, Adam Comer, Everett Smith, John Caddle, Nichl. Newton, Wm. Gardner.**

1180. 1788, Feb 19-20,22 -- 1784-1795 Court of Pleas and Quarter Sessions, Moore County, NC Page 184-186,188
[Deeds] **Wm. Argoe** to **Jesse Henley** was proven by **Wm. Searcy**
John Williamson to **Hardy Davis** acknowledged
Richardson Feagin to **Wm. Harden** was proven by **Saml. Dunn**
[Bill of sale] **Thos. Muse** to **Lydda Muse** was acknowledged
Wm. Barrett and **Anny Barrett** to **Jesse Writter** was duly acknowledged by **Wm. Barrett**
Hugh Gilmore to **Charles Seal** was proven by **Wm. Seal Jr.**
Richardson Feagin to **John Wilkins** was acknowledged
Two deeds from **John Howell** to **Wm. Beasley** were proven by **James Caddle**

1181. 1788, Feb 22 -- 1784-1795 Court of Pleas and Quarter Sessions, Moore County, NC Page 188
Ordered that **Saml. Dunn** be appointed overseer of the road in place of **Zachy. Smith.**

1182. 1788, Feb 22 -- 1784-1795 Court of Pleas and Quarter Sessions, Moore County, NC Page 189
Ordered that **Jesse Muse, Benj. Shields** and **Jas. Collins** be appointed to value the estate of **Geo. Glascock** Dec'd.

1183. 1788, Mar 10 -- 1784-1797 Land Entries, Moore County, NC
#129 **Nicholas Newton** entered 50 acres east of Wet Creek adjoining **John Smith.**

1184. 1788, Mar 10 -- Land Grant #230, Moore County, NC
Christian Jackson received 50 acres located west of Juniper Creek adjoining her own line. **Murdoch Bethune** and **William Dunn** were chain carriers.

1185. 1788, Mar 12 -- Land Grant #261, Moore County, NC
Jesse Muse received 25 acres located on McLendons Creek including his own improvement. **Hymrick Hill** and **Thomas Muse** were chain carriers.

1186. 1788, Mar 12 -- Land Grant #355, Moore County, NC
Jesse Muse received 25 acres located on Richland Creek and both sides of the Wagon Road including Porch Corn Hill. **Thomas Muse** and **Hymrick Hill** were chain carriers.

1187. 1788, Mar 19 -- Land Grant #220, Moore County, NC
Samuel Perry received 50 acres located north of Deep River. **Peter Graves** and **Willis Brewer** were chain carriers.

1188. 1788, Mar 19 -- Land Grant #229, Moore County, NC
Samuel Perry received 100 acres located south of Deep River including his own improvement. **William Phillips** and **Willis Brewer** were chain carriers.

1189. 1788, Mar 20 -- 1784-1797 Land Entries, Moore County, NC
#130 **Solomon Barrett** entered 15 acres on both sides of McLendons Creek adjoining **Patience Barrett, McLeod** and **Robert Graham** and including his own improvement.

1190. 1788, Mar 20 -- 1784-1797 Land Entries, Moore County, NC
#131 **Joseph Dunn Sr.** entered 100 acres adjoining White Lick Quarry.

A. 1788, Mar 20 -- Land Grant #1069, Chatham County, NC
Carter Hendrick received 100 acres located on Fall Creek. **Henry Persons** and **Joel Hendrick** were chain carriers.

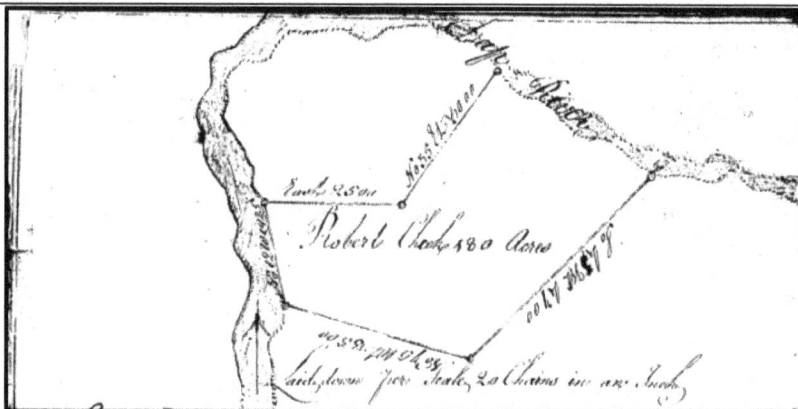

1191. 1788, Mar 21 -- Land Grant #243, Moore County, NC
Robert Cheek received 180 acres located north of Deep River adjoining his own line and **James Collins**. **Richard Cheek** and **Amos Cheek** were chain carriers.

1192. 1788, Mar 22 -- Land Grant #233, Moore County, NC
William Davis received 50 acres located north of Deep River adjoining his own line. **Benjamin Seals [Shields]** and **Patrick Dowd** were chain carriers.

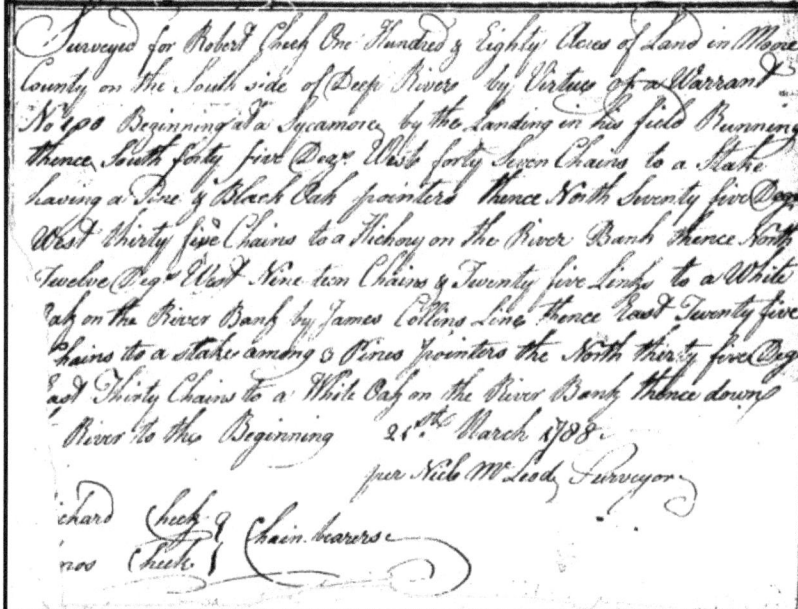

1193. 1788, Mar 27 -- Deed Book 3, Page 279, Randolph County, NC
James Presnal deeded **William Spencer** 100 acres located on Little River of P.D. adjoining **John Knight**. Granted to **William Searcy** and **Hughet** and sold to **Presnal**. **Tryon Patterson** and **Absolom Presnal** were witnesses.

B. 1788, Apr 15 -- Land Grant #964, Chatham County, NC
William Finley received 528 acres located on Tysons Creek adjoining **William England** and **Benjamin Sanders**. **Lewis Brady** and **Nicholas Brewer** were chain carriers.

C. 1788, Apr 16 -- Land Grant #954, Chatham County, NC
William Finley received 640 acres located on Fall Creek and Tysons Creek adjoining his own line and **Sanders**. **Sion Phillips** and **Even Hughs** were chain carriers.

D. 1788, Apr 20 -- Land Grant #961, Chatham County, NC
William Finley received 640 acres located on Flat Creek and Cedar Creek adjoining **Mincher Litle**, **John Powers** and his own line. **John Powers** and **James Daton** were chain carriers.

1194. 1788, Apr 20 -- 1784-1797 Land Entries, Moore County, NC
#136 **John Dunlap** entered 100 acres east of McLendons Creek adjoining **Elijah Bettis** and his own line.

A. 1788, Apr 22 -- Land Grant #963, Chatham County, NC
William Finley received 640 acres located on Flat Creek adjoining **Mincher Litle** and his own line. **John Powers** and **James Daton** were chain carriers.

B. 1788, Apr 23 -- Land Grant #956, Chatham County, NC
William Finley received 640 acres located on Cedar Branch of Fall Creek adjoining **Shearing**. **Dinnis Phillips** and **Sampson Brewer** were chain carriers.

C. 1788, Apr 23 -- Land Grant #960, Chatham County, NC

William Finley received 640 acres located on Tysons Creek adjoining **Shearing**. **Dinnis Phillips** and **Sampson Brewer** were chain carriers.

1195. 1788, Apr 24 -- Bible of David Kennedy and Joanna Moore, Moore County, NC
David Kennedy and **Joaner Moore** were married.

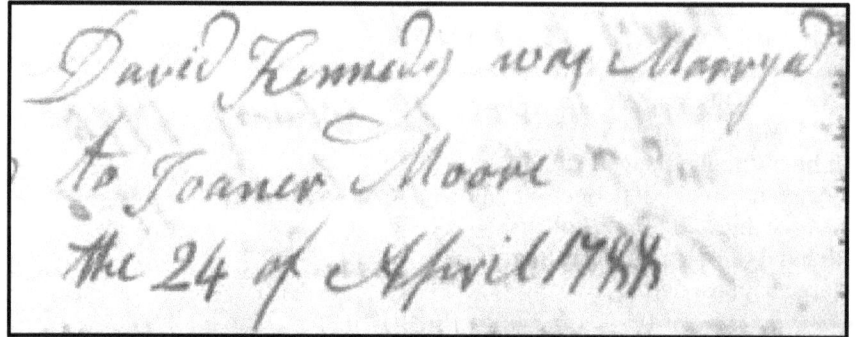

1196. 1788, May 13 -- 1784-1797 Land Entries, Moore County, NC
#138 **Zachariah Smith** entered 50 acres on both sides of Buffalo Creek where the road crosses between **McLendon**'s and **Thomas Smith**'s.

> *David Kennedy was Marryd*
> *to Joaner Moore*
> *the 24 of April 1788*

1197. 1788, May 19 -- 1784-1795 Court of Pleas and Quarter Sessions, Moore County, NC
[*jury duty - selected participants*] **Alex. Autery, John Caddle, Evrd. Smith, Adam Comer, Wm. Manus, Jesse Ritter, James Hill, Thos. Kee.** [*jury duty next term - selected participants*] **William Smith, Saml. Dun, Geo. Cagle, Leonard Cagle, Leonard Furr, Joseph Cockman, Absolam Autrey, Joseph Allen.**

1198. 1788, May 20 -- 1784-1795 Court of Pleas and Quarter Sessions, Moore County, NC Page 192
Ordered that **Tignar Wade** be bound to **John Gardner** for eight years he being now about thirteen years to learn the art of a planter.

1199. 1788, May 20 -- 1784-1795 Court of Pleas and Quarter Sessions, Moore County, NC Page 192
Jesse Muse Exr. v. **James Caddle**

1200. 1788, May 20-21 -- 1784-1795 Court of Pleas and Quarter Sessions, Moore County, NC Page 191,192,195
[Deeds] **Aaron Feagan** to **Richardson Feagan** was proven by **Philip Alston**
Edw. Moore to **John Gardner** acknowledged
William and **Zilly Smith** [no grantee named] was acknowledged by **Daniel McNeill**
Robert Patterson to **Hector McLain** was proven by **Neil McLeod**
Bill of sale from **John Overton Senr.** to **Thomas Collins** was proven by **Wm. Seal Senr.**

1201. 1788, May 20 -- 1784-1795 Court of Pleas and Quarter Sessions, Moore County, NC Page 196
Ordered that **Sterling Carroll** sell the estate of **Robert Moore**, Dec'd.

A. 1788, May 23 -- 1784-1795 Court of Pleas and Quarter Sessions, Moore County, NC Page 196-197
The will of **William Davis** was proven by **Benj. Shields** and **Sar. Cooper**. **William Davis** and **Benj. Shields** were duly qualified as executors.

1202. 1788, Jun 2 -- Deed Book 3, Page 326, Randolph County, NC
William Searcy deeded **Richard Cox** 200 acres located near the head of Fork Creek. **William Bowdon, Edmond Wade** and **William Harvey** were witnesses.

1203. 1788, Jun 5 -- Land Grant #519, Randolph County, NC
William Smitherman received 200 acres on Fork Creek adjoining **Cost. John Needham** and **James Lethem** were chain carriers.

1204. 1788, Jun 9-19 -- Deed Book 3, Page 272, 273, 275, Randolph County, NC
Robert McLean, Sheriff deeded **Nicholas Nall** three tracts that were granted to **William Searcy** and sold by bid for debt: [1] 500 acres located on Deep River adjoining **Charles Goldston, Arthur Read** and **Searcy**. [2] 300 acres located on Fork Creek adjoining **Adam Andrews** and the [Randolph] county line. [3] 640 acres located on Deep River adjoining **Charles Goldston** and Cumberland [Moore] County line and Chatham County line. **Thomas Dougan** was a witness.

A. 1788, Jun 10 -- Land Grant #1146, Chatham County, NC

William Harper received 300 acres located on Fall Creek adjoining his own line. **Sampson Brewer** and **Dennis Phillips** were chain carriers.

1205.   1788, Jul 3 -- Land Grant #354, Moore County, NC
John Ritter received 50 acres located on Locust Branch. **John Ritter** and **Everid Ritter** were chain carriers.

1206.   1788, Jul 12 -- Land Grant #258, Moore County, NC
John McAulay received 60 acres located west of Wet Creek adjoining his own line. **Angus McAulay** and **Murdock McAulay** were chain carriers.

1207.   1788, Aug 18 -- 1784-1795 Court of Pleas and Quarter Sessions, Moore County, NC
[*jury duty - selected participants*] **Edw. Moore, Saml. Dun, Geo. Cagle, Leonard Cagle, Leonard Furr, Wm. Manus, James Caddle, Absolam Autery, Joseph Cockman, Joseph Allen, John Caddle, Geo. Carrinor, Owen Carpenter, John Keys.** [*jury duty next term - selected participants*] **William Smith, John Morgan, William Morgan, William Dun** (Wet Creek), **Richard Dunn, Hardy Davis, Peter Shamburger, William Smith Senr., John Hair, John Shuffel Junr.**

1208.   1788, Aug 19 -- 1784-1795 Court of Pleas and Quarter Sessions, Moore County, NC Page 200
Will of **Simon Hart**, Dec'd. was proven by **John Cagle** and **George Cagle**.

1209.   1788, Aug 19 -- 1784-1795 Court of Pleas and Quarter Sessions, Moore County, NC Page 202
A bill of sale from **James Pearl** to **John Jackson** was proven by **Geo. Jackson**.

1210.   1788, Aug 19 -- 1784-1795 Court of Pleas and Quarter Sessions, Moore County, NC Page 202
Ordered that **Lewis Gardner** be appointed overseer in place of **Danl. Manus**.

1211.   1788, Aug 19 -- 1784-1795 Court of Pleas and Quarter Sessions, Moore County, NC Page 202
Ordered that **Leonard Cagle** be appointed overseer of the road from **Searcy**'s Ford to **Cotton**'s from Bear Creek at **Wm. Gardner**'s to the County line and have the following hands to work: **Wm. Gardner, Peter Gardner, William Wilson, John Hare, Adam Comer** and **Leonard Cagle**'s sons.

1212.   1788, Aug 19 -- 1784-1795 Court of Pleas and Quarter Sessions, Moore County, NC Page 202
John Shuffle, Junr. appointed overseer of the road which leads by Mr. **Nall**'s from Bear Creek to Randolph County and work the following hands: **Owen Carpenter**'s hands, **Nichl. Nall**'s hands, **Robert Bird, Thomas Smitherman, Andrew White** and **Peter Shamburger**.

1213.   1788, Aug 19 -- 1784-1795 Court of Pleas and Quarter Sessions, Moore County, NC Page 203
Ordered that a road be laid from road that will be laid from the Chatham County courthouse to the Moore courthouse and have the following hands to work: **John Overton Senr., John Dunlap, Jos. Gilbert, John Carrol, Thomas Tison, Thomas Overton, Jas. Collins, James Muse, Willis Dickinson, Wm. Handcock, Rand. Cheek, John Phillips, Edw. Moore, Gabl. Harden, Richd. Street, Leonard Thomas, Rich. Feagan, Elijah Bettis, Jesse Muse** and **Saml. Dun.**

1214.   1788, Aug 19 -- 1784-1795 Court of Pleas and Quarter Sessions, Moore County, NC Page 203
Ordered that a road be laid from near **Saml. Person**'s to the courthouse in Carthage and the following hands to work: **William Davis, Benj. Shields, Jas. Collins, Lenear Brewer, John Hargrove, James Brady, Henry Person, Saml. Person, John Blanchett, Joseph McGee, Joseph Duckworth, William Harden, Benj. Cooper, William**

Handcock, **Saml. Dun**, **Joseph Dun**, **Jesse Muse**, **Saml. Perry**, **Peter Graves**, **Drury Richardson** and **William Richardson**.

1215. 1788, Aug 19 -- 1784-1797 Land Entries, Moore County, NC
#142 **Nicholas Nall** entered 250 acres south of Bear Creek adjoining **Drury Richardson**.

1216. 1788, Aug 19 -- 1784-1797 Land Entries, Moore County, NC
#143 **Drury Richardson** entered 50 acres on Buffalow Creek adjoining his own line.

1217. 1788, Aug 20 -- 1784-1795 Court of Pleas and Quarter Sessions, Moore County, NC Page 203
Ordered that **Mary Wallis** be exempted from paying poll tax for 1787.

1218. 1788, Aug 20 -- 1784-1795 Court of Pleas and Quarter Sessions, Moore County, NC Page 204
State v. **Lewis** and **Bradley Gardner**

1219. 1788, Aug 20 -- 1784-1795 Court of Pleas and Quarter Sessions, Moore County, NC Page 200, 204
Ordered that **Donald McQueen** and **Geo. Carringer** be exempted from a poll tax for 1788.

1220. 1788, Aug 20 -- 1784-1795 Court of Pleas and Quarter Sessions, Moore County, NC Page 205
Ordered that **Nicholas Nall** Esq., have liberty to build a grist mill on his own land upon Bear Creek above the Public Road leading to Fayetteville.

1221. 1788, Aug 20 -- 1784-1795 Court of Pleas and Quarter Sessions, Moore County, NC Page 205
Nicholas Nall Esq. records his mark to be a swallow fork in each ear.

1222. 1788, Sep 10 -- Land Grant #244, Moore County, NC
Solomon Barrett received 15 acres located on McLendons Creek adjoining **Robert Graham**, **Patience Barrett** and including his own improvement. **Elijah Been** and **Richard Been** were chain carriers.

1223. 1788, Sep 12 -- 1784-1797 Land Entries, Moore County, NC
#146 **Leonard Cagle** entered 50 acres northwest of [blank] Creek including his vacant land and mill and adjoining his own line and **William Garner**.

A. 1788, Sep 12 -- Deed Book D Page 581-582, Chatham County, NC
Mary Dowd (of Moore County) deeded **Sampson Brewer** 150 acres located on Fall Creek adjoining **Golston**. The land was granted to **Connor Dowd**. **Edw. Griffin** and **Joseph Robson** were witnesses.

1224. 1788, Oct 27 -- 1784-1797 Land Entries, Moore County, NC
#148 **Leonard Furr** entered 50 acres located on the head of Long Meadows adjoining **Solomon Barrett**.

1225. 1788, Nov -- 1785-1868 Index to Trial Docket, Moore County, NC Page 16
Willm. Mainess v. **Jas. Jamieson**

1226. 1788, Nov 17 -- 1784-1795 Court of Pleas and Quarter Sessions, Moore County, NC
[*jury duty - selected participants*] **Richard Dun**, **John Shuffle Junr.**, **Hardy Davis**, **William Morgan**, **Jesse Brown**, **John Keys**, **James Caddle**, **Leonard Furr**, **John Hair**, **Thomas Key**, **Drury Richardson**. [*jury duty next term - selected participants*] **John Morgan**, **Peter Shamburger**, **George Cagle**, **Leonard Cagle**, **Adam Comer**, **Lewis Sowell**.

1227.   1788, Nov 17 -- 1784-1797 Land Entries, Moore County, NC
#151 **William Barrett** entered 100 acres on Suck Creek adjoining his own line, **McIver**, **McCaskle** and **Graham**.

1228.   1788, Nov 17, 19-20 -- 1784-1795 Court of Pleas and Quarter Sessions, Moore County, NC Page 209, 211-212
[Deeds] **William Seal** to **John McDuffie** was proven **John Black**
Christopher Yow to **John Boyd** proven by **Owen Carpenter**
William Harden to **Joseph McGee** was acknowledged
John Cox to **William Morgan** was proven by **John Jackson**

1229.   1788, Nov 18 -- 1784-1797 Land Entries, Moore County, NC
#154 **Jesse Brown** entered 50 acres on Richardsons Creek adjoining **Hezekiah Dunn**.

1230.   1788, Nov 19 -- 1784-1797 Land Entries, Moore County, NC
#155 **John Argo** entered 100 acres adjoining his own line and Chatham County line.

1231.   1788, Nov 19 -- 1784-1797 Land Entries, Moore County, NC
#157 **John Hargrove** entered 70 acres on Richland Creek adjoining his own line.

1232.   1788, Nov 19 -- 1784-1797 Land Entries, Moore County, NC
#158 **Roger Cagle** entered 100 acres on on Wolf Creek adjoining **John Hancock**.

1233.   1788, Nov 19 -- 1784-1797 Land Entries, Moore County, NC
#159 **Kenneth McKenzie** entered 50 acres on a branch of Buffalo Creek adjoining his own line.

1234.   1788, Nov 19 -- 1784-1797 Land Entries, Moore County, NC
#160 **Allen Morrison** entered 90 acres on Sings Creek adjoining his own line, **Newton** and **Waddle**.

1235.   1788, Nov 19 -- 1784-1797 Land Entries, Moore County, NC
#161 **Jacob Cagle** entered 200 acres on Deep Creek adjoining his own line and including **Mary Morrison**'s improvement.

A.   1788, Nov 20 -- 1784-1795 Court of Pleas and Quarter Sessions, Moore County, NC Page 212
Hardy Davis recorded his mark to be two under slopes, one in each ear

1236.   1788, Nov 21 -- 1784-1795 Court of Pleas and Quarter Sessions, Moore County, NC Page 214
Ordered that the following work on the road from McClendon's Creek bridge to Dunham's Creek: **Benj. Fry**, **Benj. Caddle**, **Danl. Caddle**, **Wm. Caddle**, **Julius Glascock**, **Jesse Muse**, **James Muse**, **Him. Hill**, **Thomas Muse** and **George Ludes**.

1237.   1788, Nov 21 -- 1784-1795 Court of Pleas and Quarter Sessions, Moore County, NC Page 214
Ordered that **Joseph McGee** be appointed overseer of the road from **John McDaniel**'s old place to Bear Creek and have the following hands to work: **Joseph McGee**, **Levi Atkins**, **Francis Myrick**, **Wm. Richardson**, **Leaven Ainsworth**, **Wm. Harden Sr.**, **Benj. Cooper**, **Peter Graves**, **Saml. Perry**, **Joseph McGee**, **Zachy. Smith**, **Stephen Richardson**, **Wm. McDaniel** and **John McDaniel**'s boys.

A.   1788, Nov 21 -- 1784-1795 Court of Pleas and Quarter Sessions, Moore County, NC Page 215
Ordered that **John Dunlap** be appointed tax collector in District #1; **Samuel Jackson** in District #2 and **Daniel McQueen** in Wm. Coxes District.

1238.   1788, Nov 22 -- 1784-1797 Land Entries, Moore County, NC
#163 **Drury Richardson** entered 50 acres southeast of Buffalo Creek adjoining his own line.

1239.   1788, Nov 22 -- 1784-1797 Land Entries, Moore County, NC
#164 **Donald McQueen** entered [blank] acres on both sides of Richland Creek adjoining his own line and **William Dunn.**

1240.   1788, Nov 23 -- 1784-1797 Land Entries, Moore County, NC
#165 **Benjamin Cooper** entered 50 acres located on both sides of Bear Creek adjoining **Mainer** and **Nicholas Nall.**

1241.   1788, Nov 24 -- 1784-1797 Land Entries, Moore County, NC
#166 **William Cook** entered 200 acres north of Deep River between Little and Big Cedar Creeks adjoining **Argo.**

1243.   1788, Nov 25 -- Land Grant #2609, Moore County, NC
Joseph McGee received 150 acres located on Blans Branch and drains of the Glade of Richland Creek. **William Harris** and **Teaser L. Sowell** were chain carriers.

1244.   1788, Nov 25 -- 1784-1797 Land Entries, Moore County, NC
#167 **Joseph McGee** entered 150 acres on Blans Branch and the drains of the Glade of Richland Creek.

1245.   1788, Nov 30 -- Land Grant #347, Moore County, NC
Jesse Brown received 50 acres located on Richardson Branch adjoining **Ezekiah Dunn. Mathais Williams** and **Ancel Melton** were chain carriers.

1246.   1788, Dec 25 -- 1784-1797 Land Entries, Moore County, NC
#170 **John Stutts** entered 50 acres above the mouth of Dry Creek of Bear [Cabin] Creek.

1247.   1788, Dec 25 -- 1784-1797 Land Entries, Moore County, NC
#171 **Drury Richardson** entered 50 acres at the Ford of Buffalow Creek adjoining **Zachariah Smith** and his own line.

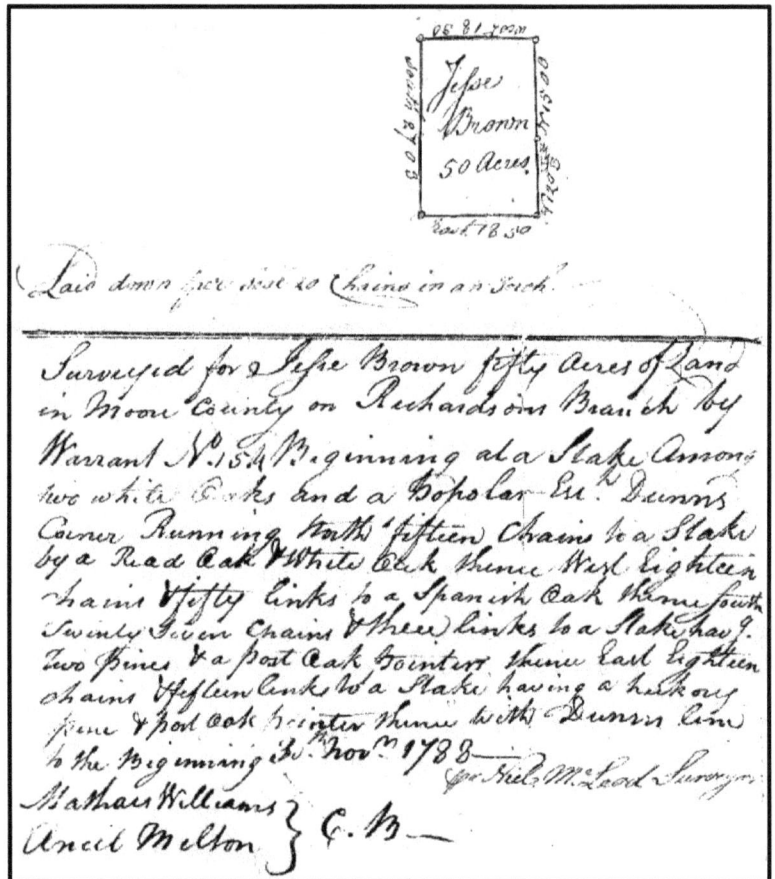

1248.   1785, Dec 25 -- Land Grant #552, Randolph County, NC
Heirs of **Edmon Mash** received 240 acres located on Fork Creek and **Southerland**'s old road adjoining his own line, **Andrews** and **Pearce. Uriah Mash** and **Michael Andrews** were chain carriers.

1249.   1788, Dec 26 -- Land Grant #556, Randolph County, NC
Adam Andrews received 313 acres located on Fork Creek adjoining **Pearce. Michael Andrews** and **Uriah Mash** were chain carriers.

1250.   1788, Dec 27 -- 1784-1797 Land Entries, Moore County, NC
#178 **Hardy Davis** entered 100 acres on Bear Creek adjoining his own 200 acre tract.

1251.   1789, Jan 27 -- Land Grant #295, Moore County, NC

William Feagan received 250 acres located on Killets Creek adjoining **George Fry, Benjamin Fry, George Glascock**, his own line and **Killetts** and **Wiers** old fields. **John Salter** and **John Inzor** were chain carriers.

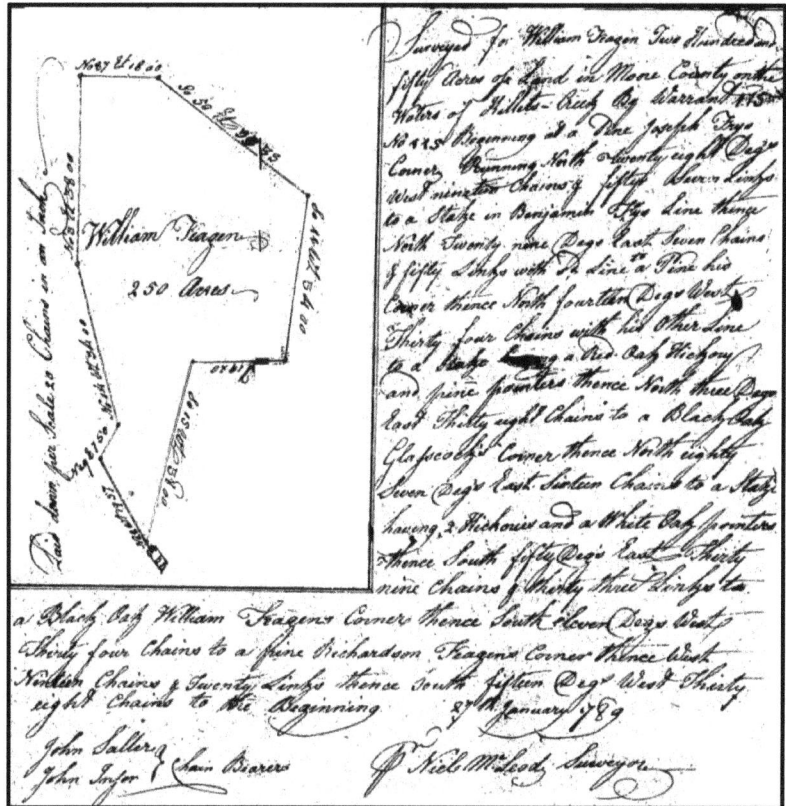

1252. 1789, Jan 27 -- Land Grant #345, Moore County, NC
Kenneth McKenzie received 50 acres located on Gum Branch of Buffalo Creek adjoining his own line. **William Richardson** and **Robert Richardson** were chain carriers.

1253. 1789, Feb 4 -- Land Grant #551, Randolph County, NC
John Pierce [assignee of **Windsor Pearce**] received 250 acres located on Deep River adjoining **Nall, Bowdon, Searcy** and **Samuel Perry**. **Wm. Pierce** and **Thos. Waddle** were chain carriers.

1254. 1789, Feb 4 -- Land Grant #553, Randolph County, NC
John Hawkins [assignee of **Samuel Perry**] received 330 acres located on both sides of Fork Creek and Deep River including his own improvement and adjoining **Adam Andrews, Pearce, Nall** and **Garner**. **Wm. Sercy** and **Thomas Waddle** were chain carriers.

1255. 1789, Feb 6 -- Land Grant #534, Randolph County, NC
Joseph Hicks [assignee of **William Searcy Sr.**] received 300 acres located on Deep River adjoining **Joseph Kerr** and **John Needham**. **Arthur Smith** and **Wm. Harris** were chain carriers.

A. 1789, Feb 6 -- Deed Book 1 Page 173, Montgomery County, NC
Jeremiah Manaschon deeded **Jonathan Carpenter** 100 acres on a branch of Cabbin Creek including **Charles Sowell's** improvement. **Joseph Parsons** and **Abraham Cochran** were witnesses.

1256. 1789, Feb 10 -- Land Grant #356, Moore County, NC
Jacob Cagle received 20 acres located on Deep Creek adjoining his own line and including **Mary Morison's** improvement. **Donald McDonald** and **Neil McLean** were chain carriers.

1257. 1789, Feb 16 -- 1784-1795 Court of Pleas and Quarter Sessions, Moore County, NC
[*jury duty - selected participants*] **Drury Richardson, John Morgan, Leonard Cagle, Jon. Caddle, Lewis Sowell, Adam Comer, Jesse Ritter, Samuel Dunn, Solomon Barrettt, Thos. Kees, John Kees, Peter Shamburger, Jas. Caddle, Owen Carpenter.** [*jury duty next term - selected participants*] **John Garner** (Capt.), **Wm. Garner, John Cagle, Samuel Dun, Joseph Dun Junr., Zachriah Smith, Edw. Moore** (Deep River), **Jacob Stutts, Leonard Furr, Geo. Carringer, Wm. Manus, Isaac Dunn, Hezeh. Dunn.**

1258. 1789, Feb 16-21 -- 1784-1795 Court of Pleas and Quarter Sessions, Moore County, NC Page 218,220,223-225
[Deeds] **Levi Pennington** to **James Dunbar** acknowledged
Stephen and **Alisabeth Richardson** to **Henry Cagle** was proven by **Wm. Dunn**.
John Cox to **Reubin Freeman** proven by **Murdo. Martin**
Peter and **Caterine Funcannon** to **Peter Hare** proven by **Owen Carpenter**
Philip Alston to **James Alston** proven by **John Carrell**
John Cox to **Peter McLean** was proven by **Murdoch Bethune**
Corns. Dowd to **Thomas Overton** acknowledged
Patrick Dowd to **Thomas Overton** acknowledged

Richardson Feagin to **William Hardin** was proven by **B. Shields**

1259.		1789, Feb 16 -- 1784-1795 Court of Pleas and Quarter Sessions, Moore County, NC Page 218
Ordered that the following hands work on the road from the **Widow Muse**'s bridge to Dunham's Creek: **Joseph Fry**, **Nathan Fry**, **John Caddle**, **Alex. McLeod** and **Neil McLeod**.

A.		1789, Feb 16 -- 1784-1795 Court of Pleas and Quarter Sessions, Moore County, NC Page 218
Ordered that **John McDaniel** be appointed Constable in **Capt. Barrett's** District in place of **Thomas Graham.**

1260.		1789, Feb 16 -- 1784-1795 Court of Pleas and Quarter Sessions, Moore County, NC Page 218
The Will of **John Jackson** Dec'd. was proven by **Christian Jackson**.

1261.		1789, Feb 17 -- 1784-1795 Court of Pleas and Quarter Sessions, Moore County, NC Page 219
Ordered that **Wm. Harden (Buck)** be appointed overseer of the road in room of **William Handcock**.

1262.		1789, Feb 17 -- 1784-1795 Court of Pleas and Quarter Sessions, Moore County, NC Page 220
Ordered that **John Keys** be appointed overseer of the road [no designation provided].

1263.		1789, Feb 17 -- 1784-1795 Court of Pleas and Quarter Sessions, Moore County, NC Page 220
Ordered that **Benj. Caddle** be appointed Constable in **Capt. Cox**'s District

1264.		1789, Feb 18 -- 1784-1795 Court of Pleas and Quarter Sessions, Moore County, NC Page 221
Ordered that the following be appointed to lay off a road from **John Overton**'s road near **William Cappes Junr.** continuing along an old road commonly called **Neil Tison**'s road to Deep River at the mouth of Governor's Creek where **Anthony Street** now lives continuing said road to where it comes into the Gulph Road near Pocket [?] Creek: **Thos. Cole**, **Andrew Cole**, **Thos. Overton**, **Edwd. Moore**, **Wm. Payne**, **Joseph Fry**, **Elijah Batis**, **Jno. Dunlap**, **Jno. Overton Senr.**, **James Hill**, **Richard Street**, **James Cadwell Senr.**, **Mathew Cogins**, **Benjn. Fry**, **Richardson Fagin**, **James Muse**, **Neil McLeod**, **Wm. Martin** and **Leonard Thomas**.

1265.		1789, Feb 17 -- 1784-1795 Court of Pleas and Quarter Sessions, Moore County, NC Page 222
Ordered that **Joseph Duckworth** be appointed overseer of the road in the room of **Saml. Dunn**.

1266.		1789, Feb 18 -- 1784-1795 Court of Pleas and Quarter Sessions, Moore County, NC Page 222
James Caddle v. **Saml. Gilmore**

1267.		1789, Mar 3 -- Land Grant #338, Moore County, NC
Roger Cagle received a 100 acre Land Grant located on Wolf Creek adjoining **John Hunzacker**. **Johnson Lathem** and **George Brazel** were chain carriers.

1268.		1789, Mar 3 -- Land Grant #344, Moore County, NC
Leonard Cagle received 50 acres located on Bear Creek including his mill and adjoining his own line and **William Garner**. **Adam Comer** and **George Cagle** were chain carriers.

1269.		1789, Mar 3 -- Land Grant #1595 and #0184, Moore County, NC
Leonard Furr received 50 acres located on the head of Long Meadow adjoining **Solomon Barret**. **John Spivy** and **Jacob Stuts** were chain carriers.

1270.		1789, Mar 4 -- Land Grant #353, Moore County, NC
Nicholas Nall received 250 acres located east of Bear Creek adjoining **Richardson**. **David Davidson** and **James Mainers** were chain carriers.

1271.		1789, Mar 6 -- Deed Book 3, Page 351, Randolph County, NC
Joseph Carr deeded **John Powers** 200 acres located on Flat Creek. **Richard Bird** and **Winsor Perce** were witnesses.

A.		1789, Mar 11 -- Land Grant #541, Montgomery County, NC
Thomas Ward received 100 acres located on both sides of Little River including his own improvement adjoining **Nathan Smith** and **Littleberry Hicks**. **John Ward** and **Nathan Smith** were chain carriers.

1272. 1789, Mar 13 -- 1784-1797 Land Entries, Moore County, NC
#184 **James Riddle** entered 104 acres on Bear Creek of Upper Little River adjoining his 200 acres.

1273. 1789, Mar 13 -- 1784-1797 Land Entries, Moore County, NC
#185 **Nicholas Nall** entered 150 acres on both sides of Bear Creek adjoining **John Sheffield Sr.**

1274. 1789, Mar 20 -- Land Grant #349, Moore County, NC
John Argo received 100 acres located on Cedar Creek adjoining his own line and the Chatham County line. **Gabriel Harden** and **William Cook** were chain carriers.

1275. 1789, Apr 18 -- Land Grant #351, Moore County, NC
Allen Morison received 90 acres located northwest of Sings Creek adjoining **Key**, **Newton**, **Waddle** and his own line. **Norman Morison** and **Alexander Morison** were chain carriers.

1276. 1789, May 5 -- Will Book A Page 240-241, Moore County, NC
Will of **John Williamson**, Dec'd. Heirs: son **William Williamson** [*all my land except the tract given to Nancy*], daughter **Nancy Manus** wife of **Daniel Manus** [*tract where they now live*], daughter **Elizabeth**, **John Williamson**, **Briggart Care**, **Sarah Shuffle** and **Jenney Medlin**. Executors: **Nicholas Nall** and **Joseph Care**. Witnesses: **Nicholas Nall** and **Polley Nall**.

1277. 1789, May 17 -- Land Grant #1370 & #0287, Moore County, NC
Murdock Bethune received 150 acres located on Sings Creek adjoining **John Key** and **Morrison**. **Alexander Morrison** and **Allen Morrison** were chain carriers.

1278. 1789, May 18 -- Land Grant #518, Randolph County, NC
Hardy Davis received 75 acres located on Fork Creek adjoining **Cost**. **John Pierce** and **Rolly Spinks** were chain carriers.

1279. 1789, May 18 -- 1784-1795 Court of Pleas and Quarter Sessions, Moore County, NC
[*jury duty - selected participants*] **John Gardner**, **John Cagle**, **Samuel Dunn**, **Zachy. Smith**, **Isaac Dunn**, **Leonard Furr**, **Jacob Stutts**, **William Manus**, **Wm. Smith**, **Jesse Brown**, **Ambrose Brown**, **Daniel Manus**, **John Keys**, **Jonathan Caddle**, **James Hill**. [*jury duty next term - selected participants*] **Wm. Dunn** (Wet Creek), **John Sheffield Junr.**, **Joseph Allen**, **Lewis Sowell**.

1280. 1789, May 18 -- 1784-1795 Court of Pleas and Quarter Sessions, Moore County, NC Page 228
Ordered that the road from the ford of the [Deep] River near **Willis Dickinsons** as lately moved by him shall be deemed the public road and that the hands who formerly worked on the old road shall work on this road.

1281. 1789, May 18, 20 -- 1784-1795 Court of Pleas and Quarter Sessions, Moore County, NC Page 228,230,232
[Deeds] **John Shuffield** to **Stephen Smith** was proven by **David Richardson**
John Cox to **John McKay** was acknowledged
John Overton to **John Overton** (son of **Jesse Overton**) proven by **Neil McLeod**
John Cox to **George Graham** proven by **Neil McLeod**
Daniel Muse to **Samuel Dunn** was proven by **Charity Muse**

1282. 1789, May 19 --
1784-1795 Court of Pleas and Quarter Sessions, Moore County, NC Page 229
Administration of the estate of **Joseph Gilbert** Dec'd. be granted to **Benj. Tison** with **Thomas Tison** and **Benj. Shields** as securities.

1283. 1789-1790 [undated estimate] -- Estate, Moore County, NC Will Book A, Page 346-347
Inventory of the Estate of **Joseph Gilbert**, Dec'd. by Administrator **Benjamin Tyson**. [*Editor's Note: No date given on actual inventory, but the date was estimated using County Court Minute reference above.*]

1284. 1789, May 19 -- 1784-1795 Court of Pleas and Quarter Sessions, Moore County, NC Page 230
Richard Upton v. **James Caddle**

1285. 1789, May 19 -- 1784-1795 Court of Pleas and Quarter Sessions, Moore County, NC Page 230
Administration of the Estate of **Simon Hart** Dec'd. granted to **Margret Hart** with **John Cagle** and **John Bullock** as securities.

1286. 1789, May 19 -- 1784-1795 Court of Pleas and Quarter Sessions, Moore County, NC Page 230
Ordered that **George Carrener** be exempted from poll tax for 1789.

1287. 1789, May 21 -- 1784-1795 Court of Pleas and Quarter Sessions, Moore County, NC Page 234
Ordered that the following be appointed to take the list of taxable for 1789: **Nichl. Nall**, Esq. [**Capt. Morgan**'s District]; **William Barrett**, Esq. [**Capt. Barrett**'s District]; **Thomas Overton**, Esq. [**Capt. Cheek's** District]; **James Collins** Esq. [**Capt. Dunn's** District].

1288. 1789, May 21 -- 1784-1795 Court of Pleas and Quarter Sessions, Moore County, NC Page 234
Ordered that **Robert Pattison** be appointed overseer of the road in room of **Nichl. Newton**.

1289. 1789, Jun 1 -- Will Book A Page 160, Moore County, NC
Bill of Sale from **Adam Andrews** to **William Williamson** for negro girl **Seal**. **Nicholas Nall** and **John Reed** were witnesses. Proven in county court May 1792.

1290. 1789, Jun 3 -- 1784-1797 Land Entries, Moore County, NC
#188 **Jacob Cagle** entered 50 acres on Haw Branch adjoining **Hill** and **Edwards**.

1291. 1789, Jun 4 -- 1784-1797 Land Entries, Moore County, NC
#189 **David Richardson** entered 50 acres on Mill Creek adjoining **John Morgan**.

1292. 1789, Jun 9 -- Land Grant #294, Moore County, NC
Farquard Campbell received 100 acres located on Richland Creek adjoining his own line. **Duncan McIntosh** and **Hector McNeill** were chain carriers.

1293. 1789, Jun 9 -- 1784-1797 Land Entries, Moore County, NC
#194 **Edward Moore** entered 100 acres north of Deep River adjoining his own line.

1294. 1789, Jun 11 -- Land Grant #1122, Chatham County, NC
James Deaton received 70 acres located on Cedar Creek. **James Deaton** and **John Powers** were chain carriers.

A. 1789, Jun 11 – Deed Book 4 Page 63, Randolph County, NC
John Garner (of Moore County) deeded **John Fushee Garner** 250 acres located on Richland Creek and Deep River. **Winsor Pearce** was a witness.

1295. 1789, Jun 13 -- Deed Book 4, Page 53, Randolph County, NC
John Garner (of Moore County) deeded **James Garner** 250 acres located on Richland Creek. **John Tucker Garner** and **Winsor Pearce** were witnesses.

1296. 1789, Aug 2 -- 1784-1797 Land Entries, Moore County, NC
#196 **George Brazil** entered 100 acres north of Wolf Creek adjoining **William Morgan**.

1297. 1789, Aug 4 -- 1784-1797 Land Entries, Moore County, NC
#202 **Nicholas Nall** entered 150 acres adjoining **Owen Carpenter** and the [Randolph] county line.

1298. 1789, Aug 4 -- 1784-1797 Land Entries, Moore County, NC
#203 **Thomas Ritter** entered 50 acres on a branch of Richland Creek adjoining **William Dunn** and **Malcolm McNeill**.

1299. 1789, Aug 4 -- 1784-1797 Land Entries, Moore County, NC
#204 **William Newton** entered 50 acres on Cabin Creek adjoining his own line and **Jacob Harvick**.

1300. 1789, Aug 8 -- Deed Book 4, Page 55, Randolph County, NC
James Whittel deeded **William Reed** (of Moore County) 240 acres located on Brush Creek. **William Pearce** and **Winsor Pearce** were witnesses.

1301. 1789, Aug 13 -- Deed Book 4, Page 63, Randolph County, NC
John Garner (of Moore County) deeded **John Fushee Garner** 250 acres located on Richland Creek. **James Garner** and **Winsor Pearce** were witnesses.

1302. 1789, Aug 17 -- 1784-1795 Court of Pleas and Quarter Sessions, Moore County, NC
[*jury duty - selected participants*] **John Shuffle, William Dun, Danl. Manus, William Manus, John Caddle, Jonathan Caddle.** [*jury duty next term - selected participants*] **Wm. Copelin, Ansel Melton, Thos. Kees, Jacob Harwick.**

1303. 1789, Aug 18 -- 1784-1795 Court of Pleas and Quarter Sessions, Moore County, NC Page 239-240
[Deeds] **James Jeffery** to **Katrine Carpenter** was acknowledged

John Jackson to **Absolam Autery** was proven by **Jackson**'s executors

---

1304. 1789, Aug 19 -- 1784-1795 Court of Pleas and Quarter Sessions, Moore County, NC Page 241
Ordered that **Eliz. Seal** daughter of the late **Margaret Seal** taken from the house of **John Adkins** and put under the care of **Wm. Seal** Esq.

A. 1789, Aug 19 -- 1784-1795 Court of Pleas and Quarter Sessions, Moore County, NC Page 243
Ordered that **Joseph Robson** be granted letters of administration on the estate of the late **Adam Keeling**.

1305. 1789, Aug 19 -- 1784-1795 Court of Pleas and Quarter Sessions, Moore County, NC Page 243
Ordered that **Duncan Patterson** be appointed overseer of the road from **Widow Munroe**'s on Drowning Creek to old Yadkin Road commonly called **Wm. Seal**'s Road and have the following hands to work provided that **Archd. Black** keep open the road from Seal's Road to the old Yadkin Road: **Benj. Bryant, Dougal MacFadin, John McArthur, Donald Munroe, Neill McNear, Neil Gwin, Donald McDonald, Jebez Clark, James McDaniel** and **Jacob Cagle**.

1306. 1789, Aug 20 -- 1784-1797 Land Entries, Moore County, NC
#206 **John Hargrove** entered 50 acres adjoining his own line and **Solomon Barrett**.

1307. 1789, Aug 26 -- 1784-1797 Land Entries, Moore County, NC

#209 **Hardy Davis** entered 100 acres on Bear Creek adjoining his own 200 acre tract.

1308.   1789, Aug 28 -- Will Book A Page 160, Moore County, NC
Bill of Sale from **Adam Andrews** to **Bradly Garner** for negro girl **Poll**. **Nicholas Nall**, **William Williamson** and **John Smith** were witnesses. Proven in county court May 1792.

1309.   1789, Sep 1 -- Land Grant #471, Montgomery County, NC
Joseph Allen received 100 acres located on Wolf Creek adjoining own line and **Wilkins**. **William Allen** and **Samuel Allen** were chain carriers.

1310.   1789, Sep 2 -- Land Grant #313, Moore County, NC
George Brazel received 100 acres located on Wolf Creek adjoining **William Morgan** and **Hunsucker**. **Geo. Brazel** and **Roger Cagle** were chain carriers.

1311.   1789, Sep 2 -- Land Grant #328, Moore County, NC
George Brazel received 100 acres Land Grant located on Wolf Creek including his own improvement. **Wm. Morgan** and **Roger Cagle** were chain carriers.

1312.   1789, Sep 3 -- Land Grant #299, Moore County, NC
John Morgan received 50 acres adjoining **William Morgan** and including his own improvement. **Wm. Smith** and **Wm. Morgan** were chain carriers.

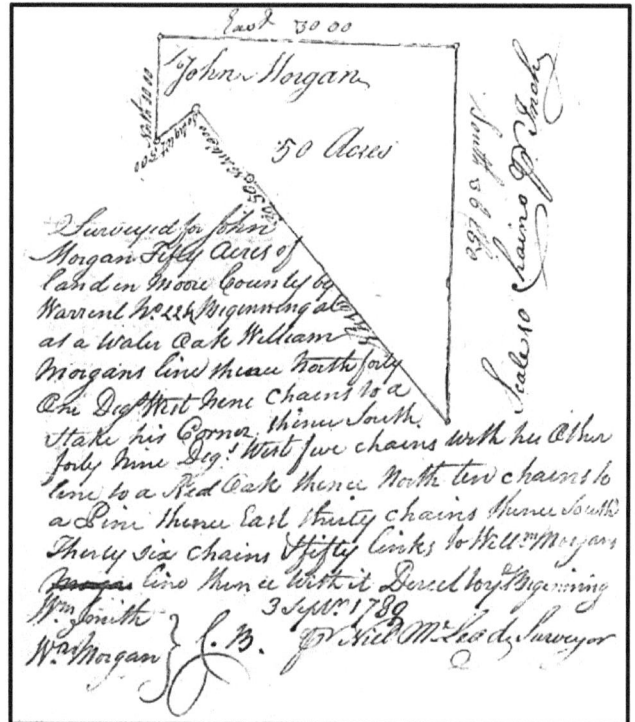

1313.   1789, Sep 3 -- Land Grant #304, Moore County, NC
William Morgan received 50 acres located northwest of Cabin Creek adjoining his own line and **Joseph Allen**. **William Smith** and **Joseph Allen** were chain carriers.

1314.   1789, Sep 3 -- Land Grant #310, Moore County, NC
David Richardson received 50 acres located on Mill Creek adjoining **John Morgan**. **William Morgan** and **John Morgan** were chain carriers.

1315.   1789, Sep 3 -- Land Grant #323, Moore County, NC
John Stutts received 50 acres located on Dry Creek. **Everet Smith** and **Nathan Smith** were chain carriers.

1316.   1789, Sep 3 -- Land Grant #334, Moore County, NC
John Morgan received 50 acres located east of Cabin Creek including his own improvement. **Davd. Richardson** and **Nathan Morgan** were chain carriers.

1317.   1789, Sep 4 -- 1784-1797 Land Entries, Moore County, NC
#212 **Neill McLeod** entered 150 acres on both sides of McLendons Creek adjoining **Sowel**.

A.   1789, Sep 18 -- Land Grant #539, Montgomery County, NC
Donald McLeod received 100 acres located on head of Cabin Creek and the Crawford Road adjoining **John Sandhill Smith**. **Norman McLeod** and **John McLeod** were chain carriers.

1318.   1789, Sep 20 -- 1784-1797 Land Entries, Moore County, NC
#219 **Hardy Davis** entered 100 acres on Grassie Creek adjoining his own line and **John Williamson**.

1319.   1789, Sep 20 -- 1784-1797 Land Entries, Moore County, NC
#220 **William Dunn** entered 50 acres on Locust Branch of Richland Creek adjoining his own line and **Donald McQueen**.

1320.   1789, Sep 20 -- 1784-1797 Land Entries, Moore County, NC
#221 **William Morgan** entered 50 acres on Cabin Creek adjoining **Joseph Allen**.

1321.   1789, Sep 20 -- 1784-1797 Land Entries, Moore County, NC
#222 **George Brazil** entered 100 acres east of Wolf Creek including his own improvement.

1322.   1789, Sep 20 -- 1784-1797 Land Entries, Moore County, NC
#223 **John Morgan** entered 50 acres south of Cabin Creek including his own improvement.

1323.   1789, Sep 21 -- 1784-1797 Land Entries, Moore County, NC
#224 **John Morgan** entered 50 acres north of Cabin Creek including his own improvement.

1324.   1789, Sep 21 -- 1784-1797 Land Entries, Moore County, NC
#225 **William Morgan** entered 100 acres between the Head of Long Branch and the Sandhill Road.

1325.   1789, Sep 21 -- 1784-1797 Land Entries, Moore County, NC
#229 **William Williamson** entered 100 acres south of Meadow Branch adjoining his own line.

1326.   1789, Sep 29 -- 1784-1797 Land Entries, Moore County, NC
#234 **William Cook** entered 150 acres on Waggon Branch north of Deep River adjoining **Lee**'s old place and **Gilmore**.

1327.   1789, Nov 7 -- Cane Creek [Quaker] Meeting Women's Minutes Page 163, Alamance County, NC
Mary Lamb formerly **Dunn** was disowned for marrying outside the unity of friends.

1328.   1789, Oct 3 -- 1784-1797 Land Entries, Moore County, NC
#144 **Norman McLeod** entered 50 acres on both sides of Sings Creek adjoining his own line.

1329.   1789, Oct 3 -- 1784-1797 Land Entries, Moore County, NC
#145 **Neill McLeod** entered 10 acres on Horse Creek.

1330.   1789, Oct 3 -- 1784-1797 Land Entries, Moore County, NC
#147 **Edward Moore** entered 50 acres on both sides of Deep River adjoining his own 100 acre tract.

A.   1789, Oct 12 -- Land Grant #491, Montgomery County, NC

William Wright received 112 acres located on North Fork of Little River including an improvement at the Bigg Branch. **Benjamin Bolin** and **Isaac Williams** were chain carriers.

B. 1789, Oct 12 -- Land Grant #530, Montgomery County, NC
Edward Duval Tyler received 50 acres located on North Fork of Little River including White Plains where he now lives and including **Samuel Graves'** improvement. **Benjamin Bolin** and **Charles Tyler** were chain carriers.

1331. 1789, Oct 13 -- Land Grant #316, Moore County, NC
Benjamin Cooper received 50 acres located on Bear Creek adjoining **Maner** and **Naul**. **Benjn. Cooper Junr.** and **Drury Richardson** were chain carriers.

1332. 1789, Oct 13 -- Land Grant #321, Moore County, NC
William Richardson received 50 acres located on Kings Street adjoining his own line. **Robt. Richardson** and **Drury Richardson** were chain carriers.

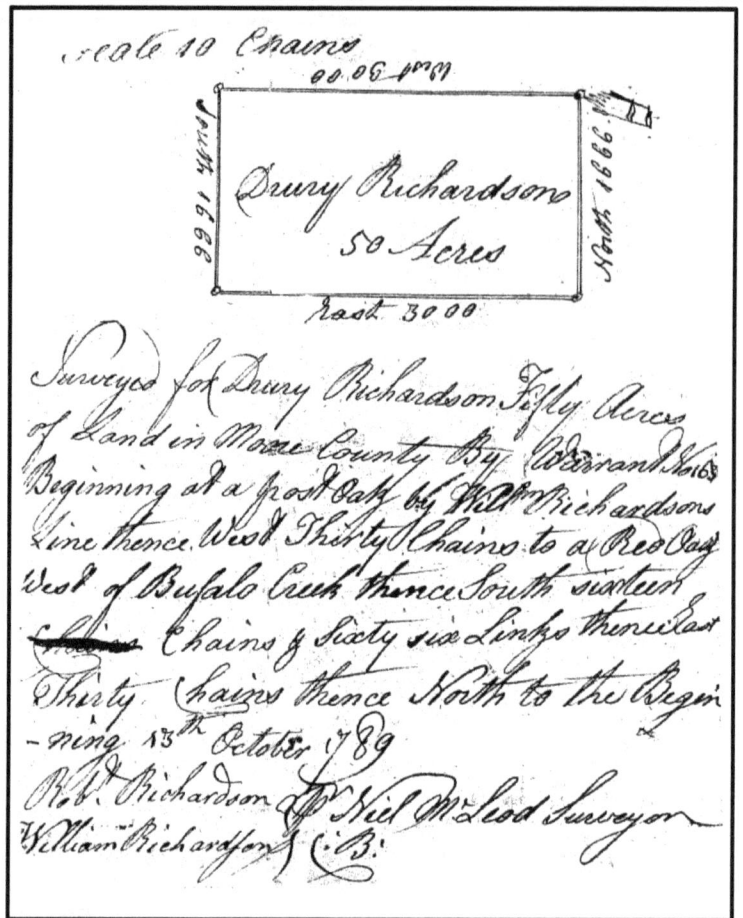

1333. 1789, Oct 13 -- Land Grant #329, Moore County, NC
Drury Richardson received 50 acres located west of Buffalo Creek adjoining **William Richardson**. **Robt. Richardson** and **William Richardson** were chain carriers.

1334. 1789, Nov 17 -- 1784-1795 Court of Pleas and Quarter Sessions, Moore County, NC
[*jury duty - selected participants*] **Ansel Melton, Thomas Keys, James Hill.** [*jury duty next term - selected participants*] **Peter Shamburrough, Leonard Cagle, George Brassell, John Morgan Sr., Richard Dunn Jur., John Hare, Zachy. Smith, Drury Richardson, Christopher Yow.**

A. 1789, Nov 17 -- 1784-1795 Court of Pleas and Quarter Sessions, Moore County, NC Page 248
Ordered that **Ambrose Brewer** pay only his single tax for 1789 – 1 poll and 100 acres.

1335. 1789, Nov 17 -- 1784-1795 Court of Pleas and Quarter Sessions, Moore County, NC Page 249
Ordered that **Joseph Dunn Junr.** be appointed overseer of the road in place of **Joseph Duckworth**.

1336. 1789, Nov 17 -- 1784-1795 Court of Pleas and Quarter Sessions, Moore County, NC Page 249
A deed from **Clem Hancock** to **Connor Dowd** was proven by **Edw. Griffen**.

1337. 1789, Nov 17 -- 1784-1795 Court of Pleas and Quarter Sessions, Moore County, NC Page 249
Mary Sowell v. **Jas. Caddle**

1338. 1789, Nov 18 -- 1784-1795 Court of Pleas and Quarter Sessions, Moore County, NC Page 251
Josiah Maples v. **Drury Richardson**

1339. 1789, Nov 20 -- Land Grant #253, Moore County, NC
William Barret received 20 acres located on Suck Creek on the old **Grove** path including a mill place adjoining **Angus McIver** and **Thomas Graham**. [illegible] and **Peter Bethune** were chain carriers.

1340. 1789, Nov 30 -- Land Grant #301, Moore County, NC

Neil McLeod received 10 acres located on Horse Creek adjoining his own line. **William Smith** and **Jacob Cagle** were chain carriers.

1341.   1789, Dec 5 -- Deed Book 4, Page 48, Randolph County, NC
James Presnall deeded **William Spencer** 100 acres located on Little River of P.D. adjoining **John Knight**, **Searcy** and **Hughet**. Granted to **Searcy** and **Hughet**. **Thomas Suggs** and **Johnston Spencer** were witnesses.

1342.   1789, Dec 11 -- Land Grant #570, Randolph County, NC
John Needham received 50 acres located on Deep River adjoining **William Searcy**. **Luke Dempsey** and **James Ledlow** were chain carriers.

1343.   1789, Dec 13 -- Land Grant #300, Moore County, NC
Nicholas Newton received 50 acres located on Wet Creek adjoining his own line and **Richard Dunn**. **Wm. Dunn** and **Thos. Kelly** were chain carriers.

1344.   1789, Dec 25 -- 1784-1797 Land Entries, Moore County, NC
#253 **Isaac Dunn** entered 100 acres between the head of Drowning Creek and Mill Creek including the White Pond.

1345.   1789, Dec 27 -- 1784-1797 Land Entries, Moore County, NC
#256 **John Key** entered 120 acres adjoining his own line.

1346.   1790, Jan 1 -- 1784-1797 Land Entries, Moore County, NC
#279 **Jesse Ritter** entered 50 acres located west of Richland Creek adjoining his own line.

1347.   1790, Jan 6 -- Land Grant #331, Moore County, NC
William Morgan Senr. received 100 acres located between the head of Long Branch and **Sandhill Smith**'s Road. **Nathan Smith** and **Jacob Harvick** were chain carriers.

1348.   1790, Jan 7 -- Land Grant #312, Moore County, NC
Nicholas Newton received 50 acres located east of Sings Creek adjoining **Jesse Brown**, his own line and **McLeod**. **William Newton** and **Ezekiah Dunn** were chain carriers.

1349.   1790, Jan 7 -- Land Grant #314, Moore County, NC
Nicholas Newton received 50 acres located east of Wet Creek adjoining his own line and **John Smith**. **William Dunn** and **Ezekiah Dunn** were chain carriers.

A.   1790, Jan 14 -- Land Grant #1157, Chatham County, NC
William Harper received 245 acres located on Fall Creek adjoining **Brewer**, **Waddle** and his own line. **Sion Phillips** and **Sampson Brewer** were chain carriers.

B.   1790, Feb 8 -- Deed Book D Page 636, Chatham County, NC
Jeremiah and **Ann Phillips** deeded **Lewis Phillips** part of the tract granted to **Jeremiah Phillips** located north of Indian Creek adjoining the path that crosses Indian Creek below the plantation and goes by **Edward Griffin's**. **Edwd. Griffin**, **Robert Phillips** and **Ezekel Hilyard** were witnesses.

1350.   1790, Feb 10 -- Land Grant #333, Moore County, NC
William Cook received 200 acres located on Cedar Creek adjoining **Goldston**, **Argo** and **Brewer**. **John Hor Goldston** and **Bunn Johnson** were chain carriers.

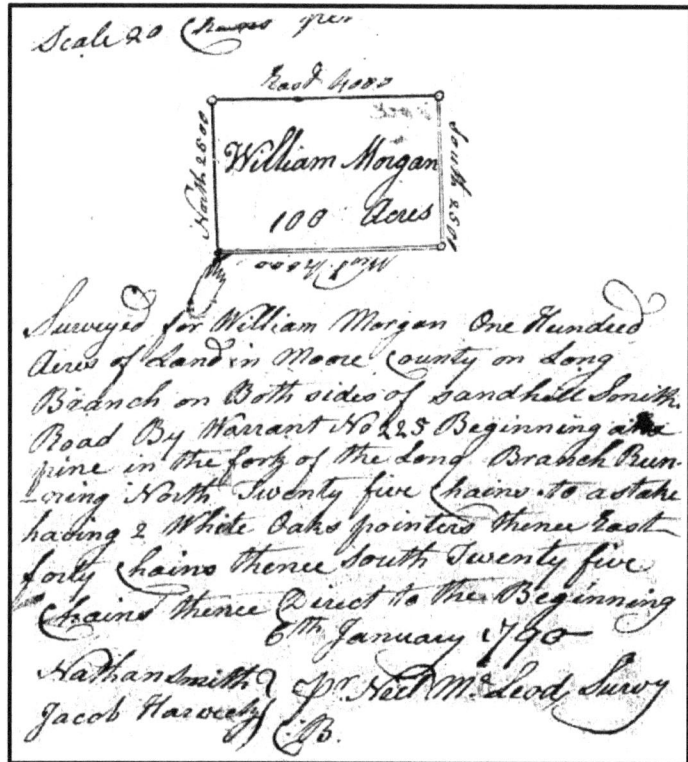

1351. 1790, Feb 16 -- 1784-1795 Court of Pleas and Quarter Sessions, Moore County, NC
[*jury duty - selected participants*] **Peter Shamburger, Drury Richardson, John Keys, Jontn. Caddell, Zachy. Smith, Saml. Dunn.** [*jury duty next term - selected participants*] **Isaac Dunn, Jesse Brown, Geo. Beassell, Edward Moore (DR), Leonard Furr, Bradley Garner, Wm. Williamson, Joseph Dunn Jr., Jesse Ritter, Wm. Gardner.**

1352. 1790, Feb 16 -- 1784-1795 Court of Pleas and Quarter Sessions, Moore County, NC Page 255,257,260
[Deeds] **John Keys** to **Thos. Keys** proven by **Ezekial Dunn**
John and **Sanna Huntsucker** to **Thomas Coash** was proven by **Owen Carpenter**.

John Cox to **James Galimore** was proven by **John Cagle**
David Lewis to **Edmond Hurley** was proven by **James Caddle**
Richard Dunn and **Isaac Dunn** to **Hezekiah Dunn** proven by **Thos. Keys**
Richard Dunn to **Hezekiah Dunn** was acknowledged
Elijah Bettis to **John Dunlap** was acknowledged

1353. 1790, Feb 16 -- 1784-1795 Court of Pleas and Quarter Sessions, Moore County, NC Page 256
David Cagle was appointed overseer of road in place of **Lew Gardner** [no location given]
Leonard Furr appointed overseer of road in place of **Joseph McGee** [no location given]

1354. 1790, Feb 16 -- 1784-1795 Court of Pleas and Quarter Sessions, Moore County, NC Page 257
Ordered that **Robert Pattison** be appointed overseer in place of **Nich. Newton** and have the following hands to work: **Wm. Dunn, Bar. Dunn, Nathl. Melton, Norman Matheson, Murdock McLeod, Hector McLean, Thos. Kee, Moses Kee, Wm. Kee, Alex Morrison, Jno. McAulay, Wm. Newton, Mur. McAulay, Ezk. Dun, Hector McLean, Thomas Graham** and **John Bethune.**

1355. 1790, Feb 16,18 -- 1784-1795 Court of Pleas and Quarter Sessions, Moore County, NC Page 256-257,263
John Cagle recorded his mark as a slope under left and cross on right.
Drury Richardson records his mark to be 2 smooth crops and 2 crops underneath.
Jacob Stutts recorded his mark as 2 crops and a hole in each ear.
Thomas Ritter recorded his mark as a swallow fork with a half moon under it in the right ear and a slit in the left ear.
John Ritter recorded his mark be recorded as a swallow fork in the left ear and a slit in the right.
Chr. Yow recorded his mark to be a swallow fork in the right ear and a crop in the left and two under nicks and the brand to be an eye in the center of a heart.
John Hare recorded his mark to be a smooth crop in the left ear and a slit in the same. J.H. branded on sheep and cattle.

1356. 1790, Feb 16 -- 1784-1795 Court of Pleas and Quarter Sessions, Moore County, NC Page 257
Ordered that **Wm. Dunn** (Wet Creek) be taken as surety for the Administration of **Simon Hart**'s estate in place of **John Cagle.**

A. 1790, Feb 20 -- Deed Book E Page 42-43, Chatham County, NC
Moses and **Rebecca Myrick** deeded **Larrance McManus** 250 acres located on Tysons Creek adjoining **Elkins** and the Moore County line. **Edwd. Griffin** was a witness.

1357. 1790, Feb 25 -- Land Grant #311, Moore County, NC

Edward Moore received 50 acres located north of Deep River adjoining England and his own line and including his own improvement. Edward Moore Junr. and George Moore were chain carriers.

1358.   1790, Feb 25 -- Land Grant #318, Moore County, NC
Edward Moore received 100 acres located north of Deep River adjoining his own line. Edward Moore Junr. and George Moore were chain carriers.

1359.   1790, Mar 3 -- Land Grant #332, Moore County, NC
Zachariah Smith received 100 acres located on Buffalo Creek where the road crosses between McDonalds and Thomas Smith adjoining his own line. John McDonald Senr. and John McDonald Junr. were chain carriers.

1360.   1790, Mar 6 -- Land Grant #320, Moore County, NC
Jacob Cagle received 50 acres located on Long Meadow including the Haw Branch and adjoining Hill and Edwards. Jno. Spivey and Jno. Stutts were chain carriers.

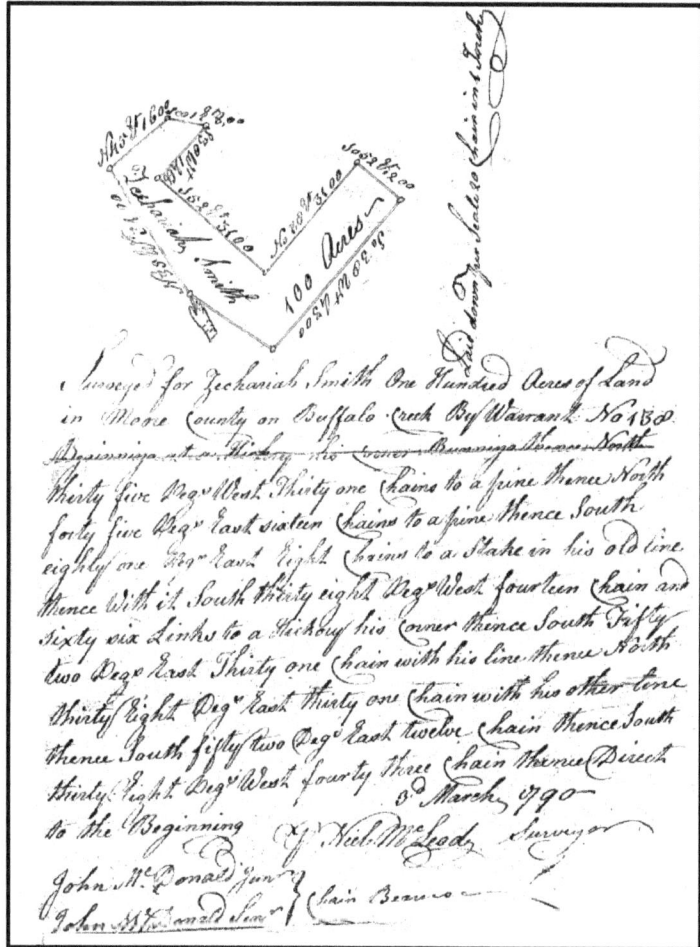

1361.   1790, Mar 6 -- Deed Book E Page 82-83, Chatham County, NC
Martha/Patty Glascock, Julius Glascock, John Milton Glascock and Martyn Glascock deeded Thomas Rubottom 240 acres located on Little Brush Creek adjoining Hugh Moffett and Hadley. Wm. Dunn and Milley Glasscock were witnesses.

1362.   1790, Mar 10 -- Land Grant #303, Moore County, NC
Murdock McAulay received 60 acres located on Wet Fork of Mill Creek adjoining his own line, McKay and Dunn. Angus McAulay and John McAulay were chain carriers.

1363.   1790, Mar 10 -- Land Grant #306, Moore County, NC
James Riddle received 127 acres located on Bear Creek of Upper Little River adjoining his own line. Angus McLeod and Duncan McIver were chain carriers.

1364.   1790, Mar 11 -- Land Grant #307, Moore County, NC
James Riddle received 104 acres located east of Bear Creek of Upper Little River adjoining his own line. Angus McLeod and Duncan McIver were chain carriers.

1365.   1790, Apr 8 -- Cane Creek [Quaker] Meeting Records (1756) Vol. 1 Page 142, Alamance County, NC
Joseph Hobson, son of William and Sarah Hobson, (of Chatham County) and Jane Tyson, daughter of Cornelius and Arcada Tison, (of Moore County) were married at the Meeting House at Deep River. Cornelius Tyson, Wm. Hobson, Jane Tyson, Lydia Tyson, Ann Tyson, George Hobson, Hannah Hobson, Aaron Tyson, William Hobson, Nathan Dixon, Hugh Moffitt, Daniel Smith and Hannah Moffitt were present and served as witnesses.

1366.   1790, Apr 17 -- 1784-1797 Land Entries, Moore County, NC
#263 Jesse Bean entered 100 acres on both sides of McLendons Creek adjoining Samuel Dunn.

1367.   1790, Apr 18 -- Land Grant #1243, Moore County, NC
Joseph McGee received 200 acres located on both sides of Scotchman Creek adjoining Powell, Malcolm McNeill, Joseph Duckworth, Allison. Joseph Duckworth and Donald McDonald were chain carriers.

A.   1790, Apr 20 -- Land Grant #1159, Chatham County, NC
Benjamin Saunders received 250 acres located on Tysons Creek adjoining **Harper** and his own line. **John Saunders** and **Benjamin Saunders Junr.** were chain carriers.

B.   1790, Apr 22 -- Land Grant #1156, Chatham County, NC
John Powers received 100 acres located on Ceder Creek adjoining his own line and **William Finley**. **William Searcey** and **Robert Harden** were chain carriers.

C.   1790, Apr 24 -- Land Grant #654, Montgomery County, NC
John Boiling Jr. received 50 acres located south of Little River adjoining **Edward Duvall Tyler**, **William Wright** and including **Benjamin Boiling's** improvement. **Tryon Patterson** and **Benjamin Bolin** were chain carriers.

1368.   1790, May 10 -- Land Grant #309, Moore County, NC
Isaac Dunn received 100 acres located on the head of Drowning Creek below the White Ponds. **Joel Atkins** and **Richard Dunn** were chain carriers.

1369.   1790, May 17 -- 1784-1795 Court of Pleas and Quarter Sessions, Moore County, NC
[*jury duty - selected participants*] **Isaac Dunn, Leonard Furr, Bradley Garner, William Williamson, Jesse Ritter, Drury Richardson, John Cagle, Hezekiah Dunn, John Caddle, James Caddle, Edward Moore, John Keys, James Hill, William Smith**. [*jury duty next term - selected participants*] **Richd. Dunn Jr., Jos. Dun Jr., Henry Cagle Sr., Hardy Davis, Roger Cagle, John Ritter, Dry. Richardson, Geo. Brazel, Thos. Ritter**.

1370.   1790, May 17-19 -- 1784-1795 Court of Pleas and Quarter Sessions, Moore County, NC Page 267, 270, 272
[Deeds] **John Sheffield Senr.** to **John Sheffield Junr.** is acknowledged
John Overton to **James Davis** proven by **Mathew Davis**
John Cox to **William Smith** was proven by **William Morgan**
Connr. Dowd to **Wm. Davis** was acknowledged
Richardson Feagin to **Gabl. Harden Junr.** was acknowledged

1371.   1790, May 17 -- 1784-1795 Court of Pleas and Quarter Sessions, Moore County, NC Page 267
The following hands were ordered to work on the road from the Montgomery County line by the Ford at Cabbin Creek to the Forks below the White Ponds: **Isaac Dunn, Richd. Dunn Jr., Rd. Dunn Sr., Ezekiah Dunn, Jesse Brown, Murk McAulay, Robert Pattison, Robert Cox, Nichl. Newton, Ansel Melton, Anguish McAulay, Donald McLeod, Norman McLeod, Joseph Allen, Wm. Morgan** and **Jacob Harvick**.

1372.   1790, May 17 -- 1784-1797 Land Entries, Moore County, NC
#265 **David Cagle** entered 100 acres south of Grassie Creek in the fork of Ceedar Branch.

1373.   1790, May 19 -- 1784-1795 Court of Pleas and Quarter Sessions, Moore County, NC Page 272
Wm. Dunn appointed to take the list of taxable for 1790 in District #3.

1374.   1790, May 19 -- 1784-1795 Court of Pleas and Quarter Sessions, Moore County, NC Page 273
Joseph Fry v. **Drury Richardson**

1375.   1790, May 22 -- Land Grant #587, Randolph County, NC
Gideon Meacon [assignee of **Capt. William Sercey**] received 200 acres located on the Fayette Road from **Hargrove's** Mill to **Widow Spinks** adjoining **Sotherland** and **Searcey**. **William Sercy** and **Enoch Spinks** were chain carriers.

1376. 1790, Jun 11 -- Deed Book J Page 116, Chatham County, NC
Zachariah Smith [of Moore County] deeded **William Tomason** [of Chatham County] 200 acres located south of Tick Creek adjoining **Hunter** and **Tomason. Joseph Stevens** and **Isaac Brooks** were witnesses.

1377. 1790, Jun 15 – 1787-1794 Court of Pleas and Quarter Sessions, Randolph County, NC Page 119
Ordered that **Matthew Hamilton** be overseer of the road from Chatham County line across Deep River at **Searcey**'s Ford and to the [Moore] County line and work the following hands: **Edmond Waddell, William Argo, Athur Reed, Joseph Rich, Jacob Routh, Charles Gray, John Reed, Richd. Bird, Robert Carr, Joseph Hix, Jesse Pits, William Searcey, James Bowdon, William Harris, Windsor Pearce, David Andrews, Wake Andrews, John Spinks, James Lathem, Howel Brewer, Nathl. Mullins, Charles Stewart, William Latham, John Argo** and **James Deaton.**

A. 1790, Jun 16 – Deed Book 4 Page 79, Randolph County, NC
Winsor Pearce [via Sheriff due to judgement] deeded **William Bowdown** 100 acres located on creek formerly called Pearces Creek and Gardner Road adjoining **Wm. Pearce.**

1378. 1790 Jul 13 -- Marriage, Moore County, NC
James Burkhead married **Charity Muse** by **William Dunn**, JP. [*Editor's Note: Found in NC Supreme Court Case #2580. Samuel Dunn produced the orginial certificate*]

1379. 1790, Aug 13 -- Land Grant #296, Moore County, NC
John Key received 120 acres adjoining his own line, **Waddle** and **Morison. Thomas Key** and **Moses Key** were chain carriers.

1380. 1790, Aug 17 -- 1784-1795 Court of Pleas and Quarter Sessions, Moore County, NC
[*jury duty - selected participants*] **Roger Cagle, George Brazell, Thomas Ritter, John Ritter, Thomas Keys, Drury Richardson, Richard Dunn Junr., Isaac Dunn, David/Davey Richardson, Richard Bean, William Smith.** [*jury duty next term - selected participants*] **Willm. Gardiner** (Dutch), **Edward Moore, William Copeland, John Morgan, Leonard Cagle, William Williamson, Stephen Richardson**

1381. 1790, Aug 17 -- 1784-1795 Court of Pleas and Quarter Sessions, Moore County, NC Page 279
Henry Cagle records his mark as an over slope in each ear.

1382. 1790, Aug 17 -- 1784-1795 Court of Pleas and Quarter Sessions, Moore County, NC Page 279
Thomas G. Mathews v. **Drury Richardson**

1383. 1790, Aug 17-19 -- 1784-1795 Court of Pleas and Quarter Sessions, Moore County, NC Page 277,278,281
[Deeds] **Jason Wadsworth** to **John Wadsworth** was acknowledged
Three deeds from **Richardson Feagin** to **John Overton Senr.** were acknowledged
John Morgan to **William Morgan** was proven by **David Richardson**

Richardson Feagin to **Malcom Buie** was acknowledged
Richard and **Mary Bean** to **John Spivey** was acknowledged
Edward Cox to **John McKay** was proven by **George Cox**

1384. 1790, Aug 17 -- 1784-1795 Court of Pleas and Quarter Sessions, Moore County, NC Page 280
Wm. Morgan was appointed overseer of the road from the Forks below the White Ponds on Yadkin Road to the [Montgomery] County line.

1385. 1790, Aug 17 -- 1784-1795 Court of Pleas and Quarter Sessions, Moore County, NC Page 285
Thomas Overton Esq. came into court and entered into bond to keep a base born child begot on the body of **Anna Jones** with **Joseph Robson** as security.

1386. 1790, Aug 19 -- 1784-1795 Court of Pleas and Quarter Sessions, Moore County, NC
Ordered that **Benjn. Caddel** be paid for attending the petit jury last session.

1387. 1790, Aug 24 -- Land Grant #365, Moore County, NC
Nicholas Nall received 150 acres located north of Bear Creek adjoining **John Shuffield Senr**. **John Shuffield** and **Adam Shuffield** were chain carriers.

1388. 1790, Aug 25 -- Land Grant #388, Moore County, NC
Hardy Davis received 100 acres located northwest of Grassy Creek adjoining his own line and **John Williamson**. **Nicholas Nall** and **William Williamson** were chain carriers.

1389. 1790, Aug 25 -- Land Grant #391, Moore County, NC
William Williamson received 100 acres located on Meadow Branch adjoining his own line. **Donald Maners** and **John Bullock** were chain carriers.

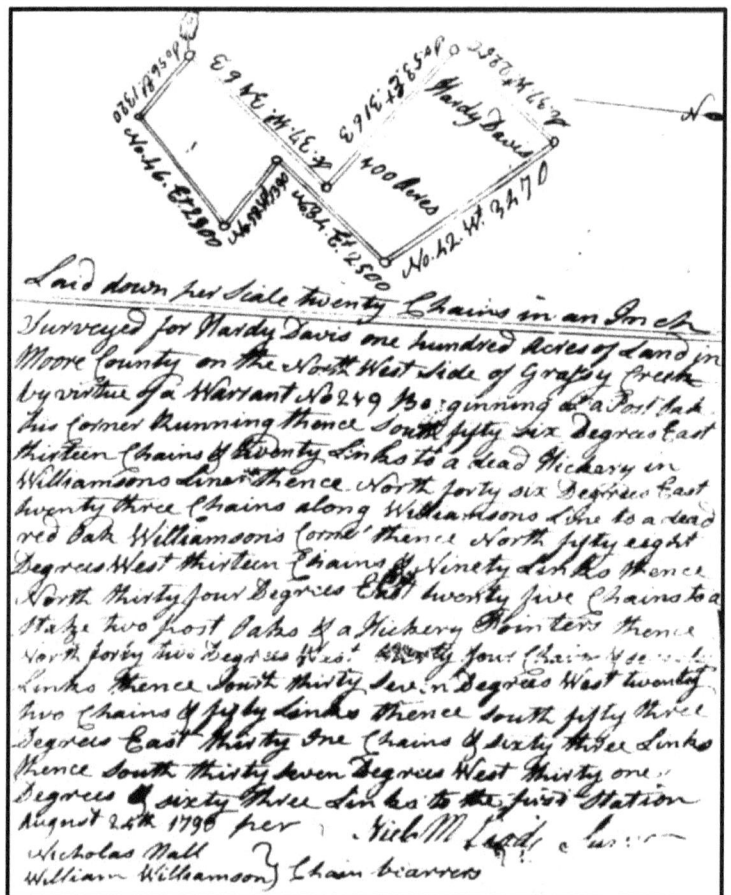

1390. 1790, Aug 26 -- Land Grant #374, Moore County, NC
Nicholas Nall received 150 acres located in the Randolph County line adjoining **Owen Carpenter**. **Wm. Williamson** and **Wm. Shearsy** were chain carriers.

1391. 1790, Sep 10 -- Deed Book 4, Page 81, Randolph County, NC
Aaron Hill deeded **Jesse Benton** a tract of land located on Deep River adjoining Chatham County line. Deeded from **William Searcy** to **Aaron Hill**. **William Bailey** and **E. Williams** were witnesses.

1392. 1790, Sep 14 – 1787-1794 Court of Pleas and Quarter Sessions, Randolph County, NC Page 125
Ordered that the following lay off a road from **Harmon Cox**'s Mill on Deep River down said river on the south side of **Garner**'s Meeting House from thense the best way to the road leading to Fayetteville: **William Bowdon, John Fushee Garner, James Garner, James Whittle, Matthew Hamilton, John Spinks, James Bowdon, Jacob Loudermilk, James Ludlow, Marmaduke Bookout, Joseph Bookout, Charles Bookout, Edmond Waddle** and **William Argo**.

1393. 1790, Oct 23 -- Land Grant #378, Moore County, NC
Hardy Davis received 100 acres located on Bear Creek adjoining his own line. **John Needham** and **Bailey Needham** were chain carriers.

1394. 1790, Nov 8 -- Deed Book G Page 71, Chatham County, NC
Mary Dowd [of Moore County] deeded **William Dunn** [of Moore County] 400 acres located on Deep River and Smith Creek adjoining **Judith Dowd**. **Reuben Sheals** and **Richard Dowd** were witnesses.

1395. 1790, Nov 16 -- Marriage Bond, Wake County, NC
Joseph Britt to **Nancy Stephens**. **Joseph Britt** was bondsman and **J. Rice** was witness. [*Editor's Note: Date of marriage occurred on or after date of marriage bond.*]

1396. 1790, Nov 16 -- 1784-1795 Court of Pleas and Quarter Sessions, Moore County, NC
[*jury duty - selected participants*] **Edw. Moore, John Morgan, John Cadwell, William Copeland, Leonard Cagle, Jesse Ritter, Richard Dunn, Stephen Richardson, James Hill, John Keys, John Ritter, Thomas Kees, Saml.**

Dunn, Daniel Caddell. [*jury duty next term - selected participants*] **Richard Dunn Junr.**, **Isaac Dun**, **Thos. Keys**, **Joseph Dunn Junr.**, **Jacob Stutts**, **Leonard Furr**, **Daniel Manus**, **Zachy. Smith**, **Lewis Sowell**, **John Morgan**, **John Shuffle Junr.**, **William Morgan**, **Solw. Dunn Junr.**

1397. 1790, Nov 16 -- 1784-1795 Court of Pleas and Quarter Sessions, Moore County, NC Page 290
Leonard Cagle records his mark as a cross and slit in right and a half cross in left.

1398. 1790, Nov 16 -- 1784-1795 Court of Pleas and Quarter Sessions, Moore County, NC Page 288, 289, 291
[Deeds] **William Seal** to **James Hogg** was proven by **Ralph Davis**
John Cox to **Allan Martin** was proven by **Murdock Martin**
Phill Alston to **James Alston** was proven by **John Carrell** Esq.

A. 1790, Nov 16 -- 1784-1795 Court of Pleas and Quarter Sessions, Moore County, NC Page 290
Ordered that **Thomas Muse** be appointed overseer of the road from McClendons Creek to **McDonald**s old field and have the same hands to work.

B. 1790, Nov 16 -- 1784-1795 Court of Pleas and Quarter Sessions, Moore County, NC Page 293
Ordered that **Hardy Davis** give **William Davis** two years schooling.

C. 1790, Nov 16 -- 1784-1795 Court of Pleas and Quarter Sessions, Moore County, NC Page 294
Ordered that hands on **John Overtons** Road on the east side of McLendons Creek are to open the road from where the last road cross[es] Deep River to where it intersects with the Gulph or Tysons Road and **John Overton** [upper] continue as overseer.

D. 1790, Nov 16 -- 1784-1795 Court of Pleas and Quarter Sessions, Moore County, NC Page 295
Ordered that **James Alston** be appointed overseer for all hands that worked on the west side of McLendons Creek on **John Benton's** road and open the road from where it crosses [Deep] River near the mouth of Governors Creek to where it intersects **John Overton's** road near **William Capps**.

1399. 1790, Nov 18 -- 1784-1795 Court of Pleas and Quarter Sessions, Moore County, NC Page 297
Ordered that **James Caddell** produce his books next court in the suit against **Patty Glascock**.

1400. 1791, Jan 1 -- 1784-1797 Land Entries, Moore County, NC
#279 **Jesse Ritter** entered 50 acres west of Richland Creek adjoining his own line where he now lives.

1401. 1791, Jan 1 -- 1784-1797 Land Entries, Moore County, NC
#281 **Murdock Martin** entered 80 acres on McLendons Creek adjoining **Campbell** and **John Cox**.

1402. 1791, Jan 4 -- 1784-1797 Land Entries, Moore County, NC
#285 **Murdock McAuley** entered 50 acres on Wet Creek adjoining **Bartholomew Dunn** and **Waddle**.

1403. 1791, Jan 4 -- 1784-1797 Land Entries, Moore County, NC
#287 **Owen Carpenter** entered 150 acres adjoining **John Garner**, **Christopher Yew** and **Richd. Bird**.

1404. 1791, Jan 6 -- Land Grant #377, Moore County, NC
Benjamin Tyson received 640 acres located on Deep River and Smiths Creek adjoining **Gabriel Johnston**. **Charles Dowd** and **Duncan Murry** were chain carriers.

1405. 1791, Jan 6 -- 1784-1797 Land Entries, Moore County, NC
#291 **Ambrose Manes** entered 100 acres located on Bear Creek below the Waggon Road adjoining **Nall**, **Brewer** 1405and **Drury Richardson**.

Land granted on Wet Creek, Cabin Creek, Wolf Creek, Mill Creek, Dry Creek by the 1790s-1800s
Map prepared utilizing early land grants
[for more information see www.MooreCountyWallaces.com]

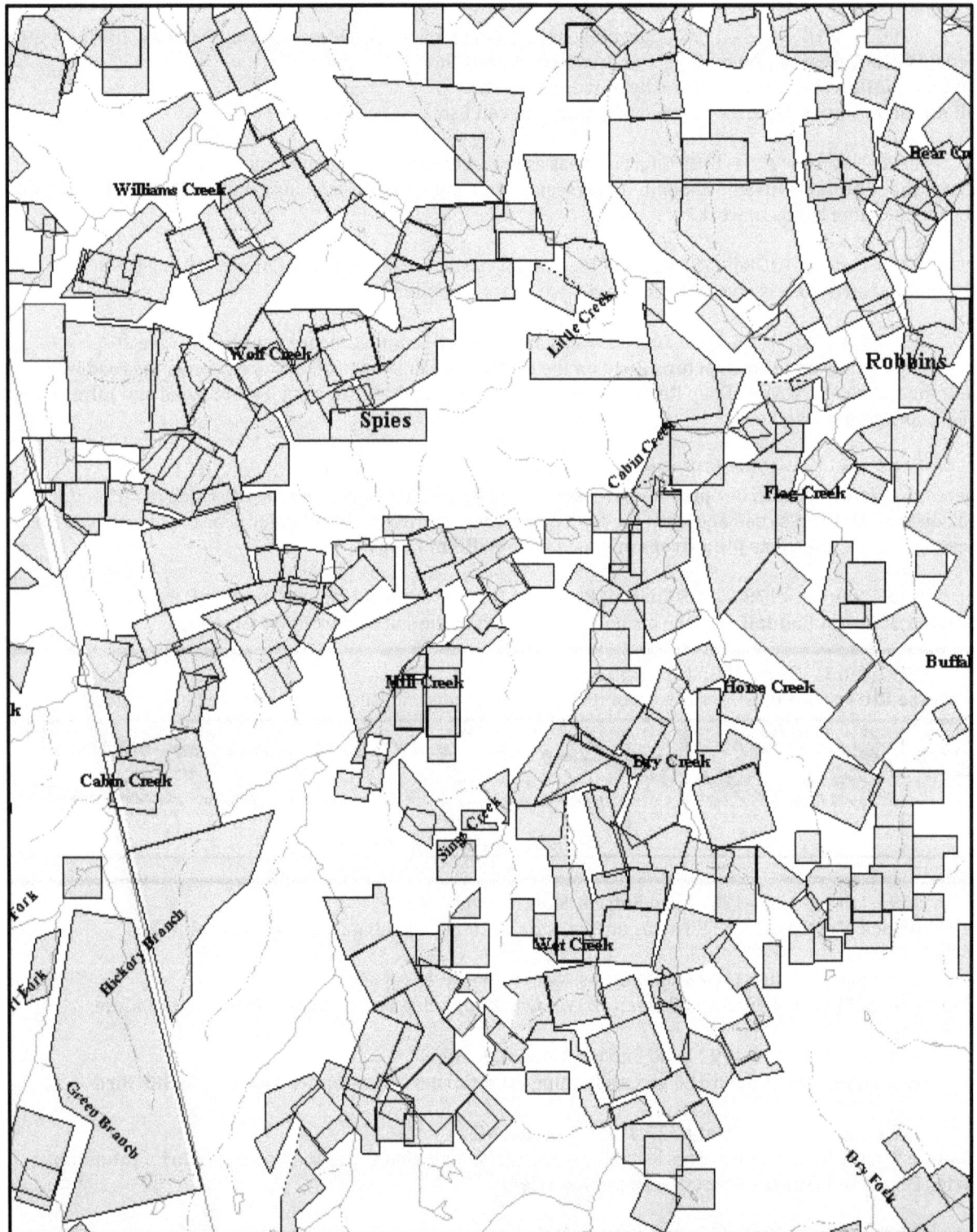

1406. 1791, Jan 7 -- 1784-1797 Land Entries, Moore County, NC
#293 **William Dunn** entered 50 acres east of Richland Creek adjoining his own line and **Donald McQueen**.

1407. 1791, Jan 7 -- 1784-1797 Land Entries, Moore County, NC
#294 **George Graham** entered 50 acres adjoining **Murdock Martin**, **John Cox** and his own line.

1408. 1791, Jan 8 -- 1784-1797 Land Entries, Moore County, NC
#296 **William Dunn** entered 100 acres east of Drowning Creek at Huff's Ford adjoining the county line.

1409. 1791, Jan 11-- 1784-1797 Land Entries, Moore County, NC
#297 **John Spyvey** entered 60 acres on Buffalow Creek including his own improvement and adjoining **Jacob Stutts**.

1410. 1791, Jan 11 -- 1784-1797 Land Entries, Moore County, NC
#298 **James Brady** entered 150 acres north of Deep River including his own improvement.

1411. 1791, Jan 12 -- 1784-1797 Land Entries, Moore County, NC
#302 **John McAuley Jr.** entered 50 acres on both sides of west prong of Sings Creek adjoining **Archd. McKeesick**'s 200 acre and the path from **Donald McLeod**'s to **McKeesicks'** improvement including the spring near the old field.

1412. 1791, Jan 13 -- 1784-1797 Land Entries, Moore County, NC
#305 **John McKay** entered 100 acres between the Willow Meadow and Little Meadow Creeks on both sides of the Rutherford Road adjoining **Alexr. McKay**.

1413. 1791, Jan 13 -- Land Grant #1669, Moore County, NC
John Overton Senr. received 640 acres located on Deep River between McLendons Creek and Governors Creek being the land entered by **Robert Cobb** adjoining **John Dunlap**, **Dowd** and own line. **John Dunlap** and **John Overton Junr.** were chain carriers.

1414. 1791, Jan 18-- 1784-1797 Land Entries, Moore County, NC
#306 **Niell McLeod** entered 60 acres south of Deep River adjoining **Traps** and **Barton**'s old field.

1415. 1791, Jan 20-- 1784-1797 Land Entries, Moore County, NC
#308 **Niell McLeod** entered 150 acres on drains of Wolf Creek and the old Yadkin Road adjoining **William Morgan Jr.**

1416. 1791, Jan 21-- 1784-1797 Land Entries, Moore County, NC
#310 **Norman McKinnon** entered 50 acres east of Dry Fork of Mill Creek adjoining his own line.

1417. 1791, Jan 21-- 1784-1797 Land Entries, Moore County, NC
#311 **Henry Cagle** entered 100 acres on both sides of Bear Creek including his own improvement and adjoining **Constable**'s 100 acres and **Gilmore**'s 100 acres.

1418. 1791, Jan 22-- 1784-1797 Land Entries, Moore County, NC
#312 **Robert Cox** entered 60 acres west of Dry Fork of Mill Creek adjoining **Norman McKinnon** and **Niell McLeod**.

1419. 1791, Jan 22 -- 1784-1797 Land Entries, Moore County, NC
#313 **Daniel Mannars** entered 120 acres located southwest of Grassie Creek adjoining his **John Williamson** and **Hardy Davis**.

1420. 1791, Jan 22-- 1784-1797 Land Entries, Moore County, NC
#314 **Hector McLaine** entered 100 acres northwest of Horse Creek adjoining his own line, **Newton**, **Smith** and the Sandhill Place.

1421.   1791, Jan 22-- 1784-1797 Land Entries, Moore County, NC
#315 **Edward Smith** entered 50 acres on Buffalow Creek including **Mary Haynes'** improvement adjoining the place he bought of **William Smith** and **Bean**.

1422.   1791, Jan 22-- 1784-1797 Land Entries, Moore County, NC
#316 **Bartholomew Dunn** entered 50 acres east of Flag Creek adjoining **Smith** and including **Hart's** improvement.

1423.   1791, Jan 22 -- 1784-1797 Land Entries, Moore County, NC
#317 **Mary Hines** entered 50 acres located on Persimmon Branch of Flag Creek including **Nicholas Wallace's** improvement.

1424.   1791, Jan 22 -- 1784-1797 Land Entries, Moore County, NC
#318 **Roger Cagle** entered 50 acres located on both sides of Wolf Creek adjoining his own line and **John Hansuckor**.

1425.   1791, Jan 24-- 1784-1797 Land Entries, Moore County, NC
#321 **Daniel McLeod** entered 60 acres east of Wet Creek adjoining **Waddill** and **John Key**.

1426.   1791, Jan 24-- 1784-1797 Land Entries, Moore County, NC
#322 **Niell McLeod** entered 60 acres west of Richland Creek adjoining his own line and **Kenneth Murchison**.

1427.   1791, Jan 24-- 1784-1797 Land Entries, Moore County, NC
#323 **Niell McLeod** entered 150 acres east of Richland Creek adjoining his own line and **Morrison**.

1428.   1791, Jan 24-- 1784-1797 Land Entries, Moore County, NC
#325 **Norman Morrison** entered 50 acres northeast of Drowning Creek adjoining his own line.

1429.   1791, Jan 24-- 1784-1797 Land Entries, Moore County, NC
#326 **John McCaskill** entered 50 acres on the drains of Richland Creek including his own improvement.

A.   1791, Jan 24 – Deed Book E Page 137-138, Chatham County, NC
Hermon Husband Junr. (of PA) deeded **Edmond Waddill** (of Randolph County) 225 acres located north of Deep River near Wilcox's Ironwork. **Bryan Boroughs**, **John Husband** and **John Argo** were witnesses.

1430.   1791, Jan 25-- 1784-1797 Land Entries, Moore County, NC

#327 **Jesse Upton** and **Richard Upton** entered 100 acres on McCallums Fork of Richland Creek including **Benjamin Atkinson**'s improvement.

1431. 1791, Jan 25-- 1784-1797 Land Entries, Moore County, NC
#328 **Joseph Dunn Sr.** entered 100 acres on McCallums Fork of Richland Creek including **Thomas Atkinson**'s improvement.

1432. 1791, Jan 25 -- 1784-1797 Land Entries, Moore County, NC
#329 **Niell McLeod** and **Jesse Ritter** entered 100 acres located on both sides of Richland Creek adjoining **Ferquhart Campbell** and **Nathan Smith**.

1433. 1791, Jan 25-- 1784-1797 Land Entries, Moore County, NC
#330 **Niell McLeod** entered 80 acres east of Richland Creek adjoining **Ferquhard Campbell** and **McKinnon**.

1434. 1791, Jan 26-- 1784-1797 Land Entries, Moore County, NC
#331 **William Smith** entered 50 acres on Long Branch of Cabin Creek adjoining **Richard Dunn**.

1435. 1791, Jan 26-- 1784-1797 Land Entries, Moore County, NC
#332 **Niell McLeod** entered 50 acres on head of Deep Creek known as Poplar Spring and the Old Yadkin Road.

1436. 1791, Jan 26-- 1784-1797 Land Entries, Moore County, NC
#333 **William Morgan** entered 50 acres on both sides of Mill Creek adjoining his own line and **James Gallemore**.

1437. 1791, Jan 26-- 1784-1797 Land Entries, Moore County, NC
#334 **William Smith Jr.** entered 30 acres on a branch of Bear Creek adjoining his own line.

1438. 1791, Jan 26-- 1784-1797 Land Entries, Moore County, NC
#335 **John Carrol** entered 100 acres adjoining **Agerton** and **Peter Smith**.

1439. 1791, Jan 28 -- Bible of Wyatt Williamson, Moore County, NC
John Williamson died at age 102.

1440. 1791, Jan 28-- 1784-1797 Land Entries, Moore County, NC
#346 **John McAulay** entered 50 acres west of Wet Creek adjoining **John McKinnon, Hezekiah Dunn, William Barrett** and **John McAulay Sr.**

1441. 1791, Jan 29 -- Land Grant #405, Moore County, NC
Richard Dowd received 640 acres located south of Deep River on the Chatham County line adjoining **Benjamin Tyson** and **Conner Dowd. Charles Dowd** and **Seth** [page torn] were chain carriers.

1442. 1791, Feb 21 -- 1784-1795 Court of Pleas and Quarter Sessions, Moore County, NC
[*jury duty - selected participants*] **Richd. Dunn Junr., Thomas Keys, Jesse Ritter, John Keys, Daniel Manus, Jacob Stutts, Lewis Sowell, Joseph Dunn Junr.** [*jury duty next term - selected participants*] **Jonathan Caddle, John Ritter, Soln. Barrett, John Stutts, Capt. William Morgan, Adam Comer, Christopher Yow, William Williamson.**

1443. 1791, Feb 21 -- 1784-1795 Court of Pleas and Quarter Sessions, Moore County, NC Page 299
Ordered that a road be laid out from the **Widow Muses** to the nearest course near **Joseph Duckworths** and son to the Island Ford and from thence to Chatham County line leading on a direct course towards **Conner** settlement and the following work on the road: **Joseph Duckworth, Joseph McGee Senr., Joseph McGee Junr., Drury Richerson, Wm. Harden, John Blanchet, James Brady, Benj. Elkins, Saml. Perry, Wm. Cook, Near Brewer, Saml. Person, Benj. Cooper, Wm. Richerson, Wm. Teague, Robert Davis, Benj. Shields** and **John Goldston.** [*Editor's Note: this entire entry was stuck through in the original records*]

1444. 1791, Feb 21-- 1784-1797 Land Entries, Moore County, NC
#349 **Jacob Harvick** entered 25 acres on Cabin Creek adjoining his own line, **Richard Dunn** and **Thomas Gilmore.**

1445.   1791, Feb 22 -- 1784-1795 Court of Pleas and Quarter Sessions, Moore County, NC Page 300
Ordered that **Stephen Davis** be bound to **Jesse Brown** to learn the trade of a hatter for a term of his being of age, which will be Nov 14, 1794.

1446.   1791, Feb 22-23 -- 1784-1795 Court of Pleas and Quarter Sessions, Moore County, NC Page 300-302
[Deeds] **William Barrett** to **Col. Thomas Armstrong** was proven by **Alexr. McIver**
Lewis Sowell to **Nicholas Newton** was proven by **Bartholomew Dunn**
Jesse Ritter to **Donald Beaton** was proven by **William Marten**
Richardson Fagan to **John Carell** was acknowledged
James Garner and wife **Betty** to **James Hogg** was acknowledged
George Lucas to **Everat Smith** was proven by **Nicholas Nall**
Isaac Dunn to **Ezekia Dunn** was proven by **Richard Dunn**
Isaac Dunn to **John McKinnon** was proven by **John McAuley**
John Stephens to **James Smith** was proven by **Solomon Barrett**

1447.   1791, Feb 23 -- 1784-1795 Court of Pleas and Quarter Sessions, Moore County, NC Page 301
Ordered that **Stephen Richardson** be appointed overseer of road in place of **Leonard Furr**

A.   1791, Feb 23 -- 1784-1795 Court of Pleas and Quarter Sessions, Moore County, NC Page 302
Ordered that **Daniel McQueen** be appointed constable in **Capt. Dunn's** District with **Wm. Martin** and **Wm. Dunn** as securities.

1448.   1791, Feb 23 -- 1784-1795 Court of Pleas and Quarter Sessions, Moore County, NC Page 302
Ordered that a road be laid from near Deep River at county line to the Black Ponds and have the following hands to work: **John Morgan, Wm. Morgan, Capt. Wm. Morgan Junr., Wm. Smith, Averett Smith, John Cagle, Lewis Sowell, Geo. Brazell, John Allen, Murdoch McAuley, Anguish McAuley, Jacob Harvick, John Shuffle Senr.,**

John Shuffle Junr., Thomas Dunn and **Robert Cox.**

1449.   1791, Feb 21-- 1784-1797 Land Entries, Moore County, NC #350 **Benjamin Cooper** entered 150 acres north of Bear Creek including **Caddel's** [?] old field.

1450.   1791, Feb 23 -- 1784-1797 Land Entries, Moore County, NC
#351 **Jesse Ritter** entered 50 acres located south of Richland Creek adjoining **Donald McQueen** and his own line.

1451.   1791, Feb 21-- 1784-1797 Land Entries, Moore County, NC
#352 **Samuel Dunn** entered 50 acres east of Richland Creek and both sides of the Waggon Road.

1452.   1791, Mar 15 – 1787-1794 Court of Pleas and Quarter Sessions, Randolph County, NC Page 143
David Andrews appointed overseer of the road from the Chatham line leading across Deep River at **Searcy's** Ford and to the [Moore] County line with the following hands: **Edmond Waddell, William Argo, Arthur Read,**

Jacob Read, John Read, Richard Bird, Robert Carr, Jesse Pits, Joseph Carr, William Searcey, Michael Andrews, Howel Brewer, Charles Stewart, John Argo and John Deaton.

1453.　　　1791, Mar 15 – 1787-1794 Court of Pleas and Quarter Sessions, Randolph County, NC Page 143
John Spinks appointed overseer of the road from Cedar Creek to the [Moore] County line at **Garner**'s Meeting House with the following hands: **James Ledlow, Reubin Hicks, Joseph Hicks, James Garner, Bradley Garner, William Mallett, James Latham, William Latham, Charles Latham, James Bowdon, William Bowdon, Winsor Pearce, William Hoskins** and **Nathan Mullins**.

A.　　　1791, Mar 23 -- Deed, Moore County, NC
Thomas Ritter and **Margaret Ritter** deeded **John Sowell** 300 acres located on McLendons Creek formerly sold by **Jacob McLendon** to **Isaac Sowell**. **Neill McLeod** and **Jesse Ritter** were witnesses. Proven by **Neill McLeod** Aug 1792. [*Editor's Note: Located in NC Supreme Court Case #2744, Thomas Ritter and wife Margaret v. William Barrett*]

B.　　　1791, May 1 -- Land Grant #1465, Randolph County, NC
James Lathem received 600 acres located on Fork Creek. **Richd. Larrance** and **Peter Larrance** were chain carriers.

1454.　　　1791, May 7-- 1784-1797 Land Entries, Moore County, NC
#362 **John McKay** entered 150 acres on both sides of McLendons Creek adjoining his own line.

1455.　　　1791, May 10-- 1784-1797 Land Entries, Moore County, NC
#363 **Thomas Smith** entered 50 acres north of Buffalow Creek adjoining **Zachariah Smith** and including a field and a cabin where **Mary Smith** lives.

| 362 | John McKay 7th May 1791 | 150 | On McLendens Creek both sides and Near or Joining his Own Two lines. |
| 303 | Thomas Smith 10th May 1791 | 50 | Near or Joining Zachariah Smiths line On the North side including a field and Cabin where Mary Smith now lives on the North side of Buffalow Creek. |

1456.　　　1791, May 12 -- Land Grant #372, Moore County, NC
George Graham received 19.5 acres located east of McLendons Creek adjoining **Cox** and **Murdock Martin**. **Thomas Grahams** and **Augustin Lanceford** were chain carriers.

1457.　　　1791, May 17 -- 1784-1795 Court of Pleas and Quarter Sessions, Moore County, NC
[*jury duty - selected participants*] **Wm. Williamson, Jona. Caddle, John Stutts, John Ritter, Adam Comer, Wm. Morgan, Christr. Yow, Jesse Ritter, John Caddell, Thomas Ritter, Rd. Dunn, Drury Richardson.** [*jury duty next term - selected participants*] **Zack. Smith, Joseph Dunn, William Smith, William Richardson Jr., Leonard Cagle, Near Brewer.**

1458.　　　1791, May 17-- 1784-1797 Land Entries, Moore County, NC
#368 **James Deeton** entered 200 acres adjoining the county line, **Phillips** and **Morgan**'s old field.

1459.　　　1791, May 17-18 -- 1784-1795 Court of Pleas and Quarter Sessions, Moore County, NC Page 306-308,310
[Deeds] **James Dunbar** to **Cornl. Dowd** was acknowledged
Farquard Campbell to **Thomas Rubottom** was proven by **William Dunn**
William Barrett to **Benjamin Caddell** was proven by **James Caddell**
Two deeds from **Joseph Robson** to **William Harden** were acknowledged

John Caddell to **Benjm. Cooper** was proven by **Samuel Persons**
Cornelius Dowd, Mary Dowd and **Cornelius Tyson** to **William Berriman** was acknowledged
[Power of Attorney] **William Smith** to **William Mears** was proven by Honorable **Spruce McCay** J.S.C.L.E.

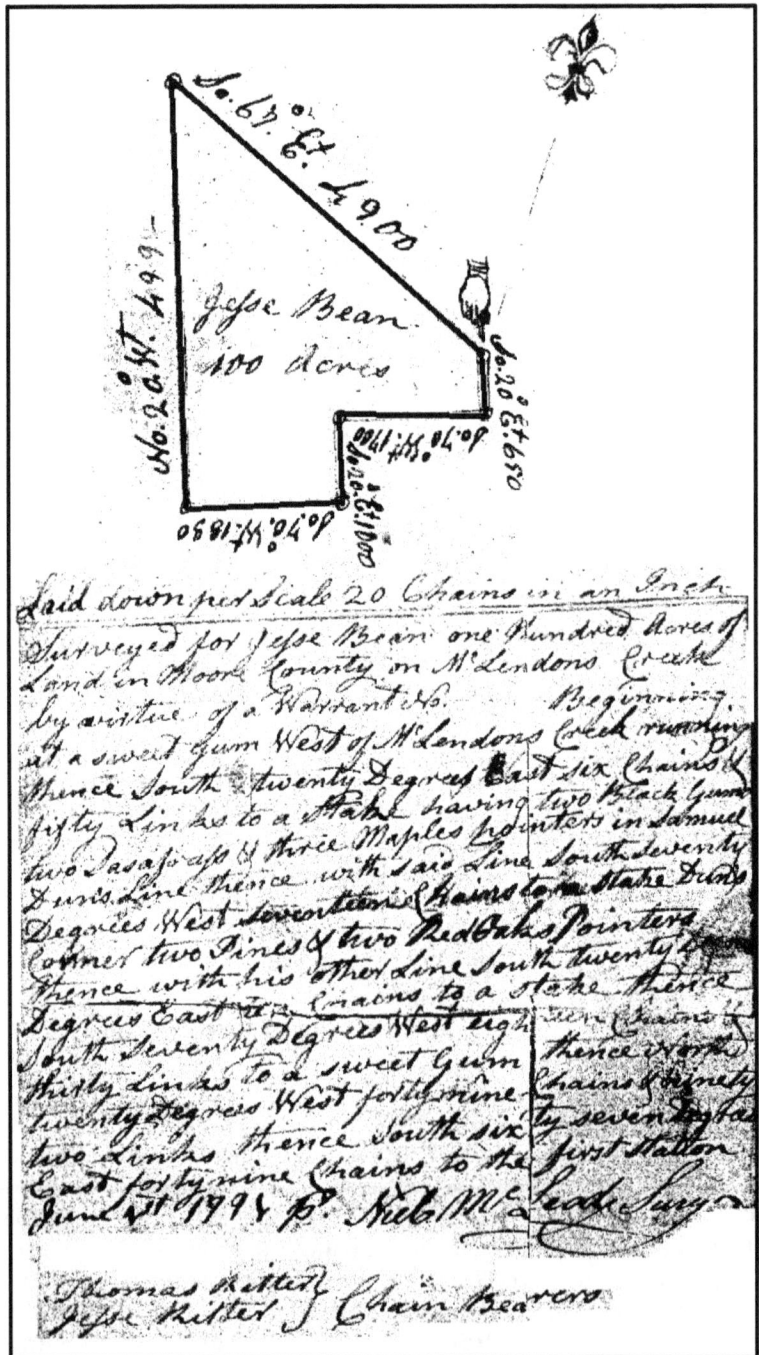

Cornelius Dowd to **William Teague** was proven by another **William Teague**

1460. 1791, May 18 -- 1784-1795 Court of Pleas and Quarter Sessions, Moore County, NC Page 307
Ordered that the following take the list of taxable property for 1791: **Nicholas Nall**, Esq. [**Capt. Morgans** District]; **William Dunn**, Esq. [**Capt. Dunn**'s District]; **Thomas Tyson**, Esq. [**Capt. Cheek's** District].

1461. 1791, May 18 -- 1784-1795 Court of Pleas and Quarter Sessions, Moore County, NC Page 308
Ordered that the following tracts of land be sold by the Sheriff: **James McDonald** on Rogers Creek and **Jno. Harden** on Cane Patch Creek

1462. 1791, May 18 -- 1784-1795 Court of Pleas and Quarter Sessions, Moore County, NC Page 309
Ordered that the Administration of the estate of **Simon Hart** be void and all papers belonging to anyone be given to **Bartholomew Dunn** except the administration bond which should be given to **John Cagle**.

1463. 1791, Jun 1 -- Land Grant #399, Moore County, NC
Jesse Bean received 100 acres located west of McLendons Creek adjoining **Samuel Dunn**. **Thomas Ritter** and **Jesse Ritter** were chain carriers.

A. 1791, Jun 21 -- Land Grant #1259, Chatham County, NC
Jonathan Barnes received 200 acres located on Indian Creek adjoining **Moses Myrick, Starling Carrell, Barbie** and **Wilkie**. **John Barnes** and **John Wilkie** were chain carriers.

1464. 1791, Jun 22 -- Land Grant #581,

Montgomery County, NC
Hezekiah Dun received 100 acres located on Drowning Creek and the Moore County line adjoining **John English**. **John Thomas** and **Hezekiah Dun** were chain carriers.

1465.   1791, Jun 25 -- Land Grant #403, Moore County, NC
Murdock Martin received 80 acres located on McLendons Creek adjoining **John Cox**, **George Graham** and **Campbell**. **Thomas Graham** and **Augustine Lunsford** were chain carriers.

1466.   1791, Jun 28 -- Land Grant #357, Moore County, NC
William Dunn received 50 acres located on Locust Branch of Richland Creek adjoining his own line and **Donald McQueen**. **Thomas Ritter** and **Jesse Ritter** were chain carriers.

1467.   1791, Jun 28 -- Land Grant #358, Moore County, NC
William Dunn received 50 acres located on Locust Branch of Richland Creek adjoining his own line and **Donald McQueen**. **Thomas Ritter** and **Jesse Ritter** were chain carriers.

1468.   1791, Jun 28 -- Land Grant #382, Moore County, NC
Thomas Ritter received 50 acres located on both sides of Richland Creek adjoining **William Dunn** and **Malcolm McNeill**. **Jesse Bean** and **Jesse Ritter** were chain carriers.

1469.   1791, Jul 1 -- Land Grant #404, Moore County, NC
Roger Cagle received a 50 acre Land Grant located on Wolf Creek adjoining **John Hensucker** and his own line. **George Cagle** and **John Andrews** were chain carriers.

1470.   1791, Jul 9-- 1784-1797 Land Entries, Moore County, NC
#378 **Jonathan Coddell** entered 100 acres in the fork of Mill Creek adjoining **James Muse**.

1471.   1791, Jul 9-- 1784-1797 Land Entries, Moore County, NC
#379 **Christopher Cagle** entered 100 acres on Bear Creek including his own improvement and adjoining **Gilmore**'s 200 acre tract.

1472.   1791, Jul 15 -- 1784-1797 Land Entries, Moore County, NC
#381 **Simon Rheubottom** entered 50 acres located north of Richland Creek adjoining **Donald McQueen** and **Jesse Ritter**.

1473.   1791, Jul 15-- 1784-1797 Land Entries, Moore County, NC
#382 **Richard Dunn Jr**. entered 60 acres on Sings Creek adjoining his own line and **Norman McLeod**.

A.   1791, Aug 8 -- 1781-1785 Court of Pleas and Quarter Sessions Page 96-97, Chatham County, NC
Benjamin and **Aaron Tyson** have leave to keep a ferry over Deep River at the place **Jonathan Barns** formerly did and enter into bond with **Corneleous Dowd**. **Benjamin** and **Aaron Tyson** have leave to build a water grist mill at the place **Conner Dowd**'s Mill formerly stood.

1474.   1791, Aug 18 -- 1784-1795 Court of Pleas and Quarter Sessions, Moore County, NC
[*jury duty - selected participants*] **Wm. Richardson Jr.**, **Leonard Cagle**. [*jury duty next term - selected participants*] **Wm. Williamson**, **Christr. Yow**, **Wm. Manus**, **Thos. Keys**, **Stephen Richardson**, **John Caddell**, **Wm. Copeland**.

1475.   1791, Aug 18 -- 1784-1795 Court of Pleas and Quarter Sessions, Moore County, NC Page 313,315,316
[Deeds] **Joseph** and **Ruth Dunn** to **Benj. Lamb** was acknowledged
Solomon Barrett to **John McDaniel** was acknowledged
Solomon Barrett to **William McDaniel** was acknowledged
Corn. Dowd to **Richard Cheek** was acknolwedged
Wm. Smith to **John Hargrove** was acknowledged
James Alston and **John Carrell** to **Thomas Overton** was acknowledged
Robert Cox to **Murdock McAuly** was acknowledged
John Wilkins to **John Records** was proven by **John Carrell**

A.   1791, Aug 18 -- 1784-1795 Court of Pleas and Quarter Sessions, Moore County, NC Page 314

Ordered that tracts belonging to **Chas. Sherring** levied by **Reuben Shields** and tract of **James Harden** lying on Cane Patch be sold by Sheriff.

1476.   1791, Aug 18 -- 1784-1795 Court of Pleas and Quarter Sessions, Moore County, NC Page 315
Ordered that the road from **Widow Muses** to the Chatham County line at **Saml. Persons** be revived and turned across Deep River at the Island Ford. **Joseph Duckworth** appointed overseer and have the following hands to work: **Joseph Dunn Junr.**, **Francis Myrick**, **Joseph McGee**, **William Teague**, **Robt. Davis**, **Robt. Cheek**, **James Collins**, **Joseph McGee Jr.**, **Wm. Harden**, **Gabriel Harden**, **Benjn. Cooper**, **Saml. Perry**, **Richd. Upton**, **Joseph Dunn Sr.** and **Henry Powers**.

1477.   1791, Aug 18 -- 1784-1795 Court of Pleas and Quarter Sessions, Moore County, NC Page 315
Ordered that **Near Brewer** be appointed overseer of the road on the other side of the River to the Chatham line and have the following hands to work: **Benjn. Shields**, **Wm. Davis**, **Sarah Davis**, **James Brady**, **Kial Johnston**, **Wm. Cook**, **Benjn. Elkins**, **Isaac Teague**, **Drury Brewer** and **Micajah Brewer**.

1478.   1791, Aug 18 -- 1784-1797 Land Entries, Moore County, NC
#388 **Thomas Ritter** entered 50 acres adjoining **Ferquhard Campbell** and **John McSwain**.

1479.   1791, Sep 2 -- Land Grant #396, Moore County, NC
Richardson Feagan received 100 acres located on both sides of Race Path Branch of Killets Creek near the branch that runs by the courthouse adjoining his own line. **Malcom McNeill** and **Donald Munk** were chain carriers.

1480.   1791, Sep 3 -- Land Grant #381, Moore County, NC
Richardson Feagan received 50 acres located on Muses Road south of the Waggon Road near the cross path from **James Muses** to the courthouse. **Thomas Mathews** and **Needham Temples** were chain carriers.

1481.   1791, Sep 23 -- Land Grant #998, Randolph County, NC

Henry Branson [assignee of John Lathem] received 550 acres on Bear Creek adjoining Elisha Lolley. Wm. Lethem and Thos. Cost were chain carriers.

1482.   1791, Oct 2 -- Land Grant #375, Moore County, NC
William Smith Junr. received 30 acres located on south prong of Cabin Creek adjoining his own line. William Morgan and James Morgan were chain carriers.

1483.   1791, Oct 6 -- Land Grant #401, Moore County, NC
John Spivey received 60 acres located on Buffalo Creek adjoining Richard Bean and including his own house and spring. Leonard Furr and Jacob Stuts were chain carriers.

1484.   1791, Oct 7 -- Land Grant #384, Moore County, NC
Drury Richardson received 50 acres located on Buffalo Creek adjoining Zachariah Smith. Cayal Johnson and William Richardson were chain carriers.

A.   1791, Nov 16 – Deed Book E Page 231, Chatham County, NC
William Goldston deeded Elizabeth Hancock 100 acres located on Fall Creek.

1485.   1791, Nov 21-- 1784-1797 Land Entries, Moore County, NC
#395 Alexr. McIver entered 50 acres on Wet Creek adjoining John McLeod and his own line.

1486.   1791, Nov 22 -- 1784-1795 Court of Pleas and Quarter Sessions, Moore County, NC
[jury duty - selected participants] Wm. Williamson, Cristopher Yow, Wm. Mainus, Wm. Copeland, Jonathan Caddell, Zachry Smith, Jesse Ritter, John Caddell, Saml. Dunn, Solomon Barrett, Ambrose Brewer, Thomas Dunn, William Richardson, John Keys. [jury duty next term - selected participants] Zach Smith, Jos. Dunn Jr., Wm. Smith

1487.   1791, Nov 22 -- 1784-1795 Court of Pleas and Quarter Sessions, Moore County, NC Page 321
Ordered that Thomas Ritter be appointed overseer of the road in place of Thomas Muse.

1488.   1791, Nov 22-24 -- 1784-1795 Court of Pleas and Quarter Sessions, Moore County, NC Page 322,323-329
[Deeds] Two deeds from William Barrett to John McKay were proven by Archd. McBryde
Phillip and Temperance Alston to Thomas Harding Perkins was proven by Col. Richard Street
John Overton Junior to John Overton (son of Aaron) was acknowledged
William Teague to Robt. Cheek was proven by Robt. Davis
[Bill of Sale] Ralph Davis to Wm. Seal's children
William Barrett to William Baston Whitford was proven by Archd. McBryde
John Overton Senr. to John Overton Junior was acknowledged
Matthew Coggen to James Caddell was proven by Neil McLeod Esq.
Joseph McGee to Robert Davis was proven by William Teague
Leaven Hainsworth to Joseph McGee was proven by Joseph Duckworth
William Harden to Leaven Hainsworth was proven by William Davis Esq.
Cornelius Dowd to Reuben Shields was proven by Richardson Feagin

1489.   1791, Nov 22-- 1784-1797 Land Entries, Moore County, NC
#396 John Quimbey entered 100 acres on McLendons Creek adjoining Niell McLeod and Campbell.

1490.   1791, Nov 24 -- 1784-1795 Court of Pleas and Quarter Sessions, Moore County, NC Page 328
Ordered that the following be appointed to lay off a road from Moore courthouse to Chatham line: Thomas Overton, Richard Street, Richardson Feagin, James Muse, Reuben Shields, Hardy Perkins, Cornelius Dowd, Patrick Dowd, James Elkins, John Overton Jur., Josiah Maples, Thomas Muse, Elijah Bettis, John Dunlap, Samuel Elkins, William King, John Overton (son of Aaron) and Elijah Bettis Junior.

1491.   1791, Nov 24 -- 1784-1795 Court of Pleas and Quarter Sessions, Moore County, NC Page 330

Letters of Administration are granted to **James Alston** for the estate of his father, **Philip Alston** Dec'd.

1492.   1791, Dec 12 -- Land Grant #920, Moore County, NC
Hector McLean received 100 acres located on the waters of Horse Creek adjoining his own line, **William Smith**, **Newton** and the Sandhill Place. **Norman Matheson** and **Hector McLean** were chain carriers.

1493.   1791, Dec 15 -- Land Grant #359, Moore County, NC
William Barret received 25 acres located west of McLendons Creek adjoining his own line and **Farquard Campbell**. **Benjamin Caddell** and **Thomas Ritter** were chain carriers.

1494.   1792, Jan 2 -- 1784-1797 Land Entries, Moore County, NC
#403 **John Ritter** entered 100 acres located on the Morter Glade adjoining **Hinson**, **Matthews** and **McLeod**.

1495.   1792, Jan 2 -- 1784-1797 Land Entries, Moore County, NC
#405 **Niell Matthison** entered 100 acres between Horse Creek and Buffalo Creek adjoining **Newton**.

1496.   1792, Jan 4 -- Land Grant #749, Randolph County, NC
Charles Stewart received 200 acres located on Fork Creek adjoining **Mash** and **Adam Andrews**. **Luke Dempsey** and **John Lowdermilk** were chain carriers.

1497.   1792, Jan 5 -- 1784-1797 Land Entries, Moore County, NC
#406 **Hector McNiell** entered 50 acres on both sides of Buffalo Creek.

1498.   1792, Jan 5 -- 1784-1797 Land Entries, Moore County, NC
#407 **William Barrett** entered 50 acres on Suck Creek adjoining his mill land.

1499.   1792, Jan 5 -- 1784-1797 Land Entries, Moore County, NC
#408 **William Barrett** entered 50 acres south of Richland Creek adjoining **McCaskill** and **Kenneth Murchison**.

A.   1792, Jan 28 -- Will, Chatham County, NC
Will of **John Vanderford**, Dec'd. Heirs: wife **Minta**, children: **Richd.**, **John**, **Elizabeth**, **Mary**, **Salley**, **Ann**, **Hanner**, **William**, **Eli** and **Susannah**. Executors: **Minta Vanderford** and **Edmd. Waddill**. Witnesses: **Isaac Teague** and **James Deaton**. Probated Feb 1792.

1500.   1792, Feb -- 1785-1868 Index to Trial Docket, Moore County, NC Page 16
Joseph Morgan v. **John Gillum**

1501.   1792, Feb 14 -- Will Book A Page 159, Moore County, NC
Bill of Sale from **Windsor Pearce** and **Robert Anderson** to **William Williamson** for negro **Charles**. **Nicholas Nall** and **Thomas Graham** were witnesses.
Bill of Sale from **Lewis Spinks**, **Edward Moore Jur.**, **William Pearce** and **Molly Pearce** to **William Williamson** for negro **Charles**. **Hardy Davis** and **Cornelius Lathom** were witnesses. Proven in county court May 1792.

1502.   1792, Feb 14 -- Bible of Wyatt Williamson, Moore County, NC
Jemima Williamson, wife of **John Williamson**, died.

1503.   1792, Feb 15 -- Land Grant #445, Moore County, NC
Normand Morison received 50 acres located northeast of Drowning Creek adjoining his own line including his own improvement. **Donald Bethune** and **Normand Morison** were chain carriers.

1504.   1792, Feb 20 -- 1784-1795 Court of Pleas and Quarter Sessions, Moore County, NC
[*jury duty - selected participants*] **Zachy. Smith**, **Wm. Richardson Junr.**, **Joseph Dunn Jur.**, **William Smith**, **Drury Richardson**, **John Ritter**, **William Manus**, **Jacob Cagle**, **Samuel Dunn**. [*jury duty next term - selected participants*] **John Bullock**, **John Morgan**, **Leonard Furr**, **George Brazel**.

1505.   1792, Feb 20,23 -- 1784-1795 Court of Pleas and Quarter Sessions, Moore County, NC Page 333,340,345
[Deeds] **Richard Dunn** to **Joseph Allen** was acknowledged
Elijah Bettis Senr. to **Elijah Bettis Junr.** was acknowledged
Willian Dunn to **Jacob Cagle** was acknowledged

John M. Glascock to **John McNeill** was proven by **William Dunn**
Solomon Barrett to **Robert Graham** proven by **Thomas Graham**
Isaac Hill to **James Melton** proven by **Joseph Robson**
James Muse to **John Wadsworth** was proven by **Thomas Wadsworth**
William Dun to **Stephen Richardson** proven by **Jacob Cagle**

1506. 1792, Feb 21 -- 1784-1795 Court of Pleas and Quarter Sessions, Moore County, NC Page 336

Ordered that **Thomas Ritter** be appointed overseer of the road that leads by the **Widow Muses** and have the following hands to work: **Wm. Dunn** & hands, **Saml. Dunn, Ida Upton, Jesse Upton, Edward Upton, Richd. Upton, Jno. Dannelly, John Atkinson, Thos. Muse, Saml. Elkins, Jacob Stutts, Jno. Ritter, Everet Ritter, Jesse Bean, John Sowell, Jno. Quimby, Jno. McCaskill, Alexr. McCaskill, Jno. Hargrove, Kenneth Murchison, Duncan McIntosh, Martin Martin, Neil McIntosh, Simon Rheubottom** and **Ezekl. Rheubottom**.

1507. 1792, Feb 21 -- 1784-1795 Court of Pleas and Quarter Sessions, Moore County, NC Page 336
Jesse Brown came into court and was duly qualified as a Justice of the Peace.

1508. 1792, Feb 21 -- 1784-1797 Land Entries, Moore County, NC
#423 **Hardy Davis** entered 50 acres adjoining the county line and his own line.

1509. 1792, Feb 22 -- 1784-1795 Court of Pleas and Quarter Sessions, Moore County, NC Page 338-339
Isaac Dunn v. **John Cox**
Joseph Morgan v. **John Gillium**

1510. 1792, Feb 22 -- 1784-1797 Land Entries, Moore County, NC
#426 **Thomas Key** entered 100 acres west of Wet Creek.

1511. 1792, Feb 22 -- 1784-1797 Land Entries, Moore County, NC
#427 **Jacob Stutts Jr.** entered 50 acres on both sides of a path that runs from **Duncan McIntosh**'s to Long Meadow adjoining his own line.

1512. 1792, Feb 22 -- 1784-1797 Land Entries, Moore County, NC
#428 **John McKinnon** entered 50 acres west of Wet Creek adjoining his own line.

1513. 1792, Feb 23 -- 1784-1795 Court of Pleas and Quarter Sessions, Moore County, NC Page 340
Ordered that **Joseph Duckworth** be appointed overseer of the road as before and have the following hands to work: **William Davis** and hands, **Robt. Davis** and his hands, **Wm. Teague** and hands, **Jos. McGee** and hands, **Jos. Duckworth** and hands, **James Brady, Saml. Perry** and hands, **Jos. Dunn Jur.** and hands and **Francis Myrick**.

1514. 1792, Feb 23 -- 1784-1795 Court of Pleas and Quarter Sessions, Moore County, NC Page 343
Ordered that **Jno. Milton Glascock** be appointed overseer of the road in place of **Neil McLeod**
Ordered that **William Richardson** be appointed overseer of the road in place of **Stephen Richardson**.

1515. 1792, Feb 23 -- 1784-1795 Court of Pleas and Quarter Sessions, Moore County, NC Page 346

Ordered that **James Muse** be appointed overseer of the new road from the courthouse to the road near **Ruben Sheal**'s and have the following hands: **Thomas Matthews**, **William Caddell** and **John Carroway**'s hands.

1516.　1792, Mar 6 -- 1784-1797 Land Entries, Moore County, NC
#429 **Norman Mattison** entered 50 acres on Horse Creek adjoining his own line.

A.　1792, Mar 12 -- Deed Book G Page 216-217, Chatham County, NC
Jonathan Barnes (of Chatham County) deeded **Benjamin Tyson** and **Aaron Tyson** (of Moore County) 1 acre located north of Deep River including the **Barns'** Meeting House for the benefit and privilege of the Quaker society adjoining **John Wilkins**. **Josnan. Barns**, **Jeremiah Barns** and **Archd. McBryde** were witnesses.

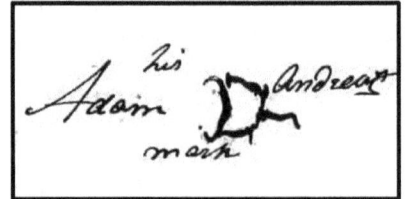

1517.　1792, Mar 24 -- Will, Randolph County, NC
Will of **Adam Andrews**, Dec'd. Heirs: wife **Peggy Andrews**, daughter **Peggy Andrews**, deceased son **Coonrod Andrews**, daughter and son-in-law **James Ludlo**, daughter **Catherine Andrews**, son **David Andrews**, son **Michael Andrews**, daughter **Susanna Lathrom**, daughter **Barberby Garner** and husband **Bradley Garner**. Executors: **William Williamson**, **Bradley Garner** and **Michael Andrews**. Witnesses: **Nicholas Nall**, **Polley Nall** and **Morah Williamson**. Proven Dec 1792.

1518.　1792, Mar 30 -- Land Grant #1782, Moore County, NC
Daniel Caddell received 100 acres located west of Wadsworth Creek. **Hugh Black Sr.** and **Hugh Black Jr.** were chain carriers.

1519.　1792, Mar 30 -- Land Grant #1785, Moore County, NC
Micajah Caddell received 150 acres located on Odom Branch of Wadsworth Creek near the Meeting House and adjoining **Thomas Wadsworth**. **Hugh Black Sr.** and **Hugh Black Jr.** were chain carriers.

1520.　1792, Mar 30 -- 1784-1797 Land Entries, Moore County, NC
#436 **Elijah Otray** entered 150 acres northwest of Bear Creek adjoining **John Bullock**.

1521.　1792, Mar 30 -- 1784-1797 Land Entries, Moore County, NC
#437 **James Key** entered 50 acres on Old Roads Branch of the Gutt, a branch of Drowning Creek adjoining **Archibald McMillan** and **James Ray**.

1522.　1792, Apr 9 -- Land Grant #459, Moore County, NC
William Newton received 50 acres located east of Cabin Creek adjoining **Cotton**, his own line and **Jacob Harvick**. **Richard Dunn Junr.** and **Edward Dudley** were chain carriers.

1523.　1792, Apr 20 -- Land Grant #1739, Moore County, NC
William Smith Junr. received 50 acres located on Big Branch of Cabin Creek below the Waggon Ford adjoining **Richard Dunn**.

1524.　1792, Apr 23 -- 1784-1797 Land Entries, Moore County, NC
#442 **John Thornton** entered 100 acres located south of Bear Creek adjoining **Ambrose Mainer**.

Land Granted on Grassy Creek, Bear Creek, Buffalo Creek, Flag Creek, Cabin Creek and Meadow Branch by the 1790s-1800s
Map prepared utilizing early land grants
[for more information see www.MooreCountyWallaces.com]

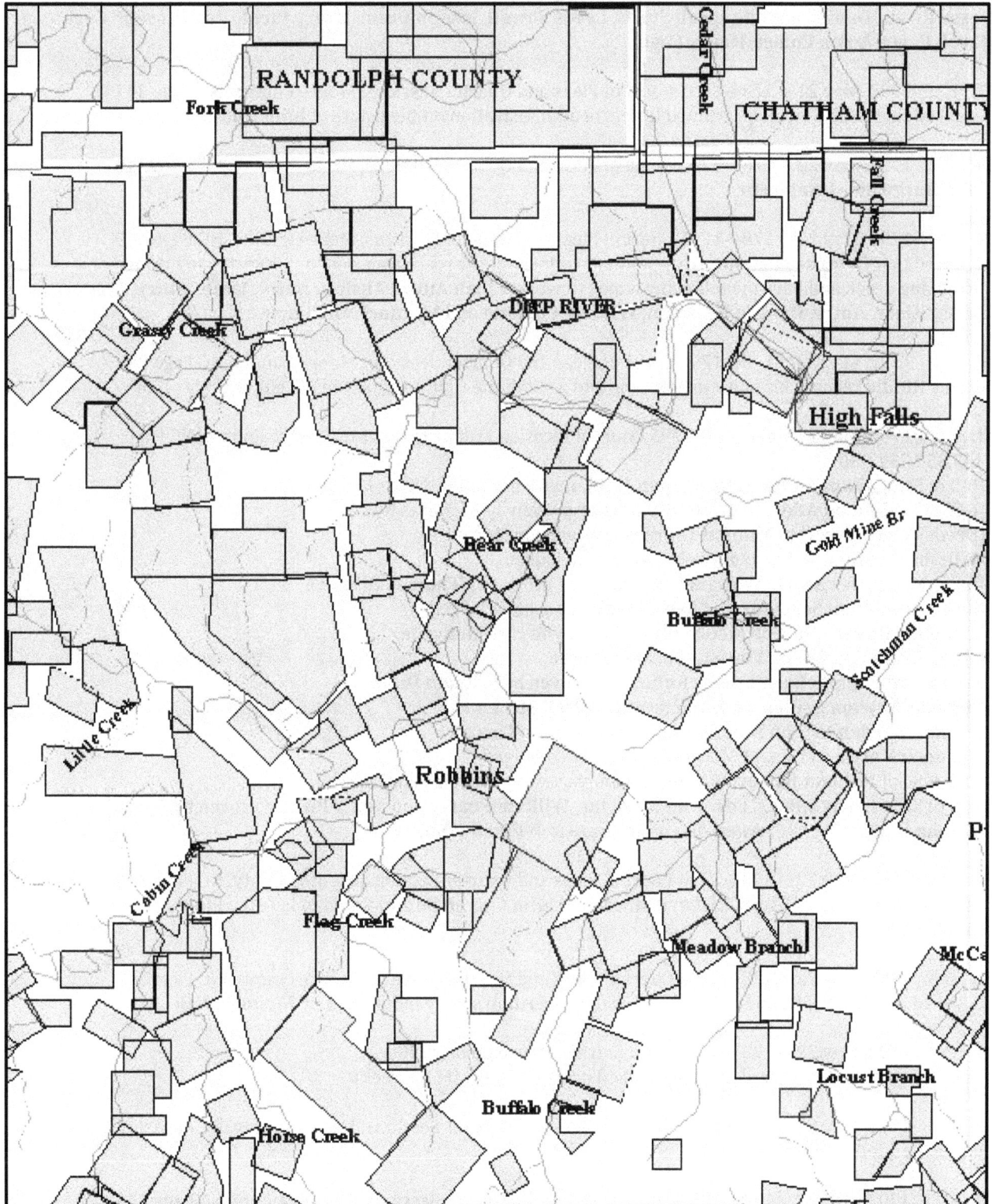

1525. 1792, May 21 -- 1784-1797 Land Entries, Moore County, NC
#448 **Isam Shuffield** entered 100 acres located east of Rattlesnake Branch of Bear Creek adjoining **John Shuffield**.

1526. 1792, May 21 -- 1784-1795 Court of Pleas and Quarter Sessions, Moore County, NC
[*jury duty - selected participants*] **Leonard Furr, John Bullock, Solm. Barrett, Drury Richardson, Thomas Ritter, John Caddell, Saml. Dunn.** [*jury duty next term - selected participants*] **Richd. Dunn Jur., Thomas Keys, Jesse Rittar, Daniel Manous, Jacob Stutts, Lewis Sowell, Joseph Dunn, Drury Richardson, Joseph Cockman, Jacob Cagle, Adam Comer, Henry Cagle.**

1527. 1792, May 21 -- 1784-1795 Court of Pleas and Quarter Sessions, Moore County, NC Page 347
Ordered that **John Sowell** be granted letters of administration on the estate of **John Quimby** Dec'd.

1528. 1792, May 22 -- 1784-1795 Court of Pleas and Quarter Sessions, Moore County, NC Page 348
John Burgwin v. **Joseph Furr**

1529. 1792, May 22 -- 1784-1795 Court of Pleas and Quarter Sessions, Moore County, NC Page 349
Ordered that **Dempsey Pelman** be appointed overseer of the road from the Poplar Spring to **Eddins'** on Drowning Creek and have the following hands to work: **Elijah Autry, Abslom Autry, James Autry, Frederick Autry, Alexr. Autry, Duncan Peterson, William Copland** and **Murdock McKenzie**

1530. 1792, May 22 -- 1784-1795 Court of Pleas and Quarter Sessions, Moore County, NC Page 350
James Riddle records his mark to be a crop and a slit in the right ear and the left ear entirely whole.

1531. 1792, May 22-24 -- 1784-1795 Court of Pleas and Quarter Sessions, Moore County, NC Page 347,350,352,356
[Bill of Sale] **Adam Andrews** to **William Williamson** proven by **Nicholas Nall**
[Bill of Sale] **Adam Andrews** to **Bradly Garner** proven by **Nicholas Nall**
[Deeds] **Wm. Barrett** to **Thomas Gilmore** was acknowledged
William Seal Junr. to **Lewis Bowell** was acknowledged
[Release] **Charles Seal** to **William Seal Junr.** was proven by **Thomas Gilmore**
[Release] **William Seal Junr.** to **Charles Seal** was acknowledged
Cornelius Dowd to **Joseph McGee** was proven by **Archd. McBryde**
James Caddell to **Adam White** was acknowledged
Ferquhard Campbell to **Thomas Rubottom** proven by **William Dunn**
Nicholas Newton to **Richard Dunn** proven by **Neil McLeod**
William Harden to **John Dunlap** was proven by **John Carroll**
Murdock Martin to **Donald McQueen** was acknowledged
[Bill of Sale] **William Barrett** to **Williamson** proven by **Nicholas Nall** Esq.
[Bill of Sale] **Lewis Spinks, Edward Moore Jur, William Pearce** and **Molly Pearce** proven by **Cornelius Latham** [*Editor's Note: Previous bills of sale were to **William Williamson**]

A. 1792, May 22 -- 1784-1795 Court of Pleas and Quarter Sessions, Moore County, NC Page 349
Ordered that **Thomas Tison, Richard Street** and **John Carrell** be appointed to lay off widow's dowry for **Jos. Gilbert,** Dec'd.

B. 1792, May 22 -- 1784-1795 Court of Pleas and Quarter Sessions, Moore County, NC Page 349
Ordered that tract of **Reuben Shields** be sold by Sheriff to satisfy judgement by **Nicholas Nall**

1532. 1792, May 22 -- 1784-1795 Land Entries, Moore County, NC
#451 **Everet Wallis** entered 50 acres located on Little Creek [Flag Creek].

1533. 1792, May 23 -- 1784-1795 Court of Pleas and Quarter Sessions, Moore County, NC Page 352
James Caddell v. **Patty Glascock**

1534. 1792, May 23 -- 1784-1795 Court of Pleas and Quarter Sessions, Moore County, NC Page 353
Letters of Administration on the estate of **John Quimby** issued to **John Sowell**.

1535. 1792, May 23 -- Land Grant #432, Moore County, NC

Mary Hines received 50 acres located on Possimond [Persimmon] Branch of Flag Creek including **Nicholas Wallace**'s improvement. **Michael Bryant** and **James Hines** were chain carriers.

1536. 1792, May 24 -- 1784-1795 Court of Pleas and Quarter Sessions, Moore County, NC Page 355
Ordered the following take the list of taxables for 1792: **Wm. Dunn** in **Barrett**'s District; **Jesse Brown** in **Morgan**'s District;

1537. 1792, May 24 -- 1784-1795 Court of Pleas and Quarter Sessions, Moore County, NC Page 357
Ordered that **Richardson Feagin** be allowed a tavern license with Col. **Thomas Overton** and **Thomas Graham** as securities.

A. 1792, Jun 5 -- Land Grant #595, Montgomery County, NC
Francis Jordan received 100 acres located on both sides of Dicks Creek adjoining his own line and **Little Berry Hicks**. **John Jordan** and **Thomas Jordan** were chain carriers.

1538. 1792, Jun 11 -- 1784-1797 Land Entries, Moore County, NC
#453 **David Davidson** entered 50 acres south of Bear Creek adjoining **Nicholas Nall**.

1539. 1792, Jun 20 -- 1784-1797 Land Entries, Moore County, NC
#458 **Allen Martin** entered 70 acres on both sides of McLendons Creek adjoining his own line.

1540. 1792, Jul 3 -- 1784-1797 Land Entries, Moore County, NC
#468 **David Kennedy** entered 100 acres on Grassie Creek adjoining **George Carriner** and **England**.

1541. 1792, Jul 3 -- 1784-1797 Land Entries, Moore County, NC
#470 **William Rite** entered 150 acres east of Wolf Creek including his own improvement and adjoining **George Brazil**.

1542. 1792, Jul 17 -- Land Grant #455, Moore County, NC
Joseph Dunn Senr. received 100 acres located on McCallums Fork of Richland Creek including **Thomas Atkinson**'s improvement. **Joseph Dunn** and **John Atkinson** were chain carriers.

1543. 1792, Jul 17 -- Land Grant #469, Moore County, NC
Joseph Dunn Senr. received 10 acres including the White Luck Quarry. **Joseph Dunn Junr.** and **John Atkinson** were chain carriers.

1544.	1792, Jul 17 -- Land Grant #470, Moore County, NC
Jesse Upton and **Richard Upton** received 100 acres located on Long Branch of McCallums Fork including **Benjamin Atkinson**'s improvement. **Joseph Dunn Junr.** and **John Atkinson** were chain carriers.

1545.	1792, Jul 23 -- 1784-1797 Land Entries, Moore County, NC
#471 **Christian McIntosh** entered 50 acres east of Richland Creek including her own improvement and adjoining **Niell McLeod**.

1546.	1792, Jul 31 -- Land Grant #431, Moore County, NC
Jacob Stutts Junr. received 50 acres located on Fork of Buffalo Creek on both sides of the path running from **Duncan McIntosh**'s to the Long Meadow adjoining **Duncan McIntosh**. **Jesse Ritter** and **John Ritter** were chain carriers.

1547.	1792, Aug 1 -- Land Grant #416, Moore County, NC
Neil Matheson received 100 acres located between Horse Creek and Buffalo Creek adjoining **Nicholas Newton**. **John Hargrove** and **Norman Morison** were chain carriers.

1548.	1792, Aug 8 -- Land Grant #460, Moore County, NC
Hector McNeill received 50 acres located on both sides of Buffalo Creek. **John Hargrove** and **Norman Matheson** were chain carriers.

1549.	1792, Aug 12 -- 1784-1797 Land Entries, Moore County, NC
#476 **James Mainer** entered 50 acres located on the drains of Bear Creek including his own improvement.

1550.	1792, Aug 12 -- Land Grant #425, Moore County, NC
Robert Cheek received 100 acres located on Deep River adjoining his own line and **John May**. **James Cheek** and **Amos Cheek** were chain carriers.

Survey plat and note:

East 34 25 / North 32.00 / Jesse & Richard Upton 100 Acres / South 32.00 / Laid down per Scale / Twenty Chains to an Inch / S 31° E ...

Pursuant to Warrant #432 Surveyed for Jesse Upton & Richard Upton one hundred Acres of Land in Moore County Beginning at a Pine on the ridge between the Long Branch of McCollums fork running thence North thirty two Chains to a Pine thence East thirty one Chains & twenty five Links thence South thirty two Chains thence West thirty one Chains & twenty five Links to the first Station July 17th 1792 per Niel McLeod Sur

Joseph (Dunn) Junr / John Atkinson — CB

1551.	1792, Aug 16 -- Land Grant #897, Moore County, NC
Neil McLeod received 100 acres located on Dry Fork of Juniper including **Overton** and **McQueens** improvement adjoining **Martin** and **Murdock McQueen**. **Shedrick Rogers** and **Jno. Fields** were chain carriers.

1552.	1792, Aug 20 -- 1784-1795 Court of Pleas and Quarter Sessions, Moore County, NC
[*jury duty - selected participants*] **Jesse Ritter, Jacob Stutts, Drury Richardson, Joseph Cockman, Jacob Cagle, Henry Cagle, John Caddell, Zachariah Smith** [*jury duty next term - selected participants*] **William Smith, James Hill, Adam Comer, John Sheffield Jr., Francis Bullock, George Carriner.**

1553.	1792, Aug 20 -- 1784-1795 Court of Pleas and Quarter Sessions, Moore County, NC Page 360
Ordered that **Robert Davis** be appointed overseer in room of **Jos. Duckworth**.

1554.	1792, Aug 20,22-23 -- 1784-1795 Court of Pleas and Quarter Sessions, Moore County, NC Page 361-362,365,368
[Deeds] **Zachariah Smith** to **Thomas Smith** was acknowledged
Eleazer Burkhead to **Jason Wordsworth** was acknowledged
Thomas Ritter and **Margaret Ritter** to **John Sowell** was proven by **Neil McLeod**

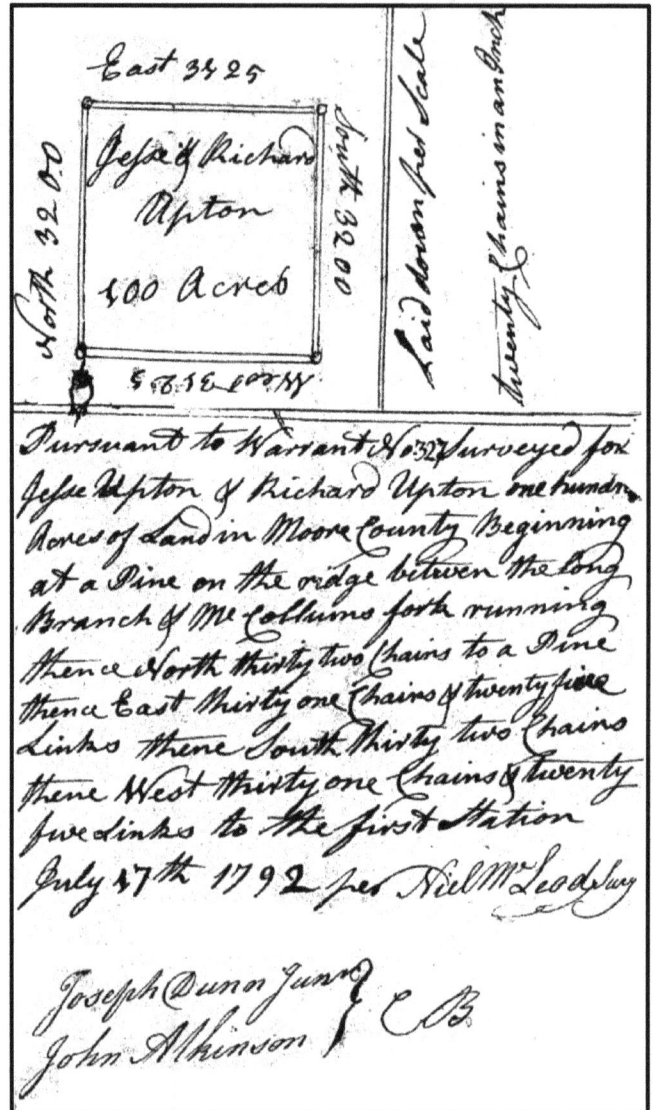

Wm. Barrett to **Robt. Davis** proven by **William Dunn**
William Finley to **Francis Bullock** proven by **Col. Thomas Overton**
Thomas Overton to **Thomas McReynolds** was acknowledged
[Bill of Sale] **Henry Person** to **Jesse Griffin** was acknowledged

1555.   1792, Aug 21 -- 1784-1795 Court of Pleas and Quarter Sessions, Moore County, NC Page 363
Ordered that **James Muse** [be appointed] overseer of the road that leads by his house and have the former hands
[to work] and **Thomas Tyner**, **Matthew Coggin** and **John Blanchet**.

1556.   1792, Aug 22 -- 1784-1795 Court of Pleas and Quarter Sessions, Moore County, NC Page 367
Ordered that **Thomas Gilmore**, **William Martin** and **John Carrel** settle with **Thos. Tyson**, **Thos. Mathews** and
Ralph Davis, administrators of **Josiah Williams'** estate.

1557.   1792, Aug 29 -- Land Grant #1319, Moore County, NC
Neil McLeod received 30 acres located on both sides of Wet Creek adjoining **Thomas Key**, **William Key**,
Murdock Bethune, **John Key** and **Donald McLeod**. **William Key** and **Thomas Key** were chain carriers.

1558.   1792, Sep 8 -- Land Grant #434, Moore County, NC
Allen Martin received 70 acres located on both sides of McLendons Creek adjoining his own line. **Donald**
McDonald and **Donald Buchanan** were chain carriers.

1559.   1792, Sep 8 -- 1784-1797 Land Entries, Moore County, NC
#479 **Ambrose Mainer** entered 50 acres located on Rocky Branch of Bear Creek adjoining his own line.

1560.   1792, Sep 18 -- 1784-1797 Land Entries, Moore County, NC
#484 **William Barrett** entered 100 acres north of Suck Creek adjoining **York**'s Cabin.

1561.   1792, Sep 26 -- 1784-1797 Land Entries, Moore County, NC
#489 **John Bullock** entered 100 acres on Persimmon Branch below where **Yew**'s and **Carriner**'s Road crosses
the branch.

1562.   1792, Sep 27 -- Land Grant #451, Moore County, NC
Nathan Fry received 100 acres located on Journey Branch of Killetts Creek adjoining **William Mears**, **James**
Muse and **James Caddell**. **Julius Glascock** and **Joseph Fry** were chain carriers.

1563.   1792, Sep 27 -- Land Grant #456, Moore County, NC
Joseph Fry received 100 acres located on Killetts Creek adjoining his own line. **Nathan Fry** and **John Milton**
Glascock were chain carriers.

1564.   1792, Sep 27 -- Land Grant #406, Moore County, NC
Patty Glascock received 100 acres located on both sides of the Waggon Road adjoining **Richardson Feagin**.
Julius Glascock and **Joseph Fry** were chain carriers.

1565.   1792, Sep 28 -- Land Grant #442, Moore County, NC
George Glascock received 50 acres adjoining his own line (formerly **Peter Salter**) and **James Muse**. **Julius**
Glascock and **Joseph Fry** were chain carriers.

1566.   1792, Oct 1 -- 1784-1797 Land Entries, Moore County, NC
#493 **John Garner** entered 100 acres adjoining **Christopher Yew**, the [Randolph] county line and his own line.

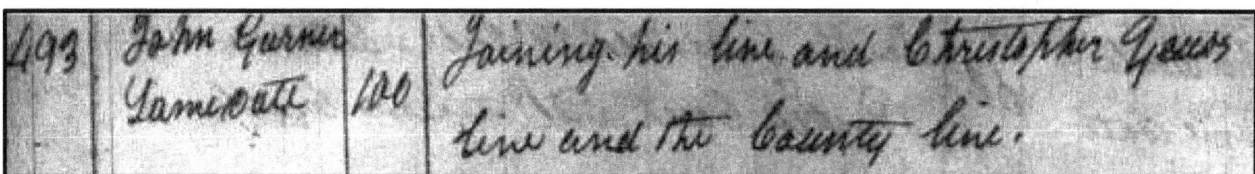

1567.   1792, Oct 7 -- Land Grant #505, Moore County, NC

Norman McKinnon received 48 acres located on Dry Fork of Mill Creek adjoining his own line. **Murdock McAulay** and **John McKinnon** were chain carriers.

1568. 1792, Oct 8 -- Land Grant #419, Moore County, NC
William Barret received 100 acres located on Suck Creek adjoining his own line, **McCaskill**, **Graham** and **McIver**. **William Martin** and **Kenneth Murchison** were chain carriers.

1569. 1792, Oct 8 -- Land Grant #2026, Moore County, NC
William Barret received 50 acres located on the drains of Richland Creek adjoining **Neil McLeod**, **McCaskill** and **Kenneth Murchison**. **John McCaskill** and **Kenneth Murchison** were chain carriers.

1570. 1792, Oct 12 -- Land Grant #415, Moore County, NC
Robert Davis received 200 acres located on Deep River adjoining **Charles Shearing**, **Robert Cheek** and his own line. **James Cheek** and **Amos Cheek** were chain carriers.

1571. 1792, Oct 20 -- 1784-1797 Land Entries, Moore County, NC
#504 **Daniel Caddell** entered 100 acres in the fork of the Dry Fork of Thomas Wadsworths Creek.

1572. 1792, Oct 25 -- Land Grant #410, Moore County, NC
John McAulay received 50 acres adjoining his own line, **Barrett**, **Dunn** and **McKinnon**. **Joel Atkins** and **Alexander Morrison** were chain carriers.

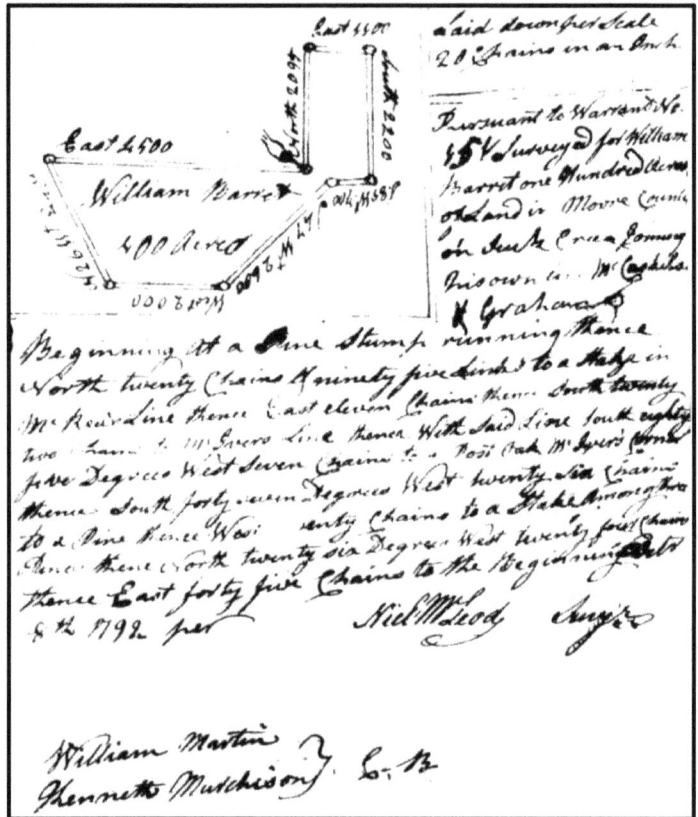

1573. 1792, Oct 29 -- Land Grant #2027, Moore County, NC
William Barret received 50 acres located on Suck Creek adjoining his mill land. **William Martin** and **Kenneth Murchison** were chain carriers.

1574. 1792, Oct 29 -- 1784-1797 Land Entries, Moore County, NC
#506 **William Martin** entered 150 acres on Yadkin Road including the place where the road from Moore Court House to Allen's Ferry crosses road where **Sam Williams** kept a store.

1575. 1792, Nov 3 -- 1784-1797 Land Entries, Moore County, NC
#509 **Michael Caddell** entered 50 acres on Adam Branch adjoining **Thomas Wadsworth** below the meeting house.

1576. 1792, Nov 6 -- Land Grant #428, Moore County, NC
John Carrel received 100 acres adjoining **Thomas Agerton** and **Peter Smith**. **Mathew Davis** and **Thomas Agerton** were chain carriers.

A. 1792, Nov 12-Dec 28 – Estate, Chatham County, NC
Estate of **William Harper** Dec'd. by Administrator **Aaron Tyson**

1577. 1792, Nov 19 -- 1784-1795 Court of Pleas and Quarter Sessions, Moore County, NC
[*jury duty - selected participants*] **James Hill**, **Adam Comer**, **William Smith**.

1578. 1792, Nov 20 -- 1784-1795 Court of Pleas and Quarter Sessions, Moore County, NC Page 371
Ordered **John Hargrove** be appointed road overseer in place of **Thos. Ritter**.

Ordered that **Wm. Brooks** be appointed road overseer in place of **Near Brewer**.

1579. 1792, Nov 20 -- 1784-1797 Land Entries, Moore County, NC
#510 **Jesse Ritter** entered 50 acres located on Locust Branch of Richland Creek adjoining **John Ritter**.

1580. 1792, Nov 20 -- 1784-1797 Land Entries, Moore County, NC
#511 **John Fushu Garner** entered 200 acres on Bear Creek adjoining **James Hogg**.

1581. 1792, Nov 20 -- 1784-1797 Land Entries, Moore County, NC
#512 **Stephen Smith** entered 50 acres on a branch of Dry Creek including **Lunsford**'s improvement.

1582. 1792, Nov 20 -- 1784-1797 Land Entries, Moore County, NC
#515 **William Martin** entered 50 acres on Yadkin Road where the road Forks that leads to **Absolam Ottray**'s commonly called Harrison's Road.

1583. 1792, Nov 20 -- 1784-1797 Land Entries, Moore County, NC
#516 **Patience Barrett** entered 50 acres on East Fork of Dry Creek of McLendons Creek adjoining **William Barrett** (now **John McLeod**).

1584. 1792, Nov 21 -- 1784-1795 Court of Pleas and Quarter Sessions, Moore County, NC Page 372
William Williamson be appointed overseer instead of **David Cagle**.

1585. 1792, Nov 20-22 -- 1784-1795 Court of Pleas and Quarter Sessions, Moore County, NC Page 370, 372, 374
[Deeds] **William Argo** to **Isaac Teague** was proven by **James Deaton**
[Bill of Sale] **Patty Glascock** to **Martin** and **Julius Glascock** was acknowledged
[Bill of Sale] **Solomon Barrett** to **Patience Barrett** was proven by **William Martin**
Anthony Seal to **William Seal** was proven by **Charles Seal**
William Barrett to **Murdock Martin** was proven by **William Martin**
Joseph Chason to **William Richardson** was proven by **John Ritter**
Solomon Barrett to **Eliza Smith** was proven by **Benj. Caddell**

A. 1792, Dec 12 -- Land Grant #724, Montgomery County, NC
William Spencer received 100 acres located west of Little River adjoining his own line. **Thos. Jinkins** and **John Simmons** were chain carriers.

B. 1792, Dec 12 -- Land Grant #739, Montgomery County, NC
William Spencer received 50 acres located east of Little River adjoining his own line (formerly **Thos. Sugg**). **Thos. Jenkins** and **Wm. Spencer** were chain carriers.

C. 1792, Dec 14 -- Land Grant #727, Montgomery County, NC
James Presnell received 150 acres located on Little River adjoining **William Wright**, Randolph County line and including **Absalom Presnell's** improvement. **Abs. Presnell** and **Benjn. Page** were chain carriers.

D. 1792, Dec 14 -- Land Grant #795, Montgomery County, NC
Edward Duval Tyler received 139 acres located on North Fork of Little River adjoining his own line and Muddy Branch. **Benjamin Page** and **Benjamin Bowling** were chain carriers.

E.   1792, Dec 15 -- Land Grant #737, Montgomery County, NC
Harbard Suggs received 100 acres located on Alder Branch of Dicks Creek. **Equilly Sugg** and **Thomas Sugg** were chain carriers.

1586.   1792, Dec 22 -- Land Grant #916, Moore County, NC
Donald McLeod received 60 acres located east of Wet Creek adjoining **John Key**, **Waddle**. **Murdock Bethune** and **Donald McLeod** were chain carriers.

1587.   1793 -- Tax List [partial], Moore County, NC
List of supernumerary taxes collected by Sheriff **Malcom McNeill** for 1793 [selected residents]: **Thomas Ritter** 1 poll and 150 acres; **James Hill** 100 acres; **Ancil Melton** 1 poll and 50 acres; **William Needham** 100 acres; **William Garner (Dutch)** 100 acres; **Robert Davis** 570 acres; **Matthews Davis** (horses); **John Cheek** (horses); **Jams. Caddwell** (horses); **Henry Cagle** (horses); **Bradly Garner** (horses); **William Cook** (horses); **William Smith** (horses). <u>**Insolvents**</u>: **James Muse** 1 poll; **Ambrose Brown** 1 poll; **William Keys** 1 poll; **William Newton** 1 poll.

1588.   1793 -- Tax List, Wake County, NC, **Captain A. Hogan**'s District [selected residents]
Joseph Britt listed 100 acres 1 white poll; **Benjn. Britt** listed 100 acres 1 white poll; **Rials Britt** listed 150 acres 1 white poll

1589.   1793, Jan 3 -- 1784-1797 Land Entries, Moore County, NC
#532 **Christopher Stutts** entered 150 acres on Club Branch of Flag Creek adjoining **Bartholomew Dunn Sr.** and **Mary Hynes**.

1590.   1793, Jan 3 -- 1784-1797 Land Entries, Moore County, NC
#538 **Alexander Kennedy** entered 100 acres adjoining **David Kennedy** and including his own improvement where he lives.

1591.   1793, Jan 3 -- 1784-1797 Land Entries, Moore County, NC
#539 **Alexander Kennedy** entered 50 acres on Persimmon Branch.

1592.   1793, Jan 3 -- 1784-1797 Land Entries, Moore County, NC
#542 **Norman Mathison** entered 50 acres on Horse Creek adjoining the Sandhill Place.

1593.   1793, Jan 5 -- 1784-1797 Land Entries, Moore County, NC
#553 **Kenneth Murchison** entered 50 acres south of Richland Creek adjoining **William Barrett**, **Niell McLeod**, **Angus McCaskill** and his own line.

1594.   1793, Jan 5 -- 1784-1797 Land Entries, Moore County, NC
#554 **Kenneth Murchison** entered 50 acres adjoining his own line and **John Hargrove**.

1595.   1793, Jan 6 -- 1784-1797 Land Entries, Moore County, NC
#558 **Thomas Ritter** entered 50 acres located on both sides of Richland Creek adjoining **McNeill**.

1596.   1793, Jan 10 -- 1784-1797 Land Entries, Moore County, NC
#563 **William Richardson** entered [blank] acres on Morter Glade and Buffalo Creek adjoining **Joseph Chason**.

1597.   1793, Jan 12 -- 1784-1797 Land Entries, Moore County, NC
#566 **Peter Hair** entered 50 acres north of Wolf Creek adjoining his own line.

A.   1793, Jan 12 -- Deed Book H Page 95-96, Chatham County, NC
Mary Dowd (of Moore County) deeded **Sampson Brewer** 300 acres located on Fall Creek adjoining **Golston**. The land was granted to **Connor Dowd**. **Archd. McBryde**, **Rosana Dowd** and **Edw. Griffin** were chain carriers.

1598.   1793, Jan 12 -- 1784-1797 Land Entries, Moore County, NC
#567 **William Richardson** entered 100 acres on Kings Street adjoining **Chason**.

1599. 1793, Jan 15 -- 1784-1797 Land Entries, Moore County, NC
#568 **Joseph Dunn** entered 150 acres on both sides of Richland Creek adjoining his own line.

1600. 1793, Jan 18 -- Land Grant #479, Moore County, NC
Thomas Key received 100 acres adjoining his own line. **Thos. Ward** and **John Key** were chain carriers.

1601. 1793, Jan 18 -- 1784-1797 Land Entries, Moore County, NC
#570 **Reubin Freeman** entered 100 acres on both sides of Wolf Creek adjoining his own line.

A. 1793, Jan 30 -- Deed Book G Page 262, Chatham County, NC
Edward Stuart deeded **Aaron Lindly** 40 acres located on Cain Creek adjoining **William McPherson** and **Braxton**. **Thomas Lindly** and **Wm. Lindly** were witnesses.

B. 1793, Feb 1 -- Land Grant #1261, Chatham County, NC
John Wilkins received 600 acres located on both sides of Line Creek adjoining his own line, the [Moore] County line, **Barns**, **Myrick** and **Gilbert**. **Seth Barnes** and **John Records** were chain carriers.

1602. 1793, Feb 7 -- 1784-1797 Land Entries, Moore County, NC
#579 **William Richardson** entered 50 acres north of Buffalo Creek adjoining **Zachariah Smith** or the line where he formerly lived.

1603. 1793, Feb 7 -- 1784-1797 Land Entries, Moore County, NC
#580 **Drury Richardson** entered 50 acres north of Buffalo Creek adjoining **William Richardson**.

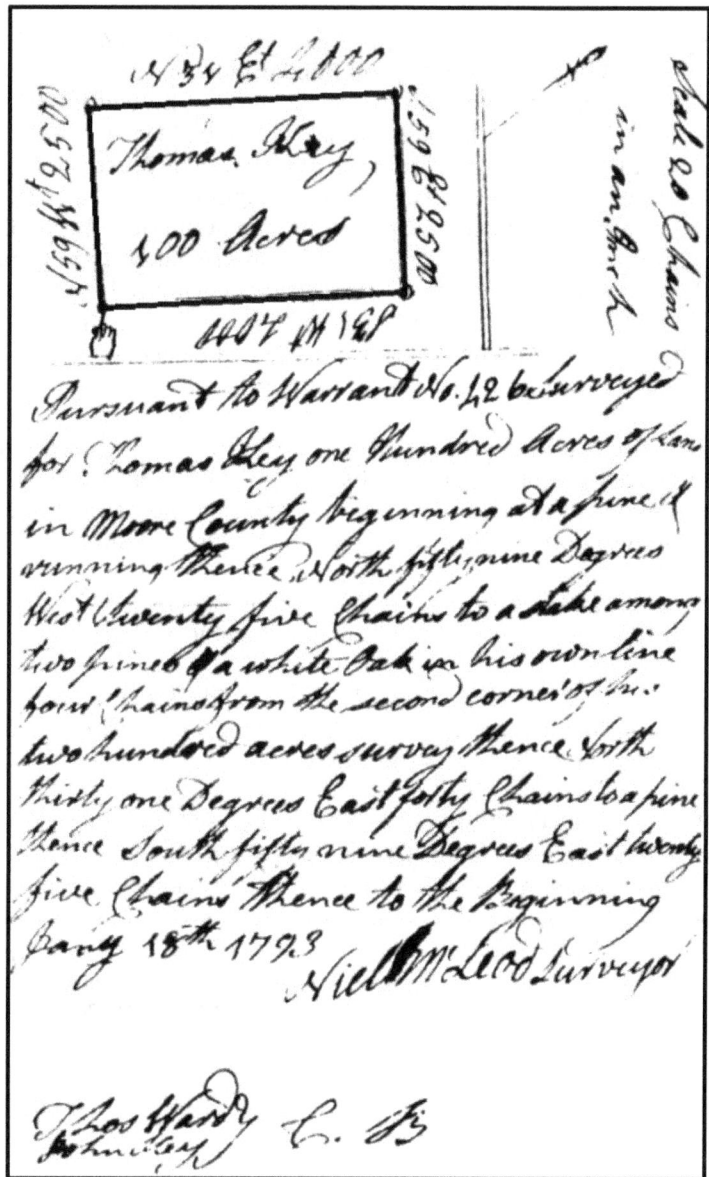

1604. 1793, Feb 18 -- 1784-1795 Court of Pleas and Quarter Sessions, Moore County, NC
[*jury duty - selected participants*] **Leonard Furr, Samuel Dunn, John Caddell, Jonathan Caddell**. [*jury duty next term - selected participants*] **William Dunn, Francis Myrick, James Hill, Lewis Sowell, Bartholomew Dunn Jur.**

A. 1793, Feb 18 -- Deed Book G Page 28-29, Chatham County, NC
Samuel Person (of Moore County) deeded **Ely McManus** 250 acres located on Fall Creek of Deep River. **Larrance McManus** and **Nathan McManus** were witnesses.

B. 1793, Feb 18 -- 1784-1795 Court of Pleas and Quarter Sessions, Moore County, NC Page 376
Robert Cheek records his mark as a crop and a slit in the left ear and an under half moon in the right

1605. 1793, Feb 19 -- 1784-1795 Court of Pleas and Quarter Sessions, Moore County, NC Page 377
Francis Bullock and **Lewis Gardiner** were duly qualified and subscribed the test. [*Editor's Note: Sworn in as Justice of the Peace.*]

1606. 1793, Feb 19 -- 1784-1795 Court of Pleas and Quarter Sessions, Moore County, NC Page 378
The following were appointed constable**s: Benjamin Caddell** and **Donald McQueen** [District #6]; **Benjamin Cooper** and **David Cagle** [District #8].

1607. 1793, Feb 19-21 -- 1784-1795 Court of Pleas and Quarter Sessions, Moore County, NC Page 378,386-390
[Deeds] **William Barrett** to **John Buchannon** was proven by **Angus Campbell**
Peter Salter to **James Caddell** was proven by **John Caddell**
William Hancock to **Samuel Dunn** was acknowledged
William Barrett to **John Johnston** was proven by **Murdoch McIntosh**
George and **Mary Brazell** to **William Wright** was proven by **Roger Cagle**
John Phillips to **Mark Phillips** was proven by **Thomas Tyson** Esq.
William Barrett to **William Hancock** was proven **William Dunn**
Richard Dunn to **William Newton** was acknowledged
Gabriel Harden to **William Davis** proven by **Jesse Griffin**
John McLeod to **Richard Dunn** was acknowledged
Richard Dunn Senr. to **Richard Dunn Jur.** proven by **Hezekiah Dunn**
William Barrett to **Angus Campbell** was proven by **John Buchannon**
William Stroud to **Leinear Brewer** was proven by **Edmond Waddell**
Jesse Healy to **Bryan Borroughs** proven by **William Waddell**
William Stroud to **Edmond Waddill** proven by **Leinear Brewer**
John Johnston to **John Lawley** proven by **James Gardiner**

1608. 1793, Feb 19 -- 1784-1797 Land Entries, Moore County, NC
#581 **John Bullock** entered 50 acres south of Bear Creek.

1609. 1793, Feb 20 -- 1784-1795 Court of Pleas and Quarter Sessions, Moore County, NC Page 379
William Dickinson gave bond with **William Davis** and **Willis Dickenson** securities for the baseborn child begotton on the body of **Sarah Harris**.

1610. 1793, Feb 20-21 -- 1784-1795 Court of Pleas and Quarter Sessions, Moore County, NC Page 381,384
Ordered that **Col. Thomas Overton**, **Malcolm McNeill** and **Neil McLeod** settle with **Nicholas Nall**, Executor of **John Williamson**, Dec'd. Return of the estate made by **Nicholas Nall** be returned and filed.

1611. 1793, Feb 20 -- 1784-1795 Court of Pleas and Quarter Sessions, Moore County, NC Page 383
Saml. Dunn records his mark to be a crop and a hole in the left ear and a swallow fork in the right ear

1612. 1793, Feb 21 -- 1784-1795 Court of Pleas and Quarter Sessions, Moore County, NC Page 384
Nichl. Nall Esq. came into court and delivered **Hardy Davis** as his security for a writ brought by **James Lowdlo** against **Davis** who gives **Derius Ramage** in his stead.

1613. 1793, Feb 21 -- 1784-1797 Land Entries, Moore County, NC
#587 **Peter Shamburger** entered 75 acres on the head of Grassie Creek near the mouth of Haw Branch.

1614. 1793, Mar 8 -- Deed Book 7 Page 211, Randolph County, NC
Aaron Hill deeded **Keziah Searcy** 30 acres located south of Deep River called the mine land that **William Searcy** sold to **Aaron Hill** adjoining **Nicholas Nall**. Proven by **Edmond Waddell** Aug 1797.

1615. 1793, Mar 13 -- Land Grant #941, Moore County, NC
Patience Barrett received 50 acres located on east prong of McLendons Creek adjoining **John McLeod** and **William Barrett**. **Murdoch Martin** and **John McLeod** were chain carriers.

1616. 1793, Mar 16 -- Land Grant #514, Moore County, NC
Jacob Harvick received 25 acres located on Cabin Creek adjoining **Thomas Gilmore**, **Richard Dunn** and his own line.

1617. 1793, Mar 20 -- Land Grant #1516, Moore County, NC
Angus McQueen received 150 acres located on north of Deep River on Tysons Creek and the Chatham County line adjoining **Robert Cheek**. **Wm. Phillips** and **James Collins** were chain carriers.

1618. 1793, Mar 25 -- Deed, Book 5 Page 78-79, Orange County, NC
George Horner Senr. deeded **George Horner Junr.** 100 acres on Mill Creek of Little River adjoining **Abercrombie**, **Dunnegan**, **Thomas Gray** and **Horn**. **John Watson** and **Joseph Brittan** were witnesses. Proven Feb 1794.

1619. 1793, Apr 10 -- Land Grant #1549, Moore County, NC
Hardy Davis received 19.5 acres located on Bear Creek and the Randolph County line adjoining **Michael Hart**, his own line. **Bailey Needham** and **William Davis** were chain carriers.

1620. 1793, Apr 15 -- Land Grant #1547, Moore County, NC
Christopher Cagle received 100 acres located north of Bear Creek including his improvement and adjoining **Gilmore**. **Henry Cagle** and **William Cagle** were chain carriers. **Hardy Davis** attested that the purchase money for the land had been paid.

1621. 1793, Apr 19 -- 1784-1797 Land Entries, Moore County, NC
#601 **Thomas Ritter** entered 50 acres located on McLendons Creek adjoining **John McKinnon**.

1622. 1793, Apr 20 -- 1784-1797 Land Entries, Moore County, NC
#602 **William Barrett** entered 50 acres on McLendons Creek adjoining **McRae** and **Widow Bathune**.

1623. 1793, May 20 -- 1784-1795 Court of Pleas and Quarter Sessions, Moore County, NC
[*jury duty - selected participants*] **Lewis Sowell**, **Francis Myrick**, **Bartholomew Dunn**, **Zachariah Smith**, **William Smith**, **John Caddell**, **Jonathan Caddell**, **Christopher Yew**, **John Spivy**, **James Caddell**.

1624. 1793, May 21-23 -- 1784-1795 Court of Pleas and Quarter Sessions, Moore County, NC Page 396,400-402
[Deeds] **William Barrett** to **Alexr. McLeod** was proven by **Archd. McBryde**
Thomas Tyson to **Samuel Womble** was acknowledged
Thomas Collins to **William Barret** was proven by **John Cameron** Esq.
William Barrett to **Norman McDonald** was proven by **John Cameron** Esq.
Robert Paterson to **William Dunn** proven by **Jesse Griffin**
William Barrett to **Thos. Cole** proven by **Robert Boals**
William Barrett to **Robert Boals** proven by **Thos. Cole**

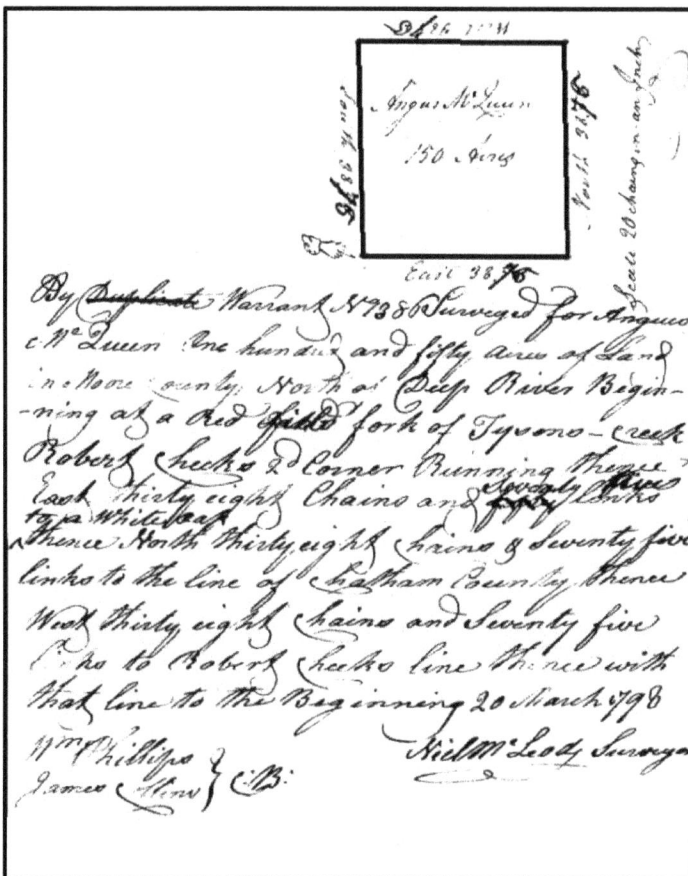

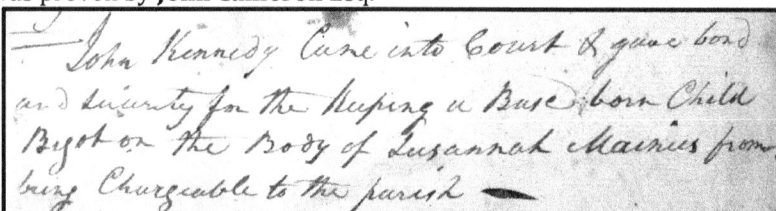

1625. 1793, May 21-Aug 22 -- 1784-1795 Court of Pleas and Quarter Sessions, Moore County, NC Page 396,416
John Kennedy gave bond for a base born child begot on the body of **Susannah Mainess**.

1626.　　1793, May 21 -- 1784-1795 Court of Pleas and Quarter Sessions, Moore County, NC Page 397
Alexr. Kennedy was appointed constable in District #8.

1627.　　1793, May 21 -- 1784-1795 Court of Pleas and Quarter Sessions, Moore County, NC Page 397
Joseph Furr listed as being exempt from poll Tax in 1792.

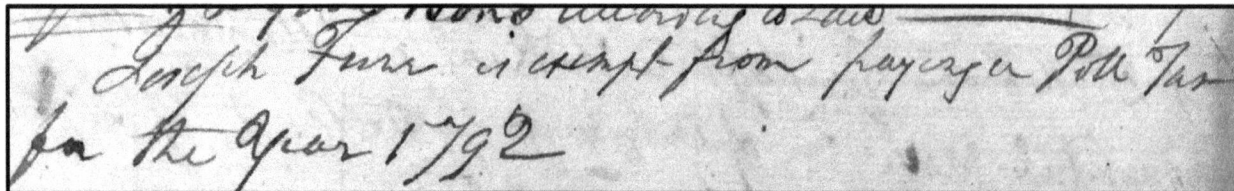

1628.　　1793, May 21 -- 1784-1797 Land Entries, Moore County, NC
#603 **Jesse Ritter** entered 100 acres adjoining his own line and **John McSwain**.

1629.　　1793, May 21 -- 1784-1797 Land Entries, Moore County, NC
#605 **Neill McLeod** entered 150 acres adjoining **Nicholas Nall**, **Richard Bird**, **Williamson** and **Leonard Hart**.

1630.　　1793, May 21 -- 1784-1797 Land Entries, Moore County, NC
#606 **William Barrett** entered 100 acres south of McLendons Creek adjoining **James Caddell**.

1631.　　1793, May 22 -- 1784-1795 Court of Pleas and Quarter Sessions, Moore County, NC Page 400
Ordered that **John Jackson**'s land and property be valued by **Neil McLeod**, **Edward Cox** and **Thos. Graham**.

1632.　　1793, May 23 -- 1784-1795 Court of Pleas and Quarter Sessions, Moore County, NC Page 403
Ordered the following take the list of taxables: **Francis Bullock** [District #8].

1633.　　1793, May 23 -- 1784-1795 Court of Pleas and Quarter Sessions, Moore County, NC Page 404
Ordered that a road be laid from the County line near **Mr. Gardiners** to the White Ponds and have the following hands to work: **Lewis Gardener, David Kennedy, John Morgan, John Sheffield Jur., Jno. Sheffield Senr., William Morgan (Capt.), Peter Shamburger, William Williamson, William Smith Jur., Lewis Sowell, Everet Smith, Thos. Key, John Morgan** and **Danl. Manners**.

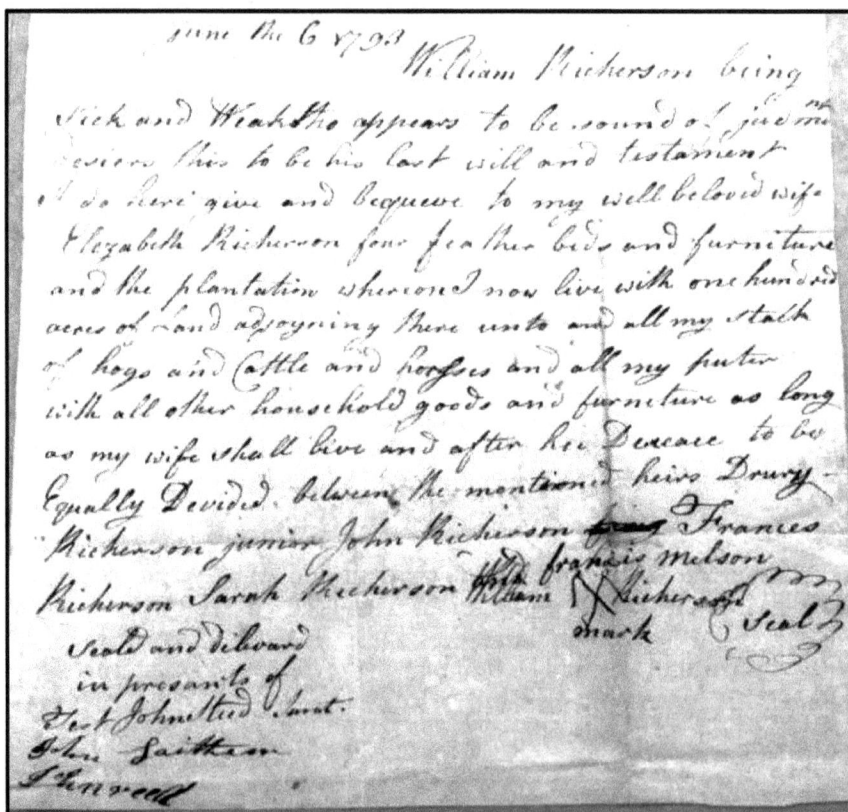

1634.　　1793, Jun 1 -- Deed Book G Page 117, Chatham County, NC
John Argo [of Randolph County] deeded **Zachariah Smith** [of Moore County] 250 acres located on Cedar Creek and [Moore] County line. **Edmd. Waddill** and **Isaac Smith** were witnesses.

1635.　　1793, Jun 6-- Will, Randolph County, NC
Will of **William Richardson**, Dec'd. Heirs: wife **Elizabeth** [*plantation and 100 acres*], **Drury Richardson Junior**,

John Richardson, **Francis Richardson**, **Sarah Richardson** and **Frances Melson**. Witnesses: **John Steed**, **John Latham** and **John Reed**. Proven Mar 1794.

1636.　　1793, Jun 8 -- Land Grant #1793a, Moore County, NC
William Davis received 150 acres located north of Deep River on Big Branch adjoining **Howel Brewer**. **Jesse Griffin** and **Henry Parson** were chain carriers.

1637.　　1793, Jun 12 -- Deed Book 5, Page 73, Randolph County, NC
Richard Cox deeded **Benjamin Page** 100 acres located near the head of Fork Creek. Granted to **William Searcy**. **Caleb Cox, Junr.** and **William Bland** were witnesses.

1638.　　1793, Jul 15 -- Land Grant #1088, Moore County, NC
John Ritter received 100 acres located on Morter Glade adjoining **Hinson** and **Mathews**. **William Richardson** and **Jesse Ritter** were chain carriers.

A.　　1793, Jul 16 -- Land Grant #1258, Chatham County, NC
John Powers received 100 acres located on waters of Deep River adjoining his own line, **Vanderford** and the Randolph County line. **Gilliam Powers** and **David Powers** were chain carriers.

1639.　　1793, Jul 23 -- 1784-1797 Land Entries, Moore County, NC
#613 **Mary Sowel** entered 50 acres on Suck Creek adjoining **Barrett**, her own line, **McRae** and **McKaskel**.

1640.　　1793, Jul 29 -- Land Grant #1719, Moore County, NC
George Williams received 50 acres located on Flag Creek including his improvement adjoining **Bartholomew Dunn**. **James Williams** and **George Cagle** were chain carriers. [*Editor's Note: **Jeremiah Williams**, **Thomas Williams**, **James Williams** and **Bartholomew Dunn** deeded to **William Williams** 1823 --> **William Williams** and **Nancy Sowell** deeded to **George Davis** 1830*]

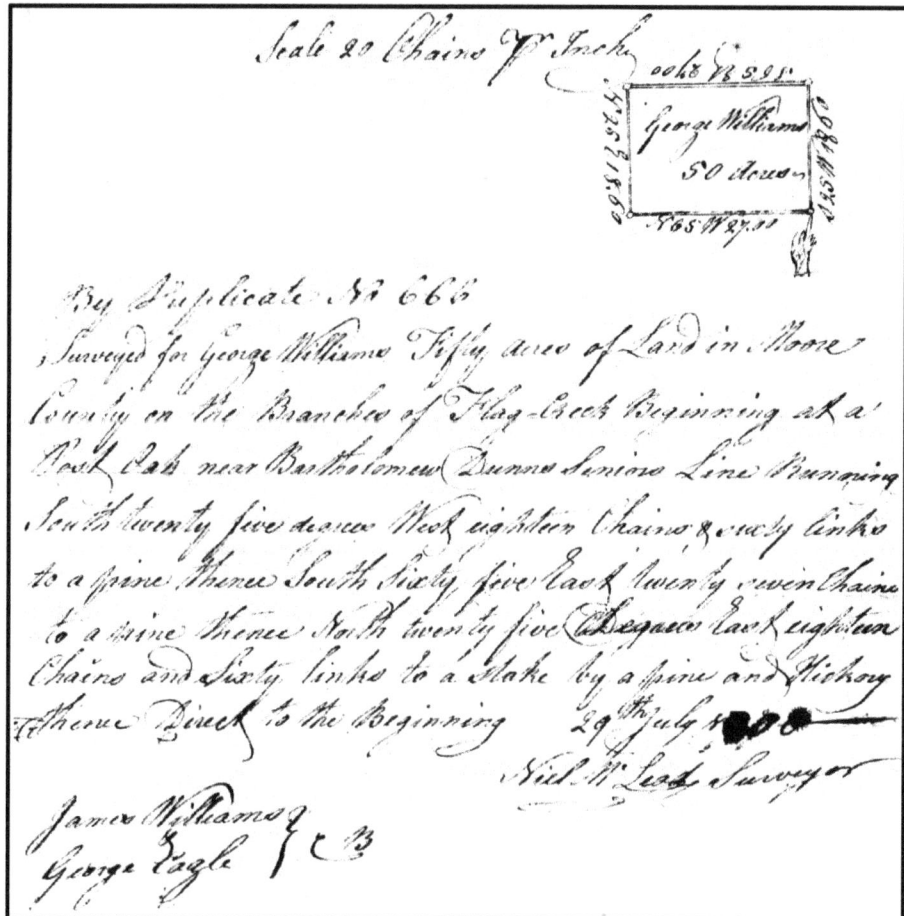

1641.　　1793, Aug 3 -- Cane Creek [Quaker] Meeting Women's Minutes Page 181, Alamance County, NC
Hannah Atkinson formerly **Dunn** was disowned for marrying outside the unity of friends.

1642.　　1793, Aug 9 -- 1784-1797 Land Entries, Moore County, NC
#616 **Bryan Burroughs** entered 100 acres on Buffalo Creek including the Good Spring.

1643.　　1793, Aug 9 -- 1784-1797 Land Entries, Moore County, NC
#617 **James Thornton** entered 50 acres west of Grassie Creek adjoining **Benjamin Cooper**.

1644.　　1793, Aug 9 -- 1784-1797 Land Entries, Moore County, NC
#618 **James Thornton** entered 50 acres north of Buffalow Creek adjoining his own line.

1645.   1793, Aug 9 -- 1784-1797 Land Entries, Moore County, NC
#619 **Robert Bird** entered 50 acres adjoining his own line including the Paley Bridge.

1646.   1793, Aug 9 -- 1784-1797 Land Entries, Moore County, NC
#622 **John McLeod** entered 50 acres between Horse Creek and Deep Creek at the Big Branch.

1647.   1793, Aug 9 -- 1784-1797 Land Entries, Moore County, NC
#623 **John McLeod** entered 50 acres on the Yadkin Road between the head of Horse Creek and the branches of Joes Creek.

1648.   1793, Aug 9 -- 1784-1797 Land Entries, Moore County, NC
#624 **Darius Ramage** entered 100 acres on the road the west side of the White Pond.

1649.   1793, Aug 12 -- 1784-1797 Land Entries, Moore County, NC
#625 **Samuel Perry** entered 100 acres on both sides of Buffalow Creek at the Steep Bottom Ford adjoining **John Askins**.

1650.   1793, Aug 12 -- 1784-1797 Land Entries, Moore County, NC
#626 **Samuel Perry** entered 100 acres south of Deep River adjoining **William England**'s big fall tract and the old **Benton** [**Barton**?] field.

1651.   1793, Aug 12 -- 1784-1797 Land Entries, Moore County, NC
#627 **Samuel Perry** entered 25 acres adjoining his own line where he now lives.

1652.   1793, Aug 14 -- Land Grant #526, Moore County, NC
Darius Ramage received 60 acres located east of Drowning Creek on the School House Branch adjoining his own line. **Alexr. Otrey** and **Simon Fraser** were chain carriers.

1653.   1793, Aug 14 -- Land Grant #1779, Moore County, NC
James McDowel received 100 acres located on Rogers Creek and the Chatham County line and Cox's old road adjoining the **Betty Phillips** place. **James Harden** and **John Stinson** were chain carriers.

1654.   1793, Aug 19 -- 1784-1795 Court of Pleas and Quarter Sessions, Moore County, NC
[*jury duty - selected participants*] **Jesse Ritter, Jacob Stutts, Joseph Cockman, Joseph Dunn, Thomas Keys, Richd. Dunn, Danl. Mainus, Adam Comer, William Smith, Absalom Autry, Hardy Davis.** [*jury duty next term - selected participants*] **Joseph Allen Jr., David Kennedy, John Hair, William Wright, Jacob Cagle.**

1655.   1793, Aug 20 -- 1784-1797 Land Entries, Moore County, NC
#630 **David Kennedy** entered 50 acres at the Green Spring adjoining his own line.

1656.   1793, Aug 21 -- 1784-1795 Court of Pleas and Quarter Sessions, Moore County, NC Page 408

Ordered that a road be laid from **John Garner**'s to **Nall**'s Mill and work the following hands: **John Garner, Alexander Kennedy, George Carriner, Christopher Yew, Owen Carpenter, Edward Moore, William Cook, Ambrose Brewer, Benjamin Cooper, Ambrose Mainus, Hardy Davis, Samuel Perry, Bryan Boroughs, Benjamin Elkins, Kial Johnston** and **Samuel Martindale**.

1657.   1793, Aug 21 -- 1784-1795 Court of Pleas and Quarter Sessions, Moore County, NC Page 410

Ordered that **Joseph McGee Jur**. be appointed overseer of the road from **Nall**'s Mill downwards instead of **Leonard Furr** and have the same hands.

1658.   1793, Aug 21 -- 1784-1795 Court of Pleas and Quarter Sessions, Moore County, NC Page 411
Mary McDonald v. **James Caddell**. Petition for Dower. After hearing petition and two deeds from the Sheriff of Cumberland and from **Warner** to **Cadell**, the court determines that's **McDonald** is not eligible for dower.

1659.   1793, Aug 21 -- 1784-1795 Court of Pleas and Quarter Sessions, Moore County, NC Page 414
Ordered that the following hands work on the road from the County line near **John Garner** to the Black Ponds: **John Sheffield Jur., Lewis Sowell, Joseph Allen, William Smith Jur., William Newton, John Hair, Thomas Keys, Wm. Williamson, Danl. Mainus, David Kennedy, Wm. Morgan Jur., Wm. Morgan (Capt), Geo. Cagle** (son of **John**) and **William Mainus**.

1660.   1793, Aug 22 -- 1784-1795 Court of Pleas and Quarter Sessions, Moore County, NC Page 416
[Deeds] **Jesse Muse** to **John Wadsworth** was acknowledged
Aaron Tyson to **Patrick Dowd** was prove by **Archibald McBryde**

1661.   1793, Aug 22 -- 1784-1795 Court of Pleas and Quarter Sessions, Moore County, NC Page 419
Ordered that the children of the late **John Jackson** be delivered to **Geo. Jackson** his executor.

A.   1793, Sep 2 – Deed Book G Page 129, Chatham County, NC
Lawrence McManus deeded **Benjamin Williams** (of Randolph County) 400 acres located on Fall Creek and the mouth of Ocony Branch having been deeded to **McManus** from **Matthew Ramsey** and formerly owned by **Fox Farmer**. **John Lambert Senior** and **J. Lambert** were witnesses.

1662.   1793, Sep 7 -- Land Grant #502, Moore County, NC
John Overton Junr. received 100 acres located on Watery Branch including **Reuben Shealdes**' improvement. **Elijah Bettis** and **Reuben Sheals** were chain carriers.

1663.   1793, Sep 7 -- Land Grant #506, Moore County, NC
John Overton Junr. received 150 acres located on Governors Creek adjoining **John Overton Senr**. **Elijah Bettis** and **Reuben Sheales** were chain carriers.

1664.   1793, Sep 10 -- 1784-1797 Land Entries, Moore County, NC
#638 **Jeremiah Wilson** entered 100 acres on Grassie Creek adjoining **Peter Shamburger** and his own line on the Haw Branch.

1665.   1793, Sep 10 -- 1784-1797 Land Entries, Moore County, NC
#639 **William Williamson** entered 100 acres adjoining **Richard Bird**.

1666.   1793, Sep 10 -- 1784-1797 Land Entries, Moore County, NC
#640 **Lewis Spinks** entered 100 acres south of Reedy Creek adjoining the county line and **Cash**.

1667.   1793, Sep 10 -- 1784-1797 Land Entries, Moore County, NC
#641 **George Carriner** entered 50 acres southwest of Grassie Creek adjoining his own line and **Christopher Yew**.

1668.   1793, Sep 12 -- Land Grant #494, Moore County, NC
William Hancock received 100 acres located on south of Deep River adjoining **Robert Cheek**. **Benjamin Gilbert** and **Jas.** [page torn] were chain carriers.

1669.   1793, Sep 12 -- Land Grant #1108, Moore County, NC
Randolph Cheek received 150 acres located on north of Deep River adjoining his own line and **Gabriel Johnston**. **Benjamin Gilbert** and **William Hancock** were chain carriers.

1670.   1793, Sep 13 -- Land Grant #1735, Moore County, NC
John Dunlap received 250 acres located on both sides of McLendons Creek below confluence of Richland Creek adjoining **John Overton**. **Robert Dickinson** and **John Dunlap** were chain carriers.

1671.   1793, Sep 16 -- Deed Book 1, Page 141, Randolph County, NC
Charity Andrews, **Roger** and **Catherine Cagle**, **Elizabeth Curtis**, **David Andrews** and **Eve Andrews** deeded **William Armstead** 100 acres located on Fork Creek at the mouth of Rock Creek. Part of a tract granted to **Adam Andrews** Dec'd. and willed to heirs of **Conrad Andrews**. **Winsor Pearce** was a witness.

1672.   1793, Sep 19 -- Land Grant #484, Moore County, NC
Ambrose Maness received 50 acres located in the Rocky Branch of Bear Creek adjoining his own line. **David Kennedy** and **John Kennedy** were chain carriers.

1673.   1793, Sep 19 -- Land Grant #508, Moore County, NC
Everet Wallace received 50 acres located in the fork of Little Creek[Flag Creek]. **John Spivey** and **Neil McLeod** were chain carriers.

1674.   1793, Sep 19 -- Land Grant #1780, Moore County, NC
Ambrose Maness received 100 acres located west of Bear Creek below the Waggon Road adjoining **Nall**, **Brewer** and **Drury Richardson**. **David Kennedy** and **John Kennedy** were chain carriers.

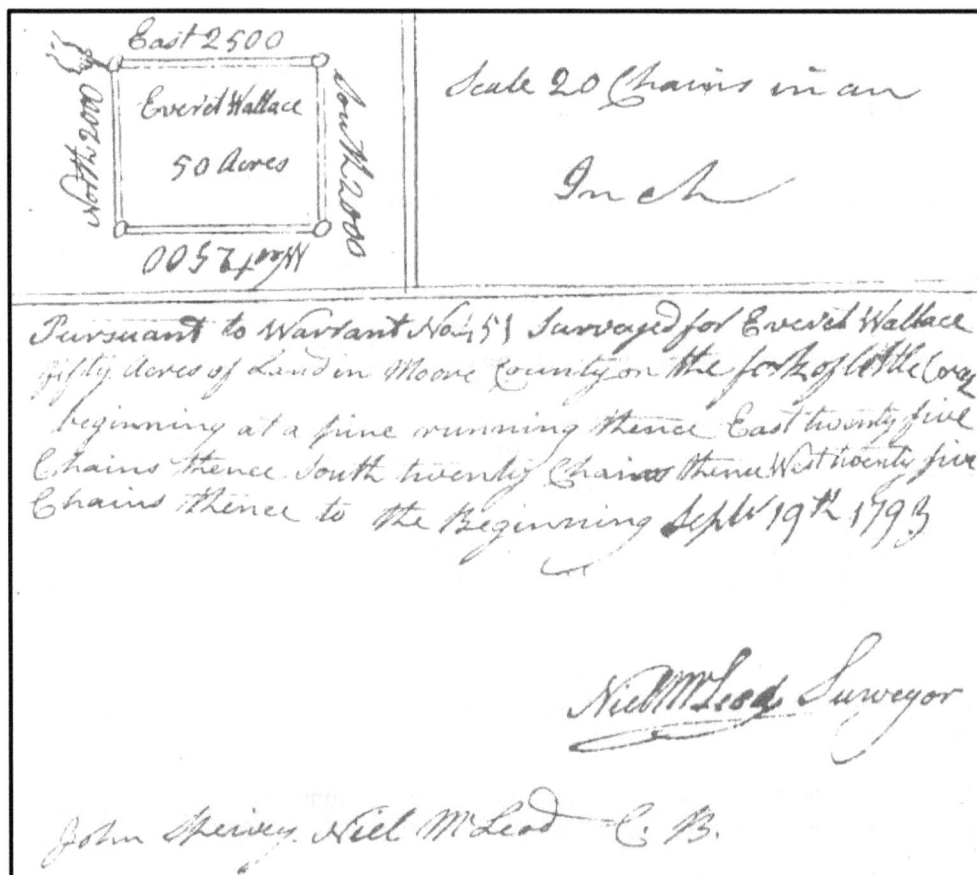

1675.   1793, Sep 20 -- Land Grant #497, Moore County, NC
Alexander Kennedy received 100 acres including his own improvement and where he now lives adjoining **George Carringer** and **David Kennedy**.

1676.   1793, Sep 21 -- Land Grant #480, Moore County, NC

Alexander Kennedy received 50 acres located on Possimond Branch adjoining **George Carriner**. **Bailey Loving** and **Alexr. Kennedy** were chain carriers.

1677.   1793, Sep 29 -- Deed Book 5, Page 90, Randolph County, NC
John Powers deeded **James Powers** 200 acres located on Flat Creek adjoining Chatham County line. **William Searcy**, **Arthur Reed** and **Sarah Searcy** were witnesses.

1678.   1793, Sep 25 -- Land Grant #486, Moore County, NC
Peter Hair received 50 acres adjoining his own line, **Freeman** and **John Hair**. **John Hare** and **Reuben Freeman** were chain carriers.

1679.   1793, Sep 25 -- Land Grant #488, Moore County, NC
Reuben Freeman received 100 acres adjoining **Armstrong**. **John Hare** and **Peter Hare** were chain carriers.

1680.   1793, Sep 25 -- Land Grant #492, Moore County, NC
Isom Shuffield received 100 acres located east of Rattlesnake Branch adjoining **John Shuffield**. **Everet Shuffield** and **Isom Shuffield** were chain carriers.

1681.   1793, Sep 26 -- 1784-1797 Land Entries, Moore County, NC
#646 **John Hair** entered 100 acres located on both sides of Wolf Creek adjoining **John Sheffield**.

1682.   1793, Sep 26 -- 1784-1797 Land Entries, Moore County, NC
#647 **John Hair** entered 50 acres on both sides of Wolf Creek adjoining his own line and **John Sheffield**.

1683.   1793, Sep 26 -- 1784-1797 Land Entries, Moore County, NC
#648 **John Hair** entered 50 acres south of Wolf Creek adjoining his own line.

1684.   1793, Sep 28 -- 1784-1797 Land Entries, Moore County, NC
#649 **George Carriner** entered 50 acres on Grassie Creek including **Willis Brewer**'s improvement.

1685.   1793, Sep 28 -- 1784-1797 Land Entries, Moore County, NC
#650 **George Carriner** entered 50 acres located north of Grassie Creek adjoining his own line, **Honsucker** and **Lewis Garner**.

1686.   1793, Sep 28 -- 1784-1797 Land Entries, Moore County, NC
#651 **Christopher Yew** entered 200 acres north of Grassie Creek adjoining **Leonard Hart**, **Richard Bird** and **William Williamson**.

1687.   1793, Oct 3 -- 1784-1797 Land Entries, Moore County, NC
#652 **Christopher Yew** entered 100 acres on both sides of Grassie Creek adjoining **Leonard Hart** and **William Williamson**.

1688.   1793, Oct 3 -- 1784-1797 Land Entries, Moore County, NC
#653 **William Williamson** entered 100 acres south of Grassie Creek adjoining his own line and **Christopher Yew**.

1689.   1793, Oct 3 -- 1784-1797 Land Entries, Moore County, NC

#654 **George Carriner** entered 50 acres north of Grassie Creek adjoining his own line and **Christopher Yew** including part of his old field.

1690.   1793, Oct 3 -- 1784-1797 Land Entries, Moore County, NC
#655 **John Garner** entered 100 acres near the county line adjoining his own line, **George Carriner**, **Yew** and **Carpenter**.

1691.   1793, Oct 12 -- Land Grant #997, Moore County, NC
William Wright received 150 acres located northwest of Wolf Creek adjoining **John Hunsacur**, **William Morgan**, **George Brazel** and including his own improvement. **Uriah Wright** and **Nathan Morgan** were chain carriers.

1692.   1793, Oct 18 -- 1784-1797 Land Entries, Moore County, NC
#664 **Daniel Manes** entered 100 acres located on Grassie Creek adjoining his own line (formerly **John Bullock**).

1693.   1793, Oct 22 -- Land Grant #874, Moore County, NC
Murdock McAulay received 50 acres located east of Wet Creek adjoining **Waddle**, **Bartholomew Dunn**. **John McAulay** and **Murdock McAulay** were chain carriers.

1694.   1793, Oct 26 -- 1784-1797 Land Entries, Moore County, NC
#666 **George Williams** entered 50 acres between Flag Creek and Bear Creek including his improvement.

1695.   1793, Nov 7 -- 1784-1797 Land Entries, Moore County, NC
#671 **Hector McNeill** entered 50 acres between the drains of Richland Creek and the Long Meadow and on both sides of Rutherford Road adjoining his own line.

1696.   1793, Nov 18 -- 1784-1795 Court of Pleas and Quarter Sessions, Moore County, NC
[*jury duty - selected participants*] **David Kennedy**, **John Haire**, **William Wright**, **Jacob Cagle**, **Jesse Ritter**, **Joseph Dunn**, **Saml. Dunn**. [*jury duty next term - selected participants*] **Joseph Dunn Jur.**, **Leonard Furr**, **Zachariah Smith**, **Christopher Yew**, **Richard Dunn Jur.**, **William Copland**, **Joseph Allen**, **Jacob Stutts Jur.**, **William Williamson**, **George Cagle**.

1697.   1793, Nov 19 -- Land Grant #1461, Moore County, NC
James Ditton received 200 acres on the Randolph County line adjoining **Phillips** and **Morgan**'s old field. **John Argo** and **Wm. Waddle** were chain carriers.

1698.   1793, Nov 19 -- 1784-1797 Land Entries, Moore County, NC
#673 **Samuel Perry** entered 100 acres on both sides of Buffalow Creek adjoining **Cooper** and the **Lawson** Place.

1699.   1793, Nov 19 -- 1784-1797 Land Entries, Moore County, NC
#675 **Dennis Carpenter** entered 100 acres on Williamson [Williams] Creek adjoining **Comer** and **Ledlow** and including **Comer**'s hog pen.

1700.   1793, Nov 19 -- 1784-1797 Land Entries, Moore County, NC
#677 **Peter Shamburger** entered 75 acres on Grassie Creek adjoining **Hardy Davis**, **Daniel Maner** and **Nall**.

1701.   1793, Nov 19-21 -- 1784-1795 Court of Pleas and Quarter Sessions, Moore County, NC Page 423,426,430
[Deeds] **Hardy Davis** and wife **Sally** to **Nicholas Nall** was acknowledged
William Ricket/Picket to **John Argo** proven by **William Argo**
George Carriner to **David Kennedy** proven by **Vincent Davis**
Hardy Davis to **Richard Cox** proven by **Nicholas Nall** Esq.
Thomas Overton to **Malcom Gilchrist** proven by **John Gilchrist**

1702.   1793, Nov 19 -- 1784-1795 Court of Pleas and Quarter Sessions, Moore County, NC Page 424
Letters of Administration granted to **Ezekiel Rheubottom** on the estate of **Thomas Rheubottom** Dec'd. with **William Dunn** and **Simon Rheubottom** as securities.

[Handwritten note:] Ordered by the Court that Letters of Administration ipue to Ezekiel Rheubottom on the Estate Thomas Rheubottom Deceased he havin Given Bond in the Sum of Two Thousand Pounds with William Dunn and Simon Rheubottom Suretties who are approved by the Court

1703. 1793, Nov 20 -- 1784-1795 Court of Pleas and Quarter Sessions, Moore County, NC Page 428
James Ludlo v. **Hardy Davis**

1704. 1793, Nov 21 -- 1784-1795 Court of Pleas and Quarter Sessions, Moore County, NC Page 430
James Hill records his mark to be a swallow fork in the right ear and a slop in the left.
Benjamin Caddell records his ear mark to be an overslit in the right ear and a swallow fork in the left.

1705. 1793, Nov 21 -- 1784-1795 Court of Pleas and Quarter Sessions, Moore County, NC Page 430
James Hines was discharged from custody on charge of horse stealing.

1706. 1793, Nov 22 -- 1784-1795 Court of Pleas and Quarter Sessions, Moore County, NC Page 432
James Caddell records his ear mark to be a smooth crop in the right ear and a smooth crop and a slit in the left and his brand to be "IC".

A. 1793, Nov 24 -- Land Grant #1367, Chatham County, NC
Sabra Gilbert received 50 acres located on Line Creek adjoining **Joseph Gilbert**, Dec'd. **Robert Moore** and **Benjn. Gilbert** were chain carriers.

1707. 1793, Nov 26 -- Land Grant #418, Moore County, NC
William Barret received 50 acres located on the drains of Richland Creek adjoining **Neill McLeod**.

1708. 1793, Nov 26 -- Land Grant #422, Moore County, NC
William Barret received 50 acres located on Suck Creek adjoining his own mill land.

1709. 1793, Nov 27 -- Land Grant #898, Moore County, NC
Neil McLeod received 150 acres located east of Mill Creek adjoining **Norman McKinnon**, **Robert Cox**, near County line. **Norman McKinnon** and **Murdock McAulay** were chain carriers.

1710. 1793, Dec 3 -- Land Grant #521, Moore County, NC
James Holcombe received 21 acres located on Cox's Mill Creek adjoining his own line, **James Muse** and **Jason Wadsworth**. **Jesse Muse** and **Jason Wadsworth** were chain carriers.

1711. 1793, Dec 20 -- Land Grant #1458, Moore County, NC
William Morgan received 50 acres located on Mill Creek adjoining his own line and **James Gallemore**. **Wm. Smith** and **Jno. Morgan** were chain carriers.

1712. 1793, Dec 21 -- Deed Book 7, Page 33, Randolph County, NC
John Hawkins (of Granville County) deeded **John Macon** 230 acres located on Fork Creek adjoining **Nall**. Proven by **Windsor Pearce** Nov 1796.

1713. 1793, Dec-Jan 1794 -- General Assembly Session Records
Petition to form Alfordstown as County Seat for Moore County, NC. The following residents [selected signers] signed the petition: **James Gallemore**; **John Gilliam**; **Christopher Bathune**; **Lewis Sowel Snr.**; **George Mor**; **Robert Bird**; *George Carringer; Daniel L. Caringer; Peter Caringer; Lewis Garner, JP.* ; **Alexander Morison**; **Allan Morison**; **John Morison**; **Lewis Sowel**; **Stephen Richardson**; **Ryal Brewer**; **John Smith**; **Willis Brewer**; **Ruben Brewer**; **Howel Brewer**; **Christopher Yew**; **Bradly Garner**; **John Garner**; **William Dickinson**, Jesse

Carroll, Alexander Carroll, James Dowd, Jas. Collins, John Carrel, Willis Davis; Benjn. Shields; *William Dunn; Bartholomew Dunn; John Sheffield; John Stuts*; Thos. Smith; Wm. Upton; Drury Richardson; Edward Richardson; *Joseph Cockman; Averit Walis*; John Baton; Alen Baton; William Caddell; Daniel Caddell; Matthew Davis; Arthur Davis; Kinsey Brient; John Sowell; John Upton; Niclas Newton; *John Newton; Bartholomew Dun; Ansel Melton; John Gilliam; Adam Shufel; John Shufel*; John Daniley; Mikel Briant; Jno. McAulay; *Jesse Brown; James Melton; Ansel Melton; Stephen Davis; Thomas Keys; Matthias Williams; Wm. Keys; John Keys; Cornelius Keys*; Willis Dickinson; *John Cagle; George Cagle; Henry Cable; Wm. Smith; George Williams*; Vincent Davis; *William Brewer; George Hunsucker; Shadrach Maness; Henry Cagil; Leonard Stutts; Levi Deeton; Andrew White; William Needham; William Deton; David Cagle; Benja. Caddell; Thos. Davis; Ruben Freman*; Normand Matheson; John Matheson; Donald Monrow; Neil Matheson; Normand McKinnon; Hector McLane; Hector McLane; Murdock McAulay; Donald Matheson; Angus McAulay; *John Morgin; John Bullack Jun.; Ambres Manes; Christopher Yow*; John McKinnon; Jno. McAuley Senr.; *Ezekial Rubottom*; John Smith; John Cox. [*Editor's Note: the petition failed. In 1796 the NC General Assembly established Carthage as the county seat. In 1806, it was changed to Faginsville to honor Richardson Fagin. The name was changed back to Carthage in 1814*]

1714. 1793, Dec 21 -- Deed Book 7, Page 34, Randolph County, NC
John Hawkins (of Granville County) deeded **Allen Bullock** a tract located on Fork Creek and the [Moore] County line adjoining **Andrews**, **Garner** and **Macon**. Proven by **Windsor Pearce** Nov 1796.

1715. 1794 -- Tax List, Wake County, NC, **Captain A. Hogan**'s District [selected residents]
Joseph Britt listed 100 acres and 1 white poll; **Benjamin Britt** listed 125 acres and 1 white poll; **Ryals Britt** listed 125 acres and 1 white poll

1716. 1794, Jan 6 -- Will Book A Page 181-182, Moore County, NC
Will of **Cornelius Tyson**, Dec'd. Heirs: wife **Jane Tyson**, son **Aaron Tyson** [*along with Benjamin the river land where I now live adjoining **Dowd** and Chatham County line; tract of land on Spring Branch adjoining previous tract and **Dowd** and **Johnston**], daughter **Sarah Stinson**, daughter **Rebecca Mirick**, son **Richard Tyson** [*tract of land where he now lives*], daughter **Sabra Gilbert**, son **Benjamin Tyson** [*along with **Aaron**, the river land where I now live adjoining **Dowd** and Chatham County line*], daughter **Jane Womble**, son **Thomas Tyson**, grandson **Thomas Tyson** and granddaughter **Elizabeth Tyson**. Executors: son **Benjamin Tyson** and son **Aaron Tyson**. Witnesses: **Seth Barnes**, **Jno. Porterfield** and **Jas. Collins**. Proven May 1795.

A. 1794, Jan 22 – Deed Book K Page 68-69, Chatham County, NC
William Finley deeded **Samuel Guthrie** 1100 acres located on Tyson Creek and the Moore County line adjoining **Cheek** and **Shearing**. Being the two tracts granted to **William Finley** 11 Jul 1788. **Beverly Guthrie**, **Clabourn Guthrie** and **German Guthrie** were witnesses.

1717. 1794, Jan 30 -- Land Grant #1588, Moore County, NC
George Carringer received 50 acres located on both sides of Grassy Creek adjoining his own line, **Hunsucker** and **Luis Gardner**. **George Carringer Jr.** and **Christopher Yow** were chain carriers.

1718. 1794, Jan 30 -- Deed Book 5, Page 156, Randolph County, NC
Joseph Carr deeded **Rolly Spinks** a tract of land located at the mouth of Flat Creek adjoining **William Carr** and including 100 acres **Joseph Carr** purchased from **John Needham**. **William Carr** and **Windsor Pierce** were witnesses.

1719. 1794, Jan 30 -- Deed Book 5, Page 157, Randolph County, NC
Joseph Carr deeded **William Kerr** 250 acres located on Deep River at the mouth of Flat Creek adjoining **William Reed Senr.** and **Joseph Kerr**. Granted to **Thomas Graves**. **Rolley Spinks** and **Windsor Pierce** were witnesses.

1720. 1794, Feb 4 -- Land Grant #903, Montgomery County, NC
James Allen received 50 acres located on Wolf Creek adjoining **Joseph Allen**, his own line and **Wilkins**. **William Allen** and **George** were chain carriers.

[Editor's Note: Signatures and marks above highlighted on previous page]

Original Carthage Town Plat with Land Grants 1790-1800

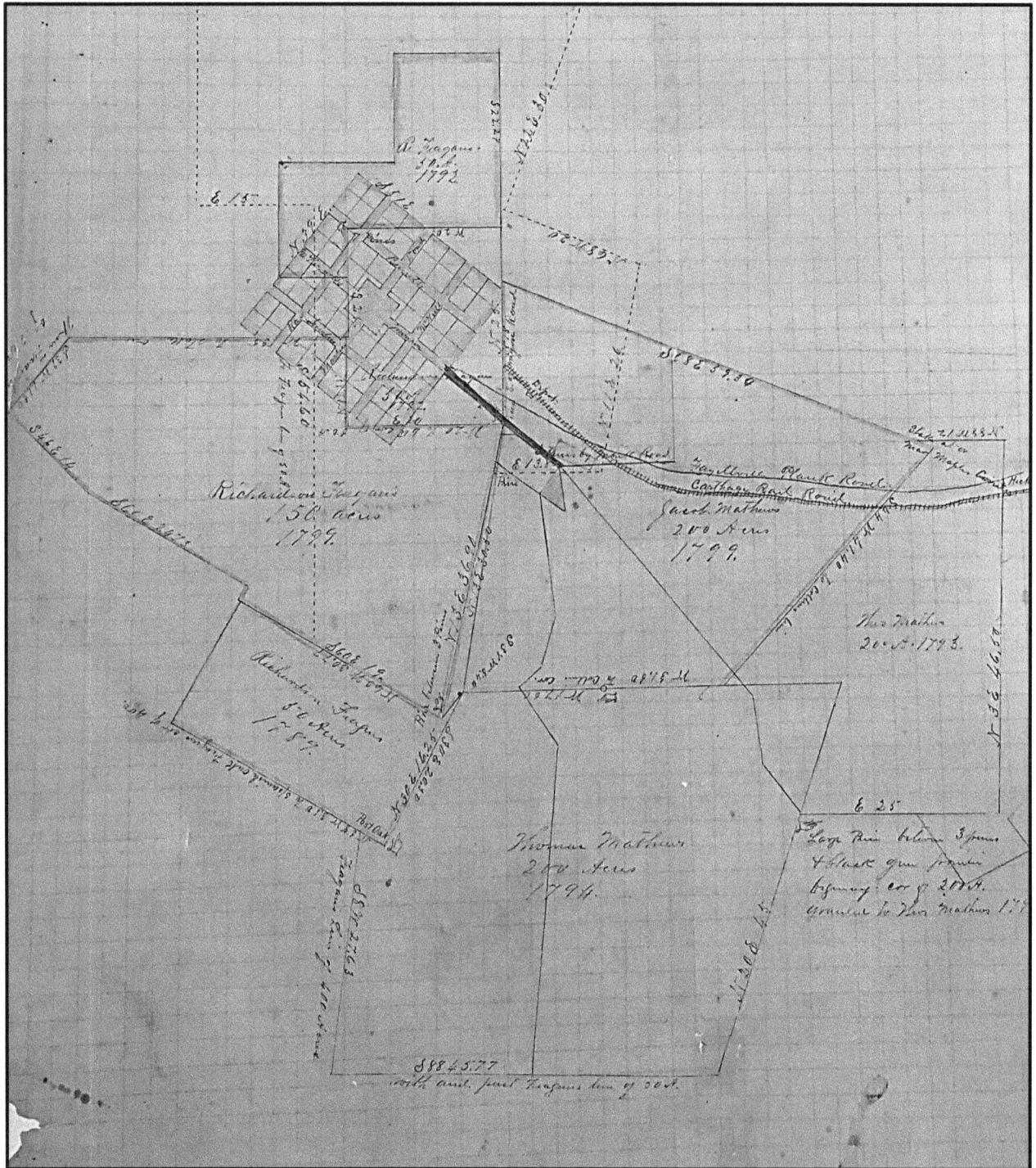

Plat by Rassie Wicker - Courtesy of the NC Archives
MC.195.C.326.1889ba and MC.195.C.326.1889bb

1728. 1794, Feb 9 -- Will Book A Page 173, Moore County, NC
Will of **Joseph McGee**, Dec'd. Heirs: wife **Milly**; children -- **Abraham McGee** [*under 20*]; **Suckey McGee**; **Jacob McGee**; **Penny McGee**, **Tempy McGee**, **Macajah McGee**, **Elizabeth McGee**, **Chiles McGee**, **Judith McGee**, **Joseph McGee**. Executors: **Edmond Wadill** and **Benjamin Tyson**. Witnesses: **Jam. Person** and **Elizabeth Person**. Proven Feb 1794.

1729. 1794, Feb 10 -- 1784-1797 Land Entries, Moore County, NC
#700 **Evan Lawler** entered 50 acres north of Deep River on both sides of Ceder Creek adjoining **George Feagan** and **Trap**.

1730. 1794, Feb 11 -- 1784-1797 Land Entries, Moore County, NC
#709 **John McAulay** entered 50 acres on the drains of Sings Creek adjoining his own line and **Donald McLeod**.

1731. 1794, Feb 11 -- 1784-1797 Land Entries, Moore County, NC
#710 **Angus McAulay** entered 84 acres on both sides of Tan Trough Branch of Mill Creek adjoining his own line.

A. 1794, Feb 11 -- Land Grant #906, Montgomery County, NC
Harbard Suggs received 400 acres located on Suggs Creek adjoining **Horatio Suggs**, **William Spencer** and **Rasha Suggs**. **William Bolin** and **Equille Sugg** were chain carriers.

1732. 1794, Feb 12 -- 1784-1797 Land Entries, Moore County, NC
#711 **Angus McAulay** entered 50 acres on the drains of Sings Creek adjoining **Arcd. McKay** on both sides of the Yadkin Road.

1733. 1794, Feb 12 -- 1784-1797 Land Entries, Moore County, NC
#712 **Benjamin Cooper** entered 130 acres on Bear Creek including **Caddle**'s old fields.

1734. 1794, Feb 12 -- 1784-1797 Land Entries, Moore County, NC
#713 **Leonard Furr** entered 50 acres located on both sides of Buffalow Creek adjoining **Leonard Cagle Sr**.

1735. 1794, Feb 12 -- 1784-1797 Land Entries, Moore County, NC
#714 **Joseph Cockman** entered 100 acres on the Long Meadow adjoining his own line.

1736. 1794, Fcb 12 -- 1784-1797 Land Entries, Moore County, NC

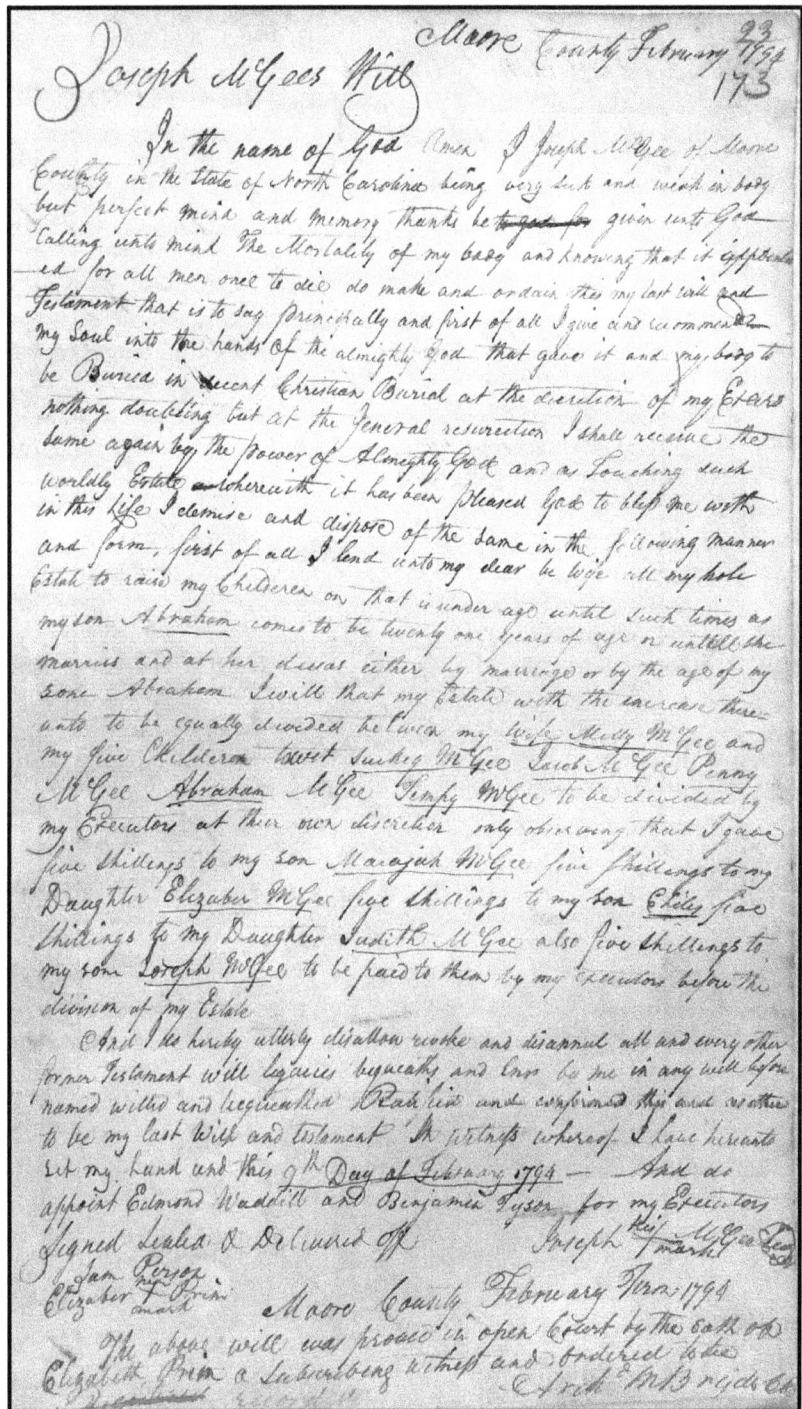

#715 **Edward Moore** entered 100 acres north of Deep River adjoining **James Moore** west of the Waggon Branch.

1737.   1794, Feb 12 -- 1784-1797 Land Entries, Moore County, NC
#716 **Niel McLeod** entered 100 acres on the Dry Fork of McLendons Creek adjoining **Donald McDonald**.

1738.   1794, Feb 12 -- 1784-1797 Land Entries, Moore County, NC
#717 **Niell McLeod** entered 100 acres on Dry Creek adjoining **Paterson** and **Hector McLaine**.

1739.   1794, Feb 12 -- 1784-1797 Land Entries, Moore County, NC
#718 **Niell McLeod** entered 60 acres on both sides of Cabin Creek adjoining **Carpenter**'s line known as the Pocket.

1740.   1794, Feb 12 -- 1784-1797 Land Entries, Moore County, NC
#719 **William Cagle** entered 100 acres on Bear Creek adjoining **Henry Cagle** and including his improvement.

1741.   1794, Feb 12 -- 1784-1797 Land Entries, Moore County, NC
#723 **Neill McLeod** entered 120 acres on the head of a branch of Wet Creek and Drowning Creek and both sides of the Uharie Road including the fork of the road with the Yadkin Road.

1742.   1794, Feb 12 -- 1784-1797 Land Entries, Moore County, NC
#724 **Peter Shamburger** entered 100 acres on Grassie Creek near Mark's Folley.

1743.   1794, Feb 12 -- 1784-1797 Land Entries, Moore County, NC
#727 **William Manes** entered 100 acres located south of Bear Creek adjoining his own line.

A.   1794, Feb 13 -- Land Grant #797, Montgomery County, NC
Johnson Spencer received 100 acres located on the head of Reedy Branch, west of Neds Mountain adjoining **Presley**. **Johnston Randle** and **Nathaniel Tucker** were chain carriers.

1744.   1794, Feb 14 -- Land Grant #1336, Randolph County, NC
Lewis Spinks [assignee of **William Sercy** and **Nicholas Nall**] received 100 acres located north of Fork Creek adjoining his own line, **Sutherland** and **Mash**. **Cornelus Lethem** and **Wm. Asbell** were chain carriers.

1745.   1794, Feb 15 -- Deed Book 5, Page 175, Randolph County, NC
John and **Sally Spinks** deeded **Nicholas Nall** 150 acres located on Deep River adjoining **William Reed**. Granted to **William Searcy**, sold to **Enoch Spinks** and willed to his son **John Spinks**. **Charles Stewart** and **George Street** were witnesses.

A.   1794, Feb 15 -- Land Grant #859, Randolph County, NC
John Needham received 200 acres located on Fork Creek and Reedy Creek adjoining **Spinks**. **Lewis Spinks** and **Wm. Asbel** were chain carriers.

B.   1794, Feb 15 -- Land Grant #1513, Randolph County, NC
Cornelius Lathem received 250 acres located on Fork Creek and Meadow Branch adjoining **John Needham**. **Lewis Spinks** and **William Asbel** were chain carriers.

1746.   1794, Feb 17 -- 1784-1795 Court of Pleas and Quarter Sessions, Moore County, NC
[*jury duty - selected participants*] **Joseph Dunn, Richd. Dunn, Zachry Smith, William Copland, George Cagle, Christopher Yew, Leonard Furr, Joseph Allen, Jacob Stutts** [*jury duty next term - selected participants*] **Nicholas Nall, Bryan Borroughs, Samuel Dunn, William Smith** (Cab. Crk.), **Jesse Ritter, Ancil Melton Senr., William Morgan Senr., David Cagle, William Dunn** (Wet), **Everet Smith**.

1747.   1794, Feb 17 -- Land Grant #813, Randolph County, NC
Thomas Cost received 60 acres on Reed Creek adjoining his own line and the [Moore] County line. **Manuel Asbel** and **Christopher Asbel** were chain carriers.

1748.   1794, Feb 17 -- Land Grant #1744, Randolph County, NC

Manuel Asbel received 200 acres on Reedy Creek adjoining Edmound Marsh. Thomas Cosh and Cornelius Lethem were chain carriers.

1749.　　1794, Feb 18-22 -- 1784-1795 Court of Pleas and Quarter Sessions, Moore County, NC Page 436, 442, 450, 452
[Deeds] William Reed to James Deaton proven by Windsor Pierce
John Sowell to William Barrett proven by Thomas Ritter
William Barrett to Patty Glascock proven by Archibald McBryde
James Muse and John Wadsworth to Thomas Matthews proven by Overton Shields
John Overton and Mary Dowd to Aaron Tyson proven by Archibald McBryde
John Rogers, Enoch Rogers and Ruth Rogers to Aaron Tyson proven by Archibald McBryde
James Alston to Samuel Womble was acknowledged
Joseph McGee to Joseph Duckworth was acknowledged
Mark Phillips to Aaron Tyson proven by Archibald McBryde
[Bill of Sale] Sarah Davis to Willis Davis proven by Archibald Shields

1750.　　1794, Feb 18 -- 1784-1795 Court of Pleas and Quarter Sessions, Moore County, NC Page 438
David Kennedy is appointed overseer of the road in place of William Williamson.

1751.　　1794, Feb 18 -- 1784-1795 Court of Pleas and Quarter Sessions, Moore County, NC Page 440
John Bullock appointed constable for 1794 in Morgan's District; Reuben Shields in Cheek's District, Thos. Graham in Dunn's District

1752.　　1794, Feb 19 -- Land Grant #861, Randolph County, NC
Enoch Spinks received 260 acres on Cow Branch of Fork Creek. Moses George and Garret Spinks were chain carriers.

1753.　　1794, Feb 19 -- 1784-1795 Court of Pleas and Quarter Sessions, Moore County, NC Page 440
Ordered that orphan Elijah Brown (age 11) be bound to Capt. William Morgan to learn the Cooper trade until he reaches full age. Thomas Key served as security.

1754.　　1794, Feb 19 -- 1784-1795 Court of Pleas and Quarter Sessions, Moore County, NC Page 442
Samuel Person is appointed overseer of the road instead of William Brooks.

1755.　　1794, Feb 19 -- 1784-1795 Court of Pleas and Quarter Sessions, Moore County, NC Page 443

Ancel Milton records his ear mark to be a crop and 2 slits in the right ear and a crop and 1 slit in the left ear.
Adam Sheffield records his mark to be a crop and a half moon in the right ear and a swallow fork in the left.

1756.　　1794, Feb 19-20 -- 1784-1795 Court of Pleas and Quarter Sessions, Moore County, NC Page 443,448
Benjamin Caddell is appointed constable in Brown's District with James Caddle and Daniel Caddle serving as securities. John Bullock is appointed constable in Morgan's District with Francis Bullock and Archibald Ray as securities. Reuben Shields is appointed constable in Cheek's District with James Holcomb and William Dunn as securities.

1757.　　1794, Feb 19 -- 1784-1795 Court of Pleas and Quarter Sessions, Moore County, NC Page 446
Aaron Tyson appointed overseer of the road from the Chatham [County] line to John McLennons house and have all the hands below Perkins Road except the hands under John McLennon.
John Stinson appointed overseer of the road instead of John Record and have all the former hands except those under Aaron Tyson and John McLennon.

A. 1794, Feb 19 -- Land Grant #881, Montgomery County, NC
Elias Spencer received 150 acres located east of Little River adjoining **William Spencer** and **Edward Duvall Tyler**. **William Spencer** and **Semore Spencer** were chain carriers.

B. 1794, Feb 20 -- Land Grant #864, Montgomery County, NC
Sarah Spencer received 300 acres located on Williams Creek. **Elias Spencer** and **Semore Spencer** were chain carriers.

1758. 1794, Feb 20 -- 1784-1795 Court of Pleas and Quarter Sessions, Moore County, NC Page 449
Ordered that **Jesse Muse** be appointed overseer of the road from McLendon's Creek at the **Widow Muse**'s to the fork of **Overton**'s Road and have the following hands to work: **Julius Glascock, Martin Glascock, William Caddill, William Feagin, Asa Hannon, Hymereck Hill, Alexander McDeed, Neil McLeod, William Trader, Samuel Elkins, Michael Dickinson, Thomas Hannon Jr., Hardy Harden** and **John Melton Glascock**.

1759. 1794, Feb 20 -- 1784-1795 Court of Pleas and Quarter Sessions, Moore County, NC Page 449
Ordered that the Letters of Administration with the will be annexed issue to **Milly McGee** and **Joseph McGee Junr.** on the estate of **Joseph McGee Senr.** with **Richardson Feagin** and **William Dunn** as securities.

1761. 1794, Feb 21 -- 1784-1795 Court of Pleas and Quarter Sessions, Moore County, NC Page 451
Francis Bullock records his mark to be two half moons in the right and a smooth crop in the left and his brand to be "FB".

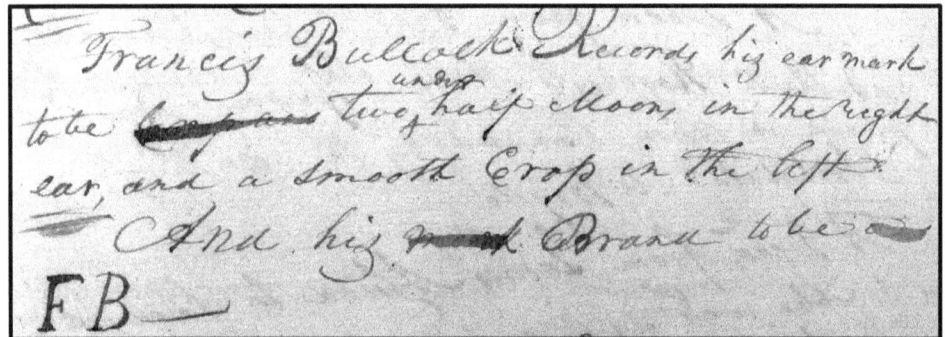

1762. 1794, Feb 21 -- 1784-1795 Court of Pleas and Quarter Sessions, Moore County, NC Page 452
Ordered that part of the road which **Josiah Maples** was formerly overseer of be put under two overseers: **Mark Phillips** from the Chatham line to McLendons Creek and **William King** from McLendons Creek as far as **Josiah Maples** was overseer of.

1763. 1794, Feb 21 -- 1784-1795 Court of Pleas and Quarter Sessions, Moore County, NC Page 453
John Hair is appointed road overseer in place of **John Sheffield**.

1764. 1794, Feb 21 -- 1784-1795 Court of Pleas and Quarter Sessions, Moore County, NC Page 453
Ordered that **Hardy Davis** be appointed overseer of the road from his house to **Williamson**'s old place and have the following hands to work: **Jeremiah Wilson, Isham Sheffield, Everet Sheffield, Thomas Davis** and **Christian Cagle**.

1765. 1794, Feb 25 -- 1784-1797 Land Entries, Moore County, NC #734 **Donald McQueen** entered 100 acres adjoining **Benjamin Atkinson** and **Honsucker**.

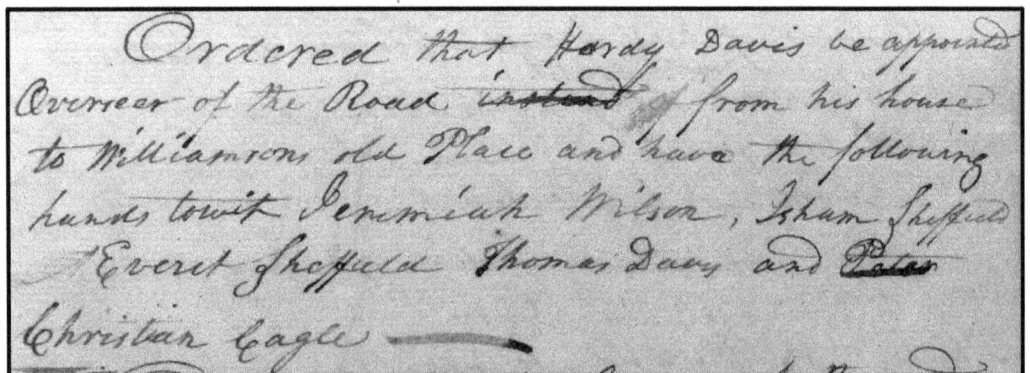

1766. 1794, Feb 25 -- 1784-1797 Land Entries, Moore County, NC
#742 **John Sowell** entered 200 acres adjoining his own line, **Rittar, Quimbey, Barrett, Edwards** and **McKay**.

1767. 1794, Feb 25 -- 1784-1797 Land Entries, Moore County, NC
#743 **Niell McLeod** entered 100 acres on Buffalo Creek adjoining **Edwards** and **Cagle**.

1768. 1794, Feb 25 -- 1784-1797 Land Entries, Moore County, NC
#744 **Thomas Ritter** entered 50 acres located on McLendons Creek adjoining his own line.

1769. 1794, Feb 25 -- 1784-1797 Land Entries, Moore County, NC
#745 **Jesse Brown** entered 100 acres on the drains of Flag Creek including **Ambrose Brown**'s improvement.

1770. 1794, Feb 25 -- 1784-1797 Land Entries, Moore County, NC
#746 **George Cagle** entered 100 acres west of Wolf Creek including his own improvement.

1771. 1794, Feb 28 -- Land Grant #1191, Moore County, NC
Benjamin Caddle [assignee of **William Barret**] received 100 acres located on the drains of McLendons Creek adjoining **James Muse** and **James Caddell**. **James White** and **James Muse** were chain carriers.

A. 1794, Mar 4 -- Land Grant #877, Montgomery County, NC
John Allen received 50 acres located on Bigg Branch and the mouth of Reedy Branch of Cabin Creek adjoining **William Allen**. **John Allen** and **Jesse Simmons** were chain carriers.

1772. 1794, Mar 8 -- Deed Book 5, Page 159, Randolph County, NC
Joseph Carr deeded **Robert Kerr** 150 acres adjoining **Arthur Smith**. **Rolley Spinks** and **William Carr** were witnesses.

A. 1794, Mar 12 -- Land Grant #867, Montgomery County, NC
Berry Hicks received 100 acres located on Crooked Creek and Little River adjoining **Jacob Humble** and **Francis Jordan**. **Francis Jordan** and **John Jordan** were chain carriers.

B. 1794, Mar 12 -- Land Grant #915, Montgomery County, NC
Berry Hix received 50 acres located on Dicks Creek adjoining **John Sowell** and his own line improvement. **John Jordan** and **William Hix** were chain carriers.

C. 1794, Mar 13 -- Land Grant #850, Montgomery County, NC
Berry Hicks received 50 acres located on Dicks Creek adjoining **Lias Butler Jr**. **Francis Jordan** and **John Jordan** were chain carriers.

D. 1794, Mar 13 -- Land Grant #914, Montgomery County, NC
John Jordan received 100 acres located on the head of Dicks Creek adjoining **Littleberry Hix**. **Litteberry Hix** and **Thos. Jordan** were chain carriers.

1773. 1794, Mar 14 -- Deed Book 5, Page 178, Randolph County, NC
Deed from **James Alston**, **John Alston**, **Phillip Alston**, **Drewery Alston** and **Smith Alston** (heirs of **Phillip Alston** Dec'd.) to **Edmond Waddill**. Also including tract of land from **James Alston** to **Edmond Waddill** located north of Deep River adjoining **Nall**, **William Bowdown**, **William Searcy** (Dec'd.) and **William Argo**. **Thomas Waddill** and **Murdock McKensey** were witnesses.

1774. 1794, Mar 18 -- Land Grant #1198, Moore County, NC
John Hare received 50 acres located east of Wolf Creek on Bear Branch adjoining his own line, **Peter Hare**, **John Sheffield**. **Reuben Freeman** and **Peter Hare** were chain carriers.

1775. 1794, Mar 19 -- Land Grant #785, Moore County, NC
Elijah Otery received 150 acres located on Bear Creek adjoining **John Bullock**. **Francis Bullock** and **John Shuffle** were chain carriers.

1776. 1794, Mar 19 -- Land Grant #1253, Moore County, NC
William Williamson received 100 acres located south of Grassy Creek adjoining **John Williamson**, his own line and **Christopher Yow**. **Christopher Yow Sr.** and **Christopher Yow Jr.** were chain carriers.

1777. 1794, Mar 20 -- Land Grant #1539, Moore County, NC

Henry Kagle Senr. received 100 acres located on Bear Creek adjoining **Michael Hart**, **James Gillmore**. **Christopher Cagle** and **William Cagle** were chain carriers.

1778. 1794, Mar 22 -- Land Grant #1141, Moore County, NC
Jeremiah Wilson received 100 acres located on Haw Branch of Grassy Creek adjoining **Peter Shamburger**. **Peter Shamburger** and **John Shamburger** were chain carriers.

1779. 1794, Mar 22 -- Land Grant #1163, Moore County, NC
Peter Shamburger received 75 acres located on both sides of Grassie Creek near the mouth of Haw Branch adjoining **Jeremiah Wilson**. **Jeremiah Wilson** and **John Shamburger** were chain carriers.

1780. 1794, Mar 24 -- Land Grant #908, Moore County, NC
Neil McLeod received 156 acres located on both sides of McLendons Creek adjoining **Jamima McLendon**, **Thomas Night**, **Barrett**, **Major McRea**, **Jacob McLendon** and **Sowell**. **Donald McLeod** and **Jno. McDonald** were chain carriers.

1781. 1794, Mar 24 -- Land Grant #782, Moore County, NC
William Martin received 150 acres located on the Yadkin Road including where the road that leads from Moore Court House to Allen's Ferry crosses the road below where **Samuel Williams** kept store. **Allen Morison** and **John McCaskill** were chain carriers.

1782. 1794, Mar 24 -- Land Grant #1791, Moore County, NC
Owen Carpenter received 150 acres located north of Grassy Creek and the Randolph County line adjoining his own line, **John Gardner**, **Christopher Yow** and **Richard Bird**. **Michael Andrews** and **Bradley Garner** were chain carriers.

1783. 1794, Mar 29 -- Land Grant #1602, Moore County, NC
Joseph McGee [assignee of **William Richardson**] received 50 acres located north of Buffalo Creek adjoining **Zachariah Smith** where he formerly lived and his own line. **Zachariah Smith** and **John Ritter** were chain carriers.

1784. 1794, Mar 30 -- Land Grant #996, Moore County, NC
William Williamson received 100 acres located south of Grassy Creek adjoining **Bullock**, his own line, **Christopher Yow**. **John Bullock** and **Christopher Yow** were chain carriers.

1785. 1794, Apr 2 -- Land Grant #956, Moore County, NC
Nathan Fry received 50 acres located on Killetts Creek adjoining his own line. **Hugh Black** and **Hugh Black** were chain carriers.

1786. 1794, Apr 2 -- 1784-1797 Land Entries, Moore County, NC
#759 **Niell McLeod** entered 50 acres adjoining **McLennon**, **Barrett** and where **McLeod** now lives.

1787. 1794, Apr 2 -- 1784-1797 Land Entries, Moore County, NC

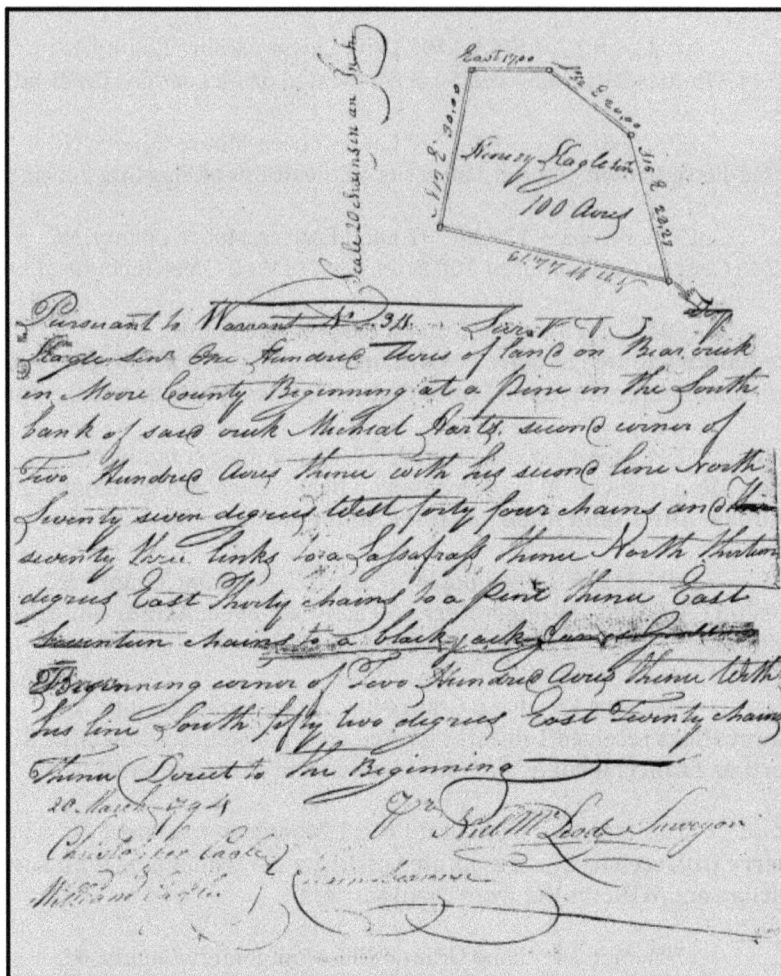

#760 **Niell McLeod** entered 100 acres on Dry Creek adjoining **William Smith** and **Malcolm Morrison**.

1788. 1794, Apr 10 -- Land Grant #1462, Moore County, NC
David Kennedy received 100 acres located south of Deep River adjoining **Pennington**, **Hunsaker**, **George Carringer** and **England**. **Alexr. Kennedy** and **George Carringer** were chain carriers.

1789. 1794, Apr 13 -- Deed Book 6, Page 182, Randolph County, NC
William Armstead deeded **James Ledlow** 70 acres located on Deep River. Proven by **John Needham Jr**. Nov 1795.

1790. 1794, Apr 13 -- Deed Book 6, Page 207, Randolph County, NC
William Armstead deeded **James Ledlow** 50 acres located on Deep River. Proven by **John Needham Jr**. Nov 1795.

A. 1794, Apr 16 -- Land Grant #778, Montgomery County, NC
Elijah Spencer received 300 acres located on Williams Creek and the head of Long Branch adjoining Crawford Road, **Thomas Mainyard** and **Sarah Spencer**. **William Spencer** and **Semore Spencer** were chain carriers.

B. 1794, Apr 16 -- Land Grant #897, Montgomery County, NC
Elijah Spencer received 200 acres located on Bear Creek adjoining **William Spencer**, **Elias Spencer** and Crawford Road. **William Spencer** and **Semore Spencer** were chain carriers.

1791. 1794, May 2 -- 1784-1797 Land Entries, Moore County, NC #768 **Joseph Allen** entered 50 acres north of Cabbin Creek adjoining his own line (formerly **Jacob Harvick**) and **Francis Bullock**.

1792. 1794, May 2 -- 1784-1797 Land Entries, Moore County, NC #774 **William Barrett** entered 50 acres south of McLendons Creek adjoining his own line and **George Jackson**.

1793. 1794, May 10 -- Land Grant #952, Moore County, NC **Jonathan Caddell** received 100 acres located on Mill Swamp adjoining **Thos. Collins** and **James Muse**. **James Muse** and **John Wadsworth** were chain carriers.

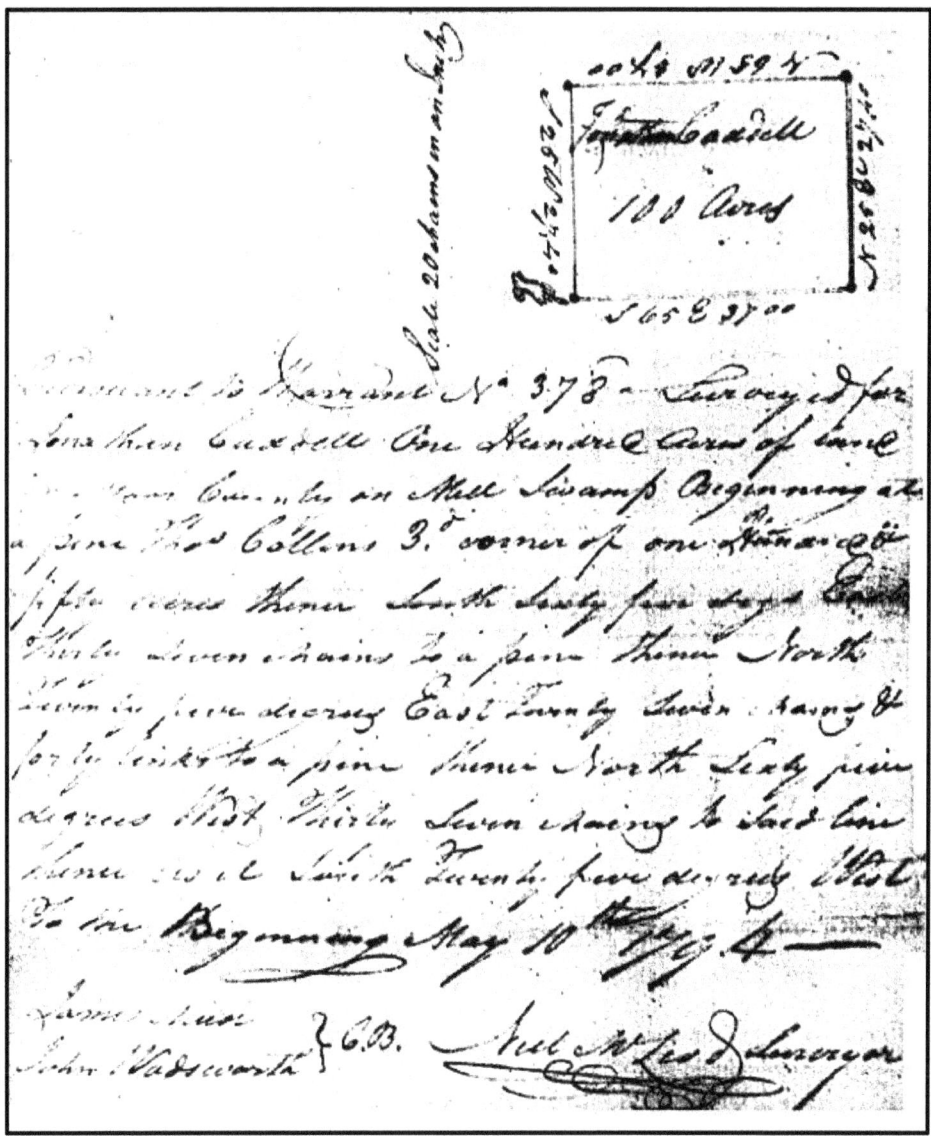

1794. 1794, May 19 -- 1784-1795 Court of Pleas and Quarter Sessions, Moore County, NC [*jury duty - selected participants*] **Bryan Borroughs, Samuel Dunn, Jesse Ritter, Ancel Milton Sr., William Dunn** (Wet Creek), **William Smith** (Cabbin Creek), **Everet Smith, David Cagle, Zachary Smith, Jacob Cagle** and **Jesse Bean**. [*jury duty next term - selected participants*] **Joseph Allan, John Haire, David Kennedy, William Wright** and **William Morgan**.

1795. 1794, May 19 -- 1784-1795 Court of Pleas and Quarter Sessions, Moore County, NC Page 454
Ordered that **Benjamin Gilbert** appointed overseer of the road instead of **John Stinson**.

1796. 1794, May 19,22 -- 1784-1795 Court of Pleas and Quarter Sessions, Moore County, NC Page 455,461,469
[Deeds] **Allan Morrison** to **Alexander Morrison** proven by **Richard Dunn**
William Barret to **Niel Hughes** was proven by **John McNeill**
John Carroll Esq. to **Robert Davis** was acknowledged
Richard Cox to **Hardy Davis** proven by **Nicholas Nall**
Benjamin Caddell to **Robert Dickinson** proven by **Thomas Tyson**, Esq.

1797. 1794, May 19 -- 1784-1795 Court of Pleas and Quarter Sessions, Moore County, NC Page 457

A Deed from Benjamin Caddell to Robert Dickinson was duly proved in open court by the oath of Thomas Tyson Esq. and was ordered to be Registered

Owen Carpenter came into court and gave up **Owen Carpenter Jur., John Carpenter** and **Sarah Carpenter** who were bound to him by the court.

1798. 1794, May 20 -- 1784-1795 Court of Pleas and Quarter Sessions, Moore County, NC Page 458
A writ of Fe Fi and ignoramus bill of indictment against **Jacob Cagle**

1799. 1794, May 21 -- 1784-1795 Court of Pleas and Quarter Sessions, Moore County, NC Page 462
Jesse Muse be appointed overseer of the road from McLendons Creek at the **Widow Muses** to Dunhams Creek and have the former hands to work under him and **Neil Munroe**. **Munroe** is exempted in consideration of keeping a path way open leading by his house towards **Kinchen Kitchen**.

1800. 1794, May 21 -- 1784-1795 Court of Pleas and Quarter Sessions, Moore County, NC Page 465
Ordered that the following take a list of taxable for 1794: **Francis Bullock** [District #8].

1801. 1794, May 21 -- 1784-1795 Court of Pleas and Quarter Sessions, Moore County, NC Page 465
Richard Bean v. **Arthur Davis**

1802. 1794, May 22 -- Land Grant #1456, Moore County, NC
Peter Shamburger received 100 acres located on the waters of Grassy Creek near Mark's Folly adjoining his own line and **Jeremiah Wilson**. **John Bullock** and **John Shamburger** were chain carriers.

1803. 1794, May 22 -- 1784-1795 Court of Pleas and Quarter Sessions, Moore County, NC Page 469
State v. **Thomas Ritter**

1804. 1794, May 24 -- Deed Book 6, Page 184, Randolph County, NC
James Ledlow deeded **John Needham** 50 acres adjoining **Ledlow**. Proven by **John Needham Jr.** Nov 1795.

1805. 1794, May 24 -- Deed Book 6, Page 187, Randolph County, NC
James Ledlow deeded **John Needham** 70 acres on Deep River. Proven by **John Needham Jr.** Nov 1795.

1806. 1794, Jun 4 -- 1784-1797 Land Entries, Moore County, NC
#794 **Jesse Muse** entered 100 acres on both sides of McLendons Creek adjoining his own line and where his mother (**Widow Muse**) now lives.

1807. 1794, Jun 6 -- Criminal Actions, Randolph County, NC, 1794-B

Capias issued against **James Bowdon** on a charge that he stole a quantity of apples and pears and leather from **Joseph Hicks**. **John Garner**, **Winsor Pearce** and **Edmond Waddel** were witnesses for plaintiff. **Joseph Carr** and **Charles Gray** for defendant.

1808.   1794, Jun 10 -- Land Grant #1667, Moore County, NC
Benjamin Gilbert [assignee of **James Collins**] received 100 acres located north of Deep River adjoining **James McDonald**. **Benjamin Brown** and **Samuel Womble** were chain carriers.

1809.   1794, Jun 12 -- Land Grant #923, Moore County, NC
Thomas Ritter received 50 acres located west of McLendons Creek adjoining his own line, **Jas. Ritter** and **Jesse Ritter** were chain carriers.

1810.   1794, Jun 29 -- Land Grant #392, Moore County, NC
Donald McQueen received 50 acres located on Locust Branch of Richland Creek adjoining his own line and **William Dunn**.

1811.   1794, Jun 30 -- Land Grant #402, Moore County, NC
Bartholomew Dunn Sr. received 50 acres located on Flag Creek adjoining **Smith** including **Hart**'s improvement. **Henry Cagle** and **James Hynes** were chain carriers.

A.   1794, Jul 1 – Deed Book G Page 343-344, Chatham County, NC
Edmond Waddill (of Randolph County) deeded his son **Thomas Waddill** 225 acres located north of Deep River. **Arch. McBryde** and **William Waddill** were witnesses.

1812.   1794, Jul 11 -- Land Grant #921, Moore County, NC
James Murray received 200 acres located on Cedar Creek adjoining **John Argo**, **James Moore**. **William Cook** and **James Ditton** were chain carriers.

1813.   1794, Aug -- Criminal Actions, Randolph County, NC, 1794-B
Presentment of **James Bowdown**, laborer, on a charge of stealing a piece of leather from **Winsor Peirse** on Jul 30, 1794.

1814.   1794, Aug 1 -- 1784-1797 Land Entries, Moore County, NC
#809 **Murdoch Martin** entered 70 acres northeast of Dry Creek adjoining **Jacob McLendon** and **Thomas Matthews**.

1815.   1794, Aug 1 -- 1784-1797 Land Entries, Moore County, NC
#810 **William Martin** entered 100 acres on McLendons Creek adjoining his own line, **John McNeill** and **Robert Graham** (now **Thomas Graham**).

1816.   1794, Aug 1 -- 1784-1797 Land Entries, Moore County, NC
#813 **Murdoch Martin** entered 30 acres on both sides of Jacobs Branch of McLendons Creek including where the road crosses the branch adjoining **Campbell** and **Christopher Bathune**.

1817.   1794, Aug 2 -- 1784-1797 Land Entries, Moore County, NC
#817 **John McAulay Jr.** entered 100 acres located south of Bear Creek adjoining **Nicholas Nall**, **Ambrose Manes**, **Drury Richardson** and **James Thornton**.

1818.   1794, Aug 3 -- 1784-1797 Land Entries, Moore County, NC
#829 **Christopher Yew** entered 100 acres south of Deep River adjoining **John Gardner** and **William England**.

1819.   1794, Aug 5 -- 1784-1797 Land Entries, Moore County, NC
#844 **Joseph McGee** entered 150 acres east of Buffalow Creek adjoining **William McDonald** and **John McDonald**.

1820.   1794, Aug 8 -- 1784-1797 Land Entries, Moore County, NC
#862 **James Riddle** entered 150 acres adjoining **John Shepherd Senr.**, **McKay** and **Jacob Stuthern**.

1821.   1794, Aug 10 -- 1784-1797 Land Entries, Moore County, NC
#889 **John Porterfield** (for **David Allison**) entered 640 acres located above Carrols Bridge on Horse Creek.

1822.   1794, Aug 10 -- 1784-1797 Land Entries, Moore County, NC
#890 **John Porterfield** (for **David Allison**) entered 640 acres located on Horse Creek adjoining his own line.

1823.   1794, Aug 10 -- 1784-1797 Land Entries, Moore County, NC
#891 **John Porterfield** (for **David Allison**) entered 640 acres located on Horse Creek adjoining **McLeod**.

1824.   1794, Aug 10 -- 1784-1797 Land Entries, Moore County, NC
#892 **John Porterfield** (for **David Allison**) entered 640 acres located on Horse Creek adjoining **McLeod**

1825.   1794, Aug 10 -- 1784-1797 Land Entries, Moore County, NC
#893 **John Porterfield** (for **David Allison**) entered 640 acres located east of Horse Creek adjoining **McLeod** and **Paterson**.

1826.   1794, Aug 10 -- 1784-1797 Land Entries, Moore County, NC
#894 **John Porterfield** (for **David Allison**) entered 640 acres located on Horse Creek adjoining **Paterson**'s old place.

1827.   1794, Aug 10 -- 1784-1797 Land Entries, Moore County, NC
#912 **John Porterfield** (for **David Allison**) entered 640 acres located south of Mill Creek on the Yadkin Road.

1828.   1794, Aug 10 -- 1784-1797 Land Entries, Moore County, NC
#913 **John Porterfield** (for **David Allison**) entered 640 acres located on Mill Creek above the Sandhill Mill.

1829.   1794, Aug 10 -- 1784-1797 Land Entries, Moore County, NC
#914 **John Porterfield** (for **David Allison**) entered 640 acres located on Mill Creek east of the Sandhill Mill.

1830.   1794, Aug 10 -- 1784-1797 Land Entries, Moore County, NC
#915 **John Porterfield** (for **David Allison**) entered 320 acres located west of Buffalow Creek adjoining **Leonard Furr**.

1831.   1794, Aug 10 -- 1784-1797 Land Entries, Moore County, NC
#916 **John Porterfield** (for **David Allison**) entered 590 acres located south of Cabbin Creek adjoining **Everet Smith**.

1832.   1794, Aug 10 -- 1784-1797 Land Entries, Moore County, NC
#917 **John Porterfield** (for **David Allison**) entered 400 acres located west of Buffalow Creek adjoining **Alexr. Munroe**.

1833.   1794, Aug 10 -- 1784-1797 Land Entries, Moore County, NC
#918 **John Porterfield** (for **David Allison**) entered 276 acres located north of Cabbin Creek adjoining **Everet Smith**.

1834.   1794, Aug 10 -- 1784-1797 Land Entries, Moore County, NC
#919 **John Porterfield** (for **David Allison**) entered 337 acres located north of Cabin Creek adjoining **William Smith**.

1835.   1794, Aug 10 -- 1784-1797 Land Entries, Moore County, NC
#920 **John Porterfield** (for **David Allison**) entered 778 acres located south of Bear Creek adjoining **John Sheffield**.

1836.   1794, Aug 10 -- 1784-1797 Land Entries, Moore County, NC
#921 **John Porterfield** (for **David Allison**) entered 756 acres located north of Cabin Creek adjoining **John Morgan**.

1837.   1794, Aug 10 -- 1784-1797 Land Entries, Moore County, NC
#922 **John Porterfield** (for **David Allison**) entered 200 acres located south of Wolf Creek adjoining **Peter Hair**.

1838.   1794, Aug 10 -- 1784-1797 Land Entries, Moore County, NC
#923 **John Porterfield** (for **David Allison**) entered 620 acres located north of Cabin Creek adjoining **William Morgan**.

1839.   1794, Aug 10 -- 1784-1797 Land Entries, Moore County, NC
#924 **John Porterfield** (for **David Allison**) entered 520 acres located on Wolf Creek adjoining **William Rite**.

1840.   1794, Aug 10 -- 1784-1797 Land Entries, Moore County, NC
#925 **John Porterfield** (for **David Allison**) entered 600 acres located south of Wolf Creek adjoining the county line.

1841.   1794, Aug 10 -- 1784-1797 Land Entries, Moore County, NC
#926 **John Porterfield** (for **David Allison**) entered 900 acres located between Sings Creek and Mill Creek.

1842.   1794, Aug 10 -- 1784-1797 Land Entries, Moore County, NC
#927 **John Porterfield** (for **David Allison**) entered 640 acres located between Sings Creek and Mill Creek adjoining **Thomas Key**.

1843.   1794, Aug 10 -- 1784-1797 Land Entries, Moore County, NC
#928 **John Porterfield** (for **David Allison**) entered 640 acres located south of Bear Creek and in the fork of Little Creek.

1844.   1794, Aug 10 -- 1784-1797 Land Entries, Moore County, NC
#929 **John Porterfield** (for **David Allison**) entered 660 acres located west of Buffalow Creek adjoining **Jacob Stutts**.

1845.   1794, Aug 10 -- 1784-1797 Land Entries, Moore County, NC
#930 **John Porterfield** (for **David Allison**) entered 640 acres located west of Buffalow Creek adjoining **Nicholas Nall**.

1846.   1794, Aug 10 -- 1784-1797 Land Entries, Moore County, NC
#931 **John Porterfield** (for **David Allison**) entered 546 acres located on the head of Richland Creek adjoining **Niell McLeod**.

1847.   1794, Aug 10 -- 1784-1797 Land Entries, Moore County, NC
#932 **John Porterfield** (for **David Allison**) entered 734 acres located south of **Nicholas Newton** near the Race Path.

1848.   1794, Aug 10 -- 1784-1797 Land Entries, Moore County, NC
#933 **John Porterfield** (for **David Allison**) entered 731 acres located on the head of Wet Creek adjoining **Richard Dunn**.

1849.   1794, Aug 10 -- 1784-1797 Land Entries, Moore County, NC
#935 **John Porterfield** (for **David Allison**) entered 816 acres located south of Wet Creek adjoining **Richard Dunn**.

1850.   1794, Aug 10 -- 1784-1797 Land Entries, Moore County, NC
#936 **John Porterfield** (for **David Allison**) entered 492 acres located southeast of **Nicholas Newton**'s place.

1851.   1794, Aug 10 -- 1784-1797 Land Entries, Moore County, NC
#937 **John Porterfield** (for **David Allison**) entered 502 acres located west of Wet Creek adjoining **Angus McAuley**.

1852.   1794, Aug 10 -- 1784-1797 Land Entries, Moore County, NC
#938 **John Porterfield** (for **David Allison**) entered 605 acres located between the head of Drowning Creek and Wet Creek.

1853.   1794, Aug 10 -- 1784-1797 Land Entries, Moore County, NC

#939 John Porterfield (for **David Allison**) entered 728 acres located on the head of the west fork of Mill Creek adjoining **Archibald Gillis**.

1854.   1794, Aug 10 -- 1784-1797 Land Entries, Moore County, NC
#940 John Porterfield (for **David Allison**) entered 624 acres located between the head of Drowning Creek and Wet Creek adjoining **Wilson**'s place.

1855.   1794, Aug 10 -- 1784-1797 Land Entries, Moore County, NC
#941 John Porterfield (for **David Allison**) entered 513 acres located on both sides of the Tan Trough adjoining **Angus McAuley**.

1856.   1794, Aug 10 -- 1784-1797 Land Entries, Moore County, NC
#942 John Porterfield (for **David Allison**) entered 655 acres located on the head of Wet Creek near **McIver**.

1857.   1794, Aug 10 -- 1784-1797 Land Entries, Moore County, NC
#944 John Porterfield (for **David Allison**) entered 529 acres located east of Horse Creek adjoining **Leonard Furr**.

1858.   1794, Aug 10 -- 1784-1797 Land Entries, Moore County, NC
#945 John Porterfield (for **David Allison**) entered 417 acres located on McLendons Creek adjoining **George Grimes** and **Michael Brians**[Bryant].

1859.   1794, Aug 10 -- 1784-1797 Land Entries, Moore County, NC
#946 John Porterfield (for **David Allison**) entered 648 acres located on Richland Creek adjoining **William Dunn**.

1860.   1794, Aug 10 -- 1784-1797 Land Entries, Moore County, NC
#947 John Porterfield (for **David Allison**) entered 752 acres located on McCallums Fork adjoining **Joseph Dunn**.

1861.   1794, Aug 10 -- 1784-1797 Land Entries, Moore County, NC
#948 John Porterfield (for **David Allison**) entered 602 acres located on Buffalow Creek.

1862.   1794, Aug 10 -- 1784-1797 Land Entries, Moore County, NC
#949 John Porterfield (for **David Allison**) entered 531 acres located between Buffalow Creek and Lick Creek.

1863.   1794, Aug 10 -- 1784-1797 Land Entries, Moore County, NC
#950 John Porterfield (for **David Allison**) entered 680 acres located on the head of McCollums Fork.

1864.   1794, Aug 10 -- 1784-1797 Land Entries, Moore County, NC
#951 John Porterfield (for **David Allison**) entered 458 acres located west of McLendons Creek.

1865.   1794, Aug 10 -- 1784-1797 Land Entries, Moore County, NC
#952 John Porterfield (for **David Allison**) entered 442 acres located on both sides of Buffalow Creek.

1866.   1794, Aug 10 -- 1784-1797 Land Entries, Moore County, NC
#953 John Porterfield (for **David Allison**) entered 634 acres located near **Joseph Dunn Junr**.

1867.   1794, Aug 10 -- 1784-1797 Land Entries, Moore County, NC
#954 John Porterfield (for **David Allison**) entered 538 acres located on both sides of Richland Creek.

1868.   1794, Aug 10 -- 1784-1797 Land Entries, Moore County, NC
#955 John Porterfield (for **David Allison**) entered 605 acres located between Deep River and McLendons Creek.

1869.   1794, Aug 10 -- 1784-1797 Land Entries, Moore County, NC
#957 John Porterfield (for **David Allison**) entered 530 acres located on the head of McCallums Fork and Lick.

1870.   1794, Aug 10 -- 1784-1797 Land Entries, Moore County, NC

#958 **John Porterfield** (for **David Allison**) entered 407 acres located on the head of Lick including the White Lick.

1871. 1794, Aug 10 -- 1784-1797 Land Entries, Moore County, NC
#959 **John Porterfield** (for **David Allison**) entered 570 acres located on both sides of the head of Richland Creek.

1872. 1794, Aug 10 -- 1784-1797 Land Entries, Moore County, NC
#960 **John Porterfield** (for **David Allison**) entered 332 acres located on both sides of Buffalow Creek.

1873. 1794, Aug 10 -- 1784-1797 Land Entries, Moore County, NC
#961 **John Porterfield** (for **David Allison**) entered 536 acres located between the Long Meadow and Richland Creek.

1874. 1794, Aug 10 -- 1784-1797 Land Entries, Moore County, NC
#978 **John Porterfield** (for **David Allison**) entered 405 acres located north of McLendons Creek adjoining **Robert Edwards**.

1875. 1794, Aug 10 -- 1784-1797 Land Entries, Moore County, NC
#981 **John Porterfield** (for **David Allison**) entered 640 acres located on Mill Creek.

1876. 1794, Aug 10 -- 1784-1797 Land Entries, Moore County, NC
#982 **John Porterfield** (for **David Allison**) entered 793 acres located south of Bear Creek.

1877. 1794, Aug 10 -- 1784-1797 Land Entries, Moore County, NC
#983 **John Porterfield** (for **David Allison**) entered 880 acres located south of Cabbin Creek adjoining **Joseph Allen**.

1878. 1794, Aug 10 -- 1784-1797 Land Entries, Moore County, NC
#984 **John Porterfield** (for **David Allison**) entered 348 acres located near **Lewis Sowell**'s Mill.

1879. 1794, Aug 10 -- 1784-1797 Land Entries, Moore County, NC
#985 **John Porterfield** (for **David Allison**) entered 494 acres located south of Cabbin Creek adjoining **Jos. Allen**.

1880. 1794, Aug 10 -- 1784-1797 Land Entries, Moore County, NC
#986 **John Porterfield** (for **David Allison**) entered 215 acres located west of Huffman Creek adjoining **Huffman**.

1881. 1794, Aug 10 -- 1784-1797 Land Entries, Moore County, NC
#987 **John Porterfield** (for **David Allison**) entered 220 acres located west of Mill Creek adjoining **John Morgan**.

1882. 1794, Aug 10 -- 1784-1797 Land Entries, Moore County, NC
#988 **John Porterfield** (for **David Allison**) entered 300 acres located northwest of Wolf Creek.

1883. 1794, Aug 10 -- 1784-1797 Land Entries, Moore County, NC
#989 **John Porterfield** (for **David Allison**) entered 189 acres located northwest of Wolf Creek near **Wm. Wright**.

1884. 1794, Aug 10 -- 1784-1797 Land Entries, Moore County, NC
#990 **John Porterfield** (for **David Allison**) entered 424 acres located in the fork of Cabbin Creek adjoining the [Montgomery] county line.

1885. 1794, Aug 10 -- 1784-1797 Land Entries, Moore County, NC
#991 **John Porterfield** (for **David Allison**) entered 720 acres located north of Bear Creek on the [Randolph] county line near **Hardy Davis**.

1886. 1794, Aug 10 -- 1784-1797 Land Entries, Moore County, NC
#992 **John Porterfield** (for **David Allison**) entered 590 acres located north of Bear Creek.

1887.   1794, Aug 10 -- 1784-1797 Land Entries, Moore County, NC
#993 **John Porterfield** (for **David Allison**) entered 640 acres located north of Bear Creek.

1888.   1794, Aug 10 -- 1784-1797 Land Entries, Moore County, NC
#994 **John Porterfield** (for **David Allison**) entered 520 acres located north of Dry Fork of Mill Creek near the county line.

1889.   1794, Aug 10 -- 1784-1797 Land Entries, Moore County, NC
#995 **John Porterfield** (for **David Allison**) entered 558 acres located east of McLendons Creek adjoining **John Overton**.

1890.   1794, Aug 10 -- 1784-1797 Land Entries, Moore County, NC
#997 **John Porterfield** (for **David Allison**) entered 590 acres located north of Bear Creek adjoining **Thomas Smitherman**.

1891.   1794, Aug 10 -- 1784-1797 Land Entries, Moore County, NC
#998 **John Porterfield** (for **David Allison**) entered 707 acres located north of Bear Creek on the county line.

1892.   1794, Aug 10 -- 1784-1797 Land Entries, Moore County, NC
#999 **John Porterfield** (for **David Allison**) entered 670 acres located north of Bear Creek near **William Garner Senr.**

1893.   1794, Aug 10 -- 1784-1797 Land Entries, Moore County, NC
#1000 **John Porterfield** (for **David Allison**) entered 476 acres located in the fork of Cabin Creek and Mill Creek.

1894.   1794, Aug 10 -- 1784-1797 Land Entries, Moore County, NC
#1001 **John Porterfield** (for **David Allison**) entered 470 acres located east of McLendons Creek adjoining **John Overton**.

1895.   1794, Aug 10 -- 1784-1797 Land Entries, Moore County, NC
#1003 **John Porterfield** (for **David Allison**) entered 640 acres located west of Wolf Creek on the county line.

1896.   1794, Aug 10 -- 1784-1797 Land Entries, Moore County, NC
#1004 **John Porterfield** (for **David Allison**) entered 914 acres located north of Williamson [Williams] Creek on the county line.

1897.   1794, Aug 10 -- 1784-1797 Land Entries, Moore County, NC
#1006 **John Porterfield** (for **David Allison**) entered 391 acres located northwest of McLendons Creek near **Kenneth McDonald**.

1898.   1794, Aug 10 -- 1784-1797 Land Entries, Moore County, NC
#1007 **John Porterfield** (for **David Allison**) entered 430 acres located on a branch of McLendons Creek near **Allen Martin**.

1899.   1794, Aug 10 -- 1784-1797 Land Entries, Moore County, NC
#1008 **John Porterfield** (for **David Allison**) entered 614 acres located on a branch of McLendons Creek adjoining **John McNeill**.

1900.   1794, Aug 10 -- 1784-1797 Land Entries, Moore County, NC
#1009 **John Porterfield** (for **David Allison**) entered 453 acres located on the head of a branch of the Dry Fork of McLendons Creek.

1901.   1794, Aug 10 -- 1784-1797 Land Entries, Moore County, NC
#1013 **John Porterfield** (for **David Allison**) entered 640 acres located north of Suck Creek adjoining **William Barrett**.

1902.   1794, Aug 10 -- 1784-1797 Land Entries, Moore County, NC
#1018 **John Porterfield** (for **David Allison**) entered 589 acres located on McLendons Creek adjoining **Allen Martin**.

**Land Granted on Lower McLendons Creek, Lower Richland Creek, Killetts Creek,
Suck Creek and the Juniper by the 1790s-1800s**
Map prepared utilizing early land grants
[for more information see www.MooreCountyWallaces.com]

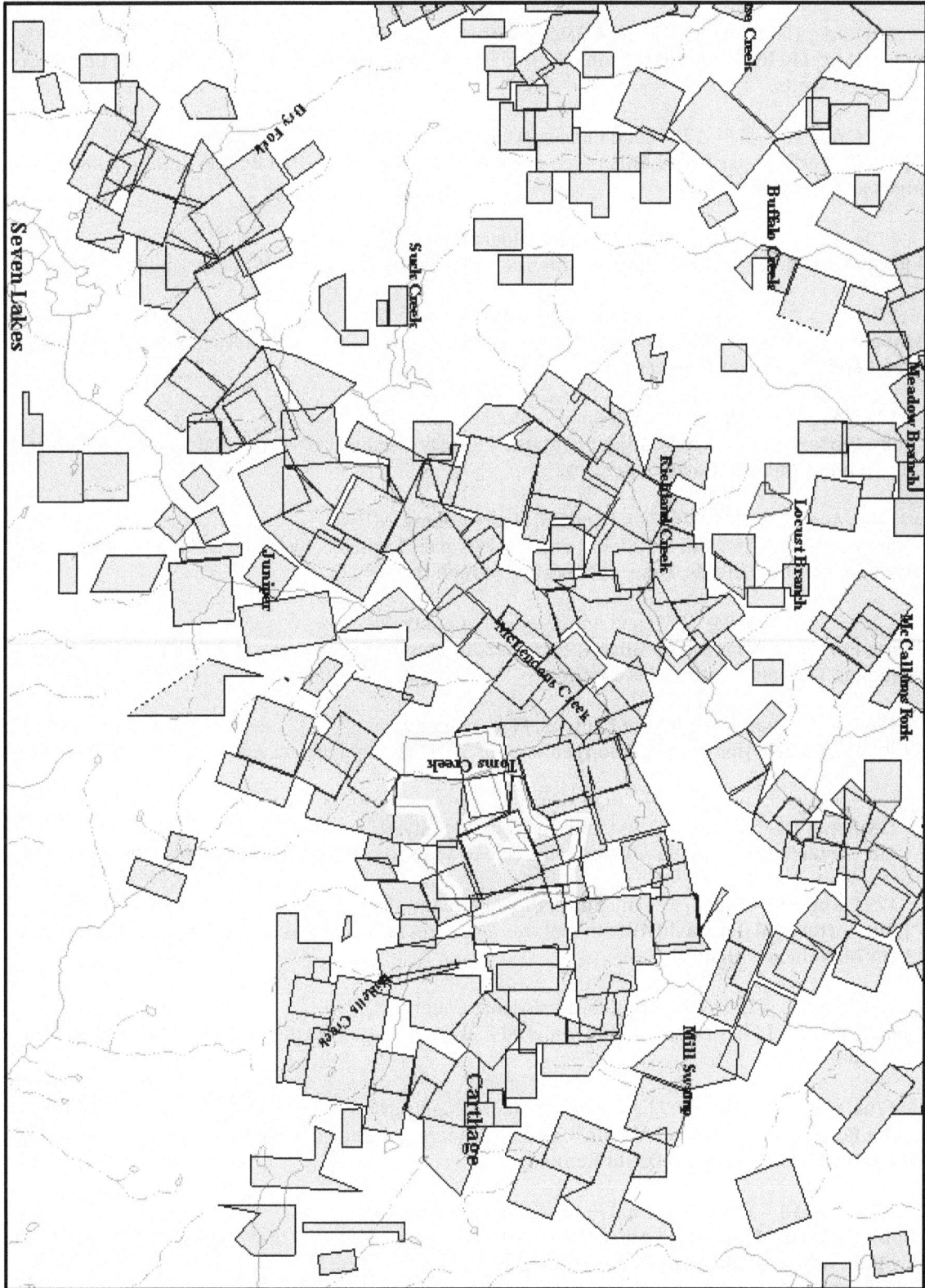

1903.   1794, Aug 10 -- 1784-1797 Land Entries, Moore County, NC
#1133 **John Porterfield** (for **David Allison**) entered 640 acres located on Little River adjoining **Caddell**.

1904.   1794, Aug 10 -- 1784-1797 Land Entries, Moore County, NC
#1134 **John Porterfield** (for **David Allison**) entered 640 acres located on Little River adjoining **Micajah Caddell**.

1905.   1794, Aug 10 -- 1784-1797 Land Entries, Moore County, NC
#1187 **John Porterfield** (for **David Allison**) entered 640 acres located between Bear Creek and Buffalo Creek adjoining **Jacob Stutts**.

1906.   1794, Aug 10 -- 1784-1797 Land Entries, Moore County, NC
#1188 **John Porterfield** (for **David Allison**) entered 495 acres located west of Buffalo Creek adjoining **Bryan Burroughs** and **Harman Brewer**.

1907.   1794, Aug 10 -- 1784-1797 Land Entries, Moore County, NC
#1189 **John Porterfield** (for **David Allison**) entered 435 acres located east of Wet Creek adjoining **Thos. Key**.

1908.   1794, Aug 10 -- 1784-1797 Land Entries, Moore County, NC
#1190 **John Porterfield** (for **David Allison**) entered 420 acres located on both sides of Horse Creek adjoining **Widow McLeod** and **Murdoch McLeod**.

1909.   1794, Aug 10 -- 1784-1797 Land Entries, Moore County, NC
#1191 **John Porterfield** (for **David Allison**) entered 284 acres located between Buffalow Creek and Bear Creek adjoining **Nicholas Nall** and **Harman Brewer**.

1910.   1794, Aug 10 -- 1784-1797 Land Entries, Moore County, NC
#1225 **John Porterfield** (for **David Allison**) entered 570 acres located between McLendons Creek and Richland Creek adjoining **Reubin Shields**, **Thomas Muse** and **Joseph Dunn**.

1911.   1794, Aug 10 -- 1784-1797 Land Entries, Moore County, NC
#1229 **John Porterfield** (for **David Allison**) entered 280 acres located between McLendons Creek and Richland Creek adjoining **Thomas Muse** and his own line.

1912.   1794, Aug 10 -- 1784-1797 Land Entries, Moore County, NC
#1234 **John Porterfield** (for **David Allison**) entered 635 acres located on McLendons Creek adjoining **Thomas Muse**.

1913.   1794, Aug 10 -- 1784-1797 Land Entries, Moore County, NC
#1251 **John Porterfield** (for **David Allison**) entered 640 acres located on Richland Creek and Lick Creek.

1914.   1794, Aug 10 -- 1784-1797 Land Entries, Moore County, NC
#1277 **John Porterfield** (for **David Allison**) entered 270 acres located between north of Bear Creek his own line, **Hector McNeill** and **Nicholas Nall**.

1915.   1794, Aug 10 -- 1784-1797 Land Entries, Moore County, NC
#1296 **John Porterfield** (for **David Allison**) entered 230 acres located northwest Williamson [Williams] Creek adjoining **Adam Comer**.

1916.   1794, Aug 10 -- 1784-1797 Land Entries, Moore County, NC
#1302 **John Porterfield** (for **David Allison**) entered 250 acres located between Persimmon Branch and Grassie Creek adjoining **Nicholas Nall** and **David Kennedy**.

1917.   1794, Aug 10 -- 1784-1797 Land Entries, Moore County, NC
#1304 **John Porterfield** (for **David Allison**) entered 340 acres located west of Williamson [Williams] Creek adjoining **John Hair** and **Adam Comer**.

1918.   1794, Aug 10 -- 1784-1797 Land Entries, Moore County, NC

#1305 **John Porterfield** (for **David Allison**) entered 400 acres located north of Bear Creek adjoining **Nicholas Nall**, **Leonard Furr** and **Everett Smith**.

1919.   1794, Aug 10 -- 1784-1797 Land Entries, Moore County, NC
#1306 **John Porterfield** (for **David Allison**) entered 269 acres located south of Bear Creek and east of Williams Creek adjoining **Adam Comer**.

1920.   1794, Aug 10 -- 1784-1797 Land Entries, Moore County, NC
#1307 **John Porterfield** (for **David Allison**) entered 300 acres located on Little Creek south of Bear Creek.

1921.   1794, Aug 10 -- 1784-1797 Land Entries, Moore County, NC
#1309 **John Porterfield** (for **David Allison**) entered 350 acres located in the fork of Bear and Cabbin Creek adjoining **Everett Smith**.

1922.   1794, Aug 10 -- 1784-1797 Land Entries, Moore County, NC
#1311 **John Porterfield** (for **David Allison**) entered 250 acres located between McLendons Creek and the Juniper adjoining **Thomas Graham** at the crossroads.

1923.   1794, Aug 10 -- 1784-1797 Land Entries, Moore County, NC
#1312 **John Porterfield** (for **David Allison**) entered 450 acres located east of McLendons Creek adjoining **McLendon**, **Barret**, **Jackson** and **Sowell**.

1924.   1794, Aug 10 -- 1784-1797 Land Entries, Moore County, NC
#1314 **John Porterfield** (for **David Allison**) entered 245 acres located south of Bear Creek adjoining **Leonard Furr**.

1925.   1794, Aug 10 -- 1784-1797 Land Entries, Moore County, NC
#1316 **John Porterfield** (for **David Allison**) entered 295 acres adjoining the Randolph County line near where **Nicholas Nall** lives and where **Robert Bird** lives.

1926.   1794, Aug 10 -- 1784-1797 Land Entries, Moore County, NC
#1317 **John Porterfield** (for **David Allison**) entered 400 acres located on the head of Bear Creek adjoining the Randolph County line and **Henry Cagle**.

1927.   1794, Aug 10 -- 1784-1797 Land Entries, Moore County, NC
#1322 **John Porterfield** (for **David Allison**) entered 313 acres located north of Bear Creek adjoining **Everett Smith**, **Francis Bullock** and **Attry**.

1928.   1794, Aug 10 -- 1784-1797 Land Entries, Moore County, NC
#1327 **John Porterfield** (for **David Allison**) entered 325 acres located on the head of Bear Creek adjoining the Randolph County line and **Henry Cagle**.

1929.   1794, Aug 10 -- 1784-1797 Land Entries, Moore County, NC
#1328 **John Porterfield** (for **David Allison**) entered 175 acres located between Cabbin Creek and Wolf Creek on both sides of the Yadkin Road.

1930.   1794, Aug 10 -- 1784-1797 Land Entries, Moore County, NC
#1329 **John Porterfield**'s [for **David Allison**] entered 235 acres adjoining **Nicholas Nall**, **William Manes'**place and **David Kennaday**.

1931.   1794, Aug 10 -- 1784-1797 Land Entries, Moore County, NC
#1331 **John Porterfield** (for **David Allison**) entered 130 acres located east of Mill Creek adjoining his own line and **Lewis Sowell**.

1932.   1794, Aug 10 -- 1784-1797 Land Entries, Moore County, NC
#1332 **John Porterfield** (for **David Allison**) entered 170 acres located between Richardson Branch and Wet Creek adjoining **Hezekiah Dunn**.

1933.   1794, Aug 12 -- Land Grant #1033, Moore County, NC

Thomas Tyson received 150 acres located on south of Deep River and both sides of the Waggon Road adjoining **Benjamin Tyson**. **Joshua Tyson** and **Archd. McBride** were chain carriers.

1934.   1794, Aug 18 -- 1784-1795 Court of Pleas and Quarter Sessions, Moore County, NC
[*jury duty - selected participants*] **William Morgan, John Haire, James Hill, Jonathan Caddill, Jesse Ritter, Zachry Smith, David Kennedy, Jacob Cagle, Samuel Dunn, John Sowell, Thomas Ritter, Jesse Bean** and **Elijah Autry**. [*jury duty next term - selected participants*] **Christopher Yow, William Williamson, George Cagle, Joseph Dunn Jr., Leonard Furr, Peter Haire, David Richardson, Zachary Smith, Richard Dunn Jur., William Copland, Joseph Allan, Jacob Stutts, Stephen Smith** and **Reuben Freeman**.

1935.   1794, Aug 18,21 -- 1784-1795 Court of Pleas and Quarter Sessions, Moore County, NC Page 470-481
[Deeds] **William Davis** to **Robert Davis** was proven by another **Robert Davis**

John Argo to **Isaac Teague** proven by **Zachariah Smith**
James Muse to **John Wadsworth** was proven by **William Mears** Esq.
Lanear Brewer to **John Lawler** proven by **Isaac Teague**
Hardy Davis to **Nichl. Nall** proven by **Robert Byrde**
Batholomew Dunn to **John Allan** was acknowledged
[Bill of Sale] **George Jackson** as Executor of **John Jackson** Dec'd. to **William Dunn** proven by **Joseph Robson**

1936.   1794, Aug 18 -- 1784-1795 Court of Pleas and Quarter Sessions, Moore County, NC Page 472-473
James Caddell v. **Geo. Glascock** heirs
John Caddell v. **Joseph Robson**

1937.   1794, Aug 18 -- Land Grant #930, Moore County, NC
Neil McLeod received 60 acres located on both sides of Cabin Creek adjoining **James Jeffreys, Carpenter**.

1938.   1794, Aug 19 -- 1784-1795 Court of Pleas and Quarter Sessions, Moore County, NC Page 474
Ordered that **William Davis** be appointed overseer of the road instead of **Robert Davis**.

1939.   1794, Sep 1 -- 1784-1797 Land Entries, Moore County, NC
#1334 **John Morgan Junr.** entered 100 acres on both sides of Cabbin Creek adjoining his own line.

1940.   1794, Sep 1 -- 1784-1797 Land Entries, Moore County, NC
#1335 **Nathan Smith Junr.** entered 100 acres on both sides of Cabbin Creek adjoining **John Morgan**.

1941.   1794, Sep 1 -- 1784-1797 Land Entries, Moore County, NC
#1336 **John Morgan Senr.** entered 50 acres on both sides of Cabbin Creek adjoining his own line.

1942.   1794, Sep 22 -- Land Grant #0195, Moore County, NC
Beyhue Sowell [assignee of **John Hargrove**] received 100 acres located on Buffalo Creek adjoining **John Hargrove**. **Lenard Furr** and **James Morgin** were chain carriers. [*Editor's Note: Never granted*]

1943.   1794, Sep 24 -- Land Grant #918, Moore County, NC
Peter Graves received 50 acres located south of Deep River adjoining **Traps** and **Barton**'s Old Field. **John Perry** and **Samuel Perry** were chain carriers.

1944.   1794, Sep 30 -- 1784-1797 Land Entries, Moore County, NC
#1340 **Leonard Furr** entered 50 acres west of Flag Creek adjoining his own line.

1945.   1794, Sep 30 -- 1784-1797 Land Entries, Moore County, NC
#1341 **John McAulay** entered 50 acres located southeast of Bear Creek and Mainers Branch adjoining **James Mainer** and **Christopher Stutts**.

1946.   1794, Sep 30 -- 1784-1797 Land Entries, Moore County, NC
#1342 **John Hargrove** entered 100 acres on Buffalow Creek adjoining his own line.

1947.   1794, Sep 30 -- 1784-1797 Land Entries, Moore County, NC
#1343 **Niell McLeod** and **John Hargrove** entered 100 acres on the head of the Persimmon Glade adjoining **John Dunlap**.

A.   1794, Oct 2 -- Land Grant #993, Montgomery County, NC
Edward Duval Tyler received 100 acres located on north fork of Little River adjoining his own line. **Richard Bean** and **Peter Bean** were chain carriers.

1948.   1794, Oct 8 -- Land Grant #1512, Randolph County, NC
Nicholas Nall [assignee of **John Spinks**] received 138 acres located on Deep River adjoining **John Spinks** and **Pearce**. **Cornelius Lathum** and **Moses George** were chain carriers.

1949.   1794, Oct 21 -- Deed Book H Page 230-231, Chatham County, NC
Zachariah Smith [of Moore County] deeded **Eli Lawler** [of Chatham County] 100 acres located on Cedar Creek and [Moore] County line. **Saml. Person**, **Isaac Teague** and **James Scott** were witnesses.

1950.   1794, Oct 21 -- Deed Book J Page 237, Chatham County, NC
Zachariah Smith [of Moore County] deeded **Isaac Teague** [of Moore County] 100 acres located on Cedar Creek and [Moore] County line adjoining **Eli Lawler**. **Eli Lawler** and **Sam. Person** were witnesses.

1951.   1794, Oct 24 -- Land Grant #1259, Moore County, NC
Hector McNeil received 50 acres located south of Deep River between the drains of Richland Creek and Long Meadow adjoining **Solomon Barrett**. **Jacob Cagle** and **Neal McIntosh** were chain carriers.

1952.   1794, Oct 28 -- Land Grant #912, Moore County, NC
John McKay received 100 acres located on both sides of Willow Meadow. **Jacob Cagle** and **Neal McIntosh** were chain carriers.

A.   1794, Oct 30 -- Land Grant #851, Montgomery County, NC
John Jordan received 50 acres adjoining **Berry Hicks** (formerly **James Cotton** Dec'd.). **Berry Hix** and **John Sowell** were chain carriers.

1953.   1794, Oct 30 -- Land Grant #957, Moore County, NC
Nathan Fry received 60 acres located on Killetts Creek including his own improvement and adjoining **Joseph Fry**. **Joseph Fry** and **Nathan Fry** were chain carriers.

A.   1794, Nov 4 -- Land Grant #1719, Chatham County, NC
Sion Phillips [assignee of **William Meroney**] received 100 acres located on Tysons Creek adjoining **Benjamin Saunders** and **Harper**. **Sampson Brewer** and **Willis Phillips** were chain carriers.

1954.   1794, Nov 11 -- Land Grant #538, Moore County, NC
David Allison received 680 acres located on the head of McCallums Fork, the branches of Buffaloe Creek and the Waggon Road adjoining **McGee**, **Cockman**, **John Riter**, **Zachariah Smith** and **John McKoy**. **Jacob Cagle** and **Neal McIntosh** were chain carriers.

1955.   1794, Nov 11 -- Land Grant #539, Moore County, NC
David Allison received 538 acres located on Richland Creek, the Persimmon Glade and both sides of Toms Creek. **Jacob Cagle** and **Neal McIntosh** were chain carriers.

1956.   1794, Nov 11 -- Land Grant #540, Moore County, NC
David Allison received 630 acres located on the head of McCallums Fork of Richland Creek and the Fork of Leek Creek adjoining **Frances Merrick**, his own line and **Zachariah Smith**. **Jacob Cagle** and **Neal McIntosh** were chain carriers.

1957.   1794, Nov 11 -- Land Grant #541, Moore County, NC

David Allison received 600 acres located on Persimmon Glade of McLendons Creek. **Jacob Cagle** and **Neal McIntosh** were chain carriers.

1958.   1794, Nov 11 -- Land Grant #633, Moore County, NC
David Allison received 590 acres located between Cabin Creek and Horse Creek adjoining his own line, **Thomas Graham**, **Everet Smith** improvement. **John McDonald** and **Angus McIver** were chain carriers.

1959.   1794, Nov 11 -- Land Grant #634, Moore County, NC
David Allison received 320 acres located on the drains of Flag Creek, west of Buffalo Creek adjoining **Leonard Furr**. **John McDonald** and **Angus McIver** were chain carriers.

1960.   1794, Nov 12 -- Land Grant #542, Moore County, NC
David Allison received 581 acres located between Leeck Creek and Buffalo Creek adjoining **McKinzie** and **Frances Merrick**. **Jacob Cagle** and **Neal McIntosh** were chain carriers.

1961.   1794, Nov 12 -- Land Grant #543, Moore County, NC
David Allison received 442 acres located on both sides of Buffalo Creek adjoining **Alxr. Monroe** and **Neal Matheson**. **Jacob Cagle** and **Neal McIntosh** were chain carriers.

1962.   1794, Nov 13 -- Land Grant #545, Moore County, NC
David Allison received 698 acres located on Richland Creek between McCollums Fork and Locust Branch adjoining **William Dunn** and **Donald McQueen**. **Jacob Cagle** and **Neal McIntosh** were chain carriers.

1963.   1794, Nov 13 -- Land Grant #546, Moore County, NC
David Allison received 634 acres located on Richland Creek in the fork of Blands Branch adjoining **Joseph Dunn Junr**. **Jacob Cagle** and **Neal McIntosh** were chain carriers.

1964.   1794, Nov 13 -- Land Grant #635, Moore County, NC
David Allison received 337 acres located north of Cabin Creek adjoining his own line, **William Smith**. **John McDonald** and **Angus McIver** were chain carriers.

1965.   1794, Nov 14 -- Land Grant #548, Moore County, NC
David Allison received 762 acres located on McCollums Fork of Richland Creek and the fork of Blands Branch adjoining **Joseph Dunn** and **Upton**. **Jacob Cagle** and **Neal McIntosh** were chain carriers.

1966.   1794, Nov 14 -- Land Grant #549, Moore County, NC
David Allison received 602 acres located on Buffalo Creek adjoining **Leonard Furr**, **Neil McLeod**, **James Melton**, **John McKoy**. **Jacob Cagle** and **Neal McIntosh** were chain carriers.

1967.   1794, Nov 14 -- Land Grant #550, Moore County, NC
David Allison received 500 acres located on both sides of Persimmon Glade of McLendons Creek adjoining **John Dunlap**. **Jacob Cagle** and **Neal McIntosh** were chain carriers.

1968.   1794, Nov 14 -- Land Grant #636, Moore County, NC
David Allison received 400 acres located west of Buffalo Creek adjoining **Alexander Munroe**. **John McDonald** and **Angus McIver** were chain carriers.

1969.   1794, Nov 14 -- Land Grant #594, Moore County, NC
David Allison received 640 acres located north of Suck Creek adjoining **William Barrett**. **Daniel McSween** and **Alexander McIntosh** were chain carriers.

1970.   1794, Nov 15 -- Land Grant #637, Moore County, NC
David Allison received 546 acres located on the head of Richland Creek adjoining **Neill McLeod**. **John McDonald** and **Angus McIver** were chain carriers.

1971.   1794, Nov 15 -- Land Grant #639, Moore County, NC
David Allison received 640 acres located on Watery Branch of Buffalo Creek adjoining his own line and **Nicholas Nall**. **John McDonald** and **Angus McIver** were chain carriers.

1972. 1794, Nov 15 -- Land Grant #649, Moore County, NC **David Allison** received 660 acres located west of Buffalo Creek adjoining his own line and **Jacob Stutts'** improvement. **John McDonald** and **Angus McIver** were chain carriers.

1973. 1794, Nov 15 -- Land Grant #0190, Moore County, NC **James Hines** [assignee of **Edward Smith**] received 50 acres located on Buffalo Creek adjoining his own line (formerly **William Smith**) and **Bean** and including his own improvement. **Donald McLeod** and **John Campbell** were chain carriers. [*Editor's Note: Never granted*]

1974. 1794, Nov 16 -- Land Grant #640, Moore County, NC **David Allison** received 734 acres south of the Race Paths adjoining **Nicholas Newton**. **John McDonald** and **Angus McIver** were chain carriers.

1975. 1794, Nov 17 -- 1784-1795 Court of Pleas and Quarter Sessions, Moore County, NC [*jury duty - selected participants*] **Christopher Yew, David Richardson, Jacob Stutts, Joseph Dunn, Zach Smith, George Cagle, Leonard Furr, John Stutts, Jacob Cagle, John Sowell, Bartholomew Dunn** and **Jesse Beane**. [*jury duty next term - selected participants*] **William Williamson, Willm. Copland, Joseph Allan, Hezekiah Dunn** and **Frederick Autry**.

1976. 1794, Nov 18 -- Land Grant #641, Moore County, NC **David Allison** received 640 acres located on Haw Branch of Mill Creek near Sings Creek adjoining his own line and **Thomas Key**. **John McDonald** and **Angus McIver** were chain carriers.

1977. 1794, Nov 18 -- Land Grant #642, Moore County, NC **David Allison** received 731 acres located on the head of Wet Creek adjoining **Richard Dunn** and **McIver**. **John McDonald** and **Angus McIver** were chain carriers.

1978. 1794, Nov 18 -- Land Grant #850, Moore County, NC **Joseph McGee** received 350 acres located south of Deep River adjoining **John Caralds** and **Joseph Duckworth**. **William Davis** and **Joseph McGee Jr**. were chain carriers.

1979. 1794, Nov 18-20 -- 1784-1795 Court of Pleas and Quarter Sessions, Moore County, NC Page 487-488,490, 494
[Deeds] **William Barrett** to **John McLeod** proven by **Winnifred Sowell**
Elijah Battis Sr. to **James Moore** proven by **William King**
Elijah Bettis Senr. to **Ezekial Ruebottom** proven by **Elijah Bettis Junr**.
Jesse Muse to **James Hill** was acknowledged
Jesse Griffin to **John Spivy** was acknowledged
Zachariah Smith to **Joseph McGee Jr**. was acknowledged
[Bill of Sale] **Joseph McGhee** to **Milly McGhee** was acknoweldged

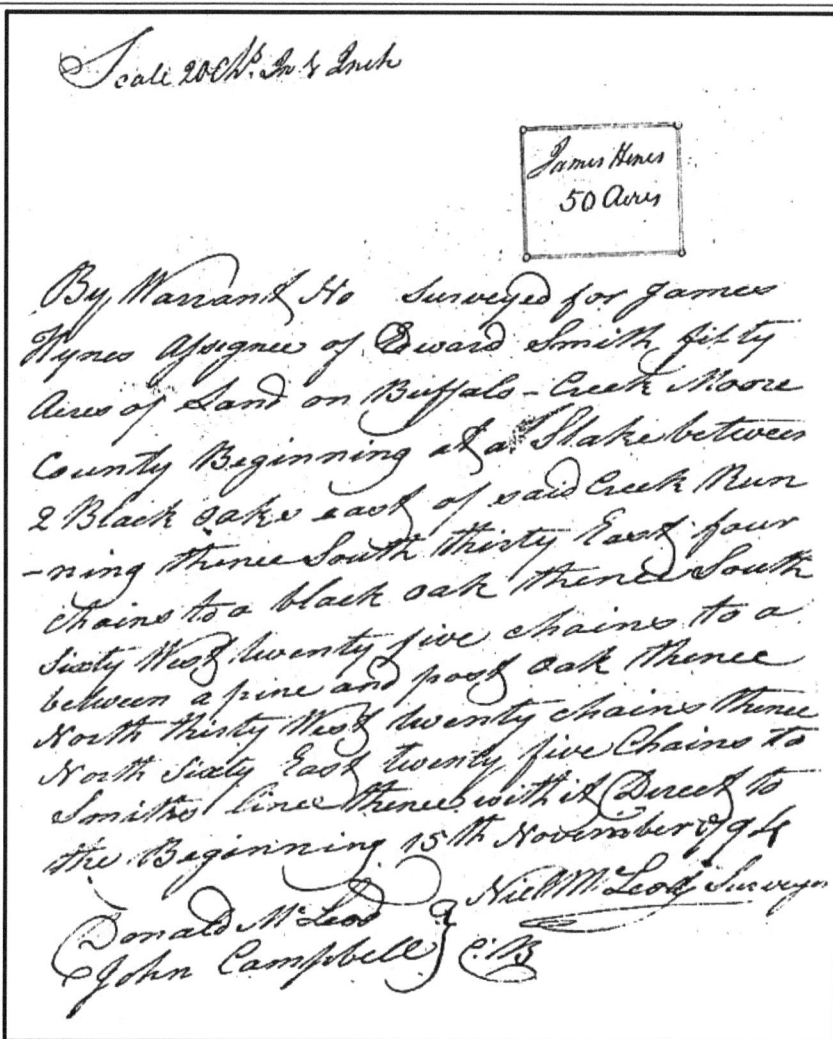

1980. 1794, Nov 19 -- Land Grant #554, Moore County, NC
David Allison received 332 acres located on Buffalo Creek adjoining **Alexander Monroe** and **John Hargrove**. **Jacob Cagle** and **Neal McIntosh** were chain carriers.

1981. 1794, Nov 19 -- 1784-1795 Court of Pleas and Quarter Sessions, Moore County, NC Page 487
Administration of the estate of **Thomas Moore** Dec'd. granted to widow **Phibe Moore** with **Jesse Griffin** and **Lewis Garner** as securities.

1982. 1794, Nov 19 -- 1784-1795 Court of Pleas and Quarter Sessions, Moore County, NC Page 490

Ordered that **John Sowell** be appointed overseer of the road in place of **Kenneth Murchison** and have the same hands to work.

1983. 1794, Nov 20 -- Land Grant #645, Moore County, NC **David Allison** received 600 acres located south of Wolf Creek and the [Montgomery] county line. **John McDonald** and **Angus McIver** were chain carriers.

1984. 1794, Nov 20 -- Land Grant #1190, Moore County, NC **Joseph Cockman** received 100 acres located on Long Meadow adjoining his own line and **James Melton**. **William McDonald** and **James Milton** were chain carriers.

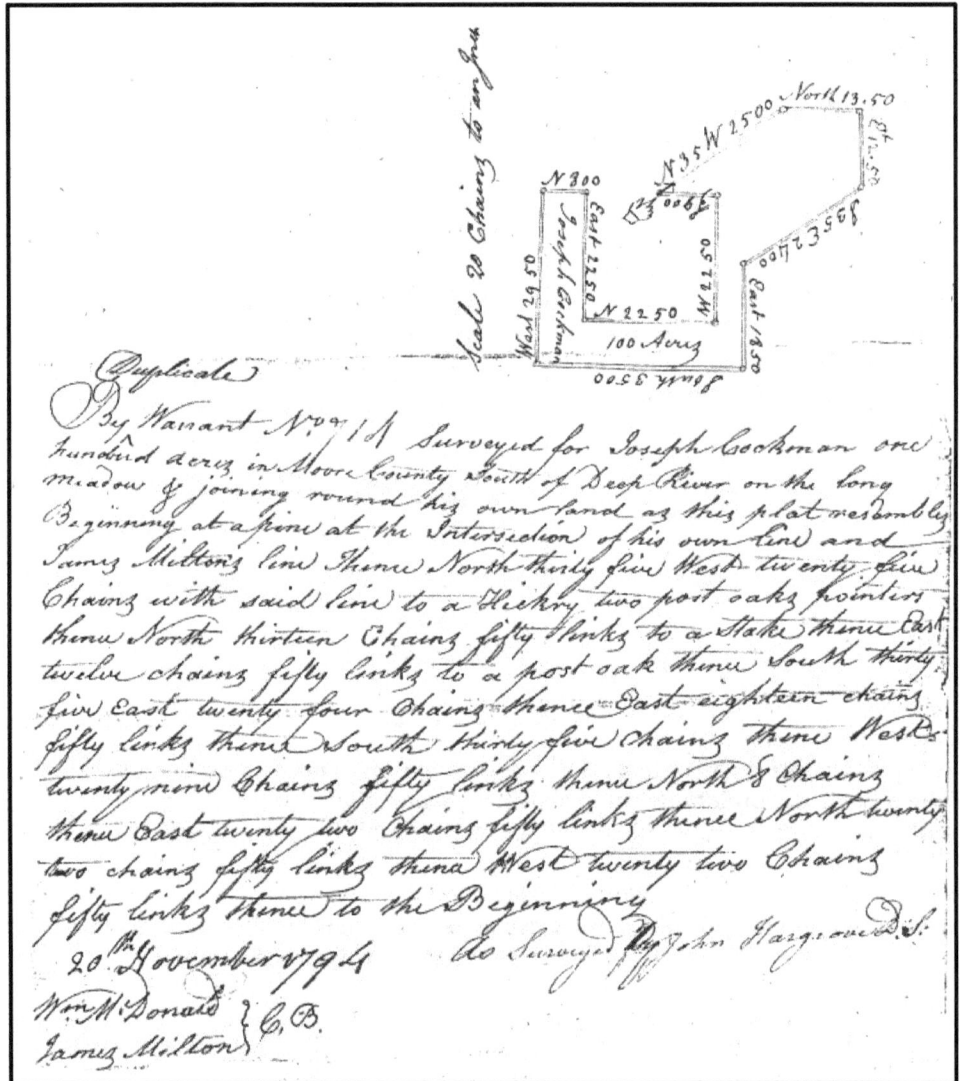

1985. 1794, Nov 21 -- Land Grant #555, Moore County, NC
David Allison received 536 acres located on Richland Creek and Long Meadow adjoining **Jesse Ritter**, **John McKoy** and **Jacob Stutts**. **Jacob Cagle** and **Neal McIntosh** were chain carriers.

1986. 1794, Nov 21 -- Land Grant #556, Moore County, NC
David Allison received 670 acres located on both sides of Richland Creek near the head adjoining **Neil McLeod** and **McDonald**. **Jacob Cagle** and **Neal McIntosh** were chain carriers.

1987. 1794, Nov 23 -- Land Grant #605, Moore County, NC
David Allison received 640 acres located west of Mill Creek near the county line adjoining his own line. **Donald McSween** and **Alexander McIntosh** were chain carriers.

1988. 1794, Nov 23 -- Land Grant #606, Moore County, NC
David Allison received 520 acres located northwest of Mill Creek near the county line adjoining **Wilson** Place and **Lewis Sowell**. **Donald McSween** and **Alexander McIntosh** were chain carriers.

1989.   1794, Nov 24 -- Land Grant #607, Moore County, NC
David Allison received 880 acres located on Half Mile Branch of Cabin Creek adjoining **Joseph Allen**. **Donald McSween** and **Alexander McIntosh** were chain carriers.

1990.   1794, Nov 24 -- Land Grant #608, Moore County, NC
David Allison received 348 acres located west of Mill Creek adjoining **Lewis Sowell**'s Mill . **Donald McSween** and **Alexander McIntosh** were chain carriers.

1991.   1794, Nov 24 -- Land Grant #609, Moore County, NC
David Allison received 494 acres located south of Cabin Creek adjoining **Joseph Allen**. **Donald McSween** and **Alexander McIntosh** were chain carriers.

1992.   1794, Nov 24 -- Land Grant #610, Moore County, NC
David Allison received 220 acres located on Half Mile Branch of Mill Creek and the Yadkin Road adjoining **John Morgan**. **Donald McSween** and **Alexander McIntosh** were chain carriers.

1993.   1794, Nov 25 -- Land Grant #611, Moore County, NC
David Allison received 476 acres located on Fork of Cabin Creek and Mill Creek adjoining **William Morgan**. **Donald McSween** and **Alexander McIntosh** were chain carriers.

1994.   1794, Nov 25 -- Land Grant #643, Moore County, NC
David Allison received 900 acres located northwest of Sings Creek near Mill Creek adjoining **James Gallemore**. **John McDonald** and **Angus McIver** were chain carriers.

1995.   1794, Nov 26 -- Land Grant #749, Moore County, NC
David Allison received 600 acres located between McLendons Creek and Richland Creek adjoining **Joseph Dunn**. **Thos. Muse** and **Jesse Muse** were chain carriers.

1996.   1794, Nov 27 -- Land Grant #612, Moore County, NC
David Allison received 424 acres located on Fork of Cabin Creek near the [Montgomery] county line. **Donald McSween** and **Alexander McIntosh** were chain carriers.

1997.   1794, Nov 27 -- Land Grant #1168, Moore County, NC
Joseph Dunn received 150 acres located on both sides of Richland Creek adjoining his own line and **Campbell**. **Thomas Muse** and **Kindred Muse** were chain carriers.

1998.   1794, Nov 28 -- Land Grant #613, Moore County, NC
David Allison received 640 acres located on Cow Branch of Wolf Creek and the [Montgomery] county line adjoining **William Right**. **Donald McSween** and **Alexander McIntosh** were chain carriers.

1999.   1794, Nov 28 -- Land Grant #644, Moore County, NC
David Allison received 520 acres located south of Wolf Creek adjoining **William Wright**. **John McDonald** and **Angus McIver** were chain carriers.

2000.   1794, Nov 28 -- Land Grant #855, Moore County, NC
Norman Matheson received 50 acres located on Horse Creek adjoining **Nicholas Newton** and the Sandhill Place. **Neal Matheson** and **Donald Buchanan** were chain carriers.

2001.   1794, Nov 28 -- Land Grant #857, Moore County, NC
Norman Matheson received 50 acres located south of Deep River adjoining **Neal Matheson**. **Neal Matheson** and **Donald Buchanan** were chain carriers.

2002.   1794, Nov 28 -- Land Grant #899, Moore County, NC
Neil McLeod received 100 acres located on Haw Branch of Long Meadow adjoining **Jacob Cagle**, **Hill** or **Furr** and **Edwards**.

2003.   1794, Nov 29 -- Land Grant #614, Moore County, NC

David Allison received 798 acres located on Leak Branch of Bear Creek. **Donald McSween** and **Alexander McIntosh** were chain carriers.

2004.   1794, Nov 29 -- Land Grant #615, Moore County, NC
David Allison received 720 acres located north of Bear Creek near the [Randolph] county line adjoining **Hardy Davis**. **Donald McSween** and **Alexander McIntosh** were chain carriers.

2005.   1794, Nov 29 -- Land Grant #616, Moore County, NC
David Allison received 596 acres located north of Bear Creek. **Donald McSween** and **Alexander McIntosh** were chain carriers.

2006.   1794, Nov 29 -- Land Grant #617, Moore County, NC
David Allison received 596 acres located north of Bear Creek adjoining **Thos. Smitherman**. **Donald McSween** and **Alexander McIntosh** were chain carriers.

2007.   1794, Nov 29 -- Land Grant #618, Moore County, NC
David Allison received 707 acres located north of Bear Creek near the [Randolph] county line adjoining his own line. **Donald McSween** and **Alexander McIntosh** were chain carriers.

2008.   1794, Nov 29 -- Land Grant #619, Moore County, NC
David Allison received 670 acres located on Rocky Branch of Bear Creek adjoining **William Gardner**. **Donald McSween** and **Alexander McIntosh** were chain carriers.

2009.   1794, Nov 29 -- Land Grant #620, Moore County, NC
David Allison received 914 acres located on Lick Branch of Williams Creek near the [Montgomery] county line adjoining **Owen Carpenter**. **Donald McSween** and **Alexander McIntosh** were chain carriers.

2010.   1794, Nov 29 -- Land Grant #646, Moore County, NC
David Allison received 620 acres located north of Cabin Creek adjoining **William Morgan**. **John McDonald** and **Angus McIver** were chain carriers.

2011.   1794, Nov 29 -- Land Grant #647, Moore County, NC
David Allison received 756 acres located on Middle Meadow Branch of Cabin Creek adjoining his own line, **John Morgan**. **John McDonald** and **Angus McIver** were chain carriers.

2012.   1794, Nov 30 -- Land Grant #621, Moore County, NC
David Allison received 215 acres located northwest of Huffmans Creek adjoining **Huffman**. **Donald McSween** and **Alexander McIntosh** were chain carriers.

2013.   1794, Nov 30 -- Land Grant #622, Moore County, NC
David Allison received 300 acres located on northwest of Wolf Creek, Rocky Branch and Meadow Branch adjoining **Bullock**'s Cabin. **Donald McSween** and **Alexander McIntosh** were chain carriers.

2014.   1794, Nov 30 -- Land Grant #623, Moore County, NC
David Allison received 189 acres located northwest of Wolf Creek adjoining his own line, **William Right** and **Presley Lovin**'s Cabin. **Donald McSween** and **Alexander McIntosh** were chain carriers.

2015.   1794, Nov 30 -- Land Grant #624, Moore County, NC
David Allison received 869 acres located north of Bear Creek near Grassy Creek. **Donald McSween** and **Alexander McIntosh** were chain carriers.

2016.   1794, Nov 30 -- Land Grant #638, Moore County, NC
David Allison received 778 acres located south of Bear Creek adjoining **John Shuffield**. **John McDonald** and **Angus McIver** were chain carriers.

2017.   1794, Nov 30 -- Land Grant #648, Moore County, NC
David Allison received 276 acres located north of Cabin Creek adjoining **Everet Smith**. **John McDonald** and **Angus McIver** were chain carriers.

2018.   1794, Nov 30 -- Land Grant #650, Moore County, NC
David Allison received 200 acres located south of Wolf Creek adjoining his own line and **Peter Hare**. **John McDonald** and **Angus McIver** were chain carriers.

2019.   1794, Nov 30 -- Land Grant #651, Moore County, NC
David Allison received 640 acres located on Little Creek adjoining his own line. **John McDonald** and **Angus McIver** were chain carriers.

2020.   1794, Dec 2 -- Land Grant #748, Moore County, NC
David Allison received 636 acres located between McLendons Creek and Richland Creek adjoining **Thomas Muse**, **Jesse Muse**, **Saml. Dunn** and **Joseph Dunn**. **Thomas Muse** and **Jesse Muse** were chain carriers.

2021.   1794, Dec 6 -- Land Grant #653, Moore County, NC
David Allison received 513 acres located on Tan Trough Branch of Mill Creek adjoining **Angus McAulay** and **Archibald Gillis**. **John McDonald** and **Angus McIver** were chain carriers.

2022.   1794, Dec 6 -- Will Book A, Moore County, NC Pages 186-187
Will of **John Sheffield**, Dec'd. Heirs: wife **Hannah Sheffield** [*100 acre plantation where I now live*], son **Mark Sheffield**, son **John Sheffield**, son **Adam Sheffield** [*100 acres on Rattlesnake Branch*], son **Isham Sheffield** [*100 acres where he now lives*], son **Averit Sheffield** [*100 acre plantation where I now live after his mother's death*], daughter **Sarah Dennis**, daughter **Mary Dun**, daughter **Lucretia Dun**, daughter **Rebekah Awtry**, daughter **Hannah Mainyard**, daughter **Elizabeth Awtry** and two youngest daughters **Lydda** and **Milly Sheffield**. Executors: wife **Hannah Sheffield** and **Averet Smith**. Witnesses: **Averet Smith**, **Isam Sheffield** and **Windsor Pearce**. Proven Feb 1796.

2023.   1794, Dec 9 -- Land Grant #654, Moore County, NC
David Allison received 655 acres located on the head of Wet Creek adjoining **Williams** Old Store and **McIver**. **John McDonald** and **Angus McIver** were chain carriers.

2024.   1794, Dec 9 -- Land Grant #655, Moore County, NC
David Allison received 605 acres located on the head of Wet Creek adjoining **Williams** Old Store and **Ezekial Dunn**. **John McDonald** and **Angus McIver** were chain carriers.

2025.   1794, Dec 10 -- Land Grant #658, Moore County, NC
David Allison received 529 acres located east of Horse Creek adjoining **Leonard Furr**. **John McDonald** and **Angus McIver** were chain carriers.

2026.   1794, Dec 10 -- Land Grant #659, Moore County, NC
David Allison received 816 acres located southeast of Wet Creek adjoining **Richard Dunn**'s Mill . **John McDonald** and **Angus McIver** were chain carriers.

2027.   1794, Dec 17 -- Land Grant #660, Moore County, NC
David Allison received 492 acres located on Dry Creek adjoining **Nicholas Newton**. **John McDonald** and **Angus McIver** were chain carriers.

2028.   1794, Dec 18 -- Land Grant #661, Moore County, NC
David Allison received 502 acres located west of Wet Creek adjoining **Angus McAulay** and **John McKinnon**. **John McDonald** and **Angus McIver** were chain carriers.

2029.   1794, Dec 20 -- Land Grant #662, Moore County, NC
David Allison received 728 acres located on Fork of Mill Creek adjoining **Archibald Gillis** and **Isaac Dunn**. **John McDonald** and **Angus McIver** were chain carriers.

2030.   1794, Dec 22 -- Land Grant #1308, Moore County, NC
Thomas Ritter received 50 acres located on both sides of Richland Creek adjoining **Robert Roan**, **Rasberry**, **McSween** and **McNeill**. **Everet Wallace** and **Jesse Bean** were chain carriers.

2031. 1795 -- Tax List [partial], Moore County, NC

List of supernumerary taxes collected by Sheriff **Malcom McNeill** for 1795 [selected residents]: **Farquhard Bethune** 50 acres; **Richard Bird** 150 acres; **Robert Bird** 200 acres; **Catharine Bethune** 50 acres; **Wm.** and **Solomon Barret** 160 acres; **Murdoch Bethune** 300 acres; **Joseph Cockman** 150 acres; **John Comer** 100 acres; **Owen Carpenter** 100 acres; **Elizabeth Carpenter** (at **Howards**) 200 acres; **Wm. Dunn** Esq. 3 polls and 300 acres; **Wm. Garner** 1 poll; **Lewis Garner** Esq. 2 polls; **Wm. Harden** 2 polls and 450 acres; **Lawson** place 100 acres; **Benjamin Lamb** 50 acres; **John Sewel** 1 poll and 400 acres; **George Williams** 1 poll and 50 acres; **George Carington** 200 acres; **James Melton** 1 poll and 100 acres; **Benjamin Melton** 100 acres; **John McAulay** 1 poll and 300 acres; **John Dunlap** 1 poll and 560 acres; **Jesse Upton** 1 poll and 50 acres

2032. 1795, Jan 2 -- Land Grant #0114, Moore County, NC
John Shuffield received 50 acres located on Beach Branch of Wolf Creek adjoining his own line and **John Hare. John Hare** and **Peter Hare** were chain carriers. [*Editor's Note: Never granted*]

2033. 1795, Jan 2 -- 1784-1797 Land Entries, Moore County, NC
#1363 **Jonathan Bullock** entered 300 acres on Bear Creek adjoining **Nicholas Nall** and **William Williamson.**

2034. 1795, Jan 2 -- 1784-1797 Land Entries, Moore County, NC
#1365 **Samuel Dunn** entered 250 acres south of Deep River adjoining **William Hancock** and **Willis Dickinson**.

2035. 1795, Jan 2 -- 1784-1797 Land Entries, Moore County, NC
#1366 **Joseph Dunn** entered 50 acres on Mill Creek adjoining his own line.

2036. 1795, Jan 3 -- 1784-1797 Land Entries, Moore County, NC
#1368 **William Wood** entered 100 acres southeast of Bear Creek adjoining his own line and **John Sheffield Senr.** and including **Dennis'** old improvement.

2037. 1795, Jan 3 -- 1784-1797 Land Entries, Moore County, NC
#1369 **John Bullock** entered 200 acres adjoining **John Garner** including where **George Carringer** now lives.

2038. 1795, Jan 5 -- 1784-1797 Land Entries, Moore County, NC
#1371 **Thomas Minyard** entered 50 acres on a branch of Williamson [Williams] Creek on the path that goes from the **Chavis** old field to the **Minyards** house including his own improvement.

2039. 1795, Jan 5 -- 1784-1797 Land Entries, Moore County, NC
#1372 **Hezekiah Dunn** entered 50 acres on the head of Wet Creek on both sides of the Yadkin Road.

2040. 1795, Jan 5 -- 1784-1797 Land Entries, Moore County, NC
#1373 **Malcolm McLeod** entered 50 acres west of McLendons Creek.

2041. 1795, Jan 5 -- 1784-1797 Land Entries, Moore County, NC
#1374 **John Morgan** entered 100 acres on Mill Creek adjoining **John Cox**'s 100 acres (now **James Gallemore**).

2042. 1795, Jan 8 -- Land Grant #1534, Moore County, NC
Richard Dunn Junr. received 60 acres located north of Sings Creek adjoining his own line and **Norman McLeod**. **Norman McLeod** and **Hezekiah Dunn** were chain carriers.

2043. 1795, Jan 12 -- 1784-1797 Land Entries, Moore County, NC
#1380 **John Hairgrove** entered 50 acres located on Buffalow Creek adjoining **Leonard Furr** and including part of **Furr**'s improvement.

2044. 1795, Jan 13 -- Land Grant #693, Moore County, NC
David Allison received 520 acres located between Bear Creek and Buffalow Creek on Maners Branch adjoining **Jacob Stuts Senr.**'s improvement. **John McLeod** and **John McDonald** were chain carriers.

2045. 1795, Jan 13 -- Land Grant #1727, Moore County, NC
John Thornton received 50 acres located east of Bear Creek adjoining **Ambrose Maines**. **John McLeod** and **John McDonald** were chain carriers.

2046. 1795, Jan 14 -- Land Grant #720, Moore County, NC
David Allison received 640 acres located between McLendons Creek and Richland Creek adjoining **Reubin Shields**, **Thomas Muse** and **Joseph Dunn**. **Thos. Cole** and **Jno. Berreman** were chain carriers.

2047. 1795, Jan 14 -- Land Grant #743, Moore County, NC
David Allison received 490 acres located west of Buffalo Creek adjoining **Bryan Boroughs** and **Harmon Brewer**. **John McLeod** and **John McDonald** were chain carriers.

2048. 1795, Jan 15 -- Land Grant #707, Moore County, NC
David Allison received 275 acres located between Buffalo Creek and Bear Creek adjoining **Nicolas Nall** and **Harmon Brewer**. **John McLeod** and **John McDonald** were chain carriers.

2049. 1795, Jan 16 -- Land Grant #714, Moore County, NC
David Allison received 417 acres located east of Wet Creek adjoining **Thomas Key**. **John McLeod** and **John McDonald** were chain carriers.

2050. 1795, Jan 17 -- Land Grant #746, Moore County, NC
David Allison received 420 acres located on both sides of Horse Creek adjoining **Widow McLeod** and **Murdock McLeod**. **John McLeod** and **John McDonald** were chain carriers.

2051. 1795, Jan 17 -- Land Grant #944, Moore County, NC
Bryant Boroughs received 100 acres located on both sides of Buffalo Creek adjoining **James Thornton** and the Good Spring. **John McLeod** and **John McDonald** were chain carriers.

A. 1795, Jan 20 -- Land Grant #1736, Moore County, NC
David Allison received 640 acres located on Pates Creek and the Chatham County line adjoining **Jesse Griffin** and **Robert Davis**. **Neill McIntosh** and **William McDonald** were chain carriers.

2052. 1795, Jan 24 -- Land Grant #1533, Moore County, NC
John McKinnon received 50 acres located west of Wet Creek adjoining his own line and **Smith**. **Angus McKinnon** and **Hezekiah Dunn** were chain carriers.

2053. 1795, Jan 26 -- 1784-1797 Land Entries, Moore County, NC
#1381 **Bryan Burroughs** entered 50 acres located on Buffalow Creek adjoining his own line and **Harman Brewer**.

2054. 1795, Jan 26 -- 1784-1797 Land Entries, Moore County, NC
#1382 **Drury Brewer** entered 50 acres located south of Bear Creek adjoining **Ambrose Brewer**.

2055. 1795, Feb 2 -- Land Grant #796, Moore County, NC
John McAulay Jr. received 50 acres located on the head of Sings Creek adjoining **Archibald McKay** and **Angus McAulay**.

2056. 1795, Feb 16 -- 1784-1795 Court of Pleas and Quarter Sessions, Moore County, NC
[jury duty - selected participants] **William Williamson, Richard Dunn, Frederick Autry, Hezekiah Dunn, Jesse Ritter, John Ritter, William Smith** and **Jesse Bean**. [jury duty next term - selected participants] **Joseph Allan, Stephen Smith, Hardy Davis, James Autry, Benjm. Caddell** and **Joseph Dunn Jr.**

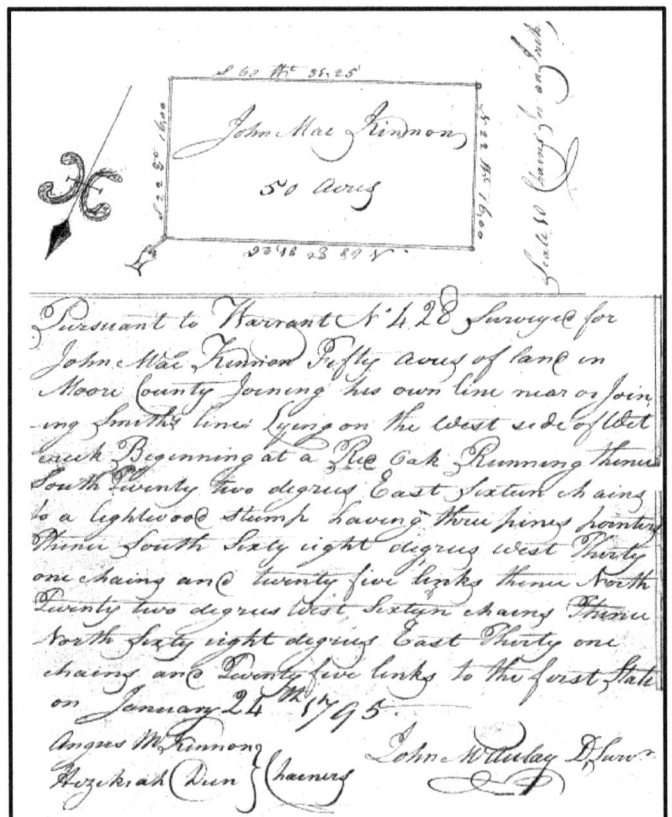

2057. 1795, Feb 17 -- 1784-1795 Court of Pleas and Quarter Sessions, Moore County, NC Page 500, 503, 506
[Deeds] **Leonard** and **Susannah Cagle** to **Thomas Smitherman** was proven by **Henry Cagle**
William Cook to **Samuel Martindale** was proven by **Jesse Griffin** Esq.
Thomas Collins to **James Collins Junr.** was acknowledged
James Collins to **Richardson Feagin** was proven by **Archd. Dalrymple**

2058. 1795, Feb 17 -- 1784-1795 Court of Pleas and Quarter Sessions, Moore County, NC Page 502
The following appointed constables: **Bartholomew Dunn** in **Brown's District #6** and **John Bullock** in **Morgan's District #8**.

2059. 1795, Feb 17 -- 1784-1795 Court of Pleas and Quarter Sessions, Moore County, NC Page 504
Burrell Deaton made oath that **Thomas Moore** died on Sep 18, 1794 and made a will ten days prior that willed his estate to his wife **Pebey Moore**. Ordered that **William Moore, Edward Moore, James Stamper** and wife **Sarah, George Wilson** and wife **Mary, David Kennedy** and wife **Joanna** appear the next court and show cause if any against the will. **Burrell Deaton** and **Edward Moore Sr.** subpoenaed to appear as witnesses to will.

2060.   1795, Feb 17 -- 1784-1795 Court of Pleas and Quarter Sessions, Moore County, NC Page 506
Ordered that **Hardy Davis** be appointed overseer of the road to be laid off from his house to **Nicholas Nall**'s and have the following hands to work: **Nicholas Nall**'s hands, **Robert Burd**, **Peter Cagle** and **Henry Cagle**'s hands.

2061.   1795, Mar 15 -- Land Grant #958, Moore County, NC
John Garner received 200 acres adjoining **Enoch Spinks**, **Leonard Hart**, **Owen Carpenter**, his own line, **George Carringer** and **Yow**. **Signal Wade** and **Bradley Garner** were chain carriers.

2062.   1795, Mar 17 -- Land Grant #1159, Moore County, NC
Donald Manners received 100 acres located southwest of Grassy Creek adjoining his own line (formerly **John Bullock**) and **John Williamson**. **Peter Shamburger** and **L. Maness** were chain carriers.

2063.   1795, Mar 18 -- Land Grant #909, Moore County, NC
Neil McLeod received 150 acres located north of Grassy Creek adjoining **Nicholas Nall**, **Richard Bird**, **Williamson** and **Leonard Hart**. **William Williamson** and **James Williamson** were chain carriers.

2064.   1795, Mar 20 -- Land Grant #1156, Moore County, NC
Nathan Smith Junr. received 100 acres located on both sides of Cabin Creek adjoining **John Morgan**. **Nathan Morgan** and **James Spivey** were chain carriers.

2065.   1795, Mar 21 -- Land Grant #1178, Moore County, NC
Leonard Furr received 50 acres located west of Flag Creek adjoining his own line. **John McDonald** and **Angus McIver** were chain carriers.

2066.   1795, Mar 22 -- Land Grant #1199, Moore County, NC
John Morgan received 100 acres located on both sides of Cabin Creek adjoining his own line. **Nathan Morgan** and **Nath. Smith** were chain carriers.

2067.   1795, Mar 23 -- Land Grant #876, Moore County, NC
Enoch Hall received 87 acres located on Tan Trough Branch of Mill Creek adjoining his own line. **Donald McAulay** and **John McAulay** were chain carriers.

2068.   1795, Mar 25 -- Land Grant #1142, Moore County, NC
Benjamin Cooper received 130 acres located north of Bear Creek adjoining **Ambrose Maness** and including **Caddel**'s [?] old field. **Ambrose Maness** and **William Cooper** were chain carriers.

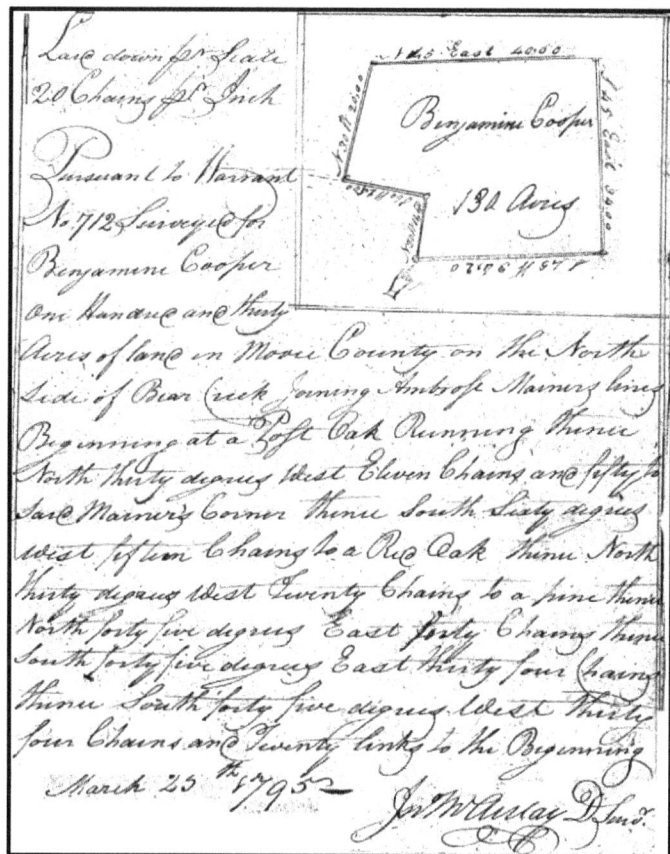

2069.   1795, Mar 25 -- Land Grant #1200, Moore County, NC
Henry Kagle, Sr. [assignee of **George Kagle**] received 100 acres located on Cow Branch of Wolf Creek. **Stephen Smith** and **John Nichols** were chain carriers.

2070.   1795, Mar 27 -- Land Grant #1054, Moore County, NC
John Morgan received 100 acres located on both sides of Cabin Creek adjoining his own line. **David Richardson** and **Nathan Morgan** were chain carriers.

A.   1795, Apr 6 – Deed Book E Page 231, Chatham County, NC
Elizabeth Hancock (of Moore County) deeded **James Scott** 100 acres located on Fall Creek. **Jesse Griffin**, **Eli Lawler** and **Marian Hancock** were witnesses.

2071. 1795, Apr 16 -- Land Grant #1288, Moore County, NC
William Cagle received 100 acres located on Fork of Bear Creek adjoining **Michael Hart**, **Henry Cagle** and including his own improvement. **Joseph Lolly** and **Henry Cagle** were chain carriers.

2072. 1795, May 6 -- Land Grant #1155, Moore County, NC
Donald McLeod [assignee of **John McAulay**] received 50 acres located on the drains of Sings Creek near the Yadkin Road adjoining **John McAulay** and own line. **Hezekiah Dunn** and **Donald McLeod** were chain carriers.

2073. 1795, May 8 -- Land Grant #1694, Moore County, NC
Edward Moore received 100 acres located north of Deep River west of Waggon Branch adjoining **William Cook**, **Neil McLeod**, **George Fagin**, **Richardson Fagin** and **James Moore**. **George Moore** and **Edward Moore** were chain carriers.

2074. 1795, May 18 -- 1784-1795 Court of Pleas and Quarter Sessions, Moore County, NC
[*jury duty - selected participants*] **Joseph Dunn**, **William Caddell**, **Jacob Cagle**, **Willm. Dunn**, **Jesse Ritter**, **William Caddell**, **Thomas Ritter**, **Benjn. Caddell**, **William Wright**, **Jonathan Caddell**, **Jacob Stutts**, **Joseph Allen** and **Stephen Smith**. [*jury duty next term - selected participants*] **Christopher Yew**, **Wm. Williamson**, **Geo. Cagle**, **Joseph Dunn Jr.**, **Leonard Furr**, **Peter Haire**, **David Richardson**, **Zachary Smith**, **Richard Dunn**, **William Copland**, **Joseph Allen**, **Stephen Smith** and **Reuben Freeman**.

2075. 1795, May 18-19 -- 1784-1795 Court of Pleas and Quarter Sessions, Moore County, NC Page 509,511
[Deeds] **Angus McAulay** to **Enoch Hall** was proven by **Instance Hall**
John Harding to **Adam Harding** was proven by **John Sowell**
Robert Davis to **Zachary Davis** was proven by **Benjn. Shields**

2076. 1795, May 18 -- 1784-1795 Court of Pleas and Quarter Sessions, Moore County, NC Page 510
The last will and testament of **Cornelius Tyson** Dec'd. was proven by **James Collins** Esq. and **Seth Barns**. An inventory of the estate of **Cornelius Tyson** was returned by **Benjamin Tyson**, one of the exectuors.

A. 1795, May 18-1813 -- Estate, Randolph County, NC
Estate of **William Bird**, Dec'd. by administrator **Margret Bird**. **Peter Shamburger** and **John F. Garner** were sureties. **John Shamburger** named guardian of **Peter Bird**.

2077. 1795, May 19 -- 1784-1795 Court of Pleas and Quarter Sessions, Moore County, NC Page 514
Ordered that the following magistrates take the list of taxables for 1795: **John McAulay** [District #6]; **Francis Bullock** [District #8].

2078. 1795, May 19 -- 1784-1795 Court of Pleas and Quarter Sessions, Moore County, NC Page 514
Ordered that **Hardy Davis** have the following hands to work on the road from his house to **Nicholas Nalls** Esquire: Nicholas Nalls hands, **Robert Bird**, **Peter Cagle**, **Henry Cagle**, **William Cagle**, **Christian Cagle**, **Leonard Cagle**, **Andrew White**, **Thomas Smitherman**, **Charles Holden**, **Adam Comer**, **Averet Sheffield** and **John Garner**.

2079. 1795, May 20 -- 1784-1795 Court of Pleas and Quarter Sessions, Moore County, NC Page 520
Ordered that **Joseph Fry** be appointed overseer of the road above **Munroe**'s which leads by the courthouse to the Wolf Pit and have the following hands: **Shadrack Rogers**, **James Smith**, **George Fry**, **Nathan Fry**, **Daniel Caddell**, **Daniel McSween**, **John Bethune**, **James Fry**, **Alexr. McLeod** and **George Jackson**'s hands.

A.   1795, May 21 -- 1784-1795 Court of Pleas and Quarter Sessions, Moore County, NC Page 521
The nuncupative will of **James Loman** Dec'd was proven by **Benjamin Shields** and **James Harden**. **Edward Epps** (the next of kin) was also present. Heirs: **Patty Epps** (daughter of **Edward Epps**) and **John Epps** (son of **Edward Epps**). **Loman** died the last day of April 1795.

2080.   1795, May 21 -- 1784-1795 Court of Pleas and Quarter Sessions, Moore County, NC Page 523
Ordered that the following persons be appointed to determine whether the road from **Instant Hall**'s plantation to the [Montgomery] County line shall go by **Thomas Dunn**'s or **Lewis Sowell**'s: **Darius Ramage**, **Norman McKennon**, **Murdo McAulay**, **Enoch Hall**, **Norman McLeod**, **Saml. Hall**, **Murdo. McAulay Jr.**, **Joseph Allen**, **William Smith Jr.**, **John McKinnon**, **Christopher Bethune**, **John Spivia**, **Hezekiah Dunn**, **Richard Dunn**, **Alexander Morrison** and **William Morgan**.

2081.   1795, May 21 -- 1784-1795 Court of Pleas and Quarter Sessions, Moore County, NC Page 523
Ordered that **Thomas Dunn** be appointed overseer of the road [above] and that the following hands to work:

William Smith Jr., **Lewis Sowell**, **John Allen**, **Donald McLeod**, **Christopher Bethune**, **Norman McLeod**, **Instant Hall**, **Enoch Hall**, **Murdo. McAulay Sen.**, **Hezekiah Dunn**, **Norman McKinnon** and **Neil McLeod**.

2082.   1795, May 21 -- 1784-1795 Court of Pleas and Quarter Sessions, Moore County, NC Page 523
Ordered that **Joseph Allen** be appointed overseer of the Yadkin Road from the County line to the fork of the road at **Instant Hall**'s plantation and have the following hands to work: **William Morgan Jr.**, **Stephen Smith**, **Nicholas Smith**, **George Cagle** (Wolf), **Peter Haire**, **Peter Garner**, **John Comber**, **Leonard Cagle**, **Moses Wilson**, **Nathan Morgan**, **George Morgan**, **Reuben Freeman** and **Henry Cagle**'s of age sons.

2083.   1795, May 21 -- 1784-1795 Court of Pleas and Quarter Sessions, Moore County, NC Page 525
Ordered that **Nicholas Nall**, **William Davis** and **William Dunn** Esq. act as commissioners to bid out the building of a bridge over McLendons Creek and another over Richland Creek where the main road crosses said creeks that leads from **Nicholas Nalls** past **Mrs. Glascocks** to Fayetteville.

2084.   1795, May 24 -- Land Grant #877, Moore County, NC
Enoch Hall received 50 acres located on Sings Creek adjoining **Archibald McKay**. **Donald McAulay** and **John McAulay** were chain carriers.

2085.   1795, May 24 -- Land Grant #869, Montgomery County, NC

John Allen received 100 acres located on Wolf Creek adjoining **Joseph Allen** and including his own improvement. **John Allen** and **Wm. Allen** were chain carriers.

2086.   1795, Jun 2 -- Land Grant #1593, Moore County, NC
Jesse Been [assignee of **Jesse Ritter**] received 50 acres located northwest of McLendons Creek and south of Richland Creek adjoining **Samuel Dunn**, **Donald McQueen** and own line. **Jesse Ritter** and **Everit Ritter** were chain carriers.

2087.   1795, Jun 24 -- Land Grant #1113, Moore County, NC
Jesse Ritter received 50 acres located on the waters of Locust Branch adjoining **John Ritter**. **John Ritter** and **Everet Ritter** were chain carriers.

A.   1795, Jul 15 -- Land Grant #876, Montgomery County, NC
James Martin received 50 acres located on Wolf Branch [Creek] adjoining Moore County line and **Wilkins**.

2088.   1795, Jul 20 -- Land Grant #885, Moore County, NC
John McAulay Jr. received 50 acres located on Sings Creek adjoining **Archibald McKay** and **Hall**. **Murdock McAulay** and **Norman McKinnon** were chain carriers.

2089.   1795, Jul 22 -- Land Grant #1027, Moore County, NC
William Barrett received 50 acres located east of McLendons Creek adjoining **McLeod** and **Sowell**. **Isaac Sowell** and **John Danaly** were chain carriers.

2090.   1795, Jul 23 -- Land Grant #1028, Moore County, NC
William Barrett received 50 acres located northwest of McLendons Creek adjoining **John Martin**, **McRae** and **Widow Bathune**. **Isaac Sowell** and **John Danaly** were chain carriers.

2091.   1795, Jul 23 -- Land Grant #1110, Moore County, NC
Thomas Ritter received 50 acres located between McLendons and Richland Creeks adjoining **John Martin** and **John McKinnon**. **Isaac Sowell** and **John Danaly** were chain carriers.

2092.   1795, Jul 23 -- Land Grant #1589, Moore County, NC
John Quimbie received 100 acres located west of McLendons Creek adjoining **Neill McLeod** and **Campbell**. **Isaac Sowel** and **John Danaly** were chain carriers.

2093.   1795, Aug 4 -- Land Grant #838, Moore County, NC
David Allison received 269 acres located south of Bear Creek adjoining **Adam Comer** and his own line. **Hezekiah Dunn** and **John Comer** were chain carriers.

2094.   1795, Aug 4 -- Land Grant #843, Moore County, NC
David Allison received 330 acres located northwest of Williams Creek adjoining **Adam Comer** and **John Hare**. **Hezekiah Dunn** and **Adam Comer** were chain carriers.

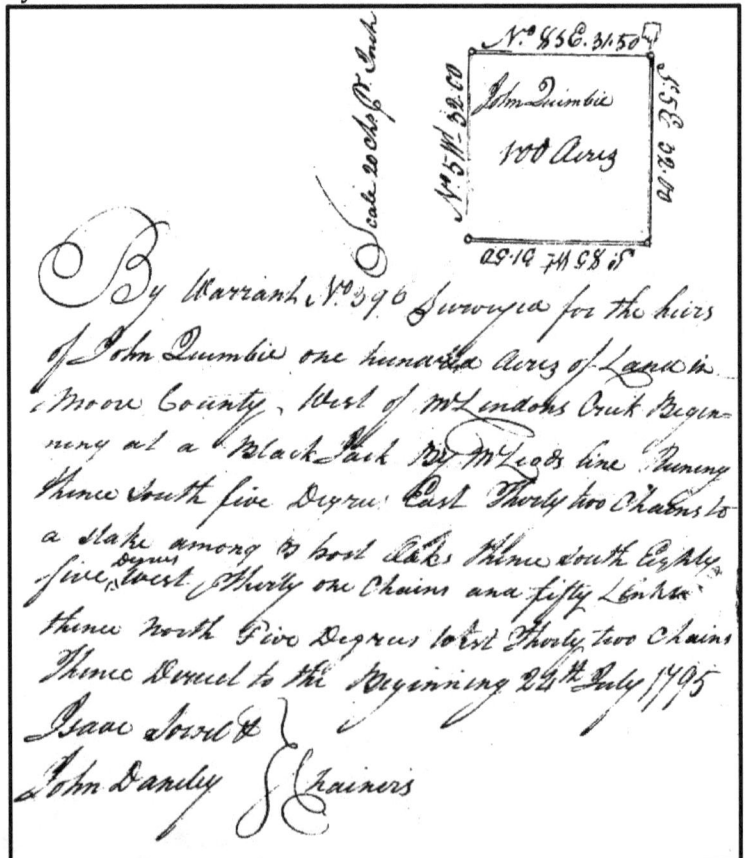

2095.   1795, Aug 5 -- Land Grant #840, Moore County, NC
David Allison received 296 acres adjoining **Lewis Spinks**, **Nicholas Nall** and **Robert Bird**. **Hezekiah Dunn** and **Robert Bird** were chain carriers.

2096.   1795, Aug 6 -- Land Grant #837, Moore County, NC
David Allison received 343 acres located on Fork of Bear Creek adjoining **Everet Smith** and his own line. **Hezekiah Dunn** and **George Cagle** were chain carriers.

2097.   1795, Aug 6 -- Land Grant #841, Moore County, NC
David Allison received 235 acres adjoining **Nicholas Nall**, **John Bullock**, **William Maness** and **David Kennedy**. **Hezekiah Dunn** and **William Maness** were chain carriers.

A.   1795, Aug 6 -- Land Grant #1378, Chatham County, NC
Joel Lawhon received 500 acres located on Flaggy Branch of Indian Creek adjoining **Moses Myrick**, **George West** and **Bray**. **Sterling Carrol** and **Daniel Carrol** were chain carriers.

2098.   1795, Aug 8 -- Land Grant #844, Moore County, NC
David Allison received 311 acres located on both sides of Little Creek adjoining his own line and **Autery**. **John McDonald** and **Angus McIver** were chain carriers.

2099.   1795, Aug 8 -- Land Grant #926, Moore County, NC
Neill McLeod received 80 acres located east of Richland Creek adjoining **Farq. Campbell**, **McLeod/Ritter** and **McKinnon**. **Zekiel Reaubotom** and **Thos. Reaubotom** were chain carriers.

2100.   1795, Aug 10 -- Land Grant #835, Moore County, NC
David Allison received 313 acres located north of Bear Creek adjoining **Everet Smith**, **Autery** and **Francis Bullock**. **Frederick Autery** and **Archibald McMillan** were chain carriers.

2101.   1795, Aug 12 -- Land Grant #842, Moore County, NC
David Allison received 160 acres located on Richardson Branch of Wet Creek adjoining **Hezekiah Dunn**. **Hezekiah Dunn** and **Murdock McAulay** were chain carriers.

2102.   1795, Aug 14 -- Land Grant #847, Moore County, NC
David Allison received 245 acres located south of Bear Creek adjoining **Leonard Furr**. **Leonard Furr** and **Jacob Furr** were chain carriers.

2103.   1795, Aug 14 -- Land Grant #904, Moore County, NC
Jesse Ritter and **Neil McLeod** received 50 acres located on Richland Creek adjoining his own line, **Farquard Campbell** and **Nathan Smith**. **Duncan McIntosh** and **Everet Ritter** were chain carriers.

2104.   1795, Aug 15 -- Land Grant #846, Moore County, NC
David Allison received 725 acres adjoining **William Maness**, **David Kennedy** and **Nicholas Nall**. **Frederick Autery** and **Archibald McMillan** were chain carriers.

2105.   1795, Aug 15 -- Land Grant #884, Moore County, NC
John McAulay Jr. received 100 acres located south of Bear Creek adjoining **James Thornton**, **Ambrose Maness**, **Drury Richardson** and **Nicolas Nall**. **Ambros Maness** and **Christopher Huntsucker** were

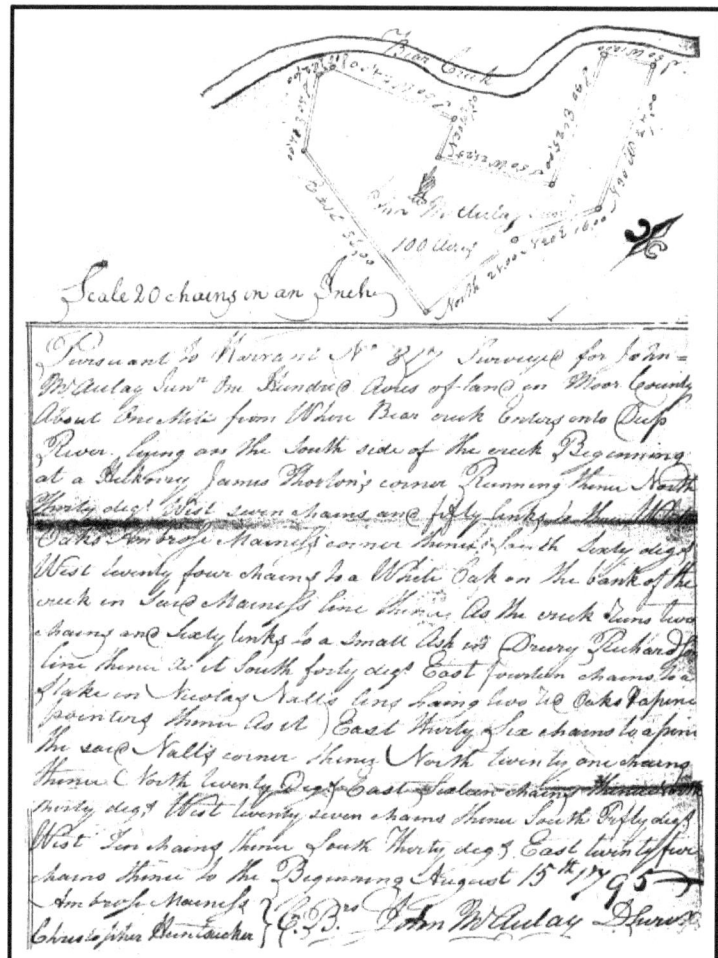

chain carriers.

2106. 1795, Aug 16 -- Land Grant #836, Moore County, NC
David Allison received 230 acres located northwest of Williams Creek adjoining **Adam Comer** and his own line. **Adam Comer** and **Hezekiah Dunn** were chain carriers.

2107. 1795, Aug 16 -- Land Grant #1532, Moore County, NC
Nicolas Nall received 200 acres located north of Bear Creek and the head of Cedar Branch. **John Bullock** and **Hezikiah Dunn** were chain carriers.

2108. 1795, Aug 17 -- 1784-1795 Court of Pleas and Quarter Sessions, Moore County, NC
[*jury duty - selected participants*] **Peter Haire, William Copland, Reuben Freeman, Leonard Furr, Stephen Smith, James Autry, Saml. Dunn, Benjn. Caddell, Stephen Richardson, Hardy Davis, Cristopher Yew, Joseph Dunn, William Dunn, William Caddell, Jesse Bean, Everet Wallace** and **Jonathn. Caddell.**

2109. 1795, Aug 17 -- 1784-1795 Court of Pleas and Quarter Sessions, Moore County, NC Page 526
[Deeds] **Archibald McKay** to **Instance Hall** was proven by **Neil McNeill**
Joseph Geson to **Zachary Smith** proven by **Willm. Richardson**
James Hill to **John Evans** proven by **Thomas Muse**
Cornelius Tyson to **Joseph Gilbert** was proven by **Benjn. Tyson**
William Barrett to **Thos. Gilmore** Esq. was acknowledged
James and **Lydia Holcombe** to **John Wadsworth** was acknowledged
Owen Carpenter Sr. to **Owen Carpenter Jr.** proven by **Nicholas Nall**
Malcom McNeill, Sheriff to **Julius Glascock** proven by **Patty Glascock**

2110. 1795, Aug 17 -- 1784-1795 Court of Pleas and Quarter Sessions, Moore County, NC Page 527
Robert Davis Sen. records his ear mark to be a crop and a slit in the right ear and a crop and two slits in the left.

2111. 1795, Aug 18 -- 1784-1795 Court of Pleas and Quarter Sessions, Moore County, NC Page 529
Administration of the estate of **Abner Lawler**, Dec'd. is granted to **John Lawler** with **Eli Lawler** as security.

2112. 1795, Aug 18 -- 1784-1795 Court of Pleas and Quarter Sessions, Moore County, NC Page 529
John Spiva records his mark to be a crop and a half crop in the right ear and a crop in the left.

A. 1795, Aug 19 -- 1784-1795 Court of Pleas and Quarter Sessions, Moore County, NC Page 533
Ordered that the following view the road that leads by **John Overton Senr.** and the county adjacent [Chatham] and determine whether it can be laid off on better ground: **James Collins, John Cheek, Richd. Street, Willis Dickinson, John Carroll Junr., William Hancock, Thomas H. Perkins, Thomas McReynolds, Malcolm Gilchrist, Patrick Dowd, Randolph Cheek, John Carroll Senr., John Philips** and **Saml. Womble.**

B. 1795, Aug 19 -- 1784-1795 Court of Pleas and Quarter Sessions, Moore County, NC Page 536
Malcolm McNeill, Sheriff reported on the sale of the following tracts sold for taxes; [blank] hundred acres on Fall Creek owned by **America Sherwood** bid off by **Archd. McBryde** and 125 acres on Richland Creek owned by **Alexr. McLeod** bid off by **John McIver.**

2113. 1795, Aug 20 -- Land Grant #839, Moore County, NC
David Allison received 112 acres located east of Mill Creek adjoining his own line, **Christopher Bethune** and **Lewis Sowell. Hezekiah Dunn** and **Murdock McAulay** were chain carriers.

2114. 1795, Aug 20 -- Land Grant #865, Moore County, NC
Lewis Spinks received 100 acres adjoining **Cost. William Asbill** and **Hezekiah Dunn** were chain carriers.

2115. 1795, Aug 20 -- Land Grant #943, Moore County, NC
Robert Bird received 50 acres including the Polly Bridge and adjoining his own line. **Hezekiah Dunn** and **Robert Bird** were chain carriers.

2116. 1795, Aug 20 -- Land Grant #1153, Moore County, NC
Joseph Allen received 50 acres located north of Cabin Creek adjoining his own line (formerly **Jacob Harwick**) and **Francis Bullock. Francis Bullock** and **Joseph Allen** were chain carriers.

2117. 1795, Aug 25 -- Land Grant #848, Moore County, NC
David Allison received 250 acres located on Persimmon Branch adjoining **Nicholas Nall**, **David Kennedy** and **William Maness**. **Frederick Autery** and **Archibald McMillan** were chain carriers.

A. 1795, Aug 27 -- Land Grant #1443, Chatham County, NC
James Culbertson received 100 acres located on Fall Creek adjoining **Person** (formerly **Powers**) and **McManess**. **John Vanderford** and **Josiah Culbertson** were chain carriers.

B. 1795, Aug 27 -- Land Grant #1571, Chatham County, NC
Willis Phillips received 150 acres located on waters of Deep River adjoining his own line. **Sion Phillips** and **Matthew Phillips** were chain carriers.

2118. 1795, Aug 28 -- Land Grant #1313, Moore County, NC
Donald McDonald received 50 acres located on Dry Creek of McLendons Creek adjoining **Murdoch Martin**, **Allen Martin** and his own line. **Murdoch Martin** and **John McDonald** were chain carriers.

2119. 1795, Aug 31 -- Land Grant #968, Moore County, NC
Thomas Graham received 50 acres located at the crossroads of Joel Road and the road that leads from the Moore Courthouse to Drowning Creek between the head of Juniper and McLendons Creek on Rocky Branch adjoining his own line and the Big Mire. **Wm. Barrett** and **Thos. Docherty** were chain carriers.

2120. 1795, Sep 16 -- Land Grant #845, Moore County, NC
David Allison received 175 acres located between Cabin Creek and Wolf Creek adjoining his own line. **Francis Bullock** and **William Morgan** were chain carriers.

2121. 1795, Sep 16 -- Land Grant #1187, Moore County, NC
John Hare [assignee of **Dennis Carpenter**] received 100 acres located south of Williams Creek adjoining his own line, **Adam Comer**, **Ludlow** and including **Adam Comer**'s hogpen. **Everet Sheffield** and **John Comer** were chain carriers.

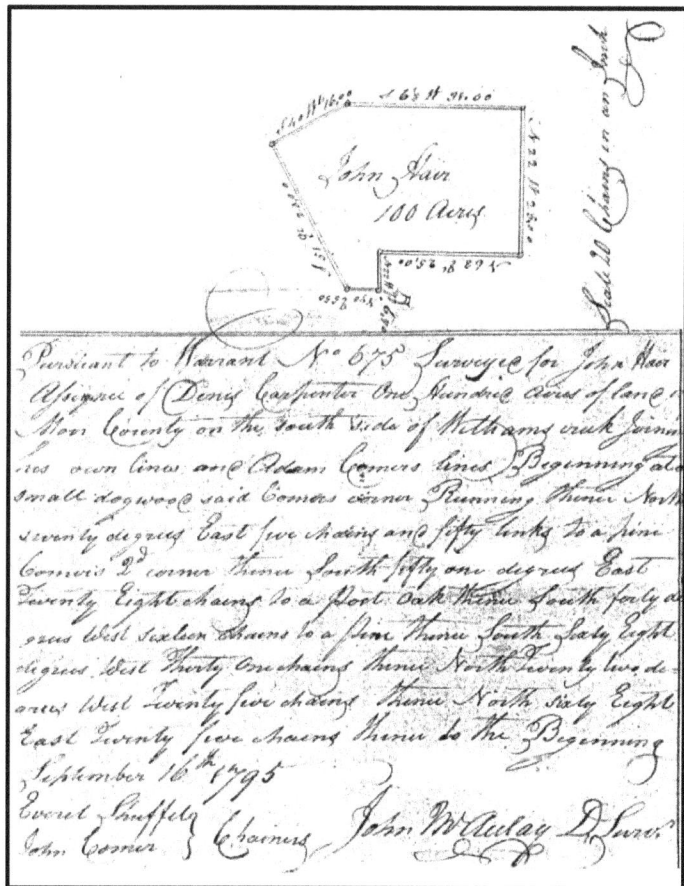

2122. 1795, Sep 20 -- Land Grant #1154, Moore County, NC
David Kennedy received 50 acres including the Green Spring adjoining **George Carringer** and his own line. **John Smith** and **John Kennedy** were chain carriers.

2123. 1795, Oct 1 -- Land Grant #982, Moore County, NC
Malcolm McNeill received 50 acres located on Williams Creek adjoining **Owen Carpenter** and **John Comer**.

2124. 1795, Oct 16 -- Land Grant #1302, Moore County, NC
Benjamin Caddell [assignee of **William Barrett**] received 100 acres located north of Suck Creek near **York**'s Cabin. **Alexander McIntosh** and **John McAulay** were chain carriers.

A. 1795, Oct 16 -- Land Grant #1374, Chatham County, NC
Joel Phillips [assignee of **Robert Cobb**] received 150 acres located on Rogers Creek including his own plantation adjoining **Jeremiah Phillips**. **Lewis Phillips** and **John Stinson** were chain carriers.

2125. 1795, Oct 20 -- 1784-1797 Land Entries, Moore County, NC
#1433 **John McAulay Jr.** entered 100 acres located on Panther Branch of Bear Creek adjoining **William Manas** and **David Kennedy**.

2126. 1795, Oct 20 -- 1784-1797 Land Entries, Moore County, NC
#1511 **John McAulay Jr.** entered 50 acres located east of Wet Creek adjoining **Waddle, Donald McLeod, Anson Melton** and **William Dunn**.

2127. 1795, Oct 25 -- Deed Book 6, Page 187, Randolph County, NC
Michael Andrews deeded **Nicholas Nall** (of Moore County) 100 acres located south of Fork Creek land formerly granted to **Adam Andrews** and left by will to his son **Michael. William Bowdon** was a witness.

2128. 1795, Oct 30 -- Land Grant #866, Moore County, NC
Philemon Hodges received 100 acres located on McLendons Creek adjoining his own line where **Alexander Morrison** formerly lived and Mrs. **Glascock** east of the road. **Daniel Moore** and **John Insor** were chain carriers.

2129. 1795, Nov 2 -- Land Grant #1281, Moore County, NC
Jesse Muse received 100 acres located on both sides of McLendons Creek near the McLendons Creek Bridge where his mother (**widow Muse**) now lives adjoining **James Muse**, his own line, **Hodges** and **Kindred Muse**. **Robert Dickenson** and **Willis Dickenson** were chain carriers.

2130. 1795, Nov 3 -- Land Grant #1231, Moore County, NC
Robert Dickinson received 50 acres located southwest of Mill Swamp adjoining his own line.

2131. 1795, Nov 16 -- 1784-1795 Court of Pleas and Quarter Sessions, Moore County, NC
[*jury duty - selected participants*] **Joseph Allan, William Wright, William Morgan, William Williamson, David Richardson, George Cagle** and **William Richardson**. [*jury duty next term - selected participants*]
Wm. Smith Junr., Peter Haire, Wm. Morgan Junr., Danl. Maines, John Sheffield, Stephen Richardson, Saml. Dunn, Drury Richardson, John Ritter, Bryan Borroughs and **Thomas Ritter**.

2132. 1795, Nov 17 -- 1784-1795 Court of Pleas and Quarter Sessions, Moore County, NC Page 538
[Deeds] **Willm. Barrett** to **Neal McKay** proven by **Jno. Sowell**
Two deeds from **Jacob Harvick** to **Joseph Allen** were proven by **William Morgan**
John and **Susannah Hunsucker** to **Nathan Smith** proven by **George Cagle**
Owen Carpenter to **John Haire** proven by **Moses Wilson**
William Wright to **Henry Cagle** was acknowledged
John McKay to **Thomas Graham** proven by **Wm. Martin**
William Newton to **Jacob Harvick** proven by **Francis Bullock**
William Barrett, Sheriff to **Patrick Dowd** proven by **John Sowell**
Benjn. Cooper to **Nancey Lakey** proven by **Mary Lakey**
Robert Graham to **Thomas Graham** proven by **Geo. Graham**

2133. 1795, Nov 17-18 -- 1784-1795 Court of Pleas and Quarter Sessions, Moore County, NC Page 540-541
The last will and testament of **Joseph Dunn** was duly proven by **Jesse Muse** and **Jesse Upton** and **Saml. Dunn** qualified as his executor.

2134. 1795, Nov 17-18 -- 1784-1795 Court of Pleas and Quarter Sessions, Moore County, NC Page 540-541
Benjamin Gilbert is appointed guardian to his three brothers: **John Gilbert, Cornelius Gilbert** and **James Gilbert** having entered bond. Settlement of the estate of **Joseph Gilbert** Dec'd. was returned by **Benjamin Tyson**, Administrator.

2135. 1795, Nov 18 -- 1784-1795 Court of Pleas and Quarter Sessions, Moore County, NC Page 541
James Collins appointed as guardian of **Susannah, Jacob, Penny, Abraham** and **Tempy McGee**, orphans of the **Joseph McGee** Dec'd.

2136. 1795, Nov 18 -- 1784-1795 Court of Pleas and Quarter Sessions, Moore County, NC Page 541
Ordered that **Francis Bullock** Esq. have leave to build a mill on his own land on Cabbin Creek.

2137. 1795, Nov 18 -- 1784-1795 Court of Pleas and Quarter Sessions, Moore County, NC Page 541
William Morgan allowed $6 annum for the wounds he received in the late war under **Capt. Cox**.

2138. 1795, Nov 18 -- 1784-1797 Land Entries, Moore County, NC
#1449 **William Manes** entered 50 acres located north of Bear Creek adjoining his own line and **David Davidson**.

2139. 1795, Nov 24 -- Will Book A, Moore County, NC Page 186-187
Will of **Nicholas Newton**, Dec'd. Heirs: wife **Meloney Newton** [*298 acres between Wet Creek and Dry Creek including the plantation where I now live, 200 acres on Sings Creek, 100 acres on Horse Creek, 50 acres on Wet Creek and negro wench Mary*], son **John Tucker Newton** [*home tract above after his mother's death*], daughter **Mary Sowel**, daughter **Meloney Dun**, daughter **Febey Melton**, son **William Newton**, son **Nicholas Smith Newton**, daughter **Hannah Carpenter**, daughter **Delaney Gibson**, daughter **Charity Newton**, daughter **Sarah Newton**, daughter **Elizabeth Newton**. Executor: **Meloney Newton**. Witnesses: **Jesse Ritter**, **John McAulay** and **Jesse Brown**. Proven Feb 1796.

2140. 1795, Dec 3 -- Deed Book 8 Page 172, Randolph County, NC
John Macon deeded **Francis Bowdown** 40 acres located north of Fork Creek on the Crooked Branch adjoining **Pearce**. Proven by **William Armstead** Aug 1800.

A. 1795, Dec 5 – Deed Book H Page 98-99, Chatham County, NC
Henry Powers deeded **Robt. Willson** 50 acres (of the 100 acres deeded by **Sampson Brewer**) located on Fall Creek and Meadow Branch adjoining **Joseph Person**, **Sampson Brewer** and **William Willson**. Peter Graves, **Samson Brewer** and **Edwd. Beeson** were witnesses.

2141. 1795, Dec 8 -- Chronicles and Records of Bensalem Presbyterian Church Page 18, Moore County, NC
Norman McLeod and **Mary Matheson** were married.

A. 1795, Dec 8 -- Deed Book H Page 94-95, Chatham County, NC
Sampson Bruer deeded **Edward Beeson** (of Randolph County) 150 acres located on Fall Creek adjoining **Goleston**. **James Culbertson** and **Robert Wilson** were witnesses.

2142. 1795, Dec 9 -- Land Grant #927, Moore County, NC
Neil McLeod received 60 acres located northwest of Richland Creek adjoining **William Smith**, **John Martin**, **Nathan Smith**, his own line and **Kenneth Murchison**. **Neill McIntosh** and **Alexander McIntosh** were chain carriers.

2143. 1795, Dec 24 -- Land Grant #851, Moore County, NC
Joseph McGee received 150 acres located east of Buffalo Creek adjoining **William McDonald** and **John McDonald**. **Jacob Cagle** and **Neal McIntoshe** were chain carriers.

2144. 1795, Dec 26 -- Land Grant #881, Moore County, NC
Christopher Stuts received 150 acres located east of Bear Creek adjoining **John Gilliam. Leonard Furr** and **James Mainers** were chain carriers. [*Editor's Note: deeded to* **Jacob C. Stutts, Mariah Stutts** *1821* --> **Martha McDonald** *deeded to* **Dempsey Stutts** *1895*]

2145. 1795, Dec 26 -- Land Grant #1795, Moore County, NC
James Maness received 50 acres located on the drains of Bear Creek including his own improvement. **Christopher Stuts** and **John Gilliam** were chain carriers.

2146. 1796, Jan 22 -- 1784-1797 Land Entries, Moore County, NC
#1477 **Ambrose Mainus** entered 100 acres located north of Bear Creek adjoining his own line, **John Bullock, Alexander Kennedy** and **Widow Kennedy**.

2147. 1796, Feb 8 -- Deed Book 7 Page 350, Randolph County, NC
Ransom Sutherland deeded **Henry Couch** 300 acres on Cow Branch of Fork Creek and the Moravian Road. Proven by **William Norwood** May 1798.

2148. 1796, Feb 11 -- 1784-1797 Land Entries, Moore County, NC
#123 **Nathaniel Melton** entered 50 acres located east of Wet Creek adjoining **Thomas Graham, Ansel Melton** and **John McAulay**.

A. 1796, Feb 12 -- Land Grant #1493, Montgomery County, NC
Little Berry Hicks received 100 acres located on Lick Fork of Cabin Creek and Maple Branch adjoining **John Higgins, Thos. Cotton** and **John Humble. James Moore** and **Little Berry Hix** were chain carriers.

2149. 1796, Feb 17 -- 1784-1797 Land Entries, Moore County, NC
#1490 **Leonard Furr** entered 100 acres located south of Bear Creek adjoining his own line, **Wm. Needham, David Allison** and **Everet Smith**.

2150. 1796, Feb 20 -- Land Grant #888, Moore County, NC
Henry Cagle Jr. received 100 acres located north of Bear Creek adjoining **John Lawley**, his own line and **Hardy Davis. Henry Cagle Sr.** and **John Cagle** were chain carriers.

A. 1796, Feb 24 -- Land Grant #1069, Montgomery County, NC
Edward Duval Tyler received 12 acres located on Muddy Branch of Little River including his own improvement called Wins Place. **William Callicot** and **George Thomas** were chain carriers.

B. 1796, Feb 24 -- Land Grant #1205, Montgomery County, NC
William Callicote received 100 acres located on north fork of Little River adjoining **John Bolin, William Wright**, Bigg Branch and **Edward D. Tylor. Edward Duval Tyler** and **George Thomas** were chain carriers.

2151. 1796, Feb 25 -- Land Grant #889, Moore County, NC
Henry Cagle Sr. received 50 acres located on Cow Branch of Wolf Creek adjoining his own line and **George Cagle. Henry Cagle** and **John Owens** were chain carriers.

2152. 1796, Feb 25 -- Marriage Bond, Wake County, NC
Ryals Britt to **Rhody Parrish. Thomas Etheredge** was bondsman and **J. Rice** was witness. [*Editor's Note: Date of marriage occurred on or after date of marriage bond.*]

2153. 1796, Mar 3 -- Will Book A Page 189-190, Moore County, NC
Will of **Jacob Stutts**, Dec'd. Heirs: wife **Elizabeth Stutts** [*200 acres where I now live*], daughter **Elizabeth Furr**, daughter **Susanna Spivey**, daughter **Mary Furr**, son **Jacob Stutts**, son **John Stutts**, son **Christian Stutts**, son **Leonard Stutts**, son **Henry Stutts** [*land where I now live after his mother's death*] and daughter **Catherine Stutts**. Executors: **Averet Smith** and **Elizabeth Stutts**. Witnesses: **Averet Smith, Stephen Richardson** and **Jacob Cagle**. Proven Nov 1796.

2154. 1796, Mar 12 -- 1784-1797 Land Entries, Moore County, NC
#1507 **Jonathan Bullock** entered 125 acres adjoining **Nall, Ambrose Mainus** and **Widow Kennedy**.

2155. 1796, Mar 13 -- Land Grant #1796a, Moore County, NC
Jonathan Bullock received 125 acres located north of Bear Creek adjoining **Nicolas Nall**, **Ambrose Mainers** and **Widow Kennedy**. **Ambrose Maness** and **Jonathan Bullock** were chain carriers.

2156. 1796, Mar 15 -- Land Grant #1555, Moore County, NC
John Bullock received 100 acres located south of Grassy Creek below where **Yew**'s and **Carringer**'s Road crosses the Persimmon Branch adjoining **George Carringer** and including **Willis Brewer**'s improvement. **Christopher Yow Sr.** and **Christopher Yow Jr.** were chain carriers.

2157. 1796, Mar 15 -- Land Grant #1587, Moore County, NC
Neil McLeod [assignee of **George Carringer Sr.**] received 50 acres located southwest of Grassy Creek adjoining **George Carringer**, **Jonathan Bullock** and including **Willis Brewer**'s improvement. **Wm. Shershe[Searcy]** and **J. Bullock** were chain carriers.

2158. 1796, Mar 16 -- Land Grant #1450, Moore County, NC
Donald Manners received 120 acres located on Grassy Creek adjoining **John Williamson** and **Hardy Davis**. **John Shamburger** and **John Bullock** were chain carriers.

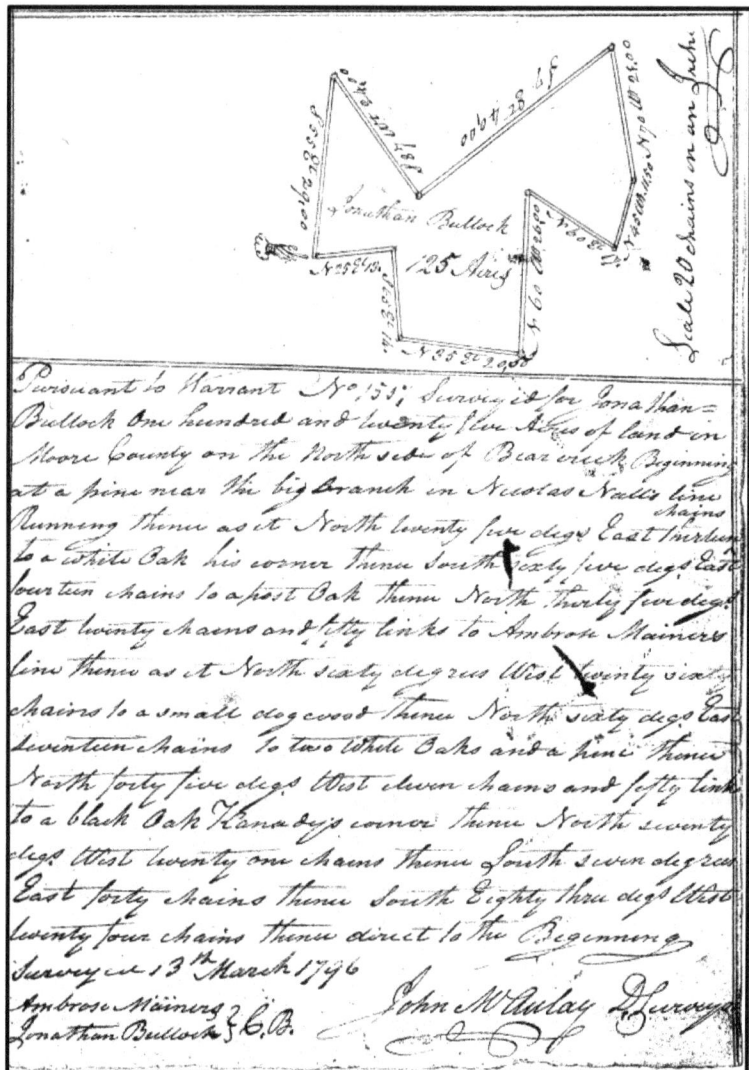

2159. 1796, Mar 17 -- Land Grant #1282, Moore County, NC
Peter Shamburger received 75 acres located south of Grassy Creek adjoining **Donald Manners**, **John Williams[on]**, **Hardy Davis**, his own line, **Nall**. **John Shamburger** and **Donald Manners** were chain carriers.

2160. 1796, Mar 21 -- Land Grant #1455, Moore County, NC
Kenneth McDonald received 50 acres located northwest of McLendons Creek adjoining **Allen Martin**, **Cox** and his own line. **Christopher Bethune** and **Allen Martin** were chain carriers.

2161. 1796, Mar 24 -- Land Grant #896, Moore County, NC
John Morrison (Taylor) received 60 acres located on Dry Fork of Mill Creek adjoining **Robert Cox**, **Norman McKinnon** and **Neil McLeod**. **Murdock McAulay** and **John McAulay** were chain carriers.

2162. 1796, Mar 24 -- Land Grant #925, Moore County, NC
Neil McLeod received 60 acres located on Dry Fork of Mill Creek adjoining **Robert Cox**, **Murdock McAulay**, **Dunn**, **Richard Tillis** (formerly **John Sandhill Smith**). **Murdock McAulay** and **Donald McLeod** were chain carriers.

2163. 1796, Apr 13 -- Land Grant #1208, Moore County, NC
John Morrison received 100 acres located McLendons Creek on the path that leads from **Glascocks** to **Hardins** adjoining **James Muse**, **John Howell** and **Glascock**. **Julius Glascock** and **William Pheagan** were chain carriers.

A. 1796, Apr 28 -- Land Grant #1095, Randolph County, NC

William Smitherman received 200 acres located on Fork Creek adjoining **Cosht** and his own line. **James Lathem** and **John Smitherman** were chain carriers.

2164.　　1796, Apr 30 -- Land Grant #844, Randolph County, NC
John Lawley received 50 acres located on Bear Creek adjoining his own line. **Hardy Davis** and **Joseph Lawly** were chain carriers.

2165.　　1796, Apr 30 -- Land Grant #849, Randolph County, NC
Joseph Lawley received 100 acres located on north fork of Bear Creek adjoining **John Lawley**. **Hardy Davis** and **John Lawly** were chain carriers.

2166.　　1796, Apr 30 -- Land Grant #865, Randolph County, NC
Joseph Lawley received 100 acres located on Bear Creek between Crawford's old road and P.D. Road adjoining **John Lawley** and his own line. **Hardy Davis** and **John Lawly** were chain carriers.

2167.　　1796, Apr 30 -- Land Grant #1290, Randolph County, NC
John Lolly received 250 acres located on Bear Creek and the [Moore] County line. **Hardy Davis** and **Joseph Lawly** were chain carriers.

2168.　　1796, Apr 30 -- Land Grant #1493, Randolph County, NC
Hardy Davis received 50 acres located on Bear Creek adjoining **John Lawley**. **Joseph Lawley** and **John Lawly** were chain carriers.

2169.　　1796, Apr 30 -- Land Grant #1494, Randolph County, NC
Hardy Davis received 50 acres located on Bear Creek below the Randolph-Moore County line adjoining **John Lawley** and including his own improvement. **Joseph Lawley** and **John Lawley** were chain carriers.

2170.　　1796, Apr 30 -- Land Grant #1495, Randolph County, NC
Hardy Davis received 100 acres located on Fork Creek adjoining his own line, **Thos. Cosht** and **John Lathem**. **Joseph Lolley** and **John Lawley** were chain carriers.

2171.　　1796, May 24 -- 1784-1797 Land Entries, Moore County, NC
#1524 **Joseph McGee** entered 100 acres located on both sides of Haw Branch adjoining **James Milton**.

2172.　　1796, Jun 2 -- Land Grant #1112, Moore County, NC
Jesse Ritter received 50 acres located west of Richland Creek adjoining his own line where he lives and **John Ritter**. **John Ritter** and **Everit Ritter** were chain carriers.

2173.　　1796, Jun 13 -- 1784-1797 Land Entries, Moore County, NC
#1559 **John Ritter** entered 100 acres located on the Morter Glade adjoining his own line.

2174.　　1796, Jun 13 -- 1784-1797 Land Entries, Moore County, NC
#1567 **Thomas Ritter** entered 50 acres located on McLendons Creek adjoining **Sowell**.

2175.　　1796, Jun 20 -- 1784-1797 Land Entries, Moore County, NC
#1581 **Niel McLeod** entered 60 acres located on Long Meadow adjoining **Leonard Furr**.

2176.　　1796, Jun 20 -- Land Grant #1094, Moore County, NC
Everid Ritter [assignee of **Jesse Ritter**] received 100 acres located between McLendons and Richland Creeks adjoining his own line and **John McSween**. **Jesse Bean** and **Jesse Ritter** were chain carriers.

2177.　　1796, Jun 20 -- Land Grant #1146, Moore County, NC
William Davis received 400 acres located north of Deep River on Big Branch adjoining **Howel Brewer** and his own line.

2178.　　1796, Jun 22 -- Land Grant #911, Moore County, NC
Neil McLeod received 114 acres located on both sides of Yadkin Road. **Enoch Hall** and **John McAulay** were chain carriers.

2179.   1796, Jun 27 -- 1784-1797 Land Entries, Moore County, NC
#1587 **Duncan McIntosh** entered 50 acres located west of Richland Creek adjoining his own line and **Jesse Ritter**.

2180.   1796, Jul 6 -- 1784-1797 Land Entries, Moore County, NC
#1602 **John McAulay** entered 100 acres located east of Wet Creek adjoining **William Dunn** and **Ansel Melton**.

2181.   1796, Jul 18 -- 1784-1797 Land Entries, Moore County, NC
#1625 **Francis Bullock** entered 100 acres located on Bear Creek adjoining **John Shuffield** and including his own improvement.

2182.   1796, Jul 28 -- Land Grant #0150, Moore County, NC
John Overton received 100 acres located northwest of McLendons Creek adjoining his own line. **Josiah Maples** and **David Overton** were chain carriers. [*Editor's Note: Never granted*]

2183.   1796, Aug -- Criminal Actions, Randolph County, NC, Box 4
Presentment of **Mary Searcy** on a charge that she assaulted **Nancy Graves** Aug 1, 1796. Prosecuted by **James Graves**. **John Arnold** and **Nancy Graves** were witnesses.

2184.   1796, Aug -- Criminal Actions, Randolph County, NC, Box 4
Presentment of **Mary Searcy**, spinster, on a charge that she stole a piece of silver from the goods of **William Bell**, as executive of **Thomas Lytle**'s last will and testament Aug 7, 1796. **Robert Gaston** was witness.

2185.   1796, Aug 10 -- Land Grant #1287, Moore County, NC
William Maples received 150 acres located on Governors Creek between the lines where **John Overton** and **Theophilus Edens** now live. **David Overton** and **John Gilchrist** were chain carriers.

2186.   1796, Aug 10 -- Land Grant #1457, Moore County, NC
Christian McIntosh received 50 acres located east of Richland Creek adjoining **Nathan Smith** and including **Neil McLeod**'s improvement. **Neil McIntosh** and **Alexr. McIntosh** were chain carriers.

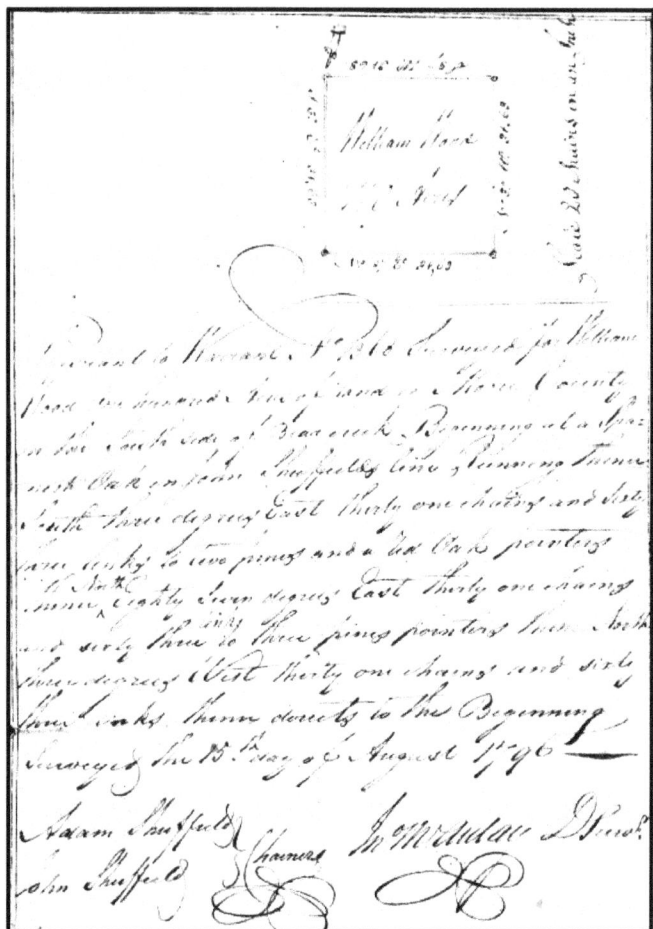

2187.   1796, Aug 12 -- 1784-1797 Land Entries, Moore County, NC
#1644 **James Williams** entered 50 acres located on Cabin Creek adjoining **John Cagle** and including his father's improvement where his father lives.

2188.   1796, Aug 14 -- Land Grant #2030, Moore County, NC
Drury Richardson received 100 acres located on Buffalo Creek adjoining his own line. **Mikijor Brewer** and **Robert Richardson** were chain carriers.

2189.   1796, Aug 15 -- Land Grant #1867, Moore County, NC
William Wood received 100 acres located south of Bear Creek adjoining **John Shuffield**, his own line and including **Dennis'** improvement. **Adam Shuffield** and **John Shuffield** were chain carriers.

2190.   1796, Aug 16 -- Land Grant #890, Moore County, NC

Henry Cagle Sr. received 100 acres located on the head of Bear Creek adjoining his own line. Peter Cagle and Henry Cagle were chain carriers.

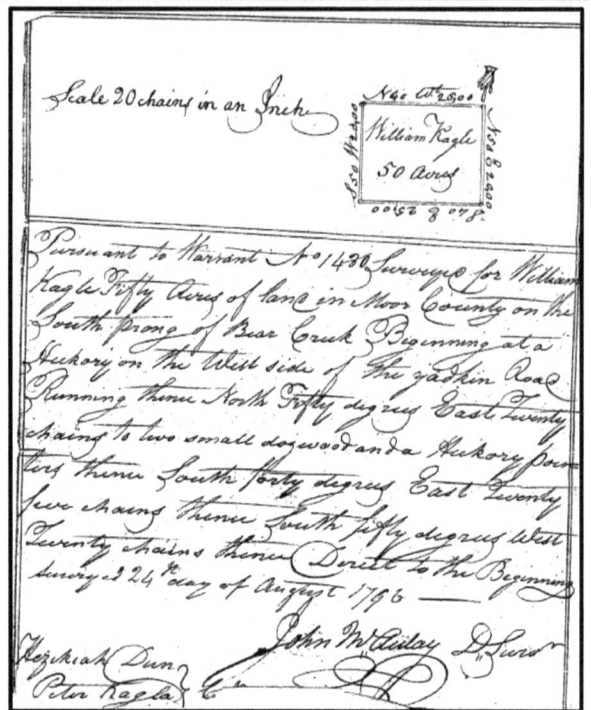

2191. 1796, Aug 18 -- Land Grant #878, Moore County, NC

Francis Bullock received 300 acres located north of Bear Creek adjoining Nicolas Nall. William Williamson and Hezekia Dunn were chain carriers.

2192. 1796, Aug 24 -- Land Grant #1499, Moore County, NC

William Kagle received 50 acres located on south prong of Bear Creek adjoining his own line. Hezekiah Dunn and Peter Kagle were chain carriers.

2193. 1796, Aug 24 -- Land Grant #1861, Moore County, NC

Charles Holden received 100 acres located in the fork of Williams Creek and Bear Creek adjoining his own line and John Gardner. Jno. Comer and Jno. Holden were chain carriers.

2194. 1796, Aug 29 -- 1784-1797 Land Entries, Moore County, NC
#10 Joseph Roberson entered 100 acres located on Governors Creek adjoining his own land known as the Melton place.

2195. 1796, Aug 29 -- Land Grant #1201, Moore County, NC
Samuel Dunn [assignee of Hezekiah Dunn] received 50 acres located on the head of Drowning Creek. Murdock McAulay and Donald McLeod were chain carriers.

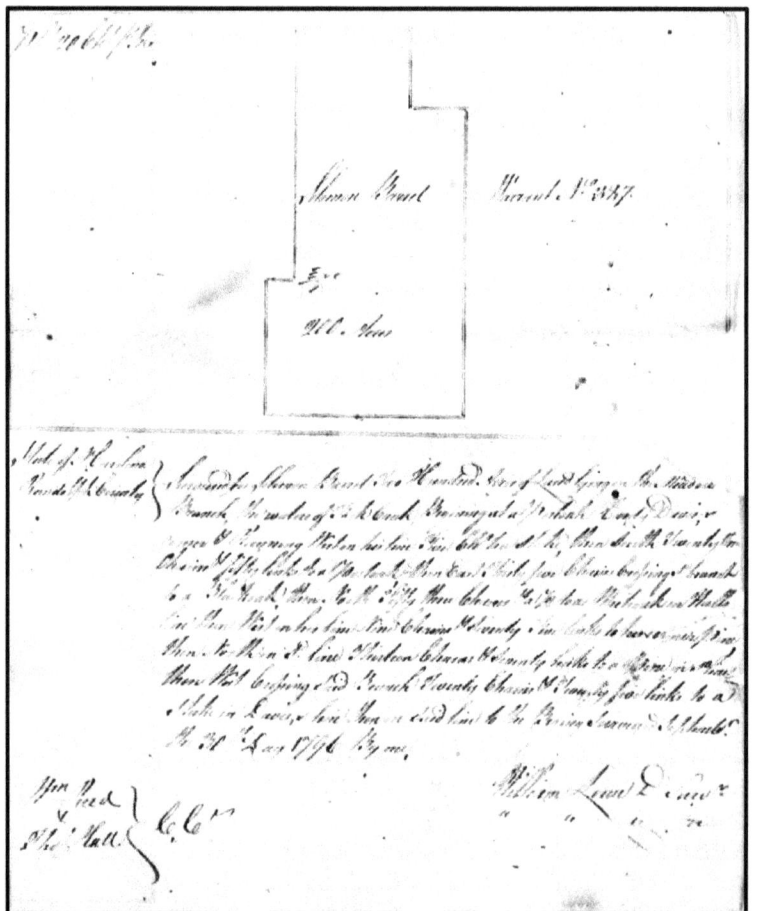

2196. 1796, Sep 3 -- Bible of David Kennedy and Joanna Moore, Moore County, NC
Mary Kennedy died.

A. 1796, Sep 7 -- Land Grant #1307, Randolph County, NC
Gabriel Hardin received 300 acres located on Barnes Creek and the Fayette Road. Michael Luther and Jacob Strider were chain carriers.

2197. 1796 Sep 12 -- 1784-1797 Land Entries, Moore County, NC
#21 John Graham entered 60 acres located on Russels prong of Governors Creek adjoining John Montgomery [formerly James Russel] and the late Jonathan Melton.

2198. 1796, Sep 30 -- Land Grant #1198, Randolph County, NC
Solomon Barret received 200 acres located on Meadow Branch adjoining Thomas Arnold, Hall and Hardy Davis including the land where Nimrod Brewer formerly lived. Wm. Reed and Thos. Hall were chain carriers.

2199.   1796, Sep 30 -- Land Grant #1470, Randolph County, NC
Thomas Hall received 100 acres located on Meadow Branch adjoining **Hardy Davis** and **Lathem**. **Solomon Barret** and **Wm. Reed** were chain carriers.

2200.   1796, Oct 24 -- Deed Book 8 Page 70, Randolph County, NC
John Johnston (of Cumberland County) deeded **William Argo** 800 acres located north of Deep River on Buffalo Branch adjoining **Searcy**. Proven by **Edmond Waddle** May 1799.

2201.   1796, Oct 24 -- Deed Book 8 Page 71, Randolph County, NC
John Johnston (of Chatham County) deeded **William Argo** 50 acres located north of Deep River on Buffalo Branch and **Goldston**'s Spring Branch. Proven by **Edmond Waddle** May 1799.

2202.   1796, Nov 15 -- Land Grant #853, Moore County, NC
William Barrett received 400 acres located on McLendons Creek adjoining **Joel McClendon**, **Jacob McClendon**, **Jemima McClendon**, **Jackson** and **John Bethune**. **Donald McDonald** and **Lauchlin McNeill** were chain carriers.

2203.   1796, Nov 22 -- 1784-1797 Land Entries, Moore County, NC
#59 **Jesse Ritter** entered 100 acres located east of Richland Creek adjoining his own line.

2204.   1796, Nov 23 -- 1784-1797 Land Entries, Moore County, NC
#69 **William Mainess** entered 100 acres located south of Bear Creek adjoining his own line.

2205.   1796, Nov 23 -- 1784-1797 Land Entries, Moore County, NC
#70 **George Carrener Sr.** entered 50 acres located on the drains of Grassy Creek adjoining his own line, **Abraham Huntsucker** and **Lewis Garner**.

2206.   1796, Nov 28 -- Land Grant #1521, Moore County, NC
Joseph Allen received 9 acres located on both sides of Cabin Creek adjoining **Thomas Graham**, his own line (formerly **Harvick**) and **Francis Bullock**. **Joseph Allen** and **James Allen** were chain carriers.

2207.   1796, Dec 7 -- 1784-1797 Land Entries, Moore County, NC
#78 **Niel McLeod** entered 50 acres located south of the Waggon Road adjoining his own line, **John Ritter** and the Speculators.

2208.   1796, Dec 16 -- 1784-1797 Land Entries, Moore County, NC
#89 **Thomas Ritter** entered 50 acres located west of McLendons Creek adjoining his own line and **Mary Sowell**.

2209.   1796, Dec 16 -- 1784-1797 Land Entries, Moore County, NC
#90 **Jesse Ritter** entered 100 acres located west of Richland Creek adjoining his own line and the Speculators.

2210.   1796, Dec 16 -- 1784-1797 Land Entries, Moore County, NC
#93 **Adam Shuffield** entered 50 acres located south of Cabin Creek adjoining his own line and **Levy Deaton**

2211.   1796, Dec 22 -- Land Grant #913, Moore County, NC
Neil McLeod received 100 acres located on Dry Creek adjoining **William Smith** and **Malcolm Morrison**. **Murdock McLeod** and **Allen McLean** were chain carriers.

2212.   1796, Dec 22 -- Land Grant #924, Moore County, NC
Neil McLeod received 100 acres located on Dry Creek adjoining **Butler**, **Hector McLean** and **Patterson**. **Murdock McLeod** and **Murdock McAulay** were chain carriers.

2213.   1796, Dec 26 -- Land Grant #1479, Moore County, NC
David Davison received 50 acres located east of Bear Creek adjoining **William Manners** and **Nall**. **David Kennedy** and **Baily Loving** were chain carriers.

2214.   1797 -- Tax List [partial], Moore County, NC
List of supernumerary taxes collected by Sheriff **Malcom McNeill** in 1797 [selected residents]: **Bryant Boroughs** 3 polls and 350 acres; **John Quimby** 100 acres; **Solom Barret** 1 poll and 265 acres; **Jesse Bean** 1 poll and 200 acres; **Jacob Cagle** 1 poll and 150 acres; **Joab Cheek** 1 poll and 150 acres; **George Carringer Junr.** 1

poll; **Daniel Caddle** 1 poll and 300 acres; **Benjn. Caddle** 1 poll and 200 acres; **Wm. McAulay** 1 poll 384 acres; **Wm. Mainess** 1 poll and 150 acres; **Hector McNeill** 1 poll and 150 acres; **John Ritter** 1 poll and 350 acres; **Nancy Williamson** 147 acres; **James Collins 1** poll and 200 acres; **Isaac Dunn** 100 acres; **Samuel Dunn** 2 polls and 600 acres; **Hardy Davis** 600 acres; **Drury Joiner** 1 poll and 300 acres; **Richardson Feagin** 3 polls and 1025 acres; **Wm. Richardson** 1 poll and 325 acres; **Christopher Stutts** 500 acres; **Jeremiah Wilson** 100 acres; **Wm. Hardin** 1 poll and 450 acres ; **Martin Nall** (stud horses); **Nicolas Nall** (stud horses)

2215. 1797-1800, 1802 -- Panosophia Masonic Lodge No. 25, Carthage, NC
Francis Bullock listed as a member.

2216. 1797, Jan 14 -- Land Grant #1544, Moore County, NC
John McKinnon received 50 acres located west of Wet Creek adjoining his own line. **Norman McKinnon** and **Angus McKinnon** were chain carriers.

2217. 1797, Jan 21 -- Land Grant #1474, Chatham County, NC
Edward Beeson received 472 acres located on Cedar Creek and Fall Creek adjoining **Vanderford**, **James Daton**, his own line, **Isaac Teague**, **Eli Lawler**, **James Culbertson**, **Michael Finley** and **Benjamin Williams. James Daton** and **Robt. White** were chain carriers.

A. 1797, Jan 23 -- Land Grant #1476, Chatham County, NC
Richard Pennington received 200 acres located on Fall Creek adjoining **Henry Powers, Carter Henry** and **Finley. James Culbertson** and **Robt. Wilson** were chain carriers.

A List of the supernumery returned from Moore County for the year 1797

B. 1797, Jan 23 -- Land Grant #1478, Chatham County, NC
Robert Wilson received 150 acres located on Fall Creek adjoining **Henry Powers, Richd. Pennington, McManus** and **Joseph Person. Robert White** and **Abner Phillips** were chain carriers.

C.   1797, Jan 24 -- Land Grant #1541, Chatham County, NC
Henry Powers received 100 acres located on Fall Creek adjoining **Edward Beeson, Benjamin Williams** and **Finley**. **James Culbertson** and **Robt. Wilson** were chain carriers.

D.   1797, Jan 24 -- Land Grant #1421, Chatham County, NC
James Culbertson received 250 acres located on Fall Creek adjoining his own line, **McManess, Henry Powers, Finley** and **Eli Lawler**. **Edward Beeson** and **John Vanderford** were chain carriers.

E.   1797, Jan 25 -- Land Grant #1452, Chatham County, NC
John Vanderford received 100 acres located on Ceder Creek adjoining **Minto Vanderford**. **Robt. Wilson** and **James Culbertson** were chain carriers.

2218.   1797, Jan 25 -- Land Grant #1484, Chatham County, NC
Edward Beeson received 200 acres located on Cedar Creek adjoining **James Daton**. **James Daton** and **Robt. Wilson** were chain carriers.

2219.   1797, Feb 6 -- 1784-1797 Land Entries, Moore County, NC
#119 **John Dun** entered 100 acres located on Buffaloe Creek adjoining **Robert Davis** at the Mill Pond and **John Ritter**.

2220.   1797, Feb 6 -- Land Grant #1341, Moore County, NC
Elijah Bettis Junr. received 92 acres adjoining **Elijah Bettis Senr.** and his mill tract, **Tomberlin** and **Goodwin**. **Solomon Holoman** and **Elisha Bettis** were chain carriers.

2221.   1797, Feb 15 -- Land Grant #1211, Moore County, NC
Simon Rheubottom received 1.5 acres located east of Richland Creek adjoining **Farquard Campbell** and **William Barrett** including his own improvement. **Byhew Sowell** and **Thos. Ritter** were chain carriers.

2222.   1797, Feb 20 -- Land Grant #892, Moore County, NC
Henry Cagle Sr. received 25 acres located on south prong of Bear Creek adjoining his own line and **James Hogg**. **Peter Cagle** and **Henry Cagle Jr.** were chain carriers.

2223.   1797, Feb 20 -- Land Grant #1427, Moore County, NC
Henry Stutts received 50 acres located west of Buffalo Creek adjoining his own line and **Jacob Stuts Senr.** **John McDonald** and **Angus McIver** were chain carriers.

2224.   1797, Feb 25 -- Land Grant #1466, Moore County, NC
Adam Comer received 100 acres located on Williams Creek adjoining **Garner** and **Smitherman** and including his own improvement. **John Comer** and **Adam Smith** were chain carriers.

2225.   1797, Feb 25 -- Land Grant #1467, Moore County, NC
Adam Comer [assignee of **John Comer**] received 100 acres located on Williams Creek adjoining **Ledlow** and his own line. **John Comer** and **Adam Smith** were chain carriers.

2226.   1797, Feb 27 -- Land Grant #1755, Moore County, NC
John Evans received 31 acres located on Cales Branch of Killetts Creek adjoining **William Caddell** and his own line. **James Hill** and **Thomas Hannon** were chain carriers.

2227.   1797, Mar 8 -- Land Grant #919, Moore County, NC
John Morrison received 100 acres located on Dry Fork of Mill Creek adjoining **Robert Cox** and **Norman McKinnon**. **Murdock McAulay** and **John McAulay** were chain carriers.

2228.   1797, Mar 11 -- Land Grant #1468 and #0230, Moore County, NC
Lewis Sowell [assignee of **John McAulay**] received 30 acres located west of Sings Creek adjoining **Christopher Bethune, John McAulay**, his own line and **Norman McLeod**. **Murdock McAulay Junr.** and **Christopher Bethune** were chain carriers.

2229.   1797, Mar 12 -- Will Book A Page 190-192, Moore County, NC
Will of **Jane Tyson**, Dec'd. Heirs: granddaughter **Jane Tyson** [of Benjamin], **Jane Tyson** [of Thomas],

granddaughter **Jane Tyson** [of Aaron], granddaughter **Jane Hopson**, granddaughter **Jane Moore**, granddaughter **Jane Stinson**, daughter **Jane Womble**, daughter **Sabra Gilbert**, daughter **Rebekah Myrick**, daughter **Sarah Stinson**, grandson **William Tyson**, son **Richard Tyson**, son **Benjamin Tyson**, son **Thomas Tyson**, son **Aaron Tyson**, and children of deceased son **Cornelius Tyson** (**Jane Hopson**, **Elizabeth Tyson** and **Thomas Tyson**). Executors: son **Benjamin Tyson** and son **Aaron Tyson**. Witnesses: **A. McBryde**, **M. McKenzie** and **Wilson Gilbert**. Proven May 1797.

2230.   1797, Mar 14 -- Land Grant #1372, Moore County, NC
George Cagle Jr. received 30 acres located between Cabin and Bear Creek adjoining **John Cagle** and **Brownlow**. **John McDonald** and **Leonard Furr** were chain carriers.

2231.   1797, Mar 14 -- 1784-1797 Land Entries, Moore County, NC
#159 **John Shuffield** entered 50 acres located on both sides of Wolf Creek adjoining his own line and **Isom Shuffield**.

2232.   1797, Mar 15 -- 1784-1797 Land Entries, Moore County, NC
#161 **Adam Shuffield** entered 50 acres located on Dry Creek adjoining his own line and **Hannah Shuffield**.

2233.   1797, Mar 19 -- Land Grant #1122, Moore County, NC
William Williamson received 72 acres located on both sides of Grassy Creek adjoining **Leonard Hart**, **John Williamson**, **Richard Bird** and **Yow**.

2234.   1797, Mar 19 -- Land Grant #1899, Moore County, NC
Francis Bullock [assignee of **David Cagle**] received 100 acres located south of Grassy Creek in fork of Cedar Branch adjoining **George Carringer**. **Christopher Yow** and **Allan Bullock** were chain carriers. **Jonathan Bullock** and **Joseph Allen** attested to the transfer of the warrant.

2235.   1797, Mar 20 -- Land Grant #915, Moore County, NC
John Comer received 100 acres located on Williams Creek adjoining **Owen Carpenter** and **James Ledlow**. **Adam Comer Sr.** and **Adam Comer Jr.** were chain carriers.

2236.   1797, Mar 24 -- Land Grant #1585, Moore County, NC
Moses Wilson received 150 acres located southeast of Williams Creek including own improvement. **Allen Morrison** and **John Gilliam Jr.** were chain carriers.

2237.   1797, Mar 30 -- Land Grant #1664, Moore County, NC
Bryant Boroughs received 75 acres located south of Deep River adjoining his own line, **Edmond Waddle** and **Perry**. **Samuel Perry** and **Samuel Martindale** were chain carriers.

2238.   1797, Apr 1 -- 1784-1797 Land Entries, Moore County, NC
#168 **Isom Shuffield** entered 50 acres located north of Bear Creek adjoining **Leonard Cagle Sr.**

2239.   1797, Apr 6 -- Land Grant #1023, Moore County, NC
Benjamin Tyson received 35 acres located south of Deep River adjoining **Thomas Tyson**, **David Allison** and **Governor Johnston**. **Thomas Tyson** and **John Graham** were chain carriers.

2240.   1797, Apr 7 -- Land Grant #1263, Moore County, NC

Samuel Perry received 100 acres located on both sides of Buffalo Creek at the Steep Bottom Ford adjoining **John Askins**. **John Perry** and **Henry Lamb** were chain carriers.

2241. 1797, Apr 19 -- Land Grant #1258, Moore County, NC
Ancel Melton [assignee of **Jesse Brown**] received 100 acres located on the drains of Flag Creek adjoining his own line and including **Ambrose Brown**'s improvement. **Jesse Brown** and **Ansel Melton** were chain carriers.

2242. 1797, Apr 19 -- Land Grant #0199, Moore County, NC
Henry Lamb received 50 acres located on both sides of Buffalo Creek adjoining his own line and **Samuel Perry**. **John Perry** and **Henry Lamb** were chain carriers. [*Editor's Note: Never granted*]

2243. 1797, Apr 24 -- Land Grant #1264, Moore County, NC
Samuel Perry received 25 acres located on both sides of Buffalo Creek adjoining his own line where he now lives. **John Perry** and **John Upton** were chain carriers.

2244. 1797, Apr 26 -- Land Grant #1149, Moore County, NC
Samuel Perry received 100 acres located on both sides of Buffalo Creek adjoining his own line, **Barton**, **Cooper** and the **Lawson** place. **John Perry** and **Henry Lamb** were chain carriers.

2245. 1797, Apr 26 -- Land Grant #1267, Moore County, NC
Samuel Perry received 100 acres located south of Deep River adjoining **Barton**, **William England**'s Big Fall tract and near the old **Benton/Barton** fields. **John Upton** and **John Perry** were chain carriers.

2246. 1797, Apr 26 -- Land Grant #1866, Moore County, NC
Samuel Perry received 50 acres located on the waters of Buffalo Creek adjoining **Cooper** and his own line. **Jno. Perry** and **Saml. Perry** were chain carriers.

2247. 1797, Apr 29 -- 1784-1797 Land Entries, Moore County, NC
#172 **Samuel Dun** and **Simon Rubottom** entered 500 acres on both sides of Deep River adjoining **Dowd**, **Perkins** and

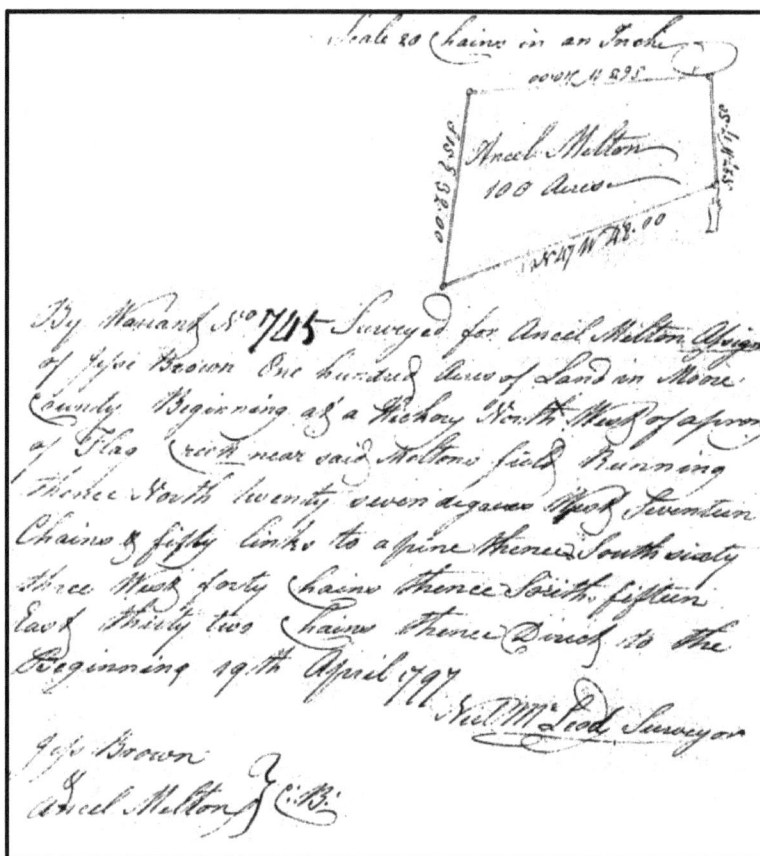

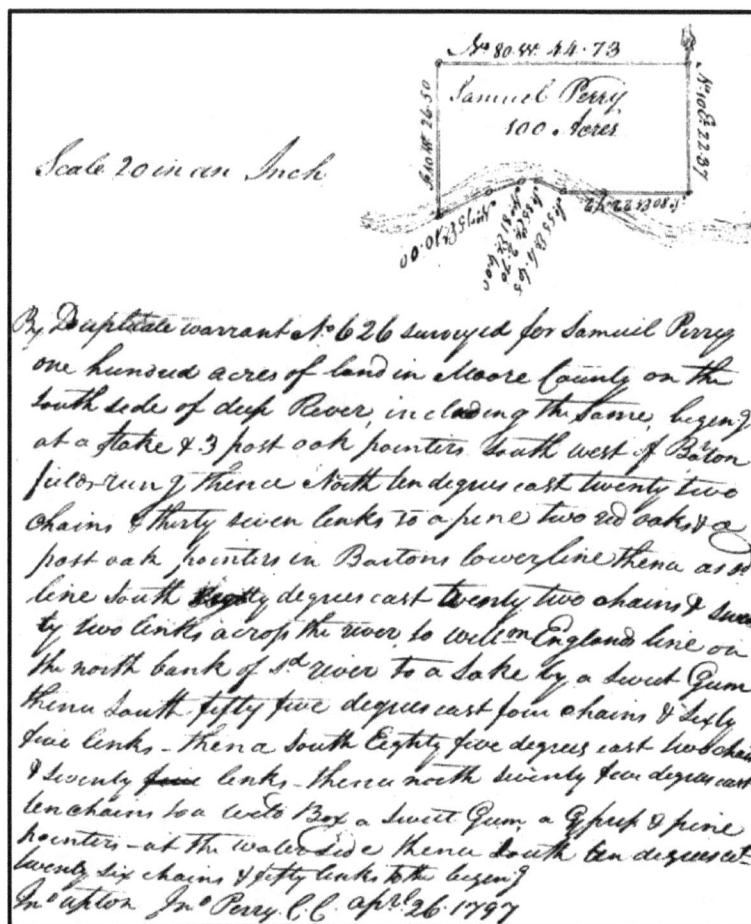

Joseph Duck including the Island Ford.

2248. 1797, May 4 -- Land Grant #1465, Moore County, NC
Nathan Morgan received 50 acres located northwest of Cabin Creek below the mouth of Mill Creek including his own improvement and **John Morgan**'s improvement adjoining **John Morgan** and his own line. **George Morgan** and **John Morgan** were chain carriers.

2249. 1797, May 4 -- Land Grant #1519, Moore County, NC
George Morgan received 50 acres located southwest of Cabin Creek adjoining **John Morgan**, **William Morgan** and his own line. **John Morgan** and **Nathan Morgan** were chain carriers.

2250. 1797, May 9 -- Land Grant #2134, Randolph County, NC
George Onslot received 200 acres located on Deep River adjoining his own line and **Robert Kerr**. **Thomas Craven** and **Eldridg Deyton** were chain carriers.

2251. 1797, May 9 -- Land Grant #1251, Randolph County, NC
William Carr received 100 acres located on Deep River adjoining his own line and **Bird**. **William Searcy** and **Robt**. **Hasdon** were chain carriers.

2252. 1797, May 10 -- Will Book A, Page 192-193, Moore County, NC
Will of **George Williams**, Dec'd. Heirs: wife **Ann Williams** [all land], son **James Williams**, daughter **Nelly Williams**, son **Jeremiah Williams**, son **Thomas Williams**, son **William Williams**, daughter **Mary Williams** and daughter **Sally Williams**. Executors: **Ann Williams** and **Leonard Furr**. Witnesses: **Everet Wallis** and **William Dunn**. Proven Aug 1797.

2253. 1797, May 13 -- 1784-1797 Land Entries, Moore County, NC
#174 **James Mainess** entered 100 acres adjoining his own line.

2254. 1797, May 15 -- Land Grant #1550, Moore County, NC
John Foushee Garner received 200 acres located on both sides of Bear Creek adjoining **Hardy Davis** and **Hogg**. **William Latham** and **Henry Cagle Jr**. were chain carriers. **Hardy Davis** attested that the purchase money for the land had been paid.

2255. 1797, May 15 -- Land Grant #1665, Moore County, NC
Adam White received 100 acres located between Lick Branch and Killetts Creek adjoining **McGathie**, **William Harden** and his own line. **Jacob White** and **James Muse** were chain carriers.

2256. 1797, May 16 -- 1784-1797 Land Entries, Moore County, NC
#178 **Malcolm Mainess** entered 125 acres located between Grassy Creek and Bear Creek adjoining his own line and **Williamson**.

2257. 1797, May 16 -- 1784-1797 Land Entries, Moore County, NC
#187 **Ambrose Maines** entered 100 acres located north of Bear Creek adjoining his own line, **Bullock** and **Kennedy**.

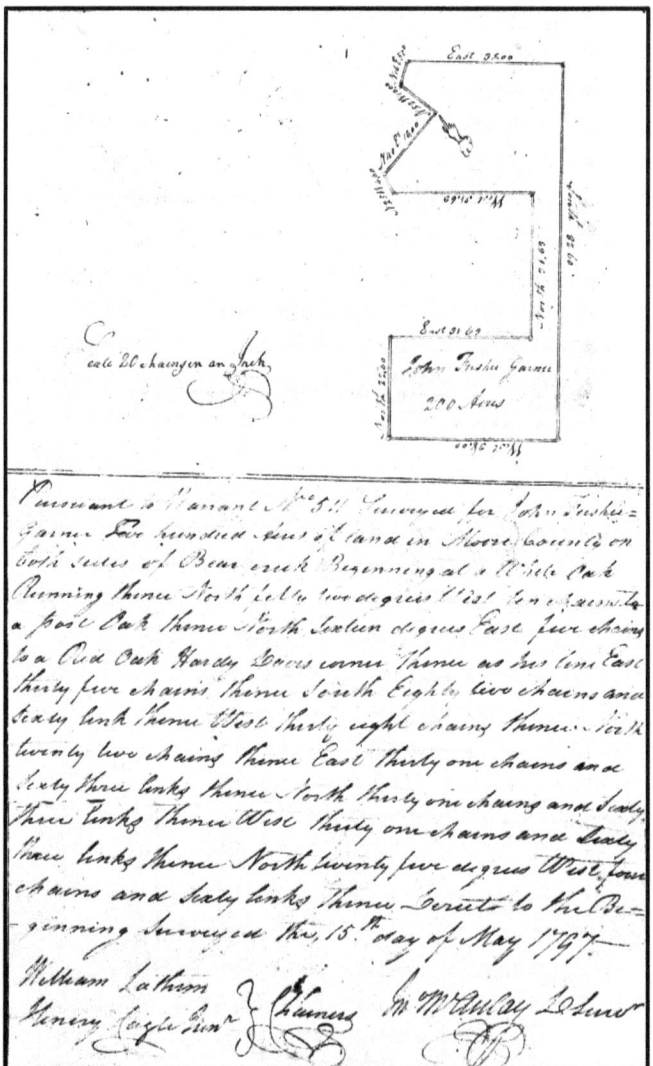

2258.   1797, May 16 -- Land Grant #1352, Moore County, NC
Samuel Dunn [assignee of **Hezekiah Dunn**] received 13 acres located west of Wet Creek adjoining his own line, **Hezekiah Dunn** and **Richard Dun** were chain carriers.

2259.   1797, May 17 -- Land Grant #1743, Moore County, NC
John Warner [assignee of **John Inzer**] received 150 acres located on both sides of the Waggon Road adjoining **Patty Glascock**. **Thomas Matthews** and **Burrel Maples** were chain carriers.

2260.   1797, May 22 -- Land Grant #1520, Moore County, NC
John Dunn received 100 acres located on both sides of Wolf Creek north of the Yadkin Waggon Road adjoining **William Morgan Jr. Reuben Freeman** and **William Morgan** were chain carriers.

2261.   1797, May 24 -- Land Grant #998, Moore County, NC
William Wright received 15 acres located on Wolf Creek adjoining his own line and **William Morgan Jr. John Dunn** and **William Wright** were chain carriers.

2262.   1797, May 27 -- Land Grant #1292, Moore County, NC
William Richardson received 50 acres located on Kings Street adjoining his own line and **Joseph Geason/Chason. Drury Richardson** and **John Ritter** were chain carriers.

2263.   1797, May 27 -- Land Grant #0108, Moore County, NC
John Ritter received 50 acres located on both sides of Morter Glade adjoining **Joseph Geason. Drury Richardson** and **Jno. Ritter** were chain carriers. [*Editor's Note: Never granted*]

2264.   1797, Jun 2 -- Land Grant #905, Moore County, NC
Neil McLeod received 50 acres located on the head of Richland Creek. **Jesse Ritter** and **John Ritter** were chain carriers.

2265.   1797, Jun 3 -- Land Grant #1385, Moore County, NC
Joseph Fry received 200 acres located on drains of Killets Creek adjoining **Jno. Insor**, own line, **Nathan Fry, Allison** and **Widow McDonald. Jas. Fry** and **Nathan Fry** were chain carriers.

2266.   1797, Jun 10 -- 1784-1797 Land Entries, Moore County, NC
#196 **Malcolm McNiel** entered 50 acres located on Williamsons [Williams] Creek adjoining his own line, **Owen Carpenter, Calicut** and including **Shuffield's** improvement.

2267.   1797, Jun 10 -- Land Grant #893, Moore County, NC
Christopher Cagle received 50 acres located north of Bear Creek adjoining his own line, **John Lawley, Christian Cagle, Henry Cagle Sr. Henry Cagle** and **John Cagle** were chain carriers.

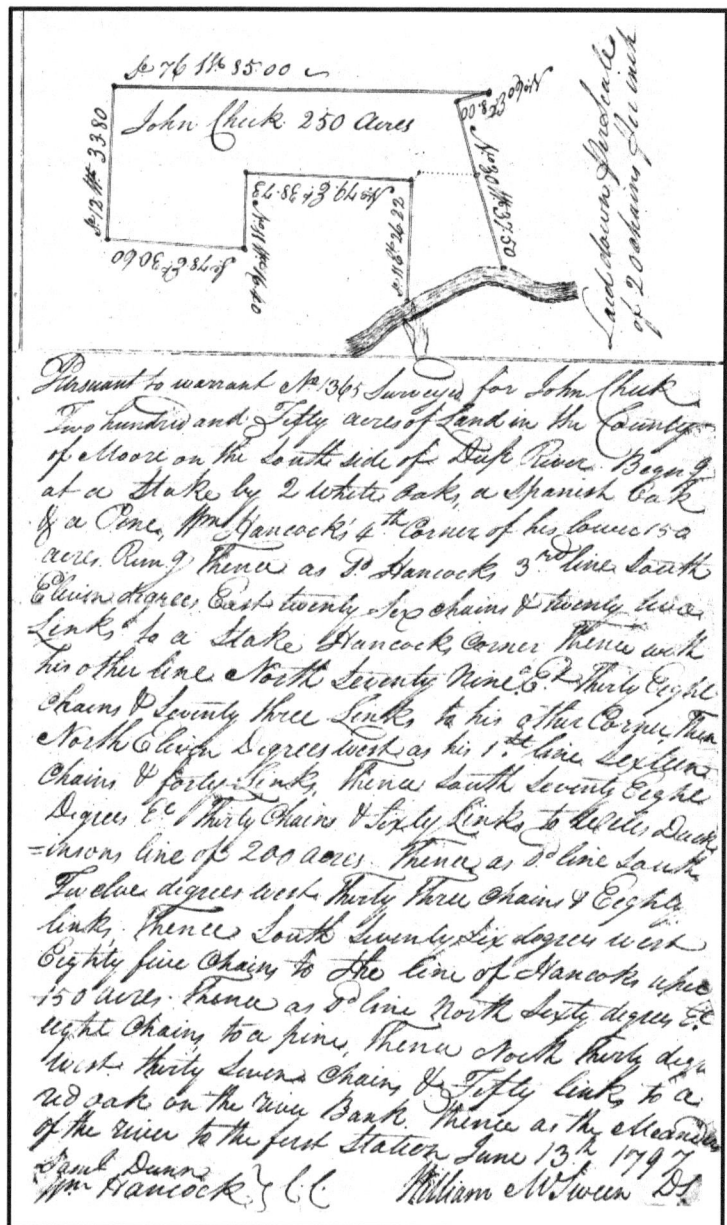

2268. 1797, Jun 13 -- Land Grant #1106, Moore County, NC *(see document on prior page)*
John Cheek [assignee of **Saml. Dunn**] received 250 acres located south of Deep River adjoining **William Hancock** and **Willis Dickinson**. **Saml. Dunn** and **Wm. Hancock** were chain carriers.

2269. 1797, Jun 14 -- Land Grant #882, Moore County, NC
Ancel Melton Senr. received 100 acres located east of Wet Creek adjoining **William Dunn**, **Graham** and his own line. **William Dunn** and **Nathaniel Melton** were chain carriers.

2270. 1797, Jun 20 -- Land Grant #1317, Moore County, NC
Neil McLeod received 50 acres located on Buffalo Creek adjoining **William Smith**, **Murdock Martin**. **Donald McLeod** and **John Hargrove** were chain carriers.

2271. 1797, Jun 22 -- Will Book A Page 204-205, Moore County, NC
Will of **John Phillips**, Dec'd. Heirs: wife **Patience**, son **Lewis Phillips** and son **John Phillips**. Executor: wife **Patience** and son **Lewis Phillips**. Witnesses: **Patrick Dowd** and **William Dickinson**. Proven Nov 1799.

2272. 1797, Jun 23 -- Land Grant #1323, Moore County, NC
Simon Rheubottom received 49 acres located northwest of Richland Creek adjoining **William Barrett**, **Farquard Campbell**, **Donald McQueen** and **Jesse Ritter**. **William Dunn** and **Everit Ritter** were chain carriers.

2273. 1797, Jun 24 -- Land Grant #1579, Moore County, NC
John Hare received 50 acres located on Wolf Creek adjoining his own line and **Peter Hare**. **John Sheffield Sr.** and **John Sheffield Jr.** were chain carriers.

2274. 1797, Jun 27 -- Land Grant #1536, Moore County, NC
Donald McDonald received 8 acres located south of McLendons Creek adjoining his own line and **Allen Martin**. **Allen Martin** and **Norman McDuffie** were chain carriers.

2275. 1797, Jul 1 -- 1784-1797 Land Entries, Moore County, NC
#206 **John Smith** entered 150 acres located on both sides of Dry Creek adjoining **Widow Tedwell**, **Adam Shuffield** and including his own improvement.

2276. 1797, Jul 3 -- Land Grant #1036, Moore County, NC
Thomas Tyson received 200 acres located on south of Deep River adjoining **Johnston**, own line and **Benjamin Tyson**. **Benjamin Tyson** and **Seth Barns** were chain carriers.

2277. 1797, Jul 4 -- Land Grant #1037, Moore County, NC
Thomas Tyson received 19 acres located on Smith's Creek of Deep River adjoining **Benjamin Tyson**, **David Allison** and **Richard Dowd**. **Kenneth Murchison** and **Danl. McRae** were chain carriers.

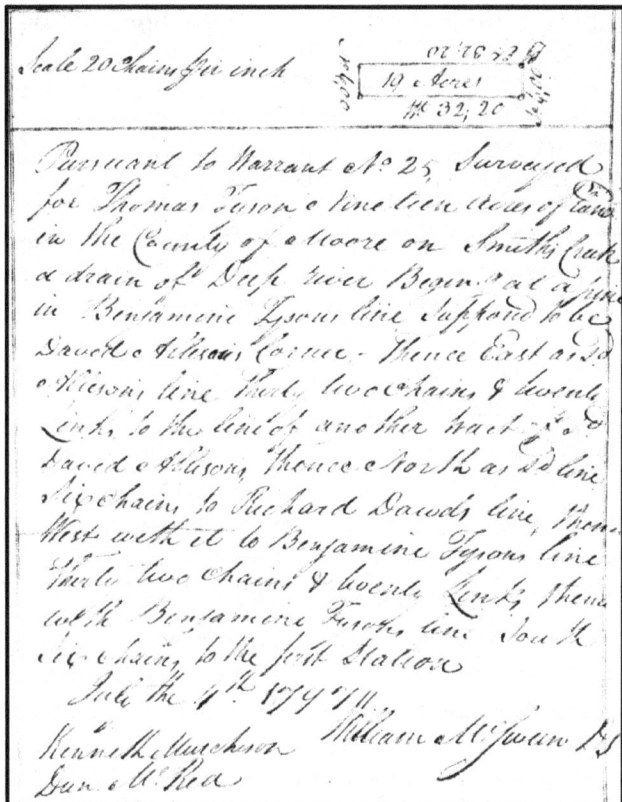

2278. 1797, Jul 4 -- Land Grant #1080, Moore County, NC
Francis Bullock received 50 acres located on Big Cedar Branch of Bear Creek. **Nathan Morgan** and **Francis Bullock** were chain carriers.

2279. 1797, Jul 4 -- Land Grant #1314, Moore County, NC
Francis Bullock received 50 acres located north of Cabin Creek adjoining his own line and **Joseph Allen**. **Joseph Allen** and **Francis Bullock** were chain carriers.

2280. 1797, Jul 4 -- Land Grant #1413, Moore County, NC
Hardy Davis received 50 acres located on both sides of Bear Creek on the [Randolph] County line adjoining his own line. **William Latham** and **John Holden** were chain carriers.

2281. 1797, Jul 8 -- Land Grant #1440, Moore County, NC
John Ritter received 50 acres located on both sides of Buffalo Creek adjoining **Pennington**, his own line (known as **Juck**'s Place). **Drury Richardson** and **Jesse Ritter** were chain carriers.

2282. 1797, Jul 11 -- Land Grant #1459, Moore County, NC
Neil McLeod received 150 acres located on both sides of Deep River adjoining **Isaac Pennington, Edward Moore, Abraham Hunsucker, England** and **Joseph Geason**. **Peter Graves** and **Samuel Elkins** were chain carriers.

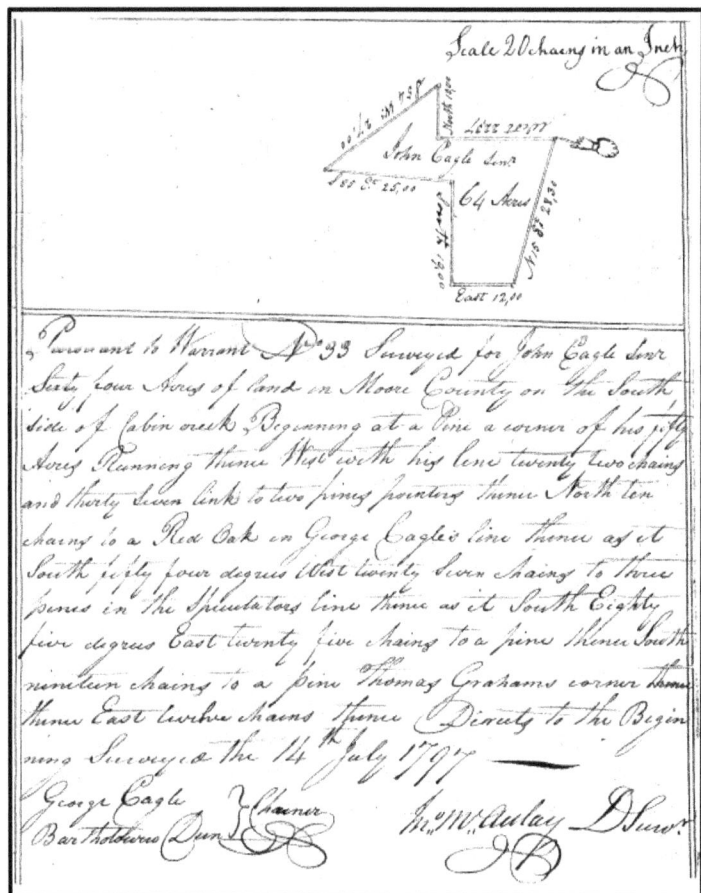

2283. 1797, Jul 13 -- Land Grant #1919, Moore County, NC
Bartholomew Dunn Senr. received 75 acres located on Flag Creek adjoining **George Williams, Christopher Stuts** and his own line. **Christopher Stuts** and **George Cagle** were chain carriers.

2284. 1797, Jul 14 -- Land Grant #1531, Moore County, NC
John Cagle Sr. received 64 acres located south of Cabin Creek adjoining his own line, **George Cagle** and **Thomas Graham**. **George Cagle** and **Bartholomew Dunn** were chain carriers.

2285. 1797, Jul 20 -- Land Grant #902, Moore County, NC

Neil McLeod received 150 acres located north of Deep River adjoining **William England**, **Samuel Perry**, **Richardson Fagin**, **William Cook**, **Hugh Gilmore**, **Barton** and **George Fagin**. **William Cook** and **Peter Graves** were chain carriers.

2286.   1797, Jul 20 -- Land Grant #910, Moore County, NC
Neil McLeod received 200 acres located north of Deep River adjoining **Edward Moore** and **James Moore**. **William Cook** and **Samuel Elkins** were chain carriers.

2287.   1797, Jul 20 -- Land Grant #1053, Moore County, NC
John Martin [assignee of **William Martin**] received 50 acres located on the Juniper adjoining **John McNeill**. **Duncan McNeill** and **Donald McLean** were chain carriers.

2288.   1797, Jul 20 -- Land Grant #1437, Moore County, NC
Thomas Armstrong [assignee of **Neil McLeod**] received 150 acres located north of Deep River on the drains of Waggon Branch and the Chatham County line adjoining **James Murray** and **James Moore**. **William Cook** and **Samuel Elkins** were chain carriers.

2289.   1797, Jul 22 -- Land Grant #929, Moore County, NC
Neil McLeod received 60 acres located north of Deep River adjoining **Isaac Pennington**, **James Barton**, **Edward Moore** and **England**. **Samuel Elkins** and **Peter Graves** were chain carriers.

2290.   1797, Jul 28 -- Land Grant #856, Moore County, NC
Neal Matheson received 100 acres located on both sides of Buffalo Creek adjoining his own line and **Hector McNeill**. **Norman Matheson** and **Donald Buchanan** were chain carriers.

2291.   1797, Jul 31 -- Criminal Actions, Randolph County, NC, Box 4
Capias against **Hardy Davis** that he assaulted **Charles Stewart** at the house of **Wm. Armistead** Jun 24, 1797. **Wm. Rains**, **Eldridge Deaton**, **Bealia Needham**, **James Smith** and **James Powers** were witnesses. Another capias was issued by **John Craven** on the same matter. **James Powers** and **Luas Needham** were witnesses.

2292.   1797, Aug 3 -- Land Grant #1470, Moore County, NC
William Morgan Senr. received 50 acres located on both sides of Calf Pen Branch north of Cabin Creek adjoining his own line. **William Morgan** and **Joseph Allen** were chain carriers.

2293.   1797, Aug 9 -- Land Grant #887, Moore County, NC
Henry. Cagle Jr. received 25 acres located south of Bear Creek adjoining his own line. **Henry Cagle Sr.** and **Peter Cagle** were chain carriers.

2294.   1797, Aug 10 -- 1784-1795 Land Entries, Moore County, NC
#229 **Everet Wallis** entered 50 acres located on drains of Flag Creek

2295.   1797, Aug 13 -- Land Grant #1021, Moore County, NC
John Morgan Medford received 50 acres located on both sides of Mill Creek adjoining **William Morgan** and including his own improvement. **Geo. Morgan** and **Joseph Bridges** were chain carriers.

2296.   1797, Aug 13 -- Land Grant #1022, Moore County, NC
John Morgan Medford received 50 acres located northwest of Mill Creek adjoining **James Gallemore** (formerly **John Cox**). **Geo. Morgan** and **Joseph Bridges** were chain carriers.

2297.   1797, Aug 18 -- Land Grant #1535, Moore County, NC
Malcolm Morrison received 50 acres located west of Dry Creek on Horse Creek adjoining **Mattheson** and his own line. **Alexr. Munroe** and **Angus Morrison** were chain carriers.

2298.   1797, Aug 18 -- 1784-1797 Land Entries, Moore County, NC
#243 **John Ritter** entered 100 acres located on Buffaloe Creek adjoining his own line, **Nier Brewer** and **Lawson**.

2299.   1797, Aug 22 -- 1784-1797 Land Entries, Moore County, NC
#255 **John Shuffield** entered 50 acres located on both sides of Wolf Creek adjoining his own line and **John Hair**.

2300. 1797, Aug 24 -- Land Grant #1121, Moore County, NC
Jacob Duckworth received 300 acres located south of Deep River and both sides of Lick Creek adjoining **Powel**, **McNeill** and **William Davis**. **Neil McIntosh** and **William McDonald** were chain carriers.

2301. 1797, Aug 25 -- Land Grant #1307, Moore County, NC
Christopher Yow received 92 acres located north of Grassy Creek adjoining **Leonard Hart**, **McLeod**, **Nall**, **Owen Carpenter**, **William Williamson** and **Richard Bird**. **William Williamson** and **James Williamson** were chain carriers.

2302. 1797, Aug 25 -- Land Grant #1151, Moore County, NC
John Hare received 100 acres located on Wolf Creek adjoining his own line and **John Sheffield**. **John Sheffield Sr.** and **John Sheffield Jr.** were chain carriers.

2303. 1797, Aug 25 -- Land Grant #1123, Moore County, NC
Mathew Ditton [assignee of **Christopher Yow**] received 84 acres located on Grassy Creek adjoining **John Williamson**, **William Williamson**, **Bullock**, **George Carringer** and **Lenard Hart**. **William Williamson** and **James Williamson** were chain carriers.

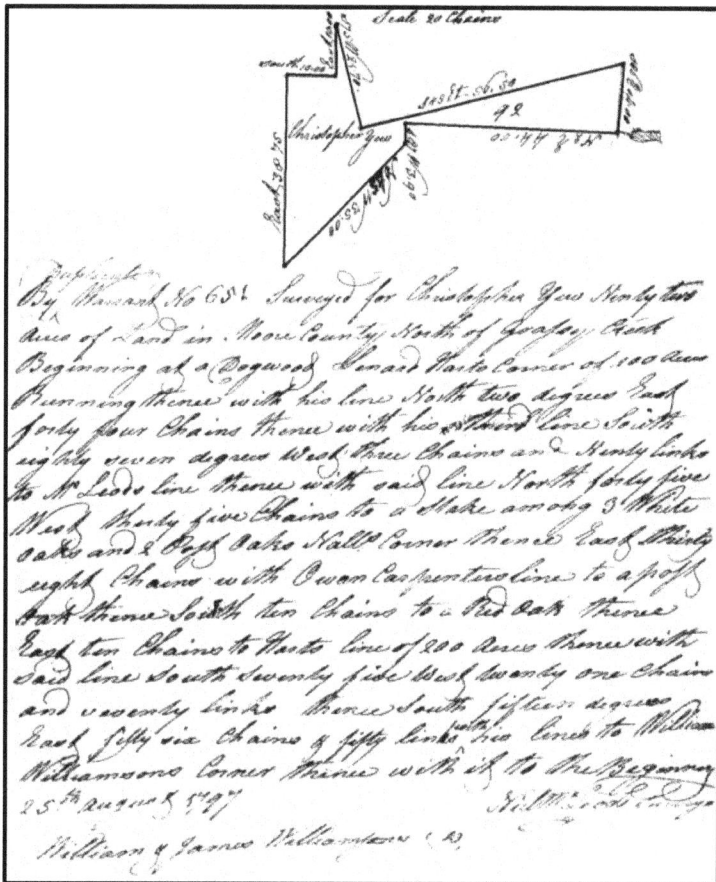

2304. 1797, Aug 26 -- 1784-1797 Land Entries, Moore County, NC
#261 **Solomon Barret** entered 100 acres located north of Bear Creek adjoining his own line, **Everet Shuffield**, **Hanna Shuffield**, **Isom Shuffield** and **Bullock**.

2305. 1797, Aug 27 -- Land Grant #1623, Moore County, NC
John Lawler received 100 acres located on drains of Fall Creek north of Deep River adjoining **William Davis**, his own line, **Beason**, **Willis Davis**, **Samuel Parson** and the Speculators. **Saml. Parson** and **Richard Beason** were chain carriers.

2306. 1797, Aug 28 -- Land Grant #894, Moore County, NC
Peter Cagle received 200 acres located on the head of Bear Creek adjoining **John Lawley** and **Henry Cagle**. **Henry Cagle** and **Peter Cagle** were chain carriers.

2307. 1797, Aug 30 -- 1784-1797 Land Entries, Moore County, NC
#262 **James Elkins** entered 150 acres located on both sides of Williams Creek adjoining **Owen Carpenter**, **William Callicoat** and including **William Shuffield**'s improvement.

2308. 1797, Aug 31 -- Land Grant #1349, Moore County, NC
Thomas Graham received 50 acres located east of McLendons Creek adjoining **Martin Martin**, **William Martin**, his own line and **William Barrett**. **Wm. Barrett** and **Thos. Docherty** were chain carriers.

2309. 1797, Sep 6 -- Land Grant #1627, Moore County, NC
William Mainess received 100 acres located south of Bear Creek adjoining his own line. **William Needom** and **William Mainess** were chain carriers.

2310. 1797, Sep 10 -- Land Grant #1316, Moore County, NC

Francis Bullock received 250 acres located north of Bear Creek on Watery Branch adjoining **Autery**. **John Sheffield** and **Francis Bullock** were chain carriers.

2311.   1797, Sep 17 -- Land Grant #1367, Moore County, NC
Keziah Thomas received 100 acres located north of Wiers Spring on a drain of Killets Creek adjoining her own line, **John Morrison**, **William Feagen** and **Glascock**. **Jesse Muse** and **Asay Hannon** were chain carriers.

2312.   1797, Sep 18 -- Land Grant #1315, Moore County, NC
Francis Bullock received 100 acres located on both sides of Bear Creek including the mouth of Lick Branch adjoining **Autery**. **John Sheffield** and **Francis Bullock** were chain carriers.

2313.   1797, Sep 19 -- 1784-1795 Land Entries, Moore County, NC
#268 **Meshack Mainess** entered 50 acres located east of Mainess Branch adjoining **William Mainess** and the Speculators.

2314.   1797, Sep 20 -- Land Grant #1075, Moore County, NC
Beyhue Sowell [assignee of **John Hargrove**] received 100 acres located on Buffalo Creek adjoining his own line. **Alexander McCaskill** and **John Cambel** were chain carriers.

2315.   1797, Sep 20 -- Land Grant #1076, Moore County, NC
Beyhue Sowell received 50 acres located on Buffalo Creek adjoining **Leonard Furr**. **Alexander McCaskill** and **John Cambel** were chain carriers.

2316.   1797, Sep 20 -- Land Grant #1119, Moore County, NC
Jno. Cheek received 250 acres located north of Deep River on the Chatham County line adjoining **Benjamin Gilbert** and **Randolph Cheek**. **William McDonald** and **Neal McIntosh** were chain carriers.

A.   1797, Sep 24 -- Will, Chatham County, NC
Will of **Abner Brown**, Dec'd. Heirs: wife **Mary Brown** (pregnant with child) [all land including three acres and mill], son **John Brown**, **Lucy Brown**, **Nancy Brown**, **Sally Brown** and **Polley Brown**. Executors: wife **Mary Brown** and **Robert Ward**. **A. Burnett**, **Harbert Lewis** and **Joseph Fooshee** were witnesses.

2317.   1797, Sep 30 -- 1784-1795 Land Entries, Moore County, NC
#273 **Levy Deaton** entered 25 acres located south of Bear Creek adjoining **William Needom** and **William Mainess**.

2318.   1797, Oct 3 -- Land Grant #891, Moore County, NC
Henry Cagle Sr. received 20 acres located north of Bear Creek adjoining his own line. **Christopher Cagle** and **John Cagle** were chain carriers.

2319.   1797, Oct 3 -- 1784-1797 Land Entries, Moore County, NC
#276 **Adam Shuffield** entered 50 acres located north of Bear Creek adjoining **William Garner**'s 400 acre tract claimed by **Dowd**.

2320.   1797, Oct 3 -- 1784-1797 Land Entries, Moore County, NC
#277 **Adam Shuffield** entered 50 acres located south of Bear Creek adjoining **William Garner**'s 400 acre tract claimed by **Dowd**.

2321.   1797, Oct 8 -- Land Grant #1460, Moore County, NC
John Argo received 200 acres located on the Sedars, Pates Creek of Deep River including Little Seadar Spring adjoining **William Davis**, **Zachariah Smith** and **David Allison**. **Jas. Harden** and **Wm. McSween** were chain carriers.

2322.   1797, Oct 9 -- Will Book A Page 194-196, Moore County, NC
Will of **William Hancock**, Dec'd. Heirs: wife [unnamed -- 200 acres adjoining *Willis Dickson*]; children: **William Hancock** [land given to wife once he becomes of age], **John Hancock** [250

acres on Deep River adjoining **Robert Cheek**], **Rhoda Hancock**, **Lydda Hancock**, **Patty Hancock**, **Elizabeth Hancock**. Executors: wife and **John Cheek**. Witnesses: **Saml. Dunn**, **Randal Cheek** and **John Cheek**. Proven Nov 1797.

2323. 1797, Oct 12 -- Land Grant #1345, Moore County, NC **Elijah Bettis Jr**. received 100 acres located in the fork of Richland Creek and McLendons Creek including the his own improvement adjoining his own line and **Elisha Bettis**. **Solomon Holomon** and **Elisha Bettis** were chain carriers.

2324. 1797, Oct 12 -- Land Grant #1350, Moore County, NC **Elijah Bettis Jr**. received 50 acres located on McLendons Creek adjoining **Tomlin/Tomberlin** and **McKay**. **Elisha Bettis** and **Archd. Ray** were chain carriers.

2325. 1797, Oct 14 -- Land Grant #1242, Moore County, NC **Joseph McGee** received 100 acres located on Long and Willow Meadow of Buffalo Creek including the Schoolhouse Spring. **Drury Joiner** and **John Martin** were chain carriers.

2326. 1797, Oct 14 -- Land Grant #1617, Moore County, NC **Elijah Bettis Jr**. [assignee of **Reuben Shields**] received 100 acres located southeast of McLendons Creek adjoining **McKay**, **Jackson** and **Tomlin/Tomberlin**. **George Jackson** and **Ezekial Rubottom** were chain carriers.

2327. 1797, Oct 16 -- Land Grant #886, Moore County, NC **John McAulay Jr**. received 200 acres located southeast of Bear Creek adjoining **David Allison**, **James Maness**, **Christopher Stuts** and **Henery Cagle**. **Christopher Stuts** and **James Maness** were chain carriers.

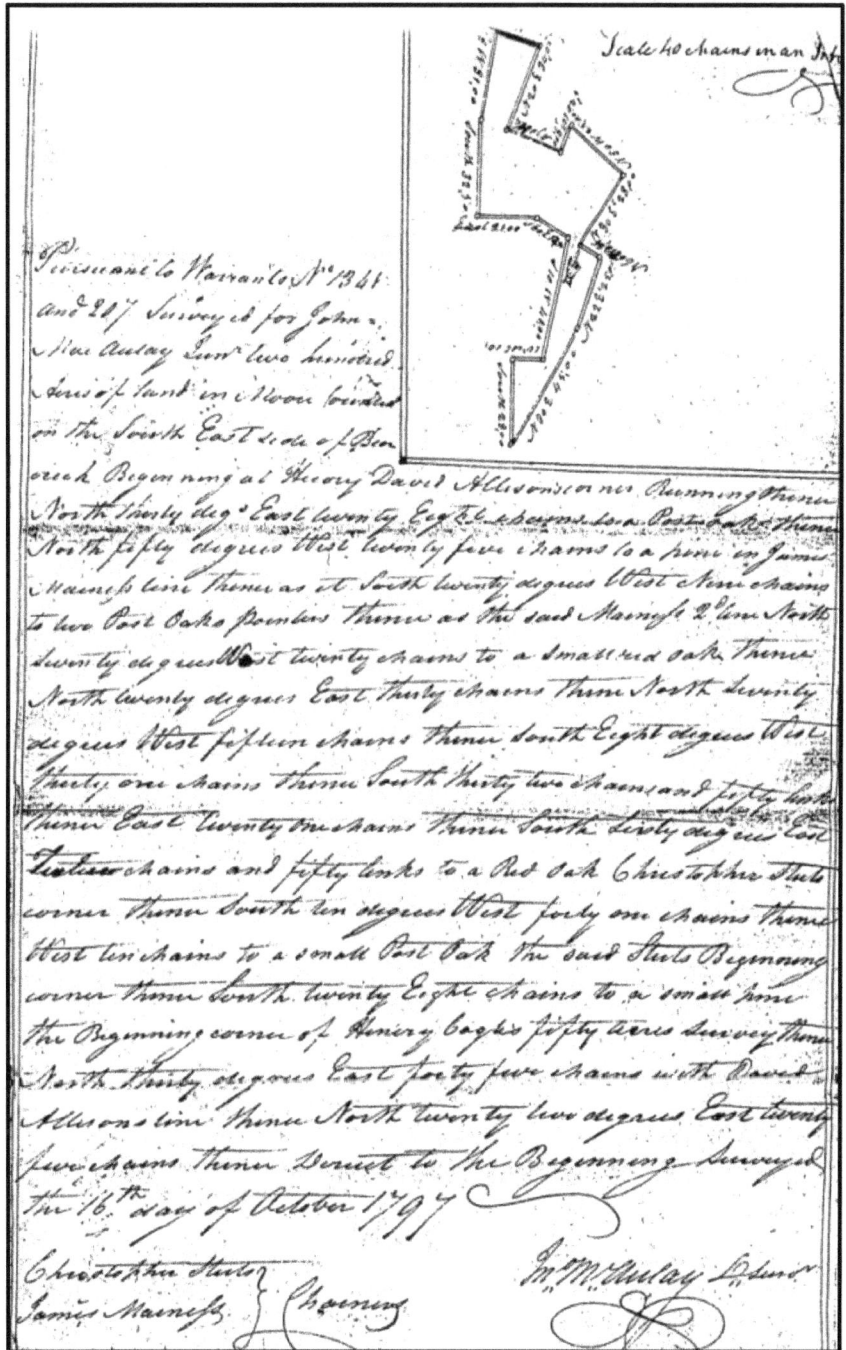

2328. 1797, Oct 20 -- Land Grant #942, Moore County, NC **William Barret** [assignee of **John Hargrove**] received 50 acres located south of Deep River adjoining his own line and **Solomon Barrett**. **William McDonald** and **John McDonald** were chain carriers.

2329. 1797, Oct 20 -- Land Grant #945, Moore County, NC **William Barret** received 70 acres located south of Deep River adjoining his own line. **William McDonald** and **John McDonald** were chain carriers.

2330.   1797, Oct 21 -- Land Grant #1388, Moore County, NC
Cornelius Dowd received 100 acres located west of McLendons Creek adjoining **Ezekial Rubottom** and his own line where he now lives called the **Duck** place. **Tom Muse** and **Ruben Sheals** were chain carriers.

2331.   1797, Oct 22 -- Land Grant #1438, Moore County, NC
Kenneth McDonald received 50 acres located northwest of McLendons Creek adjoining **Robert Cox** and his own line. **Allen Martin** and **Donald McDonald** were chain carriers.

2332.   1797, Oct 26 -- Land Grant #1433, Moore County, NC
Neill McIntosh [assignee of **John Hargrove**] received 100 acres located on the Chatham County line north of Deep River adjoining **William Phillips**, **Thomas** and **Robert Phillips**. **William Phillips** and **James Harden** were chain carriers.

2333.   1797, Nov 3 -- 1784-1797 Land Entries, Moore County, NC
#295 **Alexr. McIntosh** entered 80 acres adjoining **Widow MacIntosh** and **Thomas Ritter**.

2334.   1797, Nov 7 -- Land Grant #900, Moore County, NC
Neill McLeod received 50 acres located west of McLendons Creek adjoining **Jacob McLendon** and **Angus McIver**.

2335.   1797, Nov 8 -- Land Grant #1339, Moore County, NC
Richard Dunn Jr. received 100 acres located on both sides of Wet Creek south of Size Branch including **Elizabeth Hodges'** improvement adjoining his own line. **John McKinnon** and **Richd. Dunn** were chain carriers.

2336.   1797, Nov 8 -- Land Grant #1453, Moore County, NC
Neill McLeod received 100 acres located on Williamsons Creek adjoining **Smith** and **Carpenter**. **Stephen Smith** and **Nathan Smith** were chain carriers.

A.   1797, Nov 9 -- Land Grant #1397, Montgomery County, NC
Jesse Simmons received 100 acres located on Great Branch of Cabin Creek adjoining his own line and **William Allen**. **Jesse Simmons** and his wife were chain carriers.

B.   1797, Nov 11 – Deed Book N Page 221-222, Chatham County, NC
Henry Powers deeded **Robt. Willson** 50 acres located on Fall Creek and Meadow Branch adjoining **Parsons**, **Edwd. Beeson** and **Matthias Teague** were witnesses.

2337.   1797, Nov 13 -- Land Grant #993, Moore County, NC
Zachariah Smith received 50 acres located north of Buffalo Creek adjoining his own line. **Joseph McGee** and **William Richardson** were chain carriers.

2338.   1797, Nov 13 -- Land Grant #994, Moore County, NC
Zachariah Smith [assignee of **Thomas Smith**] received 50 acres located north of Buffalo Creek adjoining his own line, **Myre** and including a field and cabin where **Mary Smith** lives.

2339.   1797, Nov 14 -- Land Grant #1241, Moore County, NC
Drury Joiner received 50 acres located on both sides of Willow Meadow adjoining **Joseph McGee** and **McKay**. **John Martin** and **James Melton** were chain carriers.

2340.   1797, Nov 14 -- Land Grant #1270, Moore County, NC
Stephen Richardson received 100 acres located north of Buffalo Creek adjoining **Edwards**. **Joseph Cockman** and **James Melton** were chain carriers.

2341.   1797, Nov 14 -- Land Grant #1546, Moore County, NC
John Martin received 100 acres located south of Buffalo Creek adjoining **Jacob Cagle**, **Edwards** and **Stephen Richardson**. **John McGee** and **Drury Joiner** were chain carriers.

2342.   1797, Nov 14 -- Land Grant #1772, Moore County, NC

Joseph McGee received 100 acres located on the drains of Buffalo Creek on Haw Branch adjoining **Jacob Stutts**. **Drury Joiner** and **Henry Stutts** were chain carriers.

2343. 1797, Nov 14 -- Land Grant #1196, Moore County, NC **John Richardson** received 100 acres located on both sides of Buffalo Creek adjoining **Jacob Stutts**, **Stinson** and **McLeod**. **John Martin** and **Drury Joiner** were chain carriers.

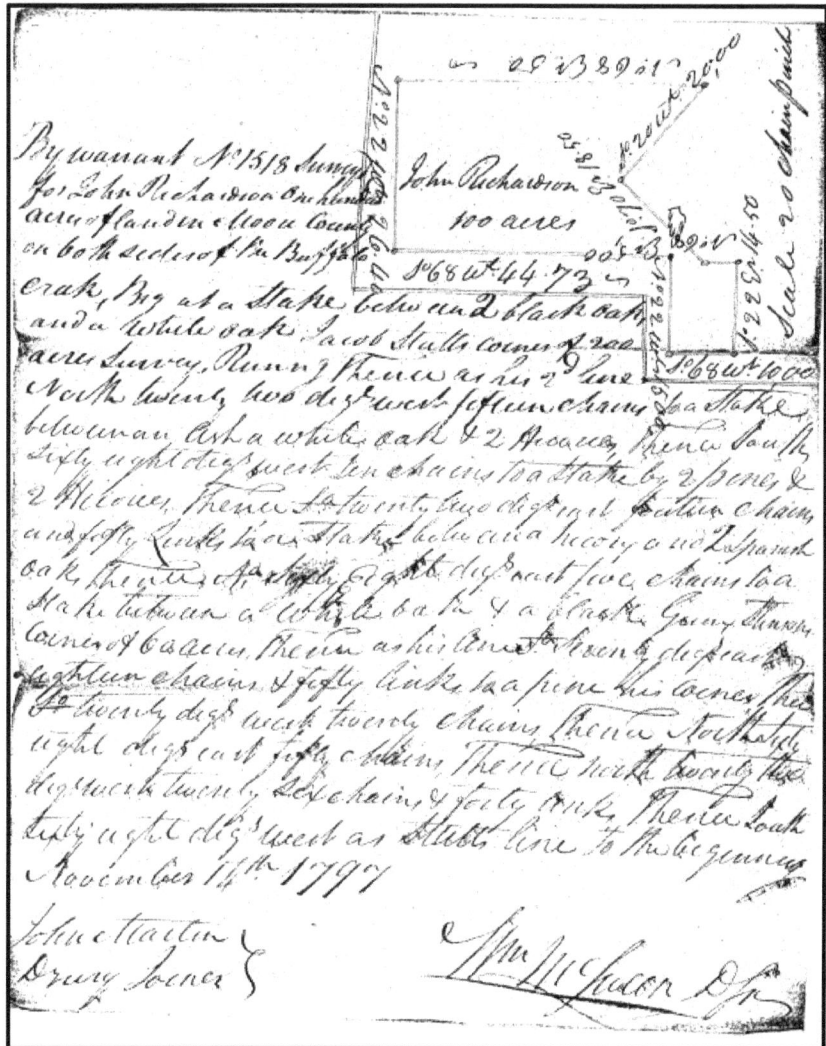

2344. 1797, Nov 15 -- Land Grant #883, Moore County, NC **John McAulay Jr.** received 100 acres located on Panther Branch of Bear Creek adjoining **David Kennedy**. **Hezekiah Dunn** and **William Maness** were chain carriers.

2345. 1797, Nov 16 -- Land Grant #875, Moore County, NC **Murdock McAulay** received 50 acres located on both sides of Wet Creek adjoining **Bartholomew Dunn**, his own line and **William Dunn**. **Murdock McAulay** and **Bartholomew Dunn** were chain carriers.

2346. 1797, Nov 16 -- Land Grant #879, Moore County, NC **Francis Bullock** received 100 acres adjoining **John Sheffield** including his own improvement. **John Sheffield** and **Francis Bullock** were chain carriers.

2347. 1797, Nov 18 -- Land Grant #0268, Moore County, NC **Neill McIntosh** received 70 acres located southeast of McLendons Creek adjoining **George Jackson**, **Wadsworth** and **Bettis'** Mill stand. **George Jackson** and **Archd. Ray** were chain carriers. [*Editor's Note: Never granted*]

2348. 1797, Nov 18 -- Land Grant #1796, Moore County, NC **Jesse Muse** received 150 acres on McLendons Creek and Jacobs Creek, west of the Cane Path adjoining his own line and **Widow Muse**. **Jeremiah Deen** and **Samuel Dunn** were chain carriers.

2349. 1797, Nov 20 -- Land Grant #1386, Moore County, NC **Joseph Fry** received 10 acres on drains of Killets Creek adjoining his own line, **William Feagan** and **Benjamin Fry**. **Jas. Fry** and **Nathan Fry** were chain carriers.

2350. 1797, Nov 22 -- Land Grant #0185, Moore County, NC **Peter Graves** received 50 acres located south of Deep River adjoining **William England** and **Edmond Waddle**. **Josua Cook** and **William Cook** were chain carriers. [*Editor's Note: Never granted*]

2351. 1797, Nov 22 -- Land Grant #1150, Moore County, NC **Malcolm McLeod** received 50 acres adjoining **Kenneth McDonald**, **Cox** and his own line. **Christopher Bethune** and **Allen Martin** were chain carriers.

A.   1797, Nov 22 -- Land Grant #1390, Montgomery County, NC
Jesse Bolin received 100 acres located on Naked Fork and Cart Fork of Cabin Creek adjoining **John Porterfield**. **John Sowell** and **Jesse Bolin** were chain carriers.

2352.   1797, Nov 23 -- Land Grant #917, Moore County, NC
Thomas Matthews received 50 acres located on Mill Swamp adjoining his own line, **Muse** and **Wadsworth**. **Daniel Fagin** and **Saml. Fagin** were chain carriers.

2353.   1797, Nov 23 -- Land Grant #1090, Moore County, NC
Joab Cheek [assignee of **Patrick Dowd**] received 50 acres located south of Deep River and east of Rogers Creek adjoining **Randolph Cheek**. **Patrick Dowd** and **Jno. McIntosh** were chain carriers.

2354.   1797, Nov 23 -- Land Grant #1269, Moore County, NC
Leonard Furr received 50 acres located on both sides of Buffalo Creek adjoining **Leonard Cagle Sr. Christopher Stuts** and **John Spivey** were chain carriers.

2355.   1797, Nov 24 -- Land Grant #1038, Moore County, NC
Bryant Boroughs received 50 acres located west of Buffalo Creek adjoining his own line and **Harmon Brewer**. **John McDonald** and **John McLeod** were chain carriers.

2356.   1797, Nov 24 -- Land Grant #1406, Moore County, NC
Hector McLean received 50 acres located west of Horse Creek adjoining his own line, **Neil McLeod** and **Brownlow**. **Murdock McLeod** and **Donald Munroe** were chain carriers.

2357.   1797, Nov 24 -- Land Grant #1537, Moore County, NC
Donald Munroe received 100 acres located between Buffalo Creek and Horse Creek adjoining **Alexr. Munroe** and **Matheson**. **Hector McLean** and **Alexr. Munroe** were chain carriers.

2358.   1797, Nov 25 -- Land Grant #1802, Moore County, NC
John McLeod received 10 acres located on Horse Creek adjoining **Neil McLeod**. **Donald Clark** and **Norman McLeod** were chain carriers.

2359.   1797, Nov 25 -- Land Grant #1804, Moore County, NC
John McLeod received 30 acres located on Horse Creek adjoining **Neil McLeod**, his own line and **Norman McLeod**. **Norman McLeod** and **Donald Clark** were chain carriers.

2360.   1797, Nov 27 -- Land Grant #1025, Moore County, NC
Robert Beason and **Isaac Wells** received 300 acres located on Fall Creek north of Deep River adjoining **Wm. Davis**, **Wells**, **Martindale**, **Lawler** and **Henley**. **Eli Lawler** and **Saml. Parsons** were chain carriers.

2361.   1797, Nov 27 -- Land Grant #1026, Moore County, NC
Isaac Wells received 200 acres located on fork of Fall Creek adjoining **William Davis**, **Richard Beason**, **Isaac Wells** and **James Brady**. **Eli Lawler** and **Saml. Parsons** were chain carriers.

2362.   1797, Nov 27 -- Land Grant #1082, Moore County, NC
John Shamburger received 100 acres located south of Reedy Creek adjoining his own line and **Robert Bird**. **Peter Shamburger Senr.** and **Peter Shamburger Junr.** were chain carriers.

2363.   1797, Nov 27 -- Land Grant #1083, Moore County, NC
John Shamburger received 100 acres located on both sides of Reedy Creek adjoining his own line and **Caster**. **Peter Shamburger Senr.** and **Peter Shamburger Junr.** were chain carriers.

2364.   1797, Nov 27 -- Land Grant #1324, Moore County, NC
Samuel Parsons received 100 acres located north of Deep River on the drains of Fall Creek and the [Chatham] County line adjoining **Isaac Teague**, **Martindale**, **Lenier Brewer** and his own line. **Edward Beason** and **Ely Lawler** were chain carriers.

2365.   1797, Nov 28 -- Land Grant #946, Moore County, NC

William Cook received 60 acres located north of Deep River adjoining George Fagin. Peter Graves and Joshua Cook were chain carriers.

2366.   1797, Nov 28 -- Land Grant #950, Moore County, NC
William Cook received 200 acres located on both sides of Fall Creek adjoining David Allison and Beason. Greenberry Cook and James Hardin were chain carriers.

2367.   1797, Nov 29 -- Land Grant #1291, Moore County, NC
Samuel Dunn received 50 acres located east of Richland Creek on both sides of the Waggon Road adjoining his own line and Lam. William Bruks and Jesse Muse were chain carriers.

2368.   1797, Nov 29 -- Land Grant #1310, Moore County, NC
William Dunn received 100 acres located east of Drowning Creek adjoining Huff's Ford and the [Montgomery] County line. Ezekiah Dunn and Richd. Dunn were chain carriers.

2369.   1797, Nov 29 -- Land Grant #1797, Moore County, NC
Jesse Muse received 50 acres located on both sides of Lick Branch of McLendons Creek adjoining James Hill, Adam White and his own line. Thomas Muse and Jeremiah Deean were chain carriers.

2370.   1797, Nov 29 -- Land Grant #1346, Moore County, NC
Samuel Dunn received 50 acres located on Barn Branch adjoining his own line and Lam. Jesse Muse and William Bruks were chain carriers.

2371.   1797, Nov 29 -- Land Grant #1353, Moore County, NC
Samuel Dunn received 100 acres located on both sides of Richland Creek adjoining Benjamin Lam and Robert Rowan. Jesse Muse and William Bruks were chain carriers.

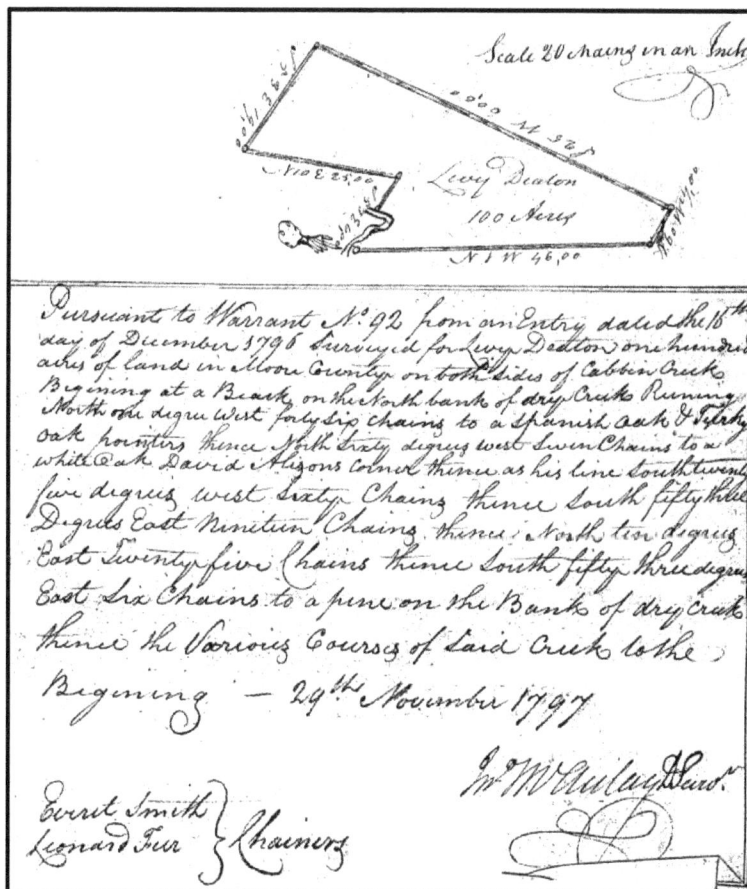

2372.   1797, Nov 29 -- Land Grant #1357, Moore County, NC
Jesse Muse received 100 acres located on both sides of Lick Branch south of McLendons Creek adjoining James Muse, Campbell and Adam White. Jeremiah Deen and Tom Muse were chain carriers.

2373.   1797, Nov 29 -- Land Grant #1423, Moore County, NC
Everet Smith Senr. received 100 acres located north of Cabin Creek adjoining David Allison and his own line. Leonard Furr and Levy Smith were chain carriers.

2374.   1797, Nov 29 -- Land Grant #1424, Moore County, NC
Levy Deaton received 100 acres located on both sides of Cabin Creek adjoining David Allison and Everet Smith. Everet Smith and Leonard Furr were chain carriers. [Editor's Note: Levy Deaton deeded to John Needham 1802]

2375.   1797, Nov 29 -- Land Grant #1715, Moore County, NC
William Cook received 100 acres located north of Deep River on the Waggon Branch adjoining his own line, Lee's old place and Gillmore. Josua Cook and Greenberry Cook were chain carriers.

2376.   1797, Nov 30 -- Land Grant #1056, Moore County, NC

John McAulay received 50 acres located east of Wet Creek adjoining **Waddle, William Dunn** and **Ancil Melton**. **Murdock McAulay** and **Donal McLeod** were chain carriers.

2377.   1797, Dec 1 -- Land Grant #1046, Moore County, NC
Kenneth Murchison [assignee of **William Martin**] received 50 acres located northwest of Richland Creek adjoining **John Martin, Neill McLeod**, his own line and **John Hargrove. Duncan McIntosh** and **John Campbell** were chain carriers.

2378.   1797, Dec 1 -- Land Grant #1426, Moore County, NC
Henry Stutts received 50 acres located west of Buffalo Creek adjoining **Jacob Stutts** and his own line and including his own improvement. **John Martin** and **John Richardson** were chain carriers.

A.   1797, Dec 1 -- Land Grant #1567, Chatham County, NC
Samuel Person received 200 acres located on Fall Creek and the Moore County line adjoining **Wilson** and his own line. **James Culbertson** and **Eli Lawler** were chain carriers.

2379.   1797, Dec 2 -- Land Grant #928, Moore County, NC
Neil McLeod received 150 acres located east of Wolf Creek adjoining **William Morgan Jr. John Morgan** and **William Morgan** were chain carriers.

2380.   1797, Dec 2 -- Land Grant #1004, Moore County, NC
Abner Lawler received 63 acres located north of Deep River adjoining **John Lawler, William Cook** and **Argo. Samuel Martindale** and **Evan Lawler** were chain carriers.

2381.   1797, Dec 2 -- Land Grant #1184, Moore County, NC
Patrick Dowd received 31 acres located west of Rogers Creek adjoining **Phillips, Aaron Tyson**, own line and **Randolph Cheek. Jno. Stinson** and **Joab Cheek** were chain carriers.

2382.   1797, Dec 2 -- Land Grant #1235, Moore County, NC
Lewis Sowell received 50 acres located east of Mill Creek adjoining **Christopher Bethune** and his own line. **Hezekiah Dunn** and **Murdock McAulay** were chain carriers.

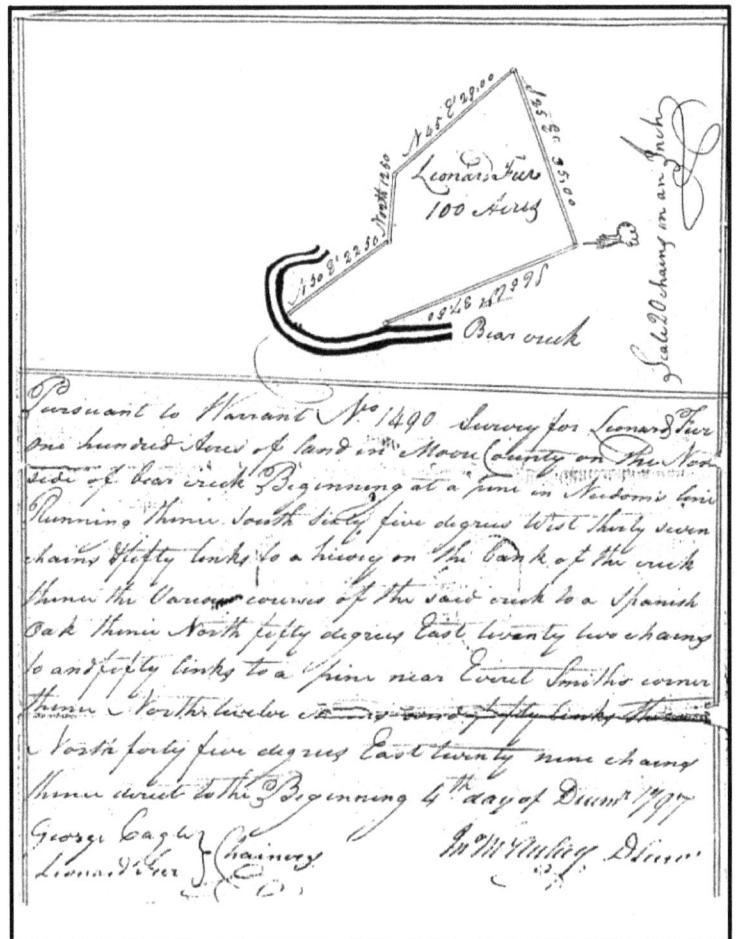

2383.   1797, Dec 4 -- Land Grant #1903, Moore County, NC
Leonard Furr received 100 acres located north of Bear Creek adjoining **William Needham, David Allison** and **Everet Smith. George Cagle** and **Leonard Furr** were chain carriers.

2384.   1797, Dec 5 -- Land Grant #1000, Moore County, NC
Samuel Dunn received 10 acres located on the drains of Richland Creek adjoining **Joseph Dunn**, his own line and **Grove. John Atkinson** and **John Upton** were chain carriers.

2385.   1797, Dec 5 -- Land Grant #1114, Moore County, NC
Robert Cheek received 22 acres located south of Deep River adjoining his own line. **Phillip Cheek** and **James Cheek** were chain carriers.

2386. 1797, Dec 6 -- Land Grant #999, Moore County, NC
Ruth Dunn received 50 acres located on Medlin Branch of Richland Creek adjoining **Joseph Dunn**. **Samuel Dunn** and **John Upton** were chain carriers.

2387. 1797, Dec 6 -- Land Grant #1478, Moore County, NC
John Stinson received 100 acres located on both sides of Rogers Creek adjoining his own line. **Patrick Dowd** and **Wm. McSween** were chain carriers.

2388. 1797, Dec 8 -- Land Grant #1024, Moore County, NC
Benjamin Tyson received 12 acres located south of Deep River adjoining **Connor Dowd**, **Governor Johnston** and **Aaron Tyson**. **Aaron Tyson** and **Seth Barnes** were chain carriers.

2389. 1797, Dec 8 -- Land Grant #1049, Moore County, NC
Murdock Martin [assignee of **William Martin**] received 70 acres located northeast of Dry Creek of McLendons Creek adjoining **Jacob McLendon**, **Thomas Mathews**, **Solomon Barrett** and the **McLeod** place. **Solomon Barret** and **Wm. Martin** were chain carriers.

2390. 1797, Dec 8 -- Land Grant #1127, Moore County, NC
Stephen Smith [assignee of **Solomon Barrett**] received 50 acres located on Dry Creek of McLendons Creek adjoining **Lunsford**'s improvement. **Wm. McSween** and **Wm. Martin** were chain carriers.

2391. 1797, Dec 8 -- Land Grant #1217, Moore County, NC
Stephen Richardson received 50 acres located on Long Meadow adjoining **Edwards**, **Myre**, **Henson** and **Furr**. **John Richardson** and **John Martin** were chain carriers.

2392. 1797, Dec 8 -- Land Grant #1249, Moore County, NC
John McNeill received 120 acres located south of McLendons Creek adjoining **Solomon Barret**, his own line, **Martin Martin** and the Speculators. **Wm. Martin** and **Malcolm Smith** were chain carriers.

2393. 1797, Dec 8 -- Deed Book 7 Page 347, Randolph County, NC
Henry Couch deeded **Lewis Spinks** 150 acres on Fork Creek and the Moravian Road/Salisbury-Cape Fear Road adjoining **Spinks**. Proven by **Sarah Ross** May 1798.

2394. 1797, Dec 8 -- Deed Book 7 Page 348, Randolph County, NC
Henry Couch deeded **John Needham** 150 acres on Cow Branch of Fork Creek adjoining **Lewis Spinks** and **Needham**. Proven by **Lewis Spinks** May 1798.

2395. 1797, Dec 8 -- Land Grant #1434, Moore County, NC
James Maness received 100 acres located east of Bear Creek adjoining his own line, **John McAulay**, **William Maness**. **Stephen Richardson** and **Parrell Sink** were chain carriers.

2396. 1797, Dec 8 -- Land Grant #1538, Moore County, NC
Donald McLeod received 41 acres located west of Sings Creek adjoining his own line, **Normand McLeod**, **Wm. Barret** and **Lewis Sowell**. **Donald McLeod** and **Wm. Martin** were chain carriers.

2397. 1797, Dec 9 -- Land Grant #1503, Moore County, NC
Duncan McIntosh received 50 acres located northwest of Richland Creek adjoining **Nathan Smith**, **Jesse Ritter**, **Neil McLeod** and **Jacob Stutts**. **Donald McDonald** and **Jacob Stutts** were chain carriers.

2398. 1797, Dec 9 -- Land Grant #1504, Moore County, NC
Duncan McIntosh received 50 acres located northwest of Richland Creek adjoining **Nathan Smith**, **Neil McLeod**, his own line and **Jesse Ritter**. **Donald McDonald** and **Jacob Stutts** were chain carriers.

2399. 1797, Dec 9 -- Land Grant #1863, Moore County, NC
Jacob Stutts received 100 acres located northwest of Richland Creek adjoining **Nathan Smith**, his own line and **Duncan McIntosh**. **Duncan McIntosh** and **Donald McDonald** were chain carriers.

2400. 1797, Dec 12 -- Land Grant #1216, Moore County, NC

Normand McLeod received 30 acres located on Sings Creek adjoining his own line and **Lewis Sowell**. **Wm. McSween** and **Donald McLeod** were chain carriers.

2401. 1797, Dec 12 -- Land Grant #1752, Moore County, NC
Thomas Hannon received 100 acres located on drains of Killetts Creek adjoining **William Feagin**, **George Glascock**, **Keziah Thomas**, **Jno. Morrison** and **Philemon Hodges**. **Wm. Feagin** and **Asay Hannon** were chain carriers.

2402. 1797, Dec 13 -- Land Grant #1152, Moore County, NC
John Morgan Medford received 100 acres located east of Mill Creek adjoining **James Gallemore** (formerly **John Cox**). **George Morgan** and **Joseph Bridges** were chain carriers.

2403. 1797, Dec 13 -- Deed Book 8 Page 116, Randolph County, NC
William Searcy deeded **William Pearce** 30 acres located north of Deep River adjoining **N. Nall**. Proven by **William Armstead** Nov 1799.

2404. 1797, Dec 14 -- Land Grant #1044, Moore County, NC
William Martin [assignee of **Solomon Barrett**] received 280 acres located on both sides of McLendons Creek including part of his mill tract adjoining his own line (formerly **Joel McLendon**), **Thomas Graham**, **Murdock Bethune**, **Solomon Barrett** and **John McNeill**. **Thomas Graham** and **John McDonald** were chain carriers.

2405. 1797, Dec 15 -- Land Grant #0152, Moore County, NC
John Atkinson received 60 acres located on the drains of Richland Creek adjoining **Joseph Dunn**, **David Allison**, **Ruth Dunn** plantation and the land where **Alexr. McDonald** now lives. **Jesse Upton** and **Saml. Dunn** were chain carriers. [*Editor's Note: Never granted*]

2406. 1797, Dec 15 -- Land Grant #1041, Moore County, NC
William Martin received 160 acres located on both sides of Mill Creek and both sides of the Yadkin Road adjoining **Thomas Dunn**, **Archd. McKay**, **Enoch Hall**, **Donald McLeod**, **Lewis Sowell**, **Neil McLeod**, **Bartholomew Dunn** and **Kenneth McLeod**. **Donald McLeod** and **John Martin** were chain carriers.

2407. 1797, Dec 18 -- Land Grant #1884, Moore County, NC

Moses Overton [assignee of **David Overton**] received 300 acres located northwest of McLendons Creek east of Wolfpen Branch and Overtons Road adjoining **David Allison**, **Street**, **Bettis**, **Dunlap** and **John Overton**. **Josiah Maples** and **David Overton** were chain carriers.

2408.   1797, Dec 19 -- Land Grant #1186, Moore County, NC
Drury Richardson received 50 acres located on both sides of Buffalo Creek adjoining his own line and **John Ritter**. **Mikagor Brewer** and **John Ritter** were chain carriers.

2409.   1797, Dec 19 -- Land Grant #1245, Moore County, NC
Joseph McGee received 100 acres located west of Buffalo Creek and both sides of the Waggon Road adjoining **Zachariah Smith**, **Drury Richardson**, **Isaac Hill**, **Thomas** and his own line. **Zachariah Smith** and **William Richardson** were chain carriers.

2410.   1797, Dec 19 -- Land Grant #1244, Moore County, NC
Joseph McGee received 100 acres located east of Buffalo Creek and both sides of the Waggon Road adjoining **Myre**, **Stephen Richardson**, **Hinson** and **Matthews**, **Drury Richardson**, **Isaac Hill**, **Zachariah Smith**, his own line, **William Richardson** and **Niel McLeod**. **John Ritter** and **William Richardson** were chain carriers.

2411.   1797, Dec 20 -- Land Grant #906, Moore County, NC
Neil McLeod received 200 acres located on both sides of Mill Creek adjoining **Lewis Sowell** and **William Morgan**. **William Morgan** and **John Morgan Medford** were chain carriers.

2412.   1797, Dec 20 -- Land Grant #907, Moore County, NC
Neil McLeod received 50 acres located on Dry Creek of Juniper adjoining **John Martin** (where **Shadrach Rogers** now lives) and his own line. **Shadrach Rogers** and **Richd. Chance** were chain carriers.

2413.   1797, Dec 21 -- Land Grant #1290, Moore County, NC
James Brady received 150 acres located north of Deep River on Fall Creek below the Great Falls including his own improvement and adjoining **William England**. **Saml. Parsons** and **Edmond Beason** were chain carriers.

2414.   1797, Dec 25 -- Deed Book 7 Page 360, Randolph County, NC
Thomas Cash Sr. deeded **John Shamburger** (of Moore County) 60 acres on Reedy Creek and the [Moore] County line. Proven by **Peter Shamburger** May 1798.

2415.   1797, Dec 26 -- Deed Book 8 Page 21, Randolph County, NC
Robert Carr deeded **Rolley Spinks** 150 acres adjoining **Arthur Smith**. Proven by **William Carr** Aug 1798.

2416.   1797, Dec 26 -- Deed Book 8 Page 22, Randolph County, NC
Robert Carr deeded **William Carr** 70 acres located on Flat Creek of Deep River part of a tract of 500 acres. Proven by **Roley Spinks** Aug 1798.

2417.   1797, Dec 26 -- Deed Book 8 Page 23, Randolph County, NC
Robert Kerr deeded **Rolley Spinks** 430 acres located on Deep River adjoining **Mullins**, **Routh** and **Onstott**. Proven by **William Kerr** Aug 1798.

2418.   1798 -- Panosophia Masonic Lodge No. 25, Carthage, NC
John Bullock was listed as a member.

2419.   1798-1800, 1802 -- Panosophia Masonic Lodge No. 25, Carthage, NC
Elijah Bettis listed as a member.

A.   1798, Jan 1 -- Deed Book J Page 300-301, Chatham County, NC
John Powers deeded **Moses Kidd** 100 acres located on Randolph County line adjoining own line, **Lend. Smith** and **Guthrie**. **Mary Searcy**, **Sarah Searcy** and **Will. Searcy** were witnesses.

B.   1798, Jan 9 -- Deed Book J Page 298-299, Chatham County, NC
Jacob Hollingsworth (of Franklin County, GA) deeded **John Record** (of Moore County) 640 acres located on Tysons Creek and granted to **Charles Shearing** Dec'd. **Robt. Wilkins** and **John Hutson** were witnesses.

2420.   1798, Jan 11 -- Land Grant #1250, Moore County, NC
John McNeill received 150 acres located on Juniper of McLendons Creek adjoining his own line of confiscated property and the Speculators. **Wm. Martin** and **Malcolm Smith** were chain carriers.

2421.   1798, Jan 30 -- Land Grant #2443, Moore County, NC
Murdock McLeod received 100 acres located on the waters of Horse Creek adjoining **Matheson**, **Meloney Newton** and the Speculators. **Hector McLean** and **Donald Monroe** were chain carriers.

2422.   1798, Feb-May -- 1798-1808 Trial and Appearance Docket, Moore County, NC
Abihu Sowell v. **Jesse Ritter**, **Senr**.

2423.   1798, Feb -- Estate, Chatham County, NC
Estate of **Edward Griffin** Dec'd. by **Corn. Dowd**, Admininstrator.

2424.   1798, Feb 1 -- Colonel **William Wofford** Survey on Georgia Frontier Settlers
Report made to Colonel Return **Jonathan Meigs**, agent to the Cherokee Indians, Southwest Point, regarding the number and condition of the Settlers living in and near the "**Wofford** Settlement", on the Frontier of Georgia and the Cherokee Nation of Indians - lying between the Currahee Mountain and the headwaters of the Oconee River. _Original Settlers in the **Nathan Smith** settlement who were left outside of Colonel **Hawkins** line_: **Nathan Smith**, **James Minyard**, **Michael Oliver**, **Stephen Smith**, **Nicholas Smith**, **Owen Carpenter**, **Jack Parker**, **Thomas Warren**, **Joseph Halcom**, **Charles Warren**, **William Thornton**, **Johnson McKinney** and **Lewis Dickenson**. [Editor's Note: Numerous Moore County families joined **Nathan Smith** and family in migrating to GA. Many continued to MS from there.]

2425.   1798, Feb 14 -- Land Grant #1447, Moore County, NC
Neil McLeod received 100 acres located on both sides of Wet Creek adjoining **Richard Grove** and **William B. Grove**. **William Gilliam** and **John Gilliam** were chain carriers.

2426.   1798, Feb 14 -- Land Grant #1740, Moore County, NC
William Smith Senr. received 100 acres located on Wet Creek adjoining his own line and **McLeod**. **William Gilliam** and **David Richardson** were chain carriers.

2427.   1798, Feb 14 -- Land Grant #1741, Moore County, NC
William Smith Senr. received 100 acres located between Wet Creek and Cabin Creek adjoining his own line and **David Allison**. **William Gilliam** and **David Richardson** were chain carriers.

2428.   1798, Feb 15 -- Land Grant #1425, Moore County, NC
John Smith received 150 acres located on both sides of Dry Creek adjoining **Widow Tedwell**, **Adam Sheffield** and including his own improvement. **Everet Smith** and **Levi Deaton** were chain carriers.

2429.   1798, Feb 16 -- Land Grant #1431, Moore County, NC
Levi Deaton received 25 acres located south of Bear Creek adjoining **William Maness** and **William Needom**. **James Mainess** and

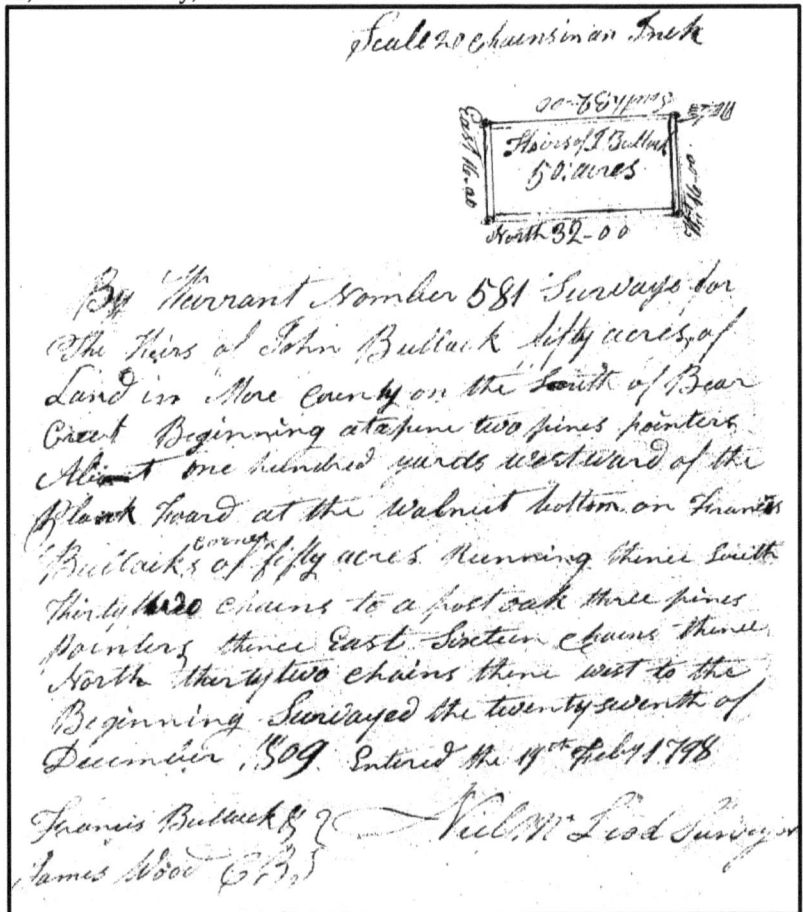

William Needom were chain carriers.

2430.　　　1798, Feb 19 -- Land Grant #2118, Moore County, NC [*see image on prior page*]
The heirs of **John Bullock** received 50 acres located south of Bear Creek including the Rocky Spring, the Walnut Bottom and the Plank Ford adjoining **Francis Bullock**. **Francis Bullock** and **James Wood** were chain carriers.

2431.　　　1798, Feb 24 -- Land Grant #1484, Moore County, NC
Adam White received 50 acres located south of McLendons Creek adjoining **James Caddle**, **Benjamin Caddle**, **Niell McGathy**, **Thomas McLendon** and **Robert Edwards**. **Jacob White** and **Benjamin Caddle** were chain carriers.

2432.　　　1798, Feb 25 -- Land Grant #1407, Moore County, NC
Jesse Bean received 25 acres located southeast of McLendons Creek adjoining **Jerom Miller**, **Danl. Muse**, **Thos. McLendon**, **Jas. Caddle**, his own line and **Adam White**. **Adam White** and **John Sowel** were chain carriers.

2433.　　　1798, Mar 10 -- Land Grant #1572, Moore County, NC
Robert Dickinson received 150 acres located west of Mill Swamp adjoining his own line and **Jason Wadsworth**. **Michael Dickinson** and **Willis Dickinson** were chain carriers.

2434.　　　1798, Mar 15 -- Land Grant #1412, Moore County, NC
Hardy Davis [assignee of **William Lathum**] received 100 acres located south of Williams Creek adjoining **William Callicutt**. **William Cagle** and **Eli Callicutt** were chain carriers.

2435.　　　1798, Mar 22 -- Land Grant #1134, Moore County, NC
Donald McDonald [assignee of **Neil McLeod**] received 100 acres located on Dry Fork of McLendons Creek adjoining his own line. **Kenneth McDonald** and **Neill McDonald** were chain carriers.

2436.　　　1798, Mar 23 -- Land Grant #922, Moore County, NC
Thomas Ritter received 50 acres located west of McLendons Creek adjoining **Sowell**. **Jas. Ritter** and **Jesse Ritter** were chain carriers.

2437.　　　1798, Apr 3 -- Land Grant #1293, Moore County, NC
John Inzor received 25 acres located on Killetts Creek adjoining **Mary McDonald**, **James Caddle** and **Joseph Fry**. **Jas. Fry** and **Joseph Fry** were chain carriers.

2438.　　　1798, Apr 17 -- Land Grant #1411, Moore County, NC
John Ritter received 100 acres located on both sides of Buffalo Creek adjoining **Bryant Boroughs**, **David Lawson**, his own line and **Nier Brewer**. **Lanier Brewer** and **Donald McDonald** were chain carriers.

2439.　　　1798, Apr 20 -- Land Grant #1196, Randolph County, NC
James Deyton received 150 acres located north of Deep River adjoining **Searcy** and **Golson**. **Eldridge Deyton** and **John Powers** were chain carriers.

2440.　　　1798, Apr 20 -- Land Grant #1247, Moore County, NC
Samuel Martindale received 100 acres located north of Deep River adjoining his own line, **Evan Lawler** (formerly **Trap**) and **David Argo**. **Samuel Perry** and **Thos. Martindale** were chain carriers.

2441.　　　1798, Apr 21 -- Land Grant #1301, Randolph County, NC
William Armistead received 350 acres adjoining **Smith**, **Wm. Pearce**, own line and **Widow Latham** (wife of **Cornelius Latham** Dec'd.). **Travis Bowdon** and **James Smith** were chain carriers.

2442.　　　1798, Apr 21 -- Land Grant #1302, Randolph County, NC
William Armistead received 150 acres adjoining **Adam Andrews**, **Windsor Pearce** or **Wm. Pearce** and **Charles Steward**. **Travis Bowdon** and **James Smith** were chain carriers.

2443.　　　1798, Apr 26 -- Land Grant #1197, Randolph County, NC
William Searcy received 500 acres located north of Deep River adjoining **Deyton**, his own line, **Golson**, **Nall**, **Reed**, **Bird**, **Kerr** and **Onslat**. **John Powers** and **Elridge Deyton** were chain carriers.

2444. 1798, May 2 -- Land Grant #368, Moore County, NC
John Dunlap received 100 acres located east of McLendons Creek adjoining his own line and **Elijah Bettis**. **John Overton** and **Reuben Sheals** were chain carriers.

2445. 1798, May 5 -- Land Grant #1522, Moore County, NC
Lewis Sowell received 20 acres located east of Mill Creek adjoining his own line and **Donald McLeod**. **Donald McLeod** and **Lewis Sowell** were chain carriers.

2446. 1798, May 10 -- Land Grant #1132, Moore County, NC
Richardson Feagan received 150 acres located on drains of Killets Creek and Waggon Road adjoining his own line and **William Feagan**. **George Feagan** and **Thomas Feagan** were chain carriers.

2447. 1798, May 11 -- Deed Book 8 Page 26, Randolph County, NC
Ransom Sutherland (of Wake County) deeded **Lewis Spinks** 1 acre of the former land of **Enoch Spinks** Dec'd. where he lived and containing the storehouse which **Sutherland** then occupied and was devised from **Enoch Spinks** to **Martha Reid**. Proven by **William Bowdown** Aug 1798.

2448. 1798, May 15 -- Land Grant #1374, Moore County, NC
Alexander Autrey received 25 acres located west of Jackson Creek adjoining **Beatis** and his own line and **Allison**. **Frederick Autrey** and **James Autrey** were chain carriers.

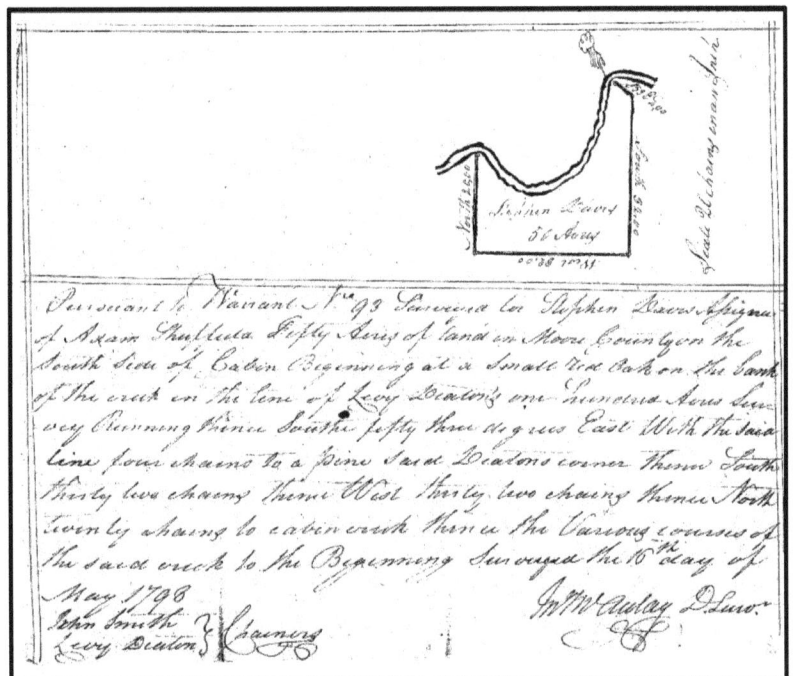

2449. 1798, May 16 -- Land Grant #1399, Moore County, NC
Isham Sheffield received 50 acres located north of Bear Creek adjoining **David Allison**, his own line and **Hannah Sheffield**. **John Sheffield** and **Thomas Davis** were chain carriers.

2450. 1798, May 16 -- Land Grant #1541, Moore County, NC
Stephen Davis [assignee of **Adam Shuffield**] received 50 acres located south of Cabin Creek adjoining **Levy Deaton** and **Adam Sheffield**. **John Smith** and **Levy Deaton** were chain carriers. [*Editor's Note: **Jeremiah Williams** deeded to **John Needham Sr.** 1804*]

2451. 1798, May 16 -- Land Grant #1542, Moore County, NC
Stephen Davis [assignee of **Adam Shuffield**] received 50 acres located east of Dry Creek adjoining his own line and **Everet Smith**. **John Smith** and **Levy Deaton** were chain carriers. [*Editor's Note: **Jeremiah Williams** deeded to **John Needham Sr.** 1804*]

2452. 1798, May 18 -- Will Book A Page 199-200, Moore County, NC
Will of **John Cagle**, Dec'd. Heirs: wife **Cathrine Cagle** [*my land and plantation until John comes of age*], son **John Cagle** [*150 acres south of Cabbin Creek and Bear Creek whereon I now live after he comes of age including 10 acres that needs to be set aside for my wife*], son **William Cagle** [*8 acres by the meeting house*], daughter **Susanna Cagle**, daughter **Dorety Cagle**, daughter **Margaret Cagle**, son **Jacob Cagle**, daughter **Elizabeth Gilmore**, son **George Cagle**, daughter **Mary Melton** and son **Henry Cagle**. Executors: **Bartholomew Dun**, **George Cagle**. Witnesses: **William Smith**, **Bartholomew Dunn** and **George Cagle**. Proven May 1799.

2453. 1798, May 21 -- Land Grant #1829, Moore County, NC

John Morgan Medford received 50 acres located east of Wolf Creek adjoining **Neil McLeod** and his own line. **William Morgan** and **Richard Holland** were chain carriers.

2454.   1798, May 22 -- Land Grant #1364, Moore County, NC
Thomas Mathews received 200 acres located on the head of a branch of Killets Creek where **Donald Munk** lives adjoining his own line and **Wadsworth**. **Malcolm McCrimmon** and **Burrel Maples** were chain carriers.

2455.   1798, Jun 1 -- Land Grant #1254, Moore County, NC
William Lathum [assignee of **Thomas Minyard**] received 50 acres located on Williams Creek on the path from goes from **Chavis'** old field to **Minyard's** house adjoining **William Callicutt**, own improvement. **William Cagle** and **William Callicutt** were chain carriers. **Adam Sheffiled** and **Wm. Morton/Martin** attested to the purchase of the entry from **Thomas Minyard**.

2456.   1798, Jun 1 -- Land Grant #1552, Moore County, NC
Lewis Davis [assignee of **Hardy Davis**] received 52.5 acres located on the drains of Bear Creek adjoining **Hardy Davis**, his own line and **Cagle**. **Thomas Smitherman** and **William Latham** were chain carriers.

2457.   1798, Jun 1 -- Land Grant #1553, Moore County, NC
Betzie Davis [assignee of **Hardy Davis**] received 100 acres located north of Bear Creek adjoining **Hardy Davis** and his own line. **Thomas Smitherman** and **William Latham** were chain carriers.

2458.   1798, Jun 1 -- Land Grant #0181, Moore County, NC
James Elkins received 50 acres adjoining the (Randolph) County line and including his own improvement where he now lives. **William Cagle** and **William Lathem** were chain carriers. [*Editor's Note: Never granted*]

2459.   1798, Jun 6 -- Land Grant #1340, Moore County, NC
William Maples received 50 acres located on drains of McLendons Creek adjoining his own line and **Bettis** including the Gooden place. **Wm. Maples** and **Thos. Maples** were chain carriers.

2460.   1798, Jun 10 -- Land Grant #1577, Moore County, NC
Michael Dickenson received 100 acres located south of McLendons Creek adjoining **Robert Dickeson** and **Kindred Muse**. **Robert Dickenson** and **Willis Dickenson** were chain carriers.

2461.   1798, Jun 15 -- Land Grant #0127, Moore County, NC
Everet Wallace received 50 acres located on the drains of Flag Creek adjoining **David Allison** and his own line. **Anselem Melton** and **William McSween** were chain carriers. [*Editor's Note: Never granted*]

2462.   1798, Jun 16 -- Will, Randolph County, NC
Will of **John Needham** Dec'd. Heirs: wife **Susannah Needham**; eldest son **William Needham** [*100 acres where he now lives and negro James*]; son **John Needham** [*negro Charles*]; son **Bailey Needham** [*100 acres where he now lives south of Deep River at the mouth of Cedar Creek adjoining Lewis Needham and negro George*]; son **Lewis Needham** [*100 acres south of Deep River at the mouth of Cedar Creek adjoining Bailey Needham and negro Ned*]; son **Garner Needham** [*100 acres east of Deep River adjoining James Whittle and negro Peter*]; son **Jesse Needham** [*100 acres east of Deep River adjoining Garner Needham and negro Ben*]; daughter **Elizabeth Spinks** [*negro Ciller*]; daughter **Susanna** [*negro Elm*]; daughter **Sarah** [*negro Joseph*]; daughter **Martha** [*negro Abraham*]; daughter **Ann** [*negro Mary*]. Executors: son **William Needham** and wife **Susannah Needham**. Witnesses: **William Bland** and **James Bland**.

2463.   1798, Jun 18 -- Land Grant #1072, Moore County, NC
John Evans received 50 acres located on Toms Creek adjoining **Edward Feagan**, **Edmond Love** and **Neil McLeod**. **Alexr. McLeod** and **Edmond Love** were chain carriers.

2464.   1798, Jun 18 -- Land Grant #1596, Moore County, NC
Niel McLeod received 200 acres located on drains of Thoms Creek of McLendons Creek adjoining **Donald Shaw**, **Edward Feagan**, **John Stephens**, **Dempsey Watts**, **Thomas Graham**, **Edward Love**, **John Evans** and where **Joseph Rouse** lives. **Jno. Evans** and **Alexr. McLeod** were chain carriers.

2465.   1798, Jun 18 -- Land Grant #1612, Moore County, NC
Adam White received 140 acres located east of McLendons Creek adjoining **Jerom Miller**, **John McSween**, **Mary Shaw**, **John McNeil**, **Malcolm Shaw**, **Benjamin Caddle**, **James Caddle**, **Jesse Bean** and his own line. **Jesse Bean** and **Jacob White** were chain carriers.

2466.   1798, Jun 20 -- Land Grant #1610, Moore County, NC
Adam White received 40 acres located on Toms Creek of McLendons Creek adjoining **Malcolm Shaw**, **Jas. Muse**, **Feagen**, **Jno. McNeill** and his own line. **James Muse** and **Jacob White** were chain carriers.

2467.   1798, Jun 20 -- Land Grant #2007, Moore County, NC
Thomas Ritter received 50 acres located west of McLendons Creek adjoining **Neil McLeod**, **Thomas Night**, **John Martin**, **Ritter** and **Sowell**. **Alexr. McIver** and **John Sowel** were chain carriers.

2468.   1798, Jun 21 -- Land Grant #1473, Moore County, NC
John Morgan Senr. received 150 acres located on both sides of Cabin Creek adjoining **Speculators** and his own line. **George Morgan** and **John Key** were chain carriers.

2469.   1798, Jun 22 -- Land Grant #1801, Moore County, NC
William Morgan received 50 acres located north of Cabin Creek on both sides of the Calf Pen Branch adjoining his own line and **Joseph Allan**. **Francis Bullock** and **John Gilliam Jr**. were chain carriers.

2470.   1798, Jun 26 -- Land Grant #1540, Moore County, NC
Nicholas Nall received 255 acres on both sides of the Fayetteville and Salisbury Waggon Road on the Randolph County line adjoining **Bird** and his own line. **Peter Shamburger** and **Richard Bird** were chain carriers.

2471.   1798, Jun 28 -- Land Grant #0238, Moore County, NC
John Morgan Senr. received 50 acres located north of Cabin Creek adjoining his own line, **George Morgan** and the Speculators. **George Morgan** and **John Key** were chain carriers. [*Editor's Note: Never granted*]

2472.   1798, Jul 10 -- Land Grant #1318, Moore County, NC
Neil McLeod received 100 acres located on Buffalo Creek adjoining **Hector McLean**, **Brumlo**, **Jesse Ritter** and **Alex. Munroe**. **Everit Ritter** and **Donald Munroe** were chain carriers.

2473.   1798, Jul 15 -- Land Grant #1055, Moore County, NC
Thomas Dunn received 28 acres located west of Wolf Creek adjoining **Francis Bullock** (formerly **Wilkins**) and **Roger Cagle**. **Joseph Bridges** and **Wm. Wright** were chain carriers.

2474.   1798, Jul 16 -- Land Grant #1347, Moore County, NC
Alexander Morrison received 50 acres located west of Sings Creek adjoining his own line, **Nicholas Newton**, **Meloney Newton**, **Murdock Bethune** and **David Allison**. **John Morrison** and **Allen Morrison** were chain carriers.

2475.   1798, Jul 18 -- Land Grant #1644, Moore County, NC
Adam Carpenter [assignee of **Neil McLeod**] received 150 acres located north of Grassy Creek and the [Randolph] County line near Fall Creek adjoining **Nicholas Nall**. **B. Garner** and **M. Andrews** were chain carriers.

2476.   1798, Jul 22 -- Land Grant #1442, Moore County, NC
Benjamin Dunn [assignee and heir of **Joseph Dunn**, Dec'd.] received 50 acres located north of Mill Creek on Little Branch adjoining **Joseph Dunn**. **Ceaser Dunn** and **Richd. Upton** were chain carriers.

2477.   1798, Jul 18 -- Land Grant #1409, Moore County, NC
Mark Phillips [assignee of **Kenneth McIver**] received 100 acres located on Wires Branch of Richland Creek adjoining his own line, **David Allison** and **John McIver**. **Jno. McIver** and **Mark Phillips Jur**. were chain carriers.

2478.   1798, Aug 11-Nov 3 -- Cane Creek Meeting [Quaker] Minutes Vol. II Page 31, Alamance County, NC
Complaint against **Ruth Dunn** and her son **John Dunn** for purchasing and holding Negroes.

2479. 1792, Sep 27 -- Land Grant #1492, Moore County, NC
Samuel Womble received 20 acres located on north of Deep River adjoining **Moses Myrick** and his own line. **Alexr. Carrol** and **Thomas Tyson Jun.** were chain carriers.

2480. 1798, Jul 28 -- Land Grant #1197, Moore County, NC
Jesse Ritter received 200 acres located between McLendons and Richland Creeks adjoining **John McSween**, **Everet Ritter**, **Donald McQueen**, **William Barrett**, **Farquard Campbell**, **McIver** (formerly **Neil McLeod**) and **John Quimby**. **Everet Ritter** and **Jesse Ritter Jur.** were chain carriers.

2481. 1798, Aug 10 -- Land Grant #1439, Moore County, NC
John McCaskill received 100 acres located east of Richland Creek adjoining **John Martin**, **Kenneth Murchison**, **John McDonald**, his own line and including his own improvement. **Alexr. McCaskill** and **Kenneth McCaskill** were chain carriers.

2482. 1798, Aug 10 -- Land Grant #1498, Moore County, NC
Batholomew Dunn Junr. received 35 acres located west of Wet Creek adjoining his own line, **Murdock McAulay**, **Samuel Dunn**, **Jesse Brown**, **Barret** and Speculators. **Nathaniel Melton** and **Bartholomew Dunn** were chain carriers.

2483. 1798, Aug 10 -- Land Grant #1501, Moore County, NC
Meloney Newton received 50 acres located on the waters of Dry Creek adjoining **John Newton**, her own line and Speculators. **Bartholomew Dunn Junr.** and **Nathaniel Melton** were chain carriers.

2484. 1798, Aug 10 -- Land Grant #1762, Moore County, NC
Joseph Allen received 45 acres located north of Cabin Creek and both sides of the Yadkin Road adjoining **William Morgan**, his own line, **William Smith**, **Francis Bullock** and the Speculators. **Francis Bullock** and **William Morgan Senr.** were chain carriers.

2485. 1798, Aug 11 -- Notice, *The North Carolina Minerva* [Fayetteville, NC] Newspaper "Sheriff's Sale: to be sold at Moore court-house, on the 17th September next, for the taxes due thereon, the following tracts of land: 100 acres on Suck Creek near **William Barrett**'s, supposed to be the property of **Captain McRee**; 100 acres on M'Lendons Creek joining **Rettar**, entered by **John Quimby**, Dec'd.; 120,000 acres entered by **John Porterfield** and transferred to

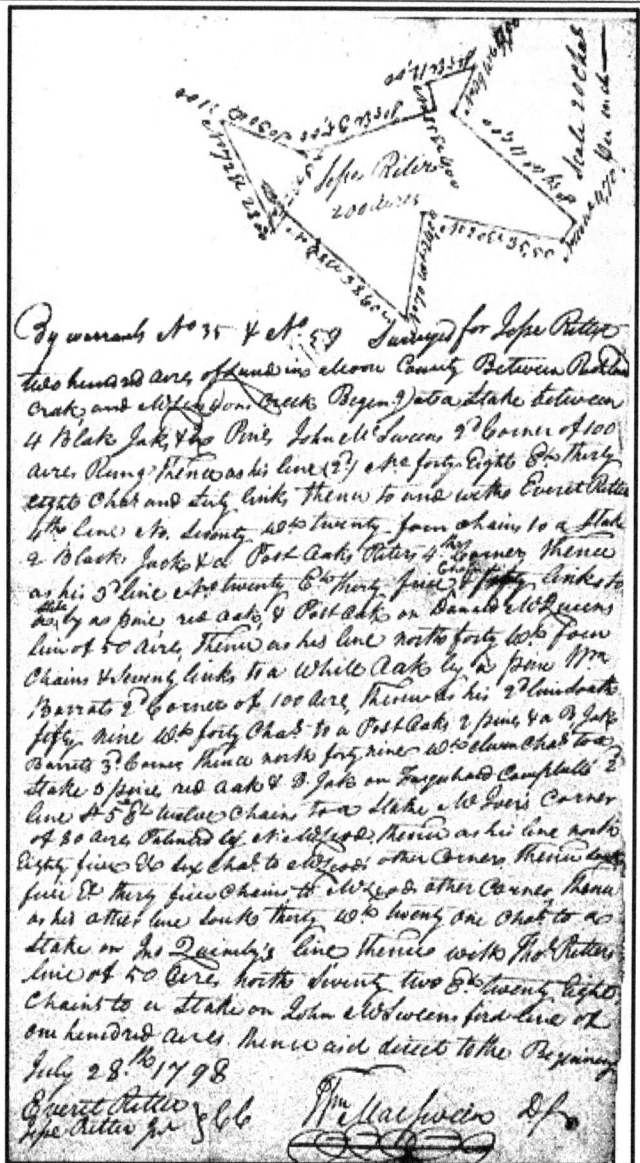

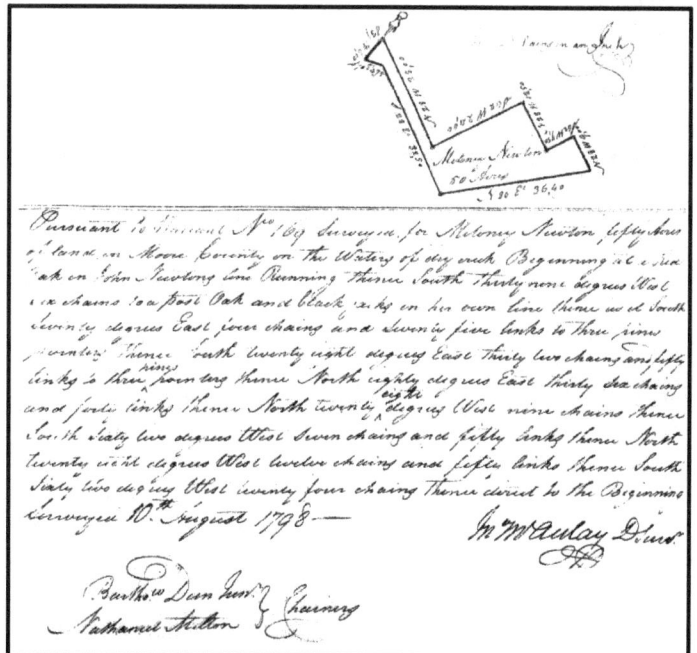

David Allison, the present proprietor unknown; 95,000 acres purchased by **Allen Morrison** and Co....**Malcolm McNeill**, Sheriff Jul 9"

2486.   1798, Aug 16 -- Land Grant #1946, Moore County, NC
Solomon Barret received 100 acres located on both sides of Bear Creek adjoining **Bullock**, **Hannah Shuffield**, his own line, **Everet Shuffield** and **Isham Shuffield**. **John Shuffield** and **Isham Shuffield** were chain carriers.

2487.   1798, Aug 20 -- Land Grant #1179, Moore County, NC
John Sowell received 209 acres adjoining **William Barrett**, **Jacob McLendon**, **Thomas Knight**, **Ritter**, **Quimby**, **Edwards** and **McKay**. **Alexander McIver** and **Thomas Ritter** were chain carriers.

2488.   1798, Sep 2 -- Land Grant #393, Moore County, NC
John Dunlap received 50 acres located east of McLendons Creek adjoining his own line and **Elijah Bettis**. **John Overton** and **Reuben Sheals** were chain carriers.

> ## SHERIFF's SALE.
> On the 17th of September next, will be sold for cash only, at the Court-house in Moore county, the following Tracts of LAND, or so much thereof as will satisfy the tax due thereon, viz.
> ONE hundred acres on Suck-creek, near William Barrett's, supposed to be the property of Captain M'Ree ; 100 do. on the waters of M'Lendon's Creek, joining Rettar's lines, entered by John Quimby, deceased ; 120,000 do. entered by John Porterfield, and by him transferred to David Allison—the present proprietor unknown ; 95,000 do. purchased at Sheriff's sale last year, by Allen Morrison & Co.
> The sale will continue from day-to day till the whole is settled.
>   **MALCOLM M'NEILL**, *Sheriff.*
> *July 9.*   21. 5*

2489.   1798, Sep 3 -- Land Grant #400, Moore County, NC
Richardson Fagin received 50 acres located on Muses Road and Fayetteville Waggon Road adjoining his own line. **Thomas Mathews** and **Needham Temples** were chain carriers.

2490.   1798, Sep 13 -- Petition to Georgia **Governor James Jackson**
The following residents of Jackson and Franklin County, GA petitioned the Governor to adjust the land boundaries to allow them to remain on their settlements: **Philip Thomas**, **John Thomas**, **Wm. Thomas**, **Philip Thomas Jr.**, **Abednego Downing**, **Geo. Waters**, **Levi Taylor**, **James Huit**, **Solomon Huitt**, **Wm. Alexander Tansey**, **Jesse Austin**, **Tho. Barnard**, **Lucas LeCroy**, **Thomas Lean**, **Equila McKrakin**, **James McKrakin**, [Mr.] **Holcom**, **Geo. Hopper**, **Wm. Weatherspoons**, **Hugh Hartgrove**, **Nathaniel Wofford**, **Richard Burkes**, **Benjamin Wofford**, **Richard Lay**, **Nicholas Smith**, **Nathan Smith**, **Oen Carpenter**, **James Minnerd**, **Nicholas Nuton**, **Stephen Smith**, (illegible signature), **Lewes Dickeson**, **Joseph Halcom**, **Jno. Parker**, **John Ratley**, **Thomas Warren**, **Robert Shipley**, **John Shipley**, **Nathaniel Shipley**, **William Little**, **Joseph Dunnegame**, **Ande Dunnegane**, **E. Dunnegame**, **Moses Terell** and **Jno. Little**. [*Editor's Note: Numerous Moore County families joined* **Nathan Smith** *and family in migrating to GA. Many continued to MS from there.*]

2491.   1798, Sep 14 -- Land Grant #1491, Moore County, NC
Sebrah Gilbert received 50 acres located north of Deep River on the Chatham County line adjoining **Joseph Gilbert**, **Governor Johnston** and **Powell Benbow**. **Ben Gilbert** and **John Upton** were chain carriers.

2492.   1798, Sep 17 -- 1798 Tax List for 1797, Moore County, NC
Mentions that Sheriff **Malcolm McNeill** sold 95,000 acres that was the former property of **Allen Morison** and 120,000 acres that was the former property of **David Allison** for non-payment of tax.

2493.   1798, Sep 18 -- Land Grant #1382, Moore County, NC
Reuben Freeman received 115 acres located east of Wolf Creek adjoining his own line, **Peter Hare**, **David Allison** and **Neil McLeod**. **William Morgan** and **John Dunn** were chain carriers.

2494.   1798, Sep 18 -- Land Grant #1403, Moore County, NC
Peter Hare received 50 acres located east of Wolf Creek adjoining his own line, **Reuben Freeman**, **David Allison**, **John Hare**. **Reuben Freeman** and **William Morgan** were chain carriers.

2495.   1798, Sep 19 -- Land Grant #1493, Moore County, NC

Jacob Matthews (assignee of Thomas Matthews) received 200 acres located on a branch of Killetts Creek adjoining Richardson Feagin, Collins, Maples, his own line and the branch Donald Munk lives on. Richardson Feagin and George Feagin were chain carriers.

2496. 1798, Sep 25 -- Land Grant #1489, Moore County, NC
Joab Cheek received 150 acres located on Rogers Creek north of Deep River on the Chatham County line adjoining John Cheek, Randolph Cheek and Stinson. Lewis Temples and Matthew Phillips were chain carriers.

2497. 1798, Sep 26 -- Land Grant #1195, Moore County, NC
Jesse Ritter Senr. received 100 acres located on Locust Branch of Richland Creek adjoining John Ritter and David Allison. Moses Ritter and Everit Ritter were chain carriers.

2498. 1798, Oct 1 -- Land Grant #1048, Moore County, NC
William Wright received 60 acres located east of Wolf Creek adjoining David Allison, Neil McLeod, William Morgan and his own line. Joseph Bridges and Thomas Dunn were chain carriers.

2499. 1798, Oct 1 -- Land Grant #1476, Moore County, NC
William Wright received 50 acres located west of Wolf Creek adjoining his own line, William Morgan Jr., David Allison and Joseph Bridges. Joseph Bridges and Thomas Dunn were chain carriers.

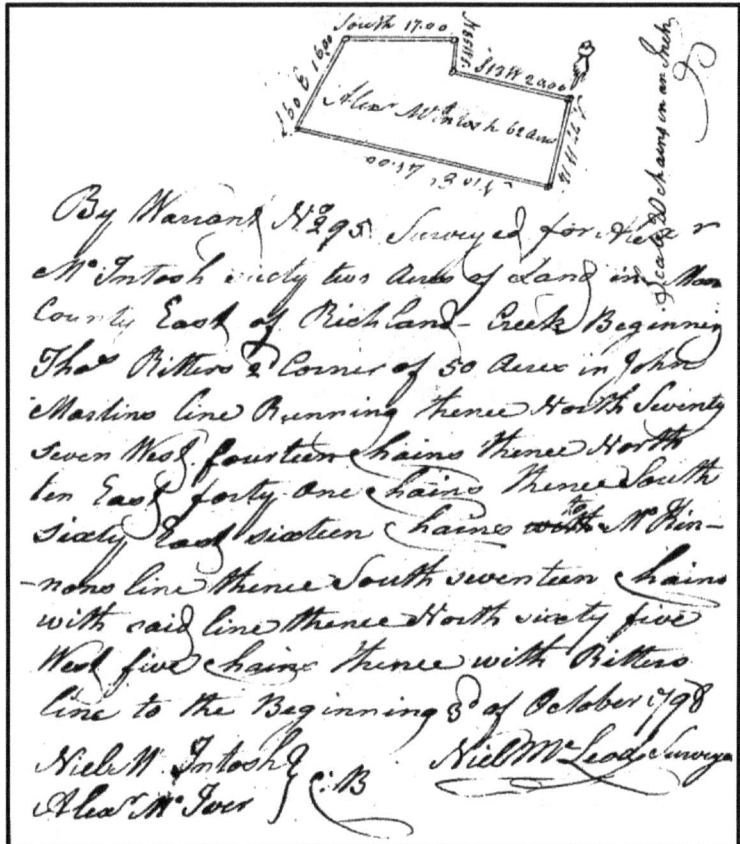

2500. 1798, Oct 3 -- Land Grant #1445, Moore County, NC
Alexander McIntosh received 62 acres located east of Richland Creek adjoining Thos. Ritter, John Martin, McKinnon and Widow McIntosh. Neill McIntosh and Alexr. McIver were chain carriers.

2501. 1798, Oct 6 -- Land Grant #1526, Moore County, NC
William Feagon received 60 acres located on the drains of Killetts Creek and the Waggon Road that leads from Monroes to Widow Muses adjoining Richardson Feagon, his own line and Patty Glascock. John Insor and Geo. Feagon were chain carriers.

2502. 1798, Sep 18 -- Land Grant #1403, Moore County, NC
Peter Hare received 50 acres located east of Wolf Creek adjoining his own line, Reuben Freeman, David Allison, John Hare. Reuben Freeman and William Morgan were chain carriers.

2503. 1798, Oct 8 -- Land Grant #1045, Moore County, NC
Kenneth Murchison [assignee of William Martin] received 50 acres located east of Richland Creek adjoining John Martin, William Barrett, Neil McLeod and Angus McCaskill. Thomas Ritter and John McCaskill were chain carriers.

2504. 1798, Oct 8 -- Land Grant #1435, Moore County, NC
Neil McLeod received 150 acres located on Richland Creek adjoining William Smith, Nathan Smith, John Martin, Christian McIntosh, his own line and Mucheson. Alex. McIntosh and Neil McIntosh were chain carriers.

2505. 1798, Oct 8 -- Land Grant #1444, Moore County, NC

William Richardson received 75 acres located on Kings Street south of Buffalo Creek adjoining **Joseph McGee**, his own line and **Joseph Geason**. **Drury Richardson** and **John Ritter** were chain carriers.

2506. 1798, Oct 9 -- Land Grant #1052, Moore County, NC
Murdock McAulay received 50 acres located on the drains of Mill Creek adjoining **Neil McLeod**, **Norman McKinnon** (formerly **Joseph Gibson**) and his own line. **Norman McKinnon** and **William Martin** were chain carriers.

2507. 1798, Oct 12 -- Land Grant #1761, Moore County, NC
Thomas Dunn received 25 acres located south of Wolf Creek adjoining **Roger Cagle**, **Wilkins** and his own line. **Joseph Bridges** and **Thomas Dunn Jr**. were chain carriers.

2508. 1798, Oct 13 -- Land Grant #1381, Moore County, NC
Reuben Freeman received 100 acres located west of Wolf Creek adjoining his own line, **Peter Hare**, **David Allison** and **John Dunn**. **William Morgan** and **Peter Hare** were chain carriers.

2509. 1798, Oct 13 -- Land Grant #1383, Moore County, NC
Adam Comer received 60 acres located on both sides of Williams Creek adjoining his own line and the Speculators. **Adam Smith** and **John Comer** were chain carriers.

2510. 1798, Oct 13 -- Land Grant #1404, Moore County, NC
Peter Hare received 100 acres located west of Wolf Creek adjoining his own line, **Reuben Freeman** and **John Hare**. **Reuben Freeman** and **William Morgan** were chain carriers.

2511. 1798, Oct 18 -- Land Grant #1464, Moore County, NC
William Morgan received 25 acres located southeast of Cabin Creek adjoining his own line. **James Morgan** and **Isaac Brown** were chain carriers.

2512. 1798, Oct 18 -- Land Grant #1471, Moore County, NC
William Morgan Senr. received 100 acres located west of Cabin Creek adjoining his own line, **George Morgan** and **Allison**. **Isaac Brown** and **James Morgan** were chain carriers.

2513. 1798, Oct 19 -- Land Grant #1050, Moore County, NC
Norman McKinnon received 50 acres located southwest of Mill Creek adjoining **Jas. Gibson** and his own line. **John Martin** and **Murdock McAulay** were chain carriers.

2514. 1798, Oct 19 -- Land Grant #1071, Moore County, NC
Malcolm McNeill received 50 acres located east of Wolf Creek adjoining **William Morgan**, **David Allison**, **John Dunn**, **Loving**'s improvement and the Yadkin Road. **William Morgan Jr**. and **Moses Wilson** were chain carriers.

2515. 1798, Oct 24 -- Land Grant #1754, Moore County, NC
John Cheek received 200 acres located on both sides of Leek Creek adjoining **Wm. Hancock**, **David Allison**, **Willis Dickinson** and his own line. **Wm. MacSween** and **Jacob Syler** were chain carriers.

2516. 1798, Nov 3-Dec 15 -- Notice, *The North Carolina Minerva* [Fayetteville, NC] Newspaper
"Sheriff's Sale: to be sold at Moore court-house on the 24th December next, for the taxes due thereon, the following tracts of land: 50 acres on Bear Creek, the property of **James Thornton**; 100 acres on Bear Creek, the property of **Gilmore...Malcolm McNeill**, Sheriff"

2517. 1798, Nov 6 -- Land Grant #1194, Moore County, NC
Robert Cheek received 110 acres located on both sides of west fork of Tysons Creek on the Chatham County line adjoining his own line. **Phillip Cheek** and **Jas. Cheek** were chain carriers.

2518. 1798, Nov 8 -- Land Grant #1793, Moore County, NC
John Sheffield received 50 acres located west of Wolf Creek adjoining his own line and **Isham Sheffield**. **John Sheffield Junr.** and **John Hare** were chain carriers.

2519. 1798, Nov 10 -- Land Grant #1568, Moore County, NC
Evan Lawler received 50 acres located on Cedar Creek adjoining **Traps**, **George Fagin** and **James Moore**. **John Lawler** and **Bryan Boroughs** were chain carriers.

2520. 1798, Nov 12 -- Land Grant #1402, Moore County, NC
John Hare received 200 acres located east of Wolf Creek adjoining **John Sheffield**, **David Allison**, **Peter Hare** and his own line. **John Sheffield** and **William Morgan Jr.** were chain carriers.

2521. 1798, Nov 17 -- Deed Book 8 Page 32, Randolph County, NC
James Bowdown (of Edgefield County, SC) deeded **William Bowdown** 17 acres located on Deep River adjoining **Nicholas Nall** and **Richard Bird**. Proven by **Travis Bowdown** Nov 1798.

2522. 1798, Nov 19 -- Land Grant #1069, Moore County, NC
Edward Beason received 300 acres located north of Deep River on the Chatham County line adjoining **Angus McQueen** and **Hargrove**. **Wm. Phillips** and **James Harden** were chain carriers.

2523. 1798, Nov 19 -- Land Grant #1448, Moore County, NC
Neil McLeod received 200 acres located north of Deep River on both sides of Tyson Creek adjoining **William Phillips**, **Neill McIntosh**, **Robert Cheek** and **Thomas**. **James Harden** and **Neil McIntosh** were chain carriers.

2524. 1798, Nov 20 -- Land Grant #1436, Moore County, NC

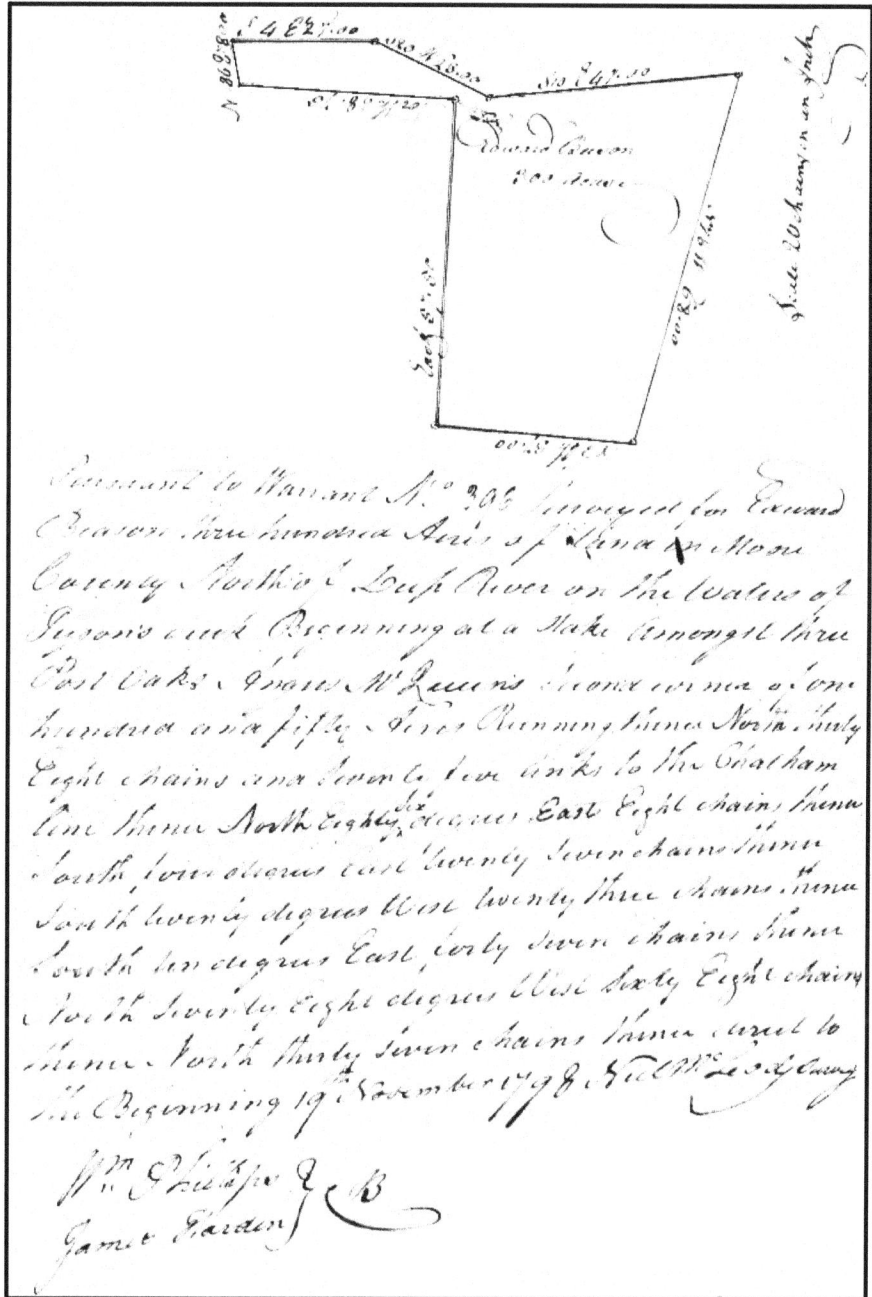

Leonard Furr received 125 acres located on Flag Creek adjoining **Peter McLean**. **Jacob Furr** and **Leonard Furr** were chain carriers.

2525. 1798, Nov 20 -- Land Grant #1500, Moore County, NC
Henry Cagle Jr. received 50 acres located on the waters of Bear Creek adjoining his own line, **John Lawley** and **Hardy Davis**. **Hardy Davis** and **Henry Cagle Sr.** were chain carriers.

2526. 1798, Nov 20 -- Land Grant #1543, Moore County, NC
William Smith Senr. [assignee of **David Richardson**] received 75 acres located on both sides of Wet Creek adjoining **Jean Tedwell**, **Neil McLeod**, **John Smith** and his own line. **Archibald McMillan** and **John Smith** were chain carriers.

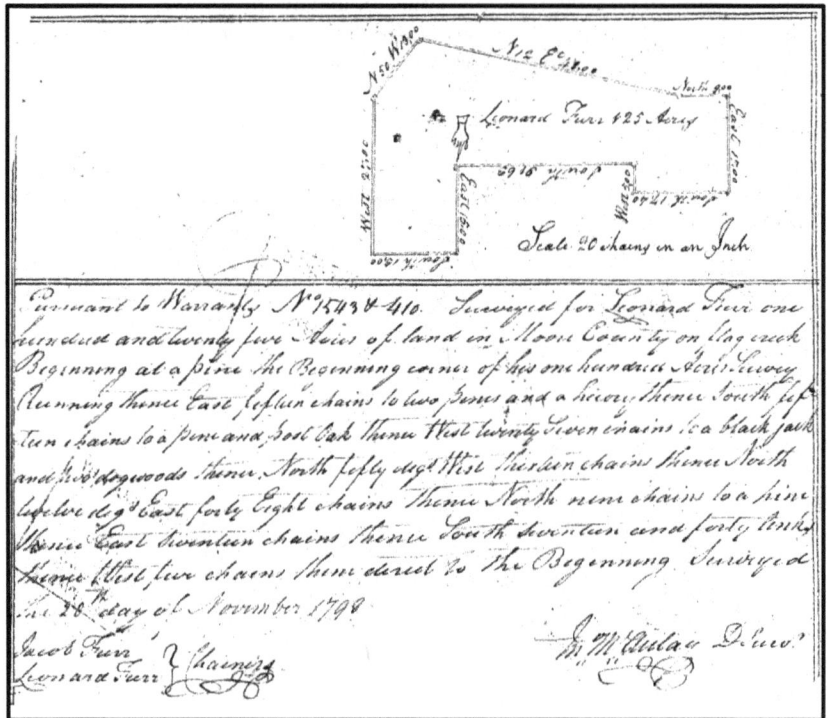

2527. 1798, Nov 20 -- Land Grant #1571, Moore County, NC
John McAulay Junr. received 60 acres located between Bear Creek and Wolf Creek adjoining **Hannah Sheffield**, **William Wood**, **Isham Sheffield** and **John Sheffield Senr.** **John Sheffield** and **Isham Sheffield Jr.** were chain carriers.

2528. 1798, Nov 22 -- Land Grant #1133, Moore County, NC
James Dyer [assignee of **James Atkins**] received 200 acres located north of Deep River adjoining **Wm. England** (formerly **John Barton**) and **Henley** (formerly **David Argo**). **Thomas Martindale** and **Willis Davis** were chain carriers.

2529. 1798, Nov 24 -- Land Grant #1649a, Moore County, NC
Heirs of **Phillip Alston** received 50 acres located west of Bear Creek south of Deep River adjoining **Ambrose Brewer** and **McNeill**. **Ambrose Brewer** and **Peter Garner** were chain carriers.

2530. 1798, Nov 26 -- Land Grant #1760, Moore County, NC
Joseph Allen received 68 acres located on both sides of Cabin Creek adjoining his own line including his improvement and **Wm. Morgan**. **Francis Bullock** and **John Gilliam Junr.** were chain carriers.

2531. 1798, Nov 28 -- Land Grant #1774, Moore County, NC
Reubin Shields [assignee of **Jesse Griffin**] received 100 acres located on the Chatham County line north of Deep River on both sides of Pates Creek near the Cane Patch Mountain. **William Cook** and **Grenbery Cook** were chain carriers.

2532. 1798, Nov 29 -- Land Grant #1067, Moore County, NC
Thomas Graham received 100 acres located south of McLendons Creek adjoining **Robert Graham Senr.**, **Patience Barrett**, **John McNeill**, **Michel Briant** and **Solomon Barret**'s hogpen. **Duncan McNeill** and **Hector McNeill** were chain carriers.

2533. 1798, Nov 30 -- Land Grant #1474, Moore County, NC
John Morgan Senr. received 100 acres located south of Cabin Creek adjoining Speculators, his own line and **David Richardson** improvement. **Nathan Smith** and **John Morgan Medford** were chain carriers.

2534. 1798, Nov 30 -- Land Grant #1475, Moore County, NC
John Morgan Senr. received 50 acres located on both sides of Mill Creek adjoining his own line, **Bridges** and the Speculators. **John Morgan Medford** and **George Morgan** were chain carriers.

2535. 1798, Dec 1 -- Land Grant #1698, Moore County, NC
Benjamin Britt [assignee of **John Morgan Medford**] received 100 acres located on both sides of Mill Creek including the mouth of the Hog Pen Branch adjoining the Speculators, **John Morgan** and **Bridges**. **John Morgan Medford** and **Ryal Britt** were chain carriers.

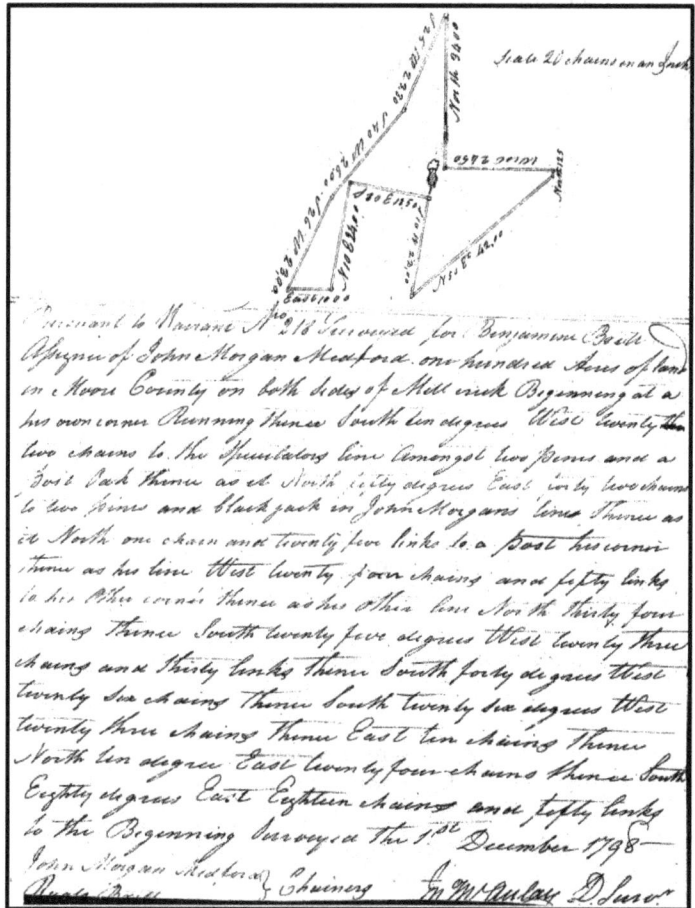

2536. 1798, Dec 1 -- Land Grant #1830, Moore County, NC
John Morgan Medford received 25 acres located west of Mill Creek adjoining **Bridges**, his own line and the Speculators. **Benjn. Britt** and **Ryal Britt** were chain carriers.

2537. 1798, Dec 1 -- Land Grant #1895, Moore County, NC
Bradley Garner [assignee of **Christopher Yew**] received 150 acres located south of Deep River including part of Barton's Island adjoining **James Barton**, **John Garner** and **William England**. **James Brady** and **Peter Graves** were chain carriers. **John Yow** and **George Carrinder** attested to the transfer of warrant.

2538. 1798, Dec 1 -- Land Grant #0257, Moore County, NC
Mary Moore received 50 acres located on the drains of Buffalo Creek adjoining **Askins** line and improvement. **Danl. McDonald** and **Fannan Moore** were chain carriers. [*Editor's Note: Never granted*]

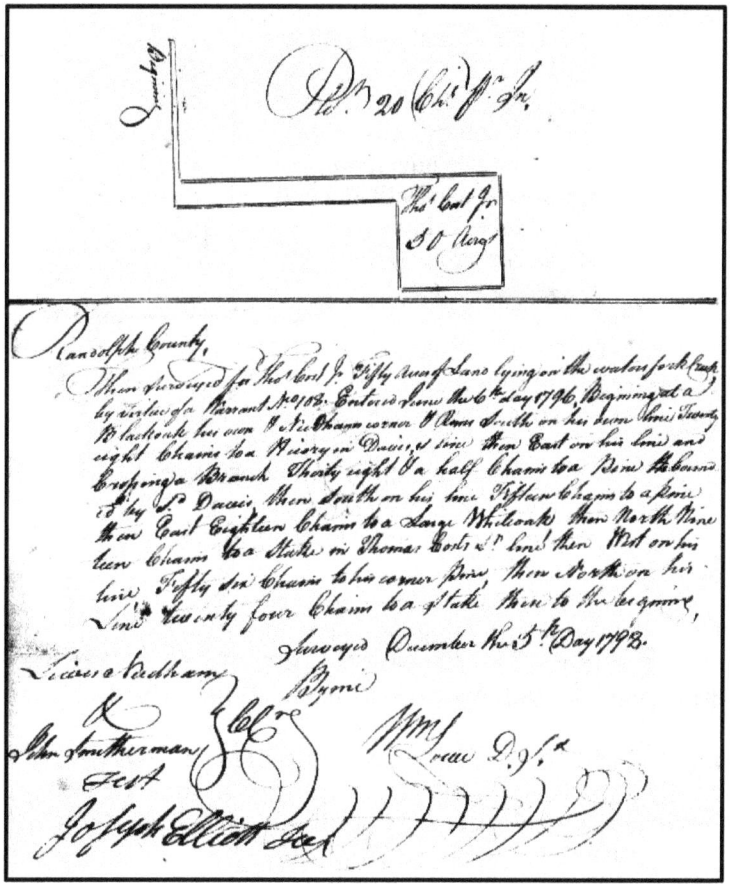

A. 1798, Dec 4 -- Land Grant #1643, Chatham County, NC
Abner Phillips received 100 acres located on Tysons Creek adjoining **Willis Philips**. **Willis Phillips** and **Meredy Phillips** were chain carriers.

B. 1798, Dec 5 -- Land Grant# 1574, Chatham County, NC
Joseph Lamb[ert] received 108 acres located on Fall Creek adjoining the Moore County line, **Beason**, **Brown**, **Guthrie**, **Parson** and **Wilson**. **Saml. Persons** and **James McCushten** were chain carriers.

2539. 1798, Dec 5 -- Land Grant #1885, Randolph County, NC
Thomas Cosht/Cost Jr. received 50 acres located on Fork Creek adjoining his own line, **Thomas Cosht Sr.** and **Hardy Davis**. **Lewis Needham** and **John Smitherman** were chain carriers.

2540. 1798, Dec 6 -- Land Grant #1040, Moore County, NC

John Bullock received 90 acres located south of Deep River adjoining **Abram Hunsucker**, Lewis Garner, Jacob **Carringer**, **John Garner**, **Christopher Yow** including where **George Carringer** now lives. **Lewis Garner** and **Bradley Garner** were chain carriers.

A. 1798, Dec 7 -- Land Grant #1759, Randolph County, NC
James Lathem Sr. received 100 acres located on Fork Creek adjoining his own line, **John Lawrence Sr.** and **William Smitherman**. **Wm. Smitherman** and **Wm. Latham** were chain carriers.

2541. 1798, Dec 8 -- Land Grant #1051, Moore County, NC
Alexander Martin received 50 acres located Juniper Creek of McLendons Creek adjoining **John McNeill**. **William Martin** and **John McNeill** were chain carriers.

2542. 1798, Dec 8 -- Land Grant #1483, Moore County, NC
Samuel Perry received 50 acres located north of Deep River adjoining **Joseph Wright**, his own line, **Boroughs**, **James Traps** and **Willis Davis**. **Samuel Martindale** and **John Perry** were chain carriers.

2543. 1798, Dec 8 -- Land Grant #0135, Moore County, NC
Mary Moore received 50 acres located on Holly Branch of Deep River adjoining **William Richardson** and **Askins'** cabin. **Danl. McDonald** and **Jas. Harden** were chain carriers. [*Editor's Note: Never granted*]

2544. 1798, Dec 11 -- Land Grant #0126, Moore County, NC
James Willey received 200 acres located on Buffalo Creek including **James Willey Senr.**'s improvement adjoining **James Hines**, **Byhugh Sowell** and **Neill McLeod**. **James Willey** and **John Tolmin** were chain carriers. [*Editor's Note: Never granted*]

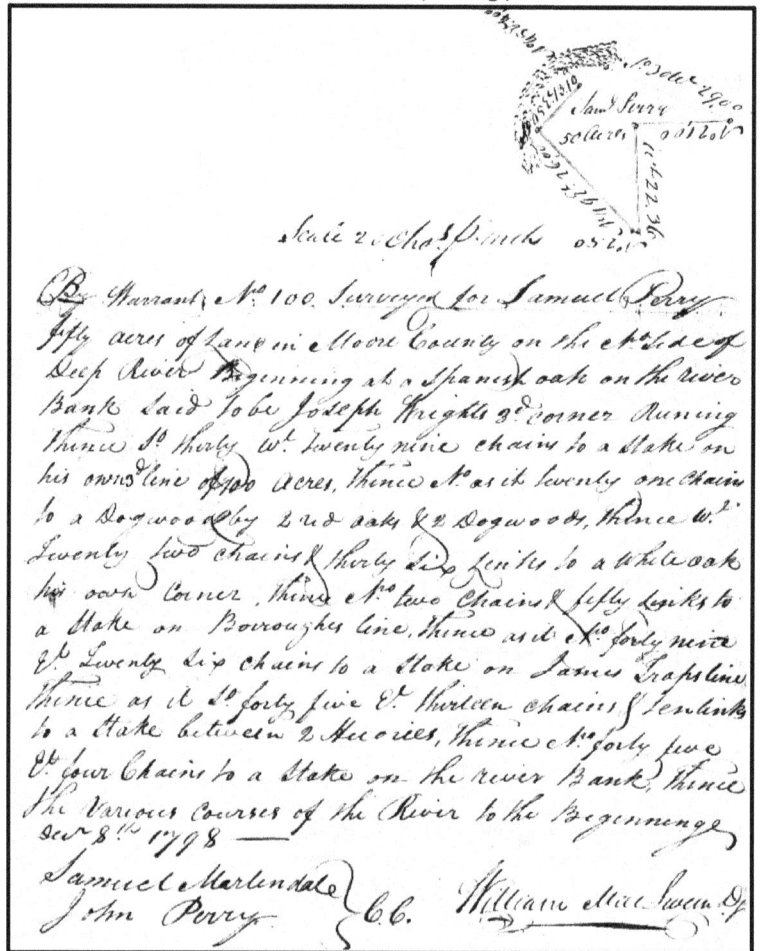

2545. 1798, Dec 13 -- Land Grant #1078, Moore County, NC
Malcolm McNeill received 50 acres adjoining his own line, **Owen Carpenter**, **Callicut** and including **Sheffield**'s improvement. **Asa Callicut** and **Eli Callicut** were chain carriers.

2546. 1798, Dec 13 -- Land Grant #1039, Moore County, NC
Mary Shaw received 100 acres located southeast of McLendons Creek adjoining **Wm. Richardson**, **Farquhard Campbell**, **Robert Edwards**, **John McNeill**, **Malcolm Shaw** and **John Stewart**. **James Fry** and **Alexr. McLeod** were chain carriers.

2547. 1798, Dec 18 -- Land Grant #2006, Moore County, NC
Thomas Ritter received 50 acres located on the drains of McLendons Creek adjoining **John McSween**, **Jesse Ritter** and **John Quimby**. **Jesse Ritter** and **William McSween** were chain carriers.

2548. 1798, Dec 18 -- Land Grant #0187, Moore County, NC
Bradly Garner received 15 acres located on the drains of Grassy Creek adjoining **Abram Huntsacre**, **Geo. Carringer**, **Lewis Garner** and **Hart**. **Lewis Garner** and **Geo. Carringer Sr.** were chain carriers. [*Editor's Note: Never granted*]

2549.   1798, Dec 20 -- Land Grant #1300, Moore County, NC
Neil McLeod [assignee of **William Martin**] received 50 acres east of Mill Creek on the Yadkin Road where the road forks that leads to **Absolom Autray**'s commonly called **Harris'** Road adjoining **Kenneth McLeod** and **John Sandhill Smith**. **Wm. Martin** and **Wm. McSween** were chain carriers.

2550.   1798, Dec 20 -- Deed Book N Page 102-103, Franklin County, GA
Joseph Neale and wife **Frances** (of Elbert County, GA) deeded **Nathan Smith** (of Franklin County, GA) 600 acres located on Hudson Fork of Broad River adjoining **Julian Neale** and **Thomas Gregg** consisting of two tracts granted to **Julian Neale** Mar 17, 1786. **Benjamin Neal** was a witness. Recorded 1799.

2551.   1798, Dec 24 -- Land Grant #0192, Moore County, NC
George Huntsucker received 100 acres located south of Deep River adjoining **David Kannady**, **Neil McLeod**, **Widow Kanady**, **Ambrose Maness**, **Alexr. Kanady**, **John Garner**, **Bradley Garner** and **Nelly Kannady**. **Ambrose Manus** and **John Carringer** were chain carriers. [*Editor's Note: Never granted*]

2552.   1799 -- Tax List, Randolph County, NC, **William Armstead**'s District [selected listing]
Name and acreage: **Charles Stewart** 1 white poll, 2 black polls, 600 acres; **John Needham** 1 white poll, 1 black poll, 300 acres; **William Larrance** 1 white poll, 150 acres; **John Shamburger** 60 acres; **Edmd. Waddell** 1 white poll, 10 black polls, 400 acres; **Allen Bullock** 1 white poll, 160 acres; **Thomas Cash** 1 white poll, 150 acres; **Isaac Redfaring** 1 white poll, 400 acres; **William Carr** 1 white poll, 2 black polls, 500 acres; **James Deeton** 1 white poll; **Roley Spinks** 1 white poll, 1 black poll, 900 acres; **Eldredge Deeton** 1 white poll, 100 acres; **Lenhard Smith** 1 white poll, 1 black poll, 90 acres; **James Leathem** 1 white poll; **William Leathem** 1 white poll, 200 acres; **Lewis Spinkes** 1 white poll, 475 acres; **William Waddell** 1 white poll; **William Pirce** 1 white poll, 875 acres; **Ruben Pirce** 1 white poll; **James Leathem** 1 white poll; **Baley Needham** 1 white poll, 1 black poll, 400 acres; **William Argoe** 1 white poll 1 black poll, 567 acres; **William Smith** 1 white poll; **Matthew Deeton** 1 white poll; **Travis Bowdoun** 1 white poll, 150 acres; **William Bowdoun** 1 white poll, 3 black polls, 313 acres; **Richard Bird** 1 white poll, 2 black polls, 200 acres; **Arther Smith** 1 white poll, 150 acres; **James Leathem** 540 acres; **John Larrance** 5 black slaves, 1224 acres; **Harday Davis** 600 acres; **Lewis Needham** 1 white poll, 1 black poll, 200 acres; **John Needham Sen.** 3 black polls, 1640 acres; **George Onstot** 200 acres; **William Armstead** 1 white poll, 6 black polls, 600 acres.

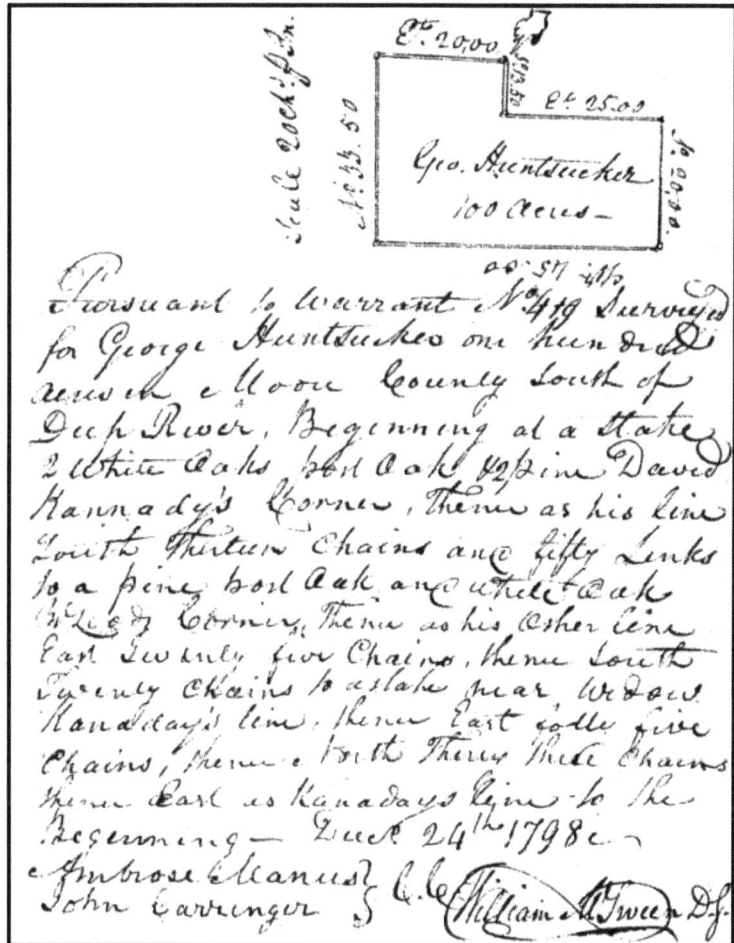

2553.   1799, Jan 8 -- Land Grant #1759, Moore County, NC
Joseph Allen received 25 acres located on a prong of Cabin Creek adjoining **James Jeffreys**, his own line and **Carpenter**. **Joseph Allen Junr.** and **Wm. McSween** were chain carriers.

2554.   1799, Jan 22 -- Land Grant #0177, Moore County, NC
Benjamin Dunn [assignee of **Kenneth McIver** and **Jason Wadsworth**] received 50 acres located west of Richland Creek adjoining **John Medlin**, where **Ruth Dunn** now lives and **Nancy Dunn**. **Jno. McIver** and **Jno. Dunn** were chain carriers. [*Editor's Note: Never granted*]

2555.   1799, Jan 24 -- Deed Book K Page 419, Chatham County, NC

Leonard Smith deeded **Matthew Caveness** 150 acres located on Cedar Creek and Randolph County line adjoining **Kidd**, **James Deaton** and **Vandaford**. **Smith** purchased the land from **John Powers**. **Will. Searcy**, **John Caveness** and **Frederick Caveness** were witnesses.

2556. 1799, Feb 1 -- Land Grant #0180, Moore County, NC
Richard Doud received 100 acres located north of Bear Creek adjoining **Peter Garner**, **Martin Ott**, **David Allison** and **Wm. Garner**. **John Comer** and **John Garner** were chain carriers. [*Editor's Note: Never granted*]

2557. 1799, Feb 6 -- Land Grant #1380, Moore County, NC
Peter Garner received 100 acres located north of Bear Creek adjoining **Martin Ott**, **David Allison**, **Dowd** (formerly **William Garner**). **Adam Comer** and **John Garner** were chain carriers.

2558. 1799, Mar 2 -- Land Grant #1781, Moore County, NC
Burrel Deaton received 7 acres located south of Dry Creek adjoining **Everet Smith**, **Stephen Davis** and **John Stutts**. **John Garner** and **Hardy Davis** were chain carriers.

2559. 1799, Mar 7 -- Land Grant #0139, Moore County, NC
Normand Matheson received 20 acres located on Horse Creek adjoining **Neal Matheson**, **Murdoch McLeod**, his own line, **Hector McNeill** and **Meloney Newton**. **Normand McLeod** and **Neil Matheson** were chain carriers. [*Editor's Note: Never granted*]

2560. 1799, Mar 11 -- Land Grant #1655, Moore County, NC
Susy Davis [assignee of **Hardy Davis**] received 100 acres located on both sides of Bear Creek adjoining **Thomas Smitherman**, **Leonard Cagle Jr.** and **Cornelius Latham**. **Leonard Cagle** and **Thomas Smitherman** were chain carriers.

2561. 1799, Mar 12 -- Land Grant #1599, Moore County, NC
Thomas Smitherman received 50 acres located north of Bear Creek adjoining his own line and **Leonard Cagle**. **John Garner** and **Leonard Cagle** were chain carriers.

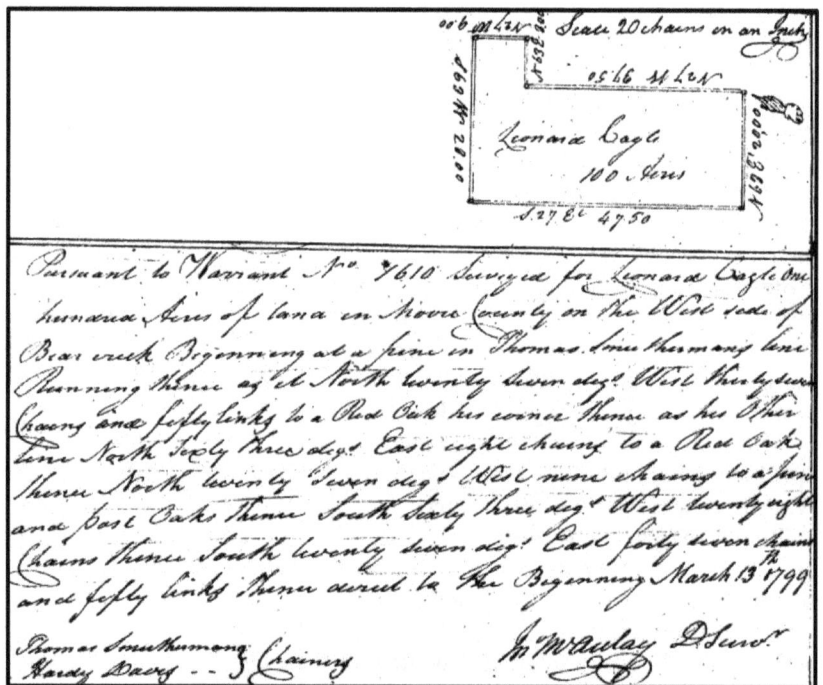

2562. 1799, Mar 13 -- Land Grant #1581, Moore County, NC
Leonard Cagle received 100 acres located west of Bear Creek adjoining **Leonard Cagle Senr.** **Thomas Smitherman**, his own line. **Thomas Smitherman** and **Hardy Davis** were chain carriers.

2563. 1799, Mar 16 -- Land Grant #1077, Moore County, NC
Beyhue Sowell [assignee of **John Hargrove**] received 100 acres located on Buffalo Creek.

2564. 1799, Mar 18 -- Land Grant #0154, Moore County, NC
Harmon Brewer received 100 acres located west of Buffalo Creek adjoining **Bryant Boroughs** and including his own improvement where he now lives. **Bryant Boroughs** and **Samuel Martindale** were chain carriers. [*Editor's Note: Never granted*]

A. 1799, Apr 21 -- Land Grant #1607, Chatham County, NC
Lemuel Smith received 150 acres located on Tysons Creek adjoining **Larrance McManus**, **Abner Phillips** and **Dinnis Phillips**. **Dinnis Phillips** and **Robert Moore** were chain carriers.

2565. 1799, Apr 22 -- Deed Book 8 Page 144, Randolph County, NC
William Argo deeded **Leonard Smith** 90 acres on a branch of Deep River. **William Waddle** proved Feb 1800.

2566. 1799, Apr 22 -- Deed Book 8 Page 268, Randolph County, NC
William Argo deeded **Charles Goldston** two tracts located north of Deep River [1] 100 acres adjoining his own line, the Moore County line and **Waddle**; [2] 320 acres adjoining the Moore County line and the Chatham County line being part of the 640 acres granted to **William Searcy** and **Charles Goldston**. Proven by **William Searcy** Aug 1801.

2567. 1799, Apr 22 -- Deed Book 8 Page 45, Randolph County, NC
William Searcey deeded **Peter Searcey** 97 acres adjoining **James Deaton**. Proven by **William Carr** May 1799.

2568. 1799, Apr 24 -- Deed Book 8 Page 45, Randolph County, NC
William Searcey deeded **Sarah Caviness** 100 acres located on Cedar Creek and the Chatham County line being part of the 500 acre grant to **Searcey** adjoining **James Deaton** and **Onstott**. Proven by **William Carr** May 1799.

2569. 1799, May 4 -- Deed Book 8 Page 70, Randolph County, NC
William Searcy deeded **Richard Bird** 50 acres located north of Deep River adjoining **William Carr**. Proven by **Edmund Waddell** May 1799.

A. 1799, May 14-Nov -- Estate, Chatham County, NC
Estate of **John Powers**, Dec'd. **David Powers** was named administrator with **Joseph Gilliland**, **James Deaton** and **John Thompson** as securities. **John Powers** died May 3, 1799. Petition for division of 200 acres located on Cedar Creek. **Edmond Waddill**, **Jos. Lambert** and **Joseph Gilliland** (with **John Argo** as witness) divided among the following heirs: widow **Susannah Powers, James Powers, David Powers, Moses** and **Karey Kidd** and **George** and **Elizabeth Railey**. _Items from the estate were purchased by_: **Susanna Powers, David Powers, Jams. Powers, Wm. Campbell, Joseph Hix, Henry Powers, Levi Lawler, Moses Kidd, Greel Norton, Wm. Searcy, Eldredg Deaton, John Vandeford** and **Benjamin Shields**.

2570. 1799, May 19 -- Will, Randolph County, NC
Will of **Leonard Smith**, Dec'd. Heirs: wife **Elizabeth**. Also mentions negro **Frank**. Witnesses: **George Onstot**, **Will. Searcy** and **Sarah Searcy**. Proven Aug 1806.

2571. 1799, Jun 10 -- Land Grant #0136, Moore County, NC
Neil Matheson received 50 acres located east of Dry Creek adjoining **Meloney Newton** and his own line. **Normand McLeod** and **Normand Matheson** were chain carriers. [_Editor's Note: Never granted_]

2572. 1799, Jun 22 -- Land Grant #1566, Moore County, NC
Neil McLeod received 100 acres located on Persimmon Glade of Richland Creek adjoining **Charles Shearin, David Allison, John Dunlap. James Hardin** and **Jacob Hardin** were chain carriers.

2573. 1799, Jul 2 -- Land Grant #1582, Moore County, NC
John Ritter [assignee of **John Dunn**] received 100 acres adjoining **Isaac Pennington**, his own line and **Robert Davis**. **Nearer Brewer** and **Michjah Brewer** were chain carriers.

2574. 1799, Jul 19 -- Land Grant #1429, Moore County, NC
Joab Cheek received 200 acres located east of Rogers Creek adjoining **John Stinson** and **Randal Cheek**.

2575. 1799, Jul 30 -- Deed Book J Page 443-444, Chatham County, NC
Mary Dowd, wife of **Connor Dowd**, deeded **Edward Griffin**, **Samuel Griffin** and **John Griffin** (heirs of **Edward Griffin**, Dec'd.) 300 acres of land located on Flaggy Branch of Indian Creek adjoining **Duncan**. **Jno. Thompson** and **Archd. McBryde** were witnesses.

2576. 1799, Aug 10 -- Land Grant #1696, Moore County, NC
Aulay McAulay received 100 acres located on Mill Swamp on Overton's Road adjoining **John Wadsworth**, **Thomas Overton** and **James Holcombe**. **Murdoch McAulay Junr.** and **Aulay McAulay** were chain carriers.

2577. 1799, Aug 26 -- Land Grant #1094, Randolph County, NC
Hardy Davis received 300 acres located on Meadow Branch of Fork Creek including **Elisha Lawley**'s improvement. **Joseph Lawley** and **John Lawly** were chain carriers.

2578. 1799, Aug 31 -- Will Book A Page 203, Moore County, NC
Will of **Ruth Dunn**, Dec'd. Heirs: daughter **Sarah Pendleton**, son **William Dunn**, heirs of son **Joseph Dunn**, daughter **Nancy McDonald**, daughter **Mary Lamb**, daughter **Elizabeth Rubotom**, daughter **Hannah Adkinson** and son **John Dunn** [*negro man Cezar and negro women Tier*]. Executor: son **John Dunn**. Witnesses: **Thos. Reynolds, Edward Upton**. Proven Nov 1799.

2579. 1799, Aug 31 -- Land Grant #1684, Moore County, NC
Francis Bullock received 100 acres located on both sides of Bear Creek adjoining **Everet Smith**. **Isaac Smith** and **Jno. Gilliam** were chain carriers.

2580. 1799, Sep 6 -- Land Grant #1862, Moore County, NC
Francis Bullock [assignee of **Jonathan Bullock**] received 150 acres located where Persimmmon Branch of Grassy Creek crosses the Waggon Road adjoining **Matthew Deaton** and **William Williamson**. **William Williamson** and **George Carringer** were chain carriers. **James Wood** attested to the transfer of the warrant.

2581. 1799, Sep 8 -- Will Book A Page 202, Moore County, NC
Will of **Josiah Frazer**, Dec'd. Heirs: wife **Elizabeth**, son **George Frazer** [*180 acres north of Deep River adjoining*

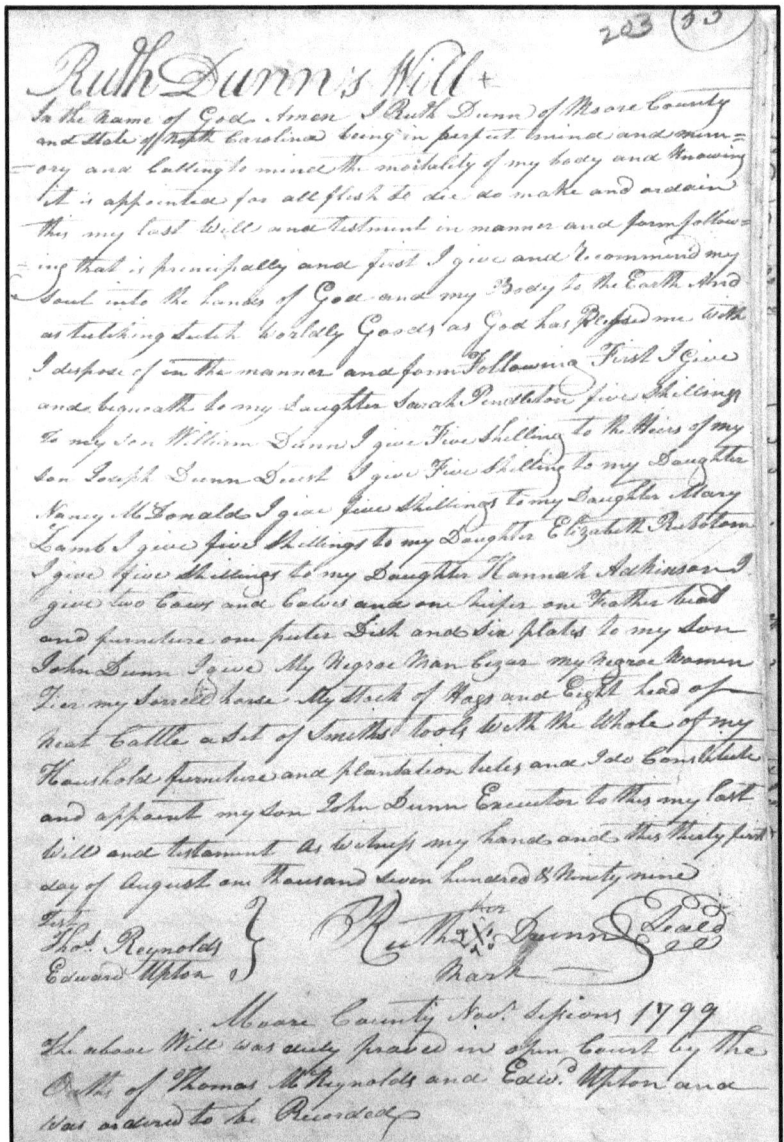

James Brady and McNeill] and daughter **Ann Frazer**. Executors: **George Frazer Junr.** and wife **Elizabeth Frazer**. Witnesses: **W. King** and **A.M. Beeson**. Proven Nov 1799.

2582. 1799, Sep 10 -- Notice, Raleigh Minerva [Raleigh, NC] Newspaper
"Sheriff's Sale: to be sold at Moore court-house, in the town of Carthage, the 30th September next, for the taxes due thereon, the following tracts of land: 200,000 acres the property of **Toreence Brady**, part of it lying on every water course in the county; 200 acres on the waters of Bear Creek joining **Cagle**'s line, property of **Gilmore**; 50 acres on Buffaloe, joining **James Williams**, the property of **James Hynes**; 100 acres on Cabin Creek, called the Black Place, supposed to be the property of **Jonathan Carpenter**; 100 acres on the south fork of Bear Creek, joining **William Cagle**, the property of **William Cole**; 50 acres at the White Ponds...**Malcolm McNeill**, Sheriff Jul 22"

SHERIFF's SALE.

TO be fold at Moore court-houfe, in the town of Carthage, the 30th of September next, for the taxes due thereon, the following tracts of Land, viz. 200,000 acres the property of Torrance Brady. part of it lying on every water courfe in the county. 200 acres on the waters of Bear creek, joning Cagle's lines, the property of —— Gilmore. 100 do. on Buffaloe, the property of Reuben Milfaps. 50 do. on Buffaloe, joining James Williams, the property of James Hynes. 100 do. on Cabin creek, called the Black Place, fuppofed to be the property of Jonathan Carpenter. 100 do. on the fouth fork of Bear creek, joining William Cagle's, the property of William Cole. 300 do. on Little-river, fuppofed to be the property of Meryl Cox and Archibald Black. 50 do. at the White ponds, joining Ramage's lines, the property of John Leggit. 150 do. on Crane's creek, joining Gilmore's line, fuppofe to be the property of Stephen Herd of Georgia. 170 do. on the waters of Drowning creek, the property of Donald M·Lain.

July 22.   MALCOLM M·NEILL, *Sheriff.*

2583. 1799, Sep 19 -- Will Book A Page 211-212, Moore County, NC
Will of **John Lawler**, Dec'd. Heirs: wife [unnamed], grandson **John Lawler** [son of **Evan**], daughter-in-law **Ann Lawler**, son **Eli Lawler**, son **Levi Lawler** and son **Evan Lawler** [*100 acre plantation where I now live*]. Executor: son **Evan Lawler**. Witnesses: **Eli Lawler** and **Mary Pitt**. Proven Nov 1800.

2584. 1799, Sep 20 -- Land Grant #1502, Moore County, NC
William Wright received 25 acres located south of Wolf Creek adjoining his own line, **Hunsucker** and **David Allison**. **William Wright Jr.** and **Francis Bullock** were chain carriers.

2585. 1799, Oct 7 -- Cane Creek [Quaker] Meeting Marriages Vol.1 Page 195, Alamance County, NC
Isaac Johnson, son of **Jesse** and **Hannah Johnson**, of Chatham County and **Elizabeth Tyson**, daughter of **Cornelius** and **Arcada Tyson**, of Moore County were married at the Friends Meeting House on Deep River. **John Johnson**, **Aaron Tyson**, **Edm. Ratliff**, **Sarah Barnes**, **Moses Myrick**, **Thomas Tyson Senr.**, **Joseph Hobson**, **Jean Hobson**, **Thomas Tyson**, **Isaac Johnson**, **Elizabeth Johnson**, **Jesse Johnson**, **Hanah Johnson** and **Benjamin Tyson** were present and served as witnesses.

A. 1799, Oct 11 -- Deed Book U Page 79-80, Chatham County, NC
John Cheek (of Moore County) deeded **Lazarus Phillips** 175 acres located on Indian Creek and the road from **Tyson's** Ferry to **Graves'** saw mill adjoining **Dowd**. Originally granted to **Joseph Robson** and sold to **William Capps** who sold to **John Cheek**. **Jacob Siler** and **Jeremiah Phillips** were witnesses.

2586. 1799, Nov 6 -- Deed Book 8 Page 199, Randolph County, NC
William Searcy deeded **William Carr** 100 acres located north of Deep River adjoining **Anstot** and **Carr**. Proven by **Rolley Spinks** Nov 1800.

A. 1799, Nov 23 -- Land Grant #1646, Chatham County, NC
Willis Phillips received 50 acres located on Tysons Creek adjoining his own line and **Sanders**. **Lindsey Poe** and **Meredith Phillips** were chain carriers.

B. 1799, Nov 23 -- Land Grant #1660, Chatham County, NC
Benjamin Sanders received 100 acres located on Indian Creek adjoining **Guthrie** and **McManus**. **Thos. Sanders** and **Benjn. Sanders** were chain carriers.

2587. 1799, Nov 26 -- Land Grant #1472, Moore County, NC
John Morgan Sr. received 50 acres located on Cabin Creek.

2588. 1799, Dec 4 -- Land Grant #1562, Moore County, NC

Drury Brewer received 50 acres located east of Bear Creek adjoining **Ambruse Brewer**, **McAulay** and his own line. **Abednego Manors** and **Jephthah Brewer** were chain carriers.

2589.   1799, Dec 4 -- Land Grant #1782, Randolph County, NC
Joseph Lawley received 100 acres located on Bear Creek adjoining his own line and **Needham**. **Absalom Presnal** and **Hardey Davis** were chain carriers.

2590.   1799, Dec 4 -- Land Grant #1786, Randolph County, NC
Christopher Asbal received 150 acres located on Reedy Creek and the Moore County line adjoining **Shamburger**, **Thomas Cosht**, **John Needham** and **Manuel Asbell**. **Wm. Smitherman** and **Wm. Asbal** were chain carriers.

A.   1799, Dec 4 -- Land Grant #1880, Randolph County, NC
Anthony Lathem received 100 acres located on both sides of Fork Creek adjoining **James Lathem Sr.**, **John Needham** and **Cornelius Lathem**. **Wm. Smitherman** and **James Latham Jr.** were chain carriers.

2591.   1799, Dec 4 -- Land Grant #1920, Randolph County, NC
Absalom Pressnal received 100 acres on Bear Creek and the Moore County line adjoining **John Lawley**. **Hardy Davis** and **Joseph Lawley** were chain carriers.

2592.   1799, Dec 5 -- Land Grant #1559, Moore County, NC
Thos. Matthews Junr. received 100 acres located on Deep River at the mouth of Fall Creek. **James Brady** and **Robert Brady** were chain carriers.

2593.   1799, Dec 5 -- Land Grant #1563, Moore County, NC
Donald McQueen received 200 acres located on McCollums Branch of Richland Creek on both sides of the Waggon Road adjoining his own line and the Speculators. **Angus McQueen** and **John McIntosh** were chain carriers.

2594.   1799, Dec 5 -- Land Grant #1564, Moore County, NC
Donald McQueen received 100 acres located on McCollums Branch on both sides of the Waggon Road adjoining his own line, **Benjamin Atkinson** and **Hunsucker**. Angus

McQueen and John McIntosh were chain carriers.

2595.   1799, Dec 7 -- Land Grant #1849, Randolph County, NC
Travis Bowden received 30 acres located south of Deep River adjoining his own line and Pearce. Wm. Searcey and James Smith were chain carriers.

2596.   1799, Dec 13 -- Land Grant #0247 and #0274, Moore County, NC
Normand McLeod received 50 acres located on both sides of Sings Creek adjoining Newton and his own line. William Dunn and Ezekiah Dunn were chain carriers. [Editor's Note: Never granted]

2597.   1799, Dec 15 -Will Book A Page 209-210, Moore County, NC
Will of John Morgan, Dec'd. Heirs: son Joseph Morgan [200 acres north of Cabbin Creek adjoining Nathan Morgan], daughter Angelina Morgan [50 acres east of Cabbin Creek adjoining Joseph Morgan], daughter Mary Morgan [50 acres on Cabbin Creek joining Joseph Morgan and Angelina Morgan], son James Morgan [200 acres with the manner plantation], son William Morgan, Jr., daughter Levicea Allen, son Nathan Morgan, daughter Elessa Dunn, daughter Deliley Dunn and son George Morgan [100 acres called the Spivey Place]. Executors: sons William Morgan, Jr. and Nathan Morgan. Witnesses: George Morgan and Richard Holland. Proven Feb 1800.

2598.   1799, Dec 17 -- Land Grant #1882, Randolph County, NC
Amanuel Asbal received 150 acres located on Mill Creek, Fayetteville Road and the Moore County line adjoining Charles Steward. Wm. Asbal and Wm. Smitherman were chain carriers.

2599.   1799, Dec 18 -- Land Grant #1709, Randolph County, NC
Hardy Davis received 50 acres located on Bear Creek and the [Moore] County line adjoining John Lawley and own line. Absalom Presnall and Joseph Lawley were chain carriers.

2600.   1799, Dec 21 -- Land Grant #1719, Randolph County, NC
William Smitherman received 350 acres located on Meadow Branch adjoining Cornelius Lathem, Needham, own line and William Lathem. Anthony Lathem and Cornelius Lathem Sr. were chain carriers.

2601.   1799, Dec 24 -- Land Grant #1884, Randolph County, NC
William Asabal received 100 acres located on Reedy Creek and the Moore County line adjoining Shambarger and Christopher Asbal. Wm. Smitherman and Jams. Lathem were chain carriers.

2602.   1799, Dec 26 -- Land Grant #1451, Moore County, NC
John Wadsworth received 100 acres located on both sides of Mill Swamp adjoining James Muse, Antony Seal and Holcombe. James Muse and Jno.than Caddle were chain carriers.

2603.   1799, Dec 28 -- Land Grant #1842, Randolph County, NC
James Lathem Sr. received 200 acres located on Meadow Branch, Reedy Creek and the [Moore] County line adjoining William Asbal, Christopher Asbal and Needham. Wm. Smitherman and Anthony Lathem were chain carriers.

2604.   1800 -- Tax List, Franklin County, GA [selected residents]
Stephen Smith 260 acres on Hudson River; Nichlas Smith 100 acres located on Hudson River; James Mainard 100 acres on Hudson River; Adam Sheffield [no acreage or location given]; Nathan Smith 300 acres on Hudson River & 350 acres on Nails Creek; Owen Carpenter 100 acres on Hudson River; William Smith [no acreage or location] and Temple Carpenter [no acreage or given].

2605.   1800, Jan 15 -- Land Grant #1556, Moore County, NC
Joseph Bridges received 50 acres located northwest of Wolf Creek adjoining William Morgan, William Wright, Hunsucker and Thomas Dunn. William Wright and James Wright were chain carriers.

2606.   1800, Feb 19-Apr 25, 1805 -- Estate, Randolph County, NC

Estate of **John Needham** Dec'd. by administrator **John Needham**. _Items were purchased by the following_: **Susanna Needham, John Needham, Baley Needham, Wm. Needham, Lewis Needham, Garner Needham, John Needham** [son of **John**]**, Hardy Davis, James Lathem Jr., Peter Garner, Enoch Spinks, James Jonston, Joseph Lawley, Peter Wright, James Latham, John Garner, John Smith, Richard Cox, Robert Bird, Wm. Rains, Wm. Tucker** and **Charles Tyler**. _Notes on the following_: **Joseph Hicks Sr.** and **Joseph Hicks Jr.** _Petition to divide land_: **Enoch** and **Elizabeth Spinks, John** and **Susannah Needham, Wm. Needham, John Needham, Bailey Needham, Lewis Needham, Garner Needham, James** and **Sarah Johnston** v. **Jesse Needham, Martha Needham** [later marries **Wm. Tucker**], **Ann Needham** [all under 21]. 2200 acres divided among 11 children on Fork Creek, Deep River, Cedar Creek and Crooked Creek of Deep River.

2607.   1800, Feb 26 -- Deed Book 8 Page 184, Randolph County, NC
William Carr deeded **Richard Bird** 50 acres adjoining **Bird** and being part of a 100 acre tract. Proven by **Arthur Reed** Aug 1800.

2608.   1800, Mar 10 -- Deed Book 8 Page 185, Randolph County, NC
James Powers (of Chatham County) deeded **Arthur Reed** 155 acres on Flat Creek of Deep River and the Chatham County line adjoining **Spinks**.

A.   1800, Mar 13 -- Land Grant #1553, Randolph County, NC
Moses Allen received 500 acres located on Reedy Creek adjoining **Hardy Davis, John Latham**, [Moore] County line and **Presnall**. **John Cavmon** and **Hugh Smitherman** were chain carriers.

2609.   1800, Mar 20 -- Land Grant #2041, Moore County, NC
David Kennedy received 50 acres located on both sides of Persimmon Branch adjoining his own line. **Everet Wallace** and **Christopher Stuts** were chain carriers.

A.   1800, Apr 8 -- Deed Book 4 Page 547-548, Moore County, NC
Alexander Campbell (of Cumberland County) deeded **Robert Graham Junr.** 150 acres located on McLendons Creek. **Wm. Martin** and **Murdock McKenzie** were witnesses.

B.   1800, Apr 12 – Deed Book O Page 169-170, Chatham County, NC
Edward Beason (of Surry County) deeded **Benjamin Williams** (of Randolph County) 150 acres located on Fall Creek adjoining **Golston**. **John Williams** and **Benjamin Williams** were witnesses.

2610.   1800, May 20 -- Land Grant #1697, Moore County, NC
Aulay McAulay received 50 acres located on Mill Swamp adjoining his own line. **Murdoch McAulay Junr.** and **Aulay McAulay** were chain carriers.

A.   1800, May 25 -- Land Grant #1631, Chatham County, NC
John Harper received 100 acres located on Mountain Branch adjoining **William Harper**. **Edwd. Harper** and **Wm. Harper** were chain carriers.

B.   1800, May 25 -- Land Grant #1731, Chatham County, NC
Joseph Lambert and **Robert Wilson** received 200 acres located on Tysons Creek adjoining **Philips** and **McManus**. **Wm. Phillips** and **Abner Phillips** were chain carriers.

C.   1800, May 27 -- Land Grant #1733, Chatham County, NC
Willis Phillips received 50 acres located on Tysons Creek adjoining own line and **Sanders**. **Lindsey Poe** and **Meredith Phillips** were chain carriers.

2611.   1800, Jun 12 -- Land Grant #1688, Moore County, NC
John McAulay Jr. received 50 acres located on Bear Creek adjoining **Leonard Furr**, where **Wm. Needom** now lives (formerly **Simon Hart**), the Speculators and **William Mainess. Amos Mainess** and **Nameliss Mainess** were chain carriers.

2612.   1800, Jul 5 -- Will Book A Page 228-229, Moore County, NC
Will of **Edward Moore** Dec'd. Heirs: son **William Moore**, son **Edward Moore** [_all land south of Deep River being the place he formerly lived on_], daughter **Sarah Stamper**, daughter **Mary Wilson**, daughter **Johana Kannedy**,

grandson **George Moore** and son-in-law **David Kannedy** [*all land north of Deep River*]. Executor: **David Kannedy**. Witnesses: **William Manus, Ambris Manus**. Proven Nov 1803.

A.	1800, Jul 18 -- Land Grant #2046, Randolph County, NC

Edward Moore's Will

Lewis Spinks [assignee of **John Winslow**] received 200 acres located on Fork Creek adjoining **Latham, Needham**, his own line, **Meacon** and **Enoch Spinks**. **James Lathem** and **Anthony Latham** were chain carriers.

2613.	1800, Jul 21 -- Land Grant #1766 and 0112, Moore County, NC
Jesse Sowell [assignee of **Mary Sowell**] received 50 acres located between Richland Creek and Suck Creek adjoining **McCaskill, Barrett, McKay**, his own line and his mother. **Jno. Sowell** and **Thos. Ritter** were chain carriers.

2614.	1800, Jul 26 -- Land Grant #1686, Moore County, NC
Murdock McLeod received 100 acres located between Dry Creek and Horse Creek adjoining **Jean Tedwell, Donald McLeod** and own line. **Allen McLean** and **David Richardson** were chain carriers.

2615.	1800, Aug-Nov 2, 1801 -- 1798-1808 Trial and Appearance Docket, Moore County, NC
Rebecca Johnston v. **George Hunsucker**

A.	1800, Sep 12 -- Land Grant #1638, Chatham County, NC
John Ramsey received 200 acres located on Tysons Creek adjoining **Record** and **Shearing**. **William Phillips** and **Dennis Phillips** were chain carriers.

2616.	1800, Sep 29 -- Land Grant #1676, Moore County, NC
Robert Bird received 75 acres located on Bull Branch of Reedy Creek adjoining Speculators and **John Shamburger**.

2617.	1800, Sep 30 -- Land Grant #1677, Moore County, NC
William Cagle received 75 acres located on the South prong of Bear Creek adjoining **Henry Cagle Sr.** and own line including his own improvement. **Henry Cagle Sr.** and **William Garner Sr.** were chain carriers.

2618.	1800, Oct 13 -- Land Grant #1769, Moore County, NC
Benjamin Shields received 100 acres located north of Deep River on Pates Creek adjoining his own line and the Speculators. **Niell Shields** and **James Shields** were chain carriers.

2619.	1800, Oct 17 -- Land Grant #1705, Moore County, NC
Robert Cheek received 79 acres located south of Deep River adjoining **William Hancock**, his own line and the Speculators. **Jas. Smith** and **Saml. Elkins** were chain carriers.

2620.	1800, Oct 20 -- Land Grant #1604, Moore County, NC
Allen McLennon received 30 acres located north of Deep River and mouth of Pates Creek adjoining **Cheek** and **Shields**. **Phillip Cheek** and **Robt. King** were chain carriers.

2621.	1800, Oct 20 -- Land Grant #1707, Moore County, NC
Henry Cagle Senr. received 21 acres located on South prong of Bear Creek adjoining his own line and **James Gilmore**. **Henry Cagle Jr.** and **John Cagle** were chain carriers.

2622.	1800, Nov 12 -- Land Grant #1682, Moore County, NC
Donald McLeod received 30 acres located east of Wet Creek adjoining **David Allison, Thomas Key** and his own line. **Murdock McAulay Junr.** and **Donald McLeod** were chain carriers.

2623.	1800, Nov 12 -- Land Grant #1590, Moore County, NC
Neill McLeod received 100 acres located between the head of Richland Creek and Little Buffalo Creek and both sides of the Flowers Road adjoining his own line. **Donald McDonald** and **Charles McKinnon** were chain carriers.

2624.	1800, Nov 18 -- Land Grant #1765, Moore County, NC

Joseph Allan received 45 acres located south of Cabin Creek adjoining **David Allison**, **William Smith**, his own line, **Richard Dunn**'s old house and **Bullock**. **Joseph Allan** and **James Allan** were chain carriers.

Moore County circa 1800

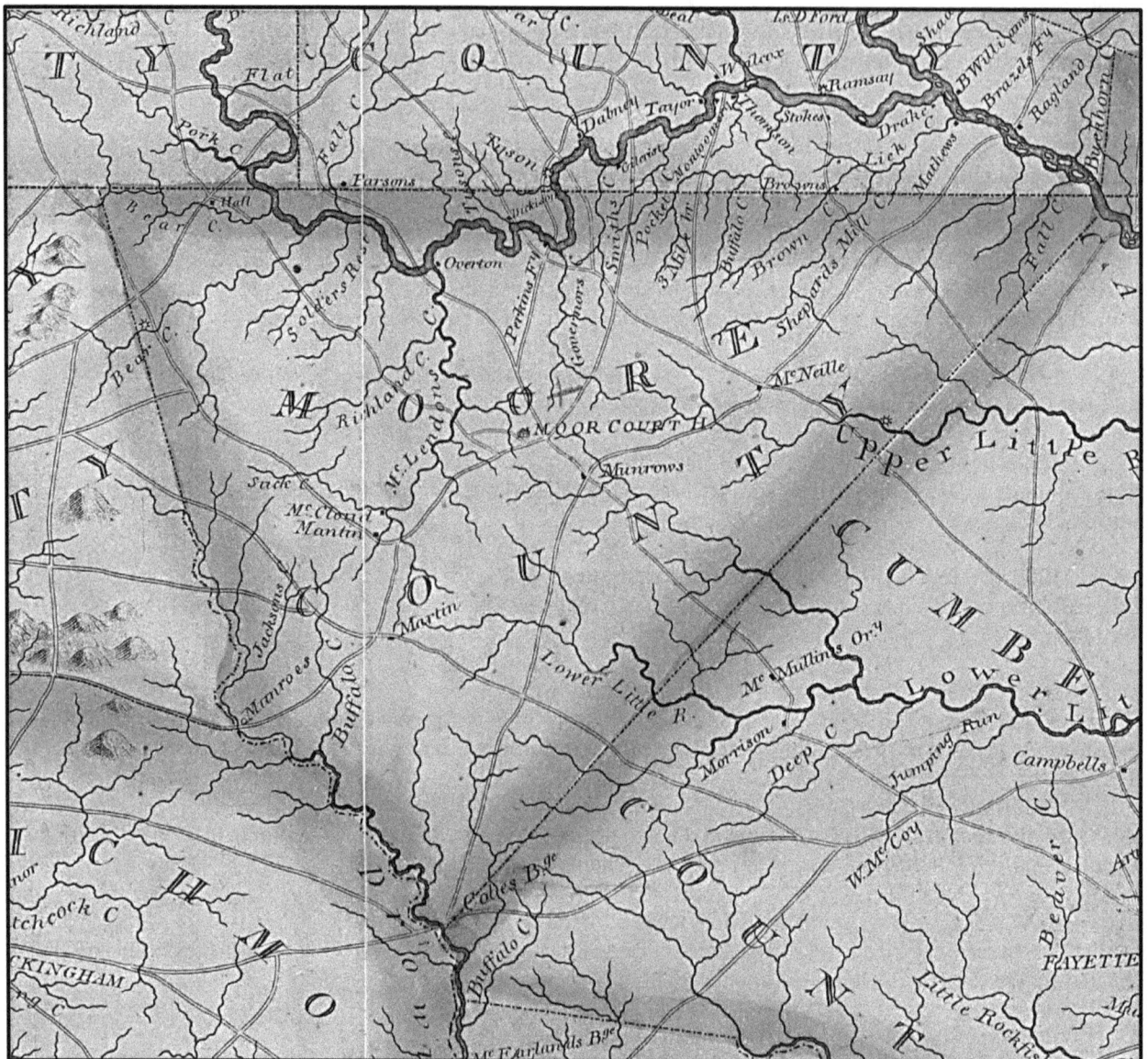

1808 Map of North Carolina by Jonathan Price and John Strother.
[Courtesy of the North Carolina Maps Digital Collection at UNC-Chapel Hill, Call Number VC912 1808p]
http://dc.lib.unc.edu/cdm/singleitem/collection/ncmaps/id/520/rec/3

2625.   1800, Nov 18 -- Land Grant #0134, Moore County, NC
James Morgan received 25 acres located on Mill Creek adjoining **Benjamin Britt**, **William Morgan** and **John Morgan Medford**. **Joseph Britt** and **James Morgan** were chain carriers. [*Editor's Note: Never granted*]

2626.   1800, Nov 18 -- Land Grant #0178, Moore County, NC
Matthew Deaton received 50 acres located south of Grassy Creek adjoining **Bullock**, **Bradly Garner** and his own line. **Christopher Yew** and **James Williamson** were chain carriers. [*Editor's Note: Never granted*]

2627.   1800, Nov 27 -- Land Grant #0102, Moore County, NC

John Paterson Jr. received 62 acres located west of Dry Creek adjoining his own line, **Thomas Graham, Ansel Melton** and the Speculators. **Ansel Melton Senr.** and **James McArthur** were chain carriers. [*Editor's Note: Never granted*]

2628.   1800, Nov 28 -- Land Grant #1887, Moore County, NC
Normand Morison received 50 acres located east of Drowning Creek and the mouth of Jacksons Branch adjoining his own line where he now lives. **Allen Morrson** and **Donald Matheson** were chain carriers.

A.   1800, Nov 29 -- Deed Book L Page 294, Chatham County, NC
Minty Vanderford deeded **William Vanderford** 100 acres located on Ceder Creek being where **William Powers** now lives and **Vanderford** purchased from **Henry Powers** and adjoining the place where **Minty Vanderford** lives. **David Powers** and **Thomas Wilson** were witnesses.

2629.   1800, Dec 9 -- Will Book A Page 213-214, Moore County, NC
Will of **Eleander Kannedy**, Dec'd. Heirs: son **George Kannedy**, son **Robert Kannedy**, daughter **Annis Smith** and daughter **Easter Kennedy**.
Executor: **Alexander Kannedy**.
Witnesses: **George Kannedy** and **Levy Smith**. Proven in Feb 1801.

Elender Kannedy's Will

A.   1800, Dec 9 – Deed Book N Page 113, Chatham County, NC
Carter Hendrick deeded **Abner Phillips** 100 acres located on Fall Creek. **Sampson Brewer** and **Peter Graves** were witnesses.

2630.   1800, Dec 15 -- Deed Book 127, Page 252, Moore County, NC
Everitt Smith deeded **Burrell Deaton** 50 acres located on Cabbin Creek adjoining **Burrell Deaton**. **Willis Davis** was a witness.

2631.   1800, Dec 16-- Land Grant #1914, Randolph County, NC
Lewis Spinks received 150 acres located on Reedy Creek and Fork Creek and the Fayetteville Road adjoining his own line, **John Needham, Mash** and **Amanuel Asbell. James Latham** and **William Bird** were chain carriers.

A.   1800, Dec 23 -- Land Grant# 1678, Chatham County, NC
John Stinson received 50 acres located on Rogers Creek adjoining his own line, **Barns** and the Moore County line. **Jno. Barnes** and **Thos. Dowdy** were chain carriers.

2632.   1801 -- Tax List, Franklin County, GA [selected residents]
Nathan Smith 300 acres on Hudson River, 1070 acres on Nail Creek; **Jas. Minard** 100 acres on Hudson River; **Niclus Smith** on Hudson River.

2633.   1801, Jan 22 -- Deed Book 8 Page 230, Randolph County, NC
Henry Branson, Edmond Wadle, Wm, Bowdown and **Charles Moffitt**, Commissioners divide the estate of **John Needham** Dec'd. [1] **Bailey Needham** 290 acres [2] **John Needham** and wife **Susannah** 370 acres [3] **Enoch Spinks** and wife **Elizabeth** 180 acres [4] **James Johnston** and wife **Sarah** 143 acres [5] **Jesse Needham** 144 acres [5] **Lewis Needham** 300 acres [6] **Gardner Needham** 250 acres [7] **Matthew Needham** 175 acres [8] **William Needham** 232 acres [9] **Anne Needham** 357 acres [10] **John Needham** 205 acres.

2634.   1801, Jan 24 -- Deed Book 8 Page 202-203 and 209, Randolph County, NC
Cornelius Lathem (of Moore County) deeded **William Smitherman** 150 acres located on Meadow Branch of Fork Creek adjoining **Smitherman** and **William Lathem**.

2635.   1801, Jan 24 -- Deed Book 8 Page 204, Randolph County, NC
Cornelius Lathem (of Moore County) deeded **William Lathem** 100 acres located on Meadow Branch of Fork Creek adjoining **Smitherman**. **William Smitherman** proved Feb 1801.

A.   1801, Jan 27 -- Deed Book L Page 293-294, Chatham County, NC
Eldredge Deaton (of Randolph County) deeded **James Powers** 56 acres located on Flat Creek and the Randolph County line adjoining **James Powers** and **Bray. Will. Searcy** and **David Powers** were witnesses.

2636. 1801, Feb 7 -- Deed Book 8, Page 158, Moore County, NC
William Wallace, Executor of **Robert Wallace**, Dec'd. (of Union County, SC) deeded **Benton Drake** of (Chatham County) 100 acres located on Little Buffalo adjoining **Andrew Reed. Wm. Willis Folsom** and **Pleasant Wicker** were witnesses.

A. 1801, Feb 9 – Deed Book L Page 274-275, Chatham County, NC
Thomas Ragland, Sheriff deeded **William Guthrie** pursuant to judgement against **Samuel Guthrie** 1100 acres located on Tyson Creek and the Moore County line adjoining **Cheek** and **Shearing**. Being the two tracts granted to **William Finley** 11 Jul 1788. **Will. Scurlock** and **F. Willis** were witnesses.

B. 1801, Feb 11 -- Deed Book L Page 232-233, Chatham County, NC
Samuel Stuart (of Moore County) deeded **Abraham Lane** 120 acres located on Little Brush Creek adjoining **Andrew Jones** and **William Graves. John Dabney, John Rumsauer** and **Edwar Stuart** were witnesses.

C. 1801, Feb 11 – Deed Book L Page 271-272, Chatham County, NC
William Guthrie deeded **John Henderson** 1100 acres located on Tyson Creek and the Moore County line adjoining **Cheek** and **Shearing**. Being the two tracts granted to **William Finley** 11 Jul 1788.

2637. 1801, Feb 16-May 1802 -- Estate, Randolph County, NC
Estate of **Gabriel Harden** Dec'd. by administrators **David Williams** and **James Harden**. _Items were purchased by the following_: **Joseph Saunders, Jacob Saunders, Jonathan Edwards, Jacob Strider, Isaac Sugs, Hardymon Rooks, James Harden, David Williams, Benjamin Harden, John Argoe, John McClendon, Bartley James, Frances Saunders, Hazle Sugs, James Randolph, Barnea Boroughs, Elisha Harden, James Harden Junr., Wm. Ford**, and **Benjn. Saunders**. Court instructed administrators to pay judgement on **Nicholas Nall** v. **Gabriel Harden**.

2638. 1801, Mar 10 -- Land Grant #1778, Moore County, NC
Alexander Autry received 62 acres located on Jacksons Creek adjoining his own line, **Elijah Autry, Archd. McMillan** and the Speculators. **Elijah Autery** and **Fredrick Autery** were chain carriers.

2639. 1801, Mar 12 -- Land Grant #1932, Randolph County, NC
William Pearce received 100 acres located on Rocky Creek adjoining **Travis Bowdon, John Pearce, Nall, William Bowdon, Armistead** and his own line. **Travis Bowdon** and **James Phillips** were chain carriers.

A. 1801, Mar 18 -- Land Grant #1690, Chatham County, NC
Joseph Lambert and **Edward Beason** received 250 acres located on Fall Creek adjoining **Beason, Guthrie, Harper** and **Brewer. Sampson Brewer** and **Henry Powers** were chain carriers.

B. 1801, Apr 20 -- Land Grant #1471, Montgomery County, NC
Harbard Suggs received 300 acres located northeast of Suggs Creek adjoining his own line. **John James** and **John Brown** were chain carriers.

2640. 1801, Apr 22 -- Deed Book 8 Page 341, Randolph County, NC
William Searcey deeded **Eldridge Deaton** 150 acres adjoining **Sarah Caviness, James Deaton** and **Richard Bird**. Proven by **William Smith** May 1802.

2641. 1801, Apr 27 -- Deed Book 8 Page 277, Randolph County, NC
William Searcey deeded **Peter Searcey** 50 acres located north of Deep River adjoining **James Deaton, Arthur Reed** and **Eldridge Deaton**. Proven by **Joseph Hicks** Nov 1801.

2642. 1801, May -- 1798-1808 Trial and Appearance Docket, Moore County, NC
Leo'd. Furr v. **William Needham** and wife
Christopher Stutts v. **James Mainus**

2643. 1801, May 4 -- Land Grant #1838, Moore County, NC
Allan Martin received 25 acres located on both sides of McLendons Creek adjoining **Kenneth McDonald**, his own line and **Robert Cox. Kenneth McDonald** and **Allan Martin** were chain carriers.

2644.   1801, May 19 -- Will Book A Page 214-216, Moore County, NC
Will of **Samuel Person**, Dec'd. Heirs: wife **Tabitha** [*plantation where I now live, negro woman Judith*], son **Thomas Person** [*negroes Sam and Selah*], son **Benjamin Person** [*negro Phil*], son **William Person** [*part of the land where I formerly lived on Fall Creek and two negroes Harry and Lette*], son **Joseph John Person** [*my land in Chatham County and negroes Will and Silvy*], daughter **Polley** and child my wife is pregnant with [*negro woman Ruth*]. Executor: **Harrson Person**, wife **Tabitha**, **David Kennedy** and **Bryan Boroughs**. Witnesses: **David Kannedy**, **B. Boroughs** and **Eli Lawler**. Proven in Aug 1801.

2645.   1801, Jun 17 -- Land Grant #1923, Moore County, NC

William Smith Senr. received 50 acres located east of Cabin Creek including the plantation where his father did live adjoining **John Cagle**. **George Cagle** and **Wm. Smith** were chain carriers. [*Editor's Note: There is confusion about whose "father" this refers to. The land was originally entered by **James Williams** in 1796 and the entry references "including his Father's improvement where his Father lives". The purchase price was ultimately not paid, and **William Smith** re-entered it in 1799. The "Father's plantation" would seem to refer to **James Williams'** father, **George Williams**, who resided nearby. But then in 1807, **William Smith** deeded all rights to this tract to **George Cagle** "except the graveyard where his father is buried." **William Smith**'s likely father, **William Smith**, purchased land adjoining this tract in 1769 from **David Cagle**.*]

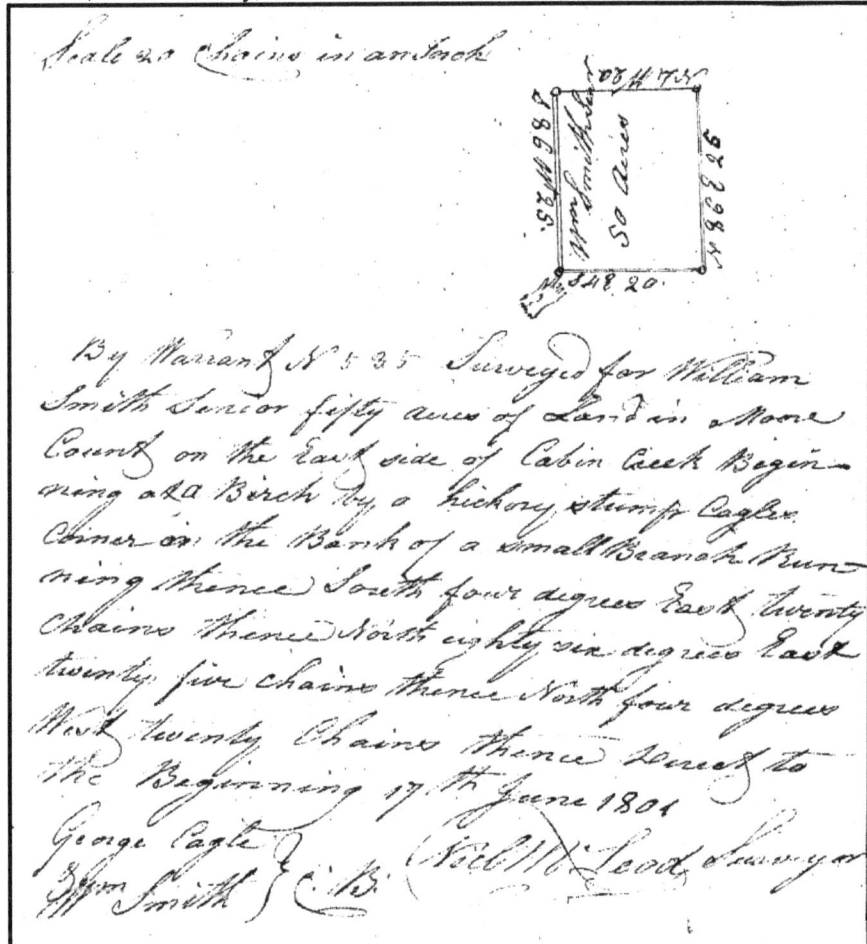

2646.   1801, Jun 18 -- Land Grant #1925, Moore County, NC
Kenneth McDonald received 67 acres located on a prong of McLendons Creek adjoining his own line, **Allan Martin** and the Speculators. **Allan Martin** and **Donald McDonald** were chain carriers.

2647.   1801, Jun 23 -- Land Grant #1706, Moore County, NC
Allan Martin received 150 acres located on McLendons Creek adjoining his own line, **Allison** and **Normand McDuffie**. **Kenneth McDonald** and **Donald McDonald** were chain carriers.

2648.   1801, Jul 1 -- Land Grant #1797a, Moore County, NC
Jesse Muse received 8 acres located on Killets Creek adjoining **William Caddell**, **James Dowd** and **McBryde**. **James Dowd** and **Jno. McIntosh** were chain carriers.

2649.   1801, Jul 17 -- Land Grant #1645, Moore County, NC
John Morgan Sr. received 25 acres located on both sides of Cabin Creek adjoining his own line. **Nathan Smith** and **Nathan Morgan** were chain carriers.

2650.   1801, Aug 21 -- Land Grant #1866, Randolph County, NC
William Green received 100 acres located on Meadow Branch adjoining **Hardy Davis**, **John Carmon** and **Hugh Smitherman**. **John Smitherman** and **Thomas Cosh** were chain carriers.

2651. 1801, Aug 27 -- Land Grant #0174, Moore County, NC
Patrick Dowd received 50 acres located on McCallums Fork adjoining **Grove**, **Lamb**, **Samuel Dunn** and **William Dunn**. **Jno. Dunn** and **Sml. Dunn** were chain carriers. [*Editor's Note: Never granted*]

2652. 1801, Aug 28 -- Land Grant #1757, Moore County, NC
Mikajah Brewer received 50 acres located on Buffalo Creek adjoining his own line and **Harden**. **Sion Hilliard** and **Jno. Ritter** were chain carriers.

2653. 1801, Aug 29 -- Land Grant #1756, Moore County, NC
Willis Davis received 50 acres located on both sides of Buffalo Creek adjoining **Samuel Perry** and his own line. **Jas. Harden** and **Robt. Richeson** were chain carriers.

A. 1801, Sep 1 – Deed Book M Page 494, Chatham County, NC
Carter Hendrick deeded **Abner Phillips** 108 acres located on Fall Creek and the Moore County line adjoining **Beason**, **Brown** and **Parsons**. **Sampson Brewer** and **Peter Graves** were witnesses.

B. 1801, Sep 20 -- Land Grant #1939, Randolph County, NC
James Lathem Sr. received 50 acres located on Fork Creek adjoining **Smitherman, William Lathem** and **Cornelius Lathem**. **James Lathem Jr.** and **Enoch Lathem** were chain carriers.

2654. 1801, Sep 29 -- Land Grant #1787a and #0229, Moore County, NC
Nathan Vick received 100 acres located on Buffalo Creek adjoining **Perry**, **John Ritter**, **Burris [Borroughs]** and the Speculators. **Sion Hilliard** and **Mikajah Brewer** were chain carriers.

A. 1801, Sep 30 -- Land Grant #1628, Randolph County, NC
William Smitherman received 50 acres located on Fork Creek adjoining **Cosht**, his own line and **Green**. **James Haddock** and **Wm. Lathem** were chain carriers.

2655. 1801, Oct 17 -- Deed Book 8 Page 285, Randolph County, NC
James Alston, John Alston and **Phillip Alston** (of Chatham County) deeded **Edmond Waddle** 330 acres north of Deep River adjoining **William Argo, Searcey** and **Reed**. Proven by **Archibald McBride** Nov 1801.

A. 1801, Oct 17 – Land Grant #1680, Chatham County, NC
John Barnes received 100 acres located on Rogers Creek and Indian Creek adjoining **Phillips** and his own line. **Merrel Hinson** and **Jno. McIntosh** were chain carriers.

2656. 1801, Oct 20 -- Land Grant #1611, Randolph County, NC
William Lathem received 100 acres located on Fork Creek adjoining **Cornelius Latham**. **James Lathem** and **William Asbal** were chain carriers.

2657. 1801, Oct 20 -- Land Grant #2239, Moore County, NC
John Smith entered 50 acres located east of Dry Creek adjoining his own line and the Speculators. **Mathew Diton** and **Isom Smith** were chain carriers.

A. 1801, Oct 27 -- Land Grant #1739, Chatham County, NC
John Record received 107 acres located on Tysons Creek adjoining **Ramsey**, his own line and **Cheek**. **Dennis Phillips** and **Hezekial Phillips** were chain carriers.

2658. 1801, Oct 28 -- Land Grant #1940, Moore County, NC
James Melton received 50 acres located on Long Meadow adjoining **Robert Sandifer**, **Neil McLeod** and own line. **Jos. Cockman** and **Jno. Martin** were chain carriers.

2659. 1801, Dec 25 -- Will Book A Page 219-220, Moore County, NC
Will of **James Riddle**, Dec'd. Heirs: wife **Temperance** [*all my land on Governors Creek and negro Isaac*], son **William**, son **John**, daughter **Mary** and daughter **Sarah**. [*also mentions 100 acres on Upper Little River to be sold by Charles McLeod to pay the debt*]. Executor: **John Worthy** and **Abraham Cole**. Witnesses: **James Campbell**, **Charles Runnalds** and **Elijah Jackson**. Proven in Feb 1802.

2660. 1802 -- Tax List, Franklin County, GA [selected residents]
Adam Sheffield [no acreage or location given]; **Stephen Smith** 345 acres on Hudson River; **Nathan Smith** 300 acres on Hudson River; **James Minyard** 90 acres on Mountain Creek; **Owen Carpenter** 100 acres on Hudson River and **Nicholas Smith** 100 acres on Hudson River.

2661. 1802, Jan 22 -- Land Grant #0197, Moore County, NC
Lewis Lawhon received 300 acres located between McLendons Creek and Richland Creek adjoining **Edwards**, **John Dannelly**, **Rone** and **Dean**. **Jesse Bean** and **Joel Lawhon** were chain carriers. [*Editor's Note: Never granted*]

2662. 1802, Feb -- Will Book A, Page 224-225, Moore County, NC
Will of **Henry Cagle**, Dec'd. Heirs: wife **Caterana Cagle** [*220 acres including the plantation where I now live adjoining the lands of **William**, **Christian** and **Henry Cagle Jr.***], eldest son **William Cagle**, son **Christian Cagle** [*50 acres adjoining where he now lives*], son **Henry Cagle**, son **Peter Cagle**, son **John Cagle** [*200 acres adjoining **Cornelius Lathem** except 22.5 acres taken up by **John McAulay***], son **Jacob Cagle** [*100 acres and 50 acres which I bought of **John McAulay** on Meadow Branch of Wolf Creek*], son **George Cagle** [*100 acres where he now lives adjoining **Peter Cagle***], last son **Martin Cagle**, daughter **Inna Caterena Cockman**, daughter **Eliza Hubbard** and daughter **Mary Auman**. Executors: wife **Caterana Cagle** and son **William Cagle**. Witnesses: **Hardy Davis**, **Peter Davis** and **Charles Tyler**. Proven Feb 1802.

2663. 1802, Feb 9 -- 1794-1802 Court of Pleas and Quarter Sessions, Randolph County, NC
Ordered that **Edmond Waddle** keep a ferry at the same place that **William Searcy** did heretofore.

> Ordered that Edmond Waddle keep a Ferry at the same place where William Searcy did heretofore. And shall be allowed the following rates for ferriage Viz. for a man & Horse Sixpence, for Carriages Sixpence pr. Wheel, for a footman Sixpence. ———

2664. 1802, Mar 2 -- Land Grant #1808, Moore County, NC
Robert Wilkerson received 16 acres located on the waters of Reedy Creek adjoining **Lewis Spinks**, his own line, **Robert Bird** and **Jno. Shamburger**. **Robert Bird** and **Wm. Bird** were chain carriers.

2665. 1802, Mar 2 -- Land Grant #1849, Moore County, NC
James Melton received 32 acres located south of Buffalo Creek adjoining **Henry Stutts**, **John Martin**, **Joseph McGee**, **Neil McLeod**, **Jacob Stutts** and **Edwards**. **Jno Martin** and **Jno. Buie** were chain carriers.

A. 1802, Mar 2 – Deed Book 8 Page 416, Randolph County, NC
David Coble Senr., **David Coble Junr.** and **Elisabeth Coble** (all of Orange County) deeded **Thomas Kosh** 240 acres located on Reedy Creek and Fork Creek. **William Needham** was a witness.

2666. 1802, Mar 9 -- Land Grant #1961, Moore County, NC
James Morgan received 50 acres located on the waters of Mill Creek adjoining his own line, the Speculators and **Neil McLeod**. **William Smith** and **John Morgan** were chain carriers.

2667. 1802, Mar 22 -- Chronicles and Records of Bensalem Presbyterian Church Page 5 & 21 Moore County, NC
Angus Morrison married **Nancy McCaskill**.

A. 1802, Mar 31 -- Land Grant #1400, Montgomery County, NC
William Spencer received 100 acres located on the mouth of Suggs Creek adjoining his own line. **Wm. Spencer** and **Seymore Spencer** were chain carriers.

2668. 1802, Apr 30 -- Criminal Actions, Randolph County, NC Box 6
Bill of complaint of **John Gilliam** accuses **William Gatlen** of making a false oath. **Suckey Davis**, **John Holden**, **Betsey Holden**, **Harday Davis** and **Lewis Davis** were witnesses for the state. **Jesse Gatlin**, **Betsey Gatlin**,

James Gatlin and Edward Gatlin were witnesses for the defense. Thomas Cash and Huke Smitherman bound for Gatlin.

2669.   1802, Apr 30 -- Deed Book 8 Page 355, Randolph County, NC
John Needham deeded Enoch Spinks 300 acres located on Bachelors Creek adjoining Samuel Cox. Proven by John Needham Aug 1803.

A.   1803, Apr 30 -- Land Grant #1676, Montgomery County, NC
William Spencer received 200 acres located on Cooks Creek and Allen's Road adjoining Benjamin Simmons and Finch's cabins. James Simmons and Elias Butler were chain carriers.

2670.   1802, May 1 -- Deed Book 8 Page 332, Randolph County, NC
Hardy Davis (of Moore County) deeded Absalom Presnell 25 acres located on Bear Creek near the [Moore] County line adjoining Presnell.

2671.   1802, May 25 -- Deed Book 8 Page 372, Randolph County, NC
Eldridge Deaton deeded John Dabney Jr. 150 acres adjoining William Carr, Anstatt, Sarah Caviness, Bird and Peter Searcey including the place where William Searcy now lives [part of 500 acres granted Jun 7, 1799]. Proven by William Searcy Nov 1803.

2672.   1802, Jun 8 -- Land Grant #1921, Moore County, NC
Jesse Ritter received 100 acres located on Locust Branch adjoining Donald McQueen, John Ritter and his own line. Jesse Ritter and Moses Ritter were chain carriers.

2673.   1802, Jun 12 -- Land Grant #1811, Moore County, NC
Robert Teaster received 100 acres located on the head of Mill Creek near the Waggon Road adjoining Neil McLeod. Neil McLeod and Nathaniel Teaster were chain carriers.

2674.   1802, Jun 17 -- Land Grant #1722, Moore County, NC
William Dunn received 50 acres located on Long Meadow adjoining Michael Hill, Robert Edwards and own line including his own improvement. Joseph Cockman and James Melton were chain carriers.

2675.   1802, Aug 16 -- Deed Book 127, Page 253, Moore County, NC
Levi Deaton deeded John Needham Sr. 100 acres located on Cabbin Creek adjoining David Allison. Allan McLain was a witness.

2676.   1802, Aug 17 -- Deed Book 127, Page 254, Moore County, NC
Burrell Deaton deeded John Needham Sr. 50 acres located on Cabbin Creek adjoining his own line. W. McCaskill was a witness.

2677.   1802, Aug 25 -- Land Grant #2074, Randolph County, NC
William Armstead Esq. received 30 acres located north of Fork Creek and west of Rock Creek adjoining Steward, Pearce and his own line. John Morris and Wm. Smith were chain carriers.

2678.   1802, Aug 25 -- Land Grant #2075, Randolph County, NC
William Armstead Esq. received 42 acres located on Fork Creek adjoining Pearce and Bowdon. Wm. Pearce and Wm. Smith were chain carriers.

A.   1802, Sep 3 – Deed Book 9 Page 350, Randolph County, NC
Moses Allen deeded Thomas Kosh Jr. 500 acres located on Reedy Creek adjoining John Latham, Hardy Davis, [Moore] County line and Presnell. Thomas Kosh was a witness.

B.   1802, Sep 15 -- Land Grant# 1669, Chatham County, NC
John McIntosh received 50 acres located on Rogers Creek adjoining Barnes, Tyson (formerly Stinson) and the Moore County line. Jno. Barnes and Thos. Dowdy were chain carriers.

2679.   1802, Sep 21 -- Land Grant #1938, Moore County, NC
Normand Matheson received 50 acres located on Buffalo Creek adjoining Hector McNeil, his own line and Murdo. McLeod. Donald Munroe and Neil Matheson were chain carriers.

2680. 1802, Sep 21 -- Land Grant #1792, Moore County, NC
Hector McNiell received 50 acres located west of Richland Creek adjoining **Solomon Barret** and his own line. **John McIntosh** and **Jacob Stuts** were chain carriers.

2681. 1802, Oct 2 -- Land Grant #1621, Moore County, NC
Patrick Dowd received 100 acres located on McCollums Fork adjoining **Grove**, **Samuel Dunn**, **Joseph Dunn**'s Mill tract. **Jesse Upton** and **John Upton** were chain carriers.

2682. 1802, Oct 7 -- Land Grant #0144, Moore County, NC
James Melton received 300 acres located on Long Meadow adjoining **Neil McLeod**, **Joseph McGee**, **Robert Wilkins** and his own line. **Jos. Cockman** and **Everet Wallis** were chain carriers. [*Editor's Note: Never granted*]

2683. 1802, Oct 8 -- Land Grant #1634, Moore County, NC
Joseph McGee received 200 acres located west of Buffalo Creek adjoining his own line, **Richardson** and **Ritter**. **D. Richardson** and **Mikajah Brewer** were chain carriers.

2684. 1802, Oct 8 -- Land Grant #2029, Moore County, NC
Mikajah Brewer received 98 acres located on both sides of Buffalo Creek adjoining **John Ritter**, **Drury Richardson** and his own line. **Jno. Ritter** and **Edwd. Richardson** were chain carriers.

A. 1802, Oct 20 – Land Grant #2030, Randolph County, NC
Absalom Presnal received 100 acres located on Bear Creek adjoining his own line and the Moore County line. **Joseph Lawler** and **Thomas Doneny** were chain carriers.

2685. 1802, Oct 29 -- Land Grant #2378, Moore County, NC
Samuel Perry received 180 acres located south of Deep River adjoining his own line, **Borroughs**, **Joseph Wright**, **Henry Lamb**, **Waddle** and the **Pood**(?) **Land**. **Henry Lamb** and **Archd. Johnson** were chain carriers.

2686. 1802, Nov 1 -- Land Grant #1805, Moore County, NC
John Danielly received 100 acres located on McLendons Creek adjoining **Jesse Bean**, **Saml. Dunn** and **McLeod**. **Joel Lawhon** and **Jesse Bean** were chain carriers.

2687. 1802, Nov 3 -- Land Grant #1643,

Moore County, NC

John Atkinson received 60 acres located east of Richland Creek adjoining **Wm. Dunn**, **Benjn. Dunn** and **Joseph Dunn Sr. Benjn. Dunn** and **Jno. Dunn** were chain carriers.

2688. 1802, Nov 3 -- Land Grant #1860, Moore County, NC
William Dunn received 50 acres located northwest of Richland Creek adjoining **Benjamin Dunn** and his own line. **Benjn. Dunn** and **Jno. Dunn** were chain carriers.

2689. 1802, Nov 4 -- Land Grant #1922, Moore County, NC
John Danielly received 100 acres located on McCallums Fork adjoining his own line and **Benjn. Dunn**. **Jesse Upton** and **Zachariah Smith** were chain carriers.

2690. 1802, Nov 4 -- Land Grant #1600, Moore County, NC
Aaron Tyson received 150 acres located east of Rogers Creek on the Chatham County line adjoining his own line (formerly **John Stinson**) and **Jno. Cheek. Jno. Cheek** and **Joab Cheek** were chain carriers.

2691. 1802, Nov8 -- Land Grant #1622, Randolph County, NC
Jesse Gatlin received 250 acres located on Meadow Branch and the Moore County line adjoining **Barrett. Wm. Asbel** and **Wm. Smitherman** were chain carriers.

2692. 1802, Nov 9 -- Land Grant #1617, Randolph County, NC
Elizabeth Asbal received 90 acres located on Meadow Branch and the Moore County line adjoining **Smitherman**, **Latham** and **Gatlin**. **Wm. Smitherman** and **Wm. Latham** were chain carriers.

2693. 1802, Nov 9 -- Land Grant #1601, Moore County, NC
James Atkins [assignee of **Robert Dyer**, only son and heir of **James Dyer**, Dec'd.] received 100 acres located on Buffalo Creek including the Cool Spring adjoining **Harmon Brewer**. **John Ritter** and **Moses Ritter** were chain carriers.

2694. 1802, Nov 12 -- Land Grant #2147, Randolph County, NC
John Shumbarger received 74 acres located on Meadow Branch of Fork Creek adjoining **Christian Asbal**, **John Needham**, **Lathem**, **Smitherman** and his own line. **Lewis Needham** and **Garner Needham** were chain carriers.

2695. 1802, Nov 20 -- Deed Book 8 Page 546, Randolph County, NC
John Garner (of Moore County) deeded **Bradley Garner** (of Moore County) 30 acres located on the [Moore] County line and Deep River near the mouth of Fork Creek. Proven by **D. Kenedy** Feb 1806.

2696. 1802, Nov 23 -- Land Grant #1625, Moore County, NC
Thomas Ritter received 100 acres located on the drains of McLendons Creek adjoining his own line, **Mary Sowell**, **John McSween**, **McKay** and **John Sowell**. **Jno. Ritter** and **Thos. Ritter** were chain carriers.

2697. 1802, Nov 23 -- Land Grant #1942, Moore County, NC
William Barret received 50 acres located on the drains of Buffalo Creek adjoining his own line and **Grove**. **Hector McLean** and **John McDonald** were chain carriers.

2698. 1802, Nov 24 -- Land Grant #1632, Moore County, NC
John McAulay and **John Martin** received 100 acres located on Scotchman Creek adjoining **Kenneth McKinzie**, **Drury Richardson**, **William Richardson**, **Thomas Smith** and the Speculators. **John McAulay** and **Neill McIntosh** were chain carriers.

2699. 1802, Nov 24 -- Land Grant #1648, Moore County, NC
The heirs of **John Bullock**, Dec'd. received 100 acres located north of Grassy Creek on both sides of the Waggon Road adjoining **Peter Shamburger**, **Hardy Davis** and **Nall. Daniel Maness** and **Peter Shamburger Junr.** were chain carriers.

2700. 1802, Nov 25 -- Land Grant #1624, Moore County, NC
The heirs of **Angus McIver** received 50 acres located west of Toms Creek adjoining **Edward Fagin**, **Jno. McNeil**, **Malcom Shaw**, **James McNeill**, **Alexr. McLeod** and his own improvement. **Alexr. McLeod** and **Wm. Smith** were chain carriers.

2701.   1802, Nov 25 -- Land Grant #2018, Moore County, NC
William Barret received 20 acres located east of McLendons Creek adjoining **Joel McLendon**, his own line and **Thomas Graham**. **Allan Morison** and **William Barret** were chain carriers.

A.   1802, Nov 25 -- Deed Book N Page 157-158, Chatham County, NC
Fox Palmer (of Bartholomew Parish, SC) deeded **Sampson Brewer** 240 acres located on both sides of Fall Creek adjoining **Elliott**. **John Elliott** and **George Smith** were chain carriers.

2702.   1802, Nov 28 -- Land Grant #0197, Moore County, NC
Lewis Lawhon received 300 acres located between McLendons and Richland Creeks adjoining **John Dannelly**, **Edwards**, **Rones** and **Dean**. **Jesse Bean** and **Joel Lawhon** were chain carriers. [*Editor's Note: Never granted*]

2703.   1802, Dec 6 -- Land Grant #1836, Moore County, NC
Henry Cagle received 25 acres located north of Bear Creek adjoining **Christopher Cagle**, his own line and **Presley**. **Cornelius Latham** and **John Cagle** were chain carriers.

2704.   1802, Dec 9 -- Will Book A Page 225-227, Moore County, NC
Will of **John Barker**, Dec'd. Heirs: wife **Mary Barker**, daughter **Miriam Scot**, son **John Barker** [*all land north of Deep River*], daughter **Sarah Williams**, son **Robert Barker** [*all land south of Deep River except 100 acres on Wolspen Branch*], daughter **Rosana Barker**, daughter **Elizabeth Barker** and son-in-law **Thomas Wilson**. Executors: wife **Mary Barker**, **James Scot** and **Eli Lawler**. Witnesses: **Robert Davis** and **Eli Lawler**. Proven Feb 1803.

2705.   1802, Dec 11 -- Land Grant #1614, Moore County, NC
John Stinson received 30 acres located east of Rogers Creek on the Chatham County line adjoining his own line. **William Kindrick** and **Joab Cheek** were chain carriers.

2706.   1802, Dec 13-Feb 1806 -- Estate, Randolph County, NC
Estate of **Thomas Cash/Cost/Kosh** Dec'd. by administrators **Dr. David Coble** and **Margaret "Peggy" Kosh/Cash**. Inventory includes negroes **Sam** and **Winny**. **Michael Harvey** and **Wm. Needham** Esq. appointed to settle with administrators. *Items were purchased by the following*: **Joseph McGee, Leonard Stuts, Saml. Barrat, Wm. Needham, Christopher Asbill, Wm. Reader, Peter Voncanon, John Guilliam, Charles Lathem** and **Thos. Davis**.

2707.   1802, Dec 24 -- Land Grant #2028, Moore County, NC
MakaJor/Kager Brewer received 50 acres located west of Buffalo Creek adjoining **Drury Richardson**.

2708.   1802, Dec 27 -- Deed Book 8 Page 352, Randolph County, NC
James Powers (of Chatham County) deeded **Rolley Spinks** 45 acres located on Flat Creek and the Chatham County line adjoining **Arthur Reed** and the tract that **Powers** currently lives on. Proven by **William Carr** Aug 1803.

A.   1802, Dec 20 -- Marriage Bond, Randolph County, NC
William Tucker and **Martha Needham** received marriage bond. **George Tucker** was bondsman. [*Editor's Note: Date of marriage occurred on or after date of marriage bond.*]

B.   1802, Dec 30 -- Marriage Bond, Randolph County, NC
Enoch Leathem and **Nancy Garner** received marriage bond. **John Garner** was bondsman. [*Editor's Note: Date of marriage occurred on or after date of marriage bond.*]

2709.   1803, Jan 12 -- Land Grant #2383, Moore County, NC
Elijah Autery received 100 acres located east of Jackson Creek on both sides of the Waggon Road adjoining **John Jackson**, **Beattis**, his own line and **Archibald McMillan**. **Alexr. Autery** and **Allen Morison** were chain carriers.

2710.   1803, Feb 18 -- Deed Book OO Page 70-71, Franklin County, GA
Thomas Gregg and wife **Anna** (of Elbert County, GA) deeded **Nathan Smith** 262 acres located on Hudson River adjoining **Nail**, **Gregg** and **Stephen Smith**. **John McGowen** and **Nimrod House** were witnesses. Recorded Oct 5, 1803.

2711.   1803, Feb 24 -- Deed Book 8 Page 365, Randolph County, NC
William Searcy deeded **William Onstat** 97 acres located south of Deep River adjoining **Arthur Reid, Peter Corey, James Deaton** and **Edmond Waddell**. Proven by **William Searcy** Nov 1803.

A.   1803, Mar 4 -- Deed Book 4 Page 549-550, Moore County, NC
Donald McLeod deeded **Donald McDonald** 83 acres located on McLendons Creek adjoining **Kenneth McDonald, Cox** and patented by **Malcolm McLeod**. **Donald McDonald** and **Neill McDonald** were witnesses.

2712.   1803, Mar 10 -- Land Grant #1807, Moore County, NC
John Patterson Junr. received 100 acres located west of Dry Creek adjoining his own line, **Ancel Melton** and **Thomas Graham**. **James McArthur** and **Ancel Melton** were chain carriers.

2713.   1803, Mar 12 -- Land Grant #1824, Moore County, NC
Neil McLeod [assignee of **John Cox**] received 50 acres located west of McLendons Creek adjoining **Cox, Malcolm McLeod, Kenneth McDonald** and his own line. **Christopher Bethune** and **Donald McDonald** were chain carriers. [*Editor's Note: deeded to* **Donald McDonald** *1804*]

2714.   1803, Mar 12 -- Land Grant #1955, Moore County, NC
Neil McDonald received 100 acres located on Dry Creek of McLendons Creek adjoining **Donald McDonald**. **Murdoch Martin** and **Donald McDonald** were chain carriers.

2715.   1803, Mar 12 -- Land Grant #2050, Moore County, NC
Murdoch Martin received 24 acres located on Dry Creek of McLendons Creek adjoining **Donald McDonald, Robert Graham** and his own line. **Donald McDonald** and **Neil McDonald** were chain carriers.

A.   1803, Apr 10 – Deed Book O Page 215-216, Chatham County, NC
Joseph Lambert deeded **Thomas Wilson** 50 acres located on Fall Creek adjoining **Brewer, Thomas Wilson, Jude Wilson, Guthrie** and **Beason**. **Abner Phillips** and **William Harper** were witnesses.

2716.   1803, May -- 1798-1808 Trial and Appearance Docket, Moore County, NC Page 3
Burrel Deaton and wife v. **Robert Melton**

2717.   1803, May 10 -- Land Grant #1886, Moore County, NC
John McLeod received 50 acres located east of Horses Creek adjoining his own line and including his own improvement. **John McLeod** and **John Paterson** were chain carriers.

2718.   1803, Jun 7 -- Land Grant #1859, Moore County, NC
Moses Wilson received 64 acres located south of Williams Creek adjoining **John Hair, Silay Hayes,** Speculators and **Adam Comer**. **Adam Comer Senr.** and **Peter Hair Junr.** were chain carriers.

A.   1803, Jun 12 -- Land Grant #1788, Chatham County, NC
Sion Phillips received 102 acres located on Tysons Creek adjoining his own line, **Sanders, Willis Phillips, Guthrie** and **Harper**. **Merrida Phillips** and **Jesse Brewer** were chain carriers.

B.   1803, Jun 13 -- Land Grant #1803, Chatham County, NC
Sampson Brewer received 92 acres located on Fall Creek adjoining **Jones** (formerly **Lambert**), **Wilson, Beason** and his own line. **Jas. Scott** and **Wm. Harper** were chain carriers.

C.   1803, Jun 13 -- Land Grant #1812, Chatham County, NC
Sampson Brewer received 59 acres located on Fall Creek adjoining **Beason** and his own line. **James Scott** and **James Harper** were chain carriers.

2719.   1803, Jul 14 -- Land Grant #1834, Moore County, NC
Wm. Copland received 50 acres located east of Drowning Creek adjoining his own line. **John Campbell** and **Richard Dunn Senr.** were chain carriers.

2720.   1803, Aug 5 -- Land Grant #1926, Moore County, NC

James Wood received 100 acres located north of Wolf Creek adjoining **Thos. Dunn**, **William Wright**, **Wm. Morgan**, **David Allison** and **Andrew Auman**. **Francis Bullock** and **John Gilliam Junr.** were chain carriers.

2721.   1803, Aug 7 -- Land Grant #0110, Moore County, NC
William Richardson received 50 acres located on Morter Glade adjoining **Zachary Smith**. **Edward Richardson** and **Zachariah Smith** were chain carriers. [*Editor's Note: Never granted*]

2722.   1803, Aug 23 -- Will Book A Page 232-233, Moore County, NC
Will of **George Carringer**, Dec'd. Heirs: son **Jacob Carringer**, granddaughter **Sally Carringer**, daughter **Caty Manes**, daughter **Peggy Manes**, daughter **Lis Autry**, daughter **Susanna Manes**, daughter **Barbary Barker**, daughter **Mary Bruer**, daughter **Dolly Rustin**, son **George Carringer**, son **John Carringer**, son **Peter Carringer**, son **Daniel Carringer** and son **David Carringer**. Executor: **William Williamson**. Witnesses: **David Kennedy** and **George Kennedy**. Proven Feb 1804.

2723.   1803, Aug 29 -- Land Grant #1885, Moore County, NC
Norman Morison received 50 acres located east of Drowning Creek and Wrights Branch adjoining his own line. **Allen Morrson** and **Angus Morison** were chain carriers.

2724.   1803, Aug 30 -- Land Grant #1812, Moore County, NC
Nathan Smith received 50 acres located on the waters of Cabin Creek adjoining his own line. **William Smith Senr.** and **Nathan Smith** were chain carriers.

2725.   1803, Aug 30 -- Land Grant #1848, Moore County, NC
Leonard Furr, Junr. received 100 acres located on both sides of Flag Creek adjoining **Jacob Furr**, his own line and **Thomas Graham**. **Leonard Furr Senr.** and **Jacob Furr** were chain carriers.

2726.   1803, Aug 30 -- Land Grant #0186, Moore County, NC
Bradly Garner received 15 acres located north of Grassy Creek adjoining **Abraham Huntsucker**, **David Kennedy**, **Geo. Carringer** and his own line. **George Kennedy** and **Bradly Garner** were chain carriers. [*Editor's Note: Never granted*]

2727.   1803, Sep 3 -- Deed Book 8 Page 528, Randolph County, NC
Lewis Needham deeded **Cornelius Lathem** 300 acres located on Meadow Branch, Fork Creek and the mouth of a branch of Mill Creek where there was formerly a millseat adjoining **Enoch Spinks**. Three tracts: 200 acres granted to **John Needham** Dec'd.; 50 acres granted to **John Needham** Dec'd.; 50 acres granted to **Enoch Spinks** Dec'd. Proven by **William Needham** Nov 1805.

2728.   1803, Sep 6 -- Land Grant #1827, Moore County, NC
John Dunn received 100 acres located east of Richland Creek adjoining **Mark Phillips** and own line. **Benjn. Dunn** and **Mark Phillips** were chain carriers.

2729.   1803, Sep 15 -- Land Grant #1850, Moore County, NC
Jacob Furr received 100 acres located east of Flag Creek adjoining **John Cox**, **Leonard Furr**, **Thos. Graham** and **Charles Sowell**. **Leonard Furr Senr.** and **Leonard Furr Junr.** were chain carriers.

2730.   1803, Sep 21 -- Land Grant #1905, Moore County, NC
Neil Matheson received 50 acres located east of Dry Creek adjoining **Melony Newton** and his own line. **Donald Munroe** and **Norman Matheson** were chain carriers.

A.   1803, Oct 7 – Land Grant #1820, Chatham County, NC
Lewis Phillips received 100 acres located on Indian Creek adjoining **Griffin** and his own line. **John Seat** and **Wm. Phillips** were chain carriers.

2731.   1803, Oct 10 -- Land Grant #1809, Moore County, NC
William Dunn received 50 acres located on Blans Branch including the Mill Stone Quarry adjoining his own line. **Mark Phillips** and **Jno. Dunn** were chain carriers.

2732.   1803, Oct 11 -- Land Grant #0125, Moore County, NC

Robert Wilkins received 65 acres located on the waters of Buffalo and Meadow adjoining his own line and **Robert Sandifer**. **Joseph Cockman** and **Daniel McQueen** were chain carriers. [*Editor's Note: Never granted*]

2733. 1803, Oct 12 -- Land Grant #1820, Moore County, NC
John White received 100 acres located south of Deep River adjoining **Robert Cheek**, **Davis**, **Andrew White** and **Adam White**. **Archd. Collins** and **Adam White** were chain carriers.

2734. 1803, Oct 12 -- Land Grant #1832, Moore County, NC
Adam White received 100 acres located north of Deep River below the mouth of Cane Patch Creek adjoining **Robert Cheek**. **Archd. Collins** and **Jno. McIntosh** were chain carriers.

2735. 1803, Oct 13 -- Land Grant #1828, Moore County, NC

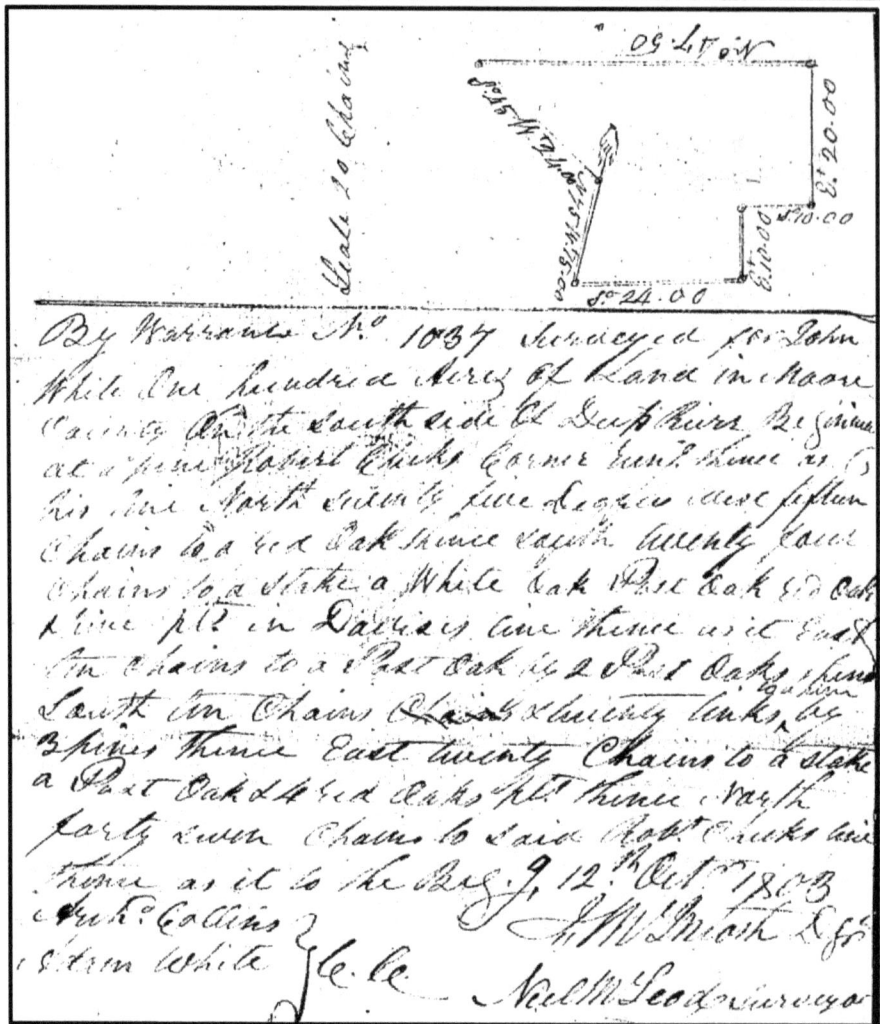

Willis Davis received 50 acres located on Buffalo Creek adjoining his own line and **Perry**. **Jas. Harden** and **Gabriel Harden** were chain carriers.

2736. 1803, Oct 13 -- Land Grant #1844, Moore County, NC
William C. Davis received 100 acres located south of Deep River adjoining **Robert Davis**, **Robt. Cheek**, **Adam White** and his own line. **Jas. Davis** and **J. McIntosh** were chain carriers.

2737. 1803, Oct 14 -- Land Grant #0115, Moore County, NC
Cornelius Shields received 20 acres located at the mouth of Buffalo Creek on Deep River adjoining **William Harden**, **Jas. Harden** and **McNeill**. **Jas. Harden** and **Fannen Moore** were chain carriers. [*Editor's Note: Never granted*]

2738. 1803, Oct 20 -- Land Grant #1902, Moore County, NC
John Richardson received 50 acres located on Buffalo Creek adjoining his own line, **Phil White** and **McGee**. **Phil White** and **S. Richardson** were chain carriers.

2739. 1803, Oct 24 -- Land Grant #1894, Moore County, NC
Eli Callicot received 100 acres located south of Williams Creek adjoining **Hardy Davis**. **Andrew Auman** and **Francis Bullock** were chain carriers.

A. 1803, Nov 2 – Land Grant #1797, Chatham County, NC
Thomas Snipes and **Eli Lawler** received 47.5 acres located on Fall Creek adjoining their own lines and **Person**. **Will. Wilson** and **John Lawler** were chain carriers.

2740. 1803, Nov 8 -- Land Grant #256, Randolph County, NC

John Gillum entered 100 acres located on Meadow Branch adjoining **William Green**, **William Smitherman**, **Thomas Cash**, **Hardy Davis** and **Adam Smith**.

2741. 1803, Nov 12 -- Land Grant #1810, Moore County, NC
John Cagle received 50 acres located south of Bear Creek adjoining **Henry Cagle Senr.**, **Henry Cagle Junr.**, **Cornelius Lathum**, his own line and **David Allison**. **Henry Cagle Junr.** and **Cornelius Latham** were chain carriers.

2742. 1803, Nov 15 -- Land Grant #1837, Moore County, NC
John Dunn received 100 acres located south of Mill Creek adjoining his own line, **John Morgan** and **David Richardson**. **William Dunn** and **John Dunn** were chain carriers.

A. 1803, Nov 19 – Deed Book M Page 517-518, Chatham County, NC
Abner Phillips deeded **Robert Wilson** two tracts totaling 150 acres: [1] located on Tyson Creek adjoining **Willis Phillips** [2] located on Tysons Creek adjoining **Willis Philips**, **Record** and **Dennis Phillips**. **Edwd. Beeson**, **Ann Perangton** [Pennington?], **Eli Lawler** and **Benj. Shields Junr.** were witnesses.

B. 1803, Nov 23 -- Deed Book 2 Page 280, Montgomery County, NC
Thomas Cotten deeded **Saml. Allen** 350 acres located on Williams Creek and Wolf Creek adjoining **John Mosler**, **George Allen**, **Saml. Allen** and **Diffie**. **George Allen** and **Meloney Allen** were witnesses.

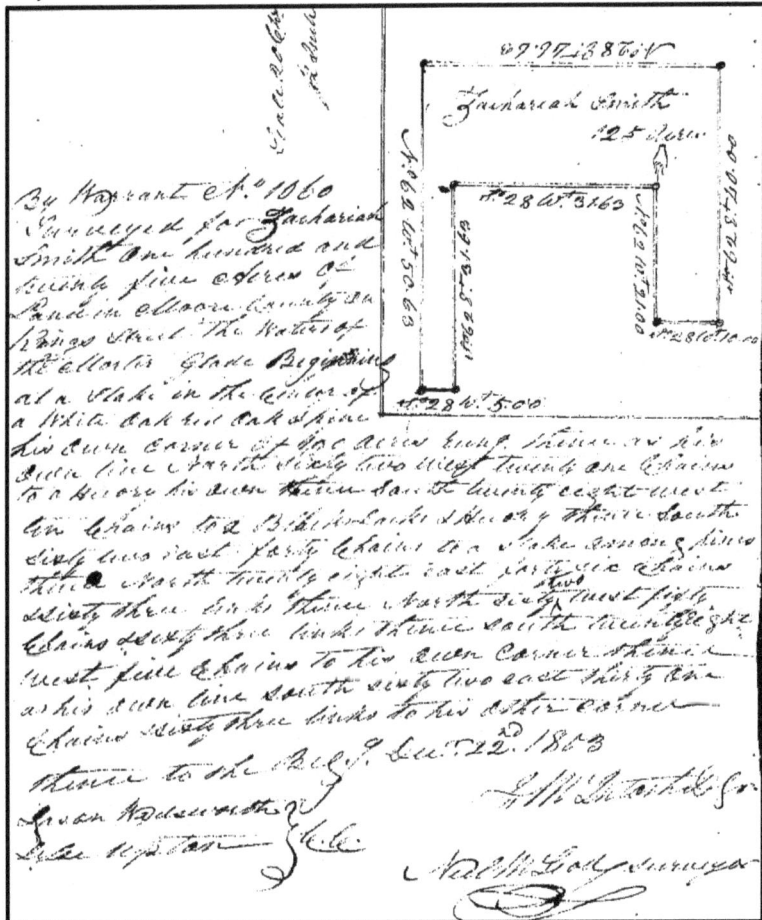

2743. 1803, Dec 13 -- Land Grant #1813, Moore County, NC
Peter Graves received 100 acres located on the waters of Fall Creek and the [Chatham] County line adjoining **Widow Parsons** and his own line. **Abner Phillips** and **Benjn. Shields** were chain carriers.

2744. 1803, Dec 13 -- Land Grant #1814, Moore County, NC
William Davis received 400 acres located north of Deep River adjoining his own line. **Robt. Wilson** and **Benjn. Shields** were chain carriers.

2745. 1803, Dec 22 -- Land Grant #1898, Moore County, NC
Zachariah Smith received 125 acres located on Kings Street/Morter Glade adjoining his own line. **Jason Wadsworth** and **Jesse Upton** were chain carriers.

2746. 1803, Dec 30 -- Deed Book 8 Page 522, Randolph County, NC
William Smotherman deeded **Cornelius Lathrem** 45 acres adjoining **Needham** and **Spinks**. Proven by **Lewis Spinks** Nov 1805.

2747. 1804 -- Colonel **William Wofford** Survey on Georgia Frontier Settlers
Updated Report made to Colonel Return **Jonathan Meigs**, agent to the Cherokee Indians, southwest Point, regarding the number and condition of the Settlers living in and near the "Wofford Settlement", on the Frontier of Georgia and the Cherokee Nation of Indians - lying between the Currahee Mountain and the headwaters of the Oconee River. *Original 1798 Settlers in the* **Nathan Smith** *settlement who were left outside of* **Colonel Hawkins** *line*: **Nathan Smith**, **James Minyard**, **Michael Oliver** [removed by 1804] **Stephen Smith** [removed by 1804] **Nicholas Smith** [removed by 1804], **Owen Carpenter**, **Jack Parker** [removed by 1804], **Thomas Warren**,

Joseph Halcom [removed by 1804], Charles Warren [removed by 1804], William Thornton [removed by 1804], Johnson McKinney [removed by 1804] and Lewis Dickenson. *New Settlers by 1804 in Nathan Smith Settlement*: Isham Smith, John Smith, Adam Sheffield, James Keys, Joseph Shelton, Samuel Spencer, William Spencer, Richard Jacks, John Huitt, Jacob Hollingsworth, Moses Alred, James Brown, Temple Carpenter, John Warren, James Hamilton, Nimrod House, James Alred, Thomas Bullen, William Newton, Snow, Asa Walker, Morgan Guest, William Smith, Averitt Smith, George Morgan and Reuben Warren. [*Editor's Note: Numerous Moore County families joined Nathan Smith and family in migrating to GA. Many continued to MS from there.*]

2748.	1804, Jan 23 -- Land Grant #2024, Moore County, NC
Jesse Muse received 100 acres located northwest of McLendons Creek on both sides of the Waggon Road adjoining **James Muse**, **Thomas Muse** and his own line. **James Muse** and **Thos. Muse** were chain carriers.

2749.	1804, Jan 31 -- Land Grant #1823, Moore County, NC
Neill McLeod received 50 acres located northwest of McLendons Creek adjoining **Edwards**, **Muse** and his own line. **James Muse** and **Jesse Muse** were chain carriers.

2750.	1804, Feb 3-- Land Grant #1890, Moore County, NC
Donald McDonald received 100 acres located on the head of Wet Creek adjoining **Dunn** and **Allan Bethune**. **Donald McDonald** and **Allan Martin** were chain carriers.

A.	1804, Feb 5 -- Land Grant #2337, Randolph County, NC
Darius Mash received 108 acres located on Fork Creek and Moore County line adjoining **Asbil** and his own line. **Charles Latham** and **Christopher Asbel** were chain carriers.

2751.	1804, Feb 29 -- Deed Book 4, Page 546, Moore County, NC
Neill McLeod deeded **Donald McDonald** 50 acres located west of McLendons Creek adjoining **Cox**, **Malcolm McLeod** and **Kenneth McDonald**. **George Hunsucker** was a witness.

2752.	1804, Mar 7 -- Land Grant #1726, Moore County, NC
Elijah Bettis Sr. [assignee of **Robert Cobb Sr.** and **Jr.**] received 230 acres located southeast of McLendons Creek adjoining **Nicholas Smith**, **John Overton** and **John Dunlap**. **Richard Ragsdale** and **Thomas Dickinson** were chain carriers.

A.	1804, Mar 7 -- Land Grant #1838, Chatham County, NC
William Green received 95.5 acres located on Tysons Creek adjoining **Wilson**, **McManus**, **Joel Phillips** and his own line. **Nimrod Phillips** and **Thos. Green** were chain carriers.

B.	1804, Mar 9 -- Deed Book 3 Page 343, Montgomery County, NC
William Dunn and **Richd. Cheek** (of Moore County) deeded **Kennith Clark** 100 acres located on Drowning Creek and the Moore County line. **Dugald McMillen** and **Norman McLeod** were witnesses.

2753.	1804, Apr 7 -- Land Grant #1953, Moore County, NC
Levi Deaton received 50 acres located east of Wet Creek adjoining **Thomas Key**, **Neil McLeod** and **Donald McLeod**. **John Key** and **Levi Deaton** were chain carriers.

2754.	1804, Apr 7 -- Land Grant #1954, Moore County, NC
Levi Deaton received 50 acres located east of Wet Creek adjoining **William Key**, **Neil McLeod**, **Groves**. **William Key** and **David Richardson** were chain carriers.

2755.	1804, Apr 18 -- Will Book A, Page 272-273, Moore County, NC
Will of **Christian Jackson**, Dec.d. Heirs: son **George Jackson** [*plantation where I now live*], eldest daughter **Mary Kachey** [*negro woman Nagin and her daughter Amie*], daughter **Martha Kachey**, grandchildren **John Dunn**,

Samuel Dunn, Jesse Overton, Samuel Overton, Martha Overton, Casey Overton, Samuel Jackson, William Jackson, Mary Jackson alias Mary McIntosh, Joseph Jackson, Christian Jackson alias Christian Lewis, Margaret Jackson, Mary Jackson and Beady Jackson (daughter of George Jackson). Executor: son George Jackson. Witnesses: Wm. Martin and Alexander MacLeod. Proven Aug 1812.

2756. 1804, Apr 18 -- Deed Book RR Page 38, Franklin County, GA
Lewis Dickerson deeded Isham Smith 200 acres located on Hudson Fork of Broad River. Originally granted to Joseph Martin Russell then deeded to Thomas Warren and then John Parker and then Dickerson. John Douglas and Caleb Griffith were witnesses. Recorded Jun 7, 1808.

2757. 1804, Apr 23 -- Land Grant #1900, Moore County, NC
Francis Bullock received 65 acres located south of Grassy Creek adjoining William Williamson Senr, Yow and Alston. Mathew Deaton and Wm. Williamson were chain carriers.

2758. 1804, May 5 -- Notice, the Minerva [Raleigh, NC] Newspaper
"Administrator's Notice - the Subscriber, having qualified as Administrator of the Estate of James Caddell, Dec'd. at last August Court, gives notice to all persons having any Demands against said Estate to bring them forward, well authenticated, within the time limited by Law, otherwise, they will be barred from Recovery and those indebted to the said Estate will please to make immediate Payment. Daniel Caddell, Moore County, NC"

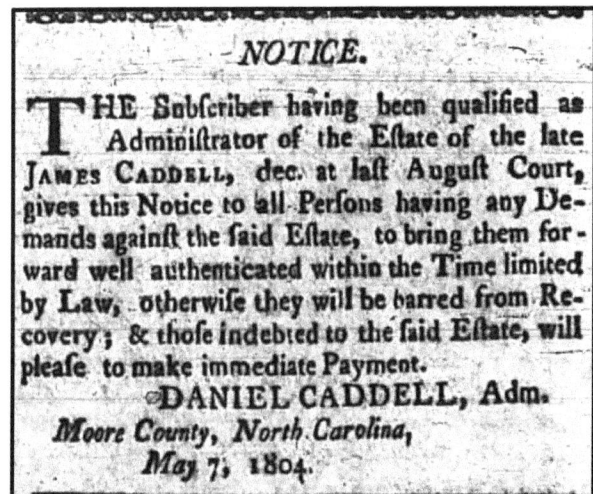

2759. 1804/1805 -- Will Book A, Page 319, Moore County, NC
Inventory of the estate of Jams. Cadwell, Dec'd. *Notes and bonds on the following*: Benjn. Davis, Michael Hunsucker, John Jinkens, James Muse Sr., George Fagon, Harday Howell, Patty Glascock, Daniel Wilson, Jack Wilson, Kenneth Stewart, John Ryans, Milton Glascock and Danl. Caddell. [*Editor's Note: Undated but based on the above notice 1804/1805 is a close approximation*]

> **NOTICE.**
>
> THE Subscriber having been qualified as Administrator of the Estate of the late James Caddell, dec. at last August Court, gives this Notice to all Persons having any Demands against the said Estate, to bring them forward well authenticated within the Time limited by Law, otherwise they will be barred from Recovery; & those indebted to the said Estate, will please to make immediate Payment.
>
> DANIEL CADDELL, Adm.
>
> *Moore County, North Carolina,*
> *May 7, 1804.*

2760. 1804, Mar 20 -- Will Book A Page 233-234, Moore County, NC
Will of Elisha Bettis, Dec'd. Heirs: Ransom Bettis [*negroes Isaac, Nich, Sal, Rachel, Fereby, Starling and Fany*], Obey Bettis, Elijah Bettis Junr., Saly Bettis and Lovy Bettis; also George Jackson, Ezekial Rubottom. Executors: Elijah Bettis Junr. and Elisha Bettis Senr.. Witnesses: John Tyson and Marchel Jones. Probated May 1804.

2761. 1804, Jun 1 -- Land Grant #1901, Moore County, NC
Francis Bullock received 100 acres located on Calf Branch of Wolf Creek adjoining James Allan, Andrew Auman and Samuel Allan. Eli Collicott and Saml. Allen were chain carriers.

A. 1804, Jun 15 – Deed Book N Page 545-546, Chatham County, NC
Juditha Wilson deeded Thomas Wilson 50 acres located on Fall Creek formerly owned by Edward Beson and Joseph Lambert adjoining Sampson Brewer, near Juditha Wilson's old house, and Guthrie. Eli Lawler was a witness.

2762. 1804, Jul 6 -- Land Grant #1878, Moore County, NC
Neil McLeod received 80 acres located north of Cabin Creek adjoining Jeffreys, Allison, his own line and Betty Carpenter. Nier Brewer and Wm. Smith were chain carriers.

2763. 1804, Aug 1 -- Estate, Randolph County, NC
Estate of John Argo, Dec'd. by Administrators Allen Bullack and Izbel Argo. *Accounts/notes/judgements listed on*: Thomas Lankford, James Braidy, James Cocker (now in SC), Jacob Wright (now in SC), John Gilliam, William Argo, James Sanders (left state), John Vandiford, Greenberry Cook (left state) and Willis Elkins. *Administrators paid the following notes*: Moses Teague, Joseph Hicks, William Searsey, Vandaford, Isaac Teague, Bradley Garner, James W. Cokers, Thomas Avery, James Garner and George Moore. Ordered Wm.

Armistead, Matthew Waddill/Waddell and William Nedham Esq. be appointed to settle with Allan v. Admr. of John Argo Dec'd.

2764.　　1804, Aug 6 - Deed Book 127 Page 255, Moore County, NC
Jeremiah Williams deeded John Needham, Sr. 3 tracts (50, 50, 50 acres) located on Cabbin Creek and Dry Creek adjoining Levi Deaton. W. N. Needham and Mathew Deton were witnesses.

A.　　1804, Aug 11-May 8, 1807 -- Estate, Chatham County, NC
Estate of Willis Phillips, Dec'd. Benjamin Sanders and Phebe Phillips were named administrators with William Phillips and A. McBryde as securities. Richd. Jones, John Sanders, Sihon Phillips and Sampson Brewer allotted widow's support to Phebe Phillips. Petition for division of 240 acres adjoining Shearing's line; 150 acres adjoining his own line; 50 acres located on Tysons Creek adjoining his own line and Sanders; 50 acres located on Tyson's Creek adjoining his own line and Record. Richd. Jones, Eli Lawler, Nathan McManus, Sugar Jones and Jno. Saunders divided among the following heirs: widow Phebe Phillips, John and Charity Deaton, Zadock and Rebecca Deaton, Matthew Phillips, Meredith Phillips, John Phillips, Labon Phillips [under 21], Benjamin Phillips [under 21], Fereby Phillips [under 21], Susanna/Sukey Phillips and Edmund Phillips [under 21]. *Items from the estate were purchased by:* George Moor, John Phillips, William Harper, William Wilson, James Deaton, Mary Mathews, Phebe Phillips, Tindsley Wade, Edward Epps, Sterling Carrol, Robert Moor, William Phillips, Daniel Brewer, Zadock Deaton, Jessee Mews, Robert Phillips, James Dunkin, Nathan McManus, John Deaton, Dennis Phillips, Lazarus Phillips, Jesse Carroll, Meredith Phillips, Sihon Phillips, Robert Wilson, Matthew Phillips, John Sanders, Joab Cheek, Joel Sanders, James Collins, Joel Lawhon, Henry Phillips, Benjamin Elkins, John Story, Robert Davis, Eli Lawler and Lewis Williamson.

2765.　　1804, Aug 26 -- Land Grant #1732, Moore County, NC
John Danielly received 100 acres located on McCallums Fork of Richland Creek adjoining Jesse Upton, Benjamin Dunn and Speculators. Jesse Upton and Jno. Upton were chain carriers.

A.　　1804, Aug 29 -- Deed Book 8 Page 437-438, Randolph County, NC
Isaac Hardin (of Greenville District, SC) deeded Benjamin Hardin 1/9 interest in 300 acres located on Barnes Creek and the Fayetteville Road. [*Editor's Note: heirs of Gabriel Hardin Dec'd.*]

B.　　1805, Oct 11 – Deed Book O Page 101, Chatham County, NC
Robert Wilson deeded Jno. Smith two tracts: [1] 100 acres located on Tysons Creek adjoining Willis Phillips [2] 50 acres located on Tysons Creek adjoining Willis Phillips, Record and Dennis Phillips. Ambrous Smith and Benjn. Shields were witnesses.

C.　　1804, Oct 16 -- Deed Book M Page 506-507, Chatham County, NC
Edward Beeson deeded Sampson Brewer 100 acres located on Fall Creek adjoining Guthry, Thomas Wilson, Sampson Brewer and Harper. Sam. Dunn and Edward Harper were chain carriers.

2766.   1804, Oct 22 -- Land Grant #1889, Moore County, NC
William Williamson Junr. received 100 acres located on the drains of Grassy Creek adjoining **Neil McLeod**, **Bullock**, his own line, **Nicolas Nall** and **William Williamson Senr. Donald Manners Senr.** and **Donald Manners Junr.** were chain carriers.

2767.   1804, Oct 22 -- Land Grant #1917, Moore County, NC
Murdock McAulay Junr. received 50 acres located on both sides of Dry Creek adjoining **Hector McLean**, **Neil McLeod**, **Butler**, **Paterson** and the Speculators. **John Paterson** and **John Morgan (Medford)** were chain carriers.

2768.   1804, Oct 30 -- Land Grant #1983, Moore County, NC
Samuel Jackson received 50 acres located North of Juniper Creek adjoining his own line, **Paterson**, **John Bethune** and **Christian Jackson. William Jackson** and **Samuel Jackson** were chain carriers.

A.   1804, Nov 14 -- Land Grant #046, Montgomery County, NC
Solomon Carpenter received 200 acres located on both sides of Cabin Creek adjoining his own line and **Robert Lax** near the crossroads. **Pleasant Gowins** and **Levy Gowins** were chain carriers. [*Editor's Note: never granted*]

2769.   1804, Nov 28 -- Land Grant #1981, Moore County, NC
Samuel Jackson received 150 acres located on the head of Suck Branches and north of Joel Road adjoining **David Sears** and his own line. **Wm. Jackson** and **Saml. Jackson** were chain carriers.

2770.   1804, Nov 28 -- Land Grant #1939, Moore County, NC
Cornelius Dowd received 100 acres located on McLendons Creek adjoining his own line and **Thomas Muse**.

2771.   1804, Nov 30 - Deed Book M Page 448, Pendleton County, SC
Burrel Deaton (of Moore County, NC) deeded **William Deaton** 105 acres located in Pendleton County, SC on the water of the Concross. **Elijah Deaton** and **Jeremi Williams** witnesses. Proven Dec 4, 1815.

A.   1804, Dec 6 -- Land Grant #1841, Chatham County, NC
John Wilkins received 640 acres located on Indian Creek and the [Moore] County line adjoining **Benjamin Tyson**, **Dowd**, **Gilbert** and own line. **Wm. Thompson** and **Wm. Kendrick** were chain carriers.

2772.   1804, Dec 11 -- Land Grant #2132, Randolph County, NC
Charles Stewart received 250 acres located on Fork Creek adjoining **Urias Mash**, **Nicholas Nall** and his own line. **William Armstead** and **John Morris** were chain carriers.

2773.   1804, Dec 28 -- Land Grant #1963, Moore County, NC
Jesse Muse received 100 acres located north of McLendons Creek on branch of Richland Creek adjoining his own line where **Jeremiah Dean** now lives. **Jesse Muse** and **Geo. Glascock** were chain carriers.

2774.   1805 -- Tax List, Franklin County, GA [selected residents]
Capt. Henry's District: **John Smith** [no acreage or location given]; **Stephen Smith** 265 acres on Hudson River; **Nichalus Nuton** [no acreage or location given]; **James Minyard** 100 acres on Hudson River; **Nicholas Smith**, agent for **Owen Carpenter**, 100 acres [no location] and 100 acres [no location]; **Isum Smith** 200 acres on Hudson River and Indian Boundary; **Nathan Smith**, agent for **Wm. Smith**, 300 acres on Hudson River and Indian Boundary and 53 acres on Hudson River and Indian Boundary.

2775.   1805-1808 [undated estimate] -- Estate, Moore County, NC Will Book A, Page 353 Inventory of the Estate of **Mary Sewell**, Dec'd. by Administrators **James Smith** and **Winefred**

Smith. [*Editor's Note: No date given on actual inventory, but the date was estimated using death date from other researchers*]

A.   1805, Jan 5 -- Deed Book O Page 371-372, Chatham County, NC
John Record (of Moore County) deeded **Bryan Boroughs** (of Moore County) two tracts: [1] 640 acres located on Tysons Creek [2] 100 acres located on Tysons Creek adjoining the prior tract and **Ramsey**. **Eli Lawler**, **Wm. Waddill** and **Wm. Aingell** were witnesses.

2776.   1805, Jan 13 -- Will, Randolph County, NC
Will of **George Onstot**, Dec'd. Heirs: **Hanner Deaton**, wife of **Eldridge Deaton**; **Sophia Deaton**, daughter of **Eldridge** and **Hanner Deaton**; son **John Onstot**. Executors: **William Carr** and **Rolley Spinks**. Witnesses: **John Dabney**, **William Smith** and **Arthur Reed**. Proven Feb 1805.

2777.   1805, Jan 22 -- Land Grant #1893, Moore County, NC
John Wadsworth Junr. received 200 acres located on Mill Swamp/Mill Creek adjoining **Jonathan Cadwel**, his own line, **Dickinson, John Wadsworth Senr.**, **Holcombe, MacIver** and **Jackson**. **John Wadsworth Senr.** and **John Whitford** were chain carriers.

2778.   1805, Jan 22 -- Land Grant #1979, Moore County, NC
John Wadsworth Junr. received 120 acres located on McLendons Creek and Mill Creek adjoining **Jonathan Cadwel**, **George Jackson** and his own line. **John Wadsworth Senr.** and **John Whitford** were chain carriers.

2779.   1805, Feb -- 1798-1808 Trial and Appearance Docket, Moore County, NC Page 10
1805, Feb -- 1785-1868 Index to Trial Docket, Moore County, NC Page 36
Charles Furr v. **Jsiah** and **John Lawhon**

A.　　　1805, Feb 3 -- Deed Book 2 Page 333, Montgomery County, NC

Robert Lax deeded **William Goin** three tracts located east of Cabin Creek: [1] 100 acres of a 200 acres tract granted to **John Fowler** and deeded to **Saml. Parson** and then to **Solomon Carpenter** including the improvement. The remaining 100 acres of the 200 acres tract located on the west side of Cabin Creek was previously deeded to **George Taylor** [2] 100 acres patented by **John Dunnaho** [3] 100 acres adjoining **Carpenter**. **J. Cochran** and **Henry Fraser** were witnesses.

2780.　　　1805, Feb 16-Mar 15 -- Will Book A Page 249-256, Moore County, NC

Will of **Aaron Tyson**, Dec'd. Heirs: wife **Lydia Tyson**, son **Aron Tyson**, son **Archibald Tyson** [under 21 years

old], son **William Tyson** [under 21], son **John Tyson**, son **Cornelius Tyson**, son **Jacob Tyson**, son **Benjamin Tyson**, daughter **Rachel**, daughter **Jane**, daughter **Lydia** and daughter **Rebecca**. _Land holdings to be divided_: 650 acres north of Deep River bought of **James Alston**; land south of Deep River in Chatham County and Moore County which were formerly the property of **James Alston, Conner Dowd, Charles Dowd, John Dowd, Owen Dowd, Work Smith** and **Richard Dowd**; plantation where I now live; lands conveyed by my father near the Mill; lands conveyed to my brother **Benjamin Tyson**; lands conveyed by **Patrick Dowd** and **Mary Dowd**; 213 acres conveyed by brother **Benjamin Tyson**; tract on Smith's Creek which I purchased at Sheriffs sale; tract on Smith's Creek conveyed by **Richard Dowd**; tract conveyed by brother **Thomas Tyson**; tract adjoining **Lewis Phillips Junr.** Executors: **Murdock McKenzie**, **Archibald McBryde**, brother **Thomas Tyson** and sons **William Tyson**, **John Tyson** and **Cornelius Tyson**. Witnesses: **Alexr. McKenzie**, **Daniel Sinclair**, **Daniel McNair** and **Saml. Womble**. Proven May 1805.

2781.　　　1805, Feb 25 -- Will, Moore County, NC

Will of **Elijah Bettis Senr.**, Dec'd. Heirs: son **Elijah Bettis Junr.** [7 negroes: **Shade, Alley, Grace, Sal, James, Liz, Cris** and 2 tracts of land], daughter **Eleanor Rheubottom** [4 negroes: **Jack, Violet, Bob, Peg** and 2 tracts of land], daughter **Jean Jackson** [*4 negroes: Harper, Jesse, Vincy, Jack and 2 tracts of land*], daughter **Sally Alston** [*5 negroes: Simon, Mingo, Nancy, Esther, Amey and a tract of land*], daughter **Lovely** [*6 negroes: Jincy, Lucy, Jonah, Charity, Ben and Phoebe (daughter of Charity)*], two youngest sons **Overton Bettis** and **Ransom Bettis**. Executor: wife **Amey Bettis** and three sons **Elijah**, **Overton** and **Ransom**. Witnesses: **A.M. McBryde**, **M. McKenzie**, **John Stinson** and **J.D. Logan**. [*Editor's Note: Copy of the original found on Ancestry.com but can not be found in any loose Wills or Will Books in Moore County*]

A. 1805, Mar 2 -- Land Grant #1852, Chatham County, NC
Sampson Brewer received 49 acres located on Fall Creek adjoining his own line and **Nancy Pendleton**. **Wm. Brewer** and **Jesse Brewer** were chain carriers.

2782. 1805, Mar 20 -- Will Book A Page 242, Moore County, NC
Nuncupative Will of **Benjamin Shields**, Dec'd. Heirs: youngest son **Patrick Shields**, youngest daughter (not named), son **Archibald Shields**, son **Cornelius Shields** and mentions eight total children. Witnesses: **James Collins**, **James Harden** and **Milly Shields**. Proven May 1805.

2783. 1805, Mar 30 -- Land Grant #0107, Moore County, NC
Jesse Ritter Senr. received 60 acres located west of Richland Creek adjoining his own line, **Donald McQueen**, **Campbell** and **James Holcom**. **Daniel Muse** and **Jacob Stuts** were chain carriers. [*Editor's Note: Never granted*]

2784. 1805, Apr 25 -- Land Grant #1950, Moore County, NC
Neil McLeod received 10 acres located south of Deep River adjoining **Abraham Hunsacur**, his own line and **John Smith**. **Bradley Garner** and **Christopher Yow** were chain carriers.

2785. 1805, Apr 29 -- Land Grant #1907, Moore County, NC
Peter Shamburger Senr. received 300 acres located on the waters of Grassy Creek adjoining his own line and **Jeremiah Wilson**. **William Shamburger** and **Henry Shamburger** were chain carriers.

2786. 1805, Apr 30 -- Land Grant #1937, Moore County, NC

Jeremiah Wilson received 83 acres located on the drains of between Grassy Creek and Reedy Creek adjoining his own line, **Robert Bird**, **Peter Shamburger**, **Neil McLeod** and **John Shamburger**. **Robert Bird Senr.** and **Robert Bird Junr.** were chain carriers.

2787.   1805, Apr 30 -- Land Grant #2022, Moore County, NC
William Bird received 50 acres located on the drains of Reedy Creek adjoining **Peter Shamburger**, **Robert Bird**, **McLeod** and his own line. **Robert Bird Senr.** and **Robert Bird Junr.** were chain carriers.

2788.   1805, May 3 -- Criminal Actions, Randolph County, NC Box 6
Bill of complaint by **William Smith** charging **Lewis Bradey** with assault against him while executing his duty as an officer on Apr 6, 1805. **Nancy Needham**, **Lenhard Stutts** and **Hardey Davis** were witnesses. **Isaac Brady** was surety for **Lewis Bradey**.

2789.   1805, May 20 -- Deed Book O Page 229-231, Chatham County, NC
Fanny Cheek and **Andrew White**, administrators of **Phillip Cheek**, Dec'd. deeded **James Cheek** (of Moore County) 1/8 share of 421 acres located on Tysons Creek of Deep River. The heirs of **Robert Cheek**, Dec'd. (**Phillip Cheek**, **Richard Cheek**, **James Cheek**, **Olive Cheek**, **Andrew White**, **Adam White** and **Nancy**) agreed to sell the land to the highest bidder and that person was **James Cheek**. **James Collins** and **Wm. Wilson** were witnesses.

2790.   1805, May 20 -- Deed Book O Page 342-344, Chatham County, NC
Richard Cheek, **Olive Cheek**, **Robert Davis** and wife **Nancy**, **Andrew White** and wife **Mary** and **Adam White** and wife **Sarah** deeded **James Cheek** (of Moore County) 150 5/8 acres [being 5/8 of 421 acres] located on Tysons Creek of Deep River. **Jas. Collins**, **Jas. Shields** and **William Cheek** were witnesses.

2791.   1805, Jun 20 -- Land Grant #1960, Moore County, NC
Jesse Sowel received 50 acres located on the drains of Suck Creek adjoining his own line and **William Barrett**. **John Sowel** and **Thomas Ritter** were chain carriers.

2792.   1805, Jul 17 -- Will Book A Page 258, Moore County, NC
Will of **Mary Lakey**, Dec'd. Heirs: daughter **Elizabeth Lake[y]**, **Nancy Lake[y]**, **Viney Overton**, **Mary Kennady**, **Lucy Stuts**, **James Lakey** and **William Lakey**. Executors: Son-in-laws **David Overton** and **Henry Stuts**. Witnesses: **David Kennady** and **Jacob Smith**. Proven Aug 1805.

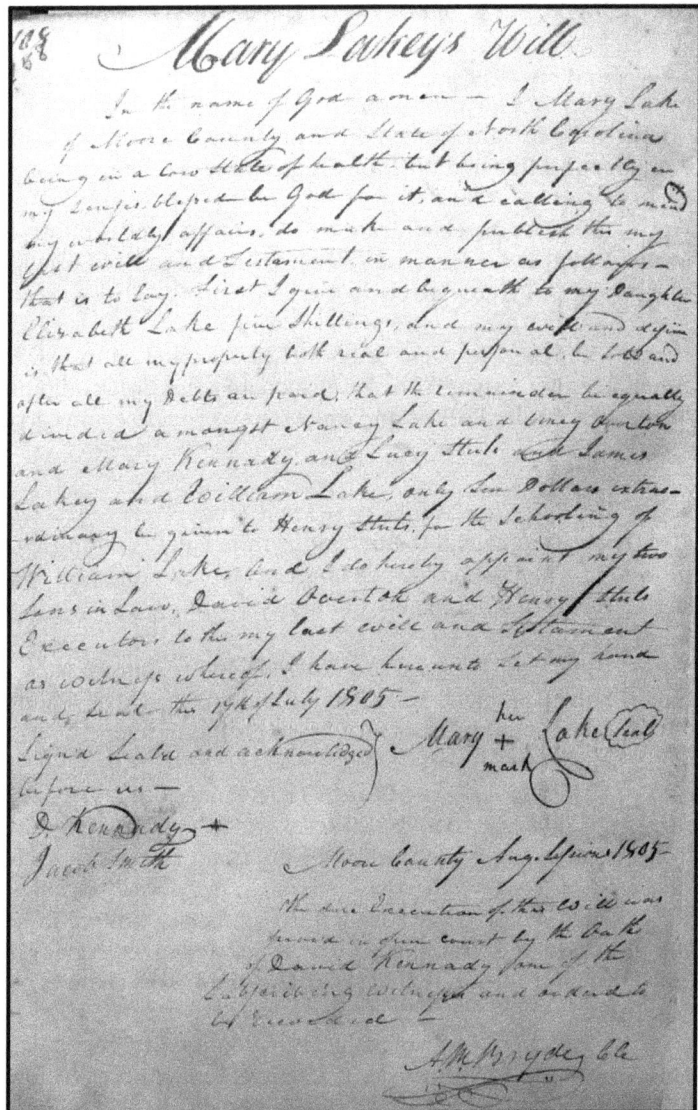

2793.   1805, Aug [undated estimate] -- Estate, Moore County, NC Will Book A, Page 356
Inventory of the Estate of **Mary Lakey**, Dec'd. [*Editor's Note: No date given on actual inventory, but the date was estimated using her will probate date.*]

2794.   1805, Aug -- Will Book A Page 259, Moore County, NC
Will of **William Richardson**, Dec'd. Heirs: wife **Margaret**, sons **John**, **Drury**, **William**, **Enoch** and **Noah**. Proven Aug 1805 by **Joseph McGee** and **B. Boroughs**.

A.   1805, Sep 9 -- Will, Chatham County, NC
Noncoperative Will of **Jeremiah Phillips Senr**. Dec'd. Heirs; daughter **Elizabeth Phillips** (and her children **Elmore** and **Alexander**), daughter **Sarah Phillips** and **Nimrod Phillips**. **Nimrod Phillips** and **Lazarus Phillips** reduced the will to writing and attested that he died Sep 9, 1805. Probated Nov 1805 on oath of **Amy Brady** and **Lazarus Phillips**.

B.   1805, Sep 18 -- Land Grant #1864, Chatham County, NC
William Wilkins received 70 acres located on Deep River and the [Moore] County line adjoining **John Wilkins** and **Gilbert**. **John Graham** and **Claborn Malden** were chain carriers.

C.   1805, Sep 18 -- Deed Book R Page 106-107, Pasquotank County, NC
Devotion Davis (of Moore County) deeded **Neil McLeod** Esq. (of Moore County) two tracts: [1] 96 acres located south of Halls Creek adjoining **Thomas Davis** and **Reuben Overman**. [2] 16 acres adjoining **Thos. Davis**, heirs of **David Davis**, Dec'd. and **Devotion Davis**. **Allen McLean** and **Edmund Davis** were witnesses. Proven Mar 1807.

2795.   1805, Oct 1 -- Land Grant #1916, Moore County, NC
William Morgan Senr. received 100 acres located south of Cabin Creek adjoining **William Lewis** and **Joseph Allan**. **Joseph Allen** and **William Singleton** were chain carriers.

A.   1805, Oct 7 -- Land Grant #1707, Montgomery County, NC
Edward Duval Tyler received 139 acres located east of Little River adjoining his own line. **William Dunning** and **Edward D. Tyler** were chain carriers.

2796.   1805, Oct 15 -- Land Grant #0129, Lincoln County, NC
Leonard Cagle received 32 acres located on Lyles Creek adjoining **Robert Philips**, **Hundsucker** and **Whittinberg**. **Robt. Philips** and **Jno. Isahower** were chain carriers. Entered Jul 2, 1805. [*Editor's Note: Never granted*]

2797.   1805, Oct 26 -- *A History of Sandy Creek Baptist Association* by George Purefoy, Page 48
Elders **Isaac Teague** and **B. Burroughs** from Fall Creek Church (Chatham County) and **Jesse Muse** and **Mark Phillips** from McLennon's Creek Church (Moore County) were delegates to the Association meeting at Chambers Meeting House in Montgomery County, NC.

2798.   1805, Oct 31 -- Land Grant #1904, Moore County, NC
Charles Sowell received 100 acres located on Flag Creek adjoining **Mary Hines** and his own line. **Thomas Williams** and **Leonard Furr Junr**. were chain carriers.

2799.   1805, Nov 1 -- Land Grant #1897, Moore County, NC
John Shuffield Senr. received 50 acres located south of Bear Creek adjoining his own line and **Nall**. **John Shuffield Junr**. and **Isaac Shuffield** were chain carriers.

2800.   1805, Nov 1 -- Land Grant #1913, Moore County, NC
John Shuffield Senr. received 100 acres located on both sides of Wolf Creek adjoining his own line and **John Hair**. **John Shuffield Junr**. and **Isaac Shuffield** were chain carriers.

A.   1805, Nov 14 -- Estate, Chatham County, NC
Estate of **Jeremiah Phillips** Dec'd. **Lazarus Phillips** named administrator with **Joab Bagley** and **Lazarus Hinson** as securities.

2801.   1805, Nov 28 -- Land Grant #1949, Moore County, NC
Neill McLeod received 100 acres located north of Deep River on Tyson Creek adjoining **Collins**, his own line and **Robert Cheek**. **James Collins** and **Richard Cheek** were chain carriers.

2802.   1805, Dec 24 -- Land Grant #1959, Moore County, NC
Thomas Ritter received 8 acres located west of McLendons Creek adjoining his own line, **John Sowell** and **McKay**. **Thos. Ritter** and **Patk. MacEachern** were chain carriers.

2803. 1806, Jan 27 -- 1796-1841 County Accounts, Moore County, NC Page 38
Charles Furr appears on a list of uncollected county debts.

2804. 1806, Feb 7 -- Land Grant #2005, Moore County, NC
Joseph Morgan received 15 acres located on Fork of between Mill Creek and Cabin Creek adjoining **Richardson**, his own line. **Nathan Morgan** and **James Morgan** were chain carriers.

2805. 1806, Feb 8 -- Land Grant #2058, Moore County, NC
Nathan Morgan received 4 acres located east of Cabin Creek adjoining his own line. **Ansel Melton** and **James Morgan** were chain carriers.

A. 1806, Feb 14 -- Deed Book O Page 105-106, Chatham County, NC
George Gee, Sheriff deeded **Murdock McKenzie** and **Archibald McBryde** of Aaron Tyson & Co. 175 acres located on the road from **Tyson**'s Ferry to **Graves'** saw mill adjoining **Dowd** (formerly **Barns**) to settle debts of **Lazarus Phillips**.

B. 1806, Feb 14 -- Deed Book W Page 317-319, Chatham County, NC
George Gee, Sheriff deeded **Murdock McKenzie** and **Archibald McBryde** of Aaron Tyson & Co. 1/9 part (33 acres) of **Jeremiah Phillips Senr.** Dec'd., 300 acres located on Indian Creek adjoining **Jonathan Barns, Ezekial Hillard** and **Griffin** to settle debts of **Lazarus Phillips**, son of **Jeremiah Phillips**.

C. 1806, Mar 18 -- Deed Book 51 Page 107-109, Moore County, NC
Neil McLeod deeded **John McLeod** 280 acres excluding 20 acres cut off by former surveys located northwest of McLendons Creek adjoining **Edwards**.

D. 1806, Mar 19 -- Deed Book P Page 208, Chatham County, NC
Sampson Brewer deeded **William Brewer** 59 acres located on Fall Creek adjoining his own line. **Wm. Brewer** paid **Elizabeth Hilyard** because **Sampson Brewer** had earlier sold this tract to his sister **Elizabeth Hilyard** and it was declared null and void. **Eli Lawler** and **Sugar Jones** were witnesses.

2806. 1806, Mar 21 -- Land Grant #1965, Moore County, NC
William Smith Junr. received 50 acres located on south prong of Cabin Creek adjoining **Joseph Allen, Thomas Graham** and **David Allison**. **George Brewer** and **John Morgan Medford** were chain carriers.

2807. 1806, Apr 3 -- Land Grant #1951, Moore County, NC
Ambrose Mainess received 100 acres located north of Bear Creek adjoining **Alexr. Kennedy** and **Benjamin Cooper**. **Alexr. Kennedy** and **Ambrose Mancss** were chain carriers.

2808. 1806, May -- 1798-1808 Trial and Appearance Docket, Moore County, NC
Jesse Ritter v. **Daniel Muse** (Levied on 50 acres -- sale ordered).

2809. 1806, Aug 27 -- Land Grant #1944, Moore County, NC
William Smith Junr. received 12 acres located on prong of Cabin Creek adjoining his own line and **David Allison**. **John Morgan Medford** and **George Brewer** were chain carriers.

2810. 1806, Aug 27 -- Land Grant #1945, Moore County, NC
William Smith Junr. received 150 acres located on both sides of Cabin Creek adjoining his own line (formerly **Allan Morrison**). **James Morgan** and **King Brewer** were chain carriers.

2811. 1806, Sep 1 -- Land Grant #2062, Moore County, NC
Cornelius Dowd and **Willis Dickison** received 200 acres located on Tysons Creek and the Chatham County line adjoining **Angus McQueen, William Phillips** and near the **Hollins** work place. **James Harden** and **Wm. Mathews** were chain carriers.

A. 1806, Sep 8 -- Deed Book O Page 313, Chatham County, NC
Sampson Brewer deeded **Robert Wilson** (of Moore County) 92 acres located on Fall Creek adjoining **Jones** (formerly **Culberts**), **Wilson** and **Beeson**. **Sugar Jones** and **Wm. Wilson** were witnesses.

B.   1806, Sep 15 -- Will, Chatham County, NC
Will of **James Deaton**, Dec'd. Heirs: wife **Obediance** [*170 acres*], children: **John Deaton** [*land he cleared on Hog Branch and the County line adjoining land John bought of Edward Beeson*], **William Deaton, Jackson Deaton** [*3 acres where Jackson lives and 70 acres in Randolph County*], **Mary Murry, James, Mathew, Thomas, Claborn, Zadock**; son-in-law **Robert Harden** and grandson **John Harden**. Executors: sons **John Deaton, Jackson Deaton** and **William Deaton**. Witnesses: **E. Lawler** and **John Vanderford**.

2812.   1806, Sep 16 -- Land Grant #1929, Moore County, NC
John Bethune received 50 acres located east of McLendons Creek adjoining his own line and **William Barrett**. **Donald Bethune** and **Thomas Hannon** were chain carriers.

2813.   1806, Oct 3 -- Deed Book Page 27-28, Franklin County, GA
James Blair deeded **Christopher Kelly** 155 acres located on Waters Creek waters of Tugalo River. Originally granted to **Samuel Ward**. **Wm. Smith, James Sparks** and **Benja. Cleveland** were witnesses.

2814.   1806, Oct 6 -- Land Grant #1969, Moore County, NC
John Matthews received 37.5 acres located east of McLendons Creek adjoining **Philemon Hodges** and **James Muse**. **Robert Dickinson** and **Michial Dickenson** were chain carriers.

2815.   1806, Oct 7 -- Land Grant #1978, Moore County, NC
Richard Cheek received 400 acres located on drains of Persimmon Glade adjoining **Shearing, Carrel, Andrew White** and **Samuel Murley**. **William Cheek** and **James Collins** were chain carriers.

A.   1806, Nov 1 -- Deed Book 51 Page 46-47, Moore County, NC
Moses Edwards (of Cumberland County) deeded **Asa Sowell** 250 acres located on both sides of McLendons Creek adjoining **Thomas McLendon** and **James Muse**. **Jason Muse** was a witness.

B.   1806, Nov 10 -- Deed Book M Page 604-605, Chatham County, NC
Aaron Shearing (of Halifax County, VA) deeded **John Record** (of TN) his claim to 640 acres located on Tysons Creek and known as the **Hollingsworth** land adjoining the heirs of **John Ramsey**, Dec'd. **A.McBryde, Thos. Waddill** and **Micajah McGee** were witnesses.

C.   1806, Nov 11 -- Deed Book M Page 605-606, Chatham County, NC
Charles Sherron (of Warren County, NC) and **Joseph Sherron** (of Iredell County, NC) deeded **John Record** (of TN) his claim to 640 acres located on Tysons Creek and known as the **Hollingsworth** land adjoining the heirs of **John Ramsey**, Dec'd. **Thos. Waddill, Micajah McGee** and **B. Boroughs** were witnesses.

D.   1806, Nov 11-Feb 1822 -- Estate, Chatham County, NC
Estate of **Sampson Brewer** Dec'd. **Edward Harper** and **Eli Lawler** named administrators with **Micajah McGee** and **Abraham Lane** as securities. **Eli Lawler** appointed guardian in 1809 to **Solomon Brewer, Stephen Brewer, Mary Brewer, Hannah Brewer** and **Ann Brewer**.

2816.   1806, Dec 5 -- Revolutionary War Pension and Bounty, File NC4 Isaac Sowell
John Sowell petitioned the NC General Assembly for the land warrant for his deceased father **Isaac Sowell**. **Isaac Sowell** died in service in SC. **Neil McLeod** and **Thomas Graham** attested to **Sowell**'s service and that he died in SC. **John McLeod** of Montgomery County, NC and **Hector McNeill** of Moore County, NC testified that they served with **Sowell** and that he died and was buried at the hospital at Ashley Hill, SC.

2817.   1807/1808 -- Tax List [partial], Moore County, NC
List of persons who failed to report their taxable property in 1807 [selected residents]: **Wm. McAuley** (retailer); **Samel Dunn** 2 polls. 1808: **Wm. McAulay** 1 poll and 650 acres (retailer); **Adam Comer** 560 acres; **Ambrose Brewer** (stud horses); **Jonathan Caddell** 200 acres

A.   1807, Jan 6 – Deed Book 11 Page 118, Randolph County, NC
Stephen Elkins (of Moore County) deeded **Susannah Cheek, Jesse Cheek** and **Lydia Cheek** (heirs of **Phillip Cheek**) 50 acres adjoining his own line, **Hudson** and **Tucker**.

2818.   1807, Jan 25 -- Chronicles and Records of Bensalem Presbyterian Church Page 11, Moore County, NC
Daniel McDonald and **Christian** (no last name given) were married

2819. 1807, Jan 27 -- Land Grant #2000, Moore County, NC
Reuben Shields received 100 acres located on Mill Swamp and both sides of the Overton Road adjoining **Aulay McAulay**, **John Wadsworth**, **Kenneth McIver** and **Peter Munroe**. **John Wadsworth Senr.** and **John Wadsworth Junr.** were chain carriers.

2820. 1807, Feb 25 -- Deed Book 65 Page 115, Moore County, NC
William Smith deeded **George Cagle** 50 acres adjoining **Cagle**. **Smith** deeded all rights to the 50 acres to **Cagle** except the "graveyard where his father is buried." **John Smith** and **Jesse Brown** were witnesses.

2821. 1807, Jun 15 -- Land Grant #2149, Moore County, NC
Cornelius Dowd received 200 acres located in the fork between McLendons and Richland Creek and **Dunlap**'s Road adjoining **John McIver**, **McKay**, **Tomberlin** and **James Carroll** (formerly **Elijah Bettis**). **Wm. Martin** and **John McIver** were chain carriers.

2822. 1807, Jul [undated estimate] -- Estate, Moore County, NC Will Book A, Page 357-361
Inventory of the Estate of **Benjamin Tyson**, Dec'd. by Administrator **Edward Moore**. [*Editor's Note: No date given on actual inventory, but the date was estimated using known date of death 30 Jun 1807.*]

A. 1807, Jul 2 – Deed Book 11 Page 185, Randolph County, NC
Hardy Davis (of Moore County) deeded **Lewis Davis** 5 tracts [75, 300, 50, 50, 50 acres] located on Bear Creek.

2823. 1807, Aug 8 -- Land Grant #2033, Moore County, NC
Shadrach Rogers received 50 acres located east of Juniper Creek adjoining **John Martin**. **Joseph Rouse** and **Donald Shears** were chain carriers.

2824. 1807, Aug 16 -- Land Grant #2085, Moore County, NC
Neil McLeod received 40 acres located on Richland Creek adjoining **Rowan**, **McNeill**, his own line and **Thomas Ritter**. **Saml. Dunn** and **Asa Sowel** were chain carriers.

2825. 1807, Sep 30 -- Land Grant #1989, Moore County, NC
Neil McLeod received 250 acres located south of Persimmon Glade near Toms Creek adjoining **Charles Shearing**, his own line and **Cheek**. **James Hardin** and **Robert Hardin** were chain carriers.

2826. 1807, Sep 30 -- Land Grant #1990, Moore County, NC
Neil McLeod received 100 acres located on the head of Persimmon Glade adjoining **John Dunlap** and **Shearing**. **James Hardin** and **Robert Hardin** were chain carriers.

A. 1807, Oct 5 -- Marriage Bond, Randolph County, NC
William Gardner and **Susanna Leatham** received marriage bond. **James Leathem** was bondsman. **W. Needham** was witness. [*Editor's Note: Date of marriage occurred on or after date of marriage bond.*]

2827. 1807, Oct 24 -- *A History of Sandy Creek Baptist Association* by George Purefoy, Page 51
Elder **Isaac Teague** and **Archibald McNeill** from Fall Creek Church (Chatham County) and **Mark Phillips** from McLennon's Creek Church (Moore County) were delegates to the Association meeting at Unity Meeting House in Randolph County, NC.

2828. 1807, Nov -- Criminal Actions, Randolph County, NC Box 6
Presentment of **Lewis Davis** on a charge of assaultling **Susanna Davis**, Oct 20, 1807. **Peter Davis** was a witness.

A. 1807, Nov 16 -- Deed Book S Page 31-32, Chatham County, NC
William Brewer (of Moore County) deeded **Elizabeth Hilyard** 59 acres located on Fall Creek adjoining **Brewer**. **Eli Lawler** and **John Lawler** were witnesses.

2829. 1807, Dec 7 -- Land Grant #1982, Moore County, NC
Samuel Jackson received 100 acres located on Suck Branch of Juniper Creek adjoining **David Sears** and **Shadarack Roger**. **Wm. Jackson** and **David Sears** were chain carriers.

2830. 1807, Dec 17 -- Notice, *Weekly Raleigh Register* [Raleigh, NC] Newspaper

Will be sold at the courthouse in Moore County, on the 23rd of Feb next, so much of a tract of land supposed to contain 43 acres, as will be sufficient to pay the taxes due thereon, (and the expenses) for the year 1806; which land is supposed to be the property of **Amos Cheek**, lying on Tyson Creek, joining the [Chatham] County line and the lands of **Archibald McBryde** and others. **John McIver**, Shff.

To be sold at the courthouse in Chatham County, on the 20th of Feb next, so much of a tract of land supposed to be the property of **Amos Cheek** as will be sufficient to pay the taxes due thereon, (and the expenses) for the year 1806; which land lies on Tyson Creek, joining the [Moore] County line and the lands of **Archibald McBryde** and others. **Geo. Gee**, Shff.

A.   1807, Dec 17 -- Marriage Bond, Randolph County, NC
Rolly Spinks and **Nancy Leatham** received marriage bond. **Jonathan Larrance** was bondsman. **W. Needham** was witness. [*Editor's Note: Date of marriage occurred on or after date of marriage bond.*]

2831.   1808 -- Tax List, Franklin County, GA
Capt. Henry's District: **Isham Smith** 200 acres on Hudson River; **Nathan Smith** on Hudson River [no acreage]; **Adam Shefield** 202.5 acres (Wilkinson County)

A.   1808, Jan 8 – Deed Book P Page 173-175, Chatham County, NC
Moses Myrick deeded **Samuel Womble** (of Moore County) 3 tracts located on Indian Creek: [1] 240 acres located on mouth of Flaggy Branch and Tally Spring Branch adjoining **Joel Lawhon** being part of the 500 acres granted to **Joel Lawhon** and sold to **Moses Myrick** 1800 [2] 100 acres adjoining **Nathaniel Powell** originally granted to **Thomas Wilkerson** and deeded by **Robert Wilkerson** to **Moses Myrick** 1801 [3] 100 acres located on Watery Branch adjoining **John Younger** and **Joel Lawhon** originally granted to **John Younger** and deeded to **Moses Myrick** 1803. **M. McKenzie** and **William Tyson** were witnesses.

2832.   1808, Feb -- 1798-1808 Trial and Appearance Docket, Moore County, NC
Neil McLeod v. **Shadrack Manus**

2833.   1808, Feb-Feb 1810 -- 1798-1808 Trial and Appearance Docket, Moore County, NC
Robert Wilson v. **Charles Furr**

2834.   1808, Feb 4 -- Bastardy Bond, Randolph County, NC
Martin Cagle fathered a child with **Caty Boling**. **Samuel Graves** and **Wm. Cagle** were securities.

A.   1808, Feb 4 -- Land Grant #1881, Chatham County, NC
Malcolm McKinsey and **Archibald McBride** (surviving partners of **Aaron Tyson** & Co.) received 115 acres located on Line Creek and the [Moore] County line adjoining their own line, **John McIntosh**, **Jonathan Barns**, **Robert Moore**, **Lazarus Phillips** and **Cornelius Gilbert**. **Jonathan Barnes** and **Soneth Barnes** were chain carriers.

B.   1808, Feb 9 -- Deed Book X Page 329-330, Chatham County, NC
George Gee, Sheriff deeded **Murdock McKenzie** and **Archibald McBryde** of Aaron Tyson & Co. 1/9 part (33 acres) of **Jeremiah Phillips Senr**. Dec'd., 300 acres located on Indian Creek to settle debts of **Nimrod Phillips**, heir of **Jeremiah Phillips**.

C.   1808, Feb 16 -- Marriage Bond, Randolph County, NC
John Lawler and **Marey Argoe** received marriage bond. **Thos. Matthews** was bondsman. **J. Bain** was witness. [*Editor's Note: Date of marriage occurred on or after date of marriage bond.*]

2835.   1808, Mar 24 -- Land Grant #2070, Moore County, NC
John Sheffield Junr. received 150 acres located on the drains of Wolf Creek adjoining **Peter Hair** and his own line. **John Sheffield Senr**. and **Isaac Sheffield** were chain carriers.

2836.   1808, Apr 4 -- Land Grant #2147, Moore County, NC
Thomas Harvel received 50 acres located east of Cabin Creek adjoining **Nathan Morgan** and **Nathan Smith**. **Joseph Morgan** and **Nathan Morgan** were chain carriers.

2837.   1808, Apr 14 -- Land Grant #2057, Moore County, NC

Nathan Morgan received 50 acres located east of Cabin Creek adjoining **Harvel**, **John Morgan**, the **Spivey** Place and **William Smith Senr**. **Joseph Morgan** and **Thomas Harvel** were chain carriers.

2838. 1808, May 7 -- Land Grant #2136 and 2209, Moore County, NC
John Cagle received 100 acres located east of Flag Creek adjoining **Charles Sowell**, **Jacob Furr**, **Everet Wallace** and **William Jones**. **Everet Wallace** and **Jacob Furr/Wm. Jones** were chain carriers.

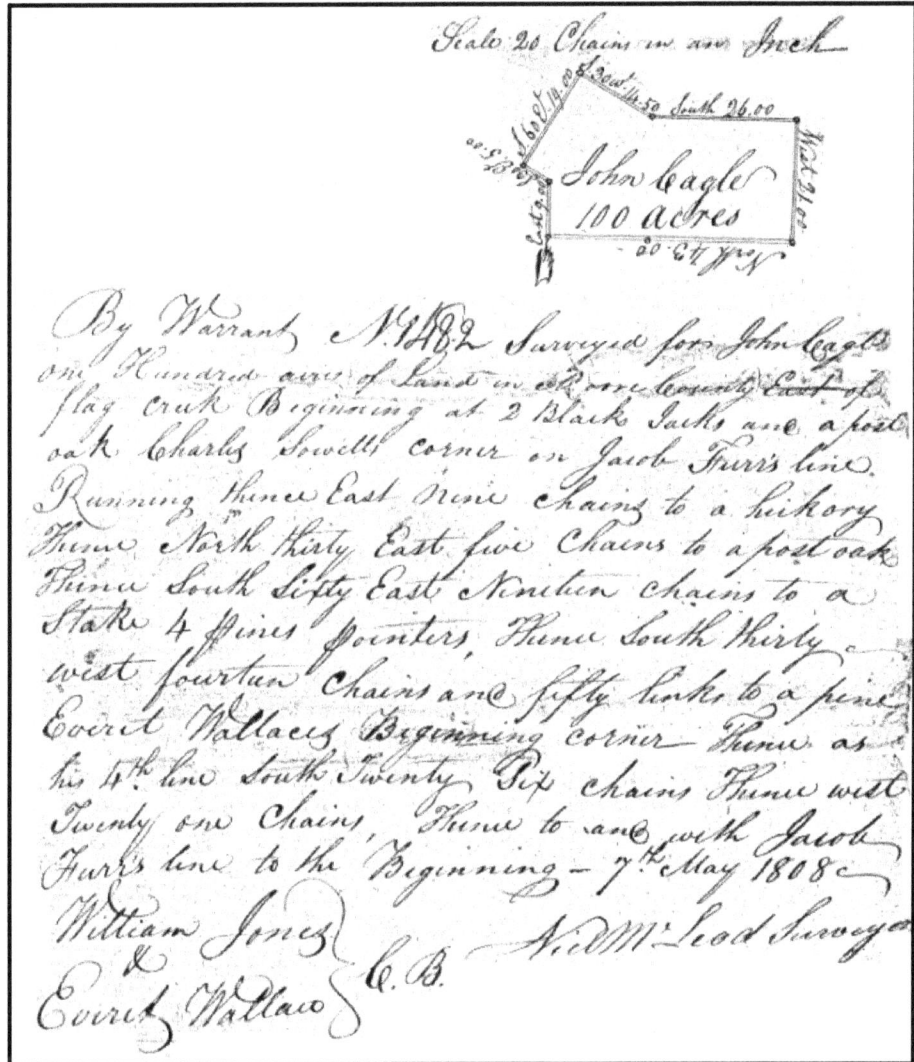

2839. 1808, May 21 -- Land Grant #2467, Moore County, NC
John Shamburger received 300 acres located north of Bear Creek adjoining **Isham Sheffield**, **McAulay**, **David Allison** and **John Sheffield**. **John Shamburger Junr.** and **Peter Shamburger** were chain carriers.

A. 1808, Jul 16 – Deed Book 13 Page 84-85, Randolph County, NC
Lewis Davis deeded **Hardy Davis Jr.** (of Moore County) a tract located on Meadow Branch adjoining **John Cannon**, his own line and **Smitherman**.

2840. 1808, Aug 10 -- Land Grant #2142, Moore County, NC
Donald McDonald received 50 acres located east of McLendons Creek adjoining **Allen Martin**, **Murdoch Martin** and **Robert Graham**. **Allen Martin** and **John McDonald** were chain carriers.

2841. 1808, Aug 22 -- Deed Book 12 Page 336, Randolph County, NC
William Smith deeded **William Pearce** 100 acres located on Rock Creek of Deep River adjoining **Searcy**. **Reuben Pearce** and **John Pearce** listed as witnesses.

2842. 1808, Sep 13 -- Land Grant #2031, Moore County, NC
Nicholas Nall received 100 acres located on the drains of Grassy Creek on Randolph County line adjoining his own line and **Bird**. **Westwood Armstead** and **Thomas Younger** were chain carriers.

2843. 1808, Sep 14 -- Land Grant #2056, Moore County, NC
William Shamburger received 100 acres located on the drains of Grassy Creek adjoining **Francis Bullock**, **Peter Shamburger Senr.** and **Nicholas Nall**. **Peter Shamburger** and **W. Shamburger** were chain carriers.

2844. 1808, Sep 14 -- Land Grant #2121, Moore County, NC
Heirs of **Mary Laky** received 19 acres located on Bear Creek adjoining **Ambrose Maner**, **Neil McLeod** and **Leonard Stutts**. **Jacob Smith** and **Jas. Laky** were chain carriers.

A. 1808, Sep 30 -- Deed Book P Page 346-347, Chatham County, NC

Abner Phillips deeded James Shields two tracts [1] 100 acres located on Fall Creek; [2] 108 acres located on Fall Creek adjoining Beeson, Brown, Parson, Wilson and the Moore County line. Jno. Saunders and James Harden were witnesses.

2845.   1808, Oct -- *A History of Sandy Creek Baptist Association* by George Purefoy, Page 52
Jesse Muse and Eli Phillips from McLennon's Creek Church (Moore County) and William Waddill and Eli Lawler from Fall Creek Church (Chatham County) were delegates to the Association meeting at Haw River Mountain Meeting House in Chatham County, NC.

2846.   1808, Oct 6-20 -- Notice, *The Raleigh Minerva* [Raleigh, NC] Newspaper
Chatham County Court of Pleas and Quarter Sessions Aug 1808. Archibald McBride v. Amoss Cheek. This petition is filed for a partition of a tract of land lying in Chatham County; and it is ordered by the court that as Amoss Cheek, who is entitled to a part of the tract of land, is an inhabitant of another state, publication shall be made for three weeks for the defendant Amoss Cheek to appear at the next court on the second Monday of November next and answer, demur, or plead to said petition, otherwise it will be taken pro confesso against him and hear Exparte. Thos. Ragland C.C.

A.   1808, Nov 5 -- Deed Book S Page 127-129, Chatham County, NC
Andrew White and wife Mary and Adam White and wife Sarah, and Robert Davis and wife Nancy (all of Moore County) deeded Archibald McBryde (of Moore County) their interest [being 3/6 of a 1/8 share of 241 acres] located on Tysons Creek and Moore County line being the interest that belonged to Amos Cheek, Dec'd. Jno. Ramsey and D. Murchison were witnesses.

B.   1808, Nov 11 -- Governor Benjamin Williams Papers, Nov 1808 Correspondence, Moore County, NC
Petition of Moore County residents on behalf of Charles Brady who was convicting of maiming and sentenced to a fine and sixty days imprisonment. The petitioners plead on behalf of Brady that the act was done in sudden affray and without any malice, the verdict was doubtful to many, Brady is very poor man with a family of small helpless children and a sickly hysterical wife and they are requesting a pardon. Signed by the following: John McIver, Richardson Fagin, Niell McLeod, Alexr. McLeod, A. McBryde, Wm. Martin, Murdo Bethune, Neill McLeod, John Sewell, John McNeill, John Martin, John Murchison, Ralph Davis, Donald McDonald, [illegible], James Melton, D. Murchison, Robt. McLauchlan, Murdoch McAulay, Geo. Jackson, Daniel Patterson, Allan Morison, Wm. Jackson, J.A. Cameron, Murdoch Martin, Corn. Dowd, Micajah Thomas, Jno. McSween, Archd. Shields, John Cameron, John Wadsworth, William Tyson, Samuel Jackson, Saml. Dunn, Daniel Buie, Edward Stuart, H. Gilmore Esq., and J. Gaster. [*see signatures on next page*]

C.   1809 -- NC General Assembly Session Law, Chapter 76
Mount Parnassus Academy was created in Moore County, NC and Bryan Boroughs, David Kennedy, William Waddle, Neil McLeod and Alexander Kennedy were appointed trustees.

D.   1809, Jan 19 -- Marriages, *Raleigh Register and NC Gazette* [Raleigh, NC] Newspaper
"In Moore County, on the 5th inst. [Jan 1809], Mr. Cornelius Tyson, of Chatham County, to Miss Ann Syler, of Moore"

2847.   1809, Feb-Feb 1810 -- 1798-1808 Trial and Appearance Docket, Moore County, NC
1810, Feb -- 1785-1868 Index to Trial Docket, Moore County, NC Page 27
Fanning Moore v. Charles Furr

2848.   1809 Feb-Feb 5, 1810 -- 1808-1819 Trial and Appearance Docket, Moore County, NC
Isaac Smith v. Wm. Brewor, Charles Brady and George Hundsucker. (Levied on George Hundsuckers land where he lives.)

A.   1809, Feb 9 -- Marriages, *Raleigh Register and NC Gazette* [Raleigh, NC] Newspaper
"In Moore County, on the 26th inst. [Jan 1809], Mr. W. Tyson, of Moore, to Miss Jane Branson"

2849.   1809, May -- Trial and Appearance Docket, Moore County, NC
Allen Morrison v. Benjn. Britt, Admstr.

2850.   1809, May-Aug 1809 -- Trial and Appearance Docket, Moore County, NC
Nicholas Nall v. Guardian of Heirs at Law of Ryals Britt

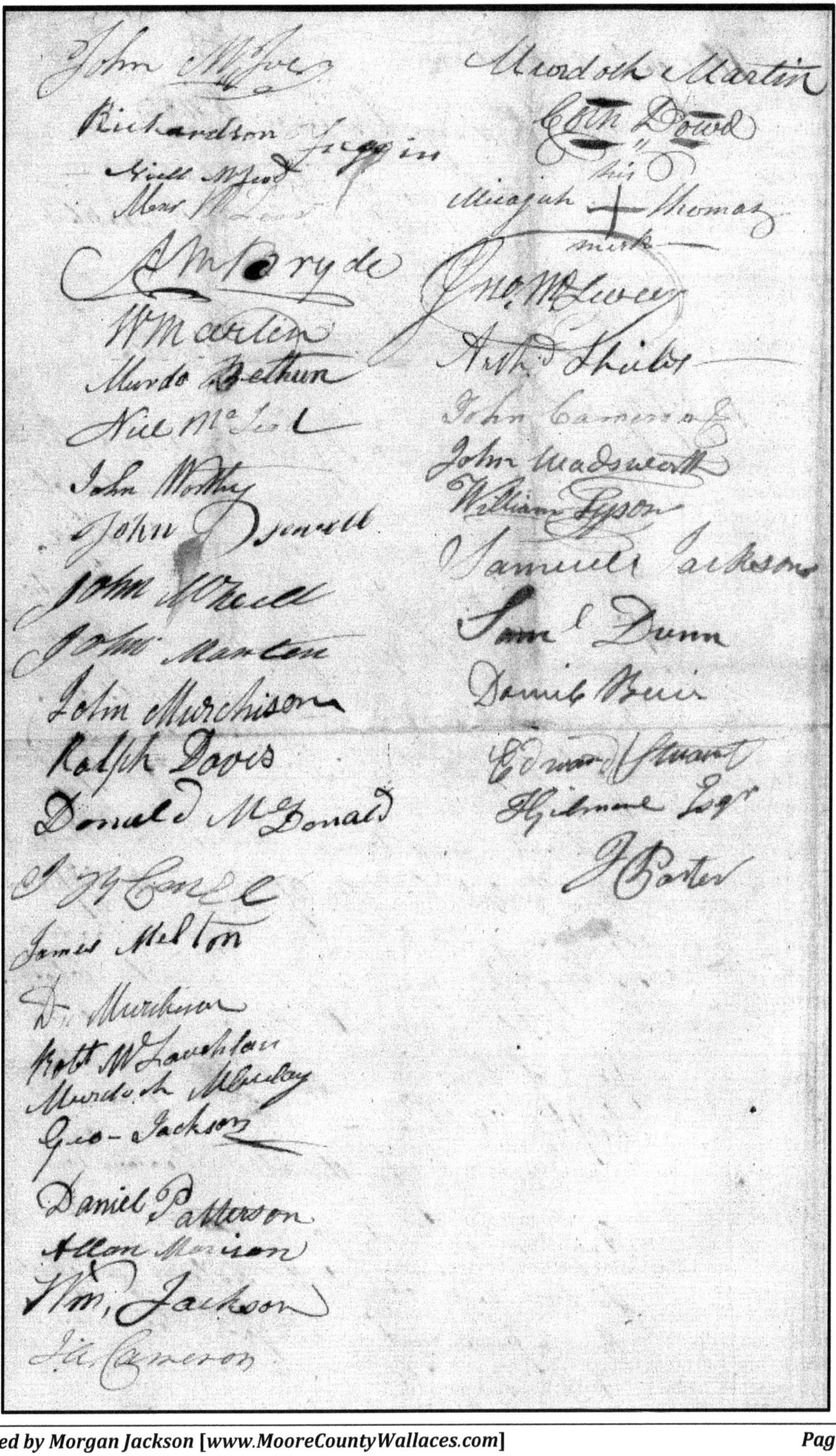

2851. 1809, May-Aug 1809 -- Trial and Appearance Docket, Moore County, NC
1809, Aug -- Index to Trial Docket, Moore County, NC
James Morgan v. Guardian of Heirs at Law of **Ryals Britt**

A. 1809, May 2 -- Marriage Bond, Randolph County, NC
Lewis Williamson and **Polly Cole** received marriage bond. **Michael Harvy** was bondsman. **Jesse Harper** was witness. [*Editor's Note: Date of marriage occurred on or after date of marriage bond.*]

2852. 1809, Jun 4 -- Will Book A Page 265, Moore County, NC
Will of **James Willey**, Dec'd. Heirs: daughter **Ann Rouse**, daughter **Milly Jones** and daughter **Betsay Bearfoot**. Witnesses: **Normon Matheson** and **Normon McLeod**. Proven Aug 1809.

2853. 1809, Jun 5 -- Land Grant #2109, Moore County, NC
Jebas York received 100 acres located on south of Deep River adjoining **Robert Davis**, **Cheek**, **Hancock** and **Andrew White**. **Adam White** and **Robert Davis** were chain carriers.

A. 1809, Jul 22 -- Deed Book 6 Page 199-201, Moore County, NC
Margaret Jackson and **William Lewis** deeded **Donald Paterson** 330 acres located between Juniper Creek and Little River adjoining **Margaret Jackson**. **Malcom McCrummen** and **John Paterson** were witnesses.

2854. 1809, Aug -- Trial and Appearance Docket, Moore County, NC
1809, Aug -- Index to Trial Docket, Moore County, NC
Allen Morrison v. Guardian of Heirs at Law of **Ryals Britt**

2855. 1809, Aug -- Trial and Appearance Docket, Moore County, NC
1809, Aug -- Index to Trial Docket, Moore County, NC
William Barrett v. Guardian of Heirs at Law of **Ryals Britt**

2856. 1809, Aug -- Trial and Appearance Docket, Moore County, NC
Rhoda Britt v. Guardian of Heirs at Law of **Ryals Britt** - Petition for Dower

2857. 1809, Sep 5 -- Land Grant #2114, Moore County, NC
Jesse Muse received 150 acres located northwest of McLendons Creek adjoining the land whereon **Thomas Muse** now lives, his own line, **James Muse** and **McIver**. **James Muse** and **Saml. Elkins** were chain carriers.

2858. 1809, Oct -- *A History of Sandy Creek Baptist Association* by George Purefoy, Page 56
Mark Phillips and **William Dowd** from McLennon's Creek Church (Moore County) and Elder **Isaac Teague** and **Allen Bullock** from Fall Creek Church (Chatham County) were delegates to the Association meeting at Abbott's Creek Meeting House in Rowan [now Davidson] County, NC.

A.   1809, Oct 18 -- Land Grant #1836, Montgomery County, NC
Semore Spencer received 100 acres located east of Little River adjoining his own line. **Jas. Munn** and **Thos. Jackson** were chain carriers.

B.   1809, Oct 18 -- Land Grant #1837, Montgomery County, NC
Semore Spencer received 50 acres located east of Little River adjoining **Elijah Spencer** and **Hannah Spencer**. **Jas. Munn** and **Thos. Jackson** were chain carriers.

C.   1809, Oct 18 -- Land Grant #1845, Montgomery County, NC
Semore Spencer received 50 acres located on northwest of Little River adjoining **William Spencer** and **Harbart Suggs**. **Jas. Munn** and **Thos. Jackson** were chain carriers.

D.   1809, Oct 19 -- Land Grant #1839, Montgomery County, NC
Harbard Suggs received 35 acres located on Suggs Creek adjoining his own line, **Elijah Spencer** and **Thomas Sugg** including his own line improvement. **Isham Wood** and **Elijah Spencer** were chain carriers.

2859.   1809, Nov 10 -- Land Grant #2150, Moore County, NC
James Fry received 40 acres located on Lick Branch adjoining **James Dowd**, **Adam White**, **Benjamin Cadwell** and **Jason Muse**. **Alexr. McLeod** and **James Muse** were chain carriers.

2860.   1809, Nov 24 -- Land Grant #2157, Moore County, NC
Michack Maner received 100 acres located north of Bear Creek adjoining **William Maner**, **Davison**, **Nall**, the Speculators and **Neil McLeod**. **Jacob Smith** and **William McLennon** were chain carriers.

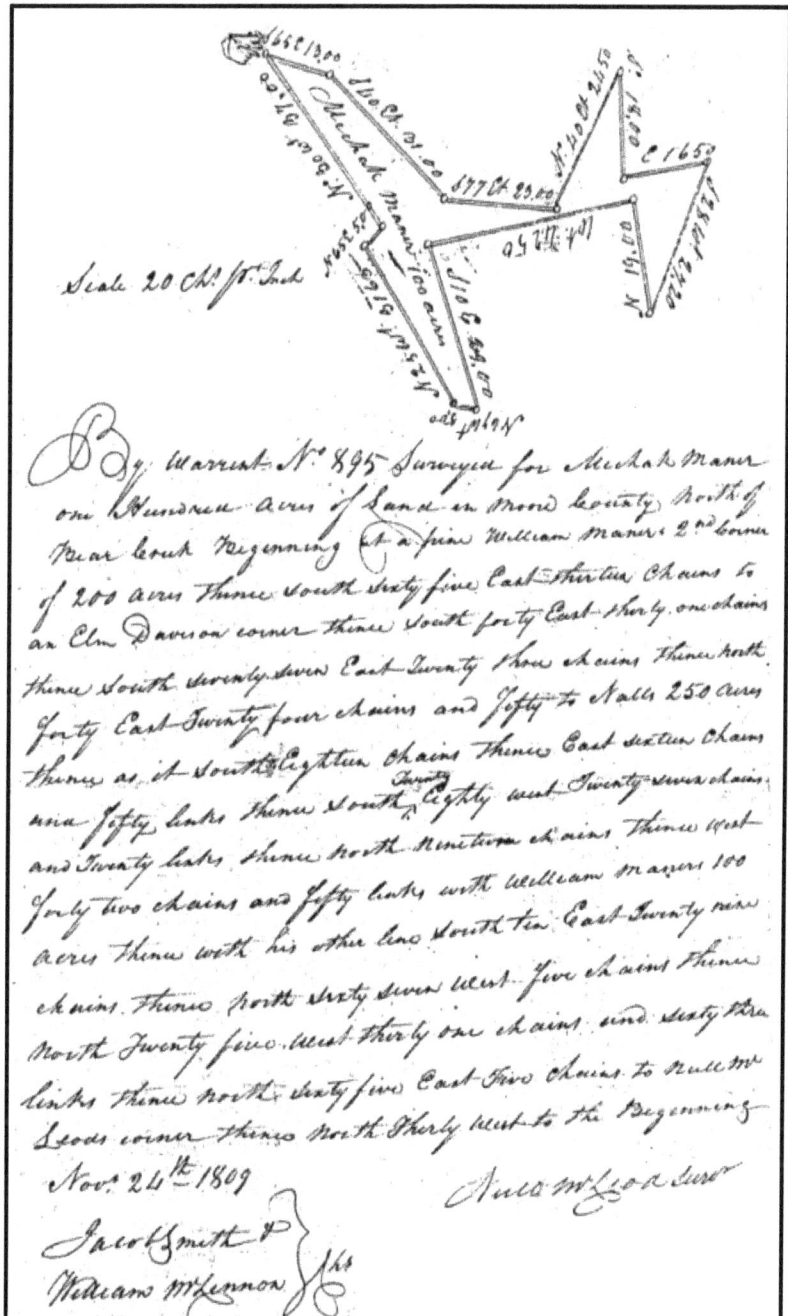

2861.   1810 -- Tax List, Franklin County, GA [selected residents]
Capt. Anderson's District: **Stephen Smith** 265 acres on Hudson River; **Isham Smith** 200 acres on Hudson River; **Nathan Smith** 300 acres on Hudson River, 100 acres on Indian Land and Hudson River, 150 acres on Hudson River; *Capt. Wofford's District*: **James Minard** 100 acres on Mountain Creek. List of Defaulters for 1810: *Capt. Anderson's District*: **John Carpenter**; **Henry Smith Sr.**; **William Smith Sr.**; **Isaac Smith**; **Andrew [Adam?] Sheffield**; **John Smith**; **Everett Smith**; **John Sheffield**; **Nicholas Smith**; **John Newton**; **Owen Carpenter**; **William Carpenter**; **Levy Smith**; **William Smith Jr.**; **Everett Sheffield** and **Nathan Carpenter**.

2862.   1810 -- Land Grant #2208, Moore County, NC
David Kennedy received 240 acres located on Persimmon Branch on both sides of the Wagon Road adjoining **Alexander Kennedy**, **Bradley Garner** and including **David Davidson**'s improvement. **Edward Kennedy** and **Alexr. Kennedy** were chain carriers.

2863. 1810-1820 [undated estimate] -- Estate, Moore County, NC Will Book A, Page 316
Inventory of the Estate of **Jesse Ritter**, Dec'd. by Administrators **Thomas Ritter** and **Jesse Sowell**. [*Editor's Note: No date given on actual inventory, but the date was estimated using the Estates that were listed before and after* **Jesse Ritter**.]

2864. 1810-1820 [undated estimate] -- Estate, Moore County, NC Will Book A, Page 324
Inventory of the Estate of **Cornelius Gilbert** Dec'd. by Administrators **Ebenezor Elliott** and **Benjn. Gilbert**. *Notes on the following:* **Willis McDuffie, James Beck, James Lawhon, Kenneth Murchison, Robert Moore** and **Edmond Wade**. [*Editor's Note: No date given on actual inventory, but the date was estimated using his appearance in the 1810 and absence in 1820.*]

2865. 1810-1820 [undated estimate] -- Estate, Moore County, NC Will Book A, Page 334
Inventory of the Estate of **Robt. Dickinson** Dec'd. by Administrator **Nancy Dickinson**. [*Editor's Note: No date given on actual inventory, but the date was estimated using his appearance in the 1810 and absence in 1820.*]

2866. 1810-1820 [undated estimate] -- Estate, Moore County, NC Will Book A, Page 362
Inventory of the Estate of **Bartholomew Dunn**, Dec'd. by Administrators **Lucretia/Creasy Dunn** and **John Dunn**. [*Editor's Note: No date given on actual inventory, but the date was estimated using the Estates that were listed before and after. Creasy Dunn was listed in the 1820 Census so it is possible that the date was between 1810-1820*]

2867. 1810, Jan 5 -- Land Grant #2507, Moore County, NC
Alexander McIntosh received 9 acres located on Locust Branch adjoining **Stephen Davis, Jesse Ritter, Donald McQueen** and **William Dunn**. **Lewis Lawhon** and **Isaac Smith** were chain carriers.

2868. 1810, Jan 11 -- Land Grant #2152, Moore County, NC
Thomas Graham received 100 acres located northwest of Juniper Creek adjoining his own line and **McNeill's** mill place. **Uriah Pope** and **James Smith** were chain carriers.

2869. 1810, Mar 29 -- Land Grant #2063, Moore County, NC
Shadrach Manes received 50 acres located southeast of Bear Creek adjoining **Neil McLeod**. **Abednego Manes** and **Howel Brewer** were chain carriers.

2870. 1810, Apr 12 -- Land Grant #2135, Moore County, NC
James Atkins received 300 acres located on Toms Creek adjoining **Harmon Brewer**, **James Dyer**, **Lamb** and **John McAulay**. **James Hardin** and **Robin Davis** were chain carriers.

2871. 1810, Apr 12 -- Deed, Moore County, NC
Jesse Ritter Senr. deeded 100 acres to his grandchildren [children of daughter **Susanna** and husband **Daniel Muse**] located between Richland and McLendons Creek being part of 200 acres adjoining **Jesse Sowell**, **Everiter Ritter**, **Donald McQueen**, **Wm. Barret**, **Farquard Campbell** and **McIver** (formerly **McLeod**). **Jesse Muse** and **Shadrach Manes** were witnesses. [*Editor's Note: Private deed in possession of **Frank Muse**, Carthage, NC*]

2872. 1810, Jun 10 -- Land Grant #2436, Moore County, NC
Adam White received 25 acres located on Killets Creek and Pond Branch adjoining his own line, the orphans of **William Harden** and **James Dowd**. **Eliazer Burket** and **John White** were chain carriers.

2873. 1810, Jul -- Deed Book HH Page 154-155, Franklin County, GA
Isom Smith deeded **Isaac Smith** 200 acres on Hudson Fork of Broad River adjoining **Hambelton** and originally granted to **Joseph Martin Russell** who conveyed to **John Parker** who conveyed to **Lewis Dickerson** who conveyed to **Smith**. **Starling Strange** and **Adam Shefield** were witnesses. Recorded Oct 10, 1817.

2874. 1810, Jul 26 --
Moore County, NC Will
Book A, Page 269
Will of **Benjamin Britt**,

Dec'd. Heirs: wife **Nancy**
(*plantation where I now live and the profits from the sale of the **Harvil** place*), children **Behuver** [**Belaver**], **Ispthu** [**Jeptha**], **Buldu**, **Edwin**, **Tinatee** [**Finity**] and **Handay**; **Rodah**, Widow of brother **Rial Britt** (*land containing*

Bent field); **Avington**, **Prulellah**, **Billasant** [**Bellison**], **Claramon** [**Cleryman**], **Becum** and **Tinsay**, orphan children of brother **Rial Britt** (*land north and west of Mill Creek that belonged to Rial*). Executor: **Joseph Allin**. Witnesses: **F. Bullock**, **Alexr. Morrison** and **Britin Britt**. Proven Aug 1810.

2875. 1810, Aug-1811 -- Moore County, NC Will Book A, Page 330
Estate of **Benjn. Britt**, Dec'd. by Administrator **Francis Bullock**. *Debts to the estate*: **George Hundsucker**, **Murdoch McAulay**, **D. Gillis**, **Richd. Hollin**, **John Kees**, **Sollomon Carpenter**, **Levy Deaton**, **Charles Sowell** and **William Kees**. [*Editor's Note: estate is undated; the belief is it took place during 1810 or 1811 given his death in Jul/Aug 1810.*]

2876. 1810, Aug -- Land Grant #2084, Moore County, NC
Neil McLeod received 80 acres located east of Bear Creek adjoining **Nicolas Nall**, **Davison** and **William Maness**.

2877. 1810, Aug 2 -- Land Grant #2115, Moore County, NC
Neil McLean received 30 acres located on Horse Creek adjoining **Duncan McLean**, his own line and **Daniel McLean**. **Neil McLean** and **Donald McLean** were chain carriers.

2878. 1810, Aug 12 -- Land Grant #2207, Moore County, NC
David Kennedy received 220 acres located north of Deep River and the [Randolph] County line adjoining **John Smith**, **Edward Moore**, **Fagin**, **Neil McLeod**, **Cavanaugh** and **James Deaton**. **Leonard Stuts** and **Benjamin Person** were chain carriers.

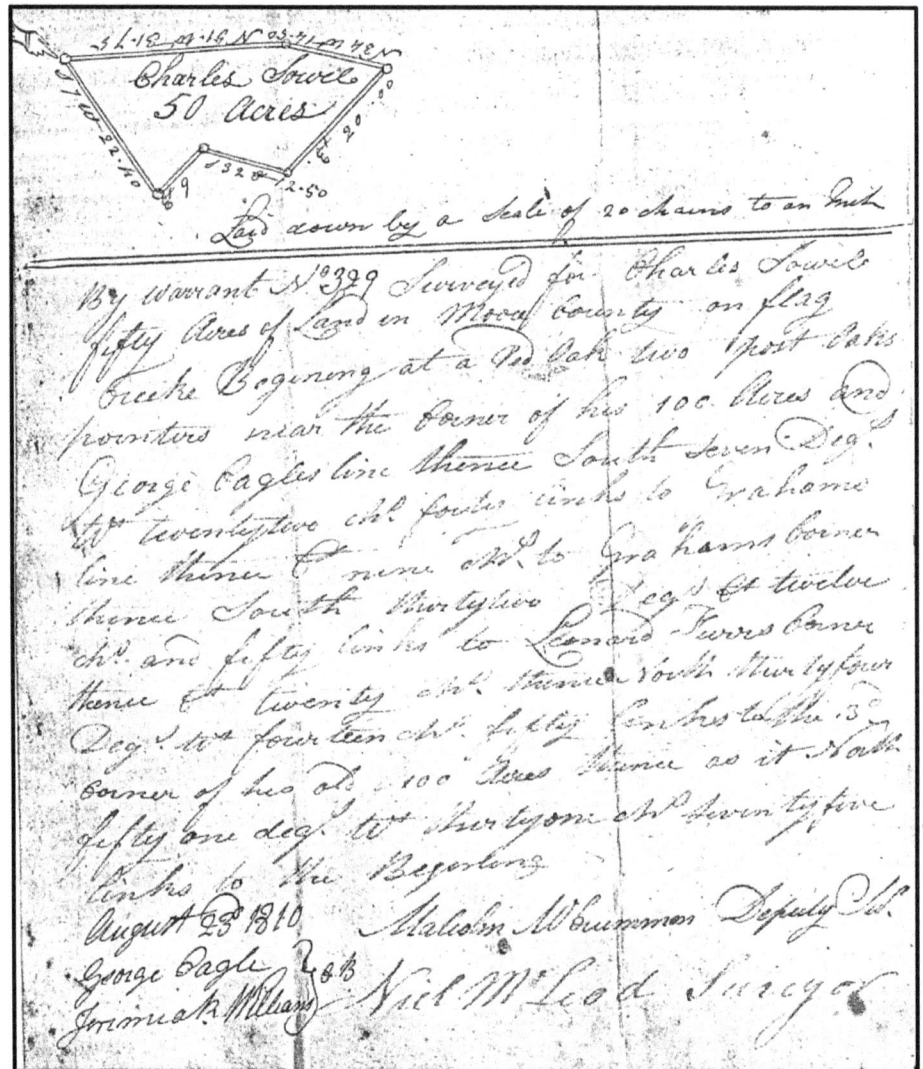

2879. 1810, Aug 18 -- Land Grant #2075, Moore County, NC
Alexander McIntosh received 50 acres located on McCollums Branch and Locust Branch on both sides of the Waggon Road adjoining **Jesse Ritter**, **Donald McQueen** and **Micajah Thomas**. **Neil McIntosh** and **John Rouse** were chain carriers.

2880. 1810, Aug 23 -- Land Grant #2034, Moore County, NC
Charles Sowell received 50 acres located on Flag Creek adjoining his own line, **George Cagle**, **Graham**, **Leonard Furr**, **Jacob Furr** and **Williams**. **George Cagle** and **Jeremiah Williams** were chain carriers. [*Editor's Note: **William Williams** deeded to **Leonard Furr** 1811 --> **George Davis** 1838*]

2881. 1810, Aug 24 -- Land Grant #2148, Moore County, NC
Normand Morison received 50 acres located on Wrights Branch east of Drowning Creek adjoining his own line. **Allan Morison** and **Angus Morison** were chain carriers.

2882. 1810, Aug 30 -- Land Grant #2032, Moore County, NC
William Barret received 300 acres located on both sides of Dry Creek adjoining **George Hunsucker, Meloney Newton, Jesse Brown, Neil Matheson, Malcolm Morrison, Chaney, John McKinnon, William Dunn** and **Cole.** **John Barret** and **Solomon Carpenter** were chain carriers.

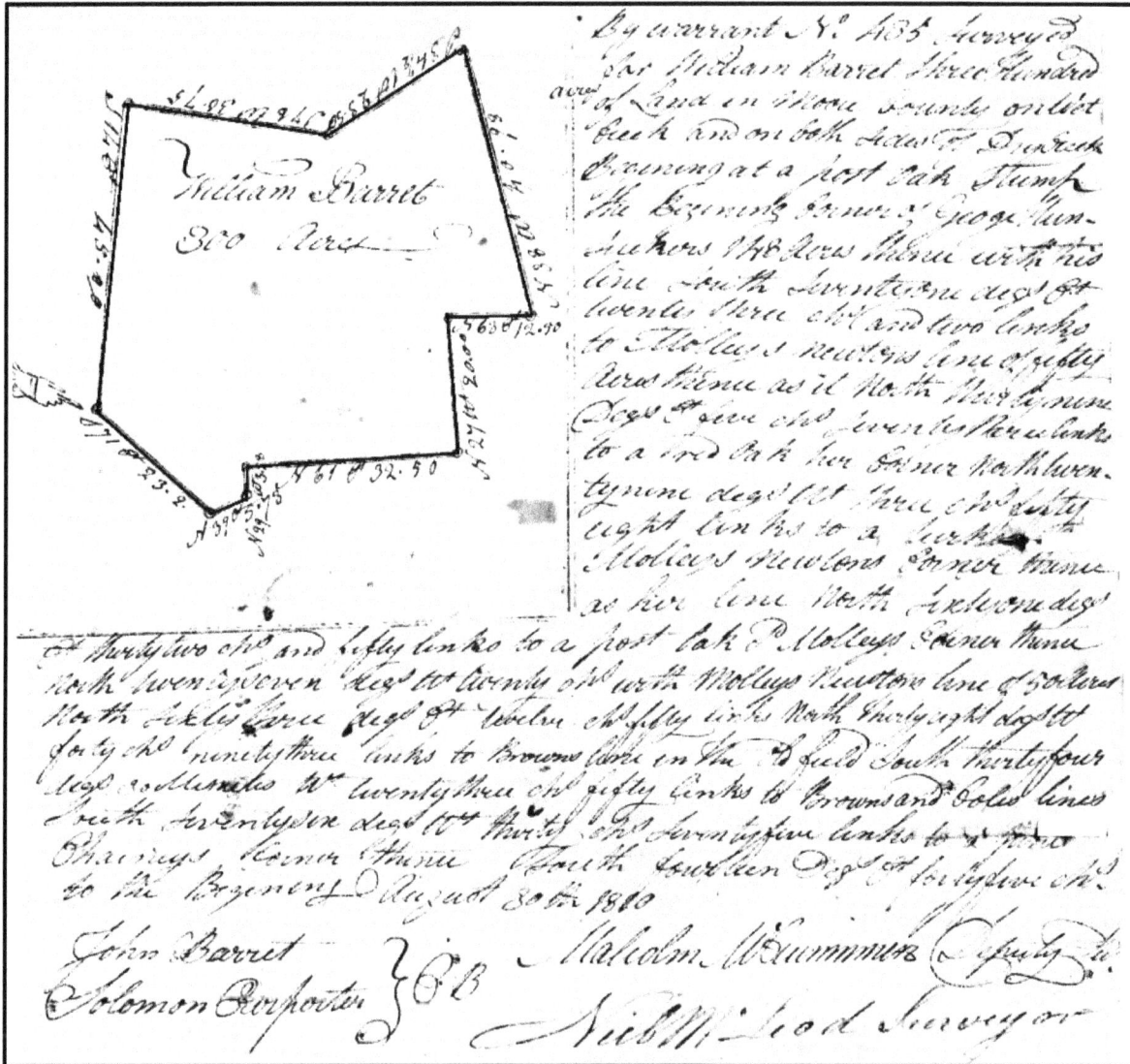

2883. 1810, Sep 3 -- Land Grant #2093, Moore County, NC
Samuel Dunn received 51 acres located on Deep River including the Big Falls above the Island Ford adjoining **Boroughs, Samuel Perry** and **Widow England. John McNeill** and **Geo. Glascock** were chain carriers.

2884. 1810, Sep 3 -- Land Grant #2094, Moore County, NC
Samuel Dunn received 51 acres located south of Deep River adjoining **Boroughs, Samuel Perry** and **Jacob Stutts. John McNeill** and **Geo. Glascock** were chain carriers.

2885. 1810, Oct -- *A History of Sandy Creek Baptist Association* by George Purefoy, Page 59
Mark Phillips and **Harden Warner** from McLennon's Creek Church (Moore County) and Elder **Isaac Teague, Bryant Boroughs** and **Lewis Spinks** from Fall Creek Church (Chatham County) were delegates to the Association meeting at George's Creek Meeting House in Chatham County, NC.

2886. 1810, Oct -- Land Grant #2173, Moore County, NC
Alexr. McLeod received 100 acres located east of McLendons Creek adjoining **Cox, John Stephens, Danl. Shaw, John Evans** and his own line. **John McSween** and **Neill McLeod** were chain carriers.

A. 1810, Oct 12 – Land Grant #1910, Chatham County, NC

Moses Myrick received 150 acres located on Flag Branch and Rocky Branch of Indian Creek adjoining his own line. **Joel Lawhon** and **Azel Myrick** were chain carriers.

2887.   1810, Oct 17 -- Will Book A, Page 285, Moore County, NC
Will of **Margaret Kosht**, Dec'd. Heirs: daughter **Barbary Garner**, daughter **Susannah Latham**, daughter **Margaret Williamson**, **Mary Freeman**, son **John Hair**, son **Peter Hair** and daughter **Elizabeth Vuncannon**. Executors: son **John Hair** and son **Peter Hair**. Witnesses: **Jeremiah Wilson** and **John Shamburger**. Proven Aug 1814.

2888.   1810, Oct 22 -- Land Grant #2125, Moore County, NC
John Shamburger received 150 acres located on Reedy Creek and the [Randolph] County line adjoining **Cornelius Lathum** and his own line. **Lewis Spinks** and **Charles Stuart** were chain carriers.

2889.   1810, Oct 23 -- Land Grant #2112, Moore County, NC
John Sheffield Junr. received 26 acres located northwest of Wolf Creek and Racoon Branch adjoining his own line and **John Sheffield Senr.** **Peter Hare** and **John Sheffield** were chain carriers.

2890.   1810, Oct 24 -- Land Grant #2172, Moore County, NC
Peter Hair received 100 acres located on Meadow Branch adjoining **Nicholas Nall** and Hare. **Isaac Shuffield** and **John Shuffield** were chain carriers.

2891.   1810, Nov 4 -- Land Grant #2092, Moore County, NC
Margaret Graham received 13 acres located west of McLendons Creek adjoining **Solomon Barret**, **Graham**, **Cox** and **McLeod**. **John McDonald** and **John Martin** were chain carriers.

2892.   1810, Nov 5 -- Deed Book 127, Page 257, Moore County, NC
John Needham deeded **Jesse Brown** 150 acres located on Cabbin Creek adjoining **Medford Owen**, **Levi Deaton** (formerly **Everet Smith**) and **Brown**. **Malcolm Patterson** and **Matthew Deton** were witnesses.

2893.   1810, Nov 6 -- Land Grant #2060, Moore County, NC
Nathaniel Melton received 43 acres located on both sides of Wet Creek adjoining **John McKinnon**, **Neil McLeod**, **Bartholomew Dunn**, **William Dunn**, **Newton** and own line. **George Hunsucker** and **John Gibson** were chain carriers.

2894.   1810, Nov 13 -- Land Grant #2055, Moore County, NC
Alexr. McIntosh received 100 acres located southeast of McLendons Creek adjoining his own line, **Michael Briant**, **Robt. Graham**, **John Cox** and **George Graham**. **Martin Martin** and **John Lewis** were chain carriers.

2895.   1810, Nov 13 -- Land Grant #2079, Moore County, NC
Alexr. McIntosh received 100 acres located east of McLendons Creek adjoining **Michael Briant**, **McNeill**, **Thos. Graham**, **Robt. Graham**, **John Cox** and **George Graham**. **Martin Martin** and **John Lewis** were chain carriers.

2896.   1810, Nov 13 -- Land Grant #2094a, Moore County, NC
Mason Harvel received 140 acres located on both sides of Cabin Creek adjoining **Nathan Smith**, **Harvel**, **James Morgan**, **Francis Bullock**, **Joseph Allen**, **Lewis**, **John Morgan** and **George Morgan**. **Richard Holland** and **Jos. Morgan** were chain carriers.

2897.   1810, Nov 14 -- Land Grant #2273, Moore County, NC
Neil McLeod received 130 acres located west of Richland Creek and the path that leads from his old place to **Hector McNeill**'s old place adjoining his own line. **John McDonald Senr.** and **John McDonald Junr.** were chain carriers.

2898.   1810, Nov 14 -- Land Grant #2275, Moore County, NC
Neil McLeod received 20 acres located west of Richland Creek adjoining his own line. **John McDonald Senr.** and **John McDonald Junr.** were chain carriers.

2899.   1810, Nov 21 -- Land Grant #2141, Moore County, NC
John McDonald received 50 acres located on Dry Fork of McLendons Creek adjoining **Neil McLeod**, **Donald McDonald Senr.**, **Robert Graham** and **George Graham**. **Donald McDonald** and **Neill McDonald** were chain carriers.

2900.   1810, Nov 21 -- Land Grant #2154, Moore County, NC
Thomas Graham received 45 acres located east of McLendons Creek adjoining **John Lewis**, **Michael Bryant**, **Robert Graham** Dec'd. and his own line. **Micheal Bryant** and **Elisha Bryant** were chain carriers.

2901.   1810, Nov 24 -- Land Grant #2110, Moore County, NC
Nancy McLeod received 100 acres located west of Horse Creek and Dry Creek adjoining **Donald McLeod**, **Hector McLean**, **Neil McLeod**, **Allen McLean** and own improvement. **Archd. McMillen** and **Donald McLean** were chain carriers.

2902.   1810, Dec 6 -- Land Grant #2187, Randolph County, NC
Christopher Asbell received 39 acres located on Reedy Creek and the Moore County line adjoining his own line and **Emanuel Asbell**. **William Lathem** and **Jesse Gatlin** were chain carriers.

A.   1810, Dec 7 -- Deed Book 48 Page 76-77, Moore County, NC
John Wadsworth and **James William Wadsworth** deeded **John Shamburger** Esq. 7/8 of an acre and a house in the town of Faginsville west of the courthouse currently occupied by **John Tyson** and **William Minter** as a shop. **John McIver** and **Daniel Feagin** were witnesses.

2903.   1810, Dec 13-1811, Jan 3 -- Notice, *The North Carolina Star* [Raleigh, NC] Newspaper
James Smith placed a notice forewarning others from trading on the Feb 7, 1807 note of debt [due Feb 6, 1811] by **William Smith** to **James Deaton** witnessed by **James Williams**, **Rollay Spinks** and **Will. Searcy**.

A FORE-WARNING.

ON or before the 6th day of February 1811, I promise to pay unto James Deaton, the sum of 135 silver dollars, it being for value received, as witness my hand and seal this the 7th of Feb. 1807.   his

Test   WILLIAM S SMITH.
James Williams,   mark
Rollay Spinks,
Will Searcy,

All persons are hereby forwarned from trading for or taking an assignment of the note of which the above is a true copy—It being obtained from me by fraud and deception, and without any valuable consideration; I therefore am resolved not to pay it.   JAMES SMITH.

Moore County, Dec. 13, 1810.   3 t

2904.   1811 -- Tax List, Franklin County, GA [selected residents]

Henry Smith Jr. 300 acres on Hudson River, [agent for **Nathan Smith**] 100 acres on Hudson River. *Capt. Anderson's District*: **Isaac Smith** 200 acres on Hudson River [for **Adam Sheffel**] 202.5 acres (Wilkinson County).

2905.   1811, Jan 24 -- Notice, *The North Carolina Star* [Raleigh, NC] Newspaper
Edward Britt of Wake County placed an ad regarding a small gray horse that strayed from the house of **Mrs. Kitchen**, about six miles from Moore courthouse on Dec 31st while he was in Moore County.

2906.   1811, Jan 24 -- Land Grant #2101, Moore County, NC
Alexander McKinnon received 50 acres located northwest of Wet Creek adjoining the heirs of **John McAulay, Junr.**, **John McKinnon** and **John Sowell**. **Alexr. Campbell** and **William McKinnon** were chain carriers.

2907.   1811, Feb -- 1785-1868 Index to Trial Docket, Moore County, NC Page 16
State v. **Shadrick Manous**

2908.   1811, Feb -- 1808-1819 Trial and Appearance Docket, Moore County, NC
Jesse Ritter v. **Angus McKinnon**

2909.   1811, Feb 11 -- Land Grant #1646, Moore County, NC
Cornelius Lathum received 100 acres located on the waters of Reedy Creek adjoining the [Randolph] County line, **John Shamburger** and his own line. **Peter Shamburger Senr.** and **William Bird** were chain carriers.

2910.   1811, Feb-Dec [undated estimate] -- Will Book A Page 327, Moore County, NC
Estate of **Neill Mathewson**, Dec'd. by Administrator **Normon Mathewson**. *Items purchased by the following:* **Murdoch Martin**, **Christian Mathewson**, **Norman Mathewson**, **Malcolm Mathewson**, **Hector McLain**, **Norman McLeod**, **Alexr. McIntosh**, **James Lakey**, **Everit Wallis**, **Benj. Caddell**, **John Cagle**, **Alexr. McLeod Senr.**, **John McSween**, **John Sowell**, **Neill McLeod Senr.**, **Kenneth McCaskill**, **Stephen Richardson**, **Neill Morrison**, **Roderick Murchison**, **Bradley Garner**, **Murdock McAulay**, **Neill McIntosh**, **Neill McLeod**, **Duncan McIntosh**, **Alexr. McLeod Senr.**, **Murdoch McDaniel**, **John McDonald**, **George Hunsucker**, **Wm. Barrott**, **George Graham** and **Samuel Barringtine**. [*Editor's Note: No date given on actual inventory, but the date was estimated using known date of death Feb 1811.*]

A.   1811, Feb 14 -- Marriage Bond, Randolph County, NC
Enoch Spinks and **Sarah Edwards** received marriage bond. **Isaac Edwards** was bondsman. **John Craven** was witness. [*Editor's Note: Date of marriage occurred on or after date of marriage bond.*]

Notice.

ONE of the representatives of Philip Cheek, dec. by his first wife by the name of Susannah Cheek, who was carried of by her mother when a small girl to South Carolina, will find it to her interest to apply to the subscriber, who has in his hands property to which the said Susannah is intitled to by the death of her father.

Also Amos Cheek, one of the representatives of Robert Cheek, will do well to apply for his interest in the estate of his father.

Proper application to the subscriber on Deep River, Moor county, North Carolina, will be attended to.

ANDREW WHITE.
80-3tp.

2911.   1811, Mar 21 -- Notice, *The Raleigh Minerva* [Raleigh, NC] Newspaper
One of the representatives of **Phillip Cheek**, Dec'd, by his first wife by the name of **Susannah Cheek**, who was carried off by her mother when a small girl to South Carolina, will find it to her interest to apply to the subscriber, who has in his hands property to which the said **Susannah** is entitled by the death of her father. Also, **Amos Cheek**, one of the representatives of **Robert Cheek**, will do well to apply for his interest in the estate of his father. Proper application to the Subscriber on Deep River, Moor County, North Carolina will be attended to. **Andrew White**

2912.   1811, Mar 29 -- Land Grant #2120, Moore County, NC
John McIver received 250 acres located between Richland Creek and McLendons Creek on the Waggon Road and Barn Branch and the Island Ford road from the Waggon Ford adjoining **Jesse Muse** (where **Samuel Elkins** lived), **Joseph Dunn**, **Jonathan Evans**, **Saml. Dunn** (where **John Richardson** now lives), **Jesse Sowel** and **Jeremiah Dean**. **Jesse Sowel** and **Thos. Muse** were chain carriers.

2913.   1811, Apr 2 -- Land Grant #2205, Moore County, NC
Jesse Ritter received 50 acres located west of Richland Creek on Locust Branch adjoining his own line, **John Ritter** and **McQueen**. **Danl. Muse** and **Moses Ritter** were chain carriers.

2914. 1811, Apr 15 -- Will Book A, Page 271, Moore County, NC
Will of **Drury Richardson**, Dec'd. Heirs: wife **Sally** [*all my land on both sides of the King Street*], daughter **Sally Writter**, son **Edward Richardson**, son **Robert Richardson**, daughter **Letha Cooper**, daughter **Eliza Writter**, daughter **Oma Brewer**, deceased son **William Richardson** and son-in-law **John Writter**. Executors: **Bryan Boroughs** and **John Writter**. Witnesses: **Aaron Smith** and **B. Boroughs**. Proven May 1811.

2915. 1811, May [undated estimate] -- Will Book A Page 332, Moore County, NC
Estate of **Drury Richardson**, Dec'd. by Administrator **John Richardson**. [*Editor's Note: No date given on actual inventory, but the date was estimated using probate date of Will above.*]

2916. 1811, May-Dec [undated estimate] -- Will Book A Page 332, Moore County, NC
Estate of **Amos Cheek** Dec'd. Only item in estate listed was "Part of **Robert Cheek** estate in the hands of the administration". [*Editor's Note: No date given on actual inventory, but the inventory appeared on same page as Richardson estate above.*]

2917. 1811, May-Dec [undated estimate] -- Will Book A Page 332, Moore County, NC
Estate of **Susannah Mcgee** Dec'd. Only item in estate listed was "1/6 part of six negroes". [*Editor's Note: No date given on actual inventory, but the inventory appeared on same page as Richardson estate above. She was the daughter of Joseph McGee mentioned in his 1794 will*]

2918. 1811, May 9 -- Land Grant #2219, Moore County, NC

Cornelius Shields received 53 acres located north of Deep River on Cane Patch Creek adjoining his own line, **White** and **Beeson**. **Fannon Moore** and **Wm. Shields** were chain carriers.

2919. 1811, May 13 -- Deed Book 95 Page 25, Moore County, NC
William Williams deeded **Leonard Furr** 50 acres located on Flag Creek adjoining **Charles Sowell**, **George Cagle**, **Graham** and **Leonard Furr**. **James Dunlap** and **Evrett Wallace** were witnesses.

2920. 1811, May 16 -- Land Grant #2095, Moore County, NC
James Smith received 50 acres located southeast of Juniper Creek adjoining **John McNeill**, **Jackson** and his own line (formerly **Martin**). **Murdo. Curry** and **Dick Gilmore** were chain carriers.

2921. 1811, May 17 -- Land Grant #2155, Moore County, NC
John Ritter received 42.5 acres located east of Buffalo Creek adjoining his own line, **Danl. McNeill** and **Jacob Stutts**. **Thos. Ritter** and **John Melton** were chain carriers.

2922. 1811, Jul 3 -- Land Grant #2167, Moore County, NC
Thomas Ritter received 28.75 acres located on the waters of Richland Creek adjoining **Neil McIntosh** (formerly **James Holcombe**), **Donald McQueen** and **Jesse Ritter**. **Jesse Sowell** and **Thos. Ritter** were chain carriers.

2923. 1811, Jul 4 -- Land Grant #2126, Moore County, NC
Peter Hair received 50 acres located north of Wolf Creek adjoining **John Sheffield Junr.**, **Reuben Freeman** and **Neil McLeod**. **John Hair** and **Peter Hair** were chain carriers.

2924. 1811, Jul 4 -- Land Grant #2139, Moore County, NC
Peter Hair received 50 acres located north of Bear Creek adjoining **Isaac Shuffield** (formerly **Nicholas Nall**). **Isaac Shuffield** and **Adam Shuffield** were chain carriers.

2925. 1811, Jul 5 -- Land Grant #2097, Moore County, NC
Adam Comber received 100 acres located north of Williams Creek adjoining his own line, **Ludlow**, **John Comber** and the heirs of **Malcom McNeill**, Dec'd. **John Comber** and **Martin Comber** were chain carriers.

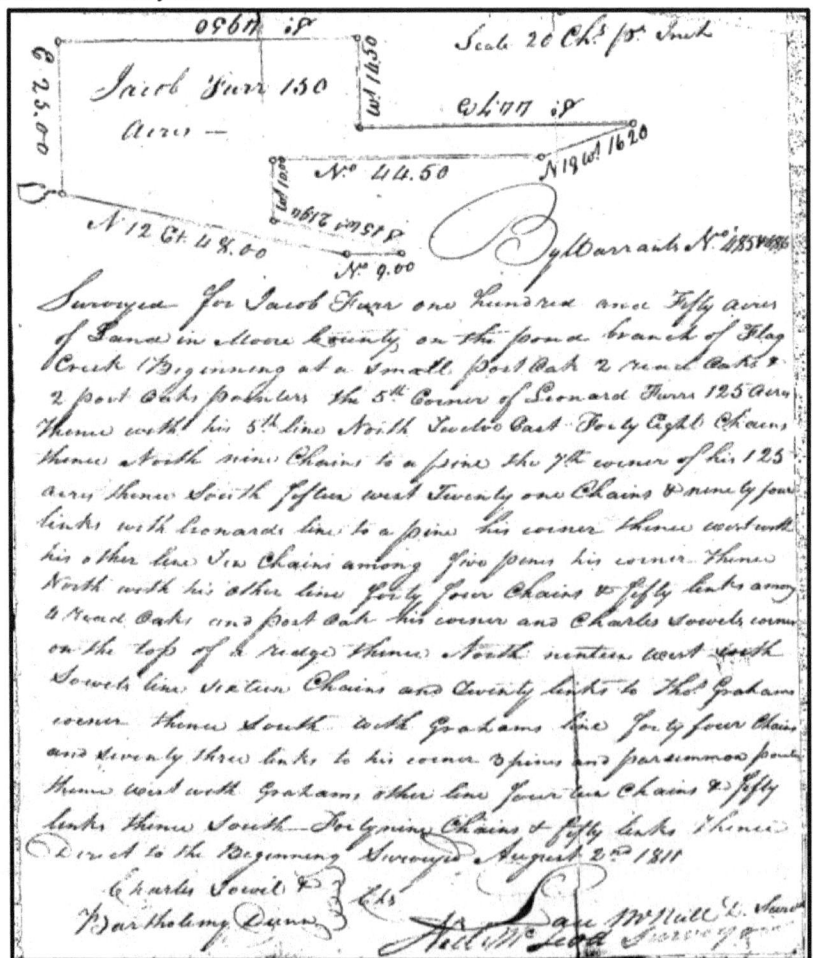

2926. 1811, Aug -- 1808-1819 Trial and Appearance Docket, Moore County, NC
Jesse Ritter v. **Angus McQueen**

2927. 1811, Aug 1 -- Land Grant #2137, Moore County, NC
Leonard Furr Senr. received 300 acres located north of Cabin Creek adjoining **Thomas Graham**, **George Cagle**, **William Cagle**, **John Cagle**, **Jesse Brown**, **John Smith**, **Matthew Deaton** and **John Needham**. **Christian Stuts** and **Isaac Cagle** were chain carriers.

2928. 1811, Aug 2 -- Land Grant #2145, Moore County, NC
Jacob Furr received 150 acres located on Pond Branch of Flag Creek adjoining **Leonard Furr Junr.**, his own line, **Charles Sowel** and **Thomas Graham**. **Charles Sowel** and **Bartholomew Dunn** were chain

carriers.

2929.   1811, Aug 14 -- Land Grant #2128, Moore County, NC
Leonard Furr Junr. received 25 acres located on both sides of Flag Creek adjoining his own line, **Ansel Melton** and **McLeod**. **Jacob Furr** and **Danl. McLean** were chain carriers.

2930.   1811, Aug 16 -- Land Grant #2119, Moore County, NC
John McKinnon received 100 acres located west of Wet Creek adjoining **Norman McKinnon Junr.**, his own line and the heirs of **John McAulay Junr. Norman McKinnon** and **Donald McKinnon** were chain carriers.

2931.   1811, Sep 14 -- Deed Book MMM Page 30, Franklin County, GA
Perry Kees deeded **Nathan Smith** 144.5 acres located on Hudson River above old boundary of **Wofford**'s Settlement adjoining **Moses Crawford** and **William Boiling**. **Archd. Ritchey** and **Joseph Hamilton**. Recorded Nov 9, 1815.

2932.   1811, Oct -- *A History of Sandy Creek Baptist Association* by George Purefoy, Page 61
Mark Phillips, **William Dowd** and **Eli Phillips** from McLennon's Creek Church (Moore County) and Elder **Isaac Teague**, **William Waddill** and **Francis Bullock** from Fall Creek Church (Chatham County) were delegates to the Association meeting at Marshal's Meeting House in Anson County, NC.

   A.   1811, Oct 28 – Land Grant #1913, Chatham County, NC
William Harper received 105 acres located on Fall Creek adjoining his own line. **James Scott** and **Joseph Harper** were chain carriers.

2933.   1811, Oct 30 -- Land Grant #2105, Moore County, NC
Samuel Jackson received 50 acres located north of Juniper Creek and the head of Whittles Branch adjoining **Barret**, **John Sowel**, **John Bethune** and his own line. **Saml. Jackson** and **Wm. Jackson** were chain carriers.

2934.   1811, Oct 30 -- Land Grant #2117, Moore County, NC
Samuel Jackson received 50 acres located on Suck Branch of Juniper Creek adjoining his own line, **McNeill** and **David Sears** (now Mrs. **Sears**). **Saml. Jackson** and **Wm. Jackson** were chain carriers.

2935.   1811, Oct 31 -- Land Grant #2677, Lincoln County, NC
Leonard Cagle received 27 acres located on Lyles Creek adjoining his own line, **Philip Backer** and **Hunsicker**. **Daniel Isenhower** and **Barnetd Fulbright** were chain carriers. Entered Jan 22, 1811.

2936.   1811, Nov -- 1808-1819 Trial and Appearance Docket, Moore County, NC
Angus McQueen v. **Shadrick Manous**

2937.   1811, Nov 9 -- Land Grant #2153, Moore County, NC
Leonard Furr Senr. received 40 acres located on both sides of Cabin Creek adjoining **William Cagle**, **Neil McLeod**, his own line and **George Cagle**.

   A.   1811, Nov 9 -- Deed Book S Page 84, Chatham County, NC
Bryan Boroughs (of Moore County) deeded **John Record** (of TN) 77 acres that was originally granted to **William Finley**. **Micajah McGee** and **Elisha Bagley** were witnesses.

2938.   1811, Nov 13 -- Land Grant #2096, Moore County, NC
James Smith received 100 acres located southeast of Juniper Creek adjoining **John McNeill**, his own line (formerly **John Martin**) and **Thomas Graham**. **Uriah Pope** and **Thos. Graham** were chain carriers.

2939.   1811, Dec 2 -- Land Grant #2122, Moore County, NC
William Barret received 100 acres located on both sides of Dry Creek below the Gum Branch adjoining **Nicholas Newton** and **Matheson**. **William Barret** and **John Dunlap** were chain carriers.

2940.   1811, Dec 3 -- Land Grant #2127, Moore County, NC
William Cagle received 37 acres located between Cabin and Bear Creek adjoining his own line (formerly **Richard Caswell**). **William Barret** and **George Cagle** were chain carriers.

2941. 1811, Dec 10 -- Deed Book 24 Page 231 Orange County, NC
George Horner to **Moses Fussell**, one negro woman named **Jude**, many items of furniture, for use of **George Horner**'s wife **Elizabeth** whom he was legally separated from and her children **Lucy King**, **Dicey Horner**, **George Wyatt Horner**. Witnesses: **Wm. Norwood**, **A. B. Bruce**.

2942. 1812/1815 -- North Carolina Militia Muster Roll
Fourth Regiment detached from the 4th and 14th Brigades: Sixth Company detached from the Moore Regiment [selected members]: **Nathaniel Tucker** (captain); **John Garner** (ensign); **Robert Kennedy**; **John Myrick**; **Drury Richardson**; **Isom Sowell**; **Joab Cheek**; **Everitt Sheffield**; **James Morgan**; **Jacob Cagle**; **Frederick Autry**; **James Owen**; **Aben [Abner?] Brown**; **James Garner**; **Edward Moore**; **Bradley Garner**; **John Richardson**; **William Williamson** and **William Key**. Rifleman 1st Company detached from the Cumberland Regiment [selected members]: **George Kenedy**; **Frederick Brewer**; **James C. Myrick**; **Jesse Ritter**; **Julius Brewer**; **John Cockman**; **John Garner**; **William Maness**; **John Melton/Milton**; **Gideon Moore** and **Louis Williamson**. Moore County 2nd Regiment [selected members]: **William Dowd** (captain); **Martin Cagle**; **Wm. Barrot**; **Merriman Britt** (fifer); **Jesse Brown**; **Henry Stuts**; **George Ritter**; **Joseph Wallis**; **Bradley Maness**; **Bartholomew Dunn**; **Wm. Smith Jun.**; **Thomas Dun**; **John Smith**; **William Britt**; **Angus McKennon**; **Wm. Jones**; **Thomas Kees**; **Wm. Milton**; **Wm. Brown**; **Joseph Owen**; **Wm. Smith**; **John Dunlop**; **William Brewer Jun.**; **Kindrick Williamson**; **Jacob Auman**; **Moses Myrick**; **Isaac Teague** and **Robert Brady**.

2943. 1812 -- Bastardy Bond, Randolph County, NC
Martin Cagle fathered a child with **Rachel Aston**. **Samuel Graves** and **Michael Harvey** were securities.

2944. 1812-1813 [undated estimate] -- Estate, Moore County, NC Will Book A, Page 313-315
Inventory of the Estate of **Lydia Tyson** Dec'd. by Administrator **William Tyson**. [*Editor's Note: No date given on actual inventory, but the date was estimated using estate note dated in 31 Oct 1812 in Chatham County Estate.*]

2945. 1812, Jan 15 -- Land Grant #2221, Moore County, NC
George Cox received 150 acres located on both sides of Juniper Creek adjoining **Jackson**, **Holden Cox**, **Wm. Cox**, **Sowel** and **Edward Cox** (formerly **McClendon**). **Ignatious Wadsworth** and **Samuel Due** were chain carriers.

2946. 1812, Feb 13 -- Land Grant #2223, Moore County, NC
Thomas P. Muse received 200 acres located northwest of McLendons Creek adjoining **Thomas Muse** and **Jesse Muse**. **Danl. H. Muse** and **James B. Muse** were chain carriers.

2947. 1812, Feb 23 -- Land Grant #2240, Moore County, NC
William Richardson received 50 acres located on the waters of Kings Street east of Burroughs Road adjoining his own line and **John Upton**. **Jesse Upton** and **Drury Richardson** were chain carriers.

2948. 1812, Mar 5 -- 1813-1828 Marriage Licenses, Moore County, NC
Alex. Leach (age 27 as of May 15, 1812) and **Christian Blue** (age 19 as of Dec 20, 1812) were married

2949. 1812, Mar 23 -- Land Grant #2187, Moore County, NC
Murdock Matheson received 20 acres located on Hucleberry Branch of Dry Creek adjoining his own line, **Ambrose Manes** and **Neil Matheson**. **Angush Morrison** and **John Gillis** were chain carriers.

2950. 1812, Mar 24 -- Land Grant #2248, Moore County, NC
Angush Morrison received 155 acres located on Dry Creek adjoining **Neil Matheson**, **Murdock Matheson**, **Malcolm Morrison**, **Daniel Gillis**, **Brown**, **McLeod**, **Thomas Graham**, **Joseph Cole** and **Paterson**. **Hector McLean** and **Norman Matheson** were chain carriers.

2951. 1812, Mar 27 -- Land Grant #2179, Moore County, NC
Murdock Matheson received 40 acres located on Dry Creek adjoining **Nathan Barret**, his own line, **Neil Matheson**, **Malcolm Morrison** and **Angus Morrison**. **Angush Morrison** and **John Gillis** were chain carriers.

2952. 1812, May 8 -- Land Grant #2186, Moore County, NC
Angush Morrison received 30 acres located on Dry Creek adjoining **Neil Matheson**, **Murdock Matheson**, **Malcolm Morrison** and **Donald Gillis**. **Murdock Matheson** and **Angush Morrison** were chain carriers.

2953. 1812, May 24 -- Land Grant #2216, Moore County, NC
Malcolm Matheson received 9 acres located east of Wet Creek adjoining **Waddle**, **John McAulay**, **George Hunsucker**, his own line (formerly **Murdock McAulay**) and **William Dunn**. **Angush Morrison** and **Murdock Matheson** were chain carriers.

2954. 1812, Jun 5 -- Land Grant #2188, Moore County, NC
George Glascock received 100 acres located east of McLendons Creek on Rocky Branch adjoining **Benjamin Williams**, **Jesse Rogers**, **Lauchlin McNeill**, **Hector McNeill**, **Tucker** and his own line where he now lives. **Julius Glascock** and **James B. Muse** were chain carriers.

2955. 1812, Jul -- NC Supreme Court Case 334
From Moore County. **John Seawell** v. **William Shomberger**. Mentions debt by **Jabez York**.

2956. 1812, Jul 28 -- Marriage Bond, Chatham County, NC
Samuel Griffin and **Rebecca Smith**. Bondsman was **Isaac Smith**. Witness was **Thomas Ragland**. [*Editor's Note: Date of marriage occurred on or after date of marriage bond.*]

2957. 1812, Aug [undated estimate] -- Estate, Moore County, NC Will Book A, Page 336
Inventory of the Estate of **Frances Tedwell**, Dec'd. by Administrator **George Jackson**. [*Editor's Note: No date given on actual inventory, but the date was estimated using Will date of probate.*]

A. 1812, Aug 7 -- Land Grant #1926, Chatham County, NC
Archibald McBryde received 167 acres located west of Tysons Creek and the [Moore] County line adjoining **William Phillips**, **Burroughs** (formerly **Record**) and own line (formerly **Cheek**). **Wm. Phillips** and **Henry Phillips** were chain carriers.

2958. 1812, Aug 10 -- Land Grant #2177, Moore County, NC
William Smith received 145 acres located north of Deep River and the Randolph County line adjoining **John Garner**, **Cavanaugh**, **Gaines** and **Morgan** (where **Smith** now lives). **Spinks Smith** and **Bryan Smith** were chain carriers.

2959. 1812, Oct -- *A History of Sandy Creek Baptist Association* by George Purefoy, Page 63
William Dowd, **Eli Phillips** and **Richard Upton** from McLennon's Creek Church (Moore County) and Elder **Isaac Teague**, **Bryant Borough** and **Archibald McNeill** from Fall Creek Church (Chatham County) were delegates to the Association meeting at Fall Creek Meeting House in Chatham County, NC.

2960. 1812, Oct 5 -- Land Grant #2174, Moore County, NC
John Dunlap received 100 acres located northeast of McLendons Creek in the fork of Martins Branch adjoining his own line (formerly **Murdoch Bethune**) and **John McNeill**. **Jesse Phillips** and **Jno. McCrimmon** were chain carriers.

A. 1812, Oct 5 -- Land Grant #1948, Chatham County, NC
Isaiah Richeson received 416 acres located on Indian Creek adjoining **Sanders**, **McManus** and **Louis Phillips**. **Nathan McManus** and **James Phillips** were chain carriers.

2961. 1812, Oct 16 -- Marriages, The Raleigh Minerva [Newspaper] Raleigh, NC
On the 11th ult. [Sep]. Mr. **Abel S. Gardner** of Guilford [County] to Miss **Mary A. Bullock** of Moore County.

2962. 1812, Nov 3 -- Land Grant #2199, Moore County, NC
Charles Brady received 100 acres located on Fall Creek adjoining **James Brady** and **Frazier**. **Frederick Brewer** and **Carroll Brady** were chain carriers.

2963. 1812, Nov 14 -- Land Grant #2212, Moore County, NC
John Dunlap Junr. received 100 acres located on both sides of Bear Creek adjoining his own line (formerly **Francis Bullock**) and **Williams**. **Jesse Brown** and **Wm. Cagle** were chain carriers.

A. 1812, Dec 3 -- Land Grant #1930, Chatham County, NC
James Hilliard received 23.5 acres located on Rocky Branch of Indian Creek adjoining **Wm. Hilyard**, own line, **Griffin** and **Phillips**. **Jesse Hilyard** and **Sion Hilyard** were chain carriers.

B.   1812, Dec 3 -- Land Grant #1936, Chatham County, NC
Lazarus Phillips received 29 acres located on Indian Creek adjoining **Ezekial Hilyard**, **McIndsey [McKenzie]**, **Jeremiah Phillips** and **Barnes**. **Jesse Hilyard** and **James Hilyard** were chain carriers.

2964.   1812, Dec 4 -- Land Grant #2196, Moore County, NC
David Kennedy received 200 acres located on both sides of Bear Creek above the road from his plantation to his mill on Bear Creek adjoining **Neil McLeod**, **Leonard Furr**, **John McAulay**, his own line and **Brown**. **Hiram Kennedy** and **William Kennedy** were chain carriers.

2965.   1812, Dec 4 -- Land Grant #2233, Moore County, NC
Nathan Smith received 25 acres located east of Wet Creek adjoining **William Smith** and his own line. **William Smith** and **Isom Cooper** were chain carriers.

2966.   1812, Dec 11 -- Land Grant #2664, Moore County, NC
Abednego Maness received 200 acres located east of Bear Creek adjoining **Neil McLeod**, **John McAulay** and **Brewer**. **Gardner Maness** and **Nathan Maness** were chain carriers.

2967.   1813 -- Tax List, Marion County, MS [selected residents]
John Cagle; **John Carpenter**; **William Carpenter**; **James Henyard [Minyard?]**; **Eli Smith**; **Henry Smith**; **Isham Smith Jr.**; **Isham Smith Sr.**; **John Smith**; **Levy Smith**; **Nathan Smith**; **Stephen Smith**; **William Smith Sr.**; **Temple Tillis** and **Willebe Tilliss**.

2968.   1813 -- Tax List, Franklin County, GA [selected residents]
Capt. Hamilton's District: **Nathan Smith** 300 acres on Hudson River, 100 acres on Hudson River, 200 acres on Hudson River, 144 acres on Hudson River; **Avarett Smith** poll; **Nicholas Newton** poll, **George Cagle** poll. *Defaults*: **Jno. Carpenter**, **Jas. Maynard**, **Templeton Carpenter** and **William Carpenter**.

2969.   1813, Jan 12 -- Land Grant #2244, Moore County, NC
Jesse Been received 23 acres located west of McLendons Creek adjoining own (formerly **Samuel Dunn**), **Joel Lawhorn**, **Jesse Sowell** and **Malcolm McCaskill**. **Lochart Fry** and **Jesse Been** were chain carriers.

2970.   1813, Jan 13 -- Land Grant #2392, Moore County, NC
Cornelius Dowd received 100 acres located north of Richland Creek and west of McLendons Creek adjoining **Mark Phillips**, **John Phillips** and his own line. **Mark Phillips** and **Harbert Cole** were chain carriers.

2971. 1813, Feb 12 -- Deed Book TTT Page 140-141, Franklin County, GA
Nathan Smith deeded **George Allen** 50 acres located on Hudson River. **Henry Smith** and **Nicholas Smith** were witnesses. Recorded Dec 18, 1813.

A. 1813, Feb 15 -- Will, Chatham County, NC
Will of **Larance McManous**, Dec'd. Heirs: wife **Cattral** [*negro Arter*], youngest son **Larrance**, son **Ely**, **Nathan**, **Aaron** and **Jonathan**, daughters **Ann Rains**, **Hannah Williams**, **Amy Rains** and **Cattrel Tommos**, granddaughters **Mary Elkins** and **Ann Barber**. Executors: sons **Nathan McManous** and **Aaron McManous**. Witnesses: **Ebenezer Elliott**, **Joseph Tillman** and **John Tillman**. Proven May 1813.

2972. 1813, Feb 26 -- Land Grant #2235, Moore County, NC
Kenneth McCaskill received 50 acres located west of Wet Creek adjoining his own line (formerly **William Key**) and **Hector McNeill**. **Danl. McKenzie** and **George Keys** were chain carriers.

2973. 1813, Mar 1 -- Land Grant #2237, Moore County, NC
George Hunsucker received 50 acres located east of Wet Creek adjoining his own line, **Meloney Newton**, **George Cox** and **Morrison**'s old place. **John Gibson** and **Soloman Carpenter** were chain carriers.

2974. 1813, Mar 5 -- Notice, The Raleigh Minerva [Newspaper] Raleigh, NC
David Kennedy wrote a special to the Minerva proposing to form a company to manufacture arms at his mills on Bear Creek in Moore County. He will donate 25 acres for the maunfactory and will be the superintendent. Plans to raise $20,000 at $25 a share.

A. 1813, Mar 29 -- Will Book D Page 517-518, Orange County, NC
Will of **William McPherson** Dec'd. Heirs: wife **Phebe**, children: **Thomas** and **Mary Braxton**, **Otheil** and **Christian McPherson**, **Ruth Thompson**, **Wm.** and **Betty McPherson**, **Daniel** and **Mary McPherson**, **Margaret** and **Jesse Pierce**, **John** and **Hannah McPherson**, **Aaron** and **Phebe Lindley**, **Mary** and **Edward Stuart**, **Ann** and **John Crutchfield**, **Edith** and **Mark Morgan**, grandson **Wm. McPherson** (son of **Enoch**), son **Enoch** and **Sarah McPherson**. Executors: **Daniel McPherson** and **John McPherson**. Witnesses: **Jacob Nugent**, **Daniel McPherson**, **Enoch McPherson** and **James Neal**. Probated Feb 1818.

2975. 1813, Mar 30 -- Land Grant #2211, Moore County, NC
Roderick Murchison received 200 acres located on Buffalo Creek adjoining **William Smith**, **Neil McLeod**, **James Dunlap**, heirs of **Malcolm McNeill** and including the place **James Willy** lived. **Danl. Murchison** and **Danl. McLean** were chain carriers.

2976. 1813, May -- 1796-1841 County Accounts, Moore County, NC Page 4
Elkin Jones v. **Leonard Furr**

2977. 1813, May -- 1785-1868 Index to Trial Docket, Moore

FOR THE MINERVA.

To the Freemen of North Carolina

Engaged in war with a great and powerful nation, destitute of the munitions of war, and consequently of the means of defence; holding among ourselves a species of population ready to fly to the standard of rebellion; in the power of our enemy to land on our coast troops of the same color, already disciplined and trained to the use of arms, are considerations that need no comment, which connected with the extraordinary appearance of the times, imperiously require that every able bodied freeman should be armed—for in a republic every freeman is a soldier.

The candid manner in which His Excellency Governor HAWKINS recommended the arming the Militia to the consideration of the legislature, at the commencement of their late session, met with the approbation of every thinking man; but, stange to tell, that a proposition, appropriating $25,000 to the purpose of arming the militia, was rejected in the senate by a small majority. While viewing this subject my heart felt indignant at that contracted policy which refuses to put our country in an attitude of defence, where so much is at stake; and the patriotism that glowed in my breast suggested a plan I shall submit to the consideration of my fellow citizens.

I would propose that a company be formed for the purpose of manufacturing arms—That the sum of 20,000 dollars be raised by subscription, at 25 dollars per share, one fourth to be paid down one fourth when the machinery, shops, work houses, &c. are ready to go into operation, the other two fourths in six months' instalments.

I am convinced that a plan of this kind, under proper regulations, would be productive of great public good, while it would afford a handsome profit to the company.

I am persuaded that muskets or rifles can be made by the company at eight or nine dollars per gun, and perhaps less, as coal, boarding and hiring of hands, &c. can be had very low, and a great part of the labor performed by water.

For the encouragement of those who are willing to assist in this laudable enterprize, I will engage for 1500 dollars to build, at my mills on Bear creek, Moore county, a Machinery to go by water that shall be sufficient to bore and grind off ten gun barrels per day; the Machinery shall also contain one water blast and trip hammer for the purpose of drawing gun scalps.

I will also give to the company 25 acres of land convenient to the machinery, and furnish pine lumber at the place, to build any number of shops and work houses, at six dollars per thousand feet. I will also engage to superintend the whole business for three years at 750 dollars per annum, and will make any kind arms, such as rifles, muskets, shot guns, pistols, swords, &c. that the company may think proper to direct.

Should this plan, or any other of the like meet the approbation of my fellow citizens, and they be desirous to engage in the business, they may rely on my greatest exertions to put the business into operation as soon as possible.

DAVID KENNEDY.

February 22, 1813.

County, NC Page 33
State v. **Vicey Hunsucker**

A.   1813, May -- Estate, Chatham County, NC
Estate of **John** and **Minty Vanderford**, Dec'd. Petition for division of 200 acres located on Cedar Creek purchased from **William Needham** and 100 acres located on Cedar Creek purchased from **Henry Person**. **Eli Lawler**, **William Underwood**, **Ab. Lane**, **Sugar Jones** and **Jehu Lawler** divided among the following heirs: **Richard Vanderford**, **Eli Vanderford**, **John Elkins** and **Elizabeth Elkins**, **John Craven** and **Mary Craven**, **John Sanders** and **Sally Sanders**, **Thomas Deaton** and **Nancy Deaton**, **John Overton** and **Susan Overton**.

2978.   1813, May 6 -- Will Book A Page 277, Moore County, NC
Nuncupative Will of **Phillip Wilson**, Dec'd. **Wilson** died May 2, 1813. Will reduced to writing May 6 by **James Shields** and **James McNeill**. Heirs: **Robert Wilson**, **Phillip Wilson**, brother **Samson Wilson** and all his brothers and sisters. Also, **Isaac Teague** mentioned. Administrator: **Robert Wilson**. Proven May 1813.

2979.   1813, May 31 -- Land Grant #2234, Moore County, NC
James Cheek received 50 acres located north of Deep River east of the Mulberry Branch on the Chatham County line adjoining **Angus McQueen**, **Robert Cheek**, **Archd. McBryde** and his own line. **William Cheek** and **Donald Brewer** were chain carriers.

2980.   1813, Jun 15 -- 1796-1841 County Accounts, Moore County, NC Page 39
George Hunsucker purchased 2 mares

2981.   1813, Oct 24 -- Land Grant #2318, Moore County, NC
Jesse Phillips received 50 acres located south of McLendons Creek adjoining **John Dunlap** and **Thomas Graham**. **John McCrummen** and **Benjamin Dunlap** were chain carriers.

2982.   1813, Oct 24 -- Land Grant #2138, Moore County, NC
John Hare received 65 acres located east of Wolf Creek on Brown Straw Branch adjoining his own line and **David Allison**. **Peter Hare** and **Owen Hare** were chain carriers.

2983.   1813, Oct 29 -- Land Grant #2241, Moore County, NC
Isom Shiffield Junr. received 50 acres located east of Wolf Creek adjoining **Everet Shiffield**, **John Shuffield Senr.** and **John McAulay**. **Murdock Currie** and **Everet Shiffield** were chain carriers.

A.   1813, Nov 9 -- Land Grant #1950, Montgomery County, NC
William Hix received 50 acres located on both sides of Dicks Creek adjoining **James Wright** and his own line. **James Wright** and **Isam Hix** were chain carriers.

B.   1813, Nov 11 -- Marriage Bond, Chatham County, NC
Richard Tomlinson (of Randolph County) and **Anne Waddill** (daughter of **Thomas** and **Margaret Waddill**) received marriage bond. **Thos. Waddill** was bondsman. [*Editor's Note: Date of marriage occurred on or after date of marriage bond.*]

2984.   1813, Nov 23 -- Land Grant #2260, Moore County, NC
Alexander McIntosh received 100 acres located northwest of Richland Creek and Locust Branch adjoining **William Dunn**, **Jesse Ritter**, his own line and **Donald McQueen**. **Allan Morison** and **Niel McIntosh** were chain carriers.

A.   1813, Nov 29 -- Land Grant #1944, Chatham County, NC
Nathan McManus received 95 acres located on Indian Creek adjoining his own line, **Joel Phillips**, **Louis Phillips** and **Richeson**. **James Phillips** and **Walter Phillips** were chain carriers.

2985.   1813, Dec 4 -- Land Grant #2242, Moore County, NC
Margaret McQueen received 14 acres located northwest of Richland Creek adjoining her own line, **Devotion Davis**, **Neill McIntosh** and **Donald McQueen**. **William Griffith** and **Angus McQueen** were chain carriers.

2986.   1813, Dec 16 -- Land Grant #2712, Moore County, NC

Isaac Sowell received 17.75 acres located on McLendons Creek adjoining McDonald, Alexander McLeod and Richard Warner (formerly Howard). Richard Warner and John Sowell were chain carriers.

2987.   1813, Dec 18 -- Land Grant #2504, Moore County, NC
Hardin Warner received 12.5 acres located east of Cabo Branch, west of Quarry Branch of Killets Creek adjoining William Cadwell and his own line. James Johnson and Hardin Warner were chain carriers.

2988.   1813, Dec 23 -- Land Grant #2570, Moore County, NC
Hiram Hill received 28 acres located north of McLendons Creek adjoining James Hill (formerly James Muse), Asa Sowell (formerly John McLeod, carpenter), Jessy Muse and his own line. Asay Sowell and Thos. P. Muse were chain carriers.

2989.   1814, Jan 3 -- Land Grant #2518, Moore County, NC
Joseph Fry received 150 acres located on Killets Creek and Dunnams Creek adjoining his own line, Fagin and the Speculators. Joseph Fry and Nathan Fry were chain carriers.

2990.   1814, Feb 1 -- Will Book B Page 27, Moore County, NC
Will of William Wright Sr., Dec'd. Heirs: wife Elisabeth, sons Joseph, Uriah, William, James and Sharod [100 acres where I now live called the old hundred], daughters Zilpha Suggs, Mary Williams, Nancy Presnall, Elisabeth Allen, Lida Shamburgor and Cealy Wards. Executors: sons Sharod Wright and William Wright. Witnesses: Burrell Deton and Edmond Holland. Proven by Edmond Hollen and Sherod Wright in May 1822.

A.   1814, Feb 12 -- Deed Book V Page 104, Chatham County, NC
Sarah Phillips deeded Murdock McKenzie and Archibald McBryde of Aaron Tyson & Co. 1/9 part (33 acres) of her father's, Jeremiah Phillips Senr. Dec'd., 300 acres located on Indian Creek adjoining Jonathan Barnes and Lazarus Phillips. John Riddle and Winson Gilbert were witnesses.

B.   1814, Feb 12 – Deed Book T Page 137, Chatham County, NC
Robert Wilson (of Moore County) deeded Sugar Jones two tracts: [1] 150 acres adjoining Henry Powers, Richard Pennington,

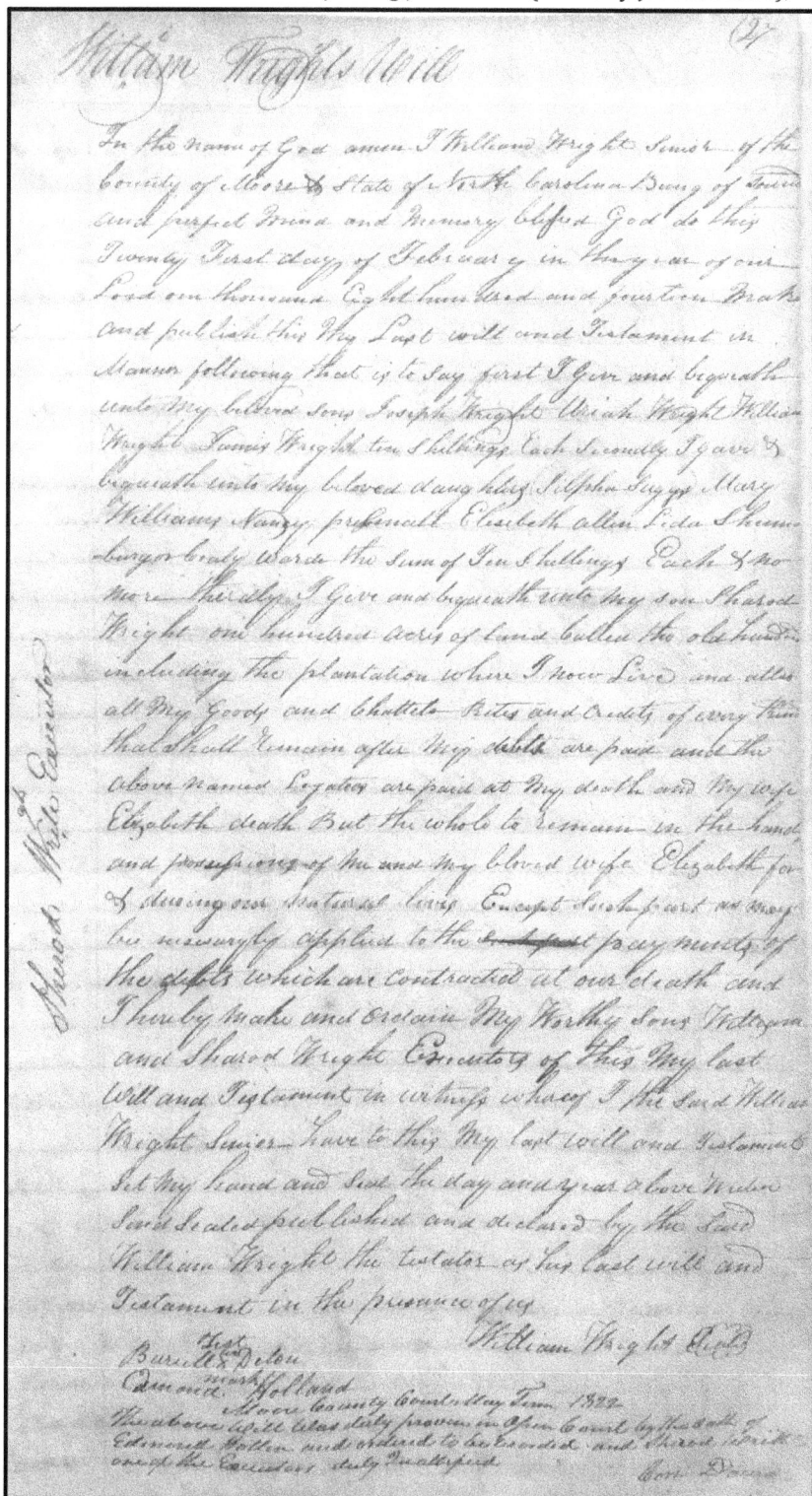

McManus, and **Joseph Parsons** [2] 92 acres adjoining **Jones** (formerly **Lambert**), **Wilson**, **Beason** and **Brewer**. **John Lawler** and **Meredith Phillips** were witnesses.

2991.   1814, Mar 4 -- Land Grant #2390, Moore County, NC
Alexander Kennedy received 250 acres located north of Bear Creek adjoining **Ambrose Brewer**, **Waddle**, **Bradley Garner**, **Neil McLeod**, his own line (formerly **Benjamin Cooper**), **David Kennedy** and **Ambrose Maness**. **Bradley Garner** and **Charles Brady** were chain carriers.

A.   1814, Mar 7 -- Deed Book 6 Page 226-227, Moore County, NC
Randal Cheek deeded **Joab Cheek** 265 acres located north of Deep River adjoining **Gregg**, **Randal Cheek**, **John Cheek** and **Joab Cheek** being ½ of the tract that **Randal Cheek** lives on. **Hector McKenzie** and **A.W. Nelson** were witnesses.

2992.   1814, Apr 4 -- Deed Book 12 Page 335, Randolph County, NC
William Pearce deeded **Reuben Pearce** 250 acres located south of Deep River adjoining **Nall** and **Bowden**. **Windsor Pearce** and **Sherwood Parrish** listed as witnesses.

2993.   1814, Apr 7 -- Land Grant #2386, Moore County, NC
John Phillips Junr. received 100 acres located on Wires Branch of Richland Creek adjoining **Mark Phillips**, **Danally**. **Mark Phillips** and **Cornelius Tyson** were chain carriers.

2994.   1814, Apr 14 -- Cane Creek [Quaker] Meeting Marriages Vol.1 Page 273, Alamance County, NC
Jesse Upton, son of **John** and **Martha Upton**, of More County and **Ann Hinshaw**, daughter of **Absolom** and **Elizabeth Hinshaw**, of Randolph County were married at the Holly Spring Friends Meeting House in Randolph County.

2995.   1814, Apr 15 -- Land Grant #2222, Moore County, NC
Cornelius Lathum received 200 acres located north of Bear Creek adjoining **Hardy Davis**, **David Allison** and his own line. **James Lathum** and **L. Tucker** were chain carriers.

2996.   1814, Apr 15 -- Obituary, *Raleigh Register and NC Gazette* [Raleigh, NC] Newspaper
"At the house of Mr. **J. Gaines**, in Moore County, (having been moved there with the hope that a change of air would be serviceable to her) Mrs. **Margaret Waddell**, in the 40th year, consort of **Thos. Waddell**, Esq. of Chatham County and youngest daughter of **John Montgomery**, Esq. A lady of amiable and moral character, leaving a disconsolate husband, with a large family of children and numerous train of relatives, to lament her loss."

2997.   1814, May 6 -- Deed, Moore County, NC
Richard Cheek, **Olive Cheek**, **Robert Davis** and wife **Nancy**, **Andrew White** and wife **Mary** and **James Cheek** deeded **Adam White** 5/8 of 5 tracts: [1] 150 acres on Deep River adjoining **Cornelius Tyson** and **John Tyson**; [2] 100 acres on Deep River adjoining **Robert Cheek**; [3] 125 acres on Tysons Creek south of Stony Hill adjoining **Robert Cheek**; [4] 100 acres near mouth of Tysons Creek adjoining **Cornelius Tyson** (now **Richard Cheek**); [5] 5 acres adjoining **Cornelius Tyson** and **John Tyson**. **Jas. Seawell** was a witness. [*Editor's Note: Original deed in possession of Patty Brinsky, descendant of Davis family*]

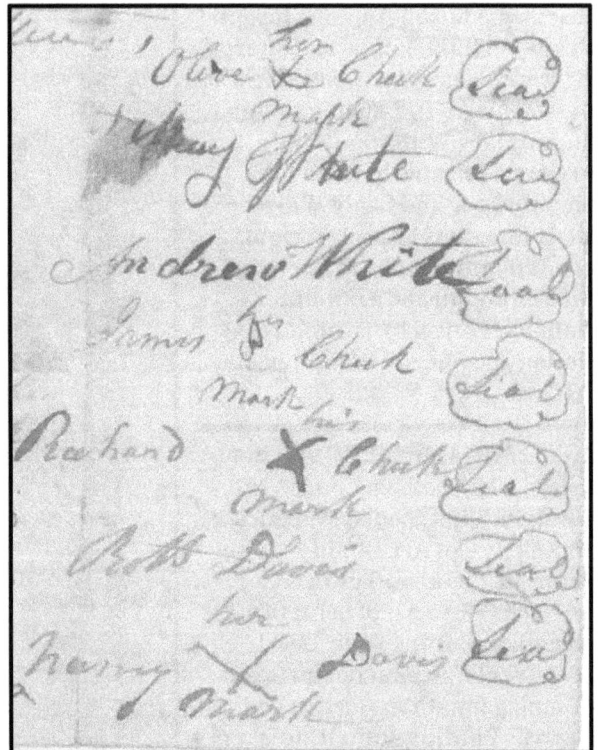

A.   1814, Aug 8 -- Governor William Hawkins Papers, Aug 1814 Correspondence, Moore County, NC
Petition of Moore County residents on behalf of **Gabriel Hardin**, **John Hardin** and **Nathan Vick** who have been convicting of killing cattle and sentenced $10 and sixty days imprisonment. The petitioners plead on behalf of these men in very moderate circumstances and no way of supporting them but by their own labors for **Governor**

Hawkins to reduce the penalty to just the fine. Signed by the following: **Francis Myrick, Wm. Waddill** JP, **Jas. Gaines, George Moore, Alexander Kennedy, Lenoard Stuts, Wm. Smith, Jesse Pearce, Howel Brewer, David Brewer, Drewry Brewer, Magor S. Johnson, Stephen Perry, Wm. Hunsucker, James Lakey, Tho. Person, Anderson B. Smith, William Kennedy, John Kennedy, Isaac Teague, William Fry, Wm. Lewis, Lockher Fry, Joseph Fry** and **Kintchn Kitching**.

2998. 1814, Oct -- *A History of Sandy Creek Baptist Association* by George Purefoy, Page 65
Elder **Isaac Teague**, **Eli Lawler** and **Archibald McNeill** from Fall Creek Church (Chatham County) were delegates to the Association meeting at Cedar Creek Meeting House in Anson County, NC.

2999. 1814, Oct 12 -- Land Grant #1968, Montgomery County, NC
George Allen Jr. received 10 acres located on Wolf Creek west of Crawford Road adjoining **Joseph Allen Sr.**, **George Allen** and **John Allen**. **Ruben Allen** and **Nathan Morgan** were chain carriers.

3000. 1814, Nov 4 -- Land Grant #2229, Moore County, NC
Allen Martin received 100 acres located on both sides of Juniper adjoining **Martin Martin** and **John McNeill**. **Allen Martin** and **Angus Martin** were chain carriers.

3001. 1814, Nov 11 -- Land Grant #2228, Moore County, NC
Daniel McNeill received 52 acres located west of Wet Creek adjoining **Grove**, **Neil McLeod**, **Thomas Harvel** and **Key**. **Phillip McNeill** and **David Richardson** were chain carriers.

3002. 1814, Nov 11 -- Land Grant #2230, Moore County, NC
Hector McNeill received 15.5 acres located east of Wet Creek adjoining his own line, **Neill McLeod** and **Grove**. **Phillip McNeill** and **David Richardson** were chain carriers.

3003. 1814, Nov 15 -- Land Grant #2231, Moore County, NC
Dugald McMillan received 50 acres located on Killets Creek and the Quarry Branch adjoining **Joseph Fry** and **Nathan Fry**. **Nathan Fry** and **James Cadwell** were chain carriers.

3004. 1814, Dec -- Chronicles and Records of Bensalem Presbyterian Church Page 20, Moore County, NC
Angus Morison and **Mary Patterson** were married. [*Editor's Note: should be* **Sarah Patterson**]

3005. 1814, Dec 1 -- Will, Randolph County, NC
Will of **Edmund Waddill Senior** Dec'd. Heirs: daughter **Lucy** [*3 negroes* **Wincy**, *her son* **Esex** *and* **Esa**]; son **John** [*land and plantation where I now live on both sides of Deep River after the death of my wife and negroes* **Elijah**, **Charles** *and* **Abraham**]; daughter **Nancy**; wife (unnamed) [*negro* **Jean**]; son **Matthew**; son **William**; son **Edmund**; son **Thomas**; daughter **Sally Boroughs**; daughter **Polly McNeill**; daughter **Lydia Goldston**. Executors: sons **William**, **Matthew**, **Edmund** and **John**. Witnesses: **Jas. Gaines** and **Isaac Teague**. Proven Feb 1815.

A. 1814, Dec 6 -- Land Grant #1959, Chatham County, NC
Lazarus Phillips received 5.5 acres adjoining **Hilyard**, **Samuel Griffin**, **Lewis Phillips** and **Jeremiah Phillips**. **Terrel Phillips** and **Wilkie Phillips** were chain carriers.

B. 1814, Dec 7 -- Land Grant #1970, Chatham County, NC
Joseph Harper received 50 acres located on Fall Creek adjoining **Elkins**, **Richard Beason** and **Sugar Jones**. **James Scott** and **Benjamin Elkins** were chain carriers.

C. 1814, Dec 7 -- Land Grant #1976, Chatham County, NC
James Scott received 168.75 acres located on Fall Creek adjoining **Findley**, **Joseph Harper** and **Edward Harper**.

D. 1814, Dec 20 -- Marriage Bond, Randolph County, NC
Robert Marsh and **Lucy Waddle** received marriage bond. **Matthew Waddill** was bondsman. **J. Craven** was a witness. [*Editor's Note: Date of marriage occurred on or after date of marriage bond.*]

3006. 1814, Dec 29 -- 1813-1828 Marriage Licenses, Moore County, NC
Angus Morrison and **Sarah Paterson** were married by **Corn. Dowd**, Clk.

3007. 1815 - Tax List, Moore County, NC [selected residents]
Name, acres and taxable amount: **Willis Dickinson** 321 acres/$640; **Wm. Dickinson** 1455/150; **Temperance Riddle** 249 acres/$300, 100 acres/$50; **George Frazier** 110 acres/$200; **Benjn. Gilbert** 650 acres/$1200; **Saml. Martindale** 330/350; **Jesse Upton** 100 acres/$50; **Lewis Phillips** 150 acres/$450; **John Handcock** 250 acres/$500; **James England** 350 acres/$700; **Eli Lawlor** 50 acres/$50; Heirs of **S. Brewer** 100 acres/$100; **Saml. Perry** 650 acres/$650; **James Brady** 100 acres/$150; **Bryan Boroughs** 662 acres; Heirs of **Jno. McAulay**

800 acres/$500; **Robt. Davis** 1300 acres/$1500; **Ambrous Brewer** 118 acres/$280, 100 acres/$100, 148 acres/$150; **Archd. Shields** 230 acres/$900, 70 acres/$30; **James Davis** 400 acres/$750, 300 acres/$70; **James Cheek** 200 acres/$200; **George Stewart** 200 acres/$200; **Patty Phillips** 160 acres/$500; **Randol Cheek** 60 acres/$100; **Cornelius Shields** 1156 acres/$1500, 166 acres/$250; **Edwd. Beason** 355 acres/$355; **Brinkley Phillips** 50 acres/$150; **Wm. England** 412 acres/$700, 100 acres/$50; **John Seat** 50 acres/$50; **Frances Myrick** 300 acres/$300; **Jonathan Caddell** 100 acres/$150; **Joab Cheek** 604 acres/$1200; **Mathew Phillips** 1560 acres/$200; **John Phillips** 100 acres/$125; **John Ritter** 640 acres/$800; **Abednego Maness** 250 acres/$250; **Jacob Stuts** 400 acres/$400; **Angus McQueen** 525 acres/$500; **Isaac Teague Jun.** 50 acres/$75; **Isaac Teague Ser.** 30 acres/$50; **Leonard Smith** 200 acres/$300; **John Danelly** 450 acres/$600; **Richd. Upton** 133 acres/$133; **William Phillips** 50 acres/$75; **Abner Lawlor** 50 acres/$75; **Roderick Murchison** 257 acres/$250, 100 acres/$20; **Gideon Seawell** 1000 acres/$2000; **Robt. Wilson** 600 acres/$1100; **Micajah Brewer** 313 acres/$250; **Harmon Brewer** 50 acres/$50; **John Upton** 220 acres/$220; **Jesse Upton** 400 acres; **Drury Richardson** 375 acres/$250; **John Cheek** 450 acres, 330 acres, 615 acres, 235 acres/$2050; **Adam White** 740 acres/$1000; **James Shields** 200 acres/$100; **Jesse Ritter** 155 acres/$250; **Wm. Dowd** 552 acres/$1000; **Corn. Dowd** 1000 acres/$1000, 445 acres/$500, 400/400; **Henry Cagle** 150 acres/$150, 100 acres/$100, 25 acres/$25, 100 acres/$100, 50 acres/$50, 25 acres/$25, 100 acres/$60; **Lewis Lawhon** 100 acres/$100; **Samuel Elkins** 75 acres/$200; **Joel Lawhon** 420 acres/$730; **Neill McIntosh** 519 acres/$650; **Thomas Ritter** 550 acres/$800; **Joseph Rouse** 50 acres/$100; **John Lawhon** 100 acres/$90; **Jesse Rodgers** 223 acres/$250, 250 acres/$50 ; **Daniel Muse** 100 acres/$150; **John Dunlap** 1300 acres/$1300; **Isaac Smith** 37 acres/$100; **Julious Glascock** 125 acres/$325; **Levin Birckhead** 100 acres/$75; **Eleazor Birckhead** 303 acres/$650; **William Caddell Sr.** 150 acres/$300; **James Muse Junr.** 94 acres/$180; **William Lewis** 400 acres/$300; **James Dowdy** 228.75 acres/$132; **Malcolm McCrummen** 100 acres/$100, 50 acres/$12; **Mark Phillips** 125 acres/$250; **John Phillips** 100 acres/$100; **Hiram Hill** 150 acres/$300; **Nehemiah Birckhead** 25 acres/$50; **Jesse F. Muse** 125 acres/$125; **Daniel Caddell** 340 acres/$680; **Thomas Muse Sr.** 100 acres/$200; **Patrick Dowd** 150 acres/$500; **Richardson Feagin** 897 acres/$1600, 200 acres/$100; **Daniel Feagin** 50 acres/$120; **Jesse Bean** 160 acres/$320; **James B. Muse** 260 acres/$500; **George Glascock** Heirs 150 acres/$250; **Jesse Sanders** 100 acres/$150, 100 acres/$150, 60 acres/$60; **Thomas Graham** 600 acres/$600, 100 acres/$100; **Isaac Sowell** 94 acres/$50; 1 acre/$50; **Jesse Sowell** 550 acres/$550; **Asa Sowell** 520 acres/$920, 149 acres/$650; **Adam Comer** 460 acres/$500; **Margaret McQueen** 200 acres/$400; **Charles Furr** 270 acres/$200; **Eli Phillips** 289 acres/$250; **Samson D. Smith** 200 acres/$300; **Benjn. Phillips** 100 acres/$200; **John Ritter** 50 acres/$40; **James Smith** 460 acres/$300; **Ann White** 950 acres/$950; **Jesse Muse Esq.** 625 acres/$1350; **Thomas P. Muse** 150 acres/$350; **William Barrett** 815 acres/$7600, 280 acres/$500, 138 acres/$40, 100 acres/$20; **Allen Morrison** 190 acres/$30, 300 acres/$20, 290 acres/$30, 160 acres/$25, 200 acres/$30, 130 acres/$25, 420 acres/$120, 109 acres/$30, 10 acres/$60, 205 acres/$200; **James McArthur** 50 acres/$50; **John Morrison** 100 acres/$100; **Alexr. Autray** 208 acres/$416; **Jeremiah Williams** 110 acres/$150; **Matthew Deaton** 313 acres/$450, 100 acres/$25, 200 acres/$200, 100 acres/$80; **John Gibson** 93 acres/$100; **Charles Seawell** 172 acres/$100; **George Hundsucker** 148 acres/$148, 60 acres/$62; **Jacob Furr** 137 acres/$137, 313 acres/$313; **John Dunn** 135 acres/$136; **Henry Stuts** 200 acres/$300, 100 acres/$50, 150 acres/$200; **Jacob Smith** 300 acres/$75; **Ezekiah Autray** 100 acres/$140; **John Lewis** 230 acres/$200; **Malcolm Morrison** 274 acres/$200; **Allin Bethune** 200 acres/$100; **Leonard Furr** 235 acres/$175, 50 acres/$37.50; **James Autray** 132 acres/$60; **Murdock McKinzie** 150 acres/$112.50, 200 acres/$50; **John Smith** 100 acres/$100; **Britton Britt** 50 acres/$60, 130 acres/$65; **William Copland** 204 acres/$204; **Abigail Harden** 50 acres/$50; **Isham Smith** 70 acres/$70; **John McNeill** 200 acres/$200, 100 acres/$100, 362 acres/$362, 300 acres/$300; **James Maness** 150 acres; **John Milton** 160 acres/$80; **Christopher Stuts** 150 acres/$400; **Hector McNeill** 164 acres/$164; **Murdoch Mathewson** 310 acres/$ 232.50; **Everet Wallis** 100 acres/$100; **Jesse Phillips** 136 acres/$136; **Alex. McKinzie** 150 acres/$150; **John Kennedy** 100 acres/$100; **George Cagle** 114 acres/$50, 100 acres/$150, 60 acres/$120, 50 acres/$25, 30 acres/$30; **Normand Mathewson** 100 acres/$50, 100 acres/$75, 100 acres/$25, 50 acres/$10, 250 acres/$200; **John McKinnon** 250 acres/$367.50, 50 acres/$50, 50 acres/$50, 150 acres/$82.50; **Normand McKinnon** 10 acres/$25; **Angus McKinnon** 60 acres/$50; **Roderick McAulay** 200 acres/$250, 100 acres/$50; **Hector McLane** 100 acres/$100, 50 acres/$25, 100 acres/$100; **John Patterson** 450 acres/$500; **John Kees** 55 acres/$82.50; **Norman Morrrison** 300 acres/$300, 150 acres/$150; **John Cockman** 100 acres/$100; **James Hains** 50 acres/$50; **Stephen Richardson** 400 acres/$600; **James Wood** 450 acres/$725; **Lewis Garner** (heirs) 425 acres/$425; **James Milton** 350 acres/$300; **Murdoch McAulay** 200 acres/$100, 65 acres/$50, 50 acres/$50; **David Richardson** 75 acres/$75; **James Dunlap** 100 acres/$150, 350 acres/$450; **Thomas Harwell** 100 acres/$100, 50 acres/$25; **Levy Deaton** 200 acres/$400, 60 acres/$100; 90 acres/$110; **Norman McKinnon** 228 acres/$228; **John McCrummen** 70 acres/$20; **Joseph Cole** 250 acres/$200; **William Smith Snr.** 50 acres/$150, 225 acres/$250; **Nathan Morgan** 169 acres/$250; **David McCrummen** 100 acres/$150, 300 acres/$300, 70 acres/$50; **Alex. McIntosh** 146 acres/$220, 200 acres/$150, 150 acres/$50, 50 acres/$25; **Hector McLain** 100

acres/$100; **William Dunn** 100 acres/$200, 64 acres/$64; **Murdock McAulay** 60 acres/$60, 150 acres/$150; **Rody Britt** 225 acres/$150; **Elijah Autray** 250 acres/$200; **Alexr. Morrison** 100 acres/$200, 72 acres/$50; **William Jones** 100 acres/$100, 125 acres/$125; **Benjn. Caddell** 100 acres/$100, 200 acres/$50, 100 acres/$50; **Bartholomew Dunn** 128 acres/$128; **William Feagin** 400 acres/$300; **Burrell Deaton** 100 acres; **Shadrick Maness** 50 acres/$70; **George Kennedy** 32 acres/$80; **Angus Morrison** 145 acres/$45; **John Smith Senr.** 125 acres/$170; **Samuel Kees** 230 acres/$300; **Catherine Cockmon** 150 acres/$150; **Solomon Barrett** 300 acres/$300; **Meloney Newton** 150 acres/$150; **Malcolm Mathewson** 50 acres/$150, 50 acres/$100 acres/$41 acres/$50; **John McKinnon** 50 acres/$25, 50 acres/$25; **Ruben Freeman** 100 acres/$100, 100 acres/$100, 89 acres/$200; **William N. Manis** 50 acres/$50; **James Garner** 133 acres/$133, 47 acres/$47.50; **William Freeman** 117 acres/$237, 100 acres/$50, 50 acres/$80; *Peter Hare Sr. 87 acres/$300, 60 acres/$140, 50 acres/$90, 50 acres/$50, 100 acres/$50, 85 acres/$25, 50 acres/$10, 100 acres/$25, 50 acres/$10; John Hare Sr. 140 acres/$420, 117 acres/$234, 100 acres/$250, 50 acres/$1--, 50 acres/$50; 65 acres/$32.50; 100 acres/$50; John Cagle 185 acres/$200; George Cagle 70 acres/$100, 100 acres/$50; John Spivay 400 acres/$400, 100 acres/$100, 100 acres/$100, 100 acres/$50; Joseph Allen 102 acres/$102, 150 acres/$150, 45 acres/$22.50, 50 acres/$25, acres/$50, 50 acres/$25, 9 acres/$9, 68 acres/$68, 50 acres/$25, 45 acres/$22.50, 50 acres/$25, 150 acres/$37.50; Mark Allen 275 acres/$275, 25 acres/$25; Allin Williamson 100 acres/$50; Everet Shuffield 172 acres/$250; Isham Shuffield 50 acres/$20, 41 acres/$50; John Caveness 200 acres/$350; William Williamson 295 acres/$886, 150 acres/$75, 70 acres/$72, 84 acres/$42, 100 acres/$50, 309 acres/$154.50, 100 acres/$25, 200 acres/$200, 100 acres/$100; Andrew Yow 100 acres/$100, 92 acres/$92; Christopher Yow (heirs) 100 acres/$100; Bradly Garner 350 acres/$350, 110 acres/$82.50, 90 acres/$45, 300 acres/$300, 88 acres/$88, 100 acres/$75, 15 acres/$11.25, 700 acres/$175; Joseph Morgan 200 acres/$300, 15 acres/$7.50, 30 acres/$15, 7 acres/$7; Jesse Brown 575 acres/$400, 50 acres/$25, 50 acres/$25; Peter Shamburger Sr. 200 acres/$150, 100 acres/$75, 300 acres/$75, 75 acres/$37.70, 75 acres/$37.50; John Kennedy 100 acres/$300; Bailey Williamson 300 acres/$150, 200 acres/$225; Martin Cagle 200 acres/$300; Nathaniel Tucker 150 acres/$300; William Shamburger 100 acres/$50; Nathan Smith 100 acres/$100, 50 acres/$25, 25 acres/$12.50, 50 acres/$50, 50 acres/$50, 10 acres/$10; Daniel Maness Sr. 100 acres/$50, 120 acres/$35, 100 acres/$50, 4 acres/$4.50; Isham Shuffield 100 acres/$75, 100 acres/$95, 50 acres/$50; Medford Owens 150 acres/$150; Edmond Hollin 100 acres/$50, 150 acres/$50; John*

Maness 100 acres/$100; Mishack Maness 100 acres/$100; Alex. Kennedy 660 acres/$1100; Charles Brady 100 acres/$100; Benjn. Persons 50 acres/$100; Edward Kennedy 50 acres/$500, 300 acres/$150; **Francis Bullock** 200 acres/$800, 150 acres/$200, 100 acres/$100, 200 acres/$200, 800 acres/$100, 240 acres/$200, 100 acres/$10, 400 acres/$200, 200 acres/$75; **Jacob Cagle** 150 acres/$150; **Richd. Holland** 90 acres/$180, 50 acres/$75, 280 acres/$160, 94 acres/$49, 189 acres/$200; **John Shuffield Junr.** 40 acres/$175, 150 acres/$123, 27 acres/$50, 26 acres/$26, 8 acres/$20, 3 acres/$6; **Henry Yow** 200 acres/$350; **Joseph Smotherman** 100 acres/$50; **Peter Shamburger Junr.** 100 acres/$385, 100 acres/$330, 100 acres/$130, 50 acres/$75, 10 acres/$3; **Angus Leatch** 200 acres/$220; **Alexr. Leatch** 124 acres/$200; **Malcolm Leatch** 336 acres/$320; **Peter Cagle** 280 acres/$250; **Peter Gardner** 94 acres/$100, 500 acres/$250, 385 acres/$96.25; **David Kennedy** 200 acres/$900, 240 acres/$240, 50 acres/$50, 50 acres/$50, 25 acres/$50, 160 acres/$160, 50 acres/$100, 3 acres/$1000, 200 acres/$100, 200 acres/$100; **Cornelius Latham** 150 acres/$250, 100 acres/$50, 200 acres/$100; **Nicholas Nall** 300 acres/$3000, 250 acres/$250, 100 acres/$100, 100 acres/$100, 90 acres/$90, 150 acres/$300; **Peter Davis** 300 acres/$900, 100 acres/$300, 100 acres/$200, 50 acres/$25, 19 acres/$10, 50 acres/$25, 100 acres/$100, 100 acres/$50; **John Shamburger** 200 acres/$750, 250 acres/$120, 60 acres/$125, 100 acres/$50, 100 acres/$50, 68 acres/$17, 300 acres/$75, 200 acres/$50, 250 acres/$200, 225 acres/$200, 150 acres/$38; **Frederick Autray** 200 acres/$500, 92 acres/$92, 89 acres/$89, 60 acres/$50; **Jeremiah Wilson** 100 acres/$300, 155 acres/$105, 83 acres/$25, 50 acres/$40, 50 acres/$40; **George Moore** 110 acres/$200, 25 acres/$100, 200 acres/$180; **Hiram Kennedy** 348 acres/$348, 300 acres/$100; **William Williamson** 100 acres/$125; **Wm. Hundsucker** 112 acres/$112; **Thomas Persons** 50 acres/$100, 69 acres/$69, 410 acres/$831; **John Dunlap Jur.** 83 acres/$100, 100 acres/$25, 80 acres/$20; **Jeremiah Williams** 150 acres/$150, 150 acres/$250; **William Right Jur.** 165 acres/$330, 50 acres/$70; **William Brown** 100 acres/$100; **William Waddell** 480 acres/$1200; **James Morgan** 100 acres/$200, 50 acres/$50, 50 acres/$50, 70 acres/$100, 50 acres/$25, 100 acres/$150; **Robert Kennedy** 200 acres/$250, 93 acres/$100; **John Shuffield Senr.** 141 acres/$150, 50 acres/$25, 50 acres/$25; **William Right Sr.** 100 acres/$200, 50 acres/$10; **Sherwood Right** 135 acres/$67.50, 60 acres/$30, 15 acres/$50, 25 acres/$12.50; **Eli Callicutt** 183 acres/$300, 100 acres/$80, 20 acres/$20; **Stephen Davis** 100 acres/$100, 189 acres/$40, 150 acres/$100, 50 acres/$15, 25 acres/$69, 15 acres/$15; **William Maness Senr.** 100 acres/$100; **Kenneth Murchison** 275 acres/$225.

A.   1815 - Tax List, Chatham County, NC [selected residents]
Name, acres and taxable amount in Capt. Lane's District: **Bryon Burroughs** 710 acres/$1000 on Tysons Creek; **Nancy Brewer** 574 acres/$692 on Fall Creek adjoining **James Scott**; **Solomon Brewer** 1 white poll; **Randal Cheek** 400 acres/$600 adjoining **James Shields**; **Jackson Deaton** 46 acres/$46 on Cedar Creek; **Clabourn Deaton** 1 white poll; **John Deaton** 130 acres/$102 on Cedar Creek and 1 white poll; **William Deaton** 230 acres/$345 on Cedar Creek and 1 white poll adjoining **John Vanderford**; **Moses Kidd** 350 acres/$800 on Cedar Creek and 1 white poll 1 black poll adjoining **Benjn. Needham**; **Eli Lawler** 124 acres/$250 on Fall Creek adjoining **William Triplet**; **John Lawler** 50 acres/$100 on Fall Creek and 1 white poll adjoining **Eli Lawler**; **Jehu Lawler** 1 white poll; **Laban Phillips** 43 acres/$86 on Tysons Creek and 1 white poll; **Sion Phillips** 304 acres/$300 on Tysons Creek and 1 white poll adjoining **Thomas Sanders**; **Meredith Phillips** 200 acres/$100 on Fall Creek and 1 white poll adjoining **Sugar Jones**; **Benjamin Phillips** 150 acres/$100 on Tysons Creek and 1 white poll adjoining **Sion Phillips**; **Phebe Phillips** 150 acres/$150 on Tysons Creek adjoining **Benjn. Sanders**; **John Vanderford** 252 acres/$252 and 1 white poll on Cedar Creek adjoining **James Culbertson**.

3008.   1815, Jan 6 -- Land Grant #2261, Moore County, NC
Donald McDonald received 50 acres located west of Dry Creek adjoining **Donald McDonald Senr.**, **John Paterson** and **Levi Deaton**. **Levi Deaton** and **John Key** were chain carriers.

3009.   1815, Feb -- 1796-1841 County Accounts, Moore County, NC Page 17
1815, May-Nov 1815 -- 1808-1819 Trial and Appearance Docket, Moore County, NC
Jacob Furr v. **Wm. Martin**, **M. Martin** and **Alexd. McLeod**, Admin.

3010.   1815, Apr 4-Nov 10 -- Civil Actions, Randolph County, NC Box 20
James Lathem and **William Lathem** sued **Samuel Allen**, **Polly Dunning**, **Jenny Dunning**, **Elizabeth Wright** (wife of **William Wright**) and **Elizabeth Wright** (wife of **Sherwood Wright**) for assaulting **William Lathem**. Bond of **Sherwood Wright**, **William Wright** and **Elizabeth Wright** secured by **Mark Wade** and **Eli Callicott** in Moore County Sep 8, 1815.

3011.   1815, Apr 26 -- Land Grant #2250, Moore County, NC
John Cheek received 200 acres located west of Rogers Creek adjoining his own line and **Phillips**. **Josiah Cheek** and **Lewis Phillips** were chain carriers.

3012. 1815, Apr 26 -- Land Grant #2252, Moore County, NC
John Cheek received 37 acres located east of Rogers Creek adjoining his own line, **Randolph Cheek** and **Joab Cheek**. **Josiah Cheek** and **Lewis Phillips** were chain carriers.

3013. 1815, May -- 1808-1819 Trial and Appearance Docket, Moore County, NC
1815, May -- 1796-1841 County Accounts, Moore County, NC Page 18
#20 **A. McQueen** v. **Jno. Melton**
#5 **Nathan Barrett** v. **John Milton**

3014. 1815, May -- 1796-1841 County Accounts, Moore County, NC Page 18
Vicy Hunsucker fines collected

3015. 1815, May 1 -- Land Grant #2470, Moore County, NC
Stephen Davis received 21 acres located on both sides of Wolf Creek adjoining **Reuben Freeman**, **Morgan**, his own line and **Eli Callicutt**. **William Davis** and **Robert Davis** were chain carriers.

A. 1815, Oct 16 -- Deed Book 63 Page 352-353, Moore County, NC
Robert Barker (of Chatham County) deeded **James Davis** 180 acres located on Deep River adjoining **James Davis**. **William C. Davis** and **Robert Davis** were witnesses. [*Editor's Note: **William Russell** also signed deed with **Robert Barker***]

3016. 1815, Oct 24 -- Land Grant #2256, Moore County, NC
John Dunlap Junr. received 80 acres located south of Bear Creek adjoining his own line (formerly **Bullock**), **Thomas Williams** (formerly **Francis Bullock**) and **Brown**. **William Brewer** and **Isaac Cagle** were chain carriers.

3017. 1815, Oct 25 -- Land Grant #2255, Moore County, NC
James Hains received 50 acres located east of Buffalo Creek adjoining his own line, **James Dunlap** and **Leonard Furr Senr.** (now known as the **Moore** Place). **Normand Matheson** and **Jeremiah Williams** were chain carriers.

3018. 1815, Oct 25 -- Land Grant #2257, Moore County, NC
Normand Matheson received 100 acres located on Willow and Long Meadow adjoining his own line (formerly **John Carrel**). **James Hains** and **Jeremiah Williams** were chain carriers.

3019. 1815, Oct 26 -- Land Grant #2339, Moore County, NC
Jeremiah Williams received 100 acres located southeast of Buffalo Creek adjoining **Henry Stutts** and own line. **Thos. Williams** and **James Hains** were chain carriers.

3020. 1815, Oct 28 -- *A History of Sandy Creek Baptist Association* by George Purefoy, Page 67

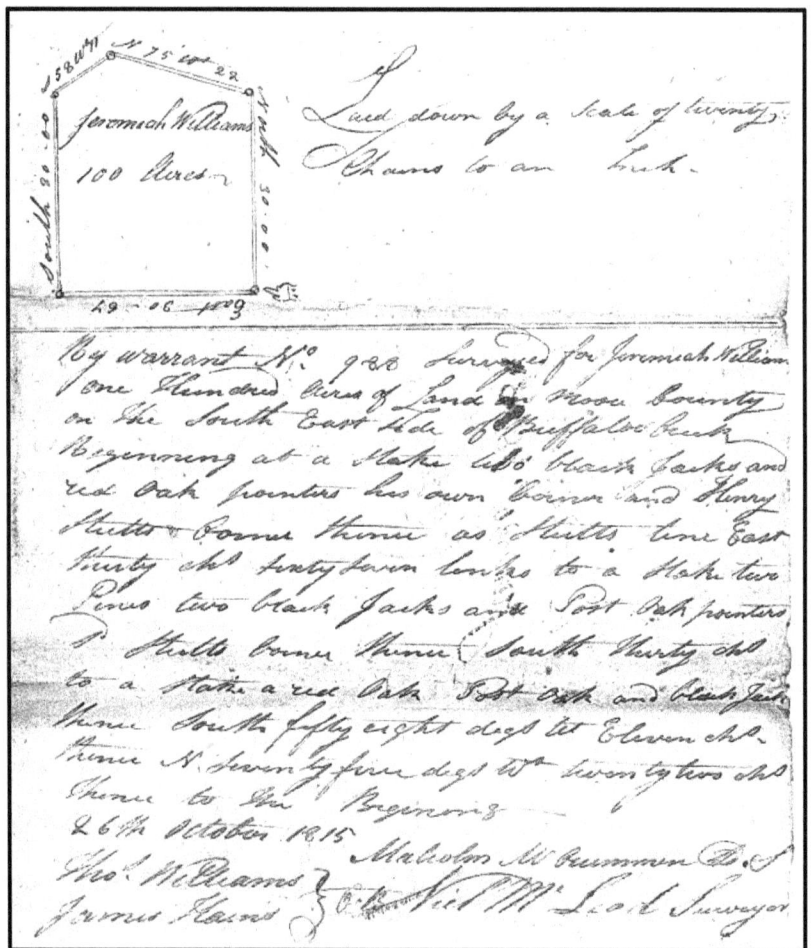

William Dowd, Jesse Muse and Holden Cox from McLennon's Creek Church (Moore County) and Elder Isaac Teague, Bryant Boroughs and Eli Lawler from Fall Creek Church (Chatham County) were delegates to the Association meeting at Rock Spring Meeting House in Chatham County, NC.

3021.	1815, Nov -- 1796-1841 County Accounts, Moore County, NC Page 4
Isaac Sowell v. T. Ritter

3022.	1815, Nov -- 1808-1819 Trial and Appearance Docket, Moore County, NC
Mishack Manus v. Benjamin Person

3023.	1815, Nov 3 -- Land Grant #2019, Montgomery County, NC
Francis Bullock received 60 acres located on both sides of Wolf Creek and the Moore County line adjoining James Callacoat's old place, Samuel Allen, McCrimon and Wilkins. Allen Bullock and John Kealin were chain carriers.

3024.	1815, Nov 3 -- Land Grant #2023, Montgomery County, NC
Francis Bullock received 100 acres located on Wolf Creek near the Moore County line adjoining Samuel Allen, his own line and John Shamburg. Allen Bullock and John Kealin were chain carriers.

3025.	1815, Nov 11 -- Land Grant #2262, Moore County, NC
Alexr. McIntosh received 50 acres located on Juniper Branch of McLendons Creek and both sides of the Waggon Road adjoining his own line and Michael Bryant. Alexr. McIntosh and Allan Martin were chain carriers.

3026.	1815, Nov 26 -- Paoli Monthly [Quaker] Meeting, Lick Creek Minutes Page 32, Orange County, IN
Simon Rubottom produced a certificate for himself and sons: namely, George, Thomas, William, Samuel, Ezekial, John and Zeno, from Cain Creek Monthly Meeting on Oct 9, 1815 and was accepted.

A.	1815, Dec 6 -- Land Grant #1938, Chatham County, NC
Edward Harper received 217 acres located on Fall Creek adjoining Findley, John Harper and William Harper. James Scott and John Scott were chain carriers.

B.	1815, Dec 22 – Deed Book V Page 28-29, Chatham County, NC
Richard Beeson deeded Meredith Phillips 200 acres located on Fall Creek adjoining Henry Powers and Findley. Eli Lawler and Edwd. Beason were witnesses.

3027.	1815, Dec 30 -- Land Grant #2373, Moore County, NC
John Seat Senr. received 10 acres located on McLendons Creek adjoining Lauchlin McNeill, Archd. Ray and Wldow Glascock. John Scat and Henry Craven were chain carriers.

3028.	1816 -- Record of Estates Book B, Moore County, NC Page 114-118
Estate of Neil McLeod, Dec'd. by Murdock Martin and Alexr. McLeod. _Accounts due on the following as of 1816 -- estate probated in 1827_: Ambrose Brewer, Bradley Garner, Leonard Stuts, John Morris, John Yow, Gabriel Harden, Susannah Brewer, Roderick McLeod, James Muse, Willis Brewer, Alexr. McCaskill, John Smith, Henry Stuts, James Hines, John Garner, George Carriner, Bartholomew Dunn, William McLennon, John McDiffie, Nathan Vick, James Williams, David Overton, Sterling Carrell, Jacob Carriner, Neill McLeod Sr., Murdock Bethune, Alexr. McLeod (Capt.), Neill McDonald (Capt.), Kenneth Murchison, Edward Stewart, Archd. McNeill, Lesh Stuts, Nathan Kenneday, John McLennon, Robert McLaughlin, William Murchison, Mary Barker, Elkins James, Angus Anderson, Duncan McIntosh, Alexr. Davidson, William Singleton, Joel Rodgers, John McDonald, John McCaskell, John Needham, Andrew Yow, Frances Myrick, Nathaniel Bostick, John Shuffield, Samuel Dunn, John Keeling, John Martin (Regt.), Winsor Pearce, Lindsay Vick, Edey Vick, Samuel Baringtine, Patrick Phillips, Howell Brewer, Henry Brewer, William Cagle, John Keller, Neill McLeod (surveyor), Nathan Barrett, Arcd. Ray Esq., William Hunsucker, Stephen Elkins, Eli Phillips, Edmd. Davis, Frederick Autray, James McArthur, Cornelius Shields, Shadrick Rodgers, John Tolmin, Nameles Maness, Charles Brady, Fanning Moore, David Richardson, James Spivay, James Garner, David Kennedy, David Brewer, Nathan Morgan, Christopher Hunsucker, Averet Wallis, Nathan Smith, Nancy McLeod, William Martindale, William Dunn, Alexr. Carrell, Moses Teague, John Wadsworth, John Martin (Long Meadow), Winson Seawell, Averet Smith, Mary Robinson, Murdy Reaves, Robert King, Ignatious Wadsworth, Jeremiah Phillips, Nicholas Maness, James Moore, Elijah Brown, Burwell Deaton, Abednego Maness, Robert Brady, George Moore, William Williams, Medford Owens, James Myers, Jabaz York, James

Right, Averet Wallis, Malcolm Mathewson, Nathan Fry, Adam White, Ruben Freeman, Neill Mathewson, Eli Lawler, Donald McLeod, Angus Morrison, Murdoch Mathewson, John Cagle, Kenneth McCaskell, Mathias Richardson, George Yow, John McDonald Jr., John Arnet, Alxr. Chisholm, Jesse Smith, Isaac Teague, Micajah Brewer, Hammer[?] Dunn, James B. Carrell, Rosannah Barker, Alexr. Autray, William Argo, George Cagle, William Needham, William Armstead, Nicholas Nall, William Russell, Burges Davis, Nancey Milton, Daniel McNeill, John McIver, Richard Cheek, Joseph Duckworth, Jason Muse, James Williamson, John Lawler, William Wilson, Urias Mash, Donald McSween, Daniel Maness and Thos. Muse Jr.

3029. 1816/1817 -- Bastardy Bond, Randolph County, NC
John Bullock (of Moore County) fathered a child with **Marab Smith**. **Thos. Cox** and **Thos. Harvey** were securities.

3030. 1816, Jan 2 -- Land Grant #2279, Moore County, NC
Jesse Brewer received 110 acres located on Fall Creek adjoining **Wells**, **Person**, **Charles Brady**, **Frazier** and **James Brady**. **Micajah Brewer** and **Bradley Brady** were chain carriers.

3031. 1816, Feb -- 1796-1841 County Accounts, Moore County, NC
Meshack Maner v. **B. Person**

3032. 1816, Feb 4 -- Land Grant #2403, Moore County, NC
John McDonald received 50 acres located on Dry Fork of McLendons Creek and Suck Branch. **Angus McAulay** and **John McDonald** were chain carriers.

3033. 1816, Feb 12-Mar 5 -- Estate, Chatham County, NC
Estate of **Randal Cheek**, Dec'd. by administrators **John Cheek** and **Joab Cheek**. **Randal Cheek** died Feb 1, 1816 owning two tracts of land: 241 acres on Tices Creek joining the [Moore] County line and 167 acres on Tices Creek adjoining the first tract and **Wm. Phillips**. Children of **Randal Cheek** listed as **John Cheek**, **Joab Cheek**, **Mary Cheek**, **Jane Gilbert**, **Patty Phillips**, **Samuel Dunn** and wife **Elizabeth**, **Matthew Phillips** and wife **Lydia**, **Thomas Parks** and wife **Anna**. **Richard Jones**, **Eli Lawler**, **Nathan McManus**, **Sugar Jones** and **Aaron McManus** were appointed to divide the land in 8 lots. *Items were purchased by the following*: **Matthew Phillips**, **Mary Cheek**, **Joab Cheek**, **Benjamin Guilbert**, **Robert Moore**, **Samuel Elliott**, **Joab Cheek Junr.**, **Archibald Shields**, **Lazurus Phillips**, **Tinzle Wade**, **Isaac Teague Seingr.**, **James Hilyard**, **Josiah Cheek**, **Roderick Murchison**, **Cornelius Shields**, **Patty Phillips**, **James Call**, **Thomas Parks**, **Adam White**, **Thomas Cheek**, **Denis Phillips**, **Edward Harper**, **Nathan McManus**, **Brinkley Phillips**, **James Hardin**, **Denis Phillips**, **Joab Cheek Seignr.**, **Henry Phillips Seignr.**, **William**

Handcock, Robert Phillips, James Phillips, William Phillips, John Murchison , James England, James Gains, John Melton, Hezekiah Phillips, Marada Phillips, Stephen Davis, Calvin Cox, Robert Wilson, Daniel McDaniel, James McNeill, Gabriel Hardin and Thomas Wilson.

3034.   1816, Mar 12 -- Land Grant #2401, Moore County, NC
Donald McDonald received 50 acres located east of McLendons Creek on Jacobs Branch adjoining John Cox, Allan Martin, Robert Graham and his own line. John McDonald and Donald McDonald were chain carriers.

A.   1816, Mar 14 -- Marriage Bond, Randolph County, NC
Hardy Davis and Rebacka Osburn received marriage bond. Absalom Millikan was bondsman. [Editor's Note: Date of marriage occurred on or after date of marriage bond.]

3035.   1816, May -- 1785-1868 Index to Trial Docket, Moore County, NC
Wm. Martin v. Abednego Maness

3036.   1816, May 7 -- Will, Jones County, GA
Will of Richardson Feagin, Dec'd. Heirs: wife Martha [negroes Sidney, Moses and Tom] and son Henry. Executors: Bryant Burroughs, Cornelius Dowd, Thomas Feagin and Samuel Feagin. Witnesses: Jesse Sanders and Sarah Feagin. Probated Aug 1818 in Jones County, GA. [Editor's Note: the will was likely written and signed in Moore County, NC and filed in Jones County, GA]

3037.   1816, May 8 -- Land Grant #2674, Moore County, NC
Sampson D. Smith received 100 acres located south of Richland Creek adjoining his own line and Roberts. Richard Upton and Cornelius Smith were chain carriers.

3038.   1816, May 21 -- Land Grant #2394, Moore County, NC
Jesse Upton Junr. received 400 acres located on the drains of McCallums Fork and the Waggon Road adjoining Angus McQueen, Solomon Brewer and John Upton. Jesse Ritter and Solo. Brewer were chain carriers.

3039.   1816, May 21 -- Land Grant #2382, Moore County, NC
George Kennedy received 100 acres located east of Bear Creek adjoining McAulay, James Manus and Stephen Richardson. Henry Stuts and Jacob Stuts were chain carriers.

3040.   1816, Jul -- Chronicles and Records of Bensalem Presbyterian Church Page 19, Moore County, NC
Allen Martin died. Husband of Margaret McDonald Martin.

A.   1816, Jul 21 -- Marriage Bond, Chatham County, NC
Benjamin Smith and Easter Argo received marriage bond. Jacob Teague was bondsman. [Editor's Note: Date of marriage occurred on or after date of marriage bond.]

3041.   1816, Aug -- 1785-1868 Index to Trial Docket, Moore County, NC Page 16
State v. Wm. Maness Jr. and Shadrick Maness Jr.

3042.   1816, Aug -- 1796-1841 County Accounts, Moore County, NC
Fines collected from Wm. and S. Maner

3043.   1816, Aug-May 1817 -- 1796-1841 County Accounts, Moore County, NC Page 20, 21
1816, Aug-Aug 3, 1817 -- 1808-1819 Trial and Appearance Docket, Moore County, NC
Wm. Hundsucker v. Roderick Murchison

3044.   1816, Aug 16 -- Land Grant #2290, Moore County, NC
John Lewis received 100 acres located east of Camp Branch adjoining his own line, Alexr. McIntosh and Benjamin Caddle. William Caddle and Wm. Lewis were chain carriers.

3045.   1816, Sep 20 -- Deed Book HH Page 154-155, Franklin County, GA
Isaac Smith and wife Elizabeth deeded James Allan 200 acres on Hudson River. William Martin and Timothy Terrell JP were witnesses. Recorded Oct 10, 1817.

3046. 1816, Sep 21-Nov 1817 -- Inventories and Sales, Surry County, NC Pages 196-198, 219
Estate of **James Ritter**, Dec'd. by **Lazarous Ritter**, Administrator. **Enoch Stone**, **Nathan Bales**, **Caleb Jesop** and **Abijah Pinson** appointed to lay off one year's allowance to **Anna Ritter**, widow of **James Ritter**. [widow is alternately listed as **Nancy Ritter**]

3047. 1816, Oct 4 -- Land Grant #2284, Moore County, NC
James Haines received 50 acres located south of Buffalo Creek adjoining his own line. **James Hains** and **Normand Matheson** were chain carriers.

3048. 1816, Oct 18 -- Land Grant #2295, Moore County, NC
Richard Cheek received 22 acres located south of Deep River adjoining **Robert Davis**, **White**, **John Hancock** and **Samuel Murley**.

3049. 1816, Oct 23 -- Land Grant #2283, Moore County, NC
Isaac Cagle received 20 acres located on both sides of Cabin Creek adjoining **George Cagle**, **Jesse Brown** and his own line. **Bartholomew Dunn** and **Wm. Brown** were chain carriers.

3050. 1816, Oct 25 -- Land Grant #2278, Moore County, NC
James Melton received 200 acres located on Long Meadow adjoining **Normand Matheson**, **Williams** and his own line. **Normand Matheson** and **Solomon Brewer** were chain carriers.

3051. 1816, Oct 26 -- *A History of Sandy Creek Baptist Association* by George Purefoy, Page 69
Elder **I. Teague**, **B. Boroughs** and **E. Lawler** from Fall Creek Church (Chatham County) were delegates to the Association meeting at Brush Creek Meeting House in Randolph County, NC.

A. 1816, Nov 10 -- Deed Book W Page 344-346, Chatham County, NC
Horace P. Bridges, Sheriff deeded **Murdock McKenzie** and **Archibald McBryde** of **Aaron Tyson** & Co. 1/9 part (33 acres) of **Jeremiah Phillips Senr.** Dec'd., 300 acres located on Indian Creek to settle debts of **Patrick Phillips**, son of **Jeremiah Phillips**.

3052. 1816, Nov 12 -- Land Grant #2289, Moore County, NC
William Barret received 25 acres located east of McLendons Creek adjoining **Goodwin**, **Elijah Bettis Jur.**, **McKenzie**, **Roberts**, **Stewart** and his own line(that he purchased from **Charles Furr**). **John Barret** and **Sterlin Carrol** were chain carriers.

3053. 1816, Nov 21 -- Deed Book HH Page 123-124, Franklin County, GA
Nathan Smith and wife **Nancy** deeded **Henry Mize** 126 acres located on Hudson Fork of Broad River being part of 600 acres granted to **Julian Nail**. **Robert S. Bailey** and **Henry Smith** were witnesses. Recorded Mar 11, 1819.

3054. 1816, Nov 28 -- Land Grant #2417, Moore County, NC
Patrick Dowd received 100 acres located north of Richland Creek adjoining **Richard Upton**, **Jesse Sowell**, **Angus McQueen** and his own line. **John Danelly** and **Calvin Cox** were chain carriers.

3055. 1817 -- Chronicles and Records of Bensalem Presbyterian Church Page 5, Moore County, NC
Alexander Leach was removed as Elder after committing adultery with a woman that was bound to him. He was prosecuted, suspended and is now a member of the Baptist Church.

3056. 1817-1818 -- Panosophia Masonic Lodge No. 25, Carthage, NC
George Kennedy was a member. Suspended between Nov 1817-Nov 1818

3057. 1817-1819 -- Pansophia Masonic Lodge No. 25, Carthage, NC
Jesse Sanders served as Treasurer

3058. 1817-1820 [undated estimate] -- Estate, Moore County, NC Will Book A, Page 327-328
Inventory of the Estate of **Adam White**, Dec'd. by Administrators **Lazarus Birckhead** and **Mrs. White**. [*Editor's Note: No date given on actual inventory, but the date was estimated using other records. Adam's last appearance was 1817 and he appeared to be deceased by 1820 Census. His estate was surrounded by others in 1810 and 1811 but Adam can be found in several records after this time suggesting his date of death was later or that there was more than one Adam White.*]

3059. 1817, Jan 4 -- Will Book A Page 295, Moore County, NC Will of **Joseph Cole**, Dec'd. Heirs: wife **Amy Cole**, son **Joseph Cole**, daughter **Sary Edins**, daughter **Elizabeth Dunlap**, son **George Cole**, son **James Cole** and daughter **Mary Jones**. Executors: **James Cole** and **John Paterson**. Witnesses: **Angus Morison** and **John Kannady**. Proven Aug 1817.

3060. 1817, Jan 7 -- Deed Book 6 Page 175, Moore County, NC **John Sowell** deeded **William Barrett Senr**. 400 acres located south of McLendons Creek adjoining **James McLeod**, **Barrett**, **John Sowell** and **David Allison**. **Aaron Sowell** and **Geo. Ritter** were witnesses.

A. 1817, Feb 26 – Deed Book 13 Page 269-270, Randolph County, NC **Lewis Davis** (of Hawkins County, TN) deeded **John Cassady** 2 tracts located on Fork Creek [1] 75 acres adjoining **Cost** [2] 100 acres **Thomas Cost Junr.** and **Latham**. **H. Moffitt** and **Peggy Moffitt** were witnesses.

B. 1817, Feb 28 – Deed Book 13 Page 170-171, Randolph County, NC **Lewis Davis** (of Hawkins County, TN) gave his power of attorney to **Peter Davis** (of Moore County) to sell all his land located in Randolph County.

3061. 1817, Mar 5 -- Land Grant #2424, Moore County, NC **John Dannelly** received 300 acres located on McCollums Fork adjoining **Patrick Dowd**, heirs of **Joseph Dunn Junr.** and **Jesse Upton**. **John Dannelly Jr.** and **Calvin Cox** were chain carriers.

3062. 1817, Mar 12 -- Land Grant #2360, Moore County, NC **James Atkins** received 200 acres located on Watery Branch between Bear Creek and Buffalo Creek adjoining **Burroughs**, his own line, **Stuts** and **Neil McLeod**. **John Ritter** and **Thos. Ritter** were chain carriers.

3063. 1817, Mar 27 -- Land Grant #2349, Moore County, NC **John Cheek** received 46 acres located north of Deep River adjoining **Benjamin Gilbert**, his own line and **Hamilton**. **Jos. Cheek** and **Josiah Cheek** were chain carriers.

3064. 1817, Mar 27 -- Land Grant #2395, Moore County, NC
John Cheek received 32 acres located on Deep River including the mouth of **Atlas Jones'** Spring Branch and an island in Deep River. **Jos. Cheek** and **Josiah Cheek** were chain carriers.

3065. 1817, Mar 30 -- Will, Randolph County, NC
Will of **John Leatham Sr.** Dec'd. Heirs: wife (unnamed) and eight children: **John** (Jr.), **Solomon**, **Richard**, **Jesse**, **Susanah**, **Salley**, **Polley** and **Betsey**. Witnesses: **Manner Brookther**, **Solomon Leatham** and **Joseph Hudson**. Proven Feb 1818.

3066. 1817, Apr 8 -- Land Grant #2306, Moore County, NC
Donald McCrummen received 70 acres located on Horse Creek adjoining **Neil McLeod**, **Murdock McLeod** and **Matthew Deaton**. **J. Britt** and **D. McCrummen** were chain carriers.

3067. 1817, Apr 10 -- Land Grant #2346, Moore County, NC
Adam White received 100 acres located on Watery Branch adjoining **Robert Davis** and **William Davis**. **James Harden** and **Jesse Willson** were chain carriers.

A. 1817, Apr 10 -- Land Grant #2348, Randolph County, NC
William Smitherman received 100 acres located on Meadow Branch and the [Moore] County line adjoining **James Latham** and his own line. **Cornelius Latham** and **Anthony Latham** were chain carriers.

3068. 1817, Apr 16 -- Land Grant #2374, Moore County, NC
John McIver received 150 acres located in the fork of McLendons Creek and Richland Creek adjoining **Carrol**, **Elijah Bettis**, **Cornelius Dowd** and **David Allison**. **William Barret** and **Tinsley Wade** were chain carriers.

3069. 1817, Apr 17 -- Land Grant #2564, Moore County, NC
Henry Stuts received 50 acres located west of Buffalo Creek adjoining **Stephen Richardson Senr.**, **Stephen Richardson Junr.**, **Jacob Stuts**, his own line and **John Richardson**. **Christopher Stuts** and **James Lacky** were chain carriers.

3070. 1817, Apr 27 -- Land Grant #2341, Moore County, NC
George Frazer received 43 acres located on Fall Creek of Deep River adjoining **Charles Brady**, his own line and **Robert Willson**. **James Hardin** and **William Matthews** were chain carriers.

3071. 1817, Apr 27 -- Land Grant #2344, Moore County, NC
Robert Willson received 100 acres located on Deep River adjoining his own line, **Charles Brady**, heirs of **John Argo** and **Cornelius Shields**. **James Hardin** and **William Matthews** were chain carriers.

3072. 1817, Apr 27 -- Deed, Moore County, NC
Frederick Siler deeded **John Oats**, **Charles Stewart**, **Archie Reed**, **William Dickerson** and **Cornelius Tyson**, Trustees of the Methodist Episcopal Chuch a tract near the Sandy Spring. **John W. Norton** and **Thomas Davis** were witnesses.
[Editor's Note: Original deed for land for Fair Promise Methodist Church. Deed located in *The John Phillips Family: Eleven Generations from Moore County, NC* by Emma Phillips Paschal]

3073. 1817, Apr 28 -- Land Grant #2391, Moore County, NC
James C. Davis received 3 acres located on

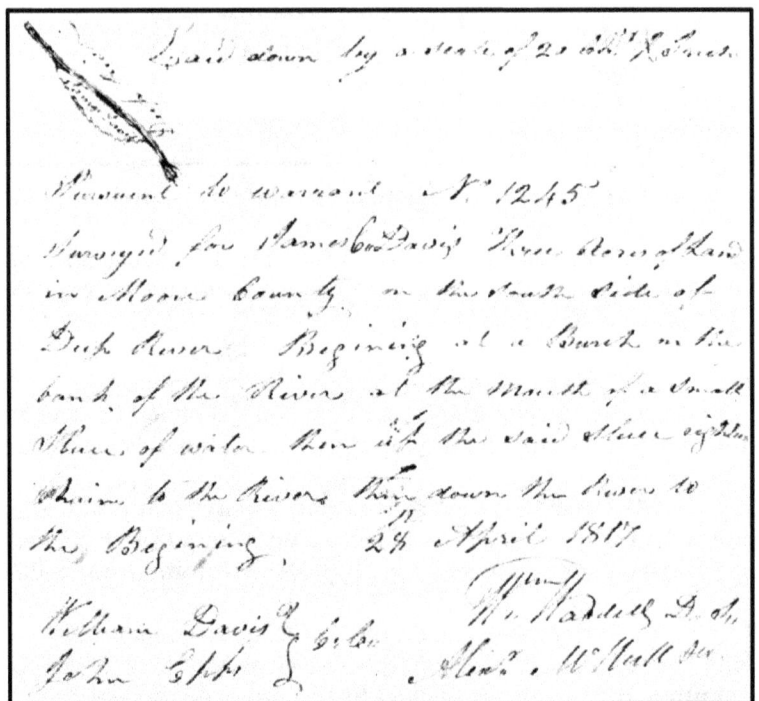

Deep River including the ford at the falls and an island below the falls adjoining his own line. **William Davis** and **John Epps** were chain carriers.

3074. 1817, Apr 30 -- Land Grant #2343, Moore County, NC
James Harden received 100 acres located on Toms Creek adjoining **Robert Davis** and **Neill McLeod**. **Adam White** and **James Davis** were chain carriers.

3075. 1817, Apr 30 -- Land Grant #2348, Moore County, NC
Adam White received 128 acres located on head of a glade of McLendons Creek adjoining **Robert Davis**, **James Harden** and **McLeod**. **James Harden** and **James Davis** were chain carriers.

A. 1817, Apr 30 -- Land Grant #2308, Moore County, NC
Archibald Shields received 24 acres located on Pates Creek adjoining **David Allison**, **James Shields**, **Argo**, **Wilson**, his own line and **Cornelius Shields**. **James Harden** and **Jesse Cheek** were chain carriers.

3076. 1817, May-Aug -- 1796-1841 County Accounts, Moore County, NC Page 21
1817, May-Aug 9, 1818 -- 1808-1819 Trial and Appearance Docket, Moore County, NC
John Richardson v. **John Melton**

A. 1817, May 7 -- Marriage Bond, Randolph County, NC
John Spinks and **Louise Jordan** received marriage bond. **James Johnston** was bondsman. **A. Gray** was witness.
[*Editor's Note: Date of marriage occurred on or after date of marriage bond.*]

B. 1817, May 30 -- Deed Book 6 Page 428-429, Moore County, NC
James Smith deeded **John Leavester** 150 acres located on Dry Fork of Juniper adjoining **McLeod** and **Rouse**. **David Brewer** and **Samuel Dew** were witnesses.

3077. 1817, Jul 1 -- Land Grant #2368, Moore County, NC
Patrick Dowd received 100 acres located on the drains of McCollums Fork adjoining **Richard Upton**, his own line and **Angus McQueen**. **Phillip Brooks** and **Calvin Cox** were chain carriers.

3078. 1817, Jul 2 -- Land Grant #2334, Moore County, NC
Jesse Upton received 100 acres on McCallums Fork of Richland Creek near the Waggon Road adjoining **Joseph Dunn Junr.** and **John Danally**. **Thomas Danally** and **Wm. Danally** were chain carriers.

3079. 1817, Jul 17 -- Land Grant #2479, Moore County, NC
John Melton received 70 acres located north of Buffalo Creek adjoining his own line. **James Melton** and **Edward Richardson** were chain carriers.

3080. 1817, Jul 18 -- Land Grant #2359, Randolph County, NC
Thomas Kosh received 44 acres on Fork Creek adjoining surplus land of **Thomas Cash** Dec'd and **Jesse Larrance**. **John Kosh** and **Thomas Kosh Junr.** were chain carriers.

A. 1817, Jul 24 – Deed Book 13 Page 268-269, Randolph County, NC
Thomas Kosh deeded **John Cassaday** 166 acres located on Fork Creek and Bear Creek adjoining **Davis** and the [Moore] County line. **H. Moffitt** and **James Gatlin** were witnesses.

B. 1817, Jul 24 – Deed Book 13 Page 270-271, Randolph County, NC
Thomas Kosh deeded **John Cassaday** 434 acres in three tracts located on Fork Creek and Bear Creek adjoining **Davis** and **Needham**. **H. Moffitt** and **Edward Gatlin** were witnesses.

3081. 1817, Jul 25 -- Land Grant #2329, Moore County, NC
Neil McKinnon received 50 acres located on Dry Fork of Mill Creek adjoining **Neil McLeod**, **John McDuffie**, **Norman McKinnon** and **Widow Buie**. **John McDuffie** and **Malcolm McDuffie** were chain carriers.

3082. 1817, Jul 28 -- Land Grant #2307, Moore County, NC
Roderick McAulay received 60 acres located west of Sings Creek adjoining **John McAulay**. **William McAulay** and **Donald McAulay** were chain carriers.

3083.   1817, Aug -- 1796-1841 County Accounts, Moore County, NC Page 23
George Moore v. **J. Ritter**

3084.   1817, Aug -- 1796-1841 County Accounts, Moore County, NC Page 22
1817, Aug -- 1785-1868 Index to Trial Docket, Moore County, NC Page 34
State v. **Moses Wallace/Wallis**

3085.   1817, Aug 5 -- Land Grant #2325, Moore County, NC
John Key received 50 acres located west of Wet Creek adjoining **Kenneth McCaskill**, his own line, **Neil Morrison**, **McLeod** and **Morgan** (formerly **Bethune**). **Vinson Key** and **Samuel Key** were chain carriers.

3086.   1817, Sep 10 -- Land Grant #2340, Moore County, NC
David Jones received 200 acres located on the Long Meadow adjoining **Widow Tolman**, **McNeill**, **Matheson** and **James Melton**. **Solomon Brewer** and **James Melton** were chain carriers.

3087.   1817, Sep 11 -- Land Grant #2324, Moore County, NC
William Jones received 25 acres located west of Flag Creek adjoining his own line, **Christopher/Christian Stutts**, **Bartholomew Dunn**, **George Williams**, **Hector McLean** and **Charles Sowell**. **Barthol. Dunn** and **Wm. Williams** were chain carriers.

3088.   1817, Sep 11 -- Land Grant #2352, Moore County, NC
Solomon Brewer received 50 acres located on Buffalo Creek adjoining **Joseph Cockman** and own line (formerly **McLeod**). **James Melton** and **Abner Brown** were chain carriers.

3089.   1817, Sep 15 -- Land Grant #2569, Moore County, NC
William Williams received 40 acres located on Flag Creek adjoining **Bartholomew Dunn**, **Leonard Furr** and **Charles Sowell**. **Barthol. Dunn** and **Charles Sowell** were chain carriers. [Editor's Note: deeded to **George Davis** 1823]

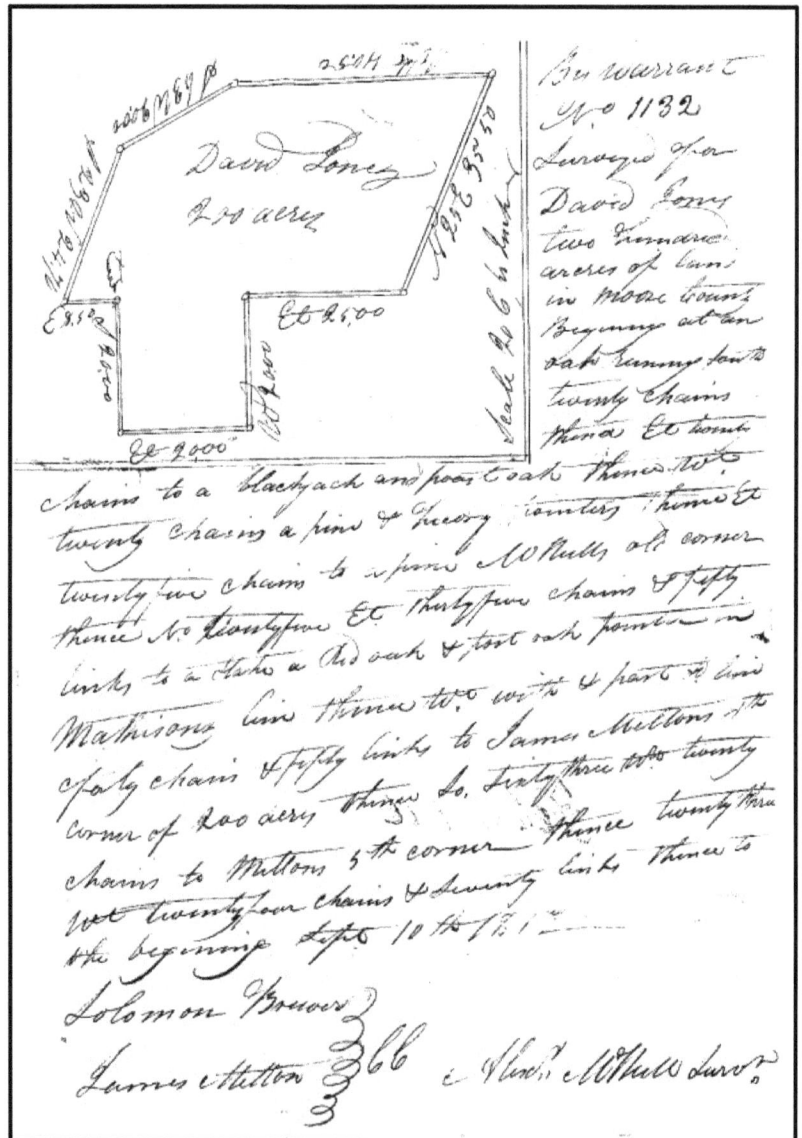

3090.   1817, Sep 17 -- Land Grant #2323, Moore County, NC
Benjamin Caddell received 200 acres located on both sides of Suck Creek adjoining his own line. **Wm. Williams** and **John Caddell** were chain carriers.

3091.   1817, Sep 17 -- Land Grant #2451, Moore County, NC
George Ritter received 250 acres adjoining **James Dowdy**. **Marble Ritter** and **Wm. Dowdy** were chain carriers.

3092.   1817, Sep 18 -- Land Grant #2327, Moore County, NC
Jesse Sowell received 200 acres adjoining **Dowd**, his own line (formerly **Neil McLeod**), **Angus McQueen** and **McIntosh**. **Isaac Sowell** and **John Sowell** were chain carriers.

3093. 1817, Oct -- Land Grant #2338, Moore County, NC
William Jackson received 50 acres located on both sides of the Juniper adjoining **Paterson**, **Allison**, **George Jackson**, **Jno. Jackson**, **McNeill** and **John Sowell**. **George Jackson** and **Samuel Jackson** were chain carriers.

3094. 1817, Oct -- Land Grant #2351, Moore County, NC
George Jackson received 15 acres located on the Juniper adjoining his own line (formerly **Christian Jackson**), **William Cox**, **Samuel Jackson** and **John Sowell**. **Samuel Jackson** and **William Cox** were chain carriers.

3095. 1817, Oct 7 -- Land Grant #2608, Moore County, NC
Alexander Carroll received 100 acres located north of Richland Creek adjoining **John Martin**, his own line, **John McIver** and **John Carroll Senr**. **Patrick Dowd** and **Conner Dowd** were chain carriers.

3096. 1817, Oct 25 -- *A History of Sandy Creek Baptist Association* by George Purefoy, Page 75
Elder **Isaac Teague**, **William Waddill** and **Eli Lawler** from Fall Creek Church (Chatham County) were delegates to the Association meeting at Bear Creek Meeting House in Chatham County, NC.

3097. 1817, Oct 28 -- Land Grant #2310, Moore County, NC
Nathan Fry received 200 acres located on the head of Dry Fork of Wads Creek adjoining his own line, **Joseph Fry Senr**. and **William Fry**. **Neill Blacke** and **Dugald McMillan** were chain carriers.

3098. 1817, Nov-May 1818 -- 1808-1819 Trial and Appearance Docket, Moore County, NC
Wm. **Lakey** v. **John Milton**

3099. 1817, Nov 3 -- Land Grant #2335, Moore County, NC
Alexander Kennedy received 2 acres located on both sides of Bear Creek including the part of the creek where he is fixing his boreing works adjoining his own line and **Abednego Maness**. **Lewis Kennedy** and ? **Craven** were chain carriers.

3100. 1817, Nov 4 -- Deed Book W Page 179, Chatham County, NC
Samuel Dunn and wife **Elizabeth** [of Montgomery County, NC] deeded **Matthew Phillips** 50 acres located on Tysons Creek. **Archd**. **Shields** and **Henry Clover** were witnesses.

3101. 1817, Nov 5 -- Land Grant #2337, Moore County, NC
Donald McLeod received 50 acres located east of Wet Creek adjoining **James McArthur**, **Waddle**, his own line, **Cole** and **Levi Deaton**. **Levi Deaton** and **Donald McLeod** were chain carriers.

A. 1817, Nov 7 -- Land Grant #2114, Montgomery County, NC
John Allen received 25 acres located on White Oak Branch adjoining his own line, **John Simmons** and **James Simmons**. **William Simmons** and **James Simmons** were chain carriers.

3102. 1817, Nov 11 -- Land Grant #2333, Moore County, NC

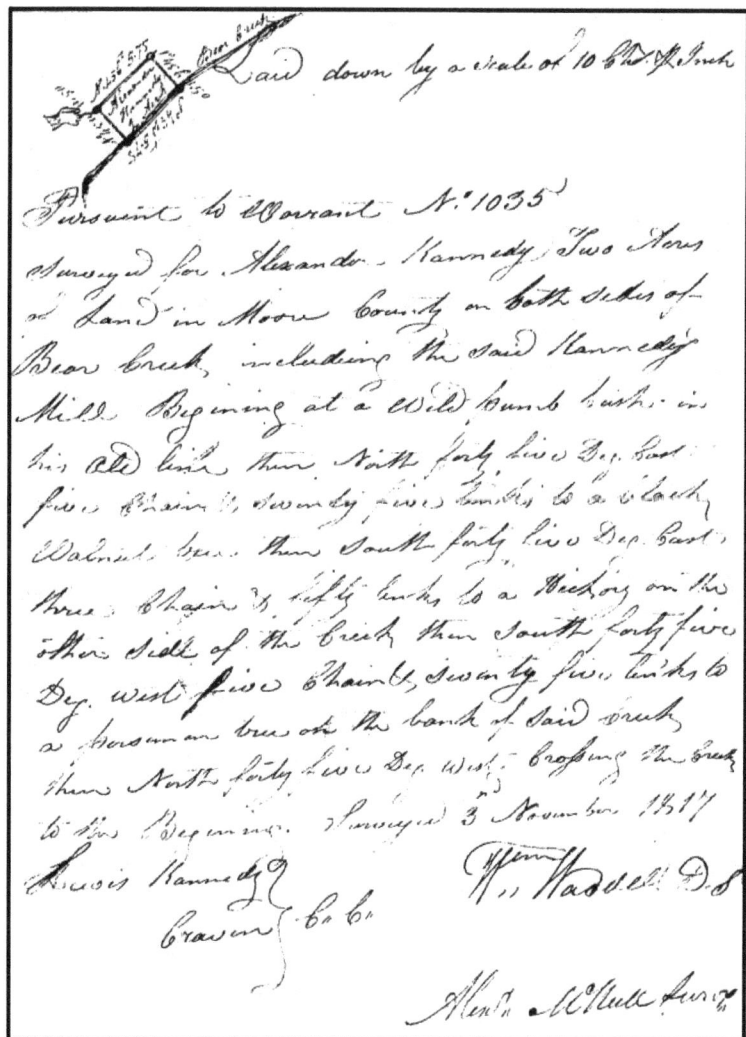

Jesse Pierce received 80 acres located south of Deep River adjoining his own line (formerly **John Russel** and **William Davis**). **John Carrell** and **Francis Myrick** were chain carriers.

3103. 1817, Nov 13 -- Land Grant #2331, Moore County, NC
John Richardson received 50 acres located between Lick Creek and the Horsepen Branch adjoining **Francis Myrick**. **Drewry Richeson** and **Jesse Ritter** were chain carriers.

3104. 1817, Nov 14 -- Bible of David Kennedy and Joanna Moore, Moore County, NC
Asa Kennedy [son of **Hiram**] died. [Born May 1, 1816]

3105. 1817, Nov 21 -- Land Grant #2315, Moore County, NC
Francis Bullock received 150 acres located south of Wolf Creek and the Montgomery County line adjoining **Wilkins**, **Wright** and **McNeill**. **Belaver Britt** and **John McKinnon** were chain carriers.

A. 1817, Nov 22 -- Deed Book V Page 37-38, Chatham County, NC
Bryan Boroughs (of Moore County) deeded **Zacheus Boroughs** two tracts [1] 320 acres located on Spring Branch of Tyson Creek adjoining **Sheron**, **Dennis Phillips** [2] 120 acres adjoining the 1st tract and **Ramsey**. **Eli Lawler Senr.** and **Eli Lawler Junr.** were witnesses.

3106. 1817, Nov 24 -- Will, Chatham County, NC
Will of **James Massey** Dec'd. Heirs: son **Thomas Massey** [*negro slaves Ben and Rachel*]; daughter **Sarah Sugg**; daughter **Margaret Bryan** [*negroes Molly, Sam and George, children of Affy and also Stephny*]; grandchildren **Jenny Guin** and **Alfred Guin**, children of **Sarah Sugg** [*negro Affy*]; daughter **Elizabeth Pearce** [*negroes Lewis and Nanny*]; daughter **Mary** [**Polly**] **Bryan** [*negroes Jack and Sucky*]; and son **Russell Massey** [*negroes Jesse and Mary*]. Executors: son **Russell Massey** and **William Scurlock**. Witnesses: **Presley George** and **Jos. W. Riddle**. Will denotes that **James Massey** died Wednesday night, April 8, 1818 at 11 o'clock.

3107. 1817, Dec 4 -- Land Grant #2320, Moore County, NC
Cornelius Dowd received 59 acres located east of McLendons Creek adjoining **George Glascock**, **McNeill** and his own line. **Conner Dowd** and **John Phillips** were chain carriers.

3108. 1817, Dec 5 -- Land Grant #2314, Moore County, NC
John Martin received 100 acres located on Blans Branch of Richland Creek adjoining **Minar**, **McLeod**, his own line (formerly **Carr**) and **Phillips**. **Jesse Sowell** and **Wm. Harris** were chain carriers.

3109. 1817, Dec 6 -- Land Grant #2319, Moore County, NC
John Martin received 100 acres located north of Richland Creek adjoining his own line and **McLeod**. **Jesse Sowell** and **Wm. Harris** were chain carriers.

3110. 1817, Dec 8 -- Land Grant #2322, Moore County, NC
Joab Cheek received 50 acres located on both sides of Rogers Creek adjoining his own line, **John Cheek** and **McKenzie** and Co. **Joab Cheek** and **John Cheek** were chain carriers.

3111. 1818-1823 -- Tax List, Moore County, NC [selected residents]
Name, acres and taxable amount: **Fredrick Autry** 1050 acres/$1050; **Elijah Autry** 250 acres/$170; **Elizabeth Autray** 100 acres/$120; **Alexander Autry** 308 acres/$475; **James Autry** 282 acres/$100; **Alexander Autry Jr.** 100 acres/$50; **Mark Allin** 300 acres/$300; **Joseph Allin** 450 acres/$675; **Allin Bullock** 715 acres/$750; **Ambrous Brewor** 366 acres/$530; **Micjah Brewor** 355 acres/$310; **Harmon Brewor** 50 acres/$50; **James Brady** 100 acres/$100; **Robert Brady** 50 acres/$50; **Charles Brady** 100 acres/50; **Eleazor Birckhead** 275 acres/$450; **Levin Birckhead** 100 acres/$210; **Jesse Brown** 675 acres/$500; **William Brown** 100 acres/$200; **Allin Bethune** 200 acres/$120; **Bryan Britt** 180 acres/$90; **Rhoday Britt** 225 acres/$110; **Michael Bryant** 660 acres/$570; **Jesse Bean** 160 acres/$320; **William Barrott** 1603 acres/$3660; **Col. Frances Bullock** 1450 acres/$1850; **Bryan Boroughs** 997 acres/$2992; **Benjamin Britt** 100 acres/$100; **Elisha Brewor** 50 acres/$100; **William Brewor** 100 acres/$10; **Eli Callicutt** 225 acres/$400; **Adam Comer** 460 acres/$400; **George Cagle** 300 acres/$350; **William Cagle** 265 acres/$400; **Jacob Cagle** 150 acres/$200; **Peter Cagle** 280 acres/$200; **Martin Cagle** 390 acres/$440; **George Cagle** 50 acres/$50; **Henry Cagle** 450 acres/$500; **Randol Cheek** 635 acres/$930; **Joab Cheek** 500 acres/$620; **John Cheek** 1395 acres/$1395; **James Cheek** 150 acres/$170; **Richard Cheek** 635 acres/$930; **John Cockmon** 100 acres/$100; **Catherine Cockmon** 150 acres/$120; **Benjamin Caddell** 400 acres/$160; **Daniel Caddell** 250 acres/$270; **Joseph Cole** 250 acres/$250;

Jonathan Caddell 200 acres/$150; Peter Davis 919 acres/$1700; James C. Davis 400 acres/$760; Robert Davis 1300 acres/$1200; Elizabeth Davis 200 acres/$500; John Danielly 450 acres/$600; Mathew Deaton 773 acres/$730; Levi Deaton 340 acres/$600; Burrell Deaton 250 acres/$160; John Dunlap Senr. 1400 acres/$1700; John Dunlap Junr. 183 acres/$150; James Dunlap 450 acres/$600; Patrick Dowd 326 acres/$600; James Dowd 250 acres/$250; John Dunn 135 acres/$200; William Dunn 100 acres/$100; Bartholomue Dunn 128 acres/$200; James Dowdy 228 acres/$132; Joseph Duckworth 200 acres/$350; Stephen Davis 300 acres/$300; Cornelius Dowd 1985 acres/$2865; Capt. William Dowd 550 acres/$800; Samuel Elkins 75 acres/$120; William England 1 lot, 512 acres/$925; Daniel Feagins 50 acres/$130; William Feagins 400 acres/$300; Rubern Freeman 290 acres/$400; William Freeman 217 acres/$350; Leonard Furr 285 acres/$400; Jacob Furr 375 acres/$400; Richardson Feagins 1088 acres/$1550; James Garner 47.5 acres/$70; Peter Gardner 1100 acres/$300; Thomas Graham 600 acres/$820; Benjamin Gilbert 550 acres/$1100; Sabra Gilbert 100 acres/$100; Geo. Glascock heirs 200 acres/$300; Patty Glascock 100 acres/$200; Julious Glascock 125 acres/$250; Bradly Garner 1677 acres/$1470; John Hare 662 acres/$1200; Peter Hare 629 acres/$800; John Handcock 250 acres/$500; James Hains 50 acres/$60; George Hundsucker 208 acres/$200; Richard Holland 642 acres/$500; Thomas Harvil 150 acres/$100; Hiram Hill 125 acres/$300; Wm. Harden heirs 250 acres/$250; Edmond Holland 200 acres/$100; William Jones 225 acres/$250; David Kennedy 1067 acres/$2600; David Kennedy (for Jacob Carringer) 112 acres/$112; Alexander Kennedy 360 acres/$900; Edward Kennedy 350 acres/$300; Robert Kennedy 300 acres/$350; Samuel Keys 230 acres/$370; John Keys 55 acres/$140; John Kennedy 100 acres/$200; Hiram Kennedy 500 acres/$400; George Kennedy 100 acres/$100; Joel Lawhon 420 acres/$730; Lewis Lawhon 100 acres/$100; Abner Lawler 100 acres/$180; John Lewis 230 acres/$300; William Lewis 300 acres/$190; Malcolm Leach and son 660 acres/$660; Malcom Morrison 274 acres/$250; Normond Morrison 450 acres/$400; Allen Morrison 2997 acres/$900; Allen Morrison (for Bethune's Estate) 1 lot/$400; John Morrison 100 acres/$100; Alexd. Morrison 170 acres/$180; Angus Morrison 185 acres/$80; Jesse Muse 600 acres/$1350; Thomas P. Muse 350 acres/$400; James Muse 90 acres/$100; Jesse F. Muse 125 acres/$150; Thomas Muse 100 acres/$100; James B. Muse 250 acres/$500; Daniel Muse 100 acres/$100; Murdo Mathewson 310 acres/$210; Normond Mathewson 350 acres/$180; Malcolm Mathewson 141 acres/$140; John Maness 100 acres/$100; Daniel Maness Senr. 324 acres/$470; Abednigo Maness 250 acres/$270; William Maness 150 acres/$150; Mishack Maness 100 acres/$150; James Manes Senr. 150 acres/$200; W. Namles Maness 50 acres/$50; James Melton 150 acres/$200; Ansel Melton 100 acres/$100; John Melton 160 acres/$100; Frances Myrick 300 acres/$300; George Moore 330 acres/$370; Fanning Moore 75 acres/$100; Samuel Martindale 330 acres/$480; James Morgan 420 acres/$620; Joseph Morgan 250 acres/$400; Nathan Morgan 179 acres/$250; Rodrick McAulay 360 acres/$550; Murdo McAulay Jr. 200 acres/$130; Murdo McAulay Esq. 317 acres/$260; James McArthur 50 acres/$50; Daniel McCrummen 490 acres/$500; John McCrummen 84 acres/$200; Malcolm McCrummen 150 acres/$150; Neill McIntosh 519 acres/$650; Alexander McIntosh 400 acres/$330; Christian McIntosh 300 acres/$500; John McKinnon 450 acres/$500; Normond McKinnon 228 acres/$250; Alexander McKinnon 74 acres/$60; Normond McKinnon Junr. 100 acres/$25; Daniel McNeill 1517 acres/$1500; John McNeill 950 acres/$950; Archd. McNeill 400 acres/$800; Lauchlin McNeill 140 acres/$200; Hector McNeill 149 acres/$170; Angus McQueen 525 acres/$500; Margaret McQueen 200 acres/$400; Thomas Maness 100 acres/$100; William McKinnon 100 acres/$50; Daniel McKinnon 93 acres/$100; Angus McKinnon 60 acres/$50; Nicholas Nall 1000 acres/$4500; Meloney Newton 150 acres/$150; Medford Owen 150 acres/$150; John Paterson Senr. 550 acres/$460; John Paterson Junr. 450 acres/$470; Lewis Phillips 200 acres/$700; Patty Phillips 160 acres/$600; Eli Phillips 289 acres/$350; Mark Phillips 100 acres/$200; Henry Powers (for S. Brewer's heirs) 100 acres/$70; Samuel Perry 610 acres/$500; William Perry 40 acres/$50; William Person 336 acres/$500; Thomas Person 500 acres/$1150; Benjamin Person 50 acres/$110; John Richardson 450 acres/$655; John Richardson (for D. Richardson's Estate) 50 acres/$160; Stephen Richardson 400 acres/$600; Stephen Richardson, Junr. 300 acres/$300; David Richardson 75 acres/$100; John Ritter 640 acres/$900; Thomas Ritter 550 acres/$800; Jesse Ritter 155 acres/$260; Moses Ritter Senr. 100 acres/$100; Moses Ritter Junr. 100 acres/$60; John Ritter Junr. 50 acres/$30; Jesse Ritter 470 acres/$300; Joseph Rouse 50 acres/$100; Druray Richardson 378 acres/$250; Gideon Seawell 1000 acres/$2000; Joseph Seawell 200 acres/$320; William Smith 275 acres/$400; James Smith 379 acres/$120; Sarah Smith 250 acres/$500; John Smith 120 acres/$150; Leonard Smith 200 acres/$450; Isham Smith 70 acres/$80; Nathan Smith 285 acres/$300; Peter Shamburger Senr. 750 acres/$700; John Shamburger 3040 acres/$1990, 1 lot Feaginsville; Peter Shamburger 360 acres/$690; William Shamburger 100 acres/$100; Isham Sheffield Senr. 250 acres/$900; John Sheffield Senr. 241 acres/$500; John Sheffield Junr. 254 acres/$400; Everet Sheffield 181 acres/$310; Isham Sheffield Junr. 91 acres/$200; Isaac Sheffield 150 acres/$270; Cornelius Shields 1859 acres/$1730; Archibald Shields 270 acres/$900; James Shields 260 acres/$80; George Stewart 225 acres/$120; Charles Stewart 50 acres/$25; George Stewart 200 acres/$200; John Sowell 1241 acres/$1350; Isaac Sowell 200 acres/$100; Asa Sowell

600 acres/$150; **Jesse Sowell** 286 acres/$360; **Charles Sowell** 172 acres/$100; **Samson D. Smith** 200 acres/$400; **Jesse Sanders** 3 lots and 107 acres/$209; **John Smith** 200 acres/$200; **Henry Stuts** 535 acres/$750; **Christian Stuts** 130 acres/$403; **Jacob Stuts** 300 acres/$250; **John Seat** 50 acres/$70; **John Spivay** 650 acres/$610; **Nathaniel Tucker** 250 acres/$375; **Isaac Teague** 50 acres/$50; **John Upton** 200 acres/$220; **Richard Upton** 133 acres/$200; **William Waddell** 480 acres/$1150; **Jeremiah Williams** 150 acres/$175; **Jeremiah Williams** 110 acres/$140; **William Williamson** 1416 acres/$2000; **Baily Williamson** 500 acres/$250; **William Williamson** 211 acres/$280; **Allin Williamson** 100 acres/$50; **Phillip Wilson** (heirs) 223 acres/$200; **Robert Wilson** 600 acres/$110; **Robert Wilson** (for **Ed. Beason**) 500 acres/$50; **Jeremiah Wilson** 438 acres/$500; **Sherwood Wright** 385 acres/$400; **William Wright** 215 acres/$400; **James Wood** 450 acres/$450; **James Wood** (for **L. Garner**'s heirs) 425 acres/$500; **Everet Wallis** 100 acres/$100; **Adam White** 475 acres/$900; **Thomas Williams** 240 acres/$240; **Henry Yow** 200 acres/$400; **Andrew Yow** 292 acres/$320; **Andrew Yow** (for **C. Yow**'s estate) 100 acres/$150 _Non-residents_: **George Frazier** 110 acres/$200; **Gabriel Harden** 200 acres/$200; **James Latham** 550 acres/$460; **Mary Teague** 50 acres/$75; **William Phillips** 200 acres/$100; **Eli Lawler** 150 acres/$200.

A.   1818, Jan 6 – Deed Book V Page 49-50, Chatham County, NC
Jacob Teague deeded **Baley Williamson** (of Moore County) 74 acres adjoining **Smith**, **John Lawler** and **Isaac Read**. **L. Smith**, **Isaac Teague** and **Eli Lawler** were witnesses.

3112.   1818, Jan 27 -- Deed Book 12 Page 33-34, Moore County, NC
Henry Stutts deeded **Bryan Boroughs** 50 acres adjoining **Bryan Boroughs**. **Wm. Boroughs** and **F. Winfield** were witnesses.

3113.   1818, Feb 10 -- Land Grant #2490, Moore County, NC
George Hunsucker received 10 acres located east of Wet Creek adjoining his own line, **John Gibson**, **John McKinnon**, **George Cox**, **Alexander McKinnon** and **Donald McKinnon**. **John Hunsucker** and **Nicholas Wallace** were chain carriers.

A.   1818, Feb 19 -- Land Grant #2569a, Moore County, NC
Robert Hardin received 100 acres located on drains of Toms Creek and Persimmon Glade adjoining **Neil McLeod**, **William Martin**, **Robert Davis** and **Jernigan**. **Edmond Wade** and **Tinsley Wade** were chain carriers.

3114.   1818, Feb 26 -- Marriage Bond, Moore County, NC
A bond for the marriage of **John Moore** and **Charlotta Barrett**. **Stephen Davis** and **Thomas Ritter** were securities and **J. Dowd** was a witness. [_Editor's Note: Found in War of 1812 Pension File 27604 for **Charlotta Moore**, widow of **John Moore**_]

3115.   1818, May -- 1796-1841 County Accounts, Moore County, NC Page 6
Furr v. **McLeod**

3116.   1818, May -- 1796-1841 County Accounts, Moore County, NC Page 23
1818, May -- 1808-1819 Trial and Appearance Docket, Moore County, NC

3117.　　　1818, May 14 -- Land Grant #2471, Moore County, NC
Ancel Melton received 20 acres located on Flag Creek adjoining **Neil McLeod** and his own line. **William Williams** and **Isaac Cagle** were chain carriers.

3118.　　　1818, May 18 -- Estate, Chatham County, NC
Estate of **James Massey** Dec'd. *Items were purchased by the following*: **Dr. John Dobson, George Dismaker, Elisha Poe, George Thompson, Joseph Foushee, Seth Thornton, Charles J. Williams, William Foushee, William Pearce, John Cocke, John Foushee, Col. James Taylor, Basel Manley** Esq., **Jo. Scurlock, Wm. W. Stedman, William Scurlock, Asa Hurley, Robert Ward, Zachariah Harman, Joseph Hackney, Hasten Poe, Ransom Poe, Presley George, Capt. Daniel Foushee, Mr. Auley Brown, Micajah Foushee, Stephen Hays, Lewis Freeman, William Caudle, Hardy Poe, Guilford Petty, Taylor Maun, Robert Thompson, Stephen Thomas, Andrew Haynes, Elijah Foushee, Mrs. Sally Sugg, Simon Foushee, Tabby Riddle** and **Saml. Parry**.

3119.　　　1818, Jun 26-Aug 7 -- Notice, *Weekly Raleigh Register* [Raleigh, NC] Newspaper

Notice is given that the Direct Tax of the United States, for 1815 and 1816, has not been paid and will be sold at the Market House in Hillsborough, Orange County on 21 Aug 1818 at 10 o'clock AM. *Moore County*: **Gabriel Harden** 250 acres, **George Horner** 350 acres, **Arch McIntire** 150 acres, **Daniel McLean** 100 acres, **Daniel Black** 100 acres, **John McIntyre** 350 acres, **Mary Finch** 350 acres.

MOORE.				
Gabriel Harden	250 do more or less			94
George Horner	350 do	do	1	41
Arch McIntire	150			71½
Daniel McLean	150			47
Daniel Black	100			47
John McIntyre	350			14
Mary Finch	350		1	17½

3120.　　　1818, Jul 9 -- Land Grant #2565, Moore County, NC
John Shamburger received 100 acres on the Randolph County line adjoining **Cagle, Peter Davis, Shamburger, Brown** and his own line. **Peter Davis** and **John Cagle** were chain carriers.

3121.　　　1818, Jul 9 -- Land Grant #2673, Moore County, NC
John Shamburger received 500 acres located north of Bear Creek on the Randolph County line adjoining his own line, **Jeremiah Wilson, Peter Shamburger, Francis Bullock, Davis** and **Ray**. **John Shamburger** and **Absolom Shamburger** were chain carriers.

3122.　　　1818, Aug -- 1796-1841 County Accounts, Moore County, NC Page 23
1818, Aug -- 1808-1819 Trial and Appearance Docket, Moore County, NC
John Melton v. **Stephen Scott**

3123.　　　1818, Aug-Feb 1819 -- 1808-1819 Trial and Appearance Docket, Moore County, NC
George Moore v. **Jesse Ritter**

3124.　　　1818, Aug 16 -- Land Grant #2485, Moore County, NC
William Martindale received 100 acres located east of Fall Creek adjoining **Mycajah Brewer, William Person/Parsons** and **Willson**. **Jas. Culbertson** and **Mycajah Brewer** were chain carriers.

A.　　　1818, Aug 22 – Deed Book 13 Page 320, Randolph County, NC
Hardy Davis (of Guilford County) deeded **Peter Davis** (of Moore County) 300 acres located on Meadow Branch being the land formerly owned by **Hardy Davis**, Dec'd. **James Davis** was a witness.

B.　　　1818, Aug 25 -- Land Grant #2252, Montgomery County, NC
Gambill Powers received 100 acres located on Cabin Creek adjoining **Milly James** and **John McCrumin**. **John McCrumin** and **John James** were chain carriers.

3125.　　　1818, Aug 26 -- Land Grant #2513, Moore County, NC
Bradley Garner received 10 acres located on Grassy Creek adjoining **Hunsucker, Kennedy, Garner**, his own line and **George Carriner**.

3126. 1818, Oct 24 -- *A History of Sandy Creek Baptist Association* by George Purefoy, Page 76
Elder **Isaac Teague** from Fall Creek Church (Chatham County) was a delegate to the Association meeting at Abbott's Creek Meeting House in Rowan [now Davidson] County, NC.

A. 1818, Oct 26 -- Land Grant #2667, Montgomery County, NC
William McLeod received 100 acres located on Cabin Creek adjoining **George Bruer**, **Milly James**, his own line, Moore County line and **Neil McLeod**. **Gambill Powers** and **Wm. James** were chain carriers.

B. 1818, Oct 28 -- Land Grant #2217, Montgomery County, NC
John Campbell received 150 acres located on Alder Bush Branch of Dicks Creek adjoining **Frances Jordan**, his own line and **Reuben Hicks'** improvement. **James Hicks** and **Archibald Campbell** were chain carriers.

3127. 1818, Nov -- Chronicles and Records of Bensalem Presbyterian Church Page 17, Moore County, NC
Daniel McKenzie and **Jennet McNeill** were married.

A. 1818, Nov 2 -- Land Grant #2190, Montgomery County, NC
Reuben Allen received 50 acres located on Lick Fork of Cotton Creek adjoining his own line and **King Brewer**. **William Allen** and **Nathan Morgan** were chain carriers.

3128. 1818, Nov 4 -- Land Grant #2384, Moore County, NC
James Melton received 100 acres located on Long Meadow adjoining **Normand Matheson**, **Williams**, **Widow Talmon**, **James Hains** and his own line. **James Laky** and **Robert Melton** were chain carriers.

3129. 1818, Nov 6 -- Land Grant #2481, Moore County, NC
Angus McDonald received 200 acres located south of McLendons Creek and the Yadkin Road adjoining **Allan Martin**, **John Cox** and his own line (formerly **Donald McDonald**). **Daniel McDonald** and **John McDonald** were chain carriers.

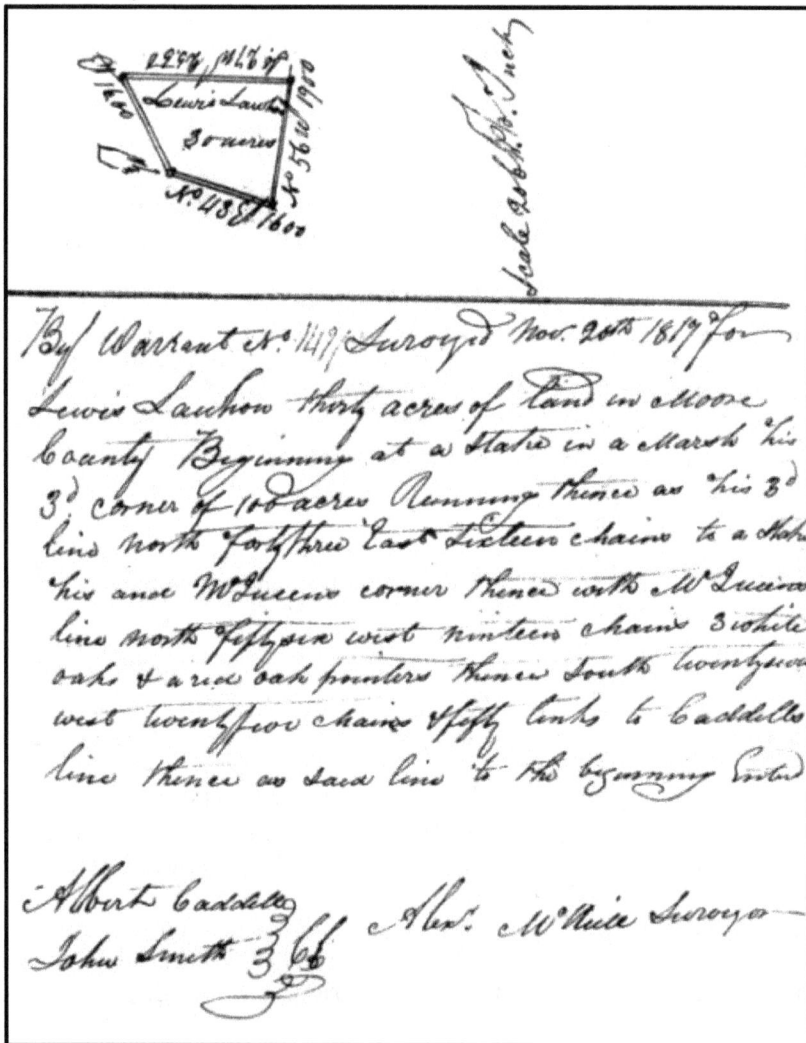

3130. 1818, Nov 12 -- Deed Book 45, Page 384, Moore County, NC
Jesse Sanders deeded **Daniel Chisholm** three tracts (100, 100, 200 acres) located on Drowning Creek adjoining **McCaller** and **Isaac Dunn**. **Shields** and **Tobias Fry** were witnesses.

3131. 1818, Nov 16 -- Deed Book 127, Page 258, Moore County, NC
Jesse Brown Sr. deeded **Jesse Brown Jr.** 100 acres located on Cabbin Creek adjoining his own line. **Abner Brown** was a witness.

3132. 1818, Nov 20 -- Land Grant #2494, Moore County, NC
Lewis Lawhon received 30 acres located on Locust Branch adjoining his own line, **Angus McQueen** and **Albert Caddell**. **Albert Caddell** and **John Smith** were chain carriers.

A. 1818, Nov 27 -- Land Grant #2311, Montgomery County, NC

James B. Hicks received 200 acres located on Alder Bush Branch of Dicks Creek adjoining **John Campbell**, **Frances Jordan** and **George Hixs'** improvement. **Frances Jordan** and **Jacob Hicks** were chain carriers.

3133.   1818, Nov 28 -- Land Grant #2421, Moore County, NC
Isaac Sowel received 220 acres located north of Richland Creek adjoining **Jesse Sowell** and **Alexr. McIntosh**. **Jesse Sowell Senr.** and **Jesse Sowell Jur.** were chain carriers.

3134.   1818, Nov 28 -- Land Grant #2431, Moore County, NC
Thomas Ritter received 10 acres located west of McLendons Creek adjoining his own line and **Obj. Sowell**. **Marvel Ritter** and **Thos. Ritter** were chain carriers.

3135.   1818, Nov 28 -- Land Grant #2432, Moore County, NC
Thomas Ritter received 50 acres located east of McLendons Creek adjoining **Edwards**, his own line, **John Sowell** and **McKay**. **William Stuts** and **Marvel Ritter** were chain carriers.

3136.   1818, Dec 1 -- Land Grant #2387, Randolph County, NC
John Cassaday received 113 acres on Ceedar Fork Creek adjoining heirs of **Hardy Davis**, his own line, **Wm. Latham**, **Wm. Brown** and **Green**. **Thomas Kosh** and **John Kosh** were chain carriers.

3137.   1818, Dec 5 -- Land Grant #2521, Moore County, NC
Mark Allen received 50 acres located north of Cabin Creek adjoining his own line. **Joseph Allen** and **Jeremiah Reynolds** were chain carriers.

3138.   1818, Dec 5 -- Land Grant #2567, Moore County, NC
Peter Shamburger received 300 acres located north of Williams Creek adjoining **Morrison** and **Martin, A.B. Smith**, **Spivey**, **Adam Comer**, **John Comer** and **McNeill**. **William Shamburger** and **John Shamburger** were chain carriers.

3139.   1818, Dec 21 -- Land Grant #2434, Moore County, NC
John Shamburger received 300 acres located north of Bear Creek adjoining **Peter Garner**, **John Spivey** and **Archibald Ray**. **John Shamburger** and **Peter Shamburger** were chain carriers.

3140.   1818, Dec 27 -- Land Grant #2594, Moore County, NC
Thomas Ritter received 50 acres adjoining **McKinnon**, **McIntosh**, **John Rouse**, his own line and **John Quimby**. **Marble Ritter** and **Dixon Ritter** were chain carriers.

3141.   1818, Dec 29 -- Land Grant #2568, Moore County, NC
Thomas Ritter received 25 acres located south of Richland Creek adjoining his own line, **McNeill** and **Mary Shaw**. **Marbell Ritter** and **Dickson Ritter** were chain carriers.

A.   1819, Jan 11 -- Deed Book W Page 129, Chatham County, NC
Aaron McMaines deeded **Josiah Cheek** 250 acres located on Tysons Creek and the Moore County line adjoining **William Phillips**. **Jesse Womble** and **John Cheek** were witnesses.

3142.   1819, Jan 15 -- Deed Book 22 Page 297-298, Moore County, NC
James Garner deeded **Thomas Ritter Jr.** 47 acres located south of Deep River adjoining **Moore** and heirs of **Lewis Garner** Dec'd. **J.A. Garner** was a witness.

3143.   1819, Feb -- 1818-1826 County Court Execution Docket, Moore County, NC
#38 Moore County v. **William Lakey**
Carrell Wallis, **Wm. Williamson**, **Wm. N. Maness** and **James C. Myrick** were witnesses.

3144.   1819, Feb -- 1796-1841 County Accounts, Moore County, NC Page 24
1819, Feb -- 1808-1819 Trial and Appearance Docket, Moore County, NC
John Melton v. **Jesse** and **Sally Ritter**

3145.   1819, Feb -- 1796-1841 County Accounts, Moore County, NC Page 25, 26
William Barrott v. **W. Hunsucker**
J.B. Kelly v. **W. Hunsucker**

3146.   1819, Feb -- 1785-1868 Index to Trial Docket, Moore County, NC Page 33
1819, Feb -- 1808-1819 Trial and Appearance Docket, Moore County, NC
1819, Feb -- 1796-1841 County Accounts, Moore County, NC Page 24
William Hunsucker v. **Abednego Maness**

3147.   1819, Feb 5 -- Marriages, *Raleigh Register & NC State Gazette* [Raleigh, NC] Newspaper
"On 20th ult. [Jan 1819] at the seat of **Nicholas Nall**, Esq. in Moore County, Mr. **Jacob Tyson** to Miss **Mary Nall**"

3148.   1819, Feb 15 -- Record of Estates Book B, Moore County, NC Page 22-23

Estate of **Devotion Davis**, Dec'd. by **Elizabeth Davis**, Administrator. **Corn. Dowd**, **Neill McIntosh** and **Joel Lawhon** appointed to lay off provision for Widow **Elizabeth Davis**. **Jesse Muse** was witness. *Items were purchased by the following*: **Elizabeth Davis**, **Stephen Davis**, **John Handcock** and **James Garner**.

3149.   1819, Feb 16-Mar 27,1820 -- U.S. Postal Records **Jesse Sanders** served as Postmaster at the Carthage Post Office

3150.   1819, Mar 7 -- Land Grant #2458, Moore County, NC
Elijah Brewer received 50 acres located south of Bear Creek adjoining **McAuley**, **Harman Brewer**, **Abednego Maness** and **Drury Brewer**. **David Brewer** and **James Manus** were chain carriers.

3151.   1819, Oct 4 -- Land Grant #2483, Moore County, NC
Lewis Phillips received 200 acres located north of Deep River adjoining **Richard Cheek**, **Neill McLeod** and his own line. **Cornelius Shields** and **John Phillips** were chain carriers.

3152.   1819, Apr 20 -- Land Grant #2464, Moore County, NC
John Deaton received 100 acres located north of Horse Creek adjoining his own line, **John Smith** and **Daniel McCrummen**. **Daniel McCrummen** and **William Deaton** were chain carriers.

3153.   1819, May-Aug 1819 -- 1808-1819 Trial and Appearance Docket, Moore County, NC
Henry Stutts v. **William Milton**

3154.   1819, May 17 -- Revolutionary War Pension and Bounty, File S41955, Mark Phillips
Mark Phillips (age 65), Moore County, NC resident living near the Carthage Courthouse, applied for a pension. **Wm. Barrett**, **James Dowd** and **John Paterson** submitted affidavits of support. On Aug 21, 1820, **Mark Phillips** (age 68) listed his occupation as farming and having three family members: wife **Rany Phillips** (age 67 and quite infirm), daughters **Polly Phillips** (age 21) and **Rany Phillips Junr.** (age 17). In 1837, a complaint was filed accusing pensioner **Mark Phillips** of having been a Tory during the

Revolutionary War. Affadavits were filed by **John Morrison**, **A.C. Curry**, **Samuel C. Bruce** and **Archibald Munroe** disputing the claim. His date of death is listed as Aug 5, 1839 in a typed letter from the Department but no other notation of death is noted in the the the file.

A. 1819, Jun 17 -- Marriage Bond, Randolph County, NC
Rolly Spinks and **Elizabeth Cassady** received marriage bond. **Dudley Willett** was bondsman. **Hugh McCain** was witness. [*Editor's Note: Date of marriage occurred on or after date of marriage bond.*]

3155. 1819, Jul 20 -- BLM General Land Office Document #298, Lincoln County, MS
Stephen Smith (of Marion County) received a tract in west of Pearl District located in southwest Quarter of Section 22, Township 7, Range 7.

3156. 1819, Aug -- Will Book B Page 3-4, Moore County, NC
Will of **Eli Callicutt**, Dec'd. Heirs: wife **Sally** [*negroes* **Lidda, Abram, Peter** and **Ephraim**], brother **John Callicutt**, sister **Polly Dillion**, brother **James Callicutt**, brother **Asa Callicutt**, sister **Nancy** (wife of **George Tucker**), sister **Clary** (wife of **Elijah Ashworth**) Executors: wife **Sally** and brother **John Callicutt**. Witnesses: **Archd. McNeill** and **Alexr. McNeill**. Proven Aug 1819.

3157. 1819, Aug -- 1796-1841 County Accounts, Moore County, NC Page 26
1819, Aug -- 1808-1819 Trial and Appearance Docket, Moore County, NC
John Milton v. **John Garner**

3158. 1819, Aug -- 1808-1819 Trial and Appearance Docket, Moore County, NC
Corn. Dowd v. **Wm. Hundsucker**
Wm. Barrett v. **Wm. Hundsucker**, **George Moore** and **Daniel McIver**
John B. Kelly v. **Wm. Hundsucker**

3159. 1819, Aug -- 1796-1841 County Accounts, Moore County, NC Page 27
Fine collected from **Charles Furr**

3160. 1819, Aug 10 -- BLM General Land Office Document #823, Copiah/Lawrence County, MS
Owen Carpenter, assignee of **William Mallite** received two fractional tracts from west of Pearl River Land Office located in Section 17/18, Township 9, Range 11.

3161. 1819, Sep 21 -- Land Grant #2456, Moore County, NC
Daniel McCrummen received 50 acres located north of Horse Creek adjoining his own line, **Neil McLeod** and **John Deaton**. **John Deaton** and **George Key** were chain carriers.

3162. 1819, Oct 4 -- Land Grant #2482, Moore County, NC
Lewis Phillips received 135 acres located south of Deep River near the Meeting House adjoining his own line and **John Phillips** (formerly **Jacob Barns**). **Cornelius Shields** and **John Phillips** were chain carriers.

A. 1819, Oct 5 -- Land Grant #2241, Montgomery County, NC
John McCrumin received 25 acres located on Wolf Creek adjoining **George Allen**, his own line. **Gambell Powers** and **George Allen** were chain carriers.

B. 1819, Oct 5 -- Land Grant #2989, Montgomery County, NC
John Smitherman received 100 acres located on Wolf Creek and Bear Creek adjoining his own line, **George Allen**. **George Allen** and **James Callicott** were chain carriers.

C. 1819, Oct 5 -- Land Grant #3468, Montgomery County, NC
James G. Allen received 100 acres located on Little River adjoining his own line and **Widow Freeman**. **Reuben Freeman** and **Branson Freeman** were chain carriers.

3163. 1819, Oct 15 -- Land Grant #2457, Moore County, NC

John McNeill received 100 acres located on both sides of Buffalo Creek adjoining **James McNeill**, **Daniel McNeill**, **Archd. McNeill**, **Hardin** and **Tabitha Person**. Francis Myrick and Phillip Brook were chain carriers.

3164. 1819, Oct 15 -- Land Grant #2460, Moore County, NC
John Ritter received 25 acres located on Buffalo Creek adjoining **Jacob Stutts**, his own line and **Boroughs** (formerly **Micajah Brewer**). **Jacob Stuts** and **Richardson Ritter** were chain carriers.

3165. 1819, Oct 15 -- Land Grant #2477, Moore County, NC
James C. Davis received 300 acres located south of Deep River adjoining **William Davis** and **McLennon**. **Phillip Brooks** and **Willian Ring** were chain carriers.

3166. 1819, Oct 15 -- Land Grant #2512, Moore County, NC
John3166, ach received 20 acres located west of Mill Creek adjoining his own line (formerly **John Smith**) and **Murdoch Bethune**. **Alexr. Leach** and **John Smith** were chain carriers.

3167. 1819, Oct 25 -- *A History of Sandy Creek Baptist Association* by George Purefoy, Page 79
Elder **Isaac Teague**, **David Kennedy** and **Bryant Boroughs** from Fall Creek Church (Chatham County) were delegates to the Association meeting at Tick Creek Meeting House in Chatham County, NC.

3168. 1819, Oct 25 -- Land Grant #2453, Moore County, NC
John Ritter received 20 acres located south of Buffalo Creek and Watery Branch adjoining his own line and **John Dannelly** (formerly **George Moore**). **Richardson Ritter** and **George Moore Jur.** were chain carriers.

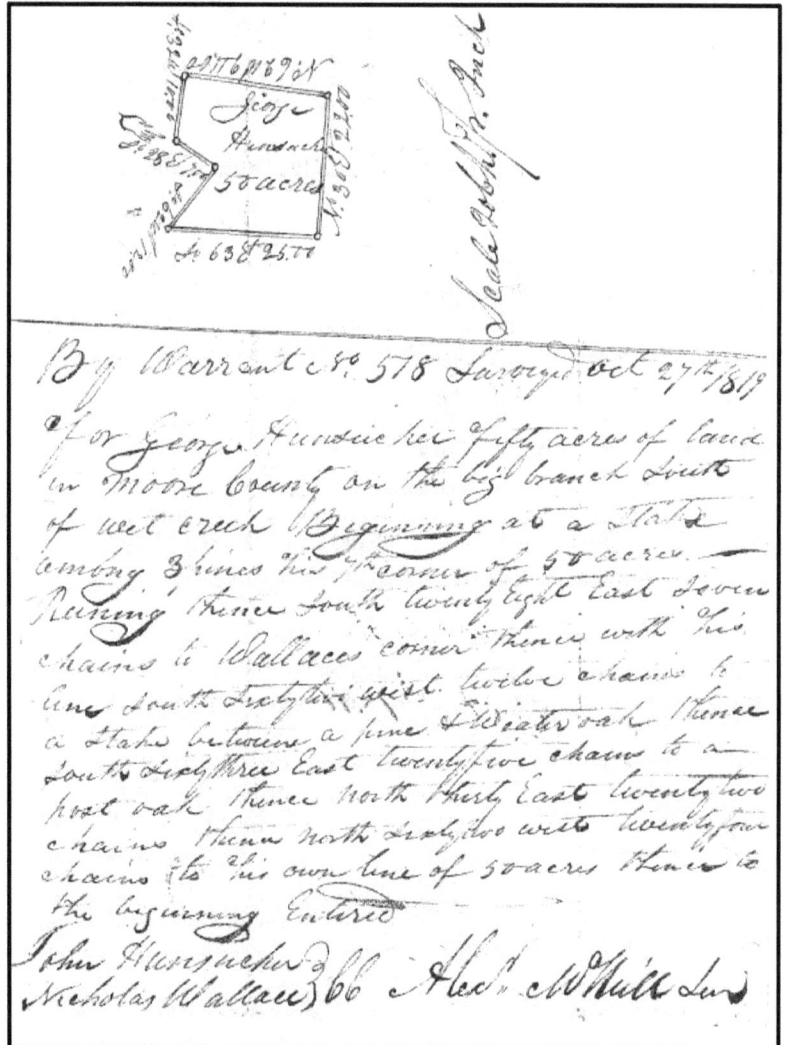

3169. 1819, Oct 25 -- Land Grant #2475, Moore County, NC
Neil McLeod received 100 acres located east of Bear Creek adjoining where **Thomas Williams** now lives (formerly **Francis Bullock**), **William Williamson** and **Jeremiah Williams**. **Thos. Williams** and **Allan Williamson** were chain carriers.

3170. 1819, Oct 27 -- Land Grant #2508, Moore County, NC
George Hunsucker received 50 acres located south of Wet Creek adjoining **Wallace**, **Neil McLeod** (formerly **Dunn**), **John Gibson**, his own line and **John McKinnon**. **John Hunsucker** and **Nicolas Wallace** were chain carriers.

3171. 1819, Oct 29 -- Land Grant #2450, Moore County, NC
Hardin Warner received 200 acres located on McLendons Creek adjoining **Leavister**, **Smith**, **Lewis**, **Neill McLeod** (Surveyor), **Neill McLeod** (Merchant) and **Alexr. McLeod**. **John Leavister** and **Edward Warner** were chain carriers.

3172. 1819, Oct 30 -- Land Grant #2525, Moore County, NC
Absalom Phillips received 12 acres located on Tysons Creek adjoining his own line and **William Phillips**. **John Phillips** and **Corn. Shields** were chain carriers.

3173.　　　1819, Oct 30 -- Land Grant #2454, Moore County, NC
James Autry received 100 acres located on Jacksons Creek adjoining **Moses Ritter. Ephraim Autry** and **John Autry** were chain carriers.

3174.　　　1819, Nov -- 1796-1841 County Accounts, Moore County, NC Page 41
M. Ritter v. **Jesse Sowell**

3175.　　　1819, Nov 19 -- Land Grant #2449, Moore County, NC
Jesse Brown received 100 acres located north of Cabin Creek adjoining his own line, **John Dunlap** and **William Brewer. Jesse Brown Jr.** and **Isaiah Brown** were chain carriers.

3176.　　　1819, Nov 19 -- Land Grant #2551, Moore County, NC
Eli Phillips received 100 acres located north of Richland Creek adjoining his own line, **Jesse Sowell, Isaac Roberts** and **Samson B. Smith. Mark Phillips** and **Jesse Sowell** were chain carriers.

3177.　　　1819, Nov 24 -- Land Grant #2511, Moore County, NC
Henry Yow received 44 acres located on the waters of Grassy Creek adjoining **Williamson**, his own line (formerly **Allen Bullock**) and **Nall. Wm. Williamson Jur.** and **Stephen Whitley** were chain carriers.

3178.　　　1819, Nov 30 -- Land Grant #2466, Moore County, NC
John Shamburger received 200 acres located north of Bear Creek adjoining his own line, **Anderson B. Smith, Robert Kennedy** and **Archibald Ray. John Shamburger** and **Peter Shamburger** were chain carriers.

3179.　　　1820 [estimated date] -- Record of Estates Book B, Moore County, NC Page 19-22
Estate of **Adam Comer** Dec'd. _Notes due on the following_: **Joseph Allen, Wm.** and **Gideon Moore** and **John Richardson**.

A.　　　1820 -- Deed Book W Page 364-366, Chatham County, NC
Horace P. Bridges, Sheriff deeded **Murdock McKenzie** and **Archibald McBryde** of **Aaron Tyson & Co.** 1/9 part (33 acres) of **Jeremiah Phillips Senr.** Dec'd., 300 acres located on Indian Creek adjoining **Jonathan Barns** and **James Hillard** to settle debts of **Robert Phillips**, son of **Jeremiah Phillips**.

3180.　　　1820, Feb 4 -- Marriages, _Raleigh Register & NC State Gazette_ [Raleigh, NC] Newspaper
"In Moore County, on the 12th ult. [Jan 1820], Mr. **Aaron Tyson** to Miss **Winfred Nall**"

3181.　　　1820, Mar 2 -- Will Book B Page 49-51, Moore County, NC
Will of **Joab Cheek**, Dec'd. Heirs: wife _Mary_ [_100 acres on Deep River and slaves Starling, Peter, Henry, Juda, Sarah and Mary_], daughter **Polly**, daughter **Betsy**, daughter **Lucy Ann**, daughter **Milly Elliot** and sons **Thomas, John, William, Blake, Joab, Brantly** and **James**. Executors: brother **John Cheek**, friend Col. **Richard Street** and son **Thomas Cheek**. Witnesses: **Atlas Jones** and **A. McKinnon**. Codicil Aug 15, 1827 names executors as brother **John Cheek** and son **Joab Cheek**. Proven Nov 1827.

3182.　　　1820, May 3 -- Land Grant #2505, Moore County, NC
Eli Phillips received 100 acres located north of Richland Creek adjoining his own line and **John Phillips. John Phillips** and **Jesse Sowell** were chain carriers.

3183.　　　1820, May 3 -- Land Grant #2530, Moore County, NC
Jesse Sowell received 1 acre located north of Richland Creek including the house where he formerly lived adjoining **Samuel Dunn, Roan, Asa Sowell** and his own line. **Wm. McIver** and **Jno. Sowell Jur.** were chain carriers.

3184.　　　1820, May 3 -- Land Grant #2532, Moore County, NC
Jesse Sowell received 8.75 acres located north of Richland Creek adjoining **Roan, Asa Sowell** and **Isaac Sowell. William McIver** and **John Sowell Jur.** were chain carriers.

3185.　　　1820, Aug 8-1833 -- Estate, Randolph County, NC
Estate of **Andrew Purvis**, Dec'd. by Administrator **Susanna Purvis** with **Hugh Moffit, Eli Bray** and **Tidince Lane** as security. **Alfred Brower**. _Items were purchased by the following_: **Harmon Bray, Abram Lane, John Bray, Saml. Redfearn, John Hutson, Eli Hix, Jesse Bray, Mathias Bray, Jackson Deaton, John Parkes, John Deaton,**

Rich Jones Esq., Thomas Willson, William Harper, Rolley Spinks, Lewis Spinks, John Caviness, Susanna Purvis, Isaac Teague, Geo. Yow, John Bowdown, Hiram Elkins, Andy Caveness, William Purvis, Banj. Haddock, Jacob Brower, George Yow, Henry Phillips, William Raines, Stephen Scott, John Lane Sr. and Joseph Lane. Andrew Purvis died in Jul 1820 with 341 acres on Flat Creek adjoining Thos. Wilson, Wm. Kerr and Moses Kid. *Petition for division of land for heirs*: James Madison Purvis; Tidence Lane, guardian of Robt. Purvis, John Purvis, Jefferson Purvis and Joseph Purvis; James Caviness, guardian for Cary Purvis. *Petition for division of slaves*: James Madison Purvis; Tidence Lane, Guardian of Robt. Purvis, John Purvis and Joseph Purvis; James Caviness, guardian for Cary Purvis; James and Susanna Caviness [widow who had remarried]. Slaves Huldah, Nancy, Barny, Dennis, Emeline and Ned.

3186.   1820, Aug 16 -- Land Grant #2520, Moore County, NC
James Bryant received 50 acres located south of McLendons Creek on Wolf Pit Branch and Joel Road adjoining Phillips, Thomas Graham (known as the crossroads tract) and Jackson. Thos. Bryant and Wm. Jackson were chain carriers.

A.   1820, Sep 15 -- Deed Book 21 Page 464-465, Moore County, NC
Lewis Lawhorn deeded Joel Lawhorn 100 acres located northwest of Richland Creek and northeast of Locust Branch adjoining William Dunn, Jesse Ritter and Alex. McIntosh. Wm. Person and Jesse Sowell were witnesses.

3187.   1820, Sep 21 -- Land Grant #2545, Moore County, NC
Robert Kennedy received 90 acres located on both sides of Bear Creek adjoining his own line (formerly William Garner) and Leonard Cagle. Peter Shamburger and Miles Jordan were chain carriers.

3188.   1820, Oct 2 -- BLM General Land Office, Lawrence County, MS
Isham Smith (of Lawrence County) received 160 acres in west of Pearl River District located in southeast Quarter of Section 8, Township 7, Range 10.

3189.   1820, Oct 12 -- Chronicles and Records of Bensalem Presbyterian Church Page 21, Moore County, NC
Neill Morison and Mary Nicholson were married.

A.   1820, Oct 21 -- Land Grant #2044, Chatham County, NC
William Tyson & Co. received 30 acres located on Indian Creek adjoining Lewis Phillips, Griffin and the land where William Melone now lives. William Melone and Horatio Phillips were chain carriers.

B.   1820, Oct 25 -- Land Grant #2506, Montgomery County, NC
John McCrumin received 125 acres located on Wolf Creek adjoining McNeill, Moore County line, his own line. Gambil Powers and William Jame were chain carriers.

3190.   1820, Oct 27 -- *A History of Sandy Creek Baptist Association* by George Purefoy, Page 80
Elder Isaac Teague, William Carr and Eli Solar [Lawler] from Fall Creek Church (Chatham County) were delegates to the Association meeting at Timber Ridge Meeting House in Randolph County, NC.

3191.   1820, Nov -- 1796-1841 County Accounts, Moore County, NC Page 41
State v. C. Furr

3192.   1820, Nov 1 -- Land Grant #2510, Moore County, NC
Josiah Culbertson received 35 acres located on Fall Creek adjoining Wells, Abner Lawler, Brewer, James England and William Martindale. John Lawler and Micajah Brewer were chain carriers.

3193.   1820, Nov 1 -- Land Grant #2517, Moore County, NC
Thos. Bryant received 100 acres located on Lackys Branch of McLendons Creek adjoining Alexr. McIntosh. Needham Bryant and Thos. Bryant were chain carriers.

3194.   1820, Nov 7 -- Land Grant #2522, Moore County, NC
Nathan Fry received 15 acres located on Killets Creek adjoining his own line, Daniel Caddle and Neil Black. James Fry and Joseph Fry were chain carriers.

3195.   1820, Nov 16 -- Record of Marriages, Wilcox County, AL

Enoch Maners married **Lidia Autry**

A.   1820, Nov 20 -- Land Grant #2333, Montgomery County, NC
George Allen received 100 acres located on East Fork of Little River, Wards Creek and Cooks Creek adjoining his own line, **John B. Callicott** and **Rubin Allen. John Allen** and **Wm. Brice** were chain carriers.

B.   1820, Nov 21 -- Land Grant #2315, Montgomery County, NC
George Allen received 200 acres located on the drains of Wolf Creek adjoining his own line, **John McRummin**, Great Lick, Crawfords Road, Cotton Creek and **Wm. Allen. Nathan Morgan** and **Wm. Brice** were chain carriers.

3196.   1820, Dec 15 -- Record of Estates Book B, Pages 31-32, 43, Moore County, NC
Estate of **John/Isham Sheffield**, Dec'd. by Administrator **Arch. McNeill. H. Kennedy, P. Shamburger** and **Wm. Hussey** appointed to lay off a year's provision for Widow **Sally Sheffield**. [*Editor's Note: Pages 31-32 lists **John** while Page 43 lists **Isham** instead -- fairly certain this is **Isham**]*

3197.   1821, Feb -- Record of Estates Book B Page 25-29 Moore County, NC
Estate of **Jesse Muse**, Dec'd. by Administrators **James B. Muse** and **Thomas P. Muse**. Inventory includes negro woman **Hannah**. Debts due the estate from the following: **John Richardson, Samuel Dunn, William Ellerbe, John Murchison** and **Lewis Elkins**. *Items purchased by the following*: Widow **Muse, Jesse Page, John B. Kelly, Nehemiah Birckhead, William Barrett**, Esq., **James B. Muse, Benjamin Phillips, Thomas M.D. Reid, Jesse Sowell**, Senr., **Joseph Johnson, William Phillips, Daniel H. Muse, James Hill, Hiram Hill, John Tyson, John Black, John Sowell**, Senr., **Joseph G. Moore, Joseph Elkins, Thomas Hannon, Alexr. McIntosh, John McIver, Wm. Cox Junr., Asa Sowell, Kindred Birckhead, James Caddell, Leonard Stuts** and **Martin Hill**.

3198.   1821, Feb 10 -- BLM General Land Office Document #1345, Lincoln County, MS
Nathan Smith, assignee of **Wyatt Allgood** received 160 acres from west of Pearl River Land Office located in northwest Quarter of Section 15, Township 7, Range 6.

3199.   1821, Feb 10 -- BLM General Land Office Document #1347, Lincoln County, MS
Stephen Smith, assignee of **Wyatt Allgood** received 160 acres from west of Pearl River Land Office located in southwest Quarter of Section 10, Township 7, Range 6.

3200.   1821, Feb 10 -- BLM General Land Office, Lawrence County, MS
Jacob Furr (of Lawrence County) received 159.75 acres from Washington Land Office located in southeast Quarter of Section 9, Township 8, Range 9.

3201.   1821, Feb 10 -- BLM General Land Office Document #1111, Lincoln County, MS
William Smith (of Lawrence County) received 160 acres from west of Pearl River Land Office located in southwest Quarter of Section 10, Township 8, Range 9.

3202.   1821, Feb 10 -- BLM General Land Office Document #1118, Lincoln County, MS
Eli Smith (of Lawrence County) received 160 acres from west of Pearl River Land Office located in southeast Quarter of Section 19, Township 7, Range 9.

3203.   1821, Feb 12 -- Estate, Chatham County, NC
Estate of **Russell Massey** Dec'd. by Administrators **William Pearce, Thomas Craven** and **Redding Bryan**

A.   1821, Feb 15 -- Marriage Bond, Randolph County, NC
Elisha Cagle and **Anna Hancock** received marriage bond. **Samuel Smithermon** was bondsman. [*Editor's Note: Date of marriage occurred on or after date of marriage bond.*]

3204.   1821, Feb 20 -- Land Grant #2571, Moore County, NC
Henry Cagle received 24 acres located on north prong of Bear Creek and Randolph County line adjoining his own line, **Davis** and **Page. Elisha Cagle** and **Henry Cagle** were chain carriers.

3205.   1821, Mar 8 -- Chronicles and Records of Bensalem Presbyterian Church Page 7, Moore County, NC
Malcolm McAuley and **Catharine McLeod** were married.

3206.   1821, Mar 13 -- Deed Book 62 Page 390, Moore County, NC

Christopher Stutts deeded **Jacob Stutts** 150 acres located on Bear Creek. **H. Kennedy** and **G. Kennedy** were witnesses.

3207. 1821, Mar 21 -- Deed Book 14 Page 80-83, Randolph County, NC
Thomas Matthews deeded **William Pearce** several tracts [1] 100 acres located north of Fork Creek adjoining **Adam Andrews**. Part of tract granted to **Adam Andrews**. [2] 150 acres located north of Fork Creek and west of Rock Creek adjoining his own line [3] 30 acres located on Rock Creek adjoining his own line and **Pearce**. [4] 350 acres located on Rock Creek adjoining his own line. **Ollave Pearce** is listed as a witness.

3208. 1821, May 10 -- Land Grant #2572, Moore County, NC
Robert Kennedy received 59 acres located south of Bear Creek adjoining **Morrison** and **Martin**, **A.B. Smith**, **Isham Davis** and his own line. **Peter Shamburger** and **Miles Jordan** were chain carriers.

3209. 1821, May 10 -- Land Grant #2574, Moore County, NC
Mark Allen received 45 acres located on Fork of Cabin Creek adjoining his own line, **Alexr. Leach**, **Neil McLeod** and **Allen**. **Jerry Reynolds** and **Alexr. Leach** were chain carriers.

3210. 1821, May 17 -- Land Grant #2581, Moore County, NC
Henry Stuts received 50 acres adjoining **George Horner**, **Stephen Richardson** and **Sink**. **Henry Stuts** and **William Stuts** were chain carriers.

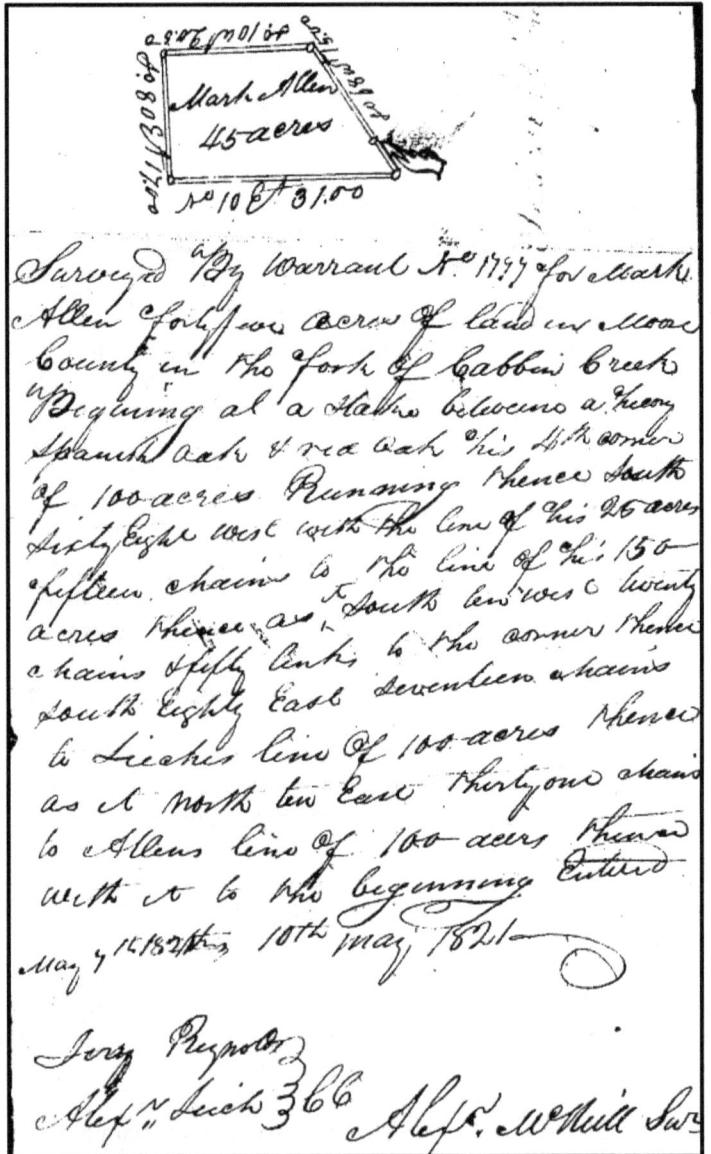

3211. 1821, May 24 -- Chronicles and Records of Bensalem Presbyterian Church Page 10, Moore County, NC
William C. Buie and **Ephemia Clark** were married

3212. 1821, Jun 4 -- BLM General Land Office, Lawrence County, MS
Caleb Dickerson, assignee of **Isham Smith Jr.** received 160 acres in west of Pearl River District located in southwest Quarter of Section 8, Township 7, Range 10.

3213. 1821, Jun 4 -- BLM General Land Office, Lincoln County, MS
William Smith, assignee of **Bailey Maners** received 156.13 acres from west of Pearl River Land Office located in northeast Quarter of Section 6, Township 7, Range 9.

3214. 1821, Jun 7 -- BLM General Land Office, Lawrence County, MS
Henry Furr, assignee of **Reuben Collins**, received 160 acres from west of Pearl River Land Office located in northwest Quarter of Section 20, Township 8, Range 9.

3215. 1821, Jun 7 -- BLM General Land Office, Lincoln County, MS
William Smith (of Lawrence County) received 160 acres from west of Pearl River Land Office located in southwest Quarter of Section 31, Township 8, Range 9.

3216. 1821, Jun 7 -- BLM General Land Office, Lincoln County, MS
Isaac Smith Senr., assignee of **Levi Smith** received 160 acres from west of Pearl River Land Office located in southwest Quarter of Section 10, Township 7, Range 8.

3217. 1821, Jun 10 -- Land Grant #2644, Moore County, NC
Neil McLeod received 100 acres located on Yadkin Road and south prong of Bear Creek adjoining **Bullock** and **Allison**. **Wm. Brewer** and **Wm. Williamson** were chain carriers.

3218. 1821, Jun 15 -- BLM General Land Office Document #1368, Lincoln County, MS
Solomon Carpenter (of Lawrence County) received 155.81 acres from west of Pearl River Land Office located in southwest Quarter of Section 24, Township 7, Range 9.

3219. 1821, Aug -- Chronicles and Records of Bensalem Presbyterian Church Page 14, Moore County, NC
John McIntosh, son of **Alexander McIntosh** and **Mary Jackson**, died.

3220. 1821, Aug 1 -- BLM General Land Office, Lincoln County, MS
Nicholas Smith (of Lawrence County) received 160 acres from west of Pearl River Land Office located in northeast Quarter of Section 9, Township 7, Range 6.

3221. 1821, Aug 25 -- Land Grant #2597, Moore County, NC
Joel Lachhorn received 27 acres located south of Richland Creek adjoining **Davis**, **Dowdy**, his own line and **McQueen**. **Jesse Bean** and **James Dowdy** were chain carriers.

3222. 1821, Sep 4 -- BLM General Land Office Document #49, Lincoln County, MS
Levi Smith., assignee of **Thomas** and **Coleman Shipp** received 80 acres from west of Pearl River Land Office located in east half of southwest Quarter of Section 11, Township 8, Range 9.

3223. 1821, Sep 4 -- BLM General Land Office Document #317, Lincoln County, MS
Levi Smith, assignee of **Thomas** and **Coleman Shipp** received 80 acres from west of Pearl River Land Office located in west half of northwest Quarter of Section 11, Township 8, Range 9.

3224. 1821, Sep 8 -- Land Grant #2645, Moore County, NC
Neil McLeod received 100 acres located northwest of Williams Creek adjoining **Carpenter**, **Allison** and his own line. **Benj. Britt** and **Wm. Diffie** were chain carriers.

3225. 1821, Fall -- 1796-1841 County Accounts, Moore County, NC Page 56
State v. **John Melton**

A. 1821, Sep 28 -- Deed Book 3 Page 494-499, Moore County, NC
Samuel Jackson deeded **William Jackson** 1226 acres: [1] 50 acres located on Juniper Creek south of McLendons Creek [2] 100 acres adjoining **Widow Jackson** [3] 200 acres adjoining **Allison** [4] 46 acres being part of 150 acres granted to **David Sears** [5] 100 acres located on Falling Branch [6] 100 acres located on the Juniper adjoining **William Sears** [7] 50 acres adjoining **Samuel Jackson** and **Patterson** [8] 50 acres located north of the Juniper adjoining **Seawell** [9] 150 acres located on Little River and north of Joel Road adjoining **David Sears** and **Samuel Jackson** [10] 100 acres located on the Suck branches of Juniper adjoining **David Sears** and **Shadrick Rogers** [11] 150 acres located on Lower Little River adjoining **Michael Johnson** (formerly **David Lewis**) and **John Jackson** [12] 100 acres located on Lower Little River and granted to **John Jackson** adjoining **Angus Campbell** [13] 50 acres located on Lower Little River including **Seal's** Cabin. **Alexr. McIntosh** and **Joseph Rouse** were witnesses.

3226. 1821, Oct 10 -- Land Grant #2566, Moore County, NC
Donald Gillis received 125 acres located east of Dry Creek adjoining his own line, **Malcolm Morrison**, **John Paterson** and (**Normand Matheson**) **Hector McLean**. **John Kennedy** and **Donald Murchison** were chain carriers.

3227. 1821, Oct 26 -- *A History of Sandy Creek Baptist Association* by George Purefoy, Page 82
Bryant Boroughs, **William Carr**, **Eli Lawler** and Elder **Isaac Teague** from Fall Creek Church (Chatham County) were delegates to the Association meeting at Sandy Field in Orange County, NC.

3228.　　1821, Nov 12 -- Land Grant #2590, Moore County, NC
Alexr. McIntosh received 15 acres located south of McLendons Creek adjoining his own line and **Bryant**. **William Lewis** and **John McIntosh** were chain carriers.

3229.　　1821, Nov 30 -- Land Grant #2583, Moore County, NC
Jesse Muse received 300 acres located north of McLendons Creek on both sides of the Waggon Road adjoining his own line, **Boroughs** and **Campbell**. **James B. Muse** and **Thos. P. Muse** were chain carriers.

3230.　　1822 (undated estimate) -- Record of Estates Book B Page 44, 66 Moore County, NC
Estate of **Thomas Ritter**, Dec'd. (includes only listing of property). **Lewis Garner** only name listed as purchasing an item.

3231.　　1822, Jan 10 -- Land Grant #2660, Moore County, NC
Robert Wilson received 50 acres located on the Kings Street waters of Buffalo Creek adjoining **John Ritter**, **Drury Richardson Sr.**, **Drury Richardson Jr.**, his own line (formerly **John Dannelly**). **Thos. Dannelly** and **John Ritter** were chain carriers.

3232.　　1822, Feb (undated estimate) -- Record of Estates Book B Page 39-40, 74-75, Moore County, NC
Estate of **Joseph Duckworth**, Dec'd. by Administrators **Hannah Duckworth** and **B. Boroughs**. Inventory includes slaves **Chain**, **Peggy**, **Jerry**, **Tempy**, **Daniel**, **Esra** and **Anderson**.

3233.　　1822, Feb 2 -- Land Grant #2622, Moore County, NC
Alexander McIntosh received 43 acres located south of Richland Creek adjoining his own line (formerly **Neill McLeod**), **Christian McIntosh**, **McKinnon** and **John Rouse**. **Neill McIntosh** and **Wm. J. McIntosh** were chain carriers.

A.　　1822, Feb 12 -- Deed Book 4 Page 550-551, Moore County, NC
George Graham deeded **John Graham** 50 acres located on McLendons Creek and Oat Patch Branch adjoining Martin's Mill Pond. **M. McCrummen** was a witness.

3234.　　1822, Feb 14 -- Record of Marriages, Wilcox County, AL
Mark Morgan married **Euphrania Hare**

A.　　1822, Feb 22 -- Land Grant #2376, Montgomery County, NC
William Autera received 80 acres located on Dicks Creek adjoining his own line and **John Jordan**. **Henry Stephens** and **William Autera** were chain carriers.

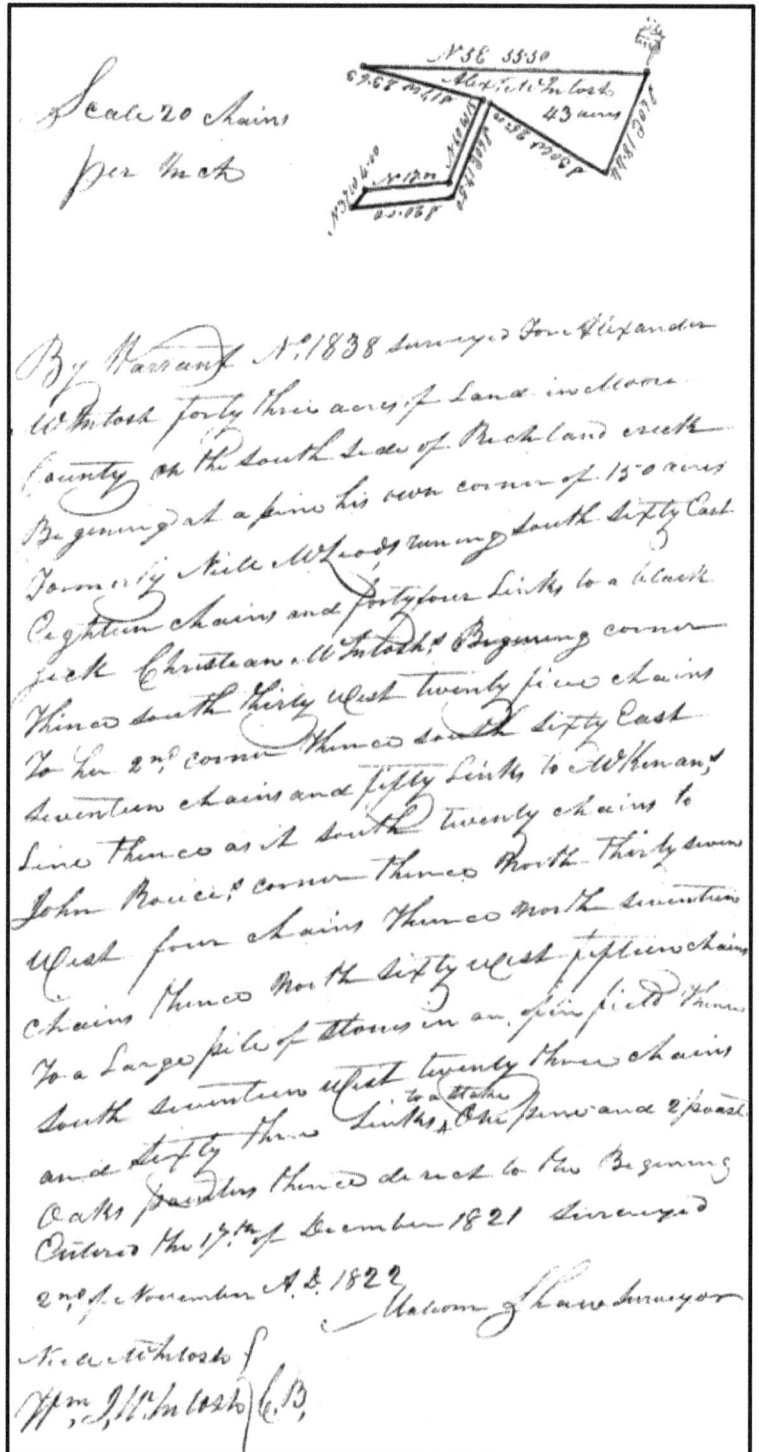

3235.   1822, Mar 14 -- Record of Estates Book B Page 40-41,69 Moore County, NC
Estate of **William Dunn**, Dec'd. by Administrator **Angus McKinnon**. *Items purchased by the following*: **Alexr. Autray, Avington Britt, Angus Morrison, Allen McLean, Bartholomew Dunn, Donald Chisholm, Donald McLeod, George Hunsucker, Hezekiah Autery, James Cole, James Keachey, John McCaskel, John Hunsucker, Jesse Brown, John Stutts, John Patterson** Esq., **Malcolm Matheson, Malcolm McCaskel, Margaret Deaton, Norman McKinnon, Nathan Coplin, Roderick McAuley, Shadrick Manes, Sarah Dunn** (Widow), **John Wallis, William Barret, William Hunsucker, Wright Deaton** and **William Nameless Manes**. *Notes due on the following*: **John Wollase, Right Deaton, John Stuts, Malcolm Mathewson, Roderick McAulay, Hezekiah Autery, William Barrett, George Hunsucker, Wm. Hunsucker, John Hunsucker, Wm. N. Maness, Shadrick Maness, Malcolm McCaskill, John Paterson, Alexr. Autray, James Keachey, Matthew Deaton** (fmr. Admin.), **William Deaton, Daniel McLeod, Bartholomew Dunn Jr., Angus McKinnon, Allen McLean, Samuel Barringtone** and **Bartholomew Dunn Sr.**

3236.   1822, Mar 15 -- Record of Estates Book B Page 42-43, Moore County, NC
Estate of **Catherine Cagle**, Dec'd. *Items purchased by the following*: **Henry Cagle, Martin Cagle, Elizabeth Boling, George Cagle, Peter Cagle, Nathaniel Tucker, John Cagle, Charles Cagle, Elisha Cagle, Jacob Cagle** and **Miles Jordan**.

3237.   1822, Apr 22 -- Land Grant #2599, Moore County, NC
Neil McLeod received 80 acres located on Blans Branch west of Richland Creek adjoining his own line. **John McLeod** and **N. McLeod** were chain carriers.

3238.   1822, May 2 -- Land Grant #2591, Moore County, NC
George Cagle received 30 acres located on both sides of Cabin Creek adjoining **John Cagle** and **Brown**. **Hiram Kennedy** and **John Cagle** were chain carriers.

3239.   1822, Aug 10 -- Land Grant #2601, Moore County, NC
Allen Bethune received 50 acres located east of Wet Creek adjoining his own line and **McIver**. **Archd. Campbell** and **Donald McAulay** were chain carriers.

A.   1822, Aug 15 -- Marriage Bond, Chatham County, NC
Silas Cheek and **Edith Phillips** received marriage bond. **Lazarus Phillips** was bondsman. [*Editor's Note: Date of marriage occurred on or after date of marriage bond.*]

3240.   1822, Aug 29 -- Land Grant #2592, Moore County, NC
Murdock Matheson received 50 acres located on Jacksons Creek adjoining **Widow McMillan**, his own line (formerly **James Autry**), **Curry** and his own line. **John Matheson** and **Newson Autrey** were chain carriers.

3241.   1822, Sep -- Chronicles and Records of Bensalem Presbyterian Church Page 10, Moore County, NC
Christian McDonald, wife of **Daniel McDonald**, died.

3242.   1822, Oct -- Chronicles and Records of Bensalem Presbyterian Church Page 16, Moore County, NC
Neill Kennedy and **Mary Kennedy** [b. Nov 19, 1815] died. **John Kennedy** died in Fall 1822 [b. Fall 1819]. All three were children of **John Kennedy** and **Margaret McKellar**.

3243.   1822, Oct 6 -- Chronicles and Records of Bensalem Presbyterian Church Page 10, Moore County, NC
Kenneth McDonald, son of **Daniel** and **Christian McDonald**, died. [Born May 9, 1819]

A.   1822, Oct 22 -- Deed Book A-A1 Page 98, Chatham County, NC
Solomon Brewer (of Randolph County) deeded **Stephen Brewer** his share of his father's **Sampson Brewer** Dec'd. land of two tracts with 350 acres located on Fall Creek. **Eli Lawler Sr.** and **Eli Lawler Jr.** were witnesses.

3244.   1822, Oct 25 -- Land Grant #2623, Moore County, NC
Alexander Plummer received 50 acres located on the waters of Bear Creek adjoining **Hammil, William Williamson** and **Allen Williamson**. **Lewis Williamson** and **Allen Williamson** were chain carriers.

3245.   1822, Oct 26 -- *A History of Sandy Creek Baptist Association* by George Purefoy, Page 84

Elder **Isaac Teague**, **B. Boroughs** and **William Waddill** from Fall Creek Church (Chatham County) were delegates to the Association meeting at May's Chapel in Orange County, NC.

3246. 1823 -- Record of Estates Book B Page 90-91, Moore County, NC
Estate of **Sherwood Wright** Dec'd. by Administrator **Levy Deaton**. _Notes due on the following_: **John Sheffield**, **Asa McLenden**, **Wilson Chalmers**, **Allen McLean**, **Daniel McLean**, **Everet Sheffield**, **Medford Owens**, **Edmond Hollan**, **Alexr. Plummer**, **John Freeman**, **Thos. Kees**, **Everet Smith**, **William Williams**, **Danl. McRummen**, **Ryland R. Miller**, **George Kees**, **Danl. McIver**, **John Arnet** and **Thomas McNeill**.

3247. 1823 -- Chronicles and Records of Bensalem Presbyterian Church Page 5, Moore County, NC
Elijah Ottery removed to Tennessee where he became blind and his son **Alexr. Ottery** followed in 1827. He acted criminally in forsaking his wife and taking up with another woman for which he was removed.

3248. 1823 -- Chronicles and Records of Bensalem Presbyterian Church Page 5, Moore County, NC
Daniel McCrimmon was removed as Elder after marrying the sister of his deceased wife in 1822. The case was carried by appeals to the highest judicatory but before it was terminated **Mr. McRummen** joined the Baptists.

3249. 1823, Jan 1 -- Land Grant #2646, Moore County, NC
Neil McLeod received 100 acres located southwest of Bear Creek adjoining **Jerry Autery**, **Bullock**, **Jeremiah Williams**, **William 3249**, and his own line. **Wm. Brewer** and **Jeremiah Williams** were chain carriers.

3250. 1823, Jan 2 -- 1813-1828 Marriage Licenses, Moore County, NC
Needham Bryant and **Margaret Black** were married by **Corn. Dowd**, Clk.

3251. 1823, Jan 4 -- Land Grant #2631, Moore County, NC
John Cockman received 13.75 acres located on Buffalo Creek adjoining **Stephen Richardson**, **Mrs. Wood**, **James Melton**, his own line and **McLeod**. **Jesse Upton** and **Drury Richardson** were chain carriers.

3252. 1823, Feb 13 -- 1813-1828 Marriage Licenses, Moore County, NC
Archd. Leach and **Catharin Patterson** were married by **Corn. Dowd**

3253. 1823, Feb 15 -- Land Grant #2693, Moore County, NC
Joseph Allen Junr. received 50 acres located south of Cabin Creek adjoining **Joseph Allen Senr.** and **Bullock**. **Jerry Reynolds** and **Mark Allen** were chain carriers.

3254. 1823, Mar 4 -- Land Grant #2614, Moore County, NC
James Autray received 50 acres located on Meadow Creek of Jacksons Creek adjoining his own line. **Malcom Ray** and **Alexr. McFarland** were chain carriers.

3255. 1823, Mar 9 -- U.S. Postal Records, Moore County, NC
Elias Kennedy appointed Postmaster of Mechanics Hill Post Office

3256. 1823, Spring -- 1796-1841 County Accounts, Moore County, NC Page 58
State v. **Wm. Hunsucker**

A. 1823, Apr 22 -- Marriage Bond, Randolph County, NC
Enoch Byrns and **Catherine Beckerdite** received marriage bond. **Nineva Beckerdite** was bondsman. [*Editor's Note: Date of marriage occurred on or after date of marriage bond.*]

3257. 1823, May 5 -- Will, Randolph County, NC
Will of **Windsor Pearce**, Dec'd. Heirs: wife **Marey**, daughters **Ollive Pearce**, **Keziah Pearce** [**Ollive** and **Keziah** to receive 250 acres where I now live and 100 acres on head of Cedar Creek called the **Jordon** Place and negro **Phiba** and her child **Classa**], **Marey Spinks** and **Pherrebee Moore**. Executors: **William Carr** and **James Johnston**. Witnesses: **William Searcy** and **John Waddill**. Proven Aug 1823

3258. 1823, May 20 -- Record of Estates Book B Page 71-72, Moore County, NC
Estate of **Mathew Deaton** Dec'd. by **Roderick McAulay**, Administrator. *Notes on the following*: **Malcolm Mathewson**, **George Kennedy**, **Neill McKinnon**, **Wm. Hunsucker**, **Abel Nicholson**, **Angus McAulay**, **Burwell Deaton** and **James Barrentine**.

3259. 1823, May 21 -- Deed Book 82 Page 41-42, Moore County, NC
Isom Sowell deeded **James Dowdy** 9 acres located on Locust Branch adjoining **Stephen Davis** and **Jesse Ritter**. **John Dowdy** and **Thomas Dowdy** were witnesses.

3260. 1823, May 25 -- Record of Marriages, Wilcox County, AL
Martin Morgan married **Cynthia Hare**

3261. 1823, Jun 10 -- Record of Marriages, Wilcox County, AL
Adam Autery married **Lydia Hare**

3262.   1823, Jul 4 -- Article, *The Star* and *NC State Gazette* [Raleigh, NC] Newspaper
"Murder -- On the 6th ult [Jun 6, 1823], about sunset, as **Mr. James Lake[y]** was returning home near Mechanic's Hill, Moore County, in a one horsewagon, he was shot dead with a rifle, by some person concealed in the woods. He was found the next morning, by his brother, in an erect position, with the whip and reins in his hands; and the horse, being very gentle, was grazing on the side of the road. Suspicion falling upon a man by the name of **Abednego Manes**, as the perpetrator of this foul and cowardly deed, he was arrested and committed to prison for trial." [*Editor's Note: Maness family tradition says that **Abednego Maness** shot and killed **James Lakey** after Lakey cheated his wife **Sukie Maness** twice. He had warned Lakey after the first time that he would kill him if he did it again. Abednego Maness was found guilty and forced to leave state -- Madison County, TN by 1830*]

3263.   1823, Jul 30 -- Land Grant #2615, Moore County, NC
John Richeson received 100 acres located south of Richland Creek and Waggon Road adjoining **Kelly**, his own line and **Rowan**. **Phillip Brooks** and **Wm. B. Smith** were chain carriers.

3264.   1823, Aug 1 -- Land Grant #2690, Moore County, NC
Hymerick Hill received 1 acre on both sides of McLendons Creek adjoining **John Tyson** and his own line. **Isac Smith** and **James B. Muse** were chain carriers.

3265.   1823, Aug 13 -- Record of Estates Book B Page 74, Moore County, NC
Estate of **John Hare, Junr.** Dec'd. by Administrator **Peter Hare**. Notes and Judgements listed on the following: **John Sheffield Jur.**, **Everet Sheffield**, **Medford Owens**, **John Sheffield Sr.**, **Mark Allen**, **Alexander Plummer**, **John Owens Sr.**, **James Williamson** and the Estate of **Isham Sheffield** Dec'd.

Murder.—On the 6th ultimo, about sunset, as Mr. James Lake was returning home, near Mechanic's Hill, Moore county, in a one horse waggon, he was shot dead with a rifle, by some person concealed in the woods. He was found next morning, by his brother, in an erect position, with the whip and reins in his hands; and the horse, being very gentle, was grazing on the side of the road. Suspicion falling upon a man by the name of Abednego Manes, as the perpetrator of this foul and cowardly deed, he was arrested and committed to prison for trial.

3266.   1823, Aug 18 -- 1823-1831 Court of Pleas and Quarter Sessions, Moore County, NC
[*jury duty - selected participants*] **George Stewart**, **William Caddell**, **Jesse Bean**, **Nathan Barrett**, **David Kennedy**, **John Manes**, **A. Sowell**, **Simon McNeill**, **Cornelius Caddell**, **John Richardson**, **Daniel Caddell**, **Dickson Ritter** and **Walter Barret**. [*jury duty next term - selected participants*] **John Shamburger** Esq., **Wm. Jones**, **Jeremiah Williams Senr.**, **Asa Sowell**, **Mark Allen**, **George Hunsucker**, **Wm. Williamson [B.]**, **James Maness**, **Merrimon Britt**, **Edmond Holland**, **Lewis Williamson**, **Danl. Caddell**, **Peter Shamburger**, **Jacob Cagle** and **George Cagle**.

3267.   1823, Aug 18 -- 1823-1831 Court of Pleas and Quarter Sessions, Moore County, NC Page 1
Ordered that an orphan child **Susan Stone** (age 7) be bound to **John Deaton**.

A.   1823, Aug 18 -- 1823-1831 Court of Pleas and Quarter Sessions, Moore County, NC Page 1
Ordered that **Elias Birckhead** be exempt from paying poll tax on account of his being a cripple.

3268.   1823, Aug 18 -- 1823-1831 Court of Pleas and Quarter Sessions, Moore County, NC Page 2
Ordered that **Peter Davis** be appointed overseer in place of **George Cagle** of the road from **Nicolas Nalls** to the county line and have the following hands to work: **George Cagle**, **Jacob Cagle**, **George Cagle**, **John Shamburger Jr.**, **John Shamburger**'s hands, **Belaver Britt**, **Thomas Shamburger**, **James Shamburgers**'s hands and **Baus Shamburger**.

3269.   1823, Aug 18 -- 1823-1831 Court of Pleas and Quarter Sessions, Moore County, NC Page 2

Ordered that **Everet Sheffield** be appointed overseer in place of **Anderson Smith** of the road from **Spivays** to **McNeill**'s Store.

3270. 1823, Aug 18 -- 1823-1831 Court of Pleas and Quarter Sessions, Moore County, NC Page 2
Ordered that **Thomas Muse** be appointed overseer in place of **Jesse Bean** of the road from Bean's Bridge to the fork at **Stodard**'s Shop.

3271. 1823, Aug 18 -- 1823-1831 Court of Pleas and Quarter Sessions, Moore County, NC Page 3
Ordered that **William Jones** be appointed overseer of the road from **Kennedy**'s Mill to the old road at **Solomon Brewers** and have the following hands to work: **Wm. Williams, Joseph Williams, Wm. Dunn, George Williams, John Wallis, John Stuts, Jacob Stuts, George Kenedy, Jacob Stuts** (son of **Henry**), **Isham Richardson, William Milton, John Williams, Thomas Williams, Jesse Melton, Henry Melton, Robert Milton** and **Joseph Wallis**.

3272. 1823, Aug 18 -- 1823-1831 Court of Pleas and Quarter Sessions, Moore County, NC Page 3
Ordered that **John Richardson** be appointed overseer in place of **Stephen Davis**.

3273. 1823, Aug 18 -- 1823-1831 Court of Pleas and Quarter Sessions, Moore County, NC Page 3
Ordered that **John Cole** [alias **Jack Cole**] be appointed overseer in place of **Neill McLeod** of the road from the **Williams'** Fork to the black rocks.

3274. 1823, Aug 18 -- 1823-1831 Court of Pleas and Quarter Sessions, Moore County, NC Page 3
Ordered that **William Ritter** be appointed overseer in place of **David Jones** of the road from Buffalow Creek to the branch at **Angus McQueens**.

A. 1823, Aug 20 -- 1823-1831 Court of Pleas and Quarter Sessions, Moore County, NC Page 5
A power of attorney from **Nicolas Nall** of the State of North Carolina and County of Moore to **Aaron Tyson** of the State of Alabama was duly acknowledged by **Nall**.

3275. 1823, Aug 20 -- 1823-1831 Court of Pleas and Quarter Sessions, Moore County, NC Page 7
Ordered that **Elijah Brewer** be appointed overseer of the road from Bear Creek to **George Moore**'s and have the following hands to work: **Abraham Stuts, Daniel Williams, George Stuts, John Ritter Jr.** and **Jacob Stuts**

A. 1823, Aug 20 -- 1823-1831 Court of Pleas and Quarter Sessions, Moore County, NC Page 7
Ordered that **William Ritter** be appointed overseer of the road from **George Moore**'s to **Angus McQueen**'s and have the following hands to work: **Samuel Reeves, John Reeves, Wm. Reeves, Wm. Danielly, John Danielly, James Jackson** and **James Upton**.

B. 1823, Aug 21 -- 1823-1831 Court of Pleas and Quarter Sessions, Moore County, NC Page 10
Ordered that **James Muse (Little)** be exempt from paying poll tax on account of his infirmities.

C. 1823, Aug 21 -- 1823-1831 Court of Pleas and Quarter Sessions, Moore County, NC Page 10
Ordered that **Nehemiah Birckhead** be appointed guardian to **Belany Birckhead** and **John Birckhead**.

3276. 1823, Aug 21 -- Deed Book 14 Page 522, Randolph County, NC
William Pearce deeded **Hugh Moffitt** 350 acres located north of Fork Creek adjoining **Nall** and **Armistead**. **Jno. K. Armistead** and **Richard Ferguson** were witnesses.

3277.   1823, Aug 22 -- 1823-1831 Court of Pleas and Quarter Sessions, Moore County, NC Page 11
[Deeds] **James Autray** to **Norman Matheson** was proven by **Murdock McKinzie**
Thomas Ritter to **John Rouse** was proven by **Miles Rouse**
Bradley Garner to **John Maness** was proven by **Bradley Garner Jr**.
Jesse Sowell to **Joel Lawhon** was acknowledged
Atlas Jones to **William Handcock** was acknowledged
Benjn. Phillips to **Zacchius Jones** was acknowledged

3278.   1823, Aug 22 -- 1823-1831 Court of Pleas and Quarter Sessions, Moore County, NC Page 12
William Jones and **Jeremiah Williams Sr**. called for jury duty next term

3279.   1823, Sep 28 --
1813-1828 Marriage
Licenses, Moore County,
NC
Ephraim Autery and
Dicy Bryant were
married by **Corn. Dowd.**

3280.   1823, Oct 1 --
BLM General Land Office
Document #274,
Lawrence County, MS
Henry Furr (of
Lawrence County)
received 80 acres from
Washington Land Office
located in east half of
northeast Quarter of
Section 19, Township 8,
Range 9.

3281.   1823, Oct 4 --
Land Grant #2692,
Moore County, NC
Phillip Brooks received
100 acres located on
Lick Creek adjoining
John Dannelly and
**Francis Myrick. John
Dannelly** and **James
Brooks** were chain
carriers.

3282.   1823, Oct 18 --
Record of Estates Book B
Page 76, Moore County,
NC
Estate of **Meloney
Newton**, Dec'd.by Administrator **Jesse Brown**. *Notes due on the following:* **William Dunn**, **Christopher Stuts**,
Nicholas Wallis and **Malcolm Mathewson**.

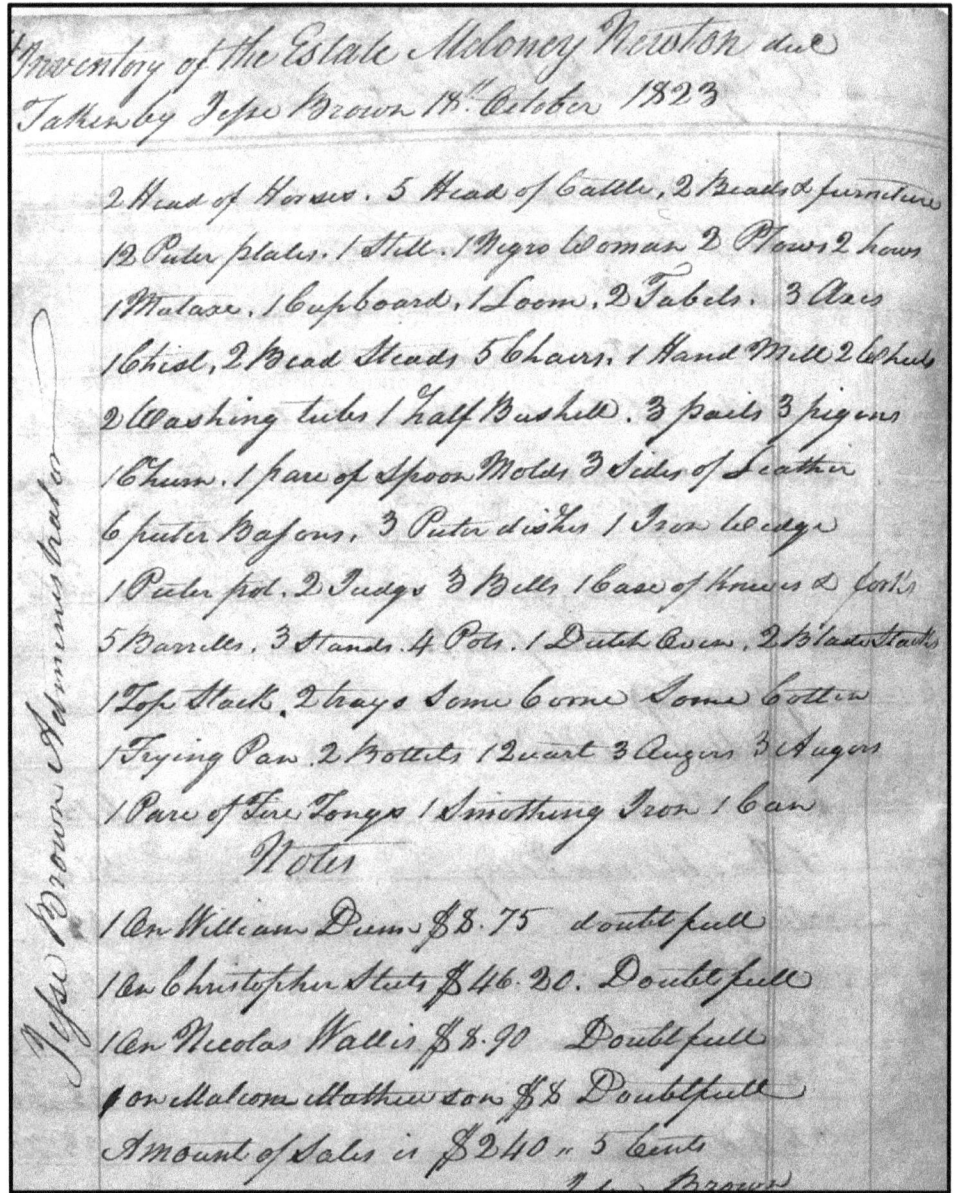

3283.   1823, Oct 25 -- *A History of Sandy Creek Baptist Association* by George Purefoy, Page 86
Elder **Isaac Teague**, **Bryant Boroughs** and **David Kennedy** from Fall Creek Church (Chatham County) and **Eli
Phillips**, **William Dowd** and **Benjamin Phillips** from Friendship Church (Moore County) were delegates to the
Association meeting at Fall Creek Meeting House in Chatham County, NC.

3284. 1823, Nov -- Estate, Randolph County, NC
Estate of **Windsor Pearce** Dec'd. by **James Johnston**, Executor [only listing of personal property]

3285. 1823, Nov 1 -- Land Grant #2616, Moore County, NC
Isaac Teague Senior received 30 acres located on Little Fall Creek adjoining **Robert Willson, Beason, Person** and **Archd. Shields. Robert Willson** and **Jesse Brewer** were chain carriers.

3286. 1823, Nov 17 -- 1823-1831 Court of Pleas and Quarter Sessions, Moore County, NC
[*jury duty - selected participants*] **George Cagle, Merrimon Britt, Jacob Cagle, Edmon Hollen, Lewis Williamson, Daniel Caddell, Peter Shamburger, James Maness, William Williamson** [B.], **Jesse Bean, William Brewer, Cornelius Caddell, Aaron Sowell, Alexr. Kennedy, John Maness, Isham Sowell, John Ritter, John Richardson** and **William Barrett Jur.** [*jury duty next term - selected participants*] **John Cagle Jur., Harmon Brewer, Alexr. Kennedy** and **Elijah Brewer.**

A. 1823, Nov 17 -- 1823-1831 Court of Pleas and Quarter Sessions, Moore County, NC Page 13
Administration of the estate of **Allin Morison** Dec'd. is granted to **Alexr. Morison.**

3287. 1823, Nov 17 -- 1823-1831 Court of Pleas and Quarter Sessions, Moore County, NC Page 14
Ordered that **William Jones** overseer of the road from **David Kennedy**'s bridge to the old road have the following additional hands to work: **David Lanckford, Enoch Wallis, Robert Melton Jr., James Milton, William Wood** and **Matthew Williams.**

3288. 1823, Nov 17 -- 1823-1831 Court of Pleas and Quarter Sessions, Moore County, NC Page 14
Ordered that **Miles Jordan** road overseer have the following additional hands to work: **Thomas Comer** and **William Cagle.**

3289. 1823, Nov 18 -- 1823-1831 Court of Pleas and Quarter Sessions, Moore County, NC Page 15
Henry Stuts recorded his mark to be a hole in the right ear and a swallow fork in the left ear.

3290. 1823, Nov 18 -- 1823-1831 Court of Pleas and Quarter Sessions, Moore County, NC Page 16
Jesse Brown Esq. granted Administration of Estate of **Meloney Newton**, Dec'd.

3291. 1823, Nov 19 -- 1823-1831 Court of Pleas and Quarter Sessions, Moore County, NC Page 17
Ordered that **Michael Bryant**, surviving administrator of **Thomas Graham**, Dec'd. be permitted to sell slaves and equally distrute process to heirs.

3292. 1823, Nov 19 -- 1823-1831 Court of Pleas and Quarter Sessions, Moore County, NC Page 17
Ordered that **William Handcock** bring to next court **Levinay Smith** who was bound to him to show cause why she shall not be taken from him and her indenture cancelled.

3293. 1823, Nov 20 -- 1823-1831 Court of Pleas and Quarter Sessions, Moore County, NC Page 20
Hiram Kennedy v. **Charles Sowell**

3294. 1823, Nov 20 -- Land Grant #2628, Moore County, NC
James B. Muse received 10 acres located south of McLendons Creek and the Big Road adjoining **Hodges, Wm. Phillips, Jesse Rodgers, Birkhead** and his own line. **James Elkins** and **Howard Muse** were chain carriers.

A. 1823, Nov 20 -- 1823-1831 Court of Pleas and Quarter Sessions, Moore County, NC Page 20
Benjn. Person; Frederick Siler; John Siler; Joseph Johnson; Eleazer Birckhead v. Heirs of **Kindred Birckhead** Dec'd. Doctr. **Kinneth B. McIver** is appointed guardian of infant heirs of **Kindred Birckhead** Dec'd to defend these suits.

3295. 1823, Nov 21 -- 1823-1831 Court of Pleas and Quarter Sessions, Moore County, NC Page 21-22
[Deeds] **George A. Muse** to **John B. Kelly** was acknowledged
Thomas P. Muse to **John B. Kelly** was acknowledged
Jesse Bean to **Susannah Bean** was acknowledged
Jesse Bean to **Daniel Caddell** was acknowledged
James B. Muse and **Jesse F. Muse** to **Isaac Smith** proven by **Benjamin Parson**
William Barrett to **Tobias Fry** proven by **Benjn. Person**

3296. 1823, Nov 27 -- Land Grant #2632, Moore County, NC
Jesse Upton received 150 acres located on the waters of Buffalo Creek adjoining **John Stutts**, **McLeod**, **Solomon Brewer**, his own line and **Drury Richardson**. **John Cockman** and **Wm. Rives** were chain carriers.

3297. 1823, Dec 3 -- Deed Book 95 Page 20, Moore County, NC
William Williams deeded **George Davis** 40 acres located on Flag Creek adjoining **Leonard Furr** and **Charles Sowell**. **William Dunn** and **Charles Sowell** were witnesses.

3298. 1823, Dec 22 -- Land Grant #2677, Moore County, NC
Thomas Ritter received 15 acres located on McLendons Creek adjoining **William Barrett Senr.**, his own line and **James Bryant**. **Dixon Ritter** and **Willeby Ritter** were chain carriers.

3299. 1823, Dec 31 --- Deed Book 95 Page 22, Moore County, NC
Jeremiah Williams, **Thomas Williams**, **James Williams**, **Bartholomew Dunn** deeded **William Williams** 2 tracts of land (100 acres and 50 acres) located on Flag Creek. **Jesse Brown Junr.** and **William Dunn** were witnesses.

3300. 1824, Feb 2 -- Land Grant #2648, Moore County, NC
Neil McLeod received 40 acres located east of Richland Creek adjoining **John Martin**. **Alexr. McCaskill** and **John McLeod** were chain carriers.

3301. 1824, Feb 17 -- 1823-1831 Court of Pleas and Quarter Sessions, Moore County, NC
[*jury duty - selected participants*] **Elijah Brewer**, **Heinrick Hill**, **Alexr. Kennedy**, **Bradly Garner**, **Asa Sowell**, **Isham Sowell**, **Simon McNeill** and **Jesse Sanders**. [*jury duty next term - selected participants*] **John Stuts**, **Neill Caddell**, **Wm. Cagle** and **Jesse Sowell**.

3302. 1824, Feb 17 -- 1823-1831 Court of Pleas and Quarter Sessions, Moore County, NC Page 23
Ordered that **Josiah Tyson** and **Eleazor Birkhead Esqs.** be appointed to examine **Polly Keys**, wife of **George Keys** and **Nancy Graham**, wife of **Andrew Graham** for voluntary consent in Deed to **Right Deaton**.

3303. 1824, Feb 17 -- 1823-1831 Court of Pleas and Quarter Sessions, Moore County, NC Page 24
Jesse Brown, **James Dunlap** and **Malcom McRummen** appointed to settle with **Michael Bryant**, Administrator of **Thos. Graham**, Dec'd.

3304. 1824, Feb 17 -- 1823-1831 Court of Pleas and Quarter Sessions, Moore County, NC Page 25
Ordered that **Emanuel Yow** be appointed overseer in place of **William Williamson** of the road from the [Randolph] County line to the Branch at **William Williamson**'s and have the following hands to work: **Henry Yow**, **Andrew Yow**, **Jas. Williamson**, **Daniel Maness**, **John Garner**, **Nicolas Nall** 1 hand, **James Gains** 2 hands, **John Cavenss Jr.**, **William Williamson**, **John Maness**, **Thomas Williams**, **Jeremeah Williams**, **William Smith** and **Gideon Moore**.

3305. 1824, Feb 17 -- 1823-1831 Court of Pleas and Quarter Sessions, Moore County, NC Page 25
Ordered that **Elijah Brewer** overseer of the road from Bear Creek to **George Moores** have the following additional hands to work: **George Moore Jr.**, **John Hunsucker**, **Edward Moore**, **Jethro Denson** and **Bradley Brady**.

3306. 1824, Feb 17 -- 1823-1831 Court of Pleas and Quarter Sessions, Moore County, NC Page 25
Ordered that **William Ritter** overseer of the road from Buffalow Creek to the branch at **McQueens** have the following additional hands to work: **John Stuts**.

3307. 1824, Feb 17 -- 1823-1831 Court of Pleas and Quarter Sessions, Moore County, NC Page 25
Ordered that **John Kennedy** overseer of the road from Bear Creek to **William Williamsons** have the following additional hands to work: **William Waddell**'s hands, **Thomas Person** and hands, **Tabitha Person**'s hands, **Major Johnson**, **Archd. McDonald**, **William Brewer** and **Robert Kennedy**'s hands.

3308. 1824, Feb 17 -- 1823-1831 Court of Pleas and Quarter Sessions, Moore County, NC Page 25

Ordered that **Henry Stuts** road overseer have the following additional hands to work: **Steven Perry**, **Garison Chavis** and **Brantley Chavis**.

3309. 1824, Feb 17 -- 1823-1831 Court of Pleas and Quarter Sessions, Moore County, NC Page 25

Ordered that **John Richardson** road overseer have the following additional hands to work: **Calvin Cox**, **Isaac Smith**, **Samson D. Smith**, **Jason Muse**, **George Fry**, **Wm. Dowdy**, **John Dowdy**, **Wm. Harris**, **Green Hill**, **Jesse Muse**, **Thomas Dowdy**, **Zack Jones**, **John Carrell**, **Kindred Phillips**, Mrs. **Davis** (**Mose** and **Jery**), **Henry Stuts**, **Marvil Ritter** and **Demsay Sowell**.

3310. 1824, Feb 18 -- 1823-1831 Court of Pleas and Quarter Sessions, Moore County, NC Page 27

Walter Barrett appointed constable in District 3
James Dunlap appointed constable in District 7
William Williams appointed constable in District 8

3311. 1824, Feb 17 -- 1823-1831 Court of Pleas and Quarter Sessions, Moore County, NC Page 27

Ordered that **Eleazor Birkhead** and **Duncan Murchison** Esqs. be appointed to examine **Elizabeth Phillips**, wife of **Brinkley Phillips** and **Charraty Phillips**, wife of **William Phillips** for voluntary consent in Deed to **John B. Kelly** for 1/6 part of land that **Jesse Muse** possessed.

3312. 1824, Feb 20 -- 1823-1831 Court of Pleas and Quarter Sessions, Moore County, NC Page 30-31

[Deeds] **Stephen Davis** to **Neil MacIntosh** was proven by **John McIntosh**
Brinkley Phillips, Elizabeth Phillips, William Phillips and **Charity Phillips** to **John B. Kelly** proven by **William Waddell**
Neil McLeod to **Asa Sowell** was acknowledged
Levi Bostick to **Neil McLeod** was proven by **Jesse Sanders**
Duncan Murchison, Sheriff to **John Phillips** was acknowledged
John Cagle to **Jesse Brown Jr.** was proven by **Jesse Brown**
Murdoch McKenzie and **Archd. McBryde** to **Mathew Deaton** proven by **William Dowd**
John Danily to **George Moore** was proven by **John Dannelly Jr.**
Daniel McNeill, Shff to **Alexd. McIntosh** proven by **Jesse Sowell**
Nathan Fry Senr. to **James Fry** was acknowledged
John Carrell to **Neill McLeod** proven by **Archd. McNeill**
Elijah Deaton to **Neil McLeod** proven by **Arch. McNeill**
Bradley Garner to **Neil McLeod** was proven by **Arch. McNeill**
Thomas Ritter to **Neil McLeod** was acknowledged
Mathew Deaton to **Daniel McKenzie** proven by **Norman McKinnon**
Nancy McLeod to **Danl. McCrimmon** proven by **John Patterson**
John McNeil to **Lauchlin McKinnon** was proven by **Hector McNeil**
John Sowell, Murdoch McKenzie and **Arch. McBryde** to **Wm. Barrett** was proven by **Wm. Barrett Jur.**
Andrew and **Nancy Graham, Matthew Deaton, Isaac Deaton, John Deaton, George** and **Polly Key** to **Right Deaton** was acknowledged
Murdock McKenzie and **Arch. McBryde** to **Mathew Deaton** was proven by **William Dowd**
James Hardin to **Robert Hardin** proven by **Hugh Hardin**
[Bills of Sale] **Kinneth McCaskel** to **Daniel McKenzie** proven by **John McCaskel**
John McIver to **Robert Davis** proven by **John Sowell**

3313. 1824, Mar 31 -- Record of Marriages, Wilcox County, AL
James Jackson married **Susan Maness**

3314. 1824, Apr 11 -- Land Grant #2658, Moore County, NC
Daniel McCrummen received 50 acres located southwest of Horse Creek adjoining his own line and **Nancy McLeod**. **Alexr. Plummer** and **Daniel McLean** were chain carriers.

3315. 1824, Apr 12 -- Land Grant #2661, Moore County, NC
John Cockman received 38 acres located on Glade of Long Meadow Branch adjoining his own line and **Solomon Brewer**. **Michael Cockman** and **David Cockman** were chain carriers.

3316. 1824, Apr 17 -- 1813-1828 Marriage Licenses, Moore County, NC
James Autery and **Nancy Batton** were married by **Corn. Dowd**.

3317. 1824, May 1 -- BLM General Land Office Document #449, Lauderdale County, AL
John Richardson, assignee of **Walter Maxey** received 80.32 acres from Huntsville Land Office located in Western half of northwest Quarter of Section 23, Township 1, Range 9.

3318. 1824, May 1 -- BLM General Land Office Document #621, Lauderdale County, AL
John Richardson, assignee of **Elisha Milton** received 79.66 acres from Huntsville Land Office located in Western half of northeast Quarter of Section 27, Township 1, Range 10.

A. 1824, May 8 -- Will Book B Page 37, Moore County, NC
Will of **Mary Montgomery** Dec'd. Heirs: daughter **Deborah Dubrutz**, mentions note on **Gabriel Dubrutz**, grandson **Joseph Dubrutz**, granddaughter **Mary Hill** (wife of **John Hill**) nephew **George Willcox** (of Chatham County), **Susannah Thompson** (widow of **John Thompson** Esq. of Chatham County), daughter **Elizabeth Gains** (wife of **James Gains**) and children of daughter **Margaret Waddell** Dec'd. Executors: **Robert Palmer** and **Archd. McBryde**. Witnesses: **A. McBryde** and **A.D. McQueen**.

3319. 1824, May 17 -- 1823-1831 Court of Pleas and Quarter Sessions, Moore County, NC
[*jury duty next term - selected participants*] **Thomas Ritter**, **Wm. Cagle**, **Henry Stuts**, **George Moore Senr.**, **William Stuts**, **Peter Cagle**, **Wm. Caddell Jr.**, **John Ritter**, **Medford Owen**, **Wm. Freeman** and **Levy Deaton**.

3320. 1824, May 18 -- Land Grant #2675, Moore County, NC
John W. Norton received 477 acres located northwest of McLendons Creek adjoining **Marley**, **Cheek**, **Davis**, **Alston**, **William Dowd** and **Street**. **Jno. D. Phillips** and **George Stewart** were chain carriers.

3321. 1824, May 18 -- 1823-1831 Court of Pleas and Quarter Sessions, Moore County, NC Page 34
Jesse Brown Esq. granted Administration of Estate of **John Smith**, Dec'd.

3322. 1824, May 18 -- 1823-1831 Court of Pleas and Quarter Sessions, Moore County, NC Page 35
Nicholas Nall appointed guardian of **Amelia Tyson**

3323. 1824, May 19 -- 1823-1831 Court of Pleas and Quarter Sessions, Moore County, NC Page 38
[Deeds] **John Cole** to **James Cole** acknowledged
Robert Davis to **William C. Davis** proven by **Daniel McNeill Junr.**
George and **Mary Keys** to **Margaret Deaton** was proven by **Wright Deaton**
John Smith to **Jesse Brown Jr.** was proven by **Jesse Brown**
Josiah Davis to **Levy Deaton** was proven by **Neill Morrison**

A. 1824, May 20 -- Notice, *Fayetteville Observer* [Fayetteville, NC] Newspaper
Gun & Rifle Manufactory. The subscriber informs the public that he still carriers on the above business at the old stand. Mechanic's Hill, NC and that he has considerably enlarged the business, by having more hands and materials engaged, which enables him somewhat to reduce the prices. Mr. **Jesse Pot's Sen**. is his agent in Fayetteville, where Guns and Riffles may be bought on the same terms as at the Factory. **David Kennedy**...May 18, 1824.

3324. 1824, May 24 -- BLM General Land Office Document #141, Wilcox County, AL

George Morgan, assignee of **Alexander Autry** received 159.90 acres from Cahaba Land Office located in southwest Quarter of Section 18, Township 12, Range 6.

3325. 1824, May 24 -- BLM General Land Office Document #142, Wilcox County, AL
George Morgan, assignee of **John Wilkerson** received 79.90 acres from Cahaba Land Office located in southwest Quarter of Section 7, Township 12, Range 6.

3326. 1824, Jun 4 -- Land Grant #2638, Moore County, NC
Drury Richardson received 50 acres located on both sides of Kings Street of Buffalo Creek adjoining his own line and **Robert Wilson**. **Enoch Richardson** and **Jno. Richardson** were chain carriers.

3327. 1824, Jun 4 -- Land Grant #2639, Moore County, NC
Drury Richison received 8 acres located on Buffalo Creek adjoining his own line and **John Stutts**. **Enoch Richison** and **Jno. Richison** were chain carriers.

3328. 1824, Jun 7 -- BLM General Land Office Document #353, Wilcox County, AL
Enoch Maner (of Monroe County) received 80.65 acres from Cahaba Land Office located in northeast Quarter of Section 22, Township 12, Range 5.

3329. 1824, Jun 8 -- Record of Marriages, Wilcox County, AL
Bailey Maness married **Sarah Hardy**

3330. 1824, Jun 10 -- Will Book B Page 36, Moore County, NC
Will of **Isaac Teague**, Dec'd. Heirs: wife **Juditha**, daughter **Rachel**, son **Jacob Teague** and son **Isaac Teague**. Executors: son **Isaac Teague** and grandson **Isaac Teague**. Witnesses: **Jno. Lawler** and **Eli Teague**. Proven Aug 1824.

A. 1811, Jun 11 -- Obituary, *The North Carolina Star* [Raleigh, NC] Newspaper
Died at the residence of **James Gaines**, Esq., in Moore County, on the 22nd ult [May 22], Mrs. **Mary Montgomery**, aged 88 years, relict of Mr. **John Montgomery** late of Chatham County.

3331. 1824, Jun 20 -- Record of Marriages, Wilcox County, AL
Peter Hair married **Mary Hair**

3332. 1824, Jun 21 -- Land Grant #2683, Moore County, NC
Alexander McNeill

received 96 acres on Toms Creek and Richland Creek adjoining **Carrol**, **Neill McLeod**, **Alston**, **Robert Hardin**. **James Mathews** and **? Mathews** were chain carriers.

3333. 1824, Jun 28 -- Record of Marriages, Wilcox County, AL
James Magee married **Susan Sheffield**

3334. 1824, Aug-Nov (undated estimate) -- Record of Estates Book B Page 83, Moore County, NC
Estate of **Allen Morrison**, Dec'd. by **Alexr. Morison**, Administrator. *Notes due on the following*: **Alexr. Morison**, **Neill Morison**, **John Morison**, **Angus Morison**, **Malcolm Bethune (R.C.)**, **Jacob Gaster**, **Wm. McLeod** and **Allen McDonald**.

3335. 1824, Aug 5 -- Land Grant #2647, Moore County, NC
Neil McLeod received 40 acres located northwest of Buffalo Creek adjoining **Henry Stuts**, **John Richardson**, **John Spivey** and his own line. **H. Stuts** and **Jno. McLeod** were chain carriers.

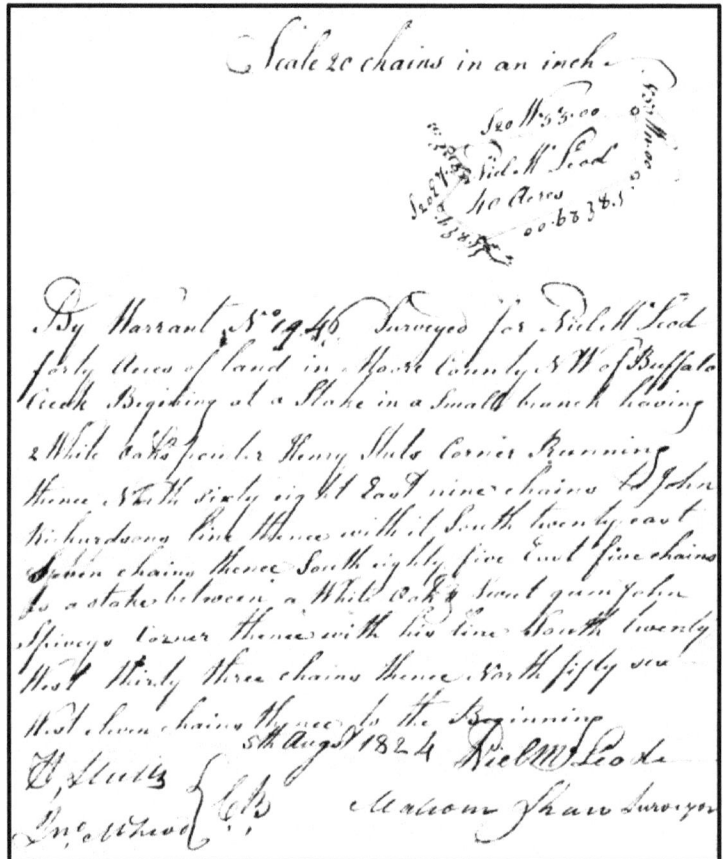

3336. 1824, Aug 16 -- 1823-1831 Court of Pleas and Quarter Sessions, Moore County, NC
[*jury duty - selected participants*] **Levy Deaton**, **Medford Owen**, **Wm. Freeman**, **John Richardson**, **Neill Caddell**, **George Stewart**, **John T. Ritter**, **Drury Richardson**, **Dickson Ritter** and **Jesse Bean**.

3337. 1824, Aug 16 -- 1823-1831 Court of Pleas and Quarter Sessions, Moore County, NC Page 39
Will of **Isaac Teague** Dec'd. was proven by **John Lawler** and **Eli Teague** and executors **Isaace Teague Sr.** and **Isaac Teague Jr.**

3338. 1824, Aug 16 -- 1823-1831 Court of Pleas and Quarter Sessions, Moore County, NC Page 40
Ordered that **George Cagle** be appointed overseer in place of **Peter Davis** of the road from **Nicholas Nall** to the [Randolph] county line and have the following hands to work: **Peter Davis**, **George Cagle**, **John Shamburger**, **James Boston**, **John Shamburger**'s hands and **Belaver Britt**.

3339. 1824, Aug 16 -- 1823-1831 Court of Pleas and Quarter Sessions, Moore County, NC Page 40
Ordered that **John Ritter Jr.** be appointed overseer in place of **Elijah Brewer** of the road from Bear Creek to **George Moore**'s and have the following hands to work: **Elijah Brewer**, **Abraham Stuts**, **Danl. Williams**, **George Stuts**, **Jacob Stuts**, **George Moore Jr.**, **John Hunsucker**, **Jethrew Denson**, **Edward Moore**, **Garner Maness** and **Bradley Brady**.

A. 1824, Aug 16 -- 1823-1831 Court of Pleas and Quarter Sessions, Moore County, NC Page 41
Ordered that **Nehemiah Birckhead** be appointed overseer of the road in place of **Thomas Muse** from Beans Bridge to the forks of the road at Stoder's Shop.

B. 1824, Aug 16 -- 1823-1831 Court of Pleas and Quarter Sessions, Moore County, NC Page 41
Ordered that **Lauchlin McNeill's** hands, **William Matthews** and **Allin Wade** be added as hands to the road that **Eli Phillips** is overseer of.

C. 1824, Aug 16 -- 1823-1831 Court of Pleas and Quarter Sessions, Moore County, NC Page 42
Ordered that **Jesse Phillips** be appointed overseer of the road in place of **Harmon Graham** from **Martin's** old store to the Wolf Pit and have the following hands to work: **Harmon Graham**, **Daniel Martin**, **Kenneth Martin**,

Robert Graham, Thos. Graham, Andrew Graham, Malcom Graham, John Lewis, William Lewis, Thomas Bryant, Elisha Bryant, John Smith and Angus Martin.

D.   1824, Aug 16 -- 1823-1831 Court of Pleas and Quarter Sessions, Moore County, NC Page 42
Ordered that **Murdoch Martin, Angus McKinnon** and **John Paterson** Esq. be appointed to settle with **Norman Mathewson**, admr. of **Malcom Mathewson,** Dec'd.

3340.   1824, Aug 16 -- 1823-1831 Court of Pleas and Quarter Sessions, Moore County, NC Page 42
Ordered that **Wm. King** be appointed overseer in place of **Jesse Sowell** of the road from the Island Ford to the Bars at **Mark Phillips** and have the same hands to work.

3341.   1824, Aug 16 -- Record of Estates Book B Page 81-82, Moore County, NC
Estate of **John Martin** Dec'd. by **Murdock Martin**, Administrator. *Items were purchased by the following*: **Angus Martin, Farquar Martin, Kenneth McCaskill, Walter Barrett** and **Murdoch McAulay.** *Notes due on the following*: **Birgis Davis, John B. Kelly, John Cheek, Jesse Womble, Jesse Sowell, Kenneth Murchison, Neil McLeod, John McLennon, John Gilbert, Roderick Murchison, Joab Cheeek, John Tyson, John Wadsworth, Nathan Barrett, Kenneth B. McIver, Donald Murchison, John Murchison, John Murchison** [Taylor]**, Simon Murchison, Alex. Curry** and wife, **Murdoch McKenzie, Donald Chisholm, James Dowd, William Martin**'s Estate, **James Dunlap, Wm. Campbell** and **Wm. Page**

A.   1824, Aug 17 -- 1823-1831 Court of Pleas and Quarter Sessions, Moore County, NC Page 43
The last will and testament of **Mary Montgomery** Dec'd. was offered and probated. Ordered that notice be given to **Thomas Waddill** (guardian of **Thomas Waddill, Caroline Waddill, James Waddill** and **Margaret Waddill**), **James Gains** Esq., **Wm. Waddill Junr.** and **John Waddill Junr.** (of Fayetteville) and that publication be made in the Carolina Observer that **Richd. Tomlinson, James Tomlinson** and **John Hill** may have notice to appear.

3342.   1824, Aug 17 -- 1823-1831 Court of Pleas and Quarter Sessions, Moore County, NC Page 44
Power of Attorney from **Nicolas Nall** to **William Nall** of the State of Alabama acknowledged

3343.   1824, Aug 17 -- 1823-1831 Court of Pleas and Quarter Sessions, Moore County, NC Page 44
Ordered that **James Gains, Archd. McNeill, Alexr. McNeill, John B. Kelly** and **John Shamburger** settle with **Nicolas Nall**, Administrator of **Jacob Tyson** Dec'd.

3344.   1824, Aug 17 -- 1823-1831 Court of Pleas and Quarter Sessions, Moore County, NC Page 44
Ordered that **John Richardson** and **William Williams** be discharged as security for **Henry Stuts** on bastardy charge as he is already in jail.

3345.   1824, Aug 17 -- 1823-1831 Court of Pleas and Quarter Sessions, Moore County, NC Page 45
Ordered that **William Waddell, James Gains** and **Hiram Kennedy** settle with **Isham Richardson** and **Dorothy Ritter**, Administrators of **Thomas Ritter** Dec'd.

3346.   1824, Aug 17 -- 1823-1831 Court of Pleas and Quarter Sessions, Moore County, NC Page 45

Ordered that **Murdoch Martin**, **Angus McKinnon** and **John McKinnon** settle with **Roderick McAulay**, Administrator of **Mathew Deaton** Dec'd.

3347.   1824, Aug 17 -- 1823-1831 Court of Pleas and Quarter Sessions, Moore County, NC Page 45
Ordered that **Polly Lakey** (13 as of Sep 10) and **Lucy Lakey** (12 as of Apr 7) be bound to **George Kennedy** until they reach age 18.

3348.   1824, Aug 17 -- 1823-1831 Court of Pleas and Quarter Sessions, Moore County, NC Page 45
Ordered that **John Deaton** be appointed guardian to **Isaac Deaton** with **William** and **Margaret Deaton** as securities. **Archd. McNeill**, **John Paterson** and **Neill Morrison** Esq. approved bond.

3349.   1824, Aug 17 -- 1823-1831 Court of Pleas and Quarter Sessions, Moore County, NC Page 46
John Paterson, **Norman Mathewson** and **Jesse Brown** appointed to settle with **Angus McKinnon** Administrator of Estate of **Wm. Dunn**, Dec'd.

3350.   1824, Aug 17 -- 1823-1831 Court of Pleas and Quarter Sessions, Moore County, NC Page 46
Ordered that **Bartholomew Dunn** be appointed overseer in place of **Neill McKinnon** of the road from Cabbin Creek to the Montgomery County line towards Rockingham and have the following hands to work: **Neill McKinnon**, **William Buie**, **Murdoch McKinnon**, **Normand McLeod**, **Angus Leach**, **Archd. Leach**, **Alexr. Leach**, **John Buie**, **Daniel McRae** and **John McDuffie**.

3351.   1824, Aug 18 -- 1823-1831 Court of Pleas and Quarter Sessions, Moore County, NC Page 47
Ordered that **Alexr. Kennedy** be named administrator and **Arch. McNeill**, **Cornelius Dunlap**, **Hugh Hammel** and **John Dunlap** be appointed to lay off a year's provision for the widow and family of **William Hussey**, Dec'd.

3352.   1824, Aug 18 -- 1823-1831 Court of Pleas and Quarter Sessions, Moore County, NC Page 48
Kenneth Clark v. Heirs at law of **Wm. Dunn**, Dec'd.and others. Appearing that **Wm. Dunn** removed to the state of Tennessee and died leaving issue whose names are unknown and reside out of state. Order that this notice be publicized in the Raleigh Star for six weeks and that the heirs appear in Carthage on the third Monday in November.

3353.   1824, Aug 19 -- 1823-1831 Court of Pleas and Quarter Sessions, Moore County, NC Page 51
Ordered to take private enumeration of **Margrate**, wife of **James Garner** and **Nancy**, wife of **Daniel McIver** to check voluntary consent on a deed

3354.   1824, Aug 19 -- 1823-1831 Court of Pleas and Quarter Sessions, Moore County, NC Page 51
Eleazor Birckhead, **James Dowd**, **Jesse Sanders** appointed to settle with **Wm. Barrett** Administrator of Estate of **George Graham**, Dec'd.

3355.   1824, Aug 19 -- 1823-1831 Court of Pleas and Quarter Sessions, Moore County, NC Page 51
Ordered that **Henry Stuts** provide maintenance to **Eltha Rodgers** for a bastard child.

3356.   1824, Aug 19 -- 1823-1831 Court of Pleas and Quarter Sessions, Moore County, NC Page 51
Ordered that **Eleazor Birckhead**, **Jesse Bean** and **Joel Lawhon** bid the building of a bridge across McLendons Creek between **Kenneth McCaskill** and **Jesse Bean** to the lowest bidder.

3357.   1824, Aug 19 -- 1823-1831 Court of Pleas and Quarter Sessions, Moore County, NC Page 51
Ordered that **John Stuts** be appointed overseer in place of **Wm. Ritter** of the road from **George Moore**'s to the branch at **Angus McQueens** and have the same hands to work.

3358.   1824, Aug 19 -- 1823-1831 Court of Pleas and Quarter Sessions, Moore County, NC Page 52
Ordered that **Daniel Caddell** be appointed overseer of the road from Bean's Bridge to Flowers Road and have the following hands to work: **Leonard Lawhon**, **John McIntosh**, **John Murchison**, **Enoch Wallis**, **Isham Wallis**, **John Rouse**, **Miles Rouse**, **Martin Rouse**, **John McDonald**, **Hugh Kelly**, **James Hill**, **Martin Hill**, **Dickson Ritter**, **James Ritter**, **Samuel Barrett**, **Wm. Barrett** Esq.'s boy, **Simon Murchison** and **Daniel Murchison**.

3359.   1824, Aug 19 -- 1823-1831 Court of Pleas and Quarter Sessions, Moore County, NC Page 52-53
[Deeds] **David Kennedy** to **Neil McLeod** was acknowledged
John Deaton to **Matthew Deaton** was acknowledged
Wright Deaton to **Matthew Deaton** was proven by **John C. Buie**
Daniel McRimmon to **William Williams** was proven by **John Paterson**
Jeremeah Williams, **Thomas Williams**, **James Williams** and **Bartholomew Dunn** to **William Williams** was proven by **Jesse Brown**
David Jones to **Cornelius Dunlap** was proven by **James Dunlap**
Hiram Kennedy to **Cornelius Dunlap** was proven by **David Kennedy**
Jesse F. Muse to **Cornelius Dowd Jr.** was acknowledged
Danl. McNeill Shff to **John Shamburger** proven by **Corn. Dowd Jr.**
[Bills of Sale] **David Kennedy** to **John Cagle** acknowledged
Archd. McBryde to **John Cheek** acknowledged

3360.   1824, Aug 19 -- 1823-1831 Court of Pleas and Quarter Sessions, Moore County, NC Page 54
Inventory of the estate of **John Smith**, Dec'd.was returned by the Administrator.

3361.   1824, Aug 19 -- 1823-1831 Court of Pleas and Quarter Sessions, Moore County, NC Page 54
Lewis Garner recorded his mark to be a half crop in the under part of the right ear and a half crop in the upper part of the left ear.

3362.   1824, Sep 4 -- BLM General Land Office Document #15.5, Lincoln County, MS
John Cagle (of Lawrence County) received 160 acres from west of Pearl River Land Office located in northeast Quarter of Section 10, Township 8, Range 9.

3363.   1824, Sep 4 -- BLM General Land Office Document #170, Lincoln County, MS
James H. Bull, assignee of **William Carpenter**, received 160 acres from west of Pearl River Land Office located in northwest Quarter of Section 30, Township 7, Range 8.

3364. 1824, Sep 4 -- BLM General Land Office Document #240, Lincoln County, MS
James H. Bull, assignee of **William Carpenter**, received 160 acres from west of Pearl River Land Office located in southeast Quarter of Section 19, Township 7, Range 8.

3365. 1824, Sep 4 -- BLM General Land Office Document #90, Lawrence County, MS
Christian Furr (of Lawrence County) received 159.75 acres from west of Pearl River Land Office located in southwest Quarter of Section 9, Township 8, Range 9.

3366. 1824, Sep 4 -- BLM General Land Office Document #137, Lawrence County, MS
John Jackson, assignee of **Isham Furr**, received 160 acres from west of Pearl River Land Office located in northeast Quarter of Section 20, Township 8, Range 9.

3367. 1824, Sep 10-Oct 15 -- *The North Carolina Star* [Raleigh, NC] Newspaper
Kinneth Clark v. Heirs at law of **Wm. Dunn**, Dec'd. and others. Petition to rectify errors in a grant. Appearing that **Wm. Dunn** removed to the state of Tennessee and died leaving issue whose names are unknown and reside out of state. Order that this notice be publicized in the Raleigh Star for six weeks and that the heirs appear in Carthage on the third Monday in November.

3368. 1824, Sep 17 -- Will Book B Page 43, Moore County, NC
Will of **William Smith**, Dec'd. Heirs: wife **Jenny Smith** [*275 acres*], children **William Smith**, **Nathan Smith**, **Everet Smith**, **Sarah Spivey**, **Jenny Cagle** and **David Richardson**. Executor: **Phillip McNeill**. Proven Feb 1826 by **Simon McNeill**

3369. 1824, Sep 30 -- Land Grant #2659, Moore County, NC
Alexander McKinnon received 50 acres located on Dry Fork of Mill Creek adjoining **Norman McKinnon** and **Neil McLeod**. **Norman McKinnon** and **Norman McLeod** were chain carriers.

3370. 1824, Oct 13 -- BLM General Land Office Document #728, Wilcox County, AL
Joseph Morgan (of Monroe County) received 80 acres from Cahaba Land Office located in east half of Section 26, Township 12, Range 5.

3371. 1824, Oct 14 -- Land Grant #2641, Moore County, NC
John D. Phillips received 242 acres located north of Deep River on the Chatham County line adjoining **William Phillips**, **Henson** [**Stinson**], **John Cheek** and **Aaron Tyson** & Co. **John Phillips Senr.** and **Dabney Phillips** were chain carriers.

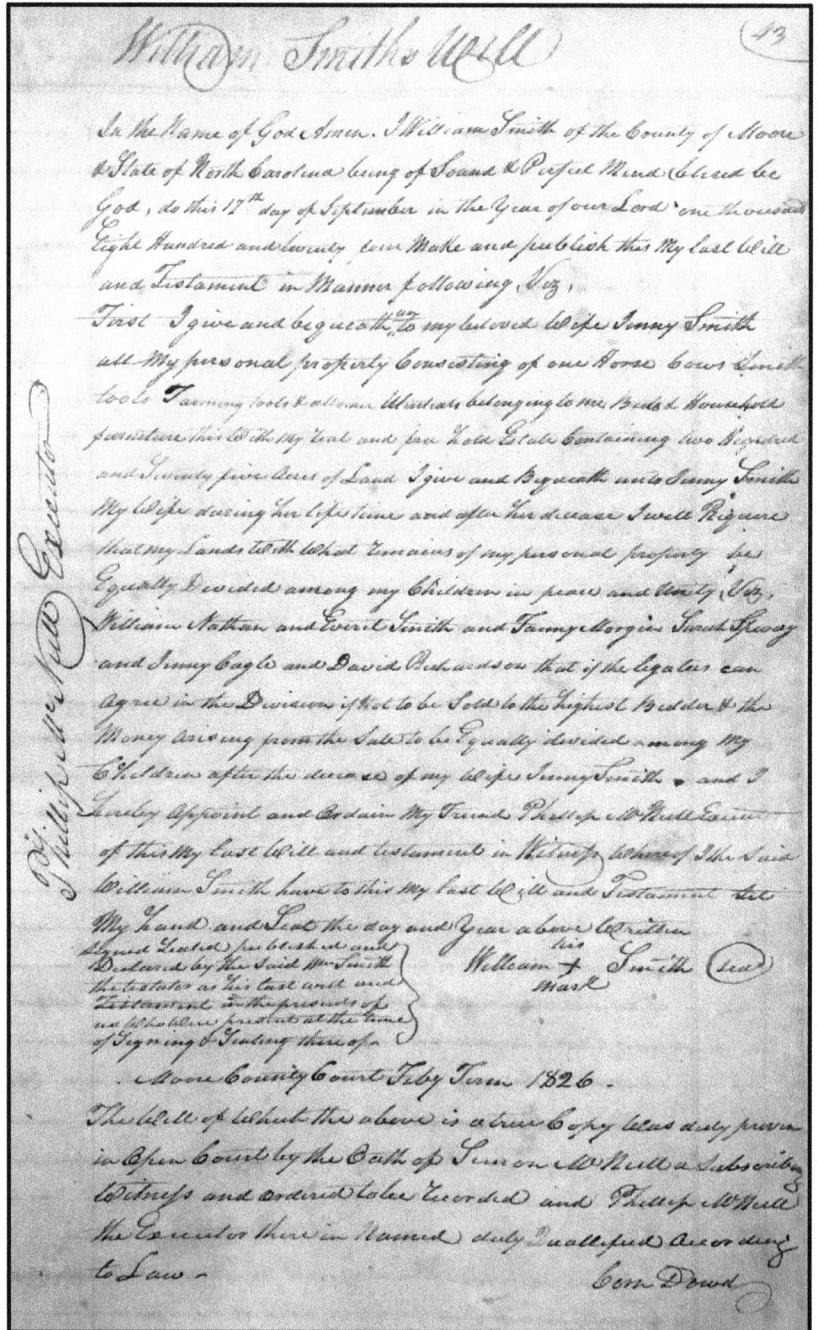

3372. 1824, Oct 23 -- *A History of Sandy Creek Baptist Association* by George Purefoy, Page 89
Bryant Boroughs, **William Waddill** and **William Carr** from Fall Creek Church (Chatham County) and **William Dowd**, **P.W. Dowd** and **Noah Richardson** from Friendship Church (Moore County) were delegates to the Association meeting at Mount Zion Meeting House in Orange [now Alamance] County, NC.

3373. 1824, Nov -- Chronicles and Records of Bensalem Presbyterian Church Page 11, Moore County, NC
Margt. Bethune became 2nd wife of **Daniel McDonald**

3374. 1824, Nov 7 -- Chronicles and Records of Bensalem Presbyterian Church Page 17, Moore County, NC
Angus McKinnon and **Mary Bethune** were married.

3375. 1824, Nov 11 -- Record of Marriages, Wilcox County, AL
Lewis Duet/Dewit married **Angelina Morgan**

3376. 1824, Nov 16 -- 1823-1831 Court of Pleas and Quarter Sessions, Moore County, NC
[*jury duty next term - selected participants*] **Jesse Brown** Esq., **Andrew Yow**, **Bartholomew Dunn**, **Wm. Ritter**, **Jacob Stuts**, **Jeremiah Williams**, **Nathan Morgan**, **Stephen Davis**, **John Richardson**, **James Morgan**, **Leonard Furr** and **John Garner**.

3377. 1824, Nov 16 -- 1823-1831 Court of Pleas and Quarter Sessions, Moore County, NC Page 56-57
Elizabeth Wright, widow and relict of **Sherwood Wright** Dec'd. renounced her right of administration of the estate and recommended **Levy Deaton** as administrator. **Deaton** appointed with **John Paterson** and **Alexr. Morison** as securities. **Neill Morrison** Esq., **Peter Shamburger**, **Donal McDonald** (SC) and **Joseph Allen** appointed to lay off a year's provision for widow and family.

A. 1823, Nov 16 -- 1823-1831 Court of Pleas and Quarter Sessions, Moore County, NC Page 57
The last will and testament of **Mary Montgomery** Dec'd. was proven by **Archd. McBryde**. Administration of the estate is granted to **Deborah Debrutz** with **Archd. McBryde** and **Duncan Murchison** as securities.

3378. 1824, Nov 16 -- 1823-1831 Court of Pleas and Quarter Sessions, Moore County, NC Page 57
Ordered that **Willis Brewer**, **Edward Boroughs** and **Robert Hollomen** work on the road under **John Ritter** in addition to his former hands.

3379. 1824, Nov 16 -- 1823-1831 Court of Pleas and Quarter Sessions, Moore County, NC Page 57
William Williamson v. Heirs at law of **Isham Sheffield**

3380. 1824, Nov 16 -- 1823-1831 Court of Pleas and Quarter Sessions, Moore County, NC Page 58
Ordered that **John Hunsucker**, **Marvel Ritter**, **Wm. Dannelly** and **James Upton** be added to work on the road from **George Moores** to **Angus McQueens**.

3381. 1824, Nov 16 -- 1823-1831 Court of Pleas and Quarter Sessions, Moore County, NC Page 58
[*jury duty next term - selected participants*] **Jesse Brown** Esq., **Jeremiah Williams**, **James Morgan** and **Leonard Furr**.

3382. 1824, Nov 16 -- 1823-1831 Court of Pleas and Quarter Sessions, Moore County, NC Page 59
[Deeds] **James Muse** to **Jesse F. Muse** was acknowledged
Benjamin Person to **Hugh Moore** proven by **Dempsey Sowell**
Executors of **Wm. Martin** Dec'd. to **Magaret Martin** proven by **Daniel Martin**
John Milton to **Emanuel Yow** is witnessed by **John Ritter**
James Kees to **Levy Deaton** was proven by **John Paterson**
[Bond] **Kindred Birckhead** to **James B. Muse** proven by **Eleazer Birckhead**

3383. 1824, Nov 16 -- 1823-1831 Court of Pleas and Quarter Sessions, Moore County, NC Page 59
The committees appointed to settle with the following returned their reports: **Benjn. W. Siler** and **Nehemiah Birckhead**, administrators for **Kindred Birckhead** Dec'd.; **Roderick McAulay** as administrator of **Mathew Deaton** Dec'd.; **Norman Mathewson** as administrator of **Malcolm Mathewson** Dec'd.; **William Barrett** as administrator of **George Graham** Dec'd.; **Alexander Morison** as administrator of **Allen Morison** Dec'd.; **Angus McKinnon** as administrator of **Wm. Dunn**, Dec'd.

3384. 1824, Nov 24 -- Land Grant #2662, Moore County, NC
Alexander McNeill received 100 acres located on Toms Creek adjoining **Jesse Sowell**, **McLeod**, **Robert Harden**, **Davis** and **Carrell**. **Hugh Harden** and **Neill Mathews** were chain carriers.

3385. 1824, Nov 27 -- Land Grant #2694, Moore County, NC
James Bryant received 50 acres located south of McLendons Creek adjoining **Jesse Phillips**, **Dunlap** and **Thomas Graham**. **Michael Bryant** and **Jesse Phillips** were chain carriers.

3386. 1824, Nov 28 -- Land Grant #2642, Moore County, NC
Neil McLeod received 60 acres located west of Horse Creek adjoining **David Allison**, **Daniel McCrummen** and his own line. **Allan McLean** and **John Patterson** were chain carriers.

3387. 1824, Nov 28 -- Land Grant #2643, Moore County, NC
Neil McLeod received 40 acres located between Dry Creek and Horse Creek adjoining his own line, **Butler** and **Allen McLean**. **Allan McLean** and **Angus Morrison** were chain carriers.

3388. 1824, Dec 8 -- Land Grant #2672, Moore County, NC
Hugh Kelly received 50 acres located on the waters of Richland Creek adjoining his own line and **Murchison**. **Angus Kelly** and **Alexr. McCaskill** were chain carriers.

3389. 1824, Dec 10 -- Land Grant #2691, Moore County, NC
Jesse F. Muse received 15 acres located east of Lick Branch of McLendons Creek adjoining heirs of **Adam White** Dec'd. and his own line. **Hyrum Hill** and **James B. Muse** were chain carriers.

3390. 1824, Dec 13 -- Land Grant #2708, Moore County, NC
George Moore received 50 acres located on the waters of Buffalo Creek and both sides of the Bigg Road adjoining **John Ritter**, **Brown**, **Emanuel Yow** and **John Dannelly**. **John Stutts** and **Thos. Dannelly** were chain carriers.

3391. 1824, Dec 13 -- Land Grant #2709, Moore County, NC
George Moore received 100 acres located on the waters of Buffalo Creek adjoining **Brown**, **Kennedy**, **Emanuel Yow** (formerly **John Melton**) and **Stephen Richardson**. **John Stutts** and **Thomas Dannelly** were chain carriers.

3392. 1824, Dec 29 -- Land Grant #2663, Moore County, NC
Robert Hardin received 53 acres located south of Deep River

adjoining **William Dowd** (formerly **Robert Cheek**), **John Hancock** and his own line. **Wm. Mathews** and **Hugh Harden** were chain carriers.

3393.   1824, Dec 26 -- Record of Marriages, Wilcox County, AL
Azariah Dumas married **Susannah Hare**

3394.   1824, Dec 29 -- Land Grant #2705, Moore County, NC
John B. Kelly received 11 acres located on both sides of McLendons Creek adjoining **Jesse Muse** Esq.and **Jesse Muse**'s Mill, **James Muse Senr.** and **Daniel Muse**. **Nathan Holloway** and **John Ferguson** were chain carriers.

3395.   1824, Dec 29 -- Land Grant #2706, Moore County, NC
John B. Kelly received 200 acres located north of McLendons Creek adjoining **Daniel H. Muse**, **John Tyson**, **Dean** (formerly **Jesse Muse**), **Sowell** (formerly **Roan**) and **Richeson**. **Nathan Holloway** and **John Ferguson** were chain carriers.

3396.   1824, Dec 29 -- Land Grant #2707, Moore County, NC
John B. Kelly received 300 acres located on both sides of the Waggon Road, west of the Island Ford Road adjoining **John Richeson**, **Dean** (formerly **Jesse Muse**) and his own line. **Nathan Holloway** and **John Ferguson** were chain carriers.

3397.   1825 -- Land Grant #2716, Moore County, NC
Bailey Williamson received 100 acres located on the waters of Cedar Creek and the Chatham County line adjoining **McLeod** and **Leonard Smith**. **John Smith** and **Isaac Teague** were chain carriers.

3398.   1825 -- Chronicles and Records of Bensalem Presbyterian Church Page 7, Moore County, NC
Nancy McKinnon McAskill, wife of **Kenneth McAskill** died. They were married in Scotland.

3399.   1825, Jan 12 -- Land Grant #2697, Moore County, NC
Gideon Seawell received 14 acres located west of Killets Creek adjoining his own line (formerly **Ann White**), **James Dowd** and **Neil Caddell**. **Alexr. Fry** and **George Cox Junr.** were chain carriers.

3400.   1825, Jan 19 -- Land Grant #2732, Moore County, NC
Cornelius Shields received 88 acres located on south prong of Tysons Creek on the Chatham County line adjoining **James Cheek**, **Beason**, own line, **Allison** and **Mathew Phillips**. **Archd. Shields** and **Robt. Shields** were chain carriers.

3401. 1825, Feb 7 -- Land Grant #2743, Moore County, NC
Levi Deaton received 50 acres located west of Wet Creek adjoining **Neil Morrison** and **John Key**. **Avington Britt** and **John Key** were chain carriers.

3402. 1825, Feb 19 -- Record of Estates Book B Page 71-72, Moore County, NC Page 93
Estate of **Isaac Teague** Dec'd.by Administrators **Isaac Teague Senr.** and **Isaac Teague Junr.** Notes on the following: **Howell Brewer** and **Isaac Teague Junr.**

3403. 1825, Feb 21 -- 1823-1831 Court of Pleas and Quarter Sessions, Moore County, NC
[jury duty - selected participants] **Nathan Morgan, Jeremiah Williams, Leonard Furr, Alexr. Leach, John Garner, John Richardson, Stephen Davis, John Stuts, George Stuts, Wm. Hill, Everet Sheffield, Wm. Barrett, Daniel Caddell, John Ritter, Jesse Bean, Thomas Williams, Wright Deaton, Edward Stewart, Danl. Maness** and **Wm. Williamson**.

3404. 1825, Feb 21 -- 1823-1831 Court of Pleas and Quarter Sessions, Moore County, NC Page 62
Ordered that **Demsay Sowell** be appointed overseer of the road in place of **John Richardson** and have the following additional hands to work: **Calvin Cox, Samson D. Smith, Jason Muse, George Fry, Wm. Dowdy, John Dowdy, Wm. Harris, Jesse Muse, Thomas Dowdy, Zacariah Jones, John Carrell, Kindred Phillips,** Mrs. Davis (**Mose** and **Jery**) and **Marvil Ritter**.

3405. 1825, Feb 22 -- 1823-1831 Court of Pleas and Quarter Sessions, Moore County, NC Page 63
Ordered that **Abner Brown** and **Wm. Danielly** be added to the road in which **John Stuts** is overseer of.

3406. 1825, Feb 22 -- 1823-1831 Court of Pleas and Quarter Sessions, Moore County, NC Page 63
Ordered that **Andrew Yow** be appointed overseer of the road from **Wm. Williamsons** to the [Randolph] County line in place of **James Garner** and have the same hands to work.

3407. 1825, Feb 22 -- 1823-1831 Court of Pleas and Quarter Sessions, Moore County, NC Page 63-64
Walter Barrett appointed constable in District 3; **James Dunlap** appointed constable in District 6; **William Williams** appointed constable in District 8
Jesse Brown, Tax Collector in District 8 and District 6 for 1823 be allowed 3 polls for insolvents

3408. 1825, Feb 23-Aug 16 -- 1823-1831 Court of Pleas and Quarter Sessions, Moore County, NC Page 66, 85
Solomon Barrett v. **Christian** and **John Stuts**

A. 1825, Feb 23 -- 1823-1831 Court of Pleas and Quarter Sessions, Moore County, NC Page 66
Ordered that **Danl. McNeill**, Sheriff deed 200 acres to **Wm. Hancock** located ½ mile below Carthage on the Fayettville Road known by the name of the **Davis** old field which was sold some time ago due to an order against **Burges Davis**.

B. 1825, Feb 23 -- 1823-1831 Court of Pleas and Quarter Sessions, Moore County, NC Page 67
Ordered that child named **Alexd. Medling** alias **Alexd. Johnson** (age 6) be bound to **Right Deaton** until he reaches age 21.

3409. 1825, Feb 24 -- 1823-1831 Court of Pleas and Quarter Sessions, Moore County, NC Page 69-70
[Deeds] **Wm. Barret** to **Lorene** and **John Alex Barrett** was proven by **Wm. Barrett Jr.**
John Hancock to **John Cheek** proven by **Atlas Jones**
Wm. C. Buie to **John C. Buie** acknowledged
John C. Buie to **Wm. C. Buie** acknowledged

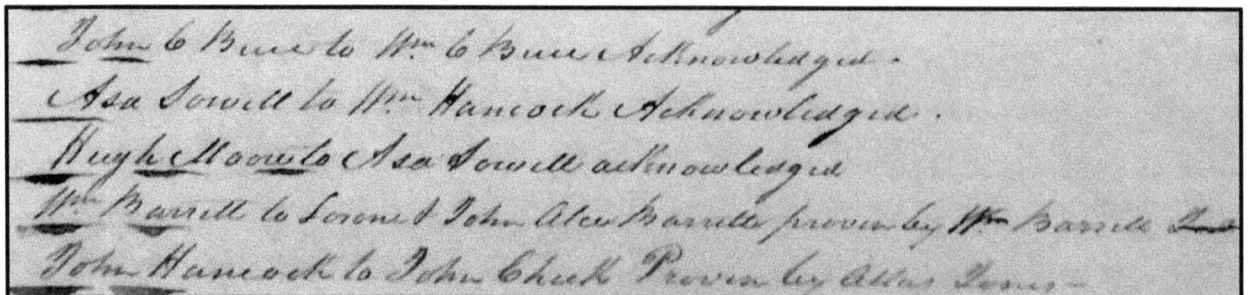

Hugh Moore to Asa Sowell was acknowledged
Asa Sowell to Wm. Hancock was acknowledged
Asa Sowell to John Tyson proven by Neil McLeod
John McIver to William Phillips proven by Absalom Phillips
Jesse Phillips to James Bryant was acknowledged
John Danelly to Wm. Rives was proven by Wm. Dannelly
Everet Sheffield to Stephen Davis was acknowledged
John R. Davis to Robert Kennedy proven by Miles Jordan
Elijah Autery and James Keahey to Angus Morison proven by Jas. Paterson
Michael and Leah Bryant to Jas. Bryant proven by M. McCrummen
John Richardson to Jeremiah Williams proven by Jesse Brown
Solomon Brewer to John Cockman is proven by Wm. Cagle
Emmanuel Yow to Abner Brown is proven by Jno Cockman
[Bills of Sale] Everet Shuffield to John Shuffield acknowledged
Roderick McAulay to Margaret Deaton acknowledged
Robert Davis to William C. Davis proven by Brant Boroughs
[Power of Attorney] James Graham to Michael Bryant proven by Thomas Bryant

---

3410.   1825, Mar 9 -- BLM General Land Office Document #618, Lincoln County, MS
Lot Smith (of Copiah County) received 79.32 acres from Jackson Land Office located in east half of northwest Quarter of Section 18, Township 8, Range 8.

3411.   1825, Mar 16 -- Land Grant #2686, Moore County, NC
Medford Owen received 100 acres located between Wolf Creek and Little Creek and Bear Branch adjoining his own line and **Everet Sheffield**. **Everet Sheffield** and **William Owen** were chain carriers.

3412.   1825, Apr 7 -- BLM General Land Office Document #480, Lincoln County, MS
William Smith (of Franklin County) received 80 acres from Washington Land Office located in east half of northwest Quarter of Section 9, Township 7, Range 6.

3413.   1825, Apr 9 -- BLM General Land Office Document #370, Lincoln County, MS
William Smith (of Lawrence County) received 76.37 acres from west of Pearl River Land Office located in east half of southeast Quarter of Section 24, Township 8, Range 8.

3414.   1825, Apr 12 -- Land Grant #2670, Moore County, NC
John T. Ritter received 100 acres located on the waters of Richland Creek adjoining **Hugh Kelly. George Muse** and **John Dannelly** were chain carriers.

3415.   1825, Apr 12 -- Land Grant #2731, Moore County, NC
William Stutts received 10 acres located southeast of Persimmon Branch adjoining **McAulay, Christopher Stutts, William Jones** and **Neil McLeod. William Jones** and **Everet Wallace** were chain carriers.

3416.   1825, Apr 14 -- Land Grant #2717, Moore County, NC
Thomas Williams received 100 acres located north of Bear Creek on the

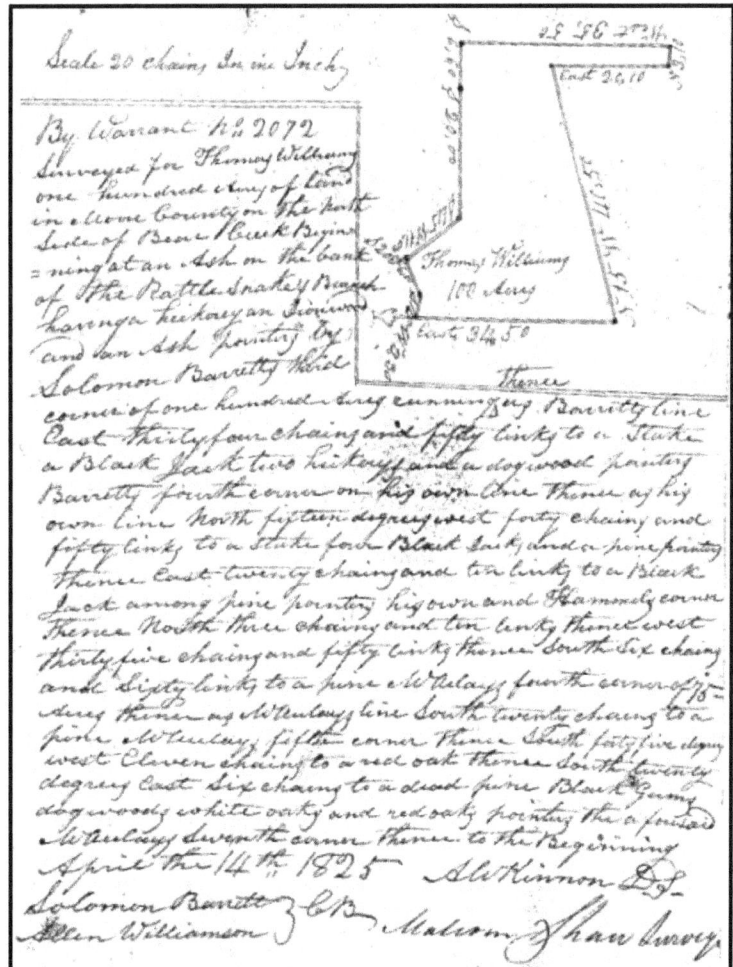

Rattlesnake Branch adjoining **Solomon Barrett**, his own line, **Hammil**, **McAulay**, **Davis** and **Sheffield**. **Soloman Barrett** and **Allen Williamson** were chain carriers.

3417.   1825, Apr 16 -- Fall Creek Baptist Church Minutes, Chatham County, NC
Ansel Melton came forward and offered his teaching for the ministry and he was permitted to exercise his gift or trial within the bounds of the church. **David Kennedy** moved to the church to have an arm of Fall Creek Church established at his schoolhouse. **Bryan Boroughs**, **Zachus Boroughs**, **John Lawler**, **William Waddille** and **Eli Lawler** appointed to review and report back May 10. [*Editor's Note: The beginnings of Mechanic's Hill Church*]

3418.   1825, Mar 1 -- Land Grant #2751, Moore County, NC
Jesse F. Muse received 50 acres located on Mill Swamp of McLendons Creek adjoining **Brinkley Phillips**, **William Phillips** and own (formerly **James B. Muse**). **Brinkley Phillips** and **James B. Muse** were chain carriers.

3419.   1825, May 5 -- Land Grant #2667, Moore County, NC
William Laky received 14 acres located on Flag Creek adjoining **Everet Wallace**, **Neil McLeod**, **William Jones** and **Furr**. **John Williams** and **Jacob Stutts** were chain carriers.

3420.   1825, May 5 -- Land Grant #2668, Moore County, NC
William Laky received 7 acres located on Flag Creek adjoining **Everet Wallace**, **Jones** and **McLeod**. **Henry Stutts** and **Jacob Stutts** were chain carriers.

3421.   1825, May 5 -- Land Grant #2688, Moore County, NC
Henry Stutts received 50 acres located north of Buffalo Creek adjoining his own line, **Horner**, **Kennedy** and **Sink**. **Jacob Stutts** and **Wm. Lakey** were chain carriers.

3422.   1825, May 6 -- Land Grant #2689, Moore County, NC
Jacob Stutts received 41 acres located south of Buffalo Creek adjoining **Jeremiah Williams**, **James Dunlap**, **Haines** and **Milton**. **Henry Stutts** and **Wm. Lakey** were chain carriers.

3423.   1825, May 7 -- Land Grant #2666, Moore County, NC

William Williamson received 4 acres located north of Bear Creek adjoining **Autery**, his own line and **John Kennedy. Allen Williamson** and **Wm. Williamson** were chain carriers.

3424. 1825, May 7 -- Land Grant #2669, Moore County, NC
William Williamson received 200 acres located south of Bear Creek adjoining **Morrison, McLeod, Bullock, Barrett, Wood**, his own line and **John Kennedy. Wm. Williams** and **Allen Williamson** were chain carriers.

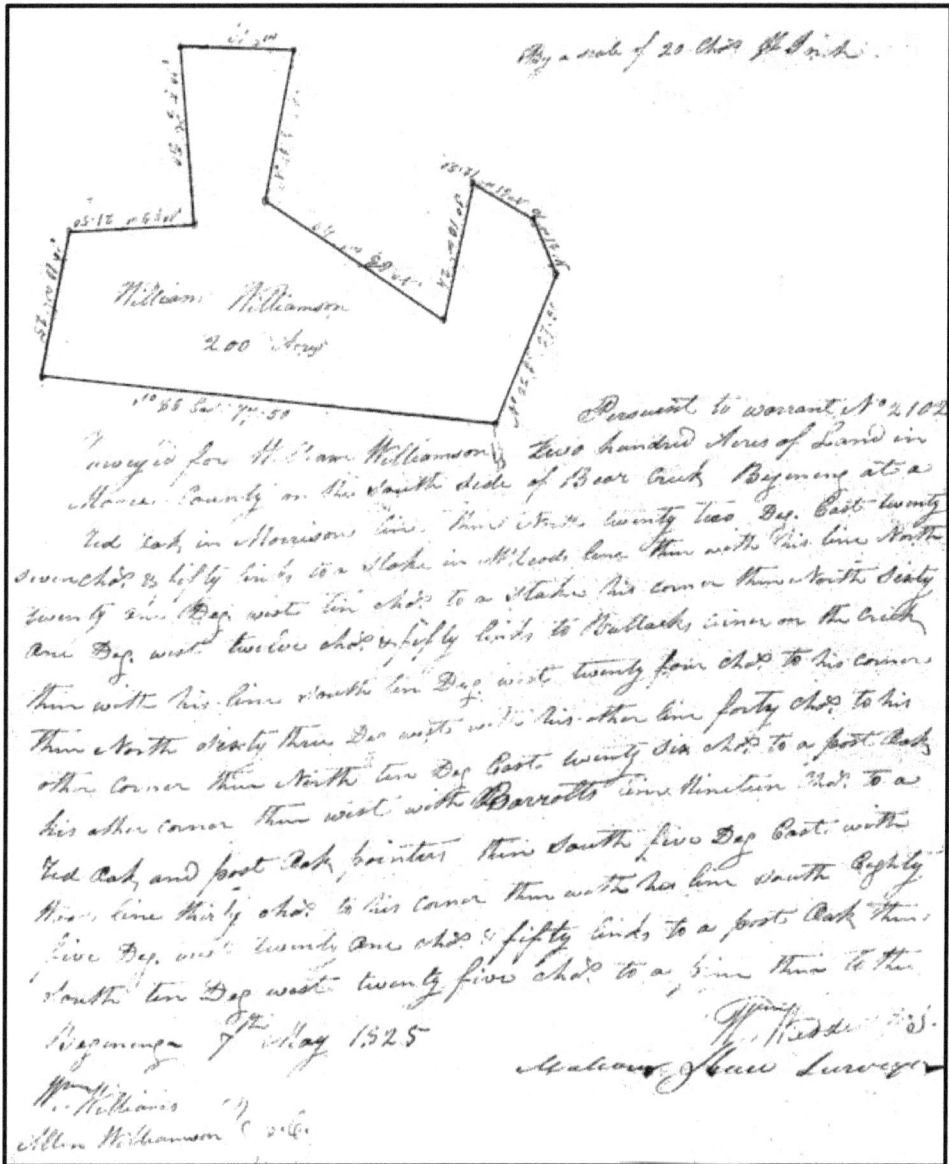

3425. 1825, May 13 -- Fall Creek Baptist Church Minutes, Chatham County, NC
D. Kennedy was among the seventeen total members of Fall Creek Baptist Church dismissed to form another church. [*Editor's Note: dismissed to Mechanic's Hill Baptist Church*]

3426. 1825, May 17 -- 1823-1831 Court of Pleas and Quarter Sessions, Moore County, NC
[*jury duty next term - selected participants*] **Angus Leach, Leonard Furr, Andrew Yow, Levy Deaton, George Kennedy, Burwell Deaton, Robt. Kennedy, Bradley Garner Sr., Martin Cagle** and **Everet Wallis**.

3427. 1825, May 17 -- 1823-1831 Court of Pleas and Quarter Sessions, Moore County, NC Page 72, 77
John Dunlap was released from bond on **Abednego Maness**. Sheriff ordered to bring **Abednego Maness** to court.

3428. 1825, May 17 -- 1823-1831 Court of Pleas and Quarter Sessions, Moore County, NC Page 72
Ordered that the following orphan children be bound until they reach age 18: **Patsey Davidson** (age 14 the 22 instant) to **Hiram Kennedy; Hiram Davidson** (age 12 as of Sep 10) and **Anderson Davidson** (age 9 as of Dec 31) to **Aaron Kennedy; Lydia Lakey** (age 6 as of Aug 22) to **George Kennedy** until she is 18.

A. 1825, May 17 -- 1823-1831 Court of Pleas and Quarter Sessions, Moore County, NC Page 74-76
Ordered that **Kinneth McKenzie** and **Dickson Ritter** be allowed fees for attending as a witness for the prosecution on behalf of the State v. **John Barrett** and **Thomas Fry**. Ordered that **John Moore** be allowed fees for attending as a witness for the prosecution on behalf of the State v. **Wm. N. Maness**. Ordered that **Carrell Brady, Alexr. Graves, Joseph Person** and **John Kid** be allowed fees for attending as a witness for the prosecution on behalf of the State v. **Wm. Martindale**.

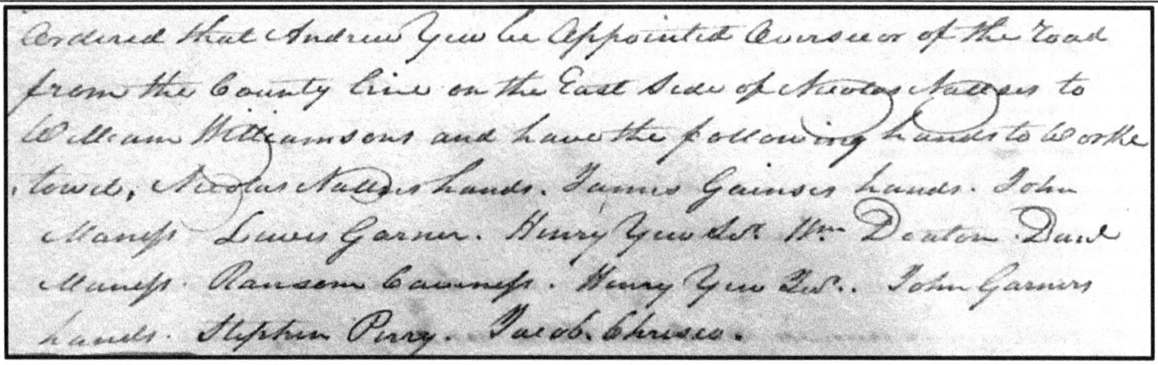

[Handwritten document image]

3429.   1825, May 17 -- 1823-1831 Court of Pleas and Quarter Sessions, Moore County, NC Page 76
Ordered that **Andrew Yow** be appointed overseer of the road from the [Randolph] county line on the east side of **Nicolas Nall** on to **William Williamsons** and have the following hands to work: **Nicolas Nalls** hands, **James Gainses'** hands, **John Maness, Lewis Garner, Henry Yow Sen., Wm. Deaton, Danl. Maness, Ransom Caveness, Henry Yow Jr., John Garner**'s hands, **Stephen Perry** and **Jacob Chrisco**.

3430.   1825, May 17 -- Land Grant #2676, Moore County, NC
John Cheek received 42 acres located south of Deep River being surplus with own 100 acres adjoining his own line and **William Dowd** (formerly **Robert Cheek**). **John Phillips** and **Jno. D. Phillips** were chain carriers.

3431.   1825, May 17 -- 1823-1831 Court of Pleas and Quarter Sessions, Moore County, NC Page 77
Ordered that **William Owens** pay **Mary Huzza** for maintenance of bastard child.

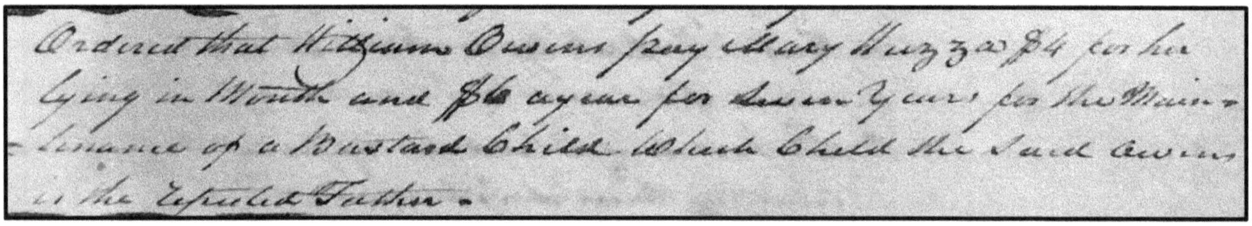

[Handwritten document image]

3432.   1825, May 18 -- 1823-1831 Court of Pleas and Quarter Sessions, Moore County, NC Page 79
[Deeds] **Henry Freeman** to **Everet Sheffield** was proven by **Wm. Brewer**
Malcolm Leach to **Alex Leach** was proven by **Angus Leach**
John Smith to **John Leach** was proven by **Angus Leach**
William Williams to **George Davis** was acknowledged
Wm. Barrett to **Samuel Jackson** was acknowledged
John Danilly Sr. to **Wm. Dannilly** was proven by **Eli Phillips**
Robert Graham to **Neill Graham** and **William Graham** was proven by **Alexr. McIntosh**

A.   1825, May 18 -- 1823-1831 Court of Pleas and Quarter Sessions, Moore County, NC Page 79
Ordered that **Benjn. Person, Joseph Johnson** and **Eleazor Birckhead** settle with **Cornelius Dowd** and **James Garner**, administrators of **Jas. Wood**, Dec'd.

3433.   1825, Jun 9 -- Article, *Fayetteville Weekly Observer* [Fayetteville, NC] Newspaper
"Horrid Murder - On the evening of the 31st May 1825, a certain **Jesse Upton** of the county of Randolph, N. C. committed one of the most horrid massacres on the person of his wife. Just at the close of the day, which we hope, has witnessed few such heart chilling scenes, this blood thirsty villain, this monster in human shape, having, no doubt, preconcerted his diabolical design, and, as it were, divested himself of every sensation of tenderness, proceeded to the execution of one of the most shocking, base and savage murders known in a civilized land. He making use of some terrifying discourse which affrighted his wife, and she wishing to make her escape, was prevented by her husband, who following her a short distance and forcing her back, commenced his abuses by striking her with his fist, then getting hold of a bench about 2 or 3 feet long, made of half a split sapling, with which he beat her on the head in a number of places, so that her brains came out at the wounds; leaving her lying on her face upon the ground, weltering in her blood, and immediately making his escape. He, the said **Upton**, is described to be between 35 and 40 years of age, nearly or about 6 feet high, middling clean or trim

built, dark complexion, dark hair and eyes, rather long visage, with somewhat of a down or sly look, and also a smooth and deceptive way of speaking. Editors of newspapers are particularly requested, whithersoever the above may come, to give it an insertion, and thereby serve the cause of humanity and justice. I do hereby certify the above statement to be true, for I was an eye witness to the disagreeable scene a few hours after the perpetrator made his escape. **H. Moffett.** I concur in the above statement. **Joseph Hinshaw.**" [*Editor's Note: **Jesse Upton** married **Ann Hinshaw** in 1814 and they were both dismissed from the Cane Creek Meeting [Quaker] in 1821 for jealousy and separating from each other. After Upton murdered his wife he later escaped to Tennessee and was plowing his field near Knoxville, TN when some passersby from North Carolina recognized him on their way home. He was taken into custody brought back to North Carolina and convicted of murder twice. He was hanged Nov 7, 1828.*]

3434. 1825, Jul 4-Feb 6, 1826 -- Record of Estates Book B Page 102-103, 105 Moore County, NC
Estate of **Richard Holland**, Dec'd. by Administrator **Edmond Holland**. *Notes due on the following*: **John Arnet, Burrell Deaton, William Craven, John Hogwood, Benjamin Stone, Harday Lawson, Nathan Smith, Belaver Britt, Mason Harvell, Elison Goff, James Right, Richard Biggs, Joseph Powell, Elijah Pou, Henry Maness** and **Silus Watson**.

3435. 1825, Aug 4 -- Land Grant #2698, Moore County, NC
Roderick McAulay received 22 acres located west of Wet Creek adjoining his own line and **Waddle. William McAulay** and **Donald McAulay** were chain carriers.

3436. 1825, Aug 4 -- Land Grant #2727, Moore County, NC
Neil Morrison received 100 acres located west of Sings Creek adjoining his own line, **Deaton** and **Alexr. Morrison. John McDonald** and **Alexr. Morrison** were chain carriers.

> **HORRID MURDER.**
>
> On the evening of the 31st May, 1825, a certain Jesse Upton of the county of Randolph, N. C. committed one of the most horrid massacres on the person of his wife. Just at the close of the day, which we hope, has witnessed few such heart chilling scenes, this blood thirsty villain, this monster in human shape, having, no doubt, preconcerted his diabolical design, and, as it were, divested himself of every sensation of tenderness, proceeded to the execution of one of the most shocking, base and savage murders known in a civilized land.
>
> He making use of some terrifying discourse which affrighted his wife, and she wishing to make her escape, was prevented by her husband, who following her a short distance and forcing her back, commenced his abuses by striking her with his fist, then getting hold of a bench about 2 or 3 feet long, made of half a split sappling, with which he beat her on the head in a number of places, so that her brains came out at the wounds; leaving her lying on her face upon the ground, weltering in her blood, and immediately making his escape. He, the said Upton, is described to be between 35 and 40 years of age, nearly or about 6 feet high, middling clean or trim built, dark complexion, dark hair and eyes, rather long visage, with somewhat of a down or sly look, and also a smooth and deceptive way of speaking.
>
> Editors of newspapers are particularly requested, whithersoever the above may come, to give it an insertion, and thereby serve the cause of humanity and justice.
>
> I do hereby certify the above statement to be true, for I was an eye witness to the disagreeable scene a few hours after the perpetrator made his escape.
>
> H. MOFFETT.
>
> I concur in the above statement.
>
> JOSEPH HINSHAW.

3437. 1825, Aug 15 -- 1823-1831 Court of Pleas and Quarter Sessions, Moore County, NC
[*jury duty - selected participants*] **George Kennedy, Robert Kennedy, Everet Wallis, Burwell Deaton, Martin Cagle, Thomas Williams, Jno. Stutts Sr., James Maness, Daniel Caddell, James Hains, John Stuts, Bradly Garner, Jesse Brewer, Wiat Williamson, Asa Sowell, Stephen Davis, John Ritter, Dickson Ritter, Alexr. Kennedy, Lewis Williamson, Thomas Williams Senr., Jesse Sanders, Wm. Williamson, Isham Sowell, Jesse Bean, Nathan Barrett, Edward Stewart, John Cockmon, Thomas Williams Junr., John T. Ritter, Isaac Smith, David Kennedy, Abram Stuts** and **Phillip McNeill**.

A. 1825, Aug 15 -- 1823-1831 Court of Pleas and Quarter Sessions, Moore County, NC Page 82
Ordered that **Wm. Phillips** be appointed overseer of the road in place of **Nehemiah Birckhead** from Beans Bridge to the forks of the road at Stoder's Shop and have the same hands to work.

3438. 1825, Aug 15 -- 1823-1831 Court of Pleas and Quarter Sessions, Moore County, NC Page 82
Ordered that **Jesse Muse** be appointed overseer of the road from Beans Bridge to the hill at the **Widow Bethune**'s and have the following hands to work: **Leonard Lawhon, John Muse, Miles Rouse, John McIntosh,**

John Rouse, James Hill, Martin Hill, Walter Barrett, Dickson Ritter, Martin Rouse, Daniel Caddell and **Enoch Wallis**.

3439. 1825, Aug 15 -- 1823-1831 Court of Pleas and Quarter Sessions, Moore County, NC Page 82
Ordered that **Danl. Murchison** be appointed overseer of the road from the hill at the **Widow Bethune**'s to Flowers Road and have the following hands to work: **John Murchison, Alexander Smith, Richmond Smith, John McDonald, Isham Wallis, Samuel Barret, Wm. Barret** Esq. **Sr.** and **Hugh Kelly**.

3440. 1825, Aug 15 -- 1823-1831 Court of Pleas and Quarter Sessions, Moore County, NC Page 82
Ordered that **George Stuts** be appointed overseer in place of **John Ritter** of the road from Bear Creek to **George Moore**'s and have the following hands to work: **John Ritter Jr., Elijah Brewer, Abraham Stuts, Danl. Williams, Jacob Stuts, George Moore Jr., John Hunsucker, Jethrew Denson, Edward Moore, Garner Maness, Bradley Brady, Willis Brewer, Edmond Boroughs** and **Robert Hollomon**.

3441. 1825, Aug 15 -- 1823-1831 Court of Pleas and Quarter Sessions, Moore County, NC Page 83
Ordered that **Peter Davis** be appointed overseer in place of **George Cagle** of the road from **Nicolas Nalls** to the County line and have the following hands to work: **George Cagle, Peter Davis** (**Jim** and **Boston**), **John Shamburger**'s hands and **Belaver Brit**.

A. 1825, Aug 15 -- 1823-1831 Court of Pleas and Quarter Sessions, Moore County, NC Page 83
Ordered that **Thomas Bryant** be appointed overseer of the road in place of **Jesse Phillips** from Martins Old Store to the Wolf Pit and have the following hands to work: **Harmon Graham, Jesse Phillips, Danl. Martin, Kinneth Martin, Robert Graham, Thomas Graham, Andrew Graham, Malcom Graham, John Lewis, Wm. Lewis, Elisha Bryant, John Smith** and **Angus Martin**.

3442. 1825, Aug 15 -- 1823-1831 Court of Pleas and Quarter Sessions, Moore County, NC Page 84
Administration of the estate of **Richard Hollan**, Dec'd. is granted to **Edmond Hollan**.

3443. 1825, Aug 16 -- 1823-1831 Court of Pleas and Quarter Sessions, Moore County, NC Page 86
Ordered that **Robartus Kennedy** be appointed overseer in place of **John Kennedy** of the road from Bear Creek to **Wm. Williamson**'s and have the following hands to work: **Stephen Maness, Archd. McDonald, Alex. Kennedy** 1 hand, **Major Johnson, Bradley Garner** 2 hands, **Bradley Garner Jr., Jeremiah Williams, John Myrick, Wm. Williamson, Wm. Deaton, Wm. Williamson Jun.** 2 hands, **Wiat Williamson, Lewas Williamson, Jno. McDonald, Hiram Williamson, Thomas Person** hands and **Tabith Person** hands.

3444. 1825, Aug 16 -- 1823-1831 Court of Pleas and Quarter Sessions, Moore County, NC Page 87
Ordered that **John Cockman** be appointed overseer of the road from **George Moore**'s to Branch near **McQueen**.

3445. 1825, Aug 16 -- 1823-1831 Court of Pleas and Quarter Sessions, Moore County, NC Page 87
Ordered that **William Dunn** be appointed overseer of the road from **Kennedy**'s Mill to the old road at **Solomon Brewers** and have the following hands to work: **Wm. Jones, John Cagle, John Stuts, John Stuts** (son of **H**),

Robert Milton, James Milton, Ansel Milton, Isah Milton, Nathan Wallis, Thomas Williams, Matthew Williams, Henry Williams, David Lankford, Jesse Collar, George Kennedy and George Davis.

A. 1825, Aug 16 -- 1823-1831 Court of Pleas and Quarter Sessions, Moore County, NC Page 87
Ordered that **Right Deaton** be appointed overseer of the road in place of **Richard Warner** from the bay ponds to the Wolf Pit and have the following hands to work: **Richard Warner, Wm. Barrett, Merrell Cox, Ervin Cox, Holden Cox, John Medling, John Martin, Levy Levister, John McSween, Angus Martin, Thomas Hannon, Wm. Jackson, Samuel Jackson** and hands of **Joseph Jackson**.

B. 1825, Aug 16 -- 1823-1831 Court of Pleas and Quarter Sessions, Moore County, NC Page 87
Ordered that the order discontinuning the road from the Election House to the Chatham County line be rescinded and that the same continue to be a public road and that **Josiah Cheek** be appointed overseer and have the following hands to work: **Josiah Cheek** and hands, **Wm. Phillips, Absolum Phillips, John Phillips, Robt. Phillips, Dabney Phillips, John Cheek** (son of **Richd.**), **John Phillips Sen., Lewis Phillips Jur., Amos Cheek, John Cheek** (son of **Joab**), **Blake Cheek, Brantly Cheek, Joab Cheek Jur., Joab Cheek's** hands, **Abner Smith, Henry Phillips, John Phillips** (his son) and **Josiah Cheek** (son of **Richd.**).

C. 1825, Aug 17 -- 1823-1831 Court of Pleas and Quarter Sessions, Moore County, NC Page 89
Ordered that **John Phillips** be appointed overseer in place of **Eli Phillips** and have the following additional hands to work: **Alexr. McNeill** one hand, **John Phillips** one hand and **Lauchlin McNeill** one hand.

D. 1825, Aug 18 -- 1823-1831 Court of Pleas and Quarter Sessions, Moore County, NC Page 91
Wm. Hancock v. **John Cheek**. Ordered that **Joab Cheek, Lewis Phillips, Richard Cheek** and **Wm. Dowd** value an acre of land on each side of Deep River, one side belonging to the plaintiff and the other side belonging to the defendant where the plaintiff intends building a mill and report the value to the next court.

3446. 1825, Aug 20 -- 1823-1831 Court of Pleas and Quarter Sessions, Moore County, NC Page 94-95
[Deeds] **Cornelius Dowd Sr.** to **Cornelius Dowd Jur.** for 470 acres was acknowledged
Murdoch Martin to **Malcom Graham** was proven by **A. Martin**
Norman McKinnon to **Alexr. McKinnon** proven by **Normon McKinnon Jur.**
Malcom Morrison to **Catharine Morrison** proven by **John Paterson**
James Dunlap to **James Hains** was acknowledged
Malcom Buie to **Bradley Garner** was acknowledged

3447. 1825, Aug 25 -- Record of Marriages, Wilcox County, AL
Alexander Jackson married **Celia Maness**

3448. 1825, Aug 28-Oct 27 -- Notice, *Fayetteville Weekly Observer* [Fayetteville, NC] Newspaper
Moore County, NC – **Benjamin Person** v. **Jesse Upton Jun.** Original attachment, levied on 400 acres of land and c[hattel]. Ordered that publication be made for two months that unless the defendant appear on or before the first day of the next term [third Monday in November] judgement final will be entered and the land will be sold to satisfy.

3449. 1825, Sep 2 -- Land Grant #2739, Moore County, NC
Leonard Furr received 44 acres located on both sides of Flag Creek north of Buffalo Creek adjoining his own line, **Neil McLeod, Ansel Melton, Laky** and **William Jones. Ansel Melton** and **Isaah Melton** were chain carriers.

3450. 1825, Sep 24 -- Land Grant #2687, Moore County, NC
James H. Muse received 150 acres located on both sides of Locust Branch of Richland Creek adjoining **Abraham Stutts**, **Griffith** and **William Caddell**.
Martin Rouse and **Everit Wallace** were chain carriers.

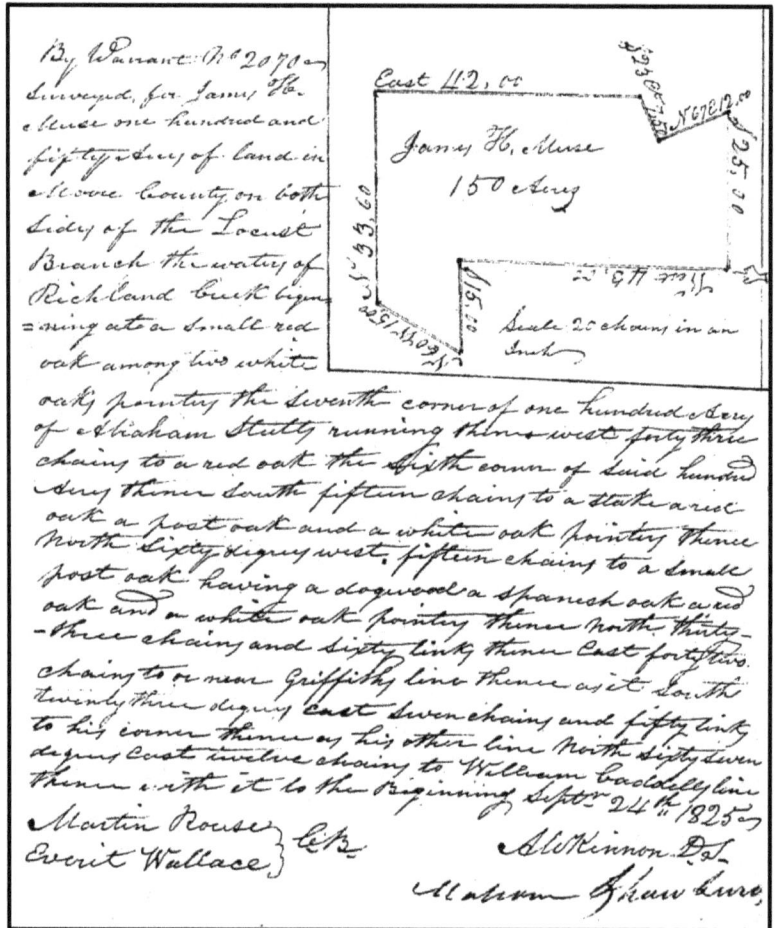

3451. 1825, Oct 1 -- BLM General Land Office Document #1676, Lauderdale County, AL
Thomas Hamm, assignee of **Matthias Richardson** received 160.04 acres from Huntsville Land Office located in southwest Quarter of Section 13, Township 1, Range 10.

3452. 1825, Oct 1 -- BLM General Land Office Document #1018, Copiah County, MS
Isaac Smith (of Copiah County) received 75.84 acres in Jackson District located in west half of northwest Quarter of Section 13, Township 9, Range 7.

3453. 1825, Oct 1 -- BLM General Land Office Document #1177, Lincoln County, MS
Stephen Smith (of Copiah County) received 152 acres from Jackson Land Office located in Section 35, Township 8, Range 6.

3454. 1825, Oct 1 -- BLM General Land Office Document #1043, Lincoln County, MS
Jeptha Britt (of Copiah County) received 159.75 acres in Choctaw District located in west half of northwest Quarter of Section 9, Township 8, Range 7.

3455. 1825, Oct 1 -- BLM General Land Office Document #1116, Copiah County, MS
John Carpenter (of Copiah County) received 79.12 acres from Jackson Land Office located in west half of northeast Quarter of Section 12, Township 9, Range 8.

3456. 1825, Oct 1 -- BLM General Land Office Document #1117, Copiah County, MS
Martin Carpenter (of Copiah County) received 73.75 acres from Jackson Land Office located in east half of northeast Quarter of Section 19, Township 10, Range 9.

3457. 1825, Oct 1 -- BLM General Land Office Document #1145, Copiah County, MS
Solomon Carpenter (of Copiah County) received 147.81 acres from Jackson Land Office located in southwest Quarter of Section 30, Township 10, Range 9.

3458. 1825, Oct 1 -- BLM General Land Office Document #1177, Lincoln County, MS
Everit Smith (of Copiah County) received 78.81 acres from Jackson Land Office located in west half of southeast Quarter of Section 4, Township 8, Range 7.

3459. 1825, Oct 1 -- BLM General Land Office Document #1217, Copiah County, MS
William Carpenter (of Copiah County) received 79.90 acres from Jackson Land Office located in west half of northwest Quarter of Section 9, Township 9, Range 9.

3460. 1825, Oct 3 -- Record of Marriages, Wilcox County, AL
Uriah B. Maness married **Henrietta Theid**

3461. 1825, Oct 5 -- Land Grant #2680, Moore County, NC
Neil McLeod received 30 acres located northwest of Richland Creek adjoining **Duncan McIntosh** and his own line. **Samuel Barrett** and **John McLeod** were chain carriers.

A. 1825, Oct 6 – Deed Book A-A1 Page 51, Chatham County, NC
Baily Williamson deeded **Isaac Teague** 124 located on Cedar Creek and the Moore County line adjoining **Balaam Fesmire**, **John Lawler** and **Jehu Lawler**. **Jehu Lawler** and **John Argo** were witnesses.

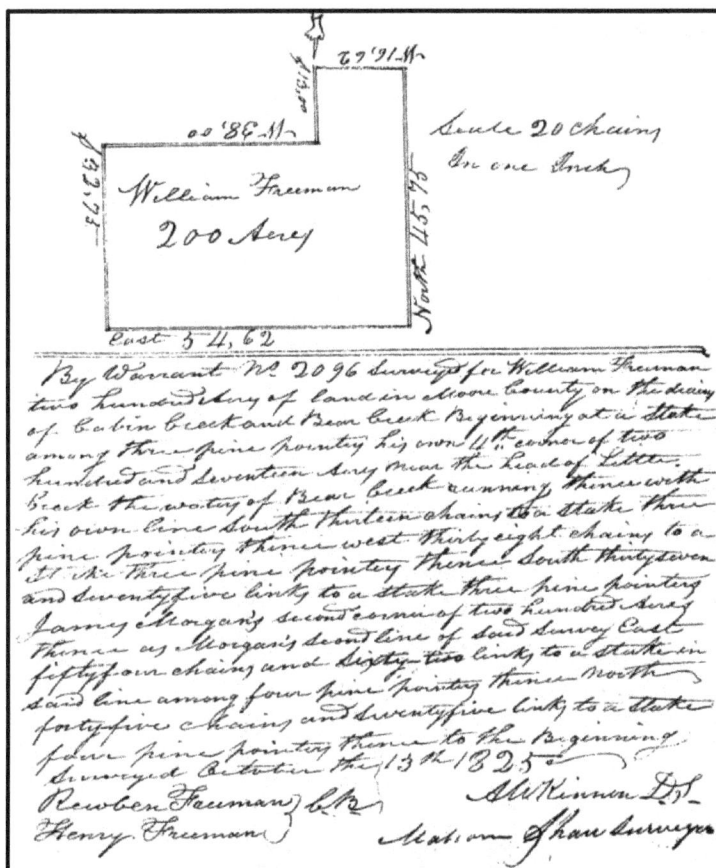

3462. 1825, Oct 13 -- Land Grant #2700, Moore County, NC
William Freeman received 200 acres located between Cabin Creek and Bear Creek adjoining his own line and **James Morgan**. **Reuben Freeman** and **Henry Freeman** were chain carriers.

3463. 1825, Oct 17 -- Land Grant #2699, Moore County, NC
Daniel McLean received 60 acres located on both sides of Dry Creek adjoining **Hector McLean**, **Daniel McCrummen**, **Neil McLeod** and his own line. **John Paterson** and **Allan McLean** were chain carriers.

3464. 1825, Oct 21 -- Land Grant #2681, Moore County, NC
William Barrett received 200 acres located northwest of Richland Creek adjoining **John Hargrove**, **Murchison**, **Kelly** and **Hiram Kennedy** (formerly **Grove**). **Samuel Barrett** and **John McLeod** were chain carriers.

3465. 1825, Oct 22 -- *A History of Sandy Creek Baptist Association* by George Purefoy, Page 92
B. Boroughs, **R. Reed** and **Zacheus Boroughs** from Fall Creek Church (Chatham County) and Elder **A. Shattuck**, Elder **William Dowd** and **William Dowdy** from Friendship Church (Moore County) and **A. Milton**, **J. Dunlap** and **Alexander Kennedy** from Mechanic's Hill Church (Moore County) were delegates to the Association meeting at Friendship Meeting House in Moore County, NC. **William Dowd**, **Artemas Shattuck** and **Eli Phillips** were ordained as ministers.

3466. 1825, Oct 26 -- Land Grant #2679, Moore County, NC
Neil McLeod received 100 acres located on both sides of Horse Creek adjoining **James Brownlow** and his own line. **Allan McLean** and **Donald McLean** were chain carriers.

3467. 1825, Nov -- County Accounts, Moore County, NC
1825, Nov -- Index to Trial Docket, Moore County, NC
State v. **Joseph Williams**

3468. 1825, Nov 15 -- Land Grant #2742, Moore County, NC
James Key received 50 acres located on Reedy Branch of Mill Creek adjoining heirs of **Ryal Britt**. **Merryman Britt** and **Angus McKinnon** were chain carriers.

A. 1825, Nov 19 – Deed Book A-A1 Page 268-269, Chatham County, NC
Josiah Culberton (of Warren County, TN), Power of Attorney for **William Culbertson**, **Joseph Culbertson**, **Laurence Culbertson**, **Andrew Culbertson**, **Aaron Culbertson** and **Jonathan Culbertson** deeded **James Culbertson** (of Montgomery County, NC) 2/3 of two tracts totaling 350 located on Fall Creek adjoining **John**

Brooks, Sugar Jones and **Eli Lawler**. Tracts their father **James Culbertson** Dec'd. was granted by state of NC. **Eli Lawler Junr.** and **Stephen Scott** were witnesses.

3469.   1825, Nov 21 -- 1823-1831 Court of Pleas and Quarter Sessions, Moore County, NC
[jury duty next term - selected participants] **John Stewart, Wm. Stuts, Jeremiah Williams Sr., John Cagle Jr., Jacob Cagle, William Brewer, Jesse Bean, Elijah Brewer, Alexd. Leach, Wm. Caddell, Hiram Hill** and **John Stuts.**

A.   1825, Nov 22 -- 1823-1831 Court of Pleas and Quarter Sessions, Moore County, NC Page 98
Ordered that **Kinneth Clark** be allowed to correct errors in a 100 acre grant to **Wm. Dunn** and deeded to **Clark** by **Wm. Dunn** and **Richd. Cheek**.

3470.   1825, Nov 22 -- 1823-1831 Court of Pleas and Quarter Sessions, Moore County, NC Page 98
Administration of the estate of **Wm. Hussey** Dec'd. formerly granted to **Alexr. Kennedy** is revoked and granted to **Mary Hussey** the widow.

A.   1825, Nov 22 -- 1823-1831 Court of Pleas and Quarter Sessions, Moore County, NC Page 98
Ordered that **Lewis Kennedy** Esq. be appointed guardian of **James Carroll** and **Diannah Carroll** infant heirs of **Starling Carroll** Dec'd.

B.   1825, Nov 22 -- 1823-1831 Court of Pleas and Quarter Sessions, Moore County, NC Page 98
Ordered that **Benjn. Person, Duncan Murchison** and **Thomas M.D. Reid**. be appointed to audit accounts of **Joab Cheek** and **Wm. Tyson**, admrs. of **Benjn. Gilbert** Dec'd.

3471.   1825, Nov 22 -- 1823-1831 Court of Pleas and Quarter Sessions, Moore County, NC Page 98
Ordered that **Wm. Wood** and **Jethrew Denson** work on the road from **Kennedy**'s Mill to **Solomon Brewer**'s old place under **Wm. Dunn** overseer in addition to the former hands.

3472.   1825, Nov 22 -- 1823-1831 Court of Pleas and Quarter Sessions, Moore County, NC Page 98
Jesse Brown, Tax Collector for Districts 6 and 8 be allowed 6 polls for insolvency for 1824

3473.   1825, Nov 22 -- 1823-1831 Court of Pleas and Quarter Sessions, Moore County, NC Page 99
Ordered that **Archd. McNeill, John Shamburger** and **William Brewer** be appointed to settle with **Peter Hair** admstr. of **John Hair** Dec'd.

3474.   1825, Nov 22 -- 1823-1831 Court of Pleas and Quarter Sessions, Moore County, NC Page 99
Ordered that **Matthew Deaton** be appointed overseer of the road called the Joel Road from the fork below **McIver**'s to Dry Creek and have the following hands to work: **James Kechey, John Wallace, Charles McArthur, Hector McCaskill, Angus McCaskill, Malcolm McCaskill, Mathew Deaton, Donald McDonald** one hand, **Roderick McAulay** one hand, **Mary McLeod** one hand, **John Deaton, Wm. Deaton, Kenneth Morrison, Archibald Munroe, Roderick McLeod** and **John McLeod.**

3475.   1825, Nov 23 -- 1823-1831 Court of Pleas and Quarter Sessions, Moore County, NC Page 100
Administration of the estate of **Joice Muse** Dec'd. is granted to **Brinkley Phillips**.

3476.   1825, Nov 23 -- 1823-1831 Court of Pleas and Quarter Sessions, Moore County, NC Page 101-102
[Deeds] **Robert Wilson** to **Absolom Phillips** proven by **Cornelius Shields**
Jesse Bean Senior to **Jesse Bean Junr.** acknowledged

Francis Myrick to **John Dannelly** proven by **William Dannelly**
Joseph Fry Jur. to **Nathan Fry Senr.** proven by **James Fry**
John C. Buie to **Wm. C. Buie** acknowledged
Wm. C. Buie to **John C. Buie** acknowledged
Malcom Morrison to **Malcolm P. Morrison** proven by **Danl. McRimmon**
Solomon Barrett to **Wm. Williamson** proven by **Wm. Brewer**
Francis Bullock to **Thomas Williams** was proven by **Wm. Brewer**
[Bills of sale] **Hannah Duckworth** to **John Dannelly Jur.** proven by **Druray Richardson**
Thomas P. Muse to **Asa Muse** acknowledged

A.   1825, Nov 23 -- 1823-1831 Court of Pleas and Quarter Sessions, Moore County, NC Page 101
Ordered that **Mary Elkins** be appointed guardian to **Darias Elkins, Mary Elkins, Samuel Elkins, Etha Elkins**
and **John W. Elkins.**

B.   1825, Nov 23 -- 1823-1831 Court of Pleas and Quarter Sessions, Moore County, NC Page 101
Ordered that **Cornelius Dowd** be appointed guardian to **Elizabeth Carrell, Thomas Carrell, Jesse Carrell,**
James Carrell and **Mary Carrell**, infant heirs of **James B. Carrell**, Dec'd.

3477.   1825, Nov 24 -- Land Grant #2729, Moore County, NC
Kenneth B. Murchison received 47 acres adjoining **Right Deaton** (formerly **McKay**), **McKenzie, Ritter,**
Jackson, Alexr. McLeod and **Jesse Bean. James Fry** and **Right Deaton** were chain carriers.

3478.   1825, Nov 30 -- BLM General Land Office Document #1856, Lauderdale County, AL
Matthias Richardson and **Jacob Stutt** (of Lauderdale County) received 79.72 acres from Huntsville Land Office
located in east half of the northeast Quarter of Section 29, Township 1, Range 9.

3479.   1825, Dec 12 -- Record of Estates Book B
Page 104-105, Moore County, NC
Estate of **Joice Muse**, Dec'd. by Administrator
Brinkley Phillips. *Notes due on the following:*

John B. Kelly and **Jesse F. Muse**. *Items were purchased by the following:* Kenneth McCaskill, Jesse Sanders,
George Cox, James Hill, Eleazor Burkhead, Danl. H. Muse, Thomas Muse Senr., Martin Hill, Alexr. McIntosh,
Danl. Muse [SP], Alex. C. Curry, James Dowd, Jane Muse, John T. Ritter, Jesse Page, John Paterson, Nathan
Holloway, John Tyson, Isaac Smith, Nathan Barrett, Stephen Davis, Lauchlin McNeill, Alexander Campbell
and **John Moore.**

3480.   1825, Dec 18 -- Land Grant #2678, Moore County, NC

Neil McLeod received 60 acres located west of Richland Creek adjoining **John Hargrove**, **Murchison** and his own line. **Samuel Barrett** and **John McLeod** were chain carriers.

A.   1825, Dec 30 -- Deed Book 37 Page 325-327, Moore County, NC
Isaac Beeson and **William Beeson** (of Randolph County) deeded **Carroll Brady** and **Bradley Brady** 500 acres located on Pates Creek being part of the 20,000 acres entered by **John Porterfield**. **William Martindale** was a witness.

3481.   1826-1838 – NC Supreme Court Case #2580, Davidson County, NC
James Burkhead and wife **Charity** v. heirs of **Joseph Colson**. Suit was brought by **Charity Muse Burkhead** claiming that her mother **Charity Muse** and her brother **Jesse Muse** illegally sold a slave **Rachel** that was bequeathed to her in her father's **James Muse**'s will. **Rachel** was sold on 6 Dec 1790 to **Joseph Colson**. She asked the court to grant her all 18 descendants of **Rachel**. Numerous affidavits and testimony were filed. **Charity Muse** presented her birthdate from the family bible. **Thomas Muse** attested that the handwriting was their father's. A marriage certificate was produced to show her marriage to **James Burkhead** on 13 Jul 1790 by **William Dunn**, JP. On Feb 15 1827, **Thomas Muse** and **Eleazer Burkhead** were examined at the home of **Thomas Muse** in Moore County, NC. The following were examined at the home of **Brinkley Phillips** in Moore County, NC on 18 Jun 1827: **Thomas Muse Senior**, James B. Muse, Betsey Muse, **Elizabeth Phillips**, Malcom Blue and **Hymrick Hill**. The following were examined in Montgomery County, NC on July 4, 1827: **Samuel Dunn** and **William Hall**. Additional affidavits were filed by **James Dowd** and **Cornelius Dowd**. *Key findings*: Samuel Dunn attested that he married the sister of **Charity Muse Burkhead** and he also stated that his daughter **Rhoda** married **Green Burkhead**, son of **James Burkhead** and **Charity Muse**. James Dowd stated that **Charity Muse**

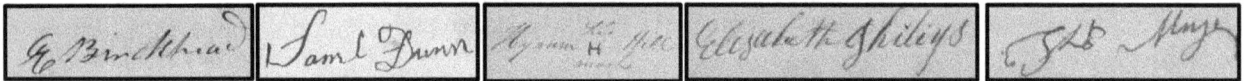

died 2 or 3 years prior to **Jesse Muse**. **Thomas Muse** attested that the last time he saw the **James Muse** family record it was in the possession of **Eleazer Burkhead**. **James B. Muse** and wife **Betsey Muse** and **Brinkley Phillips** and wife **Elizabeth Muse Phillips**, daughter of **Jesse Muse**, attested that **Charity** was given land and livestock in compensation for **Rachel**. **Thomas Muse** stated that his sister **Charity** was given 300 acres on Killetts Creek and a mare and a colt for compensation.

3482.   1826, Feb 1 -- BLM General Land Office Document #1606, Wilcox County, AL
Isham Sheffield (of Monroe County) received 80 acres from Cahaba Land Office located in southwest half of Section 26, Township 12, Range 5.

3483.   1826, Feb 1 -- BLM General Land Office Document #1606, Wilcox County, AL
Isham Sheffield (of Monroe County) received 80 acres from Cahaba Land Office located in southwest quarter of Section 26, Township 12, Range 5.

3484.   1826, Feb 1 -- BLM General Land Office Document #1607, Wilcox County, AL
Isham Sheffield (of Monroe County) received 80.45 acres from Cahaba Land Office located in northeast quarter of Section 27, Township 12, Range 5.

3485.   1826, Feb 1 -- BLM General Land Office Document #1608, Wilcox County, AL
Isham Sheffield (of Monroe County) received 80 acres from Cahaba Land Office located in east half of Section 26, Township 12, Range 5.

A.   1826, Feb 5 -- Marriage Bond, Randolph County, NC
William Cagle and **Dicey Boling** received marriage bond. **George Cagle** was bondsman. **Thos. Hancock** was witness. [*Editor's Note: Date of marriage occurred on or after date of marriage bond.*]

B.   1826, Feb 7 -- Marriage Bond, Randolph County, NC
Jacob Stuts and **Hanah Lowdermilk** received marriage bond. **Thomas Smotherman** was bondsman. [*Editor's Note: Date of marriage occurred on or after date of marriage bond.*]

3486.   1826, Feb 20 -- 1823-1831 Court of Pleas and Quarter Sessions, Moore County, NC

[*jury duty - selected participants*] **John Stuts, Hiram Hill, Wm. Caddell, John T. Ritter, Isham Sowell, Baley Williamson, Wiat Williamson, Thomas Williams, Stephen Davis, Asa Sowell, Isaac Smith, James Morgan, Daniel Caddell, Demsey Sowell, Edward Moore** and **Jesse Sanders** Esq.

3487. 1826, Feb 20 -- 1823-1831 Court of Pleas and Quarter Sessions, Moore County, NC Page 104
Hiram Kennedy, William Waddell and **Bryan Boroughs** appointed to settle with **Corn. Dowd** and **James Garner**, administrators of **James Wood** Dec'd.

3488. 1826, Feb 20 -- 1823-1831 Court of Pleas and Quarter Sessions, Moore County, NC Page 104
Ordered that **Jesse Brown Jr.** be appointed overseer of the road from **Kennedy**'s Mill to **Peter Davis'** to the 5 mile post and have the following hands to work: **David Kennedy**'s hands, **Hiram Kennedy**'s hands, **Jacob Stuts, Robert Moore, Aaron Kennedy, Jethro Denson, Wm. Cagle, John Brown, John Dunlap, Wm. Williams, Wm. Williamson** (son of **Belsay**), **Thomas Williamson Ser., Jeremiah Williams** and **William Brown.**

3489. 1826, Feb 20 -- 1823-1831 Court of Pleas and Quarter Sessions, Moore County, NC Page 106
Alexr. McKinnon is appointed guardian to **Rodrick, Nancy** and **Malcolm Mathewson** with **Angus McKinnon** and **Neill McKinnon.**

3490. 1826, Feb 21 -- 1823-1831 Court of Pleas and Quarter Sessions, Moore County, NC Page 106
Jesse Sanders qualified as Justice of the Peace

A. 1826, Feb 21 -- 1823-1831 Court of Pleas and Quarter Sessions, Moore County, NC Page 106
Administration of the estate of **Thomas Martindale**, Dec'd. granted to **Wm. Martindale.**

3491. 1826, Feb 21 -- 1823-1831 Court of Pleas and Quarter Sessions, Moore County, NC Page 107
The last will and testament of **William Smith**, Dec'd. was proven by the oath of **Simon McNeill** and ordered to be recorded and **Phillip McNeill** the Executor herein named duly qualified.

3492. 1826, Feb 22 -- 1823-1831 Court of Pleas and Quarter Sessions, Moore County, NC Page 108
Hiram Kennedy, Nathaniel Tucker, John Paterson Esq. appointed to settle with **Jesse Brown** Esq., Administrator of **Meloney Newton**, Dec'd.
Hiram Kennedy, Jesse Brown, William Brewer appointed to settle with **Peter Hair**, Administrator of **John Hair**, Dec'd.

A. 1826, Feb 22 -- Deed Book 50 Page 161-164, Moore County, NC
William Sears deeded **Daniel McCrimmon** 150 acres located on Richland Creek adjoining **Bethune** excluding 2 acres laid off for a graveyard and **Daniel Chisholm's** claim of 1/5 of the 150 acres. **Wm. Barrett Jr.** and **Duncan Murchison** were witnesses. [*Editor's Note: the graveyard referenced is the Old Scotch Graveyard*]

3493. 1826, Feb 22 -- 1823-1831 Court of Pleas and Quarter Sessions, Moore County, NC Page 108

James Dunlap appointed constable in District 6
William Williams appointed constable in District 8

3494.　　1826, Feb 22 -- 1823-1831 Court of Pleas and Quarter Sessions, Moore County, NC Page 109
State v. **Abednego Maness**. Witnesses: **Rebecca Denson, Celia Stuts, Elizabeth Ritter, Danl. Brewer, John Stuts, Wm. Lakey, Nathan Barrett, Charity McDonald, Bradley Garner, Bryan Boroughs, Isaac Maner, James Hunsucker, George Moore, Wm. Waddell, Asa Sowell, Wm. Smith Jr. (E. son), Everet Smith, John Ritter Jur., John Ritter Ser., John Tyson, David Kennedy, James Dunlap, Isaac Smith, James King, Melloney Maner, Polly Moore, Arch. Shields, Wm. Smith Senr., Edward Moore** and **Sally Denson**.

3495.　　1826, Feb 25 -- 1823-1831 Court of Pleas and Quarter Sessions, Moore County, NC Page 114
[Deeds] **John McLennon** Shff to **Daniel Caddell** proven by **Eleazor Birckhead**
Tobias Fry to **Mary Fry** proven by **Daniel Caddell**
Hector McNeill to **Brinkley Phillips** proven by **Turquill McNeill**
Thomas Fry to **Michael Bryant** and **George Graham** proven by **Benjn. Person**
Henry Stutts to **Neil McLeod** was acknowledged
James Milton to **George Kennedy** was acknowledged
Peter Davis to **John Shamburger** proven by **Benjn. Page**
Daniel McNeill Shff to **Daniel McCrummen** acknowledged
Wm. Phillips to **Brinkley Phillips** acknowledged
John Martin to **Jesse Sowell** proven by **Allen Wade**
Neill McLeod to **Jesse Sowell** acknowledged

3496.　　1826, Mar 2 -- BLM General Land Office Grant #1773, Wilcox County, AL

John Lawson, assignee of Averitt Sheffield received 79.56 acres from Cahaba Land Office located in east half of northeast Quarter of Section 11, Township 11, Range 5.

A.   1826, Mar 6 -- Deed Book 34 Page 617-619, Moore County, NC
Lewis Phillips deeded John D. Phillips 60 acres located north of Deep River on John Phillips Creek adjoining Lewis Phillips, Patrick Dowd and Fair Promise Meeting House. E. Stewart and Robert H. Phillips were witnesses.

3497.   1826, Mar 30 -- Chronicles and Records of Bensalem Presbyterian Church Page 9, Moore County, NC
John C. Buie and Margaret Martin were married.

3498.   1826, Mar 31 -- BLM General Land Office Grant #2047, Wilcox County, AL
George Morgan, assignee of John Wilkinson received 158.20 acres from Cahaba Land Office located in southeast Quarter of Section 13, Township 12, Range 5.

3499.   1826, Mar 31 -- BLM General Land Office Grant #2048, Wilcox County, AL
George Morgan (of Wilcox County) received 158.30 acres from Cahaba Land Office located in southeast Quarter of Section 12, Township 12, Range 5.

3500.   1826, Mar 31 -- BLM General Land Office Grant #2047, Wilcox County, AL
George Morgan, assignee of John Wilkinson received 79.90 acres from Cahaba Land Office located in west half of southwest Quarter of Section 7, Township 12, Range 6.

3501.   1826, Apr 5 -- Land Grant #2724, Moore County, NC
Medford Owen received 100 acres located south of Wolf Creek adjoining his own line, James Dunlap and Neil McLeod. Wm. Williamson and William Brewer were chain carriers.

3502.   1826, Apr 10 -- Land Grant #2714, Moore County, NC
Alexander McIntosh received 83 acres located south of McLendons Creek adjoining his own line. Wm. J. McIntosh and Alexr. McIntosh were chain carriers.

3503.   1826, Apr 10 -- Land Grant #2715, Moore County, NC
Alexander McIntosh received 50 acres located north of Richland Creek adjoining his own line, Duncan McIntosh and Bryant McDonald. Neill McIntosh and John J. McIntosh were chain carriers.

3504.   1826, Apr 20 -- Land Grant #2575, Moore County, NC
Alexander Leach received 100 acres located south of Cabin Creek adjoining his own line, Angus Leach and Jerry Reynolds. Jerry Reynolds and Mark Allen were chain carriers.

3505.   1826, Apr 29 -- Land Grant #2737, Moore County, NC
Norman Matheson received 32 acres located on Horse Creek adjoining his own line, Neil McLeod and Norman McLeod. John Matheson and Neil Matheson were chain carriers.

3506.   1826, May 1 -- BLM General Land Office Document #1217, Copiah County, MS
William Carpenter (of Copiah County) received 80.44 acres from Jackson Land Office located in west half of northwest Quarter of Section 33, Township 10, Range 9.

3507.   1826, May 10 -- BLM General Land Office Document #1796, Lincoln County, MS
Jeptha Britt (of Copiah County) received 79.09 acres in Choctaw District located in east half of northeast Quarter of Section 8, Township 8, Range 7.

3508.   1826, May 10 -- BLM General Land Office Document #1826, Copiah County, MS
Isaac Smith (of Copiah County) received 75.84 acres in Jackson District located in east half of northwest Quarter of Section 13, Township 9, Range 7.

3509.   1826, May 15 -- 1823-1831 Court of Pleas and Quarter Sessions, Moore County, NC
[jury duty next term - selected participants] Joel Lawhon, Wm. Caddell Jr., Mermon Britt, John Garner, Jesse Brown Jr., Nathan Morgan, George Cagle Jr., George Moore Sr., George Stewart, Mark Allen and Thomas Ritter.

A.   1826, May 15 -- 1823-1831 Court of Pleas and Quarter Sessions, Moore County, NC Page 117
Ordered that **Daniel McNeill** Esq. be appointed overseer of the road from the Island Ford to **Phillips'** Bars in place of **William King** and have the same hands.

3510.   1826, May 16 -- 1823-1831 Court of Pleas and Quarter Sessions, Moore County, NC Page 118
Ordered that orphan child **Ann Johnson** be bound to **Jesse Bean**

A.   1826, May 16 -- 1823-1831 Court of Pleas and Quarter Sessions, Moore County, NC Page 119
Ordered that **Benjn. Person** be appointed guardian of **Absolom Fry** and **Nice Fry** with **Corn. Dowd** and **Daniel McNeill** as securities.

3511.   1826, May 16 -- 1823-1831 Court of Pleas and Quarter Sessions, Moore County, NC Page 120
The following were appointed Tax Collectors for 1826 (District #3) **Jesse Sanders** (District #8) **Hiram Kennedy**.

3512.   1826, May 16 -- 1823-1831 Court of Pleas and Quarter Sessions, Moore County, NC Page 120
Ordered that **Wm. Caddell** be appointed overseer of the Raleigh Road from the Bay Pond to the Randolph Road below Carthage and have the following hands to work: **Sion Johnson, James Fry, Hardin Warner, Nathan Fry, Bryant Fry, Edwd. Fry, James Caddell, Saml. Vick, Lockart Fry, Edward Warner, John Fry** and **Green B. Caddell.**

3513.   1826, May 17 -- 1823-1831 Court of Pleas and Quarter Sessions, Moore County, NC Page 125
[Deeds] **James Birckhead** to **Jesse F. Muse** proven by **Nathan Barrett**
Susannah Bean to **Jesse Bean Sr.** proven by **Jesse Bean Jr.**

John Fry to **Jesse Bean Jr.** proven by **Wm. Caddell**
Rodrick McAulay to **John Munroe** and **Francis Munroe** proven by **William McAulay**
[Bill of sale] **Harmon Brewer** to **Lyday, John, Elizabeth, Sallay, James** and **Lusinday Brewer** proven by **Corn. Dowd**

3514.   1826, May 29 -- Bible of Wyatt Williamson, Moore County, NC
Wyatt Williamson and **Mary Myrick** were married

3515.   1826, Aug 16 -- Land Grant #2726, Moore County, NC
Daniel McAulay received 100 acres located on Wet Fork of Mill Creek adjoining **Murdock McAulay** and **Joseph Allen. Alexr. McKinnon** and **John McKinnon** were chain carriers.

3516.   1826, Aug 21 -- 1823-1831 Court of Pleas and Quarter Sessions, Moore County, NC
[*jury duty - selected participants*] **George Stewart, Thomas Ritter, George Moore Senr., Right Deaton, Bradley Garner, Abraham Stuts, George Stuts, Baley Williamson, James Maness, Cornelius Caddell, Demsy Sowell, Nathan Barrett, Bradley Garner Senr., Green Caddell, Joel Lawhon, Jesse Sowell** and **Mathew Deaton.**

3517.   1826, Aug 21 -- 1823-1831 Court of Pleas and Quarter Sessions, Moore County, NC Page 129
Ordered that **Samuel Barringtine** be appointed overseer of the road from the hill at the **Widow Bethune**'s to Flowers Road and have the following hands to work: **Alexander Smith, Isham Wallis, Samuel Barret, Wm. Barret** Esq. **Sr., Angus Kelly, Thomas Dowdy, Wm. McIntosh, John A. McIntosh, Alexander W. McIntosh**'s boy **Tim, James Haines** and **Jacob Cagle.**

3518.   1826, Aug 21 -- 1823-1831 Court of Pleas and Quarter Sessions, Moore County, NC Page 129
Ordered that **John J. McIntosh** be appointed overseer of the road from Bean's Bridge to the hill at the **Widow Bethune**'s in place of **Jesse Muse** and have the following hands to work: **Leonard Lawhon, John Muse, Miles**

Rouse, John McIntosh, John Rouse, James Hill, Martin Hill, Walter Barrett, Dickson Ritter, Martin Rouse, Donald Caddell and Enoch Wallis.

3519.　　1826, Aug 21 -- 1823-1831 Court of Pleas and Quarter Sessions, Moore County, NC Page 129
Ordered that **William Brewer** be appointed overseer in place of **Everet Sheffield** of the road from **Spivays** to **McNeill**'s store and have the same hands to work.

A.　　1826, Aug 21 -- 1823-1831 Court of Pleas and Quarter Sessions, Moore County, NC Page 129
Ordered that **Wm. Jackson** be appointed overseer in place of **Right Deaton** of the road from the Bay Pond to the Wolf Pit and have the following hands to work: **Right, Deaton, Richd. Warner, Wm. Barrett, Merrell Cox, Ervin Cox, Holdin Cox, John Medling, John Martin, Levy Leivster, John McSwain, Angus Martin, Thomas Hannon, Saml. Jackson, Wm.** and **Samuel Jackson**'s hands, **Joseph Jackson, Allin Martin, Thomas Fry, John Graham** and **Alexr. Martin**.

3520.　　1826, Aug 21 -- 1823-1831 Court of Pleas and Quarter Sessions, Moore County, NC Page 130
Ordered that **Baley Williamson** be appointed overseer of the road from **Wm. Williamsons** into the road that leads to **Kennedy**'s Bridge on Bear Creek and have the following hands to work: **Lewis Williamson, David Kennedy**'s hands, **Hiram Kennedy**'s hands, **Elias Kennedy**'s hand, **Enoch Kennedy, Anderson B. Smith** and **George Stuts**.

3521.　　1826, Aug 21 -- 1823-1831 Court of Pleas and Quarter Sessions, Moore County, NC Page 130
Ordered that **David Brewer** be appointed overseer in place of **George Stuts** of the road from Bear Creek to **George Moore**'s and have the following hands to work: **George Stuts, John Ritter Jr., Elijah Brewer, Abraham Stuts, Daniel Williams, Jacob Stuts, George Moore Jr., John Hunsucker, Jethroe Denson, Edward Moore, Garner Maness, Bradley Brady, Willis Brewer, Edmond Boroughs, Robert Hardin** and **Stephen Maness**.

3522.　　1826, Aug 22 -- 1823-1831 Court of Pleas and Quarter Sessions, Moore County, NC Page 133
Ordered that **Nathaniel Tucker** be appointed overseer of the road from the five mile post to the old road and have the following hands to work: **Martin Cagle, Elijah Hancock, Gardner Bolin, Jonathan Cagle, Wm. Cagle (son of Jacob), James Maness, Silas Wilson, Robert Kennedy, Martin Cagle Jr., Henry Cagle** and **Miles Jordan**.

3523.　　1826, Aug 22 -- 1823-1831 Court of Pleas and Quarter Sessions, Moore County, NC Page 133
Ordered that **James Gains, Hiram Kennedy** and **Wm. Waddell** be appointed to sette with **Isaac Teague Junr.**, Executor of **Isaac Teague Senr**.

3524.　　1826, Aug 22 -- 1823-1831 Court of Pleas and Quarter Sessions, Moore County, NC Page 133
Ordered that **Jacob Cagle** be appointed overseer in place of **John Cockman** of the road from **George Moore**'s to the branch near **McQueens**.

A.　　1826, Aug 22 -- 1823-1831 Court of Pleas and Quarter Sessions, Moore County, NC Page 133
Ordered that **John Cagle** be appointed overseer in place of **Wm. Dunn** of the road from **Kennedy**'s Mill to the old road at **Solomon Brewers** and have the following hands to work: **Wm. Dunn, John Stuts, John Stuts (son of H), Robert Milton, James Milton, Ansel Milton, Nathan Wallis, Matthew Williams, Henry Williams, David Lankford, Jesse Collar, George Davis, Jethrew Denson, Wm. Wood, Jno. Williams** and **Danl. McNeill**.

3525.　　1826, Aug 22 -- Land Grant #2730, Moore County, NC
James Caviness received 10 acres located north of Deep River adjoining **England, McLeod**, his own line (formerly **William Waddle**), **James Gains** and **Kelly**.

A.   1826, Aug 23 -- 1823-1831 Court of Pleas and Quarter Sessions, Moore County, NC Page 134
Administration of the estate of **Patsey Glascock** Dec'd is granted to **Jesse F. Muse**.

3526.   1826, Aug 23 -- 1823-1831 Court of Pleas and Quarter Sessions, Moore County, NC Page 137
Ordered that **Lewis Garner** be appointed overseer of the road in place of **Andrew Yow** from the [Randolph] county line on the east side of **Nicolas Nall's** to **William Williamson's**.

A.   1826, Aug 24 -- 1823-1831 Court of Pleas and Quarter Sessions, Moore County, NC Page 140
Ordered that **Jesse Sanders** and **Eleazor Birckhead** Esqs. be appointed to examine **Nancy McIver**, wife of **Daniel McIver** and **Margaret Garner**, wife of **James Garner** to confirm their voluntary consent in a deed to **Stephen Davis**.

3527.   1826, Aug 26 -- 1823-1831 Court of Pleas and Quarter Sessions, Moore County, NC Page 144
[Deeds] **Solomon Brewer** to **Stephen Brewer** was proven by **Eli Lawler**
Wm. Person to **Joseph J. Person** was proven by **Eli Lawler Jun.**
Eli Callicutt to **John Freeman** was proven by **Rich. Freeman**
John Freeman to **Edmond Holland** was proven by **Wm. Freeman**
Richard Holland to **Wm. Freeman** was proven by **Richard Freeman**
Richard Freeman to **John Freeman** was acknowledged
Edmond Holland to **Wm. Freeman** was proven by **Rich. Freeman**
Wm. Copeland to **Abigail Harden** was proven by **Nathan Copeland**
Cornelius Latham to **John Cagle** was proven by **John Shamburger**
Mary Martin to **Tobias Fry** was proven by **W.J. McIntosh**
Alexr. McIntosh to **George Graham** was proven by **M. McCrummen**
Joab Cheek to **Richd. Street** acknowledged
James Latham to **John Cagle** was proven by **John Shamburger**
Thomas Person to **Wm. Waddell** proven by **Phillip Alston**
Wm. Waddell to **Thomas Person** acknowledged
Wm. Waddell to **James Cavanest** acknowledged
[Bills of Sale] **Atlas Jones** to **John Cheek** proven by **John Murchison**
John Wilkins to **John Cheek** proven by **Lewis Phillips**

3528.   1826, Sep 13 -- Land Grant #2721, Moore County, NC
Richard Cheek received 32 acres located south of Deep River being surplus with own 400 acres adjoining his own line. **John Cheek** and **Josiah Cheek Junr.** were chain carriers.

A.   1826, Sep 18 -- Deed Book 6 Page 107-109, Moore County, NC
William Cox deeded **Samuel Jackson** and **William Jackson** 109.25 acres located on both sides of the Juniper Creek and McKoy Branch being part of the 300-acre **McCollum** tract and the 200-acre **Joel McLendon** tract. **John McKeithan** and **Benjamin Dunlap** were witnesses.

3529.   1826, Sep 20 -- Marriages, *Carolina Observer* [Fayetteville, NC] Newspaper
"In Moore County, on the 7th inst. [Sep 1826], by the Rev. Mr. **Phillips**, Mr. **Henry O. Smith** of Darlington, SC to Miss **Temperance Waddill**, daughter of **William Waddill** of Moore County, NC"

3530.   1826, Oct -- Chronicles and Records of Bensalem Presbyterian Church Page 22, Moore County, NC
Catharine McNiell Deton died. Daughter of **Hector McNeill** and **Isabel Murchison**.

3531.   1826, Oct 4 -- Marriages, *Carolina Observer* [Fayetteville, NC] Newspaper
"On the 14th ult. [Sep 1826], Mr. **Aaron Kennedy** of Moore County to Miss **Wincy Kidd** of Chatham County"

3532.   1826, Oct 12 -- Land Grant #2735, Moore County, NC
William Brewer received 50 acres located between Bear Creek and Wolf Creek adjoining **McAulay**, **John Sheffield Senr.**, **James Dunlap** and **William Williamson**. **Medford Owen** and **Everet Sheffield** were chain carriers.

3533.   1826, Oct 28 -- *A History of Sandy Creek Baptist Association* by George Purefoy, Page 93

Eli Lawler, **Bryant Boroughs** and **Zach. Boroughs** from Fall Creek Church (Chatham County) and Elder **William Dowd**, **John Dowdy** and **Alick Autry** from Friendship Church (Moore County) and **Alex. Kennedy**, **Aaron Kennedy** and **David McCrimmon** from Mechanic's Hill Church (Moore County) were delegates to the Association meeting at Brush Creek Meeting House in Randolph County, NC.

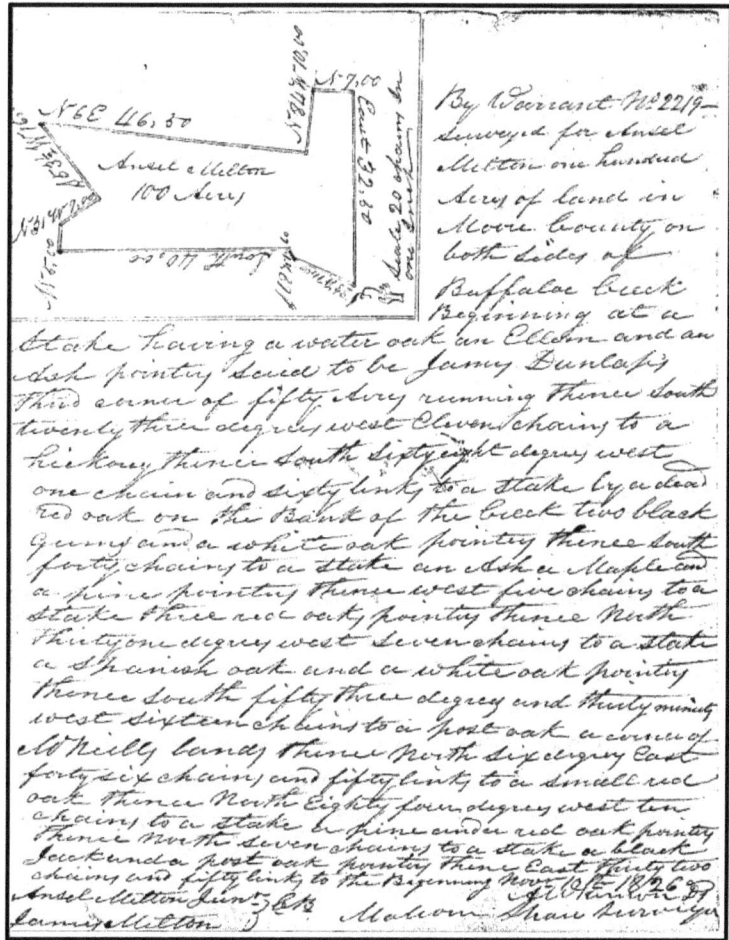

3534. 1826, Nov 7 -- Land Grant #2753, Moore County, NC
Jesse Brown received 25 acres located north of Bear Creek adjoining his own line. **Joshuah Key** and **Jesse Brown Senr.** were chain carriers.

3535. 1826, Nov 8 -- Land Grant #2734, Moore County, NC
Shadrach Manes received 16 acres located south of Bear Creek adjoining **Neil McLeod** and heirs of **John McAulay**. **Everit Manes** and **James Manes** were chain carriers.

3536. 1826, Nov 10 -- Land Grant #2754, Moore County, NC
Ancel Melton received 100 acres located on both sides of Buffalo Creek adjoining **James Dunlap** and **McNeill**. **Ansel Melton Junr.** and **James Melton** were chain carriers.

3537. 1826, Nov 13 -- Land Grant #2733, Moore County, NC
George Hunsucker received 100 acres located east of Wet Creek on Big Branch adjoining **Newton**, **Alexr. McKinnon** and heirs of **John McAulay**. **William Barrentine** and **David Hunsucker** were chain carriers.

3538. 1826, Nov 18 -- Record of Estates Book B Page 136-139, Moore County, NC
Estate of **Henry Melton**, Dec'd. by Administrator **James Dunlap**. _Accounts listed for the following_: **James Dunlap**, **James Melton**, **John Kennedy**, **Hugh Hammel**, **John Williams**, **Thomas Williams[short]** and **Robt. Melton**. _Notes due on the following_: **James Melton Jur.**, **Ansel Melton**, **Daniel Mcrimmon**, **Charles Sowell**, **James Hains**, **John Williams**, **Jesse Brown Jr.**, **Robert Melton Sr.** [son of Ansel], **William Cagle** and **David Jones**. _Items were purchased by the following_: **James Dunlap**, **Thos. Williams** [of **Chris**], **Sarah Melton**, **Jesse Brown Sr.**, **Robartis Huzza**, **William Brown/Brewer**, **Robt. Melton Sr.**, **Ansel Melton Jr.**, **Jno. Wallis**, **John McDaniel**, **James Muse**, **Edward Moore**, **Daniel McCrimmon**, **William Williamson**, **Isaac Brown**, **Isaah Melton**, **George Adams**, **Robert Melton Jr.**, **Matthew Williams**, **David Jones**, **Jesse F. Muse**, **Norman McLoud** and **George Hunsucker**.

A. 1826, Nov 20 -- 1823-1831 Court of Pleas and Quarter Sessions, Moore County, NC Page 147
The last will and testament of **Richard Street**, Dec'd. was proven by **Robert Harden** and **Joab Cheek**. **Benjamin Williams**, **Donald Street** and **Archd. L. McQueen** were named executors.

3539. 1826, Nov 21 -- Land Grant #2748, Moore County, NC
John Dannelly received 15 acres located on Lick Creek adjoining his own line, **William England** and **Brooks**. **Jno. Dannelly Jr.** and **Wm. T. England** were chain carriers.

3540. 1826, Nov 21 -- 1823-1831 Court of Pleas and Quarter Sessions, Moore County, NC
[jury duty next term - selected participants] **James Hains**, **George Hunsucker**, **William Jones** and **Lewis Williamson**.

3541. 1826, Nov 21 -- 1823-1831 Court of Pleas and Quarter Sessions, Moore County, NC Page 147

Ordered that **Jesse Bean Jr**. be appointed overseer in place of **John Fry** of the road from the Forks near **Nailors** to Bean's Bridge and have the same hands to work.

3542. 1826, Nov 21 -- 1823-1831 Court of Pleas and Quarter Sessions, Moore County, NC Page 147
Ordered that **Wm. Buie** be appointed overseer in place of **James Keys** of the road from the Montgomery County line to **Martin**'s old store have the same hands to work.

A. 1826, Nov 21 -- 1823-1831 Court of Pleas and Quarter Sessions, Moore County, NC Page 148
Benjamin Person was appointed guardian to **Alexander Carrell, Joseph Carrell, Sibbay Carrell** and **Washington Carrell**.

B. 1826, Nov 21 -- 1823-1831 Court of Pleas and Quarter Sessions, Moore County, NC Page 148
Ordered that the executor of **John Carrell** Esq., Dec'd. be allowed to sell negroes belonging to estate.

3543. 1826, Nov 21 -- 1823-1831 Court of Pleas and Quarter Sessions, Moore County, NC Page 147, 149
Sarah Milton granted Administration of the Estate of **Henry Milton**, Dec'd. **James Hains, John Paterson** Esq., **Jesse Brown** Esq., **Thomas Williams** appointed to lay off a year provision for **Sarah Milton**, Widow of **Henry Milton,** Dec'd.

3544. 1826, Nov 21 -- 1823-1831 Court of Pleas and Quarter Sessions, Moore County, NC Page 149
Ordered that **Gideon Seawell** be appointed overseer in place of **Benjn. Person** of the road from **Davis'** old place to Island Ford Road above **John B. Kellys** and have the same hands to work.

3545. 1826, Nov 21 -- 1823-1831 Court of Pleas and Quarter Sessions, Moore County, NC Page 149
Ordered that **Daniel McRimson [McCrimmon]** be appointed overseer of the road from the Randolph County Line to **John Spivay**'s and have the following hands to work: **Wm. Sheffield, E. Wallis, Jasen Muse, J. Collier, John McDonald, Thomas Williams** and **Auburn Jones**.

3546. 1826, Nov 21 -- 1823-1831 Court of Pleas and Quarter Sessions, Moore County, NC Page 150
[Deeds] **Charles Sowell** to **George Davis** was proven by **Matthew Williams**
Wm. Cox to **Samuel Jackson** and **Wm. Jackson** acknowledged
Jeremiah Williams to **Danl. McRimon** was proven by **Peter Shamburger**
John Freeman to **William Freeman** was proven by **Wm. Brewer**
Polly Elkins to **Wm. Hancock** proven by **Benjn. Person**
Asa Sowell to **Wm. Hancock** acknowledged
Samuel C. Bruce to **William Hancock** proven by **Eleazor Birckhead**

A. 1826, Dec 1 -- Land Grant #2475, Montgomery County, NC
Pleasant Simmons received 60 acres located on Dicks Creek adjoining his own line and **Angus Morrison. Malcolm Lemons** and **John Brewer** were chain carriers.

3547. 1826, Dec 15 -- Land Grant #2718, Moore County, NC
William Williams received 150 acres located north of Bear Creek adjoining **John**

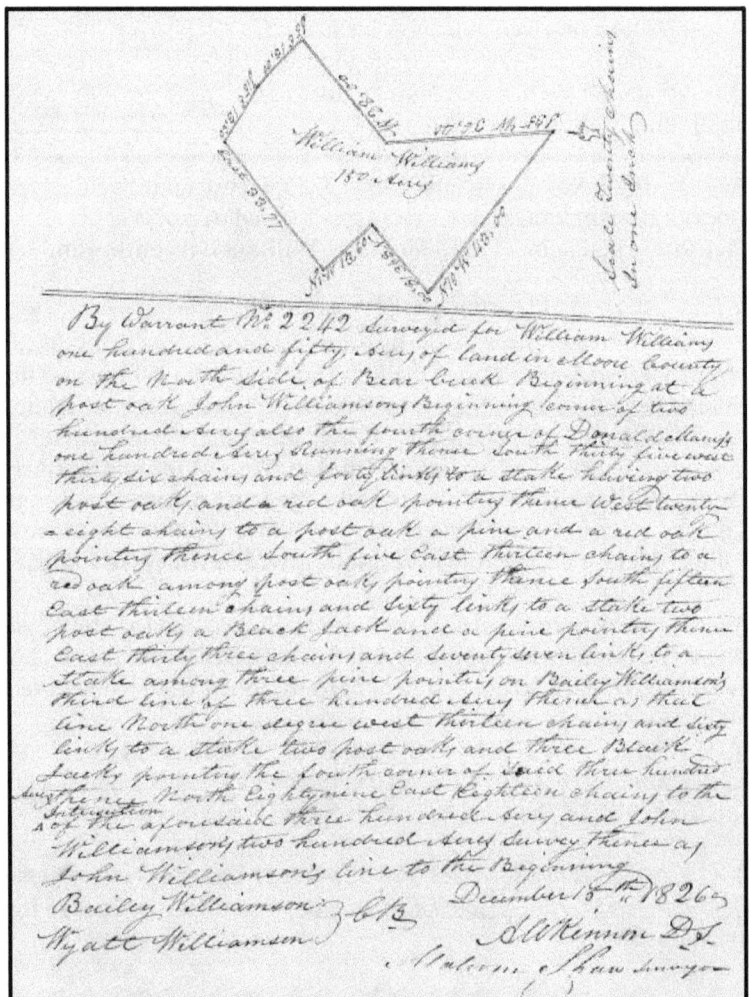

Williamson, **Donald Maness**, **Bailey Williamson** and **Shamburger**. **Bailey Williamson** and **Wyatt Williamson** were chain carriers.

A.   1826, Dec 19 -- Land Grant #2487, Montgomery County, NC
James Wright received 45 acres located on Dicks Creek adjoining his own line, **Alexander Leach** and **Joshua Cochran**. **Alexr. Leach** and **David Wright** were chain carriers.

3548.   1826, Dec 28 -- Chronicles and Records of Bensalem Presbyterian Church Page 9, Moore County, NC
John Bethune and **Mary Martin** were married

3549.   1827, Jan 4 -- Land Grant #2744, Moore County, NC
Thomas Brown received 50 acres located on both sides of Wet Creek adjoining his own line, **William Smith** and **Jesse Brown Junr. John Richardson** and **Isaiah Brown** were chain carriers.

3550.   1827, Jan 6 --- Deed, Montgomery County, NC
Saml. Dunn deeded **William Lidnum** [of Davidson County] 204 located northeast of Yadkin River and the [Davidson] County line adjoining **Barnett**. **J.W. Daniel** and **Ed. Hopkins** were witnesses.
[*Editor's Note: Original located in Stanly County Museum*]

3551.   1827, Jan 15 -- BLM General Land Office Document #1209, Warren County, MO
Jesse Ritter (of Montgomery County) received 80.84 acres located in Eastern half of southwest Quarter of Section 30, Township 47, Range 4.

3552.   1827, Jan 23 -- Land Grant #2762, Moore County, NC
John Sowell received 8 acres located south of McLendons Creek adjoining **William Barret Senr.** and **Jackson**. **Thos. Ritter** and **Isam Sowell** were chain carriers.

3553.   1827, Feb -- 1785-1868 Index to Trial Docket, Moore County, NC Page 60
Charles Furr v. **A. Sowell**

3554.   1827, Feb -- Chronicles and Records of Bensalem Presbyterian Church Page 23, Moore County, NC
Catharine McAskill Shaw, wife of **Norman Shaw**, died.

3555.   1827, Feb 19 -- 1823-1831 Court of Pleas and Quarter Sessions, Moore County, NC
[*jury duty - selected participants*] **Wm. Williamson**, **Wm. Freeman**, **Edmond Holland**, **William Jones**, **John T. Ritter**, **Lewis Garner**, **Stephen Davis**, **George Stewart**, **John Stewart**, **Wm. Williams**, **Walter Barrett**, **Nathan Barrett** and **James Milton**.

A.   1827, Feb 19 -- 1823-1831 Court of Pleas and Quarter Sessions, Moore County, NC Page 154
Peggay Deaton permitted to retail spirits at her usual place of dwelling for one year.

3556.   1827, Feb 20 -- 1823-1831 Court of Pleas and Quarter Sessions, Moore County, NC Page 155
Ordered that **Aaron Kennedy** be appointed guardian to **Polly Right**, **Betsy Right**, **Cela Right**, **Levy Write** and **William Right**, infant heirs of **Sherwood Right** Dec'd.

3557.   1827, Feb 20 -- 1823-1831 Court of Pleas and Quarter Sessions, Moore County, NC Page 155
George Hunsucker Jr. permitted to retail liquors for one year.

3558.   1827, Feb 20 -- 1823-1831 Court of Pleas and Quarter Sessions, Moore County, NC Page 156
Ordered that **John Paterson**, **Neill Morison** and **Angus McKinnon** be appointed to settle with **Levy Deaton**, administrator of **Sherwood Right**, Dec'd.

3559. 1827, Feb 20 -- 1823-1831 Court of Pleas and Quarter Sessions, Moore County, NC Page 156
Jesse Brown allowed 14 polls of insolvency for District 6 and 8 for 1825

A. 1827, Feb 20 -- 1823-1831 Court of Pleas and Quarter Sessions, Moore County, NC Page 157
Ordered that **Brinkley Phillips** be appointed overseer of the road in place of **Cornelius Dowd Jr.** from the black rocks to Carthage and have the following hands to work: **Peter Munroe, Patrick Shields, Corn. Dowd's** hands, **Willis D. Dowd, James Lewis, Thomas Fry, Joseph L. Reed, Thomas Eastridge** and son.

3560. 1827, Feb 24 -- 1823-1831 Court of Pleas and Quarter Sessions, Moore County, NC Page 165
[Deeds] **Right Deaton** to **John Deaton** was proven by **Isaac Deaton**
William Williams to **Lewis Williamson** was proven by **H. Kennedy**

3561. 1827, Mar 12-Jan 1, 1831 -- Record of Estates Book B Page 198, 275, Moore County, NC
Guardian Returns submitted for **Mary, Levi, William, Elizabeth** and **Celia Right** by guardian **Aaron Kennedy**

3562. 1827, Mar 22 -- Land Grant #2747, Moore County, NC
Henry Stutts received 6.5 acres located south of Buffalo Creek adjoining his own line, heirs of **James Wood** and **James Dunlap**. **John Stutts** and **Henry Stutts** were chain carriers.

3563. 1827, Mar 23 -- Land Grant #2766, Moore County, NC
Elizabeth McLeod received 56 acres located east of McLendons Creek adjoining **John McNeill, Angus McIver, McLendon, Alexr. McLeod, Deaton** and **Shaw. Alexr. McLeod Senr.** and **Alexr. Niel McLeod** were chain carriers.

3564. 1827, Apr 12 -- Chronicles and Records of Bensalem Presbyterian Church Page 10, Moore County, NC
Barbara Curry [daughter of **Lauchlin Curry** and **Sarah Buie**] died

3565. 1827, Apr 18 -- Will Book B Page 66, Moore County, NC
Will of **Malcolm Morrison**, Dec'd. Heirs: son **John Morrison** (of Richmond County), daughter **Margaret McLeod** (of Cumberland County and wife of **Murdoch McLeod**), daughter **Catherine Morrison**, daughter **Ann McCaskill** (wife of **Kenneth McCaskill**), son **Angus Morrison**. Executors: son **Angus Morrison**. Witnesses: **M. Martin** and **John McDonald Senr.** *[Editor's Note: no proven date but Malcolm Morrison d. 10 Jan 1829 buried at Old Scotch Cemetery]*

3566. 1827, May 21 -- 1823-1831 Court of Pleas and Quarter Sessions, Moore County, NC
[*jury duty next term - selected participants*] **Alexdr. Kennedy, Hezekiah Autry, Jesse Sanders** Esq., **Henry Stuts, Jeremiah Williams, William Cagle, Neill Caddell, James Morgan, Peter Cagle, David Kennedy, Harmon Brewer, Daniel Caddell, John Shuffield Jr., Peter Shamburger, Asa Sowell** and **John Kennedy**.

A. 1827, May 22 -- 1823-1831 Court of Pleas and Quarter Sessions, Moore County, NC Page 169
Ordered that **John Shuffied Junr.** be permitted to retail liquors at his usual place of dwelling for one year.

B. 1827, May 22 -- 1823-1831 Court of Pleas and Quarter Sessions, Moore County, NC Page 169
Ordered that **Wm. Jackson, Malcom McRimmon** and **Cornelius Dunlap** settle with **Wm. Barrett** guardian of **Malcom Graham** and **Elizabeth Graham**.

3567. 1827, May 22 -- 1823-1831 Court of Pleas and Quarter Sessions, Moore County, NC Page 171
Ordered that **Riland Miller** be appointed overseer of the road from Cabin Creek at **Leachs** to the Montgomery County line near **Archd. McNeill's** store and have the following hands to work: **Edmond Holland, Isaac Spivey, Ruben Allen, Archd. McNeill's** hands, **Stephen Davis** hands, **James Callicutt's** hands and **Mark Allen**.

3568. 1827, May 23 -- 1823-1831 Court of Pleas and Quarter Sessions, Moore County, NC Page 173-174
[Deeds] **Wm. Barrett, Mary Barrett, Andrew Graham, Malcolm Graham** and **Elizabeth Graham** to **James Bryant** proven by **Michael Bryant**
Robert Carson to **James Bryant** proven by **M. McCrummen**
Robert Carson to **Michael Bryant** proven by **James Bryant**
Joseph Buie to **Jesse Sowell** proven by **H. Kennedy**
David Kennedy to **James Gains** acknowledged
Medford Owen to **Everet Shuffield** proven by **Wm. Brewer**

William Freeman to **Reuben Freeman** was proven by **Wm. Brewer**
Reuben Freeman to **William Freeman** was proven by **Wm. Brewer**
George Hunsucker to **Abram Hunsucker** was proven by **Daniel Murchison**
Rodrick McAulay, **Malcolm McAulay**, **Ann McAulay**, **Alexr. McKinnon**, **Margaret McKinnon** to **Daniel McAulay** proven by **A. McKinnon**
William Feagan to **John Tyson** proven by **Corn. Dowd**
Daniel McNeill, Sheriff to **Levy Deaton** was proven by **Corn. Dowd**
John Richardson to **Dempsey Sowell** was acknowledged

3569.   1827, Jul 17 -- Land Grant #2796, Moore County, NC
Robert Wilson received 45 acres located north of Deep River above the Island Ford adjoining **Frazer**, **James McNeill** and **Lewis Nunnery**. **Phillip Wilson** and **James McNeill** were chain carriers.

3570.   1827, Jul 26 -- Chronicles and Records of Bensalem Presbyterian Church Page 7, Moore County, NC
Allen McAskill and **Nancy Muse** were married.

A.   1827, Aug 7 -- Obituary, *Raleigh Register and NC Gazette* [Raleigh, NC] Newspaper
"On the 16th inst. (Jul 1827), in Moore County, **John Tyson Jr.**, Esq."

B.   1827, Aug 7 -- Obituary, *Raleigh Register and NC Gazette* [Raleigh, NC] Newspaper
"At his residence in Carthage, Moore County, on the 10th instant [Dec 1828], General **Benjamin Person**, in the 35th year of his age."

3571.   1827, Aug 13 -- Land Grant #2749, Moore County, NC
Daniel Martin received 50 acres located on both sides of north prong of McLendons Creek adjoining the heirs of **Allan Martin** and **Donald McDonald**. **Angus Martin** and **Donald McDonald** were chain carriers.

3572.   1827, Aug 20 -- 1823-1831 Court of Pleas and Quarter Sessions, Moore County, NC
[jury duty - selected participants] **Daniel Caddell**, **John Shuffield**, **John Kennedy**, **Neill Caddell**, **James Morgan**, **Asa Sowell**, **David Kennedy**, **Harmon Brewer**, **John Ritter**, **Cornelius Caddell**, **Nathan Barrett**, **Hiram Hill** and **William Williams**.

3573.   1827, Aug 20 -- 1823-1831 Court of Pleas and Quarter Sessions, Moore County, NC Page 176
Ordered that **Nathan Fry** be appointed overseer in place of **Wm. Caddell** of the Raleigh Road from the Bay Pond to the Fayetteville Road below Carthage and have the following hands to work: **Wm. Caddell**, **Hardin Warner**, **Nathan Fry**, **Edward Fry**, **James Caddell**, **Saml. Vick**, **Lochart Fry**, **Edward Warner**, **Green B. Caddell**, **Sion Johnson**, **Alexr. Fry**, **John Estridge**, **Wm. Johnson**, **Jacob Fry** and **Tobias Caddell**.

3574.   1827, Aug 20 -- 1823-1831 Court of Pleas and Quarter Sessions, Moore County, NC Page 177
Ordered that **James Hill** be appointed overseer of the road from Bean's Bridge to the hill at the **Widow Bethune**'s in place of **John McIntosh** and have the following hands to work: **John J. McIntosh**, **Leonard Lawhon**, **John Muse**, **Miles Rouse**, **John McIntosh**, **John Rouse**, **Martin Hill**, **Walter Barrett**, **Dickson Ritter**, **Martin Rouse**, **Daniel Caddell** and **Enoch Wallis**.

A.   1827, Aug 20 -- 1823-1831 Court of Pleas and Quarter Sessions, Moore County, NC Page 177
Ordered that **Daniel Martin** be appointed overseer of the road from Martins Old Store to the Wolf Pit in place of **Thomas Bryant** and have the following hands to work: **Danl. Martin**, **Kinneth Martin**, **Robert Graham**, **Andrew Graham**, **Malcom Graham**, **Elisha Bryant**, **Angus Martin** and hands, **John McKeithen**, **William Gilmore**, **William Fry**, **Noah B. Fry**, **Tobias Fry** and **Margaret Martin** one hand.

3575.   1827, Aug 20 -- BLM General Land Office Document #2838, Copiah County, MS
Temple Carpenter (of Copiah County) received 79.94 acres from Jackson Land Office located in east half of southeast Quarter of Section 25, Township 10, Range 8.

3576.   1827, Aug 21 -- Land Grant #2758, Moore County, NC
Joseph G. Moore received 200 acres located on Wiers Branch adjoining **William Danely**, **Freeman** and **William Phillips**. **Charles Jones** and **George Alston** were chain carriers.

3577.   1827, Aug 21 -- 1823-1831 Court of Pleas and Quarter Sessions, Moore County, NC Page 178

John Deaton, guardian to Isaac Deaton resigned his guardianship.

3578. 1827, Aug 22 -- 1823-1831 Court of Pleas and Quarter Sessions, Moore County, NC Page 181
Ordered that **Robert Milton** be appointed overseer in place of **John Cagle** of the road from **Kennedy**'s Mill to the old road at **Solomon Brewers** and have the following hands to work: **John Cagle, Wm. Dunn, John Stuts, John Stuts** (son of H)**, Robert Milton, James Milton, Ansel Milton, Nathan Wallis, Matthew Williams, Henry Williams, David Lankford, George Davis, Jethrew Denson, Wm. Wood, John Williams, Daniel McNeill, Wm. Williams, Thomas Williams, Joseph Williams, Josiah Williams, Upshur Furr, Jason Sowell, Hiram Melton, Joseph Wallis** and **Aaron Kennedy**.

3579. 1827, Aug 22 -- 1823-1831 Court of Pleas and Quarter Sessions, Moore County, NC Page 182
Ordered that **William Daniley** be appointed overseer in place of **Jacob Cagle** of the road from **George Moores** to the branch near **McQueens** and have the same hands to work.

3580. 1827, Aug 22 -- 1823-1831 Court of Pleas and Quarter Sessions, Moore County, NC Page 182
Ordered that **Martin Cagle** be appointed overseer in place of **Nathaniel Tucker** of the road from the five mile post to the old road and have the following hands to work: **Martin Cagle, Nathaniel Tucker, Elijah Hancock, Gardner Bolin, Jonathan Cagle, Wm. Cagle** (son of Jacob)**, James Maness, Silas Wilson, Robt. Kennedy, Martin Cagle Jr., Henry Cagle** and **Miles Jordan**.

3581. 1827,.Aug 22 -- 1823-1831 Court of Pleas and Quarter Sessions, Moore County, NC Page 183
Ordered that **John Tyson** be appointed overseer of the road from Bean's Bridge to the Lick Branch at **Widow Elkins** and have the following hands to work: **Leonard Lawhon, Kindred Norden, Jesse Bean Jr., Calvin Cox** and **Edward Warner**.

A. 1827, Aug 22 -- 1823-1831 Court of Pleas and Quarter Sessions, Moore County, NC Page 183
Ordered that **Cornelius Caddell** be appointed overseer of the road from the fork near **Naylers** to the Lick Branch at **Widow Elkins** and have the following hands to work: **Nehemiah Birckhead, Benjamin Phillips, Corn. Caddell, Willis Dowd** and **Bryant Dowd**.

B. 1827, Aug 22 -- 1823-1831 Court of Pleas and Quarter Sessions, Moore County, NC Page 183
Ordered that **William Barrett Jur.** be appointed overseer of the road from the Bay Pond to the Wolf Pit in place of **Wm. Jackson** and have the following hands to work: **Right Deaton, Richd. Warner, Merrill Cox, Ervin Cox, Holden Cox, John Martin, John McSween, Angus Martin, Thomas Hannon, Wm.** and **Samuel Jacksons** hands, **Joseph Jackson, Allen Martin, Thomas Fry, John Graham** and **Alexr. Martin**.

3582. 1827, Aug 22 -- 1823-1831 Court of Pleas and Quarter Sessions, Moore County, NC Page 183
Ordered that **John Garner** be appointed overseer in place of **Lewis Garner** of the road from the [Randolph] County line on the east side of **Nicolas Nalls** to **William Williamsons** and have the same hands to work.

3583. 1827, Aug 24 -- 1823-1831 Court of Pleas and Quarter Sessions, Moore County, NC Page 187
Ordered that **Daniel McNeill**, Sheriff take in to custody at the next term an orphan **Lydia Lakey** who had been bound to **George Kennedy**. She can remain with **Kennedy** until then unless he moves out of the county.

A. 1827, Aug 24 -- 1823-1831 Court of Pleas and Quarter Sessions, Moore County, NC Page 187
Ordered that **William Davis** be appointed overseer of the road from the gate at Col. **Jones** to the Williams Fork and have the same hands to work.

3584. 1827, Aug 24 -- 1823-1831 Court of Pleas and Quarter Sessions, Moore County, NC Page 187
[Deeds] **Michael Bryant** to **Richard Gilmore** acknowledged
Medford [Owen] to **Everet Shuffield** proven by **Wm. Brewer**
John Richardson to **Phillip Brooks** acknowledged
Thomas Ritter to **Martin Hill** proven by **Eleazer Birckhead**
Thomas Graham to **Sally Graham** proven by **Andrew Graham**
Nancy McLeod to **Allan McLean** proven by **Daniel McMillan**

3585. 1827, Aug 28 -- Deed, Moore County, NC
Hiram Kennedy deeded **David Kennedy** 280 acres located on Bear Creek adjoining **Everet Smith**, **Isaac Smith**, his own line (formerly **Simon Hart**), **Anderson B. Smith** and **William Cagle**. **E.S. Kennedy** and **E.M. Kennedy** were witnesses. [*Editor's Note: located at the Moore County Library in Carthage, NC in Vertical Files*]

3586. 1827, Sep 15 -- Bible of David Kennedy and Joanna Moore, Moore County, NC
Liddy Kennedy died. [Born Dec 15, 1807]

3587. 1827, Sep 25 -- Obituary, *Raleigh Register and NC Gazette* [Raleigh, NC] Newspaper
"At Mechanics Hill, in Moore County, on the 15th instant [Sep 15, 1827]. Miss **Lydia Kennedy**, youngest daughter of Mr. **David Kennedy**, aged 19 years and 9 months. In her death her aged parents and connections have to mourn the loss of a most dutiful child and an affectionate relative. She was amiable in her disposition, moral in her conduct, agreeable in her manners and always ready to relieve distressed humanity when in reach."

3588. 1827, Oct 1 -- Land Grant #2763, Moore County, NC
Donald McDonald received 30 acres located north of McLendons Creek adjoining **John McDonald**. **Angus McDonald** and **Angus Martin** were chain carriers.

3589. 1827, Oct 1 -- BLM General Land Office Document #1177, Lincoln County, MS
William Smith, assignee of **John Carpenter** received 80 acres from west of Pearl River Land Office located in west half of southwest Quarter of Section 19, Township 8, Range 9.

3590. 1827, Oct 27 -- *A History of Sandy Creek Baptist Association* by George Purefoy, Page 92
John Lawler, **Isaac Teague** and **Stephen Scott** from Fall Creek Church (Chatham County) and Elder **Eli Phillips**, **Joseph G. Moore** and **Phillip Brooks** from Friendship Church (Moore County) and **David Kennedy**, **Samuel Dunlap** and **Daniel McKimon** from Mechanic's Hill Church (Moore County) were delegates to the Association meeting at Haw River Mountain Meeting House in Chatham County, NC.

3591. 1827, Nov 19 -- 1823-1831 Court of Pleas and Quarter Sessions, Moore County, NC
[*jury duty next term - selected participants*] **John Cockman**, **John Garner**, **William Cagle**, **Jacob Stuts**, **John Spivay**, **Jesse Sowell**, **Alexr. Kennedy**, **Bryan Boroughs** and **George Hunsucker**.

A. 1827, Nov 19 -- 1823-1831 Court of Pleas and Quarter Sessions, Moore County, NC Page 191
Ordered that **Hugh Moore** be appointed overseer of the road from **Davis'** old field to the fork of the road called the Island Ford Road near **John B. Kelly's** and have the following hands to work: **Daniel H. Muse**, **Angus McDonald**, **Asa Muse**, **Jesse Rodgers Jur.**, **Jesse F. Muse**, **Westly Nailer**, **Nathan Barrett**, **James B. Muse**,

Howard Muse, Westley Birckhead, Alexr. C. Curry, Daniel McDonald, John Morrison (Taylor), Henry Faucett, Allen McCaskill, Jesse Hedgpeth, Neill McDonald, John McNeill (Hatter), John Faucett, John Fry, Benjn. Fry, B. Smith, John Kelly (Taylor), Angus Martin, Seawell's hands Robin, Harray, Tom, Jack and Yamer, Person's hand Will and James Lewis.

B.   1827, Nov 19 -- 1823-1831 Court of Pleas and Quarter Sessions, Moore County, NC Page 191
Last will and testament of Joab Cheek, Dec'd. proven by Angus McKinnon.

3592.   1827, Nov 19 -- 1823-1831 Court of Pleas and Quarter Sessions, Moore County, NC Page 191
Jesse Brown, Wm. Brewer, Burwell Deaton appointed to settle with Edward Holland, Administrator of Estate of Richd. Holland, Dec'd.

3593.   1827, Nov 20 -- 1823-1831 Court of Pleas and Quarter Sessions, Moore County, NC Page 192
Ordered that Isaac Spivey be appointed overseer of the road in place of Wm. Brewer from Spivey to McNeill's store and have the following hands in addition: Matthew Shuffield, Enoch Wallis and Shadrach Davis.

3594.   1827, Nov 21 -- 1823-1831 Court of Pleas and Quarter Sessions, Moore County, NC Page 194
[Deeds] Joseph Allen to Mark Allen was proven by Britain Britt
John, William and Daniel McAulay to Anderson B. Smith was acknowledged
John, William and Daniel McAulay to James Dunlap was proven by Anderson B. Smith
Reuben Freeman to Wm. Freeman was proven by Alex. McKinnon
Julius Glascock to Gideon Seawell acknowledged
Baley Williamson to John M. Hodgin was proven by Wm. Brewer
Daniel McAulay and Malcolm McAulay to John McAulay was proven by power of attorney Roderick McAulay
[Bill of Sale] Hiram Kennedy to Norman Mathewson proven by David Kennedy

A.   1827, Nov 21 -- 1823-1831 Court of Pleas and Quarter Sessions, Moore County, NC Page 195
Hiram Hill, Jesse Rodgers, N. Barrett, Cornelius Caddell and Westley Naylor divided the estate of George Glascock Dec'd. located on McLendons Creek as follows: Lot #1 - 35 acres to Elizabeth Glascock; Lot #2 - 45 acres to Patsey Glascock adjoining Phillips; Lot #3 - 60 acres to Nathan Holloway; Lot#4 – 60 acres to George Glascock adjoining John B. Kelly.

3595.   1827, Nov 21 -- Land Grant #2791, Moore County, NC
Dempsey Sowell received 16 acres

located south of Richland Creek adjoining his own line, **Asa Sowell** and **Tyson**. **John Ritter** and **Jason Sowell** were chain carriers.

3596.   1827, Dec 20 -- Bible of **Jesse** and **Nancy Seawell**, Moore County, NC
E.Q. Sowell and **Mary D. Phillips** were married

3597.   1827 (undated estimate) -- Record of Estates Book B Page148-150, 215-216, Moore County, NC
Estate of **Joab Cheek**, Dec'd. by Administrators **John Cheek Senr.** and **Joab Cheek Junr.** Inventory includes five negroes: **Starling**, **Henry**, **Sudah**, **Sarah** and **Mary**. _Items were purchased by the following_: **Noah Richardson**, **Wm. B. Cheek**, **Brantly Cheek**, **Doctor Ingram**, **Wm. Hancock**, **John Cheek Junr.**, **Phillip Brooks**, **Stephen Seal**, **Lewis Phillips**, **Abner Smith**, **Mary Cheek Junr.**, **Wm. Hill**, **Angus McDonald**, **Joab Cheek Junr.**, **John Stewart**, **Mathew Phillips**, **John Hancock**, **Edward Harper**, **Abner Elkins**, **Wm. Phillips**, **Alec Phillips**, **Jesse Sowell**, **Jesse Womble**, **Edward Phillips**, **John Coal**, **John Martin**, **Lovdy Tyson** and **Daniel Campbell**.

3598.   1828, Jan 13 -- Land Grant #3114, Moore County, NC
John McLeod received 17 acres located on the drains of Buffalo Creek adjoining **John McKay** and **David Jones**. **David Jones** and **Allen Jones** were chain carriers.

3599.   1828, Feb 5 -- Land Grant #2625, Randolph County, NC
William Gardner received 45 acres located on Fork Creek and the [Moore] County line adjoining **John Shamburger** and his own line. **Medford Owen** and **James Lathem** were chain carriers.

3600.   1828, Feb 10 -- Will Book B Page 59, Moore County, NC
Nuncupative Will of **John Comer**, Dec'd. [died Feb 11, 1828]. Heirs: wife and children [unnamed]. Executors: **Neill McLeod** Esq. and **John Dunlap**. Witness: **Neill McLeod**, **John Dunlap** and **Nathaniel Tucker**. Proven Feb 20, 1828.

3601.   1828, Feb 16 -- 1813-1828 Marriage Licenses, Moore County, NC
John Johnson and **Nellay Bryant** were married by **Corn. Dowd**.

3602.   1828, Feb 19 -- 1823-1831 Court of Pleas and Quarter Sessions, Moore County, NC Page 198-199

The will of **Joseph Allen** Dec'd. was proven by **Mark Allen**, Executor and **Edmond Hollan**. Administration granted to **Mark Allen**.

3603.   1828, Feb 19 -- 1823-1831 Court of Pleas and Quarter Sessions, Moore County, NC Page 199
Ordered that **Robert Milton**, overseer of the road from **David Kennedy**'s bridge to **Solomon Brewer**'s old place and have the following additional hands to work: **Lewis Garner Jr.**, **Anderson Smith** and **Stephen Maness**.

3604.   1828, Feb 20 -- 1823-1831 Court of Pleas and Quarter Sessions, Moore County, NC Page 200
Ordered that **James Caviness** be appointed overseer of the road from Bear Creek to **Williamsons** and have the following hands to work: **Bradly Garner**'s hands, **Wm. Williamson**'s hands, **Thomas Person**'s hands, **Hiram Williamson**, **William Williamson**, **Jas. Garner**'s hands, **Wm. Gains**, **Hiram Davidson**, **John Myrick**, **Wm. Deaton**, **Edward Moore** and **Arch. McDonald**.

A.   1828, Feb 20 -- 1823-1831 Court of Pleas and Quarter Sessions, Moore County, NC Page 201
Ordered that **Dabney Phillips** be appointed overseer of the road from the Election House across the [Deep] River to the Chatham [County] line and have the usual hands to work.

3605.   1828, Feb 20 -- 1823-1831 Court of Pleas and Quarter Sessions, Moore County, NC Page 202
Ordered that **Bryan Boroughs** and **Alexr. McNeill** be appointed to settle with **Archd. Shields**, administrator of **Saml. Perry** Dec'd.

3606.   1828, Feb 20 -- 1823-1831 Court of Pleas and Quarter Sessions, Moore County, NC Page 202
Jesse Brown allowed 23 polls for insolvency for District 6 and 8 in 1826

A.   1828, Feb 22-23 -- 1823-1831 Court of Pleas and Quarter Sessions, Moore County, NC Page 206-207, 209
Administration of **John Phillips**, Dec'd. granted to **William Phillips**. **Sarah Phillips** v. heirs of **John Phillips**, Dec'd. **Lewis Phillips Senr.** appointed guardian of the infant heirs of **John Phillips**, Dec'd. for this suit. **John Cheek**, **George Stewart** and **Archd. Shields** were appointed to lay off a year's provision.

3607.   1828, Feb 23 -- 1823-1831 Court of Pleas and Quarter Sessions, Moore County, NC Page 210
[Deeds] **Joseph Allen Senr.** to **Joseph Allen Jr.** proven by **Reuben Allen**
Patty Glascock to **Jesse Hedgepth** proven by **Jesse F. Muse**
Cornelius Shields, **Mary Shields**, **James Shields**, **Susannah Shields**, **Robert Hardin** and **Jane Hardin** to

Michael Rollins and wife **Amy** proven by **Archd. Shields**
Michael Rolin and **Amy Rolin** to **James Davis** proven by **Cornelius Shields**
Jesse Sowell to **Asa Sowell** acknowledged
John McAulay, **William McAulay** and **Daniel McAulay** to **Levy Deaton** proven by **Donald McDonald**
Roderick McAulay to **John McAulay**, **William McAulay** and **Daniel McAulay** proven by **Malcolm McAulay**
[Bill of Sale] **Asa Sowell** to **Jesse Sowell** and **Wm. Barrett** acknowledged

3608.   1828, Feb 23 -- 1823-1831 Court of Pleas and Quarter Sessions, Moore County, NC Page 212
Sarah Melton, Administrator of **Henry Melton**, Dec'd. returned an inventory

3609.   1828, Mar 4 -- Will Book B Page 58-59, Moore County, NC
Will of **Richard Upton**, Dec'd. Heirs: wife, son **James**, son **George**, son **Richard** and daughter **Dorcus**. Executors: son **James Upton** and **Joseph G. Moore**. Witness: **Noah Richardson**. Proven May 1828.

3610.   1828 [estimated date] -- Record of Estates Book B Page 152-153,243, Moore County, NC

Estate of **Richard Upton**, Dec'd. by Administrators **Joseph Moore** and **Jas. Upton**. _Notes due on the following_: **Elizabeth McIver**, **John Richardson**, **Micajah Thomas**, **Isham Sewell**, **Calvin Cox** and **John Brooks**. _Items purchased by the following_: **George Upton**, **Wm. Harris**, **John Dowdy**, **Wm. Morgan**, **Angus McDonald**, **Jas. H. Muse**, **Neill McDonald**, **Dorcas Upton**, **Neill McIntosh**, **George Medling**, **Daniel McNeill**, **Jascay Phillips**, **Tolbert Russell**, **Wm. Danielly**, **John Dowd**, **Asa Muse** and **Benjn. Medling**.

3611.   1828, Mar 19 -- Obituary, _Hillsborough Recorder_ [Hillsborough, NC] Newspaper

"In Perry County, AL on the 19th ult. [Feb 19, 1828], while on a visit to his friends, Mr. **Bryan Boroughs**, of Moore County, in this state, in the 20th year of his age."

3612.   1828, Apr 6 -- Bible of Samuel Barrett and Elizabeth Graham, Moore County, NC

Samuel Barrett and **Elizabeth Graham** were married

3613.   1828, May 20 -- Land Grant #2762, Moore County, NC

Joseph Moore received 50 acres located on Wiers Branch adjoining **Wm. Danely**, **Freeman** and **William Phillips**. **Charles Jones** and **George Alston** were chain carriers.

3614.   1828, May 20 -- 1823-1831 Court of Pleas and Quarter Sessions, Moore County, NC

[_jury duty next term - selected participants_] **Wm. Brewer** Esq., **Nathan Morgan**, **Wm. Caddell**, **Hezekiah Autry**, **Asa Sowell**, **George Cagle Jr.**, **Jeremiah Williams**, **Henry Stuts Sr.**, **Wm. Williamson**, **John Ritter**, **Merimon Brit**, **Thomas Ritter**, **Peter Shamburger**, **Wm. Cagle**, **Levy Deaton**, **Wm. Cagle Jr.** and **Wm. Jones**.

A.   1828, May 20 -- 1823-1831 Court of Pleas and Quarter Sessions, Moore County, NC Page 213

The non cupertave will of **John Comer** Dec'd. was proven by **Nathaniel Tucker** Esq.

B.   1828, May 20 -- 1823-1831 Court of Pleas and Quarter Sessions, Moore County, NC Page 213

The last will and testament of **Richard Upton** Dec'd. was proven by **Noah Richardson**. **Joseph Moore** and **James Upton** named executors.

C.   1828, May 20 -- 1823-1831 Court of Pleas and Quarter Sessions, Moore County, NC Page 214

Ordered that **William Hancock** be appointed overseer of the road from Hurican gap to the ford on Deep River near Mrs. **Streets** and have the following hands to work: **Wm. Handcock** two hands, **John Handcock**, **S.D. Smith**, **Wm. Dowd's** hands, **George Stewart**, **Robert Hardin**, **Wm. Davis'** hand, **Robert Phillips**, **Lewis Phillips**, **John Cheek** (son of **Richd.**), **Archd. Shields Jur.**, **Amos Cheek**, **Leonard Cheek**, **Wm. Phillips** (son of **Lewis**), **Josiah Cheek** (son of **Richd.**), **James King**, **Stephen King**, **Wm. Stewart**, **John Carrell**, **Alexr. Carrell Jur.** and **Wm. Cole**.

3615.   1828, May 20 -- 1823-1831 Court of Pleas and Quarter Sessions, Moore County, NC Page 215

Ordered that **Mark Allen** be appointed overseer in place of **Riland Miller** of the road Cabin Creek at **Leaches** to the Montgomery County line near **Archd. McNeill**'s store and have the following hands to work: **Riland Miller, Edmond Holland, Isaac Spivay, Ruben Allen, Archd. McNeill**'s hands, **Stephen Davis'** hands, **James Callicutt**'s hands, **Thomas McNeill** and **John McNeill**.

3616.   1828, May 20 -- 1823-1831 Court of Pleas and Quarter Sessions, Moore County, NC Page 217
The following appointed to list the taxable for 1828: (District #3) **Jesse Sanders**; (District #8) **Nathaniel Tucker**.

A.   1828, May 20 -- 1823-1831 Court of Pleas and Quarter Sessions, Moore County, NC Page 217
Ordered that **Dabney Phillips** be overseer of the road from Deep River to Chatham County line and the following hands to work: **John Cheek**'s hands, **Wm. Phillips, Brantly Cheek, James Cheek, John Cheek Jur., Mary Cheek**'s hand, **Wm. B. Cheek**'s hand, **Daniel Melone, Joab Cheek** and Mr. **Linch**.

B.   1828, May 20 -- 1823-1831 Court of Pleas and Quarter Sessions, Moore County, NC Page 217
Ordered that **Wm. Davis** be overseer of the road from **Alston**'s Fork to Deep River and the following hands to work: **George Alston**'s hands, **Isaac Fields**, Mrs. **Street**'s hands, **Wm. Hill**, Mrs. **Martin**'s hands and **John Ferguson**.

C.   1828, May 21 -- 1823-1831 Court of Pleas and Quarter Sessions, Moore County, NC Page 219
The last will and testament of **Sabra Gilbert**, Dec'd. was proven by **Alexr. McNeill**.

3617.   1828, May 21 -- 1823-1831 Court of Pleas and Quarter Sessions, Moore County, NC Page 219
Ordered that **James Caveness** be appointed overseer of the road from Bear Creek to **Williamson**'s and have the following hands to work in addition to the former hands: **Jeremiah Williams, David Brewer** and **Josiah Kennedy**.

3618.   1828, May 21 -- 1823-1831 Court of Pleas and Quarter Sessions, Moore County, NC Page 220
[Deeds] **Anderson B. Smith** to **John Dunlap** acknowledged
John Sheffield to **Martin** and **Elijah Sheffield** acknowledged
[Bill of Sale] **John Shuffield** to **Martin Shuffield** acknowledged
John Shuffield to **Elijah Shuffield** acknowledged
Daniel McNeill, Sheriff to **James Dunlap** acknowledged

3619.   1828, May 21 -- BLM General Land Office Document #2296, Lauderdale County, AL
John Richardson received 159.43 acres from Huntsville Land Office located in northwest Quarter of Section 14, Township 1, Range 9.

3620.   1828, May 21 -- BLM General Land Office Document #2298, Lauderdale County, AL
John Gresham, assignee of **John Richardson** received 79.72 acres from Huntsville Land Office located in east half of the southeast Quarter of Section 14, Township 1, Range 9.

3621.   1828, May 21 -- BLM General Land Office Document #2301, Lauderdale County, AL
Thomas Gresham, assignee of **John Richardson** received 79.35 acres from Huntsville Land Office located in east half of the southeast Quarter of Section 3, Township 1, Range 9.

3622.   1828, May 28 -- Record of Estates Book B Page 141-142, Moore County, NC
Estate of **John D. Phillips**, Dec'd. by Administrator **William Phillips**. *Items purchased by the following*: **Corns. Shields, Joseph Person, Daniel McNeill, Richard Phillips, Jesse Womble, Lewis Phillips, Dabney Phillips, Widow Phillips, Brantley Cheek, Richard Gilbert, Abram Stuts, Mathew Phillips, John Hancock, Robert Harden, John Martin, Benjamin Shields, Dennis Phillips, John Cheek, Edward Carrell, Henry Phillips, Daniel Malone, Fanning Moore, George Stewart, William Hancock, Robert Phillips, N. McLarin, Lewis Phillips Senr., Widow Elkins, Blake Cheek** and **Wm. Phillips (son of Sion)**.

3623.   1828, Jun 30 -- U.S. Postal Records, Moore County, NC
Archibald Munroe appointed Postmaster of Caledonia Post Office

3624.   1828, Jul 21 -- Land Grant #2789, Moore County, NC
Daniel Muse received 200 acres located on Horsepen Branch of Richland Creek adjoining **George Ritter**, **Abraham Stutts**, **James Dowdy** and **Duncan McIntosh**. **Neil McIntosh** and **Marvel Ritter** were chain carriers.

3625.   1828, Aug 18 -- 1823-1831 Court of Pleas and Quarter Sessions, Moore County, NC
[jury duty - selected participants] **Wm. Williamson, Levy Deaton, John Ritter, Wm. Cagle, Wm. Jones, James Garner** and **Wm. Williams**.

3626.   1828, Aug 18-19 -- 1823-1831 Court of Pleas and Quarter Sessions, Moore County, NC Page 223,225
Administration of the estate of **John Ritter Senr.** Dec'd. granted to **John Ritter Jr.**
Administration of the estate of **Alexr. Kennedy** Dec'd. granted to **Elias Kennedy**
Administration of the estate of **George Moore** Dec'd. granted to **Anderson B. Smith**

3627.   1828, Aug 18 -- 1823-1831 Court of Pleas and Quarter Sessions, Moore County, NC Page 224
Ordered that **John Lakey**, age 14, be bound to **Robert Milton** until age 21

A.   1828, Aug 18 -- 1823-1831 Court of Pleas and Quarter Sessions, Moore County, NC Page 232-233
The following were appointed to lay off a portion of 369 acres located North of Deep River on John Phillips Creek and School House Spring Branch for **Sarah Phillips**, widow of **John D. Phillips** adjoining **Lewis Phillips, John Cheek Sr., John Phillips** and the branch to the Meeting House: **James C. Davis, William C. Davis, William B. Hudson, John Cheek Jr., Joab Cheek, Brantly Cheek, Wm. B. Cheek, James Cheek, Jesse Brewer, Charles Brady, James McNeill** and **John Cheek**.

B.   1828, Aug 19 -- 1823-1831 Court of Pleas and Quarter Sessions, Moore County, NC Page 224
The last will and testament of **Lydia Tyson**, Dec'd. was proven by **Henry Branson**.

3628.   1828, Aug 19 -- 1823-1831 Court of Pleas and Quarter Sessions, Moore County, NC Page 226
Ordered that **Anderson B. Smith** be appointed overseer in place of **Robert Milton** of the road from **Kennedy**'s Mill to the old road at **Solomon Brewers** and have the following hands to work: **John Cagle, Wm. Dunn, John Stuts, John Stuts** (son of H), **Robert Milton, James Milton, Ansel Milton, Nathan Wallis, Matthew Williams, Henry Williams, David Lankford, George Davis, Jethrew Denson, Wm. Wood, John Williams, Daniel McNeill, Wm. Williams, Thomas Williams, Joseph Williams, Josiah Williams, Upshur Furr, Isom Sowell, Hiram Melton, Joseph Wallis, Aaron Kennedy, Lewis Garner** and **Stephen Maness**.

A.   1828, Aug 19 -- 1823-1831 Court of Pleas and Quarter Sessions, Moore County, NC Page 227
Ordered that **Malcom Graham** be appointed overseer of the road from Martins Old Store to the Wolf Pit in place of **Daniel Martin** and have the following hands to work: **Daniel Martin, Kinneth Martin, Robert Graham, Elisha Bryant, Angus Martin** and hands, **John McKeithen, Wm. Gilmore, Wm. Fry, Noah B. Fry, Tobias Fry, Margaret Martin** one hand, **Daniel Curry, Angus McDonald** and **Normon Martin**.

B.   1828, Aug 19 -- 1823-1831 Court of Pleas and Quarter Sessions, Moore County, NC Page 227
Ordered that **Richard Warner** be appointed overseer of the road from the Bay Pond to the Wolf Pit in place of **William Barrett** and have the following hands to work: **Right Deaton, Wm. Barrett Jur., Merrill Cox, Ervin Cox, Holden Cox, John Martin, John McSween, Angus Martin, Thomas Hannon, Wm.** and **Samuel Jackson**'s hands, **Joseph Jackson, Allin Martin, Thomas Fry, John Graham, Alexr. Martin** and **Benjn. Person's** hands.

3629.   1828, Aug 19 -- 1823-1831 Court of Pleas and Quarter Sessions, Moore County, NC Page 227
Ordered that **Colin Munroe** be appointed overseer of the road from **McIvers** fork of the Joel Road to Dry Creek

and work the following hands: **John Munroe, Kenneth Morison, Angus McCaskill, John McCaskill**'s hand, **Daniel McDonald**'s hand, **Levy Deaton**'s hand, **Angus Morison, David Richardson, Wm. Deaton, John Deaton, James Cahey, Charles McArthur, Isaac Deaton** and **Matthew Deaton**.

3630. 1828, Aug 19 -- 1823-1831 Court of Pleas and Quarter Sessions, Moore County, NC Page 228
Ordered that **David Brewer** overseer of the road from Bear Creek to **George Moores** and have the following additional hands to work: **James Garner, Archd. McDonald, Hiram Davidson, Major Johnson, Ranson Stutts** and **Leonard Stutts**.

3631. 1828, Aug 19 -- 1823-1831 Court of Pleas and Quarter Sessions, Moore County, NC Page 227
Ordered that **Mark Allen** be appointed overseer in place of **Britton Britt** for the road from Mill Creek to the fork east of **Archd. McNeills** and work the following hands: **Britton Britt, Alfred Britt, Avington Britt, Daniel Munroe, Jeremiah Renolds, Joseph Allen, John Morgan, Becom Britt, Wm. Morgan, N. Lewis, John Smith** and **Hiram Deaton**.

3632. 1828, Aug 21 -- 1823-1831 Court of Pleas and Quarter Sessions, Moore County, NC Page 229
Susannah Kennedy v. **Elias Kennedy**, administrator. **Josiah Kennedy** was appointed guardian to **John, Sally** and **Sparks Kennedy**, heirs of **Alexr. Kennedy** Dec'd.

3633. 1828, Aug 22 -- 1823-1831 Court of Pleas and Quarter Sessions, Moore County, NC Page 231
[Deeds] **Asa Sowell** to **Neill McIntosh** and **John B. Kelly** proven by **Jas. H. Lewis**
Medford Owens to **Thomas Brown** was proven by **Jesse Brown**
Asa Sowell to **Samuel Jackson** proven by **Q. Sowell**
Andrew Graham and **Malcom Graham** to **Michael Bryant** proven by **Thos. Bryant**

3634. 1828, Aug 22 -- 1823-1831 Court of Pleas and Quarter Sessions, Moore County, NC Page 233
Jesse Brown Esq., **Elias Kennedy, William Jones, Lauchlin McNeill** appointed to lay off 1 years provision for **Delila Moore** and family. [*Editor's Note: Widow of George Moore*]

3635. 1828, Aug 22 -- 1823-1831 Court of Pleas and Quarter Sessions, Moore County, NC Page 233
James England, Bryan Boroughs and **Alexr. McNeill** appointed to lay off 1 years provision for **Susannah Kennedy** and family. [*Editor's Note: Widow of Alexander Kennedy*]

3636. 1828, Aug 22 -- 1823-1831 Court of Pleas and Quarter Sessions, Moore County, NC Page 233
Corn. Shields Esq., **Alexr. McNeill, Bryan Boroughs** and **Bradly Garner** appointed to lay off 1 years provision for **Elizabeth Ritter**. [*Editor's Note: Widow of John Ritter*]

3637. 1828, Aug 22 -- 1823-1831 Court of Pleas and Quarter Sessions, Moore County, NC Page 234
John Ritter Junr. returned an inventory of the estate of **John Ritter Senr**.

3638. 1828, Aug 23 -- Land Grant #2793, Moore County, NC
Jacob Cagle received 170 acres located on both sides of Bear Creek adjoining **John Shamburger, Martin Cagle** and his own line. **George Cagle** and **William Cagle** were chain carriers.

3639. 1828, Aug 26 -- Land Grant #2765, Moore County, NC
John Cockman received 150 acres located on Buffalo Creek adjoining his own line where he lives and **McKoy. Josiah Cockman** and **Michael Cockman** were chain carriers. [*Editor's Note: Noah Cockman deeded to Ann R. Burns 1895*].

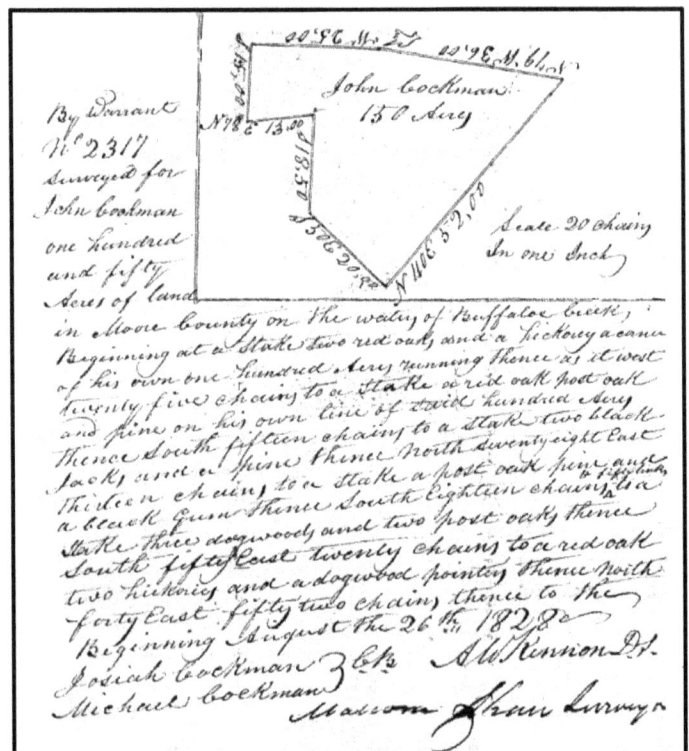

3640.　　　1828, Sep 6 -- Will Book B Page 83-86, Moore County, NC
Will of **Nicholas Nall**, Dec'd. (Amended Sep 24, 1830) Heirs: daughter **Elizabeth Tomlinson** and husband **Richard Tomlinson**, daughter **Mary Tyson** and husband **Jacob Tyson**, daughter **Ann Lee** and husband **Martin Lee**, son-in-law **Aaron Tyson**, husband of daughter **Winny** (*tract of land and mills and* **Saul, Carter, Mariah** *and* **Lucrecia**), grandson **James Goodwin Tomlinson** (*tract of land south of the road from my house to* **Aaron Tysons** *both in Randolph and Moore County*), granddaughter **Amilia Tyson** (*tract of land north of the road from my house to* **Aaron Tyson** *in Randolph County and negroes and two free holders to split with* **James Goodwin Tomlinson:** **Charles, Aleck, Pork, Dick, Silva** *and her three children* **Ann, Delina** *and* **Elesia** *and* **Sarah, Isaac, Rose, Frank, Will, Winny** *and her children* **John, Evelina, Alfred, Carolina** *and also* **Westly** *and* **Nancy**) and grandson **William Tyson**. Executors: **Hugh Moffitt** (replaced by **David Kennedy** and **James G. Tomlinson** in 1830). Witnesses: **John Shamburger** and **Andrew Yow** (1828), **Stephen Moffitt, William Moffitt** and **S.C. Bruce** (1830). Proven Aug 1833 by **John Shamburger, Andrew Yow** and **S.C. Bruce**.

3641.　　　1828, Sep 18-19 -- Record of Estates Book B, Moore County, NC Page 153, 158-162, 167, 207-208
Estate of **John Ritter Sr.**, Dec'd.by Administrator **John Ritter**. *Items were purchased by the following*: **Thomas Williams** (son of **Jer.**), **John Ritter, James H. Muse, Elizabeth Ritter, William. Ritter, Jacob Stuts** (of **Chr.**), **Wm. W. Morgan, Shadrack Maness, Alexr. McIntosh, Samuel Jackson, Martin Hill, John Stuts** (of **Jacob**), **Henry Stuts Sr., Jesse Bean Jr., Wm. Brown, James Garner, Abner Brown, Henry Maness, Aaron Kennedy, Wm. Dunn, Susan Ritter, Henry Stuts, George Hunsucker, Githroe Denson, Bryant R. McDonald, James Lewis, George Hunsucker Jr., Leonard Stuts, Robert Milton, John Hunsucker, Everet Ritter, John Stuts** (of **H**), **John Williams, Daniel Muse Jr., Henry Stuts Jr., James Ritter, Daniel Muse, George Moore** and **John Moore**. *Notes due on the following*: **L. Kennedy, Alexr. Kennedy, George Hunsucker, John T. Ritter, Wm. Hunsucker, John Milton, John Richardson, William W. Morgan, Anderson B. Smith, David Kennedy, William Waddell, Shadrick Maness, William Maness, John Ritter, David Langford, Thomas Dannelly, Nathan Wallis** and **William Cagle**.

3642.　　　1828, Oct 9-10 and Nov 14 -- Record of Estates Book B Page 163-166, 233, Moore County, NC
Estate of **Alexander Kennedy**, Dec'd. by Administrator **Elias M. Kennedy**. *Notes on the following*: **John Melton, Neill Latham, Hiram Davidson, Joseph Argo, Chrs. Stuts** and **John Stutts**. *Items purchased by the following*: **Daniel McNeill** (Sheriff), **James Hains, Anderson B. Smith, John Shamburger, Cornelusy Dowd Jur., John Lowdermilk, Edward Moore, Jeremiah Williams, Charles Brady, Josiah Kennedy, Enoch S. Kennedy, John Kennedy, Susannah Kennedy, James Keahey, James Garner, John Maness, Peter Shamburger, Aaron Kennedy, Robert Kennedy, Jesse Brown Sr., Hiram Milton, Asa Sowell, Archd. McDonald, Wm. M. Johnson, Baley Williamson, James McNeill, James Johnson, Kenneth McCaskel, Henry Bray, Abner Brown, Jacob Stuts** (**Chr.**), **Angus Morrison, Daniel Bruer, Isaac Brown, William Williamson** (**B**), **Abraham Stuts, Bradley Garner Senr., Lewis Garner, John Hunsucker, William Williams Jr., Thomas Williams, Dicy Kennedy, Lewis Williamson, Major Johnson** and **John Ritter**.

3643.　　　1828, Oct 23-Nov 17 -- Record of Estates Book B Page 162-163, 168, Moore County, NC
Estate of **Hannah Duckworth**, Dec'd. by Administrator **Daniel McNeill**. *Items purchased by the following*: **Delila Moore, William Stewart, Jesse Stafford, Leonard Stuts, Bradley Brady, Alexr. Carrell, John H. Freeman, Joseph Moore, Joab Phillips, Christian Stuts, Calvin Cox, Thomas Williams, Asa Sowell, Carrell Brady, George Stuts, Abram Stuts, James McNeill, Phillip Brooks, Charles Brady, Harbert Cole, John Danielly, Wm. Hunsucker Jun., James King, Stephen Davis, Robert Holloman, John Danielly Junr., Joseph G. Moore, John Hunsucker, John Smith, Joseph J. Person, Isham Sowell, Quimbay Sowell, George Stewart, Susanah Stuts, James Harden, James H. Muse, Patrick Shields** and **Hugh Moore**.

3644.　　　1828, Oct 28 -- *A History of Sandy Creek Baptist Association* by George Purefoy, Page 97
Zacheus Boroughs, Bryant Boroughs and **J. Teague** from Fall Creek Church (Chatham County) and Elder **Eli Phillips, James Dowdy** and **John Phillips** from Friendship Church (Moore County) and **David Kennedy**,

Thomas Williams and **Aaron Kennedy** from Mechanic's Hill Church (Moore County) were delegates to the Association meeting at Mount Gilead Meeting House in Chatham County, NC.

A.   1828, Oct 28 -- Land Grant #2525, Montgomery County, NC
John Jordan received 20 acres located on the mouth of Suggs Creek adjoining **Widow Spencer**, **Widow Suggs** and his own line. **Jacob Jordan** and **Enoch Jordan** were chain carriers.

3645.   1828, Oct 29 -- Land Grant #2794, Moore County, NC
John Stutts received 33 acres located north of Buffalo Creek adjoining **Henry Stutts**, **George Kennedy**, **James Maness** and **Sink**. **Henry Stutts** and **George Hunsucker** were chain carriers.

3646.   1828, Nov -- 1785-1868 Index to Trial Docket, Moore County, NC Page 69
A. Plummer v. **J. Wallis**

3647.   1828, Nov 9-Aug 16, 1831 -- Record of Estates Book B Page 154-157, 250-251 Moore County, NC
Estate of **George Moore Sr.**, Dec'd. by Administrator **Anderson B. Smith**. *Notes due of the following*: **David Kennedy, Wm. N. Johnson, Charles Jones, James Dannelly, William Danielly, Edmd. Wade, William Hunsucker, Warren Jones, David Jones, Phillip Brooks, Gideon Moore, John Lowdermilk, Wm. Wood, Thomas Danelly, Lewis Johnson, Wm. W. Morgan, George Stuts, Leonard Stuts, Richd. Upton, Alexr. Kennedy, Henry Brown, Daniel McNeill, Bradley Garner Jr., Jacob Stuts, White Hattter, Alexr. McNeill, Archd. Shields, Nathan Wallis, Aaron Kennedy, John Myrick, Alexr. Smith, Everet Wallis, Bennet Denson, Bradley Garner Sr., Abner Brown, Lewis Garner, David Langsford, John Cockmon, Wm. McIntosh, George Adams, Edward Moore, Phillip Brooks, Thomas Maness, Moreah Maness, Aaron Kennedy**, *Items purchased by the following*: **David Jones, Shidrack Maness, Delila Moore, Abner Brown, Daniel Muse, Edward Moore, James Williamson, John Hunsucker, Arch. Shields, George Hunsucker, A.B. Smith, John Hunsucker, Carrell Brady, Wm. W. Morgan, John Moore, Mary Moore, Henry Stuts Sr., Asa Sowell, James Caviness, Alexr. Plummer, Leonard Stuts, Jesse Rodgers, Nancy Moore, Aaron Kennedy, Johannah Hunsucker, John Ritter** and **Kenneth McCaskill**.

A.   1828, Nov 17 -- 1823-1831 Court of Pleas and Quarter Sessions, Moore County, NC Page 238-239
Letters of administration on the estate of **Hannah Duckworth**, Dec'd. were granted to **Daniel McNeill** with **Benjn. Person**, **Joseph Person** and **Malcom McNeill** as securities. **Polly Brooks** and her husband **Phillip Brooks** were recognized as next of kin.

3648.   1828, Nov 18 -- 1823-1831 Court of Pleas and Quarter Sessions, Moore County, NC Page 239
Administration of the estate of **Hugh Hammill** Dec'd. granted to **David Kennedy** with **David Reid** and **Elias Kennedy** as securities. **Jesse Brown**, **Anderson B. Smith**, **Wm. Jones** and **John Cagle** appointed to lay off 1 years provision for widow **Elizabeth Hammill**.

3649.   1828, Nov 18 -- 1823-1831 Court of Pleas and Quarter Sessions, Moore County, NC Page 239
Administration of the estate of **Thomas Person** Dec'd.granted to **Elias Kennedy** with **David Kennedy** and **Malcolm McNeill** as securities. **James Gains** Esq., **Bryan Boroughs**, **James W. England** and **Bradley Garner** appointed to lay off 1 years provision for widow **Martha Person**.

3650.   1828, Nov 18 -- 1823-1831 Court of Pleas and Quarter Sessions, Moore County, NC Page 241
Ordered that **James Garner** be appointed overseer of the road from Bear Creek to Buffalo Creek and work the same hands.

3651.   1828, Nov 18-Feb 17, 1829 -- 1823-1831 Court of Pleas and Quarter Sessions, Moore County, NC Page 241,249
Darcus Upton, widow of **Richrd. Upton** Dec'd. entered her dissent to the last will and testament.

3652.   1828, Nov 18 -- 1823-1831 Court of Pleas and Quarter Sessions, Moore County, NC Page 241

Delilay Moore v. Heirs of **George Moore** Dec'd. Ordered that publication be made in the *Fayetteville Observer* for six weeks to notify **William Moore** and **Edward Moore** (non-residents) that they are to be summoned to the court house in Carthage.

3653.   1828, Nov 18 -- 1823-1831 Court of Pleas and Quarter Sessions, Moore County, NC Page 241
Delilay Moore v. **Anderson B. Smith**, administrator. Ordered that **Cornelius Shields** Esq., **James W. England**, **Bryan Boroughs** and **Archd. Shields** be appointed to lay off 1 year's provision.

A.   1828, Nov 18 -- 1823-1831 Court of Pleas and Quarter Sessions, Moore County, NC Page 241 Ordered that **John Cheek** and **Joab Cheek**, executors of **Joab Cheek**, Dec'd. be permitted to sell negroes **Henry** and **Starling** belonging to the estate.

3654.   1828, Nov 18 -- 1823-1831 Court of Pleas and Quarter Sessions, Moore County, NC Page 242
Ordered that **James Hill** be appointed overseer of the road from **Kenneth McCaskill**'s to **George Hunsucker**'s and have the following hands to work: **William McIntosh, John McIntosh, Isham Wallis, Martin Hill, Samuel Barrett, John Lawhon, Daniel Caddell, Wm. Ritter, James Ritter, John Ritter, Wm. Barrett** Esq. one hand and **Hugh Kelly**.

3655.   1828, Nov 19 -- 1823-1831 Court of Pleas and Quarter Sessions, Moore County, NC Page 244
[*jury duty*] **James Hains**

3656.   1828, Nov 19 -- 1823-1831 Court of Pleas and Quarter Sessions, Moore County, NC Page 245
[Deeds] **Aaron Kennedy** to **John Cockmon** is proven by **Abner Brown**

Asa Sowell to **Jason Sowell** acknowledged
[Bill of sale] **Wm. Boroughs** to **John Manes** proven by **Bryan Boroughs**

3657.   1829, Jan 2-3 -- Record of Estates Book B Page 172-175, 234, Moore County, NC
Estate of **Thomas Person** Dec'd. by Administrator **Elias M. Kennedy**. *Items purchased by the following*: Hiram Williamson, Wm. Cox, John Craven, John Shamburger, Patrick Moore, Ransom Stuts, John McLeod, William Shields, Joseph Harper, John H. Hodgin, Samuel Beck, Isaac Teague, Shadrick Maness, Enoch S. Kennedy, Jeremiah Williams, Ransom Cavendish, Anderson B. Smith, Edward Harper, Stephen Perry, Aaron Tyson, James W. England, Isom Sowell, Stephen Davis, Robert Moore, John Ritter, Abram Lain, Josiah Kennedy, William B. Line, Aaron Kennedy, Harday Hardin, Tabitha Person, David Kennedy, Robert Kennedy, Wm. Martindail, John Kennedy, Charles Brady, James Garner, James M. Purvis and Joseph J. Person. *Notes due on the following*: Frances Myrick, John Kennedy, David Kennedy, Aaron Kennedy, John Smith, James Williamson, Alexr. Kennedy, Josiah Argo, Wm. Lakey, Druray Brewer, John Argo, Hammans Argo, Robert Kennedy, Thomas Maness, James Gains Esq., Charles Brady, John Waddill, Wm. M. Johnson, Bradly Garner Senr., Abraham Stuts, Samuel Martindail, Carrell Brady and Saml. C. Bruce.

A.   1829, Jan 6 -- 1823-1831 Court of Pleas and Quarter Sessions, Moore County, NC Page 260
N. Mashran, Archd. Shields, Corns. Shields, John Murchison and **Lewis Phillips** divided the estate of **Joab Cheek** Dec'd. as follows: Lot #1 - widow **Mary Cheek** 100 acres located on Randals Creek and Deep River adjoining **John Cheek**; Lot #2 – **Brantly Cheek** 112 acres adjoining **Mary Cheek** and **John Cheek**; Lot #3 – **Joab Cheek** 112 acres adjoining **Mary Cheek**; Lot #4 – **William B. Cheek** [not specified]; Lot #5 - **John Cheek** 108 acres located on Deep River adjoining **Mary Cheek** and **John Cheek Senr.**

3658. 1829, Jan 8-Feb 1 -- Criminal Actions, Randolph County, NC 1829-B
Presentment of **Johnson Pool** on the charge of assaulting **Edmond Holland** (Moore County resident) Dec 1828 at the store of **Brower** and **Troy**. **Emanuel Asbill** and **Alfred Brower** were witnesses. **James Pool Jr.**, **William Williamson Jr.** (Moore County resident) and **Alexander Pool** were also involved in general affray. **Coonrad Crisco** was surety for **James Pool**; **James Pool** was surety for **Johnson Pool** and **Abraham Brown** for **Alexander Pool**. During the examination, satisfactory evidence was presented that **Alexander Pool** did bite off **Edmund Holland**'s ear.

3659. 1829, Jan 23 -- Record of Estates Book B Page 167, Moore County, NC
Estate of **Hugh Hammill** Dec'd. by Administrator **D. Kennedy**. Items purchased by the following: **Enoch S. Kennedy**, **Elizabeth Hammill**, **Jesse Brown Senr.**, **Aaron Kennedy**, **Wm. Jones**, **Elias M. Kennedy** and **Anderson B. Smith**.

3660. 1829, Feb -- 1796-1841 County Accounts, Moore County, NC Page 89
1829, Feb -- 1785-1868 Index to Trial Docket, Moore County, NC Page 68
James Dunlap v. **Anson Melton**

3661. 1829, Feb [proven] -- Will Book B Page 63-64, Moore County, NC
Will of **Joseph Allen**, Dec'd. Heirs: wife **Elizabeth** (my land and plantation), son **Mark Allen** (land in the fork of Cabbin Creek and Popes Creek), daughter **Elizabeth "Betsy" Runalds** (tract of land lying south of Wolf Pen Branch adjoin, 366ning **Leach**), son **Reuben Allen**, son **Joseph Allen** and son **John Allen**. Executors: son **Mark Allen** and son-in-law **Jeremiah Runalds**. Witnesses: **A. McNeill** and **John McCrummen**.

3662. 1829, Feb 16 -- 1823-1831 Court of Pleas and Quarter Sessions, Moore County, NC
[*jury duty - selected participants*] **Edmond Hollin**, **George Stuts**, **John Deaton**, **Cornelius Caddell**

3663. 1829, Feb 16 -- 1823-1831 Court of Pleas and Quarter Sessions, Moore County, NC Page 246
William Caddell is released from indenture with minor orphans **Jacob Johnson** and **Harday Johnson**.

A. 1829, Feb 16 -- 1823-1831 Court of Pleas and Quarter Sessions, Moore County, NC Page 246
Ordered that **Henry Wilson** be appointed overseer of the road form the [Chatham] county line by way of Williams' Bridge and have the following hands to work: **Mary Williams'** hands, **John Murchison's** hands, **Wade Elkins, Joseph Gilbert, Jane Gilbert's** hands, **John Ingram's** hands, **Wm. Murchison, Neill Cameron, Jas. Tyson's** hands, **John Cheek's** hands, **Ths. Linch, Brantly Cheek, Blake Cheek** and hands, **John Cheek Jr., Duke** and **Buck Melone, Patrick Graham** and **Duncan Sinclair.**

3664. 1829, Feb 16 -- 1823-1831 Court of Pleas and Quarter Sessions, Moore County, NC Page 247
Ordered that **Henry Stuts**, overseer, have the following additional hands to work: **Jacob Stuts, Ransom Stuts** and **Leonard Stuts.**

A. 1829, Feb 16 -- 1823-1831 Court of Pleas and Quarter Sessions, Moore County, NC Page 247
Ordered that **Isaac Roberts** be appointed overseer in place of **William Stewart** of the road from **Williamsons** to the black rocks and work the following hands: **Wm. Stewart, Joseph L. Reid, John Stewart, Enoch Stewart, Wiley Roberts** and **Isaac Roberts'** hand.

B. 1829, Feb 16 -- 1823-1831 Court of Pleas and Quarter Sessions, Moore County, NC Page 247
Ordered that **Phillip Wilson** be appointed overseer in place of **Archd. Shields Jur.** and have the following hands to work: **Archd. Shields Jur., Robert Wilson's** hands, **James McNeill's** hands, **Corns. Shields'** hands, **Robert Moore, James Moore, Patrick Shields** and **Bryan Shields.**

3665. 1829, Feb 17 -- 1823-1831 Court of Pleas and Quarter Sessions, Moore County, NC Page 248
James Hains failed to appear for jury duty

A. 1829, Feb 17 -- 1823-1831 Court of Pleas and Quarter Sessions, Moore County, NC Page 249
Administration of estate of **Benjamin Person**, Dec'd. granted to **John Morrison** with **Gideon Seawell, Isaac Roberts, John Tyson, Josiah Tyson, Wm. Hancock, Neill Morrison** and **Wm. Jackson** as securities.

B. 1829, Feb 17 -- 1823-1831 Court of Pleas and Quarter Sessions, Moore County, NC Page 249
Ordered that **John McLeod** be appointed guardian to **Elizabeth McLeod** and **Ann McLeod,** infant heirs of **Neill McLeod,** Dec'd. with securities **Stephen Davis, Angus McKinnon, William Hancock** and **Neill Morison.**

3666. 1829, Feb 17 -- Land Grant #2841, Moore County, NC
John T. Ritter received 16 acres located south of McLendons Creek adjoining **Isaac Smith, Donald Chisholm** and **George Nailor. Samuel Jackson** and **Benjamin Phillips** were chain carriers.

3667. 1829, Feb 18 -- 1823-1831 Court of Pleas and Quarter Sessions, Moore County, NC Page 251
John B. Kelly v. **Nathan Barrett** and **Jesse Sanders**

A. 1829, Feb 19 -- Marriage Bond, Randolph County, NC
Isaac Maness and **Mary Pearce** received marriage bond. **Mason T. Brower** was bondsman. **H. Moffitt** was witness. [*Editor's Note: Date of marriage occurred on or after date of marriage bond.*]

B. 1829, Feb 19 -- 1823-1831 Court of Pleas and Quarter Sessions, Moore County, NC Page 253
Ordered that **Daniel McNeill** be appointed guardian to **Disay Carrell** and **James Carrell,** infant heirs at law of **Starling Carrell.**

3668. 1829, Feb 20 -- 1823-1831 Court of Pleas and Quarter Sessions, Moore County, NC Page 255
Jesse Sanders, Eleazer Birckhead, Eli Phillips appointed to settle with **Jesse Sowell,** Administrator of the Estate of **Charlotte Carrell,** Dec'd.

3669. 1829, Feb 20 -- 1823-1831 Court of Pleas and Quarter Sessions, Moore County, NC Page 256
Jesse Brown listed as Tax Collector in District 6 and 8 for 1827

3670. 1829, Feb 20 -- 1823-1831 Court of Pleas and Quarter Sessions, Moore County, NC Page 257
[Deeds] **William Wood** to **James Dunlap** was proven by **James Hains**
William Barrett to **Larkin N. Moore** proven by **John T. Riter**
Two deeds from **William Cagle** to **Jesse Brown Jr.** were proven by **Jesse Brown Sr.**
John McAulay an agent for **William** and **Daniel McAulay** to **William Jones** was proven by **George Davis**

William Williams to **William Jones** was proven by **George Davis**
Bradley Garner to **Wm. Brewer** was proven by **Jesse Brown Sr.**
John McAulay to **Angus Morison** proven by **Mathew Deaton**
Alexr. McKinnon to **Margaret Mathewson** was acknowledged
William Barrett to **Samuel Barrett** proven by **Martin Hill**
William Wadsworth to **Kindred Birckhead** proven by **John B. Kelly**
Everet Shuffield to **Daniel McCrumon** proven by **Wm. Brewer**

3671.　　1829, Feb 20 -- 1823-1831 Court of Pleas and Quarter Sessions, Moore County, NC Page 258
The following were appointed to lay off a portion of 685 acres on Buffalo Creek for **Elizabeth Ritter**, widow of **John Ritter**, Dec'd. adjoining **John Ritter Jr.** and **Jacob Stutts**: **Robert Wilson, Abner Brown, Archd. Shields, Henry Stuts, Robert Brady, Bradly Garner, Lewis Garner, Aaron Kennedy, William Dunn, John Cagle** and **Bradly Brady**.

3672.　　1829, Feb 20 -- 1823-1831 Court of Pleas and Quarter Sessions, Moore County, NC Page 259

The following were appointed to lay off 96 acres on Bear Creek as her allotment of 300 acres for **Susannah Kennedy**, widow of **Alexander Kennedy** Dec'd.: **John Brown, Thomas Williams, Leonard Furr, Jeremiah Williams, John Stuts, Jason Sowell, William Brown, M. Martin, Anderson B. Smith** and **John McLeod**.

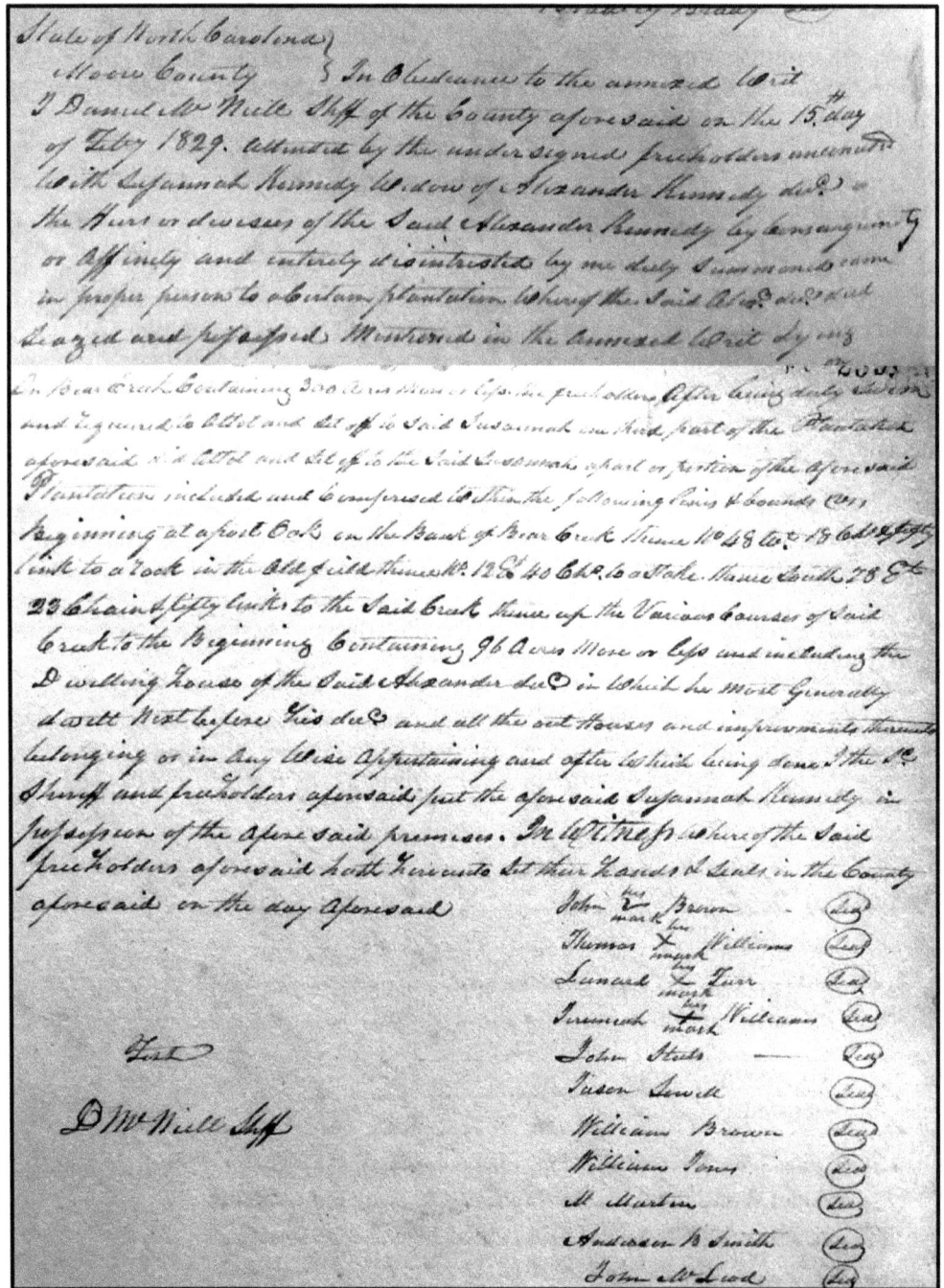

3673.　　1829, Mar 2 -- Land Grant #2771, Moore County, NC **William Ritter** received 20 acres located on the waters of Buffalo Creek adjoining heirs of **John Ritter**, Dec'd. **Robert Brady** and **Hiram Melton** were chain carriers.

3674.　　1829, Mar 6 -- Land Grant #2781, Moore County, NC **James Jackson** received 100 acres located on Dry Fork of Mill Creek and the Montgomery County line adjoining **John McDuffie, Neil McKinnon** and the heirs of **Neil McLeod**, Dec'd.

Burrell Deaton and **Neil McDuffie** were chain carriers.

3675. 1829, Mar 18 -- Land Grant #2792, Moore County, NC
Elizabeth Fry received 125 acres located south of McLendons Creek on Lackeys Branch adjoining **Thomas Bryant**, **Robert Graham** and **Lauchlin Curry**. **Lauchlin Currie** and **Thomas Bryant** were chain carriers.

3676. 1829, Mar 20 -- Land Grant #2835, Moore County, NC
Joseph J. Person received 73 acres located on the waters of Waggon Branch of Cedar Creek adjoining **Neil McLeod**, **James Moore**, **Ann Smith** and **John Hodgin**. **Wm. Martindale** and **Stephen Perry** were chain carriers.

A. 1829, Mar 21 -- Record of Estates Book B Pages 150-151,171,236, Moore County, NC
Estate of **Joseph Allen**, Dec'd. by Administrator **Mark Allen**. *Notes due on the following:* **Martin Cagle, Daniel McKenzie, Wm. Kendle, Moore Graves, John Jordan, John Deaton, Joseph/Joshua Kees, James Simmons, Burwell Deaton** and **John Kennedy**. *Items were purchased by the following:* , **Edmond Hollin, Reuben Allen, Jeremiah Runalds, Levy Deaton, Bartholomew Dunn, John Allen, William Deaton, Elizabeth Allen, Thomas Harvel, Joseph Allen, Thomas McNeill, John Smith** and **Robert Melton**.

3677. 1829, Mar 21 -- Chronicles and Records of Bensalem Presbyterian Church Page 9, Moore County, NC
Flora Ann Buie, daughter of **John C. Buie** and **Margaret Martin**, died.

3678. 1829, Mar 23 -- Land Grant #2795, Moore County, NC
John Cagle received 16 acres located south of Cabin Creek adjoining **George Cagle**, **Graham** and **Charles Sowell**. **Isaac Cagle** and **John Cagle** were chain carriers.

3679. 1829, Mar 24 -- Land Grant #0308, Moore County, NC
Isaac Maness received 100 acres located south of Bear Creek adjoining **Elijah Brewer** and **Henry Stutts**. **John McLeod** and **Isaac Manus** were chain carriers. [*Editor's Note: Never granted*]

3680. 1829, Mar 9 -- Land Grant #2772, Moore County, NC
William Barrett received 51 acres located on both sides of McLendons Creek adjoining **Thomas Knight**, **William Barrett Junr.** and **Jacob McLendon**. **David Langford** and **Jacob Stutts** were chain carriers.

3681. 1829, Apr 3 -- Land Grant #2807, Moore County, NC
William Deaton received 100 acres located south of Cabin Creek adjoining **James Cotton**, **William Smith Junr.** **Edmond Holland** and **William Deaton** were chain carriers.

A. 1829, Apr 14 -- Obituary, *Raleigh Register and NC Gazette* [Raleigh, NC] Newspaper
"On the 2nd ultimo [Mar 1829], in Moore County, **Daniel McNeill**, Esq., aged 83 years, of dropsy in the chest and constant debility.

3682. 1829, May 18 -- 1823-1831 Court of Pleas and Quarter Sessions, Moore County, NC
[*jury duty - selected participants*] **Everet Wallis**, **Danl. Caddell**

3683. 1829, May 18 -- 1823-1831 Court of Pleas and Quarter Sessions, Moore County, NC Page 263
The following were appointed to collect taxable for 1829: (District #6) **Jesse Sanders**; (District #8) **Enoch Kennedy**.

3684. 1829, May 18 -- 1823-1831 Court of Pleas and Quarter Sessions, Moore County, NC Page 263
William Barrett Esq. and **Malcolm McCrimon** Esq. were appointed to examine **Mary** and **Elizabeth Barrett**, wives of **William** and **Samuel Barrett** on deed to **Andrew** and **Malcolm Graham**.

A. 1829, May 18 -- 1823-1831 Court of Pleas and Quarter Sessions, Moore County, NC Page 263
Ordered that **Jeremiah Renalds** be appointed overseer in place of **Mark Allen** for the road from Mill Creek to the fork east of **Archd. McNeills** and work the following hands: **Mark Allen, Briton Britt, Alfred Britt, Avington Britt, Daniel Munroe, Joseph Allen, John Morgan, Becom Britt, Wm. Morgan, N. Lewis, John Smith** and **Hiram Deaton**.

B. 1829, May 19 -- 1823-1831 Court of Pleas and Quarter Sessions, Moore County, NC Page 264
Last will and testament of **Daniel McNeill Senr.**, Dec'd. was proven by **Bryan Boroughs** and **John Dannelly**. **Daniel McNeill Jun.** named executor.

3685. 1829, May 19 -- 1823-1831 Court of Pleas and Quarter Sessions, Moore County, NC Page 265
Dorcase Upton v. **Joseph Moore** and **James Upton**, Executors. **James Upton** guardian of **Richard Upton**, infant minor of **Richard Upton** Dec'd.

3686. 1829, May 19 -- 1823-1831 Court of Pleas and Quarter Sessions, Moore County, NC Page 265
Ordered that **Gideon Seawell** be appointed overseer of a new road commencing in Carthage by **G. Seawell**'s saw mill and leading into the old road at the top of the hill beyond **Daniel Caddells** and have the same hands that worked on old road from Bay Pond to Fayetteville Road.

3687. 1829, May 20 -- 1823-1831 Court of Pleas and Quarter Sessions, Moore County, NC Page 268
George Hunsucker, a musician appointed by **Col. Wm. Jackson** and **Col. Wm. Hancock** was exempt from paying poll tax.

A. 1829, May 20 -- 1823-1831 Court of Pleas and Quarter Sessions, Moore County, NC Page 269
Ordered that entry taker for county issue a duplicate warrant for **Robert Wilson** for 17 acres located on Chatham County line adjoining **Samson Brewer** it appearing that the original was lost.

B. 1829, May 20 -- 1823-1831 Court of Pleas and Quarter Sessions, Moore County, NC Page 269
Aaron Kennedy records his ear mark to be a swallow fork and a half moon under each ear.

C. 1829, May 20 -- 1823-1831 Court of Pleas and Quarter Sessions, Moore County, NC Page 270
Marriage contract for **Martha Person** and **Samuel C. Bruce** proved by **James H. Purves**

3688. 1829, May 20 -- 1823-1831 Court of Pleas and Quarter Sessions, Moore County, NC Page 270
[Deeds] **Margaret Deaton** to **Mathew Deaton** and **Isaac Deaton** proven by **A. McKinnon**
Nancy White to **Jesse Bean** proven by **Kenneth McCaskill**
Jesse and **Ann Bean** to **Edward Fry** proven by **Margaret Fry**

3689. 1829, Jun 1 -- BLM General Land Office Document #823, Lincoln County, MS
Nathaniel Smith (of Franklin County) received 80 acres from Jackson Land Office located in west half of southwest Quarter of Section 15, Township 7, Range 6.

3690. 1829, Aug 16 -- Bible of William Copeland and Mary E. Bailey, Moore County, NC
William Copeland and **Mary Bailey** were married at the residence of **Benjamin Bailey** by Rev. **Joel Harris**

3691. 1829, Aug 17 -- 1823-1831 Court of Pleas and Quarter Sessions, Moore County, NC [*jury duty - selected participants*] **Everet Wallis, Danl. Caddell, Hiram Hill, David Jones, Simon McNeill, James H. Muse**

A. 1829, Aug 18 -- 1823-1831 Court of Pleas and Quarter Sessions, Moore County, NC Page 274
Ordered that **Cornelius Dowd Jur.** be appointed guardian of **Joseph Carrell, Sabra Carrell** and **Washington Carrell** with **Corns. Dowd Senr.** and **Malcom Shaw** as securities.

B. 1829, Aug 18 -- 1823-1831 Court of Pleas and Quarter Sessions, Moore County, NC Page 274
Ordered that **Gideon Seawell** be appointed guardian of **Mary A. Person, Samuel J. Person, Murdoch Person** and **William Person,** minor orphans under the age of twenty-one years and heirs of **Benjamin Person,** Dec'd.

C. 1829, Aug 18 -- 1823-1831 Court of Pleas and Quarter Sessions, Moore County, NC Page 274
Ordered that **Isaac Fields** be appointed overseer of the road in place of **William Davis** from the Gate at Col. **Jones'** to the Williams' Fork and have the same hands to work.

D. 1829, Aug 18 -- 1823-1831 Court of Pleas and Quarter Sessions, Moore County, NC Page 276
Ordered that **Edward Warner** be appointed overseer of the road from the bay pond to the Fayetteville Road below Carthage in place of **Nathan Fry** and have the following hands to work: **Nathan Fry, Wm. Caddell, Green B. Caddell, Hopkins Fry, John Paterson, Thomas Fry, Nathan Fry, Hardin Warner, Lockart Fry, Alexd. Fry, Richd. Fry, George Fry** and **Harday Johnson.**

3692. 1829, Aug 18 -- 1823-1831 Court of Pleas and Quarter Sessions, Moore County, NC Page 276
Ordered that **John McNeill** be appointed the overseer in place of **Mark Allen** for the road from Cabin Creek at **Leaches** to the Montgomery County Line near **Arch. McNeill's** store and work the following hands: **Mark Allen, Riland Miller, Edmond Hollin, Isaac Spivay, Rubin Allen, Arch. McNeill's** hands, **Stephen Davis'** hands, **James Callicut's** hands, **Thomas McNeill's, Absalom Callicutt, Jesse Davis, John Davis** and **Britain L. Sanders.**

3693. 1829, Aug 18 -- 1823-1831 Court of Pleas and Quarter Sessions, Moore County, NC Page 277
Ordered that **Wm. Buie** be appointed the overseer of the road from the Montgomery County line to **Martin's** old store and work the following hands: **James Keys, John Smith, Wm. Smith, Joseph Smith, Simon McNeill, Isaac Smith, John McNeill, Joshua Keys, Thomas Keys, John Richardson, Isah Autray, Isham Harvill** and Mr. **McKinnon's Jim.**

3694. 1829, Aug 20 -- 1823-1831 Court of Pleas and Quarter Sessions, Moore County, NC Page 282
[Deeds] **Cornelius Keys** to **Simon McNeill** proven by **A. McKinnon**
Thomas P. Muse to **Benjn. Person** proven by **Cornelius Dowd** (son of **James**)
Levin Birckhead to **Benjn. Person** proven by **Cornelius Dowd** (son of **James**)
David Kennedy to **Bradley Garner** acknowledged

3695. 1829, Oct 1 -- Chronicles and Records of Bensalem Presbyterian Church Page 9, Moore County, NC

Mary Martin Bethune died. [wife of John Bethune]

3696. 1829, Oct 24 -- *A History of Sandy Creek Baptist Association* by George Purefoy, Page 99
Elder **Arts. Shattuck, Benjamin Phillips** and **Jno. H. Freeman** from Friendship Church (Moore County) and **Thomas Williams, Ansel Melton** and **Daniel McKimon** from Mechanic's Hill Church (Moore County) were delegates to the Association meeting at Lick Creek Meeting House in Chatham County, NC.

A. 1829, Nov 7 -- 1823-1831 Court of Pleas and Quarter Sessions, Moore County, NC Page 288-290
Ordered that **Joel Lawhon, Eleazer Birckhead Senr., Jesse Bean, Samuel Jackson, William Jackson, Hiram Hill, Leonard Lawhon, Neill Caddell, William Barrett Senr., James Dowd, Samuel Barrett** and **William Barrett Jr.** be appointed to allot the 800 acres located on McLendons Creek of **Benjn. Person** Dec'd. to widow **Ann Person:** [1] 200 acres [2] 150 acres patented by **Jacob McLennon** adjoining **Thomas McLendon** and **Jemima McLendon** [3] 150 acres patented by **Donald McDonald** located on Suck Creek adjoining **Jacob McLendon** and **Jemima McLendon** [4] 100 acres located on both sides of Suck Creek adjoining **Widow McDonald** [5] 50 acres patented by **Neill McLeod** located west of McLendons Creek adjoining **Jacob McLendon, Angus McIver** and **Joel McLendon** [6] 156 acres patented by **Neill McLeod** located on both sides of McLendons Creek adjoining **Jamima McLendon, Knight, Barrett, Major McRae, McDonald** and **Jacob McLendon**.

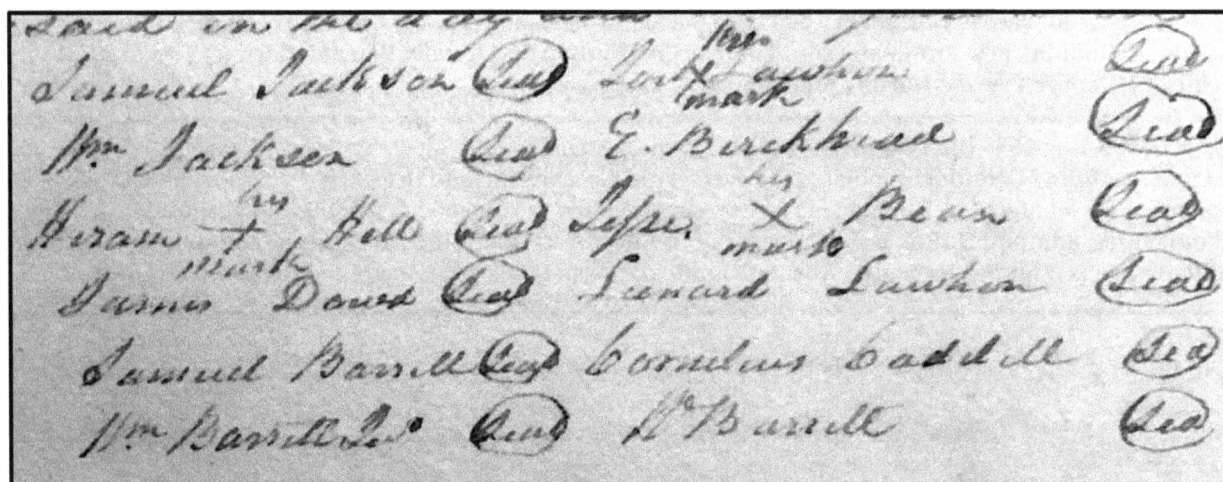

3697. 1829, Nov 10 -- Land Grant #2844, Moore County, NC
Levi Deaton received 100 acres located between Cabin Creek and Wolf Creek adjoining **Richard Holland, Mason Harvel, Edmond Holland** and his own line. **Burrell Deaton** and **Hiram Deaton** were chain carriers.

A. 1829, Nov 16 -- 1823-1831 Court of Pleas and Quarter Sessions, Moore County, NC Page 283
Administration of the estate of **William Fry**, Dec'd. is granted to **Lockart Fry** with securities **Daniel Paterson** and **James Fry**.

3698. 1829, Nov 16 -- 1823-1831 Court of Pleas and Quarter Sessions, Moore County, NC Page 283
Ordered that **James Hill** be appointed the overseer of the road from Bean's Bridge to Flowers Road and work the following hands: **Wm. McIntosh, John McIntosh, Alex. McIntosh, Alex. McIntosh Sr.**'s hand, **Wm. J. McIntosh, Samuel McIntosh, Isham Wallis, Wm. Barrett** Esq.'s hand, **Samuel Barrett, Willabe Ritter, Henry Ritter, Isaac Lawhon, Daniel Caddell, Jesse Muse, Daniel Muse, Angus Kelly** and **Alex. McCaskill**.

3699. 1829, Nov 17 -- 1823-1831 Court of Pleas and Quarter Sessions, Moore County, NC Page 284
Ordered that orphan **Kindred Davidson** [age 5] be bound to **Mark Allen**

3700. 1829, Nov 17 -- 1823-1831 Court of Pleas and Quarter Sessions, Moore County, NC Page 285
Administration of **John Lewis** Dec'd. granted to widow **Patience Lewis**

3701. 1829, Nov 17 -- Land Grant #2843, Moore County, NC
Levi Deaton received 100 acres located between Cabin Creek and Wolf Creek adjoining **Richard Holland, William Freeman** and his own line. **John Smith** and **James Holland** were chain carriers.

3702. 1829, Nov 18 -- 1823-1831 Court of Pleas and Quarter Sessions, Moore County, NC Page 286

Ordered that the road from **Daniel Caddells** to Fayetteville Road between Carthage and **Davis'** old field be discontinued.

3703. 1829, Nov 18 -- 1823-1831 Court of Pleas and Quarter Sessions, Moore County, NC Page 287
[Deeds] **Asa Sowell** to **Quimby Sowell** acknowledged
John Dannelly to **Robert Wilson** proven by **Daniel McNeill Jur.** because **Daniel McNeill Senr.** is dead
Robert Wilson to **John Ritter** proven by **Daniel McNeill Jr.**
Reuben Freeman to **Donald McCrummon** proven by **A. McKinnon**
James Smith to **John Levester** proven by **Samuel Dun**
Everet Shuffield to **Neill McIntosh** proven by **James Dunlap**

3704. 1829, Nov 18 -- 1823-1831 Court of Pleas and Quarter Sessions, Moore County, NC Page 288
Ordered that the following lay off 45 acres on McCallums Fork for **Darcus Upton**, widow of **Richard Upton**, Dec'd.: **Joseph G. Moore, Neill McIntosh, John H. Freeman, Harbart Cole, Corn. Dowd, William Caddell, Isaac Smith, John Phillips, Demsy Sowell, Isham Sowell, Leazer Sowell** and **Quimby Sowell**.

A. 1830, Jan 6 -- Marriage Bond, Randolph County, NC
Henry Yow and **Phebe Cox** received marriage bond. **Dudley Willett** was bondsman. [*Editor's Note: Date of marriage occurred on or after date of marriage bond.*]

3705. 1830, Jan 18 -- Land Grant #2824, Moore County, NC
Robert Wilson received 17 acres located north of Deep River on Chatham County line adjoining the heirs of **Sampson Brewer** and **Shields**. **Noah Brewer** and **Bradly Brady** were chain carriers.

3706. 1830, Jan 20 -- Record of Estates Book B Page 188, Moore County, NC
Estate of **John Lewis**, Dec'd. by **Patience Lewis**, Administrator. *Notes due on the following*: **John Craven**, **Tobias Fry**, **William Gilmore** and **Asa Sowell**.

3707. 1830, Feb 4 -- Will Book B Page 76, Moore County, NC
Will of **Charles Sowell**, Dec'd. Heirs: wife **Nancy**, friend **George Davis** and **Davis'** sister **Sarah**. Executors: **George Davis** and **James Hains**. Witnesses: **George Adams**, **William Cagle** and **Henry Cagle**.

3708. 1830 [undated] -- Record of Estates Book B Pages 240, Moore County, NC Estate of **Charles Sowell**, Dec'd. by Executor **George Davis**

3709. 1830, Feb 11 -- 1830-1839 Court of Pleas and Quarter Sessions, Davidson County, NC
Jesse Sulivan, an orphan boy 18 years old, was bound to as an apprentice to **Joseph Miller** until he arrives to full age and during said apprenticeship to teach or cause to be taught said apprentice to read and write well and when free, give him $30 in cash.

3710. 1830, Feb 15 -- Land Grant #2867, Moore County, NC
Jesse Stafford received 50 acres located south of Richland Creek adjoining **Moore**, **McNeill**, **Alex. Carrel**, **Allison**, **Eli Phillips**, **Sullivan** and **Cornelius Dowd**. **James Mathews** and **John Stafford** were chain carriers.

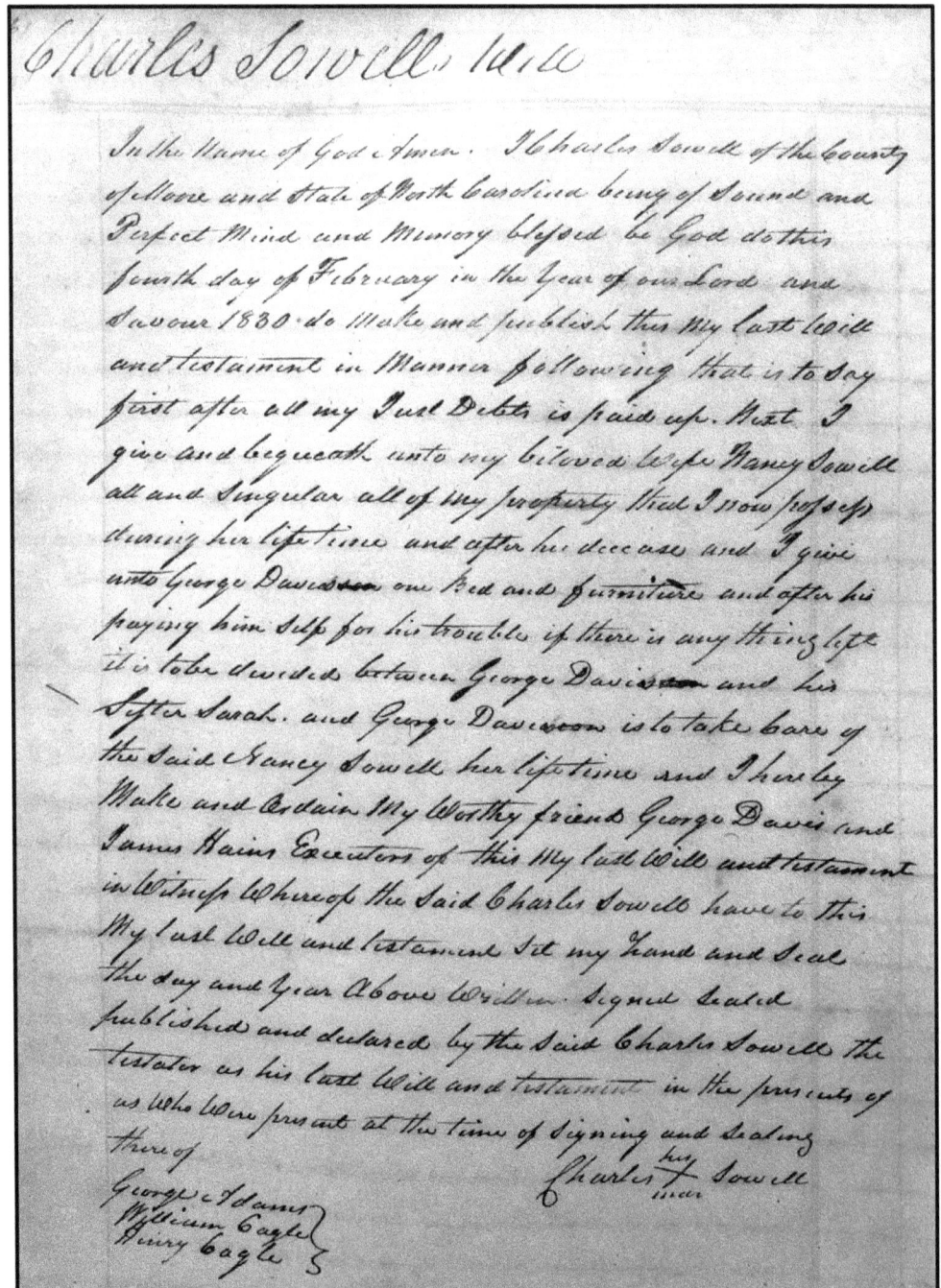

A.   1830, Feb 15 -- 1823-1831 Court of Pleas and Quarter Sessions, Moore County, NC Page 305
The following were appointed to lay off a portion of 369 acres located North of Deep River on John Phillips Creek and School House Spring Branch for **Sarah Phillips**, widow of **John D. Phillips** Dec'd. adjoining **Lewis Phillips**, **John Cheek Sr.**, **John Phillips** and the branch to the Meeting House: **John Cheek Senr.**, **John Cheek Junr.**, **George Wilcox**, **Cornelius Tyson**, **William D. Tyson**, **Harbert Cole**, **Samson D. Smith**, **Alexr. McNeill**, **William Ritter**, **John Stuts**, **William B. Cheek** and **Joab Cheek**.

3711.   1830, Feb 16 -- Land Grant #2851, Moore County, NC
Simon McNeill received 40 acres located east of Wet Creek adjoining **Thomas Key**, **Levi Deaton** and **Daniel McLean**. **Samuel Key** and **Donald McLean** were chain carriers.

3712.   1830, Feb 16 -- 1823-1831 Court of Pleas and Quarter Sessions, Moore County, NC
[*jury duty - selected participants*] **David Kennedy**, **Mark Allen**, **Simon McNeill**, **Demsy Sowell**, **Nathan Barrett**, **Angus Leach**

3713.   1830, Feb 16 -- 1823-1831 Court of Pleas and Quarter Sessions, Moore County, NC Page 294
Jesse Brown was listed as Tax Collector for District 6 and 8 for 1828

A.   1830, Feb 16 -- Deed Book 6 Page 111-113, Moore County, NC
Holden Cox and **Irvin Cox** deeded **Samuel Jackson** 150 acres located on both sides of the Juniper Creek, McKoy

Branch and Tantrough Branch being part of the 300-acre **James McCollum** tract and the 200-acre **Joel McLendon** tract adjoining **George Cox, Samuel Jackson** and the path from **William Cox's** to **Samuel Jackson's**. **M. McCrummen** and **S. Davis** were witnesses.

3714. 1830, Feb 17 -- 1823-1831 Court of Pleas and Quarter Sessions, Moore County, NC Page 297
Ordered that **Hiram Williamson** be appointed overseer in place of **James Caviness** of the road from Bear Creek to **Williamson's** and have the following hands to work: **James Caviness, Thomas Person** hands, **Wm. Williamson** hands, **Bradley Garner, Wm. Williamson, James Gaines** hands, **Wm. Gains, Hiram Davidson, John Myrick, Wm. Deaton, Edward Moore, Arch. McDonald, Jeremiah Williams, David Brewer** and **Josiah Kennedy**.

3715. 1830, Feb 18 -- 1823-1831 Court of Pleas and Quarter Sessions, Moore County, NC Page 298
Inventory of **Wm.** and **Susan Garner, Jacob** and **Polly Cagle, George** and **Nancy Cagle, John** and **Sally Cagle** was duly proven by **John Shamburger** [*Editor's Note: see Estate of **Cornelius Latham Sr.** in Bibb County, AL*]

A. 1830, Feb 18 -- 1823-1831 Court of Pleas and Quarter Sessions, Moore County, NC Page 298
Brinkley Phillips, guardian of **Ann Muse** renewed his bond with securities **Wm. Hancock** and **Wm. Phillips**.

3716. 1830, Feb 20 -- 1823-1831 Court of Pleas and Quarter Sessions, Moore County, NC Page 302
[Deeds] **James Fry** to **Jesse Sanders** was acknowledged
Nehemiah Birckhead to **James B. Muse. Nathan Holloway** (removed from state) and **Benjn. Person** (dead) were witnesses and are no longer able to attest
Nancy Sowell and **William Williams** to **George Davis** was proven by **William Jones**
Jesse Sanders to **Wm. Hill** was acknowledged
William W. Morgan to **Anderson B. Smith** acknowledged
Levy Deaton to **Simon McNeill** acknowledged
James B. Muse to **John B. Kelly** acknowledged
William Cook to **James Cook** proven by **M.G. Campbell**
Samuel Dunn to **Mathew Deaton** proven by **John McDonald Jr.**
William Barrett to **Jacob Stuts** acknowledged
Isaac Roberts to **William Barrett** proven by **Cornelius Dowd**
Jesse Rodgers to **James B. Muse** proven by **Benjamin Person**

3717. 1830, Feb 20 -- 1823-1831 Court of Pleas and Quarter Sessions, Moore County, NC Page 304-305
The 270 acres of land of **George Moore**, Dec'd. was partitioned and divided and his Widow **Delila Moore** received 90 acres located on Buffalo Creek adjoining **John Ritter**. The following commissioners were appointed: **James Melton, Abner Brown, Jos. J. Person, Neill McIntosh, James Caveness, William Ritter, John McLeod, Jethro Denson, Andrew Yow, William Dannelly, Jeremiah Williams** and **Joseph G. Moore**.

A. 1830, Feb 25 -- Notice, *Fayetteville Observer* [Fayetteville, NC] Newspaper
Pursuant to the Fall 1829 case where **John Drake** and wife and **John McNeill**, Admst. of the estate of **James**

Atkins, Dec'd. the following tracts in Cumberland & Moore counties were sold at the court house in Fayetteville on Apr 5th: [*selected tracts*] 100 acres in Moore County including the Cool Spring; 300 acres on Toms Creek; 200 acres between Buffalo and Bear Creeks; 200 acres on north side of Deep River...**W.F. Strange** Feb 15, 1830.

3718.   1830, Mar 4 -- Land Grant #2848, Moore County, NC
John Smith received 41 acres located north of Cabin Creek adjoining **Mason Harvel, Levy Deaton** and **John Morgan. Levi Deaton** and **Nathan Smith** were chain carriers.

3719.   1830, Mar 5 -- Land Grant #2806, Moore County, NC
Jesse Brown received 25 acres located north of Bear Creek adjoining his own line, **Hugh Hamill** and **William Williamson. Bailey Williamson** and **Isaac Brown** were chain carriers.

3720.   1830, Apr 5 -- Orphans Court Book A Page 268, Bibb County, AL
Decree of Distribution for Estate of **Cornelius Latham Sr.**, Dec'd. by Administrators **Cornelius Latham, Jr.** and **Enoch Lathem.** *Heirs:* wife **Elizabeth Latham;** children **John Cagle** and **Sally** his wife, late **Sally Latham; Jacob Cagle** and **Polly** his wife, late **Polly Latham; William Garner** and **Susan** his wife, late **Susan Latham; George Cagle** and **Nancy** his wife, late **Nancy Latham; John Boling** and **Patsy** his wife, late **Patsy Latham; Bellaver Britt** and **Lucretia** his wife, late **Lucretia Latham; James Latham; Cornelius Latham Jr.**, Administrator; **John Latham; Enoch Latham** Administrator; and **John Hicks** and **Catherine** his wife, late **Catharine Latham;** and grandchildren via deceased son **William Latham: John Lawley** and **Polly** his wife, late **Polly Latham; William Garner** and **Nancy** his wife, late **Nancy Latham; John Garner** and **Betsy** his wife, late **Betsy Latham; Samuel Snider** and **Mary** his wife, late **Martha Latham; Raleigh Allen** and **Sally** his wife, late **Sally Latham; Evan Howard** and **Rebecca** his wife, late **Rebecca Latham; James Latham; Jesse Latham; Margaret Latham; Amy Latham; William Latham; Andrew Latham** and grandchildren [names unknown] via deceased daughter **Elizabeth Tucker**, Dec'd., a former wife of **Jesse Tucker** of Tennessee.

A.   1830, Apr 24 -- Land Grant #2539, Montgomery County, NC
Archibald McNeill Esq. received 50 acres located on Dicks Creek adjoining his own line, **Daniel Martin** and **Joshua Cochran. William Butler** and **William McLeod** were chain carriers.

B.   1830, Apr 24 -- Land Grant #2549, Montgomery County, NC
James Wright received 75 acres located on Dry Branch of Dicks Creek adjoining **Joshua B. Cochran, A. McNeill** and his own line. **Alfred Wright** and **David Wright** were chain carriers.

3721.   1830, May 8 -- Deed Book 95 Page 26, Moore County, NC
William Williams and **Nancy Sowell** deeded **George Davis** 50 acres located on Flag Creek adjoining **Bartholomew Dunn. Joseph Williams** and **Bartholomew Dunn** were witnesses.

3722.   1830, May 17 -- 1823-1831 Court of Pleas and Quarter Sessions, Moore County, NC Page 307
Ordered that administration of estate of **Temperance Riddle** Dec'd. be granted to **William Hancock** with **Stephen Berryman** and **John Cole** as securities.

A.   1830, May 18 -- 1823-1831 Court of Pleas and Quarter Sessions, Moore County, NC Page 309
Ordered that **Samuel Barrett** be appointed the overseer of the road from Bean's Bridge to the large sassafras at Alex. **McCaskill**'s and have the following hands to work: **Neill Caddell, Isaac Lawhon, Allen McCaskill, Daniel Caddell, Jesse Muse, Daniel Muse Jr., Henry Ritter, John J. McIntosh, John Davis, Samuel McIntosh** and **James Hill.**

B.   1830, May 18 -- 1823-1831 Court of Pleas and Quarter Sessions, Moore County, NC Page 309
Ordered that **Isham Wallis** be appointed the overseer of the road from the large sassafras at **Alex. McCaskill**'s to Flowers Road and have the following hands to work: **Wm. Barrett** Esq. hands, **Hiram Melton, Angus Kelly, Alex. McIntosh** hands, **William McIntosh, John McIntosh** and **Alex McIntosh Jr.**

C.   1830, May 18 -- 1823-1831 Court of Pleas and Quarter Sessions, Moore County, NC Page 311
Ordered that **Wm. Davis** be appointed overseer in place of **Isaac Spivey** of the road from **John Spivay**'s to McNeill's store and have the following hands to work: **Isaac Spivey, Peter Shamburger** 2 hands, **John Spivay** 1 hand, **Robert Melton, Leonard Hair, Lewis Freeman, Henry Freeman, Robert Davis, Jesse Davis, Isham Hare, Thoms. Comer** and **Phillip Comer.**

D. 1830, May 18 -- 1823-1831 Court of Pleas and Quarter Sessions, Moore County, NC Page 310
Ordered that **Wm. Dawson Smith** be appointed overseer in place of **Neill Caddell** of the road from near **Naylors** to Lick Branch near **George Naylor** and have the following hands to work: **Benjn. Phillips**, **Willis Dowd**, **Benj. Dowd**, **William Dowd**, **Mark Phillips Jr.** and **Joseph Caddell**.

E. 1830, May 18 -- Land Grant #2892, Moore County, NC
James C. Davis received 61 acres located south of Deep River adjoining his own line, **Brooks** and **John Cole**. **John Cole** and **Bryant Shields** were chain carriers.

F. 1830, May 18 -- 1823-1831 Court of Pleas and Quarter Sessions, Moore County, NC Page 308
Ordered that **John Stewart** be appointed overseer of the road from Williams Fork to the Black Rocks in place of **Isaac Roberts** and have the following hands to work: **John Graham**, **Thomas Graham**, **Michael Phillips** and **Hugh Moore**'s hands.

3723. 1830, May 19 -- 1823-1831 Court of Pleas and Quarter Sessions, Moore County, NC Page 311
[Deeds] Two deeds from **Abednego Maness** to **Henry Maness** were proven by **A.C. Currie**
John Sowell to **Samuel Jackson** was proven by **Shadrack Maness**
George Cagle to **John Cagle** was proven by **Jesse Brown Sr.**
Henry Yow Sr. to **Andrew Yow** proven by **Henry Yow Jr.**
Bradly Garner to **Andrew Yow** proven by **Henry Yow Jr.**
Everet Sheffield to **Edmond Holland** proven by **Wm. Brewer**
Wesley Nailor to **Eleazer Birckhead**
Eleazer Birckhead Senr. to **Eleazer Birckhead Junr.**
John McAulay to **James Keahey** proven by **A. McKinnon**
James B. Muse to **Jesse F. Muse** proven by **Howard Muse**
Jesse F. Muse to **Samuel Smitherman** and **Willis L. Dowd** proven by **Cornelius Dowd**
William Dannelly to **Gideon Seawell** and **Henry Seawell** proven by **Sanday Fry**
William Barrett to **Gideon Seawell** and **Henry Seawell** proven by **Sanday Fry**
[Power of Attorney] **Angus Morison, Isabella Morison, Mary Morison, Nancy McDonald, Alexr. McDonald, Hector McKenzie, Margaret McKenzie, Alexr. McLeod, Catharine McLeod, Neill McLeod, Daniel McLennon, Mary McLennon, Margaret McLeod, John Morison, Alexr. Morison, Randal McDonald, John McDonald, Neill McDonald** and **Margaret Bethune** to **Neill Morison** proven by **Angus Morison**

A. 1830, Aug 17 -- 1823-1831 Court of Pleas and Quarter Sessions, Moore County, NC Page 318
Ordered that **Alex. C. Currie** be appointed overseer of the road from the west corner of John B. Kelly's fence to the **Davis** old field and have the following hands to work: **Daniel H. Muse, Abner E. Smith, Wm. Barrett Jur., Hudson Muse, Wm. A. Birckhead, Wm. Vuncannon, John Vuncannon, John T. Ritter, John B. Kelly's** hands, **Randolph McDonald, Thomas Muse (Hatter), Gideon Seawell's** hands, **Asa Muse, Jesse P. Rodgers, Jesse F. Muse, Westly Nailor, Westly Birckhead, John Morison, Jesse Hedgepeth, John McNeill (Hatter), John B. Faucett, John Fry (Hatter), Angus Martin, Causly Cox, Malcom McDonald, Duncan McIntosh, Anderson Vandaver, Wm. D. Smith, Alexr. McIver** and all other hands residing in Carthage.

3724. 1830, Aug 19 -- 1823-1831 Court of Pleas and Quarter Sessions, Moore County, NC Page 321
1830, Aug -- 1785-1868 Index to Trial Docket, Moore County, NC Page 65
State v. **Charles Furr**. **Asa Sowell** as security.

A. 1830, Aug 21 -- 1823-1831 Court of Pleas and Quarter Sessions, Moore County, NC Page 324
[Deeds] **Robert Harden** to **Harbart Cole** proven by **Wm. Mathews**
John Lawler to **Daniel McCrummen** proven by **John Tyson**
[Bill of Sale] **Asa Sowell** to **James Davis** proven by **Phillip Brooks**

3725. 1830, Aug 25 -- Land Grant #2805, Moore County, NC
Nathan Smith received 25 acres located south of Cabin Creek adjoining **William Smith Senr.**, his own line and his Mother's. **Isaac Smith** and **Joseph Smith** were chain carriers.

3726. 1830, Oct 5 -- Will, Dickson County, TN
Will of **Moses Fussell**, Dec'd. Heirs: wife **Lucy Fussell**, eldest son **Wyatt Fussell**, daughter **Elizabeth Horner** (and her children **George Wyatt Horner** and **Dicy Austin**), son **William Fussell**, daughter **Sally Horner**, daughter **Lucy Horner** (widow of **James Horner**) and daughter **Patsy Dunegan**. Executors: son **William Fussell** and **Meekins Care**. Witnesses: **Eli Crow**, **John Dunnegan** and **Elizabeth Crow**. Proven Apr 1831.

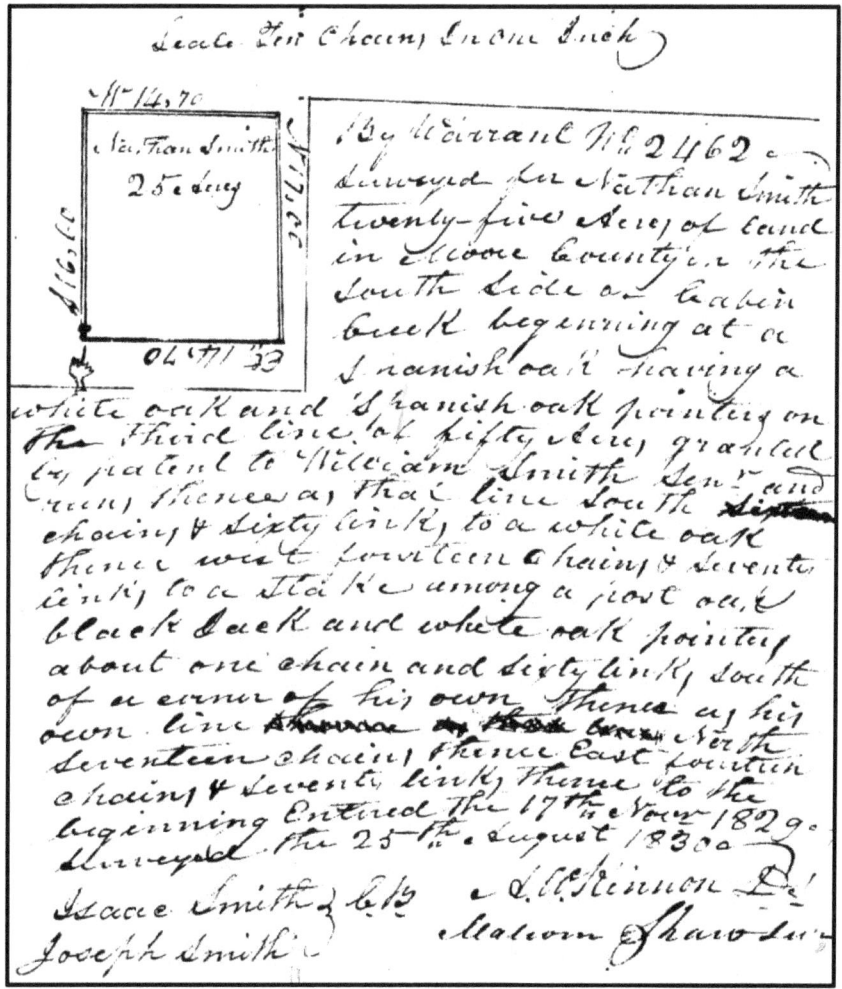

3727. 1830, Oct 15 -- Will, East Baton Rouge Parish, LA
Will of **John Overton**, Dec'd. Heirs: second wife **Susannah Overton** [*Negroes* **Jack** and **Hannah**] and their son **Thomas Jefferson Overton**; three children from his first marriage: **Samuel Overton**, **Jesse Overton** and **Cassandra Overton**. Executors: son **Samuel Overton**. Witnesses: **Wm. Brown**, **Vincent Kirkland** and **Malcolm Patterson**. Proven 19 Oct 1830.

3728. 1830, Oct 23 -- *A History of Sandy Creek Baptist Association* by George Purefoy, Page 101
Bryan Boroughs, **Jacob Teague** and **Henry Caviness** from Fall Creek Church (Chatham County) and Elder **N. Richardson**, **John Dowdy** and **James Dowdy** from Friendship Church (Moore County) and **David Kennedy** and **Cornelius Dowd** from Mechanic's Hill Church (Moore County) were delegates to the Association meeting at Love's Creek Meeting House in Chatham County, NC.

3729. 1830, Oct 30 -- Land Grant #2842, Moore County, NC
William Hill received 75 acres adjoining **William Barrett'** goldmine, **Alexander McIntosh** (formerly **Nathan Smith**), **Jacob Stutts**, **William Smith**, **McLeod**, **William Dannelly** and **Angus McQueen**. **Green Hill** and **Danl. Muse** were chain carriers.

3730. 1830, Nov 2 -- Land Grant #2801, Moore County, NC
Gideon Sowell received 200 acres located south of Richland Creek adjoining **Hugh Kelly**, **William Dannelly**, **Neil McLeod** and **John Martin**. **Alexr. McCaskill** and **Angus Kelly** were chain carriers.

3731. 1830, Nov 15 -- Record of Estates Book B Page 211-212, 226-227, Moore County, NC
Estate of **William Cook**, Dec'd. by Administrator **Joseph Cook**.

3732. 1830, Nov 15 -- 1823-1831 Court of Pleas and Quarter Sessions, Moore County, NC Page 325
Leonard Hair granted administration of **Peter Hair**, Dec'd. Bond was given by **Thomas Williams** and **Corn. Dowd Jr.**

3733. 1830, Nov 15 -- 1823-1831 Court of Pleas and Quarter Sessions, Moore County, NC Page 325

Ordered that **John Shamburger** be permitted to build a mill on Bear Creek where **William Hussey**, Dec'd. had a mill. Ordered that **James Dunlap** be permitted to build a mill on Bear Creek on his own land.

3734. 1830, Nov 15 -- 1823-1831 Court of Pleas and Quarter Sessions, Moore County, NC Page 326
Ordered that **Matthew Deaton** be appointed overseer of the Joel Road from fork near **McIvers** to Dry Creek and have the following hands to work: **James Kachey, John Munroe, Collin Munroe, John Deaton, Wm. Deaton, Isaac Deaton, Levy Deaton** 1 hand, **John McCaskill** 1 hand, **Daniel Murchinson, Kinneth Morison, Jess Collyer** and **Josiah [Isaiah] Melton.**

A. 1830, Nov 15 -- 1823-1831 Court of Pleas and Quarter Sessions, Moore County, NC Page 327
Ordered that **Isaac Spivay** be appointed overseer of the road from **John Spivay**'s to **McNeill**'s store and have the following hands to work: **Jesse Davis, John Davis, Matthew Davis, William Davis, Peter Shamburger** 2 hands, **John Spivay** 1 hand, **Robert Melton, Leonard Hare, Lewis Freeman, Henry Freeman, Robert Davis, Isham Hare, Thomas Comer** and **Phillip Comer.**

3735. 1830, Nov 15 -- BLM General Land Office Document #2960, Lauderdale County, AL
Hiram Kennedy, assignee of **James Hamm** received 159.69 acres from Huntsville Land Office located in southeast Quarter of Section 9, Township 1, Range 10.

3736. 1830, Nov 16 -- 1823-1831 Court of Pleas and Quarter Sessions, Moore County, NC Page 327
Ordered that **Henry Manas** be appointed overseer of the road from Bear Creek to Buffalo Creek in place of **James Garner** and have the following hands to work: **James Garner, James Manes, Isaac Maness, Elijah Maness, Hiram Davidson, George Stutts, Wm. Moore, John Hunsucker, John McLeod**'s hands, **Abraham Stutts, David Brewer** and **Josiah Wallis.**

3737. 1830, Nov 17 -- 1823-1831 Court of Pleas and Quarter Sessions, Moore County, NC Page 329
[Deeds] **John B. Martin**, admst. of **John Martin** Dec'd. to **Peter Shamburger** proven by **John Shamburger**
Daniel McCrimon to **Edmond Hollin** acknowledged
John Sheffield and wife to **Peter Shamburger** proven by **Wm. Brewer**
Everet Ritter to **Susannah Ritter** proven by **Corn. Shields**
[Bill of sale] **James Dunlap** to **Ansel Milton** was proven by **Corn. Dowd, Jr.**

3738. 1830, Nov 17 -- 1823-1831 Court of Pleas and Quarter Sessions, Moore County, NC Page 330
Ordered that a road be laid off from the Randolph County Line near **John Shamburgers**, as the marks to **John Shuffield**'s Mill, with marks to **James Morgan**'s on Cabin Creek, with marks to **Neill Morrison**'s, as the road opposite to the corner of **Francis Munroe**'s field where **Morrison**'s school path to **Dunn**'s old field, left to the old houseplace, left of **Autray**'s Church, as the road to **Hunsucker**'s place and work the following hands: **John Shuffield, James Morgan, N. Morison, John Keys, Danl. McKenzie, John McNeill, Daniel McDaniel, John McCaskill, Wm. Brewer, Edmond Holland, Daniel Murchison** and **Everit Shuffield.** [*See image on next page*]

3739. 1830, Nov 22 -- Land Grant #2800, Moore County, NC
John H. Hodgin received 100 acres located west of Cedar Creek adjoining his own line and heirs of **Leonard Smith. Leonard C. Smith** and **Asbury H. Hodgin** were chain carriers.

A. 1830, Nov 25 -- Marriages, *Carolina Observer* [Fayetteville, NC] Newspaper
"In Moore County, a few days ago, by **Wm. Barret**, Esq., Mr. **John Sowel**, aged 64 to Mrs. **Nancy Shaw**, aged 72."

B. 1830, Dec 9 -- Deed, Moore County, NC
John Sowell deeded **William Barrett Senr.** 50 acres located on both sides of McLendons Creek adjoining **William Barrett Junr., Thomas Night** and **William Barrett Senr. Stephen Davis** and **Wm. Cochran** were

witnesses. Proven by **Stephen Davis** Nov 1834. [*Editor's Note: Located in NC Supreme Court Case #2744, Thomas Ritter and wife Margaret v. William Barrett*]

3740.   1830, Dec 11 -- Land Grant #2864, Moore County, NC
William Hill received 56 acres located north of Richland Creek adjoining **Jacob Stutts** and **Alexr. McIntosh**. **Daniel Muse** and **Green Hill** were chain carriers.

3741.   1830, Dec 11 -- Land Grant #2865, Moore County, NC
William Hill received 40 acres adjoining **George Ritter**, **McNeill**, **Jones** and his own line (formerly **Daniel Muse**). **Daniel Muse** and **Green Hill** were chain carriers.

3742.   1830, Dec 11 -- Land Grant #2880, Moore County, NC
John A. Shaw received 102 acres located on both sides of Cedar Creek adjoining **Thomas Person**, **Smith**, **John H. Hodgin** and **McLeod**. **William Shields** and **Henry Brown** were chain carriers.

3743.   1830, Dec 30 -- Marriages, *Carolina Observer* [Fayetteville, NC] Newspaper
"In Moore County, on Thursday evening, the 9th inst. [Dec 1830], by the Rev. **T. Kelly**, Mr. **William M. Larrence** of Randolph, to Miss **Mary Shamburger**, daughter of **Peter Shamburger**, Esq."

~ *To Be Continued in Volume 2* ~

Bell, Thomas...695a
Bell, William...1122, 2184
Benbow...231
Benbow, Arcada...404
Benbow, Elizabeth...404
Benbow, Powell...3, 135, 154, 228, 230, 278, 295, 404, 449, 468, 503-504, 511, 2491
Bennett, Thomas...49, 407
Benton, Jesse...1391
Benton, John...1398d
Berryman, John...2046
Berryman, Stephen...3722
Best, Archibald...407
Bethune...862, 3085, 3111, 3492a
Bethune, Allen...1713, 2750, 3007, 3111, 3239
Bethune, Angus...668, 686, 729
Bethune, Catharine...2031
Bethune, Christian...959, 993, 1034
Bethune, Christopher...1713, 1816, 2080-2081, 2113, 2160, 2228, 2351, 2382, 2713
Bethune, Colin...666
Bethune, Donald...1446, 1503, 2812
Bethune, Farquhard...663, 666, 727, 949, 951, 2031
Bethune, John...594, 1101, 1354, 1713, 2079, 2202, 2768, 2812, 2933, 3548, 3695
Bethune, Laughlin/Lauchlin...551, 1151
Bethune, Malcolm [R.C]...3334
Bethune, Margaret...3373, 3723
Bethune, Mary...3374
Bethune, Mary Martin...3695
Bethune, Murdoch/Murdock...668, 759, 820, 861, 934-935, 1016, 1039, 1041, 1061, 1084, 1184, 1258, 1277, 1557, 1586, 2031, 2404, 2474, 2846b, 2960, 3028, 3166
Bethune, Nancy...3316
Bethune, Peter...646, 663, 668, 686, 1339
Bethune, Widow...1622, 2090, 3438-3439, 3517-3518, 3574
Bettis...2347, 2407, 2448, 2459
Bettis, Amey...2781
Bettis, Catharine...334
Bettis, E...760
Bettis, Eleanor...2781
Bettis, Elijah...48, 60, 265, 295, 322, 334-336, 370-371, 383, 433, 505, 556-557, 662, 667, 685, 728, 840, 1001, 1194, 1213, 1264, 1352, 1490, 1662-1663, 2323-2324, 2419, 2444, 2488, 2760, 2781, 2821, 3068
Bettis, Elijah Jr...1490, 1505, 1979, 2220, 2323-2324, 2326, 2760, 2781, 3052
Bettis, Elijah Sr...1505, 1979, 2220, 2752, 2781, 3052
Bettis, Elisha...48, 322, 334, 336, 2220, 2323-2324, 2760
Bettis, Elisha Sr...2760
Bettis, Francis...48, 322, 336
Bettis, Irvine...322
Bettis, Jean...2781
Bettis, John...48, 336
Bettis, Lovely/Lovy...2760, 2781
Bettis, Obey...2760
Bettis, Overton...2781
Bettis, Primus...433

Bettis, Ransom...2760, 2781
Bettis, Sally...2760, 2781
Bevill, William...543
Bigger, Robert...765
Biggs, Richard...3434
Bird...2251, 2443, 2470, 2607, 2671, 2842
Bird, John...43-44
Bird, Margaret...2076a
Bird, Peter...2076a
Bird, Richard...578, 580, 588, 661, 666, 684, 727, 744, 759, 767-769, 869-869a, 954, 1065, 1271, 1377, 1403, 1452, 1629, 1665, 1686, 1782, 2031, 2063, 2233, 2301, 2470, 2521, 2552, 2569, 2607, 2640
Bird, Robert...759, 845, 894-895, 940, 1212, 1645, 1713, 1925, 1935, 2031, 2060, 2078, 2095, 2115, 2362, 2606, 2616, 2664, 2786-2787
Bird, Robert Jr...2786-2787
Bird, Robert Sr...2786-2787
Bird, William...578-579, 869a, 2076a, 2631, 2664, 2787, 2909
Black, Archibald...1305
Black, Daniel...3119
Black, Hugh...1785
Black, Hugh Jr...1518-1519, 1785
Black, Hugh Sr...1518-1519, 1785
Black, John...444, 450-451, 1030, 1228, 3197
Black, Kenneth...444
Black, Margaret...3250
Black, Neil...3097, 3194
Black, William...336
Blair, George...3, 226-231, 277-278, 291-292, 328-329, 366, 372, 406, 503-504
Blair, James...2813
Blanchard, John...1144
Blanchet/Blanchett, John...840, 878, 972, 1086, 1162, 1214, 1443, 1555
Blanchfield, Alice...322, 334
Bland...553
Bland, James...2462
Bland, Moses...354, 502, 555
Bland, William...555, 1637, 2462
Blocker, Jacob...33
Blue, Christian...2948
Blue, Malcolm...3481
Boles, Ethro...957
Boles, Robert...1624
Boling, Benjamin...1330a-1330b, 1367c, 1585d
Boling, Caty...2834
Boling, Dicy...3485a
Boling, Elizabeth...3236
Boling, Gardner...3522, 3580
Boling, Jesse...2351a
Boling, John...455a, 2150b, 2351a, 3720
Boling, John Jr...1367c
Boling, Patsy...3720
Boling, William...1731a, 2931
Bookout, Charles...1392
Bookout, Joseph...1392
Bookout, Marmaduke...1392
Boon, James...446
Borden, William...97
Boroughs...2542, 2654, 2685, 2883-2884, 2957a, 3062, 3164, 3229
Boroughs, B...2644, 2794, 2797, 2815c, 2914, 3051, 3232, 3245, 3465

Boroughs, Barnea...2637
Boroughs, Bryan / Bryant...737i, 1429a, 1607, 1642, 1656, 1746, 1794, 1906, 2047, 2051, 2053, 2131, 2214, 2237, 2355, 2438, 2519, 2564, 2644, 2775a, 2846c, 2885, 2914, 2937a, 2959, 3007-3007a, 3020, 3036, 3105a, 3111, 3112, 3167, 3227, 3283, 3372, 3409, 3417, 3487, 3494, 3533, 3591, 3605, 3611, 3635-3636, 3644, 3649, 3653, 3656, 3684b, 3728
Boroughs, Edmond...3440, 3521
Boroughs, Edward...3378
Boroughs, Sally...3005
Boroughs, William...3112, 3656
Boroughs, Zacheus...737i, 3105a, 3417, 3465, 3533, 3644
Bostick, Levi...3312
Bostick, Nathaniel...3028
Boston, James...3338
Bowden/Bowdon...989, 1033, 1253, 2678, 2992
Bowden/Bowdon, Francis...872, 2140
Bowden/Bowdon, James...1033, 1377, 1392, 1453, 1807, 1813, 2521
Bowden/Bowdon, John...3185
Bowden/Bowdon, Travis...2441-2442, 2521, 2552, 2595, 2639
Bowden/Bowdon, William...872, 1172, 1202, 1377a, 1392, 1453, 1773, 2127, 2447, 2521, 2552, 2633, 2639
Bowell, Lewis...1531
Boyce, Arthur...429
Boyce, William...281
Boyd, John...1228
Bracey, John...171
Bradbury, Elizabeth...1067
Bradbury, George...1067
Bradbury, Hannah...1067
Bradbury, Jacob...1067
Bradbury, James...1067
Bradbury, Mary...1067
Bradbury, Rhoda...1067
Bradbury, Thomas Chambers...1067
Brady, Amy...2794a
Brady, Ann...1155
Brady, Bradley...3030, 3305, 3339, 3440, 3480a, 3521, 3643, 3671, 3705
Brady, Carrell/Carroll...2962, 3428a, 3480a, 3643, 3647, 3657
Brady, Charles...2846b, 2848, 2962, 2991, 3007, 3028, 3030, 3070-3071, 3111, 3627a, 3642-3643, 3657
Brady, Isaac...2788
Brady, James...1214, 1410, 1443, 1477, 1513, 2361, 2413, 2537, 2581, 2592, 2763, 2962, 3007, 3030, 3111
Brady, Lewis...1193a, 2788
Brady, Nathan...1155
Brady, Robert...2592, 2942, 3028, 3111, 3671, 3673
Brady, Toreence...2582
Brannon, Elizabeth...360, 625, 1128
Brannon, Terrance...346, 360, 625, 811, 848
Branson, Henry...1481, 2633, 3627b
Branson, Jane...2848a
Branson, Thomas...135
Braxton...1061a, 1601a
Braxton, Mary...2974a
Braxton, Thomas...2974a
Bray...2097a, 2635a
Bray, Eli...3185

Bray, Harmon...3185
Bray, Henry...3642
Bray, Jesse...3185
Bray, John...3185
Bray, Mathias...3185
Bray, Sarah...620
Brazel, George...380, 666, 684, 727, 921, 1007, 1020, 1267, 1296, 1310-1311, 1321, 1334, 1351, 1369, 1380, 1448, 1504, 1541, 1607, 1691
Brazel, Mary...1607
Brazel, Richard...380
Brewer...1349a, 1350, 1405, 1674, 2639a, 2715a, 2828a, 2966, 2990b, 3192
Brewer, Ambrose...1076, 1141, 1334a, 1486, 1656, 2054, 2529, 2588, 2817, 2991, 3007, 3028, 3111
Brewer, Ann...2815d
Brewer, Daniel...2764a, 3494, 3642
Brewer, David...2997a, 3028, 3076b, 3150, 3521, 3617, 3630, 3714, 3736
Brewer, Donald...2979
Brewer, Drury...1477, 2054, 2588, 2997a, 3150, 3657
Brewer, Elijah...3150, 3275, 3286, 3301, 3305, 3339, 3440, 3469, 3521, 3679
Brewer, Elisha...3111
Brewer, Elizabeth...3513
Brewer, Frederick...2942, 2962
Brewer, George...662, 667, 685, 728, 2806, 2809, 3126a
Brewer, Hannah...2815d
Brewer, Harmon...1042, 1906, 1909, 2047-2048, 2053, 2355, 2564, 2693, 2870, 3007, 3111, 3150, 3286, 3513, 3566, 3572
Brewer, Henry...914a, 3028
Brewer, Howell...19, 22, 74, 264, 314, 374, 599, 914a, 1377, 1452, 1636, 1713, 2177, 2869, 2997a, 3028, 3402
Brewer, Howell Sr...869a
Brewer, James...3513
Brewer, Jephthah...2588
Brewer, Jesse...2718a, 2781a, 3030, 3285, 3437, 3627a
Brewer, John...3513, 3546a
Brewer, Julius...2942
Brewer, King...2810, 3127a
Brewer, Lanier/Nier...295, 662, 693, 1099-1100, 1214, 1443, 1457, 1477, 1578, 1607, 1935, 2298, 2364, 2438, 2573, 2762
Brewer, Lucinda...3513
Brewer, Lydia...3513
Brewer, Mary...2722, 2815d
Brewer, Micajah/Cager...1477, 2188, 2408, 2573, 2652, 2654, 2683-2684, 2707, 3007, 3028, 3030, 3111, 3124, 3164, 3192
Brewer, Nancy...3007a
Brewer, Nehemiah...295
Brewer, Nicholas...1193a
Brewer, Nimrod...869a, 2198
Brewer, Noah...3705
Brewer, Oma...2914
Brewer, Ruben...1713
Brewer, Ryal...1713
Brewer, S...3007, 3111
Brewer, Sally...3513
Brewer, Sampson...855b, 914a, 986a, 1062a, 1194b-1194c, 1204a, 1223a,

1349a, 1597a, 1953a, 2140a, 2141a, 2629a, 2639a, 2653a, 2701a, 2718b-2718c, 2761a, 2764a, 2765c, 2781a, 2805d, 2811a, 2815d, 3243a, 3687a, 3705
Brewer, Solomon...2815d, 3007a, 3038, 3050, 3086, 3088, 3243a, 3271, 3296, 3315, 3409, 3445, 3471, 3524b, 3527, 3578, 3603, 3628
Brewer, Stephen...2815d, 3243a, 3527
Brewer, Susannah...3028
Brewer, William...1713, 2781a, 2805d, 2828a, 2848, 3016, 3111, 3175, 3217, 3249, 3286, 3307, 3432, 3469, 3473, 3476, 3492, 3501, 3519, 3532, 3538, 3546, 3568, 3584, 3592-3594, 3614, 3670, 3723, 3737-3738
Brewer, William Jr...2942
Brewer, Willis...1187-1188, 1684, 1713, 2156-2157, 3028, 3378, 3440, 3521
Brice, William...3195a-3195b
Bridges...2534-2536
Bridges, Horace P. [Sheriff]...3051a, 3179a
Bridges, Joseph...2295-2296, 2402, 2473, 2498-2499, 2507, 2605
Bridges, William...1064
Briggs, Thomas...478, 577
Britt, Alfred...3631, 3684a
Britt, Avington...2874, 3235, 3401, 3631, 3684a
Britt, Becom...2874, 3631, 3684a
Britt, Belaver...2874, 3105, 3268, 3338, 3434, 3441, 3720
Britt, Bellison...2874
Britt, Benjamin...1064, 1588, 1715, 2535-2536, 2625, 2849, 2874-2875, 3111, 3224
Britt, Britton...2874, 3007, 3594, 3631, 3684a
Britt, Bryan...3111
Britt, Buldu...2874
Britt, Cleryman...2874
Britt, Edward...2905
Britt, Edwin...2874
Britt, Finity...2874
Britt, Handay...2874
Britt, J...3066
Britt, Jeptha...2874, 3454, 3507
Britt, Joseph...702a, 710b, 1064, 1171, 1395, 1588, 1618, 1715, 2625
Britt, Lucretia...3720
Britt, Merriman...2942, 3266, 3286, 3468, 3509, 3614
Britt, Nancy...2874
Britt, Prulellah...2874
Britt, Rhoda / Rody...2856, 2874, 3007, 3111
Britt, Rial/Ryals...1064, 1588, 1715, 2152, 2535-2536, 2850-2851, 2854-2856, 2874, 3468
Britt, Tinsay...2874
Britt, William...2942
Brooks...3539, 3722e
Brooks, Isaac...1376
Brooks, James...3281
Brooks, John...3468a, 3610
Brooks, Mary...620
Brooks, Phillip...3077, 3163, 3165, 3263, 3281, 3584, 3590, 3597, 3643, 3647-3647a, 3724a
Brooks, Polly...3647a

Brooks, William...1578, 1754, 1764, 2367, 2370-2371
Brookther, Manner...3065
Brower...3658
Brower, Alfred...3185, 3658
Brower, Jacob...3185
Brower, Mason T...3667a
Brown...681, 1756, 2058, 2538b, 2653a, 2844a, 2892, 2950, 2964, 3016, 3120, 3238, 3390-3391
Brown, Aben [Abner?]...2942
Brown, Abner...656, 671a, 695a, 2316a, 2942, 3088, 3131, 3405, 3409, 3641-3642, 3647, 3656, 3671, 3717
Brown, Abraham...3658
Brown, Ambrose...656, 674, 735, 800a, 1105a, 1279, 1587, 1769, 2241
Brown, Auley...3118
Brown, Benjamin...1808
Brown, Daniel...536
Brown, Elijah...1753, 3028
Brown, Henry...97, 3647, 3742
Brown, Isaac...2511-2512, 3538, 3642, 3719
Brown, Isaiah...3175, 3549
Brown, James...2747
Brown, Jesse...656, 674, 710a, 735-736, 937, 1026, 1105a-1105b, 1226, 1229, 1245, 1279, 1348, 1351, 1371, 1445, 1507, 1536, 1713, 1769, 2139, 2241, 2482, 2820, 2882, 2892, 2927, 2942, 2963, 3007, 3049, 3111, 3131, 3175, 3235, 3282, 3290, 3303, 3312, 3321, 3323, 3349, 3359, 3376, 3381, 3407, 3409, 3472, 3492, 3534, 3543, 3559, 3592, 3606, 3633-3634, 3648, 3669, 3713, 3719
Brown, Jesse Jr...3131, 3175, 3299, 3312, 3323, 3488, 3509, 3538, 3549, 3670
Brown, Jesse Sr...3131, 3534, 3538, 3642, 3659, 3670, 3723
Brown, John...337, 656, 671a, 695a, 710a, 735-736, 2316a, 2639b, 3488, 3672
Brown, John Sr...671a
Brown, Lucy...2316a
Brown, Mary...656, 671a, 2316a
Brown, Nancy...2316a
Brown, Polly...2316a
Brown, Sally...2316a
Brown, Sampson...737e-737g
Brown, Thomas...3549, 3633
Brown, William...656, 2942, 3007, 3049, 3111, 3136, 3488, 3538, 3641, 3672, 3727
Brownlow...2230, 2356, 2472, 4090a-4090b
Brownlow, James...3466
Brownlow, John...210, 251, 295, 491, 494, 542
Bruce, A.B...2941
Bruce, S.C. [Dr.]...3640
Bruce, Samuel C...3154, 3546, 3657, 3687c
Bryan, Margaret...3106
Bryan, Mary/Polly...3106
Bryan, Redding...3203
Bryant...3228
Bryant, Benjamin...1305
Bryant, Dicy...3279
Bryant, Elisha...2900, 3339d, 3441a, 3574a, 3628a

Bryant, James...3186, 3298, 3385, 3409, 3568
Bryant, Kinsey...1713
Bryant, Leah...3409
Bryant, Michael...1535, 1713, 1858, 2532, 2894-2895, 2900, 3025, 3111, 3291, 3303, 3385, 3409, 3495, 3568, 3584, 3633
Bryant, Needham...3193, 3250
Bryant, Nellay...3601
Bryant, Thomas...3186, 3193, 3339d, 3409, 3441a, 3574a, 3633, 3675
Buchanan, Donald...1558, 2000-2001, 2290
Buchanan, John...684, 727, 759, 1607
Buchanan, Joseph...438
Buckingham, Margery...620
Buell, Michel...1067
Buie, Archibald...445
Buie, Daniel...2846b
Buie, Duncan...94
Buie, Flora Ann...3677
Buie, John...2665, 3350
Buie, John C...3359, 3409, 3476, 3497, 3677
Buie, Joseph...3568
Buie, Malcolm...445, 1383, 3446
Buie, Sarah...3564
Buie, Widow...3081
Buie, William...3350, 3542, 3693
Buie, William C...3211, 3409, 3476
Bull, James H...3363-3364
Bullard, Thomas...333, 762
Bullen, Thomas...886, 2747
Bullock...1784, 2013, 2257, 2303-2304, 2486, 2624, 2626, 2766, 3016, 3217, 3249, 3253, 3424
Bullock, Allen...1714, 2234, 2552, 2763, 2858, 3023-3024, 3111, 3177
Bullock, F...2874
Bullock, Francis...1552, 1554, 1605, 1632, 1756, 1761, 1775, 1791, 1800, 1927, 2077, 2100, 2116, 2120, 2132, 2136, 2181, 2191, 2206, 2215, 2234, 2278-2279, 2310, 2312, 2346, 2430, 2469, 2473, 2484, 2530, 2579-2580, 2584, 2720, 2739, 2757, 2761, 2843, 2875, 2896, 2932, 2963, 3007, 3016, 3023-3024, 3105, 3111, 3121, 3169, 3476
Bullock, J...2157
Bullock, John...1285, 1389, 1504, 1520, 1526, 1561, 1608, 1692, 1751, 1756, 1775, 1784, 1802, 2037, 2058, 2062, 2097, 2107, 2146, 2156, 2158, 2418, 2430, 2540, 2699, 3029
Bullock, John Jr...1713
Bullock, Jonathan...2033, 2154-2155, 2157, 2234, 2580
Bullock, Mary A...2961
Bunell, Elizabeth...438
Burgwin, John...1528
Burke, Governor...744
Burkes, Richard...2490
Burkhead...3294
Burkhead, Belany...3275c
Burkhead, Charity Muse...3481
Burkhead, Eleazer...1554, 2872, 3007, 3111, 3294a, 3302, 3311, 3354, 3356, 3382, 3432a, 3479, 3481, 3495, 3526a, 3546, 3584, 3668, 3723
Burkhead, Eleazer Jr...3723
Burkhead, Eleazer Sr...3696a, 3723

Burkhead, Elias...3267a
Burkhead, Green...3481
Burkhead, James...1378, 3481, 3513
Burkhead, John...3275c
Burkhead, Kindred...3197, 3294a, 3382-3383, 3670
Burkhead, Lazarus...3058
Burkhead, Levin...3007, 3111, 3694
Burkhead, Nehemiah...3007, 3197, 3275c, 3339a, 3383, 3437a, 3581a, 3716
Burkhead, Westley...3591a, 3723a
Burkhead, William A...3723a
Burleson, Aaron...151, 252, 399, 604
Burnett, A...2316a
Burnett, Daniel...1105b
Burns, Ann R...3639
Burns, Enoch...3256a
Burris...2654
Burt, John...697
Burt, William...223, 498, 601, 616
Burton, Richard...223
Butler...2212, 2767, 3387
Butler, Christopher...380, 501, 682, 730, 906b
Butler, Elias...682, 2669a
Butler, Elias Jr...1772c
Butler, Elizabeth...501
Butler, John...918
Butler, William...3720a
Bynum, Luke...255
Bynum, William...171
Caddell...1449, 1733, 1903, 2068
Caddell, Albert...3132
Caddell, Benjamin...942a, 1028, 1060, 1096, 1236, 1263, 1386, 1459, 1493, 1585, 1606, 1704, 1713, 1756, 1771, 1796, 2056, 2074, 2108, 2124, 2214, 2431, 2465, 2859, 2910, 3007, 3044, 3090, 3111
Caddell, Cornelius...3266, 3286, 3516, 3572, 3581a, 3594a, 3662
Caddell, Daniel...942a, 1060, 1096, 1236, 1396, 1518, 1571, 1713, 1756, 2079, 2214, 2758-2759, 3007, 3111, 3194, 3266, 3286, 3295, 3358, 3403, 3437, 3438, 3486, 3495, 3566, 3572, 3574, 3654, 3682, 3686, 3691, 3698, 3702, 3722a
Caddell, Donald...3518
Caddell, Green...3516
Caddell, Green B...3512, 3573, 3691d
Caddell, James...193, 295, 308, 411, 474, 521-522, 663, 668, 686, 724, 729, 794, 874, 915, 920, 939, 971, 1004, 1019, 1024, 1027, 1030, 1081, 1112, 1154, 1179-1180, 1199, 1207, 1226, 1257, 1266, 1284, 1337, 1352, 1369, 1399, 1459, 1488, 1531, 1533, 1562, 1587, 1607, 1623, 1630, 1658, 1706, 1756, 1771, 1936, 2431-2432, 2437, 2465, 2758-2759, 3003, 3197, 3512, 3573
Caddell, James Jr...942a, 1060, 1096
Caddell, James Sr...1085, 1264
Caddell, John...663, 922, 937, 939, 942a, 1004, 1018, 1025, 1027, 1030, 1049, 1158, 1179, 1197, 1207, 1257, 1259, 1302, 1369, 1396, 1457, 1459, 1474, 1486, 1526, 1552, 1604, 1607, 1623, 1936, 3090
Caddell, Jonathan...686, 748, 762, 834, 882, 915, 922, 939, 1003, 1257, 1279,

1302, 1351, 1442, 1457, 1470, 1486, 1604, 1623, 1793, 1934, 2074, 2108, 2602, 2777-2778, 2817, 3007, 3111
Caddell, Joseph...3722d
Caddell, Micajah...1519, 1904
Caddell, Michael...1575
Caddell, Neill...3301, 3336, 3399, 3566, 3572, 3696a, 3722a, 3722d
Caddell, Polly...937
Caddell, Tobias...3573
Caddell, William...922, 937, 1054, 1096, 1236, 1515, 1713, 1758, 2074, 2108, 2226, 2648, 2987, 3044, 3118, 3266, 3450, 3469, 3486, 3512-3513, 3573, 3614, 3663, 3691d, 3704
Caddell, William Jr...3319, 3509
Caddell, William Sr...3007
Cagle...886, 929, 1000, 1767, 2456, 2582, 2820, 3120
Cagle, Caterana...2662
Cagle, Catherine...202, 369, 1671, 2452, 3236
Cagle, Charles...128, 317, 776, 960, 3236
Cagle, Christian...1764, 2078, 2267, 2662
Cagle, Christopher...1471, 1620, 1777, 2267, 2318, 2703
Cagle, David...202, 369, 581, 766, 1353, 1372, 1584, 1606, 1713, 1746, 1794, 2234, 2645
Cagle, Dorety...2452
Cagle, Elisha...3203a-3204, 3236
Cagle, Eliza...2662
Cagle, Elizabeth...2452
Cagle, George...369, 417, 539, 661, 666, 684, 727, 759, 769, 839, 877, 922, 939, 945, 971, 1005, 1021, 1112, 1197, 1207-1208, 1226, 1268, 1469, 1640, 1659, 1696, 1713, 1746, 1770, 1934, 1975, 2069, 2074, 2082, 2096, 2131-2132, 2151, 2283-2284, 2383, 2452, 2645, 2662, 2820, 2880, 2919, 2927, 2937, 2940, 2968, 3007, 3028, 3049, 3111, 3236, 3238, 3266, 3268, 3286, 3338, 3441, 3485a, 3638, 3678, 3715, 3720, 3723
Cagle, George [son of John]...1659
Cagle, George [Wolf Creek]...2082
Cagle, George Jr...2230, 3509, 3614
Cagle, Henry...187, 295, 325, 341, 344, 475, 661, 666, 684, 727, 747, 759, 769, 879, 1258, 1381, 1417, 1526, 1552, 1587, 1620, 1713, 1740, 1777, 1811, 1926, 1928, 2057, 2060, 2069, 2071, 2078, 2082, 2132, 2151, 2190, 2267, 2306, 2327, 2452, 2662, 2703, 3007, 3111, 3204, 3236, 3522, 3580, 3707
Cagle, Henry Jr...2150, 2222, 2254, 2293, 2525, 2621, 2662, 2741
Cagle, Henry Sr...1369, 1777, 2069, 2150, 2151, 2190, 2222, 2267, 2293, 2318, 2525, 2617, 2621, 2662, 2741
Cagle, Inna Caterena...2662
Cagle, Isaac...2927, 3016, 3049, 3117, 3678
Cagle, Jacob...379, 581, 765, 882, 927, 1047, 1154, 1235, 1256, 1290, 1305, 1340, 1360, 1504-1505, 1526, 1552, 1654, 1696, 1794, 1798, 1934, 1951-1952, 1954-1957, 1960-1963, 1965-1967, 1975, 1980, 1985-1986, 2002, 2074, 2143, 2153, 2214, 2341, 2452,

2108, 2131, 2133, 2195, 2214, 2247, 2258, 2268, 2322, 2348, 2367, 2370-2371, 2384, 2386, 2405, 2482, 2651, 2681, 2686, 2755, 2765c, 2817, 2824, 2846b, 2883-2884, 2912, 2969, 3028, 3033, 3100, 3183, 3197, 3481, 3550, 3703, 3716

Dunn, Sarah...250, 300-301, 343, 421, 2578, 3235

Dunn, Thomas...892, 1120, 1176, 1448, 1486, 2080-2081, 2406, 2473, 2498-2499, 2507, 2605, 2720, 2942

Dunn, Thomas Jr...2507

Dunn, W...760

Dunn, William...295, 556, 661-662, 665-667, 673, 684-685, 705, 709, 727-728, 740, 744, 759, 769, 771-772, 785, 838, 874, 892, 906, 915, 928, 944, 1000, 1014, 1018, 1026, 1049, 1081, 1092, 1110-1112, 1120, 1136, 1154, 1184, 1207, 1239, 1258, 1298, 1302, 1319, 1343, 1349, 1354, 1361, 1373, 1378, 1394, 1406, 1408, 1447a, 1459-1460, 1466-1468, 1505-1506, 1531, 1536, 1554, 1604, 1607, 1624, 1702, 1713, 1746, 1756, 1759, 1794, 1810, 1859, 1935, 1962, 2031, 2074, 2083, 2108, 2126, 2180, 2252, 2269, 2272, 2345, 2368, 2376, 2578, 2596, 2651, 2674, 2687-2688, 2731, 2742, 2752b, 2867, 2882, 2893, 2953, 2984, 3007, 3028, 3111, 3186a, 3235, 3271, 3282, 3297, 3299, 3349, 3352, 3367, 3383, 3445, 3469a, 3471, 3481, 3524a, 3578, 3628, 3641, 3671

Dunn, William [Buffalo Creek]...1049, 1154

Dunn, William [Wet Creek]...1154, 1179, 1207, 1279, 1356, 1746, 1794

Dunnegan...1618

Dunnegan, Ande...2490

Dunnegan, Charles...870

Dunnegan, E...2490

Dunnegan, John...3726

Dunnegan, Joseph...2490

Dunnegan, Patsy...3726

Dunnegan, Richard...661

Dunning, Jenny...3010

Dunning, Polly...3010

Dunning, William...2795a

Durham, Joseph...73

Durham, Thomas...255

Dyer, James...2528, 2693, 2870

Dyer, Robert...2693

Eastridge, Thomas...3559a

Eddins...1529

Eddins, Sarah...3059

Edwards...1076, 1137, 1290, 1360, 1766-1767, 2002, 2340-2341, 2391, 2487, 2661, 2665, 2702, 2749, 2805c, 3135

Edwards, Isaac...2910a

Edwards, John...171

Edwards, Jonathan...2637

Edwards, Moses...340, 2815a

Edwards, Nancy...1170

Edwards, Robert...274-275, 299, 310, 312, 319, 330b, 340-341, 358, 385, 412-414, 473, 475, 505, 582, 618, 1874, 2431, 2546, 2674

Edwards, Sarah...2910a

Elet, Eleanor...46

Elet, Thomas...46, 457, 597-598, 639

Elkins...1356a, 3005b

Elkins, Abner...3597

Elkins, Benjamin...693, 737h, 761a-761b, 814b, 914a, 1443, 1477, 1656, 2764a, 3005b

Elkins, Darias...3176a

Elkins, Elizabeth...2977a

Elkins, Etha...3176a

Elkins, Hiram...3185

Elkins, James...1099, 1490, 2307, 2458, 3294

Elkins, John...2977a

Elkins, John W...3176a

Elkins, Joseph...2, 18, 30, 32, 80, 89, 3197

Elkins, Lewis...3197

Elkins, Mary...2971a, 3476a

Elkins, Polly...3546

Elkins, Samuel...30, 138, 1490, 1506, 1758, 2282, 2286, 2288-2289, 2619, 2857, 2912, 3007, 3111, 3476a

Elkins, Shedrick...908

Elkins, Stephen...2817a, 3028

Elkins, Wade...3663a

Elkins, Widow...3581-3581a, 3622

Elkins, Willis...2763

Ellerbe, William...3197

Elliott...737f, 2701a

Elliott, Ebenezor...2864, 2971a

Elliott, John...737g, 2701a

Elliott, Milly...3181

Elliott, Samuel...3033

Ellis, Stephen...203

Ellison, Robert...895

Elwell, John...343, 648

Elwell, Richard...343

England...966, 1118, 1140, 1357, 1540, 1788, 2282, 2289, 3525

England, James...3007, 3033, 3192, 3635

England, James W...3649, 3653, 3657

England, Widow...2883

England, William...78, 714, 739, 1055, 1193a, 1650, 1818, 2245, 2285, 2350, 2413, 2528, 2537, 3007, 3111, 3539

England, William T...3539

English, John...1464

English, Joseph...759

Epperson, John...1082

Epps, Edward...2079a, 2764a

Epps, John...2079a, 3073

Epps, Patty...2079a

Estridge, John...3573

Etheridge, Thomas...702a, 710b, 2152

Evans...556

Evans, George...287, 331

Evans, John...2109, 2226, 2463-2464, 2886

Evans, Jonathan...34, 48, 191, 215, 286-287, 295, 331, 405, 645, 2912

Evans, Theophilus...191, 287, 331, 815

Fanning, David...744, 746, 1113a

Farmer, Fox...1113a, 1661a

Farris, Frances...75

Faucett, Henry...3591a

Faucett, John...3591a

Faucett, John B...3723a

Feagin...2466, 2878, 2989

Feagin, Aaron...558, 561, 663, 667, 686, 726, 729, 962, 974, 1200

Feagin, Daniel...2352, 2902a, 3007, 3111

Feagin, Edward...295, 308, 351, 530, 543, 545, 2463-2464, 2700

Feagin, Elizabeth...7, 55

Feagin, George...7, 30, 45, 55, 283, 295, 324, 335, 419, 478, 487, 1140, 1729, 2073, 2285, 2365, 2446, 2519, 2495, 2501, 2519, 2759

Feagin, George Jr...353

Feagin, George Sr...308, 340, 409-411

Feagin, Henry...3036

Feagin, Martha...3036

Feagin, Richardson...543, 558, 561, 572, 589, 663, 668, 726, 729, 763-764, 885, 907, 910, 919, 924, 937, 977, 1002, 1082, 1105, 1113, 1133-1134, 1148-1149, 1180, 1200, 1213, 1258, 1264, 1370, 1383, 1446, 1479-1480, 1488, 1490, 1537, 1564, 1713, 1759, 2057, 2073, 2214, 2285, 2446, 2489, 2495, 2501, 2846b, 3007, 3036, 3111

Feagin, Samuel...2352, 3036

Feagin, Sarah...3036

Feagin, Thomas...2446, 3036

Feagin, William...907, 1251, 1758, 2163, 2311, 2349, 2401, 2446, 2501, 3007, 3111, 3568

Felsinger, Andrew...417

Ferguson, Alexander...661, 666

Ferguson, John...3394-3396, 3616b

Ferguson, Richard...3276

Ferrington, John...735-736, 1105a-1105b

Fesmire, Balaam...3461a

Field, Benton...1650, 2245

Field, John...666, 759

Fields, Francis...812

Fields, Isaac...3616b, 3691c

Fields, John...727, 759, 1551

Fields, Lewis...1007

Finch...2669a

Finch, Mary...3119

Finelson, John...759

Finley...2217a, 2217c-2217d, 3005c, 3026a-3026b

Finley, Charles...5, 87, 133, 137, 139

Finley, James...2, 89, 138

Finley, Mary...2, 138

Finley, Michael...2217

Finley, Susan...137

Finley, William...886, 914, 938, 1129, 1193a-1193c, 1194a-1194c, 1367b, 1554, 1695a, 1716a, 2141a, 2636a, 2636c, 2937a

Finnison, William...744

Fletcher, Angush...727

Folds, George...253, 337

Foleman, James...766

Folk, George...545

Folsom, William Willis...2636

Ford, William...2637

Foreman, Benjamin...9, 24, 99, 116, 126

Foushee, Daniel [Captain]...3118

Foushee, Elijah...3118

Foushee, John...3118

Foushee, Joseph...2316a, 3118

Foushee, Micajah...3118

Foushee, Simon...3118

Foushee, William...3118

Fowler, John...641, 2779a

Franklin, Thomas...67

Frazier...2962, 3030, 3569

Frazier, Ann...2581

Gibson, William...666, 742, 906c
Gilbert...504, 1601a, 2771a, 2794b
Gilbert, Benjamin...1668-1669, 1706a, 1795, 1808, 2134, 2316, 2491, 2864, 3007, 3033, 3063, 3111, 3470b
Gilbert, Cornelius...2134, 2834a, 2864
Gilbert, Gidean...135, 154
Gilbert, James...2134
Gilbert, Jane...3033, 3663a
Gilbert, John...2134, 3341
Gilbert, Joseph...3, 154, 449, 503, 511, 662, 667, 685, 728, 977, 1075a, 1147, 1213, 1282-1283, 1531a, 1706a, 2109, 2134, 2491, 3663a
Gilbert, Mary...154, 1046
Gilbert, Richard...3622
Gilbert, Sabra...404, 1706a, 1716, 2229, 2491, 3111, 3616c
Gilbert, Wilson...2229
Gilbert, Winson...2990a
Gilchrist, John...1701, 2185
Gilchrist, Malcom...1701, 2112a
Gilliam, John...1500, 1509, 1713, 2144-2145, 2425, 2579, 2668, 2706, 2740, 2763
Gilliam, John Jr...2236, 2469, 2530, 2720
Gilliam, William...2425-2427
Gilliland, Joseph...2569a
Gillis, Archibald...1853, 2021, 2029
Gillis, D...2875
Gillis, Daniel...2950
Gillis, Donald...2952, 3226
Gillis, John...2948, 2950
Gilmore...1140, 1326, 1417, 1471, 1620, 2375, 2516, 2582
Gilmore, Charles Herd...718-719
Gilmore, Dick...2920
Gilmore, Elizabeth...2452
Gilmore, H...2846b
Gilmore, Hugh...208, 718-719, 1180, 2285
Gilmore, James...482, 1777, 2621
Gilmore, John...259, 517, 597, 639
Gilmore, Richard...3584
Gilmore, Samuel...1266
Gilmore, Stephen...208, 268, 293, 342
Gilmore, Thomas...775, 834a, 964, 996, 1132, 1155, 1444, 1531, 1556, 1616, 2109
Gilmore, William...35-36, 39, 304, 3574a, 3628a, 3706
Glascock...2163, 2311
Glascock, Elizabeth...3594a
Glascock, George...937, 943a, 979, 1004, 1037, 1057, 1078-1079, 1082-1084, 1097, 1104a, 1113, 1129, 1130, 1182, 1251, 1565, 1936, 2401, 2773, 2883-2884, 2954, 3107, 3111, 3594a
Glascock, John M...937
Glascock, John Melton/Milton...1079, 1128a, 1153, 1361, 1505, 1514, 1563, 1758, 2759
Glascock, Julius...1084, 1236, 1361, 1562, 1564-1565, 1585, 1758, 2109, 2163, 2954, 3007, 3111, 3594
Glascock, Martha/Patty...1129, 1130, 1361, 1399, 1533, 1564, 1585, 1749, 2109, 2259, 2501, 2759, 3111, 3525a, 3594a, 3607
Glascock, Martin...1361, 1758
Glascock, Milley...1361
Glascock, Widow...2083, 2128, 3027

Godfrey, Thomas...666
Goff, Ellison...3434
Goffey, William...97
Goins, Levi...2768a
Goins, Pleasant...2768a
Goins, William...2779a
Gold, Daniel...822
Goldman, Gunroad...170
Goldman, John...166-167, 183, 220, 260
Goldston...737e, 1002, 1105, 1223a, 1350, 1597a, 2141a, 2201, 2439, 2443, 2609b
Goldston, Charles...689, 702, 755, 756, 776a, 855b, 988, 1074, 1143, 1204, 2566
Goldston, John...448, 662, 667, 719, 737, 990, 1089, 1443
Goldston, John Hor...1350
Goldston, Lydia...3005
Goldston, William...737c-737d, 741a, 743, 746, 763a, 1484a
Gooden...752, 2459
Goodwin...2220, 3052
Goodwin, John...116
Gordon, John...670, 709
Gordon, Joseph...631
Gould...127a
Gould, Daniel...670, 743
Graham...360, 625, 1227, 1568, 2269, 2880, 2891, 2919, 3678
Graham, Andrew...3302, 3312, 3339c, 3441a, 3568, 3574a, 3584, 3633, 3684
Graham, Elizabeth...3566b, 3568, 3612
Graham, George...933, 1281, 1407, 1456, 1465, 1858, 2132, 2894-2895, 2899, 2910, 3233a, 3354, 3383, 3495, 3527
Graham, Harmon...3339c, 3441a
Graham, James...488, 518-519, 595-596, 625, 3409
Graham, Jamima...497
Graham, John...144, 152, 346, 418, 2197, 2239, 2794b, 3233a, 3519a, 3581b, 3628b, 3722f
Graham, Malcolm...3339c, 3441a, 3446, 3566b, 3568, 3574a, 3628a, 3633, 3684
Graham, Margaret...2891
Graham, Nancy...3302, 3312
Graham, Neill...3432
Graham, Patrick...3663a
Graham, Robert...61, 360, 488, 625, 661, 666, 727, 759, 800, 811, 824, 847-848, 885, 1066, 1155, 1189, 1222, 1505, 1815, 2132, 2715, 2840, 2894-2895, 2899-2900, 3034, 3339c, 3432, 3441a, 3574a, 3628a, 3675
Graham, Robert Jr...2609a
Graham, Robert Sr...2532
Graham, Sally...3584
Graham, Thomas...684, 727, 759, 847-848, 850-852, 861-863, 871, 885, 891, 896-897, 901, 964, 967-968, 991, 1013, 1036, 1045, 1066, 1131, 1259a, 1339, 1354, 1456, 1465, 1501, 1505, 1537, 1631, 1751, 1815, 1922, 1958, 2119, 2132, 2148, 2206, 2284, 2308, 2404, 2464, 2532, 2627, 2701, 2712, 2725, 2729, 2806, 2816, 2868, 2895, 2900, 2927-2928, 2938, 2950, 2981, 3007,

3111, 3186, 3291, 3303, 3339c, 3385, 3441a, 3584, 3722f
Graham, William...3432
Granbery, Josiah...503-504
Grantham, Elizabeth...1067
Grantham, Thomas...1067
Graves...2585a, 2805a
Graves, Alexander...3428a
Graves, James...209, 510, 642, 688, 2183
Graves, John...132
Graves, Moore...3676a
Graves, Nancy...2183
Graves, Peter...662, 667, 693, 1187, 1214, 1237, 1943, 2140a, 2282, 2285, 2289, 2350, 2365, 2537, 2629a, 2653a, 2743
Graves, Samuel...1330b, 2834, 2943
Graves, Thomas...52, 132, 642, 659, 1719
Graves, William...2636b
Gray, A...3076a
Gray, Charles...1377, 1807
Gray, Thomas...1618
Green...2654a, 3136
Green, Farn...95
Green, Jeresth...19, 374
Green, Rachel...1046
Green, Thomas...525, 619, 2752a
Green, William...374, 2650, 2740, 2752a
Green, Zachariah...19, 74, 312, 374, 396, 398
Gregg...1150, 2710, 2991a
Gregg, Anna...2710
Gregg, Frederick...7, 19, 279, 311-312, 364, 396-398, 574-575
Gregg, Thomas...2550, 2710
Gregory, Edward...490, 544
Gresham, John...3620
Gresham, Thomas...3621
Griffin...2730a, 2805b, 2963a, 3189a
Griffin, Edward...447, 514, 536, 599, 737e, 737j, 1223a, 1336, 1349b, 1356a, 1597a, 2423, 2575
Griffin, Jesse...1554, 1607, 1624, 1636, 1979, 1981, 2051a, 2057, 2070a, 2531
Griffin, John...2575
Griffin, Samuel...2575, 2956, 3005a
Griffin, William...97, 171, 255
Griffith...3450
Griffith, Caleb...2756
Griffith, Edward...3
Griffith, Roger [Sheriff]...776a, 821a
Griffith, William...2985
Grove...867, 986, 1339, 2384, 2651, 2681, 2697, 2754, 3001-3002, 3464
Grove, Richard...196-197, 282, 315, 2425
Grove, William...899, 935
Grove, William B...2425
Guest, Henry...42, 67
Guest, Henry Jr...56
Guest, Morgan...2747
Guin, Alfred...3106
Guin, Jenny...3106
Gunter, John...255
Guthrie...2419a, 2538b, 2586b, 2639a, 2715a, 2718a, 2761a, 2765c
Guthrie, Beverly...1716a
Guthrie, Clabourn...1716a
Guthrie, German...1716a
Guthrie, Samuel...1716a, 2636a

Haygood, James...171
Hays, Stephen...3118
Healy, Jesse...1607
Heard, Charles...123
Heard, John...57
Hearing, William...41
Hedgepath, Jesse...3591a, 3607, 3723a
Held, John...684
Heller, Michael...417
Henderson, John...2636c
Hendrick, Carter...1190a, 2217a, 2629a, 2653a
Hendrick, Joel...1190a
Hendry, George...50, 154
Henley...2360, 2528
Henley, Jesse...1180
Henry, Captain...2774, 2831
Henry, Carter...2217a
Henry, John...223
Henry, Micajah...1071
Herd, Stephen...565
Heron, Phillip...635
Hewitt...1193, 1341
Hewitt, James...2490
Hewitt, John...2747
Hewitt, Solomon...2490
Hewitt, William...788-789
Hicks, Adryan...512a
Hicks, Berry...1168a, 1772a-1772c, 1952a
Hicks, Catherine...3720
Hicks, Eli...3185
Hicks, George...3132a
Hicks, Isam...2983a
Hicks, Jacob...3132a
Hicks, James...3126b
Hicks, James B...3132a
Hicks, John...3720
Hicks, Joseph...689, 869a, 1255, 1377, 1453, 1807, 2569a, 2606, 2641, 2763
Hicks, Joseph Jr...2606
Hicks, Joseph Sr...2606
Hicks, Littleberry...906b, 1168a, 1271a, 1537a, 1772d, 2148a
Hicks, Reuben...1453, 3126b
Hicks, William...1772b, 2983a
Higgins, John...157, 2148a
Hile, John...364
Hill...761, 780, 1047, 1290, 1360, 2002
Hill, Aaron...688, 1074, 1391, 1614
Hill, Benjamin...316
Hill, Green...3309, 3729, 3740-3741
Hill, Hiram/ Hyman / Hymrick...1060, 1096-1097, 1185-1186, 1236, 1758, 2988, 3007, 3111, 3197, 3264, 3301, 3389, 3469, 3481, 3486, 3572, 3594a, 3691, 3696a
Hill, Isaac...42, 188-189, 295, 475, 520, 662, 667, 671, 685, 728, 761, 769, 1505, 2409-2410
Hill, James...295, 527, 663, 668, 729, 857, 885, 1021, 1030, 1040, 1081, 1112, 1197, 1264, 1279, 1334, 1369, 1396, 1552, 1577, 1587, 1604, 1704, 1934, 1979, 2109, 2226, 2369, 2988, 3197, 3358, 3438, 3479, 3518, 3574, 3654, 3698, 3722a
Hill, John...3318a, 3341a
Hill, Joseph...1122
Hill, Martin...3197, 3358, 3438, 3479, 3518, 3574, 3584, 3641, 3654, 3670
Hill, Mary...541, 3318a

Hill, Michael...759, 827, 905-906, 1000, 1045, 1047-1048, 2674
Hill, Seth...755-757
Hill, Thomas...291
Hill, William...3403, 3597, 3616b, 3716, 3729, 3740-3741
Hillen, Nathaniel...7b
Hilliard...3005a
Hilliard, Elizabeth...2805d, 2828a
Hilliard, Ezekial...737a-737b, 737k, 801b, 1170a, 1349b, 2805b, 2963b
Hilliard, James...2963a-2963b, 3033, 3179a
Hilliard, Jesse...2963a-2963b
Hilliard, Samuel...914a
Hilliard, Sion...2652, 2654, 2963a
Hilliard, William...2963a
Hines [see Hynes]
Hinshaw, Absolom...2994
Hinshaw, Ann...2994, 3433
Hinshaw, Elizabeth...2994
Hinshaw, Joseph...3433
Hinson...1494, 1638, 2410
Hinson, J...929
Hinson, John...886, 1000
Hinson, Lazarus...2800a
Hinson, Merrel...2655a
Hinsworth [see Ainsworth]
Hinwelt, Ralph...209
Hix [see Hicks]
Hobson, George...1365
Hobson, Hannah...1365
Hobson, Jean...2585
Hobson, Joseph...1365, 2585
Hobson, Sarah...1365
Hobson, William...1365
Hodges...1037, 2129, 3294
Hodges, Elizabeth...2335
Hodges, John...661, 666
Hodges, Philemon...2128, 2401, 2814
Hodgin, Asbury H...3739
Hodgin, John...3676
Hodgin, John H...3657, 3739, 3742
Hodgin, John M...3594
Hodgson, Robert...1046
Hogan, A. [Captain]...1588, 1715,
Hogan, Isaiah...656
Hogg...2254
Hogg, James...1398, 1446, 1580, 2222
Hoggard, Hannah...1046
Hoggard, Margaret...1046
Hoggard, William...1046
Hogwood, James...255
Hogwood, John...3434
Holcombe...2490, 2602, 2777
Holcombe, James...1710, 1756, 2109, 2576, 2783, 2922
Holcombe, Joseph...2424, 2490, 2747
Holcombe, Lydia...2109
Holden, Betsey...2668
Holden, Charles...2078, 2193
Holden, John...2193, 2280, 2668
Holland, Edmond...2990, 3007, 3111, 3246, 3266, 3286, 3434, 3442, 3527, 3555, 3567, 3602, 3615, 3658, 3662, 3676a, 3681, 3692, 3697, 3723, 3737-3738
Holland, Edward...3592
Holland, James...3701
Holland, Richard...2453, 2597, 2875, 2896, 3007, 3111, 3434, 3442, 3527, 3592, 3697, 3701
Hollingsworth...2815b-2815c

Hollingsworth, Jacob...2419b, 2747
Hollins...2811
Hollomon, Robert...3378, 3440, 3643
Hollomon, Solomon...2220, 2323
Holloway, Ann...660
Holloway, Brigett...660
Holloway, Elizabeth...660
Holloway, Jane...660
Holloway, Litici...660
Holloway, Martha...660
Holloway, Mary...660
Holloway, Nathan...3394-3396, 3479, 3594a, 3716
Holloway, Priscilla...660
Holloway, Rachell...660
Holloway, Robert...660
Holloway, Ruth...660
Holloway, Samuel...660
Holloway, Steven...660
Holloway, Susannah...660
Holmes, Thomas...12, 29
Hood, William...82
Hooper, William...28, 375
Hooton, Elijah...573
Hooton, John...573
Hopkins, Ed...3550
Hopper, George...2490
Hopson, Jane...2229
Horn...1618
Horn, Henry...174
Hornaday, Hannah...995a
Horner...3421
Horner, Dicey...2941, 3726
Horner, Elizabeth...660, 842, 2941, 3726
Horner, George...842, 870, 873, 1618, 2941, 3119, 3210
Horner, George Jr...842, 870, 873, 1618
Horner, George Wyatt...2941, 3726
Horner, James...873, 3726
Horner, Lucy...3726
Horner, Sally...3726
Horser...179, 236, 628
Horser, Hezekiah...181, 402
Horser, Isaac...27, 425, 464
Horser, Joseph...840
Horser, Mary...27, 464
Hoskins, William...1453
Hough, Joseph...305
House, Nimrod...2710, 2747
Houston, John...2419b, 3185
Houton, John...626
Howard...2031, 2986
Howard, Evan...3720
Howard, Rebecca...3720
Howard, Samuel...57
Howard, Stephen...57a, 103a
Howell...555
Howell, Hardy...472, 2759
Howell, Henry...506
Howell, John...272, 284, 378, 381, 572, 741, 749, 1027, 1180, 2163
Howell, Joseph...472
Hubbard, Eliza...2662
Hudson...2817a
Hudson, Joseph...3065
Hudson, William B...3627a
Huffman...1880, 2012
Huffman, Jacob...295
Hughes, Evan...1193c
Hughes, Neil...1796
Humble, Jacob...1772a

Jones, Elkin...2976
Jones, John...135, 301
Jones, Marchel...2760
Jones, Mary...3059
Jones, Milly...2852
Jones, Rebecca...49
Jones, Richard...2764a, 3033, 3185
Jones, Sugar...2764a, 2805d, 2811a, 2977a, 2990b, 3005b, 3007a, 3033, 3468a
Jones, Thomas...29, 132
Jones, Warren...3647
Jones, William...2838, 2942, 3007, 3087, 3111, 3266, 3271, 3278, 3287, 3415, 3419, 3445, 3449, 3540, 3555, 3614, 3625, 3634, 3648, 3659, 3670, 3716
Jones, Zacariah...3404
Jones, Zacceus...3277
Jones, Zack...3309
Jordan...3257
Jordan, Enoch...3644a
Jordan, Francis...519a, 906b, 918, 1537a, 1772a, 1772c, 3126b, 3132a
Jordan, Jacob...3644a
Jordan, John...1537a, 1772a-1772d, 1952a, 3234a, 3644a, 3676a
Jordan, Louise...3076a
Jordan, Miles...3187, 3208, 3236, 3288, 3409, 3522, 3580
Jordan, Thomas...1537a, 1772d
Juck...2281
Keadle, John...251, 270-271
Keahey /Keachey, James...3235, 3409, 3474, 3629, 3642, 3723, 3734
Keahey /Keachey, Martha...2755
Keahey /Keachey, Mary...2755
Keahey /Keachey, William...498
Kealin, Adam...1304a
Kealin, John...3023-3024, 3028
Keller, John...3028
Kelly...3263, 3464, 3525
Kelly, Angus...3388, 3517, 3698, 3722b, 3730
Kelly, Christopher...2813
Kelly, Hugh...3358, 3388, 3414, 3439, 3654, 3730
Kelly, J.B...3145
Kelly, John [Tailor]...3591a
Kelly, John B...3158, 3197, 3295, 3311-3312, 3341, 3343, 3394-3396, 3479, 3544, 3591a, 3594a, 3633, 3667, 3670, 3716, 3723a
Kelly, T...3743
Kelly, Thomas...1343
Kendle, William...3676a
Kendrick, William...2771a
Kennedy...2257, 3125, 3271, 3391, 3421, 3445, 3471, 3488, 3520, 3524a, 3578, 3583, 3628
Kennedy, Aaron...3428, 3488, 3531, 3533, 3556, 3561, 3578, 3628, 3641-3642, 3644, 3647, 3656-3657, 3659, 3671, 3687b
Kennedy, Alexander...727, 759, 1590-1591, 1626, 1656, 1676, 1675-1676, 1788, 2146, 2551, 2629, 2807, 2846c, 2862, 2991, 2997a, 3007, 3099, 3111, 3286, 3301, 3351, 3437, 3443, 3465, 3470, 3533, 3566, 3591, 3626, 3632, 3635, 3641-3642, 3647, 3657, 3672
Kennedy, Asa...3104
Kennedy, D...2695, 3425, 3659

Kennedy, David...1195, 1540, 1590, 1633, 1654-1655, 1659, 1672, 1674-1675, 1696, 1701, 1750, 1788, 1794, 1916, 1930, 1934, 2059, 2097, 2104, 2117, 2122, 2125, 2196, 2213, 2344, 2551, 2609, 2612, 2644, 2722, 2726, 2792, 2846c, 2862, 2878, 2964, 2974, 2991, 3007, 3028, 3111, 3167, 3266, 3283, 3287, 3323a, 3359, 3417, 3437, 3488, 3494, 3520, 3566, 3568, 3572, 3585-3587, 3590, 3594, 3603, 3640-3641, 3644, 3647-3649, 3657, 3694, 3712, 3728
Kennedy, Dicy...3642
Kennedy, E.M...3585
Kennedy, E.S...3585
Kennedy, Easter...2629
Kennedy, Edward...2862, 3007, 3111
Kennedy, Eleander...2629
Kennedy, Elias...3255, 3520, 3626, 3632, 3634, 3648-3649
Kennedy, Elias M...3642, 3657, 3659
Kennedy, Enoch...3520, 3683
Kennedy, Enoch S...3642, 3657, 3659
Kennedy, G...3206
Kennedy, George...2629, 2722, 2726, 2942, 3007, 3039, 3056, 3111, 3258, 3271, 3347, 3426, 3428, 3437, 3445, 3495, 3583, 3645
Kennedy, H...3196, 3206, 3560, 3568
Kennedy, Hiram...2964, 3007, 3111, 3238, 3293, 3345, 3359, 3428, 3464, 3487-3488, 3492, 3511, 3520, 3523, 3585, 3594, 3735
Kennedy, Joanna...2059, 2612
Kennedy, John...1625, 1672, 1674, 2122, 2997a, 3007, 3059, 3111, 3226, 3242, 3307, 3423-3424, 3443, 3538, 3566, 3572, 3632, 3642, 3657, 3676a
Kennedy, Josiah...3617, 3632, 3642, 3657, 3714
Kennedy, L...3641
Kennedy, Lewis...3099, 3470a
Kennedy, Liddy...3586
Kennedy, Lydia...3587
Kennedy, Margaret...3242
Kennedy, Mary...2196, 2792, 3242
Kennedy, Nathan...3028
Kennedy, Neill...3242
Kennedy, Nelly...2551
Kennedy, Robartus...3443
Kennedy, Robert...2629, 2942, 3007, 3111, 3178, 3187, 3208, 3307, 3409, 3426, 3437, 3443, 3522, 3580, 3642, 3657
Kennedy, Sally...3632
Kennedy, Sparks...3632
Kennedy, Susannah...3632, 3635, 3642, 3672
Kennedy, Widow...2146, 2154-2155, 2551
Kennedy, William...2964, 2997a
Kenney, John...457, 597-598, 639, 775
Kerr...510, 767, 954, 2443, 2586
Kerr, James...690
Kerr, Jane...510
Kerr, John...688, 690
Kerr, Joseph...153, 235, 286, 303, 405, 474, 523, 565a, 642, 645, 659, 689-690, 702, 758, 869, 869a, 1255, 1271, 1452, 1718-1719, 1772, 1807
Kerr, Josiah...510
Kerr, Nathaniel...690

Kerr, Robert...689, 758, 869, 869a, 1377, 1452, 1772, 2250, 2415-2417
Kerr, William...690, 1718-1719, 1772, 2251, 2415-2417, 2552, 2567-2569, 2586, 2607, 2671, 2708, 2776, 3185, 3190, 3227, 3257, 3372
Key...1016, 1275, 3001
Key, Cornelius...1713, 3694
Key, George...2972, 3161, 3246, 3302, 3312, 3323
Key, James...1018, 1521, 2747, 3382a, 3468, 3542, 3693
Key, John...295, 488, 592, 661, 666, 684, 727, 759, 856, 874, 876, 934, 1003, 1049, 1061, 1081, 1112, 1154, 1179, 1207, 1226, 1257, 1262, 1277, 1279, 1345, 1351-1352, 1369, 1379, 1396, 1425, 1442, 1486, 1557, 1586, 1600, 1713, 2468, 2471, 2753, 2875, 3007, 3008, 3085, 3111, 3401, 3738
Key, Joseph/Joshua...3676a
Key, Joshua...3534, 3693
Key, Mary...690, 937, 3323
Key, Moses...1354, 1379
Key, Perry...2931
Key, Polly...3302, 3312
Key, Samuel...3007, 3085, 3111, 3711
Key, Thomas...313, 315, 365, 488, 661, 673, 759, 856, 874-875, 935, 971, 1003, 1049, 1081, 1112, 1154, 1179, 1197, 1226, 1257, 1302, 1334, 1352, 1354, 1379-1380, 1396, 1442, 1474, 1510, 1526, 1557, 1600, 1633, 1654, 1659, 1713, 1753, 1842, 1907, 1976, 2049, 2622, 2753, 2942, 3246, 3693, 3711
Key, Vinson...3085
Key, William...117, 162, 221, 295, 592, 666, 684, 727, 1354, 1557, 1587, 1713, 2754, 2875, 2942, 2972
Kickson, Walter...281
Kidd...2555
Kidd, Carey/Carah...2569a
Kidd, John...3428a
Kidd, Moses...2419a, 2569a, 3007a, 3185
Kidd, Wincy...3531
Kilercas, John...92
Killett...378, 558, 726, 907, 1251
Killett, Andrew...88, 281, 353, 411, 460, 643, 648, 763
Killett, Mary...88, 281
Killett, William...23, 25-26, 30, 40, 70, 220, 263, 281, 283-284, 295, 410, 565
Kindrick, William...2705
King, James...3494, 3614c, 3643
King, Lucy...2941
King, Robert...2620, 3028
King, Stephen...3614c
King, W...2581
King, William...788, 1490, 1762, 1979, 3340, 3509a
Kirk, Joseph...171
Kirk, Lewis...710a, 800a
Kirkland, Vincent...3727
Kirksey, Christian...97
Kirksey, Christopher...171, 255
Kirksey, Isaac...255
Kitchen, Kinchen...1799, 2997a
Kitchen, Mrs...2905
Knight...3696a
Knight, J...1035
Knight, John...1193, 1341

Knight, Thomas...64, 109, 114, 134, 144, 454, 1780, 2467, 2487, 3680, 3739b
Kosh/Kost [see Cash]
Lakey...3449
Lakey, Elizabeth...2792
Lakey, James...2792, 2844, 2910, 2997a, 3069, 3128, 3262
Lakey, John...3627
Lakey, Lucy...2792, 3347
Lakey, Lydia...3428, 3583
Lakey, Mary...2132, 2792-2793, 2844
Lakey, Nancy...2132, 2792
Lakey, Polly...3347
Lakey, Viney...2792
Lakey, William...2792, 3098, 3143, 3419-3422, 3494, 3657
Lamb...2367, 2370, 2651, 2870
Lamb, Benjamin...1475, 2031, 2371
Lamb, Henry...2240, 2242, 2244, 2685
Lamb, Mary...1327, 2578
Lamb, Robert...1046
Lambert...2718b, 2990b
Lambert, J...1661a
Lambert, John Sr...1661a
Lambert, Joseph...2538b, 2569a, 2610b, 2639a, 2715a, 2761a
Lammonds, Malcolm...3546a
Lane...3007a
Lane, Abraham/Abram...2636b, 2815d, 2977a, 3185, 3657
Lane, John...3185
Lane, John Sr...3185
Lane, Joseph...3185
Lane, Tidence...3185
Lankford, Augustin...1456
Lankford, David...3287, 3445, 3524a, 3578, 3628, 3641, 3647, 3680
Lankford, Thomas...2763
Latham...2199, 2612a, 2692, 2694, 3060a
Latham, Amy...3720
Latham, Andrew...3720
Latham, Anthony...2590a, 2600, 2603, 2612a, 3067a
Latham, Betsy...3065, 3720
Latham, Catharine...3720
Latham, Charles...1453, 2706, 2750a
Latham, Cornelius...744, 746, 777, 869-869a, 1035, 1501, 1531, 1744, 1745b, 1748, 1948, 2441, 2560, 2590a, 2600, 2634-2635, 2653b, 2656, 2662, 2703, 2727, 2741, 2746, 2888, 2909, 2995, 3007, 3067a, 3527, 3720
Latham, Cornelius Jr...565a, 688, 3720
Latham, Cornelius Sr...565a, 688, 2600, 3715, 3720
Latham, Elizabeth...3720
Latham, Enoch...2653b, 2708b, 3720
Latham, James...115, 327, 565a, 688, 938, 1072, 1203, 1377, 1453, 1453b, 2163a, 2552, 2601, 2606, 2612a, 2631, 2656, 2826a, 2995, 3010, 3067a, 3111, 3527, 3599, 3720
Latham, James Jr...869a, 2590a, 2606, 2653b
Latham, James Sr...869a, 2540a, 2590a, 2603, 2653b
Latham, Jesse...3065, 3720
Latham, John...869a, 1481, 1635, 2170, 2608a, 2678a, 3065, 3720
Latham, John Jr...3065
Latham, John Sr...3065

Latham, Johnson...773, 869a, 1267
Latham, Lucretia...3720
Latham, Margaret...3720
Latham, Martha...3720
Latham, Mary...869
Latham, Nancy...2830a, 3720
Latham, Neill...3642
Latham, Patsy...3720
Latham, Polly...3065, 3720
Latham, Rebecca...3720
Latham, Richard...3065
Latham, Sally...3065, 3720
Latham, Solomon...3065
Latham, Susan...3720
Latham, Susannah...1517, 2826a, 2887, 3065
Latham, Widow...2441
Latham, William...869a, 1377, 1453, 1481, 2254, 2280, 2434, 2455-2458, 2540a, 2552, 2600, 2634-2635, 2653b, 2654a, 2656, 2692, 2902, 3010, 3136, 3720
Law, Robert...1113a
Lawhorn, Isaac...3698, 3722a
Lawhorn, Isiah...2779
Lawhorn, James...2864
Lawhorn, Joel...737a-737b, 2097a, 2661, 2686, 2702, 2764a, 2831a, 2886a, 2969, 3007, 3111, 3148, 3186a, 3221, 3277, 3356, 3509, 3516, 3696a
Lawhorn, John...2779, 3007, 3654
Lawhorn, Leonard...3358, 3438, 3518, 3574, 3581, 3696a
Lawhorn, Lewis...685, 728, 2661, 2702, 2867, 3007, 3111, 3132, 3186a
Lawler...995a, 2360
Lawler, Abner...2111, 2380, 3007, 3111, 3192
Lawler, Ann...2583
Lawler, E...2811b, 3051
Lawler, Eli...1173c, 1949-1950, 2070a, 2111, 2217, 2217d, 2360-2361, 2364, 2378a, 2583, 2644, 2704, 2739a, 2742a, 2761a, 2764a, 2775a, 2805d, 2815d, 2828a, 2845, 2977a, 2998, 3007-3007a, 3020, 3026b, 3028, 3033, 3096, 3111-3111a, 3190, 3227, 3417, 3468a, 3527, 3533
Lawler, Eli Jr...3105a, 3243a, 3468a, 3527
Lawler, Eli Sr...3105a, 3243a
Lawler, Evan...1729, 2380, 2440, 2519, 2583
Lawler, Jehu...2977a, 3007a, 3461a
Lawler, John...1935, 2111, 2305, 2380, 2519, 2583, 2739a, 2828a, 2834c, 2990b, 3007a, 3028, 3111a, 3192, 3330, 3337, 3417, 3461a, 3590, 3724a
Lawler, Joseph...2684a
Lawler, Levi...2569a, 2583
Lawley, Elisha...1481, 2577
Lawley, John...481-482, 1607, 2150, 2164-2170, 2267, 2306, 2525, 2577, 2591, 2599, 2828a, 3720
Lawley, Joseph...2071, 2164-2170, 2577, 2589, 2591, 2599, 2606
Lawley, Polly...3720
Lawrence, Jesse...3080
Lawrence, John...113a, 115, 209, 438, 483, 565a, 637-638, 869, 2552
Lawrence, John Sr...2540a
Lawrence, Jonathan...2830a
Lawrence, Peter...1453b

Lawrence, Richard...1453b
Lawrence, William...814, 925, 963, 2552
Lawrence, William M...3743
Lawson...1698, 2031, 2244, 2298
Lawson, David...295, 564, 662, 667, 683, 699, 711, 715, 2438
Lawson, Harday...3434
Lawson, John...3496
Lawson, Mary...564
Lawson, Susannah...233
Lax, Robert...2768a, 2779a
Lay, Richard...2490
Leach...3567, 3615, 3661, 3692
Leach, Alexander...2948, 3007, 3055, 3166, 3209, 3350, 3403, 3432, 3469, 3504, 3547a
Leach, Angus...3007, 3350, 3426, 3432, 3504, 3712
Leach, Archibald...3252, 3350
Leach, John...3166, 3432
Leach, Malcolm...3007, 3111, 3432
Lean, Thomas...2490
Leavenston, Robert...1004
LeCroy, Lucas...2490
Ledbetter, Arthur...684, 727
Ledbetter, Mathew...682, 778, 849
Ledford, Nicholas...1122
Ledlow [see Ludlow]
Lee...386, 1326, 2375
Lee, Abel...7, 55, 78, 111, 114, 127, 192, 221, 364, 400, 436, 471, 478
Lee, Ann...78, 192, 400, 3640
Lee, Martin...3640
Lee, Robert...127
Lee, William...661
Leggett, John...446
Lengle, Henry...776
Leverett, John...135a
Levin...1035
Levister...3171
Levister, John...3076b, 3171, 3703
Levister, Levy...3445a, 3519a
Lewis...2896, 3171
Lewis, Christian...2755
Lewis, David...885, 1352, 3225a
Lewis, Harbert...2316a
Lewis, James...3559a, 3591a, 3641
Lewis, James H...3633
Lewis, John...2894-2895, 2900, 3007, 3044, 3111, 3339c, 3441a, 3700, 3706
Lewis, N...3631, 3684a
Lewis, Patience...3700, 3706
Lewis, William...2795, 2853a, 2997a, 3007, 3044, 3111, 3228, 3339c, 3441a
Lick...2312
Lidnum, William...3550
Lindly, Aaron...1601a, 2974a
Lindly, Charles...99
Lindly, Phebe...2974a
Lindly, Thomas...1601a
Lindly, William...1601a
Line, William B...3657
Lithgo [see Lethco]
Little, John...2490
Little, Mincher...1193c, 1194a
Little, Thomas...2184
Little, William...2490
Logan, J.D...2781
Lolly [see Lawley]
Loman, James...2079a
Long...2325
Long, William...171

Massey, Elizabeth...3106
Massey, James...3106, 3118
Massey, Margaret...3106
Massey, Mary / Polly...3106
Massey, Russell...3106, 3203
Massey, Sarah...3106
Massey, Thomas...3106
Matheson...985, 2297, 2357, 2421, 2939, 3086
Matheson, Christian...2910
Matheson, Daniel...759
Matheson, Donald...1713, 2628
Matheson, John...1713, 3240, 3505
Matheson, Malcolm...2910, 2953, 3007, 3028, 3111, 3235, 3258, 3282, 3339d, 3383, 3489
Matheson, Margaret...3670
Matheson, Mary...2141
Matheson, Murdock...2949-2953, 3007, 3028, 3111, 3240
Matheson, Nancy...3489
Matheson, Neil...666, 759, 802, 947, 1138, 1495, 1547, 1713, 1961, 2000-2001, 2290, 2559, 2571, 2679, 2730, 2882, 2910, 2949-2952, 3028, 3505
Matheson, Norman...1138, 1354, 1492, 1516, 1548, 1592, 1713, 2000-2001, 2290, 2559, 2571, 2679, 2730, 2852, 2910, 2950, 3007, 3017-3018, 3047, 3050, 3111, 3128, 3226, 3277, 3339d, 3349, 3383, 3505, 3594
Matheson, Roderick...3489
Matheson, William...879
Matthews...1494, 1638, 2410, 3332
Matthews, Andra...765
Matthews, Jacob...2495
Matthews, James...3332, 3710
Matthews, John...268, 2814
Matthews, Mary...46, 268, 2764a
Matthews, Neill...802, 3384
Matthews, Sarah...517
Matthews, Thomas...46, 152, 236, 360, 425, 526, 625, 643, 709, 748, 929, 977, 1000, 1113, 1131, 1133, 1480, 1515, 1556, 1749, 1814, 2259, 2352, 2389, 2454, 2489, 2495, 2834c, 3207
Matthews, Thomas G...1382
Matthews, Thomas Jr...46, 268, 457, 517, 597-598, 639, 2592
Matthews, Thomas Sr...46, 268, 457, 517, 597-598, 639
Matthews, William...2811, 3070-3071, 3339b, 3392, 3724a
Mauldin, Claborn...2794b
Mauldin, Richard...125
Maultsby, James...331
Maultsby, William...191
Maun, Taylor...3118
Mauney, Jacob...744
Maxey, Walter...3317
May...541
May, Elisabeth...387, 499
May, John...19, 22, 78, 312, 314, 374, 396-397, 436, 447, 471, 489, 492, 499, 1550
May, John Jr...311, 387
Maynard [see also Minyard / Manor]
Maynard, Hannah...2022
Maynard, James...285-286, 2604, 2968
Maynor, Ann...620
Maynor, Henry...620
Maynor, Jane...620
Maynor, Rachel...154

McArthur, Charles...3474, 3629
McArthur, James...2627, 2712, 3007, 3028, 3101, 3111
McArthur, John...1305
McAulay...2588, 2839, 3039, 3150, 3415-3416, 3532
McAulay, Angus...981, 997, 1121, 1124, 1206, 1362, 1371, 1448, 1713, 1731, 1732, 1851, 1855, 2021, 2028, 2055, 2075, 3032, 3258
McAulay, Ann...3568
McAulay, Aulay...2576, 2610, 2819
McAulay, Daniel...3515, 3568, 3594, 3607, 3670
McAulay, Donald...2067, 2084, 3082, 3239, 3435
McAulay, John...779, 932, 949, 998, 1039, 1167, 1176, 1206, 1354, 1362, 1440, 1446, 1572, 1693, 1713, 1730, 1945, 2031, 2067, 2072, 2077, 2084, 2124, 2139, 2148, 2161, 2178, 2180, 2227-2228, 2376, 2395, 2662, 2698, 2870, 2953, 2964, 2966, 2983, 3007, 3082, 3535, 3537, 3594, 3607, 3670, 3723
McAulay, John Jr...981, 1411, 1817, 2055, 2088, 2105, 2125-2126, 2327, 2344, 2527, 2611, 2906, 2930
McAulay, John Sr...1440, 1713
McAulay, Malcolm...3205, 3568, 3594, 3607
McAulay, Murdock...959, 1088, 1121, 1124, 1206, 1354, 1362, 1371, 1402, 1448, 1475, 1567, 1693, 1709, 1713, 2080, 2088, 2101, 2113, 2161-2162, 2195, 2212, 2227, 2345, 2376, 2382, 2482, 2506, 2513, 2846b, 2875, 2910, 2953, 3007, 3111, 3341, 3515
McAulay, Murdock Jr...2080, 2228, 2576, 2610, 2622, 2767, 3111
McAulay, Murdock Sr...2081
McAulay, Roderick...3007, 3082, 3111, 3235, 3258, 3346, 3383, 3409, 3435, 3474, 3513, 3568, 3594, 3607
McAulay, William...2214, 2817, 3082, 3435, 3513, 3594, 3607
McBryde...2648
McBryde, A...2229, 2764a, 2815b, 2846b, 3318a
McBryde, A.M...2781
McBryde, Archibald...1488, 1516a, 1531, 1597a, 1624, 1660, 1749, 1811a, 1933, 2112b, 2575, 2655, 2780, 2805a-2805b, 2830, 2834a-2834b, 2846-2846a, 2957a, 2979, 2990a, 3051a, 3179a, 3312, 3318a, 3359, 3377a
McCabe, Patrick...101
McCain, Hugh...3154a
McCaller...3130
McCalley, John...759
McCallum...3528a
McCallum, James...16-17, 37-38, 49, 125, 149, 168, 3713a
McCaskill...1227, 1499, 1568-1569, 1639, 2613
McCaskill, Alexander...1506, 2314-2315, 2481, 3028, 3300, 3388, 3698, 3722a-3722b, 3730
McCaskill, Allen...3570, 3591a, 3722a
McCaskill, Angus...1593, 2503, 3474, 3629
McCaskill, Ann...3565
McCaskill, Catherine...3554

McCaskill, Hector...3474
McCaskill, John...1142, 1429, 1506, 1569, 1781, 2481, 2503, 3028, 3235, 3312, 3629, 3734, 3738
McCaskill, Kenneth...2481, 2910, 2972, 3028, 3085, 3312, 3341, 3356, 3398, 3479, 3565, 3642, 3647, 3654, 3688
McCaskill, Malcolm...2969, 3235, 3474
McCaskill, Nancy...2667
McCaskill, Nancy McKinnon...3398
McCaskill, W...2676
McCay, Spruce...1459
McCrimmon...3023, 3248
McCrimmon, D...3066
McCrimmon, Daniel...3111, 3152, 3161, 3246, 3248, 3312, 3314, 3359, 3386, 3463, 3476, 3492a, 3495, 3538, 3545-3546, 3670, 3724a, 3737
McCrimmon, David...3007, 3533
McCrimmon, Donald...3066, 3703
McCrimmon, John...2960, 2981, 3007, 3111, 3124b, 3162a, 3189b, 3195b, 3661
McCrimmon, M...3233a, 3409, 3527, 3568, 3713a
McCrimmon, Malcolm...2454, 2853a, 3007, 3111, 3303, 3566b, 3684a
McCullough, William...842
McCurry, Angush...727
McCurry, John...3116
McCurry, Lauchlin...666, 727
McCushten, James...2538b
McDaniel, Daniel...825, 3033, 3738
McDaniel, James...1305
McDaniel, John...759, 1237, 1259a, 1475, 3538
McDaniel, Kenneth...759
McDaniel, Murdoch...2910
McDaniel, William...1237, 1475
McDeed, Alexander...1758
McDiffie, John...3028
McDonald...952, 1017, 1034, 1135, 1146, 1359, 1398a, 1986, 2986, 3696a
McDonald, Alexander...2405, 3723
McDonald, Allen...871, 3334
McDonald, Angus...1101, 3129, 3588, 3591a, 3597, 3610, 3628a
McDonald, Archibald...608-609, 3307, 3443, 3604, 3630, 3642, 3714
McDonald, Bryant...3503
McDonald, Bryant R...3641
McDonald, Charity...3494
McDonald, Christian...2818, 3241, 3243
McDonald, Daniel...88, 457, 684, 727, 759, 853, 858, 871, 2538, 2543, 2818, 3129, 3241, 3243, 3373, 3591a, 3629
McDonald, Donald...59, 283, 378, 426, 460-461, 518-519, 551, 554, 584, 594, 630, 636, 1256, 1305, 1367, 1558, 1737, 2118, 2202, 2274, 2331, 2397-2399, 2435, 2438, 2623, 2646-2647, 2711a, 2713-2715, 2750, 2751, 2840, 2846b, 2899, 3008, 3034, 3129, 3474, 3571, 3588, 3607, 3696a
McDonald, Donald [SC]...3377
McDonald, Donald Sr...2899, 3008
McDonald, James...88, 309, 353, 458, 514, 573, 611, 623, 635, 643, 658, 692, 763, 764, 939a, 1461, 1808
McDonald, John...995, 1041, 1780, 1819, 1958-1959, 1964, 1968, 1970-

2954, 2972, 3002, 3007, 3111, 3312, 3495, 3530

McNeill, Isabella...3530

McNeill, James...2700, 2978, 3033, 3163, 3569, 3627a, 3642-3643, 3664b

McNeill, Jennet...3127

McNeill, John...27, 464, 528-530, 552-553, 569, 666, 807, 826, 841, 859-860, 862, 965, 987, 995, 1152-1153, 1505, 1796, 1815, 1899, 2287, 2392, 2404, 2420, 2465-2466, 2532, 2541, 2546, 2700, 2846b, 2883-2884, 2920, 2938, 2960, 3000, 3007, 3111, 3163, 3312, 3563, 3615, 3692-3693, 3717a, 3738

McNeill, John [Hatter]...3591a, 3723a

McNeill, Lauchlin...2202, 2954, 3027, 3111, 3339b, 3445c, 3479, 3634

McNeill, Malcolm...84, 651, 718, 823, 1298, 1367, 1468, 1479, 1610, 2123, 2266, 2514, 2545, 2925, 2975, 3647a, 3649

McNeill, Malcolm [Sheriff]...1587, 2031, 2109, 2112b, 2214, 2485, 2492, 2516, 2582

McNeill, Neill...569, 2109

McNeill, Phillip...3001-3002, 3368, 3437, 3491

McNeill, Polly...3005

McNeill, Simon...3266, 3301, 3368, 3491, 3691, 3693-3694, 3711-3712, 3716

McNeill, Thomas...3246, 3615, 3676a, 3692

McNeill, Torquill/Turquill...3495

McPherson, Ann...2974a

McPherson, Betty...2974a

McPherson, Christian...2974a

McPherson, Daniel...2974a

McPherson, Edith...2974a

McPherson, Enoch...1061a, 2974a

McPherson, Hannah...2974a

McPherson, John...336, 548, 2974a

McPherson, Margaret...2974a

McPherson, Mary...1080, 2974a

McPherson, Otheil...2974a

McPherson, Phebe...2974a

McPherson, Ruth...2974a

McPherson, Sarah...2974a

McPherson, William...1061a, 1601a, 2974a

McQueen...1551, 2913, 3221, 3306, 3444, 3524, 3579

McQueen, A...3013

McQueen, A.D...3318a

McQueen, Angus...1617, 2522, 2593-2594, 2811, 2926, 2936, 2979, 2985, 3007, 3038, 3054, 3077, 3092, 3111, 3132, 3274, 3275a, 3357, 3380, 3729

McQueen, Archibald L...3538a

McQueen, Daniel...799, 851, 880, 1237a, 1447a, 2732

McQueen, Donald...1102, 1219, 1239, 1319, 1406, 1450, 1466-1467, 1472, 1531, 1606, 1765, 1810, 1962, 2086, 2272, 2480, 2593-2594, 2672, 2783, 2867, 2871, 2867, 2871, 2879, 2922, 2984-2985

McQueen, John...759, 948

McQueen, Margaret...2985, 3007, 3111

McQueen, Murdock...529, 584, 650, 1551

McRae...1622, 1639, 2090

McRae, Alexander...286, 645

McRae, Captain...2485

McRae, Daniel...2277, 3350

McRae, Donald...287, 815

McRae, Griffith John...1151-1152

McRae, John...527, 646, 815, 879

McRae, Major...1780, 3696a

McReynolds, Thomas...1554, 2112a

McSwain/McSween...1107, 1142, 2030

McSwain/McSween, Daniel...727, 759, 780, 802, 946, 1969, 2079

McSwain/McSween, Donald...947, 1987-1993, 1996, 1998, 2003-2009, 2012-2015, 3028

McSwain/McSween, Evan...352, 515, 521

McSwain/McSween, John...790, 1101, 1478, 1628, 2176, 2465, 2480, 2547, 2696, 2846b, 2886, 2910, 3445a, 3519a, 3581b, 3628b

McSwain/McSween, William...2321, 2387, 2390, 2400, 2461, 2515, 2547, 2549, 2553

McVay, John...1104b

Meacon...2612a

Meacon, Gideon...1375

Mears [see also Myers]

Mears, John...324-325, 335

Mears, William...186, 195, 253, 283, 304, 324, 333, 335, 337, 378, 453, 460, 467, 473, 1004, 1160, 1459, 1562, 1935

Medford, Jeptha /Jeffery...443, 666, 669, 684, 727, 759, 918

Medford, John...443, 1007

Medford, John Morgan...2295-2296, 2402, 2411, 2453, 2533-2536, 2625, 2767, 2806, 2809

Medlin, Alexander...3408b

Medlin, Benjamin...3610

Medlin, George...3610

Medlin, Jenny...1276

Medlin, John...270, 355, 2554, 3445a, 3519a

Meigs, Jonathan...2424, 2747

Melson, Frances...1635

Melton...809, 950, 2194, 3422

Melton, A...3465

Melton, Ancel / Ansel / Anson...81, 97, 255, 537, 674, 681, 684, 705, 727, 735-736, 759, 780, 785, 892, 915, 922, 946, 948, 950, 1018, 1026, 1081, 1112, 1245, 1302, 1334, 1371, 1587, 1713, 1755, 2126, 2148, 2180, 2241, 2376, 2461, 2627, 2712, 2805, 2929, 3111, 3117, 3417, 3445, 3449, 3524a, 3536, 3538, 3578, 3628, 3660, 3696, 3737

Melton, Ancel Jr...3536, 3538

Melton, Ancel Sr...1746, 1794, 2269, 2627

Melton, Archelius...81, 97

Melton, David...571, 593, 662, 667, 685, 695, 697, 728, 754, 817

Melton, Elisha...3318

Melton, Febey...2139

Melton, Henry...3271, 3538, 3543, 3608

Melton, Hercules...97

Melton, Hiram...3578, 3628, 3642, 3673, 3722b

Melton, Isaiah...3445, 3449, 3538, 3734

Melton, Isham...81

Melton, James...81, 1505, 1713, 1966, 1984, 2031, 2171, 2339-2340, 2658, 2665, 2674, 2682, 2846b, 3007, 3050, 3079, 3086, 3088, 3111, 3128, 3251, 3287, 3445, 3495, 3524a, 3536, 3538, 3555, 3578, 3628, 3717

Melton, James Jr...3538

Melton, Jeremiah...704a

Melton, Jesse...3271

Melton, John...2921, 2942, 3007, 3013, 3033, 3076, 3079, 3098, 3111, 3122, 3144, 3157, 3225, 3382, 3391, 3642

Melton, Jonathan...2197

Melton, Josiah [Isaiah]...3734

Melton, Mary...937, 2452

Melton, Mourning...175

Melton, Nancy...3028

Melton, Nathan...51, 68, 81, 83, 97, 671a

Melton, Nathaniel...81, 171, 255, 962, 974, 1073, 1354, 2148, 2269, 2482-2483, 2893

Melton, Oneal...97

Melton, Robert ...31, 51, 68, 81, 83, 97, 175, 563, 2716, 3128, 3271, 3445, 3524a, 3538, 3578, 3603, 3627-3628, 3641, 3676a, 3722c, 3734a

Melton, Robert Jr...3287, 3538

Melton, Robert Sr...3538

Melton, Robert Sr. [son of Ansel]...3538

Melton, Sarah...3538, 3543, 3608

Melton, William...2942, 3153, 3271

Meredith, Lewis...612

Meroney, William...1953a

Merrick, Frances...1956, 1960

Messer, Peter...446

Miller, James...648

Miller, Jerome...248, 263, 284, 352, 376, 411, 515, 648, 2432, 2465

Miller, Joseph...3709

Miller, Riland...3567, 3615, 3692

Miller, Riland R...3246

Miller, Robert...284

Miller, William...284

Millikin, Absalom...3034a

Mills, William H...322

Milner, Ja...503-504

Milton [see Melton]

Mins, Elizabeth...253, 333

Minter, William...2902a

Minyard [see also Maynard]...405, 645, 2038, 2455, 3108

Minyard, James...2424, 2490, 2632, 2660, 2747, 2774, 2861, 2967

Minyard, Mary...153, 303

Minyard, Thomas...153, 303, 1790a, 2038, 2455

Minzes, William...344

Misha, John...384

Mishoe, John...333

Mize, Henry...3053

Moffitt, Charles...2633

Moffitt, H...3060a, 3080a-3080b, 3433, 3667a

Moffitt, Hannah...1365

Moffitt, Hugh...1361, 1365, 3185, 3276, 3640

Moffitt, Peggy...3060a

Moffitt, Stephen...3640

Moffitt, William...3640

Monday, Christopher...209

Monk, Archibald...666

Monk, Donald...1113, 1479, 2454, 2495

Monk, James...515

Monroe...2079, 2501

Monroe, Alexander...1832, 1961, 1968, 1980, 2297, 2357, 2472

Monroe, Archibald...3154, 3474, 3623

Monroe, Colin...3629, 3734

Monroe, Daniel...3631, 3684a

Monroe, Donald...1305, 1713, 2356-2357, 2421, 2472, 2679, 2730

Monroe, Francis...3513, 3738

Monroe, John...3513, 3629, 3734

Monroe, Malcolm...223

Monroe, Neill...1799

Monroe, Peter...2819, 3559a

Monroe, Widow...1305

Montgomery, John...855a, 1127, 2197, 2996, 3330a, 3341a

Montgomery, Mary...3330a, 3341a, 3377a

Moon, John...642

Moore...326, 3142, 3710

Moore, Betty...1086

Moore, Charlotte/Charlotta...3114

Moore, Daniel...2128

Moore, Deliah...3634, 3643, 3647, 3652-3653, 3717

Moore, Edward...93, 435, 662, 667, 685, 728, 930, 939, 1002, 1009, 1049, 1081, 1105, 1112, 1131, 1154, 1179, 1200, 1207, 1213, 1264, 1293, 1330, 1351, 1357-1358, 1369, 1380, 1396, 1656, 1736, 2059, 2073, 2282, 2286, 2289, 2612, 2822, 2878, 2942, 3305, 3339, 3440, 3486, 3494, 3521, 3538, 3604, 3642, 3647, 3652, 3714

Moore, Edward [Deep River]...1257, 1351

Moore, Edward Jr...990, 1357, 1358, 1501, 1531

Moore, Edward Sr...990, 2059

Moore, Fanning...2538, 2737, 2847, 2918, 3028, 3111, 3622

Moore, George...1357-1358, 1713, 2073, 2612, 2763, 2764a, 2997a, 3007, 3028, 3083, 3111, 3123, 3158, 3168, 3275-3275a, 3305, 3312, 3339, 3357, 3380, 3390-3391, 3440, 3444, 3494, 3521, 3524, 3579, 3626, 3630, 3634, 3641, 3652, 3717

Moore, George Jr...3168, 3305, 3339, 3440, 3521

Moore, George Sr...3319, 3509, 3516, 3647

Moore, Gideon...2942, 3179, 3304, 3647

Moore, Henry...870

Moore, Hugh...3382, 3409, 3591a, 3643, 3722f

Moore, Hugh L...5225-5225a

Moore, James...685, 728, 737, 840, 990, 1053, 1139, 1482, 1736, 1812, 1979, 2073, 2148a, 2286, 2288, 2519, 3028, 3664b, 3676

Moore, Jane...2229

Moore, Joanna...1195, 2612

Moore, John...3114, 3428a, 3479, 3641, 3647

Moore, Joseph...3610, 3613, 3614b, 3643, 3685

Moore, Joseph G...3197, 3576, 3590, 3609, 3643, 3704, 3717

Moore, Larkin N...3670

Moore, Mary...2538, 2543, 2612, 3647

Moore, Nancy...3647

Moore, Patrick...3657

Moore, Pherebee...2059, 3257

Moore, Phibe...1981, 2059

Moore, Polly...3494

Moore, Robert ...9, 126, 667, 1086-1087, 1201, 1706a, 2564a, 2764a, 2834a, 2864, 3033, 3488, 3657, 3664b

Moore, Samuel...914a

Moore, Sarah...2612

Moore, Thomas...488, 590-592, 1981, 2059

Moore, William...432, 667, 680, 712, 759, 1071, 1482, 2059, 2612, 3652, 3736

Morgan...991, 1007, 1029, 1052, 1287, 1458, 1460, 1536, 1697, 1751, 1756, 2058, 2958, 3015, 3085

Morgan, Angelina...2597, 3375

Morgan, Delilah...2597

Morgan, Edith...2974a

Morgan, Elessa...2597

Morgan, George...295, 427, 443, 666, 2082, 2248-2249, 2295-2296, 2402, 2468, 2471, 2512, 2534, 2597, 2747, 2896, 3324-3325, 3498-3500

Morgan, James...295, 368, 438, 550, 661, 666, 684, 727, 818, 833, 915, 922, 939, 971, 1007, 1049, 1081-1082, 1482, 2511-2512, 2597, 2625, 2666, 2804-2805, 2810, 2851, 2896, 2942, 3007, 3111, 3376, 3381, 3462, 3486, 3566, 3572, 3738

Morgan, John...93, 245, 295, 380, 390, 427, 661, 666, 684, 727, 759, 769, 818, 915, 967, 991, 1007, 1018, 1081, 1112, 1179, 1207, 1226, 1257, 1291, 1314, 1316, 1322-1323, 1334, 1380, 1383, 1396, 1448, 1504, 1633, 1711, 1713, 1836, 1881, 1940, 1942, 1992, 2011, 2041, 2064, 2066, 2070, 2248-2249, 2295-2296, 2379, 2471, 2535, 2597, 2666, 2742, 2837, 2896, 3631, 3684a, 3718

Morgan, John Jr...1939

Morgan, John Sr...1334, 1941, 2468, 2471, 2533-2534, 2587, 2649

Morgan, Joseph...30, 184, 217, 443, 621, 1500, 1509, 2597, 2804, 2836-2837, 2896, 3007, 3111, 3370

Morgan, Levicea...2597

Morgan, Mark...2974a, 3234

Morgan, Martin...3260

Morgan, Mary...217, 224, 306-307, 621, 632, 2597

Morgan, Mehetabel...568

Morgan, Nathan...1007, 1316, 1691, 2064, 2066, 2070, 2082, 2248-2249, 2278, 2597, 2649, 2804-2805, 2836-2837, 2999, 3007, 3028, 3111, 3127a, 3195b, 3376, 3403, 3509, 3614

Morgan, Sarah Tillis/Tullos...438

Morgan, Solomon...209, 224, 288, 306-307, 432, 448, 459, 568, 1004

Morgan, William...30, 114, 127, 145, 182, 188-189, 204, 217, 224, 295, 306-307, 368, 443, 621, 632, 661, 666, 684, 687, 727, 730, 759, 813, 939, 971, 1003, 1007-1008, 1155, 1207, 1226, 1228, 1296, 1310-1314, 1320, 1324, 1370-1371, 1383-1384, 1396, 1436, 1442,

1457, 1482, 1633, 1691, 1711, 1753, 1794, 1838, 1934, 1993, 2010, 2080, 2082, 2120, 2131-2132, 2137, 2249, 2260, 2292, 2295, 2379, 2411, 2453, 2469, 2484, 2493-2494, 2498, 2502, 2508, 2510-2511, 2514, 2530, 2605, 2625, 2720, 3610, 3631, 3684a

Morgan, William [Captain]...1442, 1448, 1633, 1659, 1753

Morgan, William Jr...427, 1007, 1415, 1448, 1659, 2082, 2131, 2260-2261, 2379, 2499, 2514, 2520, 2597

Morgan, William Sr...368, 1347, 1746, 2292, 2484, 2512, 2795

Morgan, William W...3641, 3647, 3716

Morris, Ann/Anne...58, 452

Morris, Edward...161, 163, 174, 183, 321, 323, 330b, 512a

Morris, Henry...682

Morris, John...763, 2677, 2772, 3028

Morris, Sarah...161, 323

Morris, William...58, 174, 213, 322, 334, 438, 452, 1155

Morris, William Jr...438

Morrison...572, 741, 1016, 1084, 1123, 1277, 1379, 1427, 2973, 3138, 3208, 3424, 3738

Morrison, Alexander...214, 506, 513, 545, 602, 645, 934, 1275, 1277, 1354, 1572, 1713, 1796, 2080, 2128, 2474, 2874, 3007, 3286a, 3334, 3377, 3383, 3436, 3723

Morrison, Allen...759, 782, 934-935, 1123, 1234, 1275, 1277, 1713, 1781, 1796, 2236, 2474, 2485, 2492, 2628, 2701, 2709, 2723, 2810, 2846b, 2849, 2854, 2881, 2984, 3007, 3111, 3286a, 3334, 3383

Morrison, Angus...2297, 2667, 2723, 2881, 2949-2953, 3004, 3006-3007, 3028, 3059, 3111, 3235, 3334, 3387, 3409, 3546a, 3565, 3629, 3642, 3670, 3723

Morrison, Ann...3565

Morrison, Catherine...3446, 3565

Morrison, Donald...604

Morrison, Isabella...3723

Morrison, John...351, 545, 1713, 2161, 2163, 2227, 2311, 2401, 2474, 3007, 3111, 3154, 3334, 3565, 3665a, 3723, 3723a

Morrison, John [Tailor]...2161, 3591a

Morrison, Kenneth...928, 3474, 3629, 3734

Morrison, Malcolm...759, 780, 946, 1787, 2211, 2297, 2882, 2950-2952, 3007, 3111, 3226, 3446, 3476, 3565

Morrison, Malcolm P...3476

Morrison, Margaret...3565

Morrison, Mary...1235, 1256, 3723

Morrison, N...3738

Morrison, Neill...2910, 3085, 3189, 3323, 3334, 3348, 3401, 3436, 3558, 3665a-3665b, 3723, 3738

Morrison, Norman...513, 602, 651, 684, 727, 759, 949, 951, 1275, 1428, 1503, 1547, 2628, 2723, 2881, 3007, 3111

Morton/Martin, William...2455

Mosler, John...2742b

Moulden, Richard...396-398

Mullins...1170a, 2417

Mullins, Nathaniel...1377, 1453

Munn, James...2858a-2858c
Munroe [see Monroe]
Murchison...2504, 3388, 3464, 3480
Murchison, D...2846a-2846b
Murchison, Daniel...2975, 3358, 3439, 3568, 3734, 3738
Murchison, Donald...3226, 3341
Murchison, Duncan...3311-3312, 3377a, 3470b, 3492a
Murchison, Isabel...3530
Murchison, John...2846b, 3033, 3197, 3341, 3358, 3439, 3527, 3657a, 3663a
Murchison, John [Tailor]...3341
Murchison, Kenneth...815, 841, 995, 1426, 1499, 1506, 1568-1569, 1573, 1593-1594, 1982, 2142, 2277, 2377, 2481, 2503, 2864, 3007, 3028, 3341
Murchison, Kenneth B...3477
Murchison, Roderick...2910, 2975, 3007, 3033, 3043, 3341
Murchison, Simon...3341, 3358
Murchison, William...3028, 3663a
Murley, Samuel...2815, 3048
Murphy, Joseph...161, 163, 321
Murphy, Valentine...163, 321
Murray, Duncan...1404
Murray, James...1812, 2288
Murray, Jamey...1139
Murray, Mary...2811b
Muse...238, 442, 602, 836, 857, 864-865, 944, 956, 1060, 1097, 1480, 2352, 2489, 2749
Muse, Ann...66, 3715a
Muse, Annabarbury...66
Muse, Asa...3476, 3591a, 3610, 3723a
Muse, Betsey...3481
Muse, C...760
Muse, Catherine...926, 928
Muse, Charity...729, 741, 769, 771-772, 926, 944, 958, 1057, 1078, 1093, 1281, 1378, 3481
Muse, Daniel...66, 411, 572, 589, 648, 662, 663, 667, 693, 741, 879, 884, 1040, 1281, 2432, 2783, 2808, 2871, 2913, 3007, 3394, 3111, 3394, 3624, 3641, 3647, 3698, 3729, 3740-3741
Muse, Daniel [SP]...3479
Muse, Daniel H...2946, 3197, 3395, 3479, 3591a, 3723a
Muse, Daniel Jr...3641, 3722a
Muse, Elizabeth...741, 3481
Muse, Ferriba...741
Muse, Frank...2871
Muse, George...3414
Muse, George A...3295
Muse, Howard...3294, 3591a, 3723a
Muse, Hudson...3723a
Muse, James...66, 72, 90, 114, 118, 139-140, 198, 207, 218-219, 225, 233-235, 238, 243, 272, 282-283, 295, 299, 303, 324, 326, 332, 340, 350, 355, 376, 378, 381-383, 392-393, 399, 401, 405, 414, 428, 435, 442, 453, 460-461, 467, 472-474, 489, 491, 493, 505-506, 509, 512, 520, 546, 555, 562, 572, 602-603, 633, 635, 645, 648, 662, 667, 692, 729, 741, 749, 874, 879, 884, 920, 922, 926, 939, 953, 956-958, 1004, 1026, 1031, 1044, 1057, 1060, 1078, 1128a, 1213, 1236, 1264, 1470, 1480, 1490, 1505, 1515, 1555, 1562, 1565, 1587, 1710, 1749, 1771, 1793, 1935, 2129, 2163, 2255, 2372, 2466, 2602, 2748-2749,

2759, 2814, 2815a, 2857, 2859, 2946, 2988, 3028, 3111, 3382, 3394, 3481, 3538
Muse, James (Little)...3275b
Muse, James B...2946, 2954, 3007, 3111, 3197, 3229, 3264, 3294, 3295, 3382, 3389, 3418, 3481, 3591a, 3716, 3723
Muse, James H...3450, 3610, 3641, 3643, 3691
Muse, James Jr...15, 30, 33, 3007
Muse, James Sr...5, 15, 30, 32-33, 77, 686, 2759, 3394
Muse, Jane...3479
Muse, Jason...2815a, 2859, 3028, 3309, 3404, 3545
Muse, Jesse...741, 747, 769, 771-772, 816, 837, 864-865, 874, 882-882a, 884-885, 888, 915, 922, 928, 956-957, 1026, 1030, 1040, 1060, 1091, 1096-1097, 1182, 1185-1186, 1199, 1213-1214, 1236, 1660, 1710, 1758, 1799, 1806, 1979, 1995, 2020, 2129, 2133, 2311, 2348, 2367, 2369-2371, 2648, 2748-2749, 2764a, 2773, 2797, 2845, 2857, 2871, 2912, 2946, 2988, 3007, 3020, 3111, 3148, 3197, 3229, 3309, 3311, 3394-3396, 3404, 3438, 3481, 3518, 3698, 3722a
Muse, Jesse F...3007, 3111, 3295, 3359, 3382, 3389, 3418, 3479, 3513, 3525a, 3538, 3591a, 3607, 3723-3723a
Muse, John...3438, 3518, 3574
Muse, Joyce...3475, 3479
Muse, Kindred...741, 1997, 2129, 2460
Muse, Lydia...66, 741, 1180
Muse, Martha...741
Muse, Mary...741
Muse, Nancy...3570
Muse, Ruth...603
Muse, Sophia...66, 72, 87
Muse, Susanna...2871
Muse, Thomas...66, 741, 957, 1044, 1060, 1097, 1180, 1185-1186, 1236, 1398a, 1487, 1490, 1506, 1910-1912, 1995, 1997, 2020, 2046, 2109, 2330, 2369, 2372, 2748, 2770, 2857, 2912, 2946, 3007, 3111, 3270, 3339a, 3481
Muse, Thomas [Hatter]...3723a
Muse, Thomas Jr...3028
Muse, Thomas P...2946, 2988, 3007, 3111, 3197, 3229, 3295, 3476, 3694
Muse, Thomas Sr...3007, 3479, 3481
Muse, Widow...837-838, 1095, 1259, 1443, 1476, 1506, 1758, 1799, 1806, 2129, 2348, 2501, 3197
Muse, William Ceal...66
Myatt, John...702a
Myers [see also Mears]...2338, 2391, 2410
Myers, Jacob...960
Myers, James...3028
Myers, John...150, 325, 344, 414
Myers, Susannah...325, 344
Myrick...737b, 1075a, 1601b
Myrick, Azel...2886a
Myrick, Francis...1146-1147, 1237, 1476, 1513, 1604, 1623, 2997a, 3007, 3028, 3102-3103, 3111, 3163, 3281, 3476, 3657
Myrick, James C...2942, 3143
Myrick, John...2942, 3443, 3604, 3647, 3714

Myrick, Mary...3514
Myrick, Moses...814a, 878-879, 952, 1146, 1356a, 1463a, 2097a, 2479, 2585, 2831a, 2886a, 2942
Myrick, Rebecca...1356a, 1716, 2229
Nail [see also Neal]...2710
Nail, Julian...3053
Nall...989, 1178, 1212, 1253-1254, 1331, 1405, 1656-1657, 1674, 1700, 1712, 1773, 2154, 2159, 2213, 2301, 2443, 2639, 2699, 2799, 2860, 2992, 3177, 3276
Nall, Ann...3640
Nall, Elizabeth ...3640
Nall, Martin...894, 937, 2214
Nall, Mary...3147, 3640
Nall, N...1169, 2403
Nall, Nicholas...269, 691, 776a, 831, 855a, 881, 894, 938, 940, 971, 979, 989, 1003, 1035, 1039, 1068-1069, 1071, 1074, 1112a, 1204, 1212, 1215, 1220-1221, 1240, 1270, 1273, 1276, 1287, 1289, 1297, 1308, 1387-1388, 1390, 1446, 1460, 1501, 1517, 1531, 1531b, 1538, 1610, 1612, 1614, 1629, 1701, 1744-1746, 1796, 1817, 1845, 1909, 1914, 1916, 1918, 1925, 1930, 1935, 1948, 1971, 2033, 2048, 2060, 2063, 2078, 2083, 2095, 2097, 2104-2105, 2107, 2109, 2117, 2127, 2155, 2191, 2214, 2470, 2475, 2521, 2637, 2766, 2772, 2842-2843, 2850, 2876, 2890, 2924, 3007, 3028, 3111, 3147, 3268, 3274a, 3304, 3322, 3338, 3342-3343, 3429, 3441, 3526, 3582, 3640
Nall, Polley...1276, 1517
Nall, Widow...855b
Nall, William...3342
Nall, Winfred...3180
Nall, Winny...3640
Narrimour, Edward...186, 195
Narrimour, William...172-173, 186, 253
Naylor...3541, 3581a, 3722d
Naylor, George...3666, 3722d
Naylor, Westley...3591a, 3594a, 3723-3723a
Neal, Benjamin...2550
Neal, Frances...2550
Neal, James...2974a
Neal, Joseph...2550
Neal, Julian...2550
Neats, Andrew...727
Needham...2394, 2589, 2600, 2603, 2612a, 2746, 3080b
Needham, Ann...2462, 2606, 2633
Needham, Bailey...1393, 1619, 2291, 2462, 2552, 2606, 2633
Needham, Benjamin...3007a
Needham, Elizabeth...2462
Needham, Garner...2462, 2606, 2633, 2694
Needham, James...869a
Needham, Jesse...2462, 2606, 2633
Needham, John...113a, 209, 262, 327, 439, 477, 483, 565a, 642, 659, 688, 773, 814, 869, 925, 963, 1072, 1203, 1255, 1342, 1393, 1718, 1745-1745b, 1804-1805, 2374, 2394, 2462, 2552, 2590-2590a, 2606, 2631, 2633, 2669, 2694, 2727, 2892, 2927, 3028
Needham, John [son of John]...2606

Needham, John Jr...1789-1790, 1804-1805, 2450-2451
Needham, John Sr...869a, 2552, 2675-2676, 2764
Needham, Lewis...2291, 2462, 2539, 2552, 2606, 2633, 2694, 2727
Needham, Martha...2462, 2606, 2708a
Needham, Matthew...2633
Needham, Nancy...2788
Needham, Sarah...703, 1176a, 2462
Needham, Susannah...262, 439, 2462, 2606
Needham, Thomas...688
Needham, W...2826a, 2830a
Needham, W.N...2764
Needham, William...565a, 689, 703, 814, 869a, 925, 963, 989, 1072, 1114a, 1137, 1176a, 1587, 1713, 2149, 2309, 2317, 2383, 2429, 2462, 2606, 2611, 2633, 2642, 2665a, 2706, 2727, 2763, 2977a, 3028
Nelson, A.W...2991a
Ness, Paulser...960
Newton...912, 1039, 1234, 1275, 1420, 1492, 1495, 2596, 2893, 3537
Newton, Charity...2139
Newton, Delaney...2139
Newton, Elizabeth...2139
Newton, Febey...2139
Newton, Hannah...2139
Newton, Jacob...59
Newton, John...1713, 2483, 2861
Newton, John Tucker...2139
Newton, Mary...2139
Newton, Meloney...525, 2139, 2421, 2474, 2483, 2559, 2571, 2730, 2882, 2973, 3007, 3111, 3282, 3290, 3492
Newton, N...759
Newton, Nicholas...28, 106, 129, 160, 216, 220, 295, 365, 488, 525, 537, 548, 607, 619, 661, 664, 684, 700, 727, 802, 816, 843-844, 856, 867, 890, 915, 919, 922, 939, 947, 985-986, 1049, 1073, 1081, 1112, 1123, 1138, 1179, 1183, 1288, 1343, 1348-1349, 1354, 1371, 1446, 1531, 1547, 1713, 1847, 1850, 1974, 2000, 2027, 2139, 2474, 2490, 2774, 2939, 2968
Newton, Nicholas Smith...2139
Newton, Sarah...2139
Newton, William...890, 937, 985-986, 1299, 1348, 1354, 1522, 1587, 1607, 1659, 2132, 2139, 2747
Nichol, James...33, 38
Nichols, John...2069
Nicholson, Abel...3258
Nicholson, Mary...3189
Nicholson, Neil...551
Norden, Kindred...3581
Norton, Greel...2569a
Norton, John W...3072, 3320
Norwood, Nathaniel...771-772, 953
Norwood, William...2147, 2941
Nugent, Jacob...2974a
Nunnery, Lewis...3569
Oats, John...3072
Odom, Isaac...23, 25-26, 30
Odom, William...17
Oliver, Michael...2424, 2747
Onstot...2417, 2443, 2568, 2586, 2671
Onstot, George...2250, 2552, 2570, 2776
Onstot, Hannah...2776

Onstot, John...2776
Onstot, William...2711
Orrly, Elizabeth...1067
Osborn, Rebecca...3034a
Ott, Martin...156, 357, 367, 430, 2556-2557
Overman, Reuben...2794c
Overton...265, 280, 370-371, 787, 822, 1551, 1758
Overton, Aaron...626, 1488, 1490
Overton, Casey...2755
Overton, Cassandra...3727
Overton, Cherry...1012
Overton, David...626, 2182, 2185, 2407, 2792, 3028
Overton, Isaac...1012
Overton, J...760
Overton, Jesse...626, 1281, 2755, 3727
Overton, John...6, 11, 54, 57, 60, 75, 82, 85, 110, 123, 131, 140, 158, 190, 201, 214, 222, 238, 240-241, 265, 275, 279-280, 295, 362-363, 370-373, 384, 394, 420, 424, 442, 466, 470, 513, 562, 570, 626, 647, 653-654, 662, 664, 667, 685, 694, 728, 752, 769, 787, 792, 835, 840, 937, 977, 1001, 1010a, 1078, 1108, 1113, 1150, 1264, 1281, 1370, 1398c-1398d, 1488, 1490, 1670, 1749, 1889, 1894, 2182, 2185, 2407, 2444, 2488, 2752, 2977a, 3727
Overton, John (son of Aaron)...1488, 1490
Overton, John (son of Jesse)...1281
Overton, John Jr...836, 1113, 1413, 1488, 1490, 1662-1663
Overton, John Sr...836, 915, 937, 1004, 1012, 1057, 1131, 1200, 1213, 1264, 1383, 1413, 1488, 1663, 2112a
Overton, Jude...1012
Overton, Martha...2755
Overton, Moses...626, 2407
Overton, Samuel...2755, 3727
Overton, Sarah...279
Overton, Susan...2977a
Overton, Susannah...3727
Overton, Thomas...1004, 1010a, 1113, 1258, 1264, 1287, 1385, 1475, 1490, 1537, 1554, 1610, 1701, 2576
Overton, Thomas Jefferson...3727
Overton, Viney...2792
Owen, Benjamin...423, 434
Owen, Hardy...1105b
Owen, James...47, 2942
Owen, John...2151
Owen, John Sr...3265
Owen, Joseph...2942
Owen, Medford...2892, 3007, 3028, 3111, 3246, 3265, 3319, 3336, 3411, 3501, 3532, 3568, 3584, 3599, 3633
Owen, William...55, 3411, 3431
Ozburn, Mary...1046
Ozburn, Matthew...1046
Page...3204
Page, Benjamin...1585c-1585d, 1637, 3495
Page, Jesse...3197, 3479
Page, William...3341
Pain, John...373
Pain, Joshua...310
Pain, William...840
Palmer, Fox...737f, 2701a
Palmer, Robert...3318a
Parker, Jack...2424, 2747

Parker, John...2490, 2756, 2873
Parker, Richard...81, 83
Parks, Anna...3033
Parks, John...3185
Parks, Thomas...3033
Parrish, Rhody...2152
Parrish, Sherwood...2992
Parson[s] [see Person]
Pate, John...123
Patterson...1105b, 1738, 1825-1826, 2212, 2767-2768, 2950, 3093, 3225a
Patterson, Catharine...3252
Patterson, Daniel...2846b, 3697a
Patterson, Donald...2853a
Patterson, Duncan...336, 1305
Patterson, James...97, 3409
Patterson, John...336, 498, 2717, 2767, 2853a, 3007-3008, 3059, 3111, 3154, 3226, 3235, 3312, 3339d, 3348-3349, 3359, 3377, 3382, 3386, 3446, 3463, 3479, 3492, 3543, 3558, 3691d
Patterson, John Jr...2627, 2712, 3111
Patterson, John Sr...3111
Patterson, Malcolm...450-451, 464, 2892, 3727
Patterson, Mary...3004
Patterson, Molly...937
Patterson, Robert...51, 97, 171, 255, 501, 674, 682, 684, 705-706, 727, 736, 785, 948, 1200, 1288, 1354, 1371, 1624, 1688
Patterson, Sarah...3004, 3006
Patterson, Tryon...1193, 1367c
Patterson, William...737h
Pattsull, Catherine...334
Pattsull, Hugh...334
Payne, William...1113, 1264
Pearce...287, 1248-1249, 1254, 1948, 2140, 2595, 2677-2678, 3207
Pearce, Dixon...92
Pearce, Elizabeth...3106
Pearce, Jesse...251, 271, 339, 401, 988, 2974a, 2997a, 3102
Pearce, John...756, 777, 869-869a, 887, 1035, 1065, 1068, 1074, 1143, 1172, 1253, 1278, 2639, 2841
Pearce, Keziah...3257
Pearce, Margaret...2974a
Pearce, Mary...637-638, 657, 872, 988, 3257, 3667a
Pearce, Molly...1501, 1531
Pearce, Olive...3207, 3257
Pearce, Pherebee...3257
Pearce, Reuben...2552, 2841, 2992
Pearce, William...869a, 1157, 1172, 1253, 1300, 1377a, 1501, 1531, 2403, 2441-2442, 2552, 2639, 2678, 2841, 2992, 3118, 3203, 3207, 3276
Pearce, Windsor...92, 209, 242, 483, 499, 510, 523, 549, 565a, 568, 588, 637, 649, 688, 691, 734, 757, 767-768, 804, 869-869a, 872, 988, 1033, 1035, 1063, 1074, 1114b, 1168, 1253, 1271, 1294a, 1295, 1300-1301, 1377-1377a, 1453, 1501, 1671, 1712, 1714, 1718-1719, 1749, 1807, 1813, 2022, 2442, 2992, 3028, 3257, 3284
Pearl, James...1209
Pelman, Dempsey...1529
Pen, Calf...2292, 2469
Pender, Ephraim...161, 323
Pendleton, Nancy...2781a
Pendleton, Sarah...2578

Penn, Thomas...774
Pennington...512, 1788, 2281
Pennington, Ann...2742a
Pennington, Isaac...441, 662, 667, 677-678, 685, 711-713, 716-719, 728, 1077, 1117, 1161, 2282, 2289, 2573
Pennington, Levi...348, 512, 623, 683, 715, 1258
Pennington, Levi Sr...348, 441, 459
Pennington, Martha...348, 512
Pennington, Richard...2217a-2217b, 2990b
Perkins...2247
Perkins, Hardy...1490
Perkins, Thomas Harding...1488, 2112a
Perry...2237, 2654, 2735
Perry, John...1943, 2240, 2242-2246, 2542
Perry, Samuel...1089-1090, 1105, 1187-1188, 1214, 1237, 1253-1254, 1443, 1476, 1513, 1649-1651, 1656, 1698, 1943, 2237, 2240, 2242-2246, 2285, 2440, 2542. 2653, 2685, 2883-2884, 3007, 3111, 3118, 3605
Perry, Stephen...3429, 3657, 3676
Perry, William...3111
Person...2117a, 2336b, 2538b, 2653a, 2739a, 2844a, 3030, 3285, 3591a
Person, Ann...3696a
Person, B...3031
Person, Benjamin...2644, 2878, 3007, 3022, 3111, 3294a, 3295, 3382, 3432a, 3448, 3470b, 3495, 3510a, 3542a, 3544, 3546, 3570b, 3628b, 3647a, 3665a, 3691b, 3694, 3696a, 3716
Person, Elizabeth...1728
Person, Harrison...2644
Person, Henry...1173-1174, 1190a, 1214, 1554, 1636, 2977a
Person, James...1728
Person, Joseph...906a, 1255a, 2140a, 2217b, 2990b, 3428a, 3622, 3647a
Person, Joseph J...3527, 3643, 3657, 3676, 3717
Person, Joseph John...2644
Person, Martha...3649, 3687c
Person, Mary A...3691b
Person, Murdoch...3691b
Person, Polley...2644
Person, Samuel...1099-1100, 1173a-1173b, 1214, 1443, 1459, 1476, 1604a, 1754, 1949-1950, 2305, 2360-2361, 2364, 2378a, 2413, 2538b, 2644, 2654, 2779a, 3118
Person, Samuel J...3691b
Person, Tabitha...2644, 3163, 3307, 3443, 3657
Person, Thomas...2644, 2997a, 3007, 3111, 3307, 3443, 3527, 3604, 3649, 3657, 3714, 3742
Person, Widow...2743
Person, William...2644, 3111, 3124, 3186a, 3527, 3691b
Perthys, Joseph...996
Peterson, Duncan...1529
Petty, Guilford...3118
Petty, Theophilus...840, 1004, 1131-1132
Pheman...1109
Phifer, John...377

Phillips...914a, 1458, 1697, 2381, 2610b, 2655a, 2963a, 3011, 3108, 3186, 3509a, 3529, 3594a
Phillips, Abner...2217b, 2538a, 2563a, 2610b, 2629a, 2653a, 2715a, 2742a, 2743, 2844a
Phillips, Absalom...3172, 3409, 3445b, 3476
Phillips, Alexander...2794a, 3597
Phillips, Ann...1349b
Phillips, Benjamin...2764a, 3007-3007a, 3197, 3277, 3283, 3495, 3581a, 3666, 3696, 3722d
Phillips, Betty...1653
Phillips, Brinkley...3007, 3033, 3311-3312, 3418, 3475, 3479, 3481, 3495, 3559a, 3715a
Phillips, Burrell...878, 908, 992, 1038
Phillips, Charity...2764a, 3311-3312
Phillips, Dabney...3371, 3445b, 3604a, 3616a, 3622
Phillips, Dempsey...685, 728
Phillips, Dennis...992, 1038, 1194b-1194c, 1204a, 2564a, 2615a, 2657a, 2742a, 2764a, 2765b, 3033, 3105a, 3622
Phillips, Edith...3239a
Phillips, Edmund...2764a
Phillips, Edward...3597
Phillips, Eli...2845, 2932, 2959, 3007, 3028, 3111, 3176, 3182, 3283, 3339b, 3432, 3445c, 3465, 3590, 3644, 3668, 3710
Phillips, Elizabeth...667, 2794a, 3311-3312, 3481
Phillips, Elmore...2794a
Phillips, Fereby...2764a
Phillips, Henry...2764a, 2957a, 3185, 3445b, 3622
Phillips, Henry Sr...3033
Phillips, Hezekiah...2657a, 3033
Phillips, Horatio...3189a
Phillips, J...760
Phillips, James...489, 2639, 2960a, 2984a, 3033
Phillips, Jascay...3610
Phillips, Jeremiah...737j, 801b, 914a, 1349b, 2124a, 2585a, 2800a, 2805b, 2834b, 2963b, 3005a, 3028, 3051a, 3179a
Phillips, Jeremiah Sr...2794a, 2805b, 2834b, 2990a, 3051a, 3179a
Phillips, Jesse...2960, 2981, 3007, 3339c, 3385, 3409, 3441a
Phillips, Joab...3643
Phillips, Joel...127a, 662, 667, 801b, 878, 914a, 2124a, 2752a, 2984a
Phillips, John...16, 30, 40, 125, 295, 574-575, 662, 667, 685, 728, 769, 908, 992, 1038, 1213, 1607, 2112a, 2271, 2764a, 2970, 3007, 3072, 3107, 3151, 3162, 3172, 3182, 3312, 3371, 3430, 3445b-3445c, 3606a, 3627a, 3644, 3704, 3710a
Phillips, John [son of Henry]...3445b
Phillips, John D...3320, 3371, 3430, 3496a, 3622, 3627a, 3710a
Phillips, John Jr...574, 2993
Phillips, John Sr...295, 3371, 3445b
Phillips, Kindred...3309, 3404
Phillips, Labon...2764a, 3007a

Phillips, Lazurus...2585a, 2764a, 2794a, 2800a, 2805a-2805b, 2834a, 2963b, 2990a, 3005a, 3033, 3239a
Phillips, Lewis...878, 1104b, 1349b, 2124a, 2271, 2730a, 2960a, 2984a, 3005a, 3007, 3011-3012, 3111, 3151, 3162, 3189a, 3445d, 3496a, 3527, 3597, 3614c, 3622, 3627a, 3657a, 3710a
Phillips, Lewis Jr...1170, 2780, 3445b
Phillips, Lewis Sr...1170, 3606a, 3622
Phillips, Lydia...3033
Phillips, Marada...3033
Phillips, Mark...30, 878, 1607, 1749, 1762, 2477, 2728, 2731, 2797, 2827, 2858, 2885, 2932, 2970, 2993, 3007, 3111, 3154, 3176, 3340
Phillips, Mark Jr...2477, 3722d
Phillips, Mary D...3596
Phillips, Matthew...2117b, 2496, 2764a, 3007, 3033, 3100, 3400, 3597, 3622
Phillips, Meredith...2538a, 2586a, 2610c, 2718a, 2764a, 2990b, 3007a, 3026b, 3033
Phillips, Michael...3722f
Phillips, Nathan...914a
Phillips, Nimrod...2752a, 2794a, 2834b
Phillips, Patience...2271
Phillips, Patrick...3028, 3051a
Phillips, Patty...3007, 3033, 3111
Phillips, Phebe...2764a, 3007a
Phillips, Polly...3154
Phillips, Rany...3154
Phillips, Rany Jr...3154
Phillips, Rebecca...2764a
Phillips, Richard...3622
Phillips, Robert...388, 1349b, 2332, 2764a, 2796, 3033, 3179a, 3445b, 3614c, 3622
Phillips, Robert H...3496a
Phillips, Sarah...2794a, 2990a, 3606a, 3627a, 3710a
Phillips, Sion...1193c, 1349b, 1953a, 2117b, 2718a, 2764a, 3007a
Phillips, Susanna/Sukey...2764a
Phillips, Terrell...3005a
Phillips, Walter...2984a
Phillips, Widow...3622
Phillips, Wilkie...3005a
Phillips, William...737i, 761a-761b, 801a, 914a, 986a, 1188, 1617, 2332, 2522-2523, 2610b, 2615a, 2730a, 2764a, 2811, 2957a, 3007, 3033, 3111, 3141a, 3172, 3197, 3294, 3311-3312, 3371, 3409, 3418, 3437a, 3445b, 3495, 3576, 3597, 3606a, 3613, 3616a, 3622, 3715a
Phillips, William [son of Lewis]...3614c
Phillips, William [son of Sion]...3622
Phillips, William Jr...855b
Phillips, William Sr...855b
Phillips, Willis...761b, 801a, 855b, 914a, 986a, 1953a, 2117b, 2538a, 2586a, 2610c, 2718a, 2742a, 2764a, 2765b
Picken, William...1004
Picket, William...1701
Pierce [see Pearce]
Pigg, Poll...142
Piggott, Jeremiah...620

Richardson, Noah...2794, 3372, 3597, 3609, 3614b
Richardson, Oma...2914
Richardson, Robert...1075, 1177-1178, 1252, 1332-1333, 2188, 2653, 2914
Richardson, S...2738
Richardson, Sally...2914
Richardson, Sarah...432, 1635
Richardson, Stephen...347, 629, 632, 661, 666, 759, 999, 1142, 1237, 1258, 1380, 1396, 1447, 1474, 1505, 1514, 1713, 2108, 2131, 2153, 2340-2341, 2391, 2395, 2410, 2910, 3007, 3039, 3111, 3210, 3251, 3391
Richardson, Stephen Jr...3069, 3111
Richardson, Stephen Sr...3069
Richardson, Thomas...4, 14
Richardson, William...86, 107, 111-112, 289, 295, 352, 376, 435, 515, 521, 662, 667, 684, 727, 869a, 966, 1075, 1166, 1177-1178, 1214, 1237, 1252, 1332-1333, 1443, 1484, 1486, 1514, 1585, 1596, 1598, 1602-1603, 1635, 1638, 1783, 2109, 2131, 2214, 2262, 2337, 2409-2410, 2505, 2543, 2546, 2698, 2721, 2794, 2914, 2947
Richardson, William Jr...1457, 1474, 1504, 2794
Richardson, William Sr...289, 342
Ricket, William...1701
Ricketts, Jon...171
Riddle, James...1145, 1272, 1363-1364, 1530, 1820, 2659
Riddle, John...2659, 2990a
Riddle, Joseph W...3106
Riddle, Mary...2659
Riddle, Sarah...2659
Riddle, Tabby...3118
Riddle, Temperance...2659, 3007, 3722
Riddle, William...656, 2659
Ridley, B...1109
Rigsby, James...255
Ring, William...3165
Ritchey, Archibald...2931
Rittenhouse, Jonathan...238
Ritter...1766, 2099, 2467, 2485, 2487, 2683, 3477
Ritter, Aaron...1067
Ritter, Anna...3046
Ritter, Cloey...937
Ritter, Dickson...3140-3141, 3266, 3298, 3336, 3358, 3428a, 3437-3438, 3518, 3574
Ritter, Dorothy...3345
Ritter, Eliza...2914
Ritter, Elizabeth...3494, 3636, 3641, 3671
Ritter, Everet...1205, 1506, 2086-2087, 2103, 2172, 2176, 2272, 2472, 2480, 2497, 2871, 3641, 3737
Ritter, George...2942, 3060, 3091, 3624, 3741
Ritter, Hannah...1067
Ritter, Henry...3698, 3722a
Ritter, J...3083
Ritter, James...1809, 2436, 3046, 3358, 3641, 3654
Ritter, James Bradbury...1067
Ritter, Jesse...237, 318, 365, 524, 537, 581-583, 607, 624, 661, 666, 730, 750, 759, 778, 849, 903, 936, 976, 1017-

1018, 1049, 1073, 1081-1082, 1112, 1180, 1197, 1257, 1346, 1351, 1369, 1396, 1400, 1432, 1442, 1446, 1450, 1453a, 1457, 1463, 1466-1468, 1472, 1486, 1526, 1546, 1552, 1579, 1628, 1638, 1654, 1696, 1746, 1794, 1809, 1934, 1985, 2056, 2074, 2086-2087, 2103, 2139, 2172, 2176, 2179, 2203, 2209, 2264, 2272, 2281, 2397-2398, 2436, 2472, 2480, 2547, 2672, 2808, 2863, 2867, 2879, 2908, 2913, 2922, 2926, 2942, 2984, 3007, 3038, 3103, 3111, 3123, 3144, 3186a, 3259, 3551, 4090a-4090b
Ritter, Jesse Jr...2480
Ritter, Jesse Sr...2422, 2497, 2783, 2871
Ritter, John...849, 1073, 1156, 1205, 1355, 1369, 1380, 1396, 1442, 1457, 1494, 1504, 1506, 1546, 1579, 1585, 1638, 1783, 1954, 2056, 2087, 2131, 2172-2173, 2207, 2214, 2219, 2262-2264, 2281, 2298, 2408, 2410, 2438, 2497, 2505, 2573, 2652, 2654, 2672, 2684, 2693, 2696, 2913-2914, 2921, 3007, 3062, 3111, 3164, 3168, 3231, 3286, 3319, 3378, 3382, 3390, 3403, 3437, 3440, 3494, 3572, 3595, 3614, 3625, 3636, 3641-3642, 3647, 3654, 3657, 3671, 3673, 3703, 3717
Ritter, John Jr...3111, 3275, 3339, 3440, 3494, 3521, 3626, 3637, 3671
Ritter, John Sr...3494, 3626, 3637, 3641
Ritter, John T...3336, 3414, 3437, 3479, 3486, 3555, 3641, 3666, 3670, 3723a
Ritter, Lazarus...3046
Ritter, M...3174
Ritter, Margaret...1453a, 1554
Ritter, Marvel...3091, 3134-3135, 3140-3141, 3309, 3380, 3404, 3624
Ritter, Moses...524, 2497, 2672, 2693, 2913, 3173
Ritter, Moses Jr...3111
Ritter, Moses Sr...3111
Ritter, Nancy...3046
Ritter, Richardson...3164, 3168
Ritter, Sally...2914, 3144
Ritter, Susannah...2871, 3641, 3737
Ritter, T...3021
Ritter, Thomas...936, 1298, 1355, 1369, 1380, 1453a, 1457, 1463, 1466-1468, 1478, 1487, 1493, 1506, 1526, 1554, 1578, 1587, 1595, 1621, 1749, 1768, 1803, 1809, 1934, 2030, 2074, 2091, 2131, 2174, 2208, 2221, 2333, 2436, 2467, 2487, 2500, 2503, 2547, 2613, 2696, 2791, 2802, 2824, 2863, 2921-2922, 3007, 3062, 3111, 3114, 3134-3135, 3140-3141, 3230, 3277, 3298, 3312, 3319, 3345, 3509, 3516, 3552, 3584, 3614
Ritter, Thomas Jr...849, 3142
Ritter, William...3274, 3275a, 3306, 3357, 3376, 3641, 3654, 3673, 3710a, 3717
Ritter, Willoughby...3298, 3698
Roan [see Rowan]
Roberson [see Robson]
Roberts...3037, 3052
Roberts, Isaac...3176, 3664a, 3665a, 3716, 3722f
Roberts, James...1168

Roberts, Wiley...3664a
Roberts, William...683a, 1075a
Robinson, C...7b
Robinson, Charles...127a
Robinson, Charles Jr...7b, 10a
Robinson, Charles Sr...10a
Robinson, Mary...3028
Robson, Joseph...737k, 1010a, 1043, 1113, 1223a, 1304a, 1385, 1459, 1505, 1935-1936, 2194, 2585a
Rodes, John...209
Rogers, Elizabeth...603
Rogers, Eltha...3355
Rogers, Enoch...603, 878, 982, 1749, 1760
Rogers, Jacob...16, 125, 314, 423, 502, 574, 603, 633
Rogers, Jesse...2954, 3007, 3294, 3594a, 3647, 3716
Rogers, Jesse Jr...3591a
Rogers, Jesse P...3723a
Rogers, Joel...3028
Rogers, John...574, 603, 878, 1749, 1760
Rogers, Mary Ann...603
Rogers, Ruth...603, 633, 1749, 1760
Rogers, Sarah...603
Rogers, Shadrack/Shadrick...1551, 2079, 2412, 2823, 2829, 3028, 3225a
Rollins, Amy...3607
Rollins, Michael...3607
Rooks, Hardymon...2637
Ross, Sarah...2393
Rosser, Jo...776a, 821a
Rouse...3076b
Rouse, Adam...58
Rouse, Ann...2852
Rouse, John...2879, 3140, 3233, 3277, 3358, 3438, 3518, 3574
Rouse, Joseph...2464, 2823, 3007, 3111, 3225a
Rouse, Martin...3358, 3438, 3450, 3518, 3574
Rouse, Miles...3277, 3358, 3438, 3518, 3574
Routh...2417
Routh, Jacob...1377
Rowan...2661, 2702, 2824, 3183-3184, 3263, 3395
Rowan, Robert...2030, 2371
Rowan, Robert [Sheriff]...446
Rubottom, Eleanor...2781
Rubottom, Elizabeth...2578
Rubottom, Ezekial...1506, 1702, 1713, 1979, 2099, 2326, 2330, 2760, 3026
Rubottom, George...3026
Rubottom, John...3026
Rubottom, Samuel...3026
Rubottom, Simon...1472, 1506, 1702, 2221, 2247, 2272, 3026
Rubottom, Thomas...1361, 1459, 1531, 1702, 2099, 3026
Rubottom, William...3026
Rubottom, Zeno...3026
Russell...563
Russell, James...5, 47, 135, 137, 226, 231, 291-292, 329, 372, 406, 421, 431, 489, 502, 504, 507, 563, 2197
Russell, John...3102
Russell, Joseph Martin...2756, 2873
Russell, Mary...5, 135
Russell, Michael...421, 504, 879
Russell, Tolbert...3610

Shamburger, Henry...290, 2785
Shamburger, James...3268
Shamburger, John...1778-1779, 1802, 2076a, 2158-2159, 2362-2363, 2414, 2552, 2616, 2664, 2786, 2839, 2887-2888, 2902a, 2909, 3007, 3024, 3111, 3120-3121, 3138-3139, 3178, 3266, 3268, 3338, 3343, 3359, 3441, 3473, 3495, 3527, 3599, 3638, 3640, 3642, 3657, 3715, 3733, 3737-3738
Shamburger, John Jr...2839, 3268
Shamburger, Lida...2990
Shamburger, Mary...3743
Shamburger, P...3196
Shamburger, Peter...290, 416, 462, 661, 666, 727, 759, 769, 833, 939, 945, 971, 1003, 1018, 1023, 1049, 1207, 1212, 1226, 1257, 1321, 1334, 1351, 1613, 1633, 1664, 1700, 1742, 1778-1779, 1802, 2062, 2076a, 2159, 2414, 2470, 2699, 2786-2787, 2839, 2843, 3007, 3111, 3121, 3138-3139, 3178, 3187, 3208, 3266, 3286, 3377, 3546, 3566, 3614, 3642, 3722c, 3733, 3734a, 3737, 3743
Shamburger, Peter Jr...2362-2363, 2699, 3007
Shamburger, Peter Sr...2362-2363, 2785, 2843, 2909, 3007, 3111
Shamburger, Thomas...3268
Shamburger, W...2843
Shamburger, William...2785, 2843, 2955, 3007, 3111, 3138
Shattuck, A...3465
Shattuck, Artemus...3465, 3696
Shaw...3563
Shaw, Catharine McAskill...3554
Shaw, Daniel...585, 2886
Shaw, Donald...354, 526, 545-546, 602, 619, 2464
Shaw, John...529, 650
Shaw, John A...3742
Shaw, Malcolm...807, 2465-2466, 2546, 2700, 3691a
Shaw, Mary...2465, 2546, 3141
Shaw, Nancy...3739a
Shaw, Norman...3554
Shearing...294, 761b, 1194b-1194c, 1716a, 2615a, 2636a, 2636c, 2764a, 2815, 2826, 3105a
Shearing, Aaron...2815b
Shearing, Charles...4, 261, 294-295, 311-312, 440, 489, 603, 696, 737h-737i, 743, 878, 900, 909-909b, 915, 922, 984, 1027, 1058-1059, 1475a, 1570, 2419b, 2572, 2815c, 2825
Shearing, Elizabeth...1058
Shearing, John...4, 159, 294
Shearing, Joseph...2815c
Shears, Donald...2823
Sheffield...221, 2266, 2545, 3416
Sheffield, Adam...1387, 1713, 1755, 2022, 2189, 2210, 2232, 2275, 2319-2320, 2428, 2450-2451, 2455, 2604, 2660, 2747, 2831, 2861, 2873, 2904, 2924
Sheffield, Andrew [Adam?]...2861
Sheffield, Elijah...3618
Sheffield, Elizabeth...2022
Sheffield, Everet...1680, 1764, 2022, 2078, 2121, 2304, 2486, 2861, 2942, 2983, 3007, 3111, 3246, 3265, 3269, 3403, 3409, 3411, 3432, 3496, 3519,

3532, 3568, 3584, 3670, 3703, 3723, 3738
Sheffield, Hannah...2022, 2232, 2304, 2449, 2486, 2527
Sheffield, Isaac...2799-2800, 2835, 2890, 2924, 3111
Sheffield, Isham...1525, 1680, 1764, 2022, 2231, 2238, 2304, 2449, 2486, 2518, 2527, 2839, 3007, 3196, 3265, 3379, 3482-3485
Sheffield, Isham Jr...2527, 2983, 3111
Sheffield, Isham Sr...3111
Sheffield, John...221, 276, 295, 302, 330, 437, 439, 479-480, 547, 661, 680a, 727, 759, 769, 1018, 1049, 1281, 1302, 1387, 1448, 1525, 1680-1682, 1713, 1763, 1774-1775, 1835, 2016, 2022, 2032, 2036, 2131, 2181, 2189, 2231, 2299, 2310, 2312, 2346, 2449, 2486, 2518, 2520, 2527, 2835, 2839, 2861, 2889-2890, 2983, 3007, 3028, 3196, 3246, 3409, 3572, 3618, 3737-3738
Sheffield, John Jr...666, 684, 727, 759, 1207, 1212, 1226, 1279, 1370, 1396, 1448, 1552, 1633, 1659, 2273, 2302, 2518, 2799-2800, 2835, 2889, 2923, 3007, 3111, 3265, 3566-3566a
Sheffield, John Sr...666, 1273, 1370, 1387, 1448, 1633, 2273, 2302, 2527, 2835, 2799-2800, 2889, 3007, 3111, 3265, 3532
Sheffield, Lucretia...2022
Sheffield, Lydia...2022
Sheffield, Mark...367, 2022
Sheffield, Martin...3618
Sheffield, Mary...2022
Sheffield, Matthew...3593
Sheffield, Milly...2022
Sheffield, Rebecca...2022
Sheffield, Sally...3196
Sheffield, Sarah...1276, 2022
Sheffield, Susan...3333
Sheffield, William...295, 480, 532, 534, 547, 2307, 3545
Sheffield, William Sr...666
Shelton, Joseph...2747
Shepard, John...1082
Shepherd, Alexander Jr...297
Shepherd, Jacob...637-638, 659
Shepherd, John...548
Sherwood, America...2112b
Shields...2620, 3130, 3705
Shields, Archibald...1749, 2782, 2846b, 3007, 3033, 3075a, 3100, 3111, 3285, 3400, 3494, 3605, 3606a, 3607, 3647, 3653, 3657a, 3671
Shields, Archibald Jr...3614c, 3664b
Shields, B...760, 1258
Shields, Benjamin...372, 507, 662, 667, 685, 728, 744, 977, 1082, 1129, 1174, 1182, 1201a, 1214, 1282, 1443, 1477, 1713, 2075, 2079a, 2569a, 2618, 2743-2744, 2765b, 2782, 3622
Shields, Benjamin Jr...2742a
Shields, Bryan...3664b
Shields, Bryant...3722e
Shields, Cornelius...2618, 2737, 2782, 2918, 3007, 3028, 3033, 3071, 3075a, 3111, 3151, 3162, 3172, 3400, 3476, 3607, 3622, 3636, 3653, 3657a, 3664b, 3737
Shields, James...2618, 2790, 2844a, 2978, 3007-3007a, 3075a, 3111, 3607

Shields, Mary...3607
Shields, Milly...2782
Shields, Neill...2618
Shields, Overton...1749
Shields, Patrick...2782, 3559a, 3643, 3664b
Shields, Reuben...420, 667, 685, 728, 731, 744, 1113b, 1161, 1394, 1475a, 1488, 1490, 1515, 1531b, 1662-1663, 1751, 1756, 1910, 2046, 2326, 2330, 2444, 2488, 2531, 2819
Shields, Robert...3400, 3664b
Shields, Susannah...3607
Shields, William...2918, 3657, 3742
Shipley, John...2490
Shipley, Nathaniel...2490
Shipley, Robert...2490
Shipp, Coleman...3222-3223
Shurley...318
Shurley, David...318
Sides, Doratha Elizabeth...417
Sides, Dorotha...417
Sides, Henry...417
Sides, Peter...417
Siler, Ann...2846d
Siler, Benjamin W...3383
Siler, Frederick...3072, 3294a
Siler, Jacob...2515, 2585a
Siler, John...3294a
Simmons, Benjamin...972, 2669a
Simmons, James...2669a, 3101a, 3676a
Simmons, Jesse...1771a, 2336a
Simmons, John...1585a, 3101a
Simmons, Pleasant...3546a
Simmons, William...666, 3101a
Simpson, Thomas...741a, 763a
Sims, Robert...456
Sinclair, Daniel...2780
Sinclair, Duncan...3663a
Singleton, James...472
Singleton, William...2795, 3028
Sink...3210, 3421, 3645
Sink, Parrell...2395
Smith...1119a, 1122, 1420, 1422, 1811, 2052, 2336, 2441, 2820, 2873, 2958, 3111a, 3171, 3742
Smith, A.B...3138, 3208, 3647
Smith, Aaron...2914
Smith, Abner...3445b, 3597
Smith, Abner E...3723a
Smith, Adam...2224-2225, 2509, 2740
Smith, Alexander...3439, 3517, 3647
Smith, Ambrose...914a, 2765b
Smith, Anderson...3269, 3603
Smith, Anderson B...2997a, 3178, 3520, 3585, 3594, 3618, 3626, 3628, 3641-3642, 3647-3648, 3653, 3657, 3659, 3672, 3716
Smith, Ann...348, 3676
Smith, Annis...2629
Smith, Archibald...91
Smith, Arthur...657, 689, 869a, 1255, 1772, 2415, 2552
Smith, B...3591a
Smith, Benjamin...325, 3040a
Smith, Bryan...2958
Smith, Cornelius...3037
Smith, Daniel...1365
Smith, David...41
Smith, E...759
Smith, Easter...135, 590, 823
Smith, Edmond...92

Spinks, John...483, 642, 688, 744, 767, 869-869a, 1377, 1392, 1453, 1745, 1948, 3076a

Spinks, Lewis...483, 773, 869a, 1065, 1501, 1531, 1666, 1744, 1745a-1745b, 2095, 2114, 2393-2394, 2447, 2552, 2612a, 2631, 2664, 2746, 2885, 2888, 3185

Spinks, Martha...483

Spinks, Mary...3257

Spinks, Rolley...483, 869a, 887, 1278, 1718-1719, 1772, 2415-2417, 2552, 2586, 2708, 2776, 2830a, 2903, 3154a, 3185

Spinks, Sally...1745

Spinks, Sarah...483

Spinks, Widow...894, 1375

Spivey...2597, 2837, 3138, 3269, 3519, 3593

Spivey, Bathoney...937

Spivey, Isaac...3567, 3593, 3615, 3692, 3722c, 3734a

Spivey, James...2064, 3028

Spivey, John...937, 1269, 1360, 1383, 1409, 1483, 1623, 1673, 1979, 2080, 2112, 2354, 3007, 3111, 3139, 3335, 3545, 3591, 3722c, 3734a

Spivey, Sarah...3368

Spivey, Susanna...2153

Stafford, Jesse...3643, 3710

Stafford, John...3710

Stamper, James...2059

Stamper, Sarah...2059, 2612

Stanley...318

Stanley, James...1067

Stanley, Rhoda...1067

Stanley, Stephen...1067

Stanton...435

Stanton, Abigail...93, 435

Stanton, John...93, 213, 435

Stanton, Samuel...1046

Starling, Thomas...408

Starns, Isaac...128

Steadman, William W...3118

Steed, John...1635

Steell, Sarah...135

Stephens/Stevens, Emanuel...2, 80, 89

Stephens/Stevens, Henry...3234a

Stephens/Stevens, James...295, 582, 666, 706, 948

Stephens/Stevens, John...250, 343, 354, 441, 459, 546, 585-586, 1446, 2464, 2886

Stephens/Stevens, Joseph...737c, 741a, 763a, 1376

Stephens/Stevens, Nancy...1395

Stephens/Stevens, Robert...750, 759

Stephens/Stevens, William...741a, 763a

Stewart/Stuart...2677, 3052

Stewart/Stuart, Angus...666, 684, 725, 727, 781

Stewart/Stuart, Benjamin...1050

Stewart/Stuart, Charles...671a, 695a, 869a, 1377, 1452, 1496, 1745, 2291, 2442, 2552, 2598, 2772, 2888, 3072, 3111

Stewart/Stuart, E...3496a

Stewart/Stuart, Edward...1061a, 1080, 1129a, 1601a, 2636b, 2846b, 2974a, 3028, 3403, 3437

Stewart/Stuart, Enoch...3664a

Stewart/Stuart, George...3007, 3111, 3266, 3320, 3336, 3509, 3516, 3555, 3606a, 3614c, 3622, 3643

Stewart/Stuart, John...376, 422, 2546, 3469, 3555, 3597, 3664a, 3722f

Stewart/Stuart, Joseph...656

Stewart/Stuart, Kenneth...2759

Stewart/Stuart, Mary...2974a

Stewart/Stuart, Samuel...1129a, 2636b

Stewart/Stuart, William...3614c, 3643, 3664a

Stinson...2343, 2496, 2678b, 3371

Stinson, Jane...2229

Stinson, John...937, 1653, 1757, 1795, 2124a, 2381, 2387, 2574, 2631a, 2690, 2705, 2781

Stinson, Sarah...1716, 2229

Stoddard...3270, 3339a, 3437a

Stone, Benjamin...3434

Stone, Enoch...3046

Stone, Susan...3267

Stone, William...3434

Story, John...2764a

Stouth, Andra...776

Strange, Charles...209

Strange, Starling...2873

Strange, W.F...3717a

Stratton, Mary...81, 83

Strawn, Bendall...681

Street...2407, 3320

Street, Anthony...840, 977, 1264

Street, Donald...3538a

Street, George...1745

Street, Richard...1113, 1213, 1264, 1488, 1490, 1531a, 2112a, 3181, 3527, 3538a

Street, Widow...3614c, 3616b

Stribling...460-461, 558, 561, 741

Stribling, Francis...88, 281, 283, 295, 324, 335, 353, 382-383, 453, 457, 558-561, 608-609, 643, 763

Strider, Jacob...2196a, 2637

Stringfield, Richard...196

Stroud, David...78, 192, 387, 400, 478, 499, 541, 576-577

Stroud, William...1607

Stubbs, Joseph...238

Stuthern, Jacob...1820

Stutts...3062

Stutts, Abraham / Abram...3275, 3339, 3437, 3440, 3450, 3516, 3521, 3622, 3624, 3642-3643, 3657, 3736

Stutts, Catherine...2153

Stutts, Celia...3494

Stutts, Christian...2153, 2927, 3087, 3111, 3408, 3642-3643

Stutts, Christopher...1589, 1945, 2144-2145, 2214, 2283, 2327, 2354, 2609, 2642, 3007, 3069, 3087, 3206, 3282, 3415

Stutts, Dempsey...2144

Stutts, Elizabeth...2153

Stutts, George...3275, 3339, 3403, 3440, 3516, 3520-3521, 3643, 3647, 3662, 3736

Stutts, H...3335

Stutts, Henry...2153, 2223, 2342, 2378, 2665, 2792, 2942, 3007, 3019, 3028, 3039, 3069, 3111-3112, 3153, 3210, 3289, 3308-3309, 3319, 3335, 3344, 3355, 3420-3422, 3495, 3562, 3566, 3641, 3645, 3664, 3671, 3679

Stutts, Henry Jr...3641

Stutts, Henry Sr...3614, 3641, 3647

Stutts, Jacob...316-317, 341, 379, 661, 666, 684, 727, 759, 769, 971, 1003, 1049, 1081, 1179, 1257, 1269, 1279, 1355, 1396, 1409, 1442, 1483, 1506, 1526, 1552, 1654, 1746, 1844, 1905, 1934, 1972, 1975, 1985, 2074, 2153, 2342-2343, 2378, 2397-2399, 2665, 2680, 2783, 2884, 2921, 3007, 3039, 3069, 3111, 3164, 3206, 3271, 3275, 3339, 3376, 3419-3422, 3440, 3478, 3485b, 3488, 3521, 3591, 3641-3642, 3647, 3664, 3671, 3680, 3716, 3729, 3740

Stutts, Jacob [of Chr.]...3641-3642

Stutts, Jacob [son of Henry]...3271

Stutts, Jacob C...2144

Stutts, Jacob Jr...1511, 1546, 1696

Stutts, Jacob Sr...2044, 2223

Stutts, John...937, 1246, 1315, 1360, 1442, 1457, 1713, 1975, 2153, 2558, 3235, 3271, 3296, 3301, 3306, 3327, 3357, 3390-3391, 3403, 3405, 3408, 3437, 3445, 3469, 3486, 3494, 3524a, 3562, 3578, 3628, 3641-3642, 3645, 3672, 3710a

Stutts, John [of Jacob]...3641

Stutts, John [son of H.]...3445, 3524a, 3578, 3628, 3641

Stutts, John Sr...3437

Stutts, Leonard...1713, 2153, 2706, 2788, 2844, 2878, 2997a, 3028, 3197, 3630, 3641, 3647, 3664

Stutts, Lesh...3028

Stutts, Lucy...2792

Stutts, Mariah...2144

Stutts, Mary...2153

Stutts, Ransom...3630, 3657, 3664

Stutts, Susannah...2153, 3643

Stutts, William...3135, 3210, 3319, 3415, 3469

Sugg/Suggs, Equille...1585e, 1731a

Sugg/Suggs, Harbard...1585e, 1731a, 2639b, 2858c-2858d

Sugg/Suggs, Hazle...2637

Sugg/Suggs, Horatio...1731a

Sugg/Suggs, Isaac...2637

Sugg/Suggs, Rasha...455a-455b, 1731a

Sugg/Suggs, Sally...3118

Sugg/Suggs, Sarah...3106

Sugg/Suggs, Thomas...321, 455a, 1341, 1585b, 1585e, 2858d

Sugg/Suggs, Widow...3644a

Sugg/Suggs, Zilpha...2990

Sullivan...3710

Sullivan, Jesse...3709

Surratt, Leonard...983

Surls [see Sorrells]

Swanson, Olive...1171

Swanson, Richard...1171

Tansey, William Alexander...2490

Taylor, Arthur...337

Taylor, George...2779a

Taylor, James [Colonel]...3118

Taylor, John...942a

Taylor, Joseph...1109

Taylor, Levi...2490

Taylor, Reuben...531

Teague...1095

Teague, Abraham...995a

Teague, Charity...995a

Teague, David...995a

Teague, Eli...3330, 3337
Teague, Elizabeth...995a
Teague, Hannah...995a
Teague, I...3051
Teague, Isaac...995a, 1173c, 1477, 1499a, 1585, 1935, 1949-1950, 2217, 2364, 2763, 2797, 2827, 2858, 2885, 2932, 2942, 2959, 2978, 2997a-2998, 3005, 3020, 3028, 3096, 3111-3111a, 3126, 3167, 3185, 3190, 3227, 3245, 3283, 3330, 3337, 3397, 3402, 3461a, 3590, 3657
Teague, Isaac Jr...3007, 3337, 3402, 3523
Teague, Isaac Sr...3007, 3033, 3285, 3337, 3402, 3523
Teague, Isabell...995a
Teague, J...3644
Teague, Jacob...995a, 3040a, 3111a, 3330, 3728
Teague, Juditha...3330
Teague, Mary...3111
Teague, Matthias...2336b
Teague, Mayness...1137
Teague, Moses...995a, 2763, 3028
Teague, Rachel...995a, 3330
Teague, Susannah...995a
Teague, William...995a, 1443, 1459, 1476, 1488, 1513
Tear, John...28, 101
Teaster, Nathaniel...2673
Teaster, Robert...2673
Tedwell, Francis...78, 127, 162, 185, 189, 217, 295, 313, 488, 661, 666, 684, 727, 759, 916, 923-924, 2957
Tedwell, Jean...916, 923-924, 2526, 2614
Tedwell, Samuel...313, 315, 542, 666, 759, 924
Tedwell, Widow...2275, 2428
Teer [see Tear]
Temple, Samuel...4, 743
Temples, Lewis...2496
Temples, Needham...1480, 2489
Terrell, Moses...2490
Terrell, Timothy...3045
Theid, Henrietta...3460
Thomas...2332, 2409, 2523, 3222-3223
Thomas, Cattral...2971a
Thomas, George...2150a-2150b
Thomas, John...674, 1464, 2490
Thomas, Keziah...2311, 2401
Thomas, Leonard...1030, 1213, 1264
Thomas, Micajah...2846b, 2879, 3610
Thomas, Philip...2490
Thomas, Philip Jr...2490
Thomas, Stephen...3118
Thomas, William...2490
Thompson, Benjamin...135a
Thompson, Elizabeth...523
Thompson, George...3118
Thompson, Jennings...510, 523
Thompson, John...135a, 743, 2569a, 2575, 3318a
Thompson, Robert...3118
Thompson, Ruth...2974a
Thompson, Susannah...3318a
Thompson, William...159, 278, 2771a
Thornton...610
Thornton, Dann/Donn...517, 565

Thornton, James...900, 909-909b, 937, 977, 1643, 1644, 1817, 2051, 2105, 2516
Thornton, John...977, 1524, 2045
Thornton, John Sr...264, 599
Thornton, Seth...3118
Thornton, William...2424, 2747
Tiem, Jacob...210, 319
Tillet, Giles...15
Tillis / Tullos...912, 919, 921, 1006, 1039
Tillis / Tullos, Elizabeth...71, 438, 666, 733
Tillis / Tullos, Jane...438
Tillis / Tullos, John...438
Tillis / Tullos, Richard...71, 183, 225, 243, 295, 438, 2162
Tillis / Tullos, Sarah...438
Tillis / Tullos, Tarply...438, 1026
Tillis / Tullos, Temple...71, 438, 621, 632, 733, 2967
Tillis / Tullos, Willoughby...71, 438, 733, 2967
Tillman, John...2971a
Tillman, Joseph...2971a
Tollison, John...562
Tolman, John...2544, 3028
Tolman, Widow...3086, 3128
Tomason...1376
Tomason, William...1376
Tomberlin...2220, 2324, 2326, 2821
Tomlin...201, 2324, 2326
Tomlin, Moses...34, 60, 62, 75, 94, 102, 371
Tomlinson, Elizabeth...3640
Tomlinson, James...3341a
Tomlinson, James G...3640
Tomlinson, James Goodwin...3640
Tomlinson, Richard...2983b, 3341a, 3640
Tommos, Cattrel...2971a
Toney, Marts...940
Townsend, Robinson...10a
Trader, William...1758
Traps...679, 699, 713, 1414, 1729, 1943, 2440, 2519
Traps, James...2542
Traps, John...295, 386, 478, 577
Traps, John Jr...386
Traps, John Sr...386-387
Tredwell [see Tedwell]
Trent, William...1168a
Trent, William Jr...906a
Triplett, William...3007a
Troy...3658
Tucker...2817a, 2954
Tucker, Elizabeth...3720
Tucker, George...2708a, 3156
Tucker, Jesse...3720
Tucker, L...2995
Tucker, Nancy...3156
Tucker, Nathaniel...1743a, 2942, 3007, 3111, 3236, 3492, 3522, 3580, 3600, 3614a, 3616
Tucker, Thomas...78, 173, 259, 541
Tucker, William...855b, 2606, 2708a
Tullous [see Tillis]
Turner, John...710b
Turner, Simon...710b
Tyler, Charles...1330b, 2606, 2662
Tyler, Edward Duval...1330b, 1367c, 1585d, 1757a, 1947a, 2150a-2150b, 2795a

Tyner, Thomas...1555
Tyson...599, 1147, 2585a, 2678b, 2805a, 3595
Tyson, Thomas...1607, 1796
Tyson, Aaron...1046, 1365, 1473a, 1516a, 1576a, 1660, 1716, 1749, 1757, 2229, 2381, 2388, 2585, 2690, 2780, 2805a-2805b, 2834a-2834b, 2990a, 3051a, 3179a-3180, 3274a, 3371, 3640, 3657
Tyson, Amelia...3322, 3640
Tyson, Ann...1365
Tyson, Arcada...1365, 2585
Tyson, Archibald...2780
Tyson, Benjamin...404, 610, 620, 662, 667, 685, 728, 769, 1046, 1282-1283, 1404, 1441, 1473a, 1516a, 1716, 1728, 1933, 2076, 2109, 2134, 2229, 2239, 2276-2277, 2388, 2585, 2771a, 2780, 2822
Tyson, Cornelius...3-4, 25-26, 30, 50, 62, 87a, 103-104, 135, 154, 159, 228, 230-231, 249, 261, 264, 277, 280, 294-295, 298, 301, 312, 328, 396-397, 404, 421, 423, 440, 449, 504, 511, 599, 610, 620, 662, 667, 685, 728, 769, 879, 1365, 1459, 1716, 2076, 2109, 2229, 2585, 2780, 2846d, 2993, 2997, 3072, 3710a
Tyson, Cornelius Sr...743
Tyson, Elizabeth...1716, 2229, 2585
Tyson, Jacob...2780, 3147, 3343, 3640
Tyson, James...3663a
Tyson, Jane...301, 620, 1046, 1365, 1716, 2229, 2780
Tyson, Jean...154, 404
Tyson, John...4, 159, 261, 2760, 2780, 2902a, 2997, 3197, 3264, 3341, 3395, 3409, 3479, 3494, 3568, 3581, 3665a, 3724a
Tyson, John Jr...3570a
Tyson, Joshua...1933
Tyson, Josiah...3302, 3665a
Tyson, Katharine...620
Tyson, Lovdy...3597
Tyson, Lydia...1365, 2780, 2944, 3627a
Tyson, Mary...3640
Tyson, Neil...1264
Tyson, Rachel...2780
Tyson, Rebecca...1716, 2229, 2780
Tyson, Richard...404, 620, 1716, 2229
Tyson, Sabra...154, 1716, 2229
Tyson, Sarah...620, 937, 1716, 2229
Tyson, T...760
Tyson, Thomas...309, 404, 573, 620, 662, 667, 769-770, 975, 1112a, 1213, 1282, 1460, 1531a, 1556, 1607, 1624, 1716, 1796, 1933, 2229, 2239, 2276, 2277, 2585, 2780
Tyson, Thomas Jr...2479
Tyson, Thomas Sr...2585
Tyson, W...2848a
Tyson, William...294, 2229, 2780, 2831a, 2846b, 2944, 3189a, 3470b, 3640
Tyson, William D...3710a
Underwood, James...54, 65
Underwood, John...41
Underwood, William...2977a
Upton...1965, 3433
Upton, Darcus...3609-3610, 3651, 3685, 3704
Upton, Edward...1506, 2578

Upton, George...3609-3610
Upton, Ida...1506
Upton, James...3275a, 3380, 3609-3610, 3614b, 3685
Upton, Jesse...685, 728, 869, 1135-1136, 1430, 1506, 1544, 2031, 2133, 2405, 2681, 2689, 2745, 2765, 2947, 2994, 3007, 3061, 3078, 3251, 3296, 3433
Upton, Jesse Jr...3038, 3448
Upton, John...1713, 2243, 2245, 2384, 2386, 2491, 2681, 2765, 2947, 2994, 3007, 3038, 3111
Upton, Martha...2994
Upton, Richard...252, 254, 295, 662, 667, 869, 1284, 1430, 1476, 1506, 1544, 2476, 2959, 3007, 3037, 3054, 3077, 3111, 3609-3610, 3614b, 3647, 3651, 3685, 3704
Upton, William...1713
Vanderford...1638a, 2217, 2555, 2763
Vanderford, Ann...1499a
Vanderford, Eli...1499a, 2977a
Vanderford, Elizabeth...1499a, 2977a
Vanderford, Hannah...1499a
Vanderford, John...688, 703, 869, 1176a, 1499a, 2117a, 2217d-2217e, 2569a, 2763, 2811b, 2977a, 3007a
Vanderford, Mary...1499a, 2977a
Vanderford, Minty/Minta...1173, 1499a, 2217e, 2628a, 2977a
Vanderford, Nancy...2977a
Vanderford, Richard...1173, 1499a, 2977a
Vanderford, Sally...1499a, 2977a
Vanderford, Susan/Susannah...1499a, 2977a
Vanderford, William...1499a, 2628a
Vandiver, Anderson...3723a
Vestal, Thomas...620
Vick, Edey...3028
Vick, Lindsay...3028
Vick, Nathan...2654, 2997a, 3028
Vick, Samuel...3512, 3573
Viner, John...999
Voncannon, Catharine...1258
Voncannon, Elizabeth...2887
Voncannon, John...3723a
Voncannon, Peter...156, 167, 209, 2706
Voncannon, William...3723a
Waddell...782, 934, 1234, 1275, 1349a, 1379, 1402, 1425, 1586, 1693, 2126, 2376, 2566, 2685, 2953, 2991, 3101, 3435
Waddell, Anne...2983b
Waddell, Caroline...3341a
Waddell, Edmund...3005
Waddell, Edmund...44, 988, 1035, 1377, 1392, 1429a, 1452, 1499a, 1607, 1614, 1634, 1728, 1773, 1807, 1811a, 2200-2201, 2237, 2350, 2552, 2569-2569a, 2633, 2655, 2663, 2711, 3005
Waddell, Hugh...592
Waddell, James...3341a
Waddell, John...3005, 3257, 3657
Waddell, John Jr...3341a
Waddell, Lucy...3005, 3005d
Waddell, Lydia...3005
Waddell, Margaret...2983b, 2996, 3318a, 3341a
Waddell, Matthew...2763, 3005, 3005d

Waddell, Nancy...3005
Waddell, Polly...3005
Waddell, Sally...3005
Waddell, Temperance...3529
Waddell, Thomas...869a, 1253-1254, 1773, 1811a, 2815b-2815c, 2983b, 2996, 3005, 3341a
Waddell, William...1607, 1697, 1811a, 2552, 2565, 2775a, 2845, 2846c, 2932, 2996, 2997a, 3005, 3007, 3096, 3111, 3245, 3307, 3312, 3345, 3372, 3417, 3487, 3494, 3523, 3525, 3527, 3529, 3641
Waddell, William Jr...3341a
Wade, Allen...3339b, 3495
Wade, Edmond...1202, 2864, 3113a, 3647
Wade, Mark...3010
Wade, Signal...2061
Wade, Thomas...1044
Wade, Tignar...1198
Wade, Tinsley...2764a, 3033, 3068, 3113a
Wadsowrth, John Sr...2777-2778, 2819
Wadsworth...2347, 2352, 2454
Wadsworth, Ignatious...2945, 3028
Wadsworth, James...295, 762
Wadsworth, James William...2902a
Wadsworth, Jason...295, 762, 885, 1128, 1383, 1554, 1710, 2433, 2554, 2745
Wadsworth, John...295, 1383, 1505, 1660, 1749, 1793, 1935, 2109, 2576, 2602, 2777-2778, 2819, 2846b, 2902a, 3028, 3040, 3341
Wadsworth, John Jr...2777-2778, 2819
Wadsworth, Thomas...246, 295, 552-554, 1505, 1519, 1575
Wadsworth, William...3670
Wagner, John...417
Walker, Asa...2747
Walker, Joseph...68
Walker, Stephen...744
Wallace...3170
Wallace, Carrell...3143
Wallace, E...3545
Wallace, Enoch...3287, 3358, 3438, 3518, 3574, 3593
Wallace, Everet...1532, 1673, 1713, 2030, 2108, 2252, 2294, 2461, 2609, 2682, 2838, 2910, 2919, 3007, 3028, 3111, 3415, 3419-3420, 3426, 3437, 3450, 3647, 3682, 3691
Wallace, Francis...1122
Wallace, Isham...3358, 3439, 3517, 3654, 3698, 3722b
Wallace, J...3646
Wallace, John...3235, 3271, 3474, 3538
Wallace, Joseph...2942, 3271, 3578, 3628
Wallace, Josiah...53, 108, 3736
Wallace, Mary...1217
Wallace, Moses...3084
Wallace, Nathan...3445, 3524a, 3578, 3628, 3641, 3647
Wallace, Nicholas...1423, 1535, 3113, 3170, 3282
Wallace, Richard...1122
Wallace, Robert...2636
Wallace, William...2636
Wallis [see Wallace]

Walsh, John...28, 214, 373, 375, 456, 461, 816
Ward, Jetson...220
Ward, John...1271a
Ward, Robert...2316a, 3118
Ward, Samuel...2813
Ward, Thomas...74a, 220, 260, 452, 1271a, 1600
Wards, Cealy...2990
Warner...1658
Warner, Edward...3171, 3512, 3573, 3581, 3691d
Warner, Hardin...2885, 2987, 3171, 3512, 3573, 3691d
Warner, John...1004, 2259
Warner, Richard...2986, 3445a, 3519a, 3581b, 3628b
Warren, Charles...2424, 2747
Warren, John...2747
Warren, Reuben...2747
Warren, Thomas...2424, 2490, 2747, 2756
Waters, George...2490
Watkins, Ewell / Newell...217, 621, 632, 666, 684, 727
Watkins, Neill...661
Watson, Dempsey...354, 528-529, 546, 585, 650
Watson, John...1618
Watson, Silus...3434
Watts, Dempsey...2464
Wear...270, 355, 907
Wear, John...70, 220, 252, 283, 453
Weatherspoon, William...2490
Weaver, John...453, 618, 701
Weaver, Valentine...377
Weightat, John...664, 709
Welch, Emily...4767-4767a
Wellborn, Isabell...995a
Wells...2360, 3030, 3192
Wells, Isaac...2360-2361
West, George...2097a
West, John...914a
White...2918, 3048
White, Adam...1531, 2255, 2369, 2372, 2431-2432, 2465-2466, 2733-2734, 2736, 2789-2790, 2846a, 2853, 2859, 2872, 2997, 3007, 3028, 3033, 3058, 3067, 3074-3075, 3111, 3389
White, Andrew...1212, 1713, 2078, 2733, 2789-2790, 2815, 2846a, 2853, 2911, 2997
White, Ann...3007, 3399
White, Jacob...2255, 2431, 2465-2466
White, James...1771
White, John...667, 2733, 2872
White, Mary...2790, 2846a, 2997
White, Mrs. ...3058
White, Nancy...2789, 3688
White, Olive...2789-2790, 2997
White, Phil...2738
White, Robert...2217-2217b
White, Sarah...2790, 2846a
White, William...164, 204
Whitfield, Luke...162, 217
Whitford, John...2777-2778
Whitford, William Basten...571, 1488
Whitley, Epaphroditis...410
Whitley, George...409, 529
Whitley, Stephen...3177
Whittenberg...2796
Whittle, James...657, 1300, 1392, 2462
Wicker, Littleberry...918

Name Index of African-Americans

Place Name Index

Branch, Beach...*Tributary of Wolf Creek*...2032

Branch, Bear...*Tributary of Wolf Creek*...1774, 3411

Branch, Benis/Bones Lock...*Tributary of Governors Creek*...240

Branch, Big [Cabin Creek]...*Tributary of Cabin Creek*...1523

Branch, Big [Deep River]...*Tributary of Deep River*...731, 1636, 2177

Branch, Big [Deep/Drowning Creek]...*Tributary of Deep / Drowning Creek*...1646

Branch, Big [Little River]...*Located in Montgomery County. Tributary of Little River*...1330a-1330b, 1771a, 2150a

Branch, Big [Wet Creek]...*Tributary of Wet Creek*...3537

Branch, Blans...*Tributary of Richland Creek*...1243-1244, 1965, 2731, 3108, 3237

Branch, Blue...*Tributary of Indian Creek in Chatham County*...801b

Branch, Brown Straw...*Tributary of Wolf Creek*...2982

Branch, Buckhorn...*Tributary of Grassy Creek*...578

Branch, Buffalo [Randolph County]...1143, 2200-2201

Branch, Buffalo [see Buffalo Creek]

Branch, Bull...*Tributary of Reedy Creek*...2616

Branch, Cabo...467, 2987

Branch, Cales...*Tributary of Killets Creek*...2226

Branch, Calf Pen...*Tributary of Cabin Creek*...2292, 2469

Branch, Calf...*Tributary of Wolf Creek*...2761

Branch, Camp...828, 863, 3044

Branch, Cedar [Big]...*Tributary of Bear/Grassy Creek*...1069, 1372, 2107, 2234, 2278

Branch, Cedar...*Tributary of Fall Creek in Chatham County*...1194b

Branch, Club...*Tributary of Flag Creek*...1589

Branch, Cow [Randolph]...*Tributary of Fork Creek in Randolph County*...773, 1752, 2147

Branch, Cow...*Tributary of Wolf Creek*...1998, 2069, 2151, 2394

Branch, Crooked [Randolph]...*Tributary of Fork Creek in Randolph County*...2140

Branch, Desolate...*Tributary of Indian Creek in Chatham County*...737a

Branch, Dry...*Located in Montgomery County. Tributary of Dicks Creek*...3720b

Branch, Falling...3225a

Branch, Flag/Flaggy...*Tributary of Indian Creek in Chatham County*...737j, 2070a, 2575, 2831a, 2886a

Branch, Flat [Randolph]...*Tributary of Brush Creek in Randolph County*...1137

Branch, Goldston's Spring...2201

Branch, Great...*Located in Montgomery County. Tributary of Cabin Creek*...2336a

Branch, Gum...*Tributary of Buffalo Creek*...1252, 2939

Branch, Half Mile...*Tributary of Mill/Cabin Creek*...1989, 1992

Branch, Haw [Long Meadow]...*Tributary of Meadow Branch*...2002, 2171, 2342

Branch, Haw [Mill Creek]...*Tributary of Mill Creek*...1976

Branch, Haw...*Tributary of Deep River*...1147, 1290, 1360, 1613, 1664, 1778-1779

Branch, Hog Pen...*Tributary of Mill Creek*...2535

Branch, Hog...*Chatham County*...2811b

Branch, Holly...*Tributary of Buffalo Creek*...1166, 1177, 2543

Branch, Horsepen [Lick]...*Tributary of Lick Creek*...3103

Branch, Horsepen [Richland]...*Tributary of Richland Creek*...3624

Branch, Huckleberry...*Tributary of Dry Creek*...2949

Branch, Jacksons [see Jacksons Creek]

Branch, Jacobs [see also Jacobs Creek]...*Tributary of McLendons Creek*...1816

Branch, Journey...*Tributary of Killets Creek*...1562

Branch, Juniper [Hoke County]...336

Branch, Juniper [see Juniper Creek]

Branch, Juniper [Wake County]...702a

Branch, Lackys...*Tributary of McLendons Creek*...3193, 3675

Branch, Leak/Lick [Bear Creek]...*Tributary of Bear Creek*...2003, 2312

Branch, Lick [McLendons Creek]...*Tributary of McLendons Creek*...383, 557, 2255, 2369, 2372, 3389, 3581a, 3722d

Branch, Lick [Williams Creek]...*Tributary of Williams Creek*...2009

Branch, Little...*Tributary of Mill Creek*...2476

Branch, Locust [renamed Parkwood Branch]...*Tributary of Richland Creek*...254, 485, 493, 628, 880, 1102, 1156, 1205, 1319, 1466-1467, 1579, 1810, 1962, 2087, 2497, 2672, 2867, 2879, 2913, 2984, 3132, 3186a, 3259, 3450

Branch, Long [Cabin Creek]...*Tributary of Cabin Creek*...1324, 1347, 1434

Branch, Long [McCallums Fork]...*Tributary of McCallums Fork*...1544

Branch, Long [Williams Creek]...*Located in Montgomery County. Tributary of Williams Creek*...1790a

Branch, Maness...*Tributary of Bear Creek*...1945, 2044, 2313

Branch, Maple [Cabin Creek]...*Located in Montgomery County. Tributary of Cabin Creek*...2148a

Branch, Mares...1056

Branch, Martin's...*Tributary of McLendons Creek*...2960

Branch, McCallums [see McCallums Fork]

Branch, McKoy...*Tributary of Juniper Creek*...3528a, 3713a

Branch, Meadow [also Long Meadow]...414, 475, 905-906, 1048, 1224, 1269, 1325, 1360, 1389, 1412, 1511, 1695, 1735, 1873, 1951, 1984-1985, 2002, 2175, 2325, 2391, 2603, 2634-2635, 2658, 2674, 2682, 2732, 3018, 3050, 3086, 3128, 3315

Branch, Meadow [Bear Creek]...*Tributary of Bear Creek*...2013, 2662, 2890

Branch, Meadow [Cabin Creek]...*Tributary of Cabin Creek*...2011

Branch, Meadow [Chatham County]...*Tributary of Fall Creek in Chatham County*...2140a, 2336b

Branch, Meadow [Randolph County]...*Tributary of Fork Creek in Randolph County*...1072, 1745b, 2198-2199, 2577, 2600, 2650, 2694, 2727, 2740, 2839a, 3067a, 3124a

Branch, Medlin...*Tributary of Richland Creek*...2386

Branch, Mill [Wake County]...710b

Branch, Mill Swamp [see Mill Swamp]

Branch, Mirery...*Tributary of Wet Creek*...1111

Branch, Morter Glade [see Morter Glade]

Branch, Mountain...*Tributary of Fall Creek in Chatham County*...2610a

Branch, Muddy...*Located in Montgomery County. Tributary of Little River*...1585d, 2150a

Branch, Mulberry...*Tributary of Deep River*...2979

Branch, Oat Patch...*Tributary of McLendons Creek*...3233a

Branch, Ocony...737g, 1661a

Branch, Odom...1519

Branch, Old Roads...*Tributary of the Gut of Drowning Creek*...1521

Branch, Panther...*Tributary of Bear Creek*...2125, 2344

Branch, Persimmon [Flag Creek]...*Tributary of Flag Creek*...1423, 1535, 1561, 1591, 3415

Branch, Persimmon [Grassy Creek]...*Tributary of Grassy Creek*...1676, 1916, 2117, 2156, 2580, 2609, 2862

Branch, Pond...*Tributary of Killets Creek*...2872

Branch, Poplar Springs...*Tributary of Deep River*...909, 1144

Branch, Poplar...*Tributary of Indian Creek in Chatham County*...814a

Branch, Possimond [see Persimmon Branch]

Branch, Quarry...*Tributary of McLendons Creek*...378, 392, 461, 858, 2987, 3003

Branch, Raccoon...*Tributary of Wolf Creek*...2889

Branch, Race Path...*Tributary of Killets Creek*...1479

Branch, Rattlesnake [Tysons Creek]...*Tributary of Tysons Creek in Chatham County*...737h

Branch, Rattlesnake...*Tributary of Bear Creek*...1525, 1680, 2022, 3416

Branch, Reedy [Bear Creek]...*Tributary of Bear Creek*...262

Branch, Reedy [Mill Creek]...*Tributary of Mill Creek*...3468

Branch, Reedy [Montgomery County]...1743a, 1771a

Branch, Reynolds...994

Branch, Richardson...*Tributary of Sings Creek*...1229, 1245, 1932, 2101

Branch, Rocky [Bear Creek]...*Tributary of Bear Creek*...1559, 1672, 2008, 2013

Branch, Rocky [Indian Creek]...*Tributary of Indian Creek in Chatham County*...2886a, 2963a

Branch, Rocky [McLendons Creek]...*Small tributary of McLendons Creek*...348, 441, 742, 2119, 2954

Branch, Sanders...504

Branch, School House Spring...*Tributary of Little Creek*...3627a, 3710a

Branch, Schoolhouse...*[1] Tributary of Drowning Creek. [2] Tributary of Sings Creek*...1652

Branch, Seals Mare...*Tributary of Tysons Creek in Chatham County*...771b

Branch, Second...*Chatham County. Tributary of Haw River*...51

Branch, Size...*Tributary of Wet Creek*...2335

Branch, Spring [Tysons Creek]...*Tributary of Tysons Creek in Chatham County*...3105a

Branch, Spring...1716

Branch, Suck...*Tributary of Juniper Creek*...2769, 2829, 2934, 3032, 3225a

Branch, Tally Spring...*Located in Chatham County*...2831a

Branch, Tantrough [Juniper Creek]...*Tributary of Juniper Creek*...3713a

Branch, Tantrough [Mill Creek]...*Tributary of Mill Creek*...725, 781, 997, 1121, 1731, 1855, 2021, 2067

Branch, Waggon...*Tributary of Deep River*...737, 990, 1326, 1736, 2073, 2288, 2375, 3676

Branch, Watery [Bear/Buffalo]...*Tributary located between Buffalo Creek and Bear Creek*...1971, 2310, 3062, 3067, 3168

Branch, Watery [Chatham]...*Located in Chatham County*...2831a

Branch, Watery [McLendons]...*Small tributary of McLendons Creek*...82, 1662

Branch, Weirs [also Weirs Spring Branch]...381, 399, 410, 428, 604, 2311, 2477, 2993, 3576, 3613

Branch, White Lick...*Tributary of Deep River*...677, 711

Branch, White Oak [Montgomery County]...*Located in Montgomery County. Tributary of Little River*...3101a

Branch, White Oak [Wet Creek]...*Small tributary of Wet Creek*...1041

Branch, Whittles...*Tributary of Juniper Creek*...2933

Branch, Wiggins...*Hoke County*...336

Branch, Wires [see Weirs]

Branch, Wolf Pit...*Tributary of McLendons Creek*...3186

Branch, Wolf...*Tributary of Governors Creek*...240

Branch, Wolfpen [Cabin]...*Tributary of Cabin Creek*...3661

Branch, Wolfpen [McLendons]...*Tributary of McLendons Creek*...2407

Branch, Wolspen...2704

Branch, Wrights...*Tributary of Drowning Creek*...2723, 2881

Break, Cane...*Deep River*...675, 699, 718

Bridge, Bean's...*McLendons Creek*...3270, 3356, 3358, 3438, 3541, 3574, 3581, 3698, 3722a

Bridge, Cagle's...1000

Bridge, Carroll's...*Horse Creek*...1821

Bridge, Kennedy's [David]...*Bear Creek*...3287, 3520, 3603

Bridge, McLendons Creek [*see also* Muse's Bridge]...2083, 2129, 3356

Bridge, Muse's [Widow Charity]...*McLendons Creek*...1093, 1097, 1259, 2129

Bridge, Pole's...557

Bridge, Polly...1645, 2115

Bridge, Richland Creek...2083

Bridge, Williams'...3663a

Camp, Meery Maid...4

Chapel, May's...*Baptist Meeting House located in Orange County, NC*...3245

Chapel, New Hope...*Chatham County*...255

Childsburg [see Hillsborough]

Church, Autry's...3738

Church, Bensalem Presbyterian...2141, 2666, 2818, 3004, 3040, 3055, 3127, 3189, 3205, 3211, 3219, 3241-3243, 3247-3248, 3373-3374, 3398, 3497, 3530, 3548, 3554, 3564, 3570, 3677, 3695

Church, Fair Promise Methodist...3072, 3496a

Church, Fall Creek Baptist...2797, 2827, 2845, 2858, 2885, 2932, 2959, 2998, 3004, 3020, 3051, 3096, 3126, 3167, 3190, 3227, 3283, 3372, 3417, 3425, 3465, 3533, 3590, 3644, 3728

Church, Friendship Baptist [*also see* McLennon's Creek]...3283, 3372, 3465, 3533, 3590, 3644, 3696, 3728

Church, McLennon's Creek Baptist [*also see* Friendship]...2797, 2827, 2845, 2858, 2885, 2932, 2959, 3020

Church, Mechanic's Hill Baptist...3417, 3425, 3465, 3533, 3590, 3644, 3696, 3728

Concross...*Pendleton County, SC*...2771

Courthouse, Guilford County...565a

Courthouse, Moore County [Carthage]...1030, 1096, 1213-1214, 1479-1480, 1490, 1515, 1574, 1781, 2079, 2119, 2902a, 2905, 3154

Courthouse, Randolph County...869a

Creek, Adams...*Cabarrus County*...776

Creek, Barnes...*Located in Randolph County*...2196a, 2765b

Creek, Batchelor's...*Located in Randolph County*...2669

Creek, Bear [Lee County]...*Located in Lee County. Tributary of Upper Little River*...1145, 1272, 1363-1364

Creek, Bear...*Rises near Seagrove and flows southeast towards Robbins then

northwest into Deep River. Mouth located just north of North Moore High School. Tributaries include Cabin Creek, Flag Creek/Simlin Creek, Little Creek, Wolf Creek and Williams Creek*...8, 10, 12, 28-29, 58, 95, 100-101, 167, 170, 174, 185, 196, 208, 210, 221, 239, 260, 262, 266, 269, 327, 330, 357, 367, 379, 400, 430, 439, 452, 456, 476, 479-482, 484, 533, 535, 538-539, 547, 612, 738, 742, 838-839, 855b, 886, 914, 969, 1006, 1069, 1076, 1093-1094, 1141, 1178, 1211-1212, 1215, 1220, 1237, 1240, 1246, 1250, 1268, 1270, 1273, 1307, 1331, 1387, 1393, 1405, 1417, 1437, 1449, 1471, 1481, 1520, 1524-1525, 1538, 1549, 1559, 1580, 1608, 1619-1620, 1672, 1674, 1694, 1733, 1740, 1743, 1775, 1777, 1790b, 1817, 1835, 1843, 1876, 1885-1887, 1890-1892, 1905, 1909, 1904, 1918-1921, 1927-1928, 1945, 2004-2008, 2015-2016, 2033, 2036, 2045, 2048, 2054, 2068, 2071, 2093, 2096, 2100, 2102, 2105, 2107, 2125, 2138, 2144-2146, 2149-2150, 2155, 2164-2169, 2181, 2189-2193, 2204, 2213, 2222, 2230, 2238, 2254, 2256-2257, 2267, 2278, 2280, 2293, 2304, 2306, 2309-2310, 2312, 2317-2320, 2327, 2344, 2383, 2395, 2429-2430, 2449, 2452, 2456-2457, 2486, 2516, 2525, 2527, 2529, 2556-2557, 2560-2562, 2579, 2582, 2588-2589, 2591, 2599, 2611, 2617, 2621, 2670, 2684a, 2703, 2741, 2799, 2807, 2822a, 2839, 2844, 2860, 2869, 2876, 2924, 2940, 2963-2964, 2966, 2974, 2991, 2995, 3016, 3039, 3062, 3080a-3080b, 3099, 3121, 3139, 3150, 3162b, 3169, 3178, 3187, 3206, 3208, 3244, 3249, 3275, 3305, 3307, 3339, 3416, 3423-3424, 3440, 3443, 3462, 3520-3521, 3532, 3534-3535, 3547, 3585, 3604, 3617, 3630, 3638, 3650, 3672, 3679, 3714, 3717a, 3719, 3733, 3736

Creek, Beaver...118

Creek, Brush [Little]...1361, 2636b

Creek, Brush...*Located in southeastern Randolph County. Flows south/southwest into Deep River along Randolph/Chatham County border*...91, 1137, 1300

Creek, Buck [see McLendons Creek]

Creek, Buffalo [also Little Buffalo Creek]...*Rises southeast of the Robbins Crossroads and flows north/northeast into Deep River. Mouth located east of High Falls. Tributaries include Meadow Branch, Long Meadow and Gold Mine Branch*...42, 45, 56, 67, 150, 177, 188, 288-289, 316-317, 325, 341-342, 344, 347, 414, 564, 577, 583, 617, 629, 683, 715, 717, 761, 778, 793, 830, 849, 904-906, 929, 966, 999-1000, 1075, 1077, 1117, 1166, 1177, 1196, 1216, 1233, 1238, 1247, 1252, 1333, 1359, 1409, 1421, 1455, 1483-1484, 1495, 1497, 1546-1548, 1596, 1602-1603, 1642, 1644, 1649, 1698, 1734, 1767, 1783, 1819, 1830, 1832, 1844-1845, 1861-1862, 1865, 1872, 1905-1906, 1909, 1942, 1946, 1959-1961, 1966, 1968,

1971-1973, 1980, 2043-2044, 2047-2048, 2051, 2053, 2143, 2188, 2219, 2223, 2240, 2242-2244, 2246, 2270, 2281, 2290, 2298, 2314-2315, 2325, 2337, 2340-2343, 2354-2355, 2357, 2378, 2408-2410, 2438, 2472, 2505, 2538, 2544, 2563-2564, 2582, 2623, 2636, 2652-2654, 2665, 2679, 2683-2684, 2693, 2697, 2707, 2732, 2735, 2737-2738, 2921, 2975, 3017, 3019, 3047, 3062, 3069, 3079, 3088, 3163-3164, 3168, 3231, 3251, 3274, 3296, 3306, 3326-3327, 3335, 3390-3391, 3421-3422, 3449, 3536, 3562, 3598, 3639, 3645, 3650, 3671, 3673, 3717-3717a, 3736

Creek, Buffalo [Randolph County - also **Buffalo Branch**]...*Randolph County. Tributary of Deep River*...432, 702

Creek, Bush...*Randolph County. Tributary of Deep River*...52

Creek, Cabin...*Rises north of Candor and flows northeast into Bear Creek. Mouth located just west of Robbins. Tributaries include Dry Creek, Wet Creek, Mill Creek and Cotton Creek*...10, 161, 163, 169, 217, 321, 323, 379, 390, 427, 477, 521a, 540, 544, 581, 614-615, 621, 640-641, 701, 832, 906a, 906c, 964, 1246, 1255a, 1299, 1313, 1316, 1317a, 1320, 1322-1323, 1371, 1434, 1444, 1482, 1522-1523, 1616, 1739, 1771a, 1791, 1831, 1833-1834, 1836, 1838, 1877, 1879, 1884, 1893, 1921, 1929, 1937, 1939-1941, 1958, 1964, 1989, 1991, 1993, 1996, 2010-2011, 2017, 2064, 2066, 2070, 2116, 2120, 2148a, 2187, 2206, 2210, 2230, 2248-2249, 2279, 2284, 2292, 2336a, 2351a, 2373-2374, 2427, 2450, 2452, 2468-2469, 2471, 2484, 2511-2512, 2530, 2533, 2553, 2582, 2587, 2597, 2624, 2630, 2645, 2649, 2675-2676, 2724, 2762, 2764, 2768a, 2779a, 2795, 2804-2806, 2809-2810, 2836-2837, 2892, 2896, 2927, 2937, 2940, 3049, 3124b, 3126a, 3131, 3137, 3175, 3209, 3238, 3253, 3350, 3462, 3504, 3567, 3615, 3661, 3678, 3681, 3692, 3697, 3701, 3718, 3725, 3738

Creek, Cain...**Chatham County**...1061a, 1129a, 1601a

Creek, Cane Patch/Cane Path...219, 264, 599, 909b, 1461, 1475a, 2348, 2734, 2918

Creek, Cedar [also Big Cedar]...*Rises near Bennett in Chatham County and flows south into Deep River. Mouth located northwest of High Falls*...776a, 821a, 1062a, 1114a-1114b, 1139, 1173, 1173c, 1176a, 1193c, 1241, 1274, 1294, 1350, 1367b, 1453, 1634, 1729, 1812, 1949-1950, 2217, 2217e-2218, 2321, 2462, 2519, 2555, 2568, 2569a, 2606, 2628a, 2977a, 3007a, 3257, 3397, 3461a, 3676, 3739, 3742

Creek, Cedar [Little]...*Located in Chatham County. Western fork of Cedar Creek*...680, 703-704, 1139, 1241, 2321

Creek, Cedar Fork...*Located in Randolph County*...3136

Creek, Cooks...*Located in Montgomery County. Tributary of Little River*...2669a, 3195a

Creek, Cotton...*Rises in Montgomery County between Biscoe and Star and flows east into Cabin Creek. Mouth located east of Moore/Montgomery County line*...3127a, 3195b

Creek, Cox's Mill [see **Mill Creek**]

Creek, Crains...141, 172, 304, 419

Creek, Crooked [Montgomery]...*Located in Montgomery County. Tributary of Little River*...512a, 1772a

Creek, Crooked [Randolph]...*Located in southeastern Randolph County. Tributary of Richland Creek*...53, 2606

Creek, Deep...911, 1235, 1256, 1435, 1646

Creek, Dicks...*Located in Montgomery County. Tributary of Little River*...330b, 519a, 619a, 906b, 1168a, 1537a, 1585e, 1772b-1772d, 2983a, 3126a, 3132a, 3234a, 3546a, 3547a, 3720a-3720b

Creek, Drowning...*Rises near Candor and flows southeast to form Moore/Montgomery line and then Richmond/Moore line*...136, 616, 797-798, 850, 852, 885, 1344, 1368, 1408, 1428, 1464, 1503, 1521, 1529, 1652, 1741, 1852, 1854, 2195, 2368, 2628, 2719, 2723, 2752b, 2881, 3130

Creek, Dry [Cabin Creek]...*Rises near Bensalem Church and flows north into Cabin Creek. Mouth located Southwest of Robbins. Tributaries include Horse Creek*...160, 162, 216, 274, 313, 501, 780, 791, 802, 890, 946-947, 1246, 1315, 1581, 1738, 1787, 1814, 2027, 2139, 2211-2212, 2275, 2297, 2428, 2451, 2483, 2558, 2571, 2614, 2627, 2657, 2712, 2730, 2764, 2767, 2882, 2901, 2939, 2949-2952, 3008, 3226, 3387, 3463, 3474, 3629, 3734

Creek, Dry [Juniper] [see **Dry Fork**]

Creek, Dry [McLendons Creek]...*Small tributary of McLendons Creek*...354, 585, 1583, 2118, 2389-2390, 2714-2715

Creek, Dry [Wolf Creek]...2232

Creek, Dunhams...158, 199, 211, 412, 565, 697, 775, 837, 1030, 1236, 1259, 1799, 2989

Creek, Dutch Buffalo...*Cabarrus County*...960

Creek, Fall [Little]...3285

Creek, Fall/Falls...*Rises near Harpers Crossroads in Chatham County and flows south into Deep River. Mouth located east of High Falls*...148, 387, 499, 714, 737c-737g, 741a, 763a, 1099-1100, 1173a-1173b, 1190a, 1193b, 1194b, 1204a, 1223a, 1349a, 1484a, 1597, 1604a, 1661a, 1695a, 2070a, 2112b, 2117a, 2140a, 2141a, 2217-2217d, 2305, 2336b, 2360-2361, 2364, 2366, 2378a, 2413, 2475, 2538b, 2592, 2609b, 2629a, 2644, 2653a, 2715a, 2718b-2718c, 2739a, 2743, 2761a, 2765c, 2781a, 2805d, 2811a, 2828a, 2844a, 2932a, 2962, 3005b-3005c, 3007a, 3026a-3026b, 3030, 3070, 3124, 3192, 3243a

Creek, Falling...*Wayne/Lenoir Counties*...318

Creek, Flag [renamed Simlin Creek]...*Rises southwest of Robbins Crossroads and flows north into Bear Creek. Mouth located on western edge of Robbins*...202, 369, 708, 774, 808, 897, 1422-1423, 1532, 1535, 1640, 1673, 1694, 1769, 1811, 1944, 1959, 2065, 2241, 2283, 2294, 2461, 2524, 2725, 2729, 2798, 2838, 2880, 2919, 2928-2929, 3087, 3089, 3117, 3297, 3299, 3419-3420, 3449, 3721

Creek, Flat [Randolph County/Chatham County]...*Rises in Chatham County and runs southwest into Deep River in Randolph County*...510, 523, 758, 1193c, 1194a, 1271, 1677, 1718-1719, 2416, 2608, 2635a, 2708, 3185

Creek, Flat [see also **Flag Creek**]

Creek, Fork...*Located in southeastern Randolph County. Rises north of Seagrove and flows southeast into Deep River. Mouth located north of Moore/Randolph County line. Tributaries include Reedy Creek and Meadow Branch*...108, 112, 115, 143a, 157, 483, 773, 789, 814, 854-855, 887, 925, 963, 1035, 1068, 1071-1072, 1172, 1202-1204, 1248-1249, 1254, 1278, 1453b, 1496, 1637, 1671, 1712, 1714, 1744, 1745a-1745b, 1752, 2127, 2140, 2147, 2163a, 2170, 2393-2394, 2539, 2540a, 2577, 2590a, 2606, 2612a, 2631, 2634-2635, 2653b, 2654a, 2656, 2665a, 2677-2678, 2694-2695, 2727, 2750a, 2772, 3060a, 3080-3080b, 3207, 3276, 3599

Creek, Gares...*Tributary of Little River*...69, 445

Creek, Governors...226, 240-241, 279, 362-363, 384, 406, 413, 504, 507, 563, 571, 593, 754, 792, 1264, 1398d, 1413, 1663, 2185, 2194, 2197, 2659

Creek, Grassy...*Rises southwest of Needham Grove Road and flows east near Smyrna Church into Deep River*...119-120, 147, 206, 273, 415-416, 535, 576, 579-580, 588, 652, 845, 894-895, 1318, 1372, 1388, 1419, 1540, 1613, 1643, 1664, 1667, 1684-1689, 1692, 1700, 1717, 1742, 1776, 1778-1779, 1782, 1784, 1802, 1916, 2015, 2062-2063, 2156-2159, 2205, 2233-2234, 2256, 2301, 2303, 2475, 2548, 2580, 2626, 2699, 2726, 2757, 2766, 2785-2786, 2842-2843, 3125, 3177

Creek, Grist Mill...*Small tributary of Deep River near House in the Horseshoe*...3

Creek, Halls [Pasquotank County]...2794c

Creek, Horse...*Rises southwest of Rock Hill Church Road and flows northwest into Dry Creek. Mouth located at intersection of Hwy 24/27 and Dry Creek*...274, 313, 542, 582, 706, 867, 948, 986, 1329, 1340, 1420, 1492, 1495, 1516, 1547, 1592, 1646-1647, 1821-1826, 1857, 1908, 1958, 2000, 2025, 2050, 2139, 2297, 2356-2359, 2421, 2559, 2614, 2717, 2877, 2901,

3066, 3152, 3161, 3314, 3386-3387, 3466, 3505

Creek, Huffman...1880, 2012

Creek, Indian...*Tributary of Deep River in Chatham County*...57a, 130a, 683a, 704a, 737b, 737j, 801b, 814a, 1075a, 1104b, 1349b, 1463a, 2097a, 2575, 2585a, 2586b, 2655a, 2730a, 2771a, 2805a, 2831a, 2834b, 2886a, 2960a, 2963a-2963b, 2984a, 2990a, 3051a, 3179a, 3189a

Creek, Jacksons...*Rise southwest of Seven Lakes and flows south through Jackson Springs into Drowning Creek*...136, 1011, 2448, 2628, 2638, 2709, 3173, 3240, 3254

Creek, Jacobs [*see also* **Jacobs Branch**]...*Tributary of McLendons Creek*...2348, 3034

Creek, Joes...1647

Creek, John Phillips...*Tributary of Deep River*...3496a, 3627a, 3710a

Creek, Juniper [also **Big Juniper**, **The Juniper**, **Juniper Branch**]...*Rises from Seven Lakes and flows north into McLendons Creek. Mouth located west of Carthage*...17, 49, 320, 354, 358-359, 391, 409, 455, 528-529, 553-554, 569, 585, 595-596, 608-609, 650, 753, 889, 1115, 1153, 1184, 1551, 1922, 2119, 2287, 2412, 2541, 2768, 2823, 2829, 2853a, 2868, 2920, 2933-2934, 2938, 2945, 3000, 3076b, 3093-3094, 3225a, 3528a, 3713a

Creek, Killets ...*Rises south of Carthage and flows northwest around Carthage into McLendons Creek. Mouth located west of Carthage*...238, 271, 350, 353, 378, 381, 393, 410, 461, 467, 472, 558, 561, 643, 763, 858, 893, 907, 953, 1040, 1148-1149, 1251, 1479, 1562-1563, 1785, 1953, 2226, 2255, 2265, 2311, 2349, 2401, 2437, 2446, 2454, 2495, 2501, 2648, 2872, 2987, 2989, 3003, 3194, 3399, 3481

Creek, Leek [see **Wet Creek**]

Creek, Lick [**White**]...1870

Creek, Lick...*[1] Tributary of Deep River. Mouth located near House in the Horseshoe. [2] Tributary of Scotchman Creek near Putnam. [3] Tributary of Lower Little River*...345, 600, 898, 1042, 1103, 1175, 1862, 1869-1870, 1913, 1956, 1960, 2300, 2515, 2859, 3103, 3281, 3539

Creek, Line...*Tributary of Deep River in Chatham County*...64a, 1601b, 1706a, 2834a

Creek, Little [**Moore County**]...*Tributary of Bear Creek*...1843, 1920, 2019, 2098, 3411

Creek, Little [**Wake County**]...*Wake County*...1064

Creek, Lyles...*Lincoln County*...2796, 2935

Creek, McIntyre...*Located in Guilford or Randolph County.* ...128

Creek, McLendons [formerly **Buck Creek**]...*Rises just north of Seven Lakes and flows northeast into Deep River west of Carthage. Mouth located near House in the Horseshoe. Tributaries include Richland Creek, Little Creek, Killets*

Creek, Juniper Creek and Suck Creek...1, 5, 6, 9, 11, 14, 17, 20, 23-27, 45-46, 49, 54, 59, 61, 64-65, 70, 75, 85, 88, 99, 118, 126, 133-134, 140-141, 144, 146, 152, 172, 176, 178-179, 181, 193, 201, 207, 218-219, 236, 248, 258, 263, 265, 268, 275, 280-284, 296, 299, 308, 320, 324, 332, 335, 339-340, 346, 348-349, 351-352, 354, 358, 360, 370-371, 376, 378, 382-383, 385, 391-393, 402-403, 410-411, 418, 425-426, 433, 441-442, 453, 455, 457, 460, 464, 466-467, 470, 473-474, 505-506, 515, 517-519, 526-527, 530, 543, 545-546, 551-555, 557, 559-560, 562, 566, 569-570, 572, 584, 586-587, 589, 594-598, 602, 622, 625, 627-628, 630, 634-636, 639, 643, 646, 648, 650, 653-654, 658, 694, 707, 710, 723, 726, 753, 771-772, 786-787, 790, 792, 800, 803, 805, 807, 811, 820, 822, 824-826, 840-841, 847-848, 853, 857-862, 864-865, 871, 901, 933, 944, 956-957, 959, 965, 987, 993, 995, 1013, 1017, 1034, 1037, 1066, 1084, 1091, 1101, 1107, 1142, 1151-1153, 1185, 1189, 1194, 1222, 1236, 1317, 1366, 1398a, 1398c-1398d, 1401, 1413, 1453a-1454, 1456, 1463, 1465, 1489, 1539, 1558, 1583, 1615, 1621-1622, 1630, 1670, 1737, 1762, 1768, 1771, 1780, 1792, 1799, 1806, 1809, 1815-1816, 1858, 1864, 1868, 1874, 1889, 1894, 1897-1900, 1902, 1910-1912, 1957, 1967, 1995, 2020, 2040, 2046, 2083, 2086, 2089-2092, 2118-2119, 2160, 2163, 2174, 2176, 2182, 2202, 2208, 2274, 2308, 2323-2324, 2326, 2330-2331, 2334, 2347-2348, 2369, 2372, 2389-2390, 2392, 2404, 2407, 2420, 2431-2432, 2435-2436, 2444, 2459-2460, 2464-2467, 2481, 2485, 2488, 2532, 2541, 2546-2547, 2609a, 2643, 2646-2647, 2661, 2686, 2696, 2701-2702, 2711a, 2713-2715, 2748-2749, 2751-2752, 2770, 2773, 2778, 2802, 2805c, 2812, 2814, 2815a, 2821, 2840, 2857, 2871, 2886, 2891, 2894-2895, 2899-2900, 2912, 2946, 2954, 2960, 2969-2970, 2981, 2986, 2988, 3025, 3027, 3032, 3034, 3052, 3060, 3068, 3075, 3107, 3129, 3134-3135, 3171, 3186, 3193, 3225a, 3228-3229, 3233a, 3264, 3294, 3298, 3320, 3356, 3385, 3389, 3394-3395, 3418, 3502, 3552, 3563, 3571, 3588, 3666, 3675, 3680, 3696a, 3739b

Creek, Meadow...*Tributary of Jacksons Creek*...3254

Creek, Middle...*Located in Wake County*...702a, 710b

Creek, Mill [**Cabin Creek** - also **Tillis' Mill Creek** and **Smith's Mill Creek**]...*Rises north of Samarcand and flows north/northeast into Cabin Creek. Mouth located North of Pine Grove Baptist Church, South of Spies. Tributaries include Long Branch, Dry Fork, Wet Fork and Tantrough Branch*...71, 122, 183, 243, 427, 618, 701, 812-813, 967, 991, 997, 1008, 1039, 1070, 1088, 1176, 1291, 1314, 1344, 1362, 1416, 1418, 1436, 1567, 1709, 1711, 1731, 1827-1829, 1841-

1842, 1853, 1875, 1881, 1888, 1893, 1931, 1976, 1987-1988, 1990, 1992-1994, 2029, 2041, 2067, 2113, 2128-2129, 2161-2162, 2227, 2248, 2295-2296, 2382, 2402, 2406, 2411, 2445, 2506, 2513, 2534-2536, 2549, 2625, 2666, 2673, 2742, 2804, 2874, 3081, 3166, 3369, 3515, 3630, 3674, 3684a

Creek, Mill [**McLendons Creek** - *see also* **Mill Swamp**]...*Tributary of McLendons Creek. Formerly known as Cox's Mill Creek*...70, 299, 349, 385, 622, 996, 1135, 1470, 1710, 2021, 2035, 2476, 2777-2778

Creek, Mill [**Orange County**]...1618

Creek, Mill [**Randolph County**]...2598, 2727

Creek, Mills...*Small tributary of McCallums Fork*...1165

Creek, Mountain [**Durham County**]...*Durham County*...842, 870, 2660

Creek, Mountain [**GA**]...*Tributary of Hudson River in GA*...2861

Creek, Nail/Nails...*Located in Franklin County, GA*...2604, 2632

Creek, Pates...*Tributary of Deep River*...2051a, 2321, 2531, 2618, 2620, 3075a, 3480a

Creek, Pearce's...*Randolph County. Tributary of Deep River*...637, 757, 872, 1377a

Creek, Pine Hill...*Chatham County. Tributary of Cane Creek*...1129a

Creek, Pocket...697, 1150, 1264

Creek, Popes...3661

Creek, Randalls...*Tributary of Deep River*...3657a

Creek, Reedy...*Rises north of Westmoore and flows northeast to Randolph County and into Fork Creek*...143a, 389, 845, 895, 1666, 1745a, 1747-1748, 2362-2363, 2414, 2590, 2601, 2603, 2608a, 2616, 2631, 2664, 2665a, 2678a, 2786-2787, 2888, 2909

Creek, Richardson [see **Richardson Branch**]

Creek, Richland [**Moore County**]...*Rises north of Camp Durant and flows northeast into McLendons Creek. Mouth located south of Glendon. Tributaries include Persimmon Glade, Toms Branch, McCallums Fork and Locust Branch*...34, 60, 84, 90, 102, 151, 153, 191, 214-215, 250-252, 254, 267, 270-271, 285-287, 293, 297, 303, 319, 331, 343, 355, 361, 373, 399, 401, 405, 428, 433, 485, 491, 493, 512-513, 527, 531, 551, 556, 604, 617, 645-646, 799, 801, 803, 805, 815, 851, 888, 899, 903, 936, 980, 1015, 1092, 1136, 1156, 1189, 1231, 1239, 1243-1244, 1292, 1298, 1319, 1346, 1400, 1406, 1426-1427, 1429-1433, 1450-1451, 1466-1468, 1472, 1499, 1542, 1545, 1569, 1579, 1593, 1595, 1599, 1670, 1695, 1707, 1810, 1846, 1859, 1867, 1871, 1873, 1910-1911, 1913, 1951, 1955-1956, 1962-1963, 1965, 1970, 1985-1986, 1995, 1997, 2020, 2030, 2046, 2083, 2086, 2091, 2099, 2103, 2112b, 2142, 2172, 2176, 2179, 2186, 2203,

2209, 2221, 2264, 2272, 2323, 2367,
2371, 2377, 2384, 2386, 2397-2399,
2405, 2477, 2480-2481, 2497, 2500,
2503-2504, 2554, 2572, 2593, 2613,
2623, 2661, 2680, 2687-2688, 2702,
2728, 2765, 2773, 2783, 2821, 2824,
2871, 2897-2898, 2912-2913, 2922,
2970, 2984-2985, 2993, 3037, 3054,
3068, 3078, 3095, 3108-3109, 3133,
3141, 3176, 3182-3184, 3186a, 3221,
3233, 3237, 3263, 3300, 3332, 3388,
3414, 3450, 3461, 3464, 3480, 3492a,
3503, 3595, 3624, 3710, 3730, 3740
**Creek, Richland [Randolph
County]**...*Rise in south central Randolph
County and flows southeast into Deep
River. Mouth located south of
Coleridge*...53, 113a, 1294a, 1295, 1301
Creek, Rock...*Randolph County.
Tributary of Fork Creek*...777, 854-855,
1671, 2677, 2841, 3207
Creek, Rocky...*Tributary of Bear
Creek*...166, 260, 1172, 2639
Creek, Rogers...1170a, 1461, 1653,
2124a, 2353, 2381, 2387, 2496, 2574,
2631a, 2655a, 2678b, 2690, 2705,
3011-3012, 3110
Creek, Scotchman...*Rises near Putnam
and flows northeast into Deep River.
Mouth located southeast of High Falls.
Lick Creek is a tributary*...1367, 2698
**Creek, Seale's Mill [*see also* Mill
Creek]**...996
Creek, Second...*Tributary of Haw
River*...695a
Creek, Sings...*Rises between Bensalem
Church Road and Hwy 24/27 and flows
northeast into Wet Creek*...782-783,
912-913, 932, 934, 961, 981, 998, 1039,
1123, 1234, 1275, 1277, 1328, 1348,
1411, 1473, 1730, 1732, 1841-1842,
1976, 1994, 2042, 2055, 2072, 2084,
2088, 2139, 2228, 2396, 2400, 2474,
2596, 3082, 3436
Creek, Smith...*Tributary of Deep
River*...156a, 1394, 1404, 2277, 2780
Creek, Smith's Mill [*see* Mill Creek]
Creek, Stribling's...461
Creek, Suck...*Rises east of Camp Durant
and flows east into McLendons Creek.
Feeds John Beard Lake and Nello Teer
Lake*...551, 584, 810, 866, 898, 951,
973, 1036, 1227, 1339, 1498, 1560,
1568, 1573, 1639, 1708, 1901, 1969,
2124, 2485, 2613, 2791, 2829, 3090,
3696a
Creek, Suggs...*Located in Montgomery
County. Tributary of Little River*...455a-
455b, 1731a, 2639b, 2667a, 2858d,
3644a
Creek, Thomas [*see* Toms Creek]
Creek, Tice's [*see* Tysons Creek]
Creek, Tick...*Chatham County*...1376
Creek, Tillis' Mill [*see* Mill Creek]
Creek, Toms [McLendons]...*Tributary
of McLendons Creek. Rises south of
Bethlehem Baptist Church and flows
north into McLendons Creek*...351, 530,
543, 545, 2463-2464, 2466, 2700
Creek, Toms [Richland]...*Tributary of
Richland Creek near Putnam*...1955,
2825, 2870, 3074, 3332, 3384, 3717a

Creek, Tysons...19, 155, 310, 314, 388,
395, 447, 737h-737i, 761a-761b, 801a,
814b, 986a, 1193a-1193b, 1194c,
1356a, 1367a, 1617, 1716a, 1953a,
2419b, 2517, 2523, 2538a, 2564a,
2586a, 2610b-2610c, 2615a, 2636a,
2636c, 2657a, 2718a, 2742a, 2752a,
2764a, 2765b, 2775a, 2789-2790, 2801,
2811, 2815b-2815c, 2830, 2846a,
2957a, 2997, 3007a, 3033, 3105a,
3141a, 3172, 3400
**Creek, Wadsworth/Wads
[Thomas]**...1519, 1571, 3097, 3195a
Creek, Waters...2813
Creek, Wet...*Rises north of Eagle
Springs and flows north into Cabin
Creek. Mouth located southwest of
Robbins. Tributaries include Sings
Creek*...12, 28-29, 101, 106, 117, 174,
205, 315, 365, 375, 452, 500, 525, 537,
548, 590-592, 607, 705, 721-722, 779,
784-785, 806, 816, 823, 843-844, 868,
891-892, 896, 932, 935, 949, 961, 998,
1014, 1016, 1041, 1110-1111, 1115,
1167, 1183, 1206, 1343, 1349, 1402,
1425, 1440, 1485, 1510, 1512, 1557,
1586, 1693, 1741, 1848-1849, 1851-
1852, 1854, 1856, 1907, 1932, 1977,
2023-2024, 2026, 2028, 2039, 2049,
2052, 2101, 2126, 2139, 2148, 2180,
2258, 2269, 2335, 2345, 2376, 2425-
2427, 2482, 2526, 2622, 2750, 2753-
2754, 2893, 2906, 2930, 2953, 2965,
2972-2973, 3001-3002, 3085, 3101,
3113, 3170, 3239, 3401, 3435, 3537,
3549, 3711
Creek, White Oak...*Chatham County.
Tributary of New Hope*...1109
Creek, Williams...*Rises north of Ether
and flows northeast into Bear
Creek*...367, 479, 532, 534, 680a, 819,
969, 1119a, 1699, 1757b, 1790a, 1896,
1915, 1917, 1919, 2038, 2094, 2106,
2121, 2123, 2193, 2224-2225, 2235-
2236, 2266, 2307, 2336, 2434, 2455,
2509, 2718, 2739, 2742b, 2925, 3138,
3224
**Creek, Williamsons [*see* Williams
Creek]**
Creek, Wolf...*Rises north of Star and
flows northeast into Bear Creek. Mouth
located north of Spies*...121, 156, 164-
165, 204, 276, 302, 330a, 395a, 437,
550, 1232, 1267, 1296, 1309-1311,
1321, 1415, 1424, 1469, 1541, 1597,
1601, 1682-1683, 1691, 1720, 1770,
1774, 1837, 1839-1840, 1882-1883,
1895, 1929, 1983, 1998-1999, 2013-
2014, 2018, 2032, 2069, 2085, 2087a,
2120, 2151, 2231, 2260-2261, 2273,
2299, 2302, 2379, 2453, 2473, 2493-
2494, 2498-2499, 2502, 2507-2508,
2510, 2514, 2518, 2520, 2527, 2584,
2605, 2662, 2720, 2742b, 2761, 2800,
2835, 2889, 2923, 2982-2983, 2999,
3015, 3023-3024, 3105, 3126a-3126b,
3189b, 3195b, 3411, 3501, 3532, 3697,
3701
District 1...1104a, 1112a, 1237a
District 2...1104a, 1112a, 1237a
District 3...1104a, 1112a, 3511, 3616

District 6...*Tax collection district -
northern Moore County*...3407, 3472,
3559, 3606, 3669, 3683, 3713
District 8...*Tax collection district -
northern Moore County*...3310, 3407,
3472, 3493, 3511, 3559, 3606, 3616,
3669, 3683, 3713
District, Anderson's [Capt.]...*Tax
collection district - Franklin County,
GA*...2861, 2904
**District, Barrett's [Capt.
William]**...*Tax collection district -
covered present day Carthage
Township*...1259a, 1287, 1536
District, Brown's...*Tax collection
district*...1756
District, Carroll's [Capt.]...*Tax
collection district*...244
District, Cheek's [Capt']...1287, 1460,
1751, 1756
District, Cheney's [Capt.]...*Tax
collection district*...244
District, Collins' [Capt. James]...*Tax
collection district*...943a
District, Cox's [Capt. John]...*Tax
collection district - covered present day
Sheffields and Bensalem
Townships*...661, 664, 666, 684, 700,
709, 727, 740, 748, 759, 796, 834, 882,
920a, 927, 943, 943a, 1263
District, Cox's [William]...*Tax
collection district*...1237a
District, Dowd's [Capt.]...*Tax collection
district*...1113b
**District, Duckworth's [Capt.
Jacob/Joseph]**...*Tax collection district -
covered much of present day Ritters
Township*...662, 664, 667, 685, 693,
709, 728
District, Dunn's [Capt.]...*Tax collection
district*...1287, 1447a, 1460, 1751
District, Garner's [Capt.]...*Tax
collection district - Randolph
County*...869
District, Hamilton's [Capt.]...*Tax
collection district - Franklin County,
GA*...2968
District, Henry's [Capt.]...*Tax
collection district - Franklin County,
GA*...2774, 2831
District, Hinds' [John]...*Tax collection
district - Randolph County*...689
District, Hogan's [A.]...*Tax collection
district - Wake County*...1588, 1715
District, Hunnicut's [Capt. John] ...*Tax
collection district - covered much of
present day Ritters Township*...686, 740,
748, 760, 796, 856a, 920a
**District, Morgan's [Capt.
William]**...*Tax collection district -
covered much of present day Sheffields
Township*...1287, 1460, 1536, 1751,
1756, 2058
District, Pearce's [Windsor]...*Tax
collection district - Randolph
County*...688
District, Pearl...*Lincoln County,
MS*...3155
District, Seale's [Capt. William]...*Tax
collection district - covered present day
Carthage Township*...663, 668, 729

District, Wofford's [Capt.]...*Tax collection district - Franklin County, GA*...2861

Falls, Great [Chatham County]...*Chatham County*...51

Falls, Great [Moore County]...*Located at High Falls*...7, 55, 676, 714, 732, 739, 1650, 2245, 2413, 2883, 3073

Ferry, Allen's...1574, 1781

Ferry, Barnes'...*Located near Carbonton on Deep River. Later operated as Tyson's Ferry*...855a

Ferry, Searcy's...*Located in SE corner of Randolph County near Moore County and Chatham County lines. William Searcy operated a ferry across Deep River. First known as Searcy's Ford then Searcy's Ferry. In 1802 Edmund Waddell began operating the Ferry and the place became known as Waddell's Ferry*...44, 2663

Ferry, Tyson's...2585a, 2805a

Ferry, Waddell's...*Located in SE corner of Randolph County near Moore County and Chatham County lines. William Searcy operated a ferry across Deep River. First known as Searcy's Ford then Searcy's Ferry. In 1802 Edmund Waddell began operating the Ferry and the place became known as Waddell's Ferry*...44, 2663

Field, Sandy...*Baptist Meeting House located in Orange County, NC*...3227

Fields, Haw...*Randolph County*...53

Folly, Mark's...1742, 1802

Ford, Buffalo...*Buffalo Creek*...757, 1247

Ford, Burtons...*Drowning Creek*...885

Ford, Cow...*Deep River*...675, 699

Ford, Gardner's...855b

Ford, Huff's...*Drowning Creek*...1408, 2368

Ford, Island [Chatham County]...*Haw River*...171

Ford, Island [Moore County]...*Deep River*...50, 261, 1443, 1476, 2247, 2883, 3340, 3509a, 3544, 3569

Ford, Plank...*Bear Creek*...2430

Ford, Redfields...*Haw River*...255

Ford, Rocky...*On Deep River about 2 miles above mouth of McLendons Creek*...5, 21, 194, 431, 670

Ford, Searcy's...*Located in SE corner of Randolph County near Moore County and Chatham County lines. William Searcy operated a ferry across Deep River. First known as Searcy's Ford then Searcy's Ferry. In 1802 Edmund Waddell began operating the Ferry and the place became known as Waddell's Ferry*...44, 1211, 1377, 1452

Ford, Steep Bottom...*Buffalo Creek*...1077, 1117, 1649, 2240

Ford, Waggon...9a, 1178, 1523, 2912

Fork, Alston's...3616b

Fork, Ben. Hill's...*Buffalo Creek*...316

Fork, Cart...*Tributary of Cabin/Cotton Creek in Montgomery County*...2351a

Fork, Densons...*Montgomery County*...750

Fork, Dry [Juniper Creek]...528-529, 586, 650, 1551, 2412, 3076b

Fork, Dry [McLendons Creek]...*Tributary of McLendons Creek*...425, 1737, 1900, 2435, 2899, 3032

Fork, Dry [Mill Creek]...*Tributary of Mill Creek*...618, 701, 1070, 1120, 1125, 1416, 1418, 1567, 1888, 2161-2162, 2227, 3081, 3369, 3674

Fork, Dry [Wadsworth/Wads Creek]...1571, 3097

Fork, East [Dry Creek of McLendons]...1583

Fork, East [Montgomery County]...*Located in Montgomery County. Tributary of Little River*...3195a

Fork, Gould/Gold's...*Located in Montgomery County*...127a, 135a

Fork, Hudson...*Tributary of Broad River in Franklin County, GA*...2550, 2756, 2873, 3053

Fork, Lick...*Tributary of Cabin/Cotton Creek in Montgomery County*...2148a, 3127a

Fork, McCallum's...*Tributary of Richland Creek*...251, 271, 287, 320, 339, 401, 485, 491, 493, 1165, 1430-1431, 1542, 1544, 1860, 1863, 1954, 1956, 1965, 2593-2594, 2651, 2681, 2689, 2765, 2879, 3038, 3077-3078, 3704

Fork, Naked...*Located in Montgomery County. Tributary of Cabin Creek*...2351a

Fork, North [Little River]...*Located in northeast Montgomery County*...1330a-1330b, 1585d, 1947a, 2150b

Fork, Richland...*Tributary of Tysons Creek in Chatham County*...737i

Fork, Smith's...*Tributary of Buffalo Creek*...344

Fork, Wet...*Tributary of Mill Creek*...1070, 1120, 1362, 3515

Fork, Williams'...3273, 3583a, 3691d, 3722f

GA, Elbert County...2550, 2710

GA, Franklin County...2424, 2490, 2550, 2604, 2632, 2756, 2774, 2813, 2831, 2873, 2904, 2931, 2967, 2971, 3045, 3053

GA, Jackson County...2490

GA, Jones County...3036

GA, McDuffie County...710c

GA, State of...682a, 2419b, 2747

GA, Wilkinson County...2831, 2904

Glade, Morter...717, 720, 1104, 1494, 1596, 1638, 2173, 2721, 2745

Glade, Persimmon...*Rises north of Putnam and flows east into McLendons Creek. Mouth located 1/2 half above fork of McLendons and Richland Creeks*...696, 900, 1947, 1955, 1957, 1967, 2572, 2815, 2825-2826

Glade...*Tributary of Richland Creek*...1243-1244

Goldmine, Barrett's, William...3729

Goldmine, Cagle...10

Goshen...394

Graveyard, Old Scotch...3492a

Grove, Golden...79, 129

Gut, The...*Tributary of Drowning Creek*...1521

Hill, Porch Corn...888

Hill, Stony...2997

House, Abbott's Creek Meeting...*Baptist Meeting House located in Davidson County, NC*...2858, 3126

House, Barnes Meeting...*Quaker meeting house located on Deep River*...301, 404, 1516a

House, Bear Creek Meeting...*Baptist Meeting House located in Chatham County, NC*...3096

House, Brush Creek Meeting...*Baptist Meeting House located in Randolph County, NC*...3051, 3533

House, Cagle's Meeting...2452

House, Cedar Creek Meeting...*Baptist Meeting House located in Anson County, NC*...2998

House, Chambers Meeting...*Baptist Meeting House located in Montgomery County, NC*...2797

House, Election...3445b, 3604a

House, Fall Creek Meeting...*Baptist Meeting House located in Chatham County, NC*...3283

House, Garner's Meeting...1392, 1453

House, George's Creek Meeting...*Baptist Meeting House located in Chatham County, NC*...2885

House, Haw River Mountain Meeting...*Baptist Meeting House located in Chatham County, NC*...2845, 3590

House, Holly Spring Friends Meeting...*Quaker meeting house located in Randolph County*...2994

House, Lick Creek Meeting...*Baptist Meeting House located in Chatham County, NC*...3696

House, Love's Creek Meeting...*Baptist Meeting House located in Chatham County, NC*...3728

House, Marshal's Meeting...*Baptist Meeting House located in Anson County, NC*...2932

House, Mount Gilead Meeting...*Baptist Meeting House located in Chatham County, NC*...3644

House, Mount Zion Meeting...*Baptist Meeting House located in Alamance County, NC*...3372

House, Rock Spring Meeting...*Baptist Meeting House located in Chatham County, NC*...3020

House, Tick Creek Meeting...*Baptist Meeting House located in Chatham County, NC*...3167

House, Timber Ridge Meeting...*Baptist Meeting House located in Randolph County, NC*...3190

House, Unity Meeting...*Baptist Meeting House located in Randolph County, NC*...2827

IN, Orange County...3026

Ironworks, Wilcox's...*Chatham County*...1429a

Island, Barton's...78, 111, 127, 400, 436, 541, 2537

Island, Big...*Deep River*...678, 716

Island, Hobby's...*Island on Deep River opposite the mouth of McLendons Creek*...9, 24, 99, 126

Island, Reed's...*Located in southeastern Randolph County on Deep River*...637-638, 872
Juniper [see **Juniper Creek**]
LA, East Baton Rouge Parish...3727
Landing, Cannon...*On Deep River near Barton's Island*...5, 32, 47, 139
Lick, Great...3195b
Line, Chatham County...44, 155, 177, 228, 230, 277, 291, 680, 704a, 712, 761a, 814b, 835, 914a, 988, 1074, 1095, 1100, 1114, 1147, 1173c, 1204, 1230, 1274, 1356a, 1377, 1391, 1441, 1443, 1452, 1458, 1476-1477, 1490, 1601b, 1617, 1634, 1638a, 1653, 1677, 1716-1716a, 1757, 1762, 1949-1950, 2051a, 2288, 2316, 2364, 2378a, 2419a, 2491, 2496, 2517, 2522, 2531, 2538b, 2566, 2568, 2608-2608a, 2631a, 2635a, 2636a, 2636c, 2653a, 2678b, 2690, 2705a, 2708, 2743, 2771a, 2794b, 2811-2811b, 2830, 2834a, 2844a, 2846a, 2957a, 2979, 3033, 3141a, 3371, 3397, 3400, 3461a, 3604a, 3663a, 3687a, 3705
Line, Davidson County...3550
Line, Granville [**Earl of**], **Lord Carteret**...*One of the divisional lines of the Lords Proprietors. Current northern boundary of Moore County. Earl of Granville was John Carteret [1690-1763] and the Earl of Granville District encompassed the upper half of present-day North Carolina*...3, 9, 64a, 124, 148, 155a, 156a, 249, 262, 298, 327, 388, 439, 481
Line, King's [see **Granville Line**]
Line, Lord Carteret [see **Granville Line**]
Line, Montgomery County...544, 885, 1371, 1384, 1408, 1464, 1585c, 1709, 1840, 1884, 1888, 1895, 1983, 1987-1988, 1996, 1998, 2009, 2080, 2082, 2087a, 2368, 2752b, 3023-3024, 3105, 3189b, 3350, 3542, 3567, 3615, 3674, 3692-3693
Line, Randolph County...44, 177, 481, 831, 839, 855b, 881, 894, 921, 1068, 1074, 1094, 1137, 1204, 1211, 1297, 1377, 1390, 1448, 1452-1453, 1566, 1585c, 1619, 1633, 1638a, 1659, 1666, 1690, 1697, 1714, 1747, 1782, 1885, 1891, 1896, 1925-1926, 1928, 2004, 2007, 2167, 2169, 2280, 2414, 2419a, 2458, 2470, 2475, 2555, 2566, 2568, 2590, 2598-2599, 2601, 2603, 2635a, 2670, 2678a, 2684a, 2691-2692, 2708, 2750a, 2811b, 2842, 2878, 2888, 2902, 2909, 2958, 3067a, 3080a, 3120-3121, 3204, 3268, 3304, 3338, 3406, 3429, 3441, 3526, 3545, 3582, 3599, 3738
Line, Wake County...1109
Masonic Lodge #25, Panosophia...2215, 2418-2419, 3056-3057
Meadow, Hay...*Chatham County*...801a, 986a
Meadow, Long [see **Meadow Branch**]
Meadow, Willow...*Tributary of Buffalo Creek*...1412, 1952, 2325, 2339, 3018
Meeting, Cane Creek Friends...*Regional Quaker monthly meeting located near Snow Camp,*

NC...87a, 95a, 98a, 113b, 135, 154, 300-301, 401a, 404, 620, 665, 710c, 821, 1046, 1327, 1641, 2478, 2585, 2994, 3026, 3433
Meeting, Centre Friends...*Regional Quaker monthly meeting located in Guilford County*...1046
Meeting, Dunn's Creek Friends...*Regional Quaker monthly meeting located near Fayetteville, NC*...300
Meeting, Lick Creek Friends...*Regional Quaker monthly meeting located in Orange County, IN*...3026
Meeting, Wrightsborough [**GA**] **Friends**...682a, 710c
Mill, Barrett's, William...1339, 1498, 1573, 1708
Mill, Bettis', Elijah...2220, 2347
Mill, Brown's, Abner...*Located in Chatham County*...2316a
Mill, Bullock's, Francis...2136
Mill, Cagle's, Leonard...1223, 1268
Mill, Carter's...269
Mill, Cox's, Harmon...1392
Mill, Dowd's, Conner...855a, 1473a
Mill, Dunlap's, James...3733
Mill, Dunn's, Joseph...2681
Mill, Dunn's, Richard...590, 823, 2026
Mill, England's, William...714, 739
Mill, Garner's, John...471
Mill, Graves'...2585a, 2805a
Mill, Hargrove's...1375
Mill, Hussey's, William...3733
Mill, Kennedy's, David...2964, 2974, 3271, 3445, 3471, 3488, 3524a, 3578, 3628
Mill, Killet's, William...70
Mill, Lee's, Abel...471
Mill, Martin's, John...634, 820, 861, 3233a
Mill, Martin's, William...2404
Mill, McLendon's, Joel...176, 211
Mill, McNeill's...2868
Mill, Morgan's, William...813, 1007-1008, 1030, 1052
Mill, Nall's, Nicholas...894, 1220, 1656-1657
Mill, Newberry...36
Mill, Seawell's, G. [**saw**]...3686
Mill, Shamburger's, John...3733
Mill, Sheffield's, John...3738
Mill, Smith's, John "Sandhill" [later **Tillis' Mill / Lewis Sowell's Mill**]...71, 183, 225, 243, 733, 912, 919, 921, 1006, 1039, 1119-1121, 1124-1125, 1828-1829, 1878, 1990
Mill, Tyson's...1473a, 2780
Mill, Williams'...223
Mire, Big...2119
MO, Montgomery County...3551
MO, Warren County...3551
Mountain, Cane Patch...2531
Mountain, Currahee...*State of Georgia*...2424, 2747
Mountain, Neds...*Located in Montgomery County*...1743a
MS, Copiah County...3160, 3452, 3455-3457, 3459, 3506, 3508, 3575
MS, Lawrence County...3160, 3188, 3200, 3212, 3214, 3280, 3365-3366

MS, Lincoln County...3155, 3198-3199, 3201-3202, 3213, 3215-3216, 3218, 3220, 3222-3223, 3362-3364, 3410, 3412-3413, 3453-3454, 3458, 3507, 3589, 3689
MS, Marion County...2967
NC, Alamance County...87a, 95a, 98a, 113b, 135, 154, 300-301, 401a, 404, 620, 665, 682a, 821, 1327, 1365, 1641, 2478, 2585, 2994, 3372
NC, Anson County...7b, 10a, 74a, 127a, 135a, 169, 284, 321, 323, 330a-330b, 380, 395a, 402-403, 455a-455b, 512a, 519a, 521a, 544, 615, 619a, 622, 640-641, 680a, 682, 1044, 2932, 2998
NC, Beaufort County...4
NC, Bertie County...328, 432, 503-504
NC, Bladen County...1-13, 16-19, 22-23, 28, 823
NC, Bute County...294
NC, Carthage...1214, 1713, 3149, 3154, 3352, 3367, 3408a, 3512, 3559a, 3570b, 3573, 3652, 3686, 3692d, 3702, 3723a
NC, Chatham County...44, 442, 448, 514, 536, 541, 611, 620, 656, 671a, 674, 680-682, 683a, 695a, 703-704a, 710a, 712, 735-736, 737a-737k, 741a, 744, 758a, 761a-761b, 763a, 776a, 800a, 801a-801b, 814a-814b, 821a, 835, 855a, 878, 914a, 995a, 1059, 1061a, 1062a, 1075a, 1104b, 1105a-1105b, 1109, 1114a-1114b, 1129a, 1170a, 1173-1173c, 1176a, 1190a, 1193a-1193c, 1194a-1194c, 1204a, 1213, 1294, 1349a-1349b, 1361, 1365, 1367a-1367b, 1376, 1377, 1394, 1429a, 1463a, 1473a, 1484a, 1499a, 1516a, 1576a, 1597a, 1601a-1601b, 1604a, 1661a, 1695a, 1706a, 1716a, 1811a, 1949-1950, 1953a, 2070a, 2097a, 2117a, 2124a, 2217b, 2201, 2217-2218, 2316a, 2336b, 2378a, 2419a-2419b, 2423, 2538a-2538b, 2555, 2564a, 2569a, 2575, 2585, 2586a-2586b, 2608, 2609b, 2610a-2610c, 2615a, 2628a, 2629a, 2631a, 2635a-2636c, 2639a, 2644, 2653a, 2655-2655a, 2657a, 2678b, 2701a, 2715a, 2718a-2718c, 2730a, 2739a, 2742a, 2752a, 2761a, 2764a, 2765b-2765c, 2771a, 2775a, 2780, 2781a, 2789-2790, 2794a-2794b, 2797, 2800a, 2805a-2805b, 2805d, 2811a-2811b, 2815b-2815d, 2827, 2828a, 2831a, 2834a-2834b, 2844a, 2845-2846a, 2846d, 2858, 2886a, 2932-2932a, 2937a, 2944, 2956, 2957a, 2959, 2960a, 2963a-2963b, 2971a, 2977a, 2983b, 2984a, 2990a-2990b, 2996, 3005a-3005c, 3007a, 3015a, 3020, 3026a-3026b, 3033, 3040a, 3051-3051a, 3096, 3100, 3105-3106, 3111a, 3118, 3126, 3141a, 3167, 3179a, 3189a, 3190, 3203, 3227, 3239a, 3243a, 3245, 3283, 3330a, 3372, 3445b, 3461a, 3465, 3468a, 3531, 3533, 3604a, 3644, 3663a, 3687a
NC, Chowan County...503-504
NC, Craven County...20-21, 101, 134
NC, Cross Creek...209
NC, Cumberland County...*Note: only references to Cumberland County in*

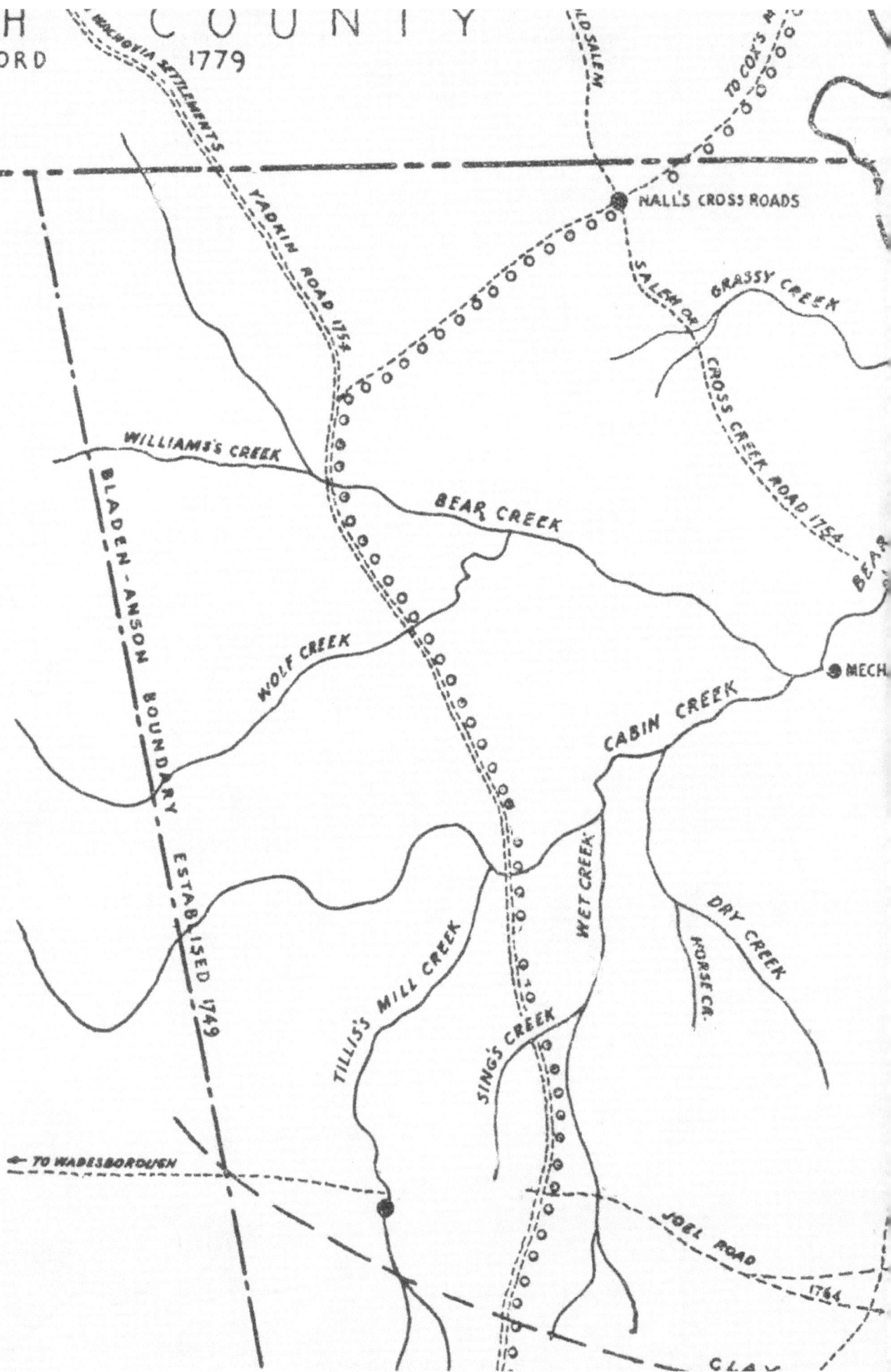

RANDOLPH COUNTY 1779
FROM GUILFORD

MORAVIAN SETTLEMENTS

OLD SALEM

TO COX'S RD.

NALL'S CROSS ROADS

GRASSY CREEK

YADKIN ROAD 1754

SALEM OR

CROSS CREEK ROAD 1754

BEAR

WILLIAM'S CREEK

BEAR CREEK

BLADEN - ANSON BOUNDARY ESTABLISHED 1749

WOLF CREEK

CABIN CREEK

MECH

WET CREEK

DRY CREEK

HORSE CR.

TILLIS'S MILL CREEK

SING'S CREEK

TO WADESBOROUGH

JOEL ROAD

1764

CLAY

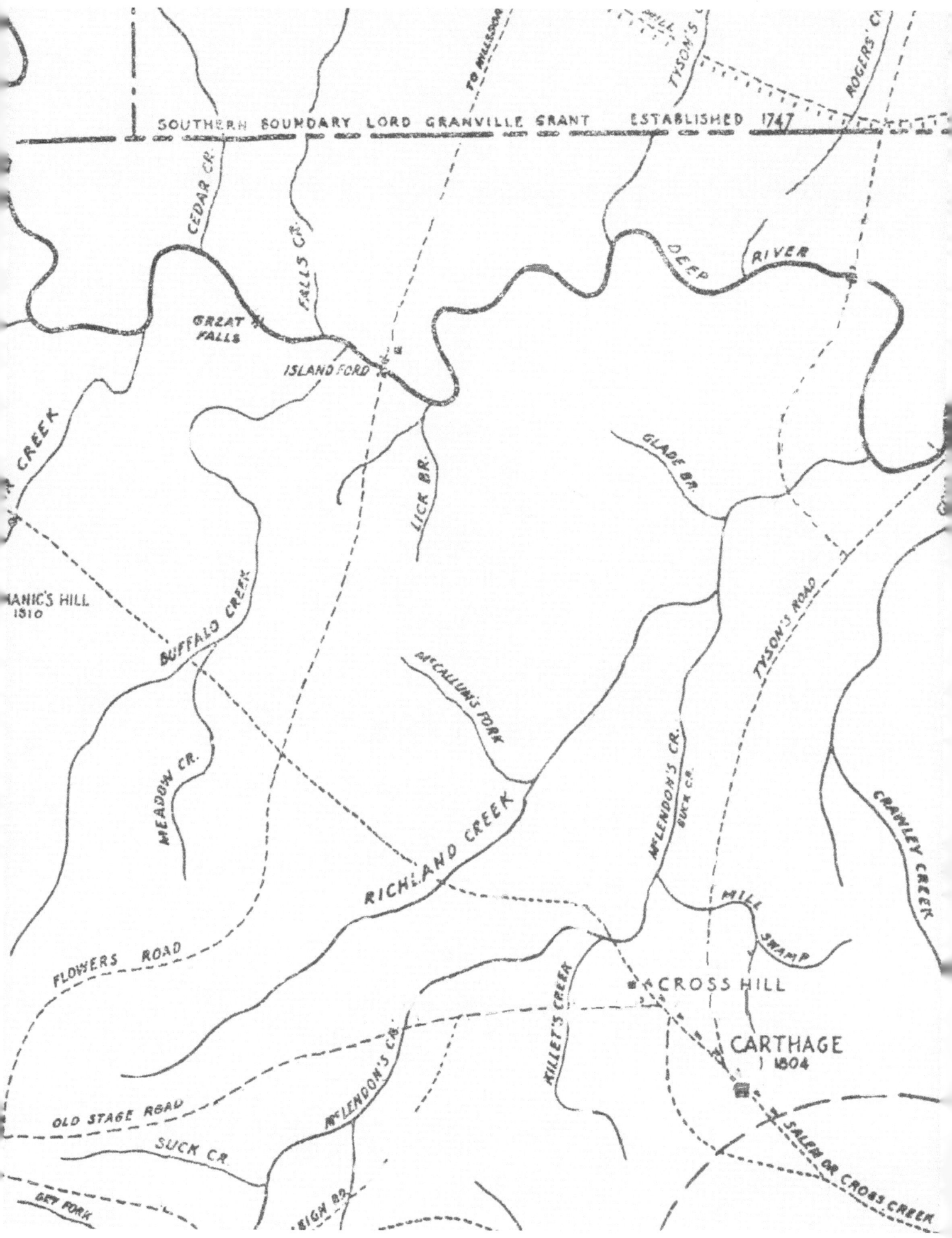

SOUTHERN BOUNDARY LORD GRANVILLE GRANT   ESTABLISHED 1747

TO MILLSORO

TYSON'S CR.

ROGERS CR.

CEDAR CR.

FALLS CR.

DEEP   RIVER

GREAT FALLS

ISLAND FORD

GLADE BR.

LICK BR.

R CREEK

ANIC'S HILL
1310

BUFFALO CREEK

McCALLUM'S FORK

TYSON'S ROAD

McLENDON'S CR.

BUCK CR.

CRAWLEY CREEK

MEADOW CR.

RICHLAND CREEK

MILL SWAMP

FLOWERS   ROAD

CROSS HILL

KILLEY'S CREEK

CARTHAGE
1804

McLENDON'S CR.

OLD STAGE ROAD

SUCK CR.

SALEM OR CROSS CREEK

EY FORK

EIGH RD.

www.ingramcontent.com/pod-product-compliance
Lightning Source LLC
Chambersburg PA
CBHW062018090426
42811CB00005B/890